P9-EMQ-166

Tax Formula for Individuals

Income (broadly defined)	$xx,xxx
Less: Exclusions	(x,xxx)
Gross income	$xx,xxx
Less: Deductions *for* adjusted gross income	(x,xxx)
Adjusted gross income	$xx,xxx
Less: The greater of—	
Total itemized deductions	
or standard deduction	(x,xxx)
Less: Personal and dependency exemptions	(x,xxx)
Taxable income	$xx,xxx
Tax on taxable income	$ x,xxx
Less: Tax credits (including Federal income tax	
withheld and prepaid)	(xxx)
Tax due (or refund)	$ xxx

Basic Standard Deduction Amounts

Filing Status	2016	2017
Single	$ 6,300	$ 6,350
Married, filing jointly	12,600	12,700
Surviving spouse	12,600	12,700
Head of household	9,300	9,350
Married, filing separately	6,300	6,350

Amount of Each Additional Standard Deduction

Filing Status	2016	2017
Single	$1,550	$1,550
Married, filing jointly	1,250	1,250
Surviving spouse	1,250	1,250
Head of household	1,550	1,550
Married, filing separately	1,250	1,250

Personal and Dependency Exemption

2016	2017
$4,050	$4,050

ROGER
CPA Review

Congratulations!

With the purchase of this Cengage textbook, you have received exclusive access to Roger CPA Review material.

Recruiting expectations demand that you pass the CPA Exam upon graduation - a rather daunting task! The earlier you expose yourself to CPA Exam materials, the more prepared you will be to pass the exam when the time comes. With the Roger CPA Review content included in your textbook, you are getting early exposure to exam topics from the leading course in the industry.

Efficient.

88%
PASS RATE

Effective.

Enjoyable.

When you're ready to take the CPA Exam, use the course you already know and love - enroll in Roger CPA Review!

877.764.4272 | rogerCPAreview.com

THOMSON REUTERS
CHECKPOINT®

3 Simple Ways Checkpoint Helps You Make Sense of All Those Taxes.

- Find what you are looking for quickly and easily online with Thomson Reuters Checkpoint®
- A comprehensive collection of primary tax law, cases and rulings, along with analytical insight you simply can't find anywhere else
- Checkpoint has built-in productivity tools to make research more efficient — a resource more tax pros use than any other

Titles that include Checkpoint Student Edition:

- **Hoffman/Young/Raabe/Maloney/Nellen,** *South-Western Federal Taxation: Individual Income Taxes, 2018 Edition*

- **Hoffman/Raabe/Young/Nellen/Maloney,** *South-Western Federal Taxation: Corporations, Partnerships, Estates & Trusts, 2018 Edition*

- **Maloney/Hoffman/Raabe/Young,** *South-Western Federal Taxation: Comprehensive Volume, 2018 Edition*

- **Raabe/Young/Nellen/Maloney,** *South-Western Federal Taxation: Essentials of Taxation: Individuals and Business Entities, 2018 Edition*

- **Murphy/Higgins,** *Concepts in Federal Taxation, 2018 Edition*

IMPORTANT INFORMATION

The purchase of this textbook includes access to Thomson Reuters Checkpoint® Student Edition for a 6-month duration.

To log in visit **checkpoint.tr.com**
You will be asked to supply a User ID and Password. Please use the following:

USER ID: CEN17-5397

PASSWORD: CEN17-5397

*PLEASE NOTE: If you have purchased a used copy of this text, the User ID and Password may have already been used. A new User ID and Password may be obtained by purchasing a new copy of this text.

 THOMSON REUTERS

ISBN-13: 978-1-337-38587-9 • ISBN-10: 1-337-38587-5

©2018 Thomson Reuters. Checkpoint is a registered trademark of Thomson Reuters (Tax & Accounting) Inc.
Other names and trademarks are properties of their respective owners.

"★★★★★"
CPA Practice Advisor
Rated 5 out of 5 stars 13 consecutive years: 2004-2016

For technical support please visit
www.cengage.com/support

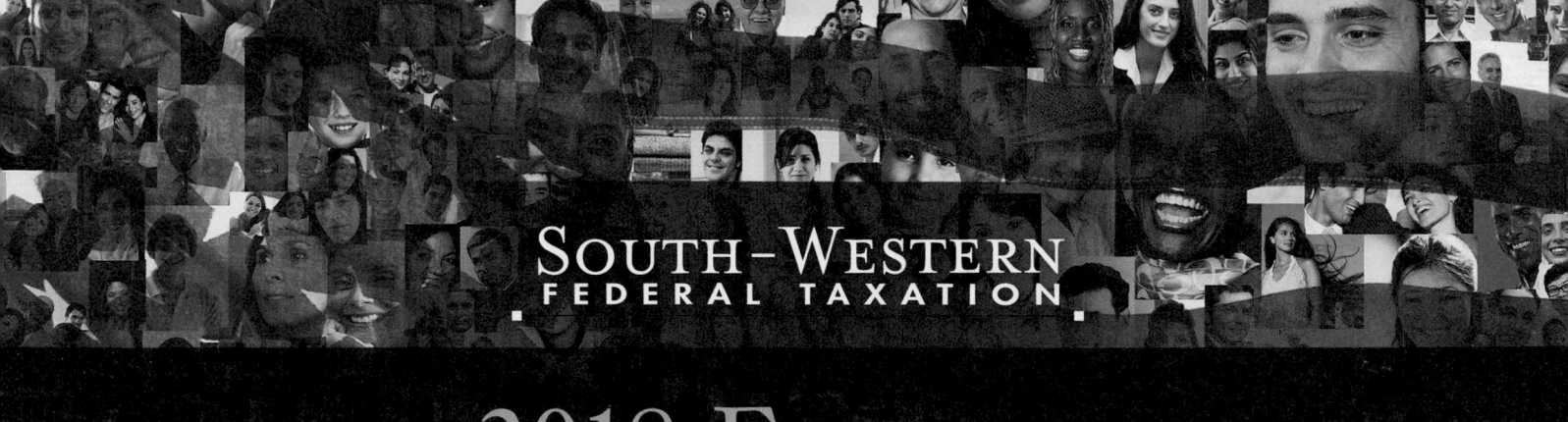

SOUTH-WESTERN FEDERAL TAXATION

2018 EDITION

INDIVIDUAL INCOME TAXES

General Editors

William H. Hoffman, Jr.
J.D., Ph.D., CPA

James C. Young
Ph.D., CPA

William A. Raabe
Ph.D., CPA

David M. Maloney
Ph.D., CPA

Annette Nellen
J.D., CPA, CGMA

Contributing Authors

James H. Boyd
Ph.D., CPA
Arizona State University

Gregory Carnes
Ph.D., CPA
University of North Alabama

D. Larry Crumbley
Ph.D., CPA
Louisiana State University

Steven C. Dilley
J.D., Ph.D., CPA
Michigan State University

Steven L. Gill
Ph.D., CPA
San Diego State University

William H. Hoffman, Jr.
J.D., Ph.D., CPA
University of Houston

David M. Maloney
Ph.D., CPA
University of Virginia

Annette Nellen
J.D., CPA, CGMA
San Jose State University

Mark B. Persellin
Ph.D., CPA, CFP
St. Mary's University

William A. Raabe
Ph.D., CPA
Milton, Wisconsin

Debra L. Sanders
Ph.D., CPA
Washington State
University, Vancouver

W. Eugene Seago
J.D., Ph.D., CPA
Virginia Polytechnic Institute
and State University

James C. Young
Ph.D., CPA
Northern Illinois University

Kristina Zvinakis
Ph.D.
The University of Texas
at Austin

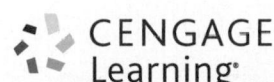

CENGAGE
Learning®

Australia • Brazil • Mexico • Singapore • United Kingdom • United States

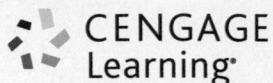

South-Western Federal Taxation: Individual Income Taxes, 2018 Edition

William H. Hoffman, Jr., James C. Young, William A. Raabe, David M. Maloney, Annette Nellen

SVP, General Manager: Social Sciences, Humanities and Business: Erin Joyner

Exec. Product Director: Mike Schenk

Product Director: Jason Fremder

Sr. Product Manager: John Barans

Content Developer: Jonathan Gross

Product Assistant: Aiyana Moore

Sr. Marketing Manager: Nathan Anderson

Content Project Manager: Nadia Saloom

Manufacturing Planner: Doug Wilke

Integrated Campaigns Project Manager, Marketing: Sarah Greber

Production Service: Cenveo Publisher Services

Sr. Art Director: Michelle Kunkler

Text and Cover Designer: Red Hangar Design

Cover Image: John Lund/Getty Images

Intellectual Property:
 Analyst: Brittani Morgan
 Project Manager: Carly Belcher

Design Images:

 Concept Summary: iStockphoto.com/
 Andrey Prokhorov

 Global Tax Issues: Andrey Prokhorov/
 Getty Images

 Bridge Discipline: iStockphoto.com/
 Andrey Prokhorov

 Ethics & Equity: iStockphoto.com/LdF

 Cumulative Problems/Tax Return Problems:
 iStockphoto.com/Pali Rao

 Financial Disclosure Insights: Vyaseleva
 Elena/Shutterstock.com

 Tax Planning Strategies: Sergey Nivens/
 Shutterstock.com

 Tax Fact: carroteater/Shutterstock.com

 Framework 1040: Tomas Urbelionis/
 Shutterstock.com

© 2018, 2017 Cengage Learning®

Unless otherwise noted, all content is © Cengage

ALL RIGHTS RESERVED. No part of this work covered by the copyright herein may be reproduced or distributed in any form or by any means, except as permitted by U.S. copyright law, without the prior written permission of the copyright owner.

For product information and technology assistance, contact us at **Cengage Learning Customer & Sales Support, 1-800-354-9706**

For permission to use material from this text or product, submit all requests online at **www.cengage.com/permissions** Further permissions questions can be emailed to **permissionrequest@cengage.com**

All tax forms within the text are: Source: Internal Revenue Service.
Tax software: Source: H&R Block
Roger CPA Review: Source: Roger CPA

ISSN: 0272-0329
2018 Annual Edition

Student Edition ISBN: 978-1-337-38589-3
Student Edition with H&R Block and RIA Checkpoint ISBN: 978-1-337-38588-6

Cengage Learning
20 Channel Center Street
Boston, MA 02210
USA

Cengage Learning is a leading provider of customized learning solutions with employees residing in nearly 40 different countries and sales in more than 125 countries around the world. Find your local representative at **www.cengage.com**.

Cengage Learning products are represented in Canada by Nelson Education, Ltd.

To learn more about Cengage Learning Solutions, visit **www.cengage.com**

Purchase any of our products at your local college store or at our preferred online store **www.cengagebrain.com**

Printed in the United States of America
Print Number: 01   Print Year: 2017

Preface

COMMITTED TO EDUCATIONAL SUCCESS

South-Western Federal Taxation (SWFT) is the **most trusted and best-selling series in college taxation.** We are focused exclusively on providing the most useful, comprehensive, and up-to-date tax texts, online study aids, tax preparation tools, and research tools to help instructors and students succeed in their tax courses and beyond.

SWFT is a comprehensive package of teaching and learning materials, significantly enhanced with each edition to meet instructor and student needs and to add overall value to learning taxation.

Individual Income Taxes, 2018 Edition provides a dynamic learning experience inside and outside of the classroom. Built with resources and tools that have been identified as the most important, our complete learning system provides options for students to achieve success.

Individual Incomes Taxes, 2018 Edition provides accessible, comprehensive, and authoritative coverage of the relevant tax code and regulations as they pertain to the individual taxpayer, as well as coverage of all major developments in Federal Taxation.

In revising the 2018 Edition, we focused on:

- *Accessibility. Clarity. Substance.* The text authors and editors made this their mantra as they revised the 2018 edition. Coverage has been streamlined to make it more accessible to students, and difficult concepts have been clarified, all without losing the substance that makes up the *South-Western Federal Taxation* series.

- *Developing professional skills.* SWFT excels in bringing students to a professional level in their tax knowledge and skills, to prepare them for immediate success in their careers. In this regard, we include development of speaking and writing communications skills, the use of tax preparation and tax research software, orientation toward success on the CPA exam, consideration of the time value of money in the tax planning process, and facility with advanced applications of spreadsheet construction.

- *CengageNOWv2 as a complete learning system.* Cengage Learning understands that digital learning solutions are central to the classroom. Through sustained research, we continually refine our learning solutions in CengageNOWv2 to meet evolving student and instructor needs. CengageNOWv2 fulfills learning and course management needs by offering a personalized study plan, video lectures, auto-graded homework, auto-graded tests, and a full eBook with features and advantages that address common challenges.

FULL-COLOR DESIGN:
We understand that students struggle with learning difficult tax code concepts and applying them to real-world scenarios. The 2018 edition uses color to bring the text to life, capture student attention, and present the tax code in a simple, yet logical format.

☐ Selected **content is streamlined** to guide students in focusing on the most important concepts for the CPA Exam while still providing in-depth coverage of topics.

☐ Examples are clearly labeled and directly follow concepts to assist with student application. An **average of over 40 examples in each chapter** use realistic situations to illustrate the complexities of the tax law and allow students to integrate chapter concepts with illustrations and examples.

COMPUTATIONAL EXERCISES: Students need lots of practice in areas such as computing
tax return problems and adjusting rates. We have developed these exercises to give students practice in calculating the solutions they need to make business decisions.

- ☐ Found in end-of-chapter section of the textbook

- ☐ CengageNOWv2 provides algorithmic versions of these problems

Computational Exercises

16. **LO.1** Sally owns real property for which the annual property taxes are $9,000. She sells the property to Kate on March 9, 2017, for $550,000. Kate pays the real property taxes for the entire year on October 1, 2017.
    a. How much of the property taxes can be deducted by Sally and how much by Kate?
    b. What effect does the property tax apportionment have on Kate's adjusted basis in the property?
    c. What effect does the apportionment have on Sally's amount realized from the sale?
    d. How would the answers in parts (b) and (c) differ if the taxes were paid by Sally?

17. **LO.1** Melba purchases land from Adrian. Melba gives Adrian $225,000 in cash and agrees to pay Adrian an additional $400,000 one year later plus interest at 5%.
    a. What is Melba's adjusted basis for the land at the acquisition date?
    b. What is Melba's adjusted basis for the land one year later?

18. **LO.1** On July 1, 2017, Katrina purchased tax-exempt bonds (face value of $75,000) for $82,000. The bonds mature in five years, and the annual interest rate is 6%. The market rate of interest is 2%.
    a. How much interest income and/or interest expense must Katrina report in 2017, assuming straight-line amortization is appropriate?
    b. What is Katrina's adjusted basis for the bonds on January 1, 2018?

ROGER CPA EXAM REVIEW QUESTIONS: The SWFT series continues to provide
the most in-depth coverage of tax concepts, and selected Roger CPA Exam Review Questions are included to further prepare students for success on the CPA Exam.

- ☐ Located in selected end-of-chapter sections

- ☐ Tagged by concept in CengageNOWv2

- ☐ Similar questions to what students would actually find on the CPA Exam

Roger CPA Review Questions

1. Stephen purchased a video game console five years ago for $500. In order to raise money for the "latest and greatest" console, Stephen sold his console for $100. Because of advances in technology, Stephen can purchase the new console for $400. What is the tax treatment of Stephen's sale of his console?
    a. Stephen recognizes a $400 loss.
    b. Stephen does not report the sale.
    c. Stephen recognizes a $300 loss.
    d. Stephen recognizes a $100 gain.

2. Uncle Ubb gave his nephew, Leroy Lamprey, a gift of stock worth $10,000. Uncle Ubb's basis in the stock was $15,000. Leroy sold the stock to an unrelated party for $11,000. What amount of gain or loss should Leroy report as a result of this sale?
    a. $0   c. $200 gain
    b. $4,000 loss   d. $1,000 gain

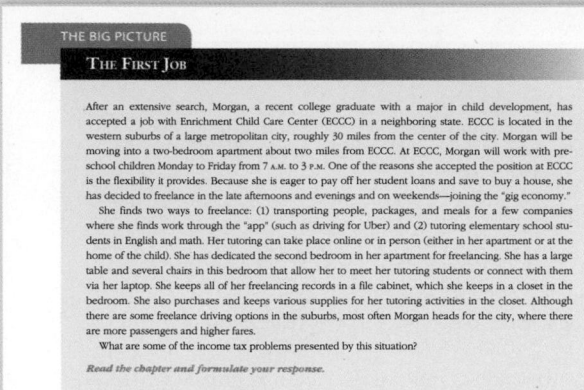

THE BIG PICTURE: Tax Solutions for the Real World. Taxation comes alive at the start of each chapter as The Big Picture Examples give a glimpse into the lives, families, careers, and tax situations of typical filers. Students will follow this one family, individual, or other taxpayer throughout the chapter showing students how the concepts they are learning play out in the real world.

Finally, to solidify student comprehension, each chapter concludes with a **Refocus on the Big Picture** summary and tax planning scenario. These scenarios apply the concepts and topics from the chapter in a reasonable and professional way.

FRAMEWORK 1040:
Fitting it all Together.
This chapter-opening feature demonstrates how topics within *Individual Income Taxes* fit together, using the Income Tax Formula for Individuals as the framework. The framework helps students organize their understanding of the chapters and topics to see how they relate to the basic tax formula and then identify where these items are reported on Form 1040. Framework 1040 helps students navigate topics by explaining how tax concepts are organized.

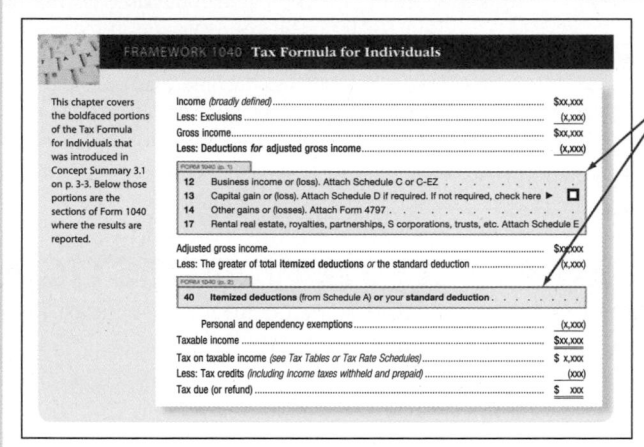

Use this chapter-opening **Framework 1040**, which shows the topics as they appear in the individual tax formula, to understand where on Form 1040 these chapter topics would appear.

FINANCIAL DISCLOSURE INSIGHTS:

Tax professionals need to understand how taxes affect the income statement and balance sheet. **Financial Disclosure Insights**, appearing throughout the text, use current data about existing taxpayers to highlight book-tax reporting differences, effective tax rates, and trends in reporting conventions.

FINANCIAL DISCLOSURE INSIGHTS Tax and Book Depreciation

A common book-tax difference relates to the depreciation amounts that are reported for GAAP and Federal income tax purposes. Typically, tax depreciation deductions are accelerated; that is, they are claimed in earlier reporting periods than is the case for financial accounting purposes.

Almost every tax law change since 1980 has included depreciation provisions that accelerate the related deductions relative to the expenses allowed under GAAP. Accelerated cost recovery deductions represent a means by which the taxing jurisdiction infuses the business with cash flow created by the reduction in the year's tax liabilities.

For instance, recently, about one-quarter of General Electric's deferred tax liabilities related to depreciation differences. For Toyota's and Ford's depreciation differences, that amount was about one-third. And for the trucking firm Ryder Systems, depreciation differences accounted for all but one percent of the deferred tax liabilities.

ETHICS & EQUITY Punching the Time Clock at Year-End

As the end of the tax year approaches, Ralph, a successful full-time real estate developer and investor, recognizes that his income tax situation for the year could be bleak. Unless he and his wife are able to generate more hours of participation in one of his real estate rental activities, they will not reach the material participation threshold. Consequently, the tax losses from the venture will not be deductible. To ensure deductibility, Ralph suggests the following plan:

- He will document the time he spends "thinking" about his rental activities.
- During the week, his wife will visit the apartment building to oversee (in a management role) the operations of the rentals.

- On weekends, he and his wife will visit the same units to further evaluate the operations.
- Also on the weekends, while they are doing their routine household shopping, they will be on the lookout for other rental properties to buy. Ralph plans to count both his and his wife's weekend hours toward the tally of total participation.

Ralph contends that the law clearly allows the efforts of one's spouse to count for purposes of the material participation tests. Likewise, nothing in the tax law requires taxpayers to be efficient in their hours of participation. How do you react?

ETHICS & EQUITY:

Most issues do not have just one correct answer. **Ethics & Equity** features will spark critical thinking and invite classroom discussion, enticing students to evaluate their own value system. Suggested answers to Ethics & Equity scenarios appear in the Solutions Manual.

TAX PLANNING:

Chapters include a separate section calling attention to how the tax law can be applied to reach the taxpayer's goals. Tax planning applications and suggestions also appear throughout each chapter.

16-7 TAX PLANNING

16-7a Importance of Capital Asset Status

Why is capital asset status important? Because of the alternative tax on net capital gain. Individuals who receive income in the form of long-term capital gains or qualified dividend income have an advantage over taxpayers who cannot receive income in these forms.

If a net capital loss results, the maximum deduction is $3,000 per year. Consequently capital gains and losses must be segregated from other types of gains and losses and must be reported separately on Schedule D of Form 1040.

GLOBAL TAX ISSUES Do Dividends from Foreign Corporations Warrant Special Treatment?

The special rates on dividends are intended to mitigate the double-tax burden—taxing income at the corporate level then taxing the dividends to the shareholder. The United States taxes foreign corporations only on the income the corporation earns in this country. Therefore, if the corporation does no business in the United States but pays dividends to shareholders subject to U.S. taxes, the corporation's income is only taxed once.

Nevertheless, special rates apply to the foreign corporation's dividends if (1) the foreign corporation's stock is traded on an established U.S. securities market or (2) the foreign corporation is eligible for the benefits of an income tax treaty between its country of incorporation and the United States. The apparent reason for the first exception is that if the corporation is listed on an established U.S. securities market, it probably does enough business in the United States to be subject to its tax. The second exception is a reciprocal arrangement: the United States confers a benefit to corporations formed in countries that exempt U.S. corporations from taxes.

GLOBAL TAX ISSUES:

The **Global Tax Issues** feature gives insight into the ways in which taxation is affected by international concerns and illustrates the effects of various events on tax liabilities across the globe.

Take your students from Motivation to Mastery with CengageNOWv2

MASTERY
APPLICATION
MOTIVATION

CengageNOWv2 is a powerful course management tool and online homework resource that elevates student thinking by providing superior content designed with the entire student workflow in mind.

- **MOTIVATION:** engage students and better prepare them for class
- **APPLICATION:** help students learn problem-solving behavior and skills to guide them to complete taxation problems on their own
- **MASTERY:** help students make the leap from memorizing concepts to actual critical thinking

Motivation —

Many instructors find that students come to class unmotivated and unprepared. To help with engagement and preparedness, CengageNOWv2 for SWFT offers:

- **"Tax Drills" test students on key concepts and applications.** With three to five questions per learning objective, these "quick-hit" questions help students prepare for class lectures or review prior to an exam.

Application —

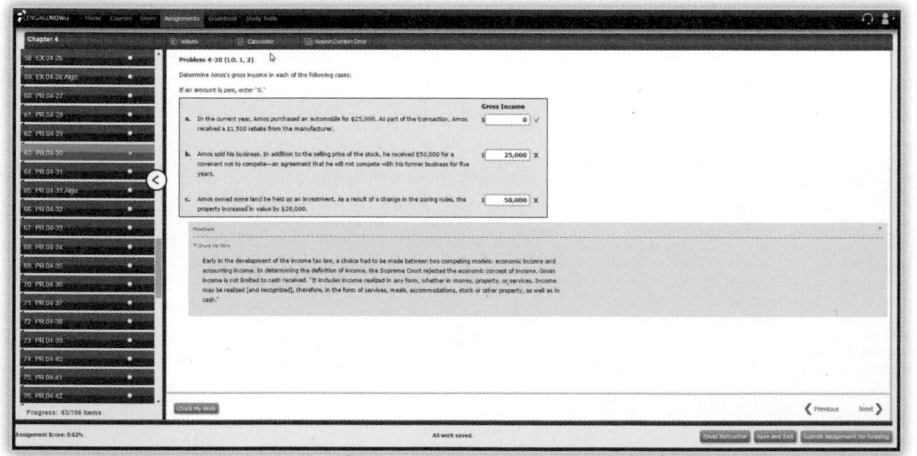

Students need to learn problem-solving behavior and skills, to guide them to complete taxation problems on their own. However, as students try to work through homework problems, sometimes they become stuck and need extra help. To reinforce concepts and keep students on the right track, CengageNOWv2 for SWFT offers the following.

- **End-of-chapter homework from the text** is expanded and enhanced to follow the workflow a professional would use to solve various client scenarios. These enhancements better engage students and encourage them to think like a tax professional.

- **Algorithmic versions** of end-of-chapter homework are available for computational exercises and at least 15 problems per chapter.

- **"Check My Work" Feedback.** Homework questions include immediate feedback so students can learn as they go. Levels of feedback include an option for "check my work" prior to submission of an assignment.

- **Post-Submission Feedback.** After submitting an assignment, students receive even more extensive feedback explaining why their answers were incorrect. Instructors can decide how much feedback their students receive and when, including the full solution.

- **Built-in Test Bank** for online assessment.

Mastery —

- **NEW! Tax Form Problems** have been added to the 2018 edition. Students can now complete the Cumulative H&R Block Problems and other homework items found in the end-of-chapter manually or in a digital environment.

- **"What-If" Questions** allow students to develop a deeper understanding of the material as they are challenged to use their prior knowledge of the tax situations and critically think through new attributes to determine how the outcome will change.

- **An Adaptive Study Plan** comes complete with an eBook, practice quizzes, crossword puzzle, glossary, and flashcards. It is designed to help give students additional support and prepare them for the exam.

CengageNOWv2 Instant Access Code ISBN:
978-1-337-38950-1

Contact your Cengage Learning Consultant about different bundle options.

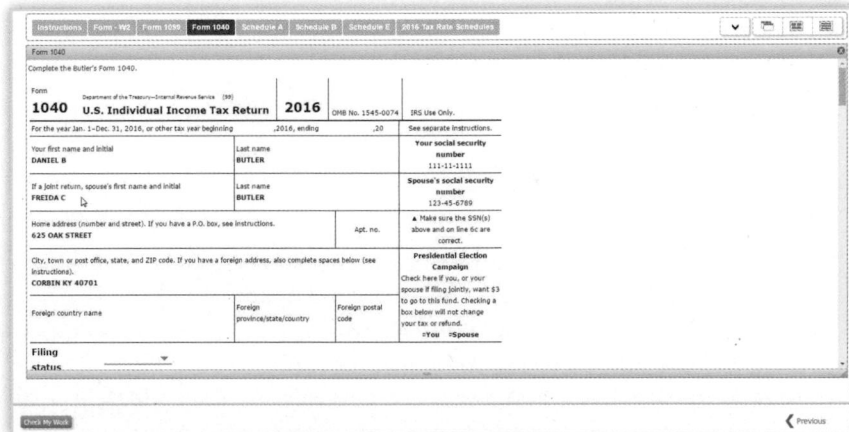

EXTENSIVELY REVISED. DEFINITIVELY UP TO DATE.

Each year the *South-Western Federal Taxation* series is updated with thousands of changes to each text. Some of these changes result from the feedback we receive from instructors and students in the form of reviews, focus groups, web surveys, and personal e-mail correspondence to our authors and team members. Other changes come from our careful analysis of the evolving tax environment. **We make sure that every tax law change relevant to the introductory taxation course was considered, summarized, and fully integrated into the revision of text and supplementary materials.**

The *South-Western Federal Taxation* authors have made every effort to keep all materials up to date and accurate. All chapters contain the following general changes for the 2018 Edition.

- Updated materials to reflect changes made by Congress through legislative action.
- Streamlined chapter content (where applicable) to clarify material and make it easier for students to understand.
- Revised numerous materials as the result of changes caused by indexing of statutory amounts.
- Revised Problem Materials, Computational Exercises, and CPA Exam problems.
- Updated Chapter Outlines to provide an overview of the material and to make it easier to locate specific topics.
- Revised *Financial Disclosure Insights* and *Global Tax Issues* as to current developments.

In addition, the following materials are available online.

- An appendix that helps instructors broaden and customize coverage of important tax provisions of the Affordable Care Act. (Instructor Companion Website at **www.cengage.com/login**)
- The Depreciation and the Accelerated Cost Recovery System (ACRS) appendix. (Instructor Companion Website at **www.cengage.com/login**)
- The Taxation in the Real World weekly blog posts for instructors. (**https://community.cengage.com/t5/Taxation-in-the-Real-World-Blog/bg-p/taxationintherealworldblog**)

Chapter 1

- "Approaching the Study of Taxation" is now the first section of the chapter and includes topics on defining "taxation," exploring the many ways taxes affect our lives, explaining the relevance of taxation to accounting and finance professionals, and offering tips for studying taxation.

- Unified the chapter sections on tax structure and tax principles into "Tax System Design." Added an exhibit illustrating how to analyze a tax proposal using principles of good tax policy.
- Updated and expanded the chapter section on proposed U.S. taxes to include brief explanations of the carbon and financial transaction taxes.
- Streamlined coverage throughout the chapter.
- Added two internet research exercises (one on tax policy and one helping students gain awareness of the taxes they pay).

Chapter 2

- Revised and clarified chapter materials.
- Updated references and citations throughout the chapter.
- Updated discussion of taxation on the CPA exam to reflect 2017 exam changes.

Chapter 3

- Updated chapter materials to reflect inflation adjustments.
- Revised and clarified materials throughout the chapter; added multiple examples to illustrate concepts.
- Reorganized materials on filing status and related filing requirements.
- Added a Form 1040 to the chapter for easy reference.

Chapter 4

- Added the new taxable prize exception for Olympic and Paralympic medals and prizes.

Chapter 5

- Updated chapter materials to reflect inflation adjustments.
- Added § 139F on damages received for wrongful incarceration, enacted in 2015.

Chapter 6

- Streamlined coverage throughout the chapter; added multiple examples to illustrate text material.

- Added a discussion of executive compensation to Tax Planning section.

- Added a new tax form problem on hobby losses (the completion of Form 1040 and Schedule A).

- Updated comprehensive tax return problems for inflation adjustments.

Chapter 7

- Revised and clarified discussion of "other casualties" and disaster area losses; added and modified several examples to clarify the rules.

- Reduced coverage of unique rules related to NOL carrybacks for casualty losses and farming losses.

- Revised end-of-chapter materials for annual inflation adjustments.

Chapter 8

- Streamlined coverage throughout the chapter; revised the Big Picture examples.

- Expanded discussion of § 179 (including several new examples), revised order of § 179 expense and additional first-year (bonus) depreciation (covering § 179 before bonus depreciation), and added new materials on using § 179 and bonus depreciation effectively (including a new Concept Summary).

- Updated materials to reflect inflation adjustment to § 179 amounts.

- Added a new tax form problem (the completion of a Form 4562).

Chapter 9

- Revised the Big Picture examples to highlight the "gig economy."

- Streamlined coverage throughout the chapter; added multiple examples illustrating text materials.

- Updated standard mileage amounts, related examples, and end-of-chapter materials.

- Added a new tax form problem (the completion of a Form 3903).

- Added new research problems on Form 1099–K related to the "gig economy."

Chapter 10

- Enhanced the presentation of the chapter coverage in the Framework 1040: Tax Formula for Individuals.

- Clarified the language concerning the medical deduction AGI floor that applies to taxpayers 65 years of age and older.

- Added a new tax form problem [the completion of a Schedule A (Form 1040)].

- Streamlined coverage throughout the chapter; refined the discussion of Health Savings Accounts.

- Rewrote a Global Tax Issues feature with a focus on the recent earthquake in central Italy.

- Updated chapter materials for inflation adjustments.

Chapter 11

- Streamlined coverage throughout the chapter.

- Adjusted the relevant interest rates and projected rates of return in the Big Picture and the associated examples to reflect the current environment.

- Clarified the discussion relating to investment expenses under the investment interest discussion.

- Added a new tax form problem (the completion of a Form 4952).

Chapter 12

- Revised discussion of the medical expense deduction for AMT purposes.

- Added example on the AMT consequences of a state tax refund.

- Added discussion regarding the utilization of the minimum tax credit.

- Improved the discussion of AMT net operating loss provisions.

Chapter 13

- Updated chapter materials for inflation adjustments.

- Streamlined and clarified coverage throughout the chapter.

- Updated Affordable Care Act materials.

Chapter 14

- Revised and clarified chapter materials; added multiple examples to illustrate concepts.

- Added a new Concept Summary on realized gains and losses and expanded discussion on this topic.

- Added a new tax form problem [the completion of a Form 8949 and a Schedule D (Form 1040)].

Chapter 15

- Revised and clarified chapter materials; added multiple examples to illustrate concepts.

- Restructured § 121 materials to focus on general rules first, followed by a discussion of the relief provision available if the two-year rules are not met.

- Removed summary material on other nonrecognition provisions (§§ 1032, 1035, 1036, 1038, 1041, and 1044).

- Added a new tax form problem (the completion of a Form 8824 for a like-kind exchange).

Chapter 16

- Updated the chapter tax return example [including the Form 8949, Schedule D (Form 1040), and the capital gains worksheet].

- Streamlined and clarified coverage throughout the chapter.

- Added a new tax form problem (the completion of a Form 8949).

- Added present value and spreadsheet components to end-of-chapter materials.

Chapter 17

- Updated the chapter tax return example, linking the example computations to placement on the various tax forms [Form 4797 and Schedule D (Form 1040)].

- Added a new tax form problem (the completion of a Form 4797).

- Added present value and spreadsheet components to end-of-chapter materials.

- Streamlined and clarified coverage throughout the chapter.

Chapter 18

- Updated Research Problem on contingent liabilities for the Third Circuit decision and IRS non-acquiescence in Giant Eagle.

Chapter 19

- Amounts updated for inflation.

Chapter 20

- Added new Learning Objective 1, Entity Choice.

- Added new text on entity choice and check-the-box.

- Added new Exhibit 20.1 (Cash Method for Inventory Exceptions Flowchart).

- Introduced corporate tax table with lower bracket taxes included.

- Revised constructive dividend section.

- Added new materials on distributions from S corporations.

- Added new materials on LLCs and qualified joint ventures in the partnership section.

TAX LAW OUTLOOK

From your SWFT Series Editors:
Concerns about complexity, income inequity, job creation, and international competitiveness will keep income tax issues at the forefront of tax-related discussions throughout 2017 and 2018. Congress is reviewing tax proposals on middle-class tax relief and tax changes for the wealthy. Federal tax treatments of income from overseas sources will also be considered, including converting from a worldwide system to a territorial one. Changes to the Affordable Care Act (ObamaCare) also are being considered. If major tax legislation is passed that affects this text, the SWFT editors will provide an update for adopters.

SUPPLEMENTS SUPPORT STUDENTS AND INSTRUCTORS

Built around the areas students and instructors have identified as the most important, our integrated supplements package offers more flexibility than ever before to suit the way instructors teach and students learn.

Online and Digital Resources for Students

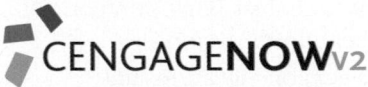

CengageNOWv2 is a powerful course management and online homework tool that provides robust instructor control and customization to optimize the student learning experience and meet desired outcomes.

CengageNOWv2 Instant Access Code ISBN:
978-1-337-38950-1

Contact your Cengage Learning Consultant about different bundle options.

THOMSON REUTERS

CHECKPOINT® **Checkpoint® Student Edition from Thomson Reuters** is the leading online tax research database used by professionals. There are three simple ways Checkpoint® helps introduce students to tax research:

- Intuitive web-based design makes it fast and simple to find what you need.
- Checkpoint® provides a comprehensive collection of primary tax law, cases, and rulings along with analytical insight you simply can't find anywhere else.
- Checkpoint® has built-in productivity tools such as calculators to make research more efficient—a resource more tax pros use than any other.

Six months' access to Checkpoint® Student Edition (after activation) is packaged automatically with every NEW copy of the textbook.*

More than software: Put the experience of H&R Block® tax professionals on your side.

- A step-by-step interview guides you through a customized process.
- Accurate calculations and 100% satisfaction—guaranteed.

- Worry-free Audit Support™ and tax advice from an H&R Block® tax professional.

Online access to H&R Block® Premium & Business software is offered with each NEW copy of the textbook—at no additional cost to students.*

CENGAGEbrain.com Students can use **CengageBrain.com** to select this textbook and access Cengage Learning content, empowering them to choose the most suitable format and giving them a better chance of success in the course. Buy printed materials, eBooks, and digital resources directly through Cengage Learning and save at **CengageBrain.com**.

Online Student Resources

Students can go to **www.cengagebrain.com** for free resources to help them study as well as the opportunity to purchase additional study aids. These valuable free study resources will help students earn a better grade:

- Flashcards use chapter terms and definitions to aid students in learning tax terminology for each chapter.
- Online glossary for each chapter provides terms and definitions from the text in alphabetical order for easy reference.
- Learning objectives can be downloaded for each chapter to help keep students on track.
- Tax tables used in the textbook are downloadable for reference.

Printed Resources for Students
Looseleaf Edition (978-1-337-38593-0)

This version provides all the pages of the text in an unbound, three-hole punched format for portability and ease of use. Online access to H&R Block® Premium & Business software is included with every NEW textbook as well as Checkpoint® Student Edition from Thomson Reuters.*

*NEW Printed copies of the textbook are automatically packaged with access to Checkpoint® Student Edition and H&R Block® tax software. If students purchase the eBook, they will not automatically receive access to Checkpoint® Student Edition and H&R Block® software. They must purchase the tax media pack offering both of these products. The ISBN is 978-1-337-55335-3 and can be purchased at **www.cengagebrain.com**.

Comprehensive Supplements Support Instructors' Needs

CENGAGENOWv2

CengageNOWv2 is a powerful course management and online homework tool that provides robust instructor control and customization to optimize the student learning experience and meet desired outcomes. In addition to the features and benefits mentioned earlier for students, CengageNOWv2 includes these features for instructors:

- **Learning Outcomes Reporting** and the ability to analyze student work from the gradebook. Each exercise and problem is tagged by topic, learning objective, level of difficulty, estimated completion time, and business program standards to allow greater guidance in developing assessments and evaluating student progress.

- **Built-in Test Bank for online assessment.** The Test Bank files are included in CengageNOWv2 so that they may be used as additional homework or tests.

Solutions Manual (978-1-337-38944-0)

Written by the **South-Western Federal Taxation** editors and authors, the Solutions Manual features solutions arranged in accordance with the sequence of chapter material.

Solutions to all homework items are tagged with their Estimated Time to Complete, Level of Difficulty, and Learning Objective(s), as well as the AACSB's and AICPA's core competencies—giving instructors more control than ever in selecting homework to match the topics covered. The Solutions Manual also contains the Solutions to Appendix E: Comprehensive Tax Return Problems and lettered answers (only) to the end-of-chapter Roger CPA Review Questions. **Available in print and on Instructor Companion Website at www.cengage.com/login.**

PowerPoint® Lectures with Notes

The Instructor PowerPoint® Lectures contain more than 30 slides per chapter, including outlines and instructor guides, concept definitions, and key points. **Available on Instructor Companion Website at www.cengage.com/login.**

Test Bank

Written by the **South-Western Federal Taxation** editors and authors, the Test Bank contains approximately 2,200 items and solutions arranged in accordance with the sequence of chapter material.

Each test item is tagged with its Estimated Time to Complete, Level of Difficulty, and Learning Objective(s), as well as the AACSB's and AICPA's core competencies—for easier instructor planning and test item selection. The 2018 Test Bank is available in Cengage's test generator software, Cognero.

Cengage Learning Testing Powered by Cognero is a flexible, online system that allows you to:

- author, edit, and manage Test Bank content from multiple Cengage Learning solutions
- create multiple test versions in an instant
- deliver tests from your LMS, your classroom, or wherever you want
- create tests from school, home, the coffee shop—anywhere with internet access (No special installs or downloads needed.)

Test Bank files in Word format as well as versions to import into your LMS are available on the Instructor Companion Website. **Cognero Test Banks available via single sign-on (SSO) account at www.cengage.com/login.**

Other Instructor Resources

All of the following instructor course materials are available online at www.cengage.com/login. Once logged into the site, instructors should select this textbook to access the online Instructor Resources.

- Instructor Guide
- Edition-to-edition correlation grids by chapter
- Detailed answer feedback for the end-of-chapter Roger CPA Review Questions in Word format (Lettered answers only are available in the Solutions Manual.)
- An appendix that helps instructors broaden and customize coverage of important tax provisions of the Affordable Care Act
- The Depreciation and the Accelerated Cost Recovery System (ACRS) appendix

Custom Solutions

Cengage Learning Custom Solutions develops personalized solutions to meet your taxation education needs. Consider the following for your adoption of **South-Western Federal Taxation 2018 Edition.**

- Remove chapters you do not cover or rearrange their order to create a streamlined and efficient text.
- Add your own material to cover new topics or information.
- Add relevance by including sections from Sawyers/Gill's *Federal Tax Research* or your state's tax laws and regulations.

ACKNOWLEDGMENTS

We want to thank all the adopters and others who participated in numerous online surveys as well as the following individuals who provided content reviews and feedback in the development of the **South-Western Federal Taxation** 2018 titles.

William H. Hoffman, Jr. / James C. Young / William A. Raabe / David M. Maloney / Annette Nellen

Lindsay G. Acker, *University of Wisconsin-Madison*

Deborah S. Adkins, *Nperspective, LLC*

Mark P. Altieri, *Kent State University*

Amy An, *University of Iowa*

Susan E. Anderson, *Elon University*

Henry M. Anding, *Woodbury University*

Jennifer A. Bagwell, *Ohio University*

George Barbi, *Lanier Technical College*

Terry W. Bechtel, *Texas A&M University – Texarkana*

Chris Becker, *LeMoyne College*

John G. Bell

Tamara Berges, *UCLA*

Ellen Best, *University of North Georgia*

Tim Biggart, *Berry College*

Rachel Birkey, *Illinois State University*

Patrick M. Borja, *Citrus College / California State University, Los Angeles*

Dianne H. Boseman, *Nash Community College*

Cathalene Bowler, *University of Northern Iowa*

Madeline Brogan, *Lone Star College – Montgomery*

Darryl L. Brown, *Illinois Wesleyan University*

Timothy G. Bryan, *University of Southern Indiana*

Robert S. Burdette, *Salt Lake Community College*

Ryan L. Burger, *Concordia University Nebraska*

Lisa Busto, *William Rainey Harper College*

Julia M. Camp, *Providence College*

Al Case, *Southern Oregon University*

Machiavelli W. Chao, *Merage School of Business University of California, Irvine*

Eric Chen, *University of Saint Joseph*

Christine Cheng, *Louisiana State University*

James Milton Christianson, *Southwestern University and Austin Community College*

Wayne Clark, *Southwest Baptist University*

Ann Burstein Cohen, *University at Buffalo, The State University of New York*

Ciril Cohen, *Fairleigh Dickinson University*

Dixon H. Cooper, *University of Arkansas*

Rick L. Crosser, *Metropolitan State University of Denver*

John P. Crowley, *Castleton University*

Richard G. Cummings, *University of Wisconsin-Whitewater*

Susan E. M. Davis, *South University*

Dwight E. Denman, *Newman University*

James M. DeSimpelare, *Ross School of Business at the University of Michigan*

John Dexter, *Northwood University*

James Doering, *University of Wisconsin – Green Bay*

Michael P. Donohoe, *University of Illinois at Urbana Champaign*

Deborah A. Doonan, *Johnson & Wales University*

Monique O. Durant, *Central Connecticut State University*

Wayne L. Edmunds, *Virginia Commonwealth University*

Rafi Efrat, *California State University, Northridge*

Charles R. Enis, *The Pennsylvania State University*

Frank J. Faber, St. Joseph's College

A. Anthony Falgiani, *University of South Carolina, Beaufort*

Jason Fiske, *Thomas Jefferson School of Law*

John Forsythe, *Eagle Gate College*

Alexander L. Frazin, *University of Redlands*

Carl J. Gabrini, *College of Coastal Georgia*

Kenneth W. Gaines, *East-West University, Chicago, Illinois*

Carolyn Galantine, *Pepperdine University*

Sheri Geddes, *Hope College*

Alexander Gelardi, *University of St. Thomas*

Daniel J. Gibbons, *Waubonsee Community College*

Martie Gillen, *University of Florida*

Charles Gnizak, *Fort Hays State University*

J. David Golub, *Northeastern University*

George G. Goodrich, *John Carroll University*

Marina Grau, *Houston Community College – Houston, TX*

Vicki Greshik, *University of Jamestown College*

Jeffrey S. Haig, *Santa Monica College*

Marcye S. Hampton, *University of Central Florida*

June Hanson, *Upper Iowa University*

Donald Henschel, *Benedictine University*

Susanne Holloway, *Salisbury University*

Susan A. Honig, *Herbert H. Lehman College*

Jeffrey L. Hoopes, *The Ohio State University*

Christopher R. Hoyt, *University of Missouri (Kansas City) School of Law*

Marsha M. Huber, *Youngstown State University*

Carol Hughes, *Asheville-Buncombe Technical Community College*

Helen Hurwitz, *Saint Louis University*

Richard R. Hutaff, *Wingate University*

Zite Hutton, *Western Washington University*

Brad Van Kalsbeek, *University of Sioux Falls*

John E. Karayan, *Woodbury University*

Carl Keller, *Missouri State University*

Cynthia Khanlarian, *Concord University*

Bob Kilpatrick, *Northern Arizona University*

Gordon Klein, *Lecturer, UCLA Anderson School*

Taylor Klett, *Sam Houston State University*

Aaron P. Knape, *Peru State College*

Cedric Knott, *Colorado State University – Global Campus*

Ausher M. B. Kofsky, *Western New England University*

Emil Koren, *Saint Leo University*

Jack Lachman, *Brooklyn College – CUNY*

Richard S. Leaman, *University of Denver*

Adena LeJeune, *Louisiana College*

Gene Levitt, *Mayville State University*

Teresa Lightner, *University of North Texas*

Sara Linton, *Roosevelt University*

Roger Lirely, *The University of Texas at Tyler*

Jane Livingstone, *Western Carolina University*

Heather Lynch, *Northeast Iowa Community College*

Michael J. MacDonald, *University of Wisconsin-Whitewater*

Mabel Machin, *Florida Institute of Technology*

Maria Alaina Mackin, *ECPI University*

Anne M. Magro, *George Mason University*

Richard B. Malamud, *California State University, Dominguez Hills*

Harold J. Manasa, *Winthrop University*

Barry R. Marks, *University of Houston – Clear Lake*

Dewey Martin, *Husson University*

Anthony Masino, *East Tennessee State University*

Norman Massel, *Louisiana State University*

Bruce W. McClain, *Cleveland State University*

Allison M. McLeod, *University of North Texas*

Meredith A. Menden, *Southern New Hampshire University*

Robert H. Meyers, *University of Wisconsin-Whitewater*
John G. Miller, *Skyline College*
Tracie L. Miller-Nobles, *Austin Community College*
Jonathan G. Mitchell, *Stark State College*
Richard Mole, *Hiram College*
Lisa Nash, *CPA, MA, Vincennes University*
Mary E. Netzler, *Eastern Florida State College*
Joseph Malino Nicassio, *Westmoreland County Community College*
Mark R. Nixon, *Bentley University*
Garth Novack, *Pantheon Heavy Industries & Foundry*
Claude R. Oakley, *DeVry University, Georgia*
Al Oddo, *Niagara University*
Sandra Owen, *Indiana University – Bloomington*
Vivian J. Paige, *Old Dominion University*
Carolyn Payne, *University of La Verne*
Ronald Pearson, *Bay College*
Thomas Pearson, *University of Hawaii at Manoa*
Nichole L. Pendleton, *Friends University*
Chuck Pier, *Angelo State University*
Lincoln M. Pinto, *DeVry University*
Sonja Pippin, *University of Nevada – Reno*
Steve Platau, *The University of Tampa*
Walfyette Powell, *Strayer University*
Dennis Price, *Samford University*
Darlene Pulliam, *West Texas A&M University*

John S. Repsis, *University of Texas at Arlington*
John D. Rice, *Trinity University*
Jennifer Hardwick Robinson, *Trident Technical College*
Shani N. Robinson, *Sam Houston State University*
Donald Roth, *Dordt College*
Richard L. Russell, *Jackson State University*
Robert L. Salyer, *Northern Kentucky University*
Rhoda Sautner, *University of Mary*
Bunney L. Schmidt, *Keiser University*
Eric D. Schwartz, *LaRoche College*
Tony L. Scott, *Norwalk Community College*
Randy Serrett, *University of Houston – Downtown*
Wayne Shaw, *Southern Methodist University*
Paul A. Shoemaker, *University of Nebraska – Lincoln*
Kimberly Sipes, *Kentucky State University*
Georgi Smatrakalev, *Florida Atlantic University*
Randy Smit, *Dordt College*
Leslie S. Sobol, *California State University Northridge*
Marc Spiegel, *University of California, Irvine*
Teresa Stephenson, *University of Wyoming*
Beth Stetson, *Oklahoma City University*
Debra Stone, *Eastern New Mexico University*
Frances A. Stott, *Bowling Green State University*
Todd S. Stowe, *Southwest Florida College*

Martin Stub, *DeVry University*
James Sundberg, *Eastern Michigan University*
Kent Swift, *University of Montana*
Robert L. Taylor, *Lees-McRae College*
Francis C. Thomas, *Richard Stockton College of New Jersey*
Randall R. Thomas, *Upper Iowa University*
Ronald R. Tidd, *Central Washington University*
MaryBeth Tobin, *Bridgewater State University*
James P. Trebby, *Marquette University*
James M. Turner, *Georgia Institute of Technology*
Anthony W. Varnon, *Southeast Missouri State University*
Adria Palacios Vasquez, *Texas A&M University – Kingsville*
Terri Walsh, *Seminole State College of Florida*
Marie Wang
Natasha R. Ware, *Southeastern University*
Mark Washburn, *Sam Houston State University*
Bill Weispfenning, *University of Jamestown (ND)*
Andrew L. Whitehair
Kent Williams, *Indiana Wesleyan University*
Candace Witherspoon, *Valdosta State University*
Sheila Woods, *DeVry University, Houston, TX*
Xinmei Xie, *Woodbury University*
Thomas Young, *Lone Star College – Tomball*

SPECIAL THANKS

We are grateful to the faculty members who have diligently worked through the problems and test questions to ensure the accuracy of the ***South-Western Federal Taxation*** homework, solutions manuals, test banks, and comprehensive tax form problems. Their comments and corrections helped us focus on clarity as well as accuracy and tax law currency. We also thank Thomson Reuters for its permission to use Checkpoint® with the text.

Sandra A. Augustine, *Hilbert College*
Bradrick M. Cripe, *Northern Illinois University*
Stephanie Lewis, *The Ohio State University*
Kate Mantzke, *Northern Illinois University*

Ray Rodriguez, *Murray State University*
George R. Starbuck, *McMurry University*
Donald R. Trippeer, *State University of New York College at Oneonta*

Raymond Wacker, *Southern Illinois University, Carbondale*
Michael Weissenfluh, *Tillamook Bay Community College*;

The South-Western Federal Taxation Series

To find out more about these books, go to www.cengagebrain.com.

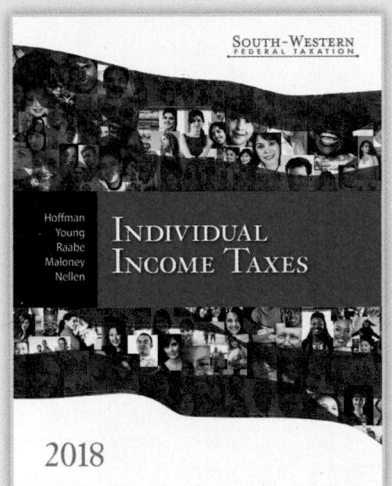

INDIVIDUAL INCOME TAXES, 2018 EDITION

(HOFFMAN, YOUNG, RAABE, MALONEY, NELLEN, Editors)
provides accessible, comprehensive, and authoritative coverage of the relevant tax code and regulations as they pertain to the individual taxpayer, as well as coverage of all major developments in Federal taxation.

(ISBN 978-1-337-38588-6)

CORPORATIONS, PARTNERSHIPS, ESTATES & TRUSTS, 2018 EDITION

(HOFFMAN, RAABE, YOUNG, NELLEN, MALONEY, Editors)
covers tax concepts as they affect corporations, partnerships, estates, and trusts. The authors provide accessible, comprehensive, and authoritative coverage of relevant tax code and regulations, as well as all major developments in Federal income taxation. This market-leading text is intended for students who have had a previous course in tax.

(ISBN 978-1-337-38594-7)

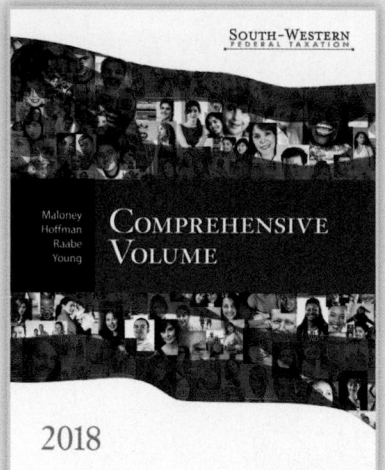

COMPREHENSIVE VOLUME, 2018 EDITION

(MALONEY, HOFFMAN, RAABE, YOUNG, Editors)
Combining the number one individual tax text with the number one corporations text, *Comprehensive Volume, 2018 Edition* is a true winner. An edited version of the first two **South-Western Federal Taxation** textbooks, this book is ideal for undergraduate or graduate levels. This text works for either a one-semester course in which an instructor wants to integrate coverage of individual and corporate taxation or for a two-semester sequence in which the use of only one book is desired.

(ISBN 978-1-337-38600-5)

ESSENTIALS OF TAXATION: INDIVIDUALS & BUSINESS ENTITIES, 2018 EDITION

(RAABE, YOUNG, NELLEN, MALONEY, Editors)
emphasizes tax planning and the multidisciplinary aspects of taxation. Formerly titled *Taxation of Business Entities*, this text is designed with the AICPA Model Tax Curriculum in mind, presenting the introductory Federal taxation course from a business entity perspective. Its **Tax Planning Framework** helps users fit tax planning strategies into an innovative pedagogical framework. The text is an ideal fit for programs that offer only one course in taxation where users need to be exposed to individual taxation, as well as corporate and other business entity taxation. This text assumes no prior course in taxation has been taken.

(ISBN 978-1-337-38617-3)

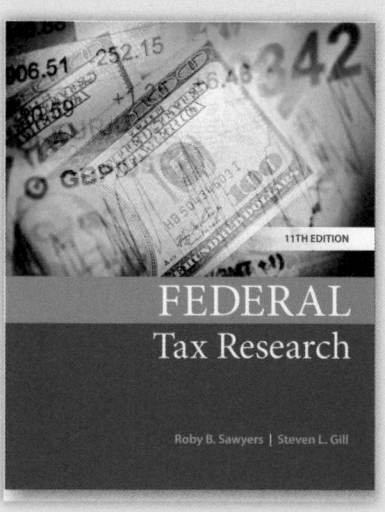

FEDERAL TAX RESEARCH, 11E

(SAWYERS AND GILL) *Federal Tax Research*, Eleventh Edition, offers hands-on tax research analysis and fully covers computer-oriented tax research tools. Also included in this edition is coverage on international tax research, a review of tax ethics, and many new real-life cases to help foster a true understanding of Federal tax law.

(ISBN 978-1-337-28298-7)

ABOUT THE EDITORS

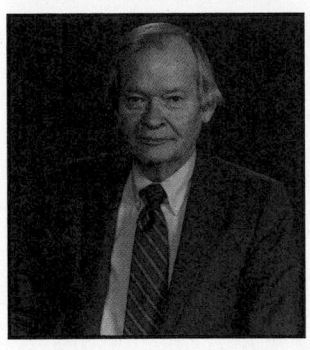

William H. Hoffman, Jr. earned B.A. and J.D. degrees from the University of Michigan and M.B.A. and Ph.D. degrees from The University of Texas. He was a licensed CPA and attorney in Texas. His teaching experience included The University of Texas (1957–1961), Louisiana State University (1961–1967), and the University of Houston (1967–1999). Professor Hoffman addressed many tax institutes and conferences and published extensively in academic and professional journals. His articles appeared in *The Journal of Taxation, The Tax Adviser, Taxes—The Tax Magazine, The Journal of Accountancy, The Accounting Review*, and *Taxation for Accountants.*

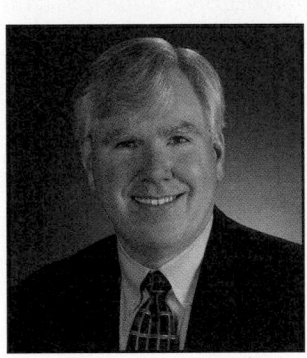

James C. Young is the Crowe Horwath Professor of Accountancy at Northern Illinois University. A graduate of Ferris State University (B.S.) and Michigan State University (M.B.A. and Ph.D.), Jim's research focuses on taxpayer responses to the income tax using archival data. His dissertation received the PricewaterhouseCoopers/American Taxation Association Dissertation Award and his subsequent research has received funding from a number of organizations, including the Ernst & Young Foundation Tax Research Grant Program. His work has been published in a variety of academic and professional journals, including the *National Tax Journal, The Journal of the American Taxation Association,* and *Tax Notes.* Jim is a Northern Illinois University Distinguished Professor, received the Illinois CPA Society Outstanding Accounting Educator Award in 2012, and has received university teaching awards from Northern Illinois University, George Mason University, and Michigan State University.

William A. Raabe, Ph.D., CPA, was the Wisconsin Distinguished Professor of Taxation. He taught at Ohio State, Arizona State, the Capital University (OH) Law School, and the Universities of Wisconsin – Milwaukee and Whitewater. A graduate of Carroll University (Wisconsin) and the University of Illinois, Dr. Raabe's teaching and research interests include international and multistate taxation, technology in tax education, personal financial planning, and the economic impact of sports teams and fine arts groups. Dr. Raabe also writes the PricewaterhouseCoopers Tax Case Studies. He has written extensively about book-tax differences in financial reporting. Dr. Raabe has been a visiting tax faculty member for a number of public accounting firms, bar associations, and CPA societies. He has received numerous teaching awards, including the Accounting Educator of the Year award from the Wisconsin Institute of CPAs. He has been the faculty adviser for student teams in the Deloitte Tax Case Competition (national finalists at three different schools) and the PricewaterhouseCoopers Extreme Tax policy competition (national finalist). For more information about Dr. Raabe, visit BillRaabeTax.com and BillRaabeTax on YouTube and Twitter.

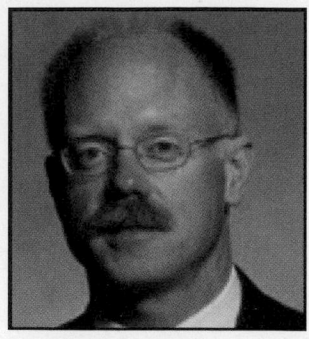

David M. Maloney, Ph.D., CPA, is the Carman G. Blough Professor of Accounting Emeritus at the University of Virginia's McIntire School of Commerce. He completed his undergraduate work at the University of Richmond and his graduate work at the University of Illinois at Urbana-Champaign. Upon joining the Virginia faculty in January 1984, Dr. Maloney taught Federal taxation in the graduate and undergraduate programs and was a recipient of major research grants from the Ernst & Young and KPMG Foundations. Dr. Maloney has published work in numerous professional journals, including *Journal of Taxation, The Tax Adviser, Tax Notes, Corporate Taxation, Accounting Horizons, Journal of Taxation of Investments,* and *Journal of Accountancy.*

Annette Nellen, CPA, CGMA, Esquire, directs San José State University's graduate tax program (MST) and teaches courses in tax research, tax fundamentals, accounting methods, property trans-actions, state taxation, employment tax, ethics, and tax policy. Professor Nellen is a graduate of CSU Northridge, Pepperdine (MBA), and Loyola Law School. Prior to joining SJSU in 1990, she was with a Big 4 firm and the IRS. At SJSU, Professor Nellen is a recipient of the Outstanding Professor and Distinguished Service Awards. Professor Nellen is an active member of the tax sections of the AICPA and American Bar Association. In 2013, she received the AICPA Arthur J. Dixon Memorial Award, the highest award given by the accounting profession in the area of taxation. Professor Nellen is the author of *BloombergBNA Tax Portfolio, Amortization of Intangibles,* and the *BloombergBNA Internet Law Resource Center, Overview of Internet Taxation Issues.* She has published numerous articles in the *AICPA Tax Insider, Tax Adviser, State Tax Notes,* and *The Journal of Accountancy.* She has testified before the House Ways & Means and Senate Finance Committees and other committees on Federal and state tax reform. Professor Nellen maintains the 21st Century Taxation website and blog (www.21stcenturytaxation.com) as well as websites on tax reform and state tax issues (www.sjsu.edu/people/annette.nellen/).

William H. Hoffman, Jr.

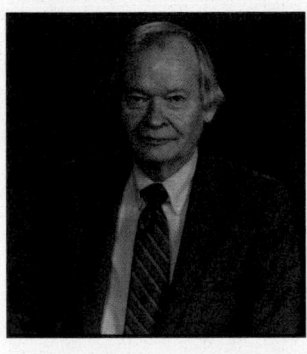

On May 1, 2016, our founding editor, valued colleague, and co-author Bill Hoffman, passed away after a brief illness. Bill was born in Casper, Wyoming, in 1929 and also lived in both Belgium and Argentina during his youth, before moving to Port Arthur, Texas. He earned both undergraduate and law degrees from the University of Michigan before serving in the Korean War as an officer in the U.S. Army's Judge Advocate General Corps. Following his return from military service, he completed both an MBA and a PhD at The University of Texas at Austin. Bill began his academic career at Louisiana State University, where he served as a professor of accounting and taxation, before moving to the University of Houston in 1967. Bill remained at Houston for the rest of his academic career, retiring in 1999.

During his time at Houston, Bill served as a professor, mentor, and doctoral advisor to countless students and colleagues. Desiring to help his students understand the intricacies of entity taxation (corporations, partnerships, and estates and trusts), he envisioned a new textbook for a second tax course in Houston's accounting program and brought together a team of authors to create the text in 1977. *South-Western Federal Taxation: Corporations, Partnerships, Estates and Trusts*—now in its forty-first edition—remains the market leader while continuing to evolve to meet the needs of twenty-first century faculty and students. The *Individual* and *Comprehensive* volumes followed shortly after the release of the *Corporations* volume, and the *Essentials* volume was added to the *SWFT Series* in 1997.

Over the past several months, we have heard from many former students and colleagues, who spoke of Bill's commitment to them, both in the classroom and in their lives, and to the tax profession at large. Here are a few of those comments.

- Through his writing and teaching, he was able to bring "to life" what could be a very challenging topic to many.

- The creation of the Corporations volume was driven by the fact that Bill needed material for his own class. This volume allowed many schools to create a second tax course and changed how accounting students prepared for a career in tax.

- Bill brought together an author team of both faculty *and* practitioners (both CPAs and attorneys); this created a unique tax series that emphasized both the law and its application. Over the years,

Bill consistently recruited new contributors, creating the strongest author team for business school tax texts.

- Bill was recognized in the profession as a dynamic and engaging teacher and was involved extensively in professional development seminars across the country.

- For me, Bill was many things, including professor, dissertation chair, mentor, editor, drinking buddy, and friend. One of my favorite memories of Bill is catching him at his desk, poring over a *BNA Daily Tax Report*, something he did unfailingly. I will miss our conversations and his keen tax insights.

- Bill was an innovator in the development of a new breed of textbooks that enabled professors to present taxation in a new and more relevant way. That pedagogy included especially the extensive use of teaching examples, forms problems, and advanced topics, so that the professor could tailor a course to local needs.

- Bill was a real pioneer in our field. His wit and enthusiasm were constant sources of amazement to me. He was always a mentor, and he shaped my academic career.

- He demanded excellence . . . and receiving a note affirming your work was truly something special.

- As my tax professor at LSU, Bill was the catalyst for my early development in tax research and writing. I owe a great deal of my success to Bill Hoffman's early advice, direction, and help. He was a tremendous writer, and he changed the teaching of taxation forever.

- He was a "giant" . . . he will be missed.

Although Bill loved the *SWFT Series* and the process of writing and creating its content, his first love was Bonnie, his wife of 64 years, and his family (which included five children and a number of grandchildren and great-grandchildren). Bonnie also made significant contributions to the *South-Western Federal Taxation Series* through the years (including keeping Bill "in line" as best she could). Together, they were an outstanding creative and editorial team.

We will miss Bill's sharp wit, his ability to clearly explain tax law (both verbally and in writing), the creativity he brought to his work, the scope of his tax knowledge, and his wonderful laugh. He truly enjoyed the competition created by rival textbooks, as he knew it would lead to a better *SWFT Series*. We will honor Bill by upholding the standards of excellence he demanded, as the *SWFT Series* continues to evolve.

Brief Contents

Part 5: Property Transactions

Part 6: Accounting Periods, Accounting Methods, and Deferred Compensation

Part 7: Corporations and Partnerships

Contents

CHAPTER 5
GROSS INCOME: EXCLUSIONS

Part 3: Deductions

CHAPTER 6
DEDUCTIONS AND LOSSES: IN GENERAL

Part 4: Special Tax Computation Methods, Payment Procedures, and Tax Credits

Part 5: Property Transactions

Part 6: Accounting Periods, Accounting Methods, and Deferred Compensation

Part 7: Corporations and Partnerships

APPENDIXES

Online Appendixes

PART 1

INTRODUCTION AND BASIC TAX MODEL

CHAPTER **1**
An Introduction to Taxation and Understanding the Federal Tax Law

CHAPTER **2**
Working with the Tax Law

CHAPTER **3**
Tax Formula and Tax Determination; An Overview of Property Transactions

Part 1 provides an introduction to taxation in the United States. Although this text focuses on income taxation, other types of taxes are also briefly discussed. The purposes of the Federal tax law are examined, and the legislative, administrative, and judicial sources of Federal tax law, including their application to the tax research process, are analyzed. Part 1 concludes by introducing the basic tax model for the individual taxpayer and providing an overview of property transactions.

CHAPTER

1

An Introduction to Taxation and Understanding the Federal Tax Law

LEARNING OBJECTIVES: *After completing Chapter 1, you should be able to:*

LO.1 Explain the importance of taxation.

LO.2 Describe some of the history and trends of the Federal income tax.

LO.3 Describe and apply principles and terminology relevant to the design of a tax system.

LO.4 Identify the different taxes imposed in the United States at the Federal, state, and local levels.

LO.5 Explain the administration of the tax law, including the audit process utilized by the IRS.

LO.6 Evaluate some of the ethical guidelines involved in tax practice.

LO.7 Recognize the economic, social, equity, and political considerations that justify various aspects of the tax law.

LO.8 Describe the role played by the IRS and the courts in the evolution of the Federal tax system.

FAMILY AND TAXES—A TYPICAL YEAR

Travis and Amy Carter are married and live in a state that imposes both a sales tax and an income tax. They have two children, April (age 17) and Martin (age 18). Travis is a mining engineer who specializes in land reclamation. After several years with a mining corporation, Travis established a consulting practice that involves a considerable amount of travel. Amy is a registered nurse who, until recently, was a homemaker. In November of this year, she decided to reenter the job market and accepted a position with a medical clinic. The Carters live only a few blocks from Ernest and Mary Walker, Amy Carter's parents. The Walkers are retired and live on interest, dividends, and Social Security benefits.

Various developments occurring during the year with possible tax ramifications are summarized below.

- The ad valorem property taxes on the Carters' residence are increased, while those on the Walkers' residence are lowered.

- When Travis registers an automobile purchased last year in another state, he is required to pay a sales tax to his home state.

- As an anniversary present, the Carters gave the Walkers a recreational vehicle (RV).

- When Travis made a consulting trip to Chicago, the client withheld Illinois state income tax from the payment made to Travis for his services.

- Travis employs his children to draft blueprints and prepare scale models for use in his work. Both April and Martin have had training in drafting and topography.

- Early in the year, the Carters are audited by the state on an income tax return filed a few years ago. Later in the year, they are audited by the IRS on a Form 1040 they filed for the same year. In each case, a tax deficiency and interest were assessed.

- The Walkers are audited by the IRS. Unlike the Carters, they did not have to deal with an agent, but settled the matter by mail.

Explain these developments and resolve the issues raised.

Read the chapter and formulate your response.

The primary objective of this chapter is to provide an overview of the Federal tax system. Among the topics discussed are the following:

- The importance and relevance of taxation and how to study taxation.
- A brief history of the Federal income tax.
- The types of taxes imposed at the Federal, state, and local levels.
- Some highlights of tax law administration.
- Tax concepts that help explain the reasons for various tax provisions.
- The influence the Internal Revenue Service (IRS) and the courts have had in the evolution of current tax law.

LO.1

Explain the importance of taxation.

1-1   APPROACHING THE STUDY OF TAXATION

1-1a   What Is Taxation?

> "Taxes are what we pay for civilized society."

This is a famous quote from U.S. Supreme Court Justice Oliver Wendell Holmes, Jr. (1841 to 1935).[1] It is engraved on the government building at 1111 Constitution Avenue in Washington, DC—headquarters of the Internal Revenue Service (IRS). This quote eloquently sums up the primary purpose of taxation—to raise revenue for government operations. Governments at all levels—national, state, and local—require funds for defense, protection (police and fire), education, roads, the court system, social services, and more. Various types of taxes provide the resources to pay for government services.

In addition, taxation is often used as a tool to influence the behavior of individuals and businesses. For example, an income tax credit (which reduces a taxpayer's tax bill) may be designed to *encourage* people to purchase a fuel-efficient car. A tobacco excise tax may *discourage* individuals from smoking by increasing the cost of tobacco products. The tax system can also be used to provide direct benefits to taxpayers, such as to help pay for health insurance.

1-1b   Taxation in Our Lives

> "Nothing is certain, except death and taxes."

Most people attribute this quote to Benjamin Franklin (1706 to 1790). Taxes permeate our society. Various types of taxes, such as income, sales, property, and excise taxes (discussed in text Section 1-4), come into play in many of the activities of individuals, businesses, nonprofit entities (like charitable organizations), and even governments.

Most directly, individuals are affected by taxes by paying them. Taxes may be paid directly or indirectly. A direct tax is paid to the government by the person who pays the tax. Examples include the personal income tax, which is paid by filing a personal income tax return (Form 1040 at the Federal level), and property taxes on one's home (paid to the local government). Individuals also pay many taxes indirectly. For example, most states impose sales tax on the purchase of tangible goods such as clothes. While this tax is collected and remitted to the government by the seller, the buyer is charged the tax along with the purchase price of the goods or services. Taxes also can be imposed indirectly when embedded in the prices charged by the seller. For example, when you buy gasoline for your car, the price you pay likely includes some of the income taxes and the gasoline excise taxes owed by the oil company.

Ultimately, all taxes are paid by individuals. The corporate income tax, for example, is paid directly by the corporation, but is really paid by individuals in their capacity as customers, investors (owners), or employees. Economists and others often study this topic to estimate the percentage of the corporate income tax borne by individuals in these

---

[1]*Compania General De Tabacos De Filipinas v. Collector of Internal Revenue*, 275 U.S. 87, 100 (1927), dissenting opinion.

different capacities. It is not easy to measure, but it is known that taxes are passed along to individuals through higher prices, lower wages, and/or lower dividends.

Taxes also affect the lives of individuals via the ballot box. Federal, state, and local elections often include initiatives that deal with taxation, such as whether state income taxes should be raised (or lowered), whether a new tax should be imposed on soda, or whether the sales tax rate should be changed. Candidates running for office often have positions on tax changes they would like to make, if elected.

Given the pervasiveness of taxation—in our roles as both direct and indirect payers of taxes, as well as citizens/voters—it is important that we understand how the tax system operates.

1-1c The Relevance of Taxation to Accounting and Finance Professionals

The top U.S. corporate income tax rate is 35 percent. State income taxes can easily constitute, on average, an additional 5 percent. So a large corporation such as a Fortune 500 company may have to devote up to 40 percent of its net income to pay income taxes. In addition, businesses are subject to employment taxes, property taxes, sales taxes, and various excise taxes. Corporations with international operations also are subject to taxation in other countries. Small businesses are also subject to a variety of taxes that affect profits and cash flows.

Given its significance, taxation is a crucial topic for accounting and finance professionals. They must understand the various types of business taxes to assist effectively with:

- *Compliance:* Ensure that the business files all tax returns and makes all tax payments on time. Mistakes will lead to penalties and interest expense.

- *Planning:* Help a business to apply favorable tax rules, such as income deferral and tax credits, to minimize tax liability (and maximize owner wealth). The time value of money concept is also important here, as is coordinating tax planning with other business goals to maximize earnings per share.

- *Controversy:* This term refers to interaction a taxpayer may have with a tax agency such as the IRS. The IRS and state and local tax agencies regularly audit tax returns that have been filed to verify that taxes were properly computed and paid.

- *Cash management:* Taxes must be paid on time to avoid penalties and interest. Income taxes must be estimated and paid quarterly and reconciled on the annual return. Other taxes may be due weekly, monthly, or semiannually. Businesses must be sure they have the funds ready when the taxes are due and have procedures to track due dates.

These tasks are also relevant to professionals such as CPAs who advise business and individual clients.

The level and depth of tax knowledge needed for any accounting or tax professional depends on his or her specific job. The vice president of tax for a company clearly needs thorough knowledge in all areas of taxation; the same is true of a partner in a CPA firm. In contrast, the corporate treasurer likely focuses more on cash management, working closely with the company's tax advisers.

Ultimately, much of taxation is transaction-based. How a transaction is structured (e.g., as a sale or a lease) has varying tax consequences that must be considered. Even the purchase of a home can result in significant change—the new mortgage interest and property tax deductions will likely mean that an individual itemizes her deductions (using Schedule A of Form 1040) rather than using the standard deduction. And life events such as marriage (and divorce) will change an individual's tax situation. Similar "life events" can also affect a corporation (e.g., acquiring a different corporation or spinning off a subsidiary).

It is essential in working with taxation to maintain a balanced perspective. A corporation that is deciding where to locate a new factory does not automatically select the city or state that offers the most generous tax benefits. Nor does the person who is retiring to a warmer climate pick Belize over Arizona because the former has no income tax while the latter does. Tax considerations should not control decisions, but they remain one of many factors to be considered (and often, one of the most significant).

1-1d **How to Study Taxation**

The goal of studying taxation is being able to recognize issues (or transactions) that have tax implications and, when possible, trying to understand the justification for them. Suppose, for example, that you come upon a situation that involves a discharge of indebtedness. If you know that forgiveness of debt results in income but there are exceptions to this rule, the battle is won! The issue has been identified, and the outcome (i.e., when an exception applies) can be resolved through research. A variety of commercial and free tools and resources are available to help you research and reach a conclusion.

You may have heard that tax is a difficult subject because of the many rules, exceptions, and definitions. You even may have heard that taxation is boring. Taxation *is* a challenging topic, but it is certainly not boring. Taxation is an important and exciting topic due to constant change by the three branches of our Federal government (as well as changes by state and local governments), the significance of taxes to the bottom line of a company and an individual's finances, and the impact on our economy and society.

Tax professionals tend to find enjoyment in their chosen field due to the intellectual challenge of dealing with tax rules for compliance and planning purposes, the opportunity to interact with colleagues or clients to help them understand the effect of taxes, and the knowledge that their work affects the financial well-being of individuals and businesses.

In studying taxation, focus on understanding the rules and the why(s) behind them (rather than memorizing the many isolated or disconnected rules and terms). The rules become more meaningful by thinking about why they exist for the particular type of tax. For example, why does the individual income tax allow for a casualty loss deduction? Why is tax depreciation different from that used for financial reporting? Also consider how the rules apply to different types of taxpayers (like employees, sole proprietors, corporations, investors, children, and retirees). Also think about how the rules apply to taxpayers of varying income levels and sophistication of transactions (a homeowner versus someone who owns assets in several countries). Aiming for understanding, rather than memorization, will make your journey into the world of taxation interesting and meaningful and will prepare you well for dealing with taxation in your accounting or finance career.

Concept Summary 1.1 illustrates the various ways that individuals deal with, and are affected by, taxes.

Concept Summary 1.1

Individuals and Taxes

The diagram to the right illustrates the many ways individuals interact with taxes. For example, as shown in the outer circle, individuals pay taxes and file tax returns (tax compliance). They also engage in tax planning as part of their desire to maximize after-tax wealth. If their tax return is audited, or they do not pay their taxes, taxpayers will deal with the IRS or their state tax agency (tax controversy). Individuals deal with tax rules and planning in their roles as consumers, employees, investors, and business owners. Tax law is designed around these various taxpayer activities. Finally, as shown by the inner circle, individuals have a personal responsibility to comply with tax laws and pay any taxes due. Individuals also have a civic responsibility to understand taxes in their role as citizens and voters. And, individuals need to understand how taxes affect their personal cash flows, consumption, and savings.

Use this diagram as you study the materials in this text, considering where in the circle various rules fit.

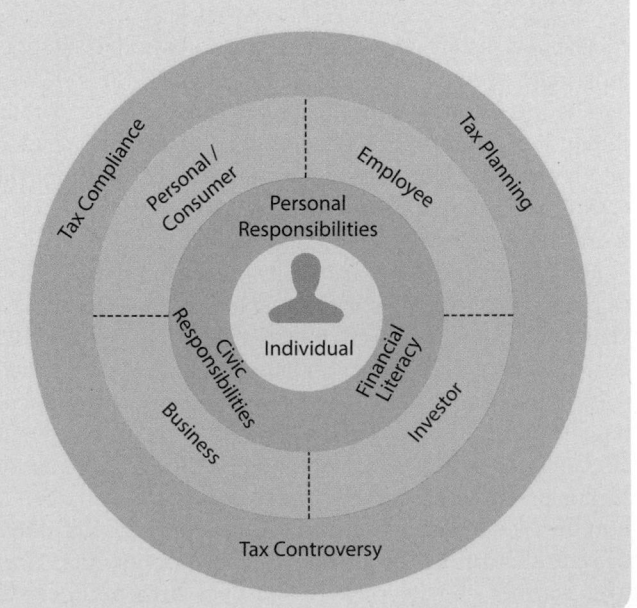

1-2 A BRIEF HISTORY OF U.S. TAXATION

LO.2

Describe some of the history and trends of the Federal income tax.

1-2a Early Periods

An income tax was first enacted in 1634 by the English colonists in the Massachusetts Bay Colony, but the Federal government did not adopt an income tax until 1861. In fact, both the Federal Union and the Confederate States of America used the income tax to raise funds to finance the Civil War.

When the Civil War ended, the need for additional revenue disappeared and the income tax was repealed. Once again the Federal government was able to finance its operations almost exclusively from customs duties (tariffs).

When a new Federal income tax on individuals was enacted in 1894, its opponents were prepared to successfully challenge its constitutionality. In *Pollock v. Farmers' Loan and Trust Co.*, the U.S. Supreme Court found that taxes on the income of real and personal property were the legal equivalent of a tax on the property involved and, therefore, required apportionment based on the population of the United States, as required by Article I, Section 8 of the Constitution.[2]

A Federal corporate income tax, enacted by Congress in 1909, fared better in the judicial system. The U.S. Supreme Court found this tax to be constitutional because it was treated as an excise tax.[3] In essence, it was a tax on the right to do business in the corporate form. So it was viewed as a form of the franchise tax.[4] Since the corporate form of doing business had been developed in the late nineteenth century, it was unknown to the framers of the U.S. Constitution. Because a corporation is an entity created under law, jurisdictions possess the right to tax its creation and operation. Using this rationale, many states still impose franchise taxes on corporations.

The ratification of the Sixteenth Amendment to the U.S. Constitution in 1913 sanctioned both the Federal individual and corporate income taxes and, as a consequence, neutralized the continuing effect of the *Pollock* decision.

1-2b Revenue Acts

After the Sixteenth Amendment was ratified by the states, Congress enacted the Revenue Act of 1913. Under this Act, the first Form 1040 was due on March 1, 1914. The law allowed various deductions and personal exemptions of $3,000 for a single individual and $4,000 for married taxpayers. These large exemptions excluded all but the more wealthy taxpayers from the new income tax.[5] Rates ranged from a low of 2 percent to a high of 6 percent. The 6 percent rate applied only to taxable income in excess of $500,000![6]

Various revenue acts were passed between 1913 and 1939. In 1939, all of these revenue laws were codified (arranged in a systematic manner) into the Internal Revenue Code of 1939. In 1954, a similar codification took place. The Internal Revenue Code of 1986, which largely carries over the provisions of the 1954 Code, is our current law. Tax law changes occur almost every year (how this happens is discussed in Chapter 2).

1-2c Historical Trends

The income tax is a major source of revenue for the Federal government. Exhibit 1.1 shows the tax revenue sources[7] and the importance of the income tax. Income tax collections from individuals and corporations amount to 61 percent of the total receipts. One revenue source missing from the Exhibit 1.1 pie chart is borrowing to cover the deficit, which in recent years has represented between 10 to 40 percent of total government revenues.

The need for revenues to finance the war effort during World War II converted the income tax into a *mass tax*. In 1939, less than 6 percent of the U.S. population was

---

[2]3 AFTR 2602, 15 S.Ct. 912 (USSC, 1895). See Chapter 2 for an explanation of the citations of judicial decisions.

[3]*Flint v. Stone Tracy Co.*, 3 AFTR 2834, 31 S.Ct. 342 (USSC, 1911).

[4]See the discussion of state franchise taxes later in text Section 1-4g.

[5]A $3,000 exemption in 1913 would be about $73,000 today, while a $4,000 exemption would be about $97,000.

[6]This should be contrasted with the highest 2017 tax rate of 39.6%, which applies once taxable income exceeds $418,400 for single taxpayers and $470,700 for married taxpayers filing a joint return.

[7]Revenue data can be found at **www.cbo.org** and **www.whitehouse.gov/omb**. The instruction booklet for Form 1040 includes a revenue pie chart that includes borrowing to cover the deficit, as well as a pie chart that shows government spending in broad categories.

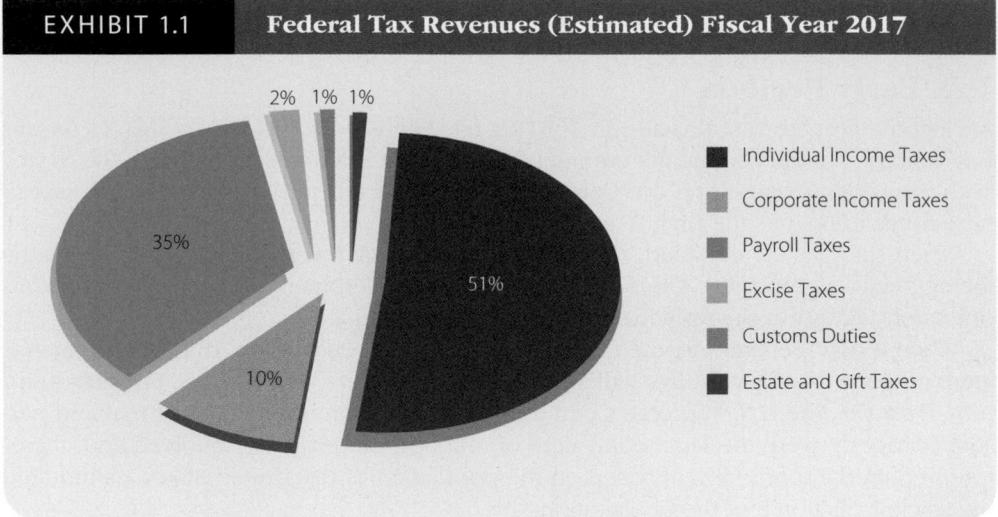

EXHIBIT 1.1   **Federal Tax Revenues (Estimated) Fiscal Year 2017**

- Individual Income Taxes
- Corporate Income Taxes
- Payroll Taxes
- Excise Taxes
- Customs Duties
- Estate and Gift Taxes

subject to the Federal income tax. By 1945, more than 74 percent of the population was subject to the Federal income tax.[8]

Certain tax law changes are important to understand. In 1943, Congress passed the Current Tax Payment Act, which provided for a pay-as-you-go tax system. A pay-as-you-go income tax system requires employers to withhold a specified portion of an employee's wages and remit them to the government to cover the worker's income taxes. Persons with income from other than wages may have to make quarterly payments to the IRS for estimated taxes due for the year.

Recently, the increasing complexity of the Federal income tax laws is causing concern. Congress has added to this complexity by frequently changing the tax laws, often adding new deductions or tax credits. This complexity forces many taxpayers to seek assistance in preparing their income tax returns. According to estimates, more than one-half of individual taxpayers who file a return pay a preparer, and one-third purchase tax software.[9]

1-3   TAX SYSTEM DESIGN

LO.3

Describe and apply principles and terminology relevant to the design of a tax system.

1-3a   Legal Foundation

Article I, Section 8 of the U.S. Constitution states in part: "The Congress shall have power to lay and collect taxes." The Constitution also provided some limits on this taxing power, which led to enactment of the Sixteenth Amendment to allow for an income tax (discussed in text Section 1-2a). This history lesson is important for a legislature or an electorate that wants to change a tax system. The jurisdiction's underlying governing documents (whether a country, state, or city) must be reviewed to determine whether they impose any restriction relevant to taxation.

For example, the California Constitution (Article 13A) states that the maximum tax rate for real property taxation is 1 percent. The Florida Constitution (Section 5) specifies limits on the imposition of income taxes on natural persons. Also, state law may impose limitations on the types or amounts of taxes that cities and counties can impose.

Thus, the governing documents of a jurisdiction must be considered as part of any effort to modify that jurisdiction's tax system to make sure the change is permissible. If a change is not permissible but desired, then the governing document must be amended, as was done with the addition of the Sixteenth Amendment to the U.S. Constitution.

---

[8]Richard Goode, *The Individual Income Tax* (Washington, D.C.: The Brookings Institution, 1964), pp. 2–4.

[9]The Tax Foundation estimates that individual taxpayers spend over $20 billion and devote about 1.35 billion hours in preparing their tax returns.

1-3b **The Basic Tax Formula**

The basic formula for any tax is:

Tax base → **X** → Tax rate → **=** → Tax liability

Tax Base

A tax base is the amount to which the tax rate is applied. In the case of the Federal income tax, the tax base is *taxable income*. As noted later in the chapter (Exhibit 1.3), taxable income is gross income reduced by certain deductions (both business and personal).

Tax Rates

Tax rates are applied to the tax base to determine a taxpayer's liability. The tax rates may be proportional or progressive. A tax is *proportional* if the rate of tax remains constant for any given income level. Examples of proportional taxes include most excise taxes, general sales taxes, and employment taxes (FICA and FUTA).

Assume that a jurisdiction applies a 30% tax rate to all taxable income. If Bill has $10,000 of taxable income, he will pay a tax of $3,000. If Sam has taxable income of $50,000, he will pay a tax of $15,000. If this constant rate is applied throughout the rate structure, the tax is *proportional*.

EXAMPLE 1

A tax is *progressive* if a higher rate of tax applies as the tax base increases. The Federal income tax, Federal gift and estate taxes, and most state income tax rate structures are progressive.

If Bill and Cora, a married couple filing jointly, have taxable income of $15,000, their Federal income tax for 2017 is $1,500 for an average tax rate of 10%. If, however, Bill and Cora's taxable income is $80,000, their Federal income tax will be $11,478 for an average tax rate of 14.3%. The tax is *progressive* because higher rates are applied to greater amounts of taxable income (see Appendix A to confirm these calculations, and note how progressivity is built into the Federal income tax).

EXAMPLE 2

The basic tax formula is relevant for both computing taxes and planning to reform a tax system. For example, if a legislator wants to lower tax rates but generate the same amount of tax revenues, the tax base must be increased. However, if she wants to increase tax revenues, the tax base can be increased *or* tax rates can be increased (or both can be increased). Changes to the tax base will depend on how it is constructed. For example, the income tax base is taxable income (income minus income exclusions minus deductions). To increase this tax base, income exclusions could be eliminated or deductions could be limited. The details of the income tax base are discussed in later chapters. Tax system changes also involve canons (or principles) of taxation, discussed next.

1-3c **Tax Principles**

In the late 1700s Adam Smith identified the following *canons (or principles) of taxation*, which are still considered today when evaluating a particular tax structure:[10]

- *Equity*. Each taxpayer enjoys fair or equitable treatment by paying taxes in proportion to his or her income level. Ability to pay a tax is one of the measures of how equitably a tax is distributed among taxpayers.
- *Certainty*. A tax should be certain rather than arbitrary. Taxpayers need to be able to understand how tax rules work so that they understand the effect of the rules on various transactions and can comply.

---

[10]*The Wealth of Nations* (New York: Dutton, 1910), Book V, Chapter II, Part II.

- *Convenience of payment.* Taxes should be imposed in a manner that involves a convenient time for payment. An advantage of the existing withholding system (pay-as-you-go) is its convenience for taxpayers.
- *Economy in collection.* A *good* tax system involves only nominal collection costs by the government and minimal compliance costs on the part of the taxpayer.

The American Institute of Certified Public Accountants (AICPA) has issued suggestions to guide tax reform and policy activities. Titled *Guiding Principles of Good Tax Policy: A Framework for Evaluating Tax Proposals*, the monograph identifies 12 principles that are commonly used as indicators of desirable tax policy. The first four principles are adapted from Adam Smith's *The Wealth of Nations*. The complete list follows.[11]

1. *Equity and Fairness.* Tax similarly situated taxpayers in a similar manner.
2. *Certainty.* Taxpayers should have certainty rather than ambiguity as to when and how a tax is paid, as well as how to calculate it.
3. *Convenience of Payment.* A tax should be due at a time and manner that is most convenient for the taxpayer.
4. *Effective Tax Administration.* Tax compliance and administrative costs should be kept to a minimum.
5. *Information Security.* Taxpayer information must be protected from improper disclosure.
6. *Simplicity.* Tax rules should be simple so that taxpayers understand them and can follow them in a cost-efficient manner.
7. *Neutrality.* The effect of tax rules on taxpayer decision making should be kept to a minimum.
8. *Economic Growth and Efficiency.* The tax system should not harm economic growth or distort economic effects among different activities and investments.
9. *Transparency and Visibility.* Taxpayers should know that a tax exists and how and when it applies to them.
10. *Minimum Tax Gap.* A tax should be structured to minimize noncompliance.
11. *Accountability to Taxpayers.* Taxpayers should have access to information on taxes, as well as proposed law changes and their rationale.
12. *Appropriate Government Revenues.* Tax rules should enable the government to predict the amount and timing of revenue production.

Exhibit 1.2 provides an application of these principles to a proposed tax law change.

LO.4

Identify the different taxes imposed in the United States at the Federal, state, and local levels.

1-4 MAJOR TYPES OF TAXES

Why does a text devoted primarily to the Federal individual income tax discuss state and local taxes? A simple illustration demonstrates the importance of non-Federal taxes.

EXAMPLE 3

Rick is employed by Flamingo Corporation in San Antonio, Texas, at a salary of $74,000. Rick's employer offers him a chance to transfer to its New York City office at a salary of $94,000.

Although Rick must consider many nontax factors before he decides on a job change, he should also evaluate the tax climate. How do state and local taxes compare? For example, neither Texas nor San Antonio imposes an income tax, but New York State and New York City do. A quick computation indicates that the additional income taxes (Federal, state, and local) involve approximately $12,000.

Consequently, what appears to be a $20,000 pay increase is actually only about $8,000 when the additional $12,000 of income taxes are taken into account. Other taxes and costs (e.g., sales taxes, property taxes, food, utilities, transportation) will also have to be factored into a decision.

---

[11]AICPA, *Guiding Principles of Good Tax Policy: A Framework for Evaluating Tax Proposals*, 2017. Similarly, see GAO, *Understanding the Tax Reform Debate: Background, Criteria, & Questions*, 2005. As "long-standing criteria," the GAO lists "equity; economic efficiency; and a combination of simplicity, transparency, and administrability."

EXHIBIT 1.2	Application of the *Guiding Principles of Good Tax Policy*

The *Guiding Principles of Good Tax Policy* can be applied to evaluate an existing tax rule or a proposed change. Here is an example of how the principles apply to a state's proposal to exempt college textbooks from sales tax.

Principle	Application	Result
Equity and fairness	While all college students would pay no sales tax on their textbooks, the effect varies among students based on their ability to pay. This proposal provides tax savings not only to lower-income students but also to higher-income students who may not need the tax break to cover school costs. Also, higher-income students might buy full-price new books rather than lower-cost used books, resulting in larger tax savings.	Not fully met
Certainty	College textbooks can be identified, such as by looking at what is listed on a course syllabus.	Met
Convenience of payment	A sales tax exemption generally means that the tax is not owed at the time of purchase. If, instead, the exemption is structured for the student to pay the sales tax and apply for a refund later, convenience of payment would not be met.	Met
Effective tax administration	Sellers will have additional record keeping and reporting requirements to separate tax-exempt textbook sales from taxable sales. Some type of system is needed to prove that the buyer is a student purchasing a book for a college class. The state tax agency will incur additional time and costs in writing rules, modifying tax forms, and auditing compliance with the new rule.	Not met
Information security	If obtaining the exemption requires students show proof to retailers that they are a student, there should be no need to provide a Social Security number. If students are required to claim the exemption with the state tax agency after purchasing the textbooks, the agency might request a student's Social Security number, which could increase the risk of identity theft.	Likely met
Simplicity	"Textbook" needs to be defined. The intent of the exemption is to benefit students. The seller needs to verify that the book is for use by a student for a class. For example, both students and nonstudents might buy a copy of *Romeo and Juliet*. Only the student purchasing it for a college class is entitled to the sales tax exemption. Complexity exists in the procedures needed to ensure that the exemption is used properly.	Not met
Neutrality	Students purchase textbooks because they are needed for class. The exemption is unlikely to change a student's behavior.	Met
Economic growth and efficiency	The exemption will reduce costs of attending college by a small amount. As a result, the change is unlikely to result in a greater number of college graduates (which might benefit the economy). Savings from not paying sales tax might be spent on other consumables. The impact on the economy is likely minor.	Met
Transparency and visibility	Students and textbook sellers are likely to be aware of the exemption because colleges will promote it as a reduction in the cost of attending college.	Met
Minimum tax gap	Students may abuse the rule by using the exemption for books that are not for class use. Nonstudents may abuse this rule by claiming they are a college student.	Not met
Accountability to taxpayers	Were students and universities, particularly those funded by the state, aware of the textbook sales tax exemption proposal? Students and universities could provide information to legislators on whether there is a need for a sales tax exemption or if other financial support would be more helpful. Bookstores would want an opportunity to provide information on the compliance costs and challenges of the exemption.	More information needed
Appropriate government revenue	Existing data on how many textbooks are purchased enables the government to estimate how much tax revenues will decrease due to the new exemption.	Met

Conclusion: While the majority of the principles are met, the ones that are not met (effective tax administration, simplicity, and minimum tax gap) are significant. If lawmakers believe this tax exemption is necessary to help lower costs for college students, they should consider alternative means of achieving the goal that are less complex. For example, grants could be offered or increased for college students in need of financial assistance.

1-4a **Property Taxes**

Correctly referred to as **ad valorem taxes** because they are based on value, property taxes are a tax on wealth, or capital. As a result, they have much in common with estate taxes and gift taxes discussed later in the chapter. Although property taxes do not tax income, the income actually derived (or the potential for any income) may be relevant if it affects the value of the property being taxed.

Property taxes fall into *two* categories: those imposed on real property (land and buildings) and those imposed on personal property (assets other than land and buildings). Both have added importance because they usually generate a deduction for Federal income tax purposes (see Chapter 10).

Ad Valorem Taxes on Real Property

Property taxes on real property are used exclusively by states and their local subdivisions (such as cities, counties, and school districts). They represent a major source of revenue for *local* governments (and school districts).

How real property is defined can have an important bearing on which assets are subject to tax. This is especially true in jurisdictions that do not impose ad valorem taxes on personal property. Real property, or, realty, generally includes real estate and any fixtures. A *fixture* is something so permanently attached to the real estate that its removal will cause irreparable damage. A built-in bookcase is likely a fixture, while a movable bookcase is not. Electrical wiring and plumbing become realty when they are installed in a building.

Here are some of the characteristics of ad valorem taxes on real property:

- Property owned by the Federal government is exempt from tax. In general, the same is true for property owned by state and local governments and by charitable organizations.

- Some states provide for lower valuations on property used for agriculture or other special uses (e.g., wildlife sanctuaries).

- States may have a homestead exemption, which makes some portion of the value of a personal residence exempt from tax.

- Lower taxes may apply to a residence owned by a taxpayer aged 65 or older.

- When non-income-producing property (e.g., a personal residence) is converted to income-producing property (e.g., a rental house), the appraised value may be increased.

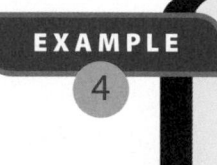

The Big Picture

EXAMPLE 4

Return to the facts of *The Big Picture* on p. 1-1. Why did the Walkers' property taxes decrease while those of the Carters increased?

A likely explanation is that one (or both) of the Walkers achieved senior citizen status, leading to a reduction of the taxes. In the case of the Carters, the assessed value of their property was probably increased (see the following discussion). Or perhaps they made significant home improvements (e.g., kitchen/bathroom renovation or addition of a deck).

In some states, property taxes have increased dramatically over the years. States have responded by either freezing the property tax valuations of personal residences or limiting their valuation increases in some way. However, these restrictions do not carry over to the new owner when the property is sold. As a result, these measures tend to lock in ownership and restrict the mobility of those who might otherwise change residences.

Ad Valorem Taxes on Personal Property

Personal property, or personalty, can be defined as all property that is not realty. There is a difference between how property is *classified* (realty or personalty) and how it is *used*. Both realty and personalty can be either business use or personal use property. Examples include a residence (realty that is personal use), an office building (realty that is business use), surgical instruments (personalty that is business use), and home furniture (personalty that is personal use).[12]

Personal property can also be classified as tangible property or intangible property. For ad valorem tax purposes, intangible personalty includes stocks, bonds, and various other securities (e.g., bank shares).

---

[12]The distinction, important for ad valorem and for Federal income tax purposes, often becomes confused when personalty is referred to as "personal" property to distinguish it from "real" property. This designation does not give a complete picture of what is involved. The description "personal" residence, however, is clearer, because a residence can be identified as being realty. What is meant in this case is realty that is personal use property.

Here are some general rules related to ad valorem taxes on personal property:

- Generally, vehicles (cars and boats, for example) are the only non-realty personal use assets subject to property tax. The value of a vehicle is typically established by a schedule based on its age and make/model (a high-priced car versus a low-priced car). Usually, any vehicle property tax is assessed and collected along with vehicle license or registration fees.

- Which jurisdiction has the authority to tax goods on rail cars (called railroad rolling stock) or on semitrailers continues to be a difficult issue.

- A few states levy an ad valorem tax on intangibles such as stocks and bonds.

1-4b **Transaction Taxes**

Transaction taxes, imposed at the manufacturer's, wholesaler's, or retailer's level, cover a wide range of transfers. Transaction taxes can be assessed by any taxing authority (Federal, state, or local government). As the description implies, these taxes cover transfers of property and normally are determined by multiplying the value by a percentage rate.

Federal Excise Taxes

In general, Federal excise taxes cover fewer items than in the past. Congress has focused (and substantially increased) the Federal excise taxes on items such as tobacco products, fuel and gasoline sales, and air travel. Other Federal excise taxes include:

- Manufacturers' excise taxes on trucks, trailers, tires, firearms, sporting equipment, medical devices, and coal and the gas guzzler tax on automobiles.[13]

- Alcohol taxes.

- Miscellaneous taxes (e.g., the tax on wagering).

When reviewing the list of both Federal and state excise taxes, recognize that these taxes may be trying to influence social behavior. For example, the gas guzzler tax is intended as an incentive for an individual to buy (and for the automobile companies to build) fuel-efficient cars.

State and Local Excise Taxes

Many state and local excise taxes parallel the Federal version. For example, all states tax the sale of gasoline, liquor, and tobacco products. However, the rates vary significantly. For gasoline products, for example, compare the 42.35 cents per gallon imposed by the state of California with the 17.3 cents per gallon levied by the state of Missouri. For tobacco sales, contrast the 17 cents per pack of 20 cigarettes in effect in Missouri with the $4.35 per pack in the state of New York.

Other excise taxes found at some state and local levels include those on admission to amusement facilities, on the sale of playing cards, and on prepared foods. Some counties impose a transaction tax on the transfer of property that requires the recording of documents (e.g., real estate sales).

Over the last few years, two types of excise taxes imposed at the local level have become increasingly popular: the hotel occupancy tax and the rental car "surcharge." The hotel occupancy tax is called a transient occupancy tax (TOT) in some areas. This tax can also apply to short-term rentals of one's home or a room in the home (such as via Airbnb). Because they tax the visitor who cannot vote, they are a political windfall and are often used to finance special projects that generate civic pride (e.g., convention centers and state-of-the-art sports arenas). These levies can be significant, as demonstrated by Houston's hotel tax of 17 percent [6 percent (state) + 7 percent (city) + 2 percent (county) + 2 percent (sports authority)].

---

[13]The gas guzzler tax is imposed on the manufacturers of automobiles (both domestic and foreign) with fuel economy under 22.5 miles per gallon. For example, a 2016 Bentley Continental GTC manages about 18 miles per gallon in combined city/highway driving and costs over $200,000. The gas guzzler tax on this vehicle is $2,600. The highest gas guzzler tax is $7,700 imposed on vehicles achieving less than 12.5 mpg. § 4064.

General Sales Taxes

The distinction between an excise tax and a general sales tax is easy to make. One is restricted to a particular transaction (e.g., the 18.4 cents per gallon Federal excise tax on the sale of gasoline), while the other covers a multitude of transactions (e.g., a 5 percent tax on *all* retail sales). In actual practice, however, the distinction is not always that clear. Some states exempt certain items from the general sales taxes (e.g., groceries, medicines, and drugs). Also, sales tax rates can vary. Many states, for example, allow lower rates for the sale of agricultural equipment or prescription drugs or apply different rates (either higher or lower than the general rate) to the sale of automobiles.

A use tax is a complement to the sales tax and is assessed at the same rate as the sales tax. A use tax is owed on property purchased outside the state but used in the state. The purpose of a use tax is to prevent the avoidance of a sales tax. For example, if you purchase clothes online and are not charged sales tax but clothes are subject to sales tax in your state, you owe use tax on the purchase. State rules vary on how use tax is collected. Many states allow individuals to pay it along with their state income tax. Alaska, Delaware, Montana, New Hampshire, and Oregon do not impose sales or use taxes. There is no Federal general sales or use tax.

The Big Picture

EXAMPLE 5

Return to the facts of *The Big Picture* on p. 1-1. The payment Travis made when he registered the car is probably a use tax.

When the car was purchased in another state, likely no (or a lesser) sales tax was levied. The current payment makes up for the amount of sales tax he would have paid had the car been purchased in his home state.

ETHICS & EQUITY   Making Good Use of Out-of-State Relatives

Marcus, a resident of Austin, Texas, has found the ideal gift for his wife in celebration of their upcoming wedding anniversary—a $22,000 diamond tennis bracelet. However, Marcus is appalled at the prospect of paying the state and local sales tax of $1,815 (combined rate of 8.25 percent). He, therefore, asks his aunt, a resident of Montana, to purchase the bracelet. The jewelry store lists the aunt as the buyer and ships the bracelet to her, with no sales tax owed on the transaction. Prior to the anniversary, Marcus receives the bracelet from his aunt. Is Marcus able to save $1,815 on the present for his wife? What can go wrong?

Local general sales taxes, over and above state sales taxes, are common. It is not unusual to find taxpayers living in the same state but paying different general sales taxes due to the location of their residence.

EXAMPLE 6

Pete and Sam both live in a state that has a general sales tax of 3%. Sam, however, resides in a city that imposes an additional general sales tax of 2%. Even though Pete and Sam live in the same state, one is subject to a rate of 3%, while the other pays a tax of 5%.

For various reasons, some jurisdictions will suspend the application of a general sales tax for a specified, brief time period. For example, a state may have a "sales tax holiday" in late summer for back-to-school clothing and supplies. Some states use sales tax holidays to encourage the purchase of energy-conserving appliances and hurricane preparedness items.

Severance Taxes

Severance taxes are transaction taxes that are based on the notion that the state has an interest in its natural resources (e.g., oil, gas, iron ore, or coal). Therefore, a tax is imposed when the natural resources are extracted. For some states, severance taxes can be a significant source of revenue.

1-4c Taxes on Transfers at Death

The right to transfer property or to receive property upon the death of the owner may be subject to estate and/or inheritance taxes. Consequently, such taxes fall into the category of excise taxes. An **estate tax** is levied on the estate of the decedent (it is a tax on the right to pass property at death). An **inheritance tax** is levied on the person receiving the property (the heir). The value of the property transferred provides the base for determining the amount of the tax.

The Federal government imposes only an estate tax. Some state governments, however, levy inheritance taxes, estate taxes, or both. Some states (e.g., Florida and Texas) levy neither tax.

At the time of her death, Wilma lived in a state that imposes an inheritance tax but not an estate tax. Mary, one of Wilma's heirs, lives in the same state. Wilma's estate is subject to the Federal estate tax, and Mary is subject to the state inheritance tax.

EXAMPLE 7

The Federal Estate Tax

The Revenue Act of 1916 incorporated the estate tax into the tax law. The tax was originally intended to prevent large concentrations of wealth from being kept in a family for many generations. Whether this objective has been accomplished is debatable. Like the income tax, estate taxes can be reduced through various planning procedures.

The gross estate includes property the decedent owned at the time of death.[14] It also includes property interests, such as life insurance proceeds paid to the estate. All property included in the gross estate is valued as of the date of death or, if the alternate valuation date is elected, six months later.[15]

Deductions from the gross estate in arriving at the taxable estate include funeral and administration expenses; certain taxes; debts of the decedent; casualty losses[16] incurred during the administration of the estate; transfers to charitable organizations; and, in some cases, the marital deduction. The *marital deduction* is available for amounts actually passing to a surviving spouse (a widow or widower).

Once the taxable estate has been determined and certain taxable gifts made by the decedent during life have been added to it, the estate tax can be computed. From this amount, various credits are subtracted to arrive at the tax, if any, that is due.[17] The most significant credit is the *unified transfer tax credit*. The main reason for this credit is to eliminate or reduce the estate tax liability for certain estates. For 2017, the credit exempts a tax base of up to $5.49 million, meaning that the vast majority of estates pass tax-free to the heirs.

Ned made no taxable gifts before his death in 2017. If Ned's taxable estate amounts to $5.49 million or less, no Federal estate tax is due because of the application of the unified transfer tax credit.

EXAMPLE 8

State Taxes on Transfers at Death

As noted earlier, some states levy an inheritance tax, an estate tax, or both. Typically, a state inheritance tax divides the heirs into classes based on their relationship to the decedent. The more closely related the heir, the lower the rates imposed and/or the greater the exemption allowed. Some states allow amounts passing to a surviving spouse to escape taxation.

---

[14]For further information on these matters, see *South-Western Federal Taxation: Corporations, Partnerships, Estates & Trusts*.

[15]See the discussion of the alternate valuation date in Chapter 14.

[16]For a definition of *casualty losses*, see the Glossary in Appendix C.

[17]For tax purposes, it is crucial to appreciate the difference between a deduction and a credit. A *credit* is a dollar-for-dollar reduction of tax liability. A *deduction*, however, benefits the taxpayer only to the extent of his or her tax bracket. A taxpayer in a 50% tax bracket, for example, would need $2 of deductions to prevent $1 of tax liability. In contrast, $1 of credit neutralizes $1 of tax liability.

1-4d **Gift Taxes**

Like taxes on transfers at death, a **gift tax** is an excise tax levied on property transfers made during the owner's life and not at death. If the recipient pays the donor for the property (but at an amount less than its fair market value), the difference is a gift.

EXAMPLE 9

Carl sells property worth $50,000 to his daughter for $1,000. Although property worth $50,000 has been transferred, only $49,000 represents a gift, because this is the portion that was not paid for.

The Federal Gift Tax

First enacted in 1932, the Federal gift tax was intended to complement the estate tax. If lifetime transfers by gift were not taxed, it would be possible to avoid the estate tax and escape taxation entirely.

Only taxable gifts are subject to the gift tax. For this purpose, a taxable gift is measured by the fair market value of the property on the date of transfer less the *annual exclusion per donee* and, in some cases, less the *marital deduction*, which allows tax-free transfers between spouses. In 2016 and 2017, each donor is allowed an annual exclusion of $14,000 for each donee.[18]

EXAMPLE 10

On December 31, 2016, Louise (a widow) gives $14,000 to each of her four married children, their spouses, and her eight grandchildren. On January 2, 2017, she repeats the procedure, again giving $14,000 to each recipient.

Due to the annual exclusion, Louise has not made a taxable gift, although she transferred $224,000 [$14,000 (annual exclusion) × 16 (donees)] in 2016 and $224,000 [$14,000 (annual exclusion) × 16 (donees)] in 2017, for a total of $448,000 ($224,000 + $224,000).

A married couple may make a special election that allows one-half of the gift made by the donor-spouse to a third party to be treated as being made by the nondonor-spouse. This *gift splitting* effectively allows the annual exclusion to double.

The Big Picture

EXAMPLE 11

Return to the facts of *The Big Picture* on p. 1-1. Although the value of the RV is not stated, it is highly likely to exceed the annual exclusion allowed of $56,000 [$14,000 (annual exclusion) × two donees (the Walkers) × two donors (the Carters)].

As a result, a taxable gift results, and a Form 709 (Gift Tax Return) must be filed. Whether any gift tax is due depends on what past taxable gifts the Carters have made and how much of their unified transfer tax credit (see the following discussion) is still available.

The gift tax and estate tax rate schedules are the same. The schedule is commonly referred to as the *unified transfer tax rate schedule*.

The Federal gift tax is *cumulative* in effect. What this means is that the tax base for current taxable gifts includes past taxable gifts. Although a credit is allowed for prior gift taxes, the result of adding past taxable gifts to current taxable gifts could force the donor into a higher tax bracket.[19] Like the Federal estate tax rates, the Federal gift tax rates are progressive (see Example 2 earlier in this chapter).

The unified transfer tax credit is available for all taxable gifts. As was the case with the Federal estate tax, the credit for 2017 is $2,141,800 (which covers taxable gifts up to $5,490,000) and for 2016 is $2,125,800 (which covers taxable gifts up to

---

[18]The purpose of the annual exclusion is to avoid the need to report and pay a tax on *modest* gifts. Without the exclusion, the IRS could face a real problem of taxpayer noncompliance. The annual exclusion is indexed as the level of inflation warrants. The exclusion was $13,000 from 2009 through 2012.

[19]For further information on the Federal gift tax, see *South-Western Federal Taxation: Corporations, Partnerships, Estates & Trusts*, Chapter 18.

$5,450,000). There is, however, only one unified transfer tax credit, and it applies to both taxable gifts and the Federal estate tax. Once the unified transfer tax credit has been used up for Federal gift tax purposes, any transfers at death will be subject to the Federal estate tax.

Making lifetime gifts of property carries several tax advantages over passing the property at death. If income-producing property is involved (e.g., marketable securities and rental real estate), a gift may shift subsequent income to donees in a lower income tax bracket. If the gift involves property that is expected to appreciate in value (e.g., life insurance policies, real estate, and artwork), future increases in value will be assigned to the donee and will not be included in the donor's estate. And due to the annual exclusion ($14,000 per donee in 2017), some of the gift can escape tax (with gift-splitting, married donors can double the annual exclusion).

Neither the actual receipt of a gift nor an inheritance will cause income tax consequences to the donee or heir.

1-4e Income Taxes

Income taxes are levied by the Federal government, most states, and some local governments. Income taxes generally are imposed on individuals, corporations, and certain fiduciaries (estates and trusts). Most jurisdictions attempt to ensure the collection of income taxes by requiring pay-as-you-go procedures, including withholding requirements for employees and estimated tax payments for all taxpayers.

Federal Income Taxes

Exhibit 1.3 illustrates the Federal income tax imposed on individuals. The individual income tax provides a framework for much of the text. Beginning with Chapter 3, each component of the formula is illustrated and explained.

Like its individual counterpart, the Federal corporate income tax is progressive in nature. However, it does not include the computation of adjusted gross income (AGI) and does not provide for the standard deduction and personal and dependency exemptions. As a result, a corporation's taxable income is the difference between gross income and deductions. While Chapters 3 through 19 cover the Federal income

EXHIBIT 1.3	Formula for Federal Income Tax on Individuals
Income (broadly defined)	$xx,xxx
Less: Exclusions (income that is not subject to tax)	(x,xxx)
Gross income (income that is subject to tax)	$xx,xxx
Less: Certain deductions (usually referred to as deductions *for* adjusted gross income)	(x,xxx)
Adjusted gross income	$xx,xxx
Less: The greater of:	
Certain personal and employee deductions (usually referred to as *itemized deductions*)	
or	
The standard deduction (including any additional standard deduction)	(x,xxx)
Less: Personal and dependency exemptions	(x,xxx)
Taxable income	$xx,xxx
Tax on taxable income (see the Tax Tables and Tax Rate Schedules in Appendix A)	$ x,xxx
Less: Tax credits (including Federal income tax withheld and other prepayments of Federal income taxes)	(xxx)
Tax due (or refund)	$ xxx

tax applicable to individuals, Chapter 20 summarizes the rules relating to corporations and partnerships.[20]

State Income Taxes

Almost all states impose an income tax on individuals.[21]

Here are some of the characteristics of state income taxes:

- With few exceptions, all states require some form of withholding procedures.

- Most states use as the tax base the income determination made for Federal income tax purposes. This is often referred to as the piggyback approach to state income taxation. Although the term *piggyback* does not lend itself to a precise definition, in this context, it means making use, for state income tax purposes, of what was done for Federal income tax purposes.

- Some states "decouple" from selected Federal tax changes passed by Congress. The purpose of the decoupling is to retain state revenue that would otherwise be lost. For example, some states do not allow the "manufacturer's deduction" or "bonus depreciation" allowed for Federal tax purposes.

- Because of the tie-ins to the Federal return, a state may be notified of any changes made by the IRS upon audit of a Federal return.

- Most states allow a deduction for personal and dependency exemptions. Some states substitute a tax credit for a deduction.

- Many state income tax returns provide checkoff boxes for donations to various causes. Many are dedicated to medical research and wildlife programs, but special projects are not uncommon. For example, Wisconsin uses one for maintenance and operating costs of Lambeau Field (home of the Green Bay Packers). These checkoff boxes have been criticized as adding complexity to the returns and misleading taxpayers.[22]

- Most states allow their residents some form of tax credit for income taxes paid to other states.

The Big Picture

EXAMPLE 12

Return to the facts of *The Big Picture* on p. 1-1. Because the income earned by Travis on his Chicago trip will be subject to tax by his home state, he probably will be able to claim an offsetting tax credit. Whether this negates the double taxation of the same income depends on the amount of credit allowed.

- The objective of most states is to tax the income of residents and those who conduct business in the state (e.g., employees sent to the state to help a client, or a professional athlete playing a game in the state).

- The due date for filing generally is the same as for the Federal income tax (for individuals, the fifteenth day of the fourth month following the close of the tax year).

- Some states have occasionally instituted amnesty programs that allow taxpayers to pay back taxes (and interest) on unreported income with no (or reduced) penalty. In many cases, the tax amnesty has generated enough revenue to warrant the authorization of follow-up programs covering future years.[23] Amnesties usually include other taxes as well (e.g., sales, franchise, and severance).

---

[20]For an in-depth treatment of the Federal income tax as it affects corporations, partnerships, estates, and trusts, see *South-Western Federal Taxation: Corporations, Partnerships, Estates & Trusts*, Chapters 2 through 9, 12, and 20.

[21]Alaska, Florida, Nevada, South Dakota, Texas, Washington, and Wyoming do not have an individual income tax. New Hampshire and Tennessee impose an individual income tax only on interest and dividends.

[22]Many taxpayers do not realize they are paying for the checkoff donation (usually with some of their income tax refund). Unlike the presidential election campaign fund available for Federal income tax purposes ($3 in this case), the contribution is *not made* by the government.

[23]Although the suggestion has been made, no comparable amnesty program has been offered for the Federal income tax. The IRS has, however, offered exemption from certain penalties for taxpayers who disclose offshore bank accounts and participation in certain tax shelters.

- Because many consumers do not pay state and local sales taxes on out-of-state purchases, state income tax returns include a separate line for reporting any use tax that is due. As a result, the income tax return serves as a means of collecting use taxes.

Nearly all states have an income tax applicable to corporations. Other states have a franchise tax (discussed later in the chapter) that can be based in part on corporate income.

Local Income Taxes

Cities imposing an income tax include, Baltimore, Cincinnati, Cleveland, Detroit, Kansas City (Missouri), New York, Philadelphia, and St. Louis. The application of a city income tax is not limited to local residents.

1-4f **Employment Taxes**

Employment taxes are a type of income tax imposed on employers and employees. We concentrate on the two major employment taxes: FICA (Federal Insurance Contributions Act—commonly referred to as the Social Security tax) and FUTA (Federal Unemployment Tax Act). Both taxes can be justified by social and public welfare considerations: FICA offers some measure of retirement security, and FUTA provides a modest source of income in the event of loss of employment.

These employment taxes come into play for employees (*not self-employed* individuals) if the particular work is covered under FICA or FUTA or both.[24]

FICA Taxes

The **FICA tax** rates and wage base have increased steadily over the years. It is difficult to imagine that the initial rate in 1937 was only 1 percent of the first $3,000 of covered wages. Thus, the maximum tax due was only $30.

The FICA tax has two components: Social Security tax (old age, survivors, and disability insurance) *and* Medicare tax (hospital insurance). The Social Security tax rate is 6.2 percent and generally does not change. The base amount usually increases each year. For 2017, the base amount is $127,200 ($118,500 for 2016).

The Medicare portion of FICA is applied at a rate of 1.45 percent and, unlike Social Security, is not subject to any dollar limitation. The Affordable Care Act (ObamaCare) imposes an additional .9 percent tax on earned income (including self-employment income) *above* $200,000 (single filers) or $250,000 (married filing jointly). Unlike the Social Security tax of 6.2 percent and the regular Medicare portion of 1.45 percent, an employer does not have to match the employees' .9 percent tax.

A spouse employed by another spouse is subject to FICA. However, children under the age of 18 who are employed in a parent's unincorporated trade or business are exempted.

The Big Picture

EXAMPLE 13

Return to the facts of *The Big Picture* on p. 1-1. Presuming that April and Martin perform meaningful services for Travis (which the facts seem to imply), they are legitimate employees. April is not subject to Social Security tax because she is under the age of 18. However, Martin is 18 and needs to be covered. Furthermore, recall that Amy Carter is now working at a medical clinic and will likewise be subject to Social Security tax. Travis, as an independent contractor, is subject to self-employment tax.

---

[24]Chapter 13 includes coverage of the self-employment tax (the Social Security and Medicare taxes for self-employed persons). See also Circular E, *Employer's Tax Guide*, issued by the IRS as Publication 15.

Taxpayers who are not employees (e.g., sole proprietors and independent contractors) may also be subject to Social Security taxes. Known as the self-employment tax, the rates are 12.4 percent for Social Security and 2.9 percent for Medicare, or twice that applicable to an employee. The additional .9 percent Medicare tax also covers situations involving high net income from self-employment. The Social Security tax is imposed on net self-employment income up to the annual base amount ($127,200 for 2017; $118,500 for 2016). The Medicare portion of the self-employment tax is not subject to any dollar limitation.

To help cover the government's cost of medical care, Congress enacted a special tax on investment income.[25] For this purpose, "investment income" is often referred to as "unearned income" because it is not generated by the performance of services. A tax of 3.8 percent is imposed on net investment income when a taxpayer's modified adjusted gross income (MAGI) exceeds certain threshold amounts.[26] The threshold amounts are $250,000 for married taxpayers and $200,000 for single taxpayers. Investment income generally includes passive income (e.g., rents, taxable interest, dividends, and capital gains). For further discussion, see Chapter 13 and the online appendix on the Affordable Care Act.

FUTA Taxes

The purpose of the **FUTA tax** is to provide funds the states can use to administer unemployment benefits. This leads to the somewhat unusual situation of one tax being handled by both Federal and state governments. This joint administration means that the employer must observe two sets of rules. State and Federal returns must be filed and payments made to both governmental units.

In 2017, FUTA is 6 percent on the first $7,000 of covered wages paid during the year to each employee. The Federal government allows a credit for FUTA paid (or allowed under a merit rating system) to the state. The credit cannot exceed 5.4 percent of the covered wages. Thus, the amount required to be paid to the Federal government could be as low as .6 percent (6.0% − 5.4%).

States reduce the unemployment tax on employers who experience stable employment, since the state pays less unemployment benefits. Thus, an employer with little or no employee turnover might find that the state rate drops to as low as .1 percent or, in some states, even to zero.

FUTA, unlike FICA, is paid entirely by the employer. A few states, however, levy a special tax on employees to provide either disability benefits or supplemental unemployment compensation or both.

1-4g Other U.S. Taxes

To complete the overview of the U.S. tax system, some missing links need to be covered that do not fit into the classifications discussed elsewhere in this chapter.

Federal Customs Duties

The tariff on imported goods,[27] also known as customs duties, together with excise taxes, provided most of the revenues needed by the Federal government during the nineteenth century. In view of present times, it is remarkable that tariffs and excise taxes alone paid off the national debt in 1835 and enabled the U.S. Treasury to pay a surplus of $28 million to the states.

In recent years, tariffs have been an instrument for carrying out protectionist policies instead of a means of generating revenue. By imposing customs duties on the importation of foreign goods that can be sold at lower prices, protectionists contend that the tariff thereby neutralizes the competitive edge held by the producer of the foreign goods.

---

[25]Enacted as part of the Health Care and Education Reconciliation Act of 2010.

[26]MAGI is adjusted gross income (see Exhibit 1.3 and the bottom of page 1 of Form 1040) plus any foreign income or excluded foreign housing costs.

An online appendix covers the net investment income tax (NIIT) and other Affordable Care Act tax provisions.

[27]Less-developed countries that rely principally on one or more major commodities (e.g., oil or coffee) are prone to favor *export* duties.

However, history shows that tariffs often lead to retaliatory action on the part of the nation or nations affected.

Miscellaneous State and Local Taxes

Most states impose a franchise tax on corporations for the right to do business in the state.[28] The tax base used varies from state to state, but most often is based on the capitalization of the corporation (either with or without certain long-term indebtedness).

Similar to the franchise tax are occupational fees that apply to various trades or businesses (e.g., a liquor store license; a taxicab permit; or a fee to practice a profession such as law, medicine, or accounting). Most of these are not significant revenue producers, and the fees are used to fund the costs of regulating the business or profession in the interest of the public good.

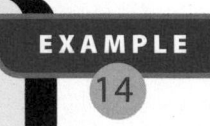

The Big Picture

EXAMPLE

14

Return to the facts of *The Big Picture* on p. 1-1. Although the facts do not mention the matter, both Travis and Amy might owe occupation or license fees—Travis for engineering and Amy for nursing.

Concept Summary 1.2 provides an overview of the major taxes existing in the United States and specifies which political jurisdiction imposes them.

Concept Summary 1.2

Overview of Taxes in the United States

Type of Tax	Imposed by Jurisdiction		
	Federal	**State**	**Local**
Property taxes:			
Ad valorem on realty	No	Yes	Yes
Ad valorem on personalty	No	Yes	Yes
Transaction taxes:			
Excise	Yes	Yes	Few*
General sales	No	Most	Some
Severance	Yes**	Most	No
Estate	Yes	Some	No
Inheritance	No	Some	No
Gift	Yes	Few	No
Income taxes:			
Corporations	Yes	Most	Few
Individuals	Yes	Most	Few
Employment taxes:			
FICA	Yes	No	No
FUTA	Yes	Yes	No
Customs duties	Yes	No	No
Franchise taxes	No	Yes	No
Occupational taxes or fees***	Yes	Yes	Yes

* An example of a local excise tax might be a tax on hotel occupancy.
** For Federal public lands and continental-shelf areas.
*** An example is a fee to operate a beauty salon or barbershop.

---

[28]Only five states do not impose a franchise tax (Michigan, Nevada, South Dakota, Washington, and Wyoming).

1-4h **Proposed U.S. Taxes**

The last major reform to the U.S. tax system was over 30 years ago (the Tax Reform Act of 1986). As that legislation developed, tax reform discussions included use of a consumption tax to replace all or a portion of the income tax. Although a consumption tax was not adopted in 1986, it continues to be part of the tax reform conversation. Consumption taxes being considered include the flat tax, a national sales tax, and a value added tax. Federal tax reform discussions have also included adding a carbon tax or a financial transactions tax. A brief description of these types of taxes follows.

Flat Tax

The flat tax, as introduced in 1981 by economists Robert Hall and Alvin Rabushka of the Hoover Institution, is a form of a consumption tax. Their proposal achieves some of the administrative advantages of a value added tax (VAT) relative to a sales tax, while also partially addressing concerns that consumption taxes impose a relatively heavier tax burden on lower-income taxpayers. It assesses a "flat" 19 percent tax on all businesses (corporate or otherwise)—identical to the VAT, except that wages, pension contributions, materials costs, and capital investments are deducted from the tax base. Individuals (or households) are assessed a 19 percent flat-rate tax on wages and pension benefits above an exemption of $25,500 for a family of four. No other income is taxable, and no other deductions are allowed. Over the past 35 years, the Hall-Rabushka proposal has served as the blueprint for a number of proposals to reform the Federal tax system.[29]

National Sales Tax

A national sales tax would operate similarly to most state sales taxes although the tax base would be larger. The rate would also be higher to generate the revenues needed to replace the Federal income tax.

A frequent proposal for a national sales tax, called the "Fair Tax," would tax all purchases, including food and medicine, real property, and many types of services, at approximately 23 percent. Exempt items include business expenses, used goods, and the costs of education. The "Fair Tax" would replace the income tax (both individual and corporate), payroll taxes (including the self-employment tax), and the gift and estate taxes. To help address the regressivity of the tax, many individuals would receive a monthly rebate to offset a portion of sales tax paid.

Value Added Tax

A value added tax (VAT) is imposed on the value added by each party in a production cycle. For example, a furniture maker is charged VAT on wood purchased to make the furniture. Customers are charged VAT when they buy the furniture. A system of credits results in the VAT ultimately only being paid by the final consumer. This form of VAT—a credit invoice VAT—is similar to a sales tax. It is viewed as more efficient than a sales tax because assessment throughout the production process better ensures collection of the tax. The credit invoice VAT is widely used throughout the world.

A VAT has been considered in the United States various times since the 1960s. In 1984, the Treasury Department released a three-volume tax reform report, with one volume devoted to the VAT.[30] In 2016, Congressman James Renacci (R-OH), introduced a proposal to replace the corporate income tax with a credit invoice VAT as part of his Simplifying America's Tax System (SATS) proposal.[31]

[29]Usually, the tax bill carries the number H.R. 1040. See R. E. Hall and A. Rabushka, *The Flat Tax*, Hoover Institution (2007).

[30]U.S. Treasury Department, *Tax Reform for Fairness, Simplicity, and Economic Growth: The Treasury Department Report to the President*, Volume 3, 1984.

[31]**http://renacci.house.gov/index.cfm/simplifying-americas-tax-system**

GLOBAL TAX ISSUES   **VAT in USA?**

The United States is the only country in the OECD (Organization of Economic Cooperation and Development) that does not have a value added tax (VAT). Over 140 countries around the world use a VAT, with rates ranging from 5 percent to 27 percent.

Is the United States out of sync with most other countries by not having a VAT? One advantage of a VAT is that it provides a significant revenue source, allowing for lower individual and corporate income tax rates. Also, unlike the income tax, a VAT is "border-adjustable," meaning that a country can impose it on imports but not exports. These are some considerations for U.S. lawmakers in evaluating the economic effects of the U.S. tax system and tax reform options in a global perspective.

One challenge of implementing a VAT in the United States is that it is a regressive tax (it has a greater impact on lower-income taxpayers relative to higher-income taxpayers). As a result, adjustments need to be implemented to protect lower-income taxpayers (e.g., expanding the earned income tax credit and/or child tax credit; both occur in the SATS proposal). Another challenge is that the Treasury Department (and IRS) will have to learn how to implement and enforce the VAT.

Carbon Tax

A carbon tax aims to help reduce carbon emissions (i.e., greenhouse gases). The tax could be applied to fossil fuels based on their level of greenhouse gas emissions. Because a significant fossil fuel is gasoline, some people suggest a higher gasoline excise tax as a simple form of a carbon tax.

Financial Transaction Tax

A financial transaction tax can take many forms. For example, it could be imposed on the value of financial instruments purchased (e.g., stocks and bonds). It could be restricted in some way (e.g., only applying to high-frequency trading). It could be imposed on the value of bank assets. Because the tax base is quite large, the tax rate would likely be low, perhaps even less than 1 percent. The primary concern with this type of tax is the possible adverse effects on financial markets.

1-5 TAX ADMINISTRATION

LO.5

Explain the administration of the tax law, including the audit process utilized by the IRS.

1-5a Internal Revenue Service

The responsibility for administering the Federal tax laws rests with the Treasury Department. The IRS is part of the Department of the Treasury and is responsible for enforcing the tax laws. The Commissioner of Internal Revenue is appointed by the President with the advice and consent of the Senate. The Commissioner is responsible for establishing policy and supervising the activities of the IRS. Here is the mission statement of the IRS:

> *Provide America's taxpayers top quality service by helping them understand and meet their tax responsibilities and enforce the law with integrity and fairness to all.*

1-5b The Audit Process

Selection of Returns for Audit

Only a small number of tax returns are audited each year. The overall audit rate for individuals is .8 percent. The audit rate for corporations is about 1.3 percent. Keep in mind, however, that the probability for audit increases for higher-income taxpayers.[32]

---

[32]Internal Revenue Service, *Data Book 2015*, Table 9a. Examination Coverage: Recommended and Average Recommended Additional Tax After Examination, by Type and Size of Return, Fiscal Year 2015.

Tax returns are selected for audit in different ways. A common technique for individuals is called information matching. For example, the IRS compares information returns it receives (e.g., a Form 1099 interest income statement from a bank related to an individual) to an individual's tax return. If the information is not reported correctly, the IRS sends a notice to the taxpayer indicating the problem and the additional tax owed. Another approach is done through computer scoring. This approach uses mathematical formulas and statistical sampling techniques to select tax returns that are most likely to contain errors and to provide significant amounts of additional tax revenues when audited. The mathematical formula yields what is called a Discriminant Index Formula (DIF) score. It is the DIF score given to a particular return that may lead to its selection for audit. Periodically, the IRS updates the DIF components by auditing a cross section of returns to determine the most likely areas of taxpayer noncompliance.

Although the IRS does not openly disclose the details of all of its audit selection techniques, here are some general comments about audit selection:

- Certain groups of taxpayers are subject to audit much more frequently than others. These groups include individuals with large amounts of gross income, self-employed individuals with substantial deductions, and taxpayers with prior tax deficiencies. The same is true for businesses that receive a large proportion of their receipts in cash (e.g., cafés and small service businesses) and thus have a high potential for tax avoidance.

Jack owns and operates a liquor store on a cash-and-carry basis. Because all of Jack's sales are for cash, he might well be a prime candidate for an audit by the IRS. Cash transactions are easier to conceal than those made on credit.

- If information returns (e.g., Form 1099 or Form W–2) are not in substantial agreement with reported income, an audit can be anticipated.
- If an individual's itemized deductions are in excess of averages established for various income levels, the probability of an audit is increased.
- Filing of a refund claim by the taxpayer may prompt an audit of the return.
- Information obtained from other sources (e.g., informants and news items) may lead to an audit.

The IRS pays rewards to persons who provide information leading to the discovery and punishment of those who violate the tax laws. The rewards may not exceed 30 percent of the taxes, fines, and penalties recovered.

Information Leading to an IRS Audit

After 15 years of service, Rita is discharged by her employer, Dr. Benjamin Smith. Shortly thereafter, the IRS receives an anonymous letter stating that Dr. Smith keeps two separate sets of books and that the one used for tax reporting substantially understates his cash receipts.

During a divorce proceeding, it is revealed that Leo, a public official, kept large amounts of cash in a shoe box at home. This information is widely disseminated by the news media and comes to the attention of the IRS. Needless to say, the IRS is interested in knowing whether these funds originated from a taxable source and, if so, whether they were reported on Leo's income tax returns.

Types of Audits

Once a return is selected for audit, the taxpayer is notified by mail. If the issue involved is minor, the matter often can be resolved simply by correspondence (a **correspondence audit**) between the IRS and the taxpayer. Approximately 78 percent of individual audits are handled via correspondence, while only about 12 percent of corporate audits are handled this way.[33]

Other examinations are generally classified as either office audits or field audits. An **office audit** usually is restricted in scope and is conducted in IRS offices. In contrast, a **field audit** involves an examination of numerous items reported on the return and is conducted at the taxpayer's location (or that of the taxpayer's representative). Exhibit 1.4 illustrates the types of audits pursued by the IRS for all tax returns filed during 2014 (individual, corporate, partnership, and exempt).

The Big Picture

Return to the facts of *The Big Picture* on p. 1-1. The audit of the Walkers by the IRS obviously was a correspondence type. The reason for the audit was probably triggered by a minor oversight by the Walkers, such as the omission of some interest or dividend income. The audit of the Carters, however, was more serious—probably a field or office type. Because the Federal audit followed a state audit that was productive (i.e., led to the assessment of a deficiency), there may have been an exchange of information between the two taxing authorities—see p. 1-16 in this chapter.

EXAMPLE
18

At the end of an audit, the examining agent issues a Revenue Agent's Report (RAR) that summarizes the findings. The RAR will result in a refund (the tax was overpaid), a deficiency (the tax was underpaid), or a no change (the tax was correct) finding. If, during the course of an audit, a special agent accompanies (or takes over from) the regular auditor, this means the IRS suspects fraud. In this case, the taxpayer should retain competent legal counsel.

Settlement Procedures

If an audit results in an assessment of additional tax and no settlement is reached with the IRS agent, the taxpayer may request an appeal within the IRS. The Appeals Division of the IRS is authorized to settle all disputes based on the *hazard of litigation* (the probability of favorable resolution of the disputed issue or issues if litigated). In some cases,

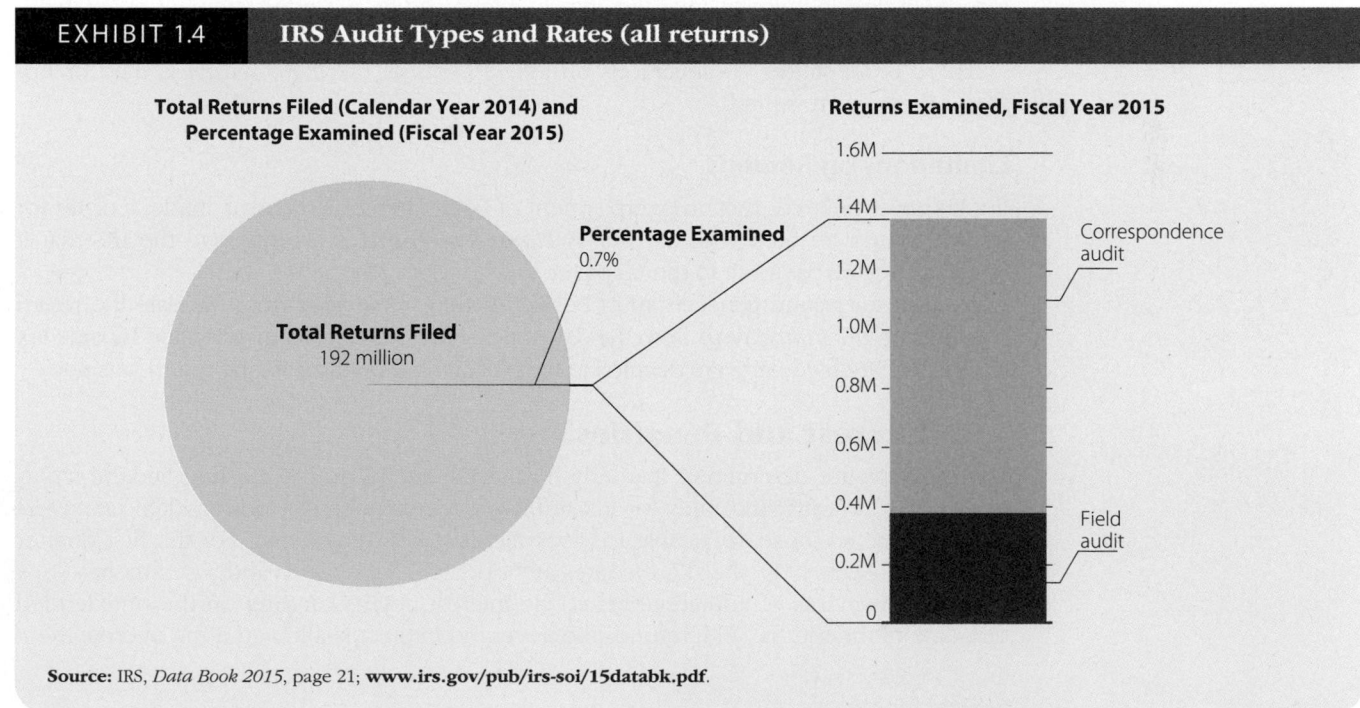

EXHIBIT 1.4   IRS Audit Types and Rates (all returns)

Total Returns Filed (Calendar Year 2014) and Percentage Examined (Fiscal Year 2015)

Total Returns Filed
192 million

Percentage Examined
0.7%

Returns Examined, Fiscal Year 2015

Correspondence audit

Field audit

Source: IRS, *Data Book 2015*, page 21; **www.irs.gov/pub/irs-soi/15databk.pdf**.

---

[33]Internal Revenue Service, *Data Book, 2015*. Table 9a.

a taxpayer may be able to obtain an overall reduction of the assessment or a favorable settlement of one or more disputed issues.

If a satisfactory settlement is not reached within the IRS, the taxpayer can litigate the case in the Tax Court, a Federal District Court, or the Court of Federal Claims. However, litigation is normally discouraged because of the legal costs involved and the uncertainty of the final outcome. Tax litigation considerations are discussed more fully in Chapter 2.

1-5c Statute of Limitations

A statute of limitations is a provision that requires any lawsuit to be brought within a reasonable period of time. Found at the state and Federal levels, such statutes cover a multitude of suits, both civil and criminal.

For the Federal income tax, there are two categories involved, which cover time limits on the assessment of additional tax deficiencies by the IRS and time limits related to refund claims by taxpayers.

Assessment by the IRS

In general, the IRS may assess an additional tax liability against a taxpayer within *three years* of the filing of the income tax return. If the return is filed early, the three-year period begins to run from the due date of the return (usually April 15 for a calendar year individual taxpayer). If the taxpayer files the return late (i.e., beyond the due date), the three-year period begins to run on the date filed.

If a taxpayer omits an amount of gross income in excess of 25 percent of the gross income reported on the return, the statute of limitations is increased to six years.

EXAMPLE 19

For 2017, Mark, a calendar year taxpayer, reported gross income of $400,000 on a timely filed income tax return. If Mark omitted more than $100,000 (25% × $400,000), the six-year statute of limitations would apply to the 2017 tax year.

The six-year provision on assessments by the IRS applies only to the omission of income; it does not cover other factors that might lead to an understatement of tax liability, such as overstatement of deductions and credits.

There is *no* statute of limitations on assessments of tax if *no return* is filed or if a *fraudulent* return is filed.

Limitations on Refunds

If a taxpayer believes that an overpayment of Federal income tax was made, a claim for refund should be filed with the IRS. A *claim for refund* is a request to the IRS that it return a tax overpayment to the taxpayer.[34]

A claim for refund generally must be filed within *three years* from the date the return was filed *or* within *two years* from the date the tax was paid, whichever is later. Income tax returns that are filed early are deemed to have been filed on the date the return was due.

1-5d Interest and Penalties

Interest rates are determined quarterly by the IRS based on the existing Federal short-term rate. Currently, the rates for tax refunds (overpayments) for individual taxpayers are the same as those applicable to assessments (underpayments). For the first quarter (January 1–March 31) of 2017, the rates are 4 percent for refunds and assessments.[35]

For assessments of additional taxes, the interest begins running on the unextended due date of the return. With refunds, however, no interest is allowed if the overpayment

---

[34]Generally, an individual filing a claim for refund should use Form 1040X.

[35]Rev. Rul. 2016–28; 2016–51 I.R.B. 805; the rates for the remainder of 2017 were not available when the text went to press.

is refunded to the taxpayer within 45 days of the date the return is filed. For this purpose, returns filed early are deemed to have been filed on the due date.

In addition to interest, the tax law provides various penalties for lack of compliance by taxpayers. Some of these penalties are summarized as follows:

- For *failure to file* a tax return by the due date (including extension—see Chapter 3), a penalty of 5 percent per month up to a maximum of 25 percent is imposed on the amount of tax shown as due on the return. Any fraction of a month counts as a full month.

- A penalty for *failure to pay* the tax due as shown on the return is imposed in the amount of .5 percent per month up to a maximum of 25 percent. Again, any fraction of a month counts as a full month. During any month in which both the failure to file penalty and the failure to pay penalty apply, the failure to file penalty is reduced by the amount of the failure to pay penalty.

EXAMPLE 20

Adam files his tax return 18 days after the due date of the return. Along with the return, he remits a check for $1,000, which is the balance of the tax he owed. Disregarding the interest element, Adam's total penalties are as follows:

Failure to pay penalty (.5% × $1,000)		$ 5
Plus:		
Failure to file penalty (5% × $1,000)	$50	
Less failure to pay penalty for the same period	(5)	
Failure to file penalty		45
Total penalties		$50

Note that the penalties for one full month are imposed even though Adam was delinquent by only 18 days. Unlike the method used to compute interest, any part of a month is treated as a whole month.

- A *negligence* penalty of 20 percent is imposed if any of the underpayment was for intentional disregard of rules and Regulations without intent to defraud. The penalty applies to just that portion attributable to the negligence.

EXAMPLE 21

Cindy underpaid her taxes in the amount of $20,000, of which $15,000 is attributable to negligence. Cindy's negligence penalty is $3,000 (20% × $15,000).

- Various penalties may be imposed in the case of *fraud*. Fraud involves specific intent on the part of the taxpayer to evade a tax. In the case of *civil* fraud, the penalty is 75 percent of the underpayment attributable to fraud. In the case of *criminal* fraud, the penalties can include large fines as well as prison sentences. The difference between civil and criminal fraud is one of degree. Criminal fraud involves the presence of willfulness on the part of the taxpayer. Also, the burden of proof, which is on the IRS in both situations, is more stringent for criminal fraud than for civil fraud. The negligence penalty is not imposed when the fraud penalty applies. For possible fraud situations, refer to Examples 16 and 17.

1-5e **Tax Practice**

If a practitioner is a member of a profession (e.g., public accounting or law), he or she must abide by certain ethical standards. Furthermore, the Internal Revenue Code imposes penalties on Federal tax return preparers who violate identified acts and procedures.

GLOBAL TAX ISSUES **Outsourcing of Tax Return Preparation**

The use of foreign nationals to carry out certain job assignments for U.S. businesses is an increasingly popular practice. Outsourcing such activities as telemarketing to India, for example, can produce the same satisfactory result as having the work done in the United States but at a lower cost.

Outsourcing is also being applied to the preparation of tax returns. Not only can this practice be expected to continue, but it probably will increase in volume. Outsourcing tax return preparation does not violate Federal law and is compatible with accounting ethical guidelines as long as three safeguards are followed: First, the practitioner must make sure client confidentiality is maintained. Second, the practitioner must verify the accuracy of the work that has been outsourced. Third, the practitioner must inform clients, preferably in writing, when any third-party contractor is used to provide professional services.

Practitioners justify outsourcing as a means of conserving time and effort that can be applied toward more meaningful tax planning on behalf of their clients.

LO.6

Evaluate some of the ethical guidelines involved in tax practice.

Ethical Guidelines

The American Institute of CPAs has issued its "Statements on Standards for Tax Services," dealing with CPAs engaged in tax practice. These pronouncements are *enforceable* as part of its Code of Professional Conduct. They include the following summarized provisions:

- Do not take questionable positions on a client's tax return in the hope the return will not be selected for audit by the IRS. Any positions taken should be supported by a good-faith belief that they have a realistic possibility of being sustained if challenged. The client should be fully advised of the risks involved and of the penalties that will result if the position taken is not successful.

- A practitioner can use a client's estimates if they are reasonable under the circumstances. If the tax law requires receipts or other verification, the client should be so advised. In no event should an estimate be given the appearance of greater accuracy than is the case. For example, an estimate of $1,000 should not be deducted on a return as $999.

- Every effort should be made to answer questions appearing on tax returns. A question need not be answered if the information requested is not readily available, the answer is voluminous, or the question's meaning is uncertain. The failure to answer a question on a return cannot be justified on the grounds that the answer could prove disadvantageous to the taxpayer.

- Upon learning of an error on a past tax return, advise the client to correct it. Do not, however, inform the IRS of the error. If the error is material and the client refuses to correct it, consider withdrawing from the engagement. This will be necessary if the error has a carryover effect and prevents the current year's tax liability from being determined correctly.

Statutory Penalties Imposed on Tax Return Preparers

In addition to ethical constraints, a tax return preparer may be subject to specific penalties, including the following:

- Various penalties involving procedural matters. Examples include failing to furnish the taxpayer with a copy of the return, endorsing a taxpayer's refund check, failing to sign the return as a preparer, failing to furnish one's identification number, and failing to keep copies of returns or maintain a client list.

- Penalty for understatement of a tax liability based on a position that lacks substantial authority. If the position has a reasonable basis, the penalty can be avoided by disclosing it on the return.

- Penalty for any willful attempt to understate taxes. This usually results when a preparer disregards or makes no effort to obtain pertinent information from a client.

- Penalty for failure to exercise due diligence in determining eligibility for, or the amount of, an earned income tax credit, the child tax credit, or the American opportunity tax credit.

1-6 UNDERSTANDING THE FEDERAL TAX LAW

LO.7

Recognize the economic, social, equity, and political considerations that justify various aspects of the tax law.

The Federal tax law reflects the three branches of our Federal government. It is a mixture of laws passed by Congress, explanations provided by the Treasury Department and the Internal Revenue Service (IRS), and interpretation of the law by the courts. Anyone who has attempted to work with this vast amount of information is familiar with its complexity. For the person who has to sift through this information to find the solution to a tax problem, it is good to know that there are reasons behind the law. Knowing these reasons is the first step toward understanding the Federal tax law.

The *primary objective* of Federal tax law is the raising of revenue. Although the fiscal needs of the government are important, other considerations (economic, social, equity, and political factors) also play a significant role. The Treasury Department, the IRS, and the courts also have significant impacts on the evolution of Federal tax law. The remainder of the chapter focuses on these topics.

1-6a Revenue Needs

Raising revenues to fund the cost of government operations is the key factor in structuring a tax system. In a perfect world, taxes raised by the government would equal the expenses incurred by government operations. However, this goal has not been achieved in the United States.

When enacting tax legislation, a deficit-conscious Congress often has been guided by the concept of revenue neutrality so that changes neither increase nor decrease the net revenues received by the government. With revenue-neutral legislation, there are likely to be both "winners" (taxpayers who see a reduction in taxes paid) and "losers" (taxpayers who see an increase in taxes paid).

In addition to making revenue-neutral changes in the tax law, several other procedures can be taken to mitigate any revenue loss. When tax reductions are involved, the full impact of the legislation can be phased in over a period of years. Or as an alternative, the tax reduction can be limited to a period of years. When the period expires, the prior law is reinstated through a sunset provision. For example, at times, Congress has allowed more rapid depreciation treatment for a specified number of years. These sunset (or temporary) provisions move legislation toward revenue neutrality (even though it is not achieved).

1-6b Economic Considerations

Sometimes tax legislation is designed to help control the economy or encourage certain activities and businesses.

Control of the Economy

Congress has used the tax depreciation rules as a means of controlling the economy. Theoretically, shorter asset lives and accelerated methods should encourage additional investment in depreciable property acquired for business use. On the other hand, longer asset lives and use of straight-line depreciation should discourage capital outlays. Congress also uses incentives like immediate expensing (§ 179) and bonus depreciation to stimulate the economy when needed.

A change in tax rates has a more immediate impact on the economy. With lower tax rates, taxpayers retain money that can be used for other purposes (e.g., purchases or savings). If, however, Congress is using the concept of revenue neutrality, these rate reductions may be offset by a reduction or elimination of deductions or credits. As a result, lower tax rates do not always mean lower taxes.

Encouragement of Certain Activities

Congress uses the tax law to encourage certain types of economic activity or segments of the economy. For example, research and development expenditures can be either deducted in the year incurred or capitalized and amortized over a period of 60 months or more. Inventions are also encouraged by tax law. Patents can qualify as capital assets, and under certain conditions, their sale results in long-term capital gain treatment.

Part of the tax law addresses the nation's energy policy—in terms of both our reliance on carbon-based fuels and the need to ease the problem of climate change. For example, a tax credit is available for installation of solar and small wind energy equipment. Residential energy credits are available for home improvements that conserve energy or make its use more efficient (e.g., solar hot water and geothermal heat pumps). Ecological considerations explain why pollution control facilities can be amortized over 60 months (rather than over the 39-year period for most business buildings).

Is saving desirable for the economy? Saving can lead to capital formation, making funds available to finance home construction and industrial expansion. The tax law encourages saving by giving private retirement plans preferential treatment. Besides contributions to certain Individual Retirement Accounts (IRAs) and Keogh (H.R. 10) plans being deductible, income from the contributions accumulates tax-free.

Encouragement of Certain Industries

Historically, agricultural activities have been favored under Federal tax law. Among the benefits are the election to expense rather than capitalize certain soil and water conservation expenditures and fertilizers and the election to defer the recognition of gain on the receipt of crop insurance proceeds.

The tax law favors the development of natural resources by permitting the use of percentage depletion and a write-off (rather than a capitalization) of certain exploration costs. The railroad and banking industries also receive special tax treatment under Federal tax law.

Encouragement of Small Business

Small business development is also encouraged under the tax law. For example, the shareholders of a small business corporation can make a special election that allows the profits (or losses) of the corporation to flow through to its shareholders, avoiding the corporate income tax.[36] Another provision allows a shareholder in a small business corporation to take an ordinary deduction (rather than a capital loss) for any loss recognized on the stock investment.

1-6c Social Considerations

Some provisions of the Federal tax law, particularly those dealing with individuals, can be explained by social considerations. Here are some notable examples:

- Certain benefits provided to employees through accident and health plans financed by employers are nontaxable to employees. It is socially desirable to encourage these plans because they provide medical benefits in the event of an employee's illness or injury. In addition, insurance companies are paying for these benefits (rather than the government).

- Most premiums paid by an employer for group term insurance covering the life of the employee are nontaxable to the employee. Life insurance proceeds (which

---

[36]Known as the S election, it is discussed in Chapter 20.

are also nontaxable) provide funds to help the family unit adjust to the loss of wages caused by the employee's death.

- A contribution made by an employer to a qualified pension or profit sharing plan for an employee may receive special treatment. The contribution and any income it generates are not taxed to the employee until the funds are distributed. This arrangement also benefits the employer by allowing a tax deduction for the contribution to the qualified plan. Private retirement plans are encouraged to supplement any Social Security payments.[37]

- A deduction is allowed for contributions to qualified charities. The deduction shifts some of the financial and administrative burden of socially desirable programs from the public (the government) to the private sector.

- A tax credit is allowed for amounts spent to furnish care for dependents to enable the taxpayer to work. For those employees who do not choose home care for their children, employers are allowed a credit for child care provided at the workplace.

- To encourage taxpayers to join the workforce even though their wages may be low, an earned income tax credit can be claimed. The credit varies depending on the number of qualifying children and the level of wages earned.

- Certain credits are made available to elderly and disabled persons. Credits also are allowed to businesses that incur expenditures to make their facilities more accessible to the disabled.

- Various tax credits, deductions, and exclusions are designed to encourage taxpayers to obtain additional education.[38]

- A tax deduction is not allowed for certain expenses deemed to be contrary to public policy. Expenses not allowed include items like fines, penalties, illegal kickbacks, bribes to government officials, and gambling losses in excess of gains.

1-6d **Equity Considerations**

The concept of equity is relative. Reasonable persons can, and often do, disagree about what is fair or unfair. In the tax area, moreover, equity is most often tied to a particular taxpayer's personal situation. To illustrate, compare the tax positions of those who rent their personal residences with those who own their homes. Renters receive no Federal income tax benefit from the rent they pay. For homeowners, however, a large portion of the house payments they make may qualify for the Federal interest and property tax deductions. Although renters may have difficulty understanding this difference in tax treatment, the encouragement of home ownership can be justified on both economic and social grounds.

Compare the tax treatment of a corporation with that of a partnership. Although the two businesses may be equal in size, similarly situated, and competitors in the production of goods or services, they are not treated comparably under the tax law. The corporation is subject to a separate Federal income tax; the partnership is not. The point is that the tax law can and does make a distinction between these business forms.

Equity, then, is not what appears fair or unfair to any one taxpayer or group of taxpayers. The concept of equity appears in tax provisions that alleviate the effect of multiple taxation and postpone the recognition of gain when the taxpayer lacks the ability or wherewithal to pay the tax. Provisions that mitigate the effect of the application of the annual accounting period concept and help taxpayers cope with the eroding results of inflation also reflect equity considerations.

---

[37]The same rationale explains the availability of similar arrangements for self-employed persons (e.g., the H.R. 10, or Keogh, plan). See Chapter 19.

[38]These provisions can also be justified under the category of economic considerations because a better-educated workforce carries a positive economic impact.

Alleviating the Effect of Multiple Taxation

Equity considerations can explain the Federal tax treatment of certain income from foreign sources. Because double taxation results when the same income is subject to both foreign and U.S. income taxes, the tax law permits the taxpayer to choose between a credit and a deduction for the foreign taxes paid.

The Wherewithal to Pay Concept

The wherewithal to pay concept recognizes the inequity of taxing a transaction when the taxpayer lacks the means (i.e., funds) to pay the tax. This concept is typically applied to transactions where the taxpayer's economic position has not changed significantly.

An illustration of the wherewithal to pay concept is the tax treatment of an involuntary conversion. An involuntary conversion occurs when property is destroyed by a casualty (e.g, a fire or hurricane) or taken by a public authority through condemnation (e.g., taking land to build a new road). If gain results from the conversion, it is deferred if the taxpayer replaces the property within a specified period of time.

EXAMPLE 22

Some of the pasture land belonging to Ron, a rancher, is condemned by the state for use as a game preserve. The condemned pasture land cost Ron $120,000, but the state pays him $150,000 (its fair market value). Shortly thereafter, Ron buys more pasture land for $150,000.

In Example 22, Ron has a realized gain of $30,000 [$150,000 (condemnation award) − $120,000 (cost of land)]. It would be inequitable to force Ron to pay a tax on this gain for two reasons. First, without selling the property acquired (the new land), Ron does not have the funds to pay the tax. Second, his economic position has not changed. If, however, the taxpayer's economic position changes in any way, tax consequences may result.

EXAMPLE 23

Assume the same facts as in Example 22, except that Ron reinvests only $140,000 of the award in new pasture land. Now Ron has a taxable gain of $10,000. Instead of ending up with only replacement property, Ron has $10,000 in cash.

Mitigating the Effect of the Annual Accounting Period Concept

All taxpayers must report their taxable income to the Federal government at regular intervals. The accounting period used to report taxable income (and settle any tax liability) is one year. Referred to as the annual accounting period concept, its effect is to divide each taxpayer's life, for tax purposes, into equal annual intervals.

The annual accounting period concept can lead to different tax treatment for taxpayers who are in the same economic position. Consider the following example.

EXAMPLE 24

José and Alicia, both sole proprietors, showed the following results during the past three years:

	Profit (or Loss)	
Year	José	Alicia
2015	$50,000	$150,000
2016	60,000	60,000
2017	60,000	(40,000)

Although José and Alicia have the same total profit of $170,000 over the three-year period, the annual accounting period concept places Alicia at a definite disadvantage for tax purposes. The net operating loss procedure offers Alicia some relief by allowing her to apply some or all of her 2017 loss to the earlier profitable years (in this case, 2015). With a net operating loss carryback, Alicia is in a position to obtain a refund for some of the taxes she paid on the $150,000 profit reported for 2015.

The reasoning used to support the net operating loss deduction can explain the special treatment the tax law accords to excess capital losses and excess charitable contributions.[39] Carryback and carryover procedures help mitigate the effect of limiting a loss or a deduction to the accounting period in which it was realized. Using these procedures, a taxpayer can salvage a loss or a deduction that might otherwise be lost.

The installment method of recognizing gain on the sale of property allows a taxpayer to spread tax consequences over the payout period.[40] The installment method is supported by the wherewithal to pay concept; recognition of gain corresponds to the collection of the cash received from the sale of the property. The tax consequences match the seller's ability to pay the tax.

Coping with Inflation

Because of the progressive nature of the income tax, a wage adjustment to compensate for inflation could place the employee in a higher income tax bracket. Known as *bracket creep*, its overall impact is an erosion of purchasing power. Congress recognized this problem and began to adjust various income tax components, such as tax brackets, standard deduction amounts, and personal and dependency exemptions, through an indexation procedure. Indexation is based on the rise in the consumer price index over the prior year.

1-6e Political Considerations

A large segment of the Federal tax law is made up of statutory provisions. Because these statutes are enacted by Congress, political considerations often influence tax law. The effect of political considerations on the tax law includes special interest legislation, political expediency situations, and state and local government influences.

Special Interest Legislation

There is no doubt that certain provisions of the tax law can largely be explained by the political influence some pressure groups have had on Congress. For example, prepaid subscription and dues income is not taxed until earned, while prepaid rents are taxed to the landlord in the year received. This exception was created because certain organizations (e.g., the American Automobile Association) convinced Congress that special tax treatment was needed for multi-year dues and subscriptions.

Another provision, sponsored by a senator from Georgia, suspended the import duties on ceiling fans. The nation's largest seller of ceiling fans is Atlanta-based Home Depot.

While some special interest legislation can be justified on economic or social grounds, in most cases, it cannot. It is, however, an inevitable product of our political system.

Political Expediency Situations

Various tax changes can be tied to the shifting moods of the American public. That Congress is sensitive to popular feeling is an accepted fact. Therefore, certain provisions of the tax law can be explained by the political climate at the time they were enacted.

Measures that deter more affluent taxpayers from obtaining so-called preferential tax treatment have always had popular appeal and, consequently, the support of Congress. Tax provisions like the imputed interest rules and the limitations on the deductibility of interest on investment indebtedness affect affluent taxpayers directly. More subtle are provisions that phase out tax breaks as income rises. These phaseouts are often called "stealth taxes," because the effects are *indirect* (and the taxpayer might not be aware of them). The tax law contains several dozen of these phaseout rules. Examples include

---

[39]The tax treatment of these items is discussed in Chapters 7, 10, and 16.

[40]Under the installment method, each payment received by the seller represents both a recovery of capital (the nontaxable portion) and profit from the sale (the taxable portion). The tax rules governing the installment method are discussed in Chapter 18.

the overall limit on itemized deductions and the phaseout of personal and dependency exemptions.

State and Local Government Influences

Political considerations played a major role in the nontaxability of interest received on state and local obligations. Somewhat less apparent has been the influence state law has had in shaping our present Federal tax law. Such was the case with community property systems. The nine states with community property systems are Arizona, California, Idaho, Louisiana, Nevada, New Mexico, Texas, Washington, and Wisconsin. The rest of the states are common law jurisdictions.[41] The difference between common law and community property systems centers around the property rights possessed by married persons. In a common law system, each spouse owns whatever he or she earns. Under a community property system, one-half of the earnings of each spouse is considered owned by the other spouse.

EXAMPLE 25

Al and Fran are married, and their only income is the $80,000 annual salary Al receives. If they live in New Jersey (a common law state), the $80,000 salary belongs to Al. If, however, they live in Arizona (a community property state), the $80,000 is divided equally, in terms of ownership, between Al and Fran.

At one time, the tax position of the residents of community property states was so advantageous that many common law states adopted community property systems. Needless to say, the political pressure placed on Congress to correct the disparity in tax treatment was considerable. To a large extent, this was accomplished in the Revenue Act of 1948, which extended many of the community property tax advantages to residents of common law jurisdictions.

Congress accomplished this by allowing married taxpayers to file joint returns and compute their tax liability as if one-half of the income had been earned by each spouse. This result is automatic in a community property state, because half of the income earned by one spouse belongs to the other spouse. The income-splitting benefits of a joint return are now incorporated as part of the tax rates applicable to married taxpayers. See Chapter 3.

1-6f **Influence of the Internal Revenue Service**

LO.8

Describe the role played by the IRS and the courts in the evolution of the Federal tax system.

The IRS has exerted its influence in many areas of the tax law. As the protector of the national revenue, the IRS has been instrumental in securing the passage of legislation designed to curtail aggressive tax avoidance practices (i.e., closing *tax loopholes*). In addition, the IRS has sought and obtained law changes to make its job easier (to attain administrative feasibility).

The IRS as Protector of the Revenue

There are many provisions in the tax law that resulted from the direct efforts of the IRS to prevent taxpayers from exploiting a tax loophole. Working within the letter of existing laws, ingenious taxpayers and their advisers devise techniques that accomplish indirectly what cannot be accomplished directly. As a result, Congress passes laws to close the loopholes that taxpayers have located and exploited.

In addition, Congress has passed laws that enable the IRS to make adjustments based on the substance of a transaction (rather than the form chosen by the taxpayer). For example, the IRS can make adjustments to a taxpayer's method of accounting when the method used by the taxpayer does not "clearly reflect income."[42]

---

[41]In Alaska, spouses can choose to have the community property rules apply. Otherwise, property rights are determined under common law rules.

[42]See Chapter 18.

EXAMPLE 26

Tina, a cash basis taxpayer, owns and operates a pharmacy. All drugs and other items acquired for resale, such as cosmetics, are charged to the purchases account and written off (expensed) for tax purposes in the year of acquisition. As this procedure does not clearly reflect income, it would be appropriate for the IRS to require that Tina establish and maintain an ending inventory account.

Administrative Feasibility

Some tax laws are created to simplify the task of the IRS in collecting the revenue and administering the law. As to collecting revenue, the IRS long ago realized the importance of placing taxpayers on a pay-as-you-go basis. Withholding procedures apply to wages, while the tax on other types of income may have to be paid via quarterly estimated payments. The IRS has been instrumental in convincing the courts that accrual basis taxpayers should, in most cases, pay taxes on prepaid income in the year received and not when earned. The approach may be contrary to generally accepted accounting principles, but prepayment is consistent with the wherewithal to pay concept.

To help the IRS collect revenues when due, Congress has passed many provisions that impose interest and penalties on taxpayers if they don't comply with the tax law. Provisions such as the penalties for failure to pay a tax or to file a return that is due, the negligence penalty for intentional disregard of rules and regulations, and various penalties for civil and criminal fraud are intended to encourage taxpayers to comply with the tax law.

The audit process conducted by the IRS is key to an effective administration of our tax system. To carry out this function, the IRS is aided by provisions that reduce the chance of taxpayer error or manipulation, thus simplifying the audit effort. For example, by increasing the standard deduction amount, the audit function is simplified because there are fewer returns with itemized deductions needing to be checked.[43]

1-6g Influence of the Courts

In addition to interpreting statutory provisions and the administrative pronouncements issued by the Treasury Department and the IRS, the Federal courts have influenced tax law in two other ways.[44] First, the courts have developed a number of judicial concepts that help guide how tax provisions are applied. Second, certain key decisions have led to changes in the Internal Revenue Code.

Judicial Concepts Relating to Tax

A leading tax concept developed by the courts deals with the interpretation of statutory tax provisions that operate to benefit taxpayers. The courts have decided that these relief provisions are to be applied narrowly. If a taxpayer wants a relief provision to apply, the taxpayer has the responsibility to meet the provision's requirements (i.e., no exceptions).

The *arm's length* concept is important here. Particularly in dealings between related parties, transactions may be tested by asking this question: Would unrelated parties have handled the transaction in the same way?

EXAMPLE 27

Rex, the sole shareholder of Silver Corporation, leases property to the corporation for a yearly rent of $60,000. To test whether the corporation should be allowed a rent deduction for this amount, the IRS and the courts will apply the arm's length concept. Would Silver Corporation have paid $60,000 a year in rent if it had leased the same property from an unrelated party (rather than from Rex)?

continued

---

[43]For a discussion of the standard deduction, see Chapter 3. The same justification was given by the IRS when it proposed to Congress the $100 limitation on personal casualty and theft losses. Imposition of the limitation eliminated many casualty and theft loss deductions and, as a consequence, saved the IRS considerable audit time. Later legislation, in addition to retaining the $100 feature, limits deductible losses to those in excess of 10% of a taxpayer's adjusted gross income. See Chapter 7.

[44]A great deal of case law is devoted to ascertaining congressional intent. The courts, in effect, ask: What did Congress have in mind when it enacted a particular tax provision?

Suppose it is determined that an unrelated third party would have charged an annual rent for the property of only $50,000. Under these circumstances, Silver Corporation will be allowed a deduction of only $50,000. The other $10,000 it paid for the use of the property represents a non-deductible dividend. Accordingly, Rex will be treated as having received rent income of $50,000 and dividend income of $10,000.

Judicial Influence on Statutory Provisions

Some court decisions have been so important that Congress incorporated them into the Internal Revenue Code. For example, many years ago the courts found that stock dividends distributed to the shareholders of a corporation were not taxable as income. This result was largely accepted by Congress, and the Code was modified to reflect the court's position.

On occasion, however, Congress reacts negatively to judicial interpretations of the tax law.

EXAMPLE 28

Nora leases unimproved real estate to Wade for 20 years. At a cost of $400,000, Wade erects a building on the land. The building is worth $150,000 when the lease terminates and Nora takes possession of the property.

Does Nora have any income either when the improvements are made or when the lease terminates? In a landmark decision, a court held that Nora must recognize income of $150,000 upon the termination of the lease.

Congress believed that the result reached in Example 28 was not consistent with the wherewithal to pay concept. As a result, the tax law was changed to provide that a landlord does not recognize any income either when the improvements are made (unless made in lieu of rent) or when the lease terminates.[45]

1-6h Summary

In addition to raising revenues, other factors have influenced the development of Federal tax law:

- *Economic considerations.* Congress uses the tax law to help regulate the economy and encourage certain activities and types of businesses.
- *Social considerations.* The tax law has been used to encourage (or discourage) certain socially desirable (or undesirable) practices.
- *Equity considerations.* The tax law can be designed to alleviate the effect of multiple taxation, recognize the wherewithal to pay concept, mitigate the effect of the annual accounting period concept, and recognize the eroding effect of inflation.
- *Political considerations.* Some tax law represents special interest legislation, reflects political expediency, or illustrates the effect of state and local law.
- *Influence of the IRS.* Laws are enacted to aid the IRS in the collection of revenue and the administration of the tax law.
- *Influence of the courts.* Court decisions have established a body of judicial concepts relating to tax law and have, on occasion, led Congress to enact laws to either clarify or negate their effect.

These factors help us understand how tax law develops (and why some provisions exist). We also must learn to work with the tax law, which is the subject of Chapter 2.

---

[45]*M.E. Blatt Co. v. U.S.*, 305 U.S. 267 (1938) and § 109.

REFOCUS ON THE BIG PICTURE

FAMILY AND TAXES—A TYPICAL YEAR

The explanation given for the difference in the ad valorem property taxes—the Carters' increase and the Walkers' decrease—seems reasonable (see Example 4). It is not likely that the Carters' increase was due to a *general* upward assessment in valuation, as the Walkers' taxes on their residence (located nearby) dropped. More business use of the Carters' residence (presuming that Travis conducts his consulting practice from his home) might be responsible for the increase, but capital improvements appear to be a more likely cause.

The imposition of the use tax when Travis registered the new automobile illustrates one of the means by which a state can preclude the avoidance of its sales tax (see Example 5).

When gifts between family members are material in amount (e.g., an RV) and exceed the annual exclusion, a gift tax return needs to be filed (see Example 11). Even though no gift tax may be due because of the availability of the unified transfer tax credit, the filing of a return starts the running of the statute of limitations.

The Carters must recognize that some of their income is subject to income taxes in two states and take advantage of whatever relief is available to mitigate the result (see Example 12).

Employment within and by the family group (e.g., children, other relatives, and domestics) has become a priority item in the enforcement of Social Security tax and income tax withholdings. Thus, the Carters must be aware of the need to cover their son, Martin (see Example 13).

Because of the double audit (i.e., both state and Federal) and the deficiency assessed, the Carters need to make sure that future returns do not contain similar errors (see Example 18). As the text suggests, taxpayers with prior deficiencies are among those whose returns may be selected for audit.

CORBIS/SUPERSTOCK

Key Terms

Ad valorem taxes, 1-9	Franchise tax, 1-19	Revenue neutrality, 1-27
Carbon tax, 1-21	FUTA tax, 1-18	Sales tax, 1-12
Correspondence audit, 1-22	Gift tax, 1-14	Severance taxes, 1-12
Employment taxes, 1-17	Indexation, 1-31	Statute of limitations, 1-24
Estate tax, 1-13	Inheritance tax, 1-13	Sunset provision, 1-27
Excise taxes, 1-11	National sales tax, 1-20	Use tax, 1-12
FICA tax, 1-17	Occupational fees, 1-19	Value added tax (VAT), 1-20
Field audit, 1-23	Office audit, 1-23	Wherewithal to pay, 1-30
Financial transaction tax, 1-21	Personalty, 1-10	
Flat tax, 1-20	Realty, 1-10	

Discussion Questions

1. **LO.1, 4** In the following independent situations, is the tax position of the taxpayer likely to change? Explain why or why not.
    a.   John started renting out a spare room in his home.

b. Theresa quit her job as a staff accountant and has established her own practice as a CPA.

c. Paul's employer transferred him from its California office to an office in Florida

Issue ID   2. **LO.1, 4** Marvin is the executor and sole heir of his aunt's estate. The estate includes her furnished home, which Marvin is considering converting to rental property to generate additional cash flow. What are some of the tax problems Marvin may confront?

3. **LO.2** The Sixteenth Amendment to the U.S. Constitution was passed to overturn a Supreme Court decision that had invalidated the Federal income tax. Do you agree? Why or why not?

4. **LO.2** World War II converted the Federal income tax into a *mass tax*. Explain.

5. **LO.2** How does the pay-as-you-go procedure apply to wage earners? To persons who have income from sources other than wages?

6. **LO.3** Jane, a tax practitioner, has reviewed the law on how State X's income tax applies to a client's web-based consulting business, but is unable to reach a conclusion for which she has a high level of confidence. Assuming Jane is a knowledgeable and experienced tax professional, which *Guiding Principles of Good Tax Policy* might not be followed by State X?

7. **LO.3** Distinguish between taxes that are *proportional* and those that are *progressive*.

Issue ID   8. **LO.4** Several years ago Ethan purchased the former parsonage of St. James Church to use as a personal residence. To date, Ethan has not received any ad valorem property tax bills from either the city or the county tax authorities.

a. What is a reasonable explanation for this oversight?

b. What should Ethan do?

Issue ID   9. **LO.4** The Adams Independent School District wants to sell a parcel of unimproved land that it does not need. Its three best offers are as follows: from the state's Department of Public Safety (DPS), $2.3 million; from the Second Baptist Church, $2.2 million; and from Baker Motors, $2.1 million. DPS would use the property for a new state highway patrol barracks, Second Baptist would start a church school, and Baker would open a car dealership. If you are the financial adviser for the school district, which offer would you prefer? Why?

10. **LO.4** The commissioners for Walker County are actively negotiating with Falcon Industries regarding the location of a new manufacturing plant in the area. As Falcon is considering several other sites, a "generous tax holiday" may be needed to influence the final choice. The local school district is opposed to any "generous tax holiday."

a. What would probably be involved in a generous tax holiday?

b. Why would the school district be opposed?

11. **LO.4** Sophia lives several blocks from her parents in the same residential subdivision. Sophia is surprised to learn that her ad valorem property taxes for the year were raised, while those of her parents were lowered. What is a possible explanation for the difference?

12. **LO.4** The Morgan family lives in Massachusetts. They moor their sailboat in Rhode Island. What might be a plausible reason for the possible inconvenience?

13. **LO.4** Is the breadth and number of Federal excise taxes increasing or decreasing? Explain.

14. **LO.4** After his first business trip to a major city, Herman is alarmed when he reviews his credit card receipts. Both the hotel bill and the car rental charge are in excess of the price he was quoted. Was Herman overcharged, or is there an explanation for the excess amounts?

15. **LO.4** What is the difference between an excise tax and a general sales tax?
   a. Do all states impose a general sales tax?
   b. Does the Federal government impose a general sales tax?

16. **LO.4** The Grays live in Clay County, which is adjacent to Jackson County. Although the retail stores in both counties are comparable, the Grays usually drive a few extra miles to shop in Jackson County. As to why the Grays might do this, consider the following:
   a. Clay County is in a different state than Jackson County.
   b. Clay County and Jackson County are in the same state.

17. **LO.4** During a social event, Muriel and Earl are discussing the home computer each   Issue ID
   recently purchased. Although the computers are identical makes and models, Muriel is surprised to learn that she paid a sales tax, while Earl did not. Comment as to why this could happen.

18. **LO.4** Distinguish between an estate tax and an inheritance tax.
   a. Do some states impose both? Neither?
   b. Which, if either, does the Federal government impose?

19. **LO.4** Jake (age 72) and Jessica (age 28) were recently married. To avoid any trans-   Issue ID
   fer taxes, Jake has promised to leave Jessica all of his wealth when he dies. Is Jake under some misconception about the operation of the Federal gift and estate taxes? Explain.

20. **LO.4** Address the following issues:
   a. What is the purpose of the unified transfer tax credit?
   b. Is the same amount available for both the Federal gift tax and the estate tax? Explain.
   c. Does the use of the credit for a gift affect the amount of credit available for the estate tax? Explain.

21. **LO.4** Elijah and Anastasia are husband and wife who have five married children and nine minor grandchildren. For 2017, what is the maximum amount they can give to their family (including the sons- and daughters-in-law) without using any of their unified transfer tax credit?

22. **LO.4** What is the difference between the Federal income tax on individuals and that imposed on corporations?

23. **LO.4** As to those states that impose an income tax, comment on the following:
   a. "Piggyback" approach and possible "decoupling" from this approach.
   b. Using IRS audit results as part of a state tax audit.
   c. Credit for taxes paid to other states.

24. **LO.4** In May 2017, Hernando, a resident of California, has his 2015 Federal income tax return audited by the IRS. An assessment of additional tax is made because he had inadvertently omitted some rental income. In October 2017, California audits his state return for the same year. Explain the coincidence.

25. **LO.4** Mike Barr was an outstanding football player in college and expects to be   Issue ID
   drafted by the NFL in the first few rounds. Mike has let it be known that he would prefer to sign with a club located in Florida, Texas, or Washington. Mike sees no reason why he should have to pay state income tax on his player's salary. Is Mike under any delusions? Explain.

Issue ID   26. **LO.4, 5** A question on a state income tax return asks the taxpayer if he or she made any out-of-state internet or mail-order catalog purchases during the year. The question requires a yes or no answer, and if the taxpayer answers yes, the amount of such purchases is to be listed.

a. Does such an inquiry have any relevance to the state income tax? If not, why is it being asked?

b. Your client, Harriet, wants to leave the question unanswered. As the preparer of her return, how do you respond?

27. **LO.4** Many state income tax returns contain checkoff boxes that allow taxpayers to make donations to a multitude of local charitable causes. On what grounds has this procedure been criticized?

28. **LO.4** Many states have occasionally adopted amnesty programs that allow taxpayers to pay back taxes with reduced penalties.

a. Besides the revenue generated, how are these programs advantageous?

b. Could an amnesty program be used by a state that does not levy an income tax?

c. Does the IRS utilize this approach?

29. **LO.4** Contrast FICA and FUTA as to the following:

a. Purpose of the tax.

b. Upon whom imposed.

c. Governmental administration of the tax.

d. Reduction of tax based on a merit rating system.

30. **LO.4** In connection with the Medicare component of FICA, comment on the following:

a. Any dollar limitation imposed.

b. The applicability of the .9% increase in the 1.45% regular tax rate.

31. **LO.4** One of the tax advantages of hiring family members to work in your business is that FICA taxes are avoided. Do you agree with this statement? Explain.

32. **LO.4** Describe the nature and purpose of the following taxes:

a. Severance taxes.

b. Franchise taxes.

c. Occupational fees.

d. Customs duties.

e. Export duties.

33. **LO.4** Regarding the value added tax (VAT), comment on the following:

a. Popularity of this type of tax.

b. Nature of the tax.

c. Effect on government spending.

34. **LO.4** Both a value added tax (VAT) and a national sales tax have been criticized as being *regressive* in their effect.

a. Explain.

b. How could this shortcoming be remedied?

35. **LO.4, 5** Serena operates a gift shop. To reduce costs of credit card transactions, she offers customers a discount if they pay in cash. For the holiday rush, she hires some short-term workers, but pays them cash and does not add them to the payroll.

a. What are some of the tax problems Serena might have?

b. Assess Serena's chances of audit by the IRS.

36. **LO.5** With regard to the IRS audit process, comment on the following:
    a. The audit is resolved by mail.
    b. The audit is conducted at the office of the IRS.
    c. A "no change" RAR results.
    d. A special agent joins the audit team.

37. **LO.5** Aldo has just been audited by the IRS. He does not agree with the agent's findings but believes that he has only two choices: pay the proposed deficiency or resort to the courts. Do you agree with Aldo's conclusion? Why or why not?

38. **LO.5** What purpose is served by a statute of limitations? How is it relevant in the case of tax controversies?

39. **LO.5** Regarding the statute of limitations on additional assessments of tax by the IRS, determine the applicable period in each of the following situations. Assume a calendar year individual with no fraud or substantial omission involved.
    a. The income tax return for 2016 was filed on February 19, 2017.
    b. The income tax return for 2016 was filed on June 25, 2017.
    c. The income tax return for 2016 was prepared on April 4, 2017, but was never filed. Through some misunderstanding between the preparer and the taxpayer, each expected the other to file the return.
    d. The income tax return for 2016 was never filed because the taxpayer thought no additional tax was due.

40. **LO.5** Brianna, a calendar year taxpayer, files her income tax return for 2016 on February 3, 2017. Although she makes repeated inquiries, she does not receive her refund from the IRS until May 28, 2017. Is Brianna entitled to interest on the refund? Explain.

41. **LO.5, 6** On a Federal income tax return filed five years ago, Andy inadvertently omitted a large amount of gross income.
    a. Andy seeks your advice as to whether the IRS is barred from assessing additional income tax in the event he is audited. What is your advice?
    b. Would your advice differ if you were the person who prepared the return in question? Explain.
    c. Suppose Andy asks you to prepare his current year's return. Would you do so? Explain.

42. **LO.5** Isabella files her income tax return 35 days after the due date of the return without obtaining an extension from the IRS. Along with the return, she remits a check for $40,000, which is the balance of the tax she owes. Disregarding the interest element, what are Isabella's penalties for failure to file and for failure to pay?

43. **LO.5** For tax year 2014, the IRS assesses a deficiency against David for $500,000. Disregarding the interest component, what is David's penalty if the deficiency is attributable to:
    a. Negligence?
    b. Fraud?

44. **LO.5, 6** In March 2017, Jim asks you to prepare his Federal income tax returns for tax years 2014, 2015, and 2016. In discussing this matter with him, you discover that he also has not filed for tax year 2013. When you mention this fact, Jim tells you that the statute of limitations precludes the IRS from taking any action as to this year.

a.   Is Jim correct about the application of the statute of limitations? Why or why not?

b.   If Jim refuses to file for 2013, should you prepare returns for 2014 through 2016? Explain.

45. **LO.5, 6** The Benson CPA firm is considering utilizing an offshore service provider to prepare many of its tax returns. In this regard, what ethical considerations must be taken into account?

46. **LO.7** In terms of tax policy, what do the following mean?

a.   Revenue neutrality.

b.   Pay-as-you-go, or "paygo."

c.   Sunset provision.

d.   Indexation.

47. **LO.7** Some tax rules can be justified on multiple grounds (e.g., economic and social). In this connection, comment on the possible justification for the rules governing the following:

a.   Pension plans.

b.   Education.

c.   Home ownership.

48. **LO.7, 8** Discuss the probable justification for each of the following aspects of the tax law:

a.   A tax credit is allowed for amounts spent to furnish care for minor children while the parent works.

b.   Deductions for interest on home mortgage and property taxes on a personal residence.

c.   The income-splitting benefits of filing a joint return.

d.   Fines and penalties are not deductible.

e.   Net operating losses of a current year can be carried back to profitable years.

f.   A taxpayer who sells property on an installment basis can recognize gain on the sale over the period the payments are received.

g.   The exclusion from Federal tax of certain interest income from state and local bonds.

h.   Prepaid income is taxed to the recipient in the year received and not in the year earned.

49. **LO.7** Mia owns a warehouse that has a cost basis to her of $80,000. The city condemns the warehouse to make room for a new fire station. It pays Mia $400,000 for the property, its agreed-to fair market value. Shortly after the condemnation, Mia purchases another warehouse as a replacement. What is her recognized gain if the new property cost:

a. $280,000?

b. $444,000?

c. $80,000?

d.   What, if any, is the justification for deferring the recognition of gain on the involuntary conversion?

50. **LO.8** A mother sells a valuable collection of antiques to her daughter for $1,000. What judicial concept might the IRS invoke to question this transaction?

Research Problems

Use internet tax resources to address the following questions. Look for reliable websites and blogs of the IRS and other government agencies, media outlets, businesses, tax professionals, academics, think tanks, and political outlets.

Research Problem 1. Using information from this chapter as well as information from the tax agency in your state (likely called the Department of Revenue) and your local government, find all of the taxes to which a sole proprietor is subject. Create a table that lists all of these taxes and the level(s) of government that imposes each tax.

Research Problem 2. Use **www.congress.gov** or another reliable website to find a proposal for a carbon tax or a financial transactions tax. Draft a summary of the tax, and analyze it against five of the principles of good tax policy.

Working with the Tax Law

LEARNING OBJECTIVES: *After completing Chapter 2, you should be able to:*

LO.1 Distinguish between the statutory, administrative, and judicial sources of the tax law and understand the purpose of each source.

LO.2 Locate and work with the appropriate tax law sources.

LO.3 Develop an awareness of tax research tools.

LO.4 Describe the tax research process.

LO.5 Communicate the results of the tax research process in a client letter and a tax file memorandum.

LO.6 Apply tax research techniques and planning procedures.

LO.7 Be aware of taxation on the CPA examination.

CHAPTER OUTLINE

MONKEY BUSINESS IMAGES/SHUTTERSTOCK.COM

THE BIG PICTURE

IMPORTANCE OF TAX RESEARCH

Early in December 2017, Fred and Megan Samuels review their financial and tax situation with their son, Sam, and daughter-in-law, Dana, who live with them. Fred and Megan are in the 28 percent tax bracket in 2017. Both Sam and Dana are age 21. Sam, a student at a nearby university, owns some publicly traded stock that he inherited from his grandmother about five years ago. A current sale would result in $8,000 of gross income ($19,000 amount realized − $11,000 basis). At this point, Fred and Megan provide about 55 percent of Sam and Dana's support. Although neither is now employed, Sam has earned $960 and Dana has earned $900 during the year. The problem: Should the stock be sold? If the stock was sold, would the sale prohibit Fred and Megan from claiming Sam and Dana as dependents? Would the stock sale in 2017 result in a tax liability for Sam and Dana?

Read the chapter and formulate your responses.

Federal tax law reflects the three branches of our Federal government. It is a mixture of laws passed by Congress, explanations provided by the Treasury Department and the Internal Revenue Service (IRS), and court decisions. Anyone who has attempted to work with this vast amount of information is familiar with its complexity. The tax research process allows us to understand, evaluate, and apply the tax law to questions that are raised by taxpayers and tax practitioners.

In addition to being able to locate and interpret tax law, a tax professional must also understand the relative *weight of authority* that each source carries. The tax law is of little significance, however, until it is applied to a set of facts and circumstances. This chapter, therefore, introduces the statutory, administrative, and judicial sources of tax law and explains how the law is applied to individual and business transactions. It also explains how to apply research techniques and use planning procedures effectively. A large part of tax research focuses on determining the intent of Congress.

Frequently, uncertainty in the tax law causes disputes between the Internal Revenue Service (IRS) and taxpayers. Due to these *gray areas* and the complexity of the tax law, a taxpayer may have more than one alternative for structuring a financial transaction. In structuring financial transactions and engaging in other tax planning activities, the tax adviser must be cognizant that the objective of tax planning is not necessarily to minimize the tax liability. Instead, a taxpayer should maximize his or her after-tax wealth, which may include maximizing nontax as well as noneconomic benefits.

2-1 TAX SOURCES

LO.1

Distinguish between the statutory, administrative, and judicial sources of the tax law and understand the purpose of each source.

Understanding taxation requires a mastery of the sources of tax law. These sources include laws passed by Congress, which are contained in the Internal Revenue Code and congressional Committee Reports, Treasury Department Regulations, other Treasury Department and IRS pronouncements, and court decisions. Thus, the *primary sources* of tax law include information from all three branches of government: legislative (or statutory), executive, and judicial.[1]

2-1a Statutory Sources of the Tax Law

Statutory sources of law include the Constitution (Article I, Sections 7, 8, and 10), the Internal Revenue Code, and tax treaties (agreements between countries to mitigate the double taxation of taxpayers subject to the tax laws of those countries). The Constitution grants Congress the power to impose and collect taxes and authorizes the creation of treaties with other countries. The power of Congress to implement and collect taxes is reflected in the Internal Revenue Code, the official title of U.S. tax law, and it is the basis for arriving at solutions to all tax questions.

Origin of the Internal Revenue Code

Before 1939, the statutory provisions relating to Federal taxation were contained in the individual revenue acts enacted by Congress. Because dealing with many separate acts was inconvenient and confusing, Congress codified all of the Federal tax laws in 1939. Known as the Internal Revenue Code of 1939, the codification arranged all Federal tax provisions in a logical sequence and placed them in a separate part of the Federal statutes. A further rearrangement took place in 1954 and resulted in the Internal Revenue Code of 1954, which continued in effect until 1986, when it was replaced by the Internal Revenue Code of 1986. Although Congress did not recodify the law in the Tax Reform Act (TRA) of 1986, the magnitude of the changes made by TRA of 1986 did provide some rationale for renaming the Federal tax law the Internal Revenue Code of 1986.[2]

---

[1]*Secondary sources* also are used by tax practitioners. These sources are not part of the tax law and include items like tax articles from professional tax journals, newsletters, and textbooks. Commentary contained in various tax research services (like Thomson Reuters *Checkpoint*) are also secondary sources.

[2]This point is important in assessing judicial decisions interpreting provisions of the Internal Revenue Code of 1939 and the Internal Revenue Code of 1954. If a provision from the 1939 or 1954 Code was included in the Internal Revenue Code of 1986 and has not been subsequently amended, the provision and the related judicial decisions have continuing validity.

The Legislative Process

Exhibit 2.1 illustrates the legislative process for enacting changes to the Internal Revenue Code of 1986. Federal tax legislation generally originates in the House of Representatives, where it is first considered by the House Ways and Means Committee.[3] Once approved by the House Ways and Means Committee, the proposed bill is referred to the entire House of Representatives for approval or disapproval. Approved bills are sent to the Senate, where they are considered by the Senate Finance Committee.[4]

After approval by the Senate Finance Committee, the bill is sent to the entire Senate. Assuming no disagreement between the House and Senate, passage by the Senate results in referral to the President for approval or veto. If the bill is approved or if

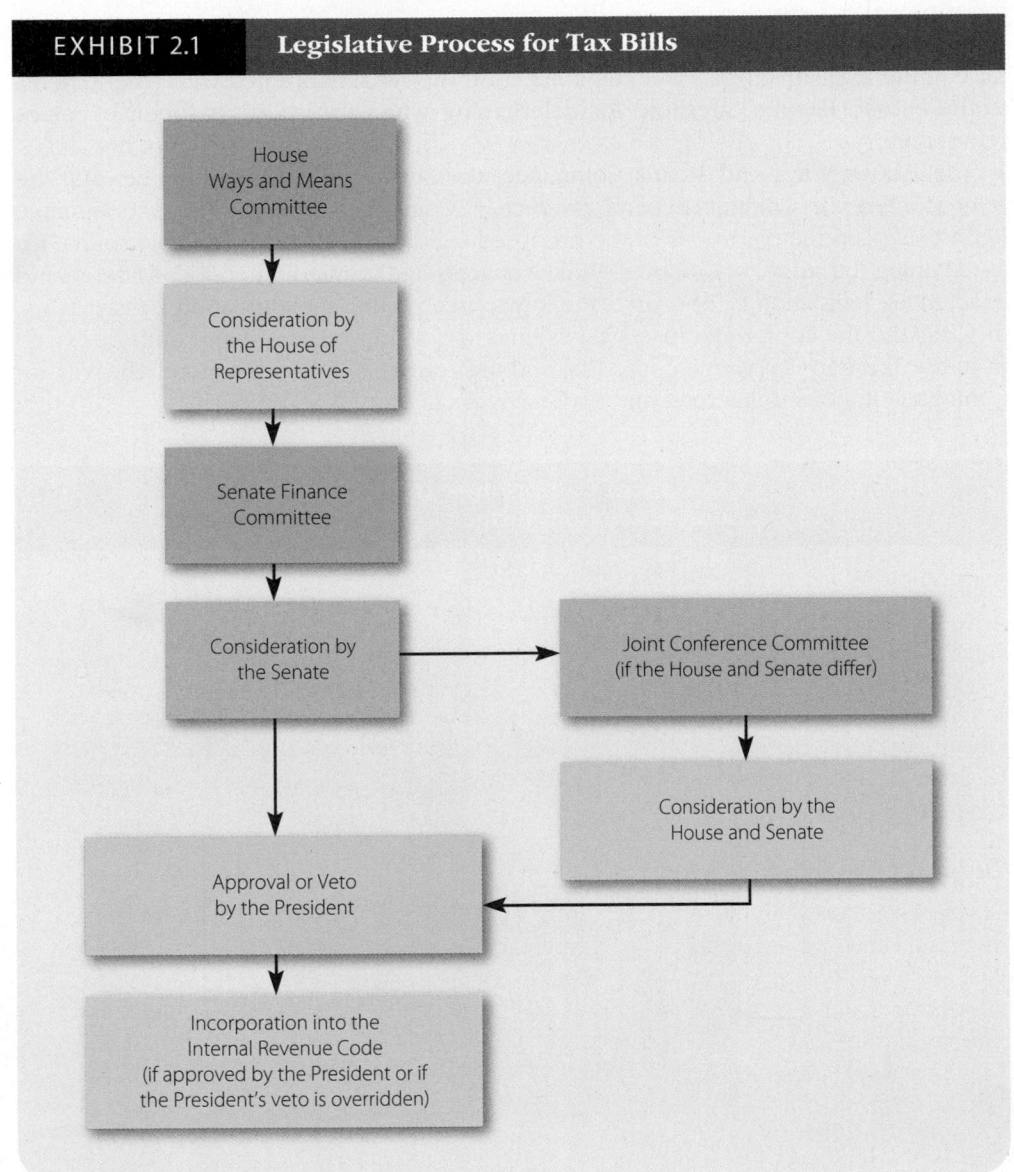

EXHIBIT 2.1	Legislative Process for Tax Bills

House Ways and Means Committee

↓

Consideration by the House of Representatives

↓

Senate Finance Committee

↓

Consideration by the Senate → Joint Conference Committee (if the House and Senate differ)

↓

Consideration by the House and Senate

Approval or Veto by the President

↓

Incorporation into the Internal Revenue Code (if approved by the President or if the President's veto is overridden)

---

[3]Congress enacts tax legislation virtually every year, and each piece of legislation contains changes to the Internal Revenue Code of 1986.

[4]Although rare, a tax bill can originate in the Senate when it is attached as a rider to a different legislative proposal. The Tax Equity and Fiscal Responsibility Act of 1982 originated in the Senate, and its constitutionality was upheld by the courts.

the President's veto is overridden, the bill becomes law and part of the Internal Revenue Code of 1986.

House and Senate versions of major tax bills frequently differ. One reason bills are often changed in the Senate is that each senator has considerable latitude to make amendments when the Senate as a whole is voting on a bill referred to it by the Senate Finance Committee.[5] In contrast, the entire House of Representatives either accepts or rejects what is proposed by the House Ways and Means Committee, and changes from the floor are rare. When the Senate version of the bill differs from that passed by the House, the Joint Conference Committee, which includes members of both the House Ways and Means Committee and the Senate Finance Committee, resolves the differences. The deliberations of the Joint Conference Committee usually produce a compromise between the two versions, which then is voted on by both the House and the Senate. If both bodies accept the bill, it is referred to the President for approval or veto.

The role of the Joint Conference Committee indicates the importance of compromise in the legislative process. Exhibit 2.2 illustrates what happened with amendments to the earned income threshold for determining when the child tax credit becomes refundable.

The House Ways and Means Committee, the Senate Finance Committee, and the Joint Conference Committee each produce a Committee Report. These Committee Reports explain the provisions of the proposed legislation and are a valuable source for ascertaining the *intent of Congress*. What Congress had in mind when it considered and enacted tax legislation is, of course, the key to interpreting the legislation by taxpayers, the IRS, and the courts. Because it takes time to develop other primary authority (e.g., from the Treasury Department, the IRS, and the courts), tax researchers rely heavily on Committee Reports to interpret and apply new tax laws.

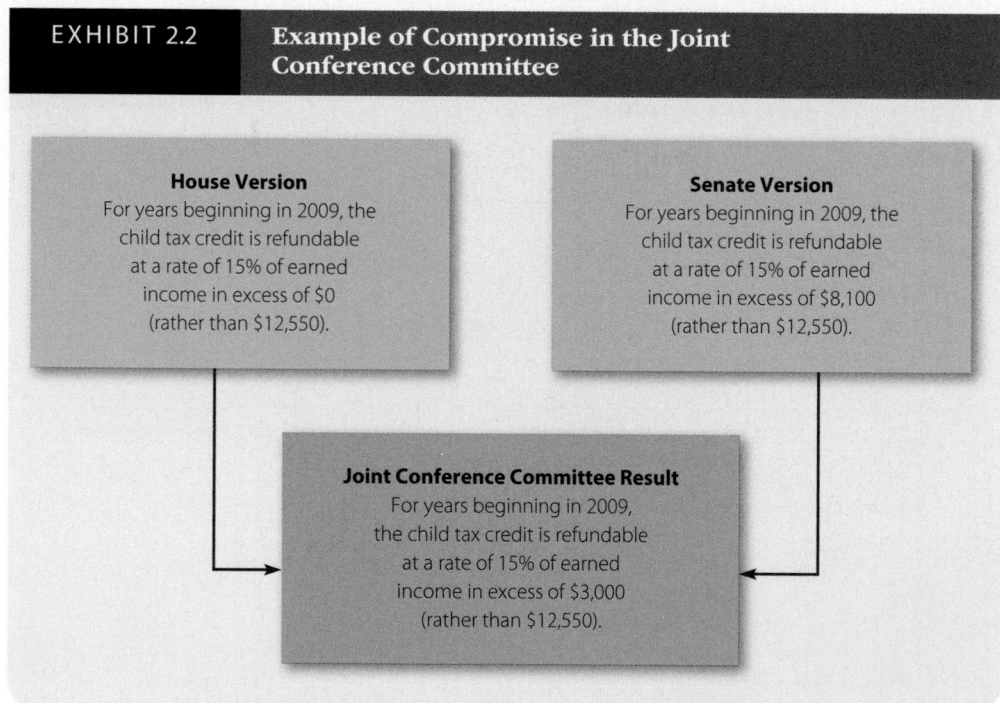

EXHIBIT 2.2	**Example of Compromise in the Joint Conference Committee**

House Version
For years beginning in 2009, the child tax credit is refundable at a rate of 15% of earned income in excess of $0 (rather than $12,550).

Senate Version
For years beginning in 2009, the child tax credit is refundable at a rate of 15% of earned income in excess of $8,100 (rather than $12,550).

Joint Conference Committee Result
For years beginning in 2009, the child tax credit is refundable at a rate of 15% of earned income in excess of $3,000 (rather than $12,550).

---

[5]During the passage of the Tax Reform Act of 1986, Senate leaders tried to make the bill *amendment proof* to avoid the normal amendment process.

Arrangement of the Internal Revenue Code

The Internal Revenue Code of 1986 is found in Title 26 of the U.S. Code. In working with the Internal Revenue Code, it helps to understand the format. Here is a partial table of contents:

> Subtitle A. Income Taxes
>   Chapter 11. Normal Taxes and Surtaxes
>   Subchapter A. Determination of Tax Liability
>   Part I. Tax on Individuals
>   Sections 1–5
>   Part II. Tax on Corporations
>   Sections 11–12

In referring to a provision of the Code, the *key* is usually the Section number. In citing a Section number, it is unnecessary to include the related Subtitle, Chapter, Subchapter, and Part. Merely mentioning the Section will suffice, because the Section numbers run consecutively and do not begin again with each new Subtitle, Chapter, Subchapter, or Part.[6]

Tax researchers often refer to specific areas of income tax law by their Subchapters. Some of the more common Subchapter designations include Subchapter C ("Corporate Distributions and Adjustments"), Subchapter K ("Partners and Partnerships"), and Subchapter S ("Tax Treatment of S Corporations and Their Shareholders").

Citing the Code

Code Sections often are broken down into subparts.[7] Section 2(a)(1)(A) serves as an example.

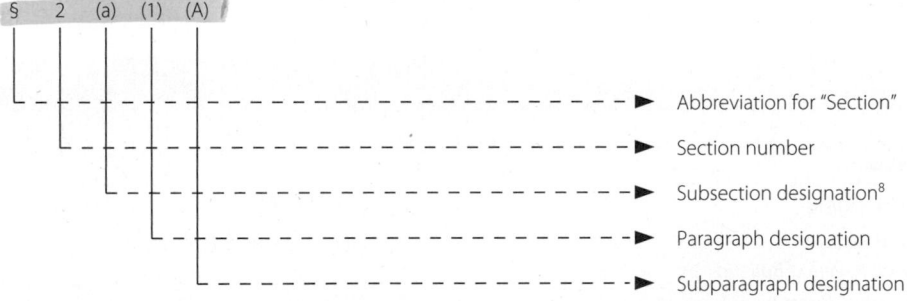

Broken down by content, § 2(a)(1)(A) becomes:

§ 2 ⟶ Definitions and special rules (relating to the income tax imposed on individuals).

(a) ⟶ Definition of a surviving spouse.

(1) ⟶ For purposes of § 1 (the determination of the applicable rate schedule), a surviving spouse must meet certain conditions.

(A) ⟶ One of the conditions necessary to qualify as a surviving spouse is that the taxpayer's spouse must have died during either of his or her two taxable years immediately preceding the present taxable year.

Throughout the text, references to the Code Sections are in the form given above. The symbols "§" and "§§" are used in place of "Section" and "Sections," respectively. The following table summarizes the format that we use:

---

[6]When the 1954 Code was drafted, some section numbers were intentionally omitted so that later changes could be incorporated into the Code without disrupting its organization. When Congress does not leave enough space, subsequent Code Sections are given A, B, C, etc., designations. A good example is the treatment of §§ 280A through 280H.

[7]Some Code Sections do not require subparts. See, for example, §§ 211 and 241.

[8]Some Code Sections omit the subsection designation and use the paragraph designation as the first subpart. See, for example, §§ 212(1) and 1222(1).

Complete Reference	Text Reference
Section 2(a)(1)(A) of the Internal Revenue Code of 1986	§ 2(a)(1)(A)
Sections 1 and 2 of the Internal Revenue Code of 1986	§§ 1 and 2
Section 2 of the Internal Revenue Code of 1954	§ 2 of the Internal Revenue Code of 1954
Section 12(d) of the Internal Revenue Code of 1939[9]	§ 12(d) of the Internal Revenue Code of 1939

2-1b Administrative Sources of the Tax Law

The administrative sources of the Federal tax law include Treasury Department Regulations, Revenue Rulings and Revenue Procedures, and various other administrative pronouncements (see Exhibit 2.3). All are issued by either the U.S. Treasury Department or the IRS.

Treasury Department Regulations

Regulations are issued by the U.S. Treasury Department under authority granted by Congress.[10] Interpretive by nature, they provide taxpayers with considerable guidance on the meaning and application of the Code. Regulations, which carry considerable authority as the official interpretation of tax law, may be issued in *proposed*, *temporary*, or *final* form.

Because Regulations interpret the Code, they are arranged in the same sequence as the Code. A number is added at the beginning, however, to indicate the type of tax or administrative, procedural, or definitional matter to which they relate.[11] For example,

EXHIBIT 2.3	Administrative Sources

Source	Location	Authority
Regulations	*Federal Register*	Force and effect of law.
Temporary Regulations	*Federal Register* *Internal Revenue Bulletin* *Cumulative Bulletin*	May be cited as a precedent.
Proposed Regulations	*Federal Register* *Internal Revenue Bulletin* *Cumulative Bulletin*	Preview of final Regulations.
Revenue Rulings Revenue Procedures Treasury Decisions Actions on Decisions	*Internal Revenue Bulletin* *Cumulative Bulletin*	Do not have the force and effect of law.
General Counsel Memoranda Technical Advice Memoranda	Tax Analysts' *Tax Notes;* Thomson Reuters *Checkpoint**; Commerce Clearing House *IntelliConnect*	May not be cited as a precedent.
Letter Rulings	Thomson Reuters and Commerce Clearing House tax services	Applicable only to taxpayer addressed. No precedential force.

* Thomson Reuters *Checkpoint* includes a wide variety of tax resources. The most significant are materials produced by the Research Institute of America (RIA), including the *Federal Tax Coordinator 2d.*

---

[9]Section 12(d) of the Internal Revenue Code of 1939 is the predecessor to § 2 of the Internal Revenue Code of 1954 and the Internal Revenue Code of 1986. Keep in mind that the 1954 Code superseded the 1939 Code, and the 1986 Code superseded the 1954 Code. Footnote 2 explains why references to the 1939 or 1954 Code are included.

[10]§ 7805.

[11]The prefix 20 designates estate tax Regulations, 25 covers gift tax Regulations, 31 relates to employment taxes, and 301 refers to procedure and administration.

the prefix 1 designates the Regulations under the income tax law. Thus, the Regulations under Code § 2 are cited as Reg. § 1.2, with subparts added for further identification. The numbering patterns of these subparts often have no correlation with the Code subsections.

ETHICS & EQUITY Reporting Tax Fraud

Maybe someone in your extended family is driving a luxury car and comments that only fools pay all of their taxes. Or maybe a contractor demands payment in cash. Or perhaps someone at work is not reporting all of his or her income. If cheating on taxes bothers you, the IRS wants to hear from you (and may make it worthwhile). The IRS has two whistleblower programs: The small-awards program is for cases involving less than $2 million of tax, and the award can be as high as 15% of collections, although it often is less. The large-awards program is more generous: For cases involving $2 million or more of tax, the reward can go as high as 30%. The IRS's tip line is 1-800-829-0433, and the appropriate form to report tax fraud is Form 3949–A (Information Referral). Would you turn in someone?

New Regulations and changes to existing Regulations are usually issued in proposed form before they are finalized. The interval between the proposal of a Regulation and its finalization permits taxpayers and other interested parties to comment on the propriety of the proposal. **Proposed Regulations** under Code § 2, for example, are cited as Prop.Reg. § 1.2. The Tax Court indicates that Proposed Regulations carry little weight. **Final Regulations** have the force and effect of law.[12]

Sometimes the Treasury Department issues **Temporary Regulations** where immediate guidance is important. These Regulations are issued without the comment period required for Proposed Regulations. Temporary Regulations, cited as Temp.Reg. §, have the same authoritative value as final Regulations and may be cited as precedents. However, Temporary Regulations must also be issued as Proposed Regulations and automatically expire within three years after the date of issuance.[13]

Proposed, Temporary, and final Regulations are published in the *Federal Register*, in the *Internal Revenue Bulletin* (I.R.B.), and by major tax services. Final Regulations are issued as Treasury Decisions (TDs).

Regulations may also be classified as *legislative, interpretive,* or *procedural.* These classifications are discussed in text Section 2-3d (Assessing the Validity of Tax Law Sources) later in the chapter.

Revenue Rulings and Revenue Procedures

Revenue Rulings are official pronouncements of the National Office of the IRS.[14] They typically provide one or more examples of how the IRS would apply a law to *specific fact situations.* Like Regulations, Revenue Rulings are designed to provide interpretation of the tax law. Although they do not carry the same legal force and effect as Regulations, because they are focused on a specific fact pattern, they provide a more detailed analysis of the law.

Although letter rulings (discussed in the next section) are not the same as Revenue Rulings, a Revenue Ruling often results from a specific taxpayer's request for a letter ruling. If the IRS believes that a letter ruling request has widespread impact, the letter ruling will be converted into a Revenue Ruling and issued. Revenue Rulings can also be issued in response to technical advice to District Offices of the IRS, court decisions, and suggestions from tax practitioner groups.

Revenue Procedures deal with the internal management practices and procedures of the IRS. For example, Rev.Proc. 2017–1 provides general instructions for taxpayers

---

[12]*F. W. Woolworth Co.*, 54 T.C. 1233 (1970); *Harris M. Miller*, 70 T.C. 448 (1978); and *James O. Tomerlin Trust*, 87 T.C. 876 (1986).

[13]§ 7805(e).

[14]§ 7805(a).

requesting letter rulings or determination letters from the IRS. A taxpayer's failure to follow a Revenue Procedure can result in unnecessary delay or, in a discretionary situation, can cause the IRS to decline to act.

Both Revenue Rulings and Revenue Procedures serve an important function by providing *guidance* to IRS personnel and taxpayers in handling routine tax matters. Revenue Rulings and Revenue Procedures generally apply retroactively and are binding on the IRS until revoked or modified by subsequent rulings or procedures, Regulations, legislation, or court decisions.

Revenue Rulings and Revenue Procedures are published weekly by the U.S. Government in the *Internal Revenue Bulletin* (I.R.B.).

The proper form for citing Revenue Rulings is as follows. Revenue Procedures are cited in the same manner, except that "Rev.Proc." is substituted for "Rev.Rul."

Rev.Rul. 2016–16, 2016–26 I.R.B. 1062.

Explanation: Revenue Ruling Number 16, appearing on page 1062 of the 26th weekly issue of the *Internal Revenue Bulletin* for 2016.

Revenue Rulings and other tax resources may be found at the IRS website: **www.irs.gov**.[15]

Letter Rulings

Letter rulings are issued for a fee upon a taxpayer's request and describe how the IRS will treat a *proposed* transaction for tax purposes. Issued by the National Office of the IRS, they apply only to the taxpayer who asks for and obtains the ruling.[16] Letter rulings can be useful to taxpayers who want to be certain of how a transaction will be taxed before proceeding with it. Letter rulings also allow taxpayers to avoid unexpected tax costs and may be the most effective way to carry out tax planning. However, the IRS limits the issuance of individual rulings to restricted, preannounced areas of taxation.[17] The IRS issues more than 2,500 letter rulings each year.

The IRS must make individual rulings available for public inspection after identifying details are deleted.[18] Published digests of private letter rulings can be found in a variety of sources, including *IRS Letter Rulings Reports* (published by CCH), Bloomberg BNA's *Daily Tax Reports,* Tax Analysts' *Tax Notes,* and electronic (online) tax research services (like Thomson Reuters *Checkpoint*).

Letter rulings are issued multidigit file numbers that indicate the year and week of issuance as well as the number of the ruling during that week. Consider, for example, Ltr.Rul. 201633025, requesting whether the beneficiaries of a trust are treated as the designated beneficiaries of an IRA.

2016	33	025
Year 2016	33rd week of 2016	25th ruling issued during the 33rd week

Other Administrative Pronouncements

Treasury Decisions (TDs) are issued by the Treasury Department to announce new Regulations, amend or change existing Regulations, or announce the position of the

---

[15]Commercial sources for Revenue Rulings and Revenue Procedures are available, usually requiring a subscription fee. Older Revenue Rulings and Revenue Procedures are often cited as being published in the *Cumulative Bulletin* (C.B.) rather than in the *Internal Revenue Bulletin* (I.R.B.).

[16]Post-1984 letter rulings may be substantial authority for purposes of the accuracy-related penalty; see pp. 2-24 and 2-25; Notice 90–20, 1990–1 C.B. 328. In this regard, letter rulings differ from Revenue Rulings, which are applicable to *all* taxpayers. A letter ruling may later lead to the issuance of a Revenue Ruling if the holding affects many taxpayers. In its Agents' Manual, the IRS indicates that letter rulings may be used as a guide with other

research materials in formulating a District Office position on an issue. The IRS is required to charge a taxpayer a fee for letter rulings, determination letters, etc.

[17]Rev.Proc. 2017–3, 2017–1 I.R.B. 130 contains a list of areas in which the IRS will not issue advance rulings. According to the IRS, the main reason they will not rule in certain areas is that specific fact-oriented situations are involved. Thus, a ruling may not be obtained on many of the problems that are particularly troublesome for taxpayers.

[18]§ 6110.

Government on selected court decisions. Like Revenue Rulings and Revenue Procedures, TDs are published in the *Internal Revenue Bulletin*.

The IRS also publishes other administrative communications in the *Internal Revenue Bulletin*, such as Announcements, Notices, IRs (News Releases), Internal Legal Memoranda (ILMs), Chief Counsel Notices (CC), and Prohibited Transaction Exemptions.

Like letter rulings, determination letters are issued at the request of taxpayers and provide guidance on the application of the tax law. They differ from letter rulings in that the issuing source is an IRS Area Director (rather than the National Office of the IRS). Also, determination letters usually involve *completed* (as opposed to proposed) transactions. Determination letters are not published and are made known only to the party making the request.

The following examples illustrate the distinction between letter rulings and determination letters:

Difference between Letter Rulings and Determination Letters

The shareholders of Red Corporation and Green Corporation want assurance that the consolidation of the corporations into Blue Corporation will be a nontaxable reorganization. The proper approach is to request that the National Office of the IRS issue a letter ruling concerning the income tax effect of the proposed transaction.

EXAMPLE 1

Chris operates a barbershop in which he employs eight barbers. To comply with the rules governing income tax and payroll tax withholdings, Chris wants to know whether the barbers working for him are employees or independent contractors. The proper procedure is to request a determination letter on their status from the appropriate Area Director.

EXAMPLE 2

A variety of internal memoranda that constitute the working law of the IRS also are released. These General Counsel Memoranda (GCMs), Technical Advice Memoranda (TAMs), Internal Legal Memoranda (ILMs), and Field Service Advice Memoranda (FSAs) are not officially published, and the IRS indicates that they may not be cited as precedents by taxpayers.[19] However, these working documents do explain the IRS's position on various issues.

The National Office of the IRS releases Technical Advice Memoranda (TAMs) weekly. TAMs resemble letter rulings in that they give the IRS's determination of an issue. However, they differ in several respects. Letter rulings deal with proposed transactions and are issued to taxpayers at their request. In contrast, TAMs deal with completed (rather than proposed) transactions. TAMs are issued by the National Office of the IRS in response to questions raised by taxpayers or IRS field personnel during audits. TAMs are not officially published and may not be cited or used as precedent.[20] They are assigned file numbers according to the same procedure used for letter rulings. For example, TAM 201624022 refers to the 22nd TAM issued during the 24th week of 2016.

The Office of Chief Counsel prepares Field Service Advice Memoranda (FSAs) to help IRS employees. These are issued in response to requests for advice, guidance, and analysis on difficult or significant tax issues and are not binding on either the taxpayer to whom they pertain or the IRS. Some FSAs are being replaced by another form of field guidance called Technical Expedited Advice Memoranda (TEAMs). The purpose of TEAMs is to expedite legal guidance to field agents as disputes are developing. FSAs are reverting to their original purpose of case-specific development of facts.[21]

---

[19]These are made available by the publishers listed in Exhibit 2.3. These internal memoranda may be substantial authority for purposes of the accuracy-related penalty for post-1984 transactions (see pp. 2-24 and 2-25; Notice 90–20, 1990–1 C.B. 328).

[20]§ 6110(j)(3). Post-1984 TAMs may be substantial authority for purposes of avoiding the accuracy-related penalty. Notice 90–20, 1990–1 C.B. 328.

[21]A TEAM guidance differs from a TAM in several ways, including a mandatory presubmission conference involving the taxpayer. In the event of a tentatively adverse conclusion for the taxpayer or the field agent, a conference of right is offered to the taxpayer and to the field agent; once the conference of right is held, no further conferences are offered.

2-1c **Judicial Sources of the Tax Law**

Five Federal courts have jurisdiction over tax disputes between the IRS and taxpayers: the U.S. Tax Court, the U.S. District Court, the U.S. Court of Federal Claims, the U.S. Court of Appeals, and the U.S. Supreme Court.

The Judicial Process in General

Once a taxpayer has exhausted the remedies available within the IRS (i.e., no satisfactory settlement has been reached at the agent or at the Appeals Division level), the dispute can be taken to the Federal courts. The trial and appellate court system for Federal tax litigation is illustrated in Exhibit 2.4.

A trial court, also known as a **court of original jurisdiction**, initially hears the case. Appeals (either by the taxpayer or the IRS) are heard by the appropriate appellate court. A taxpayer has a choice of these *four trial courts:* a **Federal District Court**, the **U.S. Court of Federal Claims**, the **U.S. Tax Court**, or the **Small Cases Division** of the U.S. Tax Court. The Small Cases Division of the U.S. Tax Court only hears cases involving amounts of $50,000 or less. The ruling of the judge is final (no appeal is available), and these rulings are not precedent for any other cases. Proceedings of the Small Cases Division are informal, and because there is no requirement that a taxpayer be represented by an attorney, they can be less costly for a taxpayer. Special trial judges, rather than Tax Court judges, preside over these hearings. Some of these cases can be found on the U.S. Tax Court website.

American law, following English law, is frequently *created* by judicial decisions. Under the doctrine of *stare decisis* ("let the decision stand"), each case has precedential value for future cases with the same set of facts. Most Federal and state appellate court decisions and some decisions of trial courts are published. Published court decisions are organized by jurisdiction (Federal or state) and level of court (trial or appellate).[22]

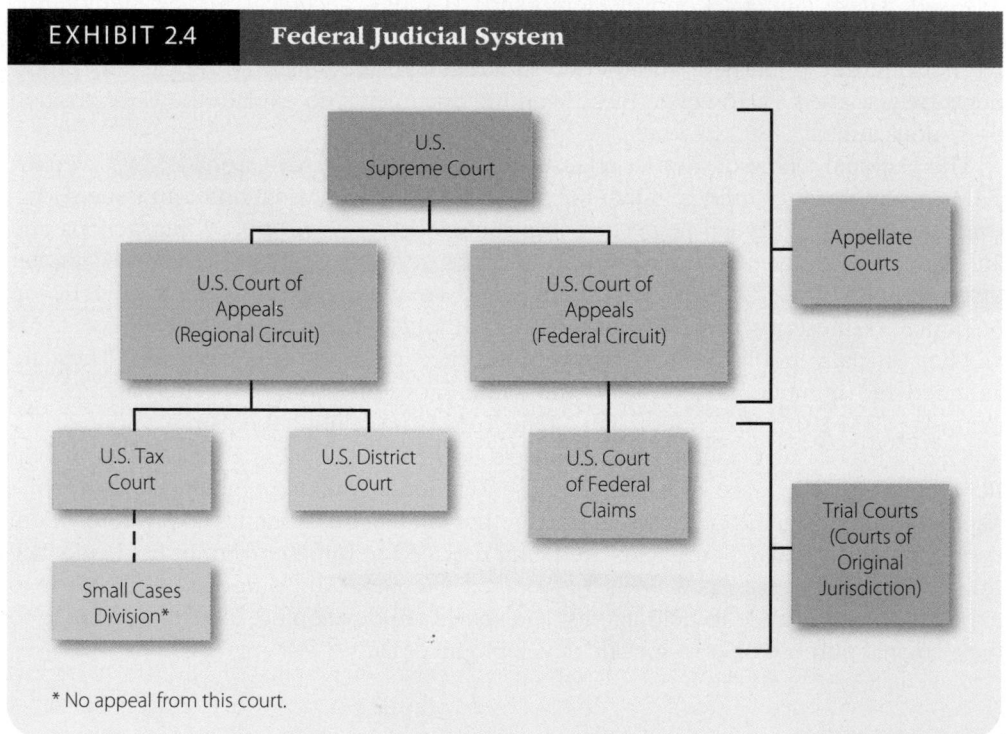

EXHIBIT 2.4   Federal Judicial System

* No appeal from this court.

---

[22]A decision of a particular court is called its holding. Sometimes a decision includes *dicta* or incidental opinions beyond the current facts. Such passing remarks, illustrations, or analogies are not essential to the current holding. Although the holding has precedential value under *stare decisis*, dicta are not binding on a future court.

Several other terms are important to understand. The *plaintiff* is the party requesting a hearing, and the *defendant* is the party being challenged. Sometimes a court uses the terms *petitioner* and *respondent* (rather than *plaintiff* and *defendant*). At the trial court level, a taxpayer is normally the plaintiff (or petitioner), and the Government is the defendant (or respondent). If the taxpayer wins and the Government appeals, it becomes the petitioner (or appellant), and the taxpayer becomes the respondent.

Trial Courts

Here are some differences between the various trial courts (courts of original jurisdiction):

- *Number of courts.* There is only one Court of Federal Claims and only one Tax Court, but there are many Federal District Courts. Federal District Courts hear cases based on where the taxpayer lives (so a taxpayer in Atlanta would have her case heard by the Atlanta Federal District Court).

- *Number of judges.* District Courts have a number of judges, but only one judge hears a case. The Court of Federal Claims has 16 judges, and the Tax Court has 19 regular judges. Typcially, Tax Court cases are heard and decided by only one of the 19 regular judges. However, if the case is viewed as important or novel tax issues are raised, the entire Tax Court might hear the case. If a case is reviewed by the full Tax Court, such an *en banc* decision has compelling authority.

- *Location.* The Court of Federal Claims meets most often in Washington, D.C. Each state has at least one District Court, and many of the more populous states have more than one. Although the Tax Court is officially based in Washington, D.C., the various judges travel to different parts of the country and hear cases at predetermined locations and dates.

- *Jurisdiction of the Tax Court and District Courts.* The Tax Court hears only tax cases and is the most popular forum for tax cases since its judges have more tax expertise; many had careers in the IRS or Treasury Department before being appointed to the Tax Court. The District Courts hear a wide variety of nontax cases as well as tax cases. As a result, District Court judges are viewed as generalists (rather than specialists) in tax law.

- *Jurisdiction of the Court of Federal Claims.* The Court of Federal Claims has jurisdiction over any claim against the United States. As a result, the Court of Federal Claims hears nontax litigation as well as tax cases. Court of Federal Claims judges are tax law generalists. This court is viewed as a stronger option when equity is an issue (as opposed to purely technical issues) or when the case requires extensive discovery of evidence. In addition, it has a pro-business orientation.[23]

- *Jury trial.* A jury trial is only available in a District Court. However, because juries can decide only questions of fact (and not questions of law), taxpayers who choose a District Court often do not request a jury trial. In that event, the judge decides all issues in a bench trial. A District Court decision carries precedential value only in its district.

- *Payment of deficiency.* Before the Court of Federal Claims or a District Court will hear a case, the taxpayer must pay any taxes assessed by the IRS and sue for a refund. This is not the case with the Tax Court. Here, a taxpayer may request a hearing without making any payments to the IRS. As a result, whether to pay the tax in advance (and limit further interest and penalties) or wait to pay the tax (and risk additional interest and penalties) becomes part of the decision-making process of selecting a venue.

---

[23]T. D. Peyser, "The Case for Selecting the Claims Court to Litigate a Federal Tax Liability," *The Tax Executive* (Winter 1988): 149.

- *Appeals.* Appeals from a District Court or a Tax Court decision are to the U.S. Court of Appeals for the circuit where the taxpayer lives. Appeals from the Court of Federal Claims go to the Court of Appeals for the Federal Circuit.

- *Bankruptcy.* When a taxpayer files a bankruptcy petition, the IRS, like other creditors, is prevented from taking action against the taxpayer. Sometimes a bankruptcy court may settle a tax claim.

- *Gray areas.* Because there are "gray areas" in the tax laws, courts may disagree as to the proper tax treatment of an item. With these differences in judicial authority, a taxpayer may have some flexibility to choose the most favorable forum to hear the case.

See Concept Summary 2.1 for a summary of various attributes of the Federal trial courts.

Concept Summary 2.1

Federal Judicial System: Trial Courts

Issue	U.S. Tax Court	U.S. District Court	U.S. Court of Federal Claims
Number of judges per court	19*	Varies	16
Payment of deficiency before trial	No	Yes	Yes
Jury trial available	No	Yes	No
Types of disputes	Tax cases only	Most criminal and civil issues	Claims against the United States
Jurisdiction	Nationwide	Location of taxpayer	Nationwide
IRS acquiescence policy	Yes	Yes	Yes
Appeal route	U.S. Court of Appeals	U.S. Court of Appeals	U.S. Court of Appeals for the Federal Circuit

*Currently, there are also 5 special trial judges and 10 senior judges (August 2016).

Appellate Courts

A trial court decision can be appealed to the appropriate Circuit Court of Appeals. The 11 geographic circuits, the circuit for the District of Columbia, and the Federal Circuit[24] appear in Exhibit 2.5. Generally, a three-judge panel hears a Court of Appeals case, but occasionally the *full* court decides more controversial cases.

If the Government loses at the trial court level (District Court, Tax Court, or Court of Federal Claims), it may decide not to appeal. However, the fact that the IRS does not appeal does not mean that the IRS agrees with the result (and it may litigate similar issues in the future).

The IRS may decide not to appeal for a number of reasons. First, the IRS may decide that available personnel should be assigned to other more important cases. Second, the IRS may decide that the taxpayer has a sympathetic position or the facts are particularly strong in his or her favor. In that event, the IRS may wait to test the legal issues with a different taxpayer (who might have a weaker case). Third, the Court of Appeals jurisdiction might matter. Based on past experience and precedent, the IRS may decide that the chance for success on a particular issue might be more promising in a different Court of Appeals.

The Federal Circuit provides the taxpayer with an alternative forum. When a particular Circuit Court of Appeals has issued an adverse decision in a similar case, the taxpayer may prefer the Court of Federal Claims route, because any appeal is to the Federal Circuit.

---

[24]The Court of Appeals for the Federal Circuit was created, effective October 1, 1982, by P.L. 97–64 (4/2/82) to hear decisions appealed from the Claims Court (now the Court of Federal Claims).

| EXHIBIT 2.5 | The Federal Courts of Appeals |

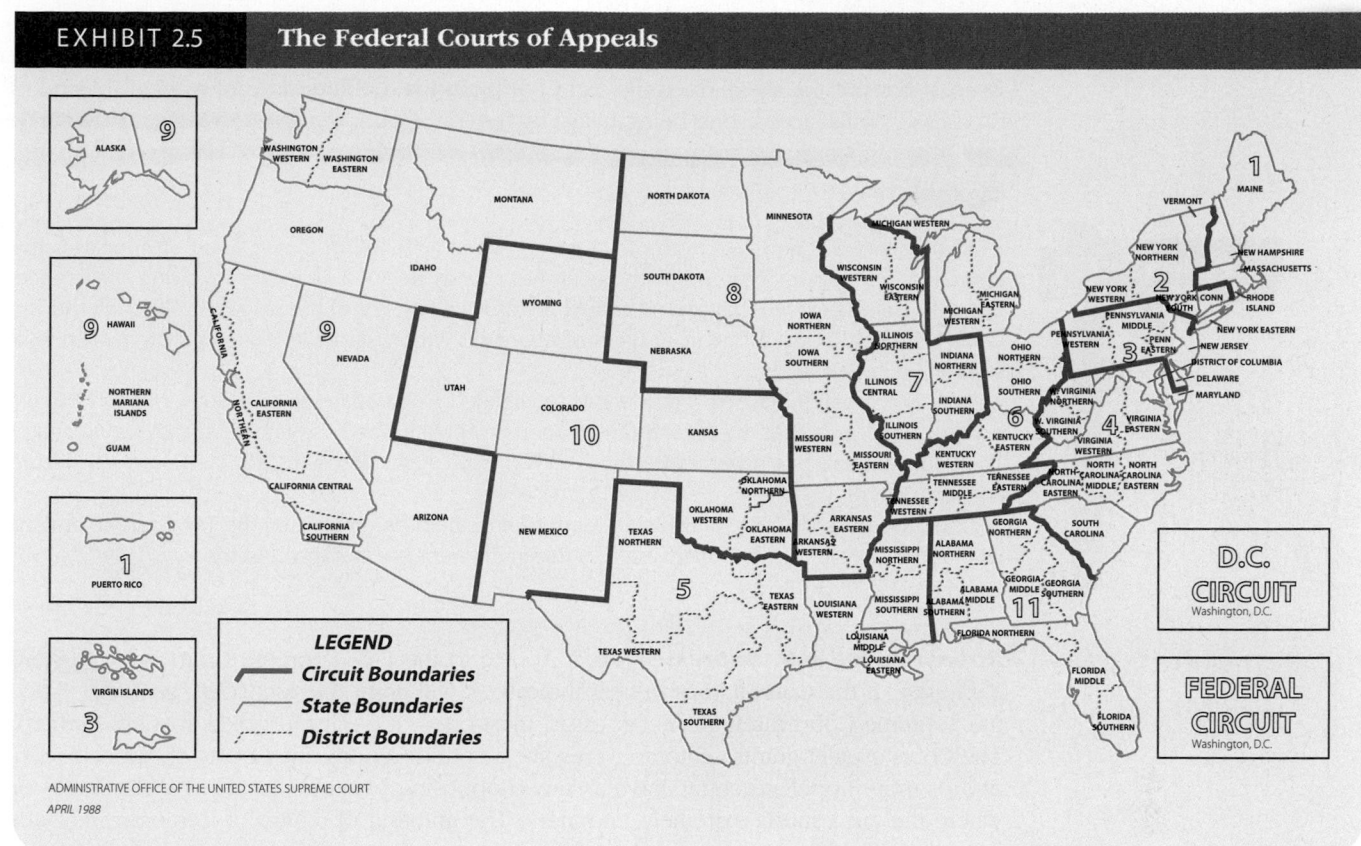

ADMINISTRATIVE OFFICE OF THE UNITED STATES SUPREME COURT
APRIL 1988

The Appellate Process

The *role* of the appellate court is usually limited to a review of whether the trial court applied the proper law in arriving at its decision. Rarely does an appellate court question a lower court's fact-finding determination. Both the Code and the Supreme Court indicate that Federal appellate courts are bound by findings of facts unless they are clearly erroneous.[25]

An appeal can have a number of possible outcomes. The appellate court may approve (affirm) or disapprove (reverse) the lower court's finding, or it may send the case back to the trial court for further consideration (remand). When many issues are involved, a mixed result is not unusual. Thus, the lower court may be affirmed (*aff'd*) on Issue A and reversed (*rev'd*) on Issue B, while Issue C is remanded (*rem'd*) for additional fact finding.

When more than one judge is involved in the decision-making process, disagreements are common. In addition to the majority view, one or more judges may concur (agree with the result reached but not with some or all of the reasoning) or dissent (disagree with the result). In any decision, of course, the majority controls. But concurring and dissenting views can have an influence on future cases or other courts.

Appellate Precedents and the Tax Court District Courts, the Tax Court, and the Court of Federal Claims must abide by the precedents set by a Court of Appeals jurisdiction. A particular Court of Appeals need not follow the decisions of another Court of Appeals. All courts, however, must follow the decisions of the U.S. Supreme Court.

This pattern of appellate precedents raises an issue for the Tax Court. Because the Tax Court is a national court, it decides cases from all parts of the country. Under a policy

---

[25]§§ 7482(a) and (c). *Comm. v. Duberstein,* 60–2 USTC ¶9515, 5 AFTR 2d 1626, 80 S.Ct. 1190 (USSC, 1960). See Rule 52(a) of the Federal Rules of Civil Procedure.

known as the *Golsen* rule, the Tax Court decides a case as it believes the law should be applied *only* if the Court of Appeals of appropriate jurisdiction has not yet ruled on the issue or has previously affirmed the Tax Court's rationale. If the Court of Appeals has ruled on a case similar to the one being heard by the Tax Court, the Tax Court will conform to the Appeals Court decision under the *Golsen* rule even though it disagrees with the decision.[26]

EXAMPLE 3

Emily lives in Texas and sues in the Tax Court on Issue A. The Fifth Circuit Court of Appeals is the appropriate appellate court. The Fifth Circuit has already decided, in a case involving similar facts but a different taxpayer, that Issue A should be resolved in favor of the taxpayer. Although the Tax Court believes that the Fifth Circuit Court of Appeals is wrong, under its *Golsen* policy, it will rule in favor of Emily.

Shortly thereafter, Rashad, a resident of New York, in a comparable case, sues in the Tax Court on Issue A. Assume that the Second Circuit Court of Appeals, the appellate court that would hear a Tax Court appeal, has never expressed itself on Issue A. As a result, the Tax Court will decide against Rashad.

Thus, it is possible for two taxpayers, both having their cases heard by the Tax Court, to end up with opposite results, merely because they live in different parts of the country.

Appeal to the U.S. Supreme Court Appeal to the U.S. Supreme Court is by Writ of Certiorari. If the Court agrees to hear the case, it will grant the Writ (*Cert. granted*). Since the Supreme Court rarely hears tax cases, most often, it denies jurisdiction (*Cert. denied*). The Court usually grants certiorari to resolve a conflict among the Courts of Appeals (e.g., two or more appellate courts have assumed opposing positions on a particular issue) or where the tax issue is extremely important. The granting of a Writ of Certiorari indicates that at least four of the nine members of the Supreme Court believe that the issue is of sufficient importance to be heard by the full Court.

Judicial Citations

LO.2

Locate and work with the appropriate tax law sources.

Court decisions are an important source of tax law, and the ability to cite and locate a case is a critical skill when working with the tax law. Judicial citations usually follow a standard pattern: case name, volume number, reporter series, page or paragraph number, court (where necessary), and year of the decision (see Concept Summary 2.2).

Judicial Citations—The U.S. Tax Court The U.S. Tax Court issues two types of decisions: Regular and Memorandum, based on the Chief Judge's determination. They differ in both substance and form. In terms of substance, *Memorandum* decisions deal with cases that involve only the application of established principles of law. *Regular* decisions involve novel issues not previously resolved by the Tax Court. In actual practice, however, both *Regular* and *Memorandum* represent the position of the Tax Court and, as such, can be relied on.[27]

The Regular and Memorandum decisions issued by the Tax Court also differ in form. Regular decisions are published by the U.S. Government in a series entitled *Tax Court of the United States Reports* (T.C.). Each volume of these *Reports* covers a six-month period (January 1 through June 30 and July 1 through December 31) and is given a succeeding volume number. Usually there is a time lag between the date a decision is rendered and the date it is published. A temporary citation may be necessary to help the researcher locate a recent Regular decision. Consider, for example, the temporary and permanent citations for *Gerd Topsnik*, a decision filed on January 20, 2016.

---

[26]*Jack E. Golsen*, 54 T.C. 742 (1970).

[27]U.S. Tax Court Small Case Division Summary Opinions carry no precedential value. Summary Opinions issued after January 9, 2001, are available on the U.S. Tax Court website.

Concept Summary 2.2

Judicial Sources

Court	Location	Authority
U.S. Supreme Court	S.Ct. Series (West)	Highest authority
	U.S. Series (U.S. Gov't.)	
	L.Ed.2d (Lawyer's Co-op.)	
	AFTR (RIA)	
	USTC (CCH)	
U.S. Courts of Appeal	Federal 3d (West)	Next highest appellate court
	AFTR (RIA)	
	USTC (CCH)	
Tax Court (Regular decisions)	U.S. Gov't. Printing Office	Highest trial court*
	RIA/CCH separate services	
Tax Court (Memorandum decisions)	RIA T.C.Memo. (RIA)	Less authority than Regular T.C. decision
	TCM (CCH)	
U.S. Court of Federal Claims**	Federal Claims Reporter (West)	Similar authority as Tax Court
	AFTR (RIA)	
	USTC (CCH)	
U.S. District Courts	F.Supp.2d Series (West)	Lowest trial court
	AFTR (RIA)	
	USTC (CCH)	
Small Cases Division of Tax Court	U.S. Tax Court website***	No precedent value

*Theoretically, the Tax Court, Court of Federal Claims, and District Courts are on the same level of authority. But some people believe that because the Tax Court hears and decides tax cases from all parts of the country (i.e., it is a national court), its decisions may be more authoritative than a Court of Federal Claims or District Court decision.

**Before October 29, 1992, the U.S. Claims Court.

***Starting in 2001.

Temporary Citation { *Gerd Topsnik*, 146 T.C. _____, No. 1 (2016).
{ *Explanation:* Page number left blank because not yet known.

Permanent Citation { *Gerd Topsnik*, 146 T.C. 1 (2016).
{ *Explanation:* Page number now available.

Both citations tell us that the case will ultimately appear in Volume 146 of the *Tax Court of the United States Reports*. But until this volume is made available, the page number must be left blank. Instead, the temporary citation identifies the decision as being the 1st Regular decision issued by the Tax Court since Volume 145 ended. With this information, the decision can easily be located in the special Tax Court services published by Commerce Clearing House (CCH) and Research Institute of America (RIA). Once Volume 146 is released, the permanent citation can be substituted and the number of the case dropped. Starting in 1995, both Regular decisions and Memorandum decisions are published on the U.S. Tax Court website (**www.ustaxcourt.gov**). Memorandum decisions, although available on the U.S. Tax Court website, are not published by the U.S. Government.

Before 1943, the Tax Court was called the Board of Tax Appeals, and its decisions were published as the *United States Board of Tax Appeals Reports* (B.T.A.). These 47 volumes cover the period from 1924 to 1942. For example, the citation *Karl Pauli*, 11 B.T.A. 784 (1928), refers to the 11th volume of the *Board of Tax Appeals Reports*, page 784, issued in 1928.

Memorandum decisions are published by both CCH and RIA. Consider, for example, the three different ways the *Nick R. Hughes* case can be cited:

Nick R. Hughes, T.C.Memo. 2009–94

> *Explanation:* The 94th Memorandum decision issued by the Tax Court in 2009.

Nick R. Hughes, 97 TCM 1488

> *Explanation:* Page 1488 of Vol. 97 of the CCH *Tax Court Memorandum Decisions*.

Nick R. Hughes, 2009 RIA T.C.Memo. ¶2009,094

> *Explanation:* Paragraph 2009,094 of the RIA *T.C. Memorandum Decisions*.

Note that the third citation contains the same information as the first. Thus, ¶2009,094 indicates both the year and decision number of the case.[28]

U.S. Tax Court Summary Opinions relate to decisions of the Tax Court's Small Cases Division.[29] These opinions may not be treated as precedent for any other case. For example, *Richard G. Braddock*, filed on August 24, 2016, is cited as follows:

Richard G. Braddock, T.C. Summary Opinion 2016–46.

If the IRS loses a decision, it may indicate whether it agrees or disagrees with the results reached by the court by publishing an **acquiescence** ("A" or "*Acq.*") or **nonacquiescence** ("NA" or "*Nonacq.*"), respectively. Until 1991, acquiescences and nonacquiescences were published only for certain Regular decisions of the Tax Court, but the IRS expanded its acquiescence program to include other tax cases. The acquiescence or nonacquiescence is published in the *Internal Revenue Bulletin* as an *Action on Decision*. The IRS can retroactively revoke an acquiescence.

Most often, the IRS issues nonacquiescences to adverse decisions that are not appealed. In this manner, the Government indicates that it disagrees with the result reached, despite its decision not to seek review of the matter in an appellate court. A nonacquiescence provides a warning to taxpayers that a similar case cannot be settled administratively. A taxpayer will incur fees and expenses while the case moves through the IRS even though the IRS may be unwilling to litigate a fact pattern similar to a nonacquiescence decision.[30]

Judicial Citations—The U.S. District Court, Court of Federal Claims, and Courts of Appeals District Court, Court of Federal Claims, Court of Appeals, and Supreme Court decisions dealing with Federal tax matters are reported in both the CCH *U.S. Tax Cases* (USTC) and the RIA *American Federal Tax Reports* (AFTR) series. Federal District Court decisions, dealing with *both* tax and nontax issues, also are published by West in its *Federal Supplement Second Series* (F.Supp.2d).[31] The following examples illustrate three different ways of citing a District Court case:

Turner v. U.S., 2004–1 USTC ¶60,478 (D.Ct. Tex., 2004).

> *Explanation:* Reported in the first volume of the *U.S. Tax Cases*, published by Commerce Clearing House, for calendar year 2004 (2004–1) and located at paragraph 60,478 (¶60,478).

Turner v. U.S., 93 AFTR 2d 2004–686 (D.Ct. Tex., 2004).

> *Explanation:* Reported in the 93rd volume of the second series of the *American Federal Tax Reports* (AFTR 2d), published by RIA, and beginning on page 686.

Turner v. U.S., 306 F.Supp.2d 668 (D.Ct. Tex., 2004).

> *Explanation:* Reported in the 306th volume of the *Federal Supplement Second Series* (F.Supp.2d), published by West, and beginning on page 668.

---

[28]In this text, the RIA citation for Memorandum decisions of the U.S. Tax Court is omitted. Thus, *Nick R. Hughes* will be cited as 97 TCM 1488, T.C. Memo. 2009–94.

[29]In 2005, the U.S. Supreme Court held that decisions of the Small Cases Division must be made public.

[30]G. W. Carter, "Nonacquiescence: Winning by Losing," *Tax Notes* (September 19, 1988): 1301–1307.

[31]Cases prior to 1999 are found in West's *Federal Supplement Series* (F.Supp.).

The case name, the reference to the Federal District Court of Texas (D.Ct. Tex.), and the year the decision was rendered (2004) appear in each of the citations.[32]

Decisions of the Court of Federal Claims[33] and the Courts of Appeals are published in the USTCs, the AFTRs, and one of two West reporters. The *Federal Third Series* (F.3d) reports Courts of Appeals decisions, while the *Federal Claims Reporter* (abbreviated as Fed.Cl.) reports Court of Federal Claims decisions.[34] The following examples illustrate the different forms:

Estate of Gribauskas v. Comm. is a decision rendered by the Second Circuit Court of Appeals in 2003 (CA–2, 2003), while *Apollo Computer, Inc.* was issued by the Court of Federal Claims in 1994 (Fed.Cl., 1994).

Judicial Citations—The U.S. Supreme Court Supreme Court decisions are published by CCH in the USTCs and by RIA in the AFTRs. The U.S. Government Printing Office also publishes these decisions in the *United States Supreme Court Reports* (U.S.), as does West in its *Supreme Court Reporter* (S.Ct.), and the Lawyer's Co-operative Publishing Company in its *United States Reports, Lawyer's Edition* (L.Ed.). The following illustrates the different ways the same decision can be cited:

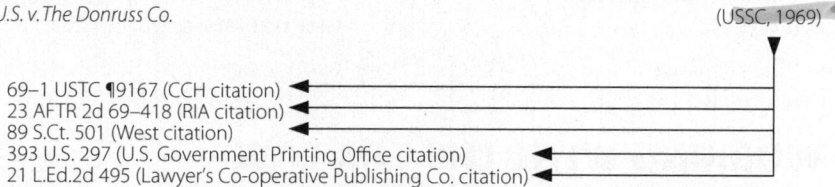

The parenthetical reference (USSC, 1969) identifies the decision as having been rendered by the U.S. Supreme Court in 1969. In this text, Supreme Court decision citations are limited to the CCH (USTC), RIA (AFTR), and West (S.Ct.) versions.

2-1d Other Sources of the Tax Law

Other sources of tax information that a tax professional may need to consult include tax treaties and tax periodicals.

Tax Treaties

The United States signs certain tax treaties (sometimes called tax conventions) with foreign countries to assist in tax enforcement and to avoid double taxation. Since 1988, when there is a direct conflict between the Code and a treaty, the most recent item takes precedence. A taxpayer must disclose on the tax return any position where a treaty overrides a tax law.[35]

---

[32]In this text, the case is cited in the following form: *Turner v. U.S.*, 2004–1 USTC ¶60,478, 93 AFTR 2d 2004–686, 306 F.Supp.2d 668 (D.Ct. Tex., 2004).

[33]Before October 29, 1992, the Court of Federal Claims was called the Claims Court. Before October 1, 1982, the Court of Federal Claims was called the Court of Claims.

[34]West's *Federal Second Series* (F.2d) contains cases prior to 1994. Beginning in October 1982, the Court of Federal Claims decisions were published in a different West reporter called the *Claims Court Reporter* (abbreviated Cl.Ct.).

[35]§ 7852(d); there is a $1,000 penalty per failure to disclose for individuals and a $10,000 per failure penalty for corporations. See Reg. §§ 301.6114–1, 301.6712–1, and 301.7701(b)(7).

Tax Periodicals

The use of tax periodicals can often shorten the research time needed to resolve a tax issue. An article relevant to the issue at hand may provide the references needed to locate the primary sources of the tax law that apply (e.g., citations to judicial decisions, Regulations, and other IRS pronouncements).

Several indexes are available for locating tax articles, including CCH's *Federal Tax Articles* (which includes a subject index, a Code Section number index, and an author's index) and the *Index to Federal Tax Articles* (published by Thomson Reuters). Both of these indexes are available by subscription.

Here are some of the more useful tax periodicals:

Journal of Taxation
Journal of International Taxation
Practical Tax Strategies
Estate Planning
Corporate Taxation
Business Entities
Taxation of Exempts
Real Estate Taxation
ria.thomsonreuters.com/journals

The Tax Executive
www.tei.org

The Tax Adviser
aicpa.org/pubs/taxadv

Tax Law Review
**www.law.nyu.edu/tax
/taxlawreview/**

Journal of the American Taxation Association
aaajournals.org/loi/atax

The ATA Journal of Legal Tax Research
aaajournals.org/loi/jltr

Oil, Gas & Energy Quarterly
**www.bus.lsu.edu/accounting
/faculty/lcrumbley/oilgas.html**

Trusts and Estates
wealthmanagement.com/te-home

Journal of Passthrough Entities
TAXES—The Tax Magazine
tax.cchgroup.com/books

Tax Notes
taxanalysts.org

Develop an awareness of tax research tools.

2-2 WORKING WITH THE TAX LAW— TAX RESEARCH TOOLS

Tax law consists of a body of legislative (e.g., Code Sections and tax treaties), administrative (e.g., Regulations and Rulings), and judicial (e.g., court cases) pronouncements. Working with the tax law requires being able to locate and use these sources effectively. A major consideration is the time required to find relevant information related to the issues identified.

Unless the problem is simple (e.g., the Code Section is known and there is a Regulation on point), the research process begins with a tax service.

2-2a Commercial Tax Services

In the past, commercial tax services could be classified as *annotated* (i.e., organized by Internal Revenue Code) or *topical* (i.e., organized by major topics). However, as tax research has become electronic, this classification system is no longer appropriate. For example, Thomson Reuters *Checkpoint* includes both the *Federal Tax Coordinator 2d* (topical) and the *United States Tax Reporter* (annotated).

Here is a partial list of the available commercial tax services:

- *Standard Federal Tax Reporter*, Commerce Clearing House.
- *CCH IntelliConnect*, Commerce Clearing House. The online version of the *Standard Federal Tax Reporter* (along with other CCH materials).
- *United States Tax Reporter*, Research Institute of America, Thomson Reuters.
- Thomson Reuters *Checkpoint*, Research Institute of America. The online versions of RIA's *Federal Tax Coordinator 2d* and *United States Tax Reporter*.

- *Practical Tax Expert*, CCH/Wolters Kluwer.
- *Tax Management Portfolios*, Bloomberg BNA.
- *Mertens Law of Federal Income Taxation*, Thomson Reuters.
- Thomson Reuters *Westlaw* and *WestlawNext*—compilations include access to *Tax Management Portfolios*, *Federal Tax Coordinator 2d*, and *Mertens*.
- LexisNexis *TaxCenter*. A compilation of primary sources and various materials taken from CCH, Matthew Bender, Kleinrock, and Bloomberg BNA.

2-2b **Using Electronic (Online) Tax Services**

A competent tax professional must become familiar and proficient with electronic research services and be able to use them to complete research projects efficiently. Following certain general procedures can simplify the research process. The following suggestions may be helpful:[36]

- Carefully choose keywords for the search. Words with a broad usage, such as *income*, are of limited value. If the researcher is interested in qualified dividend income, even *dividend income* is too broad because it finds stock dividends, constructive dividends, liquidating dividends, and more. By using *qualified dividend income* at the outset, the search is considerably narrowed. In CCH *IntelliConnect*, for example, these two modifications narrowed the search from 862,612 items to 10,919 and finally to 383. From that point, further contraction will be needed.
- Take advantage of *connectors*, such as "+" and quotation marks, to place parameters on the search and further restrict the output. Although each tax service has its own set of connectors, many are similar. Thus, quotation marks around a phrase mean "exact phrase" in both Thomson Reuters *Checkpoint* and CCH *IntelliConnect* (e.g., "personal service corporation").
- Be selective in choosing the data to search. For example, if the research project does not involve case law, do not include judicial decisions in the search.
- Use a table of contents, index, or citation when appropriate. Although the keyword approach is most frequently used, electronic databases can be searched in other ways. Using the table of contents or index may narrow the information that needs to be examined. Tax law (including annotations) can also be accessed by a citation: statutory (e.g., Code Section), administrative (e.g., Rev.Rul.), or judicial (e.g., Tax Court).

2-2c **Noncommercial Electronic (Online) Tax Services**

The internet provides a wealth of tax information in several popular forms, sometimes at no cost to the researcher. A tax professional can access a significant amount of information that can assist in the research process.

- *Websites* are provided by accounting and consulting firms, publishers, tax academics, libraries, and governmental bodies as a means of making information widely available. One of the best sites available to the tax professional is the Internal Revenue Service's home page, illustrated in Exhibit 2.6. This site offers downloadable forms and instructions, interpretations of Regulations, and news update items. Exhibit 2.7 lists some of the websites that may be most useful to tax researchers. Particularly useful is the directory at **taxsites.com**, which provides links to accounting and tax sources (including international, state, and payroll tax sources).

---

[36]For a more complete discussion of the use of Thomson Reuters *Checkpoint* and CCH *IntelliConnect* and internet research in taxation, see Sawyers, Raabe, Whittenburg, and Gill, *Federal Tax Research*, 10th ed. (Cengage Learning, 2015), Chapters 6 and 7.

EXHIBIT 2.6	The IRS's Home Page

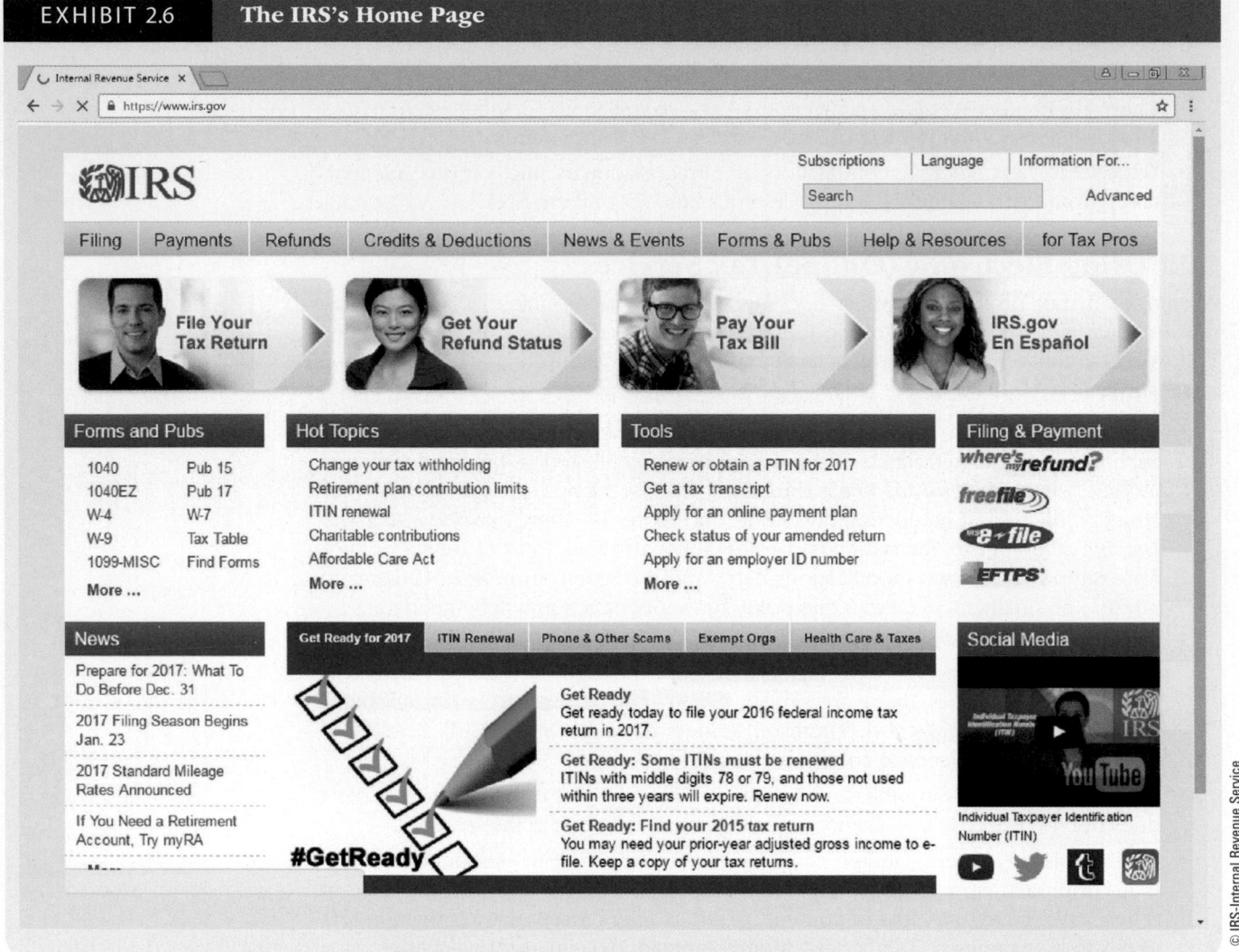

© IRS-Internal Revenue Service

- *Blogs and RSS sites* provide a means by which information related to the tax law can be exchanged among taxpayers, tax professionals, and others who subscribe to the group's services. Individuals can read the exchanges and offer replies and suggestions to inquiries. Discussions address the interpretation and application of existing law, analysis of proposals and new pronouncements, and reviews of tax software.

While tax information on the internet is plentiful, information in the public domain should not be relied upon without referring to other sources. Anyone can set up a website, and the quality of the information can be difficult for a tax professional to ascertain.

LO.4

Describe the tax research process.

2-3 WORKING WITH THE TAX LAW— TAX RESEARCH

Tax research is the process of finding a competent and professional conclusion to a tax problem. The problem may originate from completed or proposed transactions.

| EXHIBIT 2.7 | Tax-Related Websites |

Website	Web Address	Description
Accounting firms and professional organizations	For instance, the AICPA's page is at **aicpa.org**, Ernst & Young is at **ey.com**, and KPMG is at **kpmg.com**	Tax planning newsletters, descriptions of services offered and career opportunities, and exchange of data with clients and subscribers
Cengage Learning	**cengagebrain.com**	Informational updates, newsletters, support materials for students and adopters, and continuing education
Commercial tax publishers	For instance, **tax.com**, **cchgroup.com**, **tax.thomsonreuters.com**, and **bna.com**	Information about products and services available for subscription and newsletter excerpts
Court opinions	The site at **law.justia.com** covers state, Federal, and Supreme Court decisions (but not Tax Court)	A synopsis of results reached by the court
Internal Revenue Service	**irs.gov**	News releases, downloadable forms and instructions, tables, Circular 230, and e-mail
Tax Almanac	**taxalmanac.org**	Smorgasbord of tax research resources
Tax Analysts	**taxanalysts.org**	Policy-oriented readings on the tax law and proposals to change it, moderated bulletins on various tax subjects
Tax Foundation	**taxfoundation.org**	Nonprofit educational organization that promotes sound tax policy and measures tax burdens
Tax laws online	Regulations are at **law.cornell.edu/cfr**, and the Code is at **uscode.house.gov** and **law.cornell.edu/uscode**	
Tax Sites Directory	**taxsites.com**	References and links to tax sites on the internet, including state and Federal tax sites, academic and professional pages, tax forms, and software
U.S. Tax Court decisions	**ustaxcourt.gov**	Recent U.S. Tax Court decisions

Caution: Web addresses change frequently.

In the case of a completed transaction, the objective of the research is to determine the tax result of what has already taken place. For example, is a taxpayer expense deductible? When dealing with proposed transactions, tax research has a different objective: effective tax planning by determining the tax consequences of various alternatives. A large part of a tax professional's career is spent on this type of tax research.

Tax research involves the following steps:

- Identifying and refining the problem.
- Locating the appropriate tax law sources.
- Assessing the validity of the tax law sources.
- Arriving at the solution or at alternative solutions (including consideration of nontax factors).
- Effectively communicating the solution to the taxpayer.
- Updating the solution (where appropriate) in light of new developments.

This process is illustrated in Exhibit 2.8. The broken lines reflect the steps of particular interest when tax research is directed toward proposed, rather than completed, transactions.

2-3a Identifying the Problem

Problem identification starts by documenting the relevant facts involved with the issue.[37] *All* of the facts that may have a bearing on the problem must be gathered; if any facts are omitted, the solution provided will likely change. To illustrate, return to the facts of *The Big Picture* on p. 2-1 and consider what appears to be a simple problem: Can Fred and Megan claim Sam and Dana as dependents?

2-3b Refining the Problem

In the facts of *The Big Picture* on p. 2-1, the simple question of whether Fred and Megan can claim Sam and Dana as dependents becomes more complicated with the potential stock sale. Initially, it appears that Fred and Megan could *not* claim Sam and Dana as dependents if the stock was sold, because Sam would then have gross income of more than the exemption amount under § 151(d).[38] However, to determine whether a child qualifies as a dependent, the *qualifying child* requirements are examined first. Only if these requirements are not met is the *qualifying relative* test examined. The gross income test only applies under the qualifying relative test.[39] As a result, Sam could sell the stock without

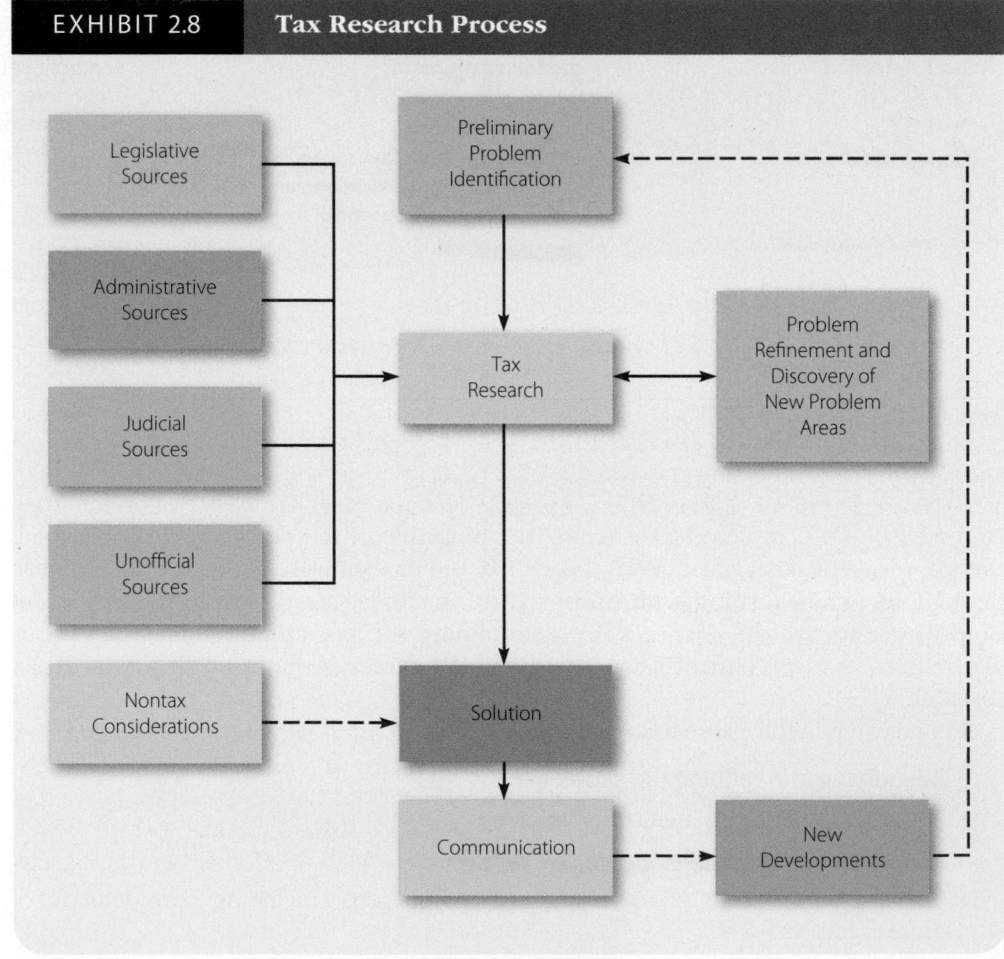

| EXHIBIT 2.8 | Tax Research Process |

---

[37]For an excellent discussion of the critical role of facts in carrying out tax research, see Gardner, Stewart, and Worsham, *Tax Research Techniques*, 10th ed. (New York: The American Institute of Certified Public Accountants, 2015), Chapter 2.

[38]§ 152(d)(2). See the related discussion in Chapter 3.

[39]Compare § 152(c) for *qualifying child* with § 152(d) for *qualifying relative*.

affecting his dependency status under the gross income test. Under the qualifying child test, however, Sam must not have provided more than one-half of his own support.[40] As a result, how Sam uses the $19,000 of stock sale proceeds is critical.

Assume, however, that further fact gathering provides the following additional information:

- Sam does not really need to spend the proceeds from the sale of the stock.
- Sam receives a sizable portion of his own support from a scholarship.

With these new facts, additional research leads to § 152(f)(5) and Regulation § 1.152–1(c), which indicate that a scholarship received by a student is ignored for purposes of the support test under the qualifying child provision. And if Sam does not spend the proceeds from the stock sale, this amount is not counted for purposes of the support test. As a result, in contrast to the initial conclusion, it appears that the parents are allowed the dependency exemptions for Sam and Dana; the qualifying child requirements are satisfied for Sam and the qualifying relative requirements are satisfied for Dana.

2-3c Locating the Appropriate Tax Law Sources

Once a problem is clearly defined, what is the next step? Although the next step is a matter of individual judgment, most tax research begins with a keyword search using an electronic tax service. If the problem is not complex, the researcher may turn directly to the Internal Revenue Code and Treasury Regulations. The Code and Regulations are accessible electronically (and also available in print from a number of publishers).[41]

2-3d Assessing the Validity of Tax Law Sources

Once a source has been located, the next step is to assess it in light of the problem at hand. Proper assessment involves careful interpretation of the tax law with consideration given to its relevance and validity. In connection with validity, an important step is to check for recent changes in the tax law.

Interpreting the Internal Revenue Code

The language of the Code can be extremely difficult to comprehend. Some of this difficulty is due to its structure (the Code follows the structure of all U.S. law), so getting used to reading (and interpreting) the Code can take time.

The Code must be read carefully for restrictive language such as "*at least* 80 percent" and "*more than* 80 percent" or "*less than* 50 percent" and "*exceeds* 50 percent." It also makes a great deal of difference, for example, whether two or more clauses are connected by *or* or by *and*.

Sometimes the Code directs the researcher elsewhere for the answer. For example, § 162(c) refers to the Foreign Corrupt Practices Act for purposes of determining when payments to foreign officials are deductible.

Definitions vary from one Code Section to another. For example, § 267 disallows losses between related parties. Brothers and sisters are included in this definition of related parties. This is not the case with § 318, which deals with the definition of related parties for certain stock redemptions. Research has shown that in one-third of the conflicts reaching the Tax Court, the court could not discern the intent of Congress by simply reading the statute (the Court had to look to Committee Reports to understand intent).[42]

If an answer is not in the Code, it may be necessary to look to other tax law, including Regulations and judicial decisions.

---

[40]§ 152(c)(1)(D).

[41]The Internal Revenue Service provides a gateway to the Internal Revenue Code, Treasury Department Regulations, and other items at: **www.irs.gov/tax-professionals/tax-code-regulations-and-official-guidance**.

[42]T. L. Kirkpatrick and W. B. Pollard, "Reliance by the Tax Court on the Legislative Intent of Congress," *The Tax Executive* (Summer 1986): 358–359.

Assessing the Validity of a Treasury Regulation

Treasury Regulations are the official interpretation of the Code and are entitled to great deference. Occasionally, however, a court invalidates a Regulation (or a portion of it) because the Regulation is contrary to the intent of Congress. Usually, courts do not question the validity of Regulations. Courts believe that "the first administrative interpretation of a provision as it appears in a new act often expresses the general understanding of the times or the actual understanding of those who played an important part when the statute was drafted."[43]

Keep the following things in mind when you assess the validity of a Regulation:

- IRS agents must give the Code and any related Regulations equal weight when dealing with taxpayers and their representatives.

- Proposed Regulations provide a preview of future final Regulations, but they are not binding on the IRS or taxpayers.

- Taxpayers have the burden of proof to show that a Regulation varies from the language of the statute and is not supported by the related Committee Reports.

- If the taxpayer challenges a Regulation and loses, a 20 percent negligence penalty may apply.[44]

- Final Regulations can be classified as procedural, interpretive, or legislative. **Procedural Regulations** are *housekeeping-type instructions* indicating information that taxpayers should provide the IRS, as well as information about the internal management and conduct of the IRS itself.

- Some **interpretive Regulations** rephrase or elaborate what Congress stated in the Committee Reports that were issued when the tax legislation was enacted. These Regulations are almost impossible to overturn because they clearly reflect the intent of Congress. Historically, an interpretive Regulation has been given less deference than a legislative Regulation.[45] The Supreme Court has told lower courts to analyze Treasury Regulations carefully before accepting the Treasury's interpretation.[46]

- In some Code Sections, Congress has given the *Treasury Secretary or his delegate* the authority to prescribe Regulations to carry out the details of administration or to otherwise complete the operating rules. In these cases, Congress is delegating its legislative powers to the Treasury Department. Regulations issued under this type of authority possess the force and effect of law and are often called **legislative Regulations**.

- Courts tend to apply a legislative reenactment doctrine. A particular Regulation is assumed to have received congressional approval if the Regulation was finalized many years earlier, and Congress has not amended the related Code Section.

Assessing the Validity of Other Administrative Sources of the Tax Law

Revenue Rulings issued by the IRS carry less weight than Treasury Department Regulations. Revenue Rulings are important, however, in that they reflect the position of the IRS on tax matters. IRS agents will follow the results reached in a Revenue Ruling that relates to the research question (or the tax return). A 1986 Tax Court decision, however, indicated that Revenue Rulings "typically do not constitute substantive authority for a position."[47] Most Revenue Rulings apply retroactively unless the ruling indicates otherwise.[48]

---

[43]*Augustus v. Comm.*, 41–1 USTC ¶9255, 26 AFTR 612, 118 F.2d 38 (CA–6, 1941).

[44]§§ 6662(a) and (b)(1). This accuracy-related penalty applies to any failure to make a reasonable attempt to comply with the tax law and any disregard of rules and Regulations [§ 6662(c)]. The term *reasonable* is not defined in the Code; the IRS looks at all of the facts and circumstances surrounding the effort of the taxpayer to report the correct tax liability.

[45]However, see *Mayo Foundation for Medical Education and Research,* 2011–1 USTC ¶50,143, 107 AFTR 2d 2011–341, 103 S.Ct. 704 (USSC, 2011), where the Supreme Court provided greater deference to interpretive Regula-

tions (and appeared to blur the line between legislative and interpretive Regulations).

[46]*U.S. v. Vogel Fertilizer Co.*, 82–1 USTC ¶9134, 49 AFTR 2d 82–491, 102 S.Ct. 821 (USSC, 1982); *National Muffler Dealers Assn., Inc.*, 79–1 USTC ¶9264, 43 AFTR 2d 79–828, 99 S.Ct. 1304 (USSC, 1979).

[47]*Nelda C. Stark*, 86 T.C. 243 (1986). See also *Ann R. Neuhoff*, 75 T.C. 36 (1980). For a different opinion, however, see *Industrial Valley Bank & Trust Co.*, 66 T.C. 272 (1976).

[48]Rev.Proc. 87–1, 1987–1 C.B. 503.

Actions on Decisions document the IRS's reaction to certain court decisions. The IRS follows a practice of either acquiescing (agreeing) or nonacquiescing (not agreeing) with selected judicial decisions.

Assessing the Validity of Judicial Sources of the Tax Law

How much reliance can be placed on a particular decision depends on the following variables:

- *The level of court.* A decision rendered by a trial court (e.g., a Federal District Court) carries less weight than one issued by an appellate court (e.g., the Fifth Circuit Court of Appeals). Unless Congress changes the Code, decisions by the U.S. Supreme Court represent the last word on any tax issue.

- *Residence of the taxpayer.* A decision of the appellate court in the taxpayer's circuit carries more weight than one rendered by an appellate court in a different circuit. If, for example, a taxpayer lives in Texas, a decision of the Fifth Circuit Court of Appeals (which would hear an appeal from a Texas trial court) means more than one rendered by the Second Circuit Court of Appeals.[49]

- *Regular or Memorandum decision.* A Tax Court Regular decision carries more weight than a Memorandum decision because the Tax Court does not consider Memorandum decisions to be binding precedents.[50] A Tax Court *reviewed* decision (where *all* of the Tax Court judges participate) carries even more weight.

- *Supreme Court certiorari.* A Circuit Court decision where *certiorari* has been requested and denied by the U.S. Supreme Court carries more weight than a Circuit Court decision that was not appealed. A Circuit Court decision heard *en banc* (all of the judges participate) carries more weight than a normal Circuit Court case.

- *Other courts' support.* A decision that is supported by cases from other courts carries more weight than a decision that is not supported by other cases.

- *Status on appeal.* The weight of a decision also can be affected by its status on appeal. For example, was the decision affirmed or overruled?

In connection with the last three variables, the use of a citator is invaluable to tax research.[51] A citator provides the history of a case, including the authority relied on (e.g., other judicial decisions) in reaching the result. Reviewing the references listed in the citator discloses whether the decision was appealed and, if so, with what result (e.g., affirmed, reversed, or remanded). It also shows other cases with the same or similar issues and how they were decided. As a result, a citator reflects on the validity of a case and may lead to other relevant judicial material.[52] If one intends to rely on a judicial decision, "citing" the case is imperative.

Assessing the Validity of Other Sources

Primary sources of tax law include the Constitution, legislative history materials, statutes, treaties, Treasury Regulations, IRS pronouncements, and judicial decisions. The IRS considers only primary sources to constitute substantial authority. However, reference to *secondary sources* such as legal periodicals, treatises, legal opinions, IRS publications, and other materials can be useful. In general, secondary sources are not authority.

Although the statement that the IRS regards only primary sources as substantial authority generally is true, there is one exception. For purposes of the accuracy-related penalty, the IRS expands the list of substantial authority *for purposes of* the accuracy-related penalty in § 6662 to include a number of secondary sources (e.g., letter rulings, General Counsel Memoranda, and the Bluebook).[53] "Authority" does not include conclusions reached in treatises, legal periodicals, and opinions rendered by tax professionals.

[49]Before October 1, 1982, an appeal from the then-named U.S. Court of Claims (the other trial court) was directly to the U.S. Supreme Court.

[50]*Severino R. Nico, Jr.,* 67 T.C. 647 (1977).

[51]The major citators are published by CCH, RIA, Westlaw, and Shepard's.

[52]The CCH citator is available online through the CCH *IntelliConnect* service; RIA's citator can be found in Thomson Reuters *Checkpoint.* Westlaw's citator (KeyCite) is part of its online service. Shepard's citator is part of LexisNexis.

[53]Notice 90–20, 1990–1 C.B. 328; see also Reg. § 1.6661–3(b)(2).

FINANCIAL DISCLOSURE INSIGHTS   Where Does GAAP Come From?

Tax law is developed by many entities, including Congress, and the legislators of other countries, the courts, and the IRS. Accounting principles also have many sources. Consequently, in reconciling the tax and financial accounting reporting of a transaction, the tax professional needs to know the hierarchy of authority of accounting principles—in particular, the level of importance to assign to a specific GAAP document. The diagram below presents the sources of GAAP arranged in a general order of authority from highest to lowest.

Professional research is conducted to find and analyze the sources of accounting reporting standards in much the same way a tax professional conducts research on an open tax question. In fact, many of the publishers that provide tax research materials also can be used to find GAAP and International Financial Reporting Standards (IFRS) documents. The Financial Accounting Standards Board (FASB) also makes its standards and interpretations available by subscription.

Highest Authority	• Financial Accounting Standards and Interpretations of the FASB. • Pronouncements of bodies that preceded the FASB, such as the Accounting Principles Board (APB).
	• FASB Technical Bulletins. • Audit and Accounting Guides, prepared by the American Institute of CPAs (AICPA) and cleared by the FASB. • Practice Bulletins, prepared by the American Institute of CPAs (AICPA) and cleared by the FASB.
	• Interpretation Guides of the FASB Staff. • Accounting Interpretations of the AICPA. • IASB Accounting Standards. • FASB Concepts Standards. • Widely accepted accounting practices, professional journals, accounting textbooks, and treatises.

A letter ruling or determination letter is substantial authority *only* for the taxpayer to whom it is issued, except for the accuracy-related penalty.

Once major tax legislation is completed, the staff of the Joint Committee on Taxation (in consultation with the staffs of the House Ways and Means and Senate Finance Committees) often prepares a General Explanation of the Act, commonly known as the Bluebook (because of the color of its cover). The IRS does not accept this detailed explanation as having legal effect, except for the accuracy-related penalty. The Bluebook does, however, provide valuable guidance to tax advisers and taxpayers until Regulations are issued.

2-3e Arriving at the Solution or at Alternative Solutions

The Big Picture on p. 2-1 raises the question of whether a taxpayer would be denied dependency exemptions for a son and a daughter-in-law if the son sold some stock near the end of the year. A refinement of the problem supplies additional information:

• Sam and Dana anticipate filing a joint return.

Section 152(b)(2) indicates that a taxpayer is not permitted a dependency exemption for a married dependent if the married individual files a joint return. As a result, it appears that a joint return filed by Sam and Dana would be problematic to the parents. However, more research uncovers two Revenue Rulings that provide an exception if the dependent files a return "solely to claim a refund of tax withheld." The Rulings indicate that each spouse must have gross income of less than the exemption amount.[54]

---

[54]Rev.Rul. 54–567, 1954–2 C.B. 108; Rev.Rul. 65–34, 1965–1 C.B. 86.

So, if Sam sells the stock and he and Dana file a joint return, the parents will lose the dependency exemption for both Sam and Dana.

If the stock is not sold until January 2018, both dependency exemptions are available to the parents in 2017 even if Sam and Dana file a joint return. However, under § 151(d)(2), if the parents claim Sam and Dana as dependents, Sam and Dana lose their personal exemptions on *their* tax return.

2-3f Communicating Tax Research

LO.5

Communicate the results of the tax research process in a client letter and a tax file memorandum.

Once the research process has been completed, the researcher will need to prepare a memo, a letter, or an oral presentation. The form of communication depends on a number of factors. For example, most firms document the results of a tax research project in a memorandum. Although the format of this memorandum can vary, certain elements appear in all memos. In addition, virtually all memos are reviewed by senior tax professionals to ensure accuracy.

How are results communicated to the client (does the client receive the tax research memo, a letter, or some other form of communication)? If an oral presentation is required, who will be the audience? Whatever form it takes, the following elements will be part of the communication:

- A clear statement of the issue.

- In more complex situations, a short review of the facts that raised the issue.

- A review of the relevant tax law sources (e.g., Code, Regulations, Revenue Rulings, and judicial authority).

- Any assumptions made in arriving at the solution.

- The solution recommended and the logic or reasoning supporting it.

- The references consulted in the research process.

A good tax research communication should tell the audience what was researched, the results of that research, and the justification for any recommendations.[55]

Exhibits 2.9, 2.10, and 2.11 present the tax file memos (internal to the firm) and the client letter associated with the facts of *The Big Picture*.

EXHIBIT 2.9	Tax File Memorandum

December 16, 2017

TAX FILE MEMORANDUM

FROM: John J. Jones
SUBJECT: Fred and Megan Samuels
          Engagement: Issues

Today I talked to Fred Samuels about his December 10, 2017 letter requesting tax assistance. He wants to know if his son, Sam, can sell stock worth $19,000 (with an $11,000 basis) without the parents losing the dependency exemptions for Sam and Sam's wife, Dana. Fred also would like to know the effect on Sam and Dana's 2017 tax liability if the stock is sold.

Fred Samuels is married to Megan, and Sam is a full-time student at a local university. Sam inherited the stock from his grandmother about five years ago. If he sells the stock, he will save the proceeds from the sale rather than spend them because he receives a $5,500 scholarship that he uses for his own support (i.e., to pay for tuition, books, and fees). Although neither Sam nor Dana is currently employed, Sam has earned income of $960 and Dana has earned income of $900 during the current year. Fred and Megan are in the 28% tax bracket and furnish approximately 55% of Sam and Dana's support.

ISSUES: If the stock is sold, would the sale prohibit Fred and Megan from claiming Sam and Dana as dependents? What is the effect on Sam and Dana's tax liability if the stock is sold in 2017? Fred would like an answer within two weeks.

---

[55]See Chapter 7 of the AICPA publication cited in Footnote 37. For oral presentations, see W. A. Raabe and G. E. Whittenburg, "Talking Tax: How to Make a Tax Presentation," *The Tax Adviser* (March 1997): 179–182.

EXHIBIT 2.10	**Tax File Memorandum**

December 18, 2017

TAX FILE MEMORANDUM

FROM: John J. Jones
SUBJECT: Fred and Megan Samuels
          Engagement: Conclusions

See the Tax File Memorandum dated December 16, 2017, which contains the facts and identifies the tax issues.

Section 152(a) provides that for a taxpayer to take a dependency exemption, the potential dependent must satisfy either the qualifying child requirements or the qualifying relative requirements (see Chapter 3). Fred and Megan provide about 55% of the support of their son, Sam, and their daughter-in-law, Dana. If Sam sells the stock in 2017, he would not need to spend the proceeds for support purposes (i.e., he would save the proceeds). Thus, the stock sale would not affect his qualifying as not self-supporting under § 152(c)(1)(D). In calculating the percentage of support provided by Fred and Megan, a $5,500 scholarship received by Sam is not counted in determining the amount of support Sam provides for himself [see § 152(f)(5) and Reg. § 1.152–1(c)]. Note, however, that if the $5,500 had been provided by student loans, it would have been included in calculating support [*Philip J. McCauley*, 56 T.C. 48 (1971)].

Section 152(d)(1)(B) provides that to qualify for a dependency exemption as a qualifying relative, the potential dependent's gross income must be less than the exemption amount (i.e., $4,050 in 2017). Without the stock sale, the gross income of both Sam ($960) and Dana ($900) will be below the exemption amount in 2017. The $5,500 Sam receives as a scholarship is excluded from his gross income under § 117(a) because he uses the entire amount to pay for his tuition, books, and fees at a local university.

Although the gross income test is not applicable to Sam (he is a qualifying child), it is applicable to Dana, the daughter-in-law (she is a qualifying relative; see Concept Summary 3.3). A key issue is whether the stock sale that produces $8,000 of recognized gain for Sam and Dana will cause the gross income test to be violated for Dana. Because the $8,000 recognized gain is from the sale of Sam's separately owned asset and they do not live in a community property state, Dana should qualify as a dependent because her gross income would be only $900.

The stock sale would result in the parents' loss of the dependency exemptions for Sam and Dana if they file a joint return for 2017 [see § 152(b)(2)]. The joint return requirement does not apply, however, if the dependent files a joint return solely to claim a refund and neither spouse had a tax liability on a separate return (Rev.Rul. 65–34, 1965–1 C.B. 86). However, sale of the stock would keep this exception from applying.

From a tax planning perspective, Sam can choose to sell the stock in 2017. However, if this choice is made, Sam and Dana need to file separate returns so as not to violate the absence of a joint return provision. Under these circumstances, the sale will not interfere with Fred and Megan's ability to claim dependency exemptions for Sam and Dana on their 2017 return. Note, however, that neither Sam nor Dana will be permitted to take a personal exemption deduction on their 2017 tax return because they are claimed as dependents on someone else's return [see § 151(d)(2)]. This disallowance of the personal exemption deduction will not produce any significant negative tax consequences for Dana because her tax liability would be $0. However, Sam's tax liability would now be $885 (see the kiddie tax discussion in Chapter 3; Sam's net unearned income is $5,900 and is a long-term capital gain taxed at a rate of 15% given his parent's marginal tax bracket). Alternatively, Sam could delay the sale of the stock until 2018. In this case, Sam and Dana's tax liability in 2017 would be $0. The disallowance of the personal exemption deductions by Sam and Dana will not produce any negative tax consequences because both Sam and Dana's tax liability would be $0.

LO.6

Apply tax research techniques and planning procedures.

2-4 WORKING WITH THE TAX LAW— TAX PLANNING

Tax research and tax planning are inseparable. The *primary* purpose of effective *tax planning* is to maximize the taxpayer's after-tax wealth. The course of action selected might not produce the lowest possible tax under the circumstances. The minimization of tax liability must be considered in context with the nontax goals of the taxpayer.

A *secondary* objective of effective tax planning is to reduce or defer the tax in the current tax year. Specifically, this objective aims to accomplish one or more of the following:

- eliminating the tax entirely;
- eliminating the tax in the current year;
- deferring the receipt of income;

EXHIBIT 2.11	Client Letter

Hoffman, Young, Raabe, Maloney, & Nellen, CPAs
5191 Natorp Boulevard
Mason, OH 45040

December 21, 2017

Mr. and Mrs. Fred Samuels
111 Boulevard
Williamsburg, VA 23185

Dear Mr. and Mrs. Samuels:

This letter is in response to your request for us to review your family's financial and tax situation. Our conclusions are based upon the facts as outlined in your December 10 letter. Any change in the facts may affect our conclusions.

You provide over 50% of the support for your son, Sam, and his wife, Dana. The scholarship Sam receives is not included in determining support. If the stock is not sold in 2017, you will qualify for a dependency exemption for both Sam and Dana.

If the stock is sold in 2017, a gain of approximately $8,000 will result. If Sam and Dana then file a joint return, you will lose the dependency exemption for Sam as a qualifying child and will lose the dependency exemption for Dana as a qualifying relative. You can avoid the loss of these two dependency exemptions if Sam and Dana file separate returns. This would result in a tax liability of $0 for Dana and $885 for Sam.

From a family tax planning and tax avoidance perspective, Sam should not sell the stock in 2017. Delaying the stock sale will enable you to claim dependency exemptions for both Sam and Dana and will enable Sam and Dana to have a $0 tax liability for 2017.

Should you need more information or need to clarify our conclusions, do not hesitate to contact me.

Sincerely yours,

John J. Jones, CPA
Partner

- converting ordinary income into capital gains;
- converting active income to passive activity income;
- converting passive activity expense to active expense;
- increasing the number of taxpayers (i.e., forming partnerships and corporations or making lifetime gifts to family members);
- eluding double taxation;
- avoiding ordinary income; or
- creating, increasing, or accelerating deductions.

However, this objective should be approached with caution. For example, a tax election in one year may reduce taxes currently but cause future years to have disadvantageous tax positions.

2-4a Nontax Considerations

There is a danger that tax considerations may impair the exercise of sound financial planning or business judgment by the taxpayer. Thus, the tax planning process can lead to ends that are economically (or socially) incorrect. Unfortunately, a tendency exists for planning to move toward the opposing extremes of placing either too little or too much emphasis on tax considerations. The goal should be a balance that recognizes the significance of taxes, but not beyond the point where planning detracts from the exercise of good business judgment. In general, if the only reason for pursuing a specific course of action is because of the tax benefits, then one should rethink that decision.

2-4b **Components of Tax Planning**

The popular perception of tax planning often is restricted to the adage "defer income and accelerate deductions." Although this timing approach does hold true and is important, meaningful tax planning involves considerably more.

Preferable to deferring income is complete *avoidance*. Consider, for example, the employee who chooses nontaxable fringe benefits (e.g., group term life insurance and health insurance) over a fully taxable future pay increase.[56] Complete avoidance of gain recognition also occurs when the owner of appreciated property transfers it by death. Here, the "step-up" (appreciation) in basis to fair market value completely escapes the income tax.[57]

If the recognition of income cannot be avoided, its deferral will postpone income tax consequences. A tax paid in the future costs less than a tax paid today because of the time value of money. *Deferral* of income can take many forms. Besides like-kind exchanges and involuntary conversions, most retirement plans postpone income tax consequences until the benefits are paid. Deferral of gain recognition also can occur when appreciated property is transferred to a newly formed corporation or partnership.[58]

A corollary to the deferral of income is the acceleration of deductions. For example, if an accrual basis, calendar year corporation authorizes a charitable contribution in 2017 and pays it on or before April 15, 2018, the deduction can be claimed for 2017.[59] Taxes also can be saved by *shifting* income to lower-bracket taxpayers. Gifts of appreciated property to lower-bracket family members can reduce the related capital gain tax rate on a later sale by 15 percentage points (from 15 percent to 0 percent).[60] For certain high-income taxpayers, the reduction is 20 percentage points.

If income cannot be avoided, deferred, or shifted, the nature of the gain can be *converted*. By changing the classification of property, income taxes can be reduced. Thus, a taxpayer who transfers appreciated inventory to a controlled corporation has converted ordinary income property (the inventory) to a capital asset (stock in the corporation). When the taxpayer's stock is later sold, preferential capital gain rates apply.

The conversion approach also can work in tax planning for losses. Properly structured, a loan to a corporation that becomes worthless can be an ordinary loss rather than a capital loss. Likewise, via § 1244, an investor in qualified small business stock can convert what would be a capital loss into an ordinary loss.[61]

Effective tax planning requires that careful consideration be given to the *choice of entity* used for conducting a business. The corporate form results in double taxation but permits shareholder-employees to be covered by fringe benefit programs. Partnerships and S corporations allow a pass-through of losses and other tax attributes, but transferring ownership interests as gifts to family members may be difficult.[62]

Although the substance of a transaction, rather than its form, generally controls, this rule is not always the case with tax planning. *Preserving formalities*, with particularly clear documentation, often is crucial to the result. Is an advance to a corporation a loan or a contribution to capital? The answer may depend on the existence of a note.

Along with preserving formalities, the taxpayer should keep records that support how a transaction is treated. Returning to the issue of loan versus contribution to capital, how is the advance listed on the books of the borrower? What do the corporate minutes say about the advance?

Finally, effective tax planning requires *consistency* on the part of taxpayers. A shareholder who treats a corporate distribution as a return of capital cannot later avoid a stock basis adjustment by contending that the distribution was really a dividend.

---

[56]See text Sections 5-6 and 5-8 and Examples 19 and 38 in Chapter 5.

[57]See Example 24 in Chapter 14.

[58]See Examples 28 and 49 in Chapter 20, and Chapter 19 in general.

[59]See Example 15 in Chapter 20.

[60]See text Section 14-3b in Chapter 14.

[61]See Example 9 in Chapter 7.

[62]See text Sections 20-5, 20-6, and 20-7c in Chapter 20.

In summary, the key components of tax planning include the following:

- *Avoid* the recognition of income (usually by resorting to a nontaxable source or nontaxable event).
- *Defer* the recognition of income (or accelerate deductions).
- *Convert* the classification of income (or deductions) to a more advantageous form (e.g., ordinary income into capital gain).
- *Choose* the business *entity* with the desired tax attributes.
- Preserve *formalities* by generating and maintaining supporting documentation.
- Act in a manner *consistent* with the intended objective.

2-4c Tax Avoidance and Tax Evasion

A fine line exists between legal tax planning and illegal tax planning—tax avoidance versus tax evasion. **Tax avoidance** is merely tax minimization through legal techniques, which is the proper objective of all tax planning. Tax evasion, while also aimed at the elimination or reduction of taxes, connotes the use of subterfuge and fraud as a means to an end. Popular usage—probably because of the common goals involved—has so linked these two concepts that many individuals are no longer aware of the true distinctions between them. Consequently, some taxpayers may not take advantage of planning possibilities. The now classic words of Judge Learned Hand in *Commissioner v. Newman* reflect the true values the taxpayer should have:

> Over and over again courts have said that there is nothing sinister in so arranging one's affairs as to keep taxes as low as possible. Everybody does so, rich or poor; and all do right, for nobody owes any public duty to pay more than the law demands: taxes are enforced extractions, not voluntary contributions. To demand more in the name of morals is mere cant.[63]

As Denis Healy, a former British Chancellor, once said, "The difference between tax avoidance and tax evasion is the thickness of a prison wall."

U.S. taxpayers spent over 8.9 billion hours (or more than one million years) preparing and filing tax returns in 2016. Considering individual, business, and employment taxes, this time amounts to about $409 billion annually in compliance costs. Of course, additional time is spent filing state tax returns each year.[64]

2-4d Follow-Up Procedures

Because tax planning usually involves a proposed (rather than a completed) transaction, being aware of if or when the law changes is critical to the tax planning process. A change in the tax law (legislative, administrative, or judicial) could alter the original conclusion. Additional research may be necessary to test the solution in light of current developments (refer to the broken lines at the right in Exhibit 2.8).

2-4e Tax Planning—A Practical Application

Returning to the facts of *The Big Picture* on p. 2-1, what could be done to protect the dependency exemptions for the parents? If Sam and Dana refrain from filing a joint return, both could be claimed by the parents.

Are there alternatives that exist related to the proposed stock sale? Sam would like to know if he could sell the stock and postpone the recognition of gain until the following year by selling short an equal number of substantially identical shares and covering the short sale in the subsequent year with the shares originally held. Selling short means that Sam sells borrowed stock (substantially identical) and repays the lender

---

[63]*Comm. v. Newman*, 47–1 USTC ¶9175, 35 AFTR 857, 159 F.2d 848 (CA–2, 1947).

[64]Scott A. Hodge, "The Compliance Costs of IRS Regulations," Tax Foundation, June 15, 2016.

with the stock held on the date of the short sale. This *short against the box* technique might allow Sam to protect his $8,000 profit and defer the closing of the sale until the following year.[65] However, additional research indicates that the short against the box technique no longer produces the desired postponement of recognized gain. That is, at the time of the short sale, Sam has a recognized gain of $8,000 from a constructive sale. Note the critical role of obtaining the correct facts in attempting to resolve the proper strategy for the taxpayers.

Throughout this text, each chapter concludes with observations on Tax Planning. These observations are not all-inclusive, but they are intended to illustrate some of the ways in which the material covered in the chapter can be effectively utilized to minimize taxes.

2-5   TAXATION ON THE CPA EXAMINATION

LO.7

Be aware of taxation on the CPA examination.

Beginning in April 2017, a revised CPA exam will be delivered. The CPA exam will continue to test in the familiar four sections—Auditing and Attestation (AUD), Business Environment and Concepts (BEC), Financial Accounting and Reporting (FAR), and Regulation (REG). However, the exam will place less emphasis on remembering-and-understanding skills, enabling higher-level analysis and evaluation skills to be tested:

- The number of task-based simulations, a highly effective way to assess higher-order skills, will increase. Task-based simulations will be added to the BEC section for the first time, and the AUD, FAR, and REG sections each will have their number of task-based simulations increased to eight or nine.

- Total testing time will increase from 14 to 16 hours. This change will accommodate increases of one hour each for the BEC and REG sections. The extra time is being allotted partly because of the increase in task-based simulations. Testing time will remain the same for the AUD and FAR sections.

- Multiple-choice questions and task-based simulations each will contribute about 50 percent toward the candidate's score in the AUD, FAR, and REG sections. In the BEC section, multiple-choice questions will contribute about 50 percent of the scoring, with 35 percent coming from task-based simulations and 15 percent from written communication.

- The revised CPA exam will place less emphasis on multiple-choice questions, which will decrease from about 60 percent to about 50 percent of the total points.

- The revised CPA exam will test remembering and understanding, application, analysis, and evaluation. The current CPA exam only tests for the first two of these items.

2-5a Preparation Blueprints

To prepare for the revised CPA exam, candidates will be able to use new AICPA-developed blueprints that will replace the current Content Specification Outline (CSO) and Skill Specification Outline (SSO).[66]

The blueprints have been drafted to provide candidates more detail about what to expect on the exam. The blueprints contain about 600 representative tasks, which are aligned with the skills required of newly licensed CPAs, across the four exam sections. The blueprints are designed to provide candidates with clearer information on the material the exam will test and will show educators what knowledge and skills candidates need as newly licensed CPAs. In addition, the blueprints will provide candidates with sample tasks that align with both the content and skill level at which the content will be tested.

---

[65]§§ 1233(a) and 1233(b)(2). See Chapter 16 for a discussion of short sales.

[66]The blueprints can be accessed at: **www.aicpa.org/BecomeACPA/ CPAExam/nextexam/DownloadableDocuments/2017-CPA-Exam-Blueprints.pdf.**

2-5b **Regulation Section**

Taxation will continue to be tested within the REG section of the CPA exam. Testing within REG is administered in five blocks called testlets, which feature multiple-choice questions (MCQs) and task-based simulations (TBSs). Candidates receive at least one research question (research-oriented TBS) that requires the candidate to search the applicable authoritative literature and find an appropriate reference.

Each of the five topics in REG includes one or more representative tasks that are not necessarily questions on the exam. For example, the exam will not specifically ask a candidate to "Calculate taxpayer penalties relating to Federal tax returns." However, identifying *situations* where a taxpayer penalty might apply would be appropriate. In addition, tasks are to be inclusive, not exclusive, of exam content. For example, the task "Calculate tax depreciation for a tangible business property…" could include the calculation of additional first-year (bonus) depreciation.

Task-based simulations are case studies that allow candidates to demonstrate their knowledge and skills by generating responses to questions rather than simply selecting an answer. They typically require candidates to use spreadsheets and/or to research authoritative literature provided in the CPA exam (e.g., Internal Revenue Code, Regulations, IRS publications, and tax forms).

There are five content areas in the REG section of the CPA exam:

- Area 1: Ethics, professional responsibilities, and Federal tax procedures (weight: 10 to 20 percent)
- Area 2: Business law (weight: 10 to 20 percent)
- Area 3: Federal taxation of property transactions (weight: 12 to 22 percent)
- Area 4: Federal taxation of individuals (weight: 15 to 25 percent)
- Area 5: Federal taxation of entities (weight: 28 to 38 percent)

Area 1 covers ethics and responsibilities in tax practice, licensing and disciplinary systems, Federal tax procedures, and legal duties and responsibilities of a CPA.

Area 3 covers Federal taxation of property transactions and Federal estate and gift taxation.

Area 4 covers the Federal income taxation of individuals from both a tax preparation and tax planning perspective (e.g., income, exclusions, deductions, retirement plans).

Area 5 covers the Federal income taxation of entities, including sole proprietorships, partnerships, limited liability companies, C corporations, S corporations, joint ventures, trusts, estates, and tax-exempt organizations, from both a tax preparation and tax planning perspective.

Accounting methods and periods and tax elections are included in Areas 3, 4, and 5. Only Area 2 does not involve taxation.

"Remembering and understanding" are tested mainly in Areas 1 and 2. Application and analysis skills are tested primarily in Areas 3, 4, and 5. These three areas contain more of the day-to-day tasks that newly licensed CPAs are expected to perform. As a result, they are tested at the higher end of the skill level continuum. Overall, the REG section will test skills as follows: remembering and learning (25 to 35 percent), application (35 to 45 percent), and analysis (25 to 35 percent). The REG section does not test any content at the Evaluation skill level as newly licensed CPAs are not expected to demonstrate that level of skill in regard to the REG content.

The REG section has 76 multiple-choice questions and 8 to 9 task-based simulations (TBSs); the key increase is in TBSs (up from 6 in the previous CPA exam). This change will allow the AICPA to assess the candidate's higher-order skills. In addition, TBSs on the CPA exam feature increased background material and data that require candidates to determine what information is or is not relevant to the question. The scoring weight of multiple-choice questions and TBSs is about 50 percent each on the REG section of the CPA exam.

Depending on the skill level being assessed, well-prepared candidates will likely spend 15 to 20 minutes for each TBS. Certain analysis and/or evaluation-level TBSs could take a well-prepared candidate up to 30 minutes to complete. Several examples of task-based simulations follow.

CPA Exam Simulation Examples

EXAMPLE 4

The *tax citation type* simulation requires the candidate to research the Internal Revenue Code and enter a Code Section and subsection.

For example, Amber Company is considering using the simplified dollar-value method of pricing its inventory for purposes of the LIFO method that is available to certain small businesses. What Code Section is the relevant authority in the Internal Revenue Code that you should use to determine whether the taxpayer is eligible to use this method? To be successful, the candidate must find § 474.

EXAMPLE 5

A *tax form completion* simulation requires the candidate to fill out a portion of a tax form. For example, Red Company is a limited liability company (LLC) for tax purposes. Complete the income section of the IRS Form 1065 for Red Company using the values found and calculated on previous tabs along with the following data:

Ordinary income from other partnerships	$ 5,200
Net gain (loss) from Form 4797	2,400
Management fee income	12,000

The candidate is provided with page 1 of Form 1065 on which to record the appropriate amounts.

Any field that requires an entry is a shaded rectangular cell. Some white rectangular cells will automatically calculate based on the entries in the shaded cell.

Candidates can learn more about the CPA examination at **www.cpa-exam.org**. This online tutorial site's topics include:

- Common tools.
- Navigation.
- Form completion.
- Numeric entry.
- Research questions.
- Authoritative literature search.
- Written communication.

The common tools are a calculator, a spreadsheet, reminder flags, and an examination clock. A 30- to 60-minute sample exam will familiarize a candidate with the types of questions on the examination.

Key Terms

Acquiescence, 2-16

Circuit Court of Appeals, 2-12

Citator, 2-25

Court of original jurisdiction, 2-10

Determination letters, 2-9

Federal District Court, 2-10

Final Regulations, 2-7

Interpretive Regulations, 2-24

Legislative Regulations, 2-24

Letter rulings, 2-8

Nonacquiescence, 2-16

Precedents, 2-13

Procedural Regulations, 2-24

Proposed Regulations, 2-7

Revenue Procedures, 2-7

Revenue Rulings, 2-7

Small Cases Division, 2-10

Tax avoidance, 2-31

Tax research, 2-20

Technical Advice Memoranda (TAMs), 2-9

Temporary Regulations, 2-7

U.S. Court of Federal Claims, 2-10

U.S. Supreme Court, 2-13

U.S. Tax Court, 2-10

Writ of Certiorari, 2-14

Discussion Questions

1. **LO.1** A large part of tax research consists of determining what?

2. **LO.1** Why do taxpayers often have more than one alternative for structuring a business transaction?

3. **LO.1** Where does Federal tax legislation generally originate?

4. **LO.2, 5** Butch Bishop operates a small international firm named Tile, Inc. A new treaty between the United States and Spain conflicts with a Section of the Internal Revenue Code. Butch asks you for advice. If he follows the treaty position, does he need to disclose this on his tax return? If he is required to disclose, are there any penalties for failure to disclose? Prepare a letter in which you respond to Butch. Tile's address is 100 International Drive, Tampa, FL 33620.   Communications

5. **LO.1, 2** Interpret this Regulation citation: Reg. § 1.163–10(a)(2).

6. **LO.1** In the citation Notice 90–20, 1990–1 C.B. 328, to what do the 20 and the 328 refer?

7. **LO.1, 4** Rank the following items from the lowest to highest authority in the Federal tax law system:
   a. Interpretive Regulation.
   b. Legislative Regulation.
   c. Letter ruling.
   d. Revenue Ruling.
   e. Internal Revenue Code.
   f. Proposed Regulation.

8. **LO.1** Interpret each of the following citations:
   a. Temp.Reg. § 1.956–2T.
   b. Rev.Rul. 2012–15, 2012–23 I.R.B. 975.
   c. Ltr.Rul. 200204051.

9. **LO.1, 5** Sally Andrews calls you on the phone. She says that she has found a 2007 letter ruling that agrees with a position she wants to take on her tax return. She asks you about the precedential value of a letter ruling. Draft a memo for the tax files outlining what you told Sally.   Communications

10. **LO.1** Sri is considering writing the IRS to find out whether a possible stock redemption would be a qualified stock redemption. Outline some relevant tax issues Sri faces in determining whether to request a letter ruling.   Issue ID

11. **LO.1** Where may private letter rulings be found?

12. **LO.1** What are the differences between Technical Advice Memoranda (TAMs) and Technical Expedited Advice Memoranda (TEAMs)?

13. **LO.1** Dwain receives a 90-day letter after his discussion with an appeals officer. He is not satisfied with the $101,000 settlement offer. Identify the relevant tax research issues facing Dwain.   Issue ID

14. **LO.1** List an advantage and a disadvantage of using the U.S. Court of Federal Claims as the trial court for Federal tax litigation.

15. **LO.1, 5** Eddy Falls is considering litigating a tax deficiency of approximately $229,030 in the court system. He asks you to provide him with a short description of his alternatives, indicating the advantages and disadvantages of each. Prepare your response to Eddy in the form of a letter. His address is 200 Mesa Drive, Tucson, AZ 85714.   Communications

16. **LO.1** List an advantage and a disadvantage of using the U.S. Tax Court as the trial court for Federal tax litigation.

17. **LO.1** A taxpayer lives in Michigan. In a controversy with the IRS, the taxpayer loses at the trial court level. Describe the appeal procedure under the following different assumptions:
    a. The trial court was the Small Cases Division of the U.S. Tax Court.
    b. The trial court was the U.S. Tax Court.
    c. The trial court was a U.S. District Court.
    d. The trial court was the U.S. Court of Federal Claims.

18. **LO.1** What is meant by the term *petitioner*?

19. **LO.1** An appellate court will often become involved in fact-finding determination. Discuss the validity of this statement.

20. **LO.1** For the U.S. Tax Court, U.S. District Court, and U.S. Court of Federal Claims, indicate the following:
    a. Number of regular judges per court.
    b. Availability of a jury trial.
    c. Whether the deficiency must be paid before the trial.

21. **LO.1** A taxpayer living in the following states would appeal a decision of the U.S. District Court to which Court of Appeals?
    a. Wyoming.
    b. Nebraska.
    c. Idaho.
    d. Louisiana.
    e. Illinois.

22. **LO.1** What precedents must each of these courts follow?
    a. U.S. Tax Court.
    b. U.S. Court of Federal Claims.
    c. U.S. District Court.

23. **LO.1** What determines the appropriate Circuit Court of Appeals for a particular taxpayer?

24. **LO.1, 4** In assessing the validity of a prior court decision, discuss the significance of the following on the taxpayer's issue:
    a. The decision was rendered by the U.S. District Court of Wyoming. Taxpayer lives in Wyoming.
    b. The decision was rendered by the U.S. Court of Federal Claims. Taxpayer lives in Wyoming.
    c. The decision was rendered by the Second Circuit Court of Appeals. Taxpayer lives in California.
    d. The decision was rendered by the U.S. Supreme Court.
    e. The decision was rendered by the U.S. Tax Court. The IRS has acquiesced in the result.
    f. Same as part (e) except that the IRS has issued a nonacquiescence as to the result.

25. **LO.2** In the citation *Schuster's Express, Inc.*, 66 T.C. 588 (1976), *aff'd* 562 F.2d 39 (CA–2, 1977), *nonacq.*, to what do the 66, 39, and *nonacq.* refer?

26. **LO.2** Is there an automatic right to appeal to the U.S. Supreme Court? If so, what is the process?

27. **LO.2** Referring to the citation only, determine which court issued these decisions.
    a. 716 F.2d 693 (CA–9, 1983).
    b. 92 T.C. 400 (1998).
    c. 70 U.S. 224 (1935).
    d. 3 B.T.A. 1042 (1926).
    e. T.C.Memo. 1957–169.
    f. 50 AFTR2d 92–6000 (Ct. Cl., 1992).
    g. Ltr.Rul. 9046036.
    h. 111 F.Supp.2d 1294 (S.D.N.Y., 2000).
    i. 98–50, 1998–1 C.B. 10.

28. **LO.2** Interpret each of the following citations:
    a. 14 T.C. 74 (1950).
    b. 592 F.2d 1251 (CA–5, 1979).
    c. 95–1 USTC ¶50,104 (CA–6, 1995).
    d. 75 AFTR2d 95–110 (CA–6, 1995).
    e. 223 F.Supp. 663 (W.D. Tex., 1963).

29. **LO.2** Give the Commerce Clearing House citation for the following courts:
    a. Small Cases Division of the Tax Court.
    b. Federal District Court.
    c. U.S. Supreme Court.
    d. U.S. Court of Federal Claims.
    e. Tax Court Memorandum decision.

30. **LO.2** Where can you locate a published decision of the U.S. Court of Federal Claims?

31. **LO.1, 2** Which of the following items can probably be found in the *Internal Revenue Bulletin*?
    a. Action on Decision.
    b. Small Cases Division of the U.S. Tax Court decision.
    c. Letter ruling.
    d. Revenue Procedure.
    e. Finalized Regulation.
    f. U.S. Court of Federal Claims decision.
    g. Acquiescences to Tax Court decisions.
    h. U.S. Circuit Court of Appeals decision.

32. **LO.3** For her tax class, Yvonne must prepare a research paper discussing the tax aspects of child support payments. Explain to Yvonne how she can research this topic using various tax research resources. **Issue ID**

33. **LO.4** Where can a researcher find the current Internal Revenue Code of 1986?

34. **LO.2, 4** You inherit a tax problem that was researched five months ago. You believe the answer is correct, but you are unfamiliar with the general area. How would you find recent articles dealing with the subject area? How do you evaluate the reliability of the authority cited in the research report? How do you determine the latest developments pertaining to the research problem? **Decision Making**

35. **LO.6** What is the primary purpose of effective tax planning? Explain.

36. **LO.7** Describe simulation questions on the CPA exam.

Problems

37. **LO.1** In which Subchapter of the Internal Revenue Code would one find information about corporate distributions?
    a. Subchapter S.
    b. Subchapter C.
    c. Subchapter P.
    d. Subchapter K.
    e. Subchapter M.

38. **LO.1** To locate an IRS Revenue Procedure that was issued during the past week, which source would you consult?
    a. *Federal Register*.
    b. *Internal Revenue Bulletin*.
    c. Internal Revenue Code.
    d. Some other source.

39. **LO.1** Which of the following items can be found in the *Federal Register*?
    a. Letter Ruling.
    b. Action on Decision.
    c. Revenue Procedure.
    d. Temporary Regulation.
    e. Technical Advice Memorandum.

40. **LO.1, 4** Rank the items below from most reliable to least reliable:
    a. Letter Ruling.
    b. Legislative Regulation.
    c. Code Section.
    d. Revenue Ruling.
    e. Proposed Regulation.
    f. Interpretive Regulation.
    g. Recent Temporary Regulation.

41. **LO.4** Using the legend provided, classify each of the following tax sources:

Legend
P = Primary tax source
S = Secondary tax source
B = Both
N = Neither

    a. Sixteenth Amendment to the U.S. Constitution.
    b. Tax treaty between the United States and India.
    c. Revenue Procedure.
    d. An IRS publication.
    e. U.S. District Court decision.
    f. *Yale Law Journal* article.
    g. Temporary Regulations (issued 2014).
    h. U.S. Tax Court Memorandum decision.
    i. Small Cases Division of the U.S. Tax Court decision.
    j. House Ways and Means Committee report.

42. **LO.1, 2** Using the legend provided, classify each of the following citations as to publisher:

Legend
RIA = Research Institute of America
CCH = Commerce Clearing House
W = West
U.S. = U.S. Government
O = Others

   a.   83–2 USTC ¶9600.
   b.   52 AFTR 2d 83–5954.
   c.   67 T.C. 293 (1976).
   d.   39 TCM 32 (1979).
   e.   416 U.S. 938.
   f.   RIA T.C. Memo. ¶80,582.
   g.   89 S.Ct. 501.
   h.   2 Cl.Ct. 600.
   i.   415 F.2d 488.
   j.   592 F.Supp. 18.
   k.   77–37, 1977–2 C.B. 568.
   l.   S. Rep. No. 1622, 83rd Cong., 2d Sess. 42 (1954).

43. **LO.6** Using the legend provided, classify each of the following statements:

Legend
A = Tax avoidance
E = Tax evasion
N = Neither

   a.   Sue writes a $707 check for a charitable contribution on December 28, 2017, but does not mail the check to the charitable organization until January 10, 2018. She takes a deduction in 2017.
   b.   Sam decides not to report interest income from a bank because the amount is only $19.75.
   c.   Harry pays property taxes on his home in December 2017 rather than waiting until February 2018.
   d.   Variet switches her investments from taxable corporate bonds to tax-exempt municipal bonds.
   e.   Mel encourages his mother to save most of her Social Security benefits so that he will be able to claim her as a dependent.

Research Problems

Note: Solutions to the Research Problems can be prepared by using the Thomson Reuters Checkpoint® Student Edition online tax research database, which accompanies this textbook. Solutions can also be prepared by using research materials found in a typical tax library.

Research Problem 1. Determine the missing data in these court decisions and rulings.

    a. *Higgens v. Comm.*, 312 U.S._____ (1941).

    b. *Talen v. U.S.*, 355 F.Supp.2d 22 (D.Ct. D.C., _____).

    c. Rev.Rul. 2008–18, 2008–13 I.R.B._____.

    d. *Pahl v. Comm.*, 150 F.3d 1124 (CA–9, _____).

    e. *Veterinary Surgical Consultants PC*, 117 T.C._____ (2001).

    f. *Yeagle Drywall Co.*, T.C.Memo. 2001_____.

Research Problem 2. Can a Tax Court Small Case Decision be treated as a precedent for other cases? Explain.

Partial list of research aids:
IRC § 7463(b).
Maria Antionette Walton Mitchell, T.C. Summ. 2004–160.

Decision Making   **Research Problem 3.** When Oprah gave away Pontiac G6 sedans to her TV audience, was the value of the cars taxable? On Labor Day weekend in 2006, World Furniture Mall in Plano, Illinois, gave away $275,000 of furniture because the Chicago Bears shut out the Green Bay Packers in the team's football season opener at Lambeau Field in Green Bay (26–0). Was the free furniture in the form of a discount or rebate taxable, or should the furniture company have handed the customers a Form 1099–MISC?

Decision Making   **Research Problem 4.** You are interviewing a client before preparing his tax return. He indicates that he did not list as income $96,000 received as a recovery for false imprisonment. What should you do with respect to this significant recovery?

Partial list of research aids:
CCA 200809001.
Daniel and Brenda Stadnyk, T.C.Memo. 2008–289.
Rev.Rul. 2007–14, 2007–1 C.B. 747.
§ 104.

Use internet tax resources to address the following questions. Look for reliable websites and blogs of the IRS and other government agencies, media outlets, businesses, tax professionals, academics, think tanks, and political outlets.

Research Problem 5. (1) Go to **www.taxalmanac.org**, and use the website to find § 61(a). What is defined in this Code Section? Is the definition broad or narrow? (2) Go to **www.legalbitstream.com**, and find the case in which Mark Spitz, the former Olympic gold medalist, is the petitioner. Answer the following questions about the case:

    a. What tax years are at issue in the case?

    b. In what year was the case decided?

    c. Did the court decide in favor of Mr. Spitz or the IRS?

    d. Were any penalties imposed on Mr. Spitz? Why or why not?

Research Problem 6. Go to the U.S. Tax Court website (**www.ustaxcourt.gov**).

    a. What different types of cases can be found on the site?

    b. What is a Summary Opinion? Find one.

    c. What is a Memorandum Opinion? Find one.

    d. Find the "Rules of Practice and Procedure."

CHAPTER

3

Tax Formula and Tax Determination; An Overview of Property Transactions

LEARNING OBJECTIVES: *After completing Chapter 3, you should be able to:*

LO.1 Recognize and apply the components of the Federal income tax formula.

LO.2 Explain the standard deduction and evaluate its choice in arriving at taxable income.

LO.3 Apply the rules for arriving at personal exemptions.

LO.4 Explain the rules for determining dependency exemptions.

LO.5 Choose the proper filing status and identify the related filing requirements.

LO.6 Demonstrate the proper procedures for determining the tax liability.

LO.7 Identify and report kiddie tax situations.

LO.8 Explain the fundamentals of property transactions.

LO.9 Evaluate tax planning opportunities associated with the individual tax formula.

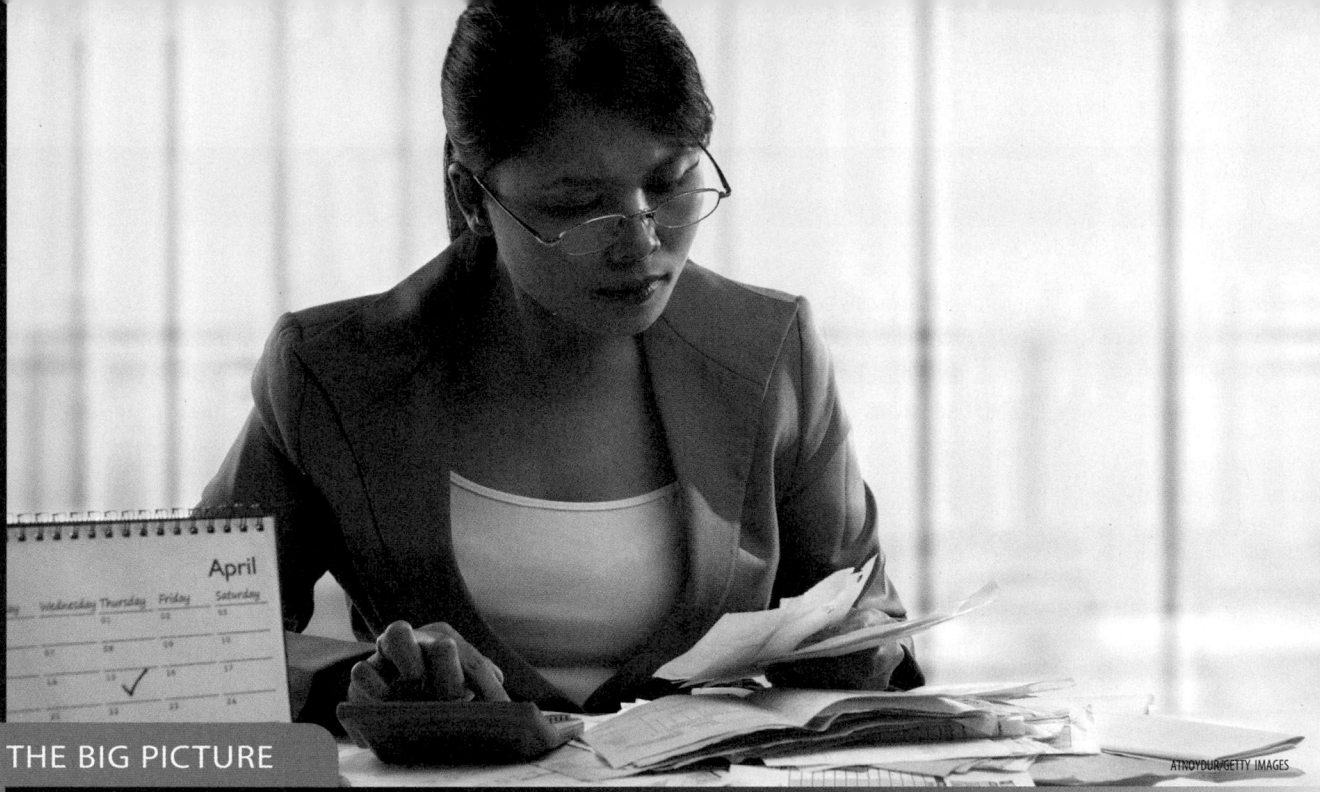

ATNOYDUR/GETTY IMAGES

THE BIG PICTURE

A DIVIDED HOUSEHOLD

Polly maintains a household in which she lives with her unemployed husband (Nick), stepdaughter (Paige), and a family friend (Maude). She provides more than half of the support for both Paige and Maude. Maude was fatally injured in an automobile accident in February, and Polly paid for her hospitalization and funeral expenses. Paige, an accomplished gymnast, graduated from high school last year. Paige has a part-time job but spends most of her time training and looking for an athletic scholarship to the "right" college. In March, Nick left for parts unknown and has not been seen or heard from since. Polly was more surprised than distressed over Nick's unexpected departure. One reaction, however, was to sell her wedding rings to a cousin who was getting married. The rings cost $11,800 and were sold for their approximate value of $9,000.

Based on these facts, what are Polly's income tax concerns for the current year?

Read the chapter and formulate your response.

FRAMEWORK 1040 **Tax Formula for Individuals**

This chapter covers the boldfaced portions of the Tax Formula for Individuals that is introduced in Concept Summary 3.1 on p. 3-3. Below those portions are the sections of Form 1040 where the results are reported.

Income *(broadly defined)*	$xx,xxx
Less: Exclusions	(x,xxx)
Gross income...	$xx,xxx
Less: **Deductions** *for* adjusted gross income..	(x,xxx)

FORM 1040 (p.1)

1 ☐ Single
2 ☐ Married filing jointly (even if only one had income)
3 ☐ Married filing separately. Enter spouse's SSN above and full name here. ▶

4 ☐ Head of household (with qualifying person). (See instructions.) If the qualifying person is a child but not your dependent, enter this child's name here. ▶
5 ☐ Qualifying widow(er) with dependent child

Adjusted gross income..	$xx,xxx
Less: The greater of total **itemized deductions** *or* the standard deduction	(x,xxx)

FORM 1040 (p. 2)

39a Check if: ☐ **You** were born before January 2, 1952,   ☐ Blind.
     ☐ **Spouse** was born before January 2, 1952,   ☐ Blind.   **Total boxes checked ▶ 39a** ☐

b If your spouse itemizes on a separate return or you were a dual-status alien, check here ▶   **39b** ☐

40 **Itemized deductions** (from Schedule A) **or** your **standard deduction** (see left margin)   . .

42 **Exemptions.** If line 38 is $155,650 or less, multiply $4,050 by the number on line 6d. Otherwise, see instructions

Personal and dependency exemptions..	(x,xxx)
Taxable income	$xx,xxx
Tax on taxable income *(see Tax Tables or Tax Rate Schedules)*............................	$ x,xxx
Less: Tax credits *(including income taxes withheld and prepaid)*	(xxx)
Tax due (or refund)	$ xxx

The tax formula provides a framework for applying the Federal income tax to individuals. It is an integral part of our U.S. tax system (i.e., local, state, and Federal). Chapter 3 provides a summary of its components, while providing a detailed discussion of several of its key components—the standard deduction, personal and dependency exemptions, and tax determination.

In addition, the tax formula establishes the framework for much of the text; its relationship to the chapters to follow are reflected in Concept Summary 3.1.

Chapter 3 also provides an overview of property transactions. When property is sold, a gain or loss results, and this can affect the determination of taxable income. Chapters 14 through 17 discuss property transactions in detail. But understanding the basic rules will help in applying other materials in the text. In addition, we discuss two concepts unique to the income tax: the difference between realized and recognized gain or loss and the classification of gain or loss (ordinary or capital).

LO.1

Recognize and apply the components of the Federal income tax formula.

3-1 **TAX FORMULA**

We begin by reviewing the various components of the income tax formula. Then we explore several components in more depth: the standard deduction, exemptions, filing status, and tax determination. The structure of the individual income tax return parallels the tax formula. The 2016 Form 1040 is included on pages 3-9 and 3-10. Be sure to review it as you read about the tax formula. (The 2017 form is not available until late 2017.)

Concept Summary 3.1

Tax Formula for Individuals (Components Integrated into the Text)

		Text Discussion
Income (broadly defined)	$xx,xxx	Chs. 3, 4
Less: **Exclusions**	(x,xxx)	Ch. 5
Gross income	$xx,xxx	Chs. 4, 16, 17
Less: **Deductions *for*** adjusted gross income	(x,xxx)	· Chs. 6–9, 11, 16, 17
Adjusted gross income	$xx,xxx	
Less: The greater of—		
Total **itemized deductions**	(x,xxx)	Chs. 6, 9, 10, 11
or **standard deduction**		Ch. 3
Less: **Personal** and **dependency exemptions**	(x,xxx)	Ch. 3
Taxable income	$xx,xxx	Chs. 3, 12, 13
Tax on taxable income	$ x,xxx	Chs. 3, 12, 13
Less: **Tax credits**	(xxx)	Ch. 13
Tax due (or refund)	$ xxx	Chs. 3, 12, 13

3-1a Components of the Tax Formula

Income (Broadly Defined)

In the tax formula, "income" is broadly defined and includes all of the taxpayer's income, both taxable and nontaxable. In general, the courts have defined "income" as *any increase in wealth*.[1] As a result, it does not include a return of capital or borrowed funds.

EXAMPLE 1

Dan decides to quit renting and buy a new house. The owner of the apartment building returns to Dan the $600 damage deposit he previously made. To make a down payment on the house, Dan sells stock for $50,000 (original cost of $28,000) and borrows $200,000 from a bank.

Only the $22,000 gain from the sale of the stock is income to Dan. The $600 damage deposit and the $28,000 cost of the stock are a return of capital. The $200,000 bank loan is not income as Dan has an obligation to repay that amount (and it does not increase his wealth).

Exclusions

For various reasons, Congress has chosen to exclude certain types of income from the income tax base. A partial list of these exclusions is shown in Exhibit 3.1. Income exclusions are covered in Chapter 5.

Gross Income

The Internal Revenue Code defines gross income broadly as "except as otherwise provided ..., all income from whatever source derived."[2] The "except as otherwise provided" phrase refers to exclusions. A partial list of items included in gross income appears in Exhibit 3.2. Gross income does not include *unrealized* gains (e.g., stock that has appreciated in value, but has not been sold). Gross income is discussed in Chapters 4 and 5.

---

[1] *Comm. v. Glenshaw Glass Co.*, 55–1 USTC ¶9308, 47 AFTR 162, 348 U.S. 426 (USSC, 1955).

[2] § 61(a).

EXHIBIT 3.1	Partial List of Exclusions from Gross Income

Accident insurance proceeds	Life insurance paid upon death
Annuities (cost element)	Meals and lodging (if furnished for employer's
Bequests	convenience)
Child support payments	Military allowances
Cost-of-living allowance (for military)	Minister's dwelling rental value allowance
Damages for personal injury or sickness	Railroad retirement benefits (to a limited
Gifts received	extent)
Group term life insurance, premium paid	Scholarship grants (to a limited extent)
by employer (for coverage up to $50,000)	Social Security benefits (to a limited extent)
Inheritances	Veterans' benefits
Interest from state and local	Welfare payments
(i.e., municipal) bonds	Workers' compensation benefits

EXAMPLE 2

Beth received the following amounts during the year:

Salary	$30,000
Interest on savings account	900
Gift from her aunt	10,000
Prize won in state lottery	1,000
Alimony from ex-husband	12,000
Child support from ex-husband	6,000
Damages for injury in auto accident	25,000
Ten $50 bills in an unmarked envelope found in an airport lounge (airport authorities could not locate anyone who claimed ownership)	500
Federal income tax refund for last year's tax overpayment	120
Increase in the value of stock held for investment	5,000

Review Exhibits 3.1 and 3.2 to determine the amount Beth must include in the computation of taxable income and the amount she may exclude.[3]

Deductions *for* Adjusted Gross Income

Individual taxpayers have two categories of deductions: (1) deductions *for* adjusted gross income (deductions from gross income to arrive at adjusted gross income) and (2) deductions *from* adjusted gross income.

Deductions *for* adjusted gross income (AGI) are sometimes called *above-the-line* deductions because on the tax return, they are taken before the "line" designating AGI. Deductions *for* AGI include, but are not limited to, the following:[4]

- Trade or business expenses.
- Part of the self-employment tax.
- Unreimbursed moving expenses.
- Contributions to traditional Individual Retirement Accounts (IRAs) and other retirement plans.

---

[3]Beth must include $44,400 in computing taxable income ($30,000 salary + $900 interest + $1,000 lottery prize + $12,000 alimony + $500 found property). She can exclude $41,000 ($10,000 gift from aunt + $6,000 child support + $25,000 damages). The $120 Federal income tax refund is excluded because it represents an adjustment (i.e., overpayment) of a nondeductible

expenditure made in the previous year. The unrealized gain on the stock held for investment also is not included in gross income.

[4]§ 62; many of these deductions are limited in some way. And, some of these deductions appear on supporting schedules or forms. For example, the business expenses of a sole proprietor appear on Schedule C (Form 1040).

EXHIBIT 3.2	**Partial List of Gross Income Items**

Alimony	Group term life insurance, premium paid
Annuities (income element)	by employer (for coverage over $50,000)
Awards	Hobby income
Back pay	Interest
Bargain purchase from employer	Jury duty fees
Bonuses	Living quarters, meals (unless furnished for
Breach of contract damages	employer's convenience)
Business income	Mileage allowance (in certain cases)
Clergy fees	Military pay (unless combat pay)
Commissions	Notary fees
Compensation for services	Partnership income
Death benefits	Pension distributions
Debts forgiven	Prizes
Director's fees	Professional fees
Dividends	Punitive damages
Embezzled funds	Rents
Employee awards (in certain	Rewards
cases)	Royalties
Employee benefits (except certain	Salaries
fringe benefits)	Severance pay
Estate and trust income	Strike and lockout benefits
Farm income	Supplemental unemployment benefits
Fees	Tips and gratuities
Gains from illegal activities	Travel allowance (in certain cases)
Gains from sale of property	Treasure trove (found property)
Gambling winnings	Wages

- College tuition and related expenses.
- Contributions to Health Savings Accounts (HSAs).
- Interest on student loans.
- Excess capital losses.
- Alimony payments.

The effect on AGI of deductions *for* AGI is illustrated below.

EXAMPLE 3

Mason, age 45, earned a salary of $78,000 in the current year. He contributed $4,000 to his traditional Individual Retirement Account (IRA), sold stock held as an investment for a short-term capital loss of $2,000, and paid $4,600 in alimony to his ex-wife. His AGI is determined as follows:

Gross income		
Salary		$ 78,000
Less: Deductions *for* AGI		
IRA contribution	$4,000	
Capital loss	2,000	
Alimony paid	4,600	(10,600)
AGI		$ 67,400

The principal deductions *for* AGI are discussed in Chapters 6, 7, 8, 9, 11, 16, and 17.

EXHIBIT 3.3	**Partial List of Itemized Deductions**

Medical expenses in excess of 10% of AGI (through 2016, 7.5% if at least age 65)

State and local income or sales taxes

Real estate taxes

Personal property taxes

Interest on home mortgage (subject to certain limitations)

Investment interest (up to the amount of net investment income)

Charitable contributions (within specified percentage limitations)

Casualty and theft losses in excess of 10% of AGI

Miscellaneous expenses (to the extent the aggregated expenses exceed 2% of AGI)

- Union dues
- Professional dues and subscriptions
- Certain educational expenses
- Tax return preparation fee
- Investment counsel fees
- Unreimbursed employee business expenses (after a percentage reduction for meals and entertainment)

Deductions *from* Adjusted Gross Income

As a general rule, personal expenses are not allowed as deductions in computing taxable income. However, Congress allows some personal expenses as deductions *from* AGI (commonly referred to as **itemized deductions**); see Exhibit 3.3 for a partial list of these deductions.

AGI is an important calculation as it is used to limit certain itemized deductions (e.g., medical expenses, charitable contributions, and casualty losses). For example, medical expenses are deductible only to the extent they exceed 10 percent of AGI, and charitable contribution deductions may not exceed 50 percent of AGI. These limitations can be described as a 10 percent *floor* under the medical expense deduction and a 50 percent *ceiling* on the charitable contribution deduction.

Assume the same facts as in Example 3, and assume that Mason had medical expenses of $8,000. Medical expenses are included in itemized deductions to the extent they exceed 10% of AGI. In computing his itemized deductions, Mason includes medical expenses of $1,260 [$8,000 medical expenses— $6,740 (10% × $67,400 AGI)].

In addition, taxpayers are allowed itemized deductions for expenses related to (1) the production or collection of income and (2) the management of property held for the production of income.[5] These expenses, sometimes referred to as *nonbusiness expenses,* are expenses incurred in connection with an income-producing activity that does *not* qualify as a trade or business.

Leo is the owner and operator of a small package delivery service. All allowable expenses that he incurs in connection with the delivery business are deductions *for* AGI. In addition, Leo has an extensive portfolio of stocks and bonds. Leo's investment activity is not treated as a trade or business. Any allowable expenses that Leo incurs in connection with these investments (e.g., subscriptions to investment publications, financial planning fees, safety deposit box rental) are itemized deductions.

Itemized deductions are discussed in Chapters 9 and 10.

---

[5]§ 212.

Nondeductible Expenses

Many expenses are not deductible and, therefore, provide no tax benefit. Here are some examples:

- Personal living expenses.
- Losses on the sale of personal use property (e.g., the furniture you own).
- Hobby losses.
- Life insurance premiums.
- Gambling losses (in excess of gains).
- Child support payments.
- Fines and penalties.
- Political contributions.
- Funeral expenses.
- Capital expenditures.

Most of these items are discussed in Chapter 6.

Standard Deduction

Instead of claiming itemized deductions, taxpayers can use the standard deduction. As discussed later in the chapter, the standard deduction varies depending on filing status, age, and blindness. The standard deduction is adjusted each year for inflation.

Personal and Dependency Exemptions

Exemptions, another type of deduction, are allowed for the taxpayer, the taxpayer's spouse, and each dependent of the taxpayer. Like the standard deduction, personal and dependency exemptions (discussed later) are adjusted each year for inflation. The exemption amount for 2017 is $4,050 (the same as in 2016).

Taxable Income

The determination of taxable income is illustrated in Example 6.

EXAMPLE
6

Grace, age 25, is single and has her disabled and dependent mother living with her. This qualifies Grace for head-of-household filing status and a standard deduction of $9,300 in 2017. In 2017, Grace earned a $42,000 salary as a high school teacher. Her other income consisted of $1,100 interest on a certificate of deposit (CD) and $500 interest on nontaxable municipal bonds that she had received as a graduation gift in 2011. During 2017, she sold stock that resulted in a $1,000 deductible capital loss. Her itemized deductions are $9,500. Grace's taxable income for the year is computed as follows:

Income (broadly defined)		
Salary	$42,000	
Interest on a CD	1,100	
Interest on municipal bonds	500	
	$43,600	
Less: Exclusion—Interest on municipal bonds	(500)	
Gross income	$43,100	
Less: Deduction *for* adjusted gross income—capital loss	(1,000)	
Adjusted gross income	$42,100	
Less: The greater of total itemized deductions ($9,500) *or* the standard deduction for head of household ($9,350)	(9,500)	
Personal and dependency exemptions (2 × $4,050)	(8,100)	
Taxable Income	$24,500	

EXHIBIT 3.4	Basic Standard Deduction Amounts	

	Standard Deduction Amount	
Filing Status	**2016**	**2017**
Single	$ 6,300	$ 6,350
Married, filing jointly	12,600	12,700
Surviving spouse	12,600	12,700
Head of household	9,300	9,350
Married, filing separately	6,300	6,350

The exclusion of $500 (i.e., interest from municipal bonds) is subtracted in determining gross income, while capital loss of $1,000 is classified as a deduction *for* AGI. Grace chose to itemize her deductions *from* AGI as they exceed the standard deduction (see Exhibit 3.4). We will determine Grace's income tax later in the chapter (in Example 49).

Tax Due (or Refund)

The last step in applying the tax formula is the determination of tax due (or refund). Tax rates (which differ based on filing status) are applied to taxable income to determine the tax liability.[6] Once the tax is computed, this amount is reduced by any taxes withheld and tax credits allowed to arrive at the additional tax due or overpayment (i.e., refund). Filing status and the tax computation are discussed later in this chapter; tax credits are the subject of Chapter 13.

3-1b Tax Formula—Correlation with Form 1040

Now that you understand the definitions used in the tax formula, review the Form 1040 included on the next two pages. The structure of individual income tax returns (Forms 1040, 1040A, or 1040EZ; see Appendix B) parallels the tax formula in Concept Summary 3.1. Like the formula, the tax return places major emphasis on adjusted gross income (AGI), which appears on the bottom of page 1 and at the top of page 2 of Form 1040. In arriving at gross income (referred to as *total income*), *most* exclusions are not reported on the tax return. Deductions *for* AGI are summarized on page 1 of Form 1040.

Deductions *from* AGI (referred to as "itemized deductions") are carried over from Schedule A to page 2 of Form 1040. The choice between the standard deduction and itemized deductions is made on page 2. This is followed by the deduction for personal and dependency exemptions to arrive at taxable income. Page 2 also contains the tax computation and reductions for tax credits and withholdings. The format of Form 1040 and its connections to the various supporting schedules containing tax formula information is illustrated in Exhibit 6.2 of Chapter 6.

---

[6]Tax Rate Schedules can be found in Appendix A. Tax Tables, developed by the IRS, are used if taxable income is less than $100,000 (these also are in Appendix A).

Form **1040**

Department of the Treasury—Internal Revenue Service (99)

U.S. Individual Income Tax Return 2016 OMB No. 1545-0074 IRS Use Only—Do not write or staple in this space.

For the year Jan. 1–Dec. 31, 2016, or other tax year beginning _____ , 2016, ending _____ , 20 ___

See separate instructions.

Your first name and initial	Last name	Your social security number

If a joint return, spouse's first name and initial	Last name	Spouse's social security number

Home address (number and street). If you have a P.O. box, see instructions. | Apt. no.

▲ Make sure the SSN(s) above and on line 6c are correct.

City, town or post office, state, and ZIP code. If you have a foreign address, also complete spaces below (see instructions).

Presidential Election Campaign
Check here if you, or your spouse if filing jointly, want $3 to go to this fund. Checking a box below will not change your tax or refund. ☐ You ☐ Spouse

Foreign country name | Foreign province/state/county | Foreign postal code

Filing Status

Check only one box.

1 ☐ Single
2 ☐ Married filing jointly (even if only one had income)
3 ☐ Married filing separately. Enter spouse's SSN above and full name here. ▶
4 ☐ Head of household (with qualifying person). (See instructions.) If the qualifying person is a child but not your dependent, enter this child's name here. ▶
5 ☐ Qualifying widow(er) with dependent child

Exemptions

6a ☐ **Yourself.** If someone can claim you as a dependent, **do not** check box 6a . . . . .
b ☐ **Spouse** . . . .

c **Dependents:**

(1) First name Last name	(2) Dependent's social security number	(3) Dependent's relationship to you	(4) ✓ if child under age 17 qualifying for child tax credit (see instructions)
			☐
			☐
			☐
			☐

If more than four dependents, see instructions and check here ▶ ☐

d Total number of exemptions claimed

Boxes checked on 6a and 6b _____
No. of children on 6c who:
• lived with you _____
• did not live with you due to divorce or separation (see instructions) _____
Dependents on 6c not entered above _____
Add numbers on lines above ▶ _____

Income

Attach Form(s) W-2 here. Also attach Forms W-2G and 1099-R if tax was withheld.

If you did not get a W-2, see instructions.

7	Wages, salaries, tips, etc. Attach Form(s) W-2	7	
8a	**Taxable** interest. Attach Schedule B if required	8a	
b	**Tax-exempt** interest. **Do not** include on line 8a . . .	8b			
9a	Ordinary dividends. Attach Schedule B if required	9a	
b	Qualified dividends	9b			
10	Taxable refunds, credits, or offsets of state and local income taxes .	10	
11	Alimony received	11	
12	Business income or (loss). Attach Schedule C or C-EZ	12	
13	Capital gain or (loss). Attach Schedule D if required. If not required, check here ▶ ☐	13	
14	Other gains or (losses). Attach Form 4797	14	
15a	IRA distributions .	15a		b Taxable amount . . .	15b	
16a	Pensions and annuities	16a		b Taxable amount . . .	16b	
17	Rental real estate, royalties, partnerships, S corporations, trusts, etc. Attach Schedule E	17	
18	Farm income or (loss). Attach Schedule F	18	
19	Unemployment compensation	19	
20a	Social security benefits	20a		b Taxable amount . . .	20b	
21	Other income. List type and amount _____	21	
22	Combine the amounts in the far right column for lines 7 through 21. This is your **total income** ▶	22	

Adjusted Gross Income

23	Educator expenses	23		
24	Certain business expenses of reservists, performing artists, and fee-basis government officials. Attach Form 2106 or 2106-EZ	24		
25	Health savings account deduction. Attach Form 8889	25		
26	Moving expenses. Attach Form 3903	26		
27	Deductible part of self-employment tax. Attach Schedule SE	27		
28	Self-employed SEP, SIMPLE, and qualified plans . .	28		
29	Self-employed health insurance deduction . . .	29		
30	Penalty on early withdrawal of savings	30		
31a	Alimony paid b Recipient's SSN ▶ _____	31a		
32	IRA deduction	32		
33	Student loan interest deduction	33		
34	Tuition and fees. Attach Form 8917	34		
35	Domestic production activities deduction. Attach Form 8903	35		
36	Add lines 23 through 35	36	
37	Subtract line 36 from line 22. This is your **adjusted gross income** . . . . . ▶	37	

For Disclosure, Privacy Act, and Paperwork Reduction Act Notice, see separate instructions. Cat. No. 11320B Form **1040** (2016)

Form 1040 (2016) Page **2**

Tax and Credits	38	Amount from line 37 (adjusted gross income)	38	

39a Check if: ☐ **You** were born before January 2, 1952, ☐ Blind. | **Total boxes** ☐ **Spouse** was born before January 2, 1952, ☐ Blind. | checked ▶ **39a** [ ]

b If your spouse itemizes on a separate return or you were a dual-status alien, check here▶ **39b** ☐

Standard Deduction for—
- People who check any box on line 39a or 39b **or** who can be claimed as a dependent, see instructions.
- All others:
Single or Married filing separately, $6,300
Married filing jointly or Qualifying widow(er), $12,600
Head of household, $9,300

Line	Description		
40	**Itemized deductions** (from Schedule A) **or** your **standard deduction** (see left margin) . .	40	
41	Subtract line 40 from line 38	41	
42	**Exemptions.** If line 38 is $155,650 or less, multiply $4,050 by the number on line 6d. Otherwise, see instructions	42	
43	**Taxable income.** Subtract line 42 from line 41. If line 42 is more than line 41, enter -0- . . .	43	
44	**Tax** (see instructions). Check if any from: **a** ☐ Form(s) 8814 **b** ☐ Form 4972 **c** ☐ [ ]	44	
45	**Alternative minimum tax** (see instructions). Attach Form 6251	45	
46	Excess advance premium tax credit repayment. Attach Form 8962	46	
47	Add lines 44, 45, and 46 . . . . ▶	47	
48	Foreign tax credit. Attach Form 1116 if required . . .	**48**	
49	Credit for child and dependent care expenses. Attach Form 2441	**49**	
50	Education credits from Form 8863, line 19 . . .	**50**	
51	Retirement savings contributions credit. Attach Form 8880	**51**	
52	Child tax credit. Attach Schedule 8812, if required . . .	**52**	
53	Residential energy credits. Attach Form 5695 . . .	**53**	
54	Other credits from Form: **a** ☐ 3800 **b** ☐ 8801 **c** ☐ [ ]	**54**	
55	Add lines 48 through 54. These are your **total credits**	55	
56	Subtract line 55 from line 47. If line 55 is more than line 47, enter -0- . . . . . ▶	56	

Other Taxes	57	Self-employment tax. Attach Schedule SE	57	

Line	Description		
58	Unreported social security and Medicare tax from Form: **a** ☐ 4137 **b** ☐ 8919	58	
59	Additional tax on IRAs, other qualified retirement plans, etc. Attach Form 5329 if required	59	
60a	Household employment taxes from Schedule H	60a	
b	First-time homebuyer credit repayment. Attach Form 5405 if required	60b	
61	Health care: individual responsibility (see instructions) Full-year coverage ☐ . . .	61	
62	Taxes from: **a** ☐ Form 8959 **b** ☐ Form 8960 **c** ☐ Instructions; enter code(s) [ ]	62	
63	Add lines 56 through 62. This is your **total tax** . . . . ▶	63	

Payments	64	Federal income tax withheld from Forms W-2 and 1099 . .	**64**	

If you have a qualifying child, attach Schedule EIC.

Line	Description		
65	2016 estimated tax payments and amount applied from 2015 return	**65**	
66a	**Earned income credit (EIC)**	**66a**	
b	Nontaxable combat pay election **66b** [ ]		
67	Additional child tax credit. Attach Schedule 8812	**67**	
68	American opportunity credit from Form 8863, line 8 . . .	**68**	
69	Net premium tax credit. Attach Form 8962	**69**	
70	Amount paid with request for extension to file	**70**	
71	Excess social security and tier 1 RRTA tax withheld . . .	**71**	
72	Credit for federal tax on fuels. Attach Form 4136 . . .	**72**	
73	Credits from Form: **a** ☐ 2439 **b** ☐ Reserved **c** ☐ 8885 **d** ☐ [ ]	**73**	
74	Add lines 64, 65, 66a, and 67 through 73. These are your **total payments** . . . ▶	74	

Refund	75	If line 74 is more than line 63, subtract line 63 from line 74. This is the amount you **overpaid**	75	

Direct deposit? See instructions.

Line	Description		
76a	Amount of line 75 you want **refunded to you.** If Form 8888 is attached, check here . . ▶ ☐	76a	
▶ b	Routing number [ ] ▶ **c** Type: ☐ Checking ☐ Savings		
▶ d	Account number [ ]		
77	Amount of line 75 you want **applied to your 2017 estimated tax** ▶ 77		

Amount You Owe	78	**Amount you owe.** Subtract line 74 from line 63. For details on how to pay, see instructions ▶	78	
	79	Estimated tax penalty (see instructions) 79		

Third Party Designee

Do you want to allow another person to discuss this return with the IRS (see instructions)? ☐ **Yes.** Complete below. ☐ **No**

Designee's name ▶ | Phone no. ▶ | Personal identification number (PIN) ▶

Sign Here

Joint return? See instructions. Keep a copy for your records.

Under penalties of perjury, I declare that I have examined this return and accompanying schedules and statements, and to the best of my knowledge and belief, they are true, correct, and accurately list all amounts and sources of income I received during the tax year. Declaration of preparer (other than taxpayer) is based on all information of which preparer has any knowledge.

Your signature | Date | Your occupation | Daytime phone number

Spouse's signature. If a joint return, **both** must sign. | Date | Spouse's occupation | If the IRS sent you an Identity Protection PIN, enter it here (see inst.)

Paid Preparer Use Only

Print/Type preparer's name | Preparer's signature | Date | Check ☐ if self-employed | PTIN

Firm's name ▶ | Firm's EIN ▶

Firm's address ▶ | Phone no.

3-2 STANDARD DEDUCTION

LO.2

Explain the standard deduction and evaluate its choice in arriving at taxable income.

The effect of the standard deduction is to exempt part of a taxpayer's income from Federal income tax liability. Congress has indicated that the standard deduction, when coupled with exemptions, should be roughly equal to the poverty level.[7]

3-2a Basic and Additional Standard Deduction

The standard deduction is the sum of two components: the *basic* standard deduction and the *additional* standard deduction.[8] Exhibit 3.4 lists the basic standard deduction allowed for taxpayers in each filing status. Certain taxpayers, however, are not allowed to claim *any* standard deduction, and the standard deduction is *limited* for others.

A taxpayer who is age 65 or over *or* blind in 2017 qualifies for an *additional standard deduction* of $1,250 or $1,550, depending on filing status (see amounts in Exhibit 3.5). Two additional standard deductions are allowed for a taxpayer who is age 65 or over *and* blind. The additional standard deduction provisions also apply for a qualifying spouse who is age 65 or over or blind, but not for a dependent.

To determine whether to itemize, the taxpayer compares the *total* standard deduction (the sum of the basic standard deduction and any additional standard deductions) with total itemized deductions. Taxpayers are allowed to deduct the *greater* of itemized deductions or the standard deduction. The choice is elective each year. For example, a taxpayer who buys a home is likely to change from using the standard deduction to itemizing deductions (because of mortgage interest and property tax deductions). The taxpayer's age can also make a difference. About two-thirds of individual tax returns filed use the standard deduction (rather than itemized deductions).

Using Itemized Deductions or Standard Deduction

Juan and Lisa Fernandez have been renting an apartment while saving money for a down payment on a house. Early in 2017, they purchased a house. Interest paid on their home mortgage in 2017 amounted $8,400, and they paid property taxes of $5,500. In addition, they had charitable contributions of $3,000.

In total, their itemized deductions amount to $16,900, and they will compute their taxable income using this amount, rather than the $12,700 standard deduction.

EXAMPLE 7

Prior to 2017, Sara, who is single, had always chosen to itemize. In 2017, however, she reaches age 65. Her itemized deductions for 2017 are $6,500, but her total standard deduction is $7,900 [$6,350 (basic standard deduction) + $1,550 (additional standard deduction)].

Sara should compute her taxable income for 2017 using the standard deduction ($7,900), because it exceeds her itemized deductions ($6,500).

EXAMPLE 8

EXHIBIT 3.5	Amount of Each Additional Standard Deduction	
Filing Status	**2016**	**2017**
Single	$1,550	$1,550
Married, filing jointly	1,250	1,250
Surviving spouse	1,250	1,250
Head of household	1,550	1,550
Married, filing separately	1,250	1,250

[7]S.Rep. No. 92–437, 92nd Cong., 1st Sess., 1971, p. 54. Another purpose of the standard deduction, discussed in Chapter 1, is to reduce the number of taxpayers who itemize their deductions. Reducing the number of taxpayers who itemize also reduces the audit effort required from the IRS.

[8]§ 63(c)(1).

3-2b Individuals Not Eligible for the Standard Deduction

Some individuals are not allowed to use the standard deduction. The following individual taxpayers must itemize:[9]

- A married individual filing a separate return where either spouse itemizes deductions.
- A nonresident alien (an individual who is neither a U.S. citizen nor a U.S. resident).

If an individual dies during a year, a full standard deduction is available for the final tax return; the deduction is not reduced because the return only covers a portion of the calendar year.

Sandy (age 80 and single) died on January 14, 2017. Her itemized deductions for 2017 amounted to $2,400. On her final income tax return, covering the period from January 1 to January 14, 2017, a standard deduction of $7,900 can be claimed (the $6,350 basic standard deduction plus the $1,550 age-related standard deduction).

3-2c Special Limitations on the Standard Deduction for Dependents

Special rules apply to the standard deduction and personal exemption of an individual who can be claimed as a dependent on another person's tax return.

When filing his or her own tax return, a *dependent's* basic standard deduction in 2017 is limited to the greater of $1,050 or the sum of the individual's earned income for the year plus $350.[10] However, if the sum of the individual's earned income plus $350 exceeds the basic standard deduction, the basic standard deduction is used (see Exhibit 3.4). A dependent who is 65 or over or blind or both is also allowed the additional standard deduction amount on his or her own return (refer to Exhibit 3.5). These provisions are illustrated in Examples 10 through 13.

Dependent Standard Deduction

Susan, who is 17 years old and single, is claimed as a dependent on her parents' tax return. During 2017, she received $1,200 interest (unearned income) on a savings account. She also earned $400 from a part-time job. When Susan files her own tax return, her standard deduction is $1,050 [the greater of $1,050 or $750 (the sum of earned income of $400 plus $350)].

Assume the same facts as in Example 10, except that Susan is 67 years old and is claimed as a dependent on her son's tax return. In this case, when Susan files her own tax return, her standard deduction is $2,600 [$1,050 (see Example 10) + $1,550 (the additional standard deduction allowed because Susan is 65 or over)].

Peggy, who is 16 years old and single, earned $800 from a summer job and had no unearned income during 2017. She is claimed as a dependent on her parents' tax return. Her standard deduction is $1,150 [the greater of $1,050 or $1,150 (the sum of $800 earned income plus $350)].

Jack, a 20-year-old, single, full-time college student, is claimed as a dependent on his parents' tax return. He worked as a musician during the summer of 2017, earning $6,500. Jack's standard deduction is $6,350 [the greater of $1,050 or $6,350 (the sum of $6,500 earned income plus $350, but limited to the $6,350 basic standard deduction for a single taxpayer)].

---

[9]§ 63(c)(6); also ineligible is an individual filing a return for a period of less than 12 months because of a change in the annual accounting period.

[10]§ 63(c)(5). Both the $1,050 amount and the $350 amount are subject to adjustment for inflation each year. In 2016 and 2015, the amounts were also $1,050 and $350.

3-3 PERSONAL EXEMPTIONS

Apply the rules for arriving at personal exemptions.

The use of exemptions in the tax system is based in part on the idea that a taxpayer with a small amount of income should be exempt from income taxation. The exemption amount ($4,050 in 2017 and 2016) is adjusted annually for inflation.

Exemptions that are allowed for the taxpayer and spouse are designated as **personal exemptions**. When a married couple files a joint return, they may claim two personal exemptions. If the married couple files separate returns, each claims one exemption.[11] Exemptions allowed for the care of other persons are called dependency exemptions and are discussed in text Section 3-4.

An individual cannot claim a personal exemption if he or she is claimed as a dependent by another.

> **EXAMPLE 14**
>
> Mark and Lisa Sanford are married and file a joint tax return in 2017. They have one dependent, Jack, their son (see Example 13). They have gross income of $118,000 and itemized deductions of $22,000. Their taxable income is $83,850, determined as follows:
>
> | | |
> |---|---:|
> | Gross income | $118,000 |
> | Less: Deductions *for* AGI | (–0–) |
> | Adjusted gross income | $118,000 |
> | Less: Greater of itemized deductions ($22,000) or standard deduction ($12,700) | (22,000) |
> | Less: Personal and dependency exemptions (3 × $4,050) | (12,150) |
> | Taxable income | $ 83,850 |
>
> On his own income tax return,[12] Jack's taxable income is $200, determined as follows:
>
> | | |
> |---|---:|
> | Gross income | $ 6,500 |
> | Less: Standard deduction | (6,300) |
> | Personal exemption | (–0–) |
> | Taxable income | $ 200 |
>
> Jack is not allowed a personal exemption because he is claimed as a dependent by his parents.

The determination of marital status generally is made at the end of the taxable year, except when a spouse dies during the year. Spouses who are divorced or legally separated before the end of the year are considered to be unmarried at the end of the taxable year.

The amount of the exemption is not reduced due to the taxpayer's death. The same rule applies to dependency exemptions. If an individual is qualified as a dependent at the time of death, the full exemption amount can be claimed.

3-4 DEPENDENCY EXEMPTIONS

Explain the rules for determining dependency exemptions.

A taxpayer may claim a **dependency exemption** ($4,050 in 2017 and 2016) for either a qualifying child or a qualifying relative. However, certain rules (e.g., the joint return test) may eliminate the exemption.

3-4a Qualifying Child

Congress has adopted a uniform definition of a qualifying child. The definition applies to the following tax provisions:

- Dependency exemption.
- Head-of-household filing status.

---

[11]§ 151(b). If a married individual files a separate return, a personal exemption may be claimed for his or her spouse only if the spouse has no gross income and is not claimed as a dependent of another taxpayer.

[12]As noted on p. 3-27 (Filing Requirements for Dependents), Jack will be required to file an income tax return.

- Earned income tax credit.
- Child tax credit.
- Credit for child and dependent care expenses.

A **qualifying child** must meet the relationship, residence, age, and support tests.[13] For dependency exemption purposes, a qualifying child must *also* satisfy the joint return test and the citizenship or residency test.

Relationship Test

The relationship test includes a taxpayer's child (son or daughter), adopted child, stepchild, eligible foster child, brother, sister, half brother, half sister, stepbrother, stepsister, or a *descendant* of any of these parties (e.g., grandchild, nephew, niece). *Ancestors* of any of these parties (e.g., uncles and aunts) and in-laws (e.g., son-in-law and brother-in-law) *are not included*.

An adopted child includes a child placed with the taxpayer even though the adoption is not final. An eligible foster child is a child who is placed with the taxpayer by an authorized placement agency or by a court order.

Maureen's household includes her mother, grandson, stepbrother, stepbrother's daughter, uncle, and sister. All meet the relationship test for a qualifying child *except* the mother and uncle.

Residence Test

A qualifying child must live with the taxpayer for more than half of the year. Temporary absences (e.g., school, vacation, medical care, military service, detention in a juvenile facility) are ignored. Special rules apply in the case of certain kidnapped children.[14]

Age Test

A qualifying child must, by the end of the tax year, be (1) under age 19 or (2) under age 24 *and* a full-time student. A full-time student is a child who was in school during any part of five months of the year.[15] The age test does not apply to a child who is disabled during any part of the year.[16] Also, a qualifying child must be younger than the taxpayer claiming him or her (e.g., a brother cannot claim his older sister as a qualifying child).

The Big Picture

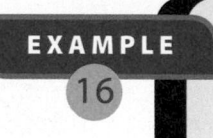

Return to the facts of *The Big Picture* on p. 3-1. Does Paige meet the requirements of a qualifying child as to Polly? Paige satisfies the relationship and residence tests, but the answer to the age test remains unclear. Because she is not a full-time student or disabled, she must be under 19 to meet the age test.

Support Test

To be a qualifying child, the individual must not be self-supporting (i.e., provide more than half of his or her own support). Support includes food, shelter, clothing, toys, medical and dental care, education, and similar items.[17] In the case of a child who is a full-time student, scholarships are not considered to be support.[18]

---

[13]A married taxpayer filing a separate return can claim two personal exemptions if his or her spouse has no income and is not claimed as the dependent of another taxpayer; § 152(c).

[14]§ 152(f)(6).

[15]§ 152(f)(2).

[16]Within the meaning of § 22(e)(3). See the discussion of the credit for the elderly or disabled in Chapter 13.

[17]A worksheet for determining support is provided in IRS Publication 501 *(Exemptions, Standard Deduction, and Filing Information)*.

[18]§ 152(f)(5).

Shawn, age 23, is a full-time student and lives with his parents and an older cousin. During 2017, Shawn receives his support from the following sources: 30% from a part-time job, 30% from a scholarship, 20% from his parents, and 20% from the cousin.

Shawn is not self-supporting and can be claimed by his parents as a dependent even though his parents contribute only 20% of his support. (Note: Shawn cannot be a qualifying child as to his cousin due to the relationship test.)

Tiebreaker Rules

In some situations, a child may be a qualifying child to more than one person. In this event, the tax law specifies which person has priority in claiming the dependency exemption.[19] Called "tiebreaker rules," these rules are summarized in Concept Summary 3.2 and are illustrated in the examples that follow.

Concept Summary 3.2

Tiebreaker Rules for Claiming Qualified Child

Persons Eligible to Claim Exemption	Person Prevailing
One of the persons is the parent.	Parent
Both persons are the parents, and the child lives longer with one parent.	Parent with the longer period of residence
Both persons are the parents, and the child lives with each the same period of time.	Parent with the higher adjusted gross income (AGI)
None of the persons is the parent.	Person with highest AGI

Qualified Child—Tiebreaker Rules

Tim, age 15, lives in the same household with his mother and grandmother. As the parent, the mother has priority as to the dependency exemption.

Jennifer, age 17, lives in the same household with her parents during the entire year. If her parents file separate returns, the one with the higher AGI has priority as to the dependency exemption.

Assume the same facts as in Example 19, except that the father moves into an apartment in November (Jennifer remains with her mother). The mother has priority as to the dependency exemption (see Concept Summary 3.2).

3-4b Qualifying Relative

In addition to a qualifying child, a **qualifying relative** can be a dependent. A qualifying relative must meet the relationship, gross income, and support tests.[20]

Relationship Test

The relationship test for a qualifying relative is more expansive than for a qualifying child. Also included are the following relatives:

- Lineal ascendants (e.g., parents and grandparents).

---

[19]§ 152(c)(4).   [20]§ 152(d).

- Collateral ascendants (e.g., uncles and aunts).
- Certain in-laws (e.g., son-, daughter-, father-, mother-, brother-, and sister-in-law).[21]

Children who do not satisfy the qualifying child definition may meet the qualifying relative criteria.

The relationship test also includes individuals who are "members of the household" (i.e., live with the taxpayer for the *entire year*). These individuals can be related or unrelated. For example, cousins are not "qualifying relatives" (cousins are not included in the list above). But a cousin can meet the relationship test if he or she is a "member of the household." Member-of-the-household status is not available for anyone who was a spouse during any part of the year.[22] However, an ex-spouse can qualify as a member of the household in a year following that of the divorce.

As the relationship test indicates, the category designation of "qualifying relative" is somewhat misleading, as persons *other than relatives* can qualify as dependents. And not all relatives will qualify (although relatives that are not listed could be a "member of the household").

The Big Picture

EXAMPLE 21

Return to the facts of *The Big Picture* on p. 3-1. Although Maude is unrelated to Polly, she qualifies as Polly's dependent by being a member of the household. Because Maude is a dependent, Polly can also claim the medical expenses she paid on Maude's behalf. The funeral expenses are not deductible. Although Maude lived for only two months, the full amount of the dependency exemption is allowed and does not have to be prorated.

Gross Income Test

A dependent's gross income must be *less* than the exemption amount—$4,050 in 2017 and 2016. Gross income is determined by any income that is taxable. In the case of scholarships, for example, include the taxable portion (e.g., amounts received for room and board) and exclude the nontaxable portion (e.g., amounts received for books and tuition).

Gross Income Test

EXAMPLE 22

Elsie provides more than half of the support of her son, Tom, who does not live with her. Tom, age 26, is a full-time student in medical school, earns $3,000 from a part-time job, and receives a $12,000 scholarship covering his tuition.

Elsie may claim Tom as a dependent because he meets the gross income test and is a qualifying relative. (Note: Tom is *not* a qualifying child; he fails both the residence and the age tests.)

EXAMPLE 23

Aaron provides more than half of the support of his widowed aunt, Myrtle, who does not live with him. Myrtle's income for the year is as follows: dividend income of $1,100, earnings from pet sitting of $1,200, nontaxable Social Security benefits of $6,000, and nontaxable interest from City of Milwaukee bonds of $8,000.

Because Myrtle's gross income is only $2,300 ($1,100 + $1,200), she meets the gross income test and can be claimed as Aaron's dependent.

---

[21]Once established by marriage, in-law status continues to exist and survives divorce.

[22]§§ 152(d)(2)(H) and (f)(3); also excluded is anyone whose relationship to the taxpayer violates local law.

Return to the facts of *The Big Picture* on p. 3-1. Assuming that Paige is not a qualifying child (see Example 16), can she be a qualifying relative for dependency exemption purposes? She meets the relationship and support tests, but what about the gross income test?

    If her income from her part-time job is less than $4,050 (the 2017 exemption amount), she does qualify and can be claimed by Polly as a dependent.

Support Test

The taxpayer must furnish over half of the qualifying relative's support. As with a qualifying child, support includes food, shelter, clothing, toys, medical and dental care, education, and similar items. However, a scholarship (both taxable and nontaxable portions) received by a student is not included for purposes of computing whether the taxpayer furnished more than half of the child's support.

Hal contributed $3,400 (consisting of food, clothing, and medical care) toward the support of his nephew, Sam, who lives with him. Sam earned $1,300 from a part-time job and received $2,000 from a student loan to attend a local university. Assuming that the other dependency tests are met, Hal can claim Sam as a dependent because Hal has contributed more than half of Sam's support.

    If the individual does not spend funds that have been received from any source, the unexpended amounts are *not* counted for purposes of the support test.

Emily contributed $3,000 to her father's support during the year. In addition, her father received $2,400 in Social Security benefits, $200 of interest, and wages of $600. Her father deposited the Social Security benefits, interest, and wages in his own savings account and did not use any of the funds for his support. Thus, the Social Security benefits, interest, and wages are not considered as support provided by Emily's father. Emily may claim her father as a dependent if the other tests are met.

    An individual's own funds, however, must be taken into account if applied toward support. The source of the funds is not relevant.

Frank contributes $8,000 toward his parents' total support of $20,000. The parents, who do not live with Frank, obtain the other $12,000 from savings and a home equity loan on their residence. Although the parents have no income, their use of savings and borrowed funds are counted as part of their support. Because Frank does not satisfy the support test, he cannot claim his parents as dependents.

    Capital expenditures for items like furniture, appliances, and automobiles are included in total support if the item does, in fact, constitute support.

Norm purchased a television set costing $950 and gave it to his mother who lives with him. The television set was placed in the mother's bedroom and was used exclusively by her. Norm should include the cost of the television set in determining the support of his mother.

Multiple Support Agreements An exception to the support test involves a multiple support agreement. A multiple support agreement allows a group of taxpayers—none of whom provide more than 50 percent of the support of a taxpayer—to designate one member of the group to claim the dependency exemption.[23] Collectively, the group must provide more than 50 percent of the support. Any person who contributed *more*

---

[23]§ 152(d)(3).

than 10 percent of the support is entitled to claim the exemption. This provision is often used by the children of aged dependent parents when none of the children meet the support test.

The person designated to claim the dependency exemption under a multiple support agreement must meet all other requirements for claiming the exemption. For example, a person who does not meet the relationship or member-of-the-household requirement cannot claim the dependency exemption under a multiple support agreement. It does not matter if he or she contributes more than 10 percent of the individual's support.

Wanda, who resides with her son, Adam, received $12,000 from various sources during the year. This constituted her entire support for the year. She received support from the following:

	Amount	Percentage of Total
Adam, a son	$ 5,760	48%
Bob, a son	1,200	10
Carol, a daughter	3,600	30
Diane, a friend	1,440	12
	$12,000	100%

If Adam and Carol file a multiple support agreement, either may claim the dependency exemption for Wanda. Bob may not claim Wanda because he did not contribute *more than 10%* of her support. Bob's consent is not required for Adam and Carol to file a multiple support agreement. Diane does not meet the relationship or member-of-the-household test and cannot be a party to the agreement. The decision as to who claims Wanda rests with Adam and Carol. It is possible for Carol to claim Wanda, even though Adam furnished more of Wanda's support.

The individual claiming the exemption must complete Form 2120 (Multiple Support Declaration) and file it with his or her tax return. In addition, every other person who qualifies under the more-than-10% rule must provide a signed statement agreeing not to claim the dependency exemption.

ETHICS & EQUITY   Discovering Lost Dependency Exemptions

For the six years prior to his death in late 2017, Jesse lived with his daughter, Hannah. Because he had no source of income, Jesse was supported by equal contributions from Hannah and his two sons, Bill and Bob. At Jesse's funeral, his surviving children are amazed to discover that none of them has been claiming Jesse as a dependent. Upon the advice of the director of the funeral home, they decide to divide among themselves the dependency exemptions for the past six years. Multiple Forms 2120 are executed, and each of the three children files amended returns for different past years. As Jesse died before the end of the current year, no deduction is planned for 2017.

Comment on the tax expectations of the parties involved.

Children of Divorced or Separated Parents Another exception to the support test applies when parents with children are divorced or separated. Unmarried parents living apart for the last six months of the year are also covered by these rules. This exception applies if the parents meet the following conditions:

- They would have been entitled to the dependency exemption(s) had they been married and filed a joint return.
- They have custody (either jointly or singly) of the child (or children) for more than half of the year.

In general, the parent having custody of the child (children) for the greater part of the year (i.e., the custodial parent) is entitled to the dependency exemption(s).[24] However, the custodial parent can sign a waiver that provides the exemption to the noncustodial parent.[25]

The waiver, Form 8332 (Release/Revocation of Release of Claim to Exemption for Child by Custodial Parent), can apply to a single year, a number of specified years, or all future years. The noncustodial parent must attach a Form 8332 to his or her return.

3-4c Other Rules for Dependency Exemptions

In addition to fitting into either the qualifying child or the qualifying relative category, a dependent must meet the joint return and the citizenship tests.

Joint Return Test

If a dependent is married, the supporting taxpayer (e.g., the parent of a married child) generally is not permitted a dependency exemption if the married individual files a joint return with his or her spouse.[26] The joint return rule does not apply, however, if the following conditions are met:

- The reason for filing is to claim a refund for tax withheld.
- No tax liability would exist for either spouse on separate returns.
- Neither spouse is required to file a return (tested using the married, filing separately rules).

See Exhibit 3.6 later in the chapter and the related discussion concerning income level requirements for filing a return.

Paul provides over half of the support of his son, Quinn. He also provides over half of the support of Vera, who is Quinn's wife. During the year, both Quinn and Vera had part-time jobs. To recover the taxes withheld, they file a joint return. If Quinn and Vera are not required to file a return, Paul is allowed to claim both as dependents.

EXAMPLE 30

Citizenship Test

To be a dependent, the individual must be a U.S. citizen, a U.S. resident, or a resident of Canada or Mexico for some part of the calendar year in which the taxpayer's tax year begins.[27]

Under an exception, an adopted child need not be a citizen or resident of the United States (or a contiguous country) as long as his or her principal residence is with a U.S. citizen.

Esther is a U.S. citizen who lives and works in Spain. She has adopted Benito, a 4-year-old Italian national, who lives with her and is a member of her household.

Although Benito does not meet the citizenship test, he is covered by the exception. Benito is a qualifying child, and Esther can claim him as a dependent.

EXAMPLE 31

3-4d Comparison of Categories for Dependency Exemptions

Concept Summary 3.3 identifies the tests for the two categories of dependency exemptions. In contrasting the two categories, here are some observations:

- As to the relationship tests, the qualifying relative category is considerably more expansive. In addition to including those identified under the qualifying child

---

[24]Reg. § 1.152–4; the general rule does not apply if a multiple support agreement is in effect.

[25]§§ 152(e)(2) and (5).

[26]§ 152(b)(2).

[27]§ 152(b)(3).

grouping, other relatives are added. Nonrelated persons who are members of the household are also included.

- The support tests are entirely different. In the case of a qualifying child, the key is that the child is *not* self-supporting.
- The qualifying child category has no gross income limitation; the qualifying relative category has no age restriction.

Concept Summary 3.3

Tests for Dependency Exemption

Test	Qualifying Child	Qualifying Relative
Relationship:		
• Children (natural, step, or adopted) and their *descendants*, and siblings and stepsiblings and their *descendants*.	X	
• Children (natural, step, or adopted) and their *descendants*, siblings and their children, parents and their *ascendants*, uncles and aunts, stepparents and stepsiblings, and certain in-laws.		X
• Member of the household (live with taxpayer for *entire* year; relative or non-relative)		X
Residence	X	
Age	X	
Support:		
• Not self-supporting ("child" furnishes half or less of his or her support)	X	
• Taxpayer furnishes over half of the support of potential dependent		X
Gross income *less* than the exemption amount		X
Joint return (potential dependent cannot file joint return)	X	X
Citizenship (potential dependent must meet test)	X	X

3-4e Phaseout of Exemptions

Several provisions of the tax law are intended to increase the tax liability of more affluent taxpayers who might otherwise enjoy some benefit of certain deductions and credits. One of these provision phases out personal and dependency exemptions.[28] The exemption phaseout occurs once AGI exceeds specified threshold amounts (indexed annually for inflation):

Filing Status	2016	2017
Married, filing jointly	$311,300	$313,800
Head of household	285,350	287,650
Single	259,400	261,500
Married, filing separately	155,650	156,900

---

[28]§ 151(d)(3); another provision phases out itemized deductions and is discussed in Chapter 10.

Exemptions (both personal and dependency) are phased out by 2 percent for each $2,500 (or portion) by which the taxpayer's AGI exceeds the threshold amounts. For a married taxpayer filing separately, the phaseout is 2 percent for each $1,250 (or portion). The allowable exemption amount can be determined with the following steps:

1. AGI − threshold amount = excess amount.
2. Excess amount ÷ $2,500 = reduction factor [rounded up to the next whole number (e.g., 18.1 = 19)] × 2 = phaseout percentage.
3. Phaseout percentage × exemption amount = phaseout amount.
4. Exemption amount − phaseout amount = allowable exemption deduction.

Brad files as a single individual in 2017. His AGI is $294,150. He is entitled to one personal exemption. Brad's allowable exemption amount is determined as follows:

1. $294,150 − $261,500 = $32,650 excess amount.
2. [($32,650 ÷ $2,500) = 13.06; rounded to 14]; 14 × 2 = 28% (phaseout percentage).
3. 28% × $4,050 = $1,134 phaseout amount.
4. $4,050 − $1,134 = $2,916 allowable exemption deduction.

Any exemptions are completely phased out when the taxpayer's AGI exceeds the threshold amount by *more than* $122,500 ($61,250 for a married taxpayer filing a separate return). With an excess amount of $122,501, the phaseout percentage is 100 percent, calculated as follows:

$$\$122,501 \div \$2,500 = 49.0004, \text{ rounded to } 50 \text{ and multiplied by } 2 = 100\%$$

Bill and Carol file a joint return in 2017 claiming two personal exemptions and two dependency exemptions for their children. Their AGI equals $445,950.

$$\$445,950 − \$313,800 = \$132,150 \text{ excess amount}$$

Since the excess amount exceeds $122,500, their exemptions are completely phased out. The loss of the full deduction for personal and dependency exemptions effectively increases Bill and Carol's tax liability by increasing their tax base—taxable income—rather than their tax rate. This is why phaseouts are sometimes referred to as "stealth taxes."

ETHICS & EQUITY Whose Qualifying Child Is He?

The Rands are successful professionals and have combined AGI of approximately $400,000. Their household includes two children: Henry (age 16) and Belinda (age 22). Belinda is not a student and has a job where she earns $15,000 a year. After a short family meeting in early April 2017, the parties decide that Belinda should claim Henry as her qualifying child. As a result, Belinda is able to deduct a full dependency exemption and claim a child tax credit and an earned income tax credit for a tax savings of more than $3,000. Had the Rands claimed Henry on their joint return, no child tax credit or earned income credit would have been available (these credits are phased out for higher-income taxpayers). And only a partial dependency exemption would have been allowed. Has the Rand family acted properly?

3-4f **Child Tax Credit**

In addition to providing a dependency exemption, a taxpayer's child may also provide a **child tax credit**. A $1,000 credit is allowed for each dependent child (including stepchildren and eligible foster children) under the age of 17.[29] For a more complete discussion of the child tax credit, see Chapter 13.

---

[29]§ 24(a).

LO.5

Choose the proper filing status and identify the related filing requirements.

3-5 FILING STATUS AND FILING REQUIREMENTS

Individuals must know their *filing status* to correctly compute both taxable income and the related income tax liability. In addition, individuals need to understand the tax return filing process. Text Sections 3-5 through 3-7 cover these important tax compliance points:

- Determination of filing status and whether a tax return must be filed (text Section 3-5).
- Computation of tax liability and adjustment for available tax credits (text Section 3-6; also see Concept Summary 3.1 and the tax formula).
- Selection of the appropriate tax form and how to file it with the IRS (text Section 3-7).

3-5a Filing Status

Every year, taxpayers must determine their **filing status**. The taxpayer's filing status is important as it is used to determine:

- The taxpayer's standard deduction (see Exhibits 3.4 and 3.5);
- Whether the taxpayer must file a tax return;
- The taxpayer's tax liability;
- Reductions of exemptions, itemized deductions, and certain tax credits; and
- Eligibility for certain provisions (e.g., some credits are not available when the married, filing separately status is used).

There are five filing statuses, and all taxpayers will file a return based on the filing status selected.

- Single
- Married, filing jointly
- Married, filing separately
- Surviving spouse (qualifying widow or widower)
- Head of household

The amount of tax varies considerably depending on which filing status is used. Consider the following example.

EXAMPLE
34

The following amounts of tax are computed using the 2017 Tax Rate Schedules for a taxpayer (or taxpayers in the case of a joint return) with $60,000 of taxable income (see Appendix A).

Filing Status	Amount of Tax
Single	$10,739
Married, filing jointly	8,068
Married, filing separately	10,739
Head of household	9,253

Single Taxpayers

A taxpayer who is unmarried (including a taxpayer who is legally separated or divorced) and does not qualify for head-of-household status (discussed below) will file as a single taxpayer.

EXAMPLE
35

Phil Jones was divorced in March and is unmarried at the end of the year. Phil has no dependents. As a result, Phil's filing status is single.

GLOBAL TAX ISSUES **Filing a Joint Return**

John Garth is a U.S. citizen and resident, but he spends much of his time in London, where his employer sends him on frequent assignments. John is married to Victoria, a citizen and resident of the United Kingdom.

Can John and Victoria file a joint return for U.S. Federal income tax purposes? Although § 6013(a)(1) specifically precludes the filing of a joint return if one spouse is a nonresident alien, another Code provision permits an exception. Under § 6013(g), the parties can elect to treat the nonqualifying spouse as a "resident" of the United States. This election would allow John and Victoria to file jointly.

But should John and Victoria make this election? If Victoria has considerable income of her own (from non-U.S. sources), the election could be ill-advised. As a nonresident alien, Victoria's non-U.S. source income *would not* be subject to the U.S. income tax. If she is treated as a U.S. resident, however, her non-U.S. source income *will be subject to U.S. tax*. Under the U.S. global approach to taxation, all income (regardless of where earned) of anyone who is a *resident* or *citizen* of the United States is subject to tax.

Married Individuals

Married couples can file tax returns together (married, filing jointly) or apart (married, filing separately). In general, marital status is determined on the last day of the year. As mentioned above, when one spouse dies during the year, the surviving spouse is considered to be married to the spouse that died at the end of the year. Most married couples will find it beneficial to file a joint return.

Married, Filing Jointly The joint filing status was originally enacted in 1948 to establish equity between married taxpayers in common law states and those in community property states. Before the joint filing status was established, taxpayers in community property states were in an advantageous position relative to taxpayers in common law states because they could split their income. For instance, in a community property state, if one spouse earned $100,000 and the other spouse was not employed, each spouse could report $50,000 of income. Splitting the income in this manner caused the total income to be subject to lower marginal tax rates; each spouse would start at the bottom of the rate structure.

Taxpayers in common law states did not have this income-splitting option, so their taxable income was subject to higher marginal rates. This inconsistency in treatment was remedied by the joint filing status. The joint return Tax Rate Schedule is constructed based on the assumption that income is earned equally by the two spouses.

A legally married same-sex couple is treated as married for Federal tax purposes no matter where they live. Registered domestic partners, however, are not "spouses" under Federal law. Therefore, they cannot file Federal tax returns using married filing jointly or married filing separately status. The same rule applies to same-sex partners in civil unions.[30]

Marital status is determined as of the last day of the tax year, except when a spouse dies during the year. In that case, marital status is determined as of the date of death.

EXAMPLE 36

Return to the facts of Example 35. Would things be different if, rather than getting a divorce, Phil's wife passed away during the year? Yes. In this case, Phil would still be "married" for tax purposes at the end of the year (and would file as a surviving spouse; discussed next).

What if Phil remarried during the year? In this case, Phil and his new spouse are a married couple (and they would file joint or separate returns). Phil's deceased spouse's filing status is married, filing separately.

---

[30]Rev.Rul. 2013–17, 2013–38 I.R.B. 201 and *U.S. v. Windsor*, 111 AFTR 2d 2013–2385, 133 S.Ct. 2675; **www.irs.gov/uac/Answers-to-Frequently-Asked-Questions-for-Registered-Domestic-Partners-and -Individuals-in-Civil-Unions**.

Filing a joint return carries the potential disadvantage of joint and several liability.[31] This means that the IRS can pursue the collection of the tax due for that year against either spouse.

Once a joint return has been filed and the due date has passed, the spouses cannot switch to separate returns for that year. However, if married persons file separately, they can change later to a joint return.

Married, Filing Separately If married individuals file separate returns, each reports only his or her own income, exemptions, deductions, and credits, and each must use the married, filing separately tax rates. In a community property state, each individual must report his or her half of the community property income.[32] Most married couples file a joint return, because the combined amount of tax is lower. However, special circumstances (e.g., significant medical expenses incurred by one spouse subject to the 10%-of-AGI limitation) may lead a married couple to file separate returns.

The Internal Revenue Code places some limitations on married persons who file separate returns. Here are some examples:

- If either spouse itemizes deductions, the other spouse must also itemize.
- The earned income credit and the credit for child and dependent care expenses cannot be claimed (see Chapter 13).
- No deduction is allowed for interest paid on qualified education loans (see Chapter 10).
- Only $1,500 of excess capital losses can be claimed by each spouse (see Chapter 16).

Surviving Spouse Joint filing status also applies for two years following the death of one spouse if the surviving spouse maintains a household for a dependent child. The child must be a son, stepson, daughter, or stepdaughter who qualifies as a dependent of the taxpayer. This is referred to as surviving spouse status.[33]

EXAMPLE 37

Fred dies in 2017, leaving Ethel with a dependent child. For the year of Fred's death (2017), Ethel files a joint return with Fred. For the next two years (2018 and 2019), Ethel, as a surviving spouse, may use the joint return rates. Beginning in 2020, Ethel may use the head-of-household rates, if she continues to maintain a household for her dependent child.

Marriage Penalty When Congress enacted the rate structure available to those filing joint returns, it generally favored married taxpayers. In certain situations, however, the parties would incur less tax if they were not married and filed as single taxpayers. The additional tax that a joint return caused, commonly called the marriage penalty, usually occurs when *both* spouses have substantial income. Long aware of the inequity of the marriage penalty, Congress reduced (but did not eliminate) the effect of the problem for some couples by increasing the standard deduction available to married filers to 200 percent of that applicable to single persons and increasing the 15 percent bracket for joint filers to 200 percent of the size of that bracket applicable to single filers. However, the marriage penalty still exists for couples who itemize their deductions and have substantial amounts of income beyond the 15 percent tax bracket.

Head of Household

Unmarried individuals who maintain a household for a dependent (or dependents) can use the head-of-household filing status.[34] The tax liability using the head-of-household rates falls between the tax liabilities for married taxpayers filing jointly and single taxpayers.

---

[31]§ 6013(d)(3).

[32]Form 8958 (Allocation of Tax Amounts Between Certain Individuals in Community Property States) is used for this purpose.

[33]§ 2(a). The IRS term for surviving spouse status is "qualifying widow(er) with dependent child."

[34]§ 2(b).

To qualify for the head-of-household filing status, a taxpayer must pay more than half the cost of maintaining a household as his or her home. The household must also be the principal home of a dependent. Except for temporary absences (e.g., school, hospitalization), the dependent must live in the taxpayer's household for over half the year.

A dependent must be either a qualifying child or a qualifying relative who meets the relationship test (other than someone who qualifies under the member-of-the-household test).

The Big Picture

EXAMPLE 38

Return to the facts of *The Big Picture* on p. 3-1. Assuming that Polly can be treated as single (i.e., not married), can Maude qualify Polly for head-of-household filing status? The answer is no. Even though Maude can be claimed as Polly's dependent (see Example 21), she does not meet the relationship test for head-of-household status (Maude qualified as a dependent under the member-of-the-household test).

EXAMPLE 39

Emma, a widow, maintains a household in which she and her aunt live. If the aunt qualifies as a dependent, Emma may file as head of household. Note that an aunt meets the relationship test.

A special rule allows taxpayers to avoid having to live with their parents. Head-of-household status still may be claimed if the taxpayer maintains a *separate home* for his or her *parent or parents* if at least one parent qualifies as a dependent of the taxpayer.[35]

EXAMPLE 40

Rick, an unmarried individual, lives in New York City and maintains a household in Detroit for his dependent parents. Rick may use the head-of-household filing status even though his parents do not reside in his New York home.

Head-of-household status is not changed during the year by the death of the dependent. As long as the taxpayer provided more than half of the cost of maintaining the household prior to the dependent's death, head-of-household status is preserved.

Abandoned Spouse Rules

When married persons file separate returns, several unfavorable tax consequences result. For example, the taxpayer must use the married filing separately tax rates. But what about a spouse who is abandoned by her husband? Since she is married, she has no choice but to file separately (a harsh result). To mitigate this outcome, Congress enacted the abandoned spouse rules. Under these rules, the taxpayer is treated as *not married* and qualifies for head-of-household status if the following conditions are met:[36]

- The taxpayer does not file a joint return.
- The taxpayer paid more than half the cost of maintaining his or her home for the tax year.
- The taxpayer's spouse did not live in the home during the last six months of the tax year.
- The home was the principal residence of the taxpayer's son, daughter, stepson, stepdaughter, foster child, or adopted child for more than half the year, and the child can be claimed as a dependent.[37]

---

[35]§ 2(b)(1)(B).

[36]§ 7703(b).

[37]§ 152(f)(1). The dependency requirement does not apply, however, if the taxpayer could have claimed a dependency exemption except for the fact

that the exemption was claimed by the noncustodial parent under a written agreement.

The Big Picture

EXAMPLE 41

Return to the facts of *The Big Picture* on p. 3-1. Can Polly qualify as an abandoned spouse? Yes, if she can claim Paige as a dependent—either as a qualifying child (see Example 16) or as a qualifying relative (see Example 24). If so, Polly can use head-of-household filing status. If not, her filing status is married filing separately.

ETHICS & EQUITY   Abandoned Spouse?

Bob and Carol have been in and out of marital counseling for the past few years. Early in 2017, they decide to separate. However, because they are barely able to get by on their current incomes, they cannot afford separate housing or the legal costs of a divorce. So Bob moves out of their house in March and takes up residence in their detached garage (which has an enclosed workshop and bathroom). Carol stays in the house with their two children and pays more than half of the costs of maintaining their residence. Bob does not enter the house for the remainder of the year. Can Carol qualify as an abandoned spouse?

3-5b Filing Requirements

General Rules

In general, an individual must file a tax return if gross income equals or exceeds the sum of the exemption amount plus the applicable standard deduction. Because the exemption and standard deduction amounts are subject to an annual inflation adjustment, the gross income amounts for determining whether a tax return must be filed normally change each year.[38] For example, a single taxpayer under age 65 must file a tax return in 2017 if gross income equals or exceeds $10,400 ($4,050 exemption plus $6,350 standard deduction). Exhibit 3.6 lists the income levels[39] that require tax returns under the general rule and under certain special rules.

EXHIBIT 3.6	Filing Requirements for Most Taxpayers	
Filing Status	**2016 Gross Income**	**2017 Gross Income**
Single		
Under 65	$10,350	$10,400
65 or older	11,900	11,950
Married, filing jointly		
Both spouses under 65	$20,700	$20,800
One spouse 65 or older	21,950	22,050
Both spouses 65 or older	23,200	23,300
Married, filing separately		
All	$ 4,050	$ 4,050
Head of household		
Under 65	$13,350	$13,400
65 or older	14,900	14,950
Qualifying widow(er)		
Under 65	$16,650	$16,750
65 or older	17,900	18,000

---

[38]See §§ 1(f), 63(c)(4), and 151(d)(3).

[39]§ 6012(a)(1).

The additional standard deduction for being age 65 or older is considered in determining the gross income filing requirements. For example, the 2017 filing requirement for a single taxpayer age 65 or older is $11,950 ($6,350 basic standard deduction + $1,550 additional standard deduction + $4,050 exemption). Except in the case of dependents, the additional standard deduction for blindness is not taken into account in determining whether a taxpayer must file a tax return (see Filing Requirements for Dependents below).

A self-employed individual with net earnings of $400 or more from a business or profession must file a tax return regardless of the amount of gross income.

Even though an individual has gross income below the filing level amounts and therefore does not owe any tax, he or she must file a return to obtain a tax refund of amounts withheld. A return is also necessary to obtain the benefits of the earned income credit (see Chapter 13).

Filing Requirements for Dependents

Computation of the gross income filing requirement for an individual who can be claimed as a dependent on another person's tax return is subject to more complex rules. These rules are tied to the amount of a dependent's standard deduction (see text Section 3-2c). For 2017, a dependent must file a return if he or she has *any* of the following:

- Earned income only and gross income that is more than the total standard deduction (including any additional standard deduction).

- Unearned income only and gross income of more than $1,050 plus any additional standard deduction.

- Both earned and unearned income and gross income of more than the larger of $1,050 or the sum of earned income plus $350 (but limited to the basic standard deduction) plus any additional standard deduction.

Dependent Filing Requirements

Tom is an unmarried dependent child who works part-time at the neighborhood pool as a lifeguard. During 2017, Tom earns $4,800 and has no other income. Must Tom file a return?

Answer: No. He had earned income only, and his gross income is less than his standard deduction of $6,350. However, if income taxes were withheld from his earnings, Tom would want to file a return to get a refund of any income taxes withheld.

EXAMPLE 42

Martha is a widow, age 68, who lives with her son (and is his dependent). In 2017, her only source of income is interest income from her bank account ($450) and tax-exempt interest income of $200. Must Martha file a return?

Answer: No. She has unearned income only and gross income of only $450 (which is less than $2,600; $1,050 plus her $1,550 additional standard deduction).

EXAMPLE 43

Return to the facts of Example 42. Tom also has $150 of interest income from his savings. Must Tom file a return?

Answer: No. He has earned income of $4,800 and gross income of $4,950. His standard deduction is $5,150 (earned income plus $350). As in Example 42, Tom will want to file a return to get a refund of any income taxes withheld.

If Tom had $400 of interest income, he would need to file a return. Now his gross income of $5,200 exceeds his $5,150 standard deduction (earned income plus $350).

EXAMPLE 44

3-6 TAX DETERMINATION

Demonstrate the proper procedures for determining the tax liability.

The computation of income tax due (or refund) involves applying the proper set of tax rates to taxable income and then adjusting for available credits. In certain cases, however, the application of the kiddie tax will change how the tax is determined (see text Section 3-6c).

3-6a Tax Rates

The basic tax rate structure is progressive, with current rates ranging from 10 percent to 39.6 percent.[40] By way of comparison, the lowest rate structure, which was in effect in 1913–1915, ranged from 1 to 7 percent, and the highest, in effect during 1944–1945, ranged from 23 to 94 percent.

Tax Table Method

The tax liability is computed using either the Tax Table method or the Tax Rate Schedule method. Most taxpayers compute their tax using the Tax Table . Eligible taxpayers compute taxable income (as shown in Concept Summary 3.1) and *must* determine their tax by reference to the Tax Table. The following taxpayers, however, may *not* use the Tax Table method:

- Individuals whose taxable income exceeds the maximum (ceiling) amount in the Tax Table. The 2016 Tax Table applies to taxable income below $100,000 for Form 1040.

- An estate or a trust.

The IRS does not release the Tax Tables until late in the year to which they apply. So the 2017 Tax Tables will be available at the end of 2017. The 2017 Tax Rate Schedules, however, were released at the end of 2016.[41] For purposes of estimating tax liability and making quarterly estimated tax payments, the Tax Rate Schedules are normally used. Because it is available, the 2016 Tax Table is used to illustrate the tax computation using the Tax Table method.

Although the Tax Table is derived from the Tax Rate Schedules (discussed next), the tax calculated using the two methods may vary slightly. This is because the tax for a particular income range in the Tax Table is based on the midpoint amount.

Linda is single and has taxable income of $30,000 for calendar year 2016. To determine Linda's tax using the Tax Table (see Appendix A), find the $30,000 to $30,050 income line. Linda's tax is $4,040. This amount is actually the tax the Tax Rate Schedule for 2016 would yield on taxable income of $30,025 (i.e., the midpoint amount between $30,000 and $30,050).

Tax Rate Schedule Method

Taxpayers who do not use the Tax Tables use the Tax Rate Schedules . The 2017 tax rate schedule for single taxpayers is reproduced in Exhibit 3.7.[42] This schedule is used to illustrate the tax computations in Examples 46 and 47.

Pat is single and had $5,870 of taxable income in 2017. His tax, based on the Tax Rate Schedule, is $587 ($5,870 × 10%).

Pat's tax, based on the Tax Table, is $588. This tax is based on taxable income of $5,875 (the midpoint between $5,850 and $5,900). As his taxable income is less than $100,000, Pat must use the Tax Table.

Several terms are used to describe tax rates. The rates in the Tax Rate Schedules are often referred to as *statutory* (or nominal) rates. The *marginal* rate is the tax rate that would be assessed on the next dollar of income for a particular taxpayer. In Example 46, the statutory rate and the marginal rate are both 10 percent.

Chris is single and had taxable income of $102,000 in 2017. Her tax is $21,541.75 [$18,713.75 + 28%($102,000 − $91,900)].

---

[40]The Tax Relief Reconciliation Act of 2001 as amended by the American Taxpayer Relief Act of 2012.

[41]Rev.Proc. 2016–55, 2016–45 I.R.B. 707. The 2016 Tax Tables and the 2017 and 2016 Tax Rate Schedules are reproduced in Appendix A. For quick reference, the rate schedules are also reproduced inside the front cover of this text.

[42]§ 1(i).

The *average* rate is equal to the tax liability divided by taxable income. In Example 47, Chris has statutory rates of 10 percent, 15 percent, 25 percent, and 28 percent and a marginal rate of 28 percent. Chris's average rate is 21.1 percent ($21,541.75 tax liability ÷ $102,000 taxable income); her marginal rate is 28 percent.

A tax is *progressive* (or graduated) if a higher rate of tax applies as the tax base increases. The progressive nature of the Federal income tax on individuals is illustrated by computing the tax in Example 47 using each rate bracket.

Tax on first $9,325 at 10%	$ 932.50
Tax on $37,950 − $9,325 at 15%	4,293.75
Tax on $91,900 − $37,950 at 25%	13,487.50
Tax on $102,000 − $91,900 at 28%	2,828.00
Total tax on taxable income of $102,000	$21,541.75

A special computation limits the effective tax rate on qualified dividends (see Chapter 4) and net long-term capital gain (see Chapter 16).

EXHIBIT 3.7	2017 Tax Rate Schedule for Single Taxpayers		

If Taxable Income Is		The Tax Is:	Of the Amount Over
Over	**But Not Over**		
$ −0−	$ 9,325	10%	$ −0−
9,325	37,950	$ 932.50 + 15%	9,325
37,950	91,900	5,226.25 + 25%	37,950
91,900	191,650	18,713.75 + 28%	91,900
191,650	416,700	46,643.75 + 33%	191,650
416,700	418,400	120,910.25 + 35%	416,700
418,400		121,505.25 + 39.6%	418,400

3-6b Computation of Net Taxes Payable or Refund Due

The pay-as-you-go feature of the Federal income tax system requires payment of all or part of the taxpayer's income tax liability during the year. These payments take the form of Federal income tax withheld by employers or estimated tax paid by the taxpayer or both.[43] The payments are applied against the tax liability to determine whether the taxpayer will get a refund or pay additional tax.

Employers are required to withhold income tax on compensation paid to their employees and to pay this tax to the government. The employer must provide each employee a Form W–2 (Wage and Tax Statement), which documents wages and taxes withheld (including income, Social Security, and Medicare taxes). An employee should receive a 2017 Form W–2 no later than January 31, 2018.

If taxpayers receive income that is not subject to withholding or income from which not enough tax is withheld, they may have to pay estimated tax. Form 1040–ES (Estimated Tax for Individuals) is used for these payments, and estimates are due quarterly (see Chapter 13 for a thorough discussion).

The income tax liability is reduced by any available tax credits (which are different from tax deductions). Tax credits reduce the tax liability dollar for dollar. Tax deductions reduce taxable income on which the tax liability is based.

---

[43]§ 3402 for withholding; § 6654 for estimated payments.

EXAMPLE 48

Gail is a taxpayer in the 25% tax bracket. As a result of incurring $1,000 in child care expenses (see Chapter 13 for details), she is entitled to a $200 child care credit ($1,000 child care expenses × 20% credit rate). She also contributed $1,000 to the American Cancer Society and included this amount in her itemized deductions.

The child care credit results in a $200 reduction of Gail's tax liability for the year. The contribution to the American Cancer Society reduces taxable income by $1,000 and results in a $250 reduction in Gail's tax liability ($1,000 reduction in taxable income × 25% tax rate).

Tax credits are discussed in Chapter 13. Some of the more common credits include:

- Earned income credit.
- Credit for child and dependent care expenses.
- Child tax credit.
- Foreign tax credit.
- Premium tax credit.

The computation of net taxes payable or refund due can be illustrated by returning to the facts of Example 6.

EXAMPLE 49

Grace is single and has her disabled and dependent mother living with her. Recall that Example 6 established that Grace has taxable income of $24,500. Further assume that she has the following: income tax withheld, $2,500; estimated tax payments, $600; and credit for dependent care expenses, $200. Grace's net taxes payable is computed as follows:

Income tax (from 2017 Tax Rate Schedule, for head of household, Appendix A)		$ 3,008 (rounded)
Less: Tax credits and prepayments—		
Credit for dependent care expenses	$ 200	
Income tax withheld	2,500	
Estimated tax payments	600	(3,300)
Net taxes payable or (refund due)		$ (292)

Because Grace maintains a home for a qualifying dependent relative, she will use head-of-household filing status. Her tax was computed using the Tax Rate Schedules rather than the Tax Tables (the text and footnote 41 explain why).

LO.7

Identify and report kiddie tax situations.

3-6c Kiddie Tax—Unearned Income of Children Taxed at Parents' Rate

At one time, a dependent child could claim an exemption on his or her own return even if claimed as a dependent by the parents. This enabled a parent to shift investment income (like interest and dividends) to a child by transferring income-producing assets. The child would pay no tax on the income to the extent that it was sheltered by the child's exemption and standard deduction amounts. And if the child did pay any tax, that tax was at the child's (lower) rates, rather than the parents' (higher) rates.

To reduce the tax savings that result from shifting income from parents to children, the net **unearned income**[44] (commonly called investment income) of certain children is taxed as if it were the parents' income. This provision, commonly referred to as the **kiddie tax**, applies to any child who is under age 19 (or under age 24 if a full-time student) and has unearned income of more than $2,100 (the same as in 2016).[45]

---

[44]Unearned income includes taxable interest, dividends, capital gains, rents, royalties, the taxable portion of scholarships, pension and annuity income, and income (other than earned income) received as the beneficiary of a trust.

[45]§ 1(g)(2). The kiddie tax does not apply if the child has earned income that exceeds half of his or her support, if the child is married and files a joint return, or if both parents are deceased.

Net Unearned Income

In 2017, net unearned income of a dependent child is computed as follows:[46]

Unearned income

Less: $1,050

Less: The greater of

- $1,050 of the standard deduction *or*
- The amount of allowable itemized deductions directly connected with the production of the unearned income

Equals: Net unearned income

If net unearned income is zero (or negative), the child's tax is computed without using the parents' rate. If net unearned income is positive, this amount is taxed at the parents' rate. The child's remaining taxable income (known as nonparental source income) is taxed at the child's rate.

Tax Determination

If a child is subject to the kiddie tax, there are two options for computing the tax on the income. A separate return may be filed for the child, or the parents may elect to report the child's income on their own return.

If a separate return is filed for the child, the tax on net unearned income (referred to as the *allocable parental tax*) is computed as though the income had been included on the parents' return. Form 8615 is used to compute the tax. The steps required in this computation are illustrated in Example 50.

> **EXAMPLE 50**
>
> Olaf and Olga have a child, Hans (age 10). In 2017, Hans received $3,200 of interest income and paid investment-related fees of $200. Olaf and Olga had $70,000 of taxable income, not including their child's investment income. The parents have no qualified dividends or capital gains. Olaf and Olga do not make the parental election (discussed below).
>
> **1. Determine Hans's net unearned income**
>
> | | |
> |---|---:|
> | Gross income (unearned) | $ 3,200 |
> | Less: $1,050 | (1,050) |
> | Less: The greater of | |
> | • $1,050 or | |
> | • Investment expense ($200) | (1,050) |
> | Equals: Net unearned income | $ 1,100 |
>
> **2. Determine allocable parental tax**
>
> | | |
> |---|---:|
> | Parents' taxable income | $70,000 |
> | Plus: Hans's net unearned income | 1,100 |
> | Equals: Revised taxable income | $71,100 |
> | Tax on revised taxable income | $ 9,733 |
> | Less: Tax on parents' taxable income | (9,568) |
> | Allocable parental tax | $ 165 |
>
> **3. Determine Hans's nonparental source tax**
>
> | | |
> |---|---:|
> | Hans's AGI | $ 3,200 |
> | Less: Standard deduction | (1,050) |
> | Less: Personal exemption | (–0–) |
> | Equals: Taxable income | $ 2,150 |
> | Less: Net unearned income | (1,100) |
> | Nonparental source taxable income | $ 1,050 |
> | Nonparental source tax ($1,050 × 10% rate) | $ 105 |
>
> *continued*

---

[46]The $1,050 amounts in the net unearned income computation are adjusted each year for inflation. The amounts were also $1,050 in 2016.

4. Determine Hans's total tax liability	
Nonparental source tax (step 3)	$ 105
Allocable parental tax (step 2)	165
Total tax	$ 270

Election to Claim Certain Unearned Income on Parent's Return

In 2017, the parent may elect to report the child's unearned income that exceeds $2,100 (the same in 2016) on the parent's own tax return if the child meets all of the following requirements:

- Gross income is from interest and dividends only.

- Gross income is more than $1,050 but less than $10,500 (for 2016, these amounts are the same).

- No estimated tax has been paid in the name and Social Security number of the child, and the child is not subject to backup withholding (see Chapter 13).

If this election is made, the child is treated as having no gross income and is not required to file a tax return. In this case, Form 8814 (Parents' Election to Report Child's Interest and Dividends) must be filed as part of the parents' tax return. The parent(s) must also pay an additional tax equal to the smaller of $105 or 10 percent of the child's gross income over $1,050.[47]

Other Rules

Here are a few other rules that apply to the kiddie tax:[48]

- If parents have more than one child subject to the tax on net unearned income, the tax for the children is computed as shown in Example 50 and then allocated to the children based on their relative amounts of income.

- For children of divorced parents, the taxable income of the custodial parent is used to determine the allocable parental tax. This parent is the one who may elect to report the child's unearned income.

- For married individuals filing separate returns, the individual with the greater taxable income is the applicable parent.

3-7 TAX RETURN FILING PROCEDURES

3-7a Selecting the Proper Form

As the 2017 tax forms had not been released when this text was published, the following comments apply to the 2016 forms.[49]

Individual taxpayers use one of three basic forms: Form 1040, Form 1040A, or Form 1040EZ. Which form is used depends on a number of factors. For example, Form 1040EZ cannot be used if:

- Taxpayer claims any dependents;

- Taxpayer (or spouse) is 65 or older or blind;

- Taxable income is $100,000 or more; or

- Taxpayer claims credits other than the earned income tax credit.

---

[47]Parents who have substantial itemized deductions based on AGI (see Chapter 10) may find that making the parental election increases total taxes for the family unit. Taxes should be calculated both with and without the parental election to determine the appropriate choice.

[48]See Chapter 31 of *Your Federal Income Tax* (IRS Publication 17) and Form 8615 (Tax for Certain Children Who Have Unearned Income).

[49]Draft tax forms are available from the IRS at **https://apps.irs.gov/app/ picklist/list/draftTaxForms.html**.

Taxpayers who have self-employment income or want to itemize deductions *from* AGI must file Form 1040 and use Schedule A (Form 1040) to document itemized deductions (Form 1040A and Form 1040EZ cannot be used). Taxpayers can use Form 1040A if their taxable income is below $100,000, they only have specific *for* AGI deductions (e.g., IRAs, student loan interest, educator expenses), and claim only specific credits (including the child care credit, the child tax credit, education credits, and the premium tax credit).

3-7b The E-File Approach

The e-file program is used by the vast majority of individual taxpayers (and is mandatory for most tax return preparers). The required tax information is transmitted to the IRS electronically either directly from the taxpayer (i.e., an "e-file online return") or indirectly through an "Authorized *e-file* Provider." These Providers are tax professionals who have been accepted into the electronic filing program by the IRS. Providers often are the preparers of the return as well.

Taxpayers can also use IRS Free File (with online fillable forms) or use commercial software to file a tax return at no cost. A number of software providers offer free e-filing services. These services are generally available only to taxpayers who have AGI of $62,000 or less. Eligibility requirements and a list of the software providers are available on the IRS website: **www.irs.gov/filing/e-file-options**.

All taxpayers and tax return preparers must attest to the returns they file. For most taxpayers, this is done through an electronic return signature using a personal identification number (a Self-Select PIN). Or the taxpayer can authorize a tax preparer to generate a PIN by signing Form 8879 (IRS e-file Signature Authorization). If certain paper documents must be submitted, a one-page form must be completed and filed when the return is e-filed. Form 8453 (U.S. Individual Income Tax Transmittal for an IRS *e-file* Return) is used to submit required attachments for both self- and practitioner-prepared electronic returns.

The *e-file* approach has two major advantages over paper filing. First, it eliminates many reporting errors. Second, it reduces the time required for processing a refund to three weeks or less.

3-7c When and Where to File

Tax returns of individuals are due on or before the fifteenth day of the fourth month following the close of the tax year. For the calendar year taxpayer, the usual filing date is on or before April 15 of the following year.[50] When the due date falls on a Saturday, Sunday, or legal holiday, the filing deadline is the next business day. If the return is mailed to the proper address with sufficient postage and is postmarked on or before the due date, it is deemed timely filed.[51] The return should be sent or delivered to the IRS Regional Service Center listed in the instructions for each type of return or contained in software applications.[52]

If a taxpayer is unable to file the return by the return's due date, a six-month extension of time can be obtained by filing Form 4868 (Application for Automatic Extension of Time to File U.S. Individual Income Tax Return) by the return's due date. Members of the U.S. Armed Forces also are allowed additional time for filing their Federal income tax returns.[53]

Although an extension provides additional time to file a return, it does not extend the deadline for paying any taxes due. If more tax is owed, it should be paid when the Form 4868 is filed. If a taxpayer does not obtain an extension of time to file and/or

---

[50]§ 6072(a); Rev.Rul. 2015–13 (2015–22 I.R.B. 1011) provides filling deadline guidance when there are unique state holidays.

[51]The Code allows the IRS to prescribe rules when taxpayers use FedEx, UPS, or a similar delivery service [§ 7502(f)]. See Notice 2016–30 (2016–18 I.R.B. 676) for the current list of "designated private delivery services" that, if used, will meet the timely filed rules.

[52]The appropriate IRS Regional Service Center address can be found at **www.irs.gov/uac/where-to-file-addresses-for-taxpayers-and-tax-professionals-filing-form-1040**.

[53]Reg. § 1.6081–4. See also *Your Federal Income Tax* (IRS Publication 17), Chapter 1.

pay any tax due, the failure to file and failure to pay penalties can be assessed (these are discussed in Chapter 1).

If an individual taxpayer needs to file an amended return (e.g., because of a failure to report income or to claim a deduction or tax credit), Form 1040X is filed. The form generally must be filed within three years of the filing date of the original return or within two years from the time the tax was paid, whichever is later.

3-7d **Modes of Payment**

Payments of any taxes due can be made in a variety of ways, including check or money order (with payment made to "United States Treasury"), IRS Direct Pay (electronic funds withdrawal from a bank account), or the Electronic Federal Tax Payment System (EFTPS). In addition, the IRS has approved the use of MasterCard, American Express, Discover, and Visa to pay Federal taxes using a payment processor (fees will apply to these transactions).

LO.8

Explain the fundamentals of property transactions.

3-8 GAINS AND LOSSES FROM PROPERTY TRANSACTIONS—IN GENERAL

Gains and losses from property transactions are discussed in detail in Chapters 14 through 17. But an overview is relevant for topics that are discussed in the intervening chapters.

When property is sold (or otherwise disposed of), a gain or loss results. This gain or loss has a tax effect on the seller when the *realized* gain or loss is *recognized* for tax purposes. Without a transaction generating realized gain or loss, there generally can be no recognized gain or loss. Realized gain or loss is computed as follows:

| Amount realized from the sale | − | Adjusted basis of the property | = | Realized gain (or loss) |

The amount realized is the selling price of the property less any costs of disposition (e.g., brokerage commissions) incurred by the seller. The adjusted basis of the property is determined as follows:

	Cost (or other original basis) at date of acquisition[54]
Add:	Capital additions
Subtract:	Depreciation (if appropriate) and other capital recoveries (see Chapter 8)
Equals:	Adjusted basis at date of sale or other disposition

In general, all realized gains are recognized (taxable). However, the tax law provides some exceptions (see, for example, Chapter 15 dealing with certain nontaxable exchanges). Realized losses may or may not be recognized (deductible) for tax purposes. Generally, losses realized from the sale of personal use property (e.g., a residence, home furnishings, clothing, sports equipment) are not recognized.

EXAMPLE

51

During the current year, Ted sells his sailboat (adjusted basis of $4,000) for $5,500. Ted also sells one of his personal automobiles (adjusted basis of $8,000) for $5,000.

Ted's realized gain of $1,500 from the sale of the sailboat is recognized. On the other hand, the $3,000 realized loss on the sale of the automobile is not recognized and will not provide Ted with any deductible tax benefit.

---

[54]Cost usually means purchase price plus expenses related to the acquisition of the property and incurred by the purchaser (e.g., brokerage commissions). For the basis of property acquired by gift or inheritance and other basis rules, see Chapter 14.

In terms of the tax formula, recognized gains from property transactions are included in gross income. If the gain is deferred (e.g., like-kind exchanges or involuntary conversions—see Chapter 15) or not recognized (e.g., sale of a residence—see Chapter 15), there is no immediate tax effect. Recognized losses from property transactions are treated as deductions *for* adjusted gross income (AGI).

If a property disposition results in a recognized gain or loss, the gain or loss must be *classified* as capital or ordinary. Although ordinary gain is fully taxable and ordinary loss is fully deductible, the same may not hold true for capital gains and capital losses.

3-9 GAINS AND LOSSES FROM PROPERTY TRANSACTIONS—CAPITAL GAINS AND LOSSES

Capital gains and losses are treated uniquely in the Federal income tax system. Capital gains are included in the determination of taxable income and may be taxed at lower (preferential) tax rates. Capital losses, on the other hand, may not be fully deductible when determining taxable income (if limited, the amount not allowed can be carried over and used in subsequent years).

3-9a Definition of a Capital Asset

Capital assets are defined in the Code as any property held by the taxpayer *other than* certain items including inventory, accounts receivable, and depreciable property or real estate used in a business (see Chapter 16 for a complete discussion). As a result, the sale or exchange of these assets normally results in ordinary income or loss (see Chapter 17).

Kelly owns a pizza parlor. During the current year, he sells an automobile that had been used as a delivery car for three years. The sale resulted in a loss of $1,000. Because this automobile is property used in his business, Kelly has an ordinary loss deduction of $1,000, rather than a capital loss deduction.

EXAMPLE 52

The principal capital assets held by an individual taxpayer include (1) assets held for personal (rather than business) use (e.g., a personal residence or an automobile), and (2) assets held for investment purposes (e.g., corporate securities or land). Capital assets generally include collectibles, which are subject to somewhat unique tax treatment. **Collectibles** include art, antiques, gems, metals, stamps, some coins and bullion, and alcoholic beverages that are held as investments.

3-9b Determination of Net Capital Gain

To arrive at a net capital gain, capital losses must be taken into account. First, capital gains and losses are categorized based on their holding period: *short-term* (held for one year or less) and *long-term* (held for more than one year). Then, gains and losses in each category are netted together. If excess losses result, they are applied to the category carrying the *highest* tax rate. A *net capital gain* occurs if the net long-term capital gain (NLTCG) exceeds the net short-term capital loss (NSTCL).

In the current year, Colin has the following capital transactions and resulting gains (losses):

Penguin Corporation stock (held for 8 months)	$ 1,000
Owl Corporation stock (held for 10 months)	(3,000)
Cardinal Corporation stock (held for 5 years)	2,000
Land (held as an investment for 3 years)	4,000

The Penguin Corporation short-term capital gain (STCG) of $1,000 is offset by the Owl Corporation short-term capital loss (STCL) of $3,000, resulting in a net STCL of $2,000. The Cardinal Corporation long-term capital gain (LTCG) and the land LTCG are combined, resulting in a net LTCG of $6,000. The net STCL offsets the net LTCG, resulting in a net capital gain of $4,000.

EXAMPLE 53

3-9c **Treatment of Net Capital Loss**

For individual taxpayers, net capital loss can be used to offset ordinary income of up to $3,000 ($1,500 for married persons filing separate returns). If a taxpayer has both short- and long-term capital losses, short-term losses are used first. Any remaining net capital loss is carried over indefinitely until used up (subject to the annual $3,000 limit). When carried over, the excess capital loss retains its classification as short- or long-term.

EXAMPLE 54

In 2017, Tina has a short-term capital loss of $2,000, a long-term capital loss of $2,500, and no capital gains. She can deduct $3,000 ($2,000 short-term + $1,000 long-term) of this amount as an ordinary loss. The remaining $1,500 is carried over to 2018 as a long-term capital loss.

The Big Picture

EXAMPLE 55

Return to the facts of *The Big Picture* on p. 3-1. Polly's sale of her wedding rings resulted in a realized capital loss of $2,800 [$9,000 (selling price) − $11,800 (cost basis)]. However, because they were personal use property, Polly cannot deduct the loss.

3-9d **Taxation of Net Capital Gain**

Net capital gains are classified and taxed as follows:

Classification	Maximum Rate
Short-term gains (held for one year or less)	39.6%
Long-term gains (held for more than one year)—	
Collectibles	28%
Certain depreciable property used in a trade or business (known as unrecaptured § 1250 gain and discussed in Chapter 17)	25%
All other long-term capital gains	20%, 15%, or 0%

The special tax rates for long-term capital gains (called the alternative tax computation) are used when the taxpayer's regular tax rate *exceeds* the alternative tax rate. When tax liability is determined, long-term capital gains are taxed last. As a result, the tax rate applied to a long-term capital gain will depend on the taxpayer's regular tax rate on other income and the size of the long-term capital gain (a large long-term capital gain may cross marginal rates brackets and, theoretically, could be taxed at 0%, 15%, and 20% rates). The 0 percent rate applies only when the taxpayer's regular tax rate is 15 percent or less. The 20 percent rate applies only when the taxpayer's regular tax rate is 39.6 percent. Special rates apply to collectibles and certain types of depreciable realty. If losses are used to offset gains, the losses are first used to offset gains with the *highest* tax rates.[55]

Net Capital Gain Tax Computation

EXAMPLE 56

During 2017, Polly is in the 15% tax bracket and has the following capital gains for the year:

Robin Corporation stock (held for 6 months)	$1,000
Crow Corporation stock (held for 13 months)	1,000

Although both transactions yield a $1,000 capital gain, the tax effects are quite different. Polly pays a tax of $150 ($1,000 × 15%) on the Robin stock gain but $0 ($1,000 × 0%) on the Crow stock gain.

---

[55]§ 1(h)(1).

Net Capital Gain Tax Computation

Assume the same facts as in Example 56, except that Polly's regular tax bracket for the year is 33% (not 15%).

Polly now pays a tax of $330 ($1,000 × 33%) on the Robin stock gain and $150 ($1,000 × 15%) on the Crow stock gain.

EXAMPLE 57

In the current year, Colin is in the 35% tax bracket and has the following capital transactions and resulting gains (losses):

Penguin Corporation stock (held for 8 months)	$ 1,000
Owl Corporation stock (held for 10 months)	(3,000)
Stamp collection (held for 5 years)	2,000
Land (held as an investment for 3 years)	4,000

The Penguin Corporation short-term capital gain (STCG) of $1,000 is offset by the Owl Corporation short-term capital loss (STCL) of $3,000, resulting in a net STCL of $2,000. This $2,000 net STCL is then applied against the stamp collection gain—a collectible long-term capital gain (LTCG) with the highest tax rate (28%). Because there is no remaining STCL, Colin has a net LTCG of $4,000 from the land sale. This is Colin's net capital gain, and it is taxed at a 15% rate.

EXAMPLE 58

3-10 TAX PLANNING

LO.9

Evaluate tax planning opportunities associated with the individual tax formula.

3-10a Maximizing the Use of the Standard Deduction

In some cases, the difference between using the standard deduction and itemizing may not be a significant amount. Here, taxes might be saved by alternating between the two options. The taxpayer does this by using the cash method to concentrate multiple years' deductions in a single year (e.g., church pledges for several years can be paid in one year). Then the standard deduction is used in alternate years.

3-10b Dependency Exemptions

The Joint Return Test

A married person can be claimed as a dependent only if that individual does not file a joint return with his or her spouse. If a joint return has been filed, the damage may be undone if separate returns are substituted on or before the due date of the return.

While preparing a client's 2016 income tax return on April 3, 2017, the tax professional discovered that the client's daughter had filed a joint return with her husband in late January 2017. Presuming that the daughter otherwise qualifies as the client's dependent, the exemption is not lost if she and her husband file separate returns on or before April 17, 2017.

If the daughter and husband attempt to file separate returns after April 17, 2017, the returns will not be accepted (the joint return election is binding).[56]

EXAMPLE 59

Keep in mind that the filing of a joint return will not affect a dependency exemption if the parties are filing solely to recover all income tax withholdings, they are not required to file a return, and no tax liability would exist on separate returns.

Support Considerations

The support of a qualifying child becomes relevant only if the child is self-supporting. In cases where the child has an independent source of funds, planning could help prevent

---

[56]Reg. § 1.6013–1(a)(1).

an undesirable result. When a qualifying relative is involved, meeting the support test is essential, as the dependency exemption is not otherwise available.

EXAMPLE 60

In 2017, Cheryl maintains a household that she shares with her son and mother. The son, Barry, is 23 years old and a full-time student in law school. The mother, Gladys, is 68 years old and active in charitable causes. Barry works part-time for a local law firm, while Gladys has income from investments. In resolving the support issue (or self-support in the case of Barry), Cheryl's contribution must be compared with that made by Barry and Gladys.[57]

What Barry and Gladys do with their funds becomes crucial. Funds that are used for nonsupport purposes (e.g., purchase of investments) or not used at all (e.g., deposited in a bank) are not considered. Limiting how much Barry and Gladys contribute to their own support enhances Cheryl's chances of claiming them as dependents. Records should be maintained showing the amount of support and its source.

Example 60 does not mention the possible application of the gross income test. Presuming that Barry is a qualifying child, the amount he earns does not matter, as the gross income test does not apply. Gladys, however, comes under the qualifying relative category, where the gross income test applies. In 2017, for her to be claimed as a dependent, her gross income must be less than $4,050.

Community Property Ramifications

In certain cases, state law can have an effect on the availability of a dependency exemption.

Dependency Exemptions: State Law Implications

EXAMPLE 61

During the year, Mitch provides more than half of the support of his son, Ross, and daughter-in-law, Connie, who live with him. Ross, age 22, is a full-time student, while Connie earns $5,000 from a part-time job. Ross and Connie do not file a joint return. All parties live in New York, a common law state. Mitch can claim Ross as a dependent, as he is a qualifying child. Connie is not a dependent because she does not meet the gross income test under the qualifying relative category.

EXAMPLE 62

Assume the same facts as in Example 61, except that all parties live in Arizona, a community property state. Now Connie also qualifies as a dependent. Because Connie's gross income is only $2,500 (half of the community income), she satisfies the gross income test.

3-10c Taking Advantage of Tax Rate Differentials

It is natural for taxpayers to be concerned about the taxes they are paying. How does a tax professional communicate information about tax rates to clients? There are several possibilities.

The *marginal rate* (refer to Examples 46 and 47) provides information that can help a taxpayer evaluate a particular course of action or structure a transaction in the most advantageous manner. For example, a taxpayer who is in the 15 percent bracket this year and expects to be in the 28 percent bracket next year should, if possible, defer payment of deductible expenses until next year to maximize the tax benefit of the deduction.

However, Congress understands these tax planning possibilities and has enacted many provisions to limit them. Some income shifting limitations are discussed in Chapters 4, 5, and 18. Limitations that affect a taxpayer's ability to shift deductions are discussed in Chapters 6 through 11 and in Chapter 18.

A taxpayer's *effective rate* can be an informative measure of the effectiveness of tax planning. The effective rate is computed by dividing the taxpayer's tax liability by the

---

[57]As part of her support contribution to Barry and Gladys, Cheryl can count the fair market value of the meals and lodging she provides.

total amount of income. A low effective rate can be considered an indication of effective tax planning.

One way of lowering the effective rate is to exclude income from the tax base. For example, a taxpayer might consider investing in tax-free municipal bonds rather than taxable corporate bonds. Although pre-tax income from corporate bonds is usually higher, after-tax income may be higher if the taxpayer invests in tax-free municipals.[58]

Another way of lowering the effective rate is to make sure the taxpayer's expenses and losses are deductible. For example, losses on investments in passive activities may not be deductible (see Chapter 11). Therefore, a taxpayer who plans to invest in an activity that will produce a loss in the early years should take steps to ensure that the business is treated as active rather than passive. Active losses are deductible, while passive activity losses are not.

3-10d Income of Certain Children

Taxpayers can use several strategies to avoid or minimize the effect of the rules that tax the unearned income of certain children at the parents' rate. Parents should consider giving a younger child assets that defer taxable income until the child reaches 19 (or 24 for full-time students). For example, U.S. government Series EE savings bonds can be used to defer income until the bonds are cashed in (see Chapter 4).

Growth stocks, which typically pay little in the way of dividends, are another option. If the child holds the stock until he or she reaches a safe age and then sells the stock at a profit, the profit is taxed at the child's low rates.

Taxpayers who own a business can employ their children. The child's earned income is sheltered by the standard deduction, and the parents' business is allowed a deduction for the wages. The kiddie tax rules have no effect on earned income, even if it is earned from the parents' business.

REFOCUS ON THE BIG PICTURE

A DIVIDED HOUSEHOLD

Of major concern to Polly is her filing status. If she qualifies as an abandoned spouse, she is entitled to file as head of household. If not, she is considered to be a married person filing separately. Moreover, to be an abandoned spouse, Polly must be able to claim Paige as a dependent. To be a dependent, Paige must meet the requirements of a qualifying child *or* a qualifying relative.

For qualifying child purposes, Paige must meet either the age (i.e., under age 19) or the full-time student (under age 24) test. (A disabled child exception seems highly unlikely.) Because Paige currently is not a full-time student, is she under age 19? If so, she is a qualifying child (see Example 16). If Paige is not a qualifying child, is she a qualifying relative? Here, the answer depends on meeting the gross income test (see Example 24). How much did Paige earn from her part-time job? If her earnings are under $4,050, she satisfies the gross income test. Thus, if Paige can be claimed as a dependent under either the qualifying child or the qualifying relative category, Polly is an abandoned spouse entitled to head-of-household filing status (see Example 41). If not, she is a married person filing separately.

Maude can be claimed as Polly's dependent because she is a member of the household. It does not matter that she died in February, and the dependency exemption amount need not be apportioned and is allowed in full. Because Maude is her

continued

---

[58]Investment in tax-free bonds will also reduce the net investment income tax (§ 1411) if the individual is subject to this additional tax (see Chapter 13).

dependent, Polly can claim the medical expenses she paid on Maude's behalf. The funeral expenses, however, are not deductible (see Example 21).

Does Maude qualify Polly for head-of-household filing status? No—although she is a dependent, Maude does not meet the relationship test (see Example 38).

The sale of the wedding rings results in a capital loss of $2,800 ($9,000 − $11,800). Because the loss is for personal use property, it cannot be claimed for tax purposes (see Example 55).

What If?

Assume that Nick left for parts unknown in *August* (not March). Now Polly cannot qualify as an abandoned spouse. Her spouse lived in the home during part of the last six months of the year. As Polly is married, she cannot qualify for head-of-household filing status. She must file as a married person filing separately. The change in when Nick left will not affect the dependency issue regarding Paige, however.

Key Terms

Abandoned spouse, 3-25	Itemized deductions, 3-6	Standard deduction, 3-7
Child tax credit, 3-21	Kiddie tax, 3-30	Surviving spouse, 3-24
Collectibles, 3-35	Marriage penalty, 3-24	Tax Rate Schedules, 3-28
Dependency exemption, 3-13	Multiple support agreement, 3-17	Tax Table, 3-28
E-file, 3-33	Personal exemptions, 3-13	Unearned income, 3-30
Filing status, 3-22	Qualifying child, 3-14	
Head-of-household, 3-24	Qualifying relative, 3-15	

Discussion Questions

Issue ID   1. **LO.1, 5, 8, 9** During the year, Addison is involved in the following transactions:

   a. Lost money gambling on a recent trip to a casino.
   b. Helped pay for her neighbor's dental bills. The neighbor is a good friend who is unemployed.
   c. Received from the IRS a tax refund due to Addison's overpayment of last year's Federal income taxes.
   d. Paid a traffic ticket received while double parking to attend a business meeting.
   e. Contributed to the mayor's reelection campaign. The mayor had promised Addison to have some of her land rezoned. The mayor was reelected and got Addison's land rezoned.
   f. Borrowed money from a bank to make a down payment on an automobile.
   g. Sold a houseboat and a camper on eBay. Both were personal use items, and the gain from one offset the loss from the other.
   h. Her dependent grandfather died on June 3 of the year.
   i. Paid for dependent grandfather's funeral expenses.
   j. Paid premiums on her dependent son's life insurance policy.

   What are the possible income tax ramifications of these transactions?

2. **LO.1** Which of the following items are *inclusions* in gross income?
   a. During the year, stock that the taxpayer purchased as an investment doubled in value.
   b. Amount an off-duty motorcycle police officer received for escorting a funeral procession.
   c. While his mother was in the hospital, the taxpayer sold her jewelry and gave the money to his girlfriend.
   d. Child support payments received.
   e. A damage deposit the taxpayer recovered when he vacated the apartment he had rented.
   f. Interest received by the taxpayer on an investment in general purpose bonds issued by IBM.
   g. Amounts received by the taxpayer, a baseball "Hall of Famer," for autographing sports equipment (e.g., balls and gloves).
   h. Tips received by a bartender from patrons. (Taxpayer is paid a regular salary by the cocktail lounge that employs him.)
   i. Taxpayer sells his Super Bowl tickets for three times what he paid for them.
   j. Taxpayer receives a new BMW from his grandmother when he passes the CPA exam.

3. **LO.1** Which of the following items are *exclusions* from gross income?
   a. Alimony payments received.
   b. Damages award received by the taxpayer for personal physical injury—none were for punitive damages.
   c. A new golf cart won in a church raffle.
   d. Amount collected on a loan previously made to a college friend.
   e. Insurance proceeds paid to the taxpayer on the death of her uncle—she was the designated beneficiary under the policy.
   f. Interest income on City of Chicago bonds.
   g. Jury duty fees.
   h. Stolen funds the taxpayer had collected for a local food bank drive.
   i. Reward paid by the IRS for information provided that led to the conviction of the taxpayer's former employer for tax evasion.
   j. An envelope containing $8,000 found (and unclaimed) by the taxpayer in a bus station.

4. **LO.1, 8, 9** In late 2017, the Polks come to you for tax advice. They are considering selling some stock investments for a loss and making a contribution to a traditional IRA. In reviewing their situation, you note that they have large medical expenses and a casualty loss, neither of which is covered by insurance. What advice would you give the Polks?   Decision Making

5. **LO.2** In choosing between the standard deduction and itemizing deductions *from* AGI, what effect, if any, does each of the following have?   Issue ID
   a. The age of the taxpayer(s).
   b. The health (i.e., physical condition) of the taxpayer.
   c. Whether taxpayers rent or own their residence.
   d. Taxpayer's filing status (e.g., single, married, filing jointly).
   e. Whether married taxpayers decide to file separate returns.
   f. The taxpayer's uninsured personal residence was recently destroyed by fire.
   g. The number of personal and dependency exemptions the taxpayer can claim.

6. **LO.2, 3, 5** In 2017, David is age 78, is a widower, and is being claimed as a dependent by his son. How does this situation affect the following?

   a. David's own individual filing requirement.

   b. David's personal exemption.

   c. The standard deduction allowed to David.

   d. The availability of any additional standard deduction.

Issue ID   7. **LO.4** Patsy maintains a household that includes a son (age 30) and a cousin (age 28). She can claim the cousin as a dependent but not her son. Explain.

8. **LO.4** Heather, age 12, lives in the same household with her mother, grandmother, and uncle.

   a. Who can qualify for the dependency exemption?

   b. Who takes precedence?

9. **LO.4** Caden and Lily are divorced on March 3, 2016. For financial reasons, however, Lily continues to live in Caden's apartment and receives her support from him. Caden does not claim Lily as a dependent on his 2016 Federal income tax return but does so on his 2017 return. Explain.

10. **LO.4** Isabella, Emma, and Jacob share equally in the support of their parents. Jacob tells his sisters to split the dependency exemptions between the two of them. Explain what Jacob means.

Issue ID   11. **LO.4** Mark and Lisa were divorced in 2016. In 2017, Mark has custody of their children, but Lisa provides nearly all of their support. Who is entitled to claim the children as dependents?

Issue ID   12. **LO.4** Mario, who is single, is a U.S. citizen and resident. He provides almost all of the support of his parents and two aunts, who are citizens and residents of Guatemala. Mario's parents and aunts are seriously considering moving to and becoming residents of Mexico. Would such a move have any impact on Mario? Why or why not?

13. **LO.3, 4** What are stealth taxes? What purpose do they serve, and why are they used?

Issue ID   14. **LO.5** Oliver is a U.S. citizen employed by a multinational corporation at its London office. Oliver is married to Regina, a British citizen, and they reside in England. Regina receives substantial rent income from real estate she owns in western Europe.

   a. Must Oliver file a U.S. income tax return?

   b. Under what circumstances might Regina be considered a resident of the United States? Would such a classification be advantageous? Disadvantageous? Explain.

15. **LO.4, 5** Comment on the availability of head-of-household filing status for 2017 in each of the following independent situations:

   a. Taxpayer lives alone but maintains the household of his parents. In July 2017, the parents use their savings to purchase a new BMW for $62,000.

   b. Taxpayer maintains a home in which she and her dependent father live. The father enters a nursing facility for treatment of a mental disorder.

   c. Taxpayer, a single parent, maintains a home in which she and her unmarried son live. The son, age 18, earns $5,000 from a part-time job.

   d. Assume the same facts as in part (c), except that the son is age 19, not 18.

   e. Taxpayer is married and maintains a household in which he and his dependent stepson live.

f. Taxpayer lives alone but maintains the household where her dependent daughter lives.

g. Taxpayer maintains a household that includes an unrelated friend who qualifies as his dependent.

16. **LO.5** In many cases, a surviving spouse ultimately becomes a head of household for filing status purposes. Explain this statement.

17. **LO.6** Jayden calculates his 2017 income tax by using both the Tax Tables and the Tax Rate Schedules. Because the Tax Rate Schedules yield a slightly lower tax liability, he plans to pay this amount.
    a. Why is there a difference?
    b. Is Jayden's approach permissible? Why or why not?

18. **LO.7** In connection with the application of the kiddie tax, comment on the following:
    a. The child has only earned income.
    b. The child has a modest amount of unearned income.
    c. The child is age 20, not a student, and not disabled.
    d. The child is married.
    e. Effect of the parental election.
    f. The result when the parental election is made and the married parents file separate returns.

19. **LO.8** During the year, Hernando has the following transactions:

    - Gain on the sale of stock held as an investment for 10 months.
    - Gain on the sale of land held as an investment for 4 years.
    - Gain on the sale of a houseboat owned for 2 years and used for family vacations.
    - Loss on the sale of a reconditioned motorcycle owned for 3 years and used for recreational purposes.

    How should Hernando treat these transactions for income tax purposes?

20. **LO.8** During the year, Brandi had the following transactions: a long-term capital gain from the sale of land, a short-term capital loss from the sale of stock, and a long-term capital gain from the sale of a gun collection.
    a. How are these transactions treated for income tax purposes?
    b. Does this treatment favor the taxpayer or the IRS? Explain.

Computational Exercises

21. **LO.2** Sam and Abby are dependents of their parents, and each has income of   Issue ID
    $2,100 for the year. Sam's standard deduction for the year is $1,050, while Abby's is $2,450. As their income is the same, what causes the difference in the amount of the standard deduction?

22. **LO.2** Compute the 2017 standard deduction for the following taxpayers.
    a. Margie is 15 and claimed as a dependent by her parents. She has $800 in dividends income and $1,400 in wages from a part-time job.
    b. Ruby and Woody are married and file a joint tax return. Ruby is age 66, and Woody is 69. Their taxable retirement income is $10,000.
    c. Shonda is age 68 and single. She is claimed by her daughter as a dependent. Her earned income is $500, and her interest income is $125.
    d. Frazier, age 55, is married but is filing a separate return. His wife itemizes her deductions.

23. **LO.4** In 2017, Dominique and Felix are married, have one dependent, and file a joint tax return. Their AGI is $316,550, and they claim three exemptions. Determine their total exemption amount for 2017.

Issue ID   24. **LO.5, 9** Paul and Sonja, who are married, had itemized deductions of $8,200 and $400, respectively, during 2017. Paul suggests that they file separately—he will itemize his deductions *from* AGI, and she will claim the standard deduction.
   a. Evaluate Paul's suggestion.
   b. What should they do?

25. **LO.6** Compute the 2017 tax liability and the marginal and average tax rates for the following taxpayers (use the 2017 tax rate schedules in Appendix A for this purpose).
   a. Chandler, who files as a single taxpayer, has taxable income of $93,000.
   b. Lazare, who files as a head of household, has taxable income of $56,000.

26. **LO.7** In 2017, Simon, age 12, has interest income of $800 and dividend income of $4,000. He has no investment expenses. His parents have taxable income of $80,200 and file a joint tax return. Assume that no parental election is made. Determine Simon's net unearned income, allocable parental tax, and total tax liability.

27. **LO.8** Rebecca sells her personal scooter for $550. She purchased the scooter for $700 three years ago. She also sells a painting for $1,200 that she acquired five years ago for $900. What are the tax implications of these sales?

28. **LO.8** During the year, Tamara had capital transactions resulting in gains (losses) as follows:

Sold stock in ABC Company (acquired two years ago)	($1,500)
Sold collectible coins (held for more than one year)	$2,000
Sold stock in XYZ Company (acquired six months ago)	($4,100)
Sold stock in LMN Company (acquired three years ago)	$500

Determine Tamara's net capital gain or loss as a result of these transactions.

Problems

29. **LO.1** Compute the taxable income for 2017 in each of the following independent situations:
   a. Drew and Meg, ages 40 and 41, respectively, are married and file a joint return. In addition to four dependent children, they have AGI of $65,000 and itemized deductions of $15,000.
   b. Sybil, age 40, is single and supports her dependent parents who live with her, as well as her grandfather who is in a nursing home. She has AGI of $80,000 and itemized deductions of $8,000.
   c. Scott, age 49, is a surviving spouse. His household includes two unmarried stepsons who qualify as his dependents. He has AGI of $75,000 and itemized deductions of $10,100.
   d. Amelia, age 33, is an abandoned spouse who maintains a household for her three dependent children. She has AGI of $58,000 and itemized deductions of $9,500.
   e. Dale, age 42, is divorced but maintains the home in which he and his daughter, Jill, live. Jill is single and qualifies as Dale's dependent. Dale has AGI of $64,000 and itemized deductions of $9,900.

   Note: Problems 30 and 31 can be solved by referring to Concept Summary 3.1, Exhibits 3.1 through 3.5, and the discussion under Deductions for Adjusted Gross Income in this chapter.

30. **LO.1, 8** Compute the taxable income for 2017 for Emily on the basis of the following information. Her filing status is single.

Salary	$85,000
Interest income from bonds issued by Xerox	1,100
Alimony payments received	6,000
Contribution to traditional IRA	5,500
Gift from parents	25,000
Short-term capital gain from stock investment	2,000
Amount lost in football office pool	500
Number of potential dependents (two cousins, who live in Canada)	?
Age	40

31. **LO.1** Compute the taxable income for 2017 for Aiden on the basis of the following information. Aiden is married but has not seen or heard from his wife since 2015.

Salary	$ 80,000
Interest on bonds issued by City of Boston	3,000
Interest on CD issued by Wells Fargo Bank	2,000
Cash dividend received on Chevron common stock	2,200
Life insurance proceeds paid upon death of aunt (Aiden was the designated beneficiary of the policy)	200,000
Inheritance received upon death of aunt	100,000
Jackson (a cousin) repaid a loan Aiden made to him in 2011 (no interest was provided for)	5,000
Itemized deductions (state income tax, property taxes on residence, interest on home mortgage, and charitable contributions)	9,700
Number of dependents (children, ages 17 and 18, and mother-in-law, age 70)	3
Age	43

32. **LO.2** Determine the amount of the standard deduction allowed for 2017 in the following independent situations. In each case, assume that the taxpayer is claimed as another person's dependent.

   a. Curtis, age 18, has income as follows: $700 interest from a certificate of deposit and $6,100 from repairing cars.

   b. Mattie, age 18, has income as follows: $600 cash dividends from a stock investment and $4,700 from handling a paper route.

   c. Mel, age 16, has income as follows: $675 interest on a bank savings account and $800 for painting a neighbor's fence.

   d. Lucy, age 15, has income as follows: $400 cash dividends from a stock investment and $500 from grooming pets.

   e. Sarah, age 67 and a widow, has income as follows: $500 from a bank savings account and $3,200 from babysitting.

33. **LO.4** Analyze each of the characteristics in considering the indicated test for dependency as a qualifying child or qualifying relative. In the last two columns, after each listed test (e.g., gross income), state whether the particular test is Met, Not Met, or Not Applicable (NA).

	Characteristic	Qualifying Child Test	Qualifying Relative Test
a.	Taxpayer's son has gross income of $7,000.	Gross income	Gross income
b.	Taxpayer's niece has gross income of $3,000.	Gross income	Gross income
c.	Taxpayer's uncle lives with him.	Relationship	Relationship

Characteristic		Qualifying Child Test	Qualifying Relative Test
d.	Taxpayer's daughter is 25 and disabled.	Age	Age
e.	Taxpayer's daughter is age 18, has gross income of $8,000, and does not live with him.	Residence Gross Income	Gross income
f.	Taxpayer's cousin does not live with her.	Relationship Residence	Relationship
g.	Taxpayer's brother does not live with her.	Residence	Relationship
h.	Taxpayer's sister has dropped out of school, is age 17, and lives with him.	Relationship Residence Age	Relationship
i.	Taxpayer's older nephew is age 23 and a full-time student.	Relationship Age	Relationship
j.	Taxpayer's grandson lives with her and has gross income of $7,000.	Relationship Residence	Relationship Gross Income

34. **LO.3, 4** For tax year 2017, determine the number of personal and dependency exemptions in each of the following independent situations:

    a. Leo and Amanda (ages 48 and 46, respectively) are husband and wife and furnish more than 50% of the support of their two children, Elton (age 18) and Trista (age 24). During the year, Elton earns $4,500 providing transportation for elderly persons with disabilities, and Trista receives a $5,000 scholarship for tuition at the law school she attends.

    b. Audry (age 45) was divorced this year. She maintains a household in which she, her ex-husband (Clint), and his mother (Olive) live and furnishes more than 50% of their support. Olive is age 91 and blind.

    c. Crystal, age 45, furnishes more than 50% of the support of her married son, Andy (age 18), and his wife, Paige (age 19) who live with her. During the year, Andy earned $8,200 from a part-time job. All parties live in Iowa (a common law state).

    d. Assume the same facts as in part (c), except that all parties live in Washington (a community property state).

35. **LO.3, 4** Compute the number of personal and dependency exemptions in each of the following independent situations:

    a. Reginald, a U.S. citizen and resident, contributes 100% of the support of his parents who are citizens of Canada and live there.

    b. Pablo, a U.S. citizen and resident, contributes 100% of the support of his parents, who are citizens of Panama. Pablo's father is a resident of Panama, and his mother is a legal resident of the United States.

    c. Gretchen, a U.S. citizen and resident, contributes 100% of the support of her parents, who are U.S. citizens but residents of Germany.

    d. Elena is a U.S. citizen and a resident of Italy. Her household includes Carlos, a 4-year-old adopted son who is a citizen of Spain.

36. **LO.3, 4** Determine how many personal and dependency exemptions would be available in each of the following independent situations. Specify whether any such exemptions would come under the qualifying child or the qualifying relative category.

    a. Andy maintains a household that includes a cousin (age 12), a niece (age 18), and a son (age 26). All are full-time students. Andy furnishes all of their support.

    b. Minerva provides all of the support of a family friend's son (age 20) who lives with her. She also furnishes most of the support of her stepmother, who does not live with her.

c. Raul, a U.S. citizen, lives in Costa Rica. Raul's household includes a friend, Helena, who is age 19 and a citizen of Costa Rica. Raul provides all of Helena's support.

d. Karen maintains a household that includes her ex-husband, her mother-in-law, and her brother-in-law (age 23 and not a full-time student). Karen provides more than half of all of their support. Karen is single and was divorced last year.

37. **LO.4** During 2017, Jenny, age 14, lives in a household with her father, uncle, and grandmother. The household is maintained by the uncle. The parties, all of whom file separate returns, have AGI as follows: father ($30,000), uncle ($50,000), and grandmother ($40,000).

a. Who is eligible to claim Jenny as a dependent?

b. Who has precedence as to the exemption?

38. **LO.3, 4** Sam and Elizabeth Jefferson file a joint return and have three children—all of whom qualify as dependents. If the Jeffersons have AGI of $335,900, what is their allowable deduction for personal and dependency exemptions for 2017?

39. **LO.4, 9** Wesley and Myrtle (ages 90 and 88, respectively) live in an assisted care facility and for 2016 and 2017 received their support from the following sources:

	Percentage of Support
Social Security benefits	16%
Son	20
Niece	29
Cousin	12
Brother	11
Family friend (not related)	12

a. Which persons are eligible to claim the dependency exemptions under a multiple support agreement?

b. Must Wesley and Myrtle be claimed by the same person(s) for both 2016 and 2017? Explain.

c. Who, if anyone, can claim their medical expenses?

40. **LO.3, 7** Taylor, age 18, is claimed as a dependent by her parents. For 2017, she has the following income: $4,000 wages from a summer job, $1,800 interest from a money market account, and $2,000 interest from City of Boston bonds.

a. What is Taylor's taxable income for 2017?

b. What is Taylor's tax for 2017? [Her parents file a joint return and have taxable income of $130,000 (no dividends or capital gains).]

41. **LO.4, 9** Walter and Nancy provide 60% of the support of their daughter (age 18) and son-in-law (age 22). The son-in-law (John) is a full-time student at a local university, while the daughter (Irene) holds various part-time jobs from which she earns $11,000. Walter and Nancy engage you to prepare their tax return for 2017. During a meeting with them in late March 2018, you learn that John and Irene have filed a joint return. What tax advice would you give based on the following assumptions:

Issue ID

Decision Making

a. All parties live in Louisiana (a community property state).

b. All parties live in New Jersey (a common law state).

42. **LO.1, 2, 3, 4, 5, 6** Charlotte (age 40) is a surviving spouse and provides all of the support of her four minor children who live with her. She also maintains the household in which her parents live and furnished 60% of their support. Besides interest on City of Miami bonds in the amount of $5,500, Charlotte's father received $2,400 from a part-time job. Charlotte has a salary of $80,000, a short-term capital loss of $2,000, a cash prize of $4,000 from a church raffle, and itemized deductions of $10,500. Using the Tax Rate Schedules, compute the 2017 tax liability for Charlotte.

43. **LO.1, 2, 3, 4, 5, 6** Morgan (age 45) is single and provides more than 50% of the support of Rosalyn (a family friend), Flo (a niece, age 18), and Jerold (a nephew, age 18). Both Rosalyn and Flo live with Morgan, but Jerold (a French citizen) lives in Canada. Morgan earns a salary of $95,000, contributes $5,000 to a traditional IRA, and receives sales proceeds of $15,000 for an RV that cost $60,000 and was used for vacations. She has $8,200 in itemized deductions. Using the Tax Rate Schedules, compute the 2017 tax liability for Morgan.

44. **LO.5** Which of the following individuals are required to file a tax return for 2017? Should any of these individuals file a return even if filing is not required? Why or why not?

    a. Patricia, age 19, is a self-employed single individual with gross income of $5,200 from an unincorporated business. Business expenses amounted to $4,900.

    b. Mike is single and is 67 years old. His gross income from wages was $10,800.

    c. Ronald is a dependent child under age 19 who received $6,500 in wages from a part-time job.

    d. Sam is married and files a joint return with his spouse, Lana. Both Sam and Lana are 67 years old. Their combined gross income was $24,250.

    e. Quinn, age 20, is a full-time college student who is claimed as a dependent by his parents. For 2017, Quinn has taxable interest and dividends of $2,500.

Decision Making   45. **LO.5, 6, 9** Roy and Brandi are engaged and plan to get married. During 2017, Roy is a full-time student and earns $9,000 from a part-time job. With this income, student loans, savings, and nontaxable scholarships, he is self-supporting. For the year, Brandi is employed and has wages of $61,000. How much income tax, if any, can Brandi save if she and Roy marry in 2017 and file a joint return?

46. **LO.5** In each of the following independent situations, determine Winston's filing status for 2017. Winston is not married.

    a. Winston lives alone, but he maintains a household in which his parents live. The mother qualifies as Winston's dependent, but the father does not.

    b. Winston lives alone but maintains a household in which his married daughter, Karin, lives. Both Karin and her husband (Winston's son-in-law) qualify as Winston's dependents.

    c. Winston maintains a household in which he and a family friend, Ward, live. Ward qualifies as Winston's dependent.

    d. Winston maintains a household in which he and his mother-in-law live. Winston's wife died in 2016.

    e. Same as part (d), except that Winston's wife disappeared (i.e., she did not die) in 2015.

47. **LO.4, 5** Christopher died in 2015 and is survived by his wife, Chloe, and their 18-year-old son, Dylan. Chloe is the executor of Christopher's estate and maintains the household in which she and Dylan live. All of their support is furnished by Chloe while Dylan saves his earnings. Dylan's status for 2015 to 2017 is as follows:

Year	Earnings	Student Status
2015	$5,000	Yes
2016	7,000	No
2017	6,000	Yes

What is Chloe's filing status for:

a. 2015?

b. 2016?

c. 2017?

48. **LO.3, 4, 5** Nadia died in 2016 and is survived by her husband, Jerold (age 44); her married son, Travis (age 22); and her daughter-in-law, Macy (age 18). Jerold is the executor of his wife's estate. He maintains the household where he, Travis, and Macy live and furnishes all of their support. During 2016 and 2017, Travis is a full-time student, while Macy earns $7,000 each year from a part-time job. Travis and Macy do not file jointly during either year. What is Jerold's filing status for 2016 and 2017 if all parties reside in:

a. Idaho (a community property state)?

b. Kansas (a common law state)?

49. **LO.1, 3, 7** Paige, age 17, is claimed as a dependent on her parents' 2017 return, on which they report taxable income of $120,000 (no qualified dividends or capital gains). Paige earned $3,900 pet sitting and $4,100 in interest on a savings account. What are Paige's taxable income and tax liability for 2017?

50. **LO.1, 3, 7** Terri, age 16, is claimed as a dependent on her parents' 2017 return. During the year, Terri earned $5,000 in interest income and $3,000 from part-time jobs.

a. What is Terri's taxable income?

b. How much of Terri's income is taxed at her rate? At her parents' rate?

c. Can the parental election be made? Why or why not?

51. **LO.8** During 2017, Inez had the following transactions involving capital assets:

Gain on the sale of unimproved land (held as an investment for 3 years)	$ 3,000
Loss on the sale of a camper (purchased 2 years ago and used for family vacations)	(5,000)
Gain on the sale of ADM stock (purchased 9 months ago as an investment)	4,000
Gain on the sale of a fishing boat and trailer (acquired 18 months ago at an auction and used for recreational purposes)	1,000

a. If Inez is in the 35% bracket, how much income tax results?

b. If Inez is in the 15% bracket, how much income tax results?

52. **LO.8** During 2017, Chester had the following transactions involving capital assets:

Gain on the sale of an arrowhead collection (acquired as an investment at different times but all pieces have been held for more than 1 year)	$ 6,000
Loss on the sale of IBM Corporation stock (purchased 11 months ago as an investment)	(4,000)
Gain on the sale of a city lot (acquired 5 years ago as an investment)	2,000

a. If Chester is in the 33% bracket, how much income tax results?

b. If Chester is in the 15% bracket, how much income tax results?

53. **LO.9** Each year, Tom and Cindy Bates normally have itemized deductions of $10,000, including a $4,000 pledge payment to their church. Upon the advice of a friend, they do the following: in early January 2017, they pay their pledge for 2016; during 2017, they pay the pledge for 2017; and in late December 2017, they prepay their pledge for 2018.

Decision Making

Communications

a. Explain what the Bateses are trying to accomplish.

b. What will be the tax saving if their marginal tax bracket is 25% for all three years? (Assume that the standard deduction amounts for 2017 and 2018 are the same.)

c. Write a letter to Tom and Cindy Bates (8212 Bridle Court, Reston, VA 20194) summarizing your analysis.

Cumulative Problems

Tax Return Problem

TAX SOFTWARE

54. Lance H. and Wanda B. Dean are married and live at 431 Yucca Drive, Santa Fe, NM 87501. Lance works for the convention bureau of the local Chamber of Commerce, while Wanda is employed part-time as a paralegal for a law firm.

During 2016, the Deans had the following receipts:

Salaries ($60,000 for Lance, $41,000 for Wanda)		$101,000
Interest income—		
City of Albuquerque general purpose bonds	$1,000	
Ford Motor company bonds	1,100	
Ally Bank certificate of deposit	400	2,500
Child support payments from John Allen		7,200
Annual gifts from parents		26,000
Settlement from Roadrunner Touring Company		90,000
Lottery winnings		600
Federal income tax refund (for tax year 2015)		400

Wanda was previously married to John Allen. When they divorced several years ago, Wanda was awarded custody of their two children, Penny and Kyle. (Note: Wanda has never issued a Form 8332 waiver.) Under the divorce decree, John was obligated to pay alimony and child support—the alimony payments were to terminate if Wanda remarried.

In July, while going to lunch in downtown Santa Fe, Wanda was injured by a tour bus. As the driver was clearly at fault, the owner of the bus, Roadrunner Touring Company, paid her medical expenses (including a one-week stay in a hospital). To avoid a lawsuit, Roadrunner also transferred $90,000 to her in settlement of the personal injuries she sustained.

The Deans had the following expenditures for 2016:

Medical expenses (not covered by insurance)		$7,200
Taxes—		
Property taxes on personal residence	$3,600	
State of New Mexico income tax (includes amount withheld from wages during 2016)	4,200	7,800
Interest on home mortgage (First National Bank)		6,000
Paid church pledge		3,600
Life insurance premiums (policy on Lance's life)		1,200
Contribution to traditional IRA (on Wanda's behalf)		5,000
Traffic fines		300
Contribution to the reelection campaign fund of the mayor of Santa Fe		500
Funeral expenses for Wayne Boyle		6,300

The life insurance policy was taken out by Lance several years ago and designates Wanda as the beneficiary. As a part-time employee, Wanda is excluded from coverage under her employer's pension plan. Consequently, she provides for her own retirement with a traditional IRA obtained at a local trust company. Because the mayor is a member of the local Chamber of Commerce, Lance felt compelled to make the political contribution.

The Deans' household includes the following, for whom they provide more than half of the support:

	Social Security Number	Birth Date
Lance Dean (age 42)	123-45-6786	12/16/1974
Wanda Dean (age 40)	123-45-6787	08/08/1976
Penny Allen (age 19)	123-45-6788	10/09/1997
Kyle Allen (age 17)	123-45-6789	05/03/1999
Wayne Boyle (age 75)	123-45-6785	06/15/1941

Penny graduated from high school on May 9, 2016, and is undecided about college. During 2016, she earned $8,500 (placed in a savings account) playing a harp in the lobby of a local hotel. Wayne is Wanda's widower father who died on January 20, 2016. For the past few years, Wayne qualified as a dependent of the Deans.

Federal income tax withheld is $5,200 (Lance) and $3,100 (Wanda). The proper amount of Social Security and Medicare tax was withheld.

Determine the Federal income tax for 2016 for the Deans on a joint return by completing the appropriate forms. They do not want to contribute to the Presidential Election Campaign Fund. All members of the family had health care coverage for all of 2016. If an overpayment results, it is to be refunded to them. Suggested software: H&R BLOCK Tax Software.

55. Logan B. Taylor is a widower whose wife, Sara, died on June 6, 2014. He lives at 4680 Dogwood Lane, Springfield, MO 65801. He is employed as a paralegal by a local law firm. During 2016, he had the following receipts:

Tax Return Problem

Decision Making

Communications

TAX SOFTWARE

Salary		$ 80,000
Interest income—		
Money market account at Omni Bank	$ 300	
Savings account at Boone State Bank	1,100	
City of Springfield general purpose bonds	3,000	4,400
Inheritance from Daniel		60,000
Life insurance proceeds		200,000
Amount from sale of St. Louis lot		80,000
Proceeds from estate sale		9,000
Federal income tax refund (for 2015 tax overpayment)		700

Logan inherited securities worth $60,000 from his uncle, Daniel, who died in 2016. Logan also was the designated beneficiary of an insurance policy on Daniel's life with a maturity value of $200,000. The lot in St. Louis was purchased on May 2, 2011, for $85,000 and held as an investment. As the neighborhood has deteriorated, Logan decided to cut his losses and sold the lot on January 5, 2016, for $80,000. The estate sale consisted largely of items belonging to Sara and Daniel (e.g., camper, boat, furniture, and fishing and hunting equipment). Logan estimates that the property sold originally cost at least twice the $9,000 he received and has declined or stayed the same in value since Sara and Daniel died.

Logan's expenditures for 2016 include the following:

Medical expenses (including $10,500 for dental)		$11,500
Taxes—		
State of Missouri income tax (includes withholdings during 2016)	$3,200	
Property taxes on personal residence	4,500	7,700
Interest on home mortgage (Boone State Bank)		4,600
Contribution to church (paid pledges for 2016 and 2017)		4,800

Logan and his dependents are covered by his employer's health insurance policy for all of 2016. However, he is subject to a deductible, and dental care is not included. The $10,500 dental charge was for Helen's implants. Helen is Logan's widowed mother, who lives with him (see below). Logan normally pledges $2,400 ($200 per month) each year to his church. On December 5, 2016, upon the advice of his pastor, he prepaid his pledge for 2017.

Logan's household, all of whom he supports, includes the following:

	Social Security Number	Birth Date
Logan Taylor (age 48)	123-45-6787	08/30/1968
Helen Taylor (age 70)	123-45-6780	01/13/1946
Asher Taylor (age 23)	123-45-6783	07/18/1993
Mia Taylor (age 22)	123-45-6784	02/16/1994

Helen receives a modest Social Security benefit. Asher, a son, is a full-time student in dental school and earns $4,500 as a part-time dental assistant. Mia, a daughter, does not work and is engaged to be married.

Part 1—Tax Computation

Using the appropriate forms and schedules, compute Logan's income tax for 2016. Federal income tax of $5,500 was withheld from his wages. If Logan has any overpayment on his income tax, he wants the refund sent to him. Assume that the proper amounts of Social Security and Medicare taxes were withheld. Logan does not want to contribute to the Presidential Election Campaign Fund. Suggested software: H&R BLOCK Tax Software.

Part 2—Follow-Up Advice

In early 2017, the following take place:

- Helen decides that she wants to live with one of her daughters and moves to Arizona.
- Asher graduates from dental school and joins an existing practice in St. Louis.
- Mia marries, and she and her husband move in with his parents.
- Using the insurance proceeds he received on Daniel's death, Logan pays off the mortgage on his personal residence.

Logan believes that these events may have an effect on his tax position for 2017. Therefore, he requests your advice.

Write a letter to Logan explaining in general terms the changes that will occur for tax purposes. Assume that Logan's salary and other factors not mentioned (e.g., property and state income taxes) will remain the same. Use the Tax Rate Schedules in projecting Logan's tax for 2017.

Research Problems

Note: Solutions to the Research Problems can be prepared by using the Thomson Reuters Checkpoint® Student Edition online tax research database, which accompanies this textbook. Solutions can also be prepared by using research materials found in a typical tax library.

Communications **Research Problem 1.** Kathy and Brett Ouray married in 1999. They began to experience marital difficulties in 2013 and, in the current year, although they are not legally separated, consider themselves completely estranged. They have contemplated getting a divorce. However, because of financial concerns and because they both want to remain involved in the lives of their three sons, they have not yet filed for divorce. In addition, their financial difficulties have meant that Kathy and Brett cannot afford to live in separate residences. So although they consider themselves emotionally estranged, they and their three sons all reside in a single-family home in Chicago, Illinois.

Although Brett earns significantly more than Kathy, both contribute financially to maintaining their home and supporting their teenage sons. In one of their few and brief conversations this year, they determined that Brett had contributed far more than Kathy to the maintenance of their home and the support of their sons. Thus, Brett has decided that for the current tax year, they will file separate Federal income tax returns and that he will claim head-of-household filing status. While they live under the same roof, Brett believes that he and Kathy should maintain separate households. Given this fact and the fact that he provides significantly more for the support of their sons, he believes that he is eligible for head-of-household filing status. Advise Brett on which filing status is most appropriate for him in the current year. His address is 16 Lahinch, Chicago, IL 60608.

Research Problem 2. John and Janet Baker are husband and wife and maintain a household in which the following persons live: Calvin and Florence Carter and Darin, Andrea, and Morgan Baker.

Decision Making

- Calvin and Florence are Janet's parents, who are retired. During the year, they receive $19,000 in nontaxable funds (e.g., disability income, interest on municipal bonds, and Social Security benefits). Of this amount, $8,000 is spent equally between them for clothing, transportation, and recreation (e.g., vacation) and the balance of $11,000 is invested in tax-exempt securities. Janet paid $1,000 for her mother's dental work and paid the $1,200 premium on an insurance policy her father owned on his own life. Calvin also had medical expenses, but he insisted on paying for them with his own funds.

- Darin is the Bakers' 18-year-old son who is not a student but operates a pool-cleaning service on a part-time basis. During the year, he earns $14,000 from the business, which he places in a savings account for later college expenses.

- Andrea is the Bakers' 19-year-old daughter who does not work or go to school. Tired of the inconvenience of borrowing and sharing the family car, during the year, she purchased a Camaro for $21,000. Andrea used funds from a savings account she had established several years ago with an inheritance from her paternal grandfather.

- Morgan is the Bakers' 23-year-old daughter. To attend graduate school at a local university, she applied for and obtained a student loan of $20,000. She uses the full amount to pay her college tuition.

The Bakers' fair rental value of their residence, including utilities, is $14,000, while their total food expense for the household is $10,500.

a. How many dependency exemptions are the Bakers entitled to claim for the year? Explain your answer.

b. From a planning standpoint, how might the Bakers have improved the tax result?

Partial list of research aids:
Reg. §§ 1.152–1(a) and –1(c).
Your Federal Income Tax (IRS Publication 17), Chapter 3.

Use internet tax resources to address the following questions. Look for reliable websites and blogs of the IRS and other government agencies, media outlets, businesses, tax professionals, academics, think tanks, and political outlets.

Research Problem 3. Locate IRS Form 2120 (at **www.irs.gov**), and answer the following questions.

a. Who must sign the form?

b. Who must file the form?

c. Can it be used for someone who is not related to the taxpayer? Explain.

Research Problem 4. What purpose is served by Form 8857? Read the directions for the form, and see IRS Publication 971 for additional information.

Research Problem 5. A nonresident alien earns money in the United States that is subject to Federal income tax. What guidance does the IRS provide about what tax form needs to be used and when it should be filed? In terms of the proper filing date, does it matter whether the earnings were subject to income tax withholding? Explain.

Roger CPA Review Questions

1. Slaton served 10 days on jury duty in 2017, for which Slaton was paid $25 per day by the county. Slaton's employer requires employees to remit to it all pay received by the county during jury duty, because Slaton's employer pays employees their normal compensation for the duration of jury duty. Slaton's W–2 income for 2017 is $40,000. What should Slaton's adjusted gross income be for 2017?

   a. $40,250   c. $39,750
   b. $40,000   d. $40,125

2. For "qualifying widow(er)" filing status, which of the following requirements must be met?

   I.   The surviving spouse does not remarry before the end of the current year
   II. The surviving spouse was eligible to file a joint tax return in the year of the spouse's death
   III. The surviving spouse maintains the cost of the principal residence for six months.

   a. I, II, and III   c. I and III, but not II
   b. I and II, but not III   d. I only

3. Which of the following prevents a husband and wife from filing a joint tax return?

   I.   The spouses have different accounting methods
   II. The spouses have different tax years, provided that both spouses are alive at the end of the year
   III. One spouse was a nonresident alien for three months during the year, and no proper election was made

   a. I and II only   c. I and III only
   b. II and III only   d. II only

4. Parker and his wife Marie would have been filing a joint tax return for 2015, however Marie died in October 2015. Parker has not remarried and continues to maintain a home for himself and his two children during 2015, 2016, 2017, and 2018. Parker's filing statuses for 2015, 2016, 2017, and 2018 are as follows:

	2015	2016	2017	2018
a.	Qualifying widower	Married filing joint return	Qualifying widower	Head of household
b.	Married filing joint return	Married filing joint return	Head of household	Qualifying widower
c.	Married filing joint return	Qualifying widower	Qualifying widower	Head of household
d.	Qualifying widower	Qualifying widower	Head of household	Qualifying widower

5. Which of the following items are included in determining the total support of a dependent?

    I.   Medical expenditures paid on behalf of the dependent
    II. Life insurance premiums paid on behalf of the dependent
    III. Fair rental value of dependent's lodging

    a. All of the above   c. I and III only
    b. I and II only   d. I only

6. Kyle and Elena Smith contributed to the support of their two children, Alexandra and Matthew, and Elena's divorced father, Nick. For 2017, Alexandra, a 22-year-old full-time college student, earned $1,700 from a part-time job. Matthew, a 27-year-old full-time graduate student, earned $23,000 from his job as a teaching assistant. Nick received $12,000 in capital gains income and $7,000 in nontaxable Social Security benefits. Alexandra, Matthew, and Nick are U.S. citizens and were over one-half supported by Kyle and Elena. How many exemptions can Kyle and Elena claim on their 2017 joint income tax return?

    a. 2   c. 4
    b. 3   d. 5

PART 2

GROSS INCOME

CHAPTER **4**

Gross Income: Concepts and Inclusions

CHAPTER **5**

Gross Income: Exclusions

Part 2 presents the income component of the basic tax model. The determination of what is income and the statutory exclusions that are permitted in calculating gross income are discussed. Because the taxpayer's accounting method and accounting period affect when income is reported, a basic discussion of these topics is also included.

CHAPTER

4

Gross Income: Concepts and Inclusions

LEARNING OBJECTIVES: *After completing Chapter 4, you should be able to:*

LO.1 Explain the concepts of gross income and realization and distinguish between the economic, accounting, and tax concepts of gross income.

LO.2 Describe choice of taxable year and the cash, accrual, and hybrid methods of accounting.

LO.3 Identify who should pay the tax on a particular item of income in various situations.

LO.4 Apply the Internal Revenue Code provisions on alimony, loans made at below-market interest rates, annuities, prizes and awards, group term life insurance, unemployment compensation, and Social Security benefits.

LO.5 Identify tax planning strategies for minimizing gross income.

CHAPTER OUTLINE

BOB DAEMMRICH/PHOTOEDIT

THE BIG PICTURE

CALCULATION OF GROSS INCOME

In 2017, Dr. Cliff Payne, age 27, opened his dental practice as a sole proprietorship with a December 31 year-end. By the beginning of February, construction on his medical building was completed. He also leased an office building and entered into a contract to make improvements. In addition, early in the year, he used $12,000 of extra money to purchase some stock.

The following financial information shows the results of Dr. Payne's first year of operation. The accounts receivable represent the amounts billed to patients.

Revenues (amounts billed patients for dental services)	$385,000
Accounts receivable: January 1	–0–
Accounts receivable: December 31	52,000

During the year, Sam Jones, a contractor who owed Dr. Payne $4,000 for dental services, satisfied the account by installing solar panels on the roof of Dr. Payne's new medical building.

As an undergraduate student, Cliff took an accounting course in which he learned that the accrual method of accounting provides a good measure of the income and expenses of a business. Therefore, based on the above financial information, Cliff concludes that the gross income for Federal income tax purposes is the $385,000 he billed his patients for the dental services rendered.

Has Dr. Payne correctly calculated the gross income of this dental practice? Is there an alternative method of accounting that would result in less taxable income in this first year?

Read the chapter and formulate your response.

FRAMEWORK 1040   Tax Formula for Individuals

This chapter covers the boldfaced portions of the Tax Formula for Individuals that was introduced in Concept Summary 3.1 on p. 3-3. Below those portions are the sections of Form 1040 where the results are reported.

Income *(broadly defined)*	$xx,xxx
Less: Exclusions	(x,xxx)
Gross income...	$xx,xxx

FORM 1040 (p. 1)

7	Wages, salaries, tips, etc. Attach Form(s) W-2	
8a	**Taxable** interest. Attach Schedule B if required	
b	**Tax-exempt** interest. **Do not** include on line 8a . . .	**8b**
9a	Ordinary dividends. Attach Schedule B if required . . .	
b	Qualified dividends	**9b**
11	Alimony received	
12	Business income or (loss). Attach Schedule C or C-EZ	
20a	Social security benefits **20a**	**b** Taxable amount . . . .
21	Other income. List type and amount ------------------------	

Less: **Deductions** *for* adjusted gross income...	(x,xxx)
Adjusted gross income...	$xx,xxx
Less: The greater of total **itemized deductions** *or* the standard deduction	(x,xxx)
Personal and dependency exemptions..	(x,xxx)
Taxable income	$xx,xxx
Tax on taxable income *(see Tax Tables or Tax Rate Schedules)*............................	$ x,xxx
Less: Tax credits *(including income taxes withheld and prepaid)*	(xxx)
Tax due (or refund)	$ xxx

This chapter addresses the first step in the computation of taxable income—the determination of gross income. Questions that are addressed include the following:

- What is income?
- When is the income recognized?
- Who must pay the tax on the gross income?

The Code provides an all-inclusive definition of gross income in § 61. Chapter 5 presents items of income that are specifically excluded from gross income (exclusions). In general terms, income is an increase in wealth, but when the increase is deemed to have occurred and who is deemed to have experienced the increase depend upon the application of tax accounting rules.

LO.1

Explain the concepts of gross income and realization and distinguish between the economic, accounting, and tax concepts of gross income.

4-1   GROSS INCOME—WHAT IS IT?

4-1a   Definition

Section 61(a) of the Internal Revenue Code defines the term gross income as follows:

> Except as otherwise provided in this subtitle, gross income means all income from whatever source derived.

This definition is based on the language of the Sixteenth Amendment to the Constitution.

GLOBAL TAX ISSUES From "All Sources" Is a Broad Definition

When § 61 refers to "income from whatever source derived," the taxing authorities are reaching far beyond the borders of the United States. Although one interpretation of "source" in this context is type of income (wages, interest, etc.), a broader interpretation revolves around the place where the income is generated. In this context, citizens and residents of the United States are subject to taxation on income earned from sources both inside and outside the country. This "worldwide income" tax base can cause potential double taxation problems, with other countries also taxing income earned within their borders, but mechanisms such as the foreign tax credit can alleviate these tax burdens.

Recently, some U.S. corporations have relocated to other countries to avoid the higher U.S. tax rates on income earned abroad. From 2014 to 2015, the number of Americans who renounced their U.S. citizenship increased by 20 percent to 4,279. See "Record Number of Americans Dump U.S. Passports," by Jethro Mullen, **http://money.cnn.com/2016/02/08/news/americans-citizenship-renunciation/**. Once per quarter, the Department of State publishes the names of U.S. citizens who have renounced their citizenship. Some of these individuals may owe Federal taxes upon renouncing. See § 877A.

Supreme Court decisions have made it clear that all sources of income are subject to tax unless Congress specifically excludes a type of income.[1]

Congress left it to the judicial and administrative branches to specifically determine the meaning of *income*.

4-1b **Recovery of Capital Doctrine**

While the Constitution grants Congress the power to tax income, it does not define the term. Thus, it would seem that Congress could simply tax gross receipts. Although Congress does allow certain deductions, they are not constitutionally required. On the other hand, the Supreme Court has held that there is no income subject to tax until the taxpayer has recovered the capital invested.[2] This concept is known as the **recovery of capital doctrine** .

In its simplest application, this doctrine means that sellers can reduce their gross receipts (selling price) by the adjusted basis of the property sold to determine the amount of gross income.[3]

The Big Picture

EXAMPLE 1

Return to the facts of *The Big Picture* on p. 4-1. Assume that Dr. Payne receives $15,000 when he sells the common stock he had purchased for $12,000. His gross receipts are $15,000, which consist of a $12,000 recovery of capital and $3,000 of gross income.

4-1c **Economic and Accounting Concepts**

The term **income** is used in the Code but is not separately defined. Thus, the courts were required to interpret "the commonly understood meaning of the term which must have been in the minds of the people when they adopted the Sixteenth Amendment to the Constitution."[4] Early in the development of the income tax law, a choice had to be made between two competing models: economic income and accounting income. In determining the definition of income, the Supreme Court rejected the economic concept of income.

Economists measure income (**economic income**) by first determining the fair market value of the individual's net assets (assets minus liabilities) at the beginning and end of the year. The difference between the beginning and ending balances is the change in

---

[1]*James v. U.S.*, 61–1 USTC ¶9449, 7 AFTR 2d 1361, 81 S.Ct. 1052 (USSC, 1961).

[2]*Doyle v. Mitchell Bros. Co.*, 1 USTC ¶17, 3 AFTR 2979, 38 S.Ct. 467 (USSC, 1916).

[3]Reg. § 1.61–3. For a definition of *adjusted basis*, see the Glossary in Appendix C.

[4]*Merchants Loan and Trust Co. v. Smietanka*, 1 USTC ¶42, 3 AFTR 3102, 41 S.Ct. 386 (USSC, 1921).

net worth for the year. Then to arrive at economic income, this change in net worth is increased by the value of the goods and services that person actually consumed during the period. Economic income also includes imputed values for such items as the rental value of an owner-occupied home and the value of food a taxpayer might grow for personal consumption.[5]

EXAMPLE 2

Helen has economic income as follows:

Fair market value of Helen's assets on December 31, 2017	$220,000	
Less liabilities on December 31, 2017	(40,000)	
Net worth on December 31, 2017		$ 180,000
Fair market value of Helen's assets on January 1, 2017	$200,000	
Less liabilities on January 1, 2017	(80,000)	
Net worth on January 1, 2017		(120,000)
Increase in net worth		$ 60,000
Consumption		
Food, clothing, and other personal expenditures		25,000
Imputed rental value of the home Helen owns and occupies		12,000
Economic income		$ 97,000

The need to value assets annually would make compliance with the tax law burdensome and would cause numerous controversies between the taxpayer and the IRS over valuation. In addition, using market values to determine income for tax purposes could result in liquidity problems. The taxpayer's assets may increase in value even though they are not readily convertible into the cash needed to pay the tax (e.g., commercial real estate). Thus, the IRS, Congress, and the courts have rejected the economic concept of income as impractical.

In contrast, the accounting concept of income is founded on the realization principle.[6] According to this principle, income (**accounting income**) is not recognized until it is realized. For realization to occur, (1) an exchange of goods or services must take place between the accounting entity and some independent, external party and (2) in the exchange, the accounting entity must receive assets that are capable of being objectively valued. Thus, income is recognized when an employee embezzles his or her employer's funds, when the income from an illegal business is realized, and when a person discovers buried treasure.[7] On the other hand, the appreciation in the market value of an asset owned is not realized and thus is not included in gross income until the asset is sold. Income is not realized when an individual creates assets for his or her own use (e.g., vegetables grown in a personal garden) because there is no exchange transaction with another party.

The Supreme Court expressed an inclination toward the accounting concept of income when it adopted the realization requirement in *Eisner v. Macomber*.[8]

In summary, *income* represents an increase in wealth recognized for tax purposes only upon realization.[9]

4-1d Comparison of the Timing of Income Rules for Tax and Accounting

Although income tax rules frequently parallel financial accounting measurement concepts, differences do exist. Of major significance, for example, is the fact that unearned

---

[5]See Henry C. Simons, *Personal Income Taxation* (Chicago: University of Chicago Press, 1933), Chapters 2–3.

[6]See the American Accounting Association Committee Report on the "Realization Concept," *The Accounting Review* (April 1965): 312–322.

[7]*Rutkin v. U.S.*, 52–1 USTC ¶9260, 41 AFTR 2d 596, 72 S.Ct. 571 (USSC, 1952); Rev.Rul. 61, 1953–1 C.B. 17.

[8]1 USTC ¶32, 3 AFTR 3020, 40 S.Ct. 189 (USSC, 1920).

[9]*Glenshaw Glass Co.*, 348 U.S. 426, 429–430, 75 S.Ct. 473, 99 L.Ed. 483 (1955).

(prepaid) income received by an accrual basis taxpayer often is taxed in the year of receipt. For financial accounting purposes, such prepayments are not treated as income until earned.[10] Because of this and other differences, many corporations report financial accounting income that is substantially different from the amounts reported for tax purposes (see Reconciliation of Corporate Taxable Income and Accounting Income in Chapter 20).

The Supreme Court provided an explanation for some of the variations between accounting and taxable income in a decision involving inventory and bad debt adjustments:

> The primary goal of financial accounting is to provide useful information to management, shareholders, creditors, and others properly interested; the major responsibility of the accountant is to protect these parties from being misled. The primary goal of the income tax system, in contrast, is the equitable collection of revenue.… Consistently with its goals and responsibilities, financial accounting has as its foundation the principle of conservatism, with its corollary that 'possible errors in measurement [should] be in the direction of understatement rather than overstatement of net income and net assets.' In view of the Treasury's markedly different goals and responsibilities, understatement of income is not destined to be its guiding light.
>
> … Financial accounting, in short, is hospitable to estimates, probabilities, and reasonable certainties; the tax law, with its mandate to preserve the revenue, can give no quarter to uncertainty.[11]

4-1e **Form of Receipt**

Gross income is not limited to cash received. "It includes income realized in any form, whether in money, property, or services. Income may be realized [and recognized], therefore, in the form of services, meals, accommodations, stock or other property, as well as in cash."[12]

Form of Receipt

Ostrich Corporation allows Bill, an employee, to use a company car for his vacation. Bill realizes income equal to the rental value of the car for the time and mileage.

EXAMPLE 3

Terry owes $10,000 on a mortgage. The creditor accepts $8,000 in full satisfaction of the debt. Terry realizes income of $2,000 from retiring the debt, the amount of his increase in net worth.[13]

EXAMPLE 4

Sam began his law practice in a building in need of repairs. Sam decided to list his services on a barter exchange. He offered to provide an hour of legal services in exchange for building repairs. A qualified carpenter performed the repairs in eight hours. The carpenter normally charges $50 an hour. Sam formed a corporation for the carpenter in exchange for the carpenter's services. Sam realized $400 (8 hours × $50) in gross income for his services.

EXAMPLE 5

---

[10]Similar differences exist in the deduction area.

[11]*Thor Power Tool Co. v. Comm.*, 79–1 USTC ¶9139, 43 AFTR 2d 79–362, 99 S.Ct. 773 (USSC, 1979).

[12]Reg. § 1.61–1(a).

[13]Reg. § 1.61–12. See *U.S. v. Kirby Lumber Co.*, 2 USTC ¶814, 10 AFTR 458, 52 S.Ct. 4 (USSC, 1931). Exceptions to this general rule are discussed in Chapter 5.

LO.2

Describe choice of taxable year and the cash, accrual, and hybrid methods of accounting.

4-2 YEAR OF INCLUSION

4-2a Taxable Year

The annual accounting period, or taxable year, is a basic component of our tax system.[14] Most individuals use a calendar year as their taxable year. Generally, an entity must use the *calendar year* to report its income. However, a *fiscal year* (a period of 12 months ending on the last day of any month other than December) can be selected if the taxpayer maintains adequate books and records. This fiscal year option generally is not available to partnerships, S corporations, and personal service corporations, as discussed in Chapter 18.[15]

In determining a person's tax liability, it is important that the income be placed in the correct tax year. The tax on the income is dependent on the applicable tax rates. The applicable rates can change between years for the following reasons:

- With a progressive rate system, a taxpayer's marginal tax rate can change from year to year.
- Congress may change the tax rates.
- The relevant rates may change because of a change in the taxpayer's status (e.g., a person may marry or a business may be incorporated).
- Several provisions in the Code are dependent on the taxpayer's gross income for the year (e.g., whether the person can be claimed as a dependent, as discussed in Chapter 3).

Even when the rates do not change between tax years, the longer payment of the tax can be postponed, the lower the present value of the tax.

4-2b Accounting Methods

The year an item of income is subject to tax often depends upon which acceptable accounting method the taxpayer regularly employs.[16] The three primary methods of accounting are (1) the cash receipts and disbursements method, (2) the accrual method, and (3) the hybrid method. Most individuals use the cash receipts and disbursements method of accounting, while large corporations use the accrual method. The Regulations require the accrual method for determining purchases and sales when inventory is an income-producing factor.[17] Some businesses use a hybrid method that is a combination of the cash and accrual methods of accounting (e.g., the accrual method for sales and cost of goods sold and the cash method for all other items of income and expenses).

In addition to these overall accounting methods, a taxpayer may choose to spread the gain from an installment sale of eligible property over the collection periods by using the *installment method* of income recognition (if applicable). Contractors may either spread profits from contracts over the periods in which the work is done (the *percentage of completion method*) or defer all profit until the year in which the project is completed (the *completed contract method*, which can be used only in limited circumstances).[18]

The IRS has the power to prescribe the accounting method to be used by the taxpayer. Section 446(b) grants the IRS broad powers to determine whether the accounting method used *clearly reflects income*:

> If no method of accounting has been regularly used by the taxpayer, or *if the method used does not clearly reflect income, the computation of taxable income shall be made under such method as, in the opinion of the Secretary … does clearly reflect income.*

A change in method of accounting requires the advance consent of the IRS.[19]

---

[14]See Accounting Periods in Chapter 18.

[15]§§ 441(a) and (d).

[16]See Accounting Methods in Chapter 18.

[17]Reg. § 1.446–1(c)(2)(i). Other circumstances in which the accrual method must be used are presented in Chapter 18. For the small business exception to the inventory requirement, see Rev.Proc. 2002–28, 2002–1 C.B. 815.

[18]§§ 453 and 460. See Chapter 18 for limitations on the use of the installment method and the completed contract method. See Appendix C for definitions of installment method and completed contract method.

[19]§ 446(e).

Cash Receipts Method

Under the cash receipts method , property or services received are included in the tax-payer's gross income in the year of actual or constructive receipt by the taxpayer or the taxpayer's agent, regardless of whether the income was earned in that year.[20] The income received need not be reduced to cash in the same year. All that is necessary for income recognition is that property or services received have a fair market value—a cash equivalent.[21] Thus, a cash basis taxpayer who receives a note in payment for services has income in the year of receipt equal to the fair market value of the note. However, a creditor's mere promise to pay (e.g., an account receivable), with no supporting note, usually is not considered to have a fair market value and therefore is not a cash equivalent.[22] Thus, the cash basis taxpayer defers income recognition until the account receivable is collected.

EXAMPLE

6

Dana, an accountant, reports her income using the cash method. In 2017, she performed an audit for Orange Corporation and billed the client for $5,000, which was collected in 2018. In 2017, Dana also performed an audit for Blue Corporation. Because of Blue's precarious financial position, Dana required Blue to issue an $8,000 secured negotiable note in payment of the fee. The note had a fair market value of $6,000. Dana collected $8,000 on the note in 2018. Dana's gross income for the two years is as follows:

	2017	2018
Fair market value of note received from Blue	$6,000	
Cash received		
From Orange on account receivable		$ 5,000
From Blue on note receivable		8,000
Less: Recovery of capital		(6,000)
Total gross income	$6,000	$ 7,000

Generally, a check received is considered a cash equivalent and, upon receipt, must be recognized as income by a cash basis taxpayer. An exception to this rule is if the person paying with the check requests that the check not be cashed until a subsequent date, the income is deferred until that later date.[23]

Accrual Method

Under the accrual method , an item is generally included in gross income for the year in which it is earned, regardless of when it is collected. The income is earned when (1) all events have occurred that fix the right to receive such income and (2) the amount to be received can be determined with reasonable accuracy.[24]

Generally, the taxpayer's rights to the income accrue when title to property passes to the buyer or the services are performed for the customer or client.[25] If the rights to the income have accrued but are subject to a potential refund claim (e.g., under a product warranty), the income is reported in the year of sale and a deduction is allowed in subsequent years when actual claims accrue.[26]

Where the taxpayer's right to the income is contested (e.g., when a contractor fails to meet specifications), the year in which the income is subject to tax depends upon whether payment has been received. If payment has not been received, no income is recognized until the claim is settled. Only then is the right to the income established.[27]

---

[20]*Julia A. Strauss*, 2 B.T.A. 598 (1925). See the Glossary in Appendix C for a discussion of the terms *cash equivalent doctrine* and *constructive receipt*.

[21]Reg. §§ 1.446–1(a)(3) and (c)(1)(i).

[22]*Bedell v. Comm.*, 1 USTC ¶359, 7 AFTR 8469, 30 F.2d 622 (CA–2, 1929).

[23]*Charles F. Kahler*, 18 T.C. 31 (1952); *Bright v. U.S.*, 91–1 USTC ¶50, 142, 67 AFTR 2d 91–673, 926 F.2d 383 (CA–5, 1991).

[24]Reg. § 1.451–1(a).

[25]*Lucas v. North Texas Lumber Co.*, 2 USTC ¶484, 8 AFTR 10276, 50 S.Ct. 184 (USSC, 1930). See also Rev.Rul. 84–31, 1984–1 C.B. 127.

[26]*Brown v. Helvering*, 4 USTC ¶1222, 13 AFTR 851, 54 S.Ct. 356 (USSC, 1933).

[27]*Burnet v. Sanford and Brooks*, 2 USTC ¶636, 9 AFTR 603, 51 S.Ct. 150 (USSC, 1931).

However, if the payment is received before the dispute is settled, a claim of right doctrine requires the taxpayer to recognize the income in the year of receipt.[28]

The Big Picture

EXAMPLE 7

Return to the facts of *The Big Picture* on p. 4-1. On completing the construction improvements to Dr. Payne's medical office building in 2017, assume that the contractor, who uses the accrual method, submitted a bill. Dr. Payne refused to pay the bill, however, claiming that the contractor had not met specifications. The contractor did not reach a settlement with Dr. Payne until 2018. No income accrues to the contractor until 2018. If Dr. Payne had paid for the work and then filed suit for damages, the contractor could not defer the income (the income would be taxable in 2017).

The measure of accrual basis income is generally the amount the taxpayer has a right to receive. Unlike the cash basis, the fair market value of the customer's obligation is irrelevant in measuring accrual basis income. The ability to defer income using the cash method is a distinct advantage over the accrual method; therefore, service businesses usually use the cash method. However, the accrual method must be used when inventories are an income-producing factor to the business.[29]

EXAMPLE 8

Assume the same facts as in Example 6, except that Dana is an accrual basis taxpayer. Dana must recognize $13,000 ($8,000 + $5,000) of gross income in 2017, the year her rights to the income accrued.

Hybrid Method

The hybrid method is a combination of the accrual method and the cash method. Generally, when the hybrid method is used, inventory is an income-producing factor. The Regulations require use of the accrual method for determining sales of inventory and cost of goods sold. Thus, the taxpayer accounts for inventory using the accrual method and uses the cash method for all other income and expense items (e.g., services and interest income). The hybrid method is primarily used by small businesses.

4-2c Special Rules Applicable to Cash Basis Taxpayers

Constructive Receipt

Income that has not actually been received by the taxpayer is taxed as though it had been received—the income is constructively received—under the following conditions:

- The amount is made readily available to the taxpayer.
- The taxpayer's actual receipt is not subject to substantial limitations or restrictions.[30]

The rationale for the constructive receipt doctrine is that if the income is available, the taxpayer should not be allowed to postpone the income recognition. For instance, a taxpayer is not permitted to defer income for December services by refusing to accept payment until January. However, determining whether the income is *readily available* and whether *substantial limitations or restrictions exist* necessitates a factual inquiry.[31] Following are some examples of the application of the constructive receipt doctrine.

EXAMPLE 9

Ted is a member of a barter club. In 2017, Ted performed services for other club members and earned 1,000 points. Each point entitles him to $1 in goods and services sold by other members of the club; the points can be used at any time. In 2018, Ted exchanged his points for a new high-definition TV. Ted must recognize $1,000 gross income in 2017 when the 1,000 points were credited to his account.[32]

---

[28]*North American Oil Consolidated Co. v. Burnet*, 3 USTC ¶943, 11 AFTR 16, 52 S.Ct. 613 (USSC, 1932).

[29]Reg. § 1.446–1(c)(2).

[30]Reg. § 1.451–2(a).

[31]*Baxter v. Comm.*, 87–1 USTC ¶9315, 59 AFTR 2d 87–1068, 816 F.2d 493 (CA–9, 1987).

[32]Rev.Rul. 80–52, 1980–1 C.B. 100.

The Big Picture

EXAMPLE 10

Return to the facts of *The Big Picture* on p. 4-1. On December 31, Dr. Payne has $10,000 in patients' checks that have not been deposited. They include a check for $3,000 from a patient who asked Dr. Payne not to deposit the check until after January 4 of next year because her account did not contain sufficient funds to pay the debt.

Under the cash method, Dr. Payne must recognize $7,000 income from the $7,000 in checks on hand in the current year because the checks are a cash equivalent that is actually received. The income from the $3,000 check is neither actually nor constructively received in the current year because an insufficient account means that the funds are not available.[33]

EXAMPLE 11

Rick has a savings account with Eagle Savings and Loan Association. Under the terms of the account, interest accrues monthly and the depositor can withdraw the funds (including accrued interest) at any time. The interest for the year is constructively received by Rick even though he does not withdraw the funds.[34]

The constructive receipt doctrine does not reach income the taxpayer is not yet entitled to receive even though the taxpayer could have contracted to receive the income at an earlier date.[35]

The Big Picture

EXAMPLE 12

Return to the facts of *The Big Picture* on p. 4-1. Assume that Dr. Payne adopted the cash basis of accounting. If he allowed patients to pay by credit card, Dr. Payne would receive immediate credit in his bank account for 96% of the charge. The other 4% would be retained by the credit card issuer. To avoid the 4% charge, Dr. Payne chose not to accept credit card payments. Instead, he established a policy of requiring all bills to be paid within 30 days after the dental services were provided. He communicated this policy to patients before he performed the services. At the end of the year, several patients who owed a combined $2,000 offered to pay with credit cards, but his office rejected their offers.

The $2,000 was not constructively received at the end of the year. Although Dr. Payne could have received payment by credit card in the current year before the dental services were performed, he contracted to receive payment at a later date. Moreover, the 4% charge by the credit card company would be a "substantial limitation." [36]

Income set apart or made available is not constructively received if its actual receipt is subject to *substantial restrictions*. The life insurance industry has used substantial restrictions as a cornerstone for designing life insurance contracts with favorable tax features. Ordinary life insurance policies provide (1) current protection—an amount payable in the event of death—and (2) a savings feature—a cash surrender value payable to the policyholder if the policy is terminated during the policyholder's life. The annual increase in cash surrender value is not taxable because the policyholder must cancel the policy to actually receive the increase in value. Because the cancellation requirement is a substantial restriction, the policyholder does not constructively receive the annual increase in cash surrender value.[37] Employees often receive from their employers property subject to substantial restrictions. Generally, no income is recognized until the restrictions lapse.[38]

EXAMPLE 13

Carlos is a key employee of Red, Inc. The corporation gives stock with a value of $10,000 to Carlos. The stock cannot be sold, however, for five years. Carlos is not required to recognize income until the restrictions lapse at the end of five years.

---

[33]*L. M. Fischer*, 14 T.C. 792 (1950).

[34]Reg. § 1.451–2(a).

[35]*Baxter v. Comm.*, 816 F.2d 493, 59 AFTR 2d 87–1068, 87–1 USTC ¶9315 (CA–9, 1997).

[36]*Cowden v. Comm.*, 61–1 USTC ¶9382, 7 AFTR 2d 1160, 289 F.2d 20 (CA–5, 1961).

[37]*Theodore H. Cohen*, 39 T.C. 1055 (1963).

[38]§ 83(a). See also Restricted Property Plans in Chapter 19.

Original Issue Discount

Lenders frequently make loans that require a payment at maturity of more than the amount of the original loan. The difference between the original amount of the loan and the amount due at maturity is actually interest but is referred to as **original issue discount** . In such an arrangement, the Code requires the original issue discount to be reported when it is earned, regardless of the taxpayer's accounting method.[39] The interest "earned" is calculated by the effective interest rate method and is applied to both cash and accrual basis lenders.

EXAMPLE 14

On January 1, 2017, Mark, a cash basis taxpayer, pays $82,645 for a 24-month certificate. The certificate is priced to yield 10% (the effective interest rate) with interest compounded annually. No interest is paid until maturity, when Mark receives $100,000. Thus, Mark's gross income from the certificate is $17,355 ($100,000 − $82,645). Mark's income earned each year is calculated as follows:

2017 (.10 × $82,645) =	$ 8,265
2018 [.10 × ($82,645 + $8,265)] =	9,090
	$17,355

The original issue discount rules do not apply to U.S. savings bonds (discussed in the following paragraphs) or to obligations with a maturity date of one year or less from the date of issue.[40] See Chapter 16 for additional discussion of the tax treatment of original issue discount.

Series E and Series EE Bonds

Certain U.S. government savings bonds (Series E before 1980 and Series EE after 1979) are issued at a discount and are redeemable for fixed amounts that increase at stated intervals. No interest payments are actually made. The difference between the purchase price and the amount received on redemption is the bondholder's interest income from the investment.

The income from these savings bonds is generally deferred until the bonds are redeemed or mature. Thus, U.S. savings bonds have attractive income deferral features not available with corporate bonds and certificates of deposit issued by financial institutions.

Of course, the deferral feature of government bonds issued at a discount is not an advantage if the investor has insufficient income to be subject to tax as the income accrues. In fact, the deferral may work to the investor's disadvantage if the investor has other income in the year the bonds mature or the bunching of the bond interest into one tax year creates a tax liability. Fortunately, U.S. government bonds have a provision for these investors. A cash basis taxpayer can elect to include in gross income the annual increment in redemption value.[41] These savings bond features can be relevant in planning with respect to reducing the kiddie tax (see Chapter 3).

EXAMPLE 15

Kate purchases Series EE U.S. savings bonds for $500 (face value of $1,000) on January 2 of the current year. If the bonds are redeemed during the first six months, no interest is paid. At December 31, the redemption value is $519.60.

If Kate elects to report the interest income annually, she must report interest income of $19.60 for the current year. If she does not make the election, she will report no interest income for the current year. When the bond matures, Kate may receive a Form 1099 from the bank for all of the interest. She should keep good records to prove that she paid the tax on the interest income over the life of the bond.

---

[39] §§ 1272(a)(3) and 1273(a).

[40] § 1272(a)(2).

[41] § 454(a).

When a taxpayer elects to report the income from the bonds on an annual basis, the election applies to all such bonds the taxpayer owns at the time of the election and to all such securities acquired subsequent to the election. A change in the method of reporting the income from the bonds requires permission from the IRS.

ETHICS & EQUITY Should the Tax Treatment of Government Bonds and Corporate Bonds Be Different?

Taxpayers are permitted to defer the original issue discount earned on U.S. Government Series EE bonds until the bonds mature, but the original issue discount on a corporate bond must be taken into gross income each year the bond is held. Is this difference in the tax treatment of income earned on government and corporate bonds defensible in terms of equity? Why or why not?

Amounts Received under an Obligation to Repay

The receipt of funds with an obligation to repay that amount in the future is the essence of borrowing. Because the taxpayer's assets and liabilities increase by the same amount, no income is realized when the borrowed funds are received. Thus, if an obligation to repay the funds exists, the receipt of deposited or borrowed funds is not a taxable event.

A landlord receives a damage deposit from a tenant. The landlord does not recognize income until the deposit is forfeited because the landlord has an obligation to repay the deposit if no damage occurs.[42] However, if the deposit is in fact a prepayment of rent, it is taxed in the year of receipt.

EXAMPLE 16

4-2d Exceptions Applicable to Accrual Basis Taxpayers

Prepaid Income

For financial reporting purposes under accrual accounting, advance payments received from customers are reflected as prepaid income and as a liability of the seller. However, for tax purposes, the prepaid income often is taxed in the year of receipt.

In December 2017, a tenant pays his January 2018 rent of $1,000. The accrual basis landlord must include the $1,000 in her 2017 gross income for tax purposes, although the unearned rent income is reported as a liability on the landlord's December 31, 2017 financial accounting balance sheet.

EXAMPLE 17

Taxpayers have repeatedly argued that deferral of income until it is actually earned properly matches revenues and expenses. Moreover, a proper matching of income with the expenses of earning the income is necessary to clearly reflect income, as required by the Code. The IRS responds that § 446(b) grants it broad powers to determine whether an accounting method clearly reflects income. The IRS further argues that generally accepted financial accounting principles should not dictate tax accounting for prepaid income because of the practical problems of collecting Federal revenues. Collection of the tax is simplest in the year the taxpayer receives the cash from the customer or client.

After a number of years of continual disputes between the IRS and taxpayers, the IRS relented and modified its rules on the prepaid income issue in some situations, as explained below.

---

[42]*John Mantell*, 17 T.C. 1143 (1952).

GLOBAL TAX ISSUES   **Tax Credit Neutralizes Foreign Income Taxes**

When a U.S. taxpayer invests in a foreign country, that investment income is subject to tax in the United States and may also be subject to tax in the foreign country. However, the taxpayer is allowed a credit on his or her U.S. Federal income tax return for income taxes paid to the foreign country. The credit system allows the taxpayer to treat the taxes paid to the foreign country as though they were paid to the United States.

If the foreign taxes paid are less than the U.S. tax on the income, the foreign taxes have cost the taxpayer nothing. On the other hand, if the foreign taxes are greater than the U.S. tax on the income, the credit is limited to the amount of the U.S. tax on the income. In this case, the taxes paid by the taxpayer will exceed what they would have been if the income had been earned in the United States.

Deferral of Advance Payments for Goods

Generally, a taxpayer can elect to defer recognition of income from *advance payments for goods* if the method of accounting for the sale is the same for tax and financial reporting purposes.[43]

EXAMPLE 18

Brown Company will ship goods only after payment for the goods has been received. In December 2017, Brown received $10,000 for goods that were not shipped until January 2018. Brown can elect to report the income for tax purposes in 2018, assuming that the company reports the income in 2018 for financial reporting purposes.

Deferral of Advance Payments for Services

Revenue Procedure 2004–34[44] permits an accrual basis taxpayer to defer recognition of income for *advance payments for services* to be performed after the end of the tax year of receipt. The portion of the advance payment that relates to services performed in the tax year of receipt is included in gross income in the tax year of receipt, matching what was reported in the taxpayer's financial statements. The portion of the advance payment that relates to services to be performed after the tax year of receipt is included in gross income in the subsequent tax year. This method of accounting may also be used for advance payments received for goods, as well as licensing of intellectual property and the sale, lease, or license of software.

EXAMPLE 19

Yellow Corporation, an accrual basis calendar year taxpayer, sells its services under 12-month, 24-month, and 36-month contracts. The corporation provides services to each customer every month. On May 1, 2017, Yellow Corporation sold the following customer contracts:

Length of Contract	Total Proceeds
12 months	$3,000
24 months	4,800
36 months	7,200

Yellow may defer until 2018 all of the income that will be earned after 2017.

Length of Contract	Income Recorded in 2017	Income Recorded in 2018
12 months	$2,000 ($3,000 × 8/12)	$1,000 ($3,000 × 4/12)
24 months	1,600 ($4,800 × 8/24)	3,200 ($4,800 × 16/24)
36 months	1,600 ($7,200 × 8/36)	5,600 ($7,200 × 28/36)

[43]Reg. § 1.451–5(b). See Reg. § 1.451–5(c) for exceptions to this deferral opportunity. The financial accounting conformity requirement is not applicable to contractors who use the completed contract method.

[44]2004–1 C.B. 991.

Revenue Procedure 2004–34 *does not* apply to prepaid rent or prepaid interest. Advance payments for these items are always taxed in the year of receipt.

4-3 INCOME SOURCES

LO.3

Identify who should pay the tax on a particular item of income in various situations.

4-3a Personal Services

It is a well-established principle of taxation that income from personal services must be included in the gross income of the person who performs the services. This principle was first established in a Supreme Court decision, *Lucas v. Earl*.[45] Mr. Earl entered into a binding agreement with his wife under which Mrs. Earl was to receive one-half of Mr. Earl's salary. Justice Holmes used the celebrated **fruit and tree metaphor** to explain that the fruit (income) must be attributed to the tree from which it came (Mr. Earl). A mere **assignment of income** does not shift the liability for the tax.

Services of an Employee

Services performed by an employee for the employer's customers are considered performed by the employer. Thus, the employer is taxed on the income from the services provided to the customer, and the employee is taxed on any compensation received from the employer.[46]

The Big Picture

EXAMPLE 20

Return to the facts of *The Big Picture* on p. 4-1. Assume that instead of operating his dental practice as a sole proprietorship, Dr. Payne incorporated his dental practice in an attempt to limit his liability. He entered into an employment contract with his corporation and was to receive a salary. All patients contract to receive their services from the corporation, and those services are provided through the corporation's employee, Dr. Payne. Thus, the corporation earned the income from patients' services and must include the patients' fees in its gross income. Dr. Payne must include his salary in his gross income. The corporation is allowed a deduction for the reasonable salary paid to Dr. Payne. (See the discussion of unreasonable compensation in Chapter 6.)

Services of a Child

In the case of a child, the Code specifically provides that amounts earned from personal services must be included in the child's gross income. This result applies even though the income is paid to other persons (e.g., the parents).[47]

4-3b Income from Property

The courts have used the fruit and tree metaphor to determine who should pay the tax on the income from property. The "tree" is the property, and income is its "fruit." The owner of the tree has control over the fruit; therefore, the owner of the property should pay tax on the income the property produces. Thus, if a father gives his daughter the right to collect the rent from his rental property, the father will be taxed on the rent because he retains ownership of the property.[48] On the other hand, if a father gives his daughter the property, she is taxed on all the income earned after she receives the property.

---

[45]2 USTC ¶496, 8 AFTR 10287, 50 S.Ct. 241 (USSC, 1930).

[46]*Sargent v. Comm.*, 91–1 USTC ¶50,168, 67 AFTR 2d 91–718, 929 F.2d 1252 (CA–8, 1991).

[47]§ 73. For circumstances in which the child's unearned income is taxed at the parents' rate, see Kiddie Tax—Unearned Income of Children Taxed at Parents' Rate in Chapter 3.

[48]*Galt v. Comm.*, 54–2 USTC ¶9457, 46 AFTR 633, 216 F.2d 41 (CA–7, 1954); *Helvering v. Horst*, 40–2 USTC ¶9787, 24 AFTR 1058, 61 S.Ct. 144 (USSC, 1940).

Interest

According to the IRS, interest accrues daily. Therefore, the interest for the period that includes the date of the transfer is allocated between the transferor and transferee based on the number of days during the period that each owned the property.

Floyd, a cash basis taxpayer, gave his son, Ethan, corporate bonds with a face amount of $12,000 and a 5% stated annual interest rate. The gift was made on February 28, 2017, and the interest was paid on the last day of each quarter. Floyd must recognize $100 of interest income (5% × $12,000 × 3/12 × 2/3) accrued at the time of the gift.

For the transferor, the timing of the recognition of the income from the property depends upon the accounting method and the manner in which the property was transferred. In the case of a gift of income-producing property, the donor must recognize his or her share of the accrued income at the time it would have been recognized had the donor continued to own the property.[49] However, if the transfer is a sale, the transferor must recognize the accrued income at the time of the sale. This results because the accrued interest will be included in the sales proceeds.

Mia purchased a corporate bond at its face amount of $10,000 on January 1, 2017. The bond pays 5% interest on each December 31. On March 31, 2017, Mia sold the bond for $10,600. Mia must recognize $125 interest income in 2017 (5% × $10,000 × 3/12). She must also recognize a $475 capital gain from the sale of the bond:

Amount received from sale	$ 10,600
Less accrued interest income	(125)
Selling price of bond less interest	$ 10,475
Less cost of the bond	(10,000)
Gain on sale	$ 475

Dividends

A corporation is taxed on its earnings, and the shareholders are taxed on the dividends paid to them from the corporation's after-tax earnings.

Corporations are permitted a dividend received deduction of from 70 percent to 100 percent of the dividends received from another domestic corporation. This is discussed in Chapter 20.

Partial relief from double taxation is provided by taxing qualified dividends received by individuals at the same rate as capital gains.[50] Individuals otherwise subject to the 10 or 15 percent marginal tax rate are eligible for a 0 percent tax on qualified dividends received. Individuals subject to the 25, 28, 33, or 35 percent marginal tax rate pay a 15 percent tax on qualified dividends received. Beginning in 2013, the maximum tax rate that applies to qualified dividends increased from 15 percent to 20 percent for high-income taxpayers—those subject to the 39.6 percent marginal tax rate.

A holding period requirement must be satisfied for the special rates to apply: the stock must have been held for more than 60 days during the 121-day period beginning 60 days before the ex-dividend date.[51] The purpose of this requirement is to prevent the taxpayer from buying the stock shortly before the dividend is paid, receiving the dividend, and then selling the stock at a loss (a short-term capital loss) after the stock goes ex-dividend. A stock's price often declines after the stock goes ex-dividend.

Note that qualified dividends are not included as capital gains in the gains and losses netting process; thus, they are *not* reduced by capital losses. Qualified dividend income

---

[49]Rev.Rul. 72–312, 1972–1 C.B. 22.
[50]§ 1(h)(11).

[51]The ex-dividend date is the date before the record date on which the corporation finalizes the list of shareholders who will receive the dividends.

GLOBAL TAX ISSUES **Do Dividends from Foreign Corporations Warrant Special Treatment?**

The special rates on dividends are intended to mitigate the double-tax burden—taxing income at the corporate level then taxing the dividends to the shareholder. The United States taxes foreign corporations only on the income the corporation earns in this country. Therefore, if the corporation does no business in the United States but pays dividends to shareholders subject to U.S. taxes, the corporation's income is only taxed once.

Nevertheless, special rates apply to the foreign corporation's dividends if (1) the foreign corporation's stock is traded on an established U.S. securities market or (2) the foreign corporation is eligible for the benefits of an income tax treaty between its country of incorporation and the United States. The apparent reason for the first exception is that if the corporation is listed on an established U.S. securities market, it probably does enough business in the United States to be subject to its tax. The second exception is a reciprocal arrangement: the United States confers a benefit to corporations formed in countries that exempt U.S. corporations from taxes.

is merely taxed at the rates that would apply to the taxpayer if he or she had an excess of net long-term capital gain over net short-term capital loss.

Stock Holding Period

EXAMPLE 23

In June 2017, Green Corporation pays a dividend of $1.50 on each share of its common stock. Madison and Daniel, two unrelated shareholders, each own 1,000 shares of the stock. Consequently, each receives a dividend of $1,500 (1,000 shares × $1.50). Assume that Daniel satisfies the 60/121-day holding period rule but Madison does not.

The $1,500 that Daniel receives is subject to preferential 0%/15%/20% treatment in 2017. The $1,500 that Madison receives, however, is not. Because Madison did not comply with the holding period rule, her dividend is not a *qualified dividend* and is taxed at ordinary income rates.

EXAMPLE 24

Assume that both Madison and Daniel in Example 23 are in the 35% tax bracket. Consequently, Madison pays a tax of $525 (35% × $1,500) on her dividend, while Daniel pays a tax of $225 (15% × $1,500) on his. The $300 saving that Daniel enjoys underscores the advantages of qualified dividend treatment.

Unlike interest, dividends do not accrue on a daily basis because the declaration of a dividend is at the discretion of the corporation's board of directors. Generally, dividends are taxed to the person who is entitled to receive them—the shareholder of record as of the corporation's record date.[52] Thus, if a taxpayer sells stock after a dividend has been declared but before the record date, the dividend generally will be taxed to the purchaser.

This rule differs in the case of a gift of stock. If a donor makes a gift of stock to someone (e.g., a family member) after the declaration date but before the record date, the Tax Court has held that the donor does not shift the dividend income to the donee. The *fruit* has sufficiently ripened as of the declaration date to tax the dividend income to the donor of the stock.[53] In a similar set of facts, the Fifth Circuit Court of Appeals concluded that the dividend income should be included in the gross income of the donee (the owner at the record date). In this case, the taxpayer gave stock to a qualified charity (a charitable contribution) after the declaration date and before the record date.[54] Thus, gifts to charities and gifts to family members are treated differently.

---

[52]Reg. § 1.61–9(c). The record date is the cutoff for determining the shareholders who are entitled to receive the dividend.

[53]*M. G. Anton*, 34 T.C. 842 (1960).

[54]*Caruth Corp. v. U.S.*, 89–1 USTC ¶9172, 63 AFTR 2d 89–716, 865 F.2d 644 (CA–5, 1989).

EXAMPLE 25

On June 20, the board of directors of Black Corporation declares a $10 per share dividend. The dividend is payable on June 30 to shareholders of record on June 25. As of June 20, Maria owned 200 shares of Black Corporation's stock. On June 21, Maria sold 100 of the shares to Norm for their fair market value and gave 100 of the shares to Sam (her son). Both Norm and Sam are shareholders of record as of June 25.

Norm (the purchaser) will be taxed on $1,000 because he is entitled to receive the dividend. However, Maria (the donor) will be taxed on the $1,000 received by Sam (the donee) because the gift was made after the declaration date but before the record date of the dividend.

4-3c **Income Received by an Agent**

Income received by the taxpayer's agent is considered to be received by the taxpayer. A cash basis principal must recognize the income at the time it is received by the agent.[55]

EXAMPLE 26

Jack, a cash basis taxpayer, delivered cattle to the auction barn in late December. The auctioneer, acting as the farmer's agent, sold the cattle and collected the proceeds in December. The auctioneer did not pay Jack until the following January. Jack must include the sales proceeds in his gross income for the year the auctioneer received the funds.

4-3d **Income from Partnerships, S Corporations, Trusts, and Estates**

A **partnership** is not a separate taxable entity. Rather, the partnership merely files an information return (Form 1065), which serves to provide the data necessary for determining the character and amount of each partner's distributive share of the partnership's income and deductions. Each partner must then report his or her distributive share of the partnership's income and deductions for the partnership's tax year ending in or with the partner's tax year. The income must be reported by each partner in the year it is earned, even if such amounts are not actually distributed to the partners. Because a partner pays tax on income as the partnership earns it, a distribution by the partnership to the partner is treated under the recovery of capital rules.[56]

EXAMPLE 27

Tara owns a one-half interest in the capital and profits of T & S Company (a calendar year partnership). For tax year 2017, the partnership earned revenue of $150,000 and had operating expenses of $80,000. During the year, Tara withdrew from her capital account $2,500 per month (for a total of $30,000).

For 2017, Tara must report $35,000 as her share of the partnership's profits [$\frac{1}{2} \times$ ($150,000 − $80,000)] even though she received distributions of only $30,000.

Contrary to the general provision that a corporation must pay tax on its income, a *small business corporation* may elect to be taxed similarly to a partnership. Thus, the shareholders rather than the corporation pay the tax on the corporation's income.[57] The electing corporation is referred to as an **S corporation**. The shareholders report their proportionate shares of the corporation's income and deductions for the year, regardless of whether the corporation actually makes any distributions to the shareholders.

The *beneficiaries of estates and trusts* generally are taxed on the income earned by the estates or trusts that is actually distributed or required to be distributed to them.[58] Any income not taxed to the beneficiaries is taxable to the estate or trust.

The taxation of income and distributions of partnerships, S corporations, and estates and trusts are compared in Concept Summary 4.1.

---

[55]Rev.Rul. 79–379, 1979–2 C.B. 204.

[56]§ 706(a) and Reg. § 1.706–1(a)(1). For further discussion, see Chapter 20.

[57]§§ 1361(a) and 1366. For further discussion, see Chapter 20.

[58]§§ 652(a) and 662(a). For further discussion of the taxation of income from partnerships, S corporations, trusts, and estates, see *South-Western Federal Taxation: Corporations, Partnerships, Estates & Trusts*, Chapters 10, 11, 12, and 20.

Concept Summary 4.1

Taxation of Income and Distributions

	Partnership	S Corporation	Estate or Trust
Share of the income for the year	Partner's share taxed when earned by the partnership.	Stockholder's share taxed when earned by the S corporation.	Undistributed income taxed to the estate or trust.
Distributions	Recovery of capital, which reduces basis in the partnership.	Recovery of capital, which reduces basis in the stock.	Beneficiary's income taxed when distributed.

4-3e Income in Community Property States

General

State law in Arizona, California, Idaho, Louisiana, Nevada, New Mexico, Texas, Washington, and Wisconsin is based upon a community property system. In Alaska, spouses can choose to have the community property rules apply. All other states have a common law property system. The basic difference between common law and community property systems centers around the property rights of married persons. Questions about community property income most frequently arise when the husband and wife file separate returns.

Under a community property system, all property is deemed either to be separately owned by the spouse or to belong to the marital community. Property may be held separately by a spouse if it was acquired before marriage or received by gift or inheritance following marriage. Otherwise, any property is deemed to be community property. For Federal tax purposes, each spouse is taxed on one-half of the income from property belonging to the community.

The laws of Idaho, Louisiana, Texas, and Wisconsin distinguish between separate property and the income it produces. In these states, the income from separate property belongs to the community. Accordingly, for Federal income tax purposes, each spouse is taxed on one-half of the income. In the remaining community property states, separate property produces separate income that the owner-spouse must report on his or her Federal income tax return.

What appears to be income, however, may really represent a recovery of capital. A recovery of capital and gain realized on separate property retain their identity as separate property. Items such as nontaxable stock dividends, royalties from mineral interests, and gains and losses from the sale of property take on the same classification as the assets to which they relate.

Bob and Jane are are married and reside in California. Among other transactions during the year, the following occurred:

- Nontaxable stock dividend received by Jane on stock that was given to her by her mother after Jane's marriage.
- Gain of $10,000 on the sale of unimproved land purchased by Bob before his marriage.
- Oil royalties of $15,000 from a lease Jane acquired with her separate funds after marriage.

Because the stock dividend was distributed on stock held by Jane as separate property, it also is her separate property. The same result occurs for the oil royalties Jane receives. All of the proceeds from the sale of the unimproved land (including the gain of $10,000) are Bob's separate property.

EXAMPLE

28

In all community property states, income from personal services (e.g., salaries, wages, and income from a professional partnership) is generally treated as if one-half is earned by each spouse.

EXAMPLE 29

Fred and Wilma are married but file separate returns. Fred received $25,000 of salary and $300 of taxable interest on a savings account he established in his name. All deposits to the savings account were made from Fred's salary that he earned since the marriage. Wilma collected $2,000 taxable dividends on stock she inherited from her father. Wilma's gross income is computed as follows under three assumptions as to the state of residency of the couple:

	California	Texas	Common Law States
Dividends	$ 2,000	$ 1,000	$2,000
Salary	12,500	12,500	–0–
Interest	150	150	–0–
	$14,650	$13,650	$2,000

Note that the savings account is a community asset because it was created with community funds (i.e., Fred's salary).

Because they have community property income and are filing separately, each spouse must include Form 8958, Allocation of Tax Amounts Between Certain Individuals in Community Property States, on his or her Form 1040.

Do not confuse community property with jointly owned property, as a number of differences can exist.

- Jointly owned property (i.e., tenants in common, joint tenants) is not limited to married couples.
- More than two owners can be involved. Thus, three brothers or two or more unrelated individuals can be joint owners of a tract of land.

Ownership interests need not be equal. Of three brothers who own a tract of land, one can hold a one-half interest, while each of the other two brothers owns a one-quarter interest.

Community Property Spouses Living Apart

The general rules for taxing the income from services performed by residents of community property states can create complications and even inequities for spouses who are living apart.

EXAMPLE 30

Mason and Lily, a married couple, have always lived in a community property state. After a bitter argument in December 2016, Lily moves in with her parents, where she remains for all of 2017. When Lily files her separate return for 2017, must she include one-half of Mason's salary? No, if she meets the requirements set forth below.

Congress has developed a simple solution to this problem. A spouse (or former spouse) is taxed only on his or her actual earnings from personal services if the following conditions are met:[59]

- The individuals live apart for the entire year.
- They do not file a joint return with each other.
- No portion of the earned income is transferred between the individuals.

LO.4

Apply the Internal Revenue Code provisions on alimony, loans made at below-market interest rates, annuities, prizes and awards, group term life insurance, unemployment compensation, and Social Security benefits.

4-4 ITEMS SPECIFICALLY INCLUDED IN GROSS INCOME

As discussed earlier, the general principles of gross income determination have occasionally yielded results that Congress found unacceptable. Thus, Congress has provided more specific rules for determining the gross income from certain sources. Some of these special rules appear in §§ 71–90 of the Code.

[59]§ 66. See Form 8958.

4-4a **Alimony and Separate Maintenance Payments**

When a married couple divorce or become legally separated, state law generally requires a division of the property accumulated during the marriage. In addition, one spouse may have a legal obligation to support the other spouse. The Code distinguishes between the support payments (alimony or separate maintenance) and the property division in terms of the tax consequences.

Alimony and separate maintenance payments are *deductible* by the party making the payments and are *includible* in the gross income of the party receiving the payments.[60] Thus, income is shifted from the income earner to the income beneficiary, who is better able to pay the tax on the amount received.

Pete and Tina are divorced, and Pete is required to pay Tina $15,000 of alimony each year. Pete earns $61,000 a year. The tax law presumes that because Tina receives the $15,000, she is better able than Pete to pay the tax on that amount. Therefore, Tina must include the $15,000 in her gross income, and Pete is allowed to deduct $15,000 from his gross income.

Property Settlements

A transfer of property *other than cash* to a former spouse under a divorce decree or agreement is not a taxable event. The transferor is not entitled to a deduction and does not recognize gain or loss on the transfer. The transferee does not recognize income and has a basis equal to the transferor's basis.[61]

Paul transfers stock to Rosa as part of a divorce settlement. The cost of the stock to Paul is $12,000, and the stock's value at the time of the transfer is $15,000. Rosa later sells the stock for $16,000. Paul is not required to recognize gain from the transfer of the stock to Rosa, and Rosa has a realized and recognized gain of $4,000 ($16,000 − $12,000) when she sells the stock.

Requirements for Alimony

To clarify whether payments are classified as support obligations (alimony) or as property of the other spouse (property settlements), Congress developed the following objective rules. Payments made under agreements and decrees are *classified as alimony* only if the following conditions are satisfied:

- The payments are in cash. (This clearly distinguishes alimony from a property division.)
- The agreement or decree does not specify that the payments are not alimony. (This allows the parties to determine by agreement whether the payments will be alimony.)
- The payor and payee are not members of the same household at the time the payments are made. (This ensures that the payments are for maintaining two households.)
- There is no liability to make the payments for any period after the death of the payee.

Front-Loading

As a further safeguard against a property settlement being disguised as alimony, special rules apply if payments in the first or second year exceed $15,000. If the change in the amount of the payments exceeds statutory limits, alimony recapture results to the extent of the excess alimony payments. In the *third* year, the payor must include the excess alimony payments for the first and second years in gross income, and the payee is allowed a deduction for these excess alimony payments. The mechanics involved in computing recapture are complex and beyond the scope of this text. Worksheets for computing the recapture are provided in *Divorced or Separated Individuals* (IRS Publication 504).

---

[60]§§ 71 and 215.

[61]§ 1041, added to the Code in 1984 to repeal the rule of *U.S. v. Davis*, 62–2 USTC ¶9509, 9 AFTR 2d 1625, 82 S.Ct. 1190 (USSC, 1962). Under the *Davis* rule, which applied to pre-1985 divorces, a property transfer incident to divorce was a taxable event.

Child Support

A taxpayer does not realize income from the receipt of child support payments made by his or her former spouse. This result occurs because the money is received subject to the duty to use the money for the child's benefit. The payor is not allowed to deduct the child support payments because the payments are made to satisfy the payor's legal obligation to support the child.

In many cases, it may be difficult to determine whether the payments are intended to be alimony or child support. The tax law resolves this issue in many cases with the following rule: if the amount of the payments would be reduced upon the happening of a contingency related to a child (e.g., the child attains age 21 or dies), the amount of the future reduction in the payment is deemed child support. In addition, if payments are less than required, they are considered to first cover the required child support with any excess treated as the required alimony payments.[62] These rules are applied even though the divorce agreement specifies other amounts for the support of the child.[63]

EXAMPLE 33

Under the divorce agreement, Matt is required to make periodic alimony payments of $500 per month to Grace. However, when Matt and Grace's child reaches age 21, marries, or dies (whichever occurs first), the payments will be reduced to $300 per month. Grace has custody of the child. Because the required contingency is the cause for the reduction in the payments, from $500 to $300, child support payments are $200 per month and alimony is $300 per month.

The tax rules relating to marital disputes are reviewed in Concept Summary 4.2.

Concept Summary 4.2

Tax Treatment of Payments and Transfers Pursuant to Divorce Agreements and Decrees

	Payor	Recipient
Alimony	Deduction from gross income.	Included in gross income.
Alimony recapture	Included in gross income of the third year.	Deducted from gross income of the third year.
Child support	Not deductible.	Not includible in gross income.
Property settlement	No income or deduction.	No income or deduction; basis for the property is the same as the transferor's basis.

4-4b Imputed Interest on Below-Market Loans

As discussed earlier in the chapter, generally no income is recognized unless it is realized. Realization usually occurs when the taxpayer performs services or sells goods, thus becoming entitled to a payment from the other party. It follows that no income is realized if the goods or services are provided at no charge (i.e., not in exchange for property or services). Under this interpretation of the realization requirement, before 1984, interest-free loans were used to shift income between taxpayers.

EXAMPLE 34

Kareem (father) is in the 50% (combined Federal and state) marginal tax bracket, and Veneia (daughter) is in the 20% marginal tax bracket. Kareem has $400,000 that he does not need, and Veneia could use the income from Kareem's excess cash. Before 1984, Kareem could transfer the cash to Veneia in exchange for a non-interest bearing demand note. Veneia could invest the cash, and the income would be taxed at her 20% tax rate. Thus, the income that Kareem could have earned on the $400,000 and that could be taxed at 50% became Veneia's income taxed at 20%. Furthermore, Kareem retained control over the principal because he could demand payment on the note at any time.

---

[62]§ 71(c)(2) and (c)(3).   [63]*Johnson v. Commissioner*, T.C.Memo. 2014–67.

The imputed interest rules prevent the income shifting illustrated in Example 34. Kareem in Example 34 is required to recognize **imputed interest** income.[64] Veneia is deemed to have incurred interest expense equal to Kareem's imputed interest income. Veneia's interest may be deductible on her return as investment interest if she itemizes deductions (see Chapter 10). In addition, Kareem is then deemed to have given Veneia the amount of the imputed interest she did not pay. The gift received by Veneia is not subject to income tax (see Chapter 5), although Kareem may be subject to the gift tax on the amount deemed given to Veneia (refer to Chapter 1).

Imputed interest is calculated using the rate the Federal government pays on new borrowings and is compounded semiannually. This Federal rate is adjusted monthly and is published by the IRS.[65] There are three Federal rates: short-term (not over three years and including demand loans), mid-term (over three years but not over nine years), and long-term (over nine years).[66]

EXAMPLE 35

Assume that the Federal rate applicable to the loan in Example 34 is 3.5% through June 30 and 4% from July 1 through December 31. Kareem made the loan on January 1, and the loan is still outstanding on December 31. Kareem must recognize interest income of $15,140, and Veneia has interest expense of $15,140. Kareem is deemed to have made a gift of $15,140 to Veneia.

Imputed interest calculations:

January 1–June 30—.035($400,000) ($1/2$ year)	$ 7,000
July 1–December 31—.04($400,000 + $7,000) ($1/2$ year)	8,140
	$15,140

If interest is charged on the loan but is less than the Federal rate, the imputed interest is the difference between the amount that would have been charged at the Federal rate and the amount actually charged.

EXAMPLE 36

Assume the same facts as in Example 35, except that Kareem charged 3% interest, compounded annually.

Interest at the Federal rate	$ 15,140
Less interest charged (.03 × $400,000)	(12,000)
Imputed interest	$ 3,140

The imputed interest rules apply to the following *types* of below-market loans:[67]

- Gift loans (made out of love, affection, or generosity, as in Example 34).
- Compensation-related loans (employer loans to employees).
- Corporation-shareholder loans (a corporation's loans to its shareholders).

The effects of these loans on the borrower and lender are summarized in Concept Summary 4.3.

Exceptions and Limitations

No interest is imputed on total outstanding *gift loans* of $10,000 or less between individuals, unless the loan proceeds are used to purchase income-producing property.[68] This exemption eliminates immaterial amounts that do not result in apparent shifts of income. However, if the proceeds of such a loan are used to purchase income-producing property, the limitations discussed in the following paragraphs apply instead.

On loans of $100,000 or less between individuals, the imputed interest cannot exceed the borrower's net investment income for the year (gross income from all investments less the related expenses).[69] Thus, the income imputed to the lender is limited to the

---

[64]§ 7872(a)(1).

[65]§§ 7872(b)(2) and (f)(2).

[66]§ 1274(d).

[67]§ 7872(c).

[68]§ 7872(c)(2).

[69]§ 7872(d).

Concept Summary 4.3

Effect of Certain Below-Market Loans on the Lender and Borrower

Type of Loan	Lender	Borrower
Gift	Interest income	Interest expense
	Gift made	Gift received
Compensation-related	Interest income	Interest expense
	Compensation expense	Compensation income
Corporation to shareholder	Interest income	Interest expense
	Dividend paid	Dividend income

borrower's net investment income. In addition, if the borrower's net investment income for the year does not exceed $1,000, no interest is imputed on loans of $100,000 or less. However, these limitations for loans of $100,000 or less do not apply if a principal purpose of a loan is tax avoidance.[70]

EXAMPLE 37

Vicki made interest-free gift loans as follows:

Borrower	Amount	Borrower's Net Investment Income	Purpose
Susan	$ 8,000	$ –0–	Education
Dan	9,000	500	Purchase of stock
Bonnie	25,000	–0–	Purchase of a business
Megan	90,000	15,000	Purchase of a residence
Olaf	120,000	–0–	Purchase of a residence

Assume that tax avoidance is not a principal purpose of any of the loans. The loan to Susan is not subject to the imputed interest rules because the $10,000 exception applies. The $10,000 exception does not apply to the loan to Dan because the proceeds were used to purchase income-producing assets. However, under the $100,000 exception, the imputed interest is limited to Dan's investment income ($500). Because the $1,000 exception also applies to this loan, no interest is imputed.

No interest is imputed on the loan to Bonnie because the $100,000 exception applies. Interest is imputed on the loan to Megan based on the lesser of (1) the borrower's $15,000 net investment income or (2) the interest as calculated by applying the Federal rate to the outstanding loan. None of the exceptions apply to the loan to Olaf because the loan was for more than $100,000.

Assume that the relevant Federal rate is 10% and that the loans were outstanding for the entire year. Vicki would recognize interest income, compounded semiannually, as follows:

Loan to Megan:	
First 6 months (.10 × $90,000 × ½ year)	$ 4,500
Second 6 months (.10 × $94,500 × ½ year)	4,725
	$ 9,225
Loan to Olaf:	
First 6 months (.10 × $120,000 × ½ year)	$ 6,000
Second 6 months (.10 × $126,000 × ½ year)	6,300
	$12,300
Total imputed interest ($9,225 + $12,300)	$21,525

---

[70]*Deficit Reduction Tax Bill of 1984: Explanation of the Senate Finance Committee* (April 2, 1984), p. 484.

As with gift loans, there is a $10,000 exemption for *compensation-related loans* and *corporation-shareholder loans*. However, the $10,000 exception does not apply if tax avoidance is one of the principal purposes of a loan.[71] This vague tax avoidance standard makes practically all compensation-related and corporation-shareholder loans suspect. Nevertheless, the $10,000 exception should apply when an employee's borrowing was necessitated by personal needs (e.g., to meet unexpected expenses) rather than tax considerations.

These exceptions to the imputed interest rules are summarized in Concept Summary 4.4.

Concept Summary 4.4

Exceptions to the Imputed Interest Rules for Below-Market Loans

Exception	Eligible Loans	Ineligible Loans and Limitations
De minimis—aggregate loans of $10,000 or less	Gift loans	Proceeds are used to purchase income-producing assets.
	Employer-employee	Principal purpose is tax avoidance.
	Corporation-shareholder	Principal purpose is tax avoidance.
Aggregate loans of $100,000 or less	Between individuals	Principal purpose is tax avoidance. For all other loans, interest is imputed to the extent of the borrower's net investment income if that income exceeds $1,000.

ETHICS & EQUITY Taxing "Made-Up" Income

Under the imputed interest rules, the taxpayer who makes a below-market loan may be required to recognize income he or she did not actually receive. For example, assume that Christian loans $200,000 to Mia, his daughter, to start a business (income-producing property).

Christian does not charge interest because Mia needs the funds to operate a struggling startup business. Why should Christian be required to pay tax on a "made-up" number (i.e., the interest he did not charge)? This type of income is sometimes referred to as "phantom" income.

4-4c Income from Annuities

Annuity contracts generally require the purchaser (the annuitant) to pay a fixed amount for the right to receive a future stream of payments. Typically, the issuer of the contract is an insurance company and will pay the annuitant a cash value if the annuitant cancels the contract. The insurance company invests the amounts received from the annuitant, and the income earned serves to increase the cash value of the annuity. No income is recognized by the annuitant at the time the cash value of the annuity increases because the taxpayer has not actually received any income. The income is not constructively received because, generally, the taxpayer must cancel the policy to receive the increase in value (the increase in value is subject to substantial restrictions).

---

[71]§ 7872(c)(3).

EXAMPLE 38

Jean, age 50, pays $30,000 for an annuity contract that is to pay her $500 per month beginning when she reaches age 65 and continuing until her death. If Jean should cancel the policy after one year, she would receive $30,200 and would include $200 ($30,200 − $30,000) in her gross income. However, if she does not cancel the policy, the $200 increase in value is not includible in her gross income, as long as she does not actually receive the $200.

The tax accounting problem associated with receiving payments under an annuity contract is one of apportioning the amounts received between recovery of capital (the original investment in the contract) and income.

Computing the Exclusion Amount

The annuitant can exclude from income (as a recovery of capital) the proportion of each payment that the investment in the contract bears to the expected return under the contract. The *exclusion amount* is calculated as follows:

$$\frac{\text{Investment}}{\text{Expected return}} \; \times \; \text{Annuity payment} \; = \; \text{Exclusion amount}$$

The *expected return* is the annual amount to be paid to the annuitant multiplied by the number of years the payments will be received. The payment period may be fixed (a *term certain*) or for the life of one or more individuals. When payments are for life, the taxpayer generally must use the annuity table published by the IRS to determine the expected return (see Exhibit 4.1). This is an actuarial table that contains life expectancies.[72] The expected return is calculated by multiplying the appropriate multiple (life expectancy) by the annual payment.

EXAMPLE 39

A taxpayer, age 60, purchases an annuity from an insurance company for $90,000. She is to receive $500 per month for life. Her life expectancy (from Exhibit 4.1) is 24.2 years from the annuity starting date. Thus, her expected return is $500 × 12 × 24.2 = $145,200, and the exclusion amount is $3,719 [($90,000 investment/$145,200 expected return) × $6,000 annual payment]. The $3,719 is a nontaxable return of capital, and $2,281 ($6,000 − $3,719) is included in gross income.

The *exclusion ratio* (investment ÷ expected return) applies until the annuitant has recovered his or her investment in the contract. Once the investment is recovered, the entire amount of subsequent payments is taxable. If the annuitant dies before recovering the investment, the unrecovered cost (adjusted basis) is deductible in the year the payments cease (usually the year of death).[73]

EXAMPLE 40

Assume that the taxpayer in Example 39 receives annuity payments for 25.2 years (302 months). For the last 12 months [302 − (12 × 24.2) = 12], the taxpayer will include $500 (the total amount received) each month in gross income. If instead the taxpayer dies after 36 months, she is eligible for a $78,843 deduction on her final tax return.

Cost of the contract	$ 90,000
Cost previously recovered $90,000/$145,200 × 36($500) =	(11,157)
Deduction	$ 78,843

---

[72]The life expectancies in Exhibit 4.1 apply for annuity investments made on or after July 1, 1986. See *General Rules for Pensions and Annuities*, IRS Publication 939 (Rev. April 2003), p. 25. See also *Pension and Annuity Income*, IRS Publication 575.

[73]§ 72(b).

EXHIBIT 4.1	Ordinary Life Annuities: One Life—Expected Return Multiples

Age	Multiple	Age	Multiple	Age	Multiple
5	76.6	42	40.6	79	10.0
6	75.6	43	39.6	80	9.5
7	74.7	44	38.7	81	8.9
8	73.7	45	37.7	82	8.4
9	72.7	46	36.8	83	7.9
10	71.7	47	35.9	84	7.4
11	70.7	48	34.9	85	6.9
12	69.7	49	34.0	86	6.5
13	68.8	50	33.1	87	6.1
14	67.8	51	32.2	88	5.7
15	66.8	52	31.3	89	5.3
16	65.8	53	30.4	90	5.0
17	64.8	54	29.5	91	4.7
18	63.9	55	28.6	92	4.4
19	62.9	56	27.7	93	4.1
20	61.9	57	26.8	94	3.9
21	60.9	58	25.9	95	3.7
22	59.9	59	25.0	96	3.4
23	59.0	60	24.2	97	3.2
24	58.0	61	23.3	98	3.0
25	57.0	62	22.5	99	2.8
26	56.0	63	21.6	100	2.7
27	55.1	64	20.8	101	2.5
28	54.1	65	20.0	102	2.3
29	53.1	66	19.2	103	2.1
30	52.2	67	18.4	104	1.9
31	51.2	68	17.6	105	1.8
32	50.2	69	16.8	106	1.6
33	49.3	70	16.0	107	1.4
34	48.3	71	15.3	108	1.3
35	47.3	72	14.6	109	1.1
36	46.4	73	13.9	110	1.0
37	45.4	74	13.2	111	.9
38	44.4	75	12.5	112	.8
39	43.5	76	11.9	113	.7
40	42.5	77	11.2	114	.6
41	41.5	78	10.6	115	.5

Simplified Method for Annuity Distributions from Qualified Retirement Plans

A simplified method is required for allocating basis to the annuity payments received under a qualified retirement plan.[74] The portion of each annuity payment that is excluded as a return of capital is the employee's investment in the contract divided by the number of anticipated monthly payments determined in accordance with Exhibit 4.2.[75]

---

[74]See Chapter 19.

[75]§ 72(d).

EXHIBIT 4.2	Number of Anticipated Monthly Annuity Payments under the Simplified Method

Age	Number of Anticipated Monthly Payments
55 and under	360
56–60	310
61–65	260
66–70	210
71 and over	160

EXAMPLE 41

Andrea, age 62, receives an annuity distribution of $500 per month for life from her qualified retirement plan beginning in January 2016. Her investment in the contract is $100,100. The excludible amount of each payment is $385 ($100,100 investment/260 monthly payments). Thus, $115 ($500 − $385) of each annuity payment is included in Andrea's gross income.

The rules for annuity payments received after the basis has been recovered by the annuitant and for the annuitant who dies before the basis is recovered are the same as under the exclusion ratio method discussed earlier.

4-4d Prizes and Awards

The fair market value of prizes and awards (other than scholarships exempted under § 117, to be discussed subsequently) must be included in gross income.[76] Therefore, TV giveaway prizes, magazine publisher prizes, door prizes, and awards from an employer to an employee in recognition of performance are fully taxable to the recipient.

A narrow exception permits a prize or an award to be excluded from gross income if *all* of the following requirements are satisfied:

- The prize or award is received in recognition of religious, charitable, scientific, educational, artistic, literary, or civic achievement (e.g., Nobel Prize, Pulitzer Prize, or faculty teaching award).
- The recipient transfers the prize or award to a qualified governmental unit or non-profit organization.
- The recipient was selected without any action on his or her part to enter the contest or proceeding.
- The recipient is not required to render substantial future services as a condition for receiving the prize or award.[77]

Because the transfer of the property to a qualified governmental unit or nonprofit organization ordinarily would be a charitable contribution (an itemized deduction as presented in Chapter 10), the exclusion produces beneficial tax consequences in the following situations:

- The taxpayer does not itemize deductions and thus would receive no tax benefit from the charitable contribution.
- The taxpayer's charitable contributions exceed the annual statutory ceiling on the deduction.

[76] § 74.
[77] § 74(b).

- Including the prize or award in gross income would reduce the amount of deductions the taxpayer otherwise would qualify for because of gross income limitations (e.g., the gross income test for a dependency exemption or the adjusted gross income limitation in calculating the medical expense deduction).

The taxpayer can avoid including prizes and awards in gross income by refusing to accept the prize or award.[78]

Another exception is provided for certain *employee achievement awards* in the form of tangible personal property (e.g., a gold watch). The awards must be made in recognition of length of service or safety achievement. Generally, the ceiling on the excludible amount for an employee is $400 per taxable year. However, if the award is a qualified plan award, the ceiling on the exclusion is $1,600 per taxable year.[79]

Yet one more exception to the taxability of prizes was added in 2016 to allow winners at the Olympic or Paralympic Games to exclude the value of the medal and any cash award. This tax advantage does not benefit all winners though, only those with income of $1 million or less. The rationale offered for this new tax preference is that the athletes "perform a valuable patriotic service."[80]

4-4e **Group Term Life Insurance**

For many years, the IRS did not attempt to tax the value of life insurance protection provided to an employee by the employer. Some companies took undue advantage of the exclusion by providing large amounts of insurance protection for executives. Therefore, Congress enacted § 79, which created a limited exclusion for `group term life insurance`. The premiums on the first $50,000 of group term life insurance protection are excludible from the employee's gross income.

The benefits of this exclusion are available only to employees. Proprietors and partners are not considered employees. The Regulations generally require broad-scale coverage of employees to satisfy the *group* requirement (e.g., shareholder-employees would not constitute a qualified group). The exclusion applies only to term insurance (protection for a period of time but with no cash surrender value) and not to ordinary life insurance (lifetime protection plus a cash surrender value that can be drawn upon before death).

As mentioned, the exclusion applies to the first $50,000 of group term life insurance protection. For each $1,000 of coverage in excess of $50,000, the employee must include the amounts indicated in Exhibit 4.3 in gross income.[81]

Finch Corporation has a group term life insurance policy with coverage equal to the employee's annual salary. Keith, age 52, is president of the corporation and receives an annual salary of $350,000. Keith must include $828 in gross income from the insurance protection for the year.

$$\frac{\$350,000 - \$50,000}{\$1,000} \times \$.23 \times 12 \text{ months} = \$828$$

EXAMPLE
42

Generally, the amount that must be included in gross income, computed from Exhibit 4.3, is much less than the price an individual would pay an insurance company for the same amount of protection. Thus, even the excess coverage provides some tax-favored income for employees when group term life insurance coverage exceeds $50,000.

If the plan discriminates in favor of certain key employees (e.g., officers), the key employees are not eligible for the exclusion. In such a case, the key employees must include in gross income the *greater* of actual premiums paid by the employer or the amount calculated from the Uniform Premiums in Exhibit 4.3. The other employees are still eligible for the $50,000 exclusion and continue to use the Uniform Premiums table to compute the income from excess insurance protection.[82]

---

[78]See Rev.Rul. 57–374, 1957–2 C.B. 69 and Rev.Proc. 87–54, 1987–2 C.B. 669.

[79]§ 74(c). Qualified plan awards are defined in § 274(j) and explained in *Business Expenses*, Chapter 2 (IRS Publication 535).

[80]P.L. 114-239 (10/7/16), adding § 74(d) effective for awards received after 2015. Also see H.R. Rep. No. 114–762 (9/20/16).

[81]Reg. § 1.79–3(d)(2).

[82]§ 79(d).

EXHIBIT 4.3	Uniform Premiums for $1,000 of Group Term Life Insurance Protection

Attained Age on Last Day of Employee's Tax Year	Cost per $1,000 of Protection for One-Month Period*
Under 25	$ .05
25–29	.06
30–34	.08
35–39	.09
40–44	.10
45–49	.15
50–54	.23
55–59	.43
60–64	.66
65–69	1.27
70 and above	2.06

*Reg. § 1.79–3, effective for coverage after June 30, 1999.

4-4f Unemployment Compensation

The unemployment compensation program is sponsored and operated by the states and Federal government to provide a source of income for people who have been employed and are temporarily (hopefully) out of work. In a series of rulings over a period of 40 years, the IRS exempted unemployment benefits from tax. These payments were considered social benefit programs for the promotion of the general welfare. After experiencing dissatisfaction with the IRS's treatment of unemployment compensation, Congress amended the Code to make the benefits taxable.[83]

4-4g Social Security Benefits

If a taxpayer's income exceeds a specified base amount, as much as 85 percent of Social Security retirement benefits must be included in gross income. The taxable amount of benefits is determined through the application of one of two formulas that utilize a unique measure of income—*modified adjusted gross income (MAGI)*.[84] MAGI is, for this purpose, the taxpayer's adjusted gross income from all sources (other than Social Security) plus the foreign earned income exclusion and any tax-exempt interest income.

In the formulas, two sets of base amounts are established. The first set is as follows:

- $32,000 for married taxpayers who file a joint return.
- $0 for married taxpayers who do not live apart for the entire year but file separate returns.
- $25,000 for all other taxpayers.

The second set of base amounts is as follows:

- $44,000 for married taxpayers who file a joint return.
- $0 for married taxpayers who do not live apart for the entire year but file separate returns.
- $34,000 for all other taxpayers.

---

[83]§ 85.

[84]§ 86. The rationale for taxing 85% of the Social Security benefits is as follows: for the average Social Security recipient, 15% of the amount received is a recovery of amounts that the individual paid into the program, and the remainder of the benefits is financed by the employer's contribution and interest earned by the Social Security trust fund.

If the sum of MAGI and 50 percent of Social Security benefits is less than or equal to the base amount from the first set of such amounts (using the applicable filing status), then none of the benefits are taxable. If MAGI plus one-half of Social Security benefits exceeds the first set of base amounts but not the second set, the taxable amount of Social Security benefits is the *lesser* of the following:

- .50(Social Security benefits).
- .50[MAGI + .50(Social Security benefits) − first base amount].

EXAMPLE 43

A married couple with adjusted gross income of $30,000, no tax-exempt interest, and $11,000 of Social Security benefits who file jointly must include $1,750 of the benefits in gross income. This works out as the lesser of the following:

1. .50($11,000) = $5,500.
2. .50[$30,000 + .50($11,000) − $32,000] = .50($3,500) = $1,750.

If instead the couple had adjusted gross income of $15,000 and their Social Security benefits totaled $5,000, none of the benefits would be taxable because .50[$15,000 + .50($5,000) − $32,000] is not a positive number.

If MAGI plus one-half of Social Security benefits exceeds the second set of base amounts, the taxable amount of Social Security benefits is the *lesser* of 1 or 2 below:

1. .85(Social Security benefits).
2. Sum of:
   a. .85[MAGI + .50(Social Security benefits) − second base amount], and
   b. Lesser of:
      - Amount included through application of the first formula.
      - $4,500 ($6,000 for married filing jointly).

EXAMPLE 44

A married couple who file jointly have adjusted gross income of $72,000, no tax-exempt interest, and $12,000 of Social Security benefits. Their includible Social Security benefits will be $10,200.
Include the lesser of the following:

1. .85($12,000) = $10,200.
2. Sum of:
   a. .85[$72,000 + .50($12,000) − $44,000] = $28,900, and
   b. Lesser of:
      - Amount calculated by the first formula, which is the lesser of:
        ‣ .50($12,000) = $6,000.
        ‣ .50[$72,000 + .50($12,000) − $32,000] = $23,000.
      - $6,000.

   The sum equals $34,900 ($28,900 + $6,000).

Because 85% of the Social Security benefits received is less than the $34,900 (the second formula amount), $10,200 is included in the couple's gross income.[85]

---

[85]To compute taxable benefits, a worksheet is provided in the instructions to Form 1040 at lines 20a and 20b and to Form 1040A at lines 14a and 14b, as well as in *Social Security and Railroad Retirement Benefits* (IRS Publication 915).

LO.5

Identify tax planning strategies for minimizing gross income.

4-5 TAX PLANNING

The materials in this chapter have focused on the following questions:

- What is income?
- When is the income recognized?
- Who is the taxpayer?

Planning strategies suggested by these materials include the following:

- Maximize economic benefits that are not included in gross income.
- Defer the recognition of income.
- Shift income to taxpayers who are in a lower marginal tax bracket.

Some specific techniques for accomplishing these strategies are discussed in the following paragraphs.

4-5a Tax Deferral

General

Because deferred taxes are tantamount to interest-free loans from the government, the deferral of taxes is a worthy goal of the tax planner. However, the tax planner must also consider the tax rates for the years the income is shifted from and to. For example, a one-year deferral of income from a year in which the taxpayer's tax rate was 28 percent to a year in which the tax rate will be 35 percent would not be advisable if the taxpayer expects to earn less than a 7 percent after-tax return on the deferred tax dollars.

The taxpayer can often defer the recognition of income from appreciated property by postponing the event triggering realization (the final closing on a sale or exchange of property). If the taxpayer needs cash, obtaining a loan by using the appreciated property as collateral may be a less costly alternative than selling the property.

EXAMPLE 45

Ira owns 100 shares of Pigeon Company common stock with a cost of $20,000 and a fair market value of $50,000. Although the stock's value has increased substantially in the past three years, Ira thinks the growth days are over. If he sells the Pigeon stock, Ira will invest the proceeds from the sale in other common stock. Assuming that Ira's marginal tax rate on the sale is 15%, he will have only $45,500 [$50,000 − .15($50,000 − $20,000)] to reinvest. The alternative investment must substantially outperform Pigeon in the future for the sale to be beneficial.

Selection of Investments

Because no tax is due until a gain has been recognized, the law favors investments that yield appreciation rather than annual income.

EXAMPLE 46

Vera can buy a corporate bond or an acre of land for $10,000. The bond pays $600 of interest (6%) each year, and Vera expects the land to increase in value 8% each year for the next 10 years. She is in the 40% (combined Federal and state) tax bracket for ordinary income and 26% for qualifying capital gains. Assuming that the bond would mature or the land would be sold in 10 years and Vera would reinvest the interest at a 6% before-tax return, she would accumulate the following amount at the end of 10 years:

continued

		Bond	Land
Original investment		$10,000	$10,000
Annual income	$ 600		
Less tax	(240)		
	$ 360		
Compound amount reinvested for			
10 years at 6%	×13.18	4,745	
		$14,745	
Compound amount, 10 years at 6%			× 1.79
			$17,900
Less tax on sale:			
26%($17,900 − $10,000)			(2,054)
			$15,846

Therefore, the value of the deferral that results from investing in the land rather than in the bond is $1,101 ($15,846 − $14,745).

Series EE bonds can also be purchased for long-term deferrals of income. In situations where the taxpayer's goal is merely to shift income one year into the future, bank certificates of deposit are useful tools. If the maturity period is one year or less, all interest is reported in the year of maturity. Bank certificates of deposit are especially useful for a taxpayer who realizes an unusually large gain from the sale of property in one year (and thus is in a high tax bracket) but expects his or her gross income to be less the following year.

Cash Basis

The timing of income from services can often be controlled through the use of the cash method of accounting. Although taxpayers are somewhat constrained by the constructive receipt doctrine (they cannot turn their backs on income), seldom will customers and clients offer to pay before they are asked. The usual lag between billings and collections (e.g., December's billings collected in January) will result in a continuous deferring of some income until the last year of operations. A salaried individual approaching retirement may contract with the employer before the services are rendered to receive a portion of compensation in the lower tax bracket retirement years.

Prepaid Income

For the accrual basis taxpayer who receives advance payments from customers, the transactions should be structured to avoid payment of tax on income before the time the income is actually earned. Revenue Procedure 2004–34 provides the guidelines for deferring the tax on prepayments for services and licensing of software and certain other items, and Regulation § 1.451–5 provides the guidelines for deferrals on sales of goods. In addition, both cash and accrual basis taxpayers can sometimes defer income by structuring the payments as deposits rather than prepaid income. For example, a landlord should require an equivalent damage deposit rather than prepayment of the last month's rent under the lease. Of course, the arrangement must meet the definition of a deposit for Federal tax purposes.[86]

---

[86]See *Commissioner v. Indianapolis Power and Light*, 494 U.S. 203 (1990).

4-5b **Reporting Conflicts**

The IRS relies upon businesses to report the amounts they paid to individuals for services. Employees receive a Form W–2, and independent contractors receive a Form 1099–MISC. The IRS attempts to match the forms they receive to the individual's income tax return. If the form submitted by the business and the individual's tax return are not in agreement, the individual has a problem, but innocent differences can occur and should be explained on the tax return.

Dr. Anders, a college professor on a cash basis, performs consulting services for Dove Corporation in early December 2017. In late December, Dove mailed a check in payment, but Anders did not receive the check until early January 2018. Dove sent Anders a Form 1099–MISC showing the payment date as 2017. If Anders did not report the income on his 2017 return, he could have a problem. Dr. Anders should include the income shown on the Form 1099–MISC and then subtract the same amount, noting that it should be properly included in 2018 income.

4-5c **Shifting Income to Relatives**

The tax liability of a family can be minimized by shifting income from higher- to lower-bracket family members. This can be accomplished through gifts of income-producing property. Furthermore, in many cases, income can be shifted with no negative effect on the family's investment plans.

Adam, who is in the 28% tax bracket, would like to save for his children's education. All of the children are under 19 years of age and are dependents of Adam. Adam could transfer income-producing properties to the children, and the children could each receive up to $1,050 of income each year (refer to Chapter 3) with no tax liability. The next $1,050 would be taxed at the child's tax rate. After a child has more than $2,100 of unearned income, there is no tax advantage to shifting more income to the child (because the income will be taxed at the parents' rate) until the child is 19 years old (or age 24 if a full-time student), when all income will be taxed according to the child's tax rate.

The Uniform Gifts to Minors Act, a model law adopted by all states (but with some variations among the states), facilitates income shifting. Under the Act, a gift of intangibles (e.g., bank accounts, stocks, bonds, and life insurance contracts) can be made to a minor but with an adult serving as custodian. Usually, a parent who makes the gift is also named as custodian. The state laws allow the custodian to sell or redeem and reinvest the principal and to accumulate or distribute the income, practically at the custodian's discretion provided there is no commingling of the child's income with the parent's property. Thus, the parent can give appreciated securities to the child, and the donor custodian can then sell the securities and reinvest the proceeds, thereby shifting both the gain and the annual income to the child. Such planning is limited by the tax liability calculation provision for a child under the age of 19 (or age 24 if a full-time student) (refer to Chapter 3).

U.S. government bonds (Series EE) can be purchased by parents for their children. When this is done, the children generally should file a return and elect to report the income on the accrual basis.

Abby pays $7,500 for Series EE bonds in 2017 and registers them in her son's name. The son, Wade, will enter college the year of original maturity of the bonds. The bonds have a maturity value of $10,000. Wade elects to report the annual increment in redemption value as income for each year the bonds are held. The first year the increase is $250, and Wade includes that amount in his gross income. If Wade has no other income, no tax will be due on the $250 bond interest because such an amount will be more than offset by his available standard deduction. The following year, the increment is $260, and Wade includes this amount in income. Thus, over the life of the bonds, Wade will include $2,500 in income ($10,000 − $7,500), none of which will result in a tax liability, assuming that he has no other income. However, if the election had not been made, Wade would have been required to include $2,500 in income on the bonds in the year of original maturity, if they had been redeemed as planned. This amount of income might result in a tax liability.

In some cases, it may be advantageous for the child not to make the accrual election. For example, a child under age 19 (or age 24 if a full-time student) with investment income of more than $2,100 each year and parents in the 25, 28, 33, 35, or 39.6 percent tax bracket would probably benefit from deferring the tax on the savings bond interest. The child would also benefit from the use of the usually lower tax rate (rather than subjecting the income to the parents' tax rate) if the bonds mature after the child is age 19 or older (or age 24 or older if a full-time student).

4-5d **Accounting for Community Property**

The classification of income as community or separate property becomes important when either of two events occurs:

- A married couple files separate income tax returns for the year.
- A married couple obtains a divorce and therefore must file separate returns for the year (refer to Chapter 3).

For planning purposes, it behooves married persons to keep track of the source of income (community or separate). To be in a position to do this effectively when income-producing assets are involved, it may be necessary to distinguish between separate and community property.[87]

4-5e **Alimony**

The person making the alimony payments favors a divorce settlement that includes a provision for deductible alimony payments. On the other hand, the recipient prefers that the payments not qualify as alimony. If the payor is in a higher tax bracket than the recipient, both parties may benefit by increasing the payments and structuring them so that they qualify as alimony.

EXAMPLE 50

Carl and Polly are negotiating a divorce settlement. Carl has offered to pay Polly $10,000 each year for 10 years, but payments would cease upon Polly's death. Polly is willing to accept the offer if the agreement will specify that the cash payments are not alimony. Carl is in the 35% tax bracket, and Polly's marginal rate is 15%.

If Carl and Polly agree that Carl will pay Polly $12,000 of alimony each year, both will have improved after-tax cash flows.

	Annual Cash Flows	
	Carl	Polly
Nonalimony payments	($10,000)	$10,000
Alimony payments	($12,000)	$12,000
Tax effects		
Tax savings [.35($12,000)]	4,200	
Tax cost [.15($12,000)]		(1,800)
After-tax cash flows	($ 7,800)	$10,200
Benefit of alimony option	$ 2,200	$ 200

Both parties benefit at the government's expense if the $12,000 alimony option is used.

---

[87]Being able to distinguish between separate and community property is crucial to the determination of a property settlement incident to a divorce. It also is vital in the estate tax area (refer to Chapter 1) because the surviving spouse's share of the community property is not included in the gross estate of the deceased spouse.

REFOCUS ON THE BIG PICTURE

CALCULATION OF GROSS INCOME

Using the accrual method of accounting, Dr. Cliff Payne has correctly calculated the gross income of his sole proprietorship. He will report the $385,000 amount on his tax return (Schedule C of Form 1040).

What If?

From a tax planning perspective, what can Dr. Payne do to decrease his gross income from the first year of operating his dental practice and thereby produce better financial results for him?

    Rather than adopt the accrual method of accounting, Dr. Payne should adopt the cash method of accounting because his dental practice is a service entity rather than a merchandising entity. His gross income for Federal income tax purposes under the cash method is calculated as follows:

Revenues	$385,000
Plus: Accounts receivable: January 1	–0–
Less: Accounts receivable: December 31	(52,000)
Gross income	$333,000

The cash method of accounting enables Dr. Payne to defer paying Federal income taxes on the unpaid accounts receivable. Furthermore, each year that Dr. Payne has accounts receivable at the end of the tax year, that income is continuously deferred. Thus, if his accounts receivable remain at $52,000 at the end of each tax year, by using the cash method of accounting rather than the accrual method, he will defer that amount of income until he terminates his practice.

BOB DAEMMRICH/PHOTOEDIT

Key Terms

Accounting income, 4-4

Accounting method, 4-6

Accrual method, 4-7

Alimony and separate maintenance payments, 4-19

Alimony recapture, 4-19

Annuity, 4-23

Assignment of income, 4-13

Cash receipts method, 4-7

Claim of right doctrine, 4-8

Community property, 4-17

Constructive receipt, 4-8

Economic income, 4-3

Fruit and tree metaphor, 4-13

Gross income, 4-2

Group term life insurance, 4-27

Hybrid method, 4-8

Imputed interest, 4-21

Income, 4-3

Original issue discount, 4-10

Partnership, 4-16

Recovery of capital doctrine, 4-3

S corporation, 4-16

Taxable year, 4-6

Discussion Questions

1. **LO.1** According to the Supreme Court, would it be good tax policy to use income as computed by financial accounting principles as the correct measure of income for Federal income tax purposes? Explain.

2. **LO.1** Compare and contrast the economist's concept used to recognize income with the concept employed in measuring taxable income.

3. **LO.1** Allen visits Reno, Nevada, once a year to gamble. This year his gambling loss   Issue ID
was $25,000. He commented to you, "At least I didn't have to pay for my air-
fare and hotel room. The casino paid that because I am such a good customer. That
was worth at least $3,000." What are the relevant tax issues for Allen?

4. **LO.1** Ben lost his job when his employer moved its plant. During the year, he collected unemployment benefits for three months, a total of $1,800. While he
was waiting to hear from prospective employers, he painted his house. If Ben had
paid someone else to paint his house, the cost would have been $3,000. The cost of
the paint Ben used was $800. What is Ben's gross income for tax purposes from the
above events?

5. **LO.1** Howard buys wrecked cars and stores them on his property. Recently, he   Issue ID
purchased a 1990 Ford Taurus for $400. If he can sell all of the usable parts,
his total proceeds from the Taurus will be over $2,500. As of the end of the year, he
has sold only the radio for $75 and he does not know how many, if any, of the
remaining parts will ever be sold. What are Howard's income recognition issues?

6. **LO.2, 3** On December 29, 2017, an employee received a $5,000 check from her
employer's client. The check was payable to the employer. The employee
did not remit the funds to the employer until December 30, 2017. The employer deposited the check on December 31, 2017, but the bank did not credit the employer's
bank account until January 2, 2018. When is the cash basis employer required to
include the $5,000 in gross income?

7. **LO.2** What is the purpose of the constructive receipt doctrine?

8. **LO.2** A Series EE U.S. government savings bond accrues 3.5% interest each year.
The bond matures in three years, at which time the principal and interest will
be paid. The bank will pay the taxpayer at a 3.5% interest rate each year if he agrees
to leave money on deposit for three years. What tax advantage does the Series EE
bond offer that is not available with the bank deposit?

9. **LO.2** The taxpayer performs services with payment due from the customer within
30 days. All customers pay within the time limit. What would be the benefit to
the taxpayer using the cash method of accounting rather than the accrual method?

10. **LO.3, 5** Wade paid $7,000 for an automobile that needed substantial repairs. He
worked nights and weekends to restore the car and spent $2,400 on parts
for it. He knows that he can sell the car for $13,000, but he is very wealthy and does
not need the money. On the other hand, his daughter, who has very little income,
needs money to make the down payment on a house.
   a. Would it matter, after taxes, whether Wade sells the car and gives the money to
his daughter or whether he gives the car to his daughter and she sells it for
$13,000? Explain.
   b. Assume that Wade gave the car to his daughter after he had arranged for
another person to buy it from his daughter. The daughter then transferred the
car to the buyer and received $13,000. Who is taxed on the gain?

11. **LO.3** Anita, a cash basis taxpayer, sued her former employer for wage discrimination. Her attorney agreed to pursue the case on a contingent fee basis—the
attorney would receive one-third of any settlement or court award. The parties
reached a settlement, and the attorney for Anita's former employer wrote a check
payable to Anita for $320,000 and a check payable to her attorney for $160,000.
Anita reasons that she and the attorney were partners in the lawsuit who shared
profits two-thirds and one-third, respectively. Therefore, she includes $320,000 in
her gross income. Is Anita's analysis correct? Explain.

12. **LO.3** Rex became a partner with a 30% interest in the partnership profits when he
invested $200,000. In 2017, the partnership generated $400,000 of taxable

income, and Rex withdrew $100,000. In 2018, the partnership had $600,000 of taxable income, and Rex withdrew $200,000. What is Rex's gross income from the partnership in 2017 and 2018?

13. **LO.4** The divorce agreement requires Alice to pay her former spouse $50,000 a year for the next ten years. Will the payments qualify as alimony? Why or why not?

Issue ID   14. **LO.4, 5** William and Abigail, who live in San Francisco, have been experiencing problems with their marriage. They have a 3-year-old daughter, April, who stays with William's parents during the day because both William and Abigail are employed. Abigail worked to support William while he attended medical school, and now she has been accepted by a medical school in Mexico. Abigail has decided to divorce William and attend medical school. April will stay in San Francisco because of her strong attachment to her grandparents and because they can provide her with excellent day care. Abigail knows that William will expect her to contribute to the cost of raising April. Abigail also believes that to finance her education, she must receive cash for her share of the property they accumulated during their marriage. In addition, she believes that she should receive some reimbursement for her contribution to William's support while he was in medical school. She expects the divorce proceedings to take several months. Identify the relevant tax issues for Abigail.

Decision Making   15. **LO.4, 5** Patrick and Eva are planning to divorce. Patrick has offered to pay Eva $12,000 each year until their 11-year-old daughter reaches age 21. Alternatively, Patrick will transfer to Eva common stock that he owns with a fair market value of $100,000. What factors should Eva and Patrick consider in deciding between these two options?

16. **LO.4** In the current year, the Rose Corporation made a $400,000 interest-free loan to John Rose, the corporation's controlling shareholder. Mr. Rose is also the corporation's chief executive officer and receives a salary of $300,000 a year. What are the tax consequences of classifying the loan as a compensation-related loan rather than as a corporation-shareholder loan?

17. **LO.4** Connor purchased an annuity that was to pay him a fixed amount each month for the remainder of his life. He began receiving payments in 2001, when he was 65 years old. In 2017, Connor was killed in an automobile accident. What are the effects of the annuity on Connor's final tax return?

18. **LO.4** An employer provides all of his employees with life insurance protection equal to twice the employee's annual salary. Melba, age 42, has an annual salary of $70,000. Is Melba required to recognize income even though she is still alive at the end of the year and thus nothing has been collected on the life insurance policy? Explain.

Issue ID   19. **LO.4** For a person who receives Social Security benefits, what effect, if any, can an increase in other income have on that person's taxable income?

Computational Exercises

20. **LO.2** On January 1, 2017, Kunto, a cash basis taxpayer, pays $46,228 for a 24-month certificate. The certificate is priced to yield 4% (the effective interest rate) with interest compounded annually. No interest is paid until maturity, when Kunto receives $50,000. In your computations:

a.   Compute Kunto's gross income from the certificate for 2017.

b.   Compute Kunto's gross income from the certificate for 2018.

Round any amounts to the nearest dollar.

21. **LO.2** Bigham Corporation, an accrual basis calendar year taxpayer, sells its services under 12-month and 24-month contracts. The corporation provides services to each customer every month. On July 1, 2017, Bigham sold the following customer contracts:

Length of Contract	Total Proceeds
12 months	$14,000
24 months	$24,000

Determine the income to be recognized in taxable income in 2017 and 2018.

Length of Contract	2017 Income	2018 Income
12 months	a. _____	c. _____
24 months	b. _____	d. _____

22. **LO.3** Simba and Zola are married but file separate returns. Simba received $80,000 of salary and $1,200 of taxable dividends on stock he purchased in his name and paid from the salary that he earned since the marriage. Zola collected $900 in taxable interest on a certificate of deposit she inherited from her aunt. Compute Zola's gross income under two assumptions as to the state of residency of the couple. If an amount is zero, enter "$0."

	Idaho (Community Property State)	South Carolina (Common Law State)
Dividends	a. _____	d. _____
Interest	b. _____	e. _____
Salary	c. _____	f. _____

23. **LO.4** Casper and Cecile are divorced this year. As part of the divorce settlement, Casper transferred stock to Cecile. Casper purchased the stock for $25,000, and it had a market value of $43,000 on the date of the transfer. Cecile sold the stock for $40,000 a month after receiving it. In addition, Casper is required to pay Cecile $1,500 a month in alimony. He made five payments to her during the year.

    What are the tax consequences for Casper and Cecile regarding these transactions?

    a. How much gain or loss does Casper recognize on the transfer of the stock?

    b. Does Casper receive a deduction for the $7,500 alimony paid?

    c. How much income does Cecile have from the $7,500 alimony received?

    d. When Cecile sells the stock, how much does she report?

24. **LO.4** Elizabeth made the following interest-free loans during the year. Assume that tax avoidance is not a principal purpose of any of the loans. Assume that the relevant Federal rate is 5% and that the loans were outstanding for the last six months of the year.

Borrower	Amount	Borrower's Net Investment Income	Purpose of Loan
Richard	$ 5,000	$800	Gift
Woody	8,000	600	Purchase stock
Irene	105,000	–0–	Purchase residence

What are the effects of the imputed interest rules on these transactions? Compute Elizabeth's gross income from each loan:

a.   Richard

b.   Woody

c.   Irene

25. **LO.4** A taxpayer, age 64, purchases an annuity from an insurance company for $50,000. She is to receive $300 per month for life. Her life expectancy is 20.8 years from the annuity starting date. Assuming that she receives $3,600 this year, what is the exclusion percentage and how much is included in her gross income? Round the exclusion percentage to two decimal places. Round the final answer for the income to the nearest dollar.

26. **LO.4** Compute the taxable Social Security benefits in each of the following situations:

a.   Erwin and Eleanor are married and file a joint tax return. They have adjusted gross income of $46,000, no tax-exempt interest, and $12,400 of Social Security benefits.

b.   Erwin and Eleanor have adjusted gross income of $12,000, no tax-exempt interest, and $16,000 of Social Security benefits.

c.   Erwin and Eleanor have adjusted gross income of $85,000, no tax-exempt interest, and $15,000 of Social Security benefits.

Problems

27. **LO.1** Determine the taxpayer's current-year (1) economic income and (2) gross income for tax purposes from the following events:

a.   Sam's employment contract as chief executive of a large corporation was terminated, and he was paid $500,000 not to work for a competitor of the corporation for five years.

b.   Elliot, a 6-year-old child, was paid $5,000 for appearing in a television commercial. His parents put the funds in a savings account for the child's education.

c.   Valery found a suitcase that contained $100,000. She could not determine who the owner was.

d.   Winn purchased a lottery ticket for $5 and won $750,000.

e.   Larry spent $1,000 to raise vegetables that he and his family consumed. The cost of the vegetables in a store would have been $2,400.

f.   Dawn purchased an automobile for $1,500 that was worth $3,500. The seller was in desperate need of cash.

Decision Making   28. **LO.1, 2, 5** Harper is considering three alternative investments of $10,000. Assume that the taxpayer is in the 25% marginal tax bracket for ordinary income and 15% for qualifying capital gains in all tax years. The selected investment will be liquidated at the end of five years. The alternatives are:

• A taxable corporate bond yielding 5.333% before tax and the interest can be reinvested at 5.333% before tax.

• A Series EE bond that will have a maturity value of $12,200 (a 4% before-tax rate of return).

• Land that will increase in value.

The gain on the land is classified and taxed as a long-term capital gain. The income from the bonds is taxed as ordinary income. How much must the land increase in value to yield a greater after-tax return than either of the bonds?

Use the future value tables in Appendix H as needed for your calculations and comparisons.

29. **LO.1** Determine the taxpayer's gross income for tax purposes in each of the following situations:

    a. Deb, a cash basis taxpayer, traded a corporate bond with accrued interest of $300 for corporate stock with a fair market value of $12,000 at the time of the exchange. Deb's cost of the bond was $10,000. The value of the stock had decreased to $11,000 by the end of the year.

    b. Deb needed $10,000 to make a down payment on her house. She instructed her broker to sell some stock to raise the $10,000. Deb's cost of the stock was $3,000. Based on her broker's advice, instead of selling the stock, she borrowed the $10,000 using the stock as collateral for the debt.

    c. Deb's boss gave her two tickets to the Rabid Rabbits rock concert because she met her sales quota. At the time she received the tickets, each ticket had a face price of $200 and was selling on eBay for $300. On the date of the concert, the tickets were selling for $250 each. Deb and her son attended the concert.

30. **LO.1, 2** Determine Amos's gross income in each of the following cases:

    a. In the current year, Amos purchased an automobile for $25,000. As part of the transaction, Amos received a $1,500 rebate from the manufacturer.

    b. Amos sold his business. In addition to the selling price of the stock, he received $50,000 for a covenant not to compete—an agreement that he will not compete with his former business for five years.

    c. Amos owned some land he held as an investment. As a result of a change in the zoning rules, the property increased in value by $20,000.

31. **LO.2, 5** Al is a medical doctor who conducts his practice as a sole proprietor. During 2017, he received cash of $280,000 for medical services. Of the amount collected, $40,000 was for services provided in 2016. At the end of 2017, Al had accounts receivable of $60,000, all for services rendered in 2017. In addition, at the end of the year, Al received $12,000 as an advance payment from a health maintenance organization (HMO) for services to be rendered in 2018. Compute Al's gross income for 2017:

    Decision Making

    a. Using the cash basis of accounting.

    b. Using the accrual basis of accounting.

    c. Advise Al on which method of accounting he should use.

32. **LO.2** Selma operates a contractor's supply store. She maintains her books using the cash method. At the end of the year, her accountant computes her accrual basis income that is used on her tax return. For 2017, Selma had cash receipts of $1.4 million, which included $200,000 collected on accounts receivable from 2016 sales. It also included the proceeds of a $100,000 bank loan. At the end of 2017, she had $250,000 in accounts receivable from customers, all from 2017 sales.

    a. Compute Selma's accrual basis gross receipts for 2017.

    b. Selma paid cash for all of the purchases. The total amount paid for merchandise in 2017 was $1.3 million. At the end of 2016, she had merchandise on hand with a cost of $150,000. At the end of 2017, the cost of merchandise on hand was $300,000. Compute Selma's gross income from merchandise sales for 2017.

Decision Making
Communications

33. **LO.2, 3, 5** Your client is a partnership, ARP Associates, which is an engineering consulting firm. Generally, ARP bills clients for services at the end of each month. Client billings are about $50,000 each month. On average, it takes 45 days to collect the receivables. ARP's expenses are primarily for salary and rent. Salaries are paid on the last day of each month, and rent is paid on the first day of each month. The partnership has a line of credit with a bank, which requires monthly financial statements. These must be prepared using the accrual method. ARP's managing partner, Amanda Sims, has suggested that the firm also use the accrual method for tax purposes and thus reduce accounting fees by $600. Assume that the partners are in the 35% (combined Federal and state) marginal tax bracket. Write a letter to your client explaining why you believe it would be worthwhile for ARP to file its tax return on the cash basis even though its financial statements are prepared on the accrual basis. ARP's address is 100 James Tower, Denver, CO 80208.

Communications

34. **LO.2** Trip Garage, Inc. (459 Ellis Avenue, Harrisburg, PA 17111), is an accrual basis taxpayer that repairs automobiles. In late December 2017, the company repaired Samuel Mosley's car and charged him $1,000. Samuel did not think the problem had been fixed and refused to pay; thus, Trip refused to release the automobile. In early January 2018, Trip made a few adjustments and convinced Samuel that the automobile was working properly. At that time, Samuel agreed to pay only $900 because he did not have the use of the car for a week. Trip said "fine," accepted the $900, and released the automobile to Samuel. An IRS agent thinks Trip, as an accrual basis taxpayer, should report $1,000 of income in 2017, when the work was done, and then deduct a $100 loss in 2018. Prepare a memo to Susan Apple, the treasurer of Trip, with the recommended treatment for the disputed income.

35. **LO.2** Determine the effects of the following on a cash basis taxpayer's gross income for 2017 and 2018.

   a. On the morning of December 31, 2017, the taxpayer received a $1,500 check from a customer. The taxpayer did not cash the check until January 3, 2018.

   b. The same as part (a), except the customer asked the taxpayer not to cash the check until January 3, 2018, after the customer's salary check could be deposited.

   c. The same as part (a), except that the check was not received until after the bank had closed on December 31, 2017.

36. **LO.2** Marlene, a cash basis taxpayer, invests in Series EE U.S. government savings bonds and bank certificates of deposit (CDs). Determine the tax consequences of the following on her 2017 gross income:

   a. On September 30, 2017, she cashed in Series EE bonds for $10,000. She purchased the bonds in 2007 for $7,090. The yield to maturity on the bonds was 3.5%.

   b. On July 1, 2016, she purchased a CD for $10,000. The CD matures on June 30, 2018, and will pay $10,816, thus yielding a 4% annual return.

   c. On July 1, 2017, she purchased a CD for $10,000. The maturity date on the CD was June 30, 2018, when Marlene would receive $10,300.

37. **LO.2** Drake Appliance Company, an accrual basis taxpayer, sells home appliances and service contracts. Determine the effect of each of the following transactions on the company's 2017 gross income assuming that the company uses any available options to defer its taxes.

   a. In December 2016, the company received a $1,200 advance payment from a customer for an appliance that Drake special ordered from the manufacturer. The appliance did not arrive from the manufacturer until January 2017, and Drake immediately delivered it to the customer. The sale was reported in 2017 for financial accounting purposes.

   b. In October 2017, the company sold a 6-month service contract for $240. The company also sold a 36-month service contract for $1,260 in July 2017.

c. On December 31, 2017, the company sold an appliance for $1,200. The company received $500 cash and a note from the customer for $700 and $260 interest, to be paid at the rate of $40 a month for 24 months. Because of the customer's poor credit record, the fair market value of the note was only $600. The cost of the appliance was $750.

38. **LO.2, 5** Freda is a cash basis taxpayer. In 2017, she negotiated her salary for 2018. Her employer offered to pay her $21,000 per month in 2018 for a total of $252,000. Freda countered that she would accept $10,000 each month for the 12 months in 2018 and the remaining $132,000 in January 2019. The employer accepted Freda's terms for 2018 and 2019.

  a. Did Freda actually or constructively receive $252,000 in 2018?

  b. What could explain Freda's willingness to spread her salary over a longer period of time?

  c. In December 2018, after Freda had earned the right to collect the $132,000 in 2019, the employer offered $133,000 to Freda at that time, rather than $132,000 in January 2019. The employer wanted to make the early payment so as to deduct the expense in 2018. Freda rejected the employer's offer. Was Freda in constructive receipt of the income in 2018? Explain.

39. **LO.2, 5** The Bluejay Apartments, a new development, is in the process of structuring its lease agreements. The company would like to set the damage deposits high enough that tenants will keep the apartments in good condition. The company is actually more concerned about damage than about tenants not paying their rent.

Decision Making

  a. Discuss the tax effects of the following alternatives:

   • $1,000 damage deposit with no rent prepayment.

   • $500 damage deposit and $500 rent for the final month of the lease.

   • $1,000 rent for the final two months of the lease and no damage deposit.

  b. Which option do you recommend? Why?

40. **LO.3** Rusty has been experiencing serious financial problems. His annual salary was $100,000, but a creditor garnished his salary for $20,000; so the employer paid the creditor (rather than Rusty) the $20,000. To prevent creditors from attaching his investments, Rusty gave his investments to his 21-year-old daughter, Rebecca. Rebecca received $5,000 in dividends and interest from the investments during the year. Rusty transferred some cash to a Swiss bank account that paid him $6,000 interest during the year. Rusty did not withdraw the interest from the Swiss bank account. Rusty also hid some of his assets in his wholly owned corporation that received $150,000 rent income but had $160,000 in related expenses, including a $20,000 salary paid to Rusty. Rusty reasons that his gross income should be computed as follows:

Salary received	$ 80,000
Loss from rental property ($150,000 − $160,000)	(10,000)
Gross income	$ 70,000

Compute Rusty's correct gross income for the year, and explain any differences between your calculation and Rusty's.

41. **LO.2, 3** Troy, a cash basis taxpayer, is employed by Eagle Corporation, also a cash basis taxpayer. Troy is a full-time employee of the corporation and receives a salary of $60,000 per year. He also receives a bonus equal to 10% of all collections from clients he serviced during the year. Determine the tax consequences of the following events to the corporation and to Troy:

  a. On December 31, 2017, Troy was visiting a customer. The customer gave Troy a $10,000 check payable to the corporation for appraisal services Troy performed during 2017. Troy did not deliver the check to the corporation until January 2018.

b.   The facts are the same as in part (a), except that the corporation is an accrual basis taxpayer and Troy deposited the check on December 31, but the bank did not add the deposit to the corporation's account until January 2018.

c.   The facts are the same as in part (a), except that the customer told Troy to hold the check until January 2018 when the customer could make a bank deposit that would cover the check.

42. **LO.3, 4** Faye, Gary, and Heidi each have a one-third interest in the capital and profits of the FGH Partnership. Each partner had a capital account of $50,000 at the beginning of the tax year. The partnership profits for the tax year were $270,000. Changes in their capital accounts during the tax year were as follows:

	Faye	Gary	Heidi	Total
Beginning balance	$ 50,000	$ 50,000	$ 50,000	$150,000
Withdrawals	(20,000)	(35,000)	(10,000)	(65,000)
Additional contributions	–0–	–0–	5,000	5,000
Allocation of profits	90,000	90,000	90,000	270,000
Ending balance	$120,000	$105,000	$135,000	$360,000

In arriving at the $270,000 of partnership profits, the partnership deducted $2,400 ($800 for each partner) in premiums paid for group term life insurance on the partners. Faye and Gary are 39 years old, and Heidi is 35 years old. Other employees are also eligible for group term life insurance equal to their annual salary. These premiums of $10,000 have been deducted in calculating the partnership profits of $270,000. Compute each partner's gross income from the partnership for the tax year.

43. **LO.3, 5** In 2017, Alva received dividends on her stocks as follows:

Amur Corporation (a French corporation whose stock is traded on an established U.S. securities market)	$60,000
Blaze, Inc., a Delaware corporation	40,000
Grape, Inc., a Virginia corporation	22,000

a.   Alva purchased the Grape stock three years ago, and she purchased the Amur stock two years ago. She purchased the Blaze stock 18 days before it went ex-dividend and sold it 20 days later at a $5,000 loss. Alva had no other capital gains and losses for the year. She is in the 35% marginal tax bracket. Compute Alva's tax on her dividend income for 2017.

b.   Alva's daughter, who is 25 and not Alva's dependent, had taxable income of $6,000, which included $1,000 of dividends on Grape, Inc. stock. The daughter had purchased the stock two years ago. Compute the daughter's tax liability on the dividends.

c.   Alva can earn 5% before-tax interest on a corporate bond or a 4% dividend on a preferred stock. Assuming that the appreciation in value is the same, which investment produces the greater after-tax income?

d.   The same as part (c), except that Alva's daughter is to make the investment.

44. **LO.3** Liz and Doug were divorced on December 31 of the current year after 10 years of marriage. Their current year's income received before the divorce was as follows:

Doug's salary	$41,000
Liz's salary	55,000
Rent on apartments purchased by Liz 15 years ago	8,000
Dividends on stock Doug inherited from his mother 4 years ago	1,900
Interest on a savings account in Liz's name funded with her salary	2,400

Allocate the income to Liz and Doug assuming that they live in:

a. California.

b. Texas.

45. **LO.4** Nell and Kirby are in the process of negotiating their divorce agreement. What should be the tax consequences to Nell and Kirby if the following, considered individually, became part of the agreement?

a. In consideration for her one-half interest in their personal residence, Kirby will transfer to Nell stock with a value of $200,000 and $50,000 of cash. Kirby's cost of the stock was $150,000, and the value of the personal residence is $500,000. They purchased the residence three years ago for $300,000.

b. Nell will receive $1,000 per month for 120 months. If she dies before receiving all 120 payments, the remaining payments will be made to her estate.

c. Nell is to have custody of their 12-year-old son, Bobby. She is to receive $1,200 per month until Bobby (1) dies or (2) attains age 21 (whichever occurs first). After either of these events occurs, Nell will receive only $300 per month for the remainder of her life.

46. **LO.4** Alicia and Rafel are in the process of negotiating a divorce agreement. They both worked during the marriage and contributed an equal amount to the marital assets. They own a home with a fair market value of $400,000 (cost of $300,000) that is subject to a mortgage of $250,000. They have lived in the home for 12 years. They also have investment assets with a cost of $160,000 and a fair market value of $410,000. Thus, the net worth of the couple is $560,000 ($400,000 − $250,000 + $410,000). The holding period for the investments is longer than one year. Alicia would like to continue to live in the house. Therefore, she has proposed that she receive the residence subject to the mortgage, a net value of $150,000. In addition, she would receive $17,600 each year for the next 10 years, which has a present value (at 6% interest) of $130,000. Rafel would receive the investment assets. If Rafel accepts this plan, he must sell one-half of the investments so that he can purchase a home. Assume that you are counseling Alicia. Explain to Alicia whether the proposed agreement would be "fair" on an after-tax basis.

Decision Making

47. **LO.4, 5** Roy decides to buy a personal residence and goes to the bank for a $150,000 loan. The bank tells him that he can borrow the funds at 4% if his father will guarantee the debt. Roy's father, Hal, owns a $150,000 CD currently yielding 3.5%. The Federal rate is 3%. Hal agrees to either of the following:

Decision Making

- Roy borrows from the bank with Hal's guarantee to the bank.
- Cash in the CD (with no penalty), and lend Roy the funds at 2% interest.

Hal is in the 33% marginal tax bracket. Roy, whose only source of income is his salary, is in the 15% marginal tax bracket. The interest Roy pays on the mortgage will be deductible by him. Which option will maximize the family's after-tax wealth?

48. **LO.2, 4** Ridge is a generous individual. During the year, he made interest-free loans to various family members when the Federal rate was 3%. What are the tax consequences of the following loans by Ridge:

a. On June 30, 2016, Ridge loaned $12,000 to his cousin, Jim, to buy a used truck. Jim's only source of income was his wages on various construction jobs during the year.

b. On August 1, 2016, Ridge loaned $8,000 to his niece, Sonja. The loan was to enable her to pay her college tuition. Sonja had $1,200 interest income from CDs her parents had given her.

c. On September 1, 2016, Ridge loaned $25,000 to his brother, Al, to start a business. Al had $220 of dividends and interest for the year.

d.   On September 30, 2016, Ridge loaned $150,000 to his mother so that she could enter a nursing home. His mother's only income was $9,000 of Social Security benefits and $500 of interest income.

49. **LO.4** Indicate whether the imputed interest rules should apply in the following situations. Assume that all of the loans were made at the beginning of the tax year unless otherwise indicated.

a.   Mike loaned his sister $90,000 to buy a new home. Mike did not charge interest on the loan. The Federal rate was 5%. Mike's sister had $900 of investment income for the year.

b.   Sam's employer maintains an emergency loan fund for its employees. During the year, Sam's wife was very ill, and he incurred unusually large medical expenses. He borrowed $8,500 from his employer's emergency loan fund for six months. The Federal rate was 5.5%. Sam and his wife had no investment income for the year.

c.   Jody borrowed $25,000 from her controlled corporation for six months. She used the funds to pay her daughter's college tuition. The corporation charged Jody 4% interest. The Federal rate was 5%. Jody had $3,500 of investment income for the year.

d.   Kait loaned her son, Jake, $60,000 for six months. Jake used the $60,000 to pay off college loans. The Federal rate was 5%, and Kait did not charge Jake any interest. Jake had dividend and interest income of $2,100 for the tax year.

50. **LO.4** Vito is the sole shareholder of Vito, Inc. He is also employed by the corporation. On June 30, 2017, Vito borrowed $8,000 from Vito, Inc., and on July 1, 2018, he borrowed an additional $10,000. Both loans were due on demand. No interest was charged on the loans, and the Federal rate was 4% for all relevant dates. Vito used the money to purchase a boat, and he had $2,500 of investment income. Determine the tax consequences to Vito and Vito, Inc., in each of the following situations:

a.   The loans are considered employer-employee loans.

b.   The loans are considered corporation-shareholder loans.

51. **LO.4** Pam retires after 28 years of service with her employer. She is 66 years old and has contributed $42,000 to her employer's qualified pension fund. She elects to receive her retirement benefits as an annuity of $3,000 per month for the remainder of her life.

a.   Assume that Pam retires in June 2017 and collects six annuity payments this year. What is her gross income from the annuity payments in the first year?

b.   Assume that Pam lives 25 years after retiring. What is her gross income from the annuity payments in the twenty-fourth year?

c.   Assume that Pam dies after collecting 160 payments. She collected eight payments in the year of her death. What are Pam's gross income and deductions from the annuity contract in the year of her death?

52. **LO.4** For each of the following, determine the amount that should be included in gross income:

a.   Peyton was selected the most valuable player in the Super Bowl. In recognition of this, he was awarded an automobile with a value of $60,000. Peyton did not need the automobile, so he asked that the title be put in his parents' names.

b.   Jacob was awarded the Nobel Peace Prize. When he was presented the check for $1.4 million, Jacob said, "I do not need the money. Give it to the United Nations to use toward the goal of world peace."

c.   Linda won the Craig County Fair beauty pageant. She received a $10,000 scholarship that paid her $6,000 for tuition and $4,000 for meals and housing for the academic year.

53. **LO.4** The LMN Partnership has a group term life insurance plan. Each partner has $150,000 of protection, and each employee has protection equal to twice his or her annual salary. Employee Alice (age 32) has $90,000 of insurance under the plan, and partner Kay (age 47) has $150,000 of coverage. Because the plan is a "group plan," it is impossible to determine the cost of coverage for an individual employee or partner.

    a. Assuming that the plan is nondiscriminatory, how much must Alice and Kay each include in gross income as a result of the partnership paying the insurance premiums?

    b. Assume that the partnership is incorporated. Kay becomes a shareholder and an employee who receives a $75,000 annual salary. The corporation provides Kay with $150,000 of group term life insurance coverage under a nondiscriminatory plan. What is Kay's gross income as a result of the corporation paying the insurance premiums?

54. **LO.2, 4** Herbert was employed for the first six months of 2017 and earned $90,000 in salary. During the next six months, he collected $8,800 of unemployment compensation, borrowed $12,000 (using his personal residence as collateral), and withdrew $2,000 from his savings account (including $60 of interest). He received dividends of $550. His luck was not all bad, for in December, he won $1,500 in the lottery on a $5 ticket. Calculate Herbert's gross income.

55. **LO.4, 5** Linda and Don are married and file a joint return. In 2017, they received $12,000 in Social Security benefits and $35,000 in taxable pension benefits and interest.

    Decision Making

    a. Compute the couple's adjusted gross income on a joint return.

    b. Don would like to know whether they should sell for $100,000 (at no gain or loss) a corporate bond that pays 8% in interest each year and use the proceeds to buy a $100,000 nontaxable State of Virginia bond that will pay $6,000 in interest each year.

    c. If Linda in part (a) works part-time and earns $30,000, how much will Linda and Don's adjusted gross income increase?

56. **LO.4** Charles E. Bennett, age 64, will retire next year and is trying to decide whether to begin collecting his Social Security benefits at that time. His monthly benefits will increase if he defers his starting date for the benefits. He has asked you to estimate how much his income tax will increase as a result of collecting Social Security. Charles and his wife Bernice B., file a joint return, have no other dependents, and claim the standard deduction. Their only income other than the Social Security benefits are:

Interest and dividends	$ 6,000
Taxable pension	$40,000

    The Social Security benefits for the year would be $12,000.

    a. Complete Worksheet 1, Figuring Your Taxable Benefits, included in IRS Publication 915 to determine the taxable portion of this couple's taxable Social Security benefits (the publication includes a blank worksheet).

    b. What is the taxable portion of the $12,000 in Social Security benefits?

57. **LO.3, 4** Donna does not think she has an income tax problem but would like to discuss her situation with you just to make sure there is no unexpected tax liability. Base your suggestions on the following relevant financial information:

    a. Donna's share of the SAT Partnership income is $150,000, but none of the income can be distributed because the partnership needs the cash for operations.

    b. Donna's Social Security benefits totaled $8,400, but Donna loaned the cash received to her nephew.

c.   Donna assigned to a creditor the right to collect $1,200 of interest on some bonds she owned.

d.   Donna and her husband lived together in California until September, when they separated. Donna has heard rumors that her husband had substantial gambling winnings since they separated.

Cumulative Problems

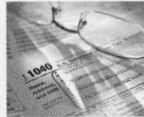

Tax Return Problem

Decision Making

Communications

TAX SOFTWARE

58. Daniel B. Butler and Freida C. Butler, husband and wife, file a joint return. The Butlers live at 625 Oak Street in Corbin, KY 40701. Dan's Social Security number is 111-11-1112, and Freida's is 123-45-6789. Dan was born on January 15, 1965, and Freida was born on August 20, 1966.

During 2016, Dan and Freida furnished over half of the total support of each of the following individuals, all of whom still live at home:

a.   Gina, their daughter, age 22, a full-time student, who married on December 21, 2016, has no income of her own and for 2016 did not file a joint return with her husband, Casey, who earned $10,600 during 2016. Gina's Social Security number is 123-45-6788.

b.   Sam, their son, age 20, who had gross income of $6,300 in 2016, dropped out of college in October 2016. He had graduated from high school in May 2016. Sam's Social Security number is 123-45-6787.

c.   Ben, their oldest son, age 26, is a full-time graduate student with gross income of $5,200. Ben's Social Security number is 123-45-6786.

Dan was employed as a manager by WJJJ, Inc. (employer identification number 11-1111111, 604 Franklin Street, Corbin, KY 40702), and Freida was employed as a salesperson for Corbin Realty, Inc. (employer identification number 98-7654321, 899 Central Street, Corbin, Ky 40701). Selected information from the W–2 Forms provided by the employers is presented below. Dan and Freida use the cash method.

Line	Description	Dan	Freida
1	Wages, tips, other compensation	$74,000	$86,000
2	Federal income tax withheld	11,000	12,400
17	State income tax withheld	2,960	3,440

Freida sold a house on December 30, 2016, and will be paid a commission of $3,100 (not included in the $86,000 reported on the W–2) on the January 10, 2017 closing date.

Other income (as reported on 1099 Forms) for 2016 consisted of the following:

Dividends on CSX stock (qualified)	$4,200
Interest on savings at Second Bank	1,600
Interest on City of Corbin bonds	900
Interest on First Bank CD	382

The $382 from First Bank was original issue discount. Dan and Freida collected $16,000 on the First Bank CD that matured on September 30, 2016. The CD was purchased on October 1, 2014, for $14,995, and the yield to maturity was 3.3%.

Dan received a Schedule K–1 from the Falcon Partnership, which showed his distributive share of income as $7,000. In addition to the above information, Dan and Freida's itemized deductions included the following:

Paid on 2016 Kentucky income tax	$ 700
Personal property tax paid	600
Real estate taxes paid	1,800
Interest on home mortgage (Corbin S&L)	4,900
Cash contributions to the Boy Scouts	800

Sales tax from the sales tax table is $1,860. Dan and Freida made Federal estimated tax payments of $8,000. All members of the family had health insurance coverage for all of 2016. Dan and Freida do not wish to contribute to the Presidential Election Campaign. The Kentucky income tax rate is 4%.

Part 1—Tax Computation
Compute Dan and Freida's 2016 Federal income tax payable (or refund due). If you use tax forms for your computations, you will need Form 1040 and Schedules A, B, and E. Suggested software: H&R BLOCK Tax Software.

Part 2—Tax Planning
Dan plans to reduce his work schedule and work only half-time for WJJJ in 2017. He has been writing songs for several years and wants to devote more time to developing a career as a songwriter. Because of the uncertainty in the music business, however, he would like you to make all computations assuming that he will have no income from songwriting in 2017. To make up for the loss of income, Freida plans to increase the amount of time she spends selling real estate. She estimates that she will be able to earn $90,000 in 2017. Assume that all other income and expense items will be approximately the same as they were in 2016. Assume that Sam will be enrolled in college as a full-time student for the summer and fall semesters. Will the Butlers have more or less disposable income (after Federal income tax) in 2017? Write a letter to the Butlers that contains your advice, and prepare a memo for the tax files.

59. Cecil C. Seymour is a 64-year-old widower. He had income for 2017 as follows:　　　Tax Computation Problem

Pension from former employer	$39,850
Interest income from Alto National Bank	5,500
Interest income on City of Alto bonds	4,500
Dividends received from IBM stock held for over one year	2,000
Collections on annuity contract he purchased from Great Life Insurance	5,400
Social Security benefits	14,000
Rent income on townhouse	9,000

The cost of the annuity was $46,800, and Cecil was expected to receive a total of 260 monthly payments of $450. Cecil has received 22 payments through 2017.

　　Cecil's 40-year-old daughter, Sarah C. Seymour, borrowed $60,000 from Cecil on January 2, 2017. She used the money to start a new business. Cecil does not charge her interest because she could not afford to pay it, but he does expect to collect the principal eventually. Sarah is living with Cecil until the business becomes profitable. Except for housing, Sarah provides her own support from her business and $1,600 in dividends on stocks that she inherited from her mother.

　　Other relevant information is presented below:

* Expenses on rental townhouse:

Utilities	$2,800
Maintenance	1,000
Depreciation	2,000
Real estate taxes	750
Insurance	700

* State income taxes paid: $3,500
* County personal property taxes paid: $2,100
* Payments on estimated 2016 Federal income tax: $5,900
* Charitable contributions of cash to Alto Baptist Church: $6,400
* Federal interest rate: 6%
* Sales taxes paid: $912

Compute Cecil's 2017 Federal income tax payable (or refund due).

Research Problems

Note: Solutions to the Research Problems can be prepared by using the Thomson Reuters Checkpoint® Student Edition online tax research database, which accompanies this textbook. Solutions can also be prepared by using research materials found in a typical tax library.

Communications   **Research Problem 1.** Tranquility Funeral Home, Inc., your client, is an accrual basis taxpayer that sells preneed funeral contracts. Under these contracts, the customer pays in advance for goods and services to be provided at the contract beneficiary's death. These payments are refundable at the contract purchaser's request, pursuant to state law, anytime until the goods and services are furnished. Tranquility, consistent with its financial accounting reporting, includes the payments in income for the year the funeral service is provided. The IRS agent insists that the payments be prepaid income subject to tax in the year of receipt. Your client believes that the amounts involved are customer deposits. Write a letter to Tranquility that contains your advice about how the issue should be resolved. The client's address is 400 Rock Street, Memphis, TN 38152.

Research Problem 2. Your client was the beneficiary of an annuity contract purchased by her stepmother. When the stepmother died, the insurance company paid the client $400,000 and sent her a Form 1099 indicating that the taxable portion (i.e., the amount in excess of the investment in the contract) was $50,000. However, according to the client, her father fraudulently convinced her that he was the intended beneficiary. She gave her father a check equal to the amount she had received from the insurance company. She did not report any of the annuity proceeds in her income tax return. She later discovered the fraud and filed a lawsuit to collect from her father. The IRS has examined your client's return and has taken the position that she must include the $50,000 in her gross income.

Evaluate the IRS's position.

Research Problem 3. Your client owns a life insurance policy on his life. He has paid $6,800 in premiums, and the cash surrender value of the policy is $30,000. He borrowed $30,000 from the insurance company, using the cash surrender value as collateral. He is considering canceling the policy in payment of the loan. He would like to know the tax consequences of canceling his policy.

Research Problem 4. Your client is a new retailer who often issues store gift (debit) cards to customers in lieu of a cash refund. You recall that the IRS issued a Revenue Procedure that provided that the prepaid income rules in Revenue Procedure 2004–34 could be applied to the income from the gift cards. Locate the Revenue Procedure authorizing the deferral of the income from gift cards.

Use internet tax resources to address the following questions. Look for reliable websites and blogs of the IRS and other government agencies, media outlets, businesses, tax professionals, academics, think tanks, and political outlets.

Research Problem 5. Lottery winnings are taxable for Federal income tax purposes. What many lottery hopefuls forget to factor into their tax considerations are that lottery winnings are also taxable in many states. Search the internet to see whether you can determine whether lottery winnings are taxable for California residents.

Communications   **Research Problem 6.** Go to the web page of a consulting firm that offers counseling services to individuals as they negotiate the terms of a divorce. What specific tax-related services do these firms offer? Suggest a new tax-related service the consulting firm could offer.

Roger CPA Review Questions

1. Smith, an individual, is required to pay Goode yearly alimony of $6,000 and yearly child support of $18,000. Smith paid Goode $20,000 in 2017. Smith's 2017 W–2 income was $50,000. Considering only the foregoing facts, what should Smith's adjusted gross income be for 2017?

   a. $30,000
   b. $45,000
   c. $48,000
   d. $50,000

2. Which of the following is excluded from gross income on an individual's 2017 tax return?

   a. January 2018 rent received in December 2017
   b. Value arising from personal use of company vehicle in 2017
   c. Dividends announced by a C corporation in December 2016 and received in January 2017
   d. Refundable security deposit received in January 2017 for a lease ending in July 2018

3. Walters, an individual, received the following in 2017:

W–2 income	$10,000
Federal tax refund for 2016	1,250
Scholarship stipend, in return for teaching assistant duties performed	25,000
Cash inheritance from deceased great-uncle	5,000

   Considering only the above, what is Walters' 2017 gross income?

   a. $35,000
   b. $36,250
   c. $15,000
   d. $16,250

4. Doran, a single individual, received $20,000 in Social Security benefits in 2017. Doran's 2017 provisional income (income plus half of the Social Security) was $65,000. Considering only these facts, what should Doran report as gross income on Doran's 2017 tax return?

   a. $75,000
   b. $72,000
   c. $57,000
   d. $65,000

5. On October 1, 2017, Cruz purchased an annuity for $90,000 in post-tax dollars, effective immediately, that pays Cruz $500 a month until death. At the date of purchase, Cruz's official life expectancy was 25 years. How much of Cruz's 2017 annuity payments should be included in Cruz's gross income for 2017?

   a. $0
   b. $900
   c. $600
   d. $1,500

Gross Income: Exclusions

LEARNING OBJECTIVES: *After completing Chapter 5, you should be able to:*

LO.1 Recognize that statutory authority is required to exclude an item from gross income.

LO.2 Identify the circumstances under which various items are excludible from gross income.

LO.3 Determine the extent to which receipts can be excluded under the tax benefit rule.

LO.4 Describe the circumstances under which income must be reported from the discharge of indebtedness.

LO.5 Identify tax planning strategies for obtaining the maximum benefit from allowable exclusions.

CHAPTER OUTLINE

EXCLUSIONS

Paul is a graduate student in the last semester of the accounting program at State University. This past summer he was an intern with a CPA firm, working in the compliance area. Paul was paid well enough for his work as an intern that he was able to pay for his meals and lodging and to save some for school. The CPA firm was so pleased with Paul's work that at the conclusion of his internship, he was given a bonus of $1,500 more than the firm had agreed to pay him. The extra amount was intended to help with his graduate school expenses. The CPA firm has offered him a full-time job after he completes his graduate program in December.

Because of his excellent academic record, the university awarded Paul a graduate assistantship that waives his tuition of $6,000 per semester and pays him $400 per month. Paul is required to teach a principles of accounting course each semester. Paul has used the $400 per month for books and for room and board.

In November, Paul was crossing a street in the pedestrian crosswalk when a delivery van struck him. The driver of the truck had a blood alcohol level of .12. Paul suffered a severe injury to his right arm that delayed his starting date for work by three months. The delivery company's insurance company settled the case by paying damages, itemized as follows:

Compensatory damages:	
Medical expenses	$ 30,000
Injury to Paul's right arm	100,000
Pain and suffering	50,000
Loss of income	15,000
Legal fees	25,000
Punitive damages	160,000
	$380,000

Paul's mother was with him in the crosswalk. Fortunately, the van did not hit her, and she was not physically injured. But she did suffer emotional distress and received $25,000 in the settlement.

Besides being Paul's friend, you also are a senior accounting major and have a keen interest in taxation. You tell Paul that you will look into the tax consequences of the settlement.

Read the chapter and formulate your response.

FRAMEWORK 1040 **Tax Formula for Individuals**

This chapter covers the boldfaced portions of the Tax Formula for Individuals that was introduced in Concept Summary 3.1 on p. 3-3. Below those portions are the sections of Form 1040 where the results are reported.

Income *(broadly defined)*	$xx,xxx
Less: Exclusions	(x,xxx)

FORM 1040 (p. 1)

8b	**Tax-exempt** interest. **Do not** include on line 8a . . .	**8b**

Gross income..	$xx,xxx

FORM 1040 (p. 1)

10	Taxable refunds, credits, or offsets of state and local income taxes . . . .
19	Unemployment compensation . . . .
21	Other income. List type and amount _____

Less: Deductions *for* adjusted gross income	(x,xxx)
Adjusted gross income...	$xx,xxx
Less: The greater of total itemized deductions *or* the standard deduction..............................	(x,xxx)
Personal and dependency exemptions	(x,xxx)
Taxable income	$xx,xxx
Tax on taxable income *(see Tax Tables or Tax Rate Schedules)*	$ x,xxx
Less: Tax credits *(including income taxes withheld and prepaid)*...	(xxx)
Tax due (or refund)	$ xxx

C hapter 4 discussed the concepts and judicial doctrines that affect the determination of gross income. If an income item is within the all-inclusive definition of gross income, the item can be excluded only if the taxpayer can locate specific authority for doing so. Chapter 5 focuses on the exclusions Congress has authorized.

LO.1

Recognize that statutory authority is required to exclude an item from gross income.

5-1 STATUTORY AUTHORITY

Sections 101 through 150 provide the authority for excluding specific items from gross income. Each exclusion has its own legislative history and reason for enactment. Certain exclusions are intended as a form of indirect welfare payments. Other exclusions prevent double taxation of income or provide incentives for socially desirable activities (e.g., nontaxable interest on certain U.S. government bonds where the owner uses the funds for educational expenses).

In some cases, Congress has enacted exclusions to rectify the effects of judicial decisions or IRS pronouncements.[1] For example, in the past, the IRS and some courts interpreted gross income to include payments the taxpayer received from his or her insurance policy to cover temporary living expenses after the person's residence was destroyed by fire. Although the IRS's and the courts' reasoning may have been a sound interpretation of the meaning of gross income, Congress determined that taxing the person under such dire circumstances was bad policy. Therefore, in 1969, Congress enacted § 123, which exempts from tax the insurance proceeds received for extraordinary living expenses when the taxpayer's home has been destroyed by fire or other casualty.[2]

---

[1]See Chapter 1, Example 28.

[2]P.L. 91–172, Tax Reform Act of 1969, Senate Report No. 91–552.

At times, Congress responds to specific events. For example, in 2001, Congress enacted § 139, Disaster Relief Payment, to ensure that victims of a *qualified disaster* (disaster resulting from a terrorist attack, Presidentially declared disaster, or common carrier accident of a catastrophic nature) would not be required to include in gross income payments received for living expenses, funeral expenses, and property damage resulting from the disaster.

For some types of transactions, the IRS does not tax what is in fact income because the revenue involved is not worth the collection effort or it is too difficult to measure the income. For example, in 2002, the IRS announced it would not attempt to tax the value of frequent flier miles earned on airline tickets purchased for business use.

5-2 GIFTS AND INHERITANCES

LO.2

Identify the circumstances under which various items are excludible from gross income.

5-2a Legislative Intent

Beginning with the Income Tax Act of 1913 and continuing to the present, Congress has allowed the recipient of a gift to exclude the value of the property from gross income. The exclusion applies to gifts made during the life of the donor (*inter vivos* gifts) and transfers that take effect upon the death of the donor (bequests and inheritances).[3] However, as discussed in Chapter 4, the recipient of a gift of income-producing property is subject to tax on the income subsequently earned from the property. Also, as discussed in Chapter 1, the donor or the decedent's estate may be subject to gift or estate taxes on the transfer.

In numerous cases, gifts are made in a business setting. For example, a salesperson gives a purchasing agent free samples, an employee receives cash from his or her employer upon retirement, or a corporation makes payments to employees who were victims of a natural disaster. In these and similar instances, it is frequently unclear whether the payment was a gift or represents compensation for past, present, or future services.

The courts have defined a gift as "a voluntary transfer of property by one to another without adequate [valuable] consideration or compensation therefrom."[4] If the payment is intended to be for services rendered, it is not a gift, even though the payment is made without legal or moral obligation and the payor receives no economic benefit from the transfer. To qualify as a gift, the payment must be made "out of affection, respect, admiration, charity or like impulses."[5] Thus, the cases on this issue have been decided on the basis of the donor's intent.

In a landmark case, *Comm. v. Duberstein*,[6] the taxpayer (Duberstein) received a Cadillac from a business acquaintance. Duberstein had supplied the businessman with the names of potential customers with no expectation of compensation. The Supreme Court concluded:

> ... despite the characterization of the transfer of the Cadillac by the parties [as a gift] and the absence of any obligation, even of a moral nature, to make it, it was at the bottom a recompense for Duberstein's past service, or an inducement for him to be of further service in the future.

Duberstein was therefore required to include the fair market value of the automobile in gross income.

5-2b Employer Payments to Employees

In the case of cash or other property *received by an employee* from his or her employer, Congress has eliminated any ambiguity. Transfers from an employer to an employee cannot be excluded as a gift.[7]

---

[3]§ 102.

[4]*Estate of D. R. Daly*, 3 B.T.A. 1042 (1926).

[5]*Robertson v. U.S.*, 52–1 USTC ¶9343, 41 AFTR 1053, 72 S.Ct. 994 (USSC, 1952).

[6]60–2 USTC ¶9515, 5 AFTR 2d 1626, 80 S.Ct. 1190 (USSC, 1960).

[7]§ 102(c). But see § 139 for qualified disaster situations.

EXAMPLE 1

Return to the facts of *The Big Picture* on p. 5-1. The $1,500 bonus paid to Paul by his summer employer was compensation for his services rather than a gift, even though the employer had not contracted to pay this additional amount. This results because the payment was most likely not motivated by the employer's generosity, but rather was made as a result of business considerations. Even if the payment had been made out of generosity, because the payment was received from his employer, Paul could not exclude the "gift."

5-2c Employee Death Benefits

Frequently, an employer makes payments (death benefits) to a deceased employee's surviving spouse, children, or other beneficiaries. If the decedent had a nonforfeitable right to the payments (e.g., the decedent's accrued salary), the amounts are generally taxable to the recipient as if the employee had lived and collected the payments. But when the employer makes voluntary payments, the gift issue arises. Generally, the IRS considers such payments to be compensation for prior services rendered by the deceased employee.[8] However, some courts have held that payments to an employee's surviving spouse or other beneficiaries are gifts if the following are true:[9]

- The payments were made to the surviving spouse and children rather than to the employee's estate.
- The employer derived no benefit from the payments.
- The surviving spouse and children performed no services for the employer.
- The decedent had been fully compensated for services rendered.
- Payments were made pursuant to a board of directors' resolution that followed a general company policy of providing payments for families of deceased employees (but not exclusively for families of shareholder-employees).

When all of the above conditions are satisfied, the payment is presumed to have been made *as an act of affection or charity*. When one or more of these conditions is not satisfied, the surviving spouse and children may still be deemed the recipients of a gift if the payment is made in light of the survivors' financial needs.[10]

Income earned by an employee that was not received by the employee prior to his or her death is not an employee death benefit. These earnings are referred to as "income in respect of a decedent"[11] and are generally taxable income to the decedent's beneficiary. This is another rare instance where the beneficiary of the income, rather than the person who earned the income, is subject to tax. For another such situation, see the discussion of Alimony and Separate Maintenance Payments in text Section 4-4a.

5-3 LIFE INSURANCE PROCEEDS

5-3a General Rule

Life insurance proceeds paid to the beneficiary because of the death of the insured are exempt from income tax.[12]

EXAMPLE 2

Mark purchases an insurance policy on his life and names his wife, Linda, as the beneficiary. Mark pays $45,000 in premiums. When he dies, Linda collects the insurance proceeds of $200,000. The $200,000 is exempt from Federal income tax.

---

[8]Rev.Rul. 62–102, 1962–2 C.B. 37.

[9]*Estate of Sydney J. Carter v. Comm.*, 72–1 USTC ¶9129, 29 AFTR 2d 332, 453 F.2d 61 (CA–2, 1972), and the cases cited there.

[10]*Simpson v. U.S.*, 58–2 USTC ¶9923, 2 AFTR 2d 6036, 261 F.2d 497 (CA–7, 1958), *cert. denied* 79 S.Ct. 724 (USSC, 1958).

[11]§ 691.

[12]§ 101(a).

Congress chose to exempt life insurance proceeds for the following reasons:

- For family members, life insurance proceeds serve much the same purpose as a nontaxable inheritance.
- In a business context (as well as in a family situation), life insurance proceeds replace an economic loss suffered by the beneficiary.

Gold Corporation purchases a life insurance policy to cover its key employee. If the proceeds were taxable, the corporation would require more insurance coverage to pay the tax as well as to cover the economic loss of the employee.

EXAMPLE 3

Thus, in general, Congress concluded that making life insurance proceeds exempt from income tax was a good policy.

5-3b **Accelerated Death Benefits**

Generally, if the owner of a life insurance policy cancels the policy and receives the cash surrender value, the taxpayer must recognize gain equal to the excess of the amount received over premiums paid on the policy (a loss is not deductible). The gain is recognized because the general exclusion provision for life insurance proceeds applies only to life insurance proceeds paid upon the death of the insured. If the taxpayer cancels the policy and receives the cash surrender value, the life insurance policy is treated as an investment by the insured.

In a limited circumstance, however, the insured is permitted to receive the benefits of the life insurance contract without having to include the gain in gross income. Under the **accelerated death benefits** rules, exclusion treatment is available for insured taxpayers who are either terminally ill or chronically ill.[13] A terminally ill taxpayer can collect the cash surrender value of the policy from the insurance company or assign the policy proceeds to a qualified third party. The resulting gain, if any, is excluded from the insured's gross income. A *terminally ill* individual is a person whom a medical doctor certifies as having an illness that is reasonably expected to cause death within 24 months.

In the case of a chronically ill patient, no gain is recognized if the proceeds of the policy are used for the long-term care of the insured. A person is *chronically ill* if he or she is certified as being unable to perform without assistance certain activities of daily living. These exclusions for the terminally ill and the chronically ill are available only to the insured. Thus, a person who purchases a life insurance policy from the insured does not qualify.

Accelerated Death Benefits

Tom owned a term life insurance policy at the time he was diagnosed as having a terminal illness. After paying $5,200 in premiums, he sold the policy to Amber Benefits, Inc., a company that is authorized by the state of Virginia to purchase such policies. Amber paid Tom $50,000. When Tom died six months later, Amber collected the face amount of the policy, $75,000. Tom is not required to include the $44,800 gain ($50,000 − $5,200) on the sale of the policy in his gross income.

EXAMPLE 4

Assume that Amber Benefits, Inc. in Example 4 paid additional premiums of $4,000 during the six months it owned the policy. When Amber collects the life insurance proceeds of $75,000, it must include the $21,000 gain [$75,000 proceeds − ($50,000 cost + $4,000 additional premiums paid)] in gross income.

EXAMPLE 5

---

[13]§ 101(g).

ETHICS & EQUITY   Should the Terminally Ill Pay Social Security Taxes?

The rationale for excluding accelerated death benefits from the gross income of the terminally ill is that they often use the funds to pay medical expenses and other costs associated with dying and do not have the ability to pay tax on the gain from the accelerated receipt of the life insurance proceeds. Yet the wages of a terminally ill person who is employed (or profits of a self-employed person) are subject to Social Security taxes. The Social Security taxes are intended to pay for retirement benefits, but a terminally ill person is unlikely to collect any Social Security benefits.

Several bills have been introduced in Congress to exempt the terminally ill from the Social Security tax. Evaluate the equity of the current tax treatment versus that in the proposed legislation.

5-3c Transfer for Valuable Consideration

A life insurance policy (other than one associated with accelerated death benefits) may be transferred after it is issued by the insurance company. If the policy is *transferred for valuable consideration*, the insurance proceeds are includible in the gross income of the transferee to the extent the proceeds received exceed the amount paid for the policy by the transferee plus any subsequent premiums paid.

EXAMPLE 6

Adam pays premiums of $4,000 for an insurance policy that has a face amount of $10,000 on the life of Beth and subsequently transfers the policy to Carol for $6,000. Upon Beth's death, Carol receives the proceeds of $10,000. The amount Carol can exclude from gross income is limited to $6,000 plus any premiums she paid subsequent to the transfer.

The Code, however, provides five exceptions to the rule illustrated in the preceding example. These exceptions permit exclusion treatment for transfers to the following:

1. The insured under the policy.
2. A partner of the insured.
3. A partnership in which the insured is a partner.
4. A corporation in which the insured is an officer or a shareholder.
5. A transferee whose basis in the policy is determined by reference to the transferor's basis.

The fifth exception applies to policies that were transferred in a tax-free exchange or were received by gift.[14]

EXAMPLE 7

When Logan's daughter Emily was born, he purchased an insurance policy on her life. Twenty-four years later after Emily graduated from college and married, Logan sold her the policy for its fair value. When Emily dies, the transfer for consideration rules will not apply.

Because the transfer was to the insured, the policy proceeds will be excluded from the recipient's gross income. The results would be the same if Logan gave (rather than sold) the policy to Emily.

Investment earnings arising from the reinvestment of life insurance proceeds are generally subject to income tax. Often the beneficiary will elect to collect the insurance proceeds in installments. The annuity rules (discussed in text Section 4-4c) are used to apportion the installment payment between the principal element (excludible) and the interest element (includible).[15]

---

[14]See the discussion of gifts in Chapter 14 and tax-free exchanges in Chapters 15 and 20. In the case of a gift, the donor's basis becomes the donee's basis.

[15]Reg. §§ 1.72–7(c)(1) and 1.101–7T.

5-4 SCHOLARSHIPS

5-4a General Information

Payments or benefits received by a student at an educational institution may be (1) compensation for services, (2) a gift, or (3) a scholarship. If the payments or benefits are received as compensation for services (past or present), the fact that the recipient is a student generally does not render the amounts received nontaxable.[16] Thus, a university teaching or research assistant is generally considered an employee, and his or her stipend is taxable compensation for services rendered. On the other hand, athletic scholarships generally are nontaxable when the individual is not required to participate in the sport.[17] In general, amounts received to be used for educational purposes (other than amounts received from family members) cannot be excluded as gifts because conditions attached to the receipt of the funds mean that the payments were not made out of "detached generosity."

The scholarship rules are intended to provide exclusion treatment for education-related benefits that cannot qualify as gifts but are not compensation for services. According to the Regulations, "a scholarship is an amount paid or allowed to, or for the benefit of, an individual to aid such individual in the pursuit of study or research."[18] The recipient must be a candidate for a degree at an educational institution.[19]

Terry enters a contest sponsored by a local newspaper. Each contestant is required to submit an essay on local environmental issues. The prize is one year's tuition at State University. Terry wins the contest. The newspaper has a legal obligation to Terry (as contest winner). Thus, the benefits are not a gift. However, because the tuition payment aids Terry in pursuing her studies, the payment is a scholarship.

As an exception to the compensation for services, nonprofit educational institutions can provide qualified tuition reduction plans for their employees and the employees can exclude the tuition from their gross income. The exclusion also applies to tuition reductions granted to the employee's spouse and the employee's dependent children.[20]

A scholarship recipient may exclude from gross income the amount used for tuition and related expenses (fees, books, supplies, and equipment required for courses), provided the conditions of the grant do not require that the funds be used for other purposes.[21]

Athletic scholarships are generally exempt from income because they are granted to assist the student in his or her education and are not considered a payment for services. In 2015, the NCAA began permitting athletic scholarships to include a "cost of attendance" amount. Now, in addition to tuition, fees, books, and room and board, the scholarship can include expenses such as academic-related supplies, transportation, and other similar items. The value of these benefits may differ from campus to campus. Only the amounts received for tuition, books, and supplies can be excluded from gross income.

Kelly received an athletic scholarship from State University. The scholarship pays her tuition, $9,000, and books and supplies, $2,400. She also received $4,500 a year for costs of attendance, which she uses to pay for housing, food, laundry, and transportation.

The tuition and the cost of books and supplies are excluded from gross income as a scholarship. The $4,500 received as costs of attendance does not qualify for the scholarship exclusion; therefore, Kelly must include that amount in her gross income.

---

[16]Reg. § 1.117–2(a). See *C. P. Bhalla*, 35 T.C. 13 (1960), for a discussion of the distinction between a scholarship and compensation. See also *Bingler v. Johnson*, 69–1 USTC ¶9348, 23 AFTR 2d 1212, 89 S.Ct. 1439 (USSC, 1969). For potential exclusion treatment, see the subsequent discussion of qualified tuition reductions.

[17]Rev.Rul. 77–263, 1977–2 C.B. 47.

[18]Prop.Reg. § 117–6(c)(3)(i).

[19]§ 117(a).

[20]§ 117(d).

[21]§ 117(b).

Some employers make scholarships available solely to the children of key employees. The tax objective of these plans is to provide a nontaxable fringe benefit to the executives by making the payment to the child in the form of an excludible scholarship. However, the IRS has ruled that the payments are generally includible in the gross income of the parent-employee.[22]

5-4b **Timing Issues**

Frequently, the scholarship recipient is a cash basis taxpayer who receives the money in one tax year but pays the educational expenses in a subsequent year. The amount eligible for exclusion may not be known at the time the money is received. In that case, the transaction is held *open* until the educational expenses are paid.[23]

EXAMPLE 10

In August 2017, Sanjay received $10,000 as a scholarship for the academic year 2017–2018. Sanjay's expenditures for tuition, books, and supplies were as follows:

August–December 2017	$3,000
January–May 2018	4,500
	$7,500

Sanjay's gross income for 2018 includes $2,500 ($10,000 − $7,500) that is not excludible as a scholarship. None of the scholarship is included in his gross income in 2017.

The Big Picture

EXAMPLE 11

Return to the facts of *The Big Picture* on p. 5-1. Paul was paid $400 a month by the university for teaching. This is reasonable compensation for his services. Although he received the assistantship because of his excellent academic record, the monthly payment of $400 must be included in his gross income because it is compensation for his services. However, the $6,000 graduate tuition reduction can be excluded from gross income.

5-5 **COMPENSATION FOR INJURIES AND SICKNESS**

5-5a **Damages**

A person who suffers harm caused by another is often entitled to compensatory damages. The tax consequences of the receipt of damages depend on the type of harm the taxpayer has experienced. The taxpayer may seek recovery for (1) a loss of income, (2) expenses incurred, (3) property destroyed, or (4) personal injury.

Generally, reimbursement for a loss of income is taxed the same as the income replaced (see the exception under Personal Injury below). The recovery of an expense is not income unless the expense was deducted. Damages that are a recovery of the taxpayer's previously deducted expenses are generally taxable under the tax benefit rule, discussed later in this chapter.

A payment for damaged or destroyed property is treated as an amount received in a sale or exchange of the property. Thus, the taxpayer has a realized gain if the damages received exceed the property's basis. Damages for personal injuries receive special treatment under the Code.

Personal Injury

The legal theory of personal injury damages is that the amount received is intended "to make the plaintiff [the injured party] whole as before the injury."[24] It follows that if the

---

[22]Rev.Rul. 75–448, 1975–2 C.B. 55; *Richard T. Armantrout*, 67 T.C. 996 (1977).

[23]Prop.Reg. § 1.117–6(b)(2).

[24]*C. A. Hawkins*, 6 B.T.A. 1023 (1928).

damages payments received were subject to tax, the after-tax amount received would be less than the actual damages incurred and the injured party would not be "whole as before the injury." In terms of personal injury damages, a distinction is made between compensatory damages and punitive damages.

ETHICS & EQUITY **Tax Treatment of Damages Not Related to Physical Personal Injury**

An individual who prevails in a personal injury claim for something other than a physical injury or sickness must include the amount of the award or settlement in gross income. In contrast, an award or settlement for a physical personal injury or sickness can be excluded (except for punitive damages) from gross income. Should damages awarded for a physical personal injury or sickness be treated more favorably than damages awarded for emotional distress or other nonphysical personal injuries such as age and sex discrimination?

Compensatory damages are intended to compensate the taxpayer for the damages incurred. Only those compensatory damages received on account of *physical personal injury or physical sickness* can be excluded from gross income.[25] Such exclusion treatment includes amounts received for loss of income associated with the physical personal injury or physical sickness. Compensatory damages awarded on account of emotional distress are not received on account of physical injury or physical sickness and thus cannot be excluded (except to the extent of any amount received for medical care) from gross income. Likewise, any amounts received for age discrimination or injury to one's reputation cannot be excluded.

Punitive damages are amounts the person who caused the harm must pay to the victim as punishment for outrageous conduct. Punitive damages are not intended to compensate the victim, but rather to punish the party who caused the harm. Thus, it follows that amounts received as punitive damages may actually place the victim in a better economic position than before the harm was experienced. Thus, punitive damages are included in gross income.

These rules are set forth in Concept Summary 5.1.

Concept Summary 5.1

Taxation of Damages

Type of Claim	Taxation of Award or Settlement
Breach of contract (generally loss of income)	Taxable.
Property damages	Gain to the extent damages received exceed basis. A loss is deductible for business property and investment property to the extent of basis over the amount realized. A loss may be deductible for personal use property (see discussion of casualty losses in Chapter 7).
Personal injury	
Physical	All compensatory amounts are excluded unless previously deducted (e.g., medical expenses). Amounts received as punitive damages are included in gross income.
Nonphysical	Compensatory damages and punitive damages are included in gross income.

---

[25]§ 104(a)(2).

The Big Picture

EXAMPLE 12

Return to the facts of *The Big Picture* on p. 5-1. The damages Paul received were awarded as a result of a physical personal injury. Therefore, all of the compensatory damages can be excluded. Note that even the compensation for the loss of income of $15,000 can be excluded. The punitive damages Paul received, however, must be included in his gross income.

Paul's mother did not suffer a personal physical injury or sickness. Therefore, the $25,000 she received must be included in her gross income.

ETHICS & EQUITY   Classifying the Amount of the Claim

Lee was injured in an automobile accident caused by a negligent driver of a commercial vehicle. Lee threatened to file a lawsuit against the company for $100,000 in damages for his physical injury and $100,000 for punitive damages. The company's insurer would not pay punitive damages. Therefore, the company advised Lee to revise his claim for $150,000 in physical damages and no punitive damages. Should Lee accept the offer?

5-5b Wrongful Incarceration

Section 139F, enacted in 2015, exempts amounts received as damages for being wrongfully incarcerated. The exclusion applies to the individual who was convicted of a Federal or state crime but is later exonerated.

5-5c Workers' Compensation

State workers' compensation laws require the employer to pay fixed amounts for specific job-related injuries. The state laws were enacted so that the employee will not have to go through the ordeal of a lawsuit (and possibly not collect damages because of some defense available to the employer) to recover the damages. Although the payments are intended, in part, to compensate for a loss of future income, Congress has specifically exempted workers' compensation benefits from inclusion in gross income.[26]

5-5d Accident and Health Insurance Benefits

The income tax treatment of accident and health insurance benefits depends on whether the policy providing the benefits was purchased by the taxpayer or the taxpayer's employer. Benefits collected under an accident and health insurance policy *purchased by the taxpayer* are excludible even though the payments are a substitute for income.[27]

Exempt Benefits

EXAMPLE 13

Bonnie purchases a medical and disability insurance policy. The insurance company pays Bonnie $1,000 per week to replace wages she loses while in the hospital. Although the payments serve as a substitute for income, the amounts received are tax-exempt benefits collected under Bonnie's insurance policy.

EXAMPLE 14

Joe's injury results in a partial paralysis of his left foot. He receives $20,000 for the injury from his accident insurance company under a policy he had purchased. The $20,000 accident insurance proceeds are tax-exempt.

---

[26]§ 104(a)(1).   [27]§ 104(a)(3).

A different set of rules applies if the accident and health insurance protection was *purchased by the individual's employer*, as discussed in the following section.

5-6 EMPLOYER-SPONSORED ACCIDENT AND HEALTH PLANS

Congress encourages employers to provide employees, retired former employees, and their dependents with accident and health benefits, disability insurance, and long-term care plans. The *premiums* are deductible by the employer and excluded from the employee's income.[28] Although § 105(a) provides the general rule that the employee has includible income when he or she collects the insurance *benefits*, two exceptions are provided.

Section 105(b) generally excludes payments received for medical care of the employee, spouse, and dependents. However, if the payments are for expenses that do not meet the Code's definition of medical care,[29] the amount received must be included in gross income. In addition, the taxpayer must include in gross income any amounts received for medical expenses that were deducted by the taxpayer on a prior return.

In 2017, Tab's employer-sponsored health insurance plan pays $4,000 for hair transplants that do not meet the Code's definition of medical care. Tab must include the $4,000 in his gross income for 2017.

EXAMPLE 15

Section 105(c) excludes payments for the permanent loss or the loss of the use of a member or function of the body or the permanent disfigurement of the employee, the spouse, or a dependent. Payments that are a substitute for salary (e.g., related to the period of time absent) are includible.

Jill loses an eye in an automobile accident unrelated to her work. As a result of the accident, Jill incurs $2,000 of medical expenses, which she deducts on her return. She collects $10,000 from an accident insurance policy carried by her employer. The benefits are paid according to a schedule of amounts that vary with the part of the body injured (e.g., $10,000 for loss of an eye and $20,000 for loss of a hand). Because the payment is for loss of a *member or function of the body*, the $10,000 is excluded from gross income. Jill is absent from work for a week as a result of the accident. Her employer provides her with insurance for the loss of income due to illness or injury. Jill collects $500, which is includible in gross income.

EXAMPLE 16

5-6a Medical Reimbursement Plans

In lieu of providing the employee with insurance coverage for hospital and medical expenses, the employer may agree to reimburse the employee for these expenses. The amounts received through the insurance coverage (insured plan benefits) are excluded from income under § 105 (as previously discussed). Unfortunately, in terms of cost considerations, the insurance companies that issue this type of policy usually require a broad coverage of employees. An alternative is to have a plan that is not funded with insurance (a self-insured arrangement). The benefits received under a self-insured plan can be excluded from the employee's income if the plan does not discriminate in favor of highly compensated employees.[30]

---

[28]§ 106, Reg. § 1.106–1, and Rev.Rul. 82–196, 1982–1 C.B. 106.

[29]See the discussion of medical care in Chapter 10.

[30]§ 105(h). Also see § 106 and Rev.Rul. 61–146, 1961–2 C.B. 25. Employers should make sure such reimbursement plans fall within the requirements

of the Affordable Care Act to avoid an excise tax. See § 4980D, Notice 2013–54, 2013–40 I.R.B. 287 and Notice 2015–17, 2015–10 I.R.B. 845.

There is also an alternative means of accomplishing a medical reimbursement plan. The employer can purchase a medical insurance plan with a high deductible (e.g., the employee is responsible for the first $2,600 of the family's medical expenses) and then make contributions to the employee's Health Savings Account (HSA).[31] The employer can make contributions each month up to the maximum contribution of 100 percent of the deductible amount. The monthly deductible amount is limited to one-twelfth of $3,400 under a high-deductible plan for self-only coverage. The monthly amount for an individual who has family coverage is limited to one-twelfth of $6,750 under a high-deductible plan. Withdrawals from the HSA must be used to reimburse the employee for the medical expenses paid by the employee that are not covered under the high-deductible plan. The employee is not taxed on the employer's contributions to the HSA, the earnings on the funds in the account, or the withdrawals made for medical expenses.[32]

5-6b **Long-Term Care Insurance Benefits**

Generally, long-term care insurance, which covers expenses such as the cost of care in a nursing home, is treated the same as accident and health insurance benefits. Thus, the employee does not recognize income when the employer pays the premiums. Also, the individual who purchases his or her own policy can exclude the benefits from gross income. However, statutory limitations (indexed for inflation) exist for the following amounts:

- Premiums paid by the employer.
- Benefits collected under the employer's plan.
- Benefits collected from the individual's policy.

The employer or insurance company generally provides the employee with information on the amount of his or her taxable benefits. The maximum amount excluded must be reduced by any amount received from third parties (e.g., Medicare, Medicaid).[33]

EXAMPLE 17

Hazel, who suffers from Alzheimer's disease, is a patient in a nursing home for the last 30 days of 2017. While in the nursing home, she incurs total costs of $7,600. Medicare pays $3,500 of the costs. Hazel receives $7,600 from her long-term care insurance policy, which pays while she is in the facility.

The amount Hazel may exclude is calculated as follows:

Greater of:		
Daily statutory amount in 2017 ($360 × 30 days)	$10,800	
Actual cost of the care	7,600	$10,800
Less: Amount received from Medicare		(3,500)
Amount of exclusion		$ 7,300

Therefore, Hazel must include $300 ($7,600 − $7,300) of the long-term care benefits received in her gross income.

The exclusion for long-term care insurance is not available if it is provided as part of a cafeteria plan or a flexible spending plan (explained later in the chapter).

---

[31] §§ 106(d) and 223. See additional coverage in Chapter 10.

[32] §§ 106(d), 223(b), and 223(d). The amounts for 2016 were $3,350 and $6,750.

[33] §§ 7702B and 213(d)(10). See IRS Publication 525 for the taxable and non-taxable amounts that the employer is required to report on the employee's W–2.

5-7 MEALS AND LODGING

5-7a General Rules for the Exclusion

As discussed in Chapter 4, income can take any form, including meals and lodging. However, § 119 excludes from income the value of meals and lodging provided to the employee and the employee's spouse and dependents under the following conditions:[34]

- The meals and/or lodging are *furnished* by the employer on the employer's *business premises* for the *convenience of the employer*.
- In the case of lodging, the *employee is required* to accept the lodging as a condition of employment.

The courts have interpreted these requirements strictly.

Furnished by the Employer

The following two questions have been raised with regard to the *furnished by the employer* requirement:

- Who is considered an *employee*?
- What is meant by *furnished*?

The IRS and some courts have reasoned that because a partner is not an employee, the exclusion does not apply to a partner. However, the Tax Court and the Fifth Circuit Court of Appeals have ruled in favor of the taxpayer on this issue.[35]

The Supreme Court held that a cash meal allowance was ineligible for the exclusion because the employer did not actually furnish the meals.[36] Similarly, one court denied the exclusion where the employer paid for the food and supplied the cooking facilities but the employee prepared the meal.[37]

On the Employer's Business Premises

The *on the employer's business premises* requirement, applicable to both meals and lodging, has resulted in much litigation. The Regulations define business premises as simply "the place of employment of the employee."[38] Thus, the Sixth Circuit Court of Appeals held that a residence, owned by the employer and occupied by an employee, two blocks from the motel that the employee managed was not part of the business premises.[39] However, the Tax Court considered an employer-owned house across the street from the hotel that was managed by the taxpayer to be on the business premises of the employer.[40] Apparently, the closer the lodging is to the business operations, the more likely the convenience of the employer is served.

For the Convenience of the Employer

The *convenience of the employer* test is intended to focus on the employer's motivation for furnishing the meals and lodging rather than on the benefits received by the employee. If the employer furnishes the meals and lodging primarily to enable the

---

[34]§ 119(a). The meals and lodging are also excluded from FICA and FUTA tax. *Rowan Companies, Inc. v. U.S.*, 81–1 USTC ¶9479, 48 AFTR 2d 81–5115, 101 S.Ct. 2288 (USSC, 1981).

[35]Rev.Rul. 80, 1953–1 C.B. 62; *Comm. v. Doak*, 56–2 USTC ¶9708, 49 AFTR 1491, 234 F.2d 704 (CA–4, 1956); but see *G. A. Papineau*, 16 T.C. 130 (1951); *Armstrong v. Phinney*, 68–1 USTC ¶9355, 21 AFTR 2d 1260, 394 F.2d 661 (CA–5, 1968).

[36]*Comm. v. Kowalski*, 77–2 USTC ¶9748, 40 AFTR 2d 6128, 98 S.Ct. 315 (USSC, 1977).

[37]*Tougher v. Comm.*, 71–1 USTC ¶9398, 27 AFTR 2d 1301, 441 F.2d 1148 (CA–9, 1971).

[38]Reg. § 1.119–1(c)(1).

[39]*Comm. v. Anderson*, 67–1 USTC ¶9136, 19 AFTR 2d 318, 371 F.2d 59 (CA–6, 1966).

[40]*J. B. Lindeman*, 60 T.C. 609 (1973).

employee to perform his or her duties properly, it does not matter that the employee considers these benefits to be a part of his or her compensation.

The Regulations give the following examples in which the tests for excluding meals are satisfied:[41]

- A restaurant requires its service staff to eat their meals on the premises during the busy lunch and breakfast hours.

- A bank furnishes meals on the premises for its tellers to limit the time the employees are away from their booths during the busy hours.

- A worker is employed at a construction site in a remote part of Alaska. The employer must furnish meals and lodging due to the inaccessibility of other facilities.

Required as a Condition of Employment

The *employee is required to accept* test applies only to lodging. If the employee's use of the housing would serve the convenience of the employer but the employee is not required to use the housing, the exclusion is not available.

EXAMPLE 18

Khalid is the manager of a large apartment complex. The employer requires Khalid to live on the premises but does not charge him rent. The rental value of his apartment is $9,600 a year. Although Khalid considers the rent-free housing a significant benefit, he is not required to include the value of the housing in his gross income.

ETHICS & EQUITY Employee Meals

Some companies famous for their products, such as Google, Facebook, and Twitter, are also famous for the perks they offer their employees. One of these benefits is free meals on the business premises. Part of the rationale for providing the food is that employees may not have food alternatives close by and business discussions may be more likely to happen when employees do not have to leave the premises. Such reasoning is intended to allow the meals to fit within the statutory exclusion of being "for the convenience of the employer." Whether excluding these meals from the employees' income will survive IRS and congressional scrutiny is uncertain. If these employees are allowed to exclude their meals from gross income, should employees whose employers do not provide meals be permitted to deduct the cost of their meals?

5-7b Other Housing Exclusions

An employee of an educational institution may be able to exclude the value of campus housing provided by the employer. Generally, the employee does not recognize income if he or she pays annual rents equal to or greater than 5 percent of the appraised value of the facility. If the rent payments are less than 5 percent of the value of the facility, the deficiency must be included in gross income.[42]

Ministers of the gospel and other religious leaders can exclude (1) the rental value of a home furnished as compensation; (2) a rental allowance paid to them as compensation, to the extent the allowance is used to rent, buy, or provide a home; or (3) the rental value of a home owned by the minister.[43] The housing or housing allowance must be provided as compensation for the conduct of religious worship, the administration

---

[41]Reg. § 1.119–1(f).

[42]§ 119(d).

[43]§ 107 and Reg. § 1.107–1.

and maintenance of religious organizations, or the performance of teaching and administrative duties at theological seminaries.

Military personnel are allowed housing exclusions under various circumstances. Authority for these exclusions generally is found in Federal laws that are not part of the Internal Revenue Code.[44]

5-8 EMPLOYEE FRINGE BENEFITS

Benefits other than wages and salary that are provided to employees by the employer are often referred to as fringe benefits . Generally, Congress decided that the availability of these benefits serves social goals. Moreover, the income tax exclusion will provide an incentive for employees to bargain for these fringe benefits in lieu of cash, thus increasing the use of this form of compensation. For example, if the employee is in the 25 percent marginal tax bracket, $100 of nontaxable fringe benefits is equivalent to $133 ($100/(1 − .25) = $133) in taxable compensation. From the employer's perspective then, it costs only $100 to provide $133 in value to that employee in the form of a tax-favored fringe benefit.

In Chapter 4 and earlier in this chapter, various fringe benefits were discussed (e.g., group term life insurance, accident and health insurance, and meals and lodging). Other employee benefits are discussed below.

5-8a **Specific Benefits**

Congress has dealt specifically with some other fringe benefits, which are summarized below.

- The employee does not have to include in gross income the value of child and dependent care services paid for by the employer and incurred to enable the employee to work. The exclusion cannot exceed $5,000 per year ($2,500 if married and filing separately). For a married couple, the annual exclusion cannot exceed the earned income of the spouse who has the lesser amount of earned income. For an unmarried taxpayer, the exclusion cannot exceed the taxpayer's earned income.[45]

- The value of the use of a gymnasium or other athletic facilities by employees, their spouses, and their dependent children may be excluded from an employee's gross income. The facilities must be on the employer's premises, and substantially all of the use of the facilities must be by employees and their family members.[46]

- Qualified employer-provided educational assistance (tuition, fees, books, and supplies) at the undergraduate and graduate level is excludible from gross income. The exclusion does not cover meals, lodging, and transportation costs. In addition, it does not cover educational payments for courses involving sports, games, or hobbies. The exclusion is subject to an annual employee statutory ceiling of $5,250.[47]

- The employee can exclude from gross income up to $13,570 of expenses incurred to adopt a child where the adoption expenses are paid or reimbursed by the employer under a qualified adoption assistance program.[48] The limit on the exclusion is the same even if the child has special needs (is not physically or mentally capable of caring for himself or herself). However, for a child with special needs, the $13,570 exclusion from gross income applies

---

[44]H. Rep. No. 99–841, 99th Cong., 2d Sess., p. 548 (1986). See § 134 and *Armed Forces Tax Guide* (IRS Publication 3).

[45]§ 129. The exclusion applies to the same types of expenses that, if paid by the employee (and not reimbursed by the employer), would be eligible for the credit for child and dependent care expense discussed in Chapter 13.

[46]§ 132(j)(4).

[47]§ 127.

[48]§ 137. A credit is also available under § 23, as discussed in Chapter 13.

even if the actual adoption expenses are less than that amount. For 2017, the exclusion is phased out as adjusted gross income increases from $203,540 to $243,540.

5-8b Cafeteria Plans

Generally, if an employee is offered a choice between cash and some other form of compensation, the employee is deemed to have constructively received the cash even when the noncash option is elected. As a result, the employee has gross income regardless of the option chosen.

An exception to this constructive receipt treatment is provided under the cafeteria plan rules. Under such a plan, the employee is permitted to choose between cash and nontaxable benefits (e.g., group term life insurance, health and accident protection, child care). If the employee chooses the otherwise nontaxable benefits, the cafeteria plan rules enable the benefits to remain nontaxable.[49] Cafeteria plans provide tremendous flexibility in tailoring the employee pay package to fit individual needs. Some employees (usually younger employees) prefer cash, while others (usually older employees) will opt for the fringe benefit program.

EXAMPLE 19

Hawk Corporation offers its employees (on a nondiscriminatory basis) a choice of any one or all of the following benefits:

Benefit	Cost
Group term life insurance	$ 200
Hospitalization insurance for family members	2,400
Child care payments	1,800
	$4,400

If a benefit is not selected, the employee receives cash equal to the cost of the benefit. Kay, an employee, has a spouse who works for another employer that provides hospitalization insurance but no child care payments. Kay elects to receive the group term life insurance, the child care payments, and $2,400 of cash. Only the $2,400 must be included in Kay's gross income.

5-8c Flexible Spending Plans

Flexible spending plans (often referred to as flexible benefit plans) operate much like cafeteria plans. Under these plans, the employee accepts lower cash compensation (as much as $2,600) in return for the employer agreeing to pay certain costs that the employer can pay without the employee recognizing gross income. For example, assume that the employer's health insurance policy does not cover dental expenses. The employee could estimate his or her dental expenses for the upcoming year and agree to a salary reduction equal to the estimated dental expenses. The employer then pays or reimburses the employee for the actual dental expenses incurred, with a ceiling of the amount of the salary reduction. If the employee's actual dental expenses are less than the reduction in cash compensation, the employee cannot recover the difference. Hence, these plans are often referred to as *use or lose* plans. To avoid forfeiture of unpaid amounts, the IRS allows a payment until March 15 of the following year to count. As is the case for cafeteria plans, flexible spending plans cannot be used to pay long-term care insurance premiums.

[49]§ 125.

5-8d **General Classes of Excluded Benefits**

An employer can confer numerous forms and types of economic benefits on employees. Under the all-inclusive concept of income, the benefits are taxable unless one of the provisions previously discussed specifically excludes the item from gross income. The amount of the income is the fair market value of the benefit.

Ryan is employed in New York as a ticket clerk for Trans National Airlines. He has a sick mother in Miami, Florida, but has no money for plane tickets. Trans National has daily flights from New York to Miami that often leave with empty seats. The cost of a round-trip ticket is $400. If Trans National allows Ryan to fly without charge to Miami, under the general gross income rules, Ryan has income equal to the value of a ticket. Therefore, Ryan must include $400 in gross income on a trip to Miami.

Because Congress believed that taxing fringe benefits often yielded harsh results, § 132 was enacted to provide exclusion treatment. This provision established seven broad classes of nontaxable employee benefits:[50]

- No-additional-cost services.
- Qualified employee discounts.
- Working condition fringes.
- *De minimis* fringes.
- Qualified transportation fringes.
- Qualified moving expense reimbursements.
- Qualified retirement planning services.

The value of the services that the employer provides its employees are nontaxable under certain circumstances.

No-Additional-Cost Services

Return to Example 20 above. This illustrates the reason for the no-additional-cost service type of fringe benefit. The services will be nontaxable if all of the following conditions are satisfied:

- The employee receives services, as opposed to property.
- The employer does not incur substantial additional cost, including forgone revenue, in providing the services to the employee.
- The services are offered to customers in the ordinary course of the business in which the employee works.[51]

In Example 20, although the airplane may burn slightly more fuel because Ryan is on board and he may receive the same snacks as paying customers, the additional costs to the airline would not be substantial. Thus, the trip could qualify as a no-additional-cost service, and the value of Ryan's flight can be excluded from his gross income.

The no-additional-cost exclusion extends to the employee's spouse and dependent children and to retired and disabled former employees.[52] However, the exclusion is not allowed to highly compensated employees unless the benefit is available on a nondiscriminatory basis.

---

[50]See, generally, § 132. Section 132 also excludes "qualified military base realignment and closure fringe," which is not discussed here.

[51]Reg. § 1.132–2.

[52]Reg. § 1.132–1(b).

Qualified Employee Discounts

When the employer sells goods or services (other than no-additional-cost benefits just discussed) to the employee for a price that is less than the price charged regular customers, the employee realizes income equal to the discount. However, the discount, referred to as a <mark>qualified employee discount</mark>, can be excluded from the gross income of the employee, subject to the following conditions and limitations:

- The exclusion is not available for real property (e.g., a house) or for personal property of the type commonly held for investment (e.g., common stocks).
- The property or services must be from the same line of business in which the employee works.
- In the case of *property*, the exclusion is limited to the *gross profit component* of the price to customers.
- In the case of *services*, the exclusion is limited to 20 percent of the customer price.

EXAMPLE 22

Silver Corporation, which operates a department store, sells a television set to a store employee for $300. The regular customer price is $500, and the gross profit rate is 25%. The corporation also sells the employee a service contract for $120. The regular customer price for the contract is $150. The employee must include $75 in gross income.

Customer price for property	$ 500
Less: Gross profit (25%)	(125)
	$ 375
Employee price	(300)
Income	$ 75
Customer price for service	$ 150
Less: 20%	(30)
	$ 120
Employee price	(120)
Income	$ –0–

As in the case of no-additional-cost benefits, the exclusion applies to employees (including service partners), employees' spouses and dependent children, and retired and disabled former employees.

Working Condition Fringes

Generally, an employee is not required to include in gross income the cost of property or services provided by the employer if the employee could deduct the cost of those items if he or she had actually paid for them. These benefits are called <mark>working condition fringes</mark>.

EXAMPLE 23

Mitch is a CPA employed by an accounting firm. The employer pays Mitch's annual dues to professional organizations. Mitch is not required to include the payment of the dues in gross income because if he had paid the dues, he would have been allowed to deduct the amount as an employee business expense (as discussed in text Section 9-8b).[53]

Unlike the other fringe benefits discussed previously, working condition fringes can be made available on a discriminatory basis and still qualify for the exclusion.

De Minimis Fringes

As the term suggests, <mark>*de minimis fringe*</mark> benefits are so small that accounting for them is impractical. The House Report contains the following examples of *de minimis* fringes:

---

[53]In many cases, this exclusion merely avoids reporting income and an off-setting deduction.

- Occasional personal use of a company copying machine, occasional company cocktail parties or picnics for employees, occasional supper money or taxi fare for employees because of overtime work, and certain holiday gifts of property with a low fair market value are excluded.

- Subsidized eating facilities (e.g., an employees' cafeteria) operated by the employer are excluded if located on or near the employer's business premises, if revenue equals or exceeds direct operating costs, and if nondiscrimination requirements are met.

When taxpayers venture beyond the specific examples contained in the House Report and the Regulations, there is obviously room for disagreement as to what is *de minimis*. According to the IRS, cash or gift cards are not considered *de minimis*.[54]

In Notice 2011–72, the IRS addressed the question of whether cell phones provided by the employer could be excluded from gross income as a working condition fringe benefit. Generally, the value of the cell phone can be excluded if it is provided for business reasons such as to enable the employee to be in contact with clients when the employee is away from the office. When the primary purpose test is satisfied, any personal use of the employer-provided cell phone will be excluded as a *de minimis* fringe benefit.

Qualified Transportation Fringes

The intent of the exclusion for qualified transportation fringes is to encourage the use of mass transit for commuting to and from work. Qualified transportation fringes encompass the following transportation benefits provided by the employer to the employee:

1. Transportation in a commuter highway vehicle between the employee's residence and the place of employment.
2. A transit pass.
3. Qualified parking.
4. Qualified bicycle commuting reimbursement.

Statutory dollar limits are placed on the amount of the exclusion. Categories (1) and (2) above are combined for purposes of applying the limit. For 2017, the inflation adjusted limit for categories (1) and (2) combined, as well as for category (3), is $255 per month ($255 in 2016, as well). The bicycle benefit is $20 per month and is not adjusted annually for inflation.

A *commuter highway vehicle* is any highway vehicle with a seating capacity of at least six adults (excluding the driver). In addition, at least 80 percent of the vehicle's use must be for transporting employees between their residences and place of employment.

Qualified parking includes the following:

- Parking provided to an employee on or near the employer's business premises.

- Parking provided to an employee on or near a location from which the employee commutes to work via mass transit, in a commuter highway vehicle, or in a carpool.

The *qualified bicycle commuting reimbursement* enables an employee to exclude up to $20 per month received from an employer as reimbursement for the cost of commuting by bicycle (i.e., bicycle purchase, improvement, repair, and storage).

Qualified transportation fringes may be provided directly by the employer or may be in the form of cash reimbursements.

EXAMPLE 24

Gray Corporation's offices are located in the center of a large city. The company pays for parking spaces to be used by the company officers. Steve, a vice president, receives $300 of such benefits each month during 2017. The parking space rental qualifies as a qualified transportation fringe. Of the $300 benefit received each month by Steve, $255 is excludible from gross income. The balance of $45 is included in his gross income. The same result would occur if Steve paid for the parking and was reimbursed by his employer.

---

[54]TAM 200437030 (9/10/04) and IRS Publication 15B (2015), *Employer's Tax Guide to Fringe Benefits*, p. 8.

Qualified Moving Expense Reimbursements

Qualified moving expenses that are reimbursed or paid by the employer are excludible from gross income. A qualified moving expense is an expense that would be deductible under § 217. See the discussion of moving expenses in text Section 9-5.

Qualified Retirement Planning Services

Qualified retirement planning services include any retirement planning advice or information that an employer who maintains a qualified retirement plan provides to an employee or the employee's spouse. Congress decided to exclude the value of such services from gross income because they are a key part of retirement income planning. Such an exclusion should motivate more employers to provide retirement planning services to their employees.

Nondiscrimination Provisions

For no-additional-cost services, qualified employee discounts, and qualified retirement planning services that are discriminatory in favor of highly compensated employees, exclusion treatment is denied. However, for the discriminatory plans, the exclusion treatment for non-highly compensated employees remains.[55]

EXAMPLE 25

Dove Company's officers are allowed to purchase goods from the company at a 25% discount. All other employees are allowed only a 15% discount. The company's gross profit margin on these goods is 30%. Because the officers receive more favorable discounts, the plan is discriminatory in favor of the officers. In regard to all other employees, the discount is "qualified" because it is available to all employees (other than the officers who receive a more favorable discount) and the discount is less than the company's gross profit.

Peggy, an officer in the company, purchased goods from the company for $750 when the price charged to customers was $1,000. Peggy must include $250 in gross income because the plan is discriminatory.

Mason, an employee of the company who is not an officer, purchased goods for $850 when the customer price was $1,000. Mason is not required to recognize gross income because he received a qualified employee discount.

De minimis (except in the case of subsidized eating facilities) and working condition fringe benefits can be provided on a discriminatory basis. The *de minimis* benefits are not subject to tax because the accounting problems that would be created are out of proportion to the amount of additional tax that would result.

A review of employee fringe benefits is set forth in Concept Summary 5.2.

5-9 FOREIGN EARNED INCOME

The United States uses a global tax system as opposed to a territorial system. Under this global system, a U.S. citizen is generally subject to tax on his or her income regardless of its economic origin. Some other countries use a territorial system; that is, a person's income is taxed only in the country in which the income was earned. Under this global system, a U.S. citizen who earns income in another country could experience double taxation: the same income would be taxed in the United States and in the foreign country. Out of a sense of fairness and to encourage U.S. citizens to work abroad (so that exports might be increased), Congress has provided alternative forms of relief from taxes on foreign earned income. The taxpayer can elect *either* (1) to include the foreign earned income in his or her taxable income and then claim a credit for foreign taxes paid or (2) to exclude up to $102,100 of foreign earned income from his or her U.S. gross income (the **foreign earned income exclusion**).[56] The foreign tax credit option is discussed in Chapter 13, but as is apparent from the following discussion, most taxpayers choose the exclusion.

---

[55]§§ 132(j)(1) and 132(m)(2).

[56]§ 911(a). The exclusion for 2016 was $101,300.

Concept Summary 5.2

Employee Fringe Benefits

Type of Benefit	Exclusion
Group term life insurance (§ 79)	Premiums on up to $50,000 of protection
Employee achievement awards (§ 74)	Up to $1,600 in a year
Accident, health, and long-term care insurance and medical reimbursement (§§ 105 and 106)	Insurance premiums paid by the employer and benefits collected
High-deductible health insurance and contributions to employee's Health Savings Account (§§ 106 and 223)	Employer premiums on high-deductible medical insurance plus contributions to Health Savings Account (statutory limits, indexed for inflation).
Meals and lodging furnished for the convenience of the employer (§ 119)	Value of meals and lodging on the employer's premises
Child care provided by the employer or reimbursement for employee's cost (§ 129)	Services provided or reimbursement of expenses up to $5,000 a year
Athletic facilities on the employer's premises (§ 132)	Value of services
Educational assistance for tuition, fees, books, and supplies (§ 127)	Limited to $5,250 per year
No-additional-cost services [e.g., use of employer's facilities (§ 132)]	Value of the use
Employee discount on purchase of goods from employer at employer's cost (§ 132)	Employer's normal profit margin
Employee discount for purchases of employer's services (§ 132)	Maximum of 20% of employer's normal price
Working condition fringes [e.g., the mechanic's tools (§ 132)]	Employer's cost
*De minimi*s items so small that the accounting effort is not warranted [e.g., use of employer telephone (§ 132)]	Value of the goods or services
Qualified transportation [e.g, transit passes and parking (§ 132)]	Statutory amounts, adjusted for inflation
Moving expense reimbursement (§ 132)	Reimbursement to the extent otherwise deductible by employee
Retirement planning services (§ 132)	Reasonable cost of services

Foreign earned income consists of the earnings from the individual's personal services rendered in a foreign country (other than as an employee of the U.S. government). To qualify for the exclusion, the taxpayer must be either of the following:

- A bona fide resident of the foreign country (or countries).
- Present in a foreign country (or countries) for at least 330 days during any 12 consecutive months.[57]

Calculating the Exclusion

EXAMPLE

26

Sandra's trips to and from a foreign country in connection with her work were as follows:

Arrived in Foreign Country	Returned to United States
March 10, 2016	February 15, 2017

During the 12 consecutive months ending on March 10, 2017, Sandra was present in the foreign country for at least 330 days (365 days less 13 days in February 2017 and 10 days in March 2017). Therefore, the income earned in the foreign country through March 10, 2017, is eligible for the exclusion.

---

[57]§ 911(d). For the definition of *resident*, see Reg. § 1.871–2(b). Under the Regulations, a taxpayer is not a resident if he or she is there for a definite period (e.g., until completion of a construction contract).

GLOBAL TAX ISSUES **Benefits of the Earned Income Exclusion Are Questioned**

The foreign earned income exclusion is intended to be a means to increase exports. But a recent GAO study questioned whether the $6 billion of lost revenue is money well spent. The report was inconclusive. It is clear that repealing the exclusion would make it more costly for U.S. companies to send their employees abroad, but there is no evidence that the benefits to the United States, in general, are worth the cost.

Source: Economic Benefits of Income Exclusion for U.S. Citizens Working Abroad Are Uncertain GAO-14-387: Published: May 20, 2014, available at **www.gao.gov/products/GAO-14-387**.

Calculating the Exclusion

EXAMPLE 27

Keith qualifies for the foreign earned income exclusion. He was present in France for all of 2017. Keith's salary for 2017 is $120,000. Because all of the days in 2017 are qualifying days, Keith can exclude $102,100 of his $120,000 salary.

Assume instead that only 342 days were qualifying days. Then Keith's exclusion is limited to $95,666, computed as follows:

$$\$102,100 \times \frac{342 \text{ days in foreign country}}{365 \text{ days in the year}} = \$95,666$$

EXAMPLE 28

In 2017, Carol, who is not married, had taxable income of $30,000 after excluding $102,100 of foreign earned income. Without the benefit of the exclusion, Carol's taxable income would have been $132,100 ($30,000 + $102,100). The tax on the taxable income of $30,000 is calculated using the marginal rate applicable to income between $101,300 and $132,100, which is 28%. Therefore, Carol's tax liability is $8,400 (.28 × $30,000).

As previously mentioned, the taxpayer may elect to include the foreign earned income in gross income and claim a credit (an offset against U.S. tax) for the foreign tax paid. The credit alternative may be advantageous if the individual's foreign earned income far exceeds the excludible amount so that the foreign taxes paid exceed the U.S. tax on the amount excluded. However, once an election is made, it applies to all subsequent years unless affirmatively revoked. A revocation is effective for the year of the change and the four subsequent years.

5-10 INTEREST ON CERTAIN STATE AND LOCAL GOVERNMENT OBLIGATIONS

At the time the Sixteenth Amendment was ratified by the states, there was some question as to whether the Federal government possessed the constitutional authority to tax interest on state and local government obligations. Taxing such interest was thought to violate the doctrine of intergovernmental immunity in that the tax would impair the state and local governments' ability to finance their operations.[58] Thus, interest on state and local government obligations was specifically exempted from Federal income taxation.[59] However, the Supreme Court has concluded that there is no constitutional prohibition against levying a nondiscriminatory Federal income tax on state and local government obligations.[60] Nevertheless, currently, the statutory exclusion still exists.

---

[58]*Pollock v. Farmer's Loan & Trust Co.*, 3 AFTR 2602, 15 S.Ct. 912 (USSC, 1895).

[59]§ 103(a).

[60]*South Carolina v. Baker III*, 88–1 USTC ¶9284, 61 AFTR 2d 88–995, 108 S.Ct. 1355 (USSC, 1988).

Obviously, the exclusion of the interest reduces the cost of borrowing for state and local governments. A taxpayer in the 35 percent tax bracket requires only a 5.2 percent yield on a tax-exempt bond to obtain the same after-tax income as a taxable bond paying 8 percent interest [5.2% ÷ (1 − .35) = 8%].

The current exempt status applies solely to state and local government bonds. Thus, income received from the accrual of interest on a condemnation award or an overpayment of state income tax is fully taxable.[61] Nor does the exemption apply to gains on the sale of tax-exempt securities.

EXAMPLE 29

Megan purchases State of Virginia bonds for $10,000 on July 1, 2016. The bonds pay $300 interest each June 30 and December 31. On March 31, 2017, Megan sells the bonds for $10,500 plus $150 for accrued interest. Megan must recognize a $500 gain ($10,500 − $10,000), but the $150 accrued interest is exempt from taxation.

Although the Internal Revenue Code excludes from Federal gross income the interest on state and local government bonds, the interest on U.S. government bonds is not excluded from the Federal tax base. Congress has decided, however, that if the Federal government is not to tax state and local bond interest, the state and local governments are prohibited from taxing interest on U.S. government bonds.[62] While this parity between the Federal and state and local governments exists in regard to taxing each other's obligations, the states are free to tax one another's obligations. Thus, some states exempt the interest on the bonds they issue, but tax the interest on bonds issued by other states.[63]

5-11 CORPORATE DISTRIBUTIONS TO SHAREHOLDERS

5-11a General Information

A corporate distribution is a payment to a shareholder with respect to his or her stock (see Chapter 4). Distributions are taxed as dividends to shareholders only to the extent the payments are made from *either* the corporation's *current earnings and profits* (similar to net income per books) or its *accumulated earnings and profits* (similar to retained earnings per books).[64] Distributions that exceed earnings and profits are treated as a nontaxable recovery of capital and reduce the shareholder's basis in the stock. Once the shareholder's basis is reduced to zero, any subsequent distributions are taxed as capital gains (see Chapters 14 and 20).[65]

Some payments are frequently referred to as dividends but are not considered dividends for tax purposes:

- Dividends received on deposits with savings and loan associations, credit unions, and banks are actually interest (a contractual rate paid for the use of money).

- Patronage dividends paid by cooperatives (e.g., for farmers) are rebates made to the users and are considered reductions in the cost of items purchased from the association. The rebates are usually made after year-end (after the cooperative has determined whether it has met its expenses) and are apportioned among members on the basis of their purchases.

- Mutual insurance companies pay dividends on unmatured life insurance policies that are considered rebates of premiums.

---

[61]*Kieselbach v. Comm.*, 43–1 USTC ¶9220, 30 AFTR 370, 63 S.Ct. 303 (USSC, 1943); *U.S. Trust Co. of New York v. Anderson*, 3 USTC ¶1125, 12 AFTR 836, 65 F.2d 575 (CA–2, 1933).

[62]31 U.S.C.A. § 742.

[63]The practice of a state exempting interest on its bonds from tax but taxing the interest on bonds issued by other states has been upheld by the Supreme Court. See *Department of Revenue of Kentucky v. Davis*, 128 S.Ct. 1801 (USSC, 2008).

[64]§ 316(a). Refer to the discussion of the beneficial tax rates for qualified dividends in Chapter 4.

[65]§ 301(c). See Chapter 5, *South-Western Federal Taxation: Corporations, Partnerships, Estates & Trusts*, for a detailed discussion of corporate distributions.

• Shareholders in a mutual investment fund are allowed to report as capital gains their proportionate share of the fund's gains realized and distributed. The capital gain and ordinary income portions are reported on the Form 1099 that the fund supplies its shareholders each year.

5-11b **Stock Dividends**

When a corporation issues a simple stock dividend (e.g., common stock issued to common shareholders), the shareholder has merely received additional shares that represent the same total investment. Thus, the shareholder does not realize income.[66] However, if the shareholder has the *option* of receiving either cash or stock in the corporation, the individual realizes gross income whether he or she receives stock or cash.[67] A taxpayer who elects to receive the stock could be deemed to be in constructive receipt of the cash he or she has rejected.[68] However, the amount of the income in this case is the value of the stock received, rather than the cash the shareholder has rejected. See Chapter 14 for a detailed discussion of stock dividends.

5-12 **EDUCATIONAL SAVINGS BONDS**

The cost of a college education has risen dramatically during the past few decades. According to U.S. Department of Education estimates, the cost of attending a publicly supported university for four years now commonly exceeds $60,000. For a private university, the cost often exceeds $200,000. Consequently, Congress has attempted to assist low- to middle-income parents in saving for their children's college education.

One of the ways Congress assists such families is through an interest income exclusion on **educational savings bonds**.[69] The interest on Series EE U.S. government savings bonds may be excluded from gross income if the bond proceeds are used to pay qualified higher education expenses.

Qualified higher education expenses consist of tuition and fees paid to an eligible educational institution for the taxpayer, spouse, or dependent. If the redemption proceeds (both principal and interest) exceed the qualified higher education expenses, only a pro rata portion of the interest will qualify for exclusion treatment.

EXAMPLE 30

Tracy's redemption proceeds from qualified savings bonds during the taxable year are $6,000 (principal of $4,000 and interest of $2,000). Tracy's qualified higher education expenses are $5,000. Because the redemption proceeds exceed the qualified higher education expenses, only $1,667 [($5,000/$6,000) × $2,000] of the interest is excludible.

The exclusion is limited by the application of the wherewithal to pay concept. That is, once the modified adjusted gross income exceeds a threshold amount, the phaseout of the exclusion begins. *Modified adjusted gross income* (*MAGI*) is adjusted gross income prior to the foreign earned income exclusion and the educational savings bond exclusion. The threshold amounts are adjusted for inflation each year. For 2017, the phaseout begins at $78,150 ($117,250 on a joint return).[70] The phaseout is completed when MAGI exceeds the threshold amount by more than $15,000 ($30,000 on a joint return). The otherwise excludible interest is reduced by the amount calculated as follows:

$$\frac{\text{MAGI} - \$78,150}{\$15,000} \otimes \xrightarrow{\text{Excludible interest}}_{\text{before phaseout}} = \xrightarrow{\text{Reduction in}}_{\text{excludible interest}}$$

On a joint return, $117,250 is substituted for $78,150 (in 2017), and $30,000 is substituted for $15,000.

---

[66]*Eisner v. Macomber*, 1 USTC ¶32, 3 AFTR 3020, 40 S.Ct. 189 (USSC, 1920); § 305(a).

[67]§ 305(b).

[68]Refer to the discussion of constructive receipt in Chapter 4.

[69]§ 135.

[70]The indexed amounts for 2016 were $77,550 and $116,300.

Assume the same facts as in Example 30, except that Tracy's MAGI for 2017 is $80,000. The phase-out results in Tracy's interest exclusion being reduced by $206 {[($80,000 − $78,150)/$15,000] × $1,667}. Therefore, Tracy's exclusion is $1,461 ($1,667 − $206).

5-13 EDUCATION SAVINGS PROGRAMS (§ 529 AND § 530 PLANS)

The Federal tax law provides two types of programs to help families save for education costs. These savings programs are referred to as the Qualified Tuition Program (§ 529 plans) and Coverdell Education Savings Accounts (§ 530 plans). Similarities between the two plans are that earnings in the accounts are not taxable if distributions are used for qualified education expenses. Also, rules govern the type of account that can be used for these savings programs, and specific rules exist regarding contributions, distributions, rollovers, and other transfers. In addition, the benefits of these plans must be coordinated with other educational tax provisions, such as nontaxable scholarships. Distributions from these accounts are reported on Form 1099–Q, Payments from Qualified Education Programs. Taxable distributions (generally those not used for qualified purposes) may be subject to an additional 10 percent tax [reported on Form 5329, Additional Taxes on Qualified Plans (Including IRAs) and Other Tax-Favored Accounts].

Significant differences between § 529 and § 530 plans are that in addition to specified higher education expenses, a Coverdell Account can also be used for specified K–12 expenses. Also, there are income limits on contributions to Coverdell Accounts as well as a dollar limit on the annual contribution per beneficiary. A beneficiary may have both § 529 and § 530 plans.

5-13a Qualified Tuition Program

Nearly all, if not all, states have created programs whereby parents can in effect prepay their child's college tuition. The prepayment serves as a hedge against future increases in tuition. Generally, if the child does not attend college, the parents are refunded their payments plus interest. Upon first impressions, these prepaid tuition programs resemble the below-market loans discussed in text Section 4-4b. That is, assuming that the tuition increases, the parent receives a reduction in the child's tuition in exchange for the use of the funds. However, Congress has created an exclusion provision for these programs.

Under a **qualified tuition program (§ 529 plan)**, the amounts contributed must be used for qualified higher education expenses. These expenses include tuition, fees, books, supplies, room and board, and equipment required for enrollment or attendance at a college, a university, or certain vocational schools. Allowable expenses also include computers and peripheral equipment, software, and internet access used primarily by the beneficiary while enrolled at an eligible educational institution. Qualified higher education expenses also include the expenses for special needs services that are incurred in connection with the enrollment and attendance of special needs students.

The earnings of the contributed funds, including the discount on tuition charged to participants, are not included in Federal gross income provided the contributions and earnings are used for qualified higher education expenses. Some states also exclude these educational benefits from state gross income.

Agnes paid $20,000 into a qualified tuition program to be used for her son's college tuition. When her son graduated from high school, the fund balance had increased to $30,000 as a result of interest credited to the account. The interest was not included in Agnes's gross income. During the current year, $7,500 of the balance in the fund was used to pay the son's tuition and fees. None of this amount is included in either Agnes's or the son's gross income.

If the parent receives a refund (e.g., child does not attend college), the excess of the amount refunded over the amount contributed by the parent is included in the parent's gross income. A special rule applies to refunded amounts recontributed to a qualified tuition program of the beneficiary.

5-13b Coverdell Education Savings Account

A Coverdell education savings account (§ 530 plan) may be used to save for K–12 education as well as postsecondary education expenses. The contributions to the plan are limited to $2,000 in any year, and the beneficiary must be under 18 or must be a special needs beneficiary in the year the contribution is made. As with the § 529 plan, contributions are nondeductible, but the income to the beneficiary is nontaxable provided the funds are used for qualified education expenses.

5-14 QUALIFIED ABLE PROGRAMS (§ 529A PLANS)

In 2014, a new type of program was created to assist individuals who became blind or disabled before age 26. The qualified ABLE program allows for § 529A plans, or ABLE (Achieving a Better Life Experience) plans, similar in concept to § 529 plans described earlier. The program must be established by a state. The ABLE account must be for the benefit of a designated beneficiary's disability expenses, and the beneficiary must have a disability certification from the government.

Contributions to the account must be in cash and may not in aggregate exceed the annual gift tax exclusion for the year ($14,000 for 2016 and 2017). Contributions to the account are not deductible. The tax benefit of an ABLE account is that its earnings are not taxable. Distributions from the account also are not taxable provided they do not exceed the qualified disability expenses of the designated beneficiary.

5-15 TAX BENEFIT RULE

LO.3

Determine the extent to which receipts can be excluded under the tax benefit rule.

Often a person will incur a cost or an expense but receive a refund or recovery in a subsequent year, which is tantamount to an adjustment to the original cost. For example, the taxpayer may purchase an item from a retailer and then receive a rebate from the manufacturer. The rebate is generally a purchase price adjustment. If the item purchased did not result in a tax deduction (e.g., the purchase of a personal automobile), the rebate does not affect taxable income. However, if the original payment resulted in a tax deduction in one year and the rebate is received in a subsequent year, the tax benefit rule will apply. Generally, if a taxpayer claims a deduction for an item in one year and in a later year recovers all or a portion of the prior deduction, the recovery is included in gross income in the year received.[71]

EXAMPLE 33

An accrual basis taxpayer deducted as a loss a $1,000 receivable from a customer when it appeared the amount would never be collected. The following year, the customer paid $800 on the receivable. The taxpayer must report the $800 as gross income in the year it is received.

However, the § 111 tax benefit rule provides that no income is recognized upon the recovery of a deduction, or the portion of a deduction, that did not yield a tax benefit in the year it was taken. If the taxpayer in Example 33 had no tax liability in the year of the deduction (e.g., itemized deductions and personal exemptions exceeded adjusted gross income), the recovery would be partially or totally excluded from gross income in the year of the recovery.[72]

---

[71]§ 111(a).

[72]Itemized deductions are discussed in Chapter 10.

Ali filed his 2016 income tax return as a single individual. His AGI for 2016 was $48,000. He had $6,650 in itemized deductions, including $1,200 in state income tax. In 2017, he received a $700 refund of the state income taxes that he paid in 2016. Because the standard deduction in 2016 was $6,300, the $1,200 of state income taxes Ali paid in 2016 yielded a tax benefit of only $350 ($6,650 itemized deductions − $6,300 standard deduction). Under the tax benefit rule, only $350 of the state income tax refund is included in gross income in 2017.

EXAMPLE 34

5-16 INCOME FROM DISCHARGE OF INDEBTEDNESS

LO.4

Describe the circumstances under which income must be reported from the discharge of indebtedness.

When a person is relieved of a debt for less than the amount owed, the debtor's net worth increases. This increase in net worth is taxable income, unless one of the exceptions discussed below applies.[73]

Kayla is unable to make her credit card payments and has negotiated a settlement with the credit card issuer. Her $40,000 debt will be settled for $25,000. Kayla must recognize income of $15,000 from the discharge of debt.

EXAMPLE 35

When property serves as security for debt, the creditor may foreclose on the property. The foreclosure is treated as a sale.[74]

Juan owns land that serves as security for a $60,000 mortgage held by State Bank. Juan does not have personal liability for the mortgage (it is nonrecourse debt). When Juan's basis in the land is $20,000 and the land's fair market value is $50,000, the bank forecloses on the loan and takes title to the land. Juan must recognize a $40,000 gain on the foreclosure, as though he sold the land for $60,000 (the amount of the nonrecourse debt). Juan has no income from discharge of indebtedness.

EXAMPLE 36

If property serves as security for the debt and the taxpayer is personally liable for the difference between the value of the property and the amount of the debt (i.e., the debt is "with recourse"), the taxpayer may have income from the discharge of the debt in addition to gain or loss from the foreclosure.

Assume the same facts in Example 36, except that Juan's debt is recourse. Juan is treated as selling the property for its fair market value ($50,000) resulting in a gain or loss. His gain is $30,000 ($50,000 sales price − $20,000 basis). In addition, Juan has $10,000 of income from discharge of indebtedness because the lender accepted the $50,000 sales price in discharging the $60,000 debt. Juan will want to determine whether any exclusion applies to his income from discharge of indebtedness (discussed next).

EXAMPLE 37

The following discharge of indebtedness situations are subject to special exclusion treatment:[75]

1. Creditors' gifts.
2. Discharges under Federal bankruptcy law.
3. Discharges that occur when the debtor is insolvent (the exclusion is limited to the amount of insolvency).
4. Discharge of the farm debt of a solvent taxpayer.
5. Discharge of qualified real property business indebtedness.
6. A seller's cancellation of the buyer's indebtedness.
7. A shareholder's cancellation of the corporation's indebtedness.
8. Forgiveness of certain loans to students.

---

[73]§ 61(a)(12) and Reg. § 1.1001–2(a).

[74]*Estate of Delman*, 73 T.C. 15 (1979).

[75]§§ 108 and 1017. See Rev.Proc. 2015–57, 2015–51 I.R.B. 863, for a special debt discharge exclusion under the U.S. Department of Education's "Defense to Repayment" program.

9. Discharge of indebtedness on the taxpayer's principal residence that occurs between January 1, 2007, and January 1, 2017, and is the result of the financial condition of the debtor.

If the creditor reduces the debt as an act of *love, affection,* or *generosity,* the debtor has simply received a nontaxable gift (situation 1). Rarely will a gift be found to have occurred in a business context. A businessperson may settle a debt for less than the amount due, but as a matter of business expediency (e.g., high collection costs or disputes as to contract terms) rather than generosity.[76]

In situations 2, 3, 4, 5, and 9, the Code allows the debtor to reduce his or her basis in the assets by the realized income from the discharge.[77] As a result, the realized income is merely deferred until the assets are sold (or depreciated). Similarly, in situation 6 (a price reduction), the debtor reduces the basis in the specific assets financed by the seller.[78]

A shareholder's cancellation of the corporation's indebtedness to him or her (situation 7) usually is considered a tax-free contribution of capital to the corporation by the shareholder. Thus, the corporation's paid-in capital is increased, and its liabilities are decreased by the same amount.[79]

Many states make loans to students on the condition that the loan will be forgiven if the student practices a profession in the state upon completing his or her studies. The amount of the loan that is forgiven (situation 8) is excluded from gross income.[80]

Identify tax planning strategies for obtaining the maximum benefit from allowable exclusions.

5-17 TAX PLANNING

The present law excludes certain types of economic gains from taxation. Therefore, taxpayers may find tax planning techniques helpful in obtaining the maximum benefits from the exclusion of such gains. Following are some of the tax planning opportunities made available by the exclusions described in this chapter.

5-17a Life Insurance

Life insurance offers several favorable tax attributes. As discussed in Chapter 4, the annual increase in the cash surrender value of the policy is not taxable (because no income has been actually or constructively received). By borrowing on the policy's cash surrender value, the owner can actually receive the policy's increase in value in cash without recognizing income.

5-17b Employee Fringe Benefits

Generally, employees view accident and health insurance, as well as life insurance, as necessities. Employees can obtain group coverage at much lower rates than individuals would have to pay for the same protection. Premiums paid by the employer can be excluded from the employees' gross income. Because of the exclusion, employees will have a greater after-tax and after-insurance income if the employer pays a lower salary but also pays the insurance premiums.

EXAMPLE 38

Pat receives a salary of $30,000. The company has group insurance benefits, but Pat is required to pay his own premiums as follows:

Hospitalization and medical insurance	$1,400
Term life insurance ($30,000 coverage)	200
Disability insurance	400
	$2,000

continued

---

[76]*Comm. v. Jacobson,* 49–1 USTC ¶9133, 37 AFTR 516, 69 S.Ct. 358 (USSC, 1949).

[77]§§ 108(a), (c), (e), and (g). Note that § 108(b) provides that other tax attributes (e.g., net operating loss) will be reduced by the realized gain from the debt discharge prior to the basis adjustment unless the taxpayer elects to apply the basis adjustment first.

[78]§ 108(e)(5).

[79]§ 108(e)(6).

[80]§ 108(f).

To simplify the analysis, assume that Pat's tax rate on income is 25%. After paying taxes of $7,500 (.25 × $30,000) and $2,000 for insurance, Pat has $20,500 remaining ($30,000 − $7,500 − $2,000) for his other living needs.

If Pat's employer reduced Pat's salary by $2,000 (to $28,000) but paid his insurance premiums, Pat's tax liability would be only $7,000 ($28,000 × .25). Thus, Pat would have $21,000 ($28,000 − $7,000) to meet his other living needs. The change in the compensation plan would save Pat $500 ($21,000 − $20,500).

Similarly, employees must often incur expenses for child care and parking. The employee can have more income for other uses if the employer pays these costs for the employee but reduces the employee's salary by the cost of the benefits.

The use of cafeteria plans has increased dramatically in recent years. These plans allow employees to tailor their benefits to meet their individual situations. As a result, where both spouses in a married couple are working, duplications of benefits can be avoided and other needed benefits can often be added. If less than all of the employee's allowance is spent, the employee can receive cash.

The meals and lodging exclusion enables employees to receive from their employer what they ordinarily must purchase with after-tax dollars. Although the requirement that the employee live on the employer's premises in order to exclude the value of the lodging limits the tax planning opportunities, the exclusion is an important factor in the employee's compensation in certain situations (e.g., hotels, motels, restaurants, farms, and ranches). The meals and lodging are clearly a benefit to the employee but are for the convenience of the employer and thus are excluded from income.

The employees' discount provision is especially important for manufacturers and wholesalers. Employees of manufacturers can avoid tax on the manufacturer's, wholesaler's, and retailer's markups. The wholesaler's employees can avoid tax on an amount equal to the wholesale and retail markups.

The exclusion of benefits is generally available only to employees. Proprietors and partners must pay tax on the same benefits their employees receive tax-free. By incorporating and becoming an employee of the corporation, the former proprietor or partner can also receive these tax-exempt benefits. Thus, the availability of employee benefits is a consideration in the decision to incorporate.

5-17c Investment Income

Tax-exempt state and local government bonds are almost irresistible investments for high-income taxpayers, who may be subject to a 39.6 percent regular tax rate plus a 3.8 percent rate on their net investment income. To realize the maximum benefit from the exemption, the investor can purchase zero-coupon bonds. Like Series EE U.S. government savings bonds, these investments pay interest only at maturity. The advantage of the zero-coupon feature for a tax-exempt bond is that the investor can earn tax-exempt interest on the accumulated principal and interest. If the investor purchases a bond that pays the interest each year, the interest received may be such a small amount that an additional tax-exempt investment cannot be made. In addition, reinvesting the interest may entail transaction costs (brokers' fees). The zero-coupon feature avoids these problems.

Series EE U.S. government savings bonds can earn tax-exempt interest if the bond proceeds are used for qualified higher education expenses. Many taxpayers can foresee these expenditures being made for their children's educations. In deciding whether to invest in the bonds, however, the investor must take into account the income limitations for excluding the interest from gross income.

REFOCUS ON THE BIG PICTURE

EXCLUSIONS

You have looked into Paul's tax situation and have the following information for him:

- *Compensation.* The amount Paul was paid for his internship is compensation for services rendered and must be included in his gross income. This includes both his base pay and the $1,500 bonus (Example 1).
- *Graduate assistantship.* The tuition waiver of $6,000 is excluded from Paul's gross income. The related payments of $400 per month are intended as a form of compensation. So Paul must include the $400 per month in his gross income (Example 11).
- *Damages.* Damages awards that relate to personal physical injury or sickness can be excluded from gross income if the payments are for compensatory damages. So all of the compensatory damages of $220,000 can be excluded from gross income. The punitive damages of $160,000 must be included in Paul's gross income. Likewise, the compensatory damages of $25,000 received by Paul's mother must be included in her gross income because emotional distress does not qualify as personal physical injury or sickness (Example 12).

What If?

From a tax planning perspective, can Paul do anything to reduce the amount of the punitive damages settlement that he must include in his gross income?

As things now stand (i.e., a completed settlement), Paul cannot reduce the $160,000 punitive damages amount he must include in gross income. However, proper tax planning might have enabled Paul to reduce the amount includible in gross income. Note that both the amount of the damages and the labels attached to the damages are negotiated. If a larger portion of the settlement had been assigned to compensatory damages rather than punitive damages, Paul could have reduced the amount he must include in his gross income.

ANDREW SHURTLEFF/NEWS.COM

Key Terms

Accelerated death benefits, 5-5

Accident and health benefits, 5-11

Cafeteria plan, 5-16

Compensatory damages, 5-9

Coverdell education savings account (§ 530 plan), 5-26

De minimis fringe, 5-18

Death benefits, 5-4

Educational savings bonds, 5-24

Flexible spending plans, 5-16

Foreign earned income exclusion, 5-20

Fringe benefits, 5-15

Health Savings Account (HSA), 5-12

Life insurance proceeds, 5-4

Long-term care insurance, 5-12

No-additional-cost service, 5-17

Punitive damages, 5-9

Qualified ABLE program, 5-26

Qualified employee discount, 5-18

Qualified real property business indebtedness, 5-27

Qualified transportation fringes, 5-19

Qualified tuition program (§ 529 plan), 5-25

Scholarship, 5-7

Tax benefit rule, 5-26

Working condition fringes, 5-18

1. **LO.2** Fred specified in his will that his nephew John should serve as executor of Fred's estate. John received $10,000 for serving as executor. Can John exclude the $10,000 from his gross income? Explain.

2. **LO.2** Leonard's home was damaged by a fire. He also had to be absent from work for several days to make his home habitable. Leonard's employer paid Leonard his regular salary, $2,500, while he was absent from work. In Leonard's pay envelope was the following note from the employer: To help you in your time of need. Leonard's fellow employees also took up a collection and gave him $900. Leonard spent over $4,000 repairing the fire damage.

   Based on the above information, how much is Leonard required to include in his gross income?

3. **LO.2** Dolly is a college student who works as a part-time server in a restaurant. Her usual tip is 20% of the price of the meal. A customer ordered a piece of pie and said that he would appreciate prompt service. Dolly abided with the customer's request. The customer's bill was $8, but the customer left a $100 bill on the table and did not ask for a receipt. Dolly gave the cashier $8 and pocketed the $100 bill. Dolly concludes that the customer thought that he had left a $10 bill, although the customer did not return to correct the apparent mistake. The customer had commented about how much he appreciated Dolly's prompt service. Dolly thinks that a $2 tip would be sufficient and that the other $98 is like "found money." How much should Dolly include in her gross income?

4. **LO.2** Carey is a waiter at a restaurant that pays a small hourly amount plus tips. Customers are not required to tip the waiter. Carey is especially attentive and friendly, and her tips average 25% of the restaurant charges. Is Carey required to include any of her tips in gross income when the customer has no legal obligation to make the payment? Explain the basis for your conclusion.

5. **LO.2** Lime Finance Company requires its customers to purchase a credit life insurance policy associated with the loans it makes. Lime is the beneficiary of the policy to the extent of the remaining balance on the loan at the time of the customer's death. In 2016, Lime wrote off as uncollectible a $5,000 account receivable from Wally, which included $1,500 of accrued interest. When Wally died in 2017, the life insurance policy was still in force and Lime received $3,500. Is the $3,500 of life insurance proceeds received by Lime included in its gross income? Explain.

6. **LO.2** Billy fell off a bar stool and hurt his back. As a result, he was unable to work for three months. He sued the bar owner and collected $100,000 for the physical injury and $50,000 for the loss of income. Billy also collected $15,000 from an income replacement insurance policy he purchased. Amber was away from work for three months following heart bypass surgery. Amber collected $30,000 under an income replacement insurance policy purchased by her employer. Are the amounts received by Billy and Amber treated the same under the tax law? Explain.

7. **LO.2** Wes was a major league baseball pitcher who earned $10 million for his 20 wins this year. Sam was also a major league baseball pitcher before a career-ending injury caused by a negligent driver. Sam sued the driver and collected $6 million as compensation for lost estimated future income as a pitcher and $4 million as punitive damages. Do the amounts that Wes and Sam receive have the same effect on their gross income? Explain.

8. **LO.2** Holly was injured while working in a factory and received $12,000 as workers' compensation while she was unable to work because of the injury. Jill, who was self-employed, was also injured and unable to work. Jill collected $12,000 on an

insurance policy she had purchased to replace her loss of income while she was unable to work. How much are Holly and Jill each required to include in their gross income?

Decision Making   9.   **LO.2, 5** Casey is in the 15% marginal tax bracket, and Jean is in the 35% marginal tax bracket. Their employer is experiencing financial difficulties and cannot continue to pay for the company's health insurance plan. The annual premiums are approximately $8,000 per employee. The employer has proposed to either (1) require the employee to pay the premiums or (2) reduce each employee's pay by $10,000 per year with the employer paying the premium. Which option is less objectionable to Casey, and which is less objectionable to Jean?

10.   **LO.2** What is the difference between a cafeteria plan and an employee flexible spending plan?

11.   **LO.2** Ted works for Azure Motors, an automobile dealership. All employees can buy a car at the company's cost plus 2%. The company does not charge employees the $300 dealer preparation fee that nonemployees must pay. Ted purchased an automobile for $29,580 ($29,000 + $580). The company's cost was $29,000. The price for a nonemployee would have been $33,900 ($33,600 + $300 preparation fee). What is Ted's gross income from the purchase of the automobile?

12.   **LO.2, 5** Wilbur has been offered a job at a salary that would put him in the 25% marginal tax bracket. In addition to his salary, he would receive health insurance coverage. Another potential employer does not offer health insurance but has agreed to match the first offer on an after-tax and insurance basis. The cost of health insurance comparable to that provided by the other potential employer is $9,000 per year. How much more in salary must the second potential employer pay so that Wilbur's financial status will be the same under both offers?

13.   **LO.2, 5** Eagle Life Insurance Company pays its employees $.30 per mile for driving their personal automobiles to and from work. The company reimburses each employee who rides the bus $100 a month for the cost of a pass. Tom collected $100 for his automobile mileage, and Mason received $100 as reimbursement for the cost of a bus pass.
   a.   What are the effects of the above on Tom's and Mason's gross income?
   b.   Assume that Tom and Mason are in the 28% marginal tax bracket and the actual before-tax cost for Tom to drive to and from work is $.30 per mile. What are Tom's and Mason's after-tax costs of commuting to and from work?

Issue ID   14.   **LO.2** Several of Egret Company's employees have asked the company to create a hiking trail that employees could use during their lunch hours. The company owns vacant land that is being held for future expansion but would have to spend approximately $50,000 if it were to make a trail. Nonemployees would be allowed to use the facility as part of the company's effort to build strong community support. What are the relevant tax issues for the employees?

15.   **LO.2** The Sage Company has the opportunity to purchase a building located next to its office. Sage would use the building as a day care center for the children of its employees and an exercise facility for the employees. Occasionally, portions of the building could be used for employees' family events such as reunions, birthday parties, and anniversaries. The company would like to know if the planned uses of the building would fit into a beneficially taxed employee compensation plan.

Decision Making   16.   **LO.2, 5** Tammy, a resident of Virginia, is considering purchasing a North Carolina bond that yields 4.6% before tax. She is in the 35% Federal marginal tax bracket and the 5% state marginal tax bracket. She is aware that State of Virginia bonds of comparable risk are yielding 4.5%. However, the Virginia bonds are exempt from Virginia tax, but the North Carolina bond interest is taxable in Virginia. Which of the two options will provide the greater after-tax return to Tammy? Tammy can deduct any state taxes paid on her Federal income tax return.

17. **LO.2** Andrea entered into a § 529 qualified tuition program for the benefit of her daughter, Joanna. Andrea contributed $15,000 to the fund. The fund balance had accumulated to $25,000 by the time Joanna was ready to enter college. However, Joanna received a scholarship that paid for her tuition, fees, books, supplies, and room and board. Therefore, Andrea withdrew the funds from the § 529 plan and bought Joanna a new car.

    a. What are the tax consequences to Andrea of withdrawing the funds?

    b. Assume instead that Joanna's scholarship did not cover her room and board, which cost $7,500 per academic year. During the current year, $7,500 of the fund balance was used to pay for Joanna's room and board. The remaining amount was left in the § 529 plan to cover her room and board for future academic years. What are the tax consequences to Andrea and to Joanna of using the $7,500 to pay for the room and board?

18. **LO.3** Dolly is a cash basis taxpayer. In 2017, she filed her 2016 South Carolina income tax return and received a $2,200 refund. Dolly took the standard deduction on her 2016 Federal income tax return, but will itemize her deductions in 2017. Molly, a cash basis taxpayer, also filed her 2016 South Carolina income tax return in 2017 and received a $600 refund. Molly had $12,000 in itemized deductions on her 2016 Federal income tax return, but will take the standard deduction in 2017. How does the tax benefit rule apply to Dolly's and Molly's situations? Explain.

19. **LO.4** Ralph has experienced financial difficulties as a result of his struggling business. He has been behind on his mortgage payments for the last six months. The mortgage holder, who is a friend of Ralph's, has offered to accept $80,000 in full payment of the $100,000 owed on the mortgage and payable over the next 10 years. The interest rate of the mortgage is 7%, and the market rate is now 8%. What tax issues are raised by the creditor's offer?

Issue ID

Computational Exercises

20. **LO.2** Valentino is a patient in a nursing home for 45 days of 2017. While in the nursing home, he incurs total costs of $13,500. Medicare pays $8,000 of the costs. Valentino receives $15,000 from his long-term care insurance policy, which pays while he is in the facility. Assume that the daily federal statutory amount for Valentino is $360.

    Of the $15,000, what amount may Valentino exclude from his gross income?

21. **LO.2** Mio was transferred from New York to Germany. He lived and worked in Germany for 340 days in 2017. Mio's salary for 2017 is $190,000. In your computation, round any division to four decimal places before converting to a percentage. For example, .473938 would be rounded to 47.39%.

    What is Mio's foreign earned income exclusion?

22. **LO.2** Ellie purchases an insurance policy on her life and names her brother, Jason, as the beneficiary. Ellie pays $32,000 in premiums for the policy during her life. When she dies, Jason collects the insurance proceeds of $500,000.

    As a result, how much gross income does Jason report?

23. **LO.2** Alfred owned a term life insurance policy at the time he was diagnosed with a terminal illness. After paying $18,300 in premiums, he sold the policy to a company that is authorized by the state of South Carolina to purchase such policies. The company paid Alfred $125,000. When Alfred died 18 months later, the company collected the face amount of the policy, $150,000.

    As a result of the sale of the policy, how much is Alfred required to include in his gross income?

24. **LO.2** Leland pays premiums of $5,000 for an insurance policy in the face amount of $25,000 upon the life of Caleb and subsequently transfers the policy to Tyler for $7,500. Over the years, Tyler pays subsequent premiums of $1,500 on the policy. Upon Caleb's death, Tyler receives the proceeds of $25,000.

    As a result, what amount is Tyler required to include in his gross income?

25. **LO.2** Jarrod receives a scholarship of $18,500 from Riggers University to be used to pursue a bachelor's degree. He spends $12,000 on tuition, $1,500 on books and supplies, $4,000 for room and board, and $1,000 for personal expenses.

    How much may Jarrod exclude from his gross income?

26. **LO.3** Myrna and Geoffrey filed a joint tax return in 2016. Their AGI was $85,000, and itemized deductions were $13,700, which included $4,000 in state income tax. In 2017, they received a $1,800 refund of the state income taxes they paid in 2016. The standard deduction for married filing jointly in 2016 was $12,600. Under the tax benefit rule, what amount of the state income tax refund is included in gross income in 2017?

Problems

27. **LO.2** Ed, an employee of the Natural Color Company, suffered from a rare disease that was very expensive to treat. The local media ran several stories about Ed's problems, and the family created a website that generated more than $10,000 in gifts from individuals to help pay the medical bills. Ed's employer provided hospital and medical insurance for its employees, but the policy did not cover Ed's illness. When it became apparent that Ed could not pay all of his medical expenses, the hospital canceled the $25,000 Ed owed at the time of his death. After Ed's death, his former employer paid Ed's widow $12,000 in "her time of need." Ed's widow also collected $50,000 on a group term life insurance policy paid for by Ed's employer. What are Ed's and his widow's gross income?

28. **LO.2** Determine the gross income of the beneficiaries in the following cases:
    a. Justin's employer was downsizing and offered employees an amount equal to one year's salary if the employee would voluntarily retire.
    b. Trina contracted a disease and was unable to work for six months. Because of her dire circumstances, her employer paid her one-half of her regular salary while she was away from work.
    c. Coral Corporation collected $1 million on a key person life insurance policy when its chief executive died. The corporation had paid the premiums on the policy of $77,000, which were not deductible by the corporation.
    d. Juan collected $40,000 on a life insurance policy when his wife, Leona, died in 2016. The insurance policy was provided by Leona's employer, and the premiums were excluded from Leona's gross income as group term life insurance. In 2017, Juan collected the $3,500 accrued salary owed to Leona at the time of her death.

Decision Making   29. **LO.2, 5** Laura was recently diagnosed with cancer and has begun chemotherapy treatments. A cancer specialist has stated that Laura has less than one year to live. She has incurred many medical bills and other general living expenses and is in need of cash. Therefore, she is considering selling stock that cost $35,000 and has a fair market value of $50,000. This amount would be sufficient to pay her medical bills. However, she has read about a company (the Vital Benefits Company) that would purchase her life insurance policy for $50,000. She has paid $30,000 in premiums on the policy.

a. Considering only the tax effects, would selling the stock or selling the life insurance policy result in more beneficial tax treatment?

b. Assume that Laura is a dependent child and that her mother owns the stock and the life insurance policy, which is on the mother's life. Which of the alternative means of raising the cash would result in more beneficial tax treatment?

30. **LO.2** What is the taxpayer's gross income in each of the following situations?

a. Darrin received a salary of $50,000 in 2017 from his employer, Green Construction.

b. In July 2017, Green gave Darrin an all-expense-paid trip to Las Vegas (value of $3,000) for exceeding his sales quota.

c. Megan received $10,000 from her employer to help her pay medical expenses not covered by insurance.

d. Blake received $15,000 from his deceased wife's employer "to help him in his time of greatest need."

e. Clint collected $50,000 as the beneficiary of a group term life insurance policy when his wife died. The premiums on the policy were paid by his deceased wife's employer.

31. **LO.2** Donald was killed in an accident while he was on the job in 2017. Darlene, Donald's wife, received several payments as a result of Donald's death. What is Darlene's gross income from the items listed below?

a. Donald's employer paid Darlene an amount equal to Donald's three months' salary ($60,000), which is what the employer does for all widows and widowers of deceased employees.

b. Donald had $20,000 in accrued salary that was paid to Darlene.

c. Donald's employer had provided Donald with group term life insurance of $480,000 (twice his annual salary), which was payable to his widow in a lump sum. Premiums on this policy totaling $12,500 had been included in Donald's gross income under § 79.

d. Donald had purchased a life insurance policy (premiums totaled $250,000) that paid $600,000 in the event of accidental death. The proceeds were payable to Darlene, who elected to receive installment payments as an annuity of $30,000 each year for a 25-year period. She received her first installment this year.

32. **LO.2** Ray and Carin are partners in an accounting firm. The partners have entered into an arm's length agreement requiring Ray to purchase Carin's partnership interest from Carin's estate if she dies before Ray. The price is set at 120% of the book value of Carin's partnership interest at the time of her death. Ray purchased an insurance policy on Carin's life to fund this agreement. After Ray had paid $45,000 in premiums, Carin was killed in an automobile accident and Ray collected $800,000 of life insurance proceeds. Ray used the life insurance proceeds to purchase Carin's partnership interest.

a. What amount should Ray include in his gross income from receiving the life insurance proceeds?

b. The insurance company paid Ray $16,000 interest on the life insurance proceeds during the period Carin's estate was in administration. During this period, Ray had left the insurance proceeds with the insurance company. Is this interest taxable?

c. When Ray paid $800,000 for Carin's partnership interest, priced as specified in the agreement, the fair market value of Carin's interest was $1 million. How much should Ray include in his gross income from this bargain purchase?

33. **LO.2** Sally was an all-state soccer player during her junior and senior years in high school. She accepted an athletic scholarship from State University. The scholarship provided the following:

Tuition and fees	$15,000
Housing and meals	6,000
Books and supplies	1,500
Transportation	1,200

a. Determine the effect of the scholarship on Sally's gross income.

b. Sally's brother, Willy, was not a gifted athlete, but he received $8,000 from their father's employer as a scholarship during the year. The employer grants the children of all executives a scholarship equal to one-half of annual tuition, fees, books, and supplies. Willy also received a $6,000 scholarship (to be used for tuition) as the winner of an essay contest related to bioengineering, his intended field of study. Determine the effect of the scholarships on Willy's and his father's gross income.

34. **LO.2** Adrian was awarded an academic scholarship to State University for the 2017–2018 academic year. He received $6,500 in August and $7,200 in December 2017. Adrian had enough personal savings to pay all expenses as they came due. Adrian's expenditures for the relevant period were as follows:

Tuition, August 2017	$3,700
Tuition, January 2018	3,750
Room and board	
August–December 2017	2,800
January–May 2018	2,500
Books and educational supplies	
August–December 2017	1,000
January–May 2018	1,200

Determine the effect on Adrian's gross income for 2017 and 2018.

35. **LO.2** Leigh sued an overzealous bill collector and received the following settlement:

Damage to her automobile that the collector attempted to repossess	$ 3,300
Physical damage to her arm caused by the collector	15,000
Loss of income while her arm was healing	6,000
Punitive damages	80,000

a. What effect does the settlement have on Leigh's gross income?

b. Assume that Leigh also collected $25,000 of damages for slander to her personal reputation caused by the bill collector misrepresenting the facts to Leigh's employer and other creditors. Is this $25,000 included in Leigh's gross income? Explain.

36. **LO.2** Determine the effect on gross income in each of the following cases:

a. Eloise received $150,000 in settlement of a sex discrimination case against her former employer.

b. Nell received $10,000 for damages to her personal reputation. She also received $40,000 in punitive damages.

c. Orange Corporation, an accrual basis taxpayer, received $50,000 from a lawsuit filed against its auditor who overcharged for services rendered in a previous year.

d. Beth received $10,000 in compensatory damages and $30,000 in punitive damages in a lawsuit she filed against a tanning parlor for severe burns she received from using its tanning equipment.

e. Joanne received compensatory damages of $75,000 and punitive damages of $300,000 from a cosmetic surgeon who botched her nose job.

37. **LO.2** Rex, age 55, is an officer of Blue Company, which provides him with the following nondiscriminatory fringe benefits in 2017:

   - Hospitalization insurance premiums for Rex and his dependents. The cost of the coverage for Rex is $2,900 per year, and the additional cost for his dependents is $3,800 per year. The plan has a $2,000 deductible, but his employer contributed $1,500 to Rex's Health Savings Account (HSA). Rex withdrew only $800 from the HSA, and the account earned $50 of interest during the year.

   - Insurance premiums of $840 for salary continuation payments. Under the plan, Rex will receive his regular salary in the event he is unable to work due to illness. Rex collected $4,500 on the policy to replace lost wages while he was ill during the year.

   - Rex is a part-time student working on his bachelor's degree in engineering. His employer reimbursed his $5,200 tuition under a plan available to all full-time employees.

   Determine the amount Rex must include in gross income.

38. **LO.2** The UVW Union and HON Corporation are negotiating contract terms.   **Communications** Assume that the union members are in the 25% marginal tax bracket and that all benefits are provided on a nondiscriminatory basis. Write a letter to the UVW Union members explaining the tax consequences of the options discussed below. The union's address is 905 Spruce Street, Washington, DC 20227.

   a. The company would eliminate the $250 deductible on medical insurance benefits. Most employees incur more than $250 each year in medical expenses.

   b. Employees would get an additional paid holiday with the same annual income (the same pay but less work).

   c. An employee who did not need health insurance (because the employee's spouse works and receives family coverage) would be allowed to receive the cash value of the coverage.

39. **LO.2, 5** Mauve Corporation has a group hospitalization insurance plan that has a   **Decision Making** $200 deductible amount for hospital visits and a $15 deductible for doctor visits and prescriptions. The deductible portion paid by employees who have children has become substantial for some employees. The company is considering adopting a medical reimbursement plan or a flexible benefits plan to cover the deductible amounts. Either of these plans can be tailored to meet the needs of the employees. What are the cost considerations to the employer that should be considered in choosing between these plans?

40. **LO.2** Belinda spent the last 60 days of 2017 in a nursing home. The cost of the services provided to her was $18,000 ($300 per day). Medicare paid $8,500 toward the cost of her stay. Belinda also received $5,500 of benefits under a long-term care insurance policy she purchased. What is the effect on Belinda's gross income?

41. **LO.2** Tim is the vice president of western operations for Maroon Oil Company and is stationed in San Francisco. He is required to live in an employer-owned home, which is three blocks from his company office. The company-provided home is equipped with high-speed internet access and several telephone lines. Tim receives telephone calls and e-mails that require immediate attention any time of day or night because the company's business is spread all over the world. A full-time administrative assistant resides in the house to assist Tim with the urgent business matters. Tim often uses the home for entertaining customers, suppliers, and employees. The fair market value of comparable housing is $9,000 per month. Tim is also provided with free parking at his company's office. The value of the parking is $350 per month. Calculate the amount associated with the company-provided housing and free parking that Tim must include in his gross income for 2017.

42. **LO.2** Does the taxpayer recognize gross income in the following situations?

  a. Ava is a filing clerk at a large insurance company. She is permitted to leave the premises for lunch, but she usually eats in the company's cafeteria because it is quick and she is on a tight schedule. On average, she pays $2 for a lunch that would cost $12 at a restaurant and it cost her employer $10 to prepare. However, if the prices in the cafeteria were not so low and the food was not so delicious, she would probably bring her lunch at a cost of $3 per day.

  b. Scott is an executive for an international corporation located in New York City. Often he works late, taking telephone calls from the company's European branch. Scott often stays in a company-owned condominium when he has a late-night work session. The condominium is across the street from the company office and has the technology needed to communicate with employees and customers throughout the world.

  c. Ira recently moved to take a job. For the first month on the new job, Ira was searching for a home to purchase or rent. During this time, his employer permitted Ira to live in an apartment the company maintains for customers during the buying season. The month that Ira occupied the apartment was not during the buying season, and the apartment would not otherwise have been occupied.

Decision Making 43. **LO.2, 5** Bertha is considering taking an early retirement offered by her employer. She would receive $3,000 per month, indexed for inflation. However, she would no longer be able to use the company's health facilities, and she would be required to pay her hospitalization insurance premiums of $8,000 each year. Bertha and her husband will file a joint return and take the standard deduction. She currently receives a salary of $55,000 a year. If she retires, she will spend approximately $300 less each month for commuting and clothing. Bertha and her husband have other sources of income and are in and will remain in the 25% marginal tax bracket. Her income tax for the current year was $8,875. She currently pays Social Security and Medicare taxes of 7.65% on her salary, but her retirement pay would not be subject to this tax. According to Bertha, she and her husband could live well if her after-tax retirement income was at least 50% of her current income. Provide Bertha with information she will need to make her decision.

Communications 44. **LO.2, 5** Finch Construction Company provides the carpenters it employs with all of the required tools. However, the company believes that this practice has led to some employees not taking care of the tools and to the mysterious disappearance of some tools. The company is considering requiring all of its employees to provide their own tools. Each employee's salary would be increased by $1,500 to compensate for the additional cost. Write a letter to Finch's management explaining the tax consequences of this plan to the carpenters. Finch's address is 300 Harbor Drive, Vermillion, SD 57069.

45. **LO.2, 5** Bluebird, Inc., does not provide its employees with any tax-exempt fringe benefits. The company is considering adopting a hospital and medical benefits insurance plan that will cost approximately $9,000 per employee. To adopt this plan, the company may have to reduce salaries and/or lower future salary increases. Bluebird is in the 35% (combined Federal and state rates) bracket. Bluebird is also responsible for matching the Social Security and Medicare taxes withheld on employees' salaries (at the full 7.65% rate). The hospital and medical benefits insurance plan will not be subject to the Social Security and Medicare taxes, and the company is not eligible for the small business credit for health insurance. The employees generally fall into two marginal tax rate groups:

Income Tax	Social Security and Medicare Tax	Total
.15	.0765	.2265
.35	.0145	.3645

The company has asked you to assist in its financial planning for the hospital and medical benefits insurance plan by computing the following:

a. How much taxable compensation is the equivalent of $9,000 of exempt compensation for each of the two classes of employees?

b. What is the company's after-tax cost of the taxable compensation computed in part (a)?

c. What is the company's after-tax cost of the exempt compensation?

d. Briefly explain your conclusions from the preceding analysis.

46. **LO.2, 5** Rosa's employer has instituted a flexible benefits program. Rosa will use the plan to pay for her daughter's dental expenses and other medical expenses that are not covered by health insurance. Rosa is in the 28% marginal tax bracket and estimates that the medical and dental expenses not covered by health insurance will be within the range of $4,000 to $5,000. Her employer's plan permits her to set aside as much as $5,000 in the flexible benefits account. Rosa does not itemize her deductions.

Decision Making

a. Rosa puts $4,000 into her flexible benefits account, and her actual expenses are $5,000. What is her cost of underestimating the expenses?

b. Rosa puts $5,000 into her flexible benefits account, and her actual expenses are only $4,000. What is her cost of overestimating her expenses?

c. What is Rosa's cost of underfunding as compared with the cost of overfunding the flexible benefits account?

d. Does your answer in part (c) suggest that Rosa should fund the account closer to the low end or to the high end of her estimates?

47. **LO.2** Sparrow Corporation would like you to review its employee fringe benefits program with regard to the tax consequences of the plan for the company's president (Polly), who is also the majority shareholder.

a. The company has a qualified retirement plan. The company pays the cost of employees attending a retirement planning seminar. The employee must be within 10 years of retirement, and the cost of the seminar is $1,500 per attendee.

b. The company owns a parking garage that is used by customers, employees, and the general public. Only the general public is required to pay for parking. The charge to the general public for Polly's parking for the year would have been $3,600 (a $300 monthly rate).

c. All employees are allowed to use the company's fixed charge long-distance telephone services, as long as the privilege is not abused. Although no one has kept track of the actual calls, Polly's use of the telephone had a value (what she would have paid on her personal telephone) of approximately $600.

d. The company owns a condominium at the beach, which it uses to entertain customers. Employees are allowed to use the facility without charge when the company has no scheduled events. Polly used the facility 10 days during the year. Her use had a rental value of $1,000.

e. The company is in the household moving business. Employees are allowed to ship goods without charge whenever there is excess space on a truck. Polly purchased a dining room suite for her daughter. Company trucks delivered the furniture to the daughter. Normal freight charges would have been $750.

f. The company has a storage facility for household goods. Officers are allowed a 20% discount on charges for storing their goods. All other employees are allowed a 10% discount. Polly's discounts for the year totaled $900.

48. **LO.2** George is a U.S. citizen who is employed by Hawk Enterprises, a global company. Beginning on June 1, 2017, George began working in London. He worked there until January 31, 2018, when he transferred to Paris. He worked in

Paris the remainder of 2018. His salary for the first five months of 2017 was $100,000, and it was earned in the United States. His salary for the remainder of 2017 was $175,000, and it was earned in London. George's 2018 salary from Hawk was $300,000, with part being earned in London and part being earned in Paris. What is George's gross income in 2017 and 2018? (Assume that the 2018 indexed amount is the same as the 2017 indexed amount.)

49. **LO.2, 3** Determine Hazel's gross income from the following receipts for the year:

Gain on sale of Augusta County bonds	$800
Interest on U.S. government savings bonds	400
Interest on state income tax refund	200
Interest on Augusta County bonds	700
Patronage dividend from Potato Growers Cooperative	350

The patronage dividend was received in March of the current year for amounts paid for her (nondeductible) garden and lawn supplies.

50. **LO.2** In January 2017, Ezra purchased 2,000 shares of Gold Utility Mutual Fund for $20,000. In June, Ezra received an additional 100 shares as a dividend, in lieu of receiving $1,000 in cash dividends. In December, the company declared a two-for-one stock split. Ezra received an additional 2,100 shares, but there was no option to receive cash. At the time of the stock dividend in December and at the end of the year, the fund shares were trading for $5 per share. Also, at the end of the year, the fund offered to buy outstanding shares for $4.50. Ezra did not sell any shares during the year.

a. What is Ezra's gross income from the 100 shares received in June?

b. What is Ezra's gross income from the receipt of the 2,100 shares as a two-for-one stock split in December?

c. Should Ezra be required to recognize gross income in 2017 even though the fair market value of his investment at the end of the year was less than the fair market value at the beginning of the year? Explain.

Decision Making 51. **LO.2** Tonya, who lives in California, inherited a $100,000 State of California bond in 2017. Her marginal Federal tax rate is 35%, and her marginal state tax rate is 5%. The California bond pays 3.3% interest, which is not subject to California income tax. She can purchase a corporate bond of comparable risk that will yield 5.2% or a U.S. government bond that pays 4.6% interest. Which investment will provide the greatest after-tax yield?

Decision Making
Communications

52. **LO.2** Lynn Swartz's husband died three years ago. Her parents have an income of over $200,000 a year and want to ensure that funds will be available for the education of Lynn's 8-year-old son, Eric. Lynn is currently earning $45,000 a year. Lynn's parents have suggested that they start a savings account for Eric. They have calculated that if they invest $4,000 a year for the next 8 years, at the end of 10 years, sufficient funds will be available for Eric's college expenses. Lynn realizes that the tax treatment of the investments could significantly affect the amount of funds available for Eric's education. She asked you to write a letter to her advising about options available to her parents and to her for Eric's college education. Lynn's address is 100 Myrtle Cove, Fairfield, CT 06824.

53. **LO.2** Starting in 2006, Chuck and Luane have been purchasing Series EE bonds in their name to use for the higher education of their daughter Susie, who currently is age 18. During the year, they cash in $12,000 of the bonds to use for freshman year tuition, fees, and room and board. Of this amount, $5,000 represents interest. Of the $12,000, $8,000 is used for tuition and fees, and $4,000 is used for room and board. Chuck and Luane's AGI, before the educational savings bond exclusion, is $120,000. Review § 135, and answer the following questions.

a. Determine the tax consequences for Chuck and Luane, who will file a joint return, and for Susie.

b.   Assume that Chuck and Luane purchased the bonds in Susie's name. Determine the tax consequences for Chuck and Luane and for Susie.

c.   How would your answer to part (a) change if Chuck and Luane filed separate returns?

54. **LO.2** Albert established a qualified tuition program for each of his twins, Kim and Jim. He started each fund with $20,000 when the children were 5 years old. Albert made no further contributions to his children's plans. Thirteen years later, both children have graduated from high school. Kim's fund has accumulated to $45,000, while Jim's has accumulated to $42,000. Kim decides to attend a state university, which will cost $60,000 for four years (tuition, fees, room and board, and books). Jim decides to go to work instead of going to college. During the current year, $7,500 is used from Kim's plan to pay the cost of her first semester in college. Because Jim is not going to college now or in the future, Albert withdraws the $42,000 plan balance and gives it to Jim to start his new life after high school.

a.   During the period since the plans were established, should Albert or the twins have been including the annual plan earnings in gross income? Explain.

b.   What are the tax consequences to Kim and Albert of the $7,500 being used for the first semester's higher education costs?

c.   Because of her participation in the qualified tuition program, Kim received a 10% reduction in tuition charges; so less than $7,500 was withdrawn from her account. Is either Albert or Kim required to include the value of this discount in gross income? Explain.

d.   What are the tax consequences to Albert and Jim of Jim's qualified tuition program being closed?

55. **LO.3** How does the tax benefit rule apply in the following cases?

a.   In 2015, the Orange Furniture Store, an accrual method taxpayer, sold furniture on credit for $1,000 to Sammy. The cost of the furniture was $600. In 2016, Orange took a bad debt deduction for the $1,000. In 2017, Sammy inherited some money and paid Orange the $1,000 he owed. Orange was in the 35% marginal tax bracket in 2015, the 15% marginal tax bracket in 2016, and the 35% marginal tax bracket in 2017.

b.   In 2016, Marvin, a cash basis taxpayer, took a $2,000 itemized deduction for state income taxes paid. This increased his itemized deductions to a total that was $800 more than the standard deduction. In 2016, Marvin received a $1,600 refund when he filed his 2016 state income tax return. Marvin was in the 15% marginal tax bracket in 2016, but was in the 35% marginal tax bracket in 2017.

c.   In 2016, Barb, a cash basis taxpayer, was in an accident and incurred $8,000 in medical expenses, which she claimed as an itemized deduction for medical expenses. Because of the 10%-of-AGI reduction, the expense reduced her taxable income by only $3,000. In 2017, Barb successfully sued the person who caused the physical injury and collected $8,000 to reimburse her for the cost of her medical expenses. Barb was in the 15% marginal tax bracket in both 2016 and 2017.

56. **LO.4, 5** Fran, who is in the 35% tax bracket, recently collected $100,000 on a life insurance policy she carried on her father. She currently owes $120,000 on her personal residence and $120,000 on business property. National Bank holds the mortgage on both pieces of property and has agreed to accept $100,000 in complete satisfaction of either mortgage. The interest rate on the mortgages is 8%, and both mortgages are payable over 10 years. What would be the tax consequences of each of the following alternatives assuming that Fran currently deducts the mortgage interest on her tax return?

Decision Making

a.   Retire the mortgage on the residence.

b.   Retire the mortgage on the business property.

Which alternative should Fran select?

57. **LO.4** Vic, who was experiencing financial difficulties, was able to adjust his debts as follows:

    a. Vic is an attorney. Vic owed his uncle $25,000. The uncle told Vic that if he serves as the executor of the uncle's estate, Vic's debt will be canceled in the uncle's will.

    b. Vic borrowed $80,000 from First Bank. The debt was secured by land that Vic purchased for $100,000. Vic was unable to pay, and the bank foreclosed when the liability was $80,000, which was also the fair market value of the property.

    c. The Land Company, which had sold land to Vic for $80,000, reduced the mortgage on the land by $12,000.

    Determine the tax consequences to Vic.

Cumulative Problems

Tax Return Problem

TAX SOFTWARE

58. Alfred E. Old and Beulah A. Crane, each age 42, married on September 7, 2014. Alfred and Beulah will file a joint return for 2016. Alfred's Social Security number is 111-11-1112. Beulah's Social Security number is 123-45-6789, and she adopted "Old" as her married name. They live at 211 Brickstone Drive, Atlanta, GA 30304.

    Alfred was divorced from Sarah Old in March 2014. Under the divorce agreement, Alfred is to pay Sarah $1,250 per month for the next 10 years or until Sarah's death, whichever occurs first. Alfred pays Sarah $15,000 in 2016. In addition, in January 2016, Alfred pays Sarah $50,000, which is designated as being for her share of the marital property. Also, Alfred is responsible for all prior years' income taxes. Sarah's Social Security number is 123-45-6788.

    Alfred's salary for 2016 is $150,000, and his employer, Cherry, Inc. (Federal I.D. No. 98-7654321), provides him with group term life insurance equal to twice his annual salary. His employer withheld $24,900 for Federal income taxes and $8,000 for state income taxes. The proper amounts were withheld for FICA taxes.

    Beulah recently graduated from law school and is employed by Legal Aid Society, Inc. (Federal I.D. No. 11-1111111), as a public defender. She receives a salary of $40,000 in 2016. Her employer withheld $7,500 for Federal income taxes and $2,400 for state income taxes. The proper amounts were withheld for FICA taxes.

    Beulah has $2,500 in qualified dividends on Yellow Corporation stock she inherited. Alfred and Beulah receive a $1,900 refund on their 2015 state income taxes. They itemized deductions on their 2015 Federal income tax return (total of $15,000). Alfred and Beulah pay $4,500 interest and $1,450 property taxes on their personal residence in 2016. Their charitable contributions total $2,400 (all to their church). They paid sales taxes of $1,400, for which they maintain the receipts. Both spouses had health insurance for all months of 2016 and do not want to contribute to the Presidential Election Campaign.

    Compute the Olds' net tax payable (or refund due) for 2016. If you use tax forms for your solution, you will need Form 1040 and Schedules A and B. Suggested software: H&R BLOCK Tax Software.

Tax Computation Problem
Decision Making
Communications

59. Martin S. Albert (Social Security number 111-11-1111) is 39 years old and is married to Michele R. Albert (Social Security number 123-45-6789). The Alberts live at 512 Ferry Road, Newport News, VA 23601. They file a joint return and have two dependent children, Charlene, age 17, and Jordan, age 18. Charlene's Social Security number is 123-45-6788, and Jordan's Social Security number is 123-45-6787. In 2017, Martin and Michele had the following transactions:

    a. Martin received $120,000 in salary from Red Steel Corporation, where he is a construction engineer. Withholding for Federal income tax was $10,750. The amounts withheld for FICA taxes were as follows: $7,049 ($113,700 × 6.2%) for

Social Security and $1,740 ($120,000 × 1.45%) for Medicare. Martin worked in Mexico from January 1, 2016, until February 15, 2017. His $120,000 salary for 2017 includes $18,000 he earned for January and one-half of February 2017 while working in Mexico.

b. Martin and Michele received $800 in qualified dividends on Green, Inc. stock and $400 interest on Montgomery County (Virginia) school bonds.

c. Martin received $2,300 interest from a Bahamian bank account.

d. Michele received 50 shares of Applegate Corporation common stock as a stock dividend. The shares had a fair market value of $2,500 at the time Michele received them, and she did not have the option of receiving cash.

e. Martin and Michele received a $1,200 refund on their 2016 Virginia income taxes. Their itemized deductions in 2016 totaled $14,000.

f. Martin paid $6,600 alimony to his former wife, Rose T. Morgan (Social Security number 123-45-6786).

g. Martin and Michele kept the receipts for their sales taxes paid of $1,100.

h. Martin and Michele's itemized deductions were as follows:

- State income tax paid and withheld totaled $5,100.

- Real estate taxes on their principal residence were $3,700.

- Mortgage interest on their principal residence was $2,500.

- Cash contributions to the church totaled $2,800.

Part 1—Tax Computation
Compute the Alberts's net tax payable (or refund due) for 2017.

Part 2—Tax Planning
The Alberts are considering buying another house. Their house mortgage payments would increase by $500 (to $1,500) per month, which includes a $250 increase in interest and a $100 increase in property tax. The Alberts would like to know how much the mortgage payments would increase net of any change in their income tax. Write a letter to the Alberts that contains your advice.

Research Problems

THOMSON REUTERS
CHECKPOINT®
Student Edition

Note: Solutions to the Research Problems can be prepared by using the Thomson Reuters Checkpoint® Student Edition online tax research database, which accompanies this textbook. Solutions can also be prepared by using research materials found in a typical tax library.

Research Problem 1. Murray reported to the Environmental Protection Agency that his employer was illegally dumping chemicals into a river. His charges were true, and Murray's employer was fined. In retaliation, Murray's employer fired him and made deliberate efforts to prevent Murray from obtaining other employment. Murray sued the employer, claiming that his reputation had been damaged. Murray won his lawsuit and received an award for "damages to his personal and professional reputation and for his mental suffering." Now he would like to know whether the award is taxable. He argues that he was awarded damages as a recovery of his human capital and that a recovery of capital is not income. Therefore, the Federal government does not have the power to tax the award.

Research Problem 2. The employees of the city of Greenville must make mandatory contributions to the city's postretirement health benefit plan. The employees' contributions are placed in a trust and are used exclusively for the employees' benefits. The employees believe that because they are required to make the contributions from their base salaries, the result should be the same as if the employer made the contribution and had reduced their salaries by the amount of the contributions. Therefore, the employees believe they should be permitted to exclude the payments from gross income. The employees have asked you to research the issue.

Research Problem 3. Your client, John Butler, is an avid Houston Astros fan. Last March at the Astros' home opener, as a result of a random drawing of those in attendance at the game, John won 300 Shipley Do-Nut coupons. Each coupon entitled him to a cup of coffee and a free doughnut or a dozen doughnut holes.

John used some of the coupons (approximately 20), but he found that eating so many doughnuts directly conflicted with his goal of losing weight. The unused coupons expired on January 1, 2017. Thus, John was surprised when he received a Form 1099 in February 2017 that valued his prize at $900. John would like to know whether the value of the doughnut coupons should be included in income and asks you to research his question. If you conclude that their value should be included in income, John also would like to know if he can reduce his gross income by including in income only the value of the coupons that he used. He has the unused coupons as documentation that neither he nor anyone else used them.

Research Problem 4. Aubrey Brown is a decorated veteran of the Vietnam War. As a result of his exposure to Agent Orange during the war, Aubrey developed lung cancer and is unable to work. He received $12,000 of Social Security disability payments in the current year. He reasons that the payments should be excluded from his gross income because the payments are compensation for the physical injury he suffered as a result of his service in the armed forces. Is Aubrey correct? Explain.

Partial list of research aids:
Rev.Rul. 77–318, 1977–2 C.B. 45.
Reimels v. Comm., 2006–1 USTC ¶50,147, 97 AFTR 2d 2006–820, 436 F.3d 344 (CA–2, 2006).

Research Problem 5. Your client works for a defense contractor and was assigned to work on a military base in Australia. As a condition of his employment, he was required to live in housing that was provided to military personnel. The housing provided was a condominium located in a civilian neighborhood that was 20 miles from the military base where he performed his services. The employer paid over $6,000 of rent while the employee was living there. Your client would like to know whether the value of the housing can be excluded from his gross income. He read an article that indicated that employees who are required to live in a "camp" in a foreign country can exclude the cost of the housing from gross income. What is the result of your research?

Use internet tax resources to address the following questions. Look for reliable websites and blogs of the IRS and other government agencies, media outlets, businesses, tax professionals, academics, think tanks, and political outlets.

Research Problem 6. Employers often use the internet as a means of attracting applications from potential employees. Locate an internet site offering employment opportunities, ideally one provided by a well-known corporation. How does the employer promote its fringe benefit and cafeteria plan packages? Compare and contrast several such sites.

Research Problem 7. One income exclusion that some states allow that the federal government does not is for lottery winnings. Does your state have an exclusion for lottery winnings? If so, how does it work? Why do you think a state might allow winnings from its own state lottery to be excluded from state income taxes?

Roger CPA Review Questions

1. In 2015 Randall suffered bodily injury while at work. On his 2015 tax return, Randall deducted related medical expenses of $10,000 and $5,000 in 2016. In 2017, Randall won a workers' compensation claim and prevailed in an injury lawsuit, both in connection with the 2015 injury. Randall received the following in 2017 as settlement:

Punitive damages	$150,000
Workers' compensation	50,000
Reimbursement for medical expenses	25,000
Compensation for emotional distress caused by the injury	15,000

    What amount of the settlement should be excluded from Randall's 2017 gross income?

    a. $ 75,000   c. $ 90,000
    b. $ 60,000   d. $165,000

2. The following pertain to Joyce in 2017:

Medical insurance premiums paid by employer	$4,800
Teacher of the Year Award, in the form of gift cards redeemable at local businesses	500
Jewelry box, received from employer for 25 years of service (FMV)	100
2016 holiday bonus awarded in December 2017, to be paid in January 2018	250

    What total amount from the above may be excluded from Joyce's 2017 gross income?

    a. $5,650   c. $5,150
    b. $350   d. $850

3. Pierce, a married individual, received the following in 2017:

Workers' compensation award	$25,000
W-2 income	20,000
Unemployment compensation	4,800
Damages awarded for emotional distress experienced as a result of workplace bodily injury	10,000

    Considering only the above, what is Pierce's 2017 gross income?

    a. $49,800   c. $30,000
    b. $34,800   d. $24,800

4. Norbert works in a beauty salon. He receives a 50% employee discount for salon services. In 2017, he used his discount to buy $1,000 of services with a fair market value of $2,000. As a result of these bargain purchases, how much should Norbert include in 2017 gross income?

    a. $1,000   c. $2,000
    b. $600   d. $0

5. Cole, a 48-year-old married individual, received the following in 2017:

S corporation stock dividends	$5,000
Interest earned on federal Treasury bills	1,000
Interest earned on municipal bonds	2,500
Interest earned on state income tax refund	50
Interest earned on Series EE savings bonds, used to help pay for room and board for dependent in college	1,500
Common stock property dividend (FMV)	3,000

In addition, Cole spent $500 on lottery scratch-off cards in 2017. All of the cards were losers except for one, from which Cole won $1,000.

Given these facts, what total amount from the above should be included in gross income on Cole's 2017 tax return?

a. $ 4,550   c. $11,050

b. $ 6,550   d. $11,550

6. Manish is a student who began working part-time as a restaurant waiter in October of 2017. He earned the following tips in 2017, with each month's tips reported in a schedule submitted to the restaurant's management by the tenth of the following month:

October	$400
November	215
December	150

In addition, Manish received a scholarship in 2017 which provided $5,000 for tuition, $5,000 for room and board, $1,000 for travel to study abroad, and $1,000 for books.

What total amount from the above should be included in Manish's 2017 gross income?

a. $5,765   c. $6,615

b. $5,615   d. $6,765

PART 3

DEDUCTIONS

Part 3 presents the deduction component of the basic tax model. Deductions are classified as business versus nonbusiness, "for" AGI versus "from" AGI, employee versus employer, active versus passive, and reimbursed versus unreimbursed. The effect of each of these classifications is analyzed. Deduction limitations and disallowances are also discussed. A separate chapter examines the special tax treatment affecting losses from investment activities.

Deductions and Losses: In General

LEARNING OBJECTIVES: *After completing Chapter 6, you should be able to:*

LO.1 Differentiate between deductions *for* and *from* adjusted gross income and describe the relevance of the differentiation.

LO.2 Describe the cash and accrual methods of accounting with emphasis on the deduction aspects.

LO.3 Apply the Internal Revenue Code deduction disallowance provisions associated with the following: public policy limitations, political activities, excessive executive compensation, investigation of

business opportunities, hobby losses, vacation home rentals, payment of others' expenses, personal expenditures, capital expenditures, related-party transactions, and expenses related to tax-exempt income.

LO.4 Identify tax planning opportunities for maximizing deductions and minimizing the disallowance of deductions.

CHAPTER OUTLINE

CALCULATION OF DEDUCTIBLE EXPENSES

Dr. Cliff Payne determines that the deductible expenses associated with his dental practice are as follows:

Salaries including FICA ($5,000 are unpaid at year-end)	$120,000
Building rent	24,000
Depreciation of dental equipment and office furnishings and equipment	52,000
Insurance (malpractice, dental equipment, and office furnishings and equipment)	22,000
Dental supplies	16,000
Office supplies	3,000
Investigation expenses	6,000
Contribution to the State Senate campaign fund of Tom Smith	1,000
Contribution to the State Senate campaign fund of Virginia White	1,000
Legal expenses associated with patient lawsuit	4,000
Fine imposed by city for improper disposal of medical waste	3,000
Dues paid to The Dental Society	10,000
Draw by Dr. Payne for living expenses ($5,000 monthly)	60,000

Has Dr. Payne correctly calculated the deductible business expenses for his dental practice?

Read the chapter and formulate your response.

FRAMEWORK 1040 **Tax Formula for Individuals**

This chapter covers the boldfaced portions of the Tax Formula for Individuals that was introduced in Concept Summary 3.1 on p. 3-3. Below those portions are the sections of Form 1040 where the results are reported.

Income *(broadly defined)*	$xx,xxx
Less: Exclusions	(x,xxx)
Gross income..	$xx,xxx
Less: **Deductions** *for* **adjusted gross income**.................................	(x,xxx)

FORM 1040 (p. 1)

12	Business income or (loss). Attach Schedule C or C-EZ	

Adjusted gross income..	$xx,xxx
Less: The greater of total **itemized deductions** *or* **the standard deduction**..........................	(x,xxx)

FORM 1040 (p. 2)

40	**Itemized deductions** (from Schedule A) **or** your **standard deduction**	

Personal and dependency exemptions	(x,xxx)
Taxable income	$xx,xxx
Tax on taxable income *(see Tax Tables or Tax Rate Schedules)*...................	$ x,xxx
Less: Tax credits *(including income taxes withheld and prepaid)*	(xxx)
Tax due (or refund)	$ xxx

T he tax law has an all-inclusive definition of income; that is, income from whatever source derived is includible in gross income. Income cannot be excluded unless there is a specific statement to that effect in the tax law.

The opposite approach is used for deductions. A deduction is allowed only if there is a specific provision in the tax law that permits it. The inclusive definition of income and the exclusive definition of deductions may not seem fair to taxpayers, but it is the structure of the tax law. The courts agree with this structure, holding that any exclusions from income and all deductions are gifts from Congress.[1]

LO.1

Differentiate between deductions *for* and *from* adjusted gross income and describe the relevance of the differentiation.

6-1 CLASSIFICATION OF DEDUCTIBLE EXPENSES

It is important to classify deductible expenses as **deductions *for* adjusted gross income** (AGI) or **deductions *from* adjusted gross income**. Deductions *for* AGI can be claimed whether or not the taxpayer itemizes. Deductions *from* AGI result in a tax benefit only if, collectively, they exceed the taxpayer's standard deduction. If itemized deductions (*from* AGI) are less than the standard deduction, they provide no tax benefit. As Example 1 illustrates, whether a deduction is classified as *for* AGI or *from* AGI can affect the benefit the taxpayer receives from the deduction.

---

[1]The courts refer to this as "legislative grace"; see *New Colonial Ice Co. v. Helvering*, 4 USTC ¶1292, 13 AFTR 1180, 54 S.Ct. 788 (USSC, 1934).

Steve is a self-employed CPA. Ralph is one of Steve's employees. During the year, Steve and Ralph incur the following expenses:

EXAMPLE 1

	Steve	Ralph
Dues to American Institute of CPAs and State Society of CPAs	$ 400	$ 300
Subscriptions to professional journals	500	200
Registration fees for tax conferences	800	800
	$1,700	$1,300

Steve does not reimburse any of his employees for dues, subscriptions, or educational programs.

Steve's expenses are classified as deductions *for* AGI because they are considered business expenses since he is a sole proprietor. Therefore, he can deduct the $1,700 on his Federal income tax return. Ralph's unreimbursed employee business expenses are classified as deductions *from* AGI.

Ralph will be able to benefit from the $1,300 of expenses on his Federal income tax return only if his itemized deductions exceed his standard deduction. If, instead, he takes the standard deduction, the $1,300 of expenses will have no effect on the calculation of his taxable income. Even if Ralph does itemize deductions, he still may not benefit from the deduction because of the 2%-of-AGI phaseout rule for certain itemized deductions.

Deductions *for* AGI may directly affect the *amount* of itemized deductions because many itemized deductions are limited to amounts in excess of specified percentages of AGI. Itemized deductions that have AGI limitations include medical expenses, personal casualty losses, and unreimbursed employee expenses.

Tina, age 36, earns a salary of $80,000 and has no other income. She itemizes her deductions during 2017. Unreimbursed medical expenses for the year are $12,000. Tina's medical expense deduction is $4,000, as computed below. Alternatively, assume that Tina receives a $10,000 bonus from her employer in 2017. Her AGI would then be $90,000 ($80,000 + $10,000), and her medical expense is reduced by $1,000 to $3,000.

EXAMPLE 2

	No Bonus	Bonus
Qualified medical expenses	$12,000	$12,000
Reduction: AGI × 10%	(8,000)	(9,000)
Deductible medical expenses	$ 4,000	$ 3,000

When Tina's income increased by $10,000, this reduced her medical expense deduction; so the total effect on taxable income is an increase of $11,000.[2]

6-1a Classifying Deductions

Two key issues must be resolved for any potential deduction. First, it must be determined whether the item is deductible, as discussed in text Section 6-1b. If the item is deductible, then the second issue is to determine if the deduction is classified as *for* AGI or *from* AGI. Deductions *for* AGI are listed in § 62. If a deduction is not listed in § 62, it is an itemized deduction. Exhibit 6.1 provides a partial list of the items classified as deductions *for* AGI.

6-1b Authority for Deductions

The specific authority for deductions is provided in many different Code sections. However, two of the most important are § 212 and § 162. To determine the proper authority

---

[2]Example 4 in Chapter 3 illustrates this same point. See Chapter 10 for additional discussion of medical expenses.

EXHIBIT 6.1	Common Deductions *for* Adjusted Gross Income	
Deduction		**Chapter**
Alimony payments		4
Expenses attributable to property held for the production of rents and royalties		6
Expenses attributable to a trade or business		9
Employee business expenses		9
Moving expenses		9
Qualified tuition and related expenses		9
Professional development and supplies (up to $250) for elementary and secondary school teachers		9
Student loan interest		9 and 10
Contributions to retirement plans		9 and 19
Medical insurance premiums paid by a self-employed taxpayer		10
Self-employment taxes		13
Losses on the sale or exchange of property		14 and 16
Penalty on premature withdrawal of funds from time savings accounts		19

for claiming a deduction, first determine what type of activity the expenditure relates to. All activities can be divided into one of the following mutually exclusive categories:

1. Investment/production of income (§ 212)
2. Trade or business (§ 162)
3. Personal activity (various Code sections)

For example, are legal expenses deductible? To make that determination, first determine whether the legal expense relates to an investment, a trade or business, or a personal activity.

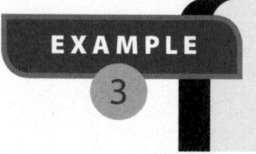

EXAMPLE 3

Darryl pays $400 to an attorney for her advice. If this payment relates to his business, it is a § 162 business expense. If the payment relates to the purchase of land that he intends to hold for profit, it is a § 212 investment/production of income expense. If the payment relates to the development of an estate plan, it is a personal expense (§ 262).

Section 212 Expenses

Section 212 allows deductions for ordinary and necessary expenses paid or incurred for:

- The production or collection of income.
- The management, conservation, or maintenance of property held for the production of income.
- Expenses paid in connection with the determination, collection, or refund of any tax.

Section 212 expenses may be *for* AGI or *from* AGI. Common examples of deductions *for* AGI are expenses related to rent and royalty income (reported on Schedule E) and professional fees paid by a sole proprietor (reported on Schedule C) or a farmer (reported on Schedule F).

All other § 212 expenses are itemized deductions (deductions *from* AGI). For example, investment-related expenses (e.g., safe deposit box rentals) are deductible as itemized deductions attributable to the production of investment income.[3]

Section 162 Trade or Business Expenses

Section 162(a) permits a deduction for all ordinary and necessary expenses paid or incurred in carrying on a trade or business. These include reasonable salaries paid for services, expenses for the use of business property, and one-half of self-employment taxes paid (see Chapter 13). These expenses are deducted *for* AGI.

---

[3]§ 62(a)(4) and Reg. § 1.212–1(g).

It is sometimes difficult to determine whether an expense is deductible as a trade or business expense. The term *trade or business* is not defined in the Code or Regulations, and the courts have not provided a satisfactory definition. One key determination is to ensure that the activity is not a hobby. If the taxpayer's operations are not extensive enough to indicate that a trade or business exists, expenses related to the activity are deductible only to the extent of the activity's income.

Section 162 *excludes* the following items from classification as trade or business expenses:

- Charitable contributions or gifts.
- Illegal bribes and kickbacks and certain treble damage payments.
- Fines and penalties.

6-1c Deduction Criteria for § 162 and § 212

Expenses under § 162 and § 212 must be `ordinary and necessary` to be deductible. In addition, compensation for services must be "reasonable" in amount.

An expense is *necessary* if a prudent businessperson would incur the same expense and the expense is expected to be appropriate and helpful in the taxpayer's business.[4] An expense is *ordinary* if it is normal, usual, or customary in the type of business conducted by the taxpayer and is not capital in nature.[5] However, an expense need not be recurring to be deductible as ordinary. For example, a business may be in a situation that is a very rare occurrence and incur an expense. If other businesses in a similar situation are likely to incur a similar expense, then the expense can be ordinary, even though it is not recurring.

Albert engaged in a mail-order business. The post office judged that his advertisements were false and misleading. Under a fraud order, the post office stamped "fraudulent" on all letters addressed to Albert's business and returned them to the senders. Albert spent $30,000 on legal fees in an unsuccessful attempt to force the post office to stop.

The legal fees (although not recurring) were ordinary business expenses because they were normal, usual, or customary in the circumstances.[6]

EXAMPLE 4

To be deductible, an expense must be both ordinary *and* necessary.

Pat purchased a business that had just been adjudged bankrupt. Because the business had a poor financial rating, Pat wanted to restore its financial reputation. Consequently, he paid off some of the debts owed by the former owners that had been canceled by the bankruptcy court.

Because Pat had no legal obligation to make these payments, the U.S. Supreme Court found that he was trying to generate goodwill. Although the payments were necessary (i.e., appropriate and helpful), they were *not* ordinary and their deduction *was not* allowed.[7]

EXAMPLE 5

The Code refers to `reasonableness` solely with respect to salaries and other compensation for services.[8] But the courts have held that for any business expense to be ordinary and necessary, it must also be reasonable in amount.[9] Example 6 illustrates the reasonableness concept for an investment expense.

Debbye is a retired pilot who owns a small portfolio of investments, including 10 shares of Robin, Inc., a publicly traded company, worth $1,000. She incurred $350 in travel expenses to attend the annual shareholders' meeting where she voted her 10 shares against the current management group.

No deduction is permitted because a 10-share investment is insignificant in value in relation to the travel expenses incurred.[10]

EXAMPLE 6

What constitutes reasonableness is a question of fact. If an expense is unreasonable, the excess amount is not allowed as a deduction.

---

[4]*Welch v. Helvering*, 3 USTC ¶1164, 12 AFTR 1456, 54 S.Ct. 8 (USSC, 1933).

[5]*Deputy v. DuPont*, 40–1 USTC ¶9161, 23 AFTR 808, 60 S.Ct. 363 (USSC, 1940).

[6]*Comm. v. Heininger*, 44–1 USTC ¶9109, 31 AFTR 783, 64 S.Ct. 249 (USSC, 1943).

[7]*Welch v. Helvering*, cited in footnote 4.

[8]§ 162(a)(1).

[9]*Comm. v. Lincoln Electric Co.*, 49–2 USTC ¶9388, 38 AFTR 411, 176 F.2d 815 (CA–6, 1949).

[10]*J. Raymond Dyer*, 36 T.C. 456 (1961).

The question of reasonableness generally arises with respect to closely held corporations since there is no separation of ownership and management. Transactions between the shareholders and the closely held company may result in the disallowance of deductions for excessive salaries and rent expense paid by the corporation to the shareholders. An unusually large salary will often be challenged by the IRS, but the courts may conclude that it is reasonable given the facts that surround a particular business.[11] If excessive payments for salaries and rents are closely related to the percentage of stock owned by the recipients, the payments are generally treated as dividends.[12] Because dividends are not deductible by the corporation, the disallowance results in an increase in the corporate taxable income.

Sparrow Corporation, a closely held corporation, is owned equally by Lupe, Carlos, and Ramon. The company has been highly profitable for several years and has not paid dividends. Lupe, Carlos, and Ramon are key officers of the company, and each receives a salary of $200,000. Salaries for similar positions in comparable companies average only $100,000.

Amounts paid to the owners in excess of $100,000 may be deemed unreasonable; if so, a total of $300,000 in salary deductions by Sparrow is disallowed. The disallowed amounts are treated as dividends rather than salary to Lupe, Carlos, and Ramon because the payments are proportional to stock ownership. Salaries are deductible by the corporation, but dividends are not.

Note that the shareholders may benefit from this reclassification. Salaries would be taxed at ordinary income rates and are subject to payroll taxes. However, dividend income would be taxed at long-term capital rates if qualified and would not be subject to payroll taxes.

6-1d **Personal Expenses**

Expenditures that are incurred in one's personal life are deductible only if a specific Code section authorizes the deduction. These expenses are usually deductions *from* AGI. Some of the more common deductions in this category include the following:

- Contributions to qualified charitable organizations.
- Medical expenses.
- Certain state and local taxes.
- Personal casualty losses.
- Certain personal interest.
- Legal fees, but only if they relate to the determination of a tax liability.

Itemized deductions are discussed in detail in Chapter 10.

Yolanda paid her doctor $650 for a medical procedure this year. She also made a charitable contribution to the United Way for $1,000. She spent $400 on uniforms for her children to wear to school.

The Internal Revenue Code specifically provides for deducting medical expenses and qualified charitable contributions, so these are deductible. Since the Code does not provide a deduction for clothing worn for personal use, the uniforms are not deductible.

6-1e **Business and Nonbusiness Losses**

Section 165 provides for a deduction for losses not compensated for by insurance. As a general rule, deductible losses of individual taxpayers are limited to those incurred in a trade or business or in a transaction entered into for profit. Individuals also are allowed to deduct losses that are the result of a casualty. Casualty losses include, but are not limited to, those caused by fire, storm, shipwreck, and theft. See Chapter 7 for a further discussion of this topic. A personal casualty loss is an itemized deduction (i.e., *from* AGI).

---

[11]*Kennedy, Jr. v. Comm.*, 82–1 USTC ¶9186, 49 AFTR 2d 82–628, 671 F.2d 167 (CA–6, 1982), *rev'g* 72 T.C. 793 (1979).

[12]Reg. § 1.162–8.

During the current year, Marcus had a series of unfortunate events happen to him. A tornado hit his personal residence in March, and he incurred a loss of $30,000. In June, he sold his car to generate cash to pay his bills. The loss on the car sale was $3,500. In October, he sold 100 shares of stock in MMM Company at a loss of $2,000.

Since the tornado is a casualty event, the $30,000 loss is potentially deductible on Schedule A. The car is a personal use asset, and the loss was not caused by a casualty, so the $3,500 loss is not deductible. The $2,000 stock loss is from an investment activity, so this is deductible as a capital loss.

6-1f **Reporting Procedures**

All deductions *for* AGI are ultimately reported on page 1 of Form 1040. Most of the deductions *for* AGI originate on supporting schedules. Examples include business expenses (Schedule C); rent, royalty, partnership, and fiduciary deductions (Schedule E); and farming expenses (Schedule F). Other deductions *for* AGI, such as contributions to traditional IRAs and Keogh retirement plans and alimony payments, are entered directly on page 1 of Form 1040.

Adjusted gross income appears on the last line of page 1 and again on the first line of page 2. Deductions *from* AGI (itemized deductions) are reported on Schedule A (Form 1040). The total of all itemized deductions is subtracted *from* AGI (unless the standard deduction is greater). Then personal and dependency exemptions are deducted to arrive at taxable income.

Exhibit 6.2 summarizes the reporting and flow of deductions on the taxpayer's return (Form 1040). See Concept Summary 6.4 later in the chapter for the classification of deductions as *for* AGI or *from* AGI.

EXHIBIT 6.2	Format of Form 1040

Form 1040, Page 1

Income from All Sources

Less: Deductions *for* AGI (partial list):
- Traditional IRAs
- Keogh Retirement Plans
- Alimony
- Moving Expenses
- Student Loan Interest
- Penalty on Early Withdrawal of Savings

Equals: Adjusted Gross Income

Schedule B
Interest and Dividends

Schedule C
Business Income

Schedule D/Form 8949
Capital Gains and Losses

Schedule E
Rents, Royalties, etc.

Schedule F
Farm Income

Form 1040, Page 2

Adjusted Gross Income

Less: Standard Deduction
or Itemized Deductions

Exemptions (Personal and Dependency)

Equals: Taxable Income

Schedule A
Medical Expenses
Taxes
Interest

Charitable Contributions

Casualty Losses

Miscellaneous Itemized Deductions

Equals: Total Itemized Deductions

Form 4952
Investment Interest

Form 8283
Noncash Charitable Contributions

Form 4684
Casualties and Thefts

Form 2106 or Form 2106 EZ
Employee Business Expenses

LO.2

Describe the cash and accrual methods of accounting with emphasis on the deduction aspects.

6-2 DEDUCTIONS AND LOSSES—TIMING OF EXPENSE RECOGNITION

6-2a Importance of Taxpayer's Method of Accounting

A taxpayer's accounting method is a major factor in determining taxable income. The method used determines when an item is includible in income and when an item is deductible on the tax return. Usually, the taxpayer's normal method of record keeping is used for income tax purposes.[13] The taxing authorities require that the method used clearly reflect income and that items be handled consistently.[14] The most common methods of accounting are the cash method and the accrual method. If a taxpayer owns multiple businesses, it may be possible to use the cash method for some and the accrual method for others.

Throughout the portions of the Code dealing with deductions, the phrase *paid or incurred* is used. *Paid* refers to the cash basis taxpayer who gets a deduction only in the year of payment. *Incurred* concerns the accrual basis taxpayer who obtains the deduction in the year in which the liability for the expense becomes certain (refer to Chapter 4).

6-2b Cash Method Requirements

The expenses of cash basis taxpayers are deductible only when they are actually paid with cash or other property. Promising to pay or issuing a note does *not* satisfy the actually paid requirement.[15] However, the payment can be made with borrowed funds. At the time taxpayers charge expenses on their credit cards, they are allowed to claim the deduction. They borrowed money from the credit card issuer and simultaneously paid the expenses.[16]

A cash basis taxpayer must have actually or constructively paid the expense. A current deduction is not allowed for capital expenditures except through amortization, depletion, or depreciation over the life of the asset. An expenditure that creates an asset having a useful life that extends substantially beyond the end of the tax year must be capitalized.[17]

The Tax Court and the IRS took the position that the cost of an asset that will expire or be consumed by the end of the tax year following the year of payment must be prorated across the years. The Ninth Circuit Court of Appeals held that these expenditures are currently deductible, however, and the Supreme Court apparently concurs (the one-year rule for prepaid expenses).[18] Generally, the deduction will be allowed if the item is recurring or was made for a business purpose rather than to manipulate income.[19] Examples 10 and 11 illustrate how this rule applies to prepaid expenses.

Prepaid Expenses

EXAMPLE 10

John, a calendar year and cash basis taxpayer, rents property from Carl. On July 1, 2017, John pays $24,000 rent for the 24 months ending June 30, 2019. The prepaid rent extends 18 months after the close of the tax year—substantially beyond the year of payment and past the end of year following payment.

As a result, John must capitalize the prepaid rent and amortize the expense on a monthly basis. His deduction for 2017 is $6,000.

---

[13]§ 446(a).

[14]§§ 446(b) and (e); Reg. § 1.446–1(a)(2).

[15]*Page v. Rhode Island Trust Co., Exr.*, 37–1 USTC ¶9138, 19 AFTR 105, 88 F.2d 192 (CA–1, 1937).

[16]Rev.Rul. 78–39, 1978–1 C.B. 73. See also Rev.Rul. 80–335, 1980–2 C.B. 170, which applies to pay-by-phone arrangements.

[17]Reg. § 1.461–1(a).

[18]*Zaninovich v. Comm.*, 80–1 USTC ¶9342, 45 AFTR 2d 80–1442, 616 F.2d 429 (CA–9, 1980), *rev'g* 69 T.C. 605 (1978). Cited by the Supreme Court in *Hillsboro National Bank v. Comm.*, 83–1 USTC ¶9229, 51 AFTR 2d 83–874, 103 S.Ct. 1134 (USSC, 1983).

[19]*Keller v. Comm.*, 84–1 USTC ¶9194, 53 AFTR 2d 84–663, 725 F.2d 1173 (CA–8, 1984), *aff'g* 79 T.C. 7 (1982).

Prepaid Expenses

Assume the same facts as in Example 10, except that John is required to pay only 12 months' rent in 2017. He pays $12,000 on July 1, 2017.

The entire $12,000 is deductible in 2017 as the benefit does not extend beyond the end of 2018.

EXAMPLE 11

The payment must be required (i.e., not a voluntary prepayment) to obtain the current deduction under the one-year rule.[20] The taxpayer must also demonstrate that allowing the current deduction will not result in a material distortion of income.

As Chapter 18 explains, not all taxpayers are allowed to use the cash method.[21] For example, in most cases, the taxpayer is required to use the accrual method for sales and cost of goods sold if inventories are an income-producing factor of the business.

6-2c **Accrual Method Requirements**

The period in which an accrual basis taxpayer can deduct an expense is determined by applying the *all events test* and the *economic performance test*. That is, a deduction cannot be claimed until (1) all of the events have occurred to create the taxpayer's liability and (2) the amount of the liability can be determined with reasonable accuracy. Once these requirements are satisfied, the deduction is permitted only if economic performance has occurred. The economic performance test is met only when the service, property, or use of property giving rise to the liability is actually performed for, provided to, or used by the taxpayer.[22]

Chris's entertainment business sponsored a jazz festival in a rented auditorium at a local college. His business is responsible for cleaning up after the festival, which took place on December 22, 2017, and reinstalling the auditorium seats. Because the college is closed over the Christmas holidays, the company hired by Chris to perform the work did not begin these activities until January 3, 2018. Chris's business cannot deduct its $1,200 labor cost until 2018, when the services are performed.

EXAMPLE 12

An exception to the economic performance requirements allows certain *recurring items* to be deducted immediately if all of the following conditions are met:

- The item is recurring in nature and is treated consistently by the taxpayer.
- Either the accrued item is not material or accruing it in the current period results in better matching of income and expenses.
- All of the events have occurred that determine the existence of the liability, and the amount of the liability can be determined with reasonable accuracy.
- Economic performance occurs within a reasonable period (but not later than $8\frac{1}{2}$ months after the close of the taxable year).[23]

Exceptions to Economic Performance Rules

Rick, an accrual basis, calendar year taxpayer, entered into a monthly maintenance contract during the year. He makes a monthly accrual at the end of every month for this service and pays the fee sometime between the first and fifteenth of the following month when services are performed. The amount involved is immaterial, and all of the other tests are met.

The December 2017 accrual is deductible in 2017 even though the service is performed on January 12, 2018.

EXAMPLE 13

---

[20]*Bonaire Development Co. v. Comm.*, 82–2 USTC ¶9428, 50 AFTR 2d 82–5167, 679 F.2d 159 (CA–9, 1982).

[21]§ 448.

[22]§ 461(h).

[23]§ 461(h)(3)(A).

Exceptions to Economic Performance Rules

EXAMPLE 14

Rita, an accrual basis, calendar year taxpayer, shipped merchandise sold on December 30, 2017, via Greyhound Van Lines on January 3, 2018, and paid the freight charges at that time.

Because Rita reported the sale of the merchandise in 2017, the shipping charge should also be deductible in 2017. This procedure results in a better matching of income and expenses.

Reserves for estimated expenses such as warranties and bad debts are often deducted for financial accounting purposes before the specific expense is identified. Generally, these reserves are not allowed for tax purposes because the economic performance test cannot be satisfied.

EXAMPLE 15

Blackbird Airlines is required by Federal law to test its engines after 3,000 flying hours. Aircraft cannot return to flight until the tests have been conducted. An unrelated aircraft maintenance company does all of the company's tests for $1,500 per engine.

For financial reporting purposes, the company accrues an expense based upon $.50 per hour of flight and credits an allowance account. The actual amounts paid for maintenance are offset against the allowance account.

For tax purposes, the economic performance test is not satisfied until the work has been done. Therefore, the reserve method cannot be used for tax purposes.

6-2d **Time Value of Tax Deductions**

Both the time value of money and marginal tax rate changes must be considered when an expense can be paid and deducted in either of two years. Cash basis taxpayers often have the choice to pay expenses at the end of the current year or at the beginning of the following year. In view of the time value of money, a tax deduction this year may be worth more than the same deduction next year. However, accelerating the payment may not be advantageous if the taxpayer's marginal tax rate is higher in the following year. Before accelerating a payment, the taxpayer also needs to forecast future cash flow to ensure that an early payment makes sense.

EXAMPLE 16

Jena pledged $50,000 to her church's special building fund. She can make the contribution in December 2017 or January 2018. Jena is in the 35% tax bracket in 2017 and in the 28% bracket in 2018. She itemizes her deductions in both years. Assume that Jena's discount rate is 5%. If she takes the deduction in 2017, she saves $4,166 ($17,500 − $13,334) due to the decrease in the tax rates and the time value of money. See Table H-2 in Appendix H.

	2017	2018
Contribution	$50,000	$50,000
Tax bracket	× .35	× .28
Tax savings	$17,500	$14,000
Discounted @ 5%	× 1.0000	× .9524
Savings in present value	$17,500	$13,334

If tax rates are changing between two years, there are several areas in which taxpayers may have discretion as to which year to make a payment to achieve tax savings. Examples include alimony payments (see Chapter 4), assets purchased and expensed under § 179 (see Chapter 8), home mortgage interest, and charitable contributions (see Chapter 10). Always remember to consider the time value of money in the analysis.

6-3 DISALLOWANCE POSSIBILITIES

Certain types of expenses are disallowed by the tax law. Without these restrictions, taxpayers might attempt to deduct items that, in reality, are personal expenditures. For example, specific tax rules are provided to determine whether an expense is for trade or business purposes or is related to a personal hobby.

6-3a Public Policy Limitation

Payments considered to be in violation of public policy are not deductible.

Justification for Denying Deductions

The courts developed the principle that a payment in violation of public policy is not a necessary expense and is not deductible.[24] Allowing a deduction would, in effect, be indirectly subsidizing a taxpayer's wrongdoing. The following expenses, which are considered contrary to public policy, are not deductible:

- Bribes and kickbacks, including those associated with Medicare or Medicaid. In the case of foreign bribes and kickbacks, only if the payments violate the U.S. Foreign Corrupt Practices Act of 1977.

- Fines and penalties paid to a government for violation of law.

- Two-thirds of the treble damage payments made to claimants resulting from violation of the antitrust law.[25]

The Big Picture

Refer to the facts of *The Big Picture* on p. 6-1. Dr. Payne had not instituted proper procedures for disposing of medical waste from his laboratory. During the current tax year, he was fined $3,000 by the city. Dr. Payne believes the fine should be deducted as an ordinary business expense.

However, because the fine was due to a violation of public policy, the $3,000 is not deductible.

To be disallowed, a bribe or kickback must be illegal under either Federal or state law and must also subject the payor to a criminal penalty or the loss of a license or privilege to engage in a trade or business. For a bribe or kickback that is illegal under state law, a deduction is denied if the state law is generally enforced.

During the year, Keith, an insurance salesperson, paid $5,000 to Karen, a real estate broker. The payment represented 20% of the commissions Keith earned from customers referred by Karen. Under state law, the splitting of commissions by an insurance salesperson is an act of misconduct that could warrant a revocation of the salesperson's license.

Keith's $5,000 payments to Karen are not deductible if the state law is generally enforced.

Legal Expenses Incurred in Defense of Civil or Criminal Penalties

To deduct legal expenses, the taxpayer must be able to show that the origin and character of the claim are directly related to (1) a trade or business, (2) an income-producing activity, or (3) the determination, collection, or refund of a tax. Personal legal expenses are not deductible. Thus, legal fees incurred in connection with a criminal defense are deductible only if the crime is associated with the taxpayer's trade or business or income-producing activity.[26]

---

[24]*Tank Truck Rentals, Inc. v. Comm.*, 58–1 USTC ¶9366, 1 AFTR 2d 1154, 78 S.Ct. 507 (USSC, 1958).

[25]§§ 162(c), (f), and (g).

[26]*Comm. v. Tellier*, 66–1 USTC ¶9319, 17 AFTR 2d 633, 86 S.Ct. 1118 (USSC, 1966).

GLOBAL TAX ISSUES   Overseas Gun Sales Result in Large Fines

The Foreign Corrupt Practices Act (FCPA) is intended to punish taxpayers who make illegal payments to foreign officials to obtain economic advantages. Not only are such payments (usually improperly recorded as business expenses) nondeductible for income tax purposes, but serious and consistent violations can lead to the imposition of fines. Severe consequences can result from violating the bribery provisions of the FCPA, as Smith & Wesson recently discovered.

Smith & Wesson is a Massachusetts-based firearms manufacturer that wanted to begin selling firearms in India, Pakistan, and other foreign countries. As a small player in this international market, company officials decided to provide gifts to government officials in these countries to encourage them to do business with Smith & Wesson. This turned out to be a costly mistake. Smith & Wesson had profits of only $100,000 from this scheme before it was uncovered, and in 2014, it agreed to pay the Securities and Exchange Commission fines of more than $2 million. Of course, the fines are not deductible because they are a violation of public policy.

Source: www.sec.gov/News/PressRelease/Detail/PressRelease/1370542384677#.

EXAMPLE 19

Debra, a financial officer of Blue Corporation, incurs legal expenses in connection with her defense in a criminal indictment for evasion of Blue's income taxes.

Debra may deduct her legal expenses because she is deemed to be in the trade or business of being an executive. The legal action impairs her ability to conduct this business activity.[27]

The following legal expenses are deductible *for* AGI:

- Ordinary and necessary expenses incurred in connection with a trade or business.
- Ordinary and necessary expenses incurred in conjunction with rental or royalty property held for the production of income.

All other deductible legal expenses are deductible *from* AGI. For example, legal expenses for tax advice relative to the preparation of an individual's income tax return are a *from* AGI deduction. On the other hand, legal fees for tax advice relative to the preparation of the portion of the tax return for a sole proprietor's trade or business (Schedule C) or an individual's rental or royalty income (Schedule E) are a *for* AGI deduction.

EXAMPLE 20

Gabriela received an invoice from GAC Law Firm for $5,000 for the following services:

- $1,200 Advising on a lawsuit filed against her sole proprietorship
- $800 Advising on a dispute with a tenant who lives in a duplex she owns and rents
- $1,300 Fees related to preparing and filing her Form 1040
- $1,700 Fees for preparing a will

The $1,700 in fees for preparing her will is a personal expense and is not deductible. The balance of the legal fees ($3,300) is deductible when paid.

The $1,200 for the sole proprietorship is deducted on Schedule C (Form 1040) as a *for* AGI deduction. The $800 related to the duplex is a rental expense and is deducted on Schedule E as a *for* AGI deduction. The $1,300 for preparing and filing her Form 1040 is a miscellaneous itemized deduction (a *from* AGI deduction subject to the 2%-of-AGI floor).

Expenses Relating to an Illegal Business

The ordinary and necessary expenses of operating an illegal business (e.g., a gambling operation) are deductible.[28] While allowing deductions for illegal activity may seem inappropriate, this is necessary because the law taxes net income from a business operation, not gross revenue. However, § 162 disallows a deduction for fines, bribes

---

[27]Rev.Rul. 68–662, 1968–2 C.B. 69.

[28]*Comm. v. Sullivan,* 58–1 USTC ¶9368, 1 AFTR 2d 1158, 78 S.Ct. 512 (USSC, 1958).

to public officials, illegal kickbacks, and other illegal payments whether these payments are part of a legal or illegal business.

EXAMPLE
21

Sam owns and operates an illegal gambling establishment. In connection with this activity, he has the following expenses during the year:

Rent	$ 60,000
Payoffs to the police	40,000
Depreciation on equipment	100,000
Wages	140,000
Interest	30,000
Criminal fines	50,000
Illegal kickbacks	10,000
Total	$430,000

All of the usual expenses (rent, depreciation, wages, and interest) are deductible; payoffs, fines, and kickbacks are not deductible. Of the $430,000 spent, $330,000 is deductible and $100,000 is not.

An exception applies to expenses incurred in illegal trafficking in drugs.[29] *Drug dealers* are not allowed a deduction for ordinary and necessary business expenses incurred in their business, except for cost of goods sold.[30]

EXAMPLE
22

Assume in Example 21 that instead of an illegal gambling business, Sam was operating an illegal drug business. Also assume that the $100,000 was not for depreciation, but for the cost of the drugs sold.

Of the $430,000 spent, only $100,000 (the cost of goods sold) is deductible. Also note that to claim the cost of goods sold as a deduction, Sam will need documentation supporting the purchases—something that is not likely to exist.

ETHICS & EQUITY Medical Marijuana: Trade or Business Activity or Illegal Operation?

Cole England operates Herbal Medical Center in Sacramento, California, as a sole proprietorship. The distribution of marijuana for medical purposes is legal in California, as follows:

> Medical patients and their designated primary caregivers may legally possess and cultivate (but not distribute or sell) marijuana under Health and Safety Code 11362.5 (Prop 215) if they have a physician's recommendation or approval.

This is Cole's first year of business operations. All of his patients have signed statements indicating that he is their designated primary caregiver. He also has on file physician's recommendations for all marijuana that was provided to his patients. Tax information for this year is as follows:

Revenues	$200,000
Cost of goods sold	120,000
Other expenses	50,000

Cole reported $30,000 of net income on Schedule C this year for Herbal Medical Center. Is this position appropriate?

6-3b **Political Contributions and Lobbying Activities**

Generally, no business deduction is allowed for direct or indirect payments for political purposes.[31] The government has been reluctant to allow these deductions since it might encourage abuses and enable businesses to have undue influence on the political process.

---

[29]§ 280E.

[30]Reg. § 1.61–3(a). Gross income is defined as sales minus cost of goods sold. Thus, while § 280E prohibits any deductions for drug dealers, it does not modify the normal definition of gross income.

[31]§ 276.

The Big Picture

EXAMPLE 23

Refer to the facts of *The Big Picture* on p. 6-1. Dr. Payne had made political contributions to the State Senate campaigns of Tom Smith and Virginia White. Dr. Payne made these contributions to encourage these senators to support a new bill that is beneficial to the state's dental profession. Therefore, he assumed that these would be deductible business expenses.

However, political contributions are not deductible, so he will receive no tax benefit from them.

Lobbying expenses incurred in attempting to influence state or Federal legislation or the actions of certain high-ranking public officials are not deductible.[32] The disallowance also applies to a pro rata portion of the membership dues of trade associations and other groups that are involved in lobbying activities.

The Big Picture

EXAMPLE 24

Refer to the facts of *The Big Picture* on p. 6-1. Dr. Payne had made contributions to The Dental Society, a trade association for dentists. The trade association estimates that 70% of its dues are allocated to lobbying activities. As a result, his deduction on Schedule C is limited to $3,000 ($10,000 × 30%).

There are three exceptions to the disallowance of lobbying expenses. First, an exception is provided for influencing local legislation (e.g., city and county governments). Second, the disallowance provision does not apply to activities devoted solely to monitoring legislation. Third, a *de minimis* exception is provided for annual in-house expenditures (lobbying expenses other than those paid to professional lobbyists or any portion of dues used by associations for lobbying) if such expenditures do not exceed $2,000. If the in-house expenditures exceed $2,000, none of the in-house expenditures can be deducted.

EXAMPLE 25

The city of Florence, Tennessee, is considering spending $1,000,000 to build a sports complex that will host youth baseball and softball tournaments. Julie, who owns a local hotel, spends $5,000 on lobbying to persuade the five members of the Florence City Council to support the project.

The $5,000 is deductible as a lobbying expense since it was not incurred to influence state or Federal legislation.

6-3c Excessive Executive Compensation

The deduction of executive compensation normally is subject to two limitations. As discussed earlier, the compensation of shareholder-employees of closely held corporations is subject to the reasonableness requirement. The second limitation, known as the millionaires' provision, applies to publicly held corporations.[33]

The millionaires' provision does not limit the amount of compensation that can be paid to an employee. Instead, it limits the amount the employer can deduct for the taxable compensation of a covered executive to $1 million annually. Covered employees as defined by the SEC are the principal executive officer (PEO), the principal financial officer (PFO), and the three other most highly compensated executives.

This disallowance does not apply to commissions based on individual performance and performance-based compensation tied to overall company performance.

EXAMPLE 26

Johnette is CEO of Lowe's Depot, a home supply store and a publicly traded corporation. For the current tax year, her compensation package consists of:

Cash compensation	$1,800,000
Taxable fringe benefits	100,000
Bonus from a qualified bonus plan tied to company performance	5,000,000

Lowe's Depot can deduct $6,000,000 of her compensation. Only $1,000,000 of the cash and fringe benefits is deductible. Since the bonus is based on a qualified bonus plan, the $5,000,000 is fully deductible.

---

[32]§ 162(e).   [33]§ 162(m).

6-3d Investigation of a Business

Investigation expenses are expenses paid or incurred to determine the feasibility of entering a new business or expanding an existing business. They include such costs as travel, engineering and architectural surveys, marketing reports, and various legal and accounting services. How such expenses are treated for tax purposes depends on a number of variables, including the following:

- The current business, if any, of the taxpayer.
- The nature of the business being investigated.
- The extent to which the investigation has proceeded.
- Whether the acquisition actually takes place.

If the taxpayer is in a business that is the *same as or similar to* that being investigated, all investigation expenses are deductible in the year paid or incurred. The tax result is the same whether or not the taxpayer acquires the business being investigated.[34]

The Big Picture

EXAMPLE 27

Refer to the facts of *The Big Picture* on p. 6-1. Dr. Payne believes that his administrative and business skills can be used to turn around dental practices whose revenues have been declining. He investigates Teeth Restoration LLC, a local dental practice that is for sale. Expenses paid to consultants and accountants as part of this investigation totaled $6,000. He determined that Teeth Restoration would not be a good investment, so he did not buy it.

The $6,000 spent to investigate this business is deductible as a business expense because Dr. Payne is already in the dental business. Expenses incurred to investigate new business opportunities in one's current trade or business are deductible as ordinary and necessary business expenses.

When the taxpayer is *not* in a business that is the same as or similar to the one being investigated, the tax result depends on whether the new business is acquired. If the business is not acquired, all investigation expenses generally are nondeductible.[35]

EXAMPLE 28

Lynn, a retired merchant, incurs expenses in traveling from Rochester, New York, to California to investigate the feasibility of acquiring several auto care centers.

If no acquisition takes place, none of the expenses are deductible.

If the taxpayer is *not* in a business that is the same as or similar to the one being investigated and actually acquires the new business, the expenses must be capitalized as **startup expenditures**. Startup expenses are not deductible under § 162 because they are incurred *before* a business begins rather than in the course of operating a trade or business. The first $5,000 of the expenses is immediately deducted. Any excess over $5,000 is amortized over a period of 180 months (15 years). In arriving at the $5,000 immediate deduction allowed, a dollar-for-dollar reduction must be made for those expenses in excess of $50,000.[36] An election can be made by the taxpayer not to deduct or amortize any portion of the startup costs. In that case, this intangible asset will remain on the balance sheet until the business is sold.

EXAMPLE 29

Tina owns and operates 10 restaurants located in various cities throughout the Southeast. She travels to Atlanta to discuss the acquisition of an auto dealership. In addition, she incurs legal and accounting costs associated with the potential acquisition. After incurring total investigation costs of $52,000, she acquires the auto dealership on October 1, 2017.

Tina may immediately deduct $3,000 [$5,000 − ($52,000 − $50,000)] and amortize the balance of $49,000 ($52,000 − $3,000) over a period of 180 months. For calendar year 2017, therefore, Tina can deduct $3,817 [$3,000 + ($49,000 × 3/180)].

Concept Summary 6.1 depicts the tax rules related to the costs involved in investigating a business.

---

[34]§ 195. *York v. Comm.*, 58–2 USTC ¶9952, 2 AFTR 2d 6178, 261 F.2d 421 (CA–4, 1958).

[35]Rev.Rul. 57–418, 1957–2 C.B. 143; *Morton Frank*, 20 T.C. 511 (1953); and *Dwight A. Ward*, 20 T.C. 332 (1953).

[36]§ 195(b).

Concept Summary 6.1

Costs of Investigating a Business

6-3e Hobby Losses

Business or investment expenses are deductible only if the taxpayer can show that the activity was entered into for the purpose of making a profit. Certain activities can have attributes that make it difficult to determine if the primary motivation for the activity is to make a profit or is for personal pleasure. Examples include raising horses and operating a farm used as a weekend residence.

While personal losses are not deductible, losses attributable to profit-seeking activities may be deducted and used to offset a taxpayer's other income. Activities that have both personal and profit-seeking motives are classified as hobbies, and the tax law limits the deductibility of **hobby losses**.

The income and deductions from a hobby are reported separately on the tax return. The revenue for the hobby is always reported as other income on page 1 of Form 1040. Deductions are reported as itemized deductions (*from* AGI deductions) and are discussed in more detail below.

General Rules

If an individual can show that an activity has been conducted with the intent to earn a profit, losses from the activity are fully deductible (and reported, along with any income, on Schedule C). The hobby loss rules apply only if the activity is *not* engaged in for profit. Hobby expenses are deductible only to the extent of hobby income.[37]

The Regulations indicate that the following nine factors should be considered in determining whether an activity is profit-seeking or is a hobby:[38]

- Whether the activity is conducted in a businesslike manner.
- The expertise of the taxpayers or their advisers.
- The time and effort expended.
- The expectation that the assets of the activity will appreciate in value.
- The taxpayer's previous success in conducting similar activities.

---

[37]§ 183(b)(2).

[38]Reg. §§ 1.183–2(b)(1) through (9).

- The history of income or losses from the activity.
- The relationship of profits earned to losses incurred.
- The financial status of the taxpayer (e.g., if the taxpayer does not have substantial amounts of other income, this may indicate that the activity is engaged in for profit).
- Elements of personal pleasure or recreation in the activity.

Whether an activity is profit-seeking or a hobby does not depend on the presence or absence of one of these factors. Rather, the decision is a subjective one that is based on an analysis of all the facts and circumstances. Exhibit 6.3 provides a list of the common activities that may likely be treated as hobbies. Concept Summary 6.2 provides more details on the nature of the nine factors identified in the Regulations.

Presumptive Rule of § 183

The Code provides a rebuttable presumption that an activity is profit-seeking if the activity shows a profit in at least three of the previous five tax years.[39] If the activity involves horses, a profit in at least two of the previous seven tax years meets the presumptive rule. If these profitability tests are met, the activity is presumed to be a trade or business rather than a personal hobby. If this is the case, the IRS must prove that the activity is personal rather than trade or business-related. On the other hand, if the three-year test (two for horses) is *not* met, then the activity is presumed to be a hobby and the taxpayer has to prove that it is profit-seeking.

EXAMPLE 30

Camille and Walter are married taxpayers who enjoy a busy lifestyle. Camille, who is an executive for a large corporation, is paid a salary of $800,000. Walter is a collector of antiques. Several years ago he opened an antique shop in a local shopping center and spends most of his time buying and selling antiques. He occasionally earns a small profit from this activity but more frequently incurs substantial losses. If Walter's losses are business-related, they are fully deductible against Camille's salary income on a joint return. In resolving this issue, consider the following:

- Initially determine whether Walter's antique activity has met the three-out-of-five years profit test.
- If the presumption is not met, the activity may nevertheless qualify as a business if Walter can show that the intent is to engage in a profit-seeking activity. It is not necessary to show actual profits.
- Attempt to fit the operation within the nine criteria prescribed in the Regulations listed previously.

EXHIBIT 6.3	**Common Activities Classified as Hobbies**	
Airplane Charter	Entertainers	Photography
Artists	Farming	Rentals
Auto Racing	Fishing	Stamp Collecting
Bowling	Gambling	Writing
Craft Sales	Horse Breeding	Yacht Charter
Direct Sales	Horse Racing	
Dog Breeding	Motorcross Racing	

Source: Internal Revenue Service Audit Technique Guide: IRC § 183: Activities Not Engaged in For Profit (Revised June 2009).

---

[39]§ 183(d).

Concept Summary 6.2

Common Questions from the IRS Concerning Hobbies/Businesses with Losses

Whether the activity is conducted in a businesslike manner.

- Is there a written business plan?
- Is there business insurance? Is it covered in the company name?
- Is there a business license to operate?

The expertise of the taxpayers or their advisers.

- Does the taxpayer have any relevant education?
- Did the taxpayer prepare for the activity by conducting research or an extensive study of its accepted business, economic, and scientific practices?

The time and effort expended.

- How many hours are spent on this activity per week? Per month? Per year? Per season?
- Who is involved with the day-to-day business operations?

The expectation that the assets of the activity will appreciate in value.

- Were the assets held prior to starting the business?
- Has anyone ever offered to buy any of the assets?

The taxpayer's previous success in conducting similar activities.

- In what other activities has the taxpayer had previous success?
- Was the business ultimately profitable?

The history of income or losses from the activity.

- Is there a trend toward profitability?
- Did the taxpayer change operating methods, adopt new techniques, or abandon nonprofitable methods in a manner consistent with intent to improve profitability?

The relationship of profits earned to losses incurred.

- Is this a highly speculative business?
- What amount of investment has the taxpayer made in the business?

The financial status of the taxpayer.

- Does the taxpayer have substantial income or capital (e.g., investments) from other sources?
- Are there other economic reasons for the taxpayer to be engaged in the activity (e.g., reduced property taxes for farmland, low-interest loans, or federal grants)?

Elements of personal pleasure or recreation in the activity.

- Are elements of fun or recreation generally associated with it by the taxpayer, by members of the taxpayer's family, or by the taxpayer's friends?
- If there are any personal benefits to being in this business, are they substantial?

Source: Internal Revenue Service Audit Technique Guide: IRC § 183: Activities Not Engaged in For Profit (Revised June 2009).

Determining the Amount of the Deduction

If an activity is a hobby, the expenses are deductible only to the extent of the gross income from the hobby. These expenses must be deducted in the following order:

- Amounts deductible under other Code sections without regard to the nature of the activity, such as property taxes and home mortgage interest.
- Amounts deductible under other Code sections if the activity had been engaged in for profit, but only if those amounts do not affect adjusted basis. Examples include maintenance, utilities, and supplies.
- Amounts for depreciation, amortization, and depletion.[40]

The last two categories of deductions are deductible *from* AGI as itemized deductions to the extent they exceed 2 percent of AGI.[41] If the taxpayer uses the standard deduction rather than itemizing, the hobby loss deductions generate no tax benefit. Even if this is the case, the revenue from a hobby still must be reported on page 1 of Form 1040.

---

[40]Reg. § 1.183–1(b)(1).   [41]Reg. § 1.67–1T(a)(1)(iv) and Rev.Rul. 75–14, 1975–1 C.B. 90.

EXAMPLE

31

Jim, the vice president of an oil company, has AGI of $80,000. He decides to pursue painting in his spare time. He uses a home studio comprising 10% of the home's square footage. During the current year, Jim incurs the following expenses:

Frames	$ 1,800
Art supplies	900
Fees paid to models	4,000
Home studio expenses:	
Total home property taxes	2,000
Total home mortgage interest	10,000
Total home maintenance and utilities	4,600
Calculated depreciation on 10% of home	500

During the year, Jim sold paintings for a total of $8,660. If the activity is held to be a hobby, Jim is allowed deductions as follows:

Gross income		$ 8,660
Deduct: Property taxes and mortgage interest (10% of $12,000)		(1,200)
Remainder		$ 7,460
Deduct: Frames	$1,800	
Art supplies	900	
Models' fees	4,000	
Maintenance and utilities (10%)	460	(7,160)
Remainder		$ 300
Deduct: Depreciation ($500, but limited to $300)		(300)
Net income		$ –0–

Jim includes the $8,660 of income in AGI, making his AGI $88,660. The taxes and interest are itemized deductions, deductible in full. The remaining $7,460 of expenses are reduced by 2% of his AGI (2% × $88,660 = $1,773), so the net deduction is $5,687. All of these deductions are reported as itemized deductions on Schedule A.

Because the property taxes and home mortgage interest are deductible even without the hobby, the net effect is a $2,973 ($8,660 less $5,687) increase in taxable income.

6-3f Rental of Vacation Homes

Restrictions on the deductions allowed for part-year rentals of personal vacation homes prevent taxpayers from deducting essentially personal expenses as rental losses. Many taxpayers who own vacation homes use the property for personal use during a portion of the year and rent the property at other times. For example, assume that a summer cabin is rented for 2 months per year, used for a family vacation for 1 month, and left vacant the rest of the year. The issue is how to treat expenses during the 9 months the cabin is vacant. If these expenses are allowed as rental expenses, a rental loss is likely to result (otherwise, personal expenses have been converted to rental expenses). Section 280A eliminates this treatment by not allowing a loss for property that is not used primarily for rental purposes. Deductions are only allowed to the extent of income received.

There are three possible tax treatments for residences used for both personal and rental purposes. The treatment depends upon the *relative time* the residence is used for personal purposes versus rental use. These rules are summarized in Concept Summary 6.3.

Primarily Personal Use

If the residence is *rented* for *fewer than 15 days* in a year, it is treated as a personal residence. The rent income is excluded from gross income, and mortgage interest and real estate taxes are allowed as itemized deductions, as with any personal residence.[42] No other expenses (e.g., depreciation, utilities, and maintenance) are deductible.

---

[42]§ 280A(g).

Concept Summary 6.3

Vacation/Rental Home

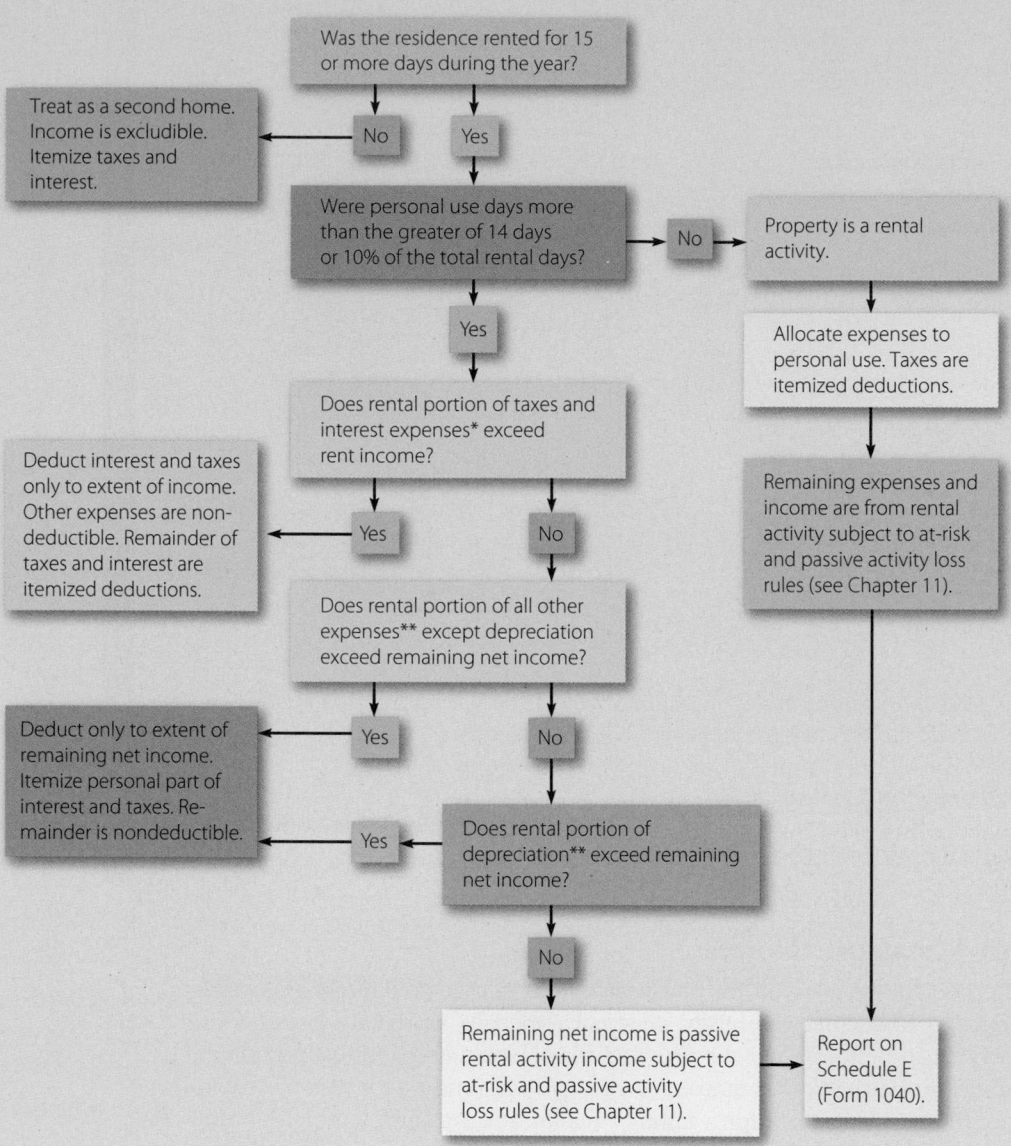

*Allocated on the basis of 365 (366 in a leap year) days (court decisions) or total days of use (IRS); see Examples 35 and 36.
**Allocated on the basis of total days of use.

EXAMPLE 32

Catherine owns a vacation cottage on the lake. During the current year, she rented it for $1,600 for two weeks, lived in it two months, and left it vacant the remainder of the year. The year's expenses amounted to $6,000 mortgage interest expense, $500 property taxes, $1,500 utilities and maintenance, and $2,400 depreciation.

Because the property was not rented for at least 15 days, the income is excluded, the mortgage interest and property tax expenses are itemized deductions, and the remaining expenses are non-deductible personal expenses.

Primarily Rental Use

If the residence is *rented* for 15 days or more in a year and is *not used* for personal purposes for more than the greater of (1) 14 days or (2) 10 percent of the total days rented, the residence is treated as rental property.[43] The expenses must be allocated between personal and rental days if there are any personal use days during the year. The real estate taxes allocated to the personal days are deductible as an itemized deduction. However, the mortgage interest allocated to the personal days cannot be deducted because the property is not a qualified residence. The deduction of the expenses allocated to rental days can exceed rent income and result in a rental loss. The loss may be deductible, subject to the at-risk and passive activity loss rules (discussed in Chapter 11).

EXAMPLE 33

Assume instead that Catherine in Example 32 used the cottage for 12 days and rented it for 48 days for $4,800. The threshold for personal use is 14 days—the greater of (1) 14 days or (2) 4.8 days (10% × 48 rental days). Because she rented the cottage for 15 days or more but did not use it for more than 14 days, the cottage is treated as rental property. The expenses must be allocated between personal and rental days.

	Percentage of Use	
	Rental 80%	Personal 20%
Income	$4,800	$ –0–
Expenses		
Mortgage interest ($6,000)	($4,800)	($1,200)
Property taxes ($500)	(400)	(100)
Utilities and maintenance ($1,500)	(1,200)	(300)
Depreciation ($2,400)	(1,920)	(480)
Total expenses	($8,320)	($2,080)
Rental loss	($3,520)	$ –0–

Catherine deducts the $3,520 rental loss *for* AGI on Schedule E (assuming that she satisfies the at-risk and passive activity loss rules, discussed in Chapter 11). She also has an itemized deduction for property taxes of $100 associated with the personal use. The mortgage interest of $1,200 associated with the personal use is not deductible as an itemized deduction because the cottage is not a qualified residence (qualified residence interest) for this purpose (see Chapter 10). The portion of utilities and maintenance and depreciation attributable to personal use is not deductible.

Personal/Rental Use

If the residence is rented for 15 days or more in a year *and* is used for personal purposes for more than the greater of (1) 14 days or (2) 10 percent of the total days rented, it is treated as a personal/rental use residence. The expenses must be allocated between personal days and rental days. Expenses are allowed only to the extent of rent income.[44]

EXAMPLE 34

Assume instead that Catherine in Example 32 rented the property for 30 days and lived in it for 30 days. The threshold for personal use is 14 days—the greater of (1) 14 days or (2) 3 days (10% × 30 rental days).

The residence is classified as personal/rental use property because she used it more than 14 days and rented it for 15 days or more. The expenses must be allocated between rental use and personal use, and the rental expenses are allowed only to the extent of rent income.

---

[43]§ 280A(d) and Prop.Reg. § 1.280A–3(c).

[44]A related issue is whether a taxpayer's primary residence is subject to the preceding rules if it is converted to rental property. If the vacation home rules apply, a taxpayer who converts a personal residence to rental property during the tax year, without any tax-avoidance motive, could have the allowable deductions limited to the rent income. To prevent this from occurring, the personal use days will not cause the property to be treated as personal/rental if once the rental period begins, the property is rented for at least 12 consecutive months at a fair rental price (a qualified rental period).

If a residence is classified as personal/rental use property, the expenses that are deductible anyway (e.g., real estate taxes and mortgage interest) must be deducted first. If a positive net income results, expenses, other than depreciation, that are deductible for rental property (e.g., maintenance, utilities, and insurance) are allowed next. Finally, if any positive balance remains, depreciation is allowed. Any disallowed expenses allocable to rental use are carried forward and used in future years subject to the same limitations. Note that these ordering rules for deductions are the same as for hobby expenses.

Expenses must be allocated between personal and rental days before the limits are applied. The courts have held that real estate taxes and mortgage interest, which accrue ratably over the year, are allocated on the basis of 365 days (366 days in a leap year).[45] The IRS, however, disagrees and allocates real estate taxes and mortgage interest on the basis of total days of use.[46] Other expenses (e.g., utilities, maintenance, depreciation) are allocated on the basis of total days used.

Personal/Rental: IRS vs. Courts

EXAMPLE 35

Jason rents his vacation home for 60 days and lives in the home for 30 days. The property is classified as personal/rental because it is rented for 15 days or more, and personal use (30 days) is greater than 14 [greater of 14 days or 6 days (10% × 60 rental days)]. Jason's gross rent income is $10,000. For the entire year, the real estate taxes are $2,190, his mortgage interest expense is $10,220, utilities and maintenance expense equals $2,400, and depreciation is $9,000.

Using the IRS approach, these amounts are deductible in this specific order:

Gross income	$10,000
Deduct: Taxes and interest ($^{60}/_{90}$ × $12,410)	(8,273)
Remainder to apply to rental operating expenses and depreciation	$ 1,727
Deduct: Utilities and maintenance ($^{60}/_{90}$ × $2,400)	(1,600)
Balance	$ 127
Deduct: Depreciation ($^{60}/_{90}$ × $9,000 = $6,000 but limited to above balance)	(127)
Net rent income	$ –0–

The nonrental use portion of real estate taxes and mortgage interest ($4,137 in this case) is deductible if the taxpayer elects to itemize (see Chapter 10). The personal use portion of utilities, maintenance, and depreciation is not deductible in any case.

Jason has a carryover of $5,873 ($6,000 − $127) of the unused depreciation, which he may be able to deduct in future years. Also note that the basis of the property is only reduced by the $127 depreciation allowed because of the above limitation. (See Chapter 14 for a discussion of the reduction in basis for depreciation allowed or allowable.)

EXAMPLE 36

Using the court's approach in allocating real estate taxes and mortgage interest, Jason, in Example 35, would have this result:

Gross income	$10,000
Deduct: Taxes and interest ($^{60}/_{365}$ × $12,410)	(2,040)
Remainder to apply to rental operating expenses and depreciation	$ 7,960
Deduct: Utilities and maintenance ($^{60}/_{90}$ × $2,400)	(1,600)
Balance	$ 6,360
Deduct: Depreciation ($^{60}/_{90}$ × $9,000 but limited to above balance.)	(6,000)
Net rent income	$ 360

Jason can deduct $10,370 ($12,410 paid − $2,040 deducted as expense in computing net rent income) of personal use mortgage interest and real estate taxes as itemized deductions.

---

[45]*Bolton v. Comm.*, 82–2 USTC ¶9699, 51 AFTR 2d 83–305, 694 F.2d 556 (CA–9, 1982).   [46]Prop.Reg. § 1.280A–3(d)(4).

Note the contrasting results in Examples 35 and 36. The IRS's approach (Example 35) results in no rental gain or loss and an itemized deduction for real estate taxes and mortgage interest of $4,137. In Example 36, Jason has net rent income of $360 and $10,370 of itemized deductions. The court's approach decreases his taxable income by $10,010 ($10,370 itemized deductions less $360 net rent income). The IRS's approach reduces his taxable income by only $4,137.

6-3g Expenditures Incurred for Taxpayer's Benefit or Taxpayer's Obligation

To be deductible, an expense must be incurred for the taxpayer's benefit or arise from the taxpayer's obligation. An individual cannot claim a tax deduction for the payment of the expenses of another individual.

EXAMPLE 37

During the current year, Fred pays the property taxes on his son Jayden's home. Neither Fred nor Jayden can take a deduction for the amount paid for Jayden's property taxes. Fred is not entitled to a deduction because the property taxes are not his obligation. Jayden cannot claim a deduction because he did not pay the property taxes.

The tax result would have been more favorable had Fred made a cash gift to Jayden and let him pay the property taxes. Then Jayden could have deducted the property taxes.

One exception to this disallowance rule is the payment of medical expenses for a dependent. Such expenses are deductible by the payor subject to the normal rules that limit the deductibility of medical expenses (see Chapters 3 and 10).[47]

6-3h Disallowance of Personal Expenditures

No deduction is allowed for personal, living, or family expenses."[48] To justify a deduction, an individual must be able to identify a particular section of the Code that permits the deduction (e.g., charitable contributions and medical expenses). Sometimes the character of a particular expenditure is not easily determined.

An example is the deduction of legal fees incurred in connection with a divorce.[49] To be deductible, an expense must relate solely to tax advice in a divorce proceeding. For example, legal fees attributable to the determination of dependency exemptions of children are deductible if the fees are distinguishable from the general legal fees incurred in obtaining a divorce. Therefore, it is advisable to request an itemization of attorney's fees to substantiate a deduction for the tax-related amounts.

EXAMPLE 38

Terry and Jack are divorced near the end of the current tax year. They had been married for 28 years and have two dependent children, Pauline (age 17) and Neal (age 18). As part of the divorce agreement, Jack paid all of the legal fees, which amounted to $24,300. The invoice from the divorce lawyer listed the following charges:

Child custody agreement and determination of amount of monthly child support	$ 3,000
Divorce decree proceedings	10,000
County court filing costs	1,800
Property settlement determination	6,000
Tax consequences of property settlement	2,000
Tax consequences of child custody and child support payments and tax filing status	1,500

Only the $3,500 ($2,000 + $1,500) paid by Jack for the charges relating to tax advice is deductible.

---

[47]§ 213(a).

[48]§ 262.

[49]Rev.Rul. 72–545, 1972–2 C.B. 179.

ETHICS & EQUITY   **Personal or Business Expenses?**

For the last eight years, Jaynice and her family have lived in a large Victorian house in New England. In the current year, Jaynice and her husband decide to convert the home into a "bed-and-breakfast." The family (including the two children and the dog) moves into the basement, which accounts for 30 percent of the square footage of the house. The basement has two bedrooms, two baths, a den, and a small kitchen. The upper two floors of the house are used for the bed-and-breakfast, which is operated as a sole proprietorship.

Jaynice hires two employees to help her run the business. Total expenses for the first year of operation are as follows:

Mortgage interest	$18,000
Real estate taxes	3,000
Salaries for two employees	40,000
Groceries for breakfast and snacks	7,000
Depreciation	10,000

For breakfast, all of the family members eat the same food that is prepared for the guests. They usually also share in the homemade cookies and cakes in the evening.

On Jaynice's Schedule C for the business, she deducts $78,000 of expenses for the current tax year. Discuss whether these deductions are appropriate.

6-3i **Disallowance of Deductions for Capital Expenditures**

A deduction is not allowed for amounts paid for new buildings or for permanent improvements or betterments that increase the value of any property.[50] Incidental repairs and maintenance of the property are not capital expenditures and can be deducted as ordinary and necessary business expenses. Repairing a roof is a deductible expense, but replacing a roof is a capital expenditure subject to depreciation deductions over its recovery period. The tune-up of a delivery truck is an expense; a complete engine overhaul probably is a capital expenditure. Adding new gravel to a gravel parking lot is a repair, but paving the parking lot is a capital expenditure because this is doing more than restoring the asset to its original condition.

All costs incurred in acquiring or producing a Unit of Property (UOP) are included in its cost, except for employee compensation and overhead costs. The taxpayer can elect to capitalize employee compensation and overhead costs (can elect separately or both). The cost includes all related expenditures incurred before the date the asset is placed in service, even if these expenditures would be repairs if incurred after the asset was placed in service. The cost of a UOP includes costs incurred to obtain a clean title and investigation costs.[51] Material or supplies that cost $200 or less can generally be deducted in the first tax year they are used or consumed.[52]

Capitalize or Expense

EXAMPLE 39

In year 1, Corporation Biz purchases 100 cell phones for its employees to use, each phone costing $130. Each cell phone is considered to be a unit of property. During year 1, 60 of the phones are put into use. The remaining phones are not used until year 2.

Since the cell phones cost less than $200, they are considered to be material and supplies. Therefore, 60 of the phones can be expensed in year 1 ($7,800). The remaining 40 phones cannot be expensed until they are put into use in year 2.

EXAMPLE 40

Jared owns a building that has 10 apartments. During the current year, one of the apartments needed a new stove. Jared paid $800 for the stove, including $75 of sales tax. He also paid $50 for the stove to be delivered and an extra $60 for it to be installed.

The stove is considered to be a unit of property, and all of these costs are included in its basis. Therefore, $910 ($800 + $50 + $60) is capitalized for the stove and this amount will be depreciated.

---

[50]§ 263(a)(1).

[51]Reg. § 1.263(a)–3(e)(1).

[52]Reg. § 1.162–3(a)(1).

A single UOP includes all components that are functionally interdependent. Thus, a building includes, for example, the walls, floors, ceilings, roof, windows, doors, electrical systems, plumbing, and heating and air systems. The major exception to this rule is that if a component is treated separately for depreciation purposes, it will not be grouped into another UOP.[53]

Taxpayers can elect under the *de minimis* safe harbor election to expense outlays for lower-cost items. The election is irrevocable. This safe harbor applies if the taxpayer:

- has written procedures in place at the beginning of the tax year that provide for the expensing of amounts below a specified dollar amount or that have a useful life of 12 months or less,

- also expenses the items for its accounting/book records, and

- ensures that items costing more than $5,000 are capitalized [$2,500 ($500 prior to 2016) if the company does not have acceptable (generally meaning audited) financial statements].

The *de minimis* safe harbor election cannot be made for inventory, land, and certain types of spare parts.[54]

> Freight Car Unlimited builds railroad cars and has adopted a written policy providing that any item purchased for $5,000 or less will be expensed for both financial reporting and tax purposes. Freight Car has audited financial statements.
>
> During the current tax year, Freight Car purchases 120 laptop computers that cost $2,700 each. These computers do not have to be capitalized and will be expensed in Freight Car's current year tax return.

EXAMPLE 41

Routine maintenance to keep UOPs operating efficiently is expensed, such as testing, cleaning, inspecting, and replacing parts. To be routine, the expectation is that the expenditure will be needed more than once during the asset's life. An expense cannot be treated as routine maintenance if it improves a UOP (treated as a betterment). A cost is treated as a betterment if it:

- enlarges or increases the capacity of a UOP, or

- materially increases the productivity, efficiency, or quality of the UOP.[55]

Qualifying small taxpayers (those with $10 million or less of average annual gross receipts in the three preceding tax years) can deduct improvements made to an eligible building property (one with an unadjusted basis of $1 million or less). The safe harbor election applies only if the total amount paid during the tax year for repairs, maintenance, improvements, and similar activities performed on the eligible building does not exceed the lesser of $10,000 or 2 percent of the building's unadjusted basis.[56]

Capitalization versus Expense

When an expenditure is for a tangible asset that has an ascertainable life, it is capitalized and may be deducted as depreciation (or cost recovery) over its depreciable life. Land is not subject to depreciation (or cost recovery) because it does not have an ascertainable life. [See Chapter 8 for a discussion of depreciation (cost recovery).]

> Stan purchased a prime piece of land located in an apartment-zoned area. Stan paid $500,000 for the property, which had an old but usable apartment building on it. He immediately had the building demolished at a cost of $100,000.
>
> The $500,000 purchase price and the $100,000 demolition costs must be capitalized, and the basis of the land is $600,000. Because land is a nondepreciable asset, no deduction is allowed.

EXAMPLE 42

---

[53]Reg. § 1.263(a)–3(e)(6).

[54]Reg. § 1.263(a)–1(f)(1).

[55]Reg. § 1.263(a)–3(i)(1).

[56]Reg. § 1.263(a)–3(h)(1); Rev.Proc. 2015–14, 2015–5 I.R.B. 450.

If the expenditure is for an intangible asset (e.g., copyright, patent, covenant not to compete, and goodwill), the capitalized expenditure can be amortized regardless of whether the intangible asset has an ascertainable life. Intangible assets, referred to as § 197 intangibles, are amortized over a 15-year statutory period using the straight-line method. See Chapter 8 for additional discussion of the amortization of intangibles.

Elite Fireworks purchased all of the assets of Interstate Fireworks for $2,000,000. The fair market value of Interstate's assets is $1,400,000.

The additional $600,000 paid is allocated to goodwill. The goodwill is a § 197 intangible asset and will be amortized over 15 years.

6-3j Transactions between Related Parties

The Code places restrictions on the recognition of gains and losses from related-party transactions. Without these restrictions, relationships created by birth, marriage, and business would provide endless possibilities for engaging in financial transactions that produce tax savings with no real economic substance or change. For example, to create an artificial loss, a wife could sell investment property to her husband at a loss and deduct the loss on their joint return. Her husband could then hold the asset indefinitely, and the family would sustain no real economic loss. A complex set of rules has been designed to eliminate these possibilities.

Relationships and Constructive Ownership

Before reviewing the tax consequences of related party sales, it is important to know the individuals and business entities that are considered to be related parties. *Related parties* include the following:

- Brothers and sisters (whether whole, half, or adopted), spouse, ancestors (parents and grandparents), and lineal descendants (children and grandchildren) of the taxpayer.

- A corporation that is owned more than 50 percent (directly or indirectly) by the taxpayer.

- Two corporations that are members of a controlled group.

- A series of other complex relationships between trusts, corporations, partnerships, and individual taxpayers.

Constructive ownership provisions are applied to determine whether the taxpayers are related. Under these provisions, stock owned by certain relatives or related entities is *deemed* to be owned by the taxpayer for purposes of applying the loss and expense deduction disallowance provisions. For example, a taxpayer is deemed to own not only his or her stock but also the stock owned by lineal descendants, ancestors, brothers and sisters or half-brothers and half-sisters, and spouse.

The stock of Sparrow Corporation is owned 20% by Ted, 30% by Ted's father, 30% by Ted's mother, and 20% by Ted's sister. Although Ted actually owns only 20% of Sparrow Corporation, he is *deemed* to own the stock owned by his father (30%), mother (30%), and sister (20%).

As a result, Ted directly and indirectly owns 100% of Sparrow Corporation, and Ted and Sparrow are related parties. The same outcome (100% direct and indirect ownership) results for all of the shareholders in this example.

Losses

Losses are disallowed from sales or exchanges of property between related parties.[57] A right of offset is created equal to the disallowed loss. When the property is subsequently sold to a nonrelated party, any gain recognized is reduced by the right of offset. However, the right of offset cannot create or increase a loss. Any right of offset is permanently lost if it is not used by the related-party buyer to offset some or all of the recognized gain on a subsequent sale or exchange to an unrelated party.

Use of Right of Offset

EXAMPLE 45

Freida sells common stock with a basis of $10,000 to her son, Bill, for its fair market value of $8,000. The $2,000 realized loss is not recognized, which creates a $2,000 right of offset. Bill sells the stock several years later for $11,000.

Freida's $2,000 loss is disallowed upon the sale to Bill, and only $1,000 of gain ($11,000 selling price − $8,000 basis − $2,000 right of offset) is taxable to him upon the subsequent sale.

EXAMPLE 46

Assume the same facts as in Example 45, except that Bill sells the stock for $9,000. Bill's gain of $1,000 ($9,000 selling price − $8,000 basis) is not recognized because of the right of offset of $2,000 from Freida's sale.

Note that the offset may result in only partial tax benefit upon the subsequent sale (as in this case). If Freida had sold the stock to an unrelated party rather than to Bill, she could have recognized a $2,000 loss. However, as a family unit, Freida and Bill recognized only $1,000 of loss.

6-3k Substantiation Requirements

The tax law is built on a voluntary compliance system. Taxpayers file their tax returns, report income and take deductions to which they are entitled, and pay their taxes through withholding or estimated tax payments during the year. The taxpayer has the burden of proof for substantiating expenses deducted on the returns and must retain adequate records. Upon audit, the IRS can disallow any undocumented or unsubstantiated deductions. These requirements have resulted in numerous conflicts between taxpayers and the IRS.

For example, *specific* and *more stringent* rules apply for deducting travel, entertainment, and gift expenses, which are discussed in Chapter 9. Certain mixed-use (both personal and business use) assets are also subject to more stringent documentation rules (see Chapter 8).

Substantiation is also important for establishing the basis of an asset (see Chapter 14). An asset's basis includes all costs incurred to place an asset in service, which includes transportation, sales tax, setup, testing, unpaid property taxes of the previous owner, and other purchase costs. Basis is used to determine gain or loss on a sale of the asset and to compute depreciation for depreciable assets. The taxpayer must document all expenses included in basis.

6-3l Expenses and Interest Relating to Tax-Exempt Income

Certain income, such as interest on municipal bonds, is tax-exempt.[58] The law also allows the taxpayer to deduct expenses incurred for the production of income.[59] However, expenses related to the production of tax-exempt income are not deductible.[60] Interest on debt used to purchase or hold tax-exempt financial instruments also is disallowed.

[57]§ 267(a)(1).
[58]§ 103.
[59]§ 212.
[60]§ 265.

EXPENSES Related to Tax-Exempt Income

EXAMPLE 47

Sandy, a taxpayer in the 35% bracket, purchased $100,000 of 6% municipal bonds. At the same time, she used the bonds as collateral on a bank loan of $100,000 at 8% interest. A positive cash flow would result from the tax benefit as follows:

Cash paid for interest expense on loan	($8,000)
Cash received as interest income from bonds	6,000
Net negative cash flow	($2,000)

Had the deduction of $8,000 been allowed for interest expense, this would have resulted in a tax benefit of $2,800 (35% × $8,000). In that case, a positive cash flow of $800 ($6,000 + $2,800 − $8,000) would have resulted.

EXAMPLE 48

In January of the current year, Alan borrowed $100,000 at 8% interest. He used the loan proceeds to purchase 5,000 shares of stock in White Corporation. In July, he sold the stock for $120,000 and reinvested the proceeds in City of Denver bonds, the income from which is tax-exempt.

Assuming that the $100,000 loan remained outstanding throughout the entire year, Alan cannot deduct the interest attributable to the period in which he held the tax-exempt bonds.

The classification of various expenses in terms of their deductibility and nondeductibility is reflected in Concept Summary 6.4.

LO.4

Identify tax planning opportunities for maximizing deductions and minimizing the disallowance of deductions.

6-4 TAX PLANNING

6-4a Vacation Homes

As previously discussed in this chapter, homes that are used for both personal and rental use can fall into one of three categories, all of which have different tax consequences. Therefore, careful tax planning often ensures that the home is classified into the category that provides the optimal tax result. For example, if a taxpayer is planning to rent a home for 15 or more days, this will subject the net income from the rental activity to taxation. If the homeowner could rent the home for 14 days or less (possibly just one less day), then all of the rental income received would escape taxation. This strategy is particularly attractive to individuals who live in areas where major sporting or entertainment events are held if there is a lack of hotel accommodations in the area.

In addition, assume that a taxpayer intends to use a home for 150 rental days and 16 personal days. Because the personal days exceed 15 (the greater of 14 days or 10% × the number of rental days), the property will be classified as *rental/personal* and a rental loss will not be allowed. However, if the owner can reduce the personal use days by only one day to 15, then the property will be classified as *rental*, and a rental loss can be allowed (subject to the passive activity loss rules).

6-4b Hobby Losses

To demonstrate that an activity has been entered into for the purpose of making a profit, a taxpayer should treat the activity as a business. The business should engage in advertising, use business letterhead stationery, and maintain a business phone.

If a taxpayer's activity earns a profit in three out of five consecutive years, the presumption is that the activity is engaged in for profit. It may be possible for a cash basis taxpayer to meet these requirements by timing the payment of expenses or the receipt of revenues. The payment of certain expenses incurred before the end of the year might be made in the following year. The billing of year-end sales might be delayed so that collections are received in the following year.

Concept Summary 6.4

Classification of Expenses

Expense Item	Deductible		Not Deductible	Applicable Code Section
	For AGI	**From AGI**		
Investment expenses				
Rent and royalty	X			§ 62(a)(4)
All other investments		X^4		§ 212
Employee expenses				
Commuting expenses			X	§ 262
Travel and transportation[1]		$X^{4,5}$		§ 162(a)(2)
Reimbursed expenses[1]	X			§ 62(a)(2)(A)
Moving expenses	X			§ 62(a)(15)
Entertainment[1]		$X^{4,5}$		§ 162(a)
Teacher professional development and supplies	X^{11}	X^4		§ 62(a)(2)(D)
All other employee expenses[1]		$X^{4,5}$		§ 162(a)
Certain expenses of performing artists	X			§ 62(a)(2)(B)
Trade or business expenses	X			§§ 162 and 62(a)(1)
Casualty losses				
Business	X			§ 165(c)(1)
Personal		X^6		§ 165(c)(3)
Tax determination				
Collection or refund expenses	X^8	X		§§ 212 and 62(a)(1) or (4)
Bad debts	X			§§ 166 and 62(a)(1) or (3)
Medical expenses		X^7		§ 213
Charitable contributions		X		§ 170
Taxes				
Trade or business	X			§§ 162, 164, and 62(a)(1)
Personal taxes				
Real property		X		§ 164(a)(1)
Personal property		X		§ 164(a)(2)
State and local income *or* sales tax		X		§§ 164(a)(3) and (b)(5)
Investigation of a business[2]	X			§§ 162 and 62(a)(1)
Interest				
Business	X			§§ 162, 163, and 62(a)(1)
Personal	X^9	X^3	X^{10}	§§ 163(a), (d), and (h)
Qualified tuition and related expenses	X			§§ 62(a)(18) and 222
All other personal expenses			X	§ 262

[1]Deduction *for* AGI if reimbursed, an adequate accounting is made, and employee is required to repay excess reimbursements.
[2]Provided certain criteria are met.
[3]Subject to the excess investment interest and the qualified residence interest provisions.
[4]Subject (in the aggregate) to a 2%-of-AGI floor imposed by § 67.
[5]Only 50% of meals and entertainment are deductible.
[6]Subject to a $100 floor per event and a 10%-of-AGI floor per tax year.
[7]Subject to a 10%-of-AGI floor.
[8]Only the portion relating to business, rental, or royalty income or losses.
[9]Only the portion relating to student loans.
[10]Other personal interest is disallowed.
[11]Subject to a statutory limit of $250.

Keep in mind that the three-out-of-five-years rule under § 183 is not absolute. All it does is shift the burden of proof. If a profit is not made in three out of five years, the losses may still be allowed if the taxpayer can show that they are due to the nature of the business. For example, success in artistic or literary endeavors can take a long time, so losses for several years in a row could occur even for a legitimate business. Also, depending on the state of the economy, full-time farmers and ranchers may have losses for several consecutive years.

Merely satisfying the three-out-of-five-years rule does not guarantee that a taxpayer is automatically home free. If the three years of profits are insignificant relative to the losses of other years or if the profits are not from the ordinary operation of the business, the taxpayer is vulnerable. The IRS may still be able to establish that the taxpayer is not engaged in an activity for profit.

EXAMPLE 49

Ashley had the following gains and losses in an artistic endeavor:

2013	($50,000)
2014	(65,000)
2015	400
2016	200
2017	125

Under these circumstances, the IRS might try to overcome the presumption that this is a business because it has profits in three of the last five years. To do this, the IRS would focus on the nine factors from the Regulations discussed in text Section 6-3e.

On the other hand, if Ashley could show conformity with the factors enumerated in the Regulations or could show evidence of business hardships (e.g., injury, death, or illness), the government might have difficulty overriding the presumption.[61]

6-4c Do Deduction Limits Affect Executive Compensation?

Only $1 million of compensation can be deducted for the CEO, the CFO, and the three other highest compensated executives of publicly traded companies. However, this limitation does not apply to performance-based compensation. One interesting issue is whether this exception is broad enough to allow publicly traded companies to pay substantial compensation to executives and still receive a tax deduction. The answer is clearly yes.

For example, in 2014, the CEO of Microsoft received a base salary of $918,917, which is just under the $1 million limitation. However, he received bonuses and stock incentives of over $80 million, which qualify to be deducted under the performance-based exception.

Fortune magazine recently reported that cash salaries account for only 10 percent of CEO compensation.[62] The remaining 90 percent consists primarily of performance incentives. This indicates that the $1 million limit does have an influence on the base salary of CEOs. However, because of the performance-based exception, this tax law appears to have had very little impact on the escalation of executives' salaries.

---

[61]*Faulconer, Sr. v. Comm.*, 84–2 USTC ¶9955, 55 AFTR 2d 85–302, 748 F.2d 890 (CA–4, 1984), *rev'g* 45 TCM 1084, T.C.Memo. 1983–165.

[62]Laura Lorenzetti, "Salaries for These CEOs Make Pay for Big Bank Bosses Look Modest," *Fortune*, September 2, 2015, **http://fortune.com/2015/09/02/pay-ratio-retail-ceos-banks/**.

CALCULATION OF DEDUCTIBLE BUSINESS EXPENSES AND TAX PLANNING

Of the expenses incurred by Dr. Payne, several comments need to be made. Being personal in nature, none of the $5,000 monthly draw is deductible. Nor is the amount involved subject to the reasonableness test (see Example 7). Dr. Payne is a sole proprietor and not in an employment relationship. The fine paid for violating waste control rules comes under the public policy limitations (see Example 17) and is specifically made nondeductible by Code § 162(f). Along the same line, the political contributions (Example 23) are made nondeductible by § 162(e). However, Dr. Payne's investigation of the practice of another dental firm (Example 27) appears reasonable and the expense incurred is deductible. The dues paid to The Dental Society are not 100 percent deductible because 70 percent of the Society's efforts relate to lobbying activities (Example 24). Although not specifically discussed in the text, his legal fees incurred in connection with a lawsuit filed by a patient appear related to his practice (Example 19). As such, they are ordinary and necessary to his trade or business.

What If?

From a tax planning perspective, should Dr. Payne calculate his deductible business expenses using the accrual method of accounting or the cash method?

In Chapter 4, we concluded that Dr. Payne could minimize his Federal income tax liability if he used the cash method of accounting. If the cash method is used for reporting the gross income of a Schedule C business, the cash method must be used for reporting the deductible business expenses that will appear on Schedule C of Form 1040.

ISTOCKPHOTO.COM/DLEWIS33

Key Terms

Accounting method, 6-8

Deductions *for* adjusted gross income, 6-2

Deductions *from* adjusted gross income, 6-2

Hobby losses, 6-16

Ordinary and necessary, 6-5

Reasonableness, 6-5

Related-party transactions, 6-26

Startup expenditures, 6-15

Vacation homes, 6-19

Discussion Questions

1. **LO.1** "All income must be reported, and all deductions are allowed unless specifically disallowed in the Code." Discuss.

2. **LO.1** Michael earned $20,000 at the K-M Resort Golf Club during the summer prior to his senior year in college. He wants to make a contribution to a traditional IRA, but the amount is dependent on whether it reduces his taxable income. If Michael is going to claim the standard deduction, will a contribution to a traditional IRA reduce his taxable income? Explain.

3. **LO.1** Classify each of the following expenditures as a deduction *for* AGI, a deduction *from* AGI, or not deductible:
   a. Sam gives cash to his father as a birthday gift.
   b. Sandra gives cash to her church.
   c. Albert pays Dr. Dafashy for medical services rendered.
   d. Mia pays alimony to Bill.
   e. Rex, who is self-employed, contributes to his pension plan.
   f. April pays expenses associated with her rental property.

4. **LO.1** Classify each of the following expenditures as a deduction *for* AGI, a deduction *from* AGI, or not deductible:
   a. Amos contributes to his H.R. 10 plan (i.e., a retirement plan for a self-employed individual).
   b. Keith pays child support to his former wife, Renee, for the support of their son, Chris.
   c. Judy pays professional dues that are *not* reimbursed by her employer.
   d. Ted pays $500 as the monthly mortgage payment on his personal residence. Of this amount, $100 represents a payment on principal, and $400 represents an interest payment.
   e. Lynn pays a moving company for moving her household goods to Detroit, where she is starting a new job. She is not reimbursed by her employer.
   f. Ralph pays property taxes on his personal residence.

5. **LO.1** Larry and Susan each invest $10,000 in separate investment activities. They each incur deductible expenses of $800 associated with their respective investments. Explain why Larry's expenses might be properly classified as deductions *from* AGI (itemized deductions) and Susan's expenses might be appropriately classified as deductions *for* AGI.

6. **LO.1** Nanette is a first-grade teacher. Potential deductions are charitable contributions of $800, personal property taxes on her car of $240, and various supplies purchased for use in her classroom of $225 (none reimbursed by her school). How will these items affect Nanette's Federal income tax return for 2017?

7. **LO.1** In the determination of whether a business expense is deductible, the reasonableness requirement applies only to salaries. Evaluate this statement.

8. **LO.1** Dave uses the second floor of a building for his residence and the first floor for his business. The uninsured building is destroyed by fire. Are the tax consequences the same for each part of the building? Explain.

9. **LO.1** Mary Kate owns a building that she leases to an individual who operates a grocery store. Rent income is $10,000, and rental expenses are $6,000. On what Form 1040 schedule or schedules are the income and expenses reported?

10. **LO.2** What is the "actually paid" requirement for the deduction of an expense by a cash basis taxpayer? Does actual payment ensure a deduction? Explain.

11. **LO.2** Aubry, a cash basis and calendar year taxpayer, decides to reduce his taxable income for 2017 by buying $65,000 worth of supplies for his business on December 27, 2017. The supplies will be used up in 2018.
    a. Can Aubry deduct the expenditure for 2017? Explain.
    b. Would your answer in part (a) change if Aubry bought the supplies because the seller was going out of business and offered a large discount on the price? Explain.

12. **LO.3** Clear, Inc., is a bottled water distributor. Clear's delivery trucks frequently are required to park in no-parking zones to make their deliveries. If the trucks are occasionally ticketed, can Clear deduct the fines that it pays? Explain.

13. **LO.3** Ted, an agent for an airline manufacturer, is negotiating a sale with a repre-   **Issue ID**
sentative of the U.S. government and with a representative of a developing country. Ted's company has sufficient capacity to handle only one of the orders. Both orders will have the same contract price. Ted believes that if his employer authorizes a $500,000 payment to the representative of the foreign country, he can guarantee the sale. He is not sure that he can obtain the same result with the U.S. government. Identify the relevant tax issues for Ted.

14. **LO.3** Stuart, an insurance salesperson, is arrested for allegedly robbing a convenience store. He hires an attorney who is successful in getting the charges dropped. Is the attorney's fee deductible? Explain.

15. **LO.3** Linda operates an illegal gambling operation. Which of the following expenses that she incurs can reduce taxable income?
    a. Bribes paid to city employees.
    b. Salaries to employees.
    c. Security cameras.
    d. Kickbacks to police.
    e. Rent on an office.
    f. Depreciation on office furniture and equipment.
    g. Tenant's casualty insurance.
    h. Utilities.

16. **LO.3** Gordon anticipates that being positively perceived by the individual who is elected mayor will be beneficial for his business. Therefore, he contributes to the campaigns of both the Democratic and the Republican candidates. The Republican candidate is elected mayor. Can Gordon deduct any of the political contributions he made?

17. **LO.3** Melissa, the owner of a sole proprietorship, does not provide health insurance for her 20 employees. She plans to spend $1,500 lobbying in opposition to legislation that would require her to provide such insurance. Discuss the tax advantages and disadvantages of paying the $1,500 to a professional lobbyist rather than spending the $1,500 on in-house lobbying expenditures.

18. **LO.3** What limits exist on the deductibility of executive compensation? Do the limits apply to all types of business entities? Are there any exceptions to the limitations? Explain.

19. **LO.3** Paul operates a restaurant in Cleveland. He travels to Columbus to investigate acquiring a business. He incurs expenses as follows: $1,500 for travel, $2,000 for legal advice, and $3,500 for a market analysis. Based on the different tax consequences listed below, describe the circumstances that were involved in Paul's investigation of the business.
    a. Paul deducts the $7,000 of expenses.
    b. Paul cannot deduct any of the $7,000 of expenses.
    c. Paul deducts $5,000 of the expenses and amortizes the $2,000 balance over a period of 180 months.

20. **LO.3** Karen and Andy own a beach house. They have an agreement with a rental   **Issue ID**
agent to rent it up to 200 days per year. For the past three years, the agent has been successful in renting it for 200 days. Karen and Andy use the beach house for one week during the summer and one week during Thanksgiving. Their

daughter, Sarah, a college student, has asked if she and some friends can use the beach house for the week of spring break. Advise Karen and Andy on how they should respond, and identify any relevant tax issues.

21. **LO.3** Hank was transferred from Arizona to North Dakota on March 1 of the current year. He immediately put his home in Phoenix up for rent. The home was rented May 1 to November 30 and was vacant during the month of December. It was rented again on January 1 for six months. What expenses related to the home, if any, can Hank deduct on his return? Which deductions are *for* AGI, and which ones are *from* AGI?

Decision Making 22. **LO.3** Ray loses his job as a result of a corporate downsizing. Consequently, he falls behind on the mortgage payments on his personal residence. His friend Ted would like to make the delinquent mortgage payments for him.

a. Could the payments be structured so that Ray can deduct the mortgage interest?

b. Could the payment arrangement deny both Ray and Ted a mortgage interest deduction?

c. Could the payments be structured so that Ted can deduct the mortgage interest?

23. **LO.3** Edna incurs various legal fees in obtaining a divorce. Which types of expenses associated with the divorce are deductible by Edna, and which are not?

Issue ID 24. **LO.3** Ella owns 60% of the stock of Peach, Inc. The stock has declined in value since she purchased it five years ago. She is going to sell 5% of the stock to a relative. Ella is also going to make a gift of 10% of the stock to another relative. Identify the relevant tax issues for Ella.

25. **LO.3** Jarret owns City of Charleston bonds with an adjusted basis of $190,000. During the year, he receives interest payments of $3,800. Jarret partially financed the purchase of the bonds by borrowing $100,000 at 5% interest. Jarret's interest payments on the loan this year are $4,900, and his principal payments are $1,100.

a. Should Jarret report any interest income this year? Explain.

b. Can Jarret deduct any interest expense this year? Explain.

Computational Exercises

26. **LO.2** Glenda, a calendar year and cash basis taxpayer, rents property from Janice. As part of the rental agreement, Glenda pays $8,400 rent on April 1, 2017, for the 12 months ending March 31, 2018.

a. How much is Glenda's deduction for rent expense in 2017?

b. Assume the same facts, except that the $8,400 is for 24 months' rent ending March 31, 2019. How much is Glenda's deduction for rent expense in 2017?

27. **LO.2** Falcon, Inc., paid salaries of $500,000 to its employees during its first year of operations. At the end of the year, Falcon had unpaid salaries of $45,000.

a. Calculate the salary deduction if Falcon is a cash basis taxpayer.

b. Calculate the salary deduction if Falcon is an accrual basis taxpayer.

28. **LO.2** Maud, a calendar year taxpayer, is the owner of a sole proprietorship that uses the cash method. On February 1, 2017, she leases an office building to use in her business for $120,000 for an 18-month period. To obtain this favorable lease rate, she pays the $120,000 at the inception of the lease. How much rent expense may Maud deduct on her 2017 tax return?

29. **LO.3** Vella owns and operates an illegal gambling establishment. In connection with this activity, he has the following expenses during the year:

Rent	$ 24,000
Bribes	40,000
Travel expenses	4,000
Utilities	18,000
Wages	230,000
Payroll taxes	13,800
Property insurance	1,600
Illegal kickbacks	22,000

What are Vella's total deductible expenses for tax purposes?

30. **LO.3** Printer Company pays a $25,000 annual membership fee to a trade association for paper wholesalers. The trade association estimates that 60% of its dues are allocated to lobbying activities.
   a. What are Printer's total deductible expenses for tax purposes?
   b. Assume the same facts as above, except that the $25,000 was incurred for in-house lobbying expenses. What are Printer's total deductible expenses for tax purposes?

31. **LO.3** Stanford owns and operates two dry cleaning businesses. He travels to Boston to discuss acquiring a restaurant. Later in the month, he travels to New York to discuss acquiring a bakery. Stanford does not acquire the restaurant but does purchase the bakery on November 1, 2017.
   Stanford incurred the following expenses:

Total investigation costs related to the restaurant	$28,000
Total investigation costs related to the bakery	51,000

What is the maximum amount Stanford can deduct in 2017 for investigation expenses?

32. **LO.3** Murphy has a brokerage account and buys on the margin, which resulted in an interest expense of $20,000 during the year. Income generated through the brokerage account was as follows:

Municipal interest	$ 50,000
Taxable dividends and interest	350,000

How much investment interest can Murphy deduct?

Problems

33. **LO.1** Amos is a self-employed tax attorney. He and Monica, his employee, attend a conference in Dallas sponsored by the American Institute of CPAs. The following expenses are incurred during the trip:

	Amos	Monica
Conference registration	$ 900	$900
Airfare	1,200	700
Taxi fares	100	–0–
Lodging in Dallas	750	300

   a. Amos pays for all of these expenses. Calculate the effect of these expenses on Amos's AGI.
   b. Would your answer to part (a) change if the American Bar Association had sponsored the conference? Explain.

Decision Making   34. **LO.1** Daniel, age 38, is single and has the following income and expenses in 2017.

Salary income	$60,000
Net rent income	6,000
Dividend income	3,500
Payment of alimony	12,000
Mortgage interest on residence	4,900
Property tax on residence	1,200
Contribution to traditional IRA	5,000
Contribution to United Church	2,100
Loss on the sale of real estate (held for investment)	2,000
Medical expenses	3,250
State income tax	300
Federal income tax	7,000

a.   Calculate Daniel's AGI.

b.   Should Daniel itemize his deductions *from* AGI or take the standard deduction? Explain.

35. **LO.1** Janice, age 22, is a student who earns $10,000 working part-time at the college ice cream shop in 2017. She has no other income. Her medical expenses for the year total $3,000. During the year, she suffers a casualty loss of $3,500 when her apartment catches on fire. Janice contributes $2,500 to her church. On the advice of her parents, Janice is trying to decide whether to contribute $1,000 to the traditional IRA her parents set up for her. What effect would the IRA contribution have on Janice's itemized deductions?

36. **LO.1** A list of the items that Peggy sold and the losses she incurred during the current tax year is as follows:

Yellow, Inc. stock	$ 1,600
Peggy's personal use SUV	8,000
Peggy's personal residence	10,000
City of Newburyport bonds	900

She also had a theft loss of $1,500 on her uninsured business use car. Calculate Peggy's deductible losses.

37. **LO.2** Duck, an accrual basis corporation, sponsored a rock concert on December 29, 2017. Gross receipts were $300,000. The following expenses were incurred and paid as indicated:

Expense		Payment Date
Rental of coliseum	$ 25,000	December 21, 2017
Cost of goods sold:		
Food	30,000	December 30, 2017
Souvenirs	60,000	December 30, 2017
Performers	100,000	January 5, 2018
Cleaning of coliseum	10,000	February 1, 2018

Because the coliseum was not scheduled to be used again until January 15, the company with which Duck had contracted did not perform the cleanup until January 8–10, 2018.

a.   Calculate Duck's net income from the concert for tax purposes for 2017.

b.   Using the present value tables in Appendix H, what is the true cost to Duck if it had to defer the $100,000 deduction for the performers until 2018? Assume a 5% discount rate and a 25% marginal rate in 2017 and 2018.

38. **LO.3** Doug incurred and paid the following expenses during the year:

- $50 for a ticket for running a red light while he was commuting to work.
- $100 for a ticket for parking in a handicapped parking space.
- $200 to an attorney to represent him in traffic court as to the two tickets.

- $500 to an attorney to draft an agreement with a tenant for a one-year lease on an apartment that Doug owns.
- $1,000 to an attorney to negotiate a reduction in his child support payments.
- $2,500 to an attorney to negotiate a reduction in his qualified alimony payments to a former spouse.

Calculate the amount of Doug's deductible expenses.

39. **LO.3** Trevor, a friend of yours from high school, works as a server at the ST Café. He asks you to help him prepare his Federal income tax return. When you inquire about why his bank deposits substantially exceed his tip income, he confides to you that he is a bookie on the side. Trevor then provides you with the following documented income and expenses for the year:

Tip income	$16,000
Gambling income	52,000
Gambling expenses	
Payouts to winners	29,000
Employee compensation	8,000
Bribe to police officer who is aware of Trevor's bookie activity	7,500

a. How will these items affect Trevor's AGI (ignore the impact of self-employment taxes)?

b. His taxable income (ignore the impact of self-employment taxes)?

40. **LO.3, 4** Amber, a publicly held corporation, currently pays its president an annual salary of $900,000. In addition, it contributes $20,000 annually to a defined contribution pension plan for him. As a means of increasing company profitability, the board of directors decides to increase the president's compensation. Two proposals are being considered. Under the first proposal, the salary and pension contribution for the president would be increased by 30%. Under the second proposal, Amber would implement a performance-based compensation program that is projected to provide about the same amount of additional compensation and pension contribution for the president.

Decision Making

Communications

a. Evaluate the alternatives from the perspective of Amber.

b. Prepare a letter to Amber's board of directors that contains your recommendations. Address the letter to the board chairperson, Agnes Riddle, whose address is 100 James Tower, Cleveland, OH 44106.

41. **LO.3** Nancy, the owner of a very successful hotel chain in the Southeast, is exploring the possibility of expanding the chain into a city in the Northeast. She incurs $35,000 of expenses associated with this investigation. Based on the regulatory environment for hotels in the city, she decides not to expand. During the year, she also investigates opening a restaurant that will be part of a national restaurant chain. Her expenses for this are $53,000. The restaurant begins operations on September 1. Determine the amount that Nancy can deduct in the current year for investigating these two businesses.

42. **LO.3** Terry traveled to a neighboring state to investigate the purchase of two hardware stores. His expenses included travel, legal, accounting, and miscellaneous expenses. The total was $52,000. He incurred the expenses in June and July 2017. Under the following circumstances, what can Terry deduct in 2017?

a. Terry was in the hardware store business and did not acquire the two hardware stores.

b. Terry was in the hardware store business and acquired the two hardware stores and began operating them on October 1, 2017.

   c.   Terry did not acquire the two hardware stores and was not in the hardware store business.

   d.   Terry acquired the two hardware stores but was not in the hardware store business when he acquired them. Operations began on October 1, 2017.

43. **LO.3** Harold Peters (Social Security number 123-45-6789) conducts a business with the following results for the year:

Revenue	$20,000
Depreciation on car	3,960
Operating expenses of car	3,100
Rent	6,000
Wages	8,200
Amortization of intangibles	680

Harold estimates that due to a depressed real estate market, the value of land owned by the business declined by $5,200.

   a.   Calculate the effect of Harold's business on his AGI.

   b.   How would your answer in part (a) change if the activity was a hobby?

   c.   Using a Form 1040 and a Schedule A, show the amounts that would be entered on these forms for the information presented, assuming that the activity is a hobby.

44. **LO.3** Alex, who is single, conducts an activity in 2017 that is appropriately classified as a hobby. The activity produces the following revenues and expenses:

Revenue	$18,000
Property taxes	3,000
Materials and supplies	4,500
Utilities	2,000
Advertising	5,000
Insurance	750
Depreciation	4,000

Without regard to this activity, Alex's AGI is $42,000. Determine the amount of income Alex must report, the amount of the expenses he is permitted to deduct, and his taxable income.

45. **LO.3** Samantha, an executive, has AGI of $100,000 before considering income or loss from her miniature horse business. Her outside income comes from prizes for winning horse shows, stud fees, and sales of yearlings. Samantha's home is on 20 acres, half of which she uses for the horse activity (i.e., stables, paddocks, fences, tack houses, and other related improvements).

   Samantha's office in her home is 10% of the square footage of the house. She uses the office exclusively for maintaining files and records on the horse activities. Her books show the following income and expenses for the current year:

Income from fees, prizes, and sales		$22,000
Expenses		
Entry fees		1,000
Feed and veterinary bills		4,000
Supplies		900
Publications and dues		500
Travel to horse shows (no meals)		2,300
Salaries and wages of employees		8,000
Depreciation		
Horse equipment	$3,000	
Horse farm improvements	7,000	
On 10% of personal residence	1,000	11,000
Total home mortgage interest		24,000
Total property taxes on home		2,200
Total property taxes on horse farm improvements		800

The mortgage interest is only on her home because the horse farm improvements are not mortgaged.

a. What are Samantha's tax consequences if the miniature horse activity is a hobby?

b. If it is a business?

46. **LO.3** Sarah owns a vacation cabin in the Tennessee mountains. Without considering the cabin, she has gross income of $65,000. During the year, she rents the cabin for two weeks for $2,500 and uses it herself for four weeks. The total expenses for the year are $10,000 mortgage interest; $1,500 property tax; $2,000 utilities, insurance, and maintenance; and $3,200 depreciation.

a. What effect does the rental of the vacation cabin have on Sarah's AGI?

b. What expenses can Sarah deduct, and how are they classified (i.e., *for* or *from* AGI)?

47. **LO.3** Adelene, who lives in a winter resort area, rented her personal residence for 14 days while she was visiting Brussels. Rent income was $5,000. Related expenses for the year were as follows:

Real property taxes	$ 3,800
Mortgage interest	7,500
Utilities	3,700
Insurance	2,500
Repairs	2,100
Depreciation	15,000

Determine the effect on Adelene's AGI.

48. **LO.3** During the year (not a leap year), Anna rented her vacation home for 30 days, used it personally for 20 days, and left it vacant for 315 days. She had the following income and expenses:

Rent income	$ 7,000
Expenses	
Real estate taxes	2,500
Interest on mortgage	9,000
Utilities	2,400
Repairs	1,000
Roof replacement (a capital expenditure)	12,000
Depreciation	7,500

a. Compute Anna's net rent income or loss and the amounts she can itemize on her tax return, using the court's approach to allocating property taxes and interest.

b. How would your answer in part (a) differ using the IRS's method of allocating property taxes and interest?

49. **LO.3** How would your answer to Problem 48 differ if Anna had rented the house for 87 days and had used it personally for 13 days?

50. **LO.1, 3** Chee, single, age 40, had the following income and expenses during 2017:

Income	
Salary	$43,000
Rental of vacation home (rented 60 days, used personally 60 days, vacant 245 days)	4,000
Municipal bond interest	2,000
Dividend from General Electric	400
Expenses	
Interest on home mortgage	8,400
Interest on vacation home	4,758
Interest on loan used to buy municipal bonds	3,100

Property tax on home	$ 2,200
Property tax on vacation home	1,098
State income tax	3,300
State sales tax	900
Charitable contributions	1,100
Tax return preparation fee	300
Utilities and maintenance on vacation home	2,600
Depreciation on rental portion of vacation home	3,500

Calculate Chee's taxable income for the year before personal exemptions. If Chee has any options, choose the method that maximizes his deductions.

Decision Making   51. **LO.1, 3, 4** Elisa and Clyde operate a retail sports memorabilia shop. For the current year, sales revenue is $55,000 and expenses are as follows:

Cost of goods sold	$21,000
Advertising	1,000
Utilities	2,000
Rent	4,500
Insurance	1,500
Wages to Boyd	8,000

Elisa and Clyde pay $8,000 in wages to Boyd, a part-time employee. Because this amount is $1,000 below the minimum wage, Boyd threatens to file a complaint with the appropriate Federal agency. Although Elisa and Clyde pay no attention to Boyd's threat, Chelsie (Elisa's mother) gives Boyd a check for $1,000 for the disputed wages. Both Elisa and Clyde ridicule Chelsie for wasting money when they learn what she has done. The retail shop is the only source of income for Elisa and Clyde.

   a.   Calculate Elisa and Clyde's AGI.
   b.   Can Chelsie deduct the $1,000 payment on her tax return? Explain.
   c.   How could the tax position of the parties be improved?

Decision Making   52. **LO.3, 4** Brittany Callihan sold stock (basis of $184,000) to her son, Ridge, for
Communications $160,000, the fair market value.

   a.   What are the tax consequences to Brittany?
   b.   What are the tax consequences to Ridge if he later sells the stock for $190,000? For $152,000? For $174,000?
   c.   Write a letter to Brittany in which you inform her of the tax consequences if she sells the stock to Ridge for $160,000. Explain how a sales transaction could be structured that would produce better tax consequences for her. Brittany's address is 32 Country Lane, Lawrence, KS 66045.

53. **LO.3** The Robin Corporation is owned as follows:

Isabelle	26%
Peter, Isabelle's husband	19%
Sonya, Isabelle's mother	15%
Reggie, Isabelle's father	25%
Quinn, an unrelated party	15%

Robin is on the accrual basis, and Isabelle and Peter are on the cash basis. Isabelle and Peter each loaned the Robin Corporation $40,000 out of their separate funds. On December 31, 2017, Robin accrued interest at 7% on both loans. The interest was paid on February 4, 2018. What is the tax treatment of this interest expense/income to Isabelle, Peter, and Robin?

54. **LO.3** For each of the following independent transactions, calculate the recognized gain or loss to the seller and the adjusted basis to the buyer.

a. Bonnie sells Parchment, Inc. stock (adjusted basis $17,000) to Phillip, her brother, for its fair market value of $12,000.

b. Amos sells land (adjusted basis $85,000) to his nephew, Boyd, for its fair market value of $70,000.

c. Susan sells a tax-exempt bond (adjusted basis $20,000) to her wholly owned corporation for its fair market value of $19,000.

d. Ron sells a business truck (adjusted basis $20,000) that he uses in his sole proprietorship to his cousin, Agnes, for its fair market value of $18,500.

e. Martha sells her partnership interest (adjusted basis $175,000) in Pearl Partnership to her adult daughter, Kim, for $220,000.

55. **LO.1, 3, 4** During the current year, Robert pays the following amounts associated with his own residence:

Decision Making

Property taxes	$3,000
Mortgage interest	8,000
Repairs	1,200
Utilities	2,700
Replacement of roof	4,000

In addition, Robert paid $1,500 of property taxes on the home that is owned and used by Anne, his daughter.

a. Which of these expenses can Robert deduct?

b. Can Anne deduct the $1,500 of property taxes?

c. Are the deductions *for* AGI or *from* AGI (itemized)?

d. How could the tax consequences be improved?

Cumulative Problems

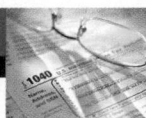

56. Roberta Santos, age 41, is single and lives at 120 Sanborne Avenue, Springfield, IL 60781. Her Social Security number is 123-45-6789. Roberta has been divorced from her former husband, Wayne, for three years. She has a son, Jason, who is 17, and a daughter, June, who is 18. Jason's Social Security number is 111-11-1112, and June's is 123-45-6788. Roberta does not want to contribute $3 to the Presidential Election Campaign Fund.

Tax Return Problem

TAX SOFTWARE

Roberta, an advertising executive, earned a salary from ABC Advertising of $80,000 in 2016. Her employer withheld $9,000 in Federal income tax and $3,100 in state income tax.

Roberta has legal custody of Jason and June. The divorce decree provides that Roberta is to receive the dependency deductions for the children. Jason lives with his father during summer vacation. Wayne indicates that his expenses for Jason are $10,500. Roberta can document that she spent $6,500 for Jason's support during 2016. In prior years, Roberta gave a signed Form 8332 to Wayne regarding Jason. For 2016, she has decided not to do so. Roberta provides all of June's support.

Roberta's mother died on January 7, 2016. Roberta inherited assets worth $625,000 from her mother. As the sole beneficiary of her mother's life insurance policy, Roberta received insurance proceeds of $300,000. Her mother's cost basis for the life insurance policy was $120,000. Roberta's favorite aunt gave her $13,000 for her birthday in October.

On November 8, 2016, Roberta sells for $22,000 Amber stock that she had purchased for $24,000 from her first cousin, Walt, on December 5, 2011. Walt's cost basis for the stock was $26,000, and the stock was worth $23,000 on December 5, 2011. On December 1, 2016, Roberta sold Falcon stock for $13,500. She had acquired the stock on July 2, 2013, for $8,000.

An examination of Roberta's records reveals that she received the following:

- Interest income of $2,500 from First Savings Bank.
- Groceries valued at $750 from Kroger Groceries for being the 100,000th customer.
- Qualified dividend income of $1,800 from Amber.
- Interest income of $3,750 on City of Springfield school bonds.
- Alimony of $16,000 from Wayne.
- Distribution of $4,800 from ST Partnership. Her distributive share of the partnership passive taxable income was $5,300. She had no prior passive activity losses.

From her checkbook records, she determines that she made the following payments during 2016:

- Charitable contributions of $4,500 to First Presbyterian Church and $1,500 to the American Red Cross (proper receipts obtained).
- Paid $5,000 to ECM Hospital for the medical expenses of a friend from work.
- Mortgage interest on her residence of $7,800 to Peoples Bank.
- Property taxes of $3,200 on her residence and $1,100 (ad valorem) on her car. $800 for landscaping expenses for residence.
- Estimated Federal income taxes of $3,800 and estimated state income taxes of $1,000.
- Medical expenses of $5,000 for her and $800 for Jason. In December, her medical insurance policy reimbursed $1,500 of her medical expenses.
- A $1,000 ticket for parking in a handicapped space.
- Attorney's fees of $500 associated with unsuccessfully contesting the parking ticket.
- Contribution of $250 to the campaign of a candidate for governor.
- Because she did not maintain records of the sales tax she paid, she calculates the amount from the sales tax table to be $994.

Calculate Roberta's net tax payable or refund due for 2016. Use the appropriate forms and schedules. Suggested software: H&R BLOCK Tax Software.

Tax Computation Problem

Decision Making

Communications

57. John and Mary Jane Diaz are married, filing jointly. Their address is 204 Shoe Lane, Blacksburg, VA 24061. John is age 35, and Mary Jane is age 30. They are expecting their first child in early 2018. John's salary in 2017 was $105,000, from which $20,800 of Federal income tax and $4,700 of state income tax were withheld. Mary Jane made $52,000 and had $3,000 of Federal income tax and $3,100 of state income tax withheld. The appropriate amounts of FICA tax and Medicare tax were withheld for John and for Mary Jane. John's Social Security number is 111-11-1111, and Mary Jane's Social Security number is 123-45-6789.

John and Mary Jane are both covered by their employer's medical insurance policies with four-fifths of the premiums being paid by the employers. The total premiums were $10,000 for John and $6,200 for Mary Jane. Mary Jane received medical benefits of $7,300 under the plan. John was not ill during 2017. Mary Jane paid non-covered medical expenses of $1,300.

John makes child support payments of $15,000 for his son, Rod, who lives with June, John's former spouse, except for two months in the summer when he visits John and Mary Jane. At the time of the divorce, John worked for a Fortune 500 company and received a salary of $225,000. As a result of corporate downsizing, he lost his job.

Mary Jane's father lived with them until his death in November. His only sources of income were salary of $2,800, unemployment compensation benefits of $3,500, and Social Security benefits of $4,100. Of this amount, he deposited $6,000 in a savings account. The remainder of his support of $9,500, which included funeral expenses of $4,500, was provided by John and Mary Jane.

Other income received by the Diazes was as follows:

Interest on certificates of deposit	$3,500
Share of S corporation taxable income (distributions from the S corporation to Mary Jane were $1,100)	1,500
Award received by Mary Jane from employer for an outstanding suggestion for cutting costs	4,000

John has always wanted to operate his own business. In October 2017, he incurred expenses of $15,000 in investigating the establishment of a retail computer franchise. With the birth of their child expected next year, however, he decides to forgo self-employment for at least a couple of years.

John and Mary Jane made charitable contributions of $3,700 during the year and paid an additional $1,800 in state income taxes in 2017 upon filing their 2016 state income tax return. Their deductible home mortgage interest was $8,200, and their property taxes came to $4,800. They paid sales taxes of $2,000, for which they have receipts. They paid a ticket of $150 that Mary Jane received for running a red light (detected by a red light camera).

Part 1—Tax Computation
Calculate John and Mary Jane's tax (or refund) due for 2017.

Part 2—Tax Planning
Assume that the Diazes come to you for advice in December 2017. John has learned that he will receive a $30,000 bonus. He wants to know if he should take it in December 2017 or in January 2018. Mary Jane will quit work on December 31 to stay home with the baby. Their itemized deductions will decrease by $3,100 because Mary Jane will not have state income taxes withheld. Mary Jane will not receive the employee award in 2018. She expects the medical benefits received to be $9,000. The Diazes expect all of their other income items to remain the same in 2018. Write a letter to John and Mary Jane that contains your advice, and prepare a memo for the tax files.

Research Problems

Note: Solutions to the Research Problems can be prepared by using the Thomson Reuters Checkpoint® Student Edition online tax research database, which accompanies this textbook. Solutions can also be prepared by using research materials found in a typical tax library.

Communications

Research Problem 1. Gray Chemical Company manufactured pesticides that were toxic. Over the course of several years, the toxic waste contaminated the air and water around the company's plant. Several employees suffered toxic poisoning, and the Environmental Protection Agency cited the company for violations. In court, the judge found Gray guilty and imposed fines of $15 million. The company voluntarily set up a charitable fund for the purpose of bettering the environment and funded it with $8 million. The company incurred legal expenses in setting up the foundation and defending itself in court. The court reduced the fine from $15 million to $7 million.

Gray Chemical Company deducted the $8 million paid to the foundation and the legal expenses incurred. The IRS disallowed both deductions on the grounds that the payment was, in fact, a fine and in violation of public policy.

Gray's president, Ted Jones, has contacted you regarding the deductibility of the $7 million fine, the $8 million payment to the foundation, and the legal fees. Write a letter to Mr. Jones that contains your advice, and prepare a memo for the tax files. Gray's address is 200 Lincoln Center, Omaha, NE 68182.

Partial list of research aids:
§§ 162(a) and (f).
Reg. § 1.162–21(b).

Research Problem 2. Rex and Agnes Harrell purchased a beach house at Duck, North Carolina, in early 2016. Although they intended to use the beach house occasionally for recreational purposes, to help pay the mortgage payments, property taxes, and maintenance costs, they also planned to rent it through the realty agency that had handled the purchase. Rex is a surgeon, and Agnes is a counselor.

The beach house was in need of substantial repairs. Rather than hiring a contractor, Rex and Agnes decided they would make the repairs themselves. During both high school and college, Rex had worked summers in construction. In addition, he had taken an advanced course in woodworking and related subjects from a local community college several years ago.

During 2016, according to a log maintained by the Harrells, they occupied the beach house 38 days and rented it 49 days. The log also indicated that on 24 of the 38 days they occupied the beach house, one or both of them were engaged in work on the beach house. Their two teenage children were with them on all of these days but did not help with the work being done. On their 2016 income tax return, Rex and Agnes, who filed a joint return, treated the beach house as a rental property and deducted a pro rata share of the property taxes, mortgage interest, utilities, maintenance and repairs, and depreciation in determining their net loss from the beach home. In the current year, after examining their return, an IRS agent has limited the deductions to the rent income. He contends that the 14-day personal use provision was exceeded and that many of the alleged repairs were capital expenditures. Advise the Harrells on how they should respond to the IRS.

Research Problem 3. Mona viewed herself as a creative individual who had chosen to go to law school for economic reasons. Mona's undergraduate majors were creative writing and American Indian studies.

Mona was very successful as an attorney and eventually was admitted to partnership in her law firm, having an expertise in negotiating settlements involving Indian water rights.

While practicing law, Mona continued her interest in the arts. She had directed plays in high school and maintained her involvement in the theater, even during law school. She belonged to local theater organizations while she practiced law. She took several courses in filmmaking and read extensively in the area. She even took several months off from her legal practice to enroll in NYU's filmmaking program. Her enrollment in the program provided her with hands-on experience and taught her about the technical aspects of filmmaking and allowed her to meet individuals who would later work with her on her documentary.

When she discovered that her husband had similar interests, she decided to create a documentary about Way to Sing America. After acquiring the rights to all of the archival footage of Way to Sing America, she hired a video production company to film interviews that she conducted with Way to Sing America alumni (over 400 hours of such interviews). She spent weekends and nights over a three-year period working on the documentary.

Once the documentary was completed, Mona began marketing it at film festivals. At some of these festivals, her documentary received awards. At the same time, she developed a business plan, hired a bookkeeper to manage the finances, and hired an accounting firm to provide tax advice.

During this three-year period, she reported the following losses:

2014	$ 30,000
2015	400,000
2016	200,000

On her tax returns for the three-year period, in each year, she offset these amounts against her law firm income of approximately $1 million.

Upon audit by the IRS, the agent concluded that her filmmaking activity is a hobby and therefore the losses cannot be deducted except to the extent of the income generated.

Who is correct? Explain.

Use internet tax resources to address the following questions. Look for reliable websites and blogs of the IRS and other government agencies, media outlets, businesses, tax professionals, academics, think tanks, and political outlets.

Research Problem 4. Sarah was contemplating making a contribution to her traditional IRA in 2016. She determined that she would contribute $5,000 in December 2016, but forgot about making the contribution until she was preparing her 2016 tax return in February 2017. Use the website of any well-known IRA provider (e.g., Fidelity, Vanguard, T. Rowe Price) to determine if Sarah can make a 2016 contribution to her IRA after the tax year has ended.

Research Problem 5. The $1 million maximum compensation deduction does not seem to have deterred large corporations from remunerating their executives at very high levels. What techniques are being used to work around the millionaires' provision? Are executives taking pay cuts, or are their salaries being deferred or changed in nature due to § 162(m)?

Roger CPA Review Questions

1. Newton, a business owner, signed a ten-year lease beginning in July of 2017 and immediately paid rent for the remainder of 2017, all of 2018, and all of 2019. How much of the rent paid at the lease signing can be declared as a business expense on Schedule C of Newton's 2017 tax return?

   a.   All of it

   b.   The July 2017–June 2018 portion only

   c.   None of it

   d.   The 2017 portion only

2. Freddy, a sole proprietor, is one of several retail business owners competing to rent space in a desirable location that rents at a rate of $2,000 per month. Freddy pays the landlord 12 months' rent up front, even though only two months' advance rent is required. The lease term begins October 1, 2017. In addition, Freddy gives the landlord a $2,500 cash gift in order to sweeten the deal. Considering only these facts, what amount is deductible on Schedule C of Freddy's 2017 tax return?

   a. $4,000   c. $6,500

   b. $6,000   d. $8,500

3. Rebecca owns and runs an auto repair shop that is assessed an environmental fine of $2,500 by the state government for failing to properly dispose of used engine oil. Rebecca incurs $1,500 in legal fees to fight this assessment, but does not prevail. She also contributes $2,000 to the political campaign of a gubernatorial candidate who is a lawyer by profession and who specifically promises to simplify the

environmental ordinance under which Rebecca's fine was assessed. Considering the above facts, what total amount is deductible on Rebecca's business tax return?

a. $0

b. $1,500

c. $3,500

d. $6,000

4. Aman, a sole proprietor and rental property owner, had the following expenses in 2017:

Payment to tax lawyer for advice related to business tax liability	$1,000
Property taxes paid on rental home	2,000
Management fee for Aman's retirement portfolio	500

Specify whether each expense would be deducted *for* adjusted gross income (AGI) or *from* AGI on Aman's 2017 tax return.

	Tax Lawyer	Property Taxes	Management Fee
a.	For	From	From
b.	For	For	From
c.	From	For	For
d.	From	From	For

5. A sale between which of the following could trigger a gain or a loss for federal tax purposes?

a. Husband and wife

b. Cousin and cousin

c. Majority shareholder and corporation

d. Ancestor and descendent

CHAPTER

7

Deductions and Losses: Certain Business Expenses and Losses

LEARNING OBJECTIVES: *After completing Chapter 7, you should be able to:*

LO.1 Determine the amount, classification, and timing of the bad debt deduction.

LO.2 State and illustrate the tax treatment of worthless securities, including § 1244 stock.

LO.3 Distinguish between deductible and nondeductible losses of individuals.

LO.4 Identify a casualty and determine the amount, classification, and timing of casualty and theft losses.

LO.5 State and apply the alternative tax treatments for research and experimental expenditures.

LO.6 Calculate the domestic production activities deduction.

LO.7 Determine the amount of the net operating loss and review the impact of the carryback and carryover provisions on previous and subsequent years' taxable income.

LO.8 Identify tax planning opportunities in deducting certain business expenses, business losses, and personal losses.

TETRA IMAGES/GETTY IMAGES

THE BIG PICTURE

LOSSES

Martha, a cash basis and calendar year taxpayer, is nearing the end of a year that she would like to forget. Several years ago she loaned $25,000 to her friend Janice to enable her to start a business. Janice had made scheduled payments of $7,000 ($1,000 of this was interest) when she unexpectedly died in January. At the time of her death, Janice was insolvent. Martha's attempts to collect on the debt were fruitless.

Last October, Martha invested $50,000 in the stock of a pharmaceutical company that previously had been profitable. However, as a result of losing a patent infringement suit, the company declared bankruptcy in May of this year. The bankruptcy trustee has informed shareholders that they should not expect to receive anything from the company.

Martha has owned and operated a bookstore as a sole proprietorship for the past 10 years. The bookstore previously produced annual profits of about $75,000. Due to the growth of online vendors and e-books, Martha's bookstore sustained a net loss of $180,000 this year.

In September, a hurricane caused a large oak tree to blow over onto Martha's house. The cost of removing the tree and making repairs was $32,000. Martha received a check for $25,000 from her insurance company in final settlement of the claim. Her adjusted basis for the house was $280,000.

In March, Martha purchased what she believed to be § 1244 stock from her friend, Peter, for $20,000. The stock's value began to decline significantly soon after its purchase. Several months after her purchase, Martha sold the stock for $12,000.

Can you help relieve Martha's feeling of despair by making her aware of beneficial loss provisions in the tax law?

Read the chapter and formulate your response.

FRAMEWORK 1040 **Tax Formula for Individuals**

This chapter covers the boldfaced portions of the Tax Formula for Individuals that was introduced in Concept Summary 3.1 on p. 3-3. Below those portions are the sections of Form 1040 where the results are reported.

Income *(broadly defined)*	$xx,xxx
Less: Exclusions	(x,xxx)
Gross income...	$xx,xxx
Less: Deductions *for* adjusted gross income...	(x,xxx)

FORM 1040 (p. 1)

12	Business income or (loss). Attach Schedule C or C-EZ	
35	Domestic production activities deduction. Attach Form 8903	

Adjusted gross income..	$xx,xxx
Less: The greater of total **itemized deductions** *or* the standard deduction	(x,xxx)

FORM 1040 (p. 2)

40	**Itemized deductions** (from Schedule A) **or** your **standard deduction** . . . .

Personal and dependency exemptions	(x,xxx)
Taxable income	$xx,xxx
Tax on taxable income *(see Tax Tables or Tax Rate Schedules)*.............................	$ x,xxx
Less: Tax credits *(including income taxes withheld and prepaid)*	(xxx)
Tax due (or refund)	$ xxx

ndividual deductions must be properly classified as either *for* adjusted gross income (AGI) or *from* AGI (itemized deductions). Business expenses and losses, along with expenses and losses related to rent and royalty activities (entered into for profit), are deducted *for* AGI. Most other investment expenses are deducted *from* AGI. The determination of the taxpayer's activity (i.e., whether the taxpayer is engaged in a trade or business, an investment, or a personal activity) is crucial in this classification process.[1]

Deductible losses on personal use property are deductions *from* AGI (as itemized deductions). Casualty and theft losses on personal use property are discussed in this chapter; other itemized deductions are discussed in Chapter 10.

In determining the amount and timing of the deduction for bad debts, proper classification is again important. A business bad debt is classified as a deduction *for* AGI, and a nonbusiness bad debt is classified as a short-term capital loss.

Other topics discussed in Chapter 7 are research and experimental expenditures, the domestic production activities deduction, and the net operating loss deduction.

7-1 BAD DEBTS

LO.1

Determine the amount, classification, and timing of the bad debt deduction.

If a taxpayer sells goods or provides services on credit and the account receivable subsequently becomes worthless, a **bad debt** deduction is permitted only if income arising from the creation of the account receivable was previously included in income.[2] No deduction is allowed, for example, for a bad debt arising from the sale of a product or service when the taxpayer is on the cash basis because no income is reported until the cash has been collected.

---

[1]See, for example, *Groetzinger v. Comm.*, 85–2 USTC ¶9622, 56 AFTR 2d 85–5683, 771 F.2d 269 (CA–7, 1985), aff'd in 87–1 USTC ¶ 9191, 59 AFTR 2d 87–532, 107 S.Ct. 980 (USSC, 1987).

[2]Reg. § 1.166–1(e).

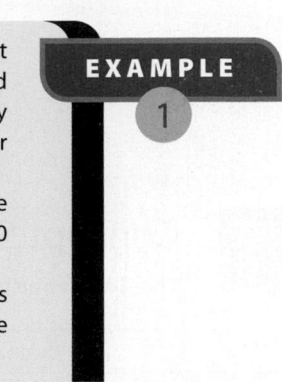

EXAMPLE 1

Tracy, a sole proprietor, operates a business named Executive Accounting and Tax Services. Last year, Pat hired Tracy to help him with the accounting for his small business. Tracy also prepared the S corporation income tax return for the business and Pat's personal income tax return. Tracy billed Pat $8,000 for the services she performed. Pat has never paid the bill, his business no longer exists, and his whereabouts are unknown.

If Tracy is an *accrual basis taxpayer*, she includes the $8,000 in income when the services are performed. When she determines that Pat's account will not be collected, she deducts the $8,000 as a bad debt expense.

If Tracy is a *cash basis taxpayer*, she does not include the $8,000 in income until payment is received. When she determines that Pat's account will not be collected, she cannot deduct the $8,000 as a bad debt expense because it was never recognized as income.

The Big Picture

EXAMPLE 2

Return to the facts of *The Big Picture* on p. 7-1. Because Martha is a cash basis taxpayer, she cannot take as a bad debt deduction any unpaid accrued interest on the loan to Janice (her friend) because it was never recognized as income.

A bad debt can also result from the nonrepayment of a loan made by the taxpayer or from purchased debt instruments.

7-1a Specific Charge-Off Method

In general, the specific charge-off method must be used for tax purposes when accounting for bad debts. Certain financial institutions are allowed to use the reserve method for computing deductions for bad debts.

A taxpayer using the specific charge-off method may claim a deduction in the year when a specific business debt becomes either partially or wholly worthless. A nonbusiness debt must be wholly worthless to claim a deduction.[3] The taxpayer must be able to document the fact that the debt is either partially or completely worthless. This is one of the more difficult tasks facing a taxpayer. Legal proceedings against the debtor are not required as long as the taxpayer can demonstrate that collection is unlikely.

In the case of a business debt, partial worthlessness can result in a deduction. If, in a later year, the balance of the debt is deemed uncollectible, it can be deducted. In the case of a nonbusiness debt, a deduction is only allowed in the year the debt becomes completely worthless.

EXAMPLE 3

In 2015, Ross loaned $1,000 to Kay, who agreed to repay the loan in two years. In 2017, Kay disappeared after the note became delinquent. If a reasonable investigation by Ross indicates that he cannot find Kay or that a suit against Kay would not result in collection, Ross can deduct the $1,000 in 2017.

Bankruptcy is generally an indication of at least partial worthlessness of a debt. Bankruptcy may create worthlessness before the settlement date. If this is the case, the deduction may be taken in the year of worthlessness.

EXAMPLE 4

In Example 3, assume that Kay filed for personal bankruptcy in 2016 and that the debt is a business debt. At that time, Ross learned that unsecured creditors (including Ross) were ultimately expected to receive 20 cents on the dollar. In 2017, settlement is made, and Ross receives only $150. He should deduct $800 ($1,000 loan − $200 expected settlement) in 2016 and $50 in 2017 ($200 balance − $150 proceeds).

---

[3]§ 166(a).

If a receivable is written off (deducted) as uncollectible and then collected in a later tax year, income will result if the deduction yielded a tax benefit in the year it was taken. See Examples 33 and 34 in Chapter 5.

Concept Summary 7.1 provides a summary of the tax treatment of bad debts using the specific charge-off method.

Concept Summary 7.1

The Tax Treatment of Bad Debts Using the Specific Charge-Off Method

	Business Bad Debts	Nonbusiness Bad Debts
Timing of deduction	A deduction is allowed when the debt becomes either partially or wholly worthless.	A deduction is allowed *only* when the debt becomes wholly worthless.
Character of deduction	The bad debt is deducted as an ordinary loss.	The bad debt is classified as a short-term capital loss, subject to the $3,000 net capital loss limitation for individuals.
Recovery of amounts previously deducted	If the account recovered was written off during the current tax year, the write-off entry is reversed. If the account was written off in a previous tax year, income is created subject to the tax benefit rule.	If the account recovered was written off during the current tax year, the write-off entry is reversed. If the account was written off in a previous tax year, income is created subject to the tax benefit rule.

7-1b Business versus Nonbusiness Bad Debts

Whether a debt is business or nonbusiness depends on the role of the lender. How the borrower uses the funds is of no consequence. A **nonbusiness bad debt** is unrelated to the lender's trade or business either when it was created or when it became worthless. Loans to relatives or friends are the most common type of nonbusiness bad debt.

The Big Picture

EXAMPLE 5

Return to the facts of *The Big Picture* on p. 7-1. Martha loaned her friend Janice $25,000. Janice used the money to start a business, which subsequently failed. When Janice died after having made payments of $7,000 on the loan, she was insolvent.

Even though the proceeds of the loan were used in a business, the loan is a nonbusiness bad debt because the business was Janice's, not Martha's, and Martha is not in the business of lending money.

The distinction between a business bad debt and a nonbusiness bad debt is important. A **business bad debt** is treated as an ordinary deduction in the year incurred. In contrast, a nonbusiness bad debt is always treated as a short-term capital loss. Since net capital loss deductions are limited to no more than $3,000 per year, a taxpayer's nonbusiness bad debt deduction could have a limited benefit (see Chapter 16 for a detailed discussion). It is assumed that any loans made by a business are related to its trade or business. A common example is credit sales to customers. Any bad debts that occur from these transactions are business bad debts.

The following example is an illustration of business bad debts adapted from the Regulations.[4]

EXAMPLE 6

In 2016, Leif sold his business but retained a claim (note or account receivable) against Bob. The claim became worthless in 2017.

Leif's loss is treated as a business bad debt because the debt was created in the conduct of his former trade or business. Leif is accorded business bad debt treatment even though he was holding the note as an investor and was no longer in a trade or business when the claim became worthless.

[4]Reg. § 1.166–5(d).

7-1c **Loans between Related Parties**

Loans between related parties (especially family members) raise the issue of whether the transaction was a *bona fide* loan or a gift. The Regulations indicate that individual circumstances must be examined to determine whether advances between related parties are gifts or loans. Some considerations are these:

- Was a note properly executed?
- Was there a reasonable rate of interest?
- Was collateral provided?
- What collection efforts were made?
- What was the intent of the parties?

EXAMPLE
7

Lana loans $2,000 to her widowed mother for an operation. Lana's mother owns no property and is not employed, and her only income consists of Social Security benefits. No note is issued for the loan, no provision for interest is made, and no repayment date is mentioned. In the current year, Lana's mother dies, leaving no estate.

Assuming that the loan is not repaid, Lana cannot take a deduction for a nonbusiness bad debt because the facts indicate that no debtor-creditor relationship existed.

See Concept Summary 7.2 for a review of the bad debt deduction rules.

Concept Summary 7.2

Bad Debt Deductions

```
                      Does a valid debt exist
No deduction   No    (a debtor-creditor relationship)?
allowed      ←────
                              │ Yes
                              ↓
                      Is the debt really
No deduction   No          worthless?
allowed      ←────
                              │ Yes
                              ↓
                      Is the debt evidenced      Yes    See § 165(g) dealing with
                         by a security?       ────→     worthless securities
                                                        (discussed on p. 7-6)
                              │ No
                              ↓
                      Is the creditor a          Yes    Business bad debt
                         corporation?         ────→     (treated as an
                                                        ordinary deduction)
                              │ No
                              ↓
                   Is the debt created or incurred   No    Nonbusiness bad
                   in connection with the creditor's ────→ debt (treated as a
                       trade or business?                  short-term capital loss)
                              │ Yes
                              ↓
                      Business bad debt
                        (treated as an
                      ordinary deduction)
```

LO.2

State and illustrate the tax treatment of worthless securities, including § 1244 stock.

7-2 WORTHLESS SECURITIES AND SMALL BUSINESS STOCK LOSSES

7-2a Worthless Securities

A loss is allowed for securities that become *completely* worthless during the year (**worthless securities**).[5] Such securities are shares of stock, bonds, notes, or other evidence of indebtedness issued by a corporation or government. The losses generated are treated as capital losses deemed to have occurred on the *last day* of the taxable year. By treating the loss as having occurred on the last day of the taxable year, a loss that would otherwise have been classified as short term (if the date of worthlessness was used) may be classified as a long-term capital loss. Capital losses may be of limited benefit due to the $3,000 net capital loss limitation.[6]

The Big Picture

EXAMPLE 8

Return to the facts of *The Big Picture* on p. 7-1. Martha owned stock in a pharmaceutical company that she acquired as an investment on October 1, 2016, at a cost of $50,000. On May 31, 2017, the stock became worthless when the company declared bankruptcy.

Because the stock is deemed to have become worthless as of December 31, 2017, Martha has a capital loss from an asset held for 15 months (a long-term capital loss).

7-2b Small Business Stock (§ 1244 Stock) Losses

In general, shareholders receive capital gain or loss treatment when they sell stock. However, it is possible to receive an ordinary loss deduction if the loss relates to **small business stock (§ 1244 stock)**. Only *individuals*[7] who acquired the stock *from* the corporation are eligible to receive ordinary loss treatment under § 1244. The ordinary loss is limited to $50,000 ($100,000 for married individuals filing jointly) per year. Losses in excess of these limits receive capital loss treatment.

The corporation issuing the stock must be a "small business corporation."[8] A corporation meets this definition if the total amount of money and other property received by the corporation for stock as a contribution to capital (or paid-in surplus) does not exceed $1 million. The $1 million test is made at the time the stock is issued. Section 1244 stock can be common or preferred stock. Section 1244 applies only to losses. If § 1244 stock is sold at a gain, the Section is not applicable and the gain is capital gain.

EXAMPLE 9

Iris, a single individual, was looking for an investment that would give some diversity to her stock portfolio. A friend suggested that she acquire some stock in Eagle Corporation, a new startup company. On July 1, 2015, Iris purchased 100 shares of Eagle Corporation for $100,000. At the time Iris acquired her stock from Eagle Corporation, the corporation had $700,000 of paid-in capital. As a result, the stock qualified as § 1244 stock. On June 20, 2017, Iris sold all of her Eagle stock for $20,000.

Because the Eagle stock is § 1244 stock, Iris has a $50,000 ordinary loss and a $30,000 long-term capital loss.

The Big Picture

EXAMPLE 10

Return to the facts of *The Big Picture* on p. 7-1. On March 8, 2017, Martha purchases what she believes is § 1244 stock from her friend Peter for $20,000. On November 2, 2017, she sells the stock in the marketplace for $12,000.

Because Martha did not acquire the stock from the corporation, the stock is not § 1244 stock to Martha. As a result, Martha has an $8,000 short-term capital loss.

---

[5]§ 165(g).
[6]§ 1211(b).

[7]The term *individuals* for this purpose does not include a trust or an estate (but could include a partnership or an LLC).
[8]§ 1244(c)(3).

7-3 **LOSSES OF INDIVIDUALS**

Distinguish between deductible and nondeductible losses of individuals.

An individual may deduct the following losses under § 165(c):

- Losses incurred in a trade or business (e.g., business loss of a sole proprietor or sale of a business asset at a loss).

- Losses incurred in a transaction entered into for profit (e.g., sale of an asset used in a rental activity at a loss).

- Losses caused by fire, storm, shipwreck, or other casualty or by theft (e.g., a residence damaged in a hurricane).

In general, losses on personal use property (e.g., a car, furniture, or a residence) are not deductible. The casualty loss rules are an exception. Although the terms *fire, storm, shipwreck,* and *theft* are easy to understand, what is meant by *other casualty*? First, it means that events similar to a fire, storm, or shipwreck qualify. In addition, accidental losses also qualify. Overall, the loss must result from an event that is (1) identifiable; (2) damaging to property; and (3) sudden, unexpected, and unusual in nature.[9] Examples include auto accidents, mine cave-ins, sonic booms, and vandalism. Weather that causes damage (e.g., drought) must be unusual and severe for the particular region. Damage must be to the taxpayer's property to qualify as a casualty loss.

A taxpayer can take a deduction for a casualty loss from an automobile accident only if the damage was not caused by the taxpayer's willful act or willful negligence.

Ted parks his car on a hill and fails to set the brake properly and to curb the wheels. As a result of Ted's negligence, the car rolls down the hill and is damaged. The repairs to Ted's car should qualify for casualty loss treatment because Ted's act of negligence does not appear to be willful.

7-3a **Events That Are Not Casualties**

Identify a casualty and determine the amount, classification, and timing of casualty and theft losses.

Not all acts of nature are treated as casualty losses for income tax purposes. Because a casualty must be sudden, unexpected, and unusual, progressive deterioration (such as erosion due to wind or rain) is not a casualty because it does not meet the suddenness test.

Examples of nonsudden events that generally do not qualify as casualties include disease and insect damage. When the damage was caused by termites over a period of several years, some courts have disallowed a casualty loss deduction.[10] Other examples of events that are not casualties are losses resulting from a decline in value rather than an actual loss of the property. No loss was allowed where the taxpayer's home declined in value as a result of a landslide that destroyed neighboring homes but did no actual damage to the taxpayer's home.[11] Similarly, a taxpayer was allowed a loss for the actual flood damage to his property but not for the decline in market value due to the property being flood-prone.[12]

7-3b **Theft Losses**

Theft includes, but is not necessarily limited to, larceny, embezzlement, and robbery.[13] Theft does not include misplaced items.[14]

Theft losses are deducted in the year of *discovery*, which may not be the same as the year of the theft. If an insurance claim exists and there is a reasonable expectation of recovering the adjusted basis of the asset from the insurance company, no deduction is permitted.[15] If in the year of settlement the recovery is less than the asset's adjusted basis,

[9]Rev.Rul. 72–592, 1972–2 C.B. 101.

[10]*Fay v. Helvering,* 41–2 USTC ¶9494, 27 AFTR 432, 120 F.2d 253 (CA–2, 1941); *U.S. v. Rogers,* 41–1 USTC ¶9442, 27 AFTR 423, 120 F.2d 244 (CA–9, 1941). The current position of the IRS is that termite damage is not deductible (Rev.Rul. 63–232, 1963 C.B. 97).

[11]*H. Pulvers v. Comm.,* 69–1 USTC ¶9222, 23 AFTR 2d 69–678, 407 F.2d 838 (CA–9, 1969).

[12]*S. L. Solomon,* 39 TCM 1282, T.C.Memo. 1980–87.

[13]Reg. § 1.165–8(d).

[14]*Mary Francis Allen,* 16 T.C. 163 (1951).

[15]Reg. §§ 1.165–1(d)(2) and 1.165–8(a)(2).

a partial deduction may be available. If the recovery is greater than the asset's adjusted basis, gain may be recognized.

Keith's new sailboat, which he uses for personal purposes, was stolen from the storage marina in December 2016. He discovered the loss on June 3, 2017, and filed a claim with his insurance company that was settled on January 30, 2018.

Assuming that there is a reasonable expectation of full recovery, no deduction is allowed in 2017 (the year of discovery). A partial deduction may be available in 2018 if the actual insurance proceeds are less than the lower of the fair market value or the adjusted basis of the asset.

7-3c **When to Deduct Casualty Losses**

General Rule

Generally, a casualty loss is deducted in the year the loss occurs. However, no casualty loss is permitted if an insurance claim with a *reasonable prospect of full recovery* exists.[16] If the taxpayer has a partial claim, only part of the loss can be claimed in the year of the casualty, and the remainder is deducted in the year the claim is settled.

Brian's new sailboat was completely destroyed by fire in 2017. Its cost and fair market value were $15,000. Brian's only claim against the insurance company was on a $10,000 policy, which was not settled by year-end. The following year, 2018, Brian settled with the insurance company for $8,000.

Brian is entitled to a $5,000 deduction in 2017 ($10,000 − $15,000) and a $2,000 deduction in 2018.

If a taxpayer receives reimbursement for a casualty loss sustained and deducted in a previous year, an amended return is *not* filed. Instead, the taxpayer includes the reimbursement in gross income when it is received to the extent the previous deduction resulted in a tax benefit.

Fran had a deductible casualty loss of $4,000 on her 2016 tax return. Fran's taxable income for 2016 was $60,000. In June 2017, Fran is reimbursed $2,750 for the prior year's casualty loss.

Fran includes the entire $2,750 in gross income for 2017 because the deduction in 2016 produced a tax benefit.

Disaster Area Losses

An exception to the general rule for the time of deduction is allowed for disaster area losses, which are casualties sustained in an area designated as a disaster area by the President of the United States.[17] In such cases, the taxpayer may *elect* to treat the loss as having occurred in the taxable year immediately *preceding* the taxable year in which the disaster actually occurred. The rationale for this exception is to provide immediate relief to disaster victims in the form of accelerated tax benefits.

The Big Picture

Return to the facts of *The Big Picture* on p. 7-1. On September 28, 2017, Martha's personal residence was damaged when a hurricane caused an oak tree to fall onto the house. The amount of her uninsured loss was $7,000 ($25,000 insurance settlement − $32,000 damages incurred). Because of the extent of the damage in the area, the President of the United States designated the area a disaster area.

Because Martha's loss is a disaster area loss, she may elect to file an amended return for 2016 and take the loss in that year. Alternatively, she may take the loss on her 2017 income tax return.

---

[16]Reg. § 1.165–1(d)(2)(i).

[17]§ 165(i). Disaster loss treatment also applies if a residence has been rendered unsafe as the result of a disaster within 120 days of the disaster loss designation [§ 165(k)].

7-3d **Measuring the Amount of Loss**

Amount of Loss

The rules for determining the amount of a loss depend in part on whether business use, income-producing use, or personal use property was involved. Another factor that must be considered is whether the property was partially or completely destroyed.

If business or rental property is *completely destroyed*, the loss is equal to the adjusted basis of the property at the time of destruction.

Vicki's business equipment, was destroyed by flood. Vicki had no flood insurance on her business. The fair market value of the equipment was $9,000 at the time of the flood, and its adjusted basis was $10,000.

Vicki is allowed a loss deduction of $10,000 (the basis of the equipment). The $10,000 loss is a deduction *for* AGI.

EXAMPLE 16

A different measurement rule applies for *partial destruction* of business or rental property and for *partial* or *complete destruction* of personal use property. In these situations, the loss is the *lesser* of the following:

- The adjusted basis of the property.
- The difference between the fair market value of the property before the event and the fair market value immediately after the event.

Kelly's uninsured automobile, which was used only for business purposes, was damaged in an accident. On the date of the accident, the fair market value of the automobile was $12,000, and its adjusted basis was $9,000. After the accident, the automobile was appraised at $4,000.

Kelly's loss deduction is $8,000 (the lesser of the adjusted basis or the decrease in fair market value). The $8,000 loss is a deduction *for* AGI.

EXAMPLE 17

If the property is used for both personal and business/rental use, the loss deduction must be computed separately for the business portion and the personal portion. If a taxpayer has insurance coverage on *personal use* property, an insurance claim must be filed to claim a casualty loss.[18]

Generally, an appraisal before and after the casualty is needed to measure the amount of the loss. However, the *cost of repairs* can be used if following criteria are met:

- The repairs are necessary to restore the property to its condition immediately before the casualty.
- The amount spent for repairs is not excessive.
- The repairs do not extend beyond the damage suffered.
- The value of the property after the repairs does not, as a result of the repairs, exceed the value of the property immediately before the casualty.[19]

ETHICS & EQUITY **Is Policy Cancellation an Escape Hatch?**

Noah's house is burglarized for the third time, and he knows that if he files a claim, the insurance company will cancel his homeowner's policy or impose a prohibitive premium. Noah does not file a claim, yet he deducts the loss on his tax return. Is his loss allowed?

---

[18]§ 165(h)(4)(E).

[19]Reg. § 1.165–7(a)(2)(ii).

Personal Use Loss Reductions: The $100-per-Event and 10%-of-AGI Floors

The amount of the loss for *personal use* property must be further reduced by a $100-*per-event* floor and a 10%-of-AGI *aggregate* floor.[20] The $100 floor applies separately to each casualty and applies to the entire loss from each casualty (e.g., if a storm damages both a taxpayer's residence and automobile, only $100 is subtracted from the total amount of the loss). The losses are then added together, and the total is reduced by 10 percent of the taxpayer's AGI. The resulting loss is the taxpayer's itemized deduction for casualty and theft losses.

Rocky, who had AGI of $30,000, was involved in a motorcycle accident in 2017. His motorcycle, which was used only for personal use and had a fair market value of $12,000 and an adjusted basis of $9,000, was completely destroyed. He received $5,000 from his insurance company.

Rocky's casualty loss deduction is $900 [$9,000 basis − $5,000 insurance recovery − $100 floor − $3,000 (10% × $30,000 AGI)]. The $900 casualty loss is an itemized deduction (*from* AGI).

When a nonbusiness casualty loss is spread between two taxable years because of an outstanding insurance claim, the loss in the second year is not reduced by the $100 floor (the "$100-per-event" reduction occurred in the first year). However, the loss in the second year is still subject to the 10 percent floor based upon the taxpayer's second-year AGI. For taxpayers who suffer qualified disaster area losses, the 10%-of-AGI floor is determined by using the AGI of the year the deduction is claimed.[21]

Brian's new *personal use* sailboat, completely destroyed by fire in 2017, had a $15,000 cost and fair market value. He only had $10,000 of insurance coverage for the boat. He filed an insurance claim and settled with the insurance company in 2018 for $8,000.

Brian is entitled to a $5,000 deduction in 2017 ($10,000 − $15,000) and a $2,000 deduction in 2018. Brian's $5,000 casualty loss deduction in 2017 is reduced first by $100 and then by 10% of his 2017 AGI. The $2,000 deduction in 2018 is reduced by 10% of his 2018 AGI.

Multiple Losses

The rules for computing loss deductions where multiple losses have occurred are explained in Examples 20 and 21.

Multiple Casualty Losses

EXAMPLE 20

During the year, Tim had the following casualty losses:

Asset	Adjusted Basis	Before the Casualty	After the Casualty	Insurance Recovery
		Fair Market Value of Asset		
A	$900	$600	$−0−	$400
B	300	800	250	100

Assets A and B were used in Tim's business at the time of the casualty. The following losses are allowed:

Asset A: $500. The complete destruction of a business asset results in a deduction of the adjusted basis of the property (reduced by any insurance recovery), regardless of the asset's fair market value.

Asset B: $200. The partial destruction of a business (or personal use) asset results in a deduction equal to the lesser of the adjusted basis ($300) or the decline in value ($550), reduced by any insurance recovery ($100).

Both the Asset A and Asset B losses are deductions *for* AGI. The $100 floor and the 10%-of-AGI floor do not apply because the assets are business assets.

Multiple Casualty Losses

During the year, Emily had AGI of $20,000 and the following casualty losses:

| | | Fair Market Value of Asset | | |
Asset	Adjusted Basis	Before the Casualty	After the Casualty	Insurance Recovery
A	$1,900	$1,400	$ –0–	$200
B	2,500	4,000	1,000	–0–
C	800	400	100	250

Assets A, B, and C were held for personal use, and the losses to these three assets are from three different casualties. The loss for each asset is computed as follows:

Asset A: $1,100. The lesser of the adjusted basis of $1,900 or the $1,400 decline in value, reduced by the insurance recovery of $200, minus the $100 floor.

Asset B: $2,400. The lesser of the adjusted basis of $2,500 or the $3,000 decline in value, minus the $100 floor.

Asset C: $0. The lesser of the adjusted basis of $800 or the $300 decline in value, reduced by the insurance recovery of $250, minus the $100 floor.

Emily's itemized casualty loss deduction for the year is $1,500:

Asset A loss	$ 1,100
Asset B loss	2,400
Asset C loss	–0–
Total loss	$ 3,500
Less: 10% of AGI (10% × $20,000)	(2,000)
Itemized casualty loss deduction	$ 1,500

EXAMPLE

21

7-3e Personal Casualty Gains and Losses

If a taxpayer has personal casualty and theft gains as well as losses, a special set of rules applies for determining the tax consequences. First, the taxpayer must net (offset) the personal casualty gains and personal casualty losses (after application of the $100 floor). If the gains exceed the losses, the gains and losses are treated as gains and losses from the sale of capital assets. The capital gains and losses are short term or long term, depending on how long the taxpayer held each of the assets (assets held more than one year are long term). In the netting process, personal casualty and theft gains and losses are not netted with the gains and losses on business and income-producing property.

During the year, Cliff had the following personal casualty gains and losses (after deducting the $100 floor):

Asset	Holding Period	Gain or (Loss)
A	Three months	($ 300)
B	Three years	(2,400)
C	Two years	3,200

Cliff computes the tax consequences as follows:

Personal casualty gain	$ 3,200
Personal casualty loss ($300 + $2,400)	(2,700)
Net personal casualty gain	$ 500

Cliff treats all of the gains and losses as capital gains and losses:

Short-term capital loss (Asset A)	$ 300
Long-term capital loss (Asset B)	2,400
Long-term capital gain (Asset C)	3,200

EXAMPLE

22

If personal casualty losses exceed personal casualty gains, all gains and losses are treated as ordinary items. The gains—and the losses to the extent of gains—are treated as ordinary income and ordinary loss in computing AGI. Losses in excess of gains are deducted as itemized deductions to the extent the losses exceed 10 percent of AGI.[22]

During the year, Hazel had AGI of $20,000 and the following personal casualty gain and loss (after deducting the $100 floor):

Asset	Holding Period	Gain or (Loss)
A	Three years	($2,700)
B	Four months	200

Hazel computes the tax consequences as follows:

Personal casualty loss	($2,700)
Personal casualty gain	200
Net personal casualty loss	($2,500)

Hazel treats the gain and the loss as ordinary items. The $200 gain and $200 of the loss are included in computing AGI. Hazel's itemized deduction for casualty losses is computed as follows:

Casualty loss in excess of gain ($2,700 − $200)	$ 2,500
Less: 10% of AGI (10% × $20,000)	(2,000)
Itemized deduction	$ 500

See Concept Summary 7.3 for a review of the tax treatment of casualty gains and losses.

Concept Summary 7.3

Casualty Gains and Losses

	Business Use or Income-Producing Property	Personal Use Property
Event creating the loss	Any event.	Casualty or theft.
Amount	The lesser of the decline in fair market value or the adjusted basis, but always the adjusted basis if the property is totally destroyed.	The lesser of the decline in fair market value or the adjusted basis.
Insurance	Insurance proceeds received reduce the amount of the loss.	Insurance proceeds received (or for which there is an unfiled claim) reduce the amount of the loss.
$100 floor	Not applicable.	Applicable per event.
Gains and losses	Gains and losses are netted (see detailed discussion in Chapter 17).	Personal casualty and theft gains and losses are netted.
Gains exceeding losses	See Chapter 17.	The gains and losses are treated as gains and losses from the sale of capital assets.
Losses exceeding gains	See Chapter 17.	The gains—and the losses to the extent of gains—are treated as ordinary items in computing AGI. The losses in excess of gains, to the extent they exceed 10% of AGI, are itemized deductions.

---

[22]§ 165(h).

7-3f Statutory Framework for Deducting Losses of Individuals

Concept Summary 7.4 provides a summary of the statutory framework of deducting losses of individuals.

Concept Summary 7.4

Statutory Framework for Deducting Losses of Individuals

	Personal Casualty/Theft Losses		Employee Casualty/Theft Losses	Production of Income Casualty/Theft Losses	Trade or Business Casualty/Theft Losses
	$100-per-Event Rule	10%-of-AGI Rule	2%-of-AGI Rule		
General Application	Reduce each casualty or theft loss by $100 when figuring the potential casualty loss deduction. Apply this rule to personal use property after the amount of the loss has been determined.	Reduce the *total* casualty or theft loss by 10% of adjusted gross income. Apply this rule to personal use property after each loss is reduced by $100 (the "$100-per-event rule"). These personal losses are not subject to the 2%-of-AGI rule.	Casualty and theft losses incurred by an employee in connection with a trade or business are deductible *for* AGI if the loss is reimbursed by the employer (with the net loss being deductible). If the loss is not reimbursed, the loss is deductible *from* AGI as a miscellaneous itemized deduction subject to the 2%-of-AGI floor. These losses are not subject to the $100-per-event rule or the 10%-of-AGI rule.[23]	Casualty and theft losses incurred by an individual in a transaction entered into for profit are not subject to the $100-per-event and the 10%-of-AGI limitations. If these losses are attributable to rents or royalties, the deduction is *for* AGI.[24] If not, they are deductions *from* AGI.	Casualty and theft losses incurred by an individual in connection with a trade or business are deductible *for* AGI.[25] These losses are not subject to the $100-per-event and the 10%-of-AGI limitations.
Single Event	Apply this rule only once to each casualty or theft event, even if many pieces of property are affected by the event.	Apply this rule only once, even if many pieces of property are affected.	Apply this rule only once, even if many pieces of property are affected.		
More Than One Event	Apply to the loss from each event.	Apply to the total of all losses from all events.	Apply to the total of all losses from all events.		

7-4 RESEARCH AND EXPERIMENTAL EXPENDITURES

State and apply the alternative tax treatments for research and experimental expenditures.

Section 174 covers the treatment of research and experimental expenditures. The Regulations define research and experimental expenditures as follows:

> all such costs incident to the development or improvement of a product (including an experimental or pilot model, a plant process, a product, a formula, an invention, or similar property). The term includes the costs of obtaining a patent, such as attorneys' fees expended in making and perfecting a patent application. Expenditures represent research and development

[23]§ 67(b)(3).
[24]§ 62(a)(4).
[25]§ 62(a)(1).

costs in the experimental or laboratory sense if they are for activities intended to discover information that would eliminate uncertainty concerning the development or improvement of a product. The term does not include expenditures such as those for the ordinary testing or inspection of materials or products for quality control or those for efficiency surveys, management studies, consumer surveys, advertising, or promotions.[26]

The law permits the following *three alternatives* for the handling of research and experimental expenditures:

- Expensed in the year paid or incurred.
- Deferred and amortized.
- Capitalized.

If the costs are capitalized, a deduction may not be available until the research project is abandoned or is deemed worthless. Because many products resulting from research projects do not have a definite and limited useful life, most taxpayers choose to write off the expenditures immediately or to defer and amortize them.[27]

7-4a **Expense Method**

A taxpayer can expense all of the research and experimental expenditures incurred provided this method is adopted for the first taxable year in which these expenditures were paid or incurred.[28] Once this method is adopted, the taxpayer must continue to expense all qualifying expenditures unless a request for a change is made to, and approved by, the IRS.

7-4b **Deferral and Amortization Method**

If elected by the taxpayer, research and experimental expenditures may be deferred and amortized ratably over a period of not less than 60 months.[29] A deduction is allowed beginning with the month in which the taxpayer first realizes benefits from the experimental expenditure. The election is binding, and a change requires permission from the IRS.

EXAMPLE 24

Gold Corporation decides to develop a new line of adhesives. The project begins in 2017. Gold incurs the following expenses in 2017 and 2018 in connection with the project:

	2017	2018
Salaries	$25,000	$18,000
Materials	8,000	2,000
Depreciation on machinery	6,500	5,700

The benefits from the project will be realized starting in March 2019. If Gold Corporation elects a 60-month deferral and amortization period, there is no deduction prior to March 2019, the month benefits from the project begin to be realized. The deduction for 2019 is $10,867, computed as follows:

Salaries ($25,000 + $18,000)	$43,000
Materials ($8,000 + $2,000)	10,000
Depreciation ($6,500 + $5,700)	12,200
Total	$65,200
$65,200 × (10 months/60 months) =	$10,867

---

[26]Reg. § 1.174–2(a)(1), (2), and (3). Expenses in connection with the acquisition or improvement of land or depreciable property are not research and experimental expenditures. Rather, they increase the basis of the land or depreciable property. However, depreciation on an asset used for research may be a research and experimental expense.

[27]A credit for increasing research expenditures is also available; § 41. See Chapter 13 for a more detailed discussion of this credit.

[28]Deductions are even allowed if incurred before actually engaging in any trade or business activity; *Snow v. Comm.*, 74–1 USTC ¶9432, 33 AFTR 2d 74–1251, 94 S.Ct. 1876 (USSC, 1974).

[29]§ 174(b)(2).

The option to defer and amortize research and experimental expenditures is usually employed when a company does not have sufficient income to offset the expenses.[30] The deferral of research and experimental expenditures should also be considered if the taxpayer expects higher tax rates in the future.

7-5 DOMESTIC PRODUCTION ACTIVITIES DEDUCTION

LO.6
Calculate the domestic production activities deduction.

A number of years ago, Congress enacted changes to a variety of tax provisions that our world trading partners regarded as allowing unfair advantage to U.S. exports. In response, Congress created a **domestic production activities deduction (DPAD)** based on the income from manufacturing activities (designated as *production activities*).[31]

7-5a Operational Rules

Calculation of the Domestic Production Activities Deduction

The DPAD is based on the following formula:[32]

9% × Lesser of ⟨ Qualified production activities income (QPAI)

Taxable (or modified adjusted gross) income or alternative minimum taxable income

Taxable income is determined without regard to the DPAD. In the case of an individual (a sole proprietorship or an owner of a flow-through entity), **modified adjusted gross income** is substituted for taxable income.[33]

The taxable income limitation is determined after the application of any net operating loss (NOL) deduction for the tax year. Thus, a taxpayer with an NOL carryforward for a tax year is ineligible for the DPAD if the carryforward eliminates current taxable income. Further, a taxpayer that has an NOL carryback may lose part or all of the DPAD benefit for that year. As taxable income is reduced by the NOL carryback, there is a corresponding reduction in the DPAD. If qualified production activities income (QPAI) cannot be used in a particular year due to the taxable income limitation, it is lost forever.

DPAD: Calculation Using QPAI

Opal, Inc., manufactures and sells costume jewelry. It also sells costume jewelry purchased from other manufacturers. During 2017, Opal had a *profit* of $200,000 (QPAI) from the sale of its own manufactured jewelry and a *loss* of $50,000 from the sale of the purchased jewelry.

Based on this information, Opal's QPAI is $200,000 and its taxable income is $150,000 ($200,000 − $50,000). Opal's DPAD becomes $13,500 [9% of the lesser of $200,000 (QPAI) or $150,000 (taxable income)].

EXAMPLE
25

Assume the same facts as in Example 25, except that Opal also has an NOL carryover from 2016 of $300,000.

As taxable income for 2017 is zero ($200,000 − $50,000 − $300,000), there is no DPAD.

EXAMPLE
26

The DPAD cannot exceed 50 percent of certain **W–2 wages** paid by the taxpayer during the tax year.[34] If no W–2 wages are paid, no DPAD will be allowed. So part of the rationale

---

[30]Another option is to deduct these expenses for regular tax purposes, but elect in any year where helpful, to capitalize and amortize the expenses over 10 years for both regular tax and alternative minimum tax purposes [§ 59(e)]. Chapter 12 includes a discussion of this option.

[31]§ 199; Section 101 of the *American Jobs Creation Act of 2004*, Public Law No. 108-357 (October 22, 2004). Form 8903 is used to report the calculation of the DPAD.

[32]§ 199(a).

[33]§ 199(d)(2). Generally, modified AGI is AGI before any DPAD.

[34]§ 199(b).

behind this limitation is to preserve U.S. manufacturing jobs and to discourage their outsourcing. An employer's W–2 wages include the sum of the aggregate amount of wages and elective deferrals required to be included on the W–2 wage statements for employees engaged in qualified production activities during the employer's taxable year.[35]

DPAD: W–2 Limitation

EXAMPLE 27

In 2017, Red, Inc., a calendar year taxpayer, has QPAI of $2 million and taxable income of $2.1 million. Because Red outsources much of its work to independent contractors, its W–2 wage base, which for Red is related entirely to production activities, is $80,000.

Although Red's DPAD normally would be $180,000 [9% of the lesser of $2 million (QPAI) or $2.1 million (taxable income)], it is limited to $40,000 [50% of $80,000 (W–2 wages)].

EXAMPLE 28

Assume the same facts as in Example 27, except that Red also pays salaries of $50,000 related to its *nonproduction* activities. Because these wages are not paid to employees engaged in production activities, the wage limitation on the DPAD remains at $40,000 [50% of $80,000 ($80,000 + $0)].

Calculation of Qualified Production Activities Income

Qualified production activities income (QPAI) is the excess of **domestic production gross receipts (DPGR)** over the sum of:

- The cost of goods sold allocated to such receipts.
- Other deductions, expenses, or losses directly allocated to such receipts.
- The ratable portion of deductions, expenses, and losses not directly allocable to such receipts or another class of income.[36]

QPAI is determined on an item-by-item basis—not on a division-by-division or a transaction-by-transaction basis. Because all items must be netted in the calculation, the final QPAI amount can be either positive or negative. The effect of the netting rule is to preclude taxpayers from selecting only profitable product lines or profitable transactions when calculating QPAI.

EXAMPLE 29

A taxpayer manufactures pants and shirts with the following QPAI results: $5 for one pair of pants and a negative $2 for one shirt. Because the two items are netted, the QPAI amount that controls is $3 ($5 − $2).

Five specific categories of DPGR qualify for the DPAD:[37]

- The lease, license, sale, exchange, or other disposition of qualified production property (QPP) that was manufactured, produced, grown, or extracted (MPGE) in the United States.
- Qualified films largely created in the United States.
- The production of electricity, natural gas, or potable water.
- Construction (but not self-construction) performed in the United States.
- Engineering and architectural services for domestic construction.

The sale of food and beverages prepared by a taxpayer at a retail establishment and the transmission or distribution of electricity, natural gas, or potable water are specifically excluded from the definition of DPGR.

7-5b **Eligible Taxpayers**

The deduction is available to a variety of taxpayers, including individuals, partnerships, S corporations, C corporations, cooperatives, estates, and trusts. For a pass-through entity

---

[35]Elective deferrals include those amounts deferred under § 457 plans (see Chapter 19).

[36]§ 199(c).

[37]§ 199(c)(4).

(e.g., partnerships and S corporations), the deduction flows through to the individual owners. In the case of a sole proprietor, a deduction *for* AGI results and is claimed on Form 1040, line 35 on page 1. A Form 8903 must be attached to support the deduction.[38]

7-6 NET OPERATING LOSSES

LO.7

Determine the amount of the net operating loss and review the impact of the carryback and carryover provisions on previous and subsequent years' taxable income.

The requirement that every taxpayer file an annual income tax return may result in inequities for taxpayers who experience income fluctuations (and losses in certain tax years) versus taxpayers with stable income levels. A loss in a particular tax year would produce no tax benefit if the Code did not provide for the carryback and carryforward of these losses to profitable years.

EXAMPLE 30

Juanita has a business and realizes the following taxable income or loss over a five-year period: year 1, $50,000; year 2, ($30,000); year 3, $100,000; year 4, ($200,000); and year 5, $380,000. She is married and files a joint return. Hubert also has a business and has a taxable income pattern of $60,000 every year. He, too, is married and files a joint return. Both Juanita and Hubert have total taxable income of $300,000 over the five-year period. Assuming that there is no provision for carryback or carryover of NOLs, Juanita and Hubert would have the following five-year tax bills:

Year	Juanita's Tax	Hubert's Tax
1	$ 6,568	$ 8,068
2	–0–	8,068
3	16,478	8,068
4	–0–	8,068
5	100,617	8,068
	$123,663	$40,340

Note: The computation of tax is made without regard to any NOL benefit. The 2017 Tax Rate Schedules are used to compute the tax.

Even though Juanita and Hubert realized the same total taxable income over the five-year period, Juanita had to pay taxes of $123,663, while Hubert paid taxes of only $40,340.

To provide partial relief from this inequitable tax treatment, a **net operating loss (NOL)** deduction is allowed.[39] NOLs for any one year can be offset against taxable income of other years. In general, only losses from the operation of a trade or business and casualty and theft losses, can create an NOL.

7-6a Carryback and Carryover Periods

General Rules

In general, an NOL can be carried back 2 tax years and forward 20 years. So it is carried first to the second prior year and then to the immediately preceding tax year (or until used up). If the loss is not fully used in the carryback period, it must be carried forward to the first year after the loss year and then forward until used (or the carryforward period expires).[40]

EXAMPLE 31

For 2017, the taxpayer and spouse have an NOL of $50,000. The NOL can be carried back 2 years (first to 2015 and then to 2016) and then carried forward 20 years (from 2018 to 2037).

---

[38]In practice, the DPAD calculation is challenging (and complicated by numerous rules and definitions contained in the Code and Regulations). Further, the additional records needed to support the deduction, along with its computational complexities, increase the tax reporting burden. For additional information on the DPAD, see Chapter 3 in *South-Western Federal Taxation: Corporations, Partnerships, Estates & Trusts*.

[39]§ 172.

[40]A three-year carryback period is available for any NOL resulting from a casualty or theft loss or small business NOLs that result from a Presidentially declared disaster. A five-year carryback is available for a farming loss.

If the loss is being carried to a preceding year, an amended return is filed on Form 1040X or a quick refund claim is filed on Form 1045. In either case, a refund of taxes previously paid is requested. When the loss is carried forward, the current return shows an NOL deduction for the prior year's loss.

Election to Forgo Carryback

A taxpayer can *irrevocably elect* not to carry back an NOL to any of the prior years. This election must be made by the due date (including extensions) for filing the taxpayer's return for the year in which the NOL occurred.[41] In that case, the loss is available as a carryover for 20 years. The election is often made when the taxpayer is in a low marginal tax bracket in the carryback years but expects to be in a high marginal tax bracket in future years.

EXAMPLE 32

For 2017, taxpayer and spouse have an NOL of $10,000. The NOL may be carried back and applied against taxable income first in 2015 and then in 2016. Any remaining NOL is carried forward to 2018 through 2037. As their marginal tax rate in 2015 and 2016 was only 10% and they expect their marginal tax rate in 2018 and later years to be at least 25%, they elect to forgo the carryback period. As a result, the NOL initially is carried to 2018 and forward through 2037, until it's completely applied (or the carryforward period expires).

NOLs and Self-Employment Taxes

An NOL can be carried back to offset taxable income and, as a result, reduce the taxpayer's income tax liability. However, an NOL *cannot* be used to reduce self-employment income. As a result, a taxpayer's self-employment tax liability will not change as the result of an NOL.[42]

7-6b Computation of the Net Operating Loss

Because the NOL provisions apply solely to business-related and casualty losses, individual taxpayers must make adjustments to their taxable income since nonbusiness deductions are allowed (e.g, personal and dependency exemptions and itemized deductions). To arrive at the NOL for an individual, taxable income must be adjusted as follows:[43]

1. No deduction is allowed for personal and dependency exemptions. These amounts must be added back.
2. The NOL carryover or carryback from another year is not allowed in the computation of the current year's NOL.
3. Capital losses and nonbusiness deductions are limited in determining the current year's NOL. These limits are as follows:
   a. The excess of nonbusiness capital losses over nonbusiness capital gains must be added back.
   b. The excess of nonbusiness deductions over the sum of nonbusiness income and *net* nonbusiness capital gains must be added back. *Net nonbusiness capital gains* are the excess of nonbusiness capital gains over nonbusiness capital losses. *Nonbusiness income* is income that is not related to a taxpayer's trade or business (e.g., dividends, investment interest, alimony received, and Social Security income). *Nonbusiness deductions* are those deductions that are not related to a taxpayer's trade or business [e.g., Individual Retirement Account (IRA) deductions, alimony paid deductions, and most itemized deductions]. Personal casualty and theft losses, losses incurred in a

[41]§ 172(b)(3).

[42]§ 1402(a).

[43]§ 172(d); Reg. § 1.172–3(a). Also see *Net Operating Losses for Individuals* (IRS Publication 536) and Forms 1045 and 1139.

transaction entered into for profit, and employee business expense deductions are allowed.

A taxpayer who does not itemize deductions computes the excess of nonbusiness deductions over nonbusiness income by substituting the standard deduction for total itemized deductions.

c. The excess of business capital losses over the sum of business capital gains and the excess of nonbusiness income and net nonbusiness capital gains over nonbusiness deductions must be added back.

d. The add-back for net nonbusiness capital losses and excess business capital losses does not include net capital losses not included in the current-year computation of taxable income because of the capital loss limitation provisions (discussed in Chapter 16).

For a review of the computation of the net operating loss for individuals, see Concept Summary 7.5.

Concept Summary 7.5

Computation of Net Operating Loss

Taxable income shown on the return

Add back:

1. Personal and dependency exemptions.

2. Net operating loss carryover or carryback from another year.

3. The excess of nonbusiness capital losses over nonbusiness capital gains.

4. The excess of nonbusiness deductions over the sum of nonbusiness income plus *net* nonbusiness capital gains.

5. The excess of business capital losses over the sum of business capital gains plus the excess of nonbusiness income and *net* nonbusiness capital gains over nonbusiness deductions.

Note: The add-back from the total of items 3 and 5 will not exceed $3,000 because of the capital loss limitation rules.

Equals: The net operating loss

The capital loss and nonbusiness deduction limits are illustrated in Examples 33 through 36.

Capital Loss and Nonbusiness Deduction Limits

For 2017, taxpayer and spouse have $6,000 of nonbusiness capital losses and $4,000 of nonbusiness capital gains.

They must add back $2,000 to taxable income ($6,000 − $4,000), which is the excess of nonbusiness capital losses over nonbusiness capital gains.

EXAMPLE 33

For 2017, taxpayer and spouse have $2,600 of nonbusiness capital gains, $1,000 of nonbusiness capital losses, $2,000 of interest income, and no itemized deductions.

They must add back $9,100 to taxable income {$12,700 standard deduction − [$2,000 interest income + $1,600 ($2,600 − $1,000) net nonbusiness capital gains]}.

Note that in this example, there is no excess of nonbusiness capital losses over nonbusiness capital gains.

EXAMPLE 34

Capital Loss and Nonbusiness Deduction Limits

EXAMPLE 35

For 2017, taxpayer and spouse have $2,600 of nonbusiness capital gains, $1,000 of nonbusiness capital losses, $15,000 of interest income, $14,500 of itemized deductions (none of which are personal casualty and theft losses), $4,000 of business capital losses, and $1,000 of business capital gains.

They must add back $900 to taxable income {$4,000 business capital losses − [$1,000 business capital gains + ($15,000 nonbusiness income + $1,600 net nonbusiness capital gains − $14,500 nonbusiness deductions)]}.

Note that in this example, there is no excess of nonbusiness capital losses over nonbusiness capital gains, nor is there an excess of nonbusiness deductions over the sum of nonbusiness income and net nonbusiness capital gains.

EXAMPLE 36

For 2017, taxpayer and spouse have $2,600 of nonbusiness capital gains, $3,000 of nonbusiness capital losses, $13,000 of interest income, $15,000 of itemized deductions (none of which are personal casualty and theft losses), $8,000 of business capital losses, and $4,000 of business capital gains.

They must add back $5,000 to taxable income:
(1) $2,000 ($15,000 − $13,000), which is the excess of nonbusiness deductions over nonbusiness income, and
(2) $3,000, which is the excess of combined capital losses because the capital loss limitation caps the loss at $3,000 in computing taxable income for the year.

Example 37 illustrates the computation of an NOL.

EXAMPLE 37

James opened a retail store in 2016 and experienced an NOL of $185 for that year. James had no taxable income for 2014 or 2015. James is married, has no dependents, and files a joint return. For 2017, James and his wife have the following taxable income:

Gross income from the business	$ 67,000	
Less: Business expenses	(73,000)	($ 6,000)
Salary from a part-time job		875
Interest on savings account		525
Nonbusiness long-term capital gain		1,000
NOL carryover from 2016		(185)
Net loss on rental property		(100)
Adjusted gross income		($ 3,885)
Less: Itemized deductions		
Interest expense on home mortgage	$ 4,600	
Taxes	7,300	
Casualty loss	2,000	
Total itemized deductions		(13,900)
Exemptions (2 × $4,050)		(8,100)
Taxable income		($25,885)

James's 2017 NOL is computed as follows:

Taxable income				($25,885)
Add:				
Net operating loss from 2016			$ 185	
Personal exemptions (2)			8,100	
Excess of nonbusiness deductions over nonbusiness income				
Total itemized deductions		$13,900		
Less: Casualty loss		(2,000)		
		$11,900		
Less: Interest income	$ 525			
Less: Long-term capital gain	1,000	(1,525)	10,375	18,660
Net operating loss				($ 7,225)

The NOL can be thought of as follows:

Business loss	($6,000)
Rental loss	(100)
Casualty loss	(2,000)
Salary income	875
Net operating loss	($7,225)

7-6c Recomputation of Tax Liability for Year to Which Net Operating Loss Is Carried

When an NOL is carried back to a nonloss year, the taxable income and income tax for the carryback year must be recomputed by including the NOL as a deduction *for* AGI. Several deductions (such as medical expenses and charitable contributions) are based on the amount of AGI. When an NOL is carried back, all such deductions *except* the charitable contributions deduction must be recomputed on the basis of the new AGI after the NOL has been applied. The deduction for charitable contributions is determined without regard to any NOL carryback but with regard to any other modification affecting AGI. Furthermore, any tax credits limited by or based upon the tax must be recomputed, based on the recomputed tax.

EXAMPLE 38

Peggy sustains an NOL of $11,000 in 2017. Peggy's loss is first carried back to 2015. For 2015, the joint income tax return of Peggy and her husband reported the following information:

Salary income		$ 15,000
Dividends (not qualified dividends)		4,000
Net short-term capital gain		1,700
Adjusted gross income		$ 20,700
Itemized deductions		
Charitable contributions	$3,810	
Medical [$2,140 − ($20,700 × 10%)]	70	
Interest expense on home mortgage	5,700	
Taxes	2,420	(12,000)
Exemptions (2 × $4,000)		(8,000)
Taxable income		$ 700
Tax (married filing jointly)		$ 70

Peggy's new tax liability for the carryback year is computed as follows:

Adjusted gross income		$ 20,700
Less: Net operating loss		(11,000)
Recomputed adjusted gross income		$ 9,700
Itemized deductions		
Charitable contributions	$3,810	
Medical [$2,140 − ($9,700 × 10%)]	1,170	
Interest expense on home mortgage	5,700	
Taxes	2,420	(13,100)
Exemptions (2 × $4,000)		(8,000)
Recomputed taxable income		($ 11,400)
Tax		$ −0−
Tax originally paid and refund claim		$ 70

7-6d Calculation of the Remaining Net Operating Loss

After computing the amount of the refund claim for the initial carryback year, it is then necessary to determine the extent to which any NOL remains to carry over to future years.[44] The amount of this carryover loss is the excess of the NOL over the taxable income of the year to which the loss is being applied. However, the taxable income of the year to which the loss is being applied must be determined with the following *modifications*:

- No deduction is allowed for excess capital losses over capital gains.
- No deduction is allowed for the NOL that is being carried back. However, deductions are allowed for NOLs occurring before the loss year.
- Any deductions claimed that are based on or limited by AGI must be determined after making the preceding adjustments. However, charitable contributions do not take into account any NOL carryback.
- No deduction is allowed for personal and dependency exemptions.

Referring to the facts in Example 38, the NOL carryover from 2015 available for future years is ($2,300), computed as follows:

Salary income		$ 15,000
Dividends (not qualified dividends)		4,000
Net short-term capital gain		1,700
Adjusted gross income		$ 20,700
Itemized deductions		
Charitable contributions	$3,810	
Medical [$2,140 − ($20,700 × 10%)]	70	
Interest expense on home mortgage	5,700	
Taxes	2,420	(12,000)
Exemptions (not allowed)		–0–
Modified taxable income		$ 8,700
Net operating loss		($ 11,000)
Modified taxable income		8,700
Net operating loss to carry forward		($ 2,300)

Because the ending figure is negative, it represents the remaining 2015 NOL. This amount can be applied to 2016 and then to 2018 and later years.

7-7 TAX PLANNING

 LO.8

Identify tax planning opportunities in deducting certain business expenses, business losses, and personal losses.

7-7a Small Business Stock (§ 1244 Stock) Losses

Because § 1244 limits the amount of loss classified as ordinary loss on a yearly basis, a taxpayer might maximize the benefits of § 1244 by selling the stock in more than one taxable year. The result could be that the losses in any one taxable year would not exceed the § 1244 limits on ordinary loss.

Mitch, a single individual, purchased small business stock in 2015 for $150,000 (150 shares at $1,000 per share). On December 20, 2017, the stock is worth $60,000 (150 shares at $400 per share). Mitch wants to sell the stock at this time. Mitch earns a salary of $80,000 a year, has no other capital transactions, and does not expect any in the future.

continued

---

[44]Taxpayers with an NOL carryover must keep records to track its use in carryback and/or carryforward years.

If Mitch sells all of the small business stock in 2017, his recognized loss will be $90,000 ($60,000 − $150,000). The loss will be characterized as a $50,000 ordinary loss and a $40,000 long-term capital loss. In computing taxable income for 2017, Mitch could deduct the $50,000 ordinary loss but could deduct only $3,000 of the capital loss. The remainder of the capital loss could be carried over and used in future years subject to the $3,000 limitation if Mitch has no capital gains.

Instead, if Mitch sells 82 shares in 2017, he will recognize an ordinary loss of $49,200 [82 × ($1,000 − $400)]. If Mitch then sells the remainder of the shares in 2018, he will recognize an ordinary loss of $40,800 [68 × ($1,000 − $400)]. Mitch could deduct the $49,200 ordinary loss in computing 2017 taxable income and the $40,800 ordinary loss in computing 2018 taxable income.

7-7b Casualty Losses

A special election is available for taxpayers who sustain casualty losses in an area designated by the President as a disaster area. This election affects only the *timing*, not the calculation, of the deduction. The benefit, of course, is a faster refund (or reduction in tax). It will also be advantageous to carry the loss back if the taxpayer's tax rate in the carryback year is higher than the tax rate in the year of the loss.

To find out if an event qualifies as a disaster area loss, one can look in any of the major tax services, the Compilation of Presidential Documents (released by the U.S. Government Publishing Office), or the *Internal Revenue Bulletin*.

7-7c Net Operating Losses

In certain instances, it may be advisable for a taxpayer to elect *not* to carry back an NOL. For an individual, the benefits from the loss carryback could be scaled down or lost due to the economic adjustments that must be made to taxable income for the year to which the loss is carried. For example, a taxpayer should attempt to minimize the number of taxable years to which an NOL is carried. The more years to which the NOL is applied, the more benefits are lost from adjustments for items such as personal and dependency exemptions.

REFOCUS ON THE BIG PICTURE

LOSSES

Martha can receive tax benefits associated with her unfortunate occurrences during the current tax year. Some of the losses, however, will provide a greater tax benefit than others as a result of different tax provisions governing the amount and the classification of the losses.

Bad Debt

Based on the facts provided, it appears that Martha's loan to her friend Janice was a bona fide debt. Otherwise, nothing would be deductible. The amount of the deduction is the unpaid principal balance of $19,000 ($25,000 − $6,000). Unfortunately, because the bad debt is a nonbusiness bad debt, it is classified as a short-term capital loss (see Example 5).

Investment Losses

The $50,000 loss from the pharmaceutical company stock is deductible. However, it appears that the loss should be classified as a long-term capital loss rather than as a

continued

TETRA IMAGES/GETTY IMAGES

short-term capital loss. Although the actual holding period was not greater than one year (October through May), the disposal date for the stock (which qualifies as a worthless security) is deemed to be the last day of the tax year (October of last year through end of December of the current year). The loss does not appear to qualify for ordinary loss treatment under § 1244 (see Example 8). The stock she purchased from her friend Peter results in an $8,000 short-term capital loss (and does not qualify under § 1244; see Example 10).

Loss from Bookstore

The $180,000 loss from the bookstore is reported on Schedule C of Form 1040. It is an ordinary loss, and it qualifies for NOL treatment. Therefore, Martha can carry any net loss back and offset it against taxable income of the past two years (starting with the earliest carryback year). Any amount not offset by carrying the loss back to the two previous taxable years can be carried forward for the next 20 years. Any carryback will produce a claim for a tax refund.

Casualty Loss

The loss on the damage to Martha's personal residence is classified as a personal casualty loss. Using the cost of repairs method, the amount of the casualty loss is $7,000 ($25,000 − $32,000). However, this amount must be reduced by the statutory materiality amounts of $100 and 10 percent of AGI.

If the President classified the area in which Martha's house is located as a disaster area, Martha has the option of deducting the casualty loss on the prior year's tax return (see Example 15).

Key Terms

Bad debt, 7-2	Modified adjusted gross income, 7-15	Small business stock (§ 1244 stock), 7-6
Business bad debt, 7-4	Net operating loss (NOL), 7-17	Specific charge-off method, 7-3
Casualty loss, 7-7	Nonbusiness bad debt, 7-4	Theft losses, 7-7
Disaster area losses, 7-8	Qualified production activities income (QPAI), 7-16	W–2 wages, 7-15
Domestic production activities deduction (DPAD), 7-15	Research and experimental expenditures, 7-13	Worthless securities, 7-6
Domestic production gross receipts (DPGR), 7-16	Reserve method, 7-3	

Discussion Questions

1. **LO.1** Explain how an account receivable can give rise to a bad debt deduction.

2. **LO.1** Ron, a cash basis taxpayer, sells his business accounts receivable of $100,000 to Mike for $70,000 (70% of the actual accounts receivable). Discuss the amount and classification of Ron's bad debt deduction.

3. **LO.1** Discuss when a bad debt deduction can be taken for a nonbusiness debt.

4. **LO.1** Discuss the treatment of a business bad debt when the business also has long-term capital gains.

5. **LO.1, 2, 3, 4, 5** Many years ago, Jack purchased 400 shares of Canary stock. During the current year, the stock became worthless. It was determined that the company "went under" because several corporate officers embezzled a large amount of company funds. Identify the relevant tax issues for Jack. Issue ID

6. **LO.2** Sean is in the business of buying and selling stocks and bonds. He has a bond of Green Corporation for which he paid $200,000. The bond is currently worth only $50,000. Discuss whether Sean can take a $150,000 loss for a business bad debt or for a worthless security.

7. **LO.2** Discuss the tax treatment of the sale of § 1244 stock at a gain.

8. **LO.3, 4** Jim discovers that his residence has extensive termite damage. Discuss whether he may take a deduction for the damage to his residence.

9. **LO.3, 4** The value of Mary's personal residence has declined significantly because of a recent forest fire in the area where she lives. Mary's house suffered no actual damage during the fire, but because much of the surrounding area was destroyed, the value of all of the homes in the area declined substantially. Discuss whether Mary can take a casualty loss for the decline in value of her residence caused by the fire.

10. **LO.4** Discuss at what point in time a theft loss generally is recognized.

11. **LO.4** Discuss the circumstances under which the cost of repairs to the damaged property can be used to measure the amount of a casualty loss.

12. **LO.4** Hazel sustained a loss on the theft of a painting. She had paid $20,000 for the painting, but it was worth $40,000 at the time of the theft. Evaluate the tax consequences of treating the painting as investment property or as personal use property.

13. **LO.4** Kelly decided to invest in Lime, Inc. common stock after reviewing Lime's public disclosures, including recent financial statements and a number of press releases issued by Lime. On August 7, 2015, Kelly purchased 60,000 shares of Lime for $210,000. In May 2016, Lime entered into a joint venture with Cherry, Inc. In November 2016, the joint venture failed, and Lime's stock began to decline in value. In December 2016, Cherry filed a lawsuit against Lime for theft of corporate opportunity and breach of fiduciary responsibility. In February 2017, Lime filed a countersuit against Cherry for fraud and misappropriation of funds. At the end of December 2017, Kelly's stock in Lime was worth $15,000. Identify the relevant tax issues for Kelly. Issue ID

14. **LO.3, 4** In 2014, John opened an investment account with Randy Hansen, who held himself out to the public as an investment adviser and securities broker. John contributed $200,000 to the account in 2014. John provided Randy with a power of attorney to use the $200,000 to purchase and sell securities on John's behalf. John instructed Randy to reinvest any gains and income earned. In 2014, 2015, and 2016, John received statements of the amount of income earned by his account and included these amounts in his gross income for these years. In 2017, it was discovered that Randy's purported investment advisory and brokerage activity was in fact a fraudulent investment arrangement known as a Ponzi scheme. In reality, John's account balance was zero, the money having been used by Randy in his scheme. Identify the relevant tax issues for John. Issue ID

15. **LO.5** Discuss under what circumstances a company would elect to amortize research and experimental expenditures rather than use the expense method.

16. **LO.6** Amos began a business, Silver, Inc., on July 1, 2014. The business extracts and processes silver ore. During 2017, Amos becomes aware of the domestic production activities deduction (DPAD) and would like to take advantage of this deduction. Identify the relevant tax issues for Silver, Inc. Issue ID

17. **LO.6** The DPAD is unlike other deductions and is designed to provide a tax benefit in a somewhat unique manner. Explain this statement.

18. **LO.7** Discuss whether unreimbursed employee business expenses can create an NOL for an individual taxpayer.

19. **LO.7** Discuss whether deductions *for* AGI can be treated as nonbusiness deductions in computing an individual's NOL.

Issue ID   20. **LO.7** Thomas believes that he has an NOL for the current year and wants to carry it back to a previous year and receive a tax refund. In determining his NOL, Thomas offset his business income by alimony payments he made to his ex-wife, contributions he made to his traditional Individual Retirement Account (IRA), and moving expenses he incurred. His reason for using these items in the NOL computation is that each item is a deduction *for* AGI. Identify the relevant tax issues for Thomas.

Computational Exercises

21. **LO.1** Last year Jane identified $50,000 as a nonbusiness bad debt. In that tax year, before considering the tax implications of the nonbusiness bad debt, Jane had $100,000 of taxable income, of which $5,000 consisted of short-term capital gains. This year Jane collected $10,000 of the amount she had previously identified as a bad debt. Determine Jane's tax treatment of the $10,000 received in the current tax year.

22. **LO.1** Bob owns a collection agency. He purchases uncollected accounts receivable from other businesses at 60% of their face value and then attempts to collect these accounts. During the current year, Bob collected $60,000 on an account with a face value of $80,000. Determine the amount of Bob's bad debt deduction.

23. **LO.2** On May 9, 2015, Calvin acquired 250 shares of stock in Aero Corporation, a new startup company, for $68,750. Calvin acquired the stock directly from Aero, and it is classified as § 1244 stock (at the time Calvin acquired his stock, the corporation had $900,000 of paid-in capital). On January 15, 2017, Calvin sold all of his Aero stock for $7,000. Assuming that Calvin is single, determine his tax consequences as a result of this sale.

24. **LO.4** Mary's diamond ring was stolen in 2016. She originally paid $8,000 for the ring, but it was worth considerably more at the time of the theft. Mary filed an insurance claim for the stolen ring, but the claim was denied. Because the insurance claim was denied, Mary took a casualty loss for the stolen ring on her 2016 tax return. In 2016, Mary had AGI of $40,000. In 2017, the insurance company had a "change of heart" and sent Mary a check for $5,000 for the stolen ring. Determine the proper tax treatment of the $5,000 Mary received from the insurance company in 2017.

25. **LO.4** Determine the treatment of a loss on rental property under the following facts:

Basis	$650,000
FMV before the loss	800,000
FMV after the loss	200,000

26. **LO.4** Belinda was involved in a boating accident in 2017. Her speedboat, which was used only for personal use and had a fair market value of $28,000 and an adjusted basis of $14,000, was completely destroyed. She received $10,000 from her insurance company. Her AGI for 2017 is $37,000. What is Belinda's casualty loss deduction (after any limitations)?

27. **LO.4** During the year, Tucker had the following personal casualty gains and losses (after deducting the $100 floor):

Asset	Holding Period	Gain or (Loss)
Asset 1	18 months	($1,200)
Asset 2	2 months	750
Asset 3	3 years	1,500

What are the tax consequences of these items to Tucker?

28. **LO.5** Sandstorm Corporation decides to develop a new line of paints. The project begins in 2017. Sandstorm incurs the following expenses in 2017 in connection with the project:

Salaries	$85,000
Materials	30,000
Depreciation on equipment	12,500

The benefits from the project will be realized starting in July 2018. If Sandstorm Corporation chooses to defer and amortize its research and experimental expenditures over a period of 60 months, what are its related deductions in 2017 and 2018?

29. **LO.6** In 2017, Loftis, Inc., a calendar year taxpayer, has QPAI of $4.5 million and taxable income of $3.1 million. Because Loftis outsources much of its work to independent contractors, its W–2 wage base, which for Loftis is related entirely to production activities, is $214,000. What is Loftis, Inc.'s DPAD for 2017?

30. **LO.7** Phillis and Trey are married and file a joint tax return. For 2017, they have $4,800 of nonbusiness capital gains, $2,300 of nonbusiness capital losses, $500 of interest income, and no itemized deductions. The standard deduction for married filing jointly is $12,700.

Based on these transactions, to arrive at the NOL, Phillis and Trey's taxable income must be adjusted by what amount?

31. **LO.7** Emily, who is single, sustains an NOL of $7,800 in 2017. The loss is carried back to 2015. For 2015, Emily's income tax information was as follows:

Adjusted gross income		$ 38,200
Itemized deductions:		
Medical [$4,855 − (10% × $38,200)]	$ 1,035	
Taxes	6,100	
Interest expense on home mortgage	11,000	(18,135)
Personal exemption		(4,000)
Taxable income		$ 16,065

As a result of the carryback, what is Emily's recomputed adjusted gross income and her recomputed taxable income?

Problems

32. **LO.1** Several years ago John Johnson, who is in the lending business, loaned Sara $30,000 to purchase an automobile to be used for personal purposes. In August of the current year, Sara filed for bankruptcy, and John was notified that he could not expect to receive more than $4,000. As of the end of the current year, John has received $1,000. John has contacted you about the possibility of taking a bad debt deduction for the current year.

Write a letter to John that contains your advice as to whether he can claim a bad debt deduction for the current year. Also prepare a memo for the tax files. John's address is 100 Tyler Lane, Erie, PA 16563.

Communications

33. **LO.1** Monty loaned his friend Ned $20,000 three years ago. Ned signed a note and made payments on the loan. Last year, when the remaining balance was $11,000, Ned filed for bankruptcy and notified Monty that he would be unable to pay the balance on the loan. Monty treated the $11,000 as a nonbusiness bad debt. Last year, before considering the tax implications of the nonbusiness bad debt, Monty had capital gains of $4,000 and taxable income of $20,000. During the current year, Ned paid Monty $10,000 in satisfaction of the debt. Determine Monty's tax treatment for the $10,000 received in the current year.

34. **LO.1** Sally is in the business of purchasing accounts receivable. Last year Sally purchased an account receivable with a face value of $80,000 for $60,000. During the current year, Sally settled the account, receiving $65,000. Determine the maximum amount of the bad debt deduction for Sally for the current year.

35. **LO.1, 2** Mable and Jack file a joint return. For the current year, they had the following items:

Salaries	$120,000
Loss on sale of § 1244 stock acquired two years ago	105,000
Gain on sale of § 1244 stock acquired six months ago	20,000
Nonbusiness bad debt	19,000

Determine their AGI for the current year.

Decision Making   36. **LO.2, 8** Mary, a single taxpayer, purchased 10,000 shares of § 1244 stock several years ago at a cost of $20 per share. In November of the current year, Mary received an offer to sell the stock for $12 per share. She has the option of either selling all of the stock now or selling half of the stock now and half of the stock in January of next year. Mary will receive a salary of $80,000 for the current year and $90,000 next year. Mary will have long-term capital gains of $8,000 for the current year and $10,000 next year. If Mary's goal is to minimize her AGI for the two years, determine whether she should sell all of her stock this year or half of her stock this year and half next year.

Decision Making   37. **LO.3, 4, 8** Olaf lives in the state of Minnesota. A tornado hit the area and damaged his home and automobile. Applicable information is as follows:

Item	Adjusted Basis	FMV before	FMV after	Insurance Proceeds
Home	$350,000	$500,000	$100,000	$280,000
Auto	60,000	40,000	10,000	20,000

Because of the extensive damage caused by the tornado, the President designated the area a disaster area.

Olaf and his wife, Anna, always file a joint return. Their 2016 tax return shows AGI of $180,000 and taxable income of $140,000. In 2017, their return shows AGI of $300,000 and taxable income (exclusive of the casualty loss deduction) of $215,000.

Determine the amount of Olaf and Anna's loss and the year in which they should take the loss.

38. **LO.3, 4** Heather owns a two-story building. The building is used 40% for business use and 60% for personal use. During 2017, a fire caused major damage to the building and its contents. Heather purchased the building for $800,000 and has taken depreciation of $100,000 on the business portion. At the time of the fire, the building had a fair market value of $900,000. Immediately after the fire, the fair market value was $200,000. The insurance recovery on the building was $600,000. The contents of the building were insured for any loss at fair market value. The business assets had an adjusted basis of $220,000 and a fair market value of $175,000. These assets were totally destroyed. The personal use assets had an adjusted basis of $50,000 and a fair market value of $65,000. These assets were also totally destroyed.

If Heather's AGI is $100,000 before considering the effects of the fire, determine her itemized deduction as a result of the fire. Also determine Heather's AGI.

39. **LO.3, 4** On July 24 of the current year, Sam Smith was involved in an accident with his business use automobile. Sam had purchased the car for $30,000. The automobile had a fair market value of $20,000 before the accident and $8,000 immediately after the accident. Sam has taken $20,000 of depreciation on the car. The car is insured for the fair market value of any loss. Because of Sam's history, he is afraid that if he submits a claim, his policy will be canceled. Therefore, he is considering not filing a claim. Sam believes that the tax loss deduction will help mitigate the loss of the insurance reimbursement. Sam's current marginal tax rate is 35%.

> Decision Making
>
> Communications

    Write a letter to Sam that contains your advice with respect to the tax and cash-flow consequences of filing versus not filing a claim for the insurance reimbursement for the damage to his car. Also prepare a memo for the tax files. Sam's address is 450 Colonel's Way, Warrensburg, MO 64093.

40. **LO.5** Blue Corporation, a manufacturing company, decided to develop a new line of merchandise. The project began in 2017. Blue had the following expenses in connection with the project:

	2017	2018
Salaries	$500,000	$600,000
Materials	90,000	70,000
Insurance	8,000	11,000
Utilities	6,000	8,000
Cost of inspection of materials for quality control	7,000	6,000
Promotion expenses	11,000	18,000
Advertising	–0–	20,000
Equipment depreciation	15,000	14,000
Cost of market survey	8,000	–0–

The new product will be introduced for sale beginning in July 2019. Determine the amount of the deduction for research and experimental expenditures for 2017, 2018, and 2019 if:

a. Blue Corporation elects to expense the research and experimental expenditures.

b. Blue Corporation elects to amortize the research and experimental expenditures over 60 months.

41. **LO.6** Sarah Ham, operating as a sole proprietor, manufactures printers in the United States. For 2017, the proprietorship has QPAI of $400,000. Sarah's modified AGI was $350,000. The W–2 wages paid by the proprietorship to employees engaged in the qualified domestic production activity were $60,000. Calculate Sarah's DPAD for 2017.

42. **LO.6** Barbara, a calendar year taxpayer, owns and operates a company that manufactures toys. For 2017, she has modified AGI of $500,000 and QPAI of $550,000. Ignoring the W–2 wage limitation, calculate Barbara's DPAD.

43. **LO.6** Red Corporation manufactures hand tools in the United States. For the current year, the QPAI derived from the manufacture of hand tools was $1 million. Red's taxable income for the current year was $2.0 million. Last year Red had an NOL of $800,000, which Red elected to carry forward. Calculate Red's DPAD for the current year.

44. **LO.6** Green Corporation manufactures skirts and blouses in the United States. The DPGR derived from the manufacture of one skirt is $12, and the DPGR from one blouse is $10. The cost of goods sold is $5 for one skirt and $6 for one blouse. Other allocated costs are $1 for one skirt and $5 for one blouse. What amount of QPAI is available to Green for calculating the DPAD?

Decision Making   45. **LO.6** In 2017, Rose, Inc., has QPAI of $4 million and taxable income of $3 million. Rose pays independent contractors $500,000. Rose's W–2 wages are $600,000, but only $400,000 of the wages are paid to employees engaged in qualified domestic production activities.

    a.   Calculate the DPAD for Rose, Inc., for 2017.

    b.   What suggestions could you make to enable Rose to increase its DPAD?

46. **LO.7** Sam, age 45, is single. For 2017, he has the following items:

Business income	$70,000
Business expenses	75,000
Alimony paid	12,000
Interest income	3,000
Itemized deductions	8,000

    a.   Determine Sam's taxable income for 2017.

    b.   Determine Sam's NOL for 2017.

47. **LO.7** Mary, a single taxpayer with two dependent children, has the following items of income and expense during 2017:

Gross receipts from business	$144,000
Business expenses	180,000
Alimony received	22,000
Interest income	3,000
Itemized deductions (no casualty or theft)	24,000

    a.   Determine Mary's taxable income for 2017.

    b.   Determine Mary's NOL for 2017.

48. **LO.7** Gus, who is married and files a joint return, owns a grocery store. In 2017, his gross sales were $276,000, and operating expenses were $320,000. Other items on his 2017 return were as follows:

Nonbusiness capital gains (short term)	$20,000
Nonbusiness capital losses (long term)	9,000
Itemized deductions (no casualty or theft)	18,000
Ordinary nonbusiness income	8,000
Salary from part-time job	10,000

In 2015, Gus had taxable income of $21,100 computed as follows:

Net business income		$ 60,000
Interest income		2,000
Adjusted gross income		$ 62,000
Less: Itemized deductions		
Charitable contributions of $40,000, limited to 50% of AGI	$31,000	
Medical expenses of $8,100, limited to the amount in excess of 10% of AGI ($8,100 − $6,200)	1,900	
Total itemized deductions		(32,900)
Exemptions (2 × $4,000)		(8,000)
Taxable income		$ 21,100

    a.   What is Gus's 2017 NOL?

    b.   Determine Gus's recomputed taxable income for 2015.

    c.   Determine the amount of Gus's 2017 NOL to be carried forward from 2015 to 2016.

49. **LO.7** During 2017, Rick and his wife, Sara, had the following items of income and expense to report:

Gross receipts from business	$400,000
Business expenses	525,000
Interest income from bank savings accounts	8,000
Sara's salary	50,000
Long-term capital gain on stock held as an investment	4,000
Itemized deductions (no casualty or theft)	15,000

a. Assuming that Rick and Sara file a joint return, what is their taxable income for 2017?

b. What is the amount of Rick and Sara's NOL for 2017?

c. To what years can Rick and Sara's NOL be carried?

d. Based on your computations, identify the components of their NOL. What is the rationale for excluding the items that do not affect the NOL computation?

50. **LO.7** Assume that in addition to the information in Problem 49, Rick and Sara had $3,700 of taxable income for 2015 computed as follows:

Salary		$ 25,000
Capital loss		(1,000)
Adjusted gross income		$ 24,000
Less: Itemized deductions		
Charitable contributions of $20,000, limited to 50% of AGI	$12,000	
Medical expenses of $2,700, limited to the amount in excess of 10% of AGI ($2,700 − $2,400)	300	
Total itemized deductions		(12,300)
Exemptions (2 × $4,000)		(8,000)
Taxable income		$ 3,700

a. Determine Rick and Sara's recomputed taxable income for 2015.

b. Determine the amount of Rick and Sara's 2017 NOL to be carried forward from 2015 to 2016.

51. **LO.7** Robert and Susan Reid had an NOL of $30,000 in 2017. They had $14,250 of taxable income for 2015 computed as follows:

Communications

Salary		$ 50,000
Capital loss		(4,000)
Adjusted gross income		$ 46,000
Less: Itemized deductions		
Charitable contributions of $24,000, limited to 50% of AGI	$23,000	
Medical expenses of $5,350, limited to the amount in excess of 10% of AGI ($5,350 − $4,600)	750	
Total itemized deductions		(23,750)
Exemptions (2 × $4,000)		(8,000)
Taxable income		$ 14,250

Write a letter to Robert and Susan informing them of the amount of the remaining NOL to be carried forward if the loss is applied against the 2015 taxable income. Also prepare a memo for the tax files. Their address is 201 Jerdone Avenue, Conway, SC 29526.

52. **LO.7** Pete and Polly are married and file a joint return. They had the following income and deductions for 2017:

Salary	$50,000
Interest from savings account	5,000
Itemized deductions (no casualty or theft)	15,000
2016 NOL carried to 2017	60,000

a. What is Pete and Polly's taxable income for 2017?

b. What is Pete and Polly's NOL for 2017?

c. What is Pete and Polly's NOL to be carried forward to 2018?

53. **LO.1, 2, 7** Soong, single and age 32, had the following items for the tax year 2017:
- Salary of $30,000.
- Interest income from U.S. government bonds of $2,000.
- Dividends from a foreign corporation of $500.
- Sale of small business § 1244 stock on October 20, 2017, for $20,000. The stock had been acquired two years earlier for $65,000.
- Business bad debt of $4,000.
- Nonbusiness bad debt of $5,000.
- Sale of small business § 1244 stock on November 12, 2017, for $4,000. The stock had been acquired on June 5, 2017, for $800.
- Sale of preferred stock on December 4, 2017, for $40,000. The stock was acquired four years ago for $18,000.
- Total itemized deductions of $25,000 (no casualty or theft).

a. Determine Soong's NOL for 2017.

b. Assuming that Soong had taxable income for each of the last five years, determine the carryback year to which the 2017 NOL should be applied.

54. **LO.1, 3** Nell, single and age 38, had the following income and expense items in 2017:

Nonbusiness bad debt	$ 6,000
Business bad debt	2,000
Nonbusiness long-term capital gain	4,000
Nonbusiness short-term capital loss	3,000
Salary	50,000
Interest income	3,000

Determine Nell's AGI for 2017.

55. **LO.1, 4** Assume that in addition to the information in Problem 54, Nell had the following items in 2017:

Personal casualty gain on an asset held for four months	$10,000
Personal casualty loss on an asset held for two years	1,000

Determine Nell's AGI for 2017.

56. **LO.1, 4, 7** Assume that in addition to the information in Problems 54 and 55, Nell had the following items in 2017:

Personal casualty loss on an asset held for five years	$60,000
Interest expense on home mortgage	15,000

Determine Nell's taxable income and NOL for 2017.

57. **LO.1, 2, 3, 4, 7** Jed, age 55, is married with no children. During 2017, Jed had the following income and expense items:

a. Three years ago, Jed loaned a friend $10,000 to help him purchase a new car. In June of the current year, Jed learned that his friend had been declared bankrupt and had left the country. There is no possibility that Jed will ever collect any of the $10,000.

b. In April of last year, Jed purchased some stock for $5,000. In March of the current year, the company was declared bankrupt, and Jed was notified that his shares of stock were worthless.

c. Several years ago Jed purchased some § 1244 stock for $120,000. This year he sold the stock for $30,000.

d. In July of this year, Jed sold some land that he had held for two years for $60,000. He had originally paid $42,000 for the land.

e. Jed received $40,000 of interest income from State of Minnesota bonds.

f. In September, Jed's home was damaged by an earthquake. Jed's basis in his home was $430,000. The value of the home immediately before the quake was $610,000. After the quake, the home was worth $540,000. Because earthquake damage was an exclusion on Jed's homeowner's insurance policy, he received no insurance recovery.

g. Jed received a salary of $80,000.

h. Jed paid home mortgage interest of $14,000.

If Jed files a joint return for 2017, determine his NOL for the year.

Cumulative Problems

58. Jane Smith, age 40, is single and has no dependents. She is employed as a legal secretary by Legal Services, Inc. She owns and operates Typing Services located near the campus of Florida Atlantic University at 1986 Campus Drive. Jane is a material participant in the business. She is a cash basis taxpayer. Jane lives at 2020 Oakcrest Road, Boca Raton, FL 33431. Jane's Social Security number is 123-45-6789. Jane indicates that she wants to designate $3 to the Presidential Election Campaign Fund. Jane had health insurance for all months of 2016. During 2016, Jane had the following income and expense items:

Tax Return Problem

Decision Making

Communications

H&R BLOCK
TAX SOFTWARE

a. $100,000 salary from Legal Services, Inc.

b. $20,000 gross receipts from her typing services business.

c. $700 interest income from Third National Bank.

d. $1,000 Christmas bonus from Legal Services, Inc.

e. $60,000 life insurance proceeds on the death of her sister.

f. $5,000 check given to her by her wealthy aunt.

g. $100 won in a bingo game.

h. Expenses connected with the typing service:

Office rent	$7,000
Supplies	4,400
Utilities and telephone	4,680
Wages to part-time typists	5,000
Payroll taxes	500
Equipment rentals	3,000

i. $9,500 interest expense on a home mortgage (paid to San Jose Savings and Loan).

j. $15,000 fair market value of silverware stolen from her home by a burglar on October 12, 2016. Jane had paid $14,000 for the silverware on July 1, 2007. She was reimbursed $1,500 by her insurance company.

k. Jane had loaned $2,100 to a friend, Joan Jensen, on June 3, 2013. Joan declared bankruptcy on August 14, 2016, and was unable to repay the loan. Assume that the loan is a bona fide debt.

l. Legal Services, Inc., withheld Federal income tax of $16,000 and the appropriate amount of FICA tax from her wages.

m. Alimony of $10,000 received from her former husband, Ted Smith.

n. Interest income of $800 on City of Boca Raton bonds.

o. Jane made estimated Federal tax payments of $1,000.

p. Sales taxes from the sales tax table of $946.

q. Property taxes on her residence of $1,100.

r. Charitable contribution of $2,500 to her alma mater, Citrus State College.

s. On November 1, 2016, Jane was involved in an automobile accident. At the time of the accident, Jane's automobile had an FMV of $45,000. After the accident, the automobile's FMV was $38,000. Jane acquired the car on May 2, 2015 at a cost of $52,000. Jane's car was covered by insurance, but because the policy had a $5,000 deduction clause, Jane decided not to file a claim for the damage.

Part 1—Tax Computation

Compute Jane Smith's 2016 Federal income tax payable (or refund due). If you use tax forms for your computations, you will need Forms 1040 and 4684 and Schedules A, C, and D. Suggested software: H&R BLOCK Tax Software.

Part 2—Tax Planning

In 2017, Jane plans to continue her job with Legal Services, Inc. Therefore, items a, d, and l will recur in 2017. Jane plans to continue her typing services business (refer to item b) and expects gross receipts of $26,000. She projects that all business expenses (refer to item h) will increase by 10%, except for office rent, which, under the terms of her lease, will remain the same as in 2016. Items e, f, g, j, k, and s will not recur in 2017. Items c, i, m, n, p, q, and r will be approximately the same as in 2016.

Jane would like you to compute the minimum amount of estimated tax she will have to pay for 2017 so that she will not have to pay any additional tax upon filing her 2017 Federal income tax return. Write a letter to Jane that contains your advice, and prepare a memo for the tax files.

Tax Computation Problem   59. Mason Phillips, age 45, and his wife, Ruth, live at 230 Wood Lane, Salt Lake City, UT 84101. Mason's Social Security number is 111-11-1111. Ruth's Social Security number is 123-45-6789. Mason and Ruth are cash basis taxpayers and had the following items for 2017:

- Salary of $140,000.
- Bad debt of $30,000 from uncollected rent.
- Collection of unpaid rent from a prior year of $6,000.
- Sale of § 1244 stock resulting in a loss of $105,000. The stock was acquired eight months ago.
- Rental income of $60,000.
- Rental expenses of $33,000.
- Casualty loss on rental property of $10,000.
- Personal casualty loss (from one event) of $20,000.
- Theft loss of $5,000 on a computer used 100% associated with their jobs.
- Theft loss of $8,000 on a painting held for investment.
- Other itemized deductions of $18,000.
- Federal income tax withheld of $3,000.

Compute Mason and Ruth's 2017 Federal income tax payable (or refund due).

Research Problems

THOMSON REUTERS
CHECKPOINT
Student Edition

Note: Solutions to the Research Problems can be prepared by using the Thomson Reuters Checkpoint® Student Edition online tax research database, which accompanies this textbook. Solutions can also be prepared by using research materials found in a typical tax library.

Research Problem 1. During 2017, John was the chief executive officer and a shareholder of Maze, Inc. He owned 60% of the outstanding stock of Maze. In 2014, John and Maze, as co-borrowers, obtained a $100,000 loan from United National Bank. This loan was secured by John's personal residence. Although Maze was listed as a co-borrower, John repaid the loan in full in 2017. On Maze's Form 1120 tax returns, no loans from shareholders were reported. Discuss whether John is entitled to a bad debt deduction for the amount of the payment on the loan.

Partial list of research aids:
U.S. v. Generes, 405 U.S. 93 (1972).
Dale H. Sundby, T.C.Memo. 2003–204.
Arrigoni v. Comm., 73 T.C. 792 (1980).
Estate of Herbert M. Rapoport, T.C.Memo. 1982–584.
Clifford L. Brody and Barbara J. DeClerk, T.C. Summary Opinion, 2004–149.

Research Problem 2. Mary Marble took out a homeowner's insurance policy on her residence. One of the policy provisions listed the insured's duties with respect to a loss. This provision required the policyholder to give notice and required an inventory of damaged personal property within 60 days of the insurance company's request and to supply proof of loss.

In November of the current year, Mary's home was damaged by a fire. Shortly after the fire, Mary reported the loss to the insurance company. In December, the insurance company generated a claim report sheet with a claim number and sent Mary a proof of loss form. Mary failed to provide the insurance company with the proof of loss form within the required 60-day period; hence, the insurance company denied Mary's claim for damages. Discuss whether Mary is entitled to a casualty loss deduction for the damage to her home caused by the fire.

Research Problem 3. Esther owns a large home on the East Coast. Her home is surrounded by large, mature oak trees that significantly increase the value of her home. In August 2016, a hurricane damaged many of the trees surrounding her home. In September 2016, Esther engaged a local arborist to evaluate and treat the trees, but five of the largest trees were seriously weakened by the storm. These trees died from disease in 2017. Esther has ascertained that the amount of the casualty loss from the death of the five trees is $25,000; however, she is uncertain in which year to deduct this loss. Discuss whether the casualty loss should be deducted in the calculation of Esther's 2016 or 2017 taxable income.

Partial list of research aids:
Reg. § 1.165–1.
Oregon Mesabi Corporation, 39 B.T.A. 1033 (1939).

Use internet tax resources to address the following questions. Look for reliable websites and blogs of the IRS and other government agencies, media outlets, businesses, tax professionals, academics, think tanks, and political outlets.

Research Problem 4. Find a newspaper article that discusses tax planning for casualty losses when a disaster area designation is made. Does the article convey the pertinent tax rules correctly? Then list all of the locations identified by the President as Federal disaster areas in the last two years.

Communications **Research Problem 5.** Many states that have corporate income taxes "piggyback" onto the Federal corporate income tax calculation. In other words, these states' corporate income tax calculations incorporate many of the Federal calculations and deductions to make both compliance and verification of tax liability easier. However, some state legislatures were concerned that the domestic production activities deduction, if allowed for state tax purposes, would result in significant revenue losses. Determine whether states with corporate income taxes allow or disallow the domestic production activities deduction in the calculation of the state's corporate income tax liability. Be sure to state the sources for your answer.

Roger CPA Review Questions

1. Glenn and Mary's house was damaged by a hurricane in 2017. The fair value of their home before the hurricane was $150,000. After the hurricane, the fair value of their home was $125,000. They received $10,000 from their homeowner's insurance policy. What is their casualty loss deduction for 2017 if their adjusted gross income was $40,000?

   a. $10,900   c. $14,900
   b. $11,000   d. $15,000

2. Hank's home is burglarized on December 22, 2017. Personal property with a fair market value of $40,000 and an adjusted basis to Hank of $25,000 is stolen. Hank paid an independent appraiser $700 on December 29 to determine the fair market value of the property at the time of the break-in. Hank's homeowner's insurance policy leads him to believe he is entitled to receive $15,000 in reimbursement for the event, but no settlement has been made with the insurance company by year-end. Hank's AGI in 2017 is $30,000. How much may Hank deduct from AGI as a result of these facts on his 2017 tax return? Assume Hank itemizes, and assume there has still been no settlement with the insurance company at the time of filing.

   a. $7,000   c. $6,900
   b. $21,900   d. $22,000

3. On the night of October 14, 2017, a hurricane caused serious damage to Paige's personal vehicle and to the roof of her personal residence, a townhome. Just prior to the hurricane, Paige had a $200,000 basis in her home and a $12,000 basis in her vehicle, which had a fair market value just prior to the hurricane of $10,000. The damage to the roof is appraised at $7,000, and the fair market value of the vehicle immediately after the hurricane is appraised at $5,000. Paige is uninsured and has a 2017 AGI of $40,000. What amount of casualty loss deduction may Paige claim on her 2017 tax return as a result of the hurricane?

   a. $9,800   c. $9,900
   b. $7,900   d. $7,800

4. Regarding the tax treatment of a business's research and experimental (R&E) expenditures, which of the following statements is true?

   a.   A common reason for electing tax deferral for such expenses is the expectation of lower tax rates in the future.

   b.   Expenses associated with the acquisition of land upon which a purpose-built R&E facility is constructed are considered R&E expenditures for tax purposes.

   c.   Companies generally prefer to expense R&E costs immediately, but may elect instead to defer and amortize such costs over a minimum of 60 months.

   d.   Companies may elect to immediately expense R&E costs incurred in the first applicable taxable year and all future years through an appropriate filing with the IRS.

5. Identify the correct statement below regarding the domestic production activities deduction (DPAD).

   a. Qualified production activities income (QPAI) is calculated by applying a percentage to net income from an IRS rate table based on specific criteria.

   b. The DPAD cannot exceed attributable W–2 wages paid.

   c. A sole proprietorship cannot claim the DPAD, but a partnership or an S corporation with more than one shareholder can.

   d. Taxable income for the purposes of calculating or amending the DPAD includes any net operating loss (NOL) deduction, such as an NOL carryforward or NOL carryback.

CHAPTER

8

Depreciation, Cost Recovery, Amortization, and Depletion

LEARNING OBJECTIVES: *After completing Chapter 8, you should be able to:*

LO.1 State the rationale for the cost consumption concept and identify the relevant time periods for depreciation, ACRS, and MACRS.

LO.2 Determine the amount of cost recovery under MACRS.

LO.3 Recognize when and how to make the § 179 expensing election and use additional first-year depreciation, calculate the amount of the deductions, and apply the effect of the elections in making the MACRS calculation.

LO.4 Identify listed property and apply the deduction limitations on listed property and on luxury automobiles.

LO.5 Determine when and how to use the alternative depreciation system (ADS).

LO.6 Report cost recovery deductions appropriately.

LO.7 Identify intangible assets that are eligible for amortization and calculate the amount of the deduction.

LO.8 Determine the amount of depletion expense, including being able to apply the alternative tax treatments for intangible drilling and development costs.

LO.9 Identify tax planning opportunities for cost recovery, amortization, and depletion.

CHAPTER OUTLINE

ERSLER DMITRY/SHUTTERSTOCK.COM

CALCULATING COST RECOVERY DEDUCTIONS

Dr. Cliff Payne purchased and placed in service $612,085 of new fixed assets in his dental practice during the current year.

Office furniture and fixtures	$ 70,000
Computers and peripheral equipment	67,085
Dental equipment	475,000

Using his financial reporting system, he concludes that the depreciation expense on Schedule C of Form 1040 is $91,298.

Office furniture and fixtures ($70,000 × 14.29%)	$10,003
Computers and peripheral equipment ($67,085 × 20%)	13,417
Dental equipment ($475,000 × 14.29%)	67,878
	$91,298

In addition, this year Dr. Payne purchased another personal residence for $480,000 and converted his original residence to a rental property. He also purchased another rental property in the current year for $170,000 near his office that he is going to rent to a third party.

Has Dr. Payne correctly calculated the depreciation expense for his dental practice? Will he be able to deduct any depreciation expense for his rental properties?

Read the chapter and formulate your response.

This chapter covers the boldfaced portions of the Tax Formula for Individuals that was introduced in Concept Summary 3.1 on p. 3-3. Below those portions are the sections of Form 1040 where the results are reported.

Income *(broadly defined)*	$xx,xxx
Less: Exclusions	(x,xxx)
Gross income...	$xx,xxx
Less: Deductions *for* adjusted gross income...	(x,xxx)

FORM 1040 (p. 1)

12	Business income or (loss). Attach Schedule C or C-EZ	

Adjusted gross income..	$xx,xxx
Less: The greater of total itemized deductions *or* the standard deduction	(x,xxx)
Personal and dependency exemptions..	(x,xxx)
Taxable income	$xx,xxx
Tax on taxable income *(see Tax Tables or Tax Rate Schedules)*..	$ x,xxx
Less: Tax credits *(including income taxes withheld and prepaid)*	(xxx)
Tax due (or refund)	$ xxx

The Internal Revenue Code allows a depreciation, cost recovery, amortization, or depletion deduction based on an asset's cost. These deductions reflect the recovery of capital doctrine (see text Section 4-1b). Cost recovery deductions are based on the idea that the asset acquired (or improvement made) benefits more than one accounting period. If not, the expenditure is deducted in the year incurred.[1]

Taxpayers may "write off" (deduct) the cost of certain assets that are used in a trade or business or held for the production of income. A write-off may take the form of depreciation (or cost recovery), depletion, or amortization. Tangible assets, other than natural resources, are *depreciated*. Natural resources, such as oil, gas, coal, and timber, are *depleted*. Intangible assets, such as copyrights and patents, are *amortized*. Generally, a deduction is allowed for an asset only if it has a determinable useful life.

Congress completely overhauled the **depreciation** rules in 1981 by creating the **accelerated cost recovery system (ACRS)**, which shortened depreciable lives and allowed accelerated depreciation methods. In 1986, Congress made substantial modifications to ACRS, which resulted in the **modified accelerated cost recovery system (MACRS)**. Although the terms *depreciation* and **cost recovery** often are used interchangeably, the former normally refers to the allocation of costs to the appropriate period for financial reporting purposes, while the latter refers to an equivalent concept for tax purposes. Concept Summary 8.1 provides an overview of the various depreciation systems and the time frames involved.

The tax law changes that have taken place since 1980 have widened the gap that exists between depreciation (for financial reporting purposes) and cost recovery (for tax purposes). The tax rules that existed prior to 1981 were similar to generally accepted accounting principles.

This chapter focuses on the MACRS rules because they cover property placed in service after 1986.[2] The chapter concludes with a discussion of the amortization of intangible property and startup expenditures and the depletion of natural resources.

---

[1]See the discussion of capitalization versus expense in text Section 6-3i.

[2]§ 168. The terms *depreciation* and *cost recovery* are used interchangeably in the text and in § 168. The ACRS rules and the pre-1981 rules are covered in the online appendix *Depreciation and the Accelerated Cost Recovery System (ACRS)*.

Concept Summary 8.1

Depreciation and Cost Recovery: Relevant Time Periods

System	Date Property Is Placed in Service
Pre-1981 depreciation	Before January 1, 1981, and *certain* property placed in service after December 31, 1980.
Accelerated cost recovery system (ACRS)	After December 31, 1980, and before January 1, 1987.
Modified accelerated cost recovery system (MACRS)	After December 31, 1986.

8-1 DEPRECIATION AND COST RECOVERY

State the rationale for the cost consumption concept and identify the relevant time periods for depreciation, ACRS, and MACRS.

8-1a Nature of Property

Property includes both realty (real property) and personalty (personal property). *Realty* generally includes land and buildings permanently affixed to the land. *Personalty* is defined as any asset that is not realty.[3] Personalty includes furniture, machinery, equipment, and any other asset that is movable or not permanently affixed to land. Personalty (or personal property) should not be confused with *personal use* property. Personal use property is any property (realty or personalty) that is held for personal use rather than for use in a trade or business or an income-producing activity. Cost recovery deductions are not allowed for personal use assets.

In summary, both realty and personalty can be either business use/income-producing property or personal use property. Examples include:

- A residence (realty that is personal use),
- An office building (realty that is business use),
- A dump truck (personalty that is business use), and
- Common clothing (personalty that is personal use).

It is critical that the distinction between the *classification* of an asset (realty or personalty) and the *use* to which the asset is put (business or personal) be understood.

Assets used in a trade or business or for the production of income are eligible for cost recovery if they are subject to wear and tear, decay or decline from natural causes, or obsolescence (e.g., an automobile that the taxpayer rents to third parties). Assets that do not decline in value on a predictable basis or that do not have a determinable useful life (e.g., land, stock, and antiques) are not eligible for cost recovery.

8-1b Placed in Service Requirement

Cost recovery begins on the date an asset is placed in service (ready and available for use), not the date of purchase. This distinction is particularly important for an asset that is purchased near the end of the tax year, but not placed in service until after the beginning of the following tax year.

8-1c Cost Recovery Allowed or Allowable

To prevent the recovery of the same cost more than once (i.e., through periodic cost recovery and on the sale of the asset), the basis of property is reduced by any cost recovery deductions taken on a tax return (this is the *allowed* cost recovery). However, the property's basis is reduced by at least the amount of cost recovery that could have been taken under the applicable cost recovery method (this is the *allowable* cost recovery). As a result, even if the taxpayer does not claim any cost recovery on property during a

---

[3]Refer to text Section 1-4a for further discussion.

particular year, the basis of the property still is reduced by the amount of cost recovery that should have been deducted (the allowable cost recovery).

EXAMPLE 1

On March 15, year 1, Jack purchased a copier, to use in his business, for $10,000. The copier is 5-year property, and Jack elected to use the straight-line method of cost recovery. Jack made the election because the business was a new undertaking and he reasoned that in the first few years of the business, a large cost recovery deduction was not needed.

Because the business was doing poorly, Jack did not claim any cost recovery deductions in years 3 and 4. In years 5 and 6, Jack deducted the proper amount of cost recovery. The allowed cost recovery (cost recovery actually deducted) and the allowable cost recovery are computed as follows.

	Cost Recovery Allowed	Cost Recovery Allowable
Year 1	$1,000	$1,000
Year 2	2,000	2,000
Year 3	–0–	2,000
Year 4	–0–	2,000
Year 5	2,000	2,000
Year 6	1,000	1,000

If Jack sold the copier for $800 in year 7, he would recognize an $800 gain ($800 amount realized − $0 adjusted basis); the adjusted basis of the copier is zero ($10,000 cost − $10,000 total *allowable* cost recovery in years 1 through 6).

8-1d Cost Recovery Basis for Personal Use Assets Converted to Business or Income-Producing Use

If personal use assets are converted to business or income-producing use, the basis for cost recovery and for loss is the *lower* of the adjusted basis or the fair market value at the time the property was converted. This rule ensures that any decline in value that occurred while the property was personal use property cannot be deducted via cost recovery.

The Big Picture

EXAMPLE 2

Return to the facts of *The Big Picture* on p. 8-1. In 2007, Dr. Payne purchased a personal residence for $250,000. In the current year, Payne found a larger home that he acquired for his personal residence. Because of the downturn in the housing market, however, he was not able to sell his original residence and recover his purchase price of $250,000. The residence was appraised at $180,000.

Instead of continuing to try to sell the original residence, Dr. Payne converted it to rental property. The basis for cost recovery of the rental property is $180,000 because the fair market value is less than the adjusted basis. The $70,000 decline in value is deemed to be personal (because it occurred while the property was held for personal use by Payne) and therefore nondeductible.

LO.2

Determine the amount of cost recovery under MACRS.

8-2 MODIFIED ACCELERATED COST RECOVERY SYSTEM (MACRS): GENERAL RULES

Under the modified accelerated cost recovery system (MACRS), the cost of an asset is recovered over a predetermined period that generally is shorter than the economic life of an asset. The MACRS rules were designed to encourage investment, improve productivity, and simplify the tax law and its administration.

MACRS provides separate cost recovery syetems for realty and personalty. Based on cost recovery periods (called class lives), methods, and conventions specified in the Internal Revenue Code, the IRS provides tables that identify cost recovery allowances for personalty and for realty. Excerpts from those tables are provided in text Section 8-7c.

Concept Summary 8.2 provides an overview of the class lives, methods, and conventions that apply under MACRS.

Concept Summary 8.2

MACRS: Class Lives, Methods, and Conventions

	Personalty	Realty
Class lives	3 to 20 years	Residential: 27.5 years Nonresidential: 39 years
Method	200% declining balance for property with class lives less than 15 years 150% declining balance for property with 15- or 20-year class lives	Straight-line
Convention	Half-year or mid-quarter	Mid-month

8-2a Personalty: Recovery Periods and Methods

Classification of Property

MACRS provides that the basis of eligible personalty (and certain realty) is recovered over 3, 5, 7, 10, 15, or 20 years. Property is classified by recovery period under MACRS through the use of Asset Depreciation Range (ADR) midpoint lives issued by the IRS.[4] See Exhibit 8.1 for examples of assets in each class.[5]

Double declining balance is used for the 3-, 5-, 7-, and 10-year classes, with a switchover to straight-line depreciation when appropriate. Cost recovery for the 15- and 20-year classes is based on the 150-percent declining balance method, with an appropriate straight-line switchover.[6] The appropriate computation methods and conventions are built into the tables. Therefore, it is generally not necessary to calculate the appropriate percentages.

EXHIBIT 8.1   Cost Recovery Periods: MACRS Personalty

Property Class	Generally Includes Assets with the Following ADR Lives	Examples
3-year	4 years or less	Tractor units for use over the road
		A racehorse that is more than 2 years old, or any other horse that is more than 12 years old, at the time it is placed in service
		Special tools used in the manufacturing of motor vehicles, such as dies, fixtures, molds, and patterns
5-year	More than 4 years and less than 10 years	Automobiles and taxis
		Light and heavy general-purpose trucks
		Calculators and copiers
		Computers and peripheral equipment
		Rental appliances, furniture, carpets
7-year	10 years or more and less than 16 years	Office furniture, fixtures, and equipment
		Agricultural machinery and equipment
10-year	16 years or more and less than 20 years	Vessels, barges, tugs, and similar water transportation equipment
		Assets used for petroleum refining or for the manufacture of grain and grain mill products, sugar and sugar products, or vegetable oils and vegetable oil products
		Single-purpose agricultural or horticultural structures
15-year	20 years or more and less than 25 years	Land improvements
		Assets used for industrial steam and electric generation and/or distribution systems
		Assets used in the manufacture of cement
20-year	25 years or more	Farm buildings except single-purpose agricultural and horticultural structures
		Water utilities

---

[4]Personalty is assigned to recovery classes based on asset depreciation range (ADR) midpoint lives (Rev.Proc. 87–56, 1987–2 C.B. 674). ADR lives generally represent estimates of an asset's useful economic life.

[5]§ 168(e).

[6]§ 168(b).

FINANCIAL DISCLOSURE INSIGHTS   Tax and Book Depreciation

A common book-tax difference relates to the depreciation amounts that are reported for GAAP and Federal income tax purposes. Typically, tax depreciation deductions are accelerated; that is, they are claimed in earlier reporting periods than is the case for financial accounting purposes.

Almost every tax law change since 1980 has included depreciation provisions that accelerate the related deductions relative to the expenses allowed under GAAP. Accelerated cost recovery deductions represent a means by which the taxing jurisdiction infuses the business with cash flow created by the reduction in the year's tax liabilities.

For instance, recently, about one-quarter of General Electric's deferred tax liabilities related to depreciation differences. For Toyota's and Ford's depreciation differences, that amount was about one-third. And for the trucking firm Ryder Systems, depreciation differences accounted for all but one percent of the deferred tax liabilities.

To determine the amount of the cost recovery allowance, simply identify the asset by class and go to the appropriate table to find the cost recovery percentage. The MACRS percentages for personalty appear in Exhibit 8.3 (see text Section 8-7c). Concept Summary 8.3 provides an overview of the various conventions that apply under the MACRS statutory percentage method.

Concept Summary 8.3

Statutory Percentage Method under MACRS

	Personal Property	Real Property*
Convention	Half-year or mid-quarter	Mid-month
Cost recovery deduction in the year of disposition**	Half-year for year of sale or half-quarter for quarter of sale	Half-month for month of sale

*Straight-line method must be used.
**A disposition can include a sale, exchange, abandonment, or retirement. For simplicity, we will assume a sale in this chapter.

Taxpayers may *elect* the straight-line method to compute cost recovery allowances for each of these classes of property. Certain property is not eligible for accelerated cost recovery and must be depreciated under an alternative depreciation system (ADS). Both the straight-line election and ADS are discussed later in the chapter.

Cost recovery for personalty generally incorporates the **half-year convention**; that is, cost recovery in the year the asset is placed in service, as well as the year it is removed from service, is based on the assumption that the asset was used for exactly one half of the year, allowing a half-year of cost recovery.[7] For example, the statutory recovery period for property with a life of three years begins in the middle of the year an asset is placed in service and ends three years later, in the fourth taxable year. In practical terms, this means that an asset's cost is actually recovered over 4, 6, 8, 11, 16, and 21 years.

Half-Year Convention

EXAMPLE 3

Kareem acquires a 5-year class asset on April 10, 2017, for $30,000. Kareem's cost recovery deduction for 2017 is computed as follows.

MACRS cost recovery [$30,000 × .20 (Exhibit 8.3)] $6,000

EXAMPLE 4

Assume the same facts as in Example 3. Kareem sells the asset on March 5, 2019. Kareem's cost recovery deduction for 2019 is $2,880 [$30,000 × ½ × .192 (Exhibit 8.3)].

[7]§ 168(d)(4)(A).

Mid-Quarter Convention

The half-year convention is based on the simplifying presumption that assets generally are acquired at an even pace throughout the tax year. However, Congress was concerned that taxpayers might defeat that presumption by placing large amounts of property in service toward the end of the taxable year (and by doing so, receive a half-year's depreciation on those large, end-of-year acquisitions).

To inhibit this behavior, Congress added the **mid-quarter convention** that applies if more than 40 percent of the value of property other than eligible real estate (see text Section 8-2b) is placed in service during the last quarter of the year.[8] Under this convention, property acquisitions are grouped by the quarter they were acquired for cost recovery purposes. Acquisitions during the first quarter are allowed 10.5 months (three and one-half quarters) of cost recovery; the second quarter, 7.5 months (two and one-half quarters); the third quarter, 4.5 months (one and one-half quarters); and the fourth quarter, 1.5 months (one-half quarter). The percentages are shown in Exhibit 8.4.

EXAMPLE 5

Silver Corporation acquires the following new 5-year class property in 2017.

Property Acquisition Dates	Cost
February 15	$ 200,000
July 10	400,000
December 5	600,000
Total	$1,200,000

Under the statutory percentage method, Silver's cost recovery allowances for the first two years are computed below. Because more than 40% ($600,000/$1,200,000 = 50%) of the acquisitions are in the last quarter, the mid-quarter convention applies.

2017

	Mid-Quarter Convention Depreciation (Exhibit 8.4)	Total Depreciation
February 15	$200,000 × .35	$ 70,000
July 10	$400,000 × .15	60,000
December 5	$600,000 × .05	30,000
		$160,000

2018

	Mid-Quarter Convention Depreciation (Exhibit 8.4)	Total Depreciation
February 15	$200,000 × .26	$ 52,000
July 10	$400,000 × .34	136,000
December 5	$600,000 × .38	228,000
		$416,000

Without the mid-quarter convention, Silver's 2017 cost recovery deduction would have been $240,000 [$1,200,000 × .20 (Exhibit 8.3)]. The mid-quarter convention slows down the taxpayer's available cost recovery deductions.

When "mid-quarter" property is sold, the property is treated as though it were sold at the midpoint of the quarter. So in the quarter when sold, cost recovery is allowed for one-half of the quarter.

---

[8]§ 168(d)(3).

EXAMPLE 6

Assume the same facts as in Example 5, except that Silver Corporation sells the $400,000 asset on November 30, 2018. The cost recovery deduction for 2018 is computed as follows (Exhibit 8.4).

February 15	$200,000 × .26	$ 52,000
July 10	$400,000 × .34 × (3.5/4)	119,000
December 5	$600,000 × .38	228,000
Total cost recovery deduction		$399,000

The tax adjusted basis of the $400,000 asset when sold is $221,000 [$400,000 (cost) − $60,000 (2017 cost recovery) − $119,000 (2018 cost recovery)].

The Big Picture

EXAMPLE 7

Return to the facts of *The Big Picture* on p. 8-1. If the placed-in-service date for the office furniture and fixtures and computers and peripheral equipment is September 29 and the placed-in-service date for the dental equipment is October 3, Dr. Payne's total cost recovery deduction is computed as follows.

Office furniture and fixtures:	
MACRS cost recovery $70,000 × .1071 (Exhibit 8.4)	$ 7,497
Computers and peripheral equipment:	
MACRS cost recovery $67,085 × .15 (Exhibit 8.4)	10,063
Dental equipment:	
MACRS cost recovery $475,000 × .0357 (Exhibit 8.4)	16,958
Total cost recovery deduction	$34,518

Note the implications of the mid-quarter convention. If the dental equipment had been placed in service before October 1 (the beginning of the fourth quarter), the total cost recovery deduction would have been $91,298 (p. 8-1).

8-2b Realty: Recovery Periods and Methods

Under MACRS, the cost of most real property is recovered using the straight-line method. The recovery period for residential rental real estate is 27.5 years. **Residential rental real estate** includes property where 80 percent or more of the gross rental revenues are from residential units (e.g., an apartment building). Hotels, motels, and similar establishments are not residential rental property. Low-income housing is classified as residential rental real estate. Nonresidential real estate is recovered over 39 years.[9]

Some items of real property are not treated as real estate for purposes of MACRS. For example, single-purpose agricultural structures are in the 10-year MACRS class. Land improvements are in the 15-year MACRS class.

All eligible real estate is depreciated using the **mid-month convention**.[10] Under this convention, one-half month's cost recovery is allowed for the month the property is placed in service. So if a calendar year taxpayer places real estate in service on June 2 of the current tax year, it will be able to deduct six and one-half months of cost recovery (June 15 to December 31). If the property is sold before the end of the recovery period, one-half month's cost recovery is permitted for the month of sale (no matter when the property is sold).

As with personalty, the IRS provides tables to assist taxpayers in computing cost recovery on realty. Cost recovery is computed by multiplying the applicable rate (Exhibit 8.8) by the cost recovery basis.

---

[9] §§ 168(b), (c), and (e). A 31.5-year life is used for nonresidential real estate placed in service before May 13, 1993.

[10] § 168(d)(1).

Real Estate Cost Recovery

Alec acquired a building on April 1, 1999, for $800,000. If the building is classified as residential rental real estate, the cost recovery deduction for 2017 is $29,088 (.03636 × $800,000).

If the building is sold on October 7, 2017, the cost recovery deduction for 2017 is $23,028 [.03636 × (9.5/12) × $800,000]. (See Exhibit 8.8 for percentage.)

EXAMPLE 8

Jane acquired a building on March 2, 1993, for $1 million. If the building is classified as non-residential real estate, the cost recovery deduction for 2017 is $31,740 (.03174 × $1,000,000).

If the building is sold on January 5, 2017, the cost recovery deduction for 2017 is $1,323 [.03174 × (.5/12) × $1,000,000]. (See Exhibit 8.8 for percentage.)

EXAMPLE 9

Mark acquired a building on November 19, 2017, for $1.2 million. If the building is classified as nonresidential real estate, the cost recovery deduction for 2017 is $3,852 [.00321 × $1,200,000 (Exhibit 8.8)]. The cost recovery deduction for 2018 is $30,768 [.02564 × $1,200,000 (Exhibit 8.8)].

If the building is sold on May 21, 2018, the cost recovery deduction for 2018 is $11,538 [.02564 × (4.5/12) × $1,200,000 (Exhibit 8.8)].

EXAMPLE 10

8-2c **Straight-Line Election**

Although MACRS requires straight-line depreciation for real estate, the taxpayer may *elect* to use the straight-line method for personal property.[11] If elected, the property is depreciated using the class life (recovery period) of the asset with a half-year convention or a mid-quarter convention, whichever applies. The election is available on a class-by-class and year-by-year basis (see Concept Summary 8.4). So, for example, a taxpayer could elect the straight-line method for 5-year MACRS assets placed in service during the current year; 5-year MACRS assets placed in service the following year are not bound by this choice. And, the choice of having 5-year MACRS assets on the straight-line method would not apply to other personalty (e.g., the 3-year and 7-year MACRS classes), unless elected by the taxpayer. The percentages for the straight-line election with a half-year convention appear in Exhibit 8.5.

Concept Summary 8.4

Straight-Line Election under MACRS

	Personal Property	Real Property*
Convention	Half-year or mid-quarter	Mid-month
Cost recovery deduction in the year of disposition**	Half-year for year of sale or half-quarter for quarter of sale	Half-month for month of sale
Elective or mandatory	Elective	Mandatory
Breadth of election	Class by class	

*Straight-line method must be used.

**A disposition can include a sale, exchange, abandonment, or retirement. For simplicity, we will assume a sale in this chapter.

---

[11]§ 168(b)(5).

The Big Picture

EXAMPLE 11

Return to the facts of *The Big Picture* on p. 8-1. If Dr. Payne elects the straight-line method of cost recovery, his total cost recovery deduction is computed as follows.

Office furniture and fixtures	
($70,000 × .0714) (Exhibit 8.5)	$ 4,998
Computers and peripheral equipment	
($67,085 × .10) (Exhibit 8.5)	6,709
Dental equipment	
($475,000 × .0714) (Exhibit 8.5)	33,915
Total cost recovery deduction	$45,622

If Payne does not elect the straight-line cost recovery method, his cost recovery deduction is $91,298 (as detailed on p. 8-1).

The Big Picture

EXAMPLE 12

Assume the same facts as in Example 11, except that Dr. Payne sells the computers and peripheral equipment on November 21, 2018. His cost recovery deduction for 2018 is $6,709 ($67,085 × .20 × 1/2) (Exhibit 8.5).

Recognize when and how to make the § 179 expensing election and use additional first-year depreciation, calculate the amount of the deductions, and apply the effect of the elections in making the MACRS calculation.

8-3 MODIFIED ACCELERATED COST RECOVERY SYSTEM (MACRS): SPECIAL RULES

A number of special rules apply under MACRS. To encourage investment in capital assets and reduce the related compliance costs, Congress has implemented two rules: immediate expensing (§ 179) and additional first-year depreciation (also called bonus depreciation). To curb potential taxpayer abuses of certain assets—particularly when the assets are used for both business and personal purposes—Congress established specific rules for "listed property." Finally, Congress also created an alternative depreciation system (ADS) that taxpayers can use instead of MACRS. The ADS must be used in certain settings (e.g., for the alternative minimum tax).

8-3a Election to Expense Assets (§ 179)

Section 179 (Election to Expense Certain Depreciable Business Assets) permits the taxpayer to deduct up to $510,000 (in 2017; $500,000 in 2016) of the acquisition cost of *tangible personal property* used in a trade or business. Amounts that are expensed under § 179 reduce the asset's basis for additional first-year depreciation (see text Section 8-3b) or cost recovery under MACRS (see text Section 8-2a).

The **§ 179 expensing** election is an annual election that applies to the acquisition cost of property placed in service that year. The immediate expense election generally is not available for real property or for property used for the production of income.[12]

Any elected § 179 expense is taken *before* additional first-year depreciation is computed (see text Section 8-3b). Any MACRS deduction is calculated on the basis of the asset net of the § 179 expense and any additional first-year depreciation.

---

[12]The § 179 amount allowed is per taxpayer, per year. On a joint return, the statutory amount applies to the couple. If the taxpayers are married and file separate returns, each spouse is eligible for 50% of the statutory amount.

The annual expense and phaseout amounts ($500,000 and $2 million, respectively) apply to 2010 and subsequent tax years. These amounts are adjusted for inflation beginning in 2016 and rounded to the nearest $10,000 multiple.

Limited types of "qualified real property," computer software, and heating and air conditioning units also are eligible for expensing.

§ 179 Election and Basis

EXAMPLE 13

Allison acquires and places in service business equipment (a 5-year class asset) on February 1, 2017, at a cost of $80,000. It is the only asset she places in service in 2017. If Allison elects § 179, she can deduct the asset's entire cost in 2017. If not, she will use MACRS to cost recover the asset's cost over six years.

- If Allison elects § 179:

2017	§ 179 deduction	$80,000

- If Allison uses MACRS (see Exhibit 8.3):

2017	$80,000 × .20	$16,000
2018	$80,000 × .32	25,600
2019	$80,000 × .192	15,360
2020	$80,000 × .1152	9,216
2021	$80,000 × .1152	9,216
2022	$80,000 × .0576	4,608
		$80,000

EXAMPLE 14

Assume the same facts as in Example 13. Allison sells the asset in 2019 for $50,000.

- If Allison elects § 179, the asset's adjusted basis is zero ($80,000 − $80,000) and she has a realized gain of $50,000.
- If Allison uses MACRS, the asset's adjusted basis is $30,720 and she has a realized gain of $19,280.

Selling price			$ 50,000
Cost		$ 80,000	
Less: Cost recovery			
2017 MACRS	$16,000		
2018 MACRS	25,600		
2019 MACRS ($15,360 × ½)	7,680	(49,280)	(30,720)
Realized gain			$ 19,280

Deduction Limitations

The § 179 expense deduction is subject to three limitations, applied in this order.

- **Ceiling Amount**. A taxpayer's § 179 deduction cannot exceed an annual ceiling amount ($510,000 in 2017; $500,000 in 2016).
- **Property Placed in Service Maximum**. The § 179 deduction ceiling amount ($510,000 in 2017) is reduced dollar for dollar when § 179 property placed in service during the taxable year exceeds a specified maximum amount ($2,030,000 in 2017; $2,010,000 in 2016). In 2017, a taxpayer who places in service $2,540,000 or more of qualifying property ($510,000 + $2,030,000) will not be able to claim a § 179 deduction.
- **Business Income Limitation**. The § 179 deduction allowed for a taxable year cannot exceed the taxpayer's business income for the year.

These limitations are discussed and illustrated below.

Ceiling Amount. A taxpayer can choose to use all, part, or none of the annual § 179 amount. If a business expects its marginal tax rate to increase in the future, it may decide not to use the § 179 deduction. In such a situation, it may be better to defer deductions to those later years. As discussed below, the business income limitation may also lead a business owner to choose not to expense assets.

In 2017, Sonya Peters places in service $450,000 of 7-year MACRS assets. Although she could immediately expense all of these assets, she would prefer to use § 179 on just $275,000 of the assets. She knows that combining this expense with regular MACRS depreciation effectively reduces her business income to zero, and she wants to defer the remaining deductions to future years when her marginal tax rate will be higher. As a result, Sonya's total cost recovery deduction for 2017 is calculated as follows.

§ 179 expense	$275,000
MACRS depreciation [($450,000 − $275,000) × .1429 (Exhibit 8.3)]	25,008
Total cost recovery deduction	$300,008

Property Placed in Service Maximum. This rule effectively restricts the application of the § 179 deduction to smaller businesses. In 2017, a business that places in service more than $2,030,000 of qualifying property will have its § 179 deduction reduced, and a business that places in service $2,540,000 or more of qualifying property will have its § 179 deduction eliminated.

§ 179: Property Placed in Service Maximum

During 2017, Madison Sanders places $645,000 of § 179 property in service for use in her marketing consultancy. Madison can take a $510,000 § 179 expense election; there is no reduction in the § 179 amount since the property placed in service maximum ($2,030,000) was not reached.

During 2017, George Krull places $2,160,000 of § 179 property in service for use in his manufacturing business (all assets are new 7-year MACRS assets). Because George placed in service more than the $2,030,000 maximum, he must reduce his § 179 deduction dollar for dollar by the amount in excess of $2,030,000 ($2,160,000 − $2,030,000 = $130,000). As a result, George's maximum § 179 deduction is $380,000 ($510,000 − $130,000). This reduction cannot be reclaimed in any way; it is permanently lost. George's total cost recovery deduction for 2017 is calculated as follows.

§ 179 expense	$380,000
MACRS depreciation [($2,160,000 − $380,000) × .1429 (Exhibit 8.3)]	254,362
Total cost recovery deduction	$634,362

Note: George can also take additional first-year (bonus) depreciation, if he chooses to do so. We will revisit this example after discussing bonus depreciation.

George also places in service a $700,000 office building during 2017. Will this have any effect on the calculation above? No. The building is not *tangible personal property* (it is MACRS *realty*). Only tangible personal property is used to determine whether the § 179 ceiling amount ($510,000 in 2017) is reduced.

Business Income Limitation. The §179 deduction allowed for a taxable year cannot exceed the taxpayer's business income for the year. For this purpose, business income is calculated by deducting all business expenses except the § 179 deduction. As a result, a taxpayer's § 179 deduction cannot create (or increase) a net operating loss. A taxpayer's "business income" includes not just income from a sole proprietorship, but also from wages and any allocated business income from a partnership or an S corporation.

During 2017, Lance Smith has a sole proprietorship through which he provides accounting and tax services that generated net income of $68,000. In addition, Lance is a 40% shareholder in a management consultancy operated as an S corporation. The S corporation pays Lance a salary of $40,000, and it recorded taxable income of $50,000. In this case, Lance's business income is $128,000 [$68,000 + $40,000 + $20,000 ($50,000 × 40%)].

Any § 179 amount in excess of taxable income is carried forward to future taxable years and added to other amounts eligible for expensing. Then the various limitations for that carryforward year are applied (i.e., the ceiling amount, the placed in service maximum amount, and the business income limitation).

Jill owns a computer service and operates it as a sole proprietorship. In 2017, taxable income is $138,000 before considering any § 179 deduction. If Jill spends $2.3 million on new equipment, her § 179 expense deduction for the year is computed as follows.

§ 179 deduction before adjustment	$ 510,000
Less: Dollar limitation reduction ($2,300,000 − $2,030,000)	(270,000)
Remaining § 179 deduction	$ 240,000
Business income limitation	$ 138,000
§ 179 deduction allowed	$ 138,000
§ 179 deduction carryforward ($240,000 − $138,000)	$ 102,000

Effect on Basis

The basis of the property for cost recovery purposes is reduced by the § 179 amount after accounting for the current-year amount of property placed in service in excess of the specified maximum amount ($2,030,000 for 2017). This adjusted amount does not reflect any business income limitation.

Assume the same facts as in Example 19. Jill's adjusted basis in the equipment for cost recovery purposes is $2,060,000 ($2,300,000 cost less the $240,000 § 179 expense amount before the business income limitation). If any portion of the $102,000 carryover (due to the business income limitation) is not deducted before the equipment is sold, this amount may be added back to the basis of the equipment in determining its adjusted basis.

Section 179 and the Mid-Quarter Convention

The mid-quarter convention generally results in smaller depreciation deductions in the asset's acquisition year. However, the basis of property used to determine whether the mid-quarter convention applies is derived *after* any § 179 immediate expense election.[13] As a result, a taxpayer may be able to avoid the mid-quarter convention by designating § 179 treatment for assets placed in service during the last quarter of the taxable year.

Dimond Manufacturing places the following assets in service during 2017. All are 5-year class assets, and they are the only assets that Dimond placed in service during the year.

Asset 1 (April 3, 2017)	$ 438,000
Asset 2 (July 17, 2017)	232,000
Asset 3 (October 22, 2017)	580,000
Total	$1,250,000

As Dimond has placed more than 40% of the assets in service during the last quarter of the taxable year, the mid-quarter convention applies ($580,000/$1,250,000 = 46.4%). As a result, Dimond's cost recovery deduction for the year is computed as follows (see Exhibit 8.4).

Asset 1	$438,000 × .25	$109,500
Asset 2	$232,000 × .15	34,800
Asset 3	$580,000 × .05	29,000
Total		$173,300

However, if Dimond elects to expense $500,000 of the October 22 acquisition under § 179, the mid-quarter convention would not apply.

Asset 1 (April 3, 2017)	$438,000
Asset 2 (July 17, 2017)	232,000
Asset 3 (October 22, 2017; $580,000 − $500,000)	80,000
Total	$750,000

continued

---

[13]Reg. § 1.168(d)–1(b)(4).

> Now Dimond has placed only 10.7% ($80,000/$750,000) of the assets in service during the last quarter of the taxable year. As a result, the mid-quarter convention does not apply, and Dimond's cost recovery deduction for the year (including the § 179 expense election) is:
>
> | | |
> |---|---|
> | MACRS depreciation ($750,000 × .20; Exhibit 8.3) | $150,000 |
> | Section 179 expense (Asset 3) | 500,000 |
> | Total cost recovery deduction | $650,000 |
>
> As a result of its effective use of § 179, Dimond has increased its 2017 cost recovery deduction and simplified its reporting and record keeping related to these assets.

Conversion to Personal Use

Conversion of the expensed property to personal use at any time results in recapture income (see text Section 17-2). A property is converted to personal use if it is not used predominantly in a trade or business.[14]

ETHICS & EQUITY   Section 179 Limitation

Joe Moran worked in the construction business throughout most of his career. In June of the current year, he sold his interest in Ajax Enterprises LLC for a profit of $300,000. Shortly thereafter, Joe started his own business, which involves the redevelopment of distressed residential real estate.

In connection with his new business venture, Joe purchased a dump truck at a cost of $70,000. The new business struggled and showed a net operating loss for the year. Joe is considering expensing the $70,000 cost of the truck under §179 on this year's tax return. Evaluate Joe's plan.

8-3b   Additional First-Year Depreciation (Bonus Depreciation)

Congress uses the tax system to stimulate the economy—especially in challenging economic times. An example is **additional first-year depreciation** (also referred to as bonus depreciation). This provision allows taxpayers to deduct an additional 50 percent cost recovery in the year qualified property is placed in service.[15]

The term *qualified property* includes most *new* depreciable assets other than buildings with a recovery period of 20 years or less. The term *new* means the original or first use of the property. Property that is used but "new to the taxpayer" does not qualify.

The additional first-year depreciation is taken in the year in which the qualifying property is placed in service; it is computed after any immediate expense (§ 179) deduction is claimed. After the additional first-year depreciation is determined, the regular MACRS cost recovery deduction is calculated by multiplying the remaining cost recovery basis (original cost recovery basis less § 179 expense and additional first-year depreciation) by the appropriate MACRS percentage. A taxpayer may elect *not* to take additional first-year depreciation.

Bonus Depreciation

EXAMPLE 22

Kelly acquires equipment (a new 5-year class asset) on February 1, 2017, at a cost of $535,000 and elects to expense $510,000 under § 179. Kelly also chooses to take bonus depreciation in addition to regular MACRS cost recovery for 2017 (see Exhibit 8.3). As a result, her total cost recovery deduction for the year is calculated as follows.

§ 179 expense	$510,000
50% additional first-year depreciation [($535,000 − $510,000) × 50%]	12,500
MACRS cost recovery [($535,000 − $510,000 − $12,500) × .20]	2,500
Total cost recovery deduction	$525,000

---

[14]See Reg. § 1.179–1(e) and related examples.

[15]§ 168(k). Additional first-year depreciation is allowed for qualified property placed in service after 2011 and before 2020. The additional first-year depreciation percentage decreases from 50% to 40% in 2018 and then to 30% in 2019. No bonus depreciation is scheduled for tax years after 2019. Different rules applied between 2008 and 2011.

Bonus Depreciation

Assume the same facts as in Example 22. Kelly sells the asset on October 22, 2018. Kelly's 2018 cost recovery deduction for the asset is $2,000 [$12,500 basis for MACRS recovery × .32 (Exhibit 8.3) × ½ (half-year convention)].

EXAMPLE

23

8-3c Using § 179 and Bonus Depreciation Effectively

Choosing Assets for Immediate Expensing

The § 179 deduction can be allocated to reduce the basis of qualifying assets in any manner the taxpayer chooses. This allows the deduction to be allocated proportionally across all assets acquired during the year or to specific assets identified by the taxpayer. This flexibility is important.

There are two general rules that might affect this choice. First, taxpayers should *not* use the § 179 election on automobiles. Automobiles are subject to special cost recovery rules (and annual limits), which we will discuss later in this chapter. Second, given the time value of money, taxpayers should accelerate deductions to the earliest year possible. This is accomplished by expensing the assets with the longest MACRS lives first.

During 2017, Dexter purchases equipment (a new 7-year MACRS asset) costing $335,000 and a computer system costing $280,000 (a new 5-year MACRS asset). As the total amount of MACRS assets placed in service for the year ($615,000; $335,000 + $280,000) is less than $2,030,000, there is no reduction in the $510,000 § 179 deduction. How should Dexter allocate his $510,000 § 179 expense election?

Dexter should expense the longest-lived MACRS asset first (the equipment; the 7-year MACRS asset). If he makes this choice, Dexter's total cost recovery deduction in 2017 is $573,000, calculated as follows.

EXAMPLE

24

Equipment (7-year MACRS asset)	
§ 179 expense	$335,000
Computer System (5-year MACRS asset)	
§ 179 expense ($510,000 − $335,000)	175,000
Additional first-year depreciation [($280,000 − $175,000) × 50%]	52,500
MACRS cost recovery [($280,000 − $175,000 − $52,500) × .2000 (Exhibit 8.3)]	10,500
Total cost recovery deduction	$573,000

If Dexter were to allocate the § 179 expense election to the machinery (MACRS 5-year property), his total cost recovery deduction in 2017 would be only $570,002, calculated as follows.

Computer System (5-year MACRS asset)	
§ 179 expense	$280,000
Equipment (7-year MACRS asset)	
§ 179 expense ($510,000 − $280,000)	230,000
Additional first-year depreciation [($335,000 − $230,000) × 50%]	52,500
MACRS cost recovery [($335,000 − $230,000 − $52,500) × .1429 (Exhibit 8.3)]	7,502
Total cost recovery deduction	$570,002

No matter which asset is expensed, after using both § 179 and bonus depreciation, $52,500 is subject to MACRS cost recovery. However, if the 7-year MACRS asset is expensed, this $52,500 is cost-recovered over six tax years (here, the $52,500 relates to the 5-year MACRS asset). If the 5-year MACRS asset is expensed, the $52,500 will be recovered over eight tax years (here, the $52,500 relates to the 7-year MACRS asset). Using the § 179 expense election on the longest-lived asset accelerates overall cost recovery deductions to earlier years, gaining a time-value-of-money advantage for the taxpayer.

Using Both § 179 and Bonus Depreciation

In general, in 2017, a business that places in service $510,000 or less of qualifying § 179 property will exclusively use § 179 to immediately expense all of those assets, while a business placing in service $2,540,000 or more of qualifying assets (the point at which the § 179 amount is completely phased out; $510,000 + $2,030,000) will qualify only for bonus depreciation. Any business placing in service between $510,000 and $2,540,000 of qualifying § 179 property will be able to use a combination of both § 179 and bonus depreciation (see Concept Summary 8.5).[16]

Concept Summary 8.5

Using § 179 and Bonus Depreciation

Use § 179 Exclusively	Use Both §179 and Bonus Depreciation	Use Bonus Depreciation Exclusively

$0 $510,000 $2,540,000

Total Qualifying Property Placed in Service (2017)

EXAMPLE 25

Return to the facts of Example 17. Given that George has placed $2,160,000 of assets in service during 2017, he can use both § 179 and additional first-year depreciation (see Concept Summary 8.5). If George uses both § 179 and bonus depreciation, his total cost recovery deduction will increase to $1,397,181, computed as follows.

§ 179 expense	$ 380,000
Additional first-year depreciation [($2,160,000 − $380,000) × 50%]	890,000
MACRS depreciation [($2,160,000 − $380,000 − $890,000) × .1429 (Exhibit 8.3)]	127,181
Total cost recovery deduction	$1,397,181

The Big Picture

EXAMPLE 26

Return to the facts of *The Big Picture* on p. 8-1 and assume that the tax year is 2017. Dr. Payne has placed $612,085 of assets in service ($70,000 + $67,085 + $475,000). Because this amount is less than $2,030,000, there is no reduction in the $510,000 maximum § 179 deduction. Further, assume that Dr. Payne has sufficient business income to avoid any § 179 limitation.

Dr. Payne should expense the longest-lived MACRS assets first (the office furniture and fixtures and the dental equipment are 7-year MACRS assets). Although he would be indifferent to expensing either of the 7-year assets, by expensing the office furniture and fixtures, he will simplify his record keeping by expensing these assets completely.

Dr. Payne can also use additional first-year depreciation. As a result, Dr. Payne's total cost recovery deduction is $570,252, calculated as follows.

continued

---

[16]This general rule applies to the vast majority of taxpayers. However, it would not apply if the § 179 taxable income limitation applies or the tax-payer chooses to defer deductions to later tax years (e.g., if the taxpayer expects marginal tax rates to increase).

Office furniture and fixtures	
§ 179 expense	$ 70,000
Dental equipment	
§ 179 expense ($510,000 − $70,000)	440,000
Additional first-year depreciation [($475,000 − $440,000) × 50%]	17,500
MACRS depreciation [($475,000 − $440,000 − $17,500) × .1429 (Exhibit 8.3)]	2,501
Computers and peripheral equipment	
Additional first-year depreciation ($67,085 × 50%)	33,543
MACRS depreciation [($67,085 − $33,543) × .2000 (Exhibit 8.3)]	6,708
Total cost recovery deduction	$570,252

If Dr. Payne chooses to use neither § 179 nor additional first-year depreciation, his cost recovery deduction will be $91,298 (as detailed on p. 8-1).

8-3d Business and Personal Use of Automobiles and Other Listed Property

LO.4

Identify listed property and apply the deduction limitations on listed property and on luxury automobiles.

Limits exist on cost recovery deductions for automobiles and other listed property that are used for both personal and business purposes.[17] If listed property is not *predominantly used* for business purposes when placed in service, it is not eligible for the accelerated methods built into MACRS, the immediate expense election (§ 179), or bonus depreciation. If not *predominantly used* for business, the listed property's cost must be recovered using the *straight-line method* (see Exhibit 8-5). Further, the straight-line method must continue to be used even if, at some later date, the property *is* predominantly used for business.

Listed property includes:

- Any passenger automobile.
- Any other property used as a means of transportation.
- Any property of a type generally used for purposes of entertainment, recreation, or amusement.
- Any computer or peripheral equipment, with the exception of equipment used exclusively at a regular business establishment, including a qualifying home office.
- Any other property specified in the Regulations.

Automobiles and Other Listed Property Used Predominantly in Business

For listed property to be considered as *predominantly used in business*, its *business use* must exceed 50 percent.[18] The use of listed property for production of income does not qualify as business use for purposes of the more-than-50% test. However, both production of income and business use percentages are used to compute the cost recovery deduction.

EXAMPLE

27

On September 1, 2017, Emma places in service listed 5-year recovery property. The property cost $10,000. She elects not to take any available additional first-year depreciation.

If Emma uses the property 40% for business and 25% for the production of income, the property is not considered as predominantly used for business. The cost is recovered using straight-line cost recovery. Emma's cost recovery allowance for the year is $650 ($10,000 × .10 × 65%).

If, however, Emma uses the property 60% for business and 25% for the production of income, the property is considered as used predominantly for business. Therefore, she may use the statutory percentage method. Emma's cost recovery allowance for the year is $1,700 ($10,000 × .20 × 85%).

In determining the percentage of business use of listed property, a mileage-based percentage is used for automobiles. For other listed property, one employs the most

---

[17]§ 280F.

[18]§ 280F(b)(3).

appropriate unit of time (e.g., hours) for which the property actually is used (rather than its availability for use).[19]

Limits on Cost Recovery for Automobiles

The law places further limits on the annual cost recovery deductions for passenger automobiles. These dollar limits were imposed on passenger automobiles because of the belief that the tax system was being used to underwrite automobiles whose cost and luxury far exceeded what was needed for the taxpayer's business use.

A *passenger automobile* is any four-wheeled vehicle manufactured for use on public streets, roads, and highways with an unloaded gross vehicle weight (GVW) rating of 6,000 pounds or less.[20] This definition specifically excludes vehicles used directly in the business of transporting people or property for compensation, [e.g., taxicabs (including autos used for Uber or Lyft), ambulances, hearses, and trucks and vans].

The following "luxury auto" depreciation limits apply.[21]

Date Placed in Service	First Year	Second Year	Third Year	Fourth and Later Years
2016*	$3,160	$5,100	$3,050	$1,875
2012–2015	$3,160	$5,100	$3,050	$1,875
2010–2011	$3,060	$4,900	$2,950	$1,775

*Because the 2017 indexed amounts were not available when we published, the 2016 amounts are used in the Examples and end-of-chapter problem materials.

For an automobile placed in service prior to 2010, the limitation for subsequent years' cost recovery is based on the limits for the year the automobile was placed in service.[22]

In the event a passenger automobile used predominantly for business qualifies for additional first-year depreciation (i.e., new property), the first-year recovery limitation is increased by $8,000.[23] Therefore, for acquisitions made in 2016, the initial-year cost recovery limitation increases from $3,160 to $11,160 ($3,160 + $8,000).[24]

The luxury auto limits must be reduced proportionally for any personal use of the auto. In addition, the limitation in the first year includes any amount the taxpayer elects to expense under § 179.[25] If the passenger automobile is used partly for personal use, the personal use percentage is ignored for the purpose of determining the unrecovered cost available for deduction in later years.

EXAMPLE 28

On July 1, 2017, Dan places in service a new automobile that cost $40,000. He does not elect § 179 expensing, and he elects not to take any available additional first-year depreciation. The car is used 80% for business and 20% for personal use in each tax year. Dan chooses the MACRS 200% declining-balance method of cost recovery (the auto is a 5-year asset).

The depreciation computation for 2017 through 2022 is summarized in the table below. The cost recovery allowed is the lesser of the MACRS amount or the recovery limitation.

Year	MACRS Amount	Recovery Limitation	Depreciation Allowed
2017	$6,400 ($40,000 × .2000 × 80%)	$2,528 ($3,160 × 80%)	$2,528
2018	$10,240 ($40,000 × .3200 × 80%)	$4,080 ($5,100 × 80%)	$4,080

continued

---

[19]Reg. § 1.280F–6T(e).

[20]§ 280F(d)(5).

[21]§ 280F(a)(1); Rev.Proc. 2016–23, 2016–16 I.R.B. 589.

[22]Cost recovery limitations for years prior to 2010 are found in IRS Publication 463.

[23]§ 168(k)(2)(F). The $8,000 amount will decrease to $6,400 in 2018 and $4,800 in 2019. No increase in the first-year recovery limitation will be allowed after 2019.

[24]There are different cost recovery limitations for trucks and vans, and for electric automobiles. Because these limitations are applied in the same manner as those imposed on passenger automobiles, we have chosen not to discuss these additional limitations.

[25]§ 280F(d)(1).

Year	MACRS Amount	Recovery Limitation	Depreciation Allowed
2019	$6,144 ($40,000 × .1920 × 80%)	$2,440 ($3,050 × 80%)	$2,440
2020	$3,686 ($40,000 × .1152 × 80%)	$1,500 ($1,875 × 80%)	$1,500
2021	$3,686 ($40,000 × .1152 × 80%)	$1,500 ($1,875 × 80%)	$1,500
2022	$1,843 ($40,000 × .0576 × 80%)	$1,500 ($1,875 × 80%)	$1,500

If Dan continues to use the car after 2022, his cost recovery is limited to the lesser of the recoverable basis or the recovery limitation (i.e., $1,875 × business use percentage). For this purpose, the recoverable basis is computed as if the full recovery limitation was allowed even if it was not. Thus, the recoverable basis as of January 1, 2023, is $23,065 ($40,000 − $3,160 − $5,100 − $3,050 − $1,875 − $1,875 − $1,875).

If Dan takes additional first-year depreciation, the calculated amount of additional first-year depreciation is $16,000 ($40,000 × 50% × 80%). However, the deduction would be limited to $8,928 [($8,000 + $3,160) × 80%].

The cost recovery limitations are maximum amounts. If the regular MACRS calculation produces a smaller amount of cost recovery, the smaller amount is used.

On April 2, 2017, Gail places in service a used automobile that cost $10,000. The car is always used 70% for business and 30% for personal use. The cost recovery allowance for 2017 is $1,400 ($10,000 × .20 MACRS table factor × 70%), and not $2,212 ($3,160 passenger auto maximum × 70%).

Special Limitation for Sport-Utility Vehicles (SUVs)

Some sport-utility vehicles (SUVs) are not considered passenger automobiles and, therefore, are not subject to the luxury automobile limitations. However, a $25,000 limit applies for the § 179 deduction when the luxury auto limits do not apply. The limit is in effect for SUVs with an unloaded GVW rating of more than 6,000 pounds and not more than 14,000 pounds.[26]

During 2017, Jay acquires and places in service a new SUV that cost $70,000 and has a GVW of 8,000 pounds. Jay uses the vehicle 100% of the time for business use. The total cost recovery deduction for 2017 with respect to the SUV is computed as follows.

§ 179 expense	$25,000
50% additional first-year depreciation [($70,000 − $25,000) × 50%]	22,500
Standard MACRS calculation [($70,000 − $25,000 − $22,500) × .20 (Exhibit 8.3)]	4,500
Total cost recovery deduction	$52,000

Automobiles and Other Listed Property Not Used Predominantly in Business

For automobiles and other listed property not used predominantly in business in the year of acquisition (i.e., 50 percent or less), the straight-line method under the alternative depreciation system is required (see text Section 8-3e).[27] Under this system, the straight-line recovery period for automobiles is five years. However, the cost recovery deduction for any passenger automobile cannot exceed the luxury auto limit.

---

[26]§ 179(b)(6).   [27]§ 280F(b)(1).

Auto Not Predominantly Used in Business

On July 27, 2017, Fred places in service an automobile that cost $20,000. The auto is used 40% for business and 60% for personal use. The cost recovery allowance for 2017 is $800 [$20,000 × .10 (Exhibit 8.7) × 40%].

Assume the same facts as in Example 31, except that the automobile cost $50,000. The cost recovery allowance for 2017 is $1,264 [$50,000 × .10 (Exhibit 8.7) = $5,000 (limited to $3,160) × 40%].

The straight-line method is used even if, at some later date, the business use of the property increases to more than 50 percent (although the cost recovery allowed will reflect the increase in business use).

Assume the same facts as in Example 31, except that in 2018, Fred uses the automobile 70% for business and 30% for personal use. Fred's cost recovery allowance for 2018 is $2,800 [$20,000 × .20 (Exhibit 8.7) × 70%], which is less than 70% of the second-year limit.

Change from Predominantly Business Use

If the business use percentage of listed property falls to 50 percent or less after the year the property is placed in service, the property is subject to *cost recovery recapture*. The amount required to be recaptured and included in the taxpayer's ordinary income is the *excess cost recovery*.

Excess cost recovery is the excess of the cost recovery deduction taken in prior years using the statutory percentage method over the amount that would have been allowed if the straight-line method had been used since the property was placed in service.[28]

EXAMPLE 34

Seth purchased a new car on January 22, 2017, at a cost of $20,000. Business use was 80% in 2017, 70% in 2018, 40% in 2019, and 60% in 2020. Seth elects not to take any available additional first-year depreciation. Seth's excess cost recovery to be recaptured as ordinary income in 2019 is:

2017

MACRS [($20,000 × .20 × 80%) (limited to $3,160 × 80%)]	$ 2,528
Straight-line [($20,000 × .10 × 80%) (limited to $3,160 × 80%)]	(1,600)
Excess	$ 928

2018

MACRS [($20,000 × .32 × 70%) (limited to $5,100 × 70%)]	$ 3,570
Straight-line [($20,000 × .20 × 70%) (limited to $5,100 × 70%)]	(2,800)
Excess	$ 770

2019

2017 excess	$ 928
2018 excess	770
Ordinary income recapture	$1,698

After the business use of the listed property drops below the more-than-50% level, the straight-line method is used for the remaining life of the property.

---

[28]§ 280F(b)(2).

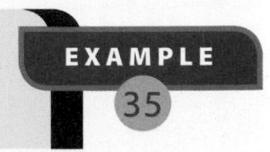

Assume the same facts as in Example 34. Seth's cost recovery deduction for 2019 and 2020 is:

2019 $1,220 [($20,000 × .20 × 40%) limited to $3,050 × 40%]
2020 $1,125 [($20,000 × .20 × 60%) limited to $1,875 × 60%]

Concept Summary 8.6 illustrates the cost recovery rules for various types of listed property.

Concept Summary 8.6

Listed Property Cost Recovery

```
                        ┌──────────────┐
                        │    Listed    │
                        │   Property   │
                        └──────┬───────┘
                               │
                   ┌───────────▼────────────┐
                   │      Is the Property    │
                   │   Used Predominantly    │
                   │       for Business?     │
                   └───┬─────────────────┬───┘
              No       │                 │       Yes
         ┌─────────────┘                 └─────────────┐
         │                                             │
  ┌──────▼──────┐                              ┌──────▼──────┐
  │ Is the Property │                          │ Is the Property │
  │  a Passenger │                             │  a Passenger │
  │  Automobile? │                             │  Automobile? │
  └──┬────────┬──┘                             └──┬────────┬──┘
  No │        │ Yes                            No │        │ Yes
```

| Straight-line cost recovery reduced by the personal use percentage | Straight-line cost recovery subject to the recovery limitations that apply (based on the year placed in service) and reduced by the personal use percentage | Regular MACRS cost recovery reduced by the personal use percentage | Regular MACRS cost recovery subject to the recovery limitations that apply (based on the year placed in service) and reduced by the personal use percentage |

Leased Automobiles

Taxpayers who lease, rather than purchase, a passenger automobile for business purposes are not subject to the luxury auto limits. To prevent taxpayers from circumventing the luxury auto limits by deducting the full amount of lease payments associated with a luxury automobile leased for business, the law requires these taxpayers to report an *inclusion amount* in gross income. The inclusion amount is computed from an IRS table for each taxable year for which the taxpayer leases the automobile.

The inclusion amount is based on the fair market value of the automobile; it is prorated for the number of days the auto is used during the taxable year. The prorated dollar amount then is multiplied by the business and income-producing use percentage.[29] The taxpayer deducts the lease payments, multiplied by the business and income-producing use percentage. In effect, the taxpayer's annual deduction for the lease payment is reduced by the inclusion amount.

---

[29]Reg. § 1.280F–7(a).

EXAMPLE

36

On April 1, 2017, Jim leases and places in service a passenger automobile worth $52,400. The lease is to be for a period of five years. During the taxable years 2017 and 2018, Jim uses the automobile 70% for business and 30% for personal use.

Assuming that the dollar amounts from the IRS table for 2017 and 2018 are $66 and $144, respectively, Jim includes in gross income:

2017 $66 × (274/365) × 70% = $35

2018 $144 × (365/365) × 70% = $101

In each year, Jim still can deduct 70% of the lease payments made, related to his business use of the auto.

Substantiation Requirements

The substantiation requirements of § 274 apply to listed property. A taxpayer must be able to prove for any business use the amount of expense or use, the time and place of use, the business purpose for the use, and the business relationship to the taxpayer of persons using the property.

Substantiation requires adequate records or sufficient evidence corroborating the taxpayer's statement. For example, to document business use of an automobile, it is expected that a taxpayer maintain a contemporaneous record of business miles driven (vs. other miles), any expenses incurred (e.g., fuel, repairs, business tolls, parking), and the business reason for the auto's use.[30]

8-3e Alternative Depreciation System (ADS)

LO.5

Determine when and how to use the alternative depreciation system (ADS).

The alternative depreciation system (ADS) must be used:[31]

- To calculate the portion of depreciation treated as an alternative minimum tax (AMT) adjustment for purposes of the corporate and individual AMT (see Chapters 12 and 20).[32]

- To compute depreciation allowances for earnings and profits purposes (see Chapter 20).

In general, ADS depreciation is computed using the straight-line method. However, for AMT, depreciation of personal property is computed using the 150 percent declining-balance method with a switch to the straight-line method when appropriate.

The taxpayer must use the half-year or the mid-quarter convention, whichever is applicable, for all property other than real estate. The mid-month convention is used for real estate. ADS cost recovery percentages are found in Exhibits 8.6, 8.7, and 8.9. Under ADS, personal property is depreciated using the appropriate asset class life (e.g., 5- or 7-year) and the 150 percent declining-balance method. Realty is depreciated over a 40-year life using straight-line depreciation.[33]

To simplify reporting, taxpayers may *elect* to use the 150 percent declining-balance method to compute cost recovery for the regular income tax (rather than the 200 percent declining-balance method that is available for personal property). If this election is made, there is no difference between the regular income tax and AMT cost recovery.[34]

---

[30]§§ 274(d) and (i). These substantiation requirements do not apply to vehicles that, by reason of their nature, are not likely to be used more than a *de minimis* amount for personal purposes.

[31]§ 168(g). ADS must also be used to compute cost recovery for property used predominantly outside the United States, used by a tax-exempt entity, and used in several other unique situations.

[32]This AMT adjustment applies for real and personal property placed in service before 1999. However, it also applies for personal property placed in

service after 1998 if the taxpayer uses the 200% declining-balance method for regular income tax purposes. See text Section 12-1c.

[33]The class life for certain properties described in § 168(e)(3) is specially determined under § 168(g)(3)(B).

[34]For personal property placed in service before 1999, taxpayers making the election use the ADS recovery periods in computing cost recovery for the regular income tax. The ADS recovery periods generally are longer than the regular recovery periods under MACRS.

On March 1, 2017, Abby purchases computer-based telephone central office switching equipment for $80,000. Abby elects not to take any available additional first-year depreciation. If Abby uses statutory percentage cost recovery (assuming no § 179 election), her deduction for 2017 is $16,000 [$80,000 × .20 (Exhibit 8.3, 5-year class property)].

If Abby elects to use ADS 150% declining-balance cost recovery for the regular income tax (assuming no § 179 election), the cost recovery allowance for 2017 is $12,000 [$80,000 × .15 (Exhibit 8.6, 5-year class property)].

EXAMPLE 37

Rather than determining depreciation under the regular MACRS method, taxpayers may *elect* straight-line under ADS. One reason for making this election is to defer cost recovery deductions to later years (presuming that marginal tax rates will be higher in those years). Another reason is to simplify record keeping, as the cost recovery deduction will be the same as earnings and profits depreciation.[35]

Polly acquires an apartment building on March 17, 2017, for $700,000. She takes the maximum cost recovery allowance for determining taxable income. For 2017, Polly deducts $20,153 [$700,000 × .02879 (Exhibit 8.8)].

However, Polly's cost recovery for computing her earnings and profits is only $13,853 [$700,000 × .01979 (Exhibit 8.9)].

EXAMPLE 38

8-4 **REPORTING PROCEDURES**

LO.6

Report cost recovery deductions appropriately.

Sole proprietors engaged in a business file a Schedule C, Profit or Loss from Business, to accompany Form 1040. A 2016 Schedule C is illustrated, as the 2017 Schedule C was not available when this text was printed.

The top part of page 1 requests certain key information about the taxpayer (e.g., name, address, Social Security number, principal business activity, and accounting method used). Part I provides for the reporting of items of income. If the business requires the use of inventories and the computation of cost of goods sold (see text Section 18-2 for when this is necessary), Part III must be completed and the cost of goods sold amount transferred to line 4 of Part I.

Part II allows for the reporting of deductions. Some of the deductions discussed in this chapter and their location on the form are depletion (line 12) and depreciation (line 13). Other expenses (line 27) include those items not already covered (see lines 8–26). An example is research and experimental expenditures.

If depreciation is claimed, it should be supported by completing Form 4562. A 2016 Form 4562 is illustrated, as the 2017 Form 4562 is not yet available. The amount listed on line 22 of Form 4562 is transferred to line 13 of Part II of Schedule C.

Thomas Andrews, Social Security number 111-11-1111, was employed as an accountant until May 2016, when he opened his own practice. His address is 279 Mountain View, Ogden, UT 84201. Andrews keeps his books on the cash basis and reported the following revenue and business expenses in 2016.

a. Revenue from accounting practice, $192,000.
b. Insurance, $5,000.
c. Office supplies, $4,000.
d. Office rent, $16,000.
e. Copier lease payments, $3,000.
f. Licenses, $2,000.
g. New furniture and fixtures were acquired on May 10, for $142,000. Thomas elects § 179 expensing and uses the statutory percentage cost recovery method.

Andrews reports the above information on Schedule C and Form 4562 as illustrated on the following pages.

EXAMPLE 39

---

[35]This straight-line election is made on a year-by-year basis. For property other than real estate, the election is made by MACRS class and applies to all assets in that MACRS class. So, for example, the election could be made for 7-year MACRS property and not for 5-year MACRS property placed in service during the same year. For real estate, the election is made on a property-by-property basis.

Form **4562**

Department of the Treasury
Internal Revenue Service (99)

Depreciation and Amortization
(Including Information on Listed Property)
▶ Attach to your tax return.
▶ Information about Form 4562 and its separate instructions is at *www.irs.gov/form4562.*

OMB No. 1545-0172

2016

Attachment
Sequence No. **179**

Name(s) shown on return	Business or activity to which this form relates	Identifying number
Thomas Andrews	*Andrews Accounting Services*	*111-11-1111*

Part I **Election To Expense Certain Property Under Section 179**
Note: If you have any listed property, complete Part V before you complete Part I.

1	Maximum amount (see instructions)	**1**	*500,000*
2	Total cost of section 179 property placed in service (see instructions)	**2**	*142,000*
3	Threshold cost of section 179 property before reduction in limitation (see instructions)	**3**	*2,010,000*
4	Reduction in limitation. Subtract line 3 from line 2. If zero or less, enter -0-	**4**	*-0-*
5	Dollar limitation for tax year. Subtract line 4 from line 1. If zero or less, enter -0-. If married filing separately, see instructions	**5**	*142,000*

6	(a) Description of property	(b) Cost (business use only)	(c) Elected cost	
	Furniture and Fixtures	*142,000*	*142,000*	

7	Listed property. Enter the amount from line 29 . . . . **7**		
8	Total elected cost of section 179 property. Add amounts in column (c), lines 6 and 7	**8**	*142,000*
9	Tentative deduction. Enter the **smaller** of line 5 or line 8	**9**	*142,000*
10	Carryover of disallowed deduction from line 13 of your 2015 Form 4562	**10**	*-0-*
11	Business income limitation. Enter the smaller of business income (not less than zero) or line 5 (see instructions)	**11**	*142,000*
12	Section 179 expense deduction. Add lines 9 and 10, but don't enter more than line 11	**12**	*142,000*
13	Carryover of disallowed deduction to 2017. Add lines 9 and 10, less line 12 ▶ **13**		

Note: Don't use Part II or Part III below for listed property. Instead, use Part V.

Part II **Special Depreciation Allowance and Other Depreciation (Don't** include listed property.) (See instructions.)

14	Special depreciation allowance for qualified property (other than listed property) placed in service during the tax year (see instructions)	**14**	
15	Property subject to section 168(f)(1) election	**15**	
16	Other depreciation (including ACRS)	**16**	

Part III **MACRS Depreciation (Don't** include listed property.) (See instructions.)

Section A

17	MACRS deductions for assets placed in service in tax years beginning before 2016	**17**	
18	If you are electing to group any assets placed in service during the tax year into one or more general asset accounts, check here . . . . ▶ ☐		

Section B—Assets Placed in Service During 2016 Tax Year Using the General Depreciation System

(a) Classification of property	(b) Month and year placed in service	(c) Basis for depreciation (business/investment use only—see instructions)	(d) Recovery period	(e) Convention	(f) Method	(g) Depreciation deduction
19a 3-year property						
b 5-year property						
c 7-year property						
d 10-year property						
e 15-year property						
f 20-year property						
g 25-year property			25 yrs.		S/L	
h Residential rental property			27.5 yrs.	MM	S/L	
			27.5 yrs.	MM	S/L	
i Nonresidential real property			39 yrs.	MM	S/L	
				MM	S/L	

Section C—Assets Placed in Service During 2016 Tax Year Using the Alternative Depreciation System

20a Class life					S/L	
b 12-year			12 yrs.		S/L	
c 40-year			40 yrs.	MM	S/L	

Part IV **Summary** (See instructions.)

21	Listed property. Enter amount from line 28	**21**	
22	**Total.** Add amounts from line 12, lines 14 through 17, lines 19 and 20 in column (g), and line 21. Enter here and on the appropriate lines of your return. Partnerships and S corporations—see instructions .	**22**	*142,000*
23	For assets shown above and placed in service during the current year, enter the portion of the basis attributable to section 263A costs **23**		

For Paperwork Reduction Act Notice, see separate instructions.   Cat. No. 12906N   Form **4562** (2016)

SCHEDULE C (Form 1040) Department of the Treasury Internal Revenue Service (99)	**Profit or Loss From Business** (Sole Proprietorship) ▶ Information about Schedule C and its separate instructions is at *www.irs.gov/schedulec*. ▶ **Attach to Form 1040, 1040NR, or 1041; partnerships generally must file Form 1065.**	OMB No. 1545-0074 20**16** Attachment Sequence No. **09**

Name of proprietor	Social security number (SSN)
Thomas Andrews	*111–11–1111*

A Principal business or profession, including product or service (see instructions)   **B** Enter code from instructions ▶

C Business name. If no separate business name, leave blank.   **D** Employer ID number (EIN), (see instr.)
Andrews Accounting Services

E Business address (including suite or room no.) ▶ *279 Mountain View*
City, town or post office, state, and ZIP code   *Ogden, UT 84201*

F Accounting method: **(1)** ☒ Cash   **(2)** ☐ Accrual   **(3)** ☐ Other (specify) ▶

G Did you "materially participate" in the operation of this business during 2016? If "No," see instructions for limit on losses   ☒ Yes   ☐ No

H If you started or acquired this business during 2016, check here   ▶ ☐

I Did you make any payments in 2016 that would require you to file Form(s) 1099? (see instructions)   ☐ Yes   ☐ No

J If "Yes," did you or will you file required Forms 1099?   ☐ Yes   ☐ No

Part I Income

1	Gross receipts or sales. See instructions for line 1 and check the box if this income was reported to you on Form W-2 and the "Statutory employee" box on that form was checked ▶ ☐	1	*192,000*
2	Returns and allowances	2	
3	Subtract line 2 from line 1	3	*192,000*
4	Cost of goods sold (from line 42)	4	
5	**Gross profit.** Subtract line 4 from line 3	5	*192,000*
6	Other income, including federal and state gasoline or fuel tax credit or refund (see instructions)	6	
7	**Gross income.** Add lines 5 and 6 ▶	7	*192,000*

Part II Expenses. Enter expenses for business use of your home **only** on line 30.

8	Advertising	8		18	Office expense (see instructions)	18	*4,000*
9	Car and truck expenses (see instructions)	9		19	Pension and profit-sharing plans	19	
10	Commissions and fees	10		20	Rent or lease (see instructions):		
11	Contract labor (see instructions)	11		a	Vehicles, machinery, and equipment	20a	*3,000*
12	Depletion	12		b	Other business property	20b	*16,000*
13	Depreciation and section 179 expense deduction (not included in Part III) (see instructions)	13	*142,000*	21	Repairs and maintenance	21	
				22	Supplies (not included in Part III)	22	
				23	Taxes and licenses	23	*2,000*
				24	Travel, meals, and entertainment:		
14	Employee benefit programs (other than on line 19)	14	*5,000*	a	Travel	24a	
15	Insurance (other than health)	15		b	Deductible meals and entertainment (see instructions)	24b	
16	Interest:			25	Utilities	25	
a	Mortgage (paid to banks, etc.)	16a		26	Wages (less employment credits)	26	
b	Other	16b		27a	Other expenses (from line 48)	27a	
17	Legal and professional services	17		b	**Reserved for future use**	27b	

28	**Total expenses** before expenses for business use of home. Add lines 8 through 27a ▶	28	*172,000*
29	Tentative profit or (loss). Subtract line 28 from line 7	29	*20,000*
30	Expenses for business use of your home. Do not report these expenses elsewhere. Attach Form 8829 unless using the simplified method (see instructions). **Simplified method filers only:** enter the total square footage of: (a) your home: _____ and (b) the part of your home used for business: _____. Use the Simplified Method Worksheet in the instructions to figure the amount to enter on line 30	30	
31	**Net profit or (loss).** Subtract line 30 from line 29. • If a profit, enter on both **Form 1040, line 12** (or **Form 1040NR, line 13**) and on **Schedule SE, line 2.** (If you checked the box on line 1, see instructions). Estates and trusts, enter on **Form 1041, line 3.** • If a loss, you **must** go to line 32.	31	*20,000*
32	If you have a loss, check the box that describes your investment in this activity (see instructions). • If you checked 32a, enter the loss on both **Form 1040, line 12,** (or **Form 1040NR, line 13**) and on **Schedule SE, line 2.** (If you checked the box on line 1, see the line 31 instructions). Estates and trusts, enter on **Form 1041, line 3.** • If you checked 32b, you **must** attach **Form 6198.** Your loss may be limited.	32a ☐ All investment is at risk. 32b ☐ Some investment is not at risk.

For Paperwork Reduction Act Notice, see the separate instructions.   Cat. No. 11334P   Schedule C (Form 1040) 2016

LO.7

Identify intangible assets that are eligible for amortization and calculate the amount of the deduction.

8-5 **AMORTIZATION**

Taxpayers can recover the costs of certain intangible assets through an amortization deduction. The amount of the deduction is determined by amortizing the adjusted basis of these intangibles ratably over a 15-year period beginning in the month in which the intangible is acquired.[36]

Section 197 covers the amortization of most intangibles. *Amortizable § 197 intangibles* include most intangibles acquired after August 10, 1993, and acquired in connection with the acquisition of a business, including goodwill, going-concern value, franchises, trademarks, copyrights, patents, and covenants not to compete. Generally, self-created intangibles are *not* § 197 intangibles.

The 15-year amortization period applies regardless of the actual useful life of an amortizable § 197 intangible. No other depreciation or amortization deduction is permitted for these intangibles.

EXAMPLE 40

On June 1, 2017, Neil purchased and began operating the Falcon Café. Of the purchase price, $90,000 is allocated to goodwill. The 2017 § 197 amortization deduction is $3,500 [($90,000/15) × (7/12)].

Startup expenditures are partially amortizable by using a § 195 election.[37] A taxpayer must make this election no later than the due date of the return for the taxable year in which the trade or business begins.[38] If no election is made, the startup expenditures are capitalized.[39]

The amortization election for startup expenditures allows the taxpayer to deduct the smaller of (1) the startup expenditures related to the trade or business or (2) $5,000. The $5,000 maximum is reduced dollar for dollar by the amount of startup expenditures in excess of $50,000. As a result, if startup expenditures equal or exceed $55,000, no immediate deduction is allowed. Any startup expenditures not deducted are amortized ratably over a 180-month period, beginning in the month in which the trade or business begins.[40]

Startup Expenditures

EXAMPLE 41

Green Corporation begins business on August 1, 2017. The corporation incurs startup expenditures of $47,000. If Green elects amortization under § 195, the total startup expenditures that Green may deduct in 2017 is computed as follows.

Deductible amount	$5,000
Amortizable amount {[($47,000 − $5,000)/180] × 5 months}	1,167
Total deduction	$6,167

EXAMPLE 42

Assume the same facts as in Example 41, except that the startup expenditures total $53,000. The 2017 deduction is computed as follows.

Deductible amount [$5,000 − ($53,000 − $50,000)]	$2,000
Amortizable amount {[($53,000 − $2,000)/180] × 5 months}	1,417
Total deduction	$3,417

---

[36]§ 197(a).

[37]§ 195(b).

[38]§ 195(d).

[39]§ 195(a).

[40]§§ 195(b)(1)(A) and (B).

Amortizable startup expenditures generally must satisfy two requirements.[41] First, the expenses must be paid or incurred in connection with:

- Creating a business,
- Investigating the creation or acquisition of a business, or
- Anticipating an activity becoming a business.

Second, the expenses must reflect those that could be deducted in an existing trade or business in the same field (see Investigation of a Business, text Section 6-3d).

The startup costs of creating a new active trade or business could include advertising; salaries and wages; travel and other expenses incurred in lining up prospective distributors, suppliers, or customers; and salaries and fees for executives, consultants, and professional services. Costs that relate to either created or acquired businesses could include expenses incurred for the analysis or survey of potential markets, products, labor supply, transportation facilities, and the like. Startup expenditures do not include allowable deductions for interest, taxes, and research and experimental costs.[42]

Amortization deductions also can be claimed for organizational expenses (see text Section 20-2d) and research and experimental expenditures (see text Section 7-4).

8-6 DEPLETION

LO.8

Determine the amount of depletion expense, including being able to apply the alternative tax treatments for intangible drilling and development costs.

Natural resources (e.g., oil, gas, coal, gravel, and timber) are subject to **depletion**, a form of cost recovery that applies to natural resources. Land generally cannot be depleted.

Although all natural resources are subject to depletion, oil and gas wells are used as an example in the following paragraphs to illustrate the related costs and issues.

In developing an oil or gas well, the producer typically makes four types of expenditures.

- Natural resource costs.
- Intangible drilling and development costs.
- Tangible asset costs.
- Operating costs.

Natural resources are physically limited, and the costs to acquire them (e.g., oil under the ground) are, therefore, recovered through depletion. Costs incurred in making the property ready for drilling, such as the cost of labor in clearing the property, erecting derricks, and drilling the hole, are **intangible drilling and development costs (IDCs)**. These costs generally have no salvage value and are a lost cost if the well is dry.

Costs for tangible assets such as tools, pipes, and engines are capitalized and recovered through depreciation (cost recovery). Costs incurred after the well is producing are operating costs. These costs include expenditures for such items as labor, fuel, and supplies. Operating costs are deductible as trade or business expenses. Depletable costs and intangible drilling and development costs receive different treatment.

8-6a Intangible Drilling and Development Costs (IDCs)

Intangible drilling and development costs can be handled in one of two ways at the option of the taxpayer. They can be *either* charged off as an expense in the year in which they are incurred *or* capitalized and written off through depletion. The taxpayer makes the election in the first year such expenditures are incurred, either by taking a deduction on the return or by adding them to the depletable basis.

Once made, the election is binding on both the taxpayer and the IRS for all such expenditures in the future. If the taxpayer fails to elect to expense IDCs on the original

---

[41]§§ 195(c)(1)(A) and (B).   [42]§ 195(c).

timely filed return for the first year in which such expenditures are incurred, an irrevocable election to capitalize them has been made.

As a general rule, it is more advantageous to expense IDCs. The obvious benefit of an immediate write-off (as opposed to a deferred write-off through depletion) is not the only advantage. Because a taxpayer can use percentage depletion, which is calculated without reference to basis (see Example 46), the IDCs may be completely lost as a deduction if they are capitalized.

8-6b Depletion Methods

There are two methods of calculating depletion. *Cost depletion* can be used on any wasting asset (and is the only method allowed for timber). *Percentage depletion* is subject to a number of limitations, particularly for oil and gas deposits. Depletion should be calculated both ways, and the method that results in the larger deduction should be used. The choice between cost depletion and percentage depletion is an annual decision; the taxpayer can use cost depletion in one year and percentage depletion in the following year.

Cost Depletion

Cost depletion resembles units-of-production depreciation.[43] The basis is divided by the estimated recoverable units of the asset (e.g., barrels and tons) to arrive at the depletion per unit. This amount then is multiplied by the number of units sold (*not* the units produced) during the year to arrive at the cost depletion allowed.

On January 1, 2017, Pablo purchases the rights to a mineral interest for $1 million. At that time, the remaining recoverable units in the mineral interest are estimated to be 200,000. The depletion per unit is $5 ($1,000,000 adjusted basis ÷ 200,000 estimated recoverable units).

If 60,000 units are mined and 25,000 are sold this year, the cost depletion is $125,000 ($5 depletion per unit × 25,000 units sold).

If the taxpayer later discovers that the original estimate was incorrect, the depletion per unit for future calculations is redetermined, using the revised estimate.[44]

Assume the same facts as in Example 43. In 2018, Pablo realizes that an incorrect estimate was made as to the capacity of the mine. The remaining recoverable units now are determined to be 400,000. Based on this new information, the revised depletion per unit is $2.1875 ($875,000 adjusted basis ÷ 400,000 estimated recoverable units). The $875,000 adjusted basis is the original cost ($1,000,000) reduced by the depletion claimed in 2017 ($125,000).

If 30,000 units are sold in 2018, the depletion for the year is $65,625 ($2.1875 depletion per unit × 30,000 units sold).

Percentage Depletion

Percentage depletion (also referred to as statutory depletion) uses a specified percentage provided by the Code. The percentage varies according to the type of mineral interest involved. A sample of these percentages is shown in Exhibit 8.2. The rate is applied to the gross income from the property, but in no event may percentage depletion exceed 50 percent of the taxable income from the property before the allowance for depletion.[45]

---

[43]§ 612.

[44]§ 611(a).

[45]§ 613(a). Special rules apply for certain oil and gas wells (e.g., the 50% ceiling is replaced with a 100% ceiling, and the percentage depletion may not exceed 65% of the taxpayer's taxable income from all sources before the allowance for depletion). § 613A.

EXHIBIT 8.2	Selected Percentage Depletion Rates

22% Depletion

Cobalt	Sulfur
Lead	Tin

15% Depletion

Copper	Oil, gas, oil shale
Gold	Silver

14% Depletion

Granite	Marble
Limestone	Potash

10% Depletion

Coal	Sodium chloride

5% Depletion

Gravel	Sand

EXAMPLE 45

CarrollCo reports gross income of $100,000 and other property-related expenses of $60,000 and uses a depletion rate of 22%. CarrollCo's depletion allowance is determined as follows.

Gross income	$100,000
Less: Other expenses	(60,000)
Taxable income before depletion	$ 40,000
Depletion allowance [the lesser of $22,000 (22% × $100,000) or $20,000 (50% × $40,000)]	(20,000)
Taxable income after depletion	$ 20,000

The adjusted basis of CarrollCo's property is reduced by $20,000, the depletion deduction allowed. If the other expenses had been only $55,000, the full $22,000 could have been deducted, and the adjusted basis would have been reduced by $22,000.

Note that percentage depletion is based on a percentage of the gross income from the property and makes no reference to cost. All other deductions detailed in this chapter are a function of the adjusted basis (cost) of the property. Thus, when percentage depletion is used, it is possible to claim aggregate depletion deductions that exceed the original cost of the property. If percentage depletion is used, however, the adjusted basis of the property (for computing cost depletion in a future tax year) is reduced by any depletion deducted, until the basis reaches zero.

EXAMPLE 46

Melissa reports the following related to her sulfur mine.

Remaining depletable basis	$ 11,000
Gross income (10,000 units)	100,000
Expenses (other than depletion)	30,000

Because cost depletion is limited to the remaining depletable basis of $11,000, Melissa would choose percentage depletion of $22,000 (a 22% depletion rate is used for sulfur). Her basis in the mine then becomes zero. In future years, however, she can continue to take percentage depletion; percentage depletion is computed without reference to the remaining basis.

LO.9

Identify tax planning opportunities for cost recovery, amortization, and depletion.

8-7 TAX PLANNING

8-7a Cost Recovery

Cost recovery schedules should be reviewed annually for possible retirements, abandonments, and obsolescence.

> **EXAMPLE 47**
>
> An examination of the cost recovery schedule of Eagle Company reveals:
>
> - Asset A was abandoned when it was discovered that the cost of repairs would be in excess of the cost of replacement. Asset A had an adjusted basis of $3,000.
> - Asset J became obsolete this year, at which point its adjusted basis was $8,000.
>
> Assets A and J should be written off, resulting in deductions of $11,000.

Because of the deductions for cost recovery, interest, and property taxes, investments in real estate can be highly attractive. When thinking about an investment in real estate, taxpayers should consider the tax savings generated by these deductions.

> **The Big Picture**
>
> **EXAMPLE 48**
>
> Return to the facts of *The Big Picture* on p. 8-1. In early January 2016, Dr. Payne purchased residential rental property for $170,000 (of which $20,000 was allocated to the land and $150,000 to the building). He made a down payment of $25,000 and assumed the seller's mortgage for the balance. Under the mortgage agreement, monthly payments of $1,000 are required and are applied toward interest, taxes, insurance, and principal.
>
> Because the property was already occupied, Payne continued to receive rent income of $1,200 per month from the tenant. He actively participates in this activity and so comes under the special rule for a rental real estate activity with respect to the limitation on passive activity losses (refer to Chapter 11). He is in the 28% tax bracket.
>
> For 2017, Payne's expenses included:
>
> | | |
> |---|---:|
> | Interest | $10,000 |
> | Taxes | 800 |
> | Insurance | 1,000 |
> | Repairs and maintenance | 2,200 |
> | Depreciation ($150,000 × .03636) | 5,454 |
> | Total expenses | $19,454 |
>
> The deductible loss from the rental property is:
>
> | | |
> |---|---:|
> | Rent income ($1,200 × 12 months) | $ 14,400 |
> | Less total expenses (see above) | (19,454) |
> | Net loss | ($ 5,054) |
>
> But what is Dr. Payne's net cash position for the year when the tax benefit of the loss is taken into account?
>
> | | | |
> |---|---:|---:|
> | Cash Inflows— | | |
> | Rent income | $14,400 | |
> | Tax savings [28% (income tax bracket) × $5,054 (loss from the property)] | 1,415 | $ 15,815 |
> | Cash Outflows— | | |
> | Mortgage payments ($1,000 × 12 months) | $12,000 | |
> | Repairs and maintenance | 2,200 | (14,200) |
> | Net cash benefit | | $ 1,615 |
>
> Should Payne cease to be an active participant in the rental activity, the passive activity loss rules would apply, and he could lose the current period benefit of the loss.

Another consideration when making decisions related to cost recovery is whether faster (or slower) cost recovery will be more beneficial for the taxpayer. If the taxpayer's goal is to recover the cost of fixed assets as quickly as possible, the following strategies should be used.

- When electing § 179 expensing, choose assets with longer lives.
- Choose accelerated cost recovery methods when available.

If a taxpayer has a new business with little income or a business with a net operating loss carryover, the taxpayer's goal may be to slow down cost recovery. In such a situation, the taxpayer should:

- Elect not to take additional first-year depreciation, if available.
- Choose the straight-line cost recovery method.
- Do not expense assets under § 179.
- Defer placing assets in service in the current tax year or postpone capital outlays until future tax years.

8-7b **Amortization**

When a business is purchased, goodwill and covenants not to compete are both subject to an amortization period of 15 years. Given that goodwill and covenants not to compete are treated the same from a tax perspective, bargaining for a covenant should be based on legal rather than tax reasons. The seller, however, may have different motives as goodwill is a capital asset, while a covenant is an ordinary income asset.

Because the amortization period for both goodwill and a covenant is 15 years, the purchaser may want to assign purchase costs to assets with shorter lives (e.g., inventory, receivables, and personalty). If, however, the purchase price will be assigned to assets with longer recovery periods (e.g., realty) or to assets not eligible for cost recovery (e.g., land), the purchaser would likely prefer costs to be assigned to goodwill or a covenant.

8-7c **Cost Recovery Tables**

Summary of Tables

Exhibit 8.3	Modified ACRS statutory percentage table for personalty.
	Applicable depreciation methods: 200 or 150 percent declining-balance switching to straight-line.
	Applicable recovery periods: 3, 5, 7, 10, 15, 20 years.
	Applicable convention: half-year.
Exhibit 8.4	Modified ACRS statutory percentage table for personalty.
	Applicable depreciation method: 200 percent declining-balance switching to straight-line.
	Applicable recovery periods: 3, 5, 7 years.
	Applicable convention: mid-quarter.
Exhibit 8.5	Modified ACRS optional straight-line table for personalty.
	Applicable depreciation method: straight-line.
	Applicable recovery periods: 3, 5, 7, 10, 15, 20 years.
	Applicable convention: half-year.
Exhibit 8.6	Alternative minimum tax declining-balance table for personalty.
	Applicable depreciation method: 150 percent declining-balance switching to straight-line.
	Applicable recovery periods: 3, 5, 7, 9.5, 10, 12 years.
	Applicable convention: half-year.

Summary of Tables

Exhibit 8.7	Alternative depreciation system straight-line table for personalty.
	Applicable depreciation method: straight-line.
	Applicable recovery periods: 5, 10, 12 years.
	Applicable convention: half-year.
Exhibit 8.8	Modified ACRS straight-line table for realty.
	Applicable depreciation method: straight-line.
	Applicable recovery periods: 27.5, 31.5, 39 years.
	Applicable convention: mid-month.
Exhibit 8.9	Alternative depreciation system straight-line table for realty.
	Applicable depreciation method: straight-line.
	Applicable recovery period: 40 years.
	Applicable convention: mid-month.

EXHIBIT 8.3   **MACRS Accelerated Depreciation for Personal Property Assuming Half-Year Convention**

For Property Placed in Service after December 31, 1986

Recovery Year	3-Year (200% DB)	5-Year (200% DB)	7-Year (200% DB)	10-Year (200% DB)	15-Year (150% DB)	20-Year (150% DB)
1	33.33	20.00	14.29	10.00	5.00	3.750
2	44.45	32.00	24.49	18.00	9.50	7.219
3	14.81*	19.20	17.49	14.40	8.55	6.677
4	7.41	11.52*	12.49	11.52	7.70	6.177
5		11.52	8.93*	9.22	6.93	5.713
6		5.76	8.92	7.37	6.23	5.285
7			8.93	6.55*	5.90*	4.888
8			4.46	6.55	5.90	4.522
9				6.56	5.91	4.462*
10				6.55	5.90	4.461
11				3.28	5.91	4.462
12					5.90	4.461
13					5.91	4.462
14					5.90	4.461
15					5.91	4.462
16					2.95	4.461
17						4.462
18						4.461
19						4.462
20						4.461
21						2.231

*Switchover to straight-line depreciation.

EXHIBIT 8.4	MACRS Accelerated Depreciation for Personal Property Assuming Mid-Quarter Convention

For Property Placed in Service after December 31, 1986 (Partial Table*)

Recovery Year	First Quarter	3-Year Second Quarter	Third Quarter	Fourth Quarter
1	58.33	41.67	25.00	8.33
2	27.78	38.89	50.00	61.11

Recovery Year	First Quarter	5-Year Second Quarter	Third Quarter	Fourth Quarter
1	35.00	25.00	15.00	5.00
2	26.00	30.00	34.00	38.00

Recovery Year	First Quarter	7-Year Second Quarter	Third Quarter	Fourth Quarter
1	25.00	17.85	10.71	3.57
2	21.43	23.47	25.51	27.55

*The figures in this table are taken from the official tables that appear in Rev.Proc. 87–57, 1987–2 C.B. 687. Because of their length, the complete tables are not presented.

EXHIBIT 8.5	MACRS Straight-Line Depreciation for Personal Property Assuming Half-Year Convention*

For Property Placed in Service after December 31, 1986

MACRS Class	% First Recovery Year	Other Recovery Years Years	%	Last Recovery Year Year	%
3-year	16.67	2–3	33.33	4	16.67
5-year	10.00	2–5	20.00	6	10.00
7-year	7.14	2–7	14.29	8	7.14
10-year	5.00	2–10	10.00	11	5.00
15-year	3.33	2–15	6.67	16	3.33
20-year	2.50	2–20	5.00	21	2.50

*The official table contains a separate row for each year. For ease of presentation, certain years are grouped in this table. In some instances, this will produce a difference of .01 for the last digit when compared with the official table.

EXHIBIT 8.6	Alternative Minimum Tax: 150% Declining-Balance Assuming Half-Year Convention

For Property Placed in Service after December 31, 1986 (Partial Table*)

Recovery Year	3-Year 150%	5-Year 150%	7-Year 150%	9.5-Year 150%	10-Year 150%	12-Year 150%
1	25.00	15.00	10.71	7.89	7.50	6.25
2	37.50	25.50	19.13	14.54	13.88	11.72
3	25.00**	17.85	15.03	12.25	11.79	10.25
4	12.50	16.66**	12.25**	10.31	10.02	8.97
5		16.66	12.25	9.17**	8.74**	7.85
6		8.33	12.25	9.17	8.74	7.33**
7			12.25	9.17	8.74	7.33
8			6.13	9.17	8.74	7.33
9				9.17	8.74	7.33
10				9.16	8.74	7.33
11					4.37	7.32
12						7.33
13						3.66

*The figures in this table are taken from the official table that appears in Rev.Proc. 87–57, 1987–2 C.B. 687. Because of its length, the complete table is not presented.
**Switchover to straight-line depreciation.

EXHIBIT 8.7	ADS Straight-Line for Personal Property Assuming Half-Year Convention

For Property Placed in Service after December 31, 1986 (Partial Table)*

Recovery Year	5-Year Class	10-Year Class	12-Year Class
1	10.00	5.00	4.17
2	20.00	10.00	8.33
3	20.00	10.00	8.33
4	20.00	10.00	8.33
5	20.00	10.00	8.33
6	10.00	10.00	8.33
7		10.00	8.34
8		10.00	8.33
9		10.00	8.34
10		10.00	8.33
11		5.00	8.34
12			8.33
13			4.17

*The figures in this table are taken from the official table that appears in Rev.Proc. 87–57, 1987–2 C.B. 687. Because of its length, the complete table is not presented. The tables for the mid-quarter convention also appear in Rev.Proc. 87–57.

EXHIBIT 8.8	MACRS Straight-Line Depreciation for Real Property Assuming Mid-Month Convention*

For Property Placed in Service after December 31, 1986: 27.5-Year Residential Real Property

Recovery Year(s)	The Applicable Percentage Is (Use the Column for the Month in the First Year the Property Is Placed in Service):											
	1	2	3	4	5	6	7	8	9	10	11	12
1	3.485	3.182	2.879	2.576	2.273	1.970	1.667	1.364	1.061	0.758	0.455	0.152
2–18	3.636	3.636	3.636	3.636	3.636	3.636	3.636	3.636	3.636	3.636	3.636	3.636
19–27	3.637	3.637	3.637	3.637	3.637	3.637	3.637	3.637	3.637	3.637	3.637	3.637
28	1.970	2.273	2.576	2.879	3.182	3.485	3.636	3.636	3.636	3.636	3.636	3.636
29	0.000	0.000	0.000	0.000	0.000	0.000	0.152	0.455	0.758	1.061	1.364	1.667

For Property Placed in Service after December 31, 1986, and before May 13, 1993: 31.5-Year Nonresidential Real Property

Recovery Year(s)	The Applicable Percentage Is (Use the Column for the Month in the First Year the Property Is Placed in Service):											
	1	2	3	4	5	6	7	8	9	10	11	12
1	3.042	2.778	2.513	2.249	1.984	1.720	1.455	1.190	0.926	0.661	0.397	0.132
2–19	3.175	3.175	3.175	3.175	3.175	3.175	3.175	3.175	3.175	3.175	3.175	3.175
20–31	3.174	3.174	3.174	3.174	3.174	3.174	3.174	3.174	3.174	3.174	3.174	3.174
32	1.720	1.984	2.249	2.513	2.778	3.042	3.175	3.175	3.175	3.175	3.175	3.175
33	0.000	0.000	0.000	0.000	0.000	0.000	0.132	0.397	0.661	0.926	1.190	1.455

For Property Placed in Service after May 12, 1993: 39-Year Nonresidential Real Property

Recovery Year(s)	The Applicable Percentage Is (Use the Column for the Month in the First Year the Property Is Placed in Service):											
	1	2	3	4	5	6	7	8	9	10	11	12
1	2.461	2.247	2.033	1.819	1.605	1.391	1.177	0.963	0.749	0.535	0.321	0.107
2–39	2.564	2.564	2.564	2.564	2.564	2.564	2.564	2.564	2.564	2.564	2.564	2.564
40	0.107	0.321	0.535	0.749	0.963	1.177	1.391	1.605	1.819	2.033	2.247	2.461

*The official tables contain a separate row for each year. For ease of presentation, certain years are grouped in these tables. In some instances, this will produce a difference of .001 for the last digit when compared with the official tables.

EXHIBIT 8.9	ADS Straight-Line for Real Property Assuming Mid-Month Convention

For Property Placed in Service after December 31, 1986

Recovery Year	Month Placed in Service											
	1	2	3	4	5	6	7	8	9	10	11	12
1	2.396	2.188	1.979	1.771	1.563	1.354	1.146	0.938	0.729	0.521	0.313	0.104
2–40	2.500	2.500	2.500	2.500	2.500	2.500	2.500	2.500	2.500	2.500	2.500	2.500
41	0.104	0.312	0.521	0.729	0.937	1.146	1.354	1.562	1.771	1.979	2.187	2.396

REFOCUS ON THE BIG PICTURE

CALCULATING COST RECOVERY DEDUCTIONS

Regardless of whether the accrual method or the cash method of accounting is used, MACRS must be used to calculate the cost recovery of fixed assets for tax purposes. Evidently, Dr. Payne's financial reporting system uses MACRS, because $91,298 is the correct amount of cost recovery. The computers and peripheral equipment are 5-year property. The office furniture and fixtures and the dental equipment are 7-year property.

Based on the IRS cost recovery tables, the following percentages are used in calculating depreciation expense for the first year of each asset's life.

5-year property	20.00%
7-year property	14.29%

Payne can deduct depreciation on the house he converted from personal use to rental use and on the rental house he purchased.

What If?

From a tax planning perspective, what can Dr. Payne do to increase the cost recovery deductions associated with the purchase of these fixed assets and reduce the amount of the business net income reported on Schedule C of Form 1040 for his dental practice?

In addition to the standard MACRS deduction using the percentages for 2017, § 179 allows the immediate expensing of fixed assets. This provision applies to personalty, but does not apply to realty (e.g., buildings). The maximum amount that can be deducted under § 179 is subject to several overall limits. First, the total amount deducted cannot exceed $510,000. Second, maximum amount is reduced dollar for dollar for any § 179 assets placed in service in excess of $2,030,000. Finally, the § 179 deduction cannot exceed the taxable income from the business.

If Payne elects § 179 treatment for some of the fixed asset purchases of his dental practice, he can reduce the Schedule C net income of his dental practice beyond the $91,298 of depreciation expense computed using MACRS to a maximum of $510,000 § 179 expense for 2017.

The remaining amount of the $612,085 purchases of § 179 assets not deducted in the current year are also eligible for additional first-year depreciation and MACRS cost recovery. The sequence of calculating the cost recovery deduction is, in order:

- § 179 immediate expensing.
- Additional first-year depreciation.
- Standard MACRS cost recovery.

ERSLER DMITRY/SHUTTERSTOCK.COM

Key Terms

Discussion Questions

1. **LO.1** Discuss whether property that is classified as personal use is subject to cost recovery.

2. **LO.1** Discuss the difference between personal property and personal use property.

3. **LO.1** Discuss whether land improvements used in a trade or business are eligible for cost recovery.

4. **LO.2** At the beginning of the current year, Henry purchased a ski resort for $10 million. Henry does not own the land on which the resort is located. The Federal government owns the land, and Henry has the right to operate the resort on the land pursuant to Special Use Permits, which are terminable at will by the Federal government, and Term Special Use Permits, which allow the land to be used for a fixed number of years.   **Issue ID**

    In preparing the income tax return for the current year, Henry properly allocated $2 million of the purchase price to the costs of constructing mountain roads, slopes, and trails. Since the acquisition, Henry has spent an additional $1 million on maintaining the mountain roads, slopes, and trails. Identify the relevant tax issues for Henry.

5. **LO.2** Identify the three factors reflected in the MACRS tables when the amount of cost recovery is determined.

6. **LO.2** Discuss the computation of cost recovery in the year an asset is placed in service when the mid-quarter convention is being used.

7. **LO.2** Discuss the computation of cost recovery in the year of sale of an asset when the mid-quarter convention is being used.

8. **LO.2** Robert purchased and placed in service $100,000 of 7-year class assets on August 10 of the current year. He also purchased and placed in service $500,000 of 5-year class assets on November 15 of the current year. He does not claim any available additional first-year depreciation. If Robert elects to use the MACRS straight-line method of cost recovery on the 7-year class assets, discuss the calculation of cost recovery for the 5-year class assets.

9. **LO.2** Jim owns a very large ranch. A large part of his business is the production and raising of breeding cattle. Jim understands that he is entitled to use MACRS cost recovery on breeding cattle. Identify the relevant tax issues for Jim with respect to taking cost recovery on his self-produced breeding cattle.   **Issue ID**

10. **LO.3** Discuss when § 179 expense must be recaptured.

11. **LO.3** Explain how the § 179 immediate expensing deduction affects the computation of MACRS cost recovery.

12. **LO.3** Discuss the treatment of a § 179 expensing carryforward.

13. **LO.3** Discuss the definition of *taxable income* as it is used in limiting the § 179 expensing amount.

14. **LO.2, 3** A professional consulting business sells professional tools and equipment and provides associated services, such as repair and maintenance, to its customer base. The company's employees include technicians, who are required to provide and maintain their own tools and equipment for performing the repairs and maintenance work. The company will reimburse a technician for amounts spent to purchase tools and equipment eligible for a § 179 deduction up to a set amount each year. Any costs for tools and equipment that exceed the set amount will not be reimbursed.   **Issue ID**

    John is a technician for the company. During the current year, he purchased equipment that qualifies for the § 179 deduction. John paid $50,000 for the equipment and was reimbursed the set amount of $40,000. Identify the relevant tax issues for John with respect to § 179 and the computation of his taxable income.

15. **LO.4** Discuss how the limits on cost recovery apply to listed property.

16. **LO.4** Discuss the tax consequences if the business use percentage of listed property falls to 50% or lower after the year the property is placed in service.

17. **LO.7** Explain the amortization period of a § 197 intangible if the actual useful life is less than 15 years.

Issue ID 18. **LO.7** Harold and Bart own 75% of the stock of Orange Motors. The other 25% of the stock is owned by Jeb. Orange Motors entered into an agreement with Harold and Bart to acquire all of their Orange stock.

In addition, Harold and Bart signed a noncompete agreement with Orange Motors. Under the terms of the noncompete agreement, Orange will pay Harold and Bart $15,000 each per year for four years. Identify the relevant tax issues for Orange Motors.

Issue ID 19. **LO.7** In May 2017, George began searching for a trade or business to acquire. In anticipation of finding a suitable aquisition, George hired an investment banker to evaluate three potential businesses. He also hired a law firm to begin drafting regulatory approval documents for a target company. Eventually, George decided to purchase all of the assets of Brash Corporation. Brash and George entered into an acquisition agreement on December 1, 2017. Identify the relevant tax issues for George.

20. **LO.8** Discuss how the cost of mineral rights enters into the calculation of cost depletion.

Computational Exercises

21. **LO.2** Euclid acquires a 7-year class asset on May 9, 2017, for $80,000. Euclid does not elect immediate expensing under § 179. She does not claim any available additional first-year depreciation. Calculate Euclid's cost recovery deduction for 2017 and 2018.

22. **LO.2** Hamlet acquires a 7-year class asset on November 23, 2017, for $100,000. Hamlet does not elect immediate expensing under § 179. He does not claim any available additional first-year depreciation. Calculate Hamlet's cost recovery deductions for 2017 and 2018.

23. **LO.2** Lopez acquired a building on June 1, 2012, for $1 million. Calculate Lopez's cost recovery deduction for 2017 if the building is:
   a.   Classified as residential rental real estate.
   b.   Classified as nonresidential real estate.

24. **LO.2** Andre acquired a computer on March 3, 2017, for $2,800. He elects the straight-line method for cost recovery. Andre does not elect immediate expensing under § 179. He does not claim any available additional first-year depreciation. Calculate Andre's cost recovery deduction for the computer for tax years 2017 and 2018.

25. **LO.2** Diana acquires, for $65,000, and places in service a 5-year class asset on December 19, 2017. It is the only asset that Diana acquires during 2017. Diana does not elect immediate expensing under § 179. She elects additional first-year deprecation. Calculate Diana's total cost recovery deduction for 2017.

26. **LO.3** McKenzie purchased qualifying equipment for his business that cost $212,000 in 2017. The taxable income of the business for the year is $5,600 before consideration of any § 179 deduction. Calculate McKenzie's § 179 expense deduction for 2017 and any carryover to 2018.

27. **LO.4** On April 5, 2017, Kinsey places in service a new automobile that cost $36,000. He does not elect § 179 expensing, and he elects not to take any available additional first-year depreciation. The car is used 70% for business and 30% for personal use in each tax year.

    Kinsey chooses the MACRS 200% declining-balance method of cost recovery (the auto is a 5-year asset). Assume the following luxury automobile limitations: year 1: $3,160; year 2: $5,100. Compute the total depreciation allowed for 2017 and 2018.

28. **LO.7** On September 30, 2017, Priscilla purchased a business. Of the purchase price, $60,000 is allocated to a patent and $375,000 is allocated to goodwill. Calculate Priscilla's 2017 § 197 amortization deduction.

29. **LO.8** On March 25, 2017, Parscale Company purchases the rights to a mineral interest for $8 million. At that time, the remaining recoverable units in the mineral interest are estimated to be 500,000 tons. If 80,000 tons are mined and 75,000 tons are sold this year, calculate Parscale's cost depletion for 2017.

30. **LO.8** Jebali Company reports gross income of $340,000 and other property-related expenses of $229,000 and uses a depletion rate of 14%. Calculate Jebali's depletion allowance for the current year.

Problems

31. **LO.1, 2** On November 4, 2015, Blue Company acquired an asset (27.5-year residential real property) for $200,000 for use in its business. In 2015 and 2016, respectively, Blue took $642 and $5,128 of cost recovery. These amounts were incorrect; Blue applied the wrong percentages (i.e., those for 39-year rather than 27.5-year assets). Blue should have taken $910 and $7,272 cost recovery in 2015 and 2016, respectively.

    On January 1, 2017, the asset was sold for $180,000. Calculate the gain or loss on the sale of the asset for that year.

32. **LO.1, 2** José purchased a house for $300,000 in 2014. He used the house as his personal residence. In March 2017, when the fair market value of the house was $400,000, he converted the house to rental property. What is José's cost recovery for 2017?

33. **LO.2** Orange Corporation acquired new office furniture on August 15, 2017, for $130,000. Orange does not elect immediate expensing under § 179. Orange claims any available additional first-year depreciation. Determine Orange's cost recovery for 2017.

34. **LO.2** Weston acquires a new office machine (7-year class asset) on November 2, 2016, for $75,000. This is the only asset Weston acquired during the year. He does not elect immediate expensing under § 179. He claims the maximum additional first-year depreciation deduction. On September 15, 2017, Weston sells the machine.
    a. Determine Weston's cost recovery for 2016.
    b. Determine Weston's cost recovery for 2017.

35. **LO.2** Juan acquires a new 5-year class asset on March 14, 2017, for $200,000. This is the only asset Juan acquired during the year. He does not elect immediate expensing under § 179. He does not claim any available additional first-year depreciation. On July 15, 2018, Juan sells the asset.
    a. Determine Juan's cost recovery for 2017.
    b. Determine Juan's cost recovery for 2018.

36. **LO.2** Debra acquired the following new assets during 2017.

Date	Asset	Cost
April 11	Furniture	$40,000
July 28	Trucks	40,000
November 3	Computers	70,000

Determine Debra's cost recovery deductions for the current year. Debra does not elect immediate expensing under § 179. She does not claim any available additional first-year depreciation.

37. **LO.2** On August 2, 2017, Wendy purchased a new office building for $3.8 million. On October 1, 2017, she began to rent out office space in the building. On July 15, 2021, Wendy sold the office building.

    a. Determine Wendy's cost recovery deduction for 2017.
    b. Determine Wendy's cost recovery deduction for 2021.

38. **LO.2** On April 3, 2017, Terry purchased and placed in service a building that cost $2 million. An appraisal determined that 25% of the total cost was attributed to the value of the land. The bottom floor of the building is leased to a retail business for $32,000. The other floors of the building are rental apartments with an annual rent of $160,000. Determine Terry's cost recovery deduction for 2017.

39. **LO.2** On May 5, 2017, Christy purchased and placed in service a hotel. The hotel cost $10.8 million, and the land cost $1.2 million ($12 million in total). Calculate Christy's cost recovery deductions for 2017 and for 2027.

40. **LO.2** Janice acquired an apartment building on June 4, 2017, for $1.6 million. The value of the land is $300,000. Janice sold the apartment building on November 29, 2023.

    a. Determine Janice's cost recovery deduction for 2017.
    b. Determine Janice's cost recovery deduction for 2023.

Decision Making   41. **LO.2, 3, 9** Lori, who is single, purchased 5-year class property for $200,000 and 7-year class property for $410,000 on May 20, 2017. Lori expects the taxable income derived from her business (without regard to the amount expensed under § 179) to be about $800,000. Lori wants to elect immediate § 179 expensing, but she doesn't know which asset she should expense under § 179. She does not claim any available additional first-year depreciation.

    a. Determine Lori's total cost recovery deduction if the § 179 expense is first taken with respect to the 5-year class asset.
    b. Determine Lori's total cost recovery deduction if the § 179 expense is first taken with respect to the 7-year class asset.
    c. What is your advice to Lori?
    d. Assume that Lori is in the 25% marginal tax bracket and that she uses § 179 on the 7-year asset. Determine the present value of the tax savings from the depreciation deductions for both assets. See Appendix H for present value factors, and assume a 6% discount rate.
    e. Assume the same facts as in part (d), except that Lori decides not to use § 179 on either asset. What is the present value of the tax savings generated by using the § 179 deduction on the 7-year asset?

42. **LO.2, 3** Olga is the proprietor of a small business. In 2017, the business's income, before consideration of any cost recovery or § 179 deduction, is $250,000.

    Olga spends $610,000 on new 7-year class assets and elects to take the § 179 deduction on them. She does not claim any available additional first-year depreciation. Olga's cost recovery deduction for 2017, except for the cost recovery with respect to the new 7-year assets, is $95,000. Determine Olga's total cost recovery for 2017 with respect to the 7-year class assets and the amount of any § 179 carryforward.

43. **LO.2, 3, 9** On June 5, 2016, Javier Sanchez purchased and placed in service a new 7-year class asset costing $550,000 for use in his landscaping business, which he operates as a single member LLC (Sanchez Landscaping LLC). During 2016, his business generated a net income of $945,780 before any § 179 immediate expense election.

   a. Determine the maximum deductions that Javier can claim with respect to this asset in 2016 and 2017.

   b. Complete Javier's Form 4562 (page 1) for 2016. His Social Security number is 123-45-6789.

44. **LO.3, 4** Jabari Johnson is considering acquiring an automobile at the beginning of 2017 that he will use 100% of the time as a taxi. The purchase price of the automobile is $35,000. Johnson has heard of cost recovery limits on automobiles and wants to know how much of the $35,000 he can deduct in the first year.

   Communications

   Write a letter to Jabari in which you present your calculations. Also prepare a memo for the tax files, summarizing your analysis. Johnson's address is 100 Morningside, Clinton, MS 39058.

45. **LO.2, 4** On October 15, 2017, Jon purchased and placed in service a used car. The purchase price was $25,000. This was the only business use asset Jon acquired in 2017. He used the car 80% of the time for business and 20% for personal use. Jon used the MACRS statutory percentage method. Calculate the total cost recovery deduction Jon may take for 2017 with respect to the car.

46. **LO.4** On June 5, 2016, Leo purchased and placed in service a new car that cost $20,000. The business use percentage for the car is always 100%. Leo claims any available additional first-year depreciation. Compute Leo's cost recovery deductions for 2016 and 2017.

47. **LO.2, 3, 4** On March 15, 2017, Helen purchased and placed in service a new Escalade. The purchase price was $62,000, and the vehicle had a rating of 6,500 GVW. The vehicle was used 100% for business. Calculate the maximum total depreciation deduction that Helen may take with respect to the vehicle for 2017.

48. **LO.2, 4** On May 28, 2017, Mary purchased and placed in service a new $20,000 car. The car was used 60% for business, 20% for production of income, and 20% for personal use in 2017. In 2018, the usage changed to 40% for business, 30% for production of income, and 30% for personal use. Mary did not elect immediate expensing under § 179. She did not claim any available additional first-year depreciation. Compute Mary's cost recovery deduction and any cost recovery recapture for 2018.

49. **LO.2, 4, 9** Sally purchased a new computer (5-year property) on June 1, 2017, for $4,000. Sally could use the computer 100% of the time in her business, or she could allow her family to use the computer as well. Sally estimates that if her family uses the computer, the business use will be 45% and the personal use will be 55%.

   Decision Making

   Determine the tax cost to Sally, in the year of acquisition, of allowing her family to use the computer. Assume that Sally would not elect § 179 immediate expensing, and that her marginal tax rate is 28%. She does not claim any available additional first-year depreciation.

50. **LO.2, 4, 9** Dennis Harding is considering acquiring a new automobile that he will use 100% for business. The purchase price of the automobile would be $48,500. If Dennis leased the car for five years, the lease payments would be $375 per month. Dennis will acquire the car on January 1, 2017. The inclusion dollar amounts from the IRS table for the next five years are $59, $128, $191, $228, and $264.

   Decision Making
   Communications

Dennis wants to know the effect on his adjusted gross income of purchasing versus leasing the car for the next five years. He does not claim any available additional first-year depreciation. Write a letter to Dennis, and present your calculations. Then prepare a memo for the tax files on these matters. Dennis's address is 150 Avenue I, Memphis, TN 38112.

51. **LO.2, 5** In 2017, Muhammad purchased a new computer for $16,000. The computer is used 100% for business. Muhammad did not make a § 179 election with respect to the computer. He does not claim any available additional first-year depreciation. If Muhammad uses the MACRS statutory percentage method, determine his cost recovery deduction for 2017 for computing taxable income and for computing his alternative minimum tax.

Decision Making   52. **LO.2, 5, 9** Jamie purchased $100,000 of new office furniture for her business in June of the current year. Jamie understands that if she elects to use ADS to compute her regular income tax, there will be no difference between the cost recovery for computing the regular income tax and the AMT.

a. Jamie wants to know the present value of the *tax cost*, after three years, of using ADS rather than MACRS. Assume that Jamie does not elect § 179 expensing, she does not claim any additional first-year depreciation, and her marginal tax rate is 28%. See Appendix H for present value factors, and assume a 6% discount rate.

b. What is the present value of the tax savings/costs that result over the life of the asset if Jamie uses MACRS rather than ADS?

Decision Making   53. **LO.2, 7, 9** Mike Saxon is negotiating the purchase of a business. The final purchase
Communications   price has been agreed upon, but the allocation of the purchase price to the assets is still being discussed. Appraisals on a warehouse range from $1.2 million to $1.5 million. If a value of $1.2 million is used for the warehouse, the remainder of the purchase price, $800,000, will be allocated to goodwill. If $1.5 million is allocated to the warehouse, goodwill will be $500,000.

Mike wants to know what effect each alternative will have on cost recovery and amortization during the first year. Under the agreement, Mike will take over the business on January 1 of next year. Write a letter to Mike in which you present your calculations and recommendation. Then prepare a memo for the tax files, addressing these matters. Mike's address is 200 Rolling Hills Drive, Shavertown, PA 18708.

54. **LO.7** Oleander Corporation, a calendar year entity, begins business on March 1, 2017. The corporation incurs startup expenditures of $64,000. If Oleander elects § 195 treatment, determine the total amount of startup expenditures that it may deduct for 2017.

55. **LO.7** Martha was considering starting a new business. During her preliminary investigations related to the new venture, she incurred the following expenditures.

Salaries	$22,000
Travel	18,000
Interest on short-term note	4,000
Professional fees	13,000

Martha begins the business on July 1 of the current year. If Martha elects § 195 treatment, determine her startup expenditure deduction for the current year.

56. **LO.8** Wes acquired a mineral interest during the year for $10 million. A geological survey estimated that 250,000 tons of the mineral remained in the deposit. During the year, 80,000 tons were mined, and 45,000 tons were sold for $12 million. Other related expenses amounted to $5 million. Assuming that the mineral depletion rate is 22%, calculate Wes's lowest taxable income, after any depletion deductions.

57. Janice Morgan, age 24, is single and has no dependents. She is a freelance writer. In January 2016, Janice opened her own office located at 2751 Waldham Road, Pleasant Hill, NM 88135. She called her business Writers Anonymous. Janice is a cash basis taxpayer. She lives at 132 Stone Avenue, Pleasant Hill, NM 88135. Her Social Security number is 123-45-6789. Janice's parents continue to provide health insurance for her under their policy. Janice wants to contribute to the Presidential Election Campaign Fund.

Tax Return Problem

TAX SOFTWARE

During 2016, Janice reported the following income and expense items connected with her business.

Income from sale of articles	$85,000
Rent	16,500
Utilities	7,900
Supplies	1,800
Insurance	5,000
Travel (including meals of $1,200)	3,500

Janice purchased and placed in service the following fixed assets for her business. Janice wants to elect immediate expensing under § 179, if possible.

- Furniture and fixtures (new) costing $21,000 on January 10.
- Computer equipment (new) costing $12,400 on July 28.

Janice's itemized deductions include:

State income tax	$2,950
Home mortgage interest paid to First National Bank	6,000
Property taxes on home	1,500
Charitable contribution to her alma mater, State College	1,200

Janice did not keep a record of the sales tax she paid. The amount from the sales tax table is $437.

Janice reports interest income of $4,000 on certificates of deposit at Second National Bank. Janice makes estimated tax payments of $3,000 for 2016.

Compute Janice Morgan's 2016 Federal income tax payable (or refund due). If you use tax forms for your computations, you will need Forms 1040 and 4562 and Schedules A, B, and C. Suggested software: H&R BLOCK Tax Software.

58. John Smith, age 31, is single and has no dependents. At the beginning of 2017, John started his own excavation business and named it Earth Movers. John lives at 1045 Center Street, Lindon, UT, and his business is located at 381 State Street, Lindon, UT. The ZIP Code for both addresses is 84042. John's Social Security number is 111-11-1111, and the business identification number is 11-1111111. John is a cash basis taxpayer. During 2017, John reports the following items in connection with his business.

Tax Computation Problem

Decision Making

Communications

Fee income for services rendered	$912,000
Building rental expense	36,000
Office furniture and equipment rental expense	9,000
Office supplies	2,500
Utilities	4,000
Salary for secretary	34,000
Salary for equipment operators	42,000
Payroll taxes	7,000
Fuel and oil for the equipment	21,000
Purchase of three new front-end loaders on January 15, 2017, for $560,000	560,000
Purchase of a new dump truck on January 18, 2017	80,000

During 2017, John recorded the following additional items.

Interest income from First National Bank	$10,000
Dividends from ExxonMobil	9,500
Quarterly estimated tax payments	11,500

John makes the election under § 179 on the three front-end loaders purchased in January. John claims any available additional first-year depreciation.

On October 8, 2017, John inherited IBM stock from his Aunt Mildred. John had been her favorite nephew. According to the data provided by the executor of Aunt Mildred's estate, the stock was valued for estate tax purposes at $110,000. John is considering selling the IBM stock for $125,000 on December 29, 2017, and using $75,000 of the proceeds to purchase an Acura ZDX. He would use the car 100% for business. John wants to know what effect these transactions would have on his 2017 adjusted gross income.

Write a letter to John in which you present your calculations, and prepare a memo for the tax files. Ignore any Federal self-employment tax implications.

Research Problems

Note: Solutions to the Research Problems can be prepared by using the Thomson Reuters Checkpoint® Student Edition online tax research database, which accompanies this textbook. Solutions can also be prepared by using research materials found in a typical tax library.

Communications

Research Problem 1. Your client, Dave's Sport Shop, sells sports equipment and clothing in three retail outlets in New York City. During 2017, the CFO decided that keeping track of inventory using a combination of QuickBooks and Excel was not an efficient way to manage the stores' inventories. So Dave's purchased an inventory management system for $9,000 that allowed the entity to keep track of inventory, as well as automate ordering and purchasing, without replacing QuickBooks for its accounting function.

The CFO would like to know whether the cost of the inventory management program can be expensed in the year of purchase. Write a letter to the CFO, Cassandra Martin, that addresses the tax treatment of purchased software. Cassandra's mailing address is 867 Broadway, New York, NY 10003.

Research Problem 2. In 2013, Jed James began planting a vineyard. The costs of the land preparation, labor, rootstock, and planting were capitalized. The land preparation costs do not include any nondepreciable land costs. In 2017, when the plants became viable, Jed placed the vineyard in service. Jed wants to know whether he can claim a deduction under § 179 on his 2017 income tax return for the 2013 costs for planting the vineyard.

Research Problem 3. Juan owns a business that acquires exotic automobiles that are high-tech, state-of-the-art vehicles with unique design features or equipment. The exotic automobiles are not licensed or set up to be used on the road. Rather, the cars are used exclusively for car shows or related promotional photography. With respect to the exotic automobiles, Juan would like to know whether he can take a cost recovery deduction on his Federal income tax return.

Partial list of research aids:
Bruce Selig, 70 TCM 1125, T.C.Memo. 1995–519.

Use internet tax resources to address the following questions. Look for reliable websites and blogs of the IRS and other government agencies, media outlets, businesses, tax professionals, academics, think tanks, and political outlets.

Research Problem 4. Locate a financial calculator program that assesses the wisdom of buying versus leasing a new car. Install the program on your computer, and become familiar with it. Use the program to work through Problem 50 in this chapter.

Research Problem 5. Changes to depreciation systems often are discussed by policy-makers and observers of the tax system. Outline the terms and policy objectives of one of the changes currently proposed by the Treasury, a member of Congress, or a tax policy think tank.

Communications

Roger CPA Review Questions

1. Quanti Co., a calendar year taxpayer, purchased small tools for $5,000 on December 21, 2017, representing the company's *only* purchase of tangible personal property that took place during 2017. On its 2017 tax return, how many months of MACRS depreciation may Quanti Co. claim on the tools, assuming that it does not use § 179 (immediate expensing)?

   a. One-and-a-half months
   b. One month
   c. Six months
   d. None

2. Which of the following is *correct* about depreciation under Federal tax law?

   I. The recovery period is longer than the useful life of the asset.
   II. There are different recovery periods for new and used property.
   III. Salvage values are ignored.

   a. I and II only
   b. II only
   c. III only
   d. I, II, and III

3. Joe purchased a van on February 1, 2017, for use in his business, Crew Airport Transport. The van was purchased for $30,000, has an estimated useful life of 10 years, and has a salvage value of $2,000. No other assets were put into service that year. What is Joe's MACRS depreciation for the van for 2017?

   a. $2,567
   b. $6,000
   c. $10,500
   d. $10,267

4. In 2017, Dolly purchased and placed into service qualifying depreciable property at a total cost of $2,280,000. Dolly has elected to take the § 179 deduction. What is Dolly's § 179 deduction for 2017?

   a. $0
   b. $260,000
   c. $510,000
   d. $1,770,000

5. In 2017, Christa purchased and placed into service five-year assets at a total cost of $2,290,000. If Christa elects both the § 179 deduction and additional first-year (bonus) depreciation, but does not elect the straight-line method, what is Christa's depreciation expense for tax purposes for the year, assuming a half-year convention?

   a. $250,000
   b. $510,000
   c. $1,270,000
   d. $1,474,000

CHAPTER 9

Deductions: Employee and Self-Employed-Related Expenses

LEARNING OBJECTIVES: *After completing Chapter 9, you should be able to:*

LO.1 Distinguish between employee and self-employed (independent contractor) status.

LO.2 Recognize deductible transportation expenses.

LO.3 Describe how travel expenses are treated.

LO.4 Determine the moving expense deduction.

LO.5 Differentiate between deductible and nondeductible education expenses.

LO.6 Explain how entertainment and meal expenses are treated.

LO.7 Identify other employee expenses.

LO.8 Compare various deductions for contributions to retirement accounts.

LO.9 Demonstrate the difference between accountable and nonaccountable employee plans.

LO.10 Apply the limitations on miscellaneous itemized deductions.

LO.11 List and evaluate tax planning ideas related to employee business expenses.

CHAPTER OUTLINE

ISTOCKPHOTO.COM/SVETIKD

THE FIRST JOB

After an extensive search, Morgan, a recent college graduate with a major in child development, has accepted a job with Enrichment Child Care Center (ECCC) in a neighboring state. ECCC is located in the western suburbs of a large metropolitan city, roughly 30 miles from the center of the city. Morgan will be moving into a two-bedroom apartment about two miles from ECCC. At ECCC, Morgan will work with pre-school children Monday to Friday from 7 A.M. to 3 P.M. One of the reasons she accepted the position at ECCC is the flexibility it provides. Because she is eager to pay off her student loans and save to buy a house, she has decided to freelance in the late afternoons and evenings and on weekends—joining the "gig economy."

She finds two ways to freelance: (1) transporting people, packages, and meals for a few companies where she finds work through the "app" (such as driving for Uber) and (2) tutoring elementary school students in English and math. Her tutoring can take place online or in person (either in her apartment or at the home of the child). She has dedicated the second bedroom in her apartment for freelancing. She has a large table and several chairs in this bedroom that allow her to meet her tutoring students or connect with them via her laptop. She keeps all of her freelancing records in a file cabinet, which she keeps in a closet in the bedroom. She also purchases and keeps various supplies for her tutoring activities in the closet. Although there are some freelance driving options in the suburbs, most often Morgan heads for the city, where there are more passengers and higher fares.

What are some of the income tax problems presented by this situation?

Read the chapter and formulate your response.

FRAMEWORK 1040 **Tax Formula for Individuals**

This chapter covers the boldfaced portions of the Tax Formula for Individuals that was introduced in Concept Summary 3.1 on p. 3-3. Below those portions are the sections of Form 1040 where the results are reported.

Income *(broadly defined)*	$xx,xxx
Less: Exclusions	(x,xxx)
Gross income	$xx,xxx
Less: **Deductions** *for* adjusted gross income	(x,xxx)

FORM 1040 (p. 1)

12	Business income or (loss). Attach Schedule C or C-EZ			
23	Educator expenses	**23**		
24	Certain business expenses of reservists, performing artists, and fee-basis government officials. Attach Form 2106 or 2106-EZ	**24**		
26	Moving expenses. Attach Form 3903	**26**		
32	IRA deduction	**32**		
34	Tuition and fees. Attach Form 8917	**34**		

Adjusted gross income	$xx,xxx
Less: The greater of total **itemized deductions** *or* the standard deduction	(x,xxx)

FORM 1040 (p. 2)

40	**Itemized deductions** (from Schedule A) **or** your **standard deduction** (see left margin)	

Personal and dependency exemptions	(x,xxx)
Taxable income	$xx,xxx
Tax on taxable income *(see Tax Tables or Tax Rate Schedules)*	$ x,xxx
Less: Tax credits *(including income taxes withheld and prepaid)*	(xxx)
Tax due (or refund)	$ xxx

onsidering the large number of taxpayers affected, the tax treatment of job-related expenses is unusually complex. To resolve this complexity, a number of key questions must be asked:

- Is the taxpayer an *employee* or *self-employed?*
- If an employee, what expenses *qualify* as deductions?
- How are the deductible expenses *classified* for tax purposes (*for* AGI or *from* AGI)?
- To the extent the expenses are classified as deductions *from* AGI, are they subject to any *limitation?*

In addition to answering these questions, the chapter also discusses tax planning opportunities to maximize the deductibility of employee and self-employed expenses.

LO.1

Distinguish between employee and self-employed (independent contractor) status.

9-1 EMPLOYEE VERSUS INDEPENDENT CONTRACTOR

When one person performs services for another, the person performing the service either is an employee or is self-employed (an independent contractor). Failure to recognize a person's work status correctly can have serious tax consequences (in addition to Federal and state labor law consequences). Tax deficiencies as well as interest and penalties may result from improper classification.

Unlike employees, self-employed persons do not have to be included in various fringe benefit programs (e.g., group term life insurance and retirement plans). Because self-employed persons are not covered by FICA and FUTA (see Chapter 1), a business also avoids these payroll costs. The IRS is very much aware of the tendency of businesses to attempt to classify workers as self-employed rather than as employees.

Employment status also makes a great deal of difference to the person who performs the services. Expenses of self-employed taxpayers, if deductible, are classified as deductions *for* AGI and are reported on Schedule C (Profit or Loss From Business) of Form 1040.[1] With the exception of reimbursement under an accountable plan (discussed later in the chapter), expenses of employees are deductions *from* AGI. They are reported on Form 2106 (Employee Business Expenses) and Schedule A (Itemized Deductions) of Form 1040.[2]

Most persons classified as employees are common law employees. The common law employee classification originated in the courts and is summarized in various IRS pronouncements.[3] Revenue Ruling 87–41, for example, lists 20 factors that can be used to determine whether a worker is a common law employee or an independent contractor (and, thus, self-employed).[4] The IRS has indicated that these 20 factors can be grouped into three broad categories: behavioral control, financial control, and the relationship of the parties.

An employee-employer relationship exists when the employer has the right to specify the end result and the ways and means by which that result is to be attained.[5] In general, this means that a worker is classified as an employee if the employer identifies *what* should be done and *how* it should be done. If an individual is told *what* to do, but is allowed to independently determine how to do it, an employee-employer relationship likely does not exist.

If a business provides the following items to a worker, a common law employee-employer relationship likely exists:

- Furnishing tools or equipment and a place to work.
- Providing support services, including the hiring of assistants to help do the work.
- Making training available to provide needed job skills.
- Allowing participation in various workplace fringe benefits (e.g., accident and health plans, group life insurance, and retirement plans).
- Paying for services based on time rather than the task performed.

Alternatively, independent contractors are more likely to have unreimbursed business expenses, a significant investment in tools and work facilities, and less permanency in their business relationships. Independent contractors, moreover, anticipate a profit from their work, make their services available to the relevant marketplace, and are likely to be paid a flat fee on a per-job basis.

In resolving employment status, each case must be tested on its own merits. But the key test is whether the business maintains the right to control the means and methods of accomplishment (both what must be done *and* how it should be done). If this is the case, an employer-employee relationship exists. Concept Summary 9.1 provides an overview of the current IRS position.

Employee *versus* Independent Contractor

EXAMPLE 1

Arnold is a lawyer whose major client accounts for 60% of his billings. He does the routine legal work and income tax returns at the client's request. He is paid a monthly retainer in addition to amounts charged for extra work. Arnold is a self-employed individual. Even though most of his income comes from one client, he still has the right to determine how the end result of his work is attained.

---

[1] In simple situations, a Schedule C–EZ can be used. Also, a Schedule SE (Self-Employment Tax) must be filed.

[2] In simple situations, a Form 2106–EZ (Unreimbursed Employee Business Expenses) can be used.

[3] See, for example, IRS Publication 15–A (*Employer's Supplemental Tax Guide*).

[4] 1987–1 C.B. 296. Also see IRS Publication 1779 (*Independent Contractor or Employee*).

[5] Reg. § 31.3401(c)–(1)(b).

Concept Summary 9.1

Employee versus Independent Contractor

Although the 20 factors identified by the Internal Revenue Service in Revenue Ruling 87–41 remain relevant, the IRS has grouped these factors into three broad categories in order to provide some clarity to a difficult area, while acknowledging that the 20 factors are not all-inclusive.

Behavioral Control	Financial Control	The Relationship of the Parties

• Does the business control (or have the right to control) what the worker does and how the worker does his or her job?
• Facts that show whether the business has **behavioral control** include:
  ➤ *Instructions.* An employee is generally told:
    1. When, where, and how to work.
    2. What equipment, tools, or processes to use.
    3. What workers can be hired to assist with the work.
    4. Where to purchase supplies and services.
    5. What work must be performed by a specified individual.
    6. What order or sequence to follow in performing the work.
  ➤ *Training.* An employee normally receives training to perform work in a particular manner.
	• Are the business aspects of the worker's job controlled by the payer?
	• Facts that show whether the business has **financial control** include:
	  ➤ The extent to which the worker has unreimbursed business expenses.
	  ➤ The extent of the worker's investment.
	  ➤ The extent to which the worker makes services available to a larger market (e.g., is the worker marketing his or her services to multiple businesses?).
	  ➤ How the business pays the worker (is it the same or different from how employees are paid?).
	  ➤ The extent to which the worker can realize a profit or loss.
		• A variety of facts and documents can show the **relationship of the parties**:
		  ➤ Written contracts describing the relationship the parties intended to create.
		  ➤ Whether the worker is provided with employee-type fringe benefits.
		  ➤ The permanency of the relationship (e.g., is the work for a specified period of time or indefinite?).
		  ➤ How integral the services are to the principal activity of the business.

Summary

1. Businesses must weigh all factors when determining whether a worker is an employee or independent contractor. Some factors might indicate that the worker is an employee, while other factors might indicate that the worker is an independent contractor.
2. No set number of factors "makes" the worker an employee or an independent contractor, and no one factor stands alone in making this determination. Also, factors that are relevant in one situation may not be relevant in a different situation.
3. Overall, one must look at the entirety of the relationship, consider the degree or extent of the right to direct and control, and document each of the factors used in coming to a decision.

Employee *versus* Independent Contractor

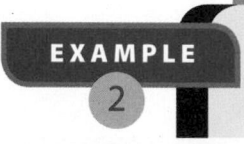

Ellen is a lawyer hired by Arnold to assist him in the performance of services for the client mentioned in Example 1. Ellen is under Arnold's supervision; he reviews her work and pays her an hourly fee. Ellen is an employee of Arnold.

When one taxpayer holds multiple jobs, it is possible to have dual status as both an employee and an independent contractor (i.e., self-employed).

Dr. Davis, DDS, is a full-time employee at the Robin University Health Center. In the evenings and on weekends, he shares a practice with another dentist who works the Monday through Friday daytime shifts. Dr. Davis is both employed and self-employed.

Certain workers who *are not* common law employees are treated as employees for employment tax purposes. Known as statutory employees, this group includes certain drivers (e.g., nondairy beverage distributors and laundry and dry cleaning pickup service), life insurance sales agents, home workers, and other salespersons. These employees are allowed to claim their business-related expenses as deductions *for* AGI by using Schedule C. The wages or commissions paid to statutory employees are not subject to Federal income tax withholding but are subject to Social Security tax.[6]

To avoid the confusion that might otherwise result in their classification, the tax law categorically treats certain categories of workers as independent contractors. Included in this group are licensed real estate agents and direct sellers. Such persons are treated as self-employed for all Federal purposes, including income and employment taxes.[7]

If a taxpayer wants to know whether employee or independent contractor status exists, the IRS will issue a determination if the taxpayer files a Form SS–8 (Determination of Worker Status for Purposes of Federal Employment Taxes and Income Tax Withholding). An adverse ruling is appealable to the U.S. Tax Court.[8]

9-2 EMPLOYEE EXPENSES—IN GENERAL

Once the employment relationship is established, employee expenses fall into one of the following categories:

- Transportation.
- Travel.
- Moving.
- Education.
- Entertainment.
- Other.

These expenses are discussed below in the order presented.

Keep in mind, however, that these expenses are not necessarily limited to employees. A deduction for business transportation, for example, is equally available to taxpayers who are self-employed.

9-3 TRANSPORTATION EXPENSES

LO.2

Recognize deductible transportation expenses.

9-3a Qualified Expenses

An employee may deduct unreimbursed employment-related transportation expenses as an itemized deduction *from* AGI. Transportation expenses include only the cost of transporting the employee from one place to another in the course of employment when the employee is *not in travel status* (discussed in text Section 9-4). Such costs include taxi fares, automobile expenses, tolls, and parking.

Commuting Expenses

Commuting between home and one's place of employment is a personal, nondeductible expense. The fact that one employee drives 30 miles to work and another employee walks six blocks to work does not matter.

---

[6]§ 3121(d)(3). See Circular E, *Employer's Tax Guide* (IRS Publication 15), for further discussion of statutory employees.

[7]§ 3508. See *Employer's Supplemental Tax Guide* (IRS Publication 15–A).

[8]§ 7436.

Geraldo is employed by Sparrow Corporation. He drives 22 miles each way to work. The 44 miles he drives each workday are nondeductible commuting expenses.

There are several exceptions to the nondeductible commuting expenses rule. An employee who uses an automobile to transport heavy tools to work and who otherwise would not drive to work is allowed a deduction, but only for the additional costs incurred to transport the tools. For example, the rental of a trailer for transporting tools is deductible, but the expenses of operating the automobile generally are not deductible.[9]

Another exception is provided for an employee who has a second job. The expenses of getting from one job to another are deductible. If the employee goes home between jobs, the deduction is based on the distance between jobs.

In the current year, Cynthia holds two jobs, a full-time job with Blue Corporation and a part-time job with Wren Corporation. Cynthia customarily leaves home at 7:30 A.M. and drives 30 miles to the Blue Corporation plant, where she works until 5:00 P.M. After dinner at a nearby café, Cynthia drives 20 miles to Wren Corporation and works from 7:00 to 11:00 P.M. The distance from the second job to Cynthia's home is 40 miles. Her deduction is based on 20 miles (the distance between jobs).

If the taxpayer is required to incur a transportation expense to travel between workstations, that expense is deductible.

Norman is the local manager for a national chain of fast-food outlets. Each workday, he drives from his home to his office to handle administrative matters. Most of his day, however, is then spent making the rounds of the retail outlets, after which he drives home.

The costs incurred in driving to his office and driving home from the last outlet are nondeductible commuting expenses. The other transportation costs are deductible.

Likewise, the commuting costs from home to a temporary workstation and from the temporary workstation to home are deductible.

Vivian works for a firm in downtown Denver and commutes to work. She occasionally works in a customer's office. On one such occasion, Vivian drove directly to the customer's office, a round-trip distance from her home of 40 miles. She did not go into her office, which is a 52-mile round-trip. Her mileage for going to and from the temporary workstation is deductible.

Also deductible is the reasonable travel cost between the general working area and a temporary workstation outside that area.

Sam, a building inspector in Minneapolis, regularly inspects buildings for building code violations for his employer, a general contractor. During one busy season, the St. Paul inspector became ill, and Sam was required to inspect several buildings in St. Paul. The expenses for transportation for the trips to St. Paul are deductible.

What constitutes the general working area depends on the facts and circumstances of each situation. Furthermore, if an employee customarily works on several temporary assignments in a localized area, that localized area becomes the regular place of employment. Transportation from home to these locations becomes a personal, nondeductible commuting expense.

---

[9]*Fausner v. Comm.*, 73–2 USTC ¶9515, 32 AFTR 2d 73–5202, 93 S.Ct. 2820 (USSC, 1973).

If a taxpayer has a home office that qualifies as a principal place of business, the transportation costs between home and various work locations are deductible (i.e., the costs are *not* a commuting expense).

The Big Picture

Return to the facts of *The Big Picture* on p. 9-1. Because Morgan will have an office in her home for her two freelancing businesses, the apartment will be her principal place of business. Thus, any transportation from her home to freelancing sites (e.g., driving to a child's home for tutoring) is *not* a commuting expense.[10] However, Morgan will have commuting expenses for the mileage between her apartment and her job at Enrichment Child Care Center.

EXAMPLE
9

9-3b Computation of Automobile Expenses

A taxpayer has two choices in determining automobile expenses: the automatic mileage method and the actual cost method. If an automobile is used for both business and personal purposes (mixed use), only the expenses related to the business use are deductible. The percentage of business use is usually arrived at by comparing the business mileage with total mileage—both business and personal.

Automatic Mileage Method

Also called the standard mileage method, the `automatic mileage method` is convenient in that it simplifies record keeping. The rate allowed per mile takes into account average operating expenses (such as gas and oil, repairs, and depreciation). Consequently, the taxpayer only has to multiply the automatic mileage rate by the business miles driven to compute the deduction.

For 2017, the deduction is based on 53.5 cents per mile for business miles.[11] This represents a one-half cent decrease from the rate of 54 cents applicable to 2016. Although the mileage rate usually remains constant for an entire year, the IRS occasionally makes mid-year changes to the rate, usually when there is a large change in the cost of fuel. As a result, it is important that the taxpayer keep records to identify when the driving took place.

Chad, a salesperson, drove his car 20,000 miles for business during 2017. To determine his standard mileage deduction, he simply multiplies his business miles by the appropriate standard mileage rate (53.5 cents per mile in 2017). So his total standard mileage deduction for the year is $10,700 (20,000 miles × 53.5 cents per mile).

EXAMPLE
10

The automatic mileage rate for deductible education expenses is the same as for business; 17 cents per mile is allowed for moving (discussed later in this chapter) and medical purposes, and the rate for the charitable contribution deduction is 14 cents a mile (see Chapter 10 for a discussion of medical and charitable deductions). Parking fees and tolls are allowed in addition to the deduction computed using the automatic mileage method.

Generally, a taxpayer may elect either method for any particular year. However, the following restrictions apply to the standard mileage method:

- The vehicle must be owned or leased by the taxpayer.
- The vehicle must not be used for hire (e.g., taxi, Uber, or Lyft).
- If five or more vehicles are in use (for business purposes) at the *same* time (not alternately), a taxpayer may not use the automatic mileage method.
- A basis adjustment for depreciation is required if the taxpayer changes from the automatic mileage method to the actual operating cost method. The depreciation adjustment for the business miles is determined using the following schedule:

---

[10]*Walter K. Strohmalter*, 113 T.C. 106 (1999).

[11]Notice 2016–79, 2016–52 I.R.B. 918 and Rev.Proc. 2010–51, 2010–51 I.R.B.883.

Year	Rate per Mile
2017	25 cents
2016	24 cents
2015	24 cents
2014	22 cents
2013	23 cents

EXAMPLE 11

Tim purchased his automobile in 2014 for $36,000. It is used 90% for business purposes. Tim drove the automobile for 10,000 business miles in 2016, 8,500 business miles in 2015, and 6,000 business miles in 2014. At the beginning of 2017, the basis of the business portion is $26,640.

Depreciable basis ($36,000 × 90%)	$32,400
Less depreciation:	
2016 (10,000 miles × 24 cents)	(2,400)
2015 (8,500 miles × 24 cents)	(2,040)
2014 (6,000 miles × 22 cents)	(1,320)
Adjusted business basis 1/1/2017	$26,640

- Use of the automatic mileage method in the first year an auto is placed in service is considered an election to exclude the auto from MACRS cost recovery (discussed in Chapter 8).
- A taxpayer may not switch to the automatic mileage method if the MACRS statutory percentage method or a § 179 expense election has been used.

Actual Cost Method

Under this method, the actual cost of operating the automobile is used to compute the deduction. Actual costs include the following expenses:

- Gas and oil, lubrication.
- Depreciation (or lease payments).
- Insurance.
- Dues to auto clubs.
- Repairs.
- Tires and other parts.
- Licenses and registration fees.
- Parking and tolls.

EXAMPLE 12

Return to the facts of Example 10. Chad drove his car a total of 25,000 miles in 2017 (20,000 for business and 5,000 for personal use). He incurred the following automobile costs (he has receipts for all of these expenses):

Lease payments ($350 per month)	$ 4,200
Fuel	2,300
Insurance	2,800
Repairs and maintenance	1,200
State registration fee	150
Total Expenses	$ 10,650
× Business use percentage (20,000 ÷ 25,000)	× 80%
Actual Cost Method Deduction	$ 8,520

As a result, Chad is better off using the automatic mileage rate method. Chad's true cost of operating the vehicle is 42.6 cents per mile ($10,650 ÷ 25,000 miles), yet the government is allowing him to deduct 53.5 cents per mile.

As noted in Chapter 8, the allowance for depreciation (or lease payments) is subject to limitations when mixed-use vehicles are involved. Interest on car loans is not deductible if the taxpayer is an employee, but it can qualify as a business expense if the taxpayer is self-employed. Sales taxes paid on the purchase of a car are added to the cost of the car and recovered by means of the MACRS deduction. In mixed-use situations, the portion of the sales tax attributable to personal use may, in some cases, be claimed as a deduction *from* AGI (see Chapter 10 and the choice required between state and local income and sales taxes).

Except for parking and tolls, none of the expenses noted previously can be separately claimed under the automatic mileage method. A deduction for parking tickets and other traffic violations is not allowed under either method because it is a violation of public policy [§ 162(f); see Chapter 6].

The Big Picture

EXAMPLE

13

Return to the facts of *The Big Picture* on p. 9-1. During Morgan's senior year in college, her parents gave her one of the family cars—a 2014 Toyota Camry. Morgan has no idea as to the car's original cost or the odometer reading at the time the car was registered in her name. She has, however, kept track of the miles driven for business since she accepted her new job. Morgan should use the automatic mileage method in claiming business use of the car.

Which Method Is Best?

Every year the American Automobile Association estimates how much it costs per mile to drive a car in the United States. Its 2016 report shows that it costs, on average, anywhere from 43.9 cents to 69.9 cents per mile to drive a sedan for 15,000 miles. Driving a minivan for 15,000 miles costs an average of 61.8 cents per mile, while an all-wheel drive SUV costs 68.4 cents per mile.[12]

The difference depends on the size (and cost) of the car and the number of miles driven during the year—the more miles driven, the less one's cost per mile.

In general, taxpayers are better off using the standard mileage rate if they drive a smaller car, particularly if they drive many business miles. And a taxpayer is likely to benefit from using the standard mileage rate if an old or inexpensive car is used. Why? Because the same fixed deduction rate applies no matter how much the car is worth. Because the standard mileage rate factors in depreciation (which does not vary), an inexpensive car might benefit more from using this method than would an expensive vehicle.

The actual cost method will likely provide a larger deduction if the taxpayer drives a more expensive car, an SUV, or a minivan. In addition, the actual cost method will normally result in a larger deduction if fewer business miles are driven.

Yet, the only way to know for sure which method is best is to keep careful track of the actual costs and the business mileage driven. Then calculations can be done under both methods, and the larger deduction can be taken.

The Big Picture

EXAMPLE

14

Return to the facts of *The Big Picture* on p. 9-1. Morgan wants to make sure she documents her business miles appropriately. She knows that the IRS expects her to keep track of her business miles on a regular basis, including where she drove and the business reason for the trip. She wonders whether there are some mobile apps that can help.

Actually, a number of mileage tracking apps are available that would allow Morgan to begin logging miles automatically every time she started a trip. Some use Bluetooth and begin as soon

continued

---

[12]American Automobile Association, *Your Driving Costs*, 2016 edition.

as the car starts moving; others (usually free) require the user to input locations. All of the apps create detailed records of all trips; the user just needs to identify the purpose of the trip. Here are a few apps that are available (with information from the developer's website):

- **MileIQ (www.mileiq.com)** tracks every trip you take automatically. Then it lets you quickly categorize a trip as business, personal, medical, charity, or a custom category you create. It also lets you log any additional information (like freeway tolls or parking fees). Trip information is backed up automatically using MileIQ's cloud servers, and its data integrates with a number of accounting/tax software programs (including QuickBooks). MileIQ is free if you track fewer than 40 trips per month and about $60 per year with unlimited trip tracking.

- **TripLog (https://triplogmileage.com)** monitors your mileage via GPS; tracks any parking, tolls, or other expenses; records fuel costs; generates IRS-ready reports; and integrates with QuickBooks. As with MileIQ, you have the option of specifying the nature of the trip (business, charity, medical, etc.), entering notes, and adding any applicable parking or toll costs. TripLog's basic features are free. Advanced features, such as Bluetooth "autostart" and automatic daily cloud backup, cost $15 per year. You can also use TripLog to estimate your gas mileage and find the best gas prices.

- Some free apps are available. **Hurdlr (https://hurdlr.com)** not only tracks mileage but also is a fairly comprehensive business and expense tracking app for freelancers, Uber/Lyft drivers, and AirBnB/VRBO owners. Like other apps, **Everlance (www.everlance.com)** uses GPS to track mileage and allows the user to categorize trips. It also includes automatic cloud storage.

9-4 TRAVEL EXPENSES

Describe how travel expenses are treated.

9-4a Definition of Travel Expenses

An itemized deduction is allowed for unreimbursed travel expenses related to a taxpayer's employment. **Travel expenses** include transportation expenses, meals and lodging, and incidental expenses while working away from home. In general, the reason for allowing a travel expense deduction is to alleviate the duplication of living expenses (where the taxpayer incurs expenses while at home and while working away from home).

Transportation expenses (discussed previously) are deductible even if the taxpayer is *not* away from home. Meals cannot be lavish or extravagant. Examples of incidental expenses include laundry, baggage fees and/or tips, and ATM fees. A deduction for travel expenses, however, is only allowed if the taxpayer is away from his or her tax home.

9-4b Away-from-Home Requirement

The crucial test for the deductibility of travel expenses is whether the employee is away from home overnight. "Overnight" need not be a 24-hour period, but it must be a period substantially longer than an ordinary day's work and must require rest, sleep, or a relief-from-work period.[13] A one-day business trip normally does not warrant travel status; therefore, meals and lodging for such a trip are not deductible.

Temporary Assignments

The employee must be away from home for a temporary period. If the taxpayer-employee is reassigned to a new location for an indefinite period of time, that new location becomes his or her tax home. *Temporary* indicates that the assignment's termination is expected within a reasonably short period of time. The position of the IRS is that the tax home is the business location of the taxpayer. Thus, travel expenses are not deductible if a taxpayer is reassigned for an indefinite period and does not move his or her place of residence to the new location.

[13]*U.S. v. Correll*, 68–1 USTC ¶9101, 20 AFTR 2d 5845, 88 S.Ct. 445 (USSC, 1967); Rev.Rul. 75–168, 1975–1 C.B. 58.

Temporary Becomes Permanent

Malcolm's employer opened a branch office in San Diego. Malcolm was assigned to the new office for three months to train a new manager and to assist in setting up the new office. He tried commuting from his home in Los Angeles for a week and decided that he could not continue driving several hours a day. He rented an apartment in San Diego, where he lived during the week. He spent weekends with his wife and children at their home in Los Angeles.

Malcolm's rent, meals, laundry, incidentals, and automobile expenses in San Diego are deductible. To the extent that Malcolm's transportation expense related to his weekend trips home exceeds what his cost of meals and lodging would have been, the excess is personal and nondeductible.

Assume that Malcolm in Example 15 was transferred to the new location to become the new manager permanently. His wife and children continued to live in Los Angeles until the end of the school year.

Malcolm is no longer "away from home" because the assignment is not temporary. His travel expenses are not deductible.

To curtail controversy in this area, the Code specifies that a taxpayer "*shall not* be treated as *temporarily* away from home during any period of employment if such period exceeds 1 year."[14]

Determining the Tax Home

In most situations, determining the location of a taxpayer's tax home is not difficult. The tax home is the area in which the taxpayer works.

It is possible for a taxpayer never to be away from his or her tax home. In other words, the tax home follows the taxpayer. In this situation, all meals and lodging remain personal and are not deductible.

Jim is single and works full-time as a long-haul truck driver. He lists his mother's home as his address and stays there during holidays. However, he contributes nothing toward its maintenance.

Because Jim has no regular place of duty or place where he regularly lives, his tax home is where he works (i.e., on the road). As an itinerant (transient), he is never away from home, and all of his meals and lodging while on the road are personal and not deductible.

The result reached in Example 17 is justified on the grounds that there is no duplication of living expenses in the case of itinerant taxpayers.[15]

When a taxpayer has more than one place of business or work, the main one is considered to be the tax home. This is determined by considering the time spent, the level of activity involved, and the income earned at each job.

Art, a physical therapist, lives with his family in Lancaster, Pennsylvania. For seven months each year, he is employed by the New Orleans Saints football team at a salary of $150,000. During this period, he rents an apartment in New Orleans. In the off-season, he works for the Lancaster YMCA at a salary of $15,000.

Art's tax home is clearly New Orleans and not Lancaster. Consequently, his living expenses while in New Orleans (i.e., food and lodging) are not deductible.

---

[14]§ 162(a).

[15]Rev.Rul. 73–529, 1973–2 C.B. 37 and *James O. Henderson*, 70 TCM 1407, T.C.Memo. 1995–559, *aff'd* by 98–1 USTC ¶50,375, 81 AFTR 2d 98–1748, 143 F.3d 497 (CA–9, 1998).

9-4c **Restrictions on Travel Expenses**

The possibility always exists that taxpayers will attempt to treat vacation or pleasure travel as deductible business travel. To prevent such practices, the law contains restrictions on certain travel expenses.

Conventions

For travel expenses to be deductible, a convention must be directly related to the taxpayer's trade or business.[16] Compare Examples 19 and 20.

Type of Convention

EXAMPLE 19

Dr. Hill, a pathologist who works for a hospital in Ohio, travels to Las Vegas to attend a two-day session on recent developments in estate planning. No deduction is allowed for Dr. Hill's travel expenses.

EXAMPLE 20

Assume the same facts as in Example 19, except that the convention deals entirely with recent developments in pathology. Now a travel deduction is allowed.

The taxpayer must attend convention sessions along with other participants in order to claim a deduction. Attendance does not include watching or listening to sessions at a later date that are recorded (video or audio) (e.g., a taxpayer cannot vacation during the convention sessions and watch the videos later). However, a deduction will be allowed for costs (other than travel, meals, and entertainment) of renting or using recorded materials related to business.

EXAMPLE 21

A CPA is unable to attend a convention at which current developments in taxation are discussed. She pays $300 to stream the recorded sessions and views them at home later. The $300 is a miscellaneous itemized deduction if the CPA is an employee. If she is self-employed, the $300 is a deduction *for* AGI.

The Code places stringent restrictions on the deductibility of travel expenses of the taxpayer's spouse or dependent.[17] Generally, there must be a business reason for the spouse or dependent to attend, and the expenses must be otherwise deductible.

EXAMPLE 22

Assume the same facts as in Example 20 with the additional fact that Dr. Hill is accompanied by Mrs. Hill. Mrs. Hill is not employed, but possesses secretarial skills and takes notes during the proceedings. No deduction is allowed for Mrs. Hill's travel expenses.

If, however, Mrs. Hill is a nurse trained in pathology and is employed by Dr. Hill as his assistant, her travel expenses become deductible.

Education

Travel as a form of education is not deductible.[18] If, however, the education qualifies as a deduction, the travel involved is allowed. Compare Examples 23 and 24.

Education Travel

EXAMPLE 23

Greta, a German teacher, travels to Germany to maintain general familiarity with the language and culture. No travel expense deduction is allowed.

---

[16]§ 274(h)(1).

[17]§ 274(m)(3).

[18]§ 274(m)(2).

Education Travel

EXAMPLE 24

Jean-Claude, a scholar of French literature, travels to Paris to do specific library research that cannot be done elsewhere and to take courses that are offered only at the Sorbonne. The travel costs are deductible, assuming that the other requirements for deducting education expenses (discussed later in the chapter) are met.

9-4d Combined Business and Pleasure Travel

To be deductible, travel expenses need not be incurred in the performance of specific job functions.

Domestic Travel for Business and Pleasure

In order to limit the possibility of a taxpayer claiming a tax deduction for what is essentially a personal vacation, several rules were created to handle deductions associated with combined business and pleasure trips. If the business/pleasure trip is entirely within the United States, the transportation expenses are deductible only if the trip is *primarily for business.*[19] Meals, lodging, and other expenses are allocated between business and personal days. If the trip is primarily for pleasure, no transportation expenses qualify as a deduction. Compare Examples 25 and 26.

Meeting the Primary Business Purpose Requirement

EXAMPLE 25

In the current year, Hana travels from Seattle to New York primarily for business. She spends five days conducting business and three days sightseeing and attending shows. Her plane and taxi fare amounts to $1,160. Her meals amount to $200 per day, and lodging and incidental expenses are $350 per day.

She can deduct the transportation charges of $1,160, because the trip is primarily for business (five days of business versus three days of sightseeing). Meals are limited to five days and are subject to a 50% reduction (see text Section 9-7a), for a total of $500 [5 days × ($200 × 50%)], and other expenses are limited to $1,750 (5 days × $350). If Hana is an employee, the unreimbursed travel expenses are miscellaneous itemized deductions.

EXAMPLE 26

Assume that Hana goes to New York for a two-week vacation. While there, she spends several hours renewing acquaintances with people in her company's New York office. Her transportation expenses are not deductible.

Foreign Travel for Business and Pleasure

When the trip is *outside the United States*, different rules apply. Transportation expenses must be allocated between business and personal unless:

1. The taxpayer is away from home for seven days or less, *or*
2. Less than 25 percent of the time was for personal purposes.

No allocation is required if the taxpayer has no substantial control over arrangements for the trip or the desire for a vacation is not a major factor in taking the trip. If the trip is primarily for pleasure, no transportation charges are deductible. Days devoted to travel are considered business days. Weekends, legal holidays, and intervening days are considered business days, provided both the day before and the day after were business days.[20] Compare Examples 27 and 28.

---

[19]Reg. § 1.162–2(b)(1).

[20]§ 274(c) and Reg. § 1.274–4. For purposes of the seven-days-or-less exception, the departure travel day is not counted.

The Amount of Nonbusiness Time Permitted

EXAMPLE 27

In the current year, Robert takes a trip from New York to Japan primarily for business purposes. He is away from home from June 10 through June 19. He spends three days vacationing and seven days (including two travel days) conducting business. His airfare is $4,000, his meals amount to $200 per day, and lodging and incidental expenses are $300 per day. Because Robert is away from home for more than seven days and more than 25% of his time is devoted to personal purposes, only 70% (7 days business/10 days total) of the transportation is deductible. His deductions are as follows:

Transportation (70% × $4,000)		$2,800
Lodging ($300 × 7)		2,100
Meals ($200 × 7)	$1,400	
Less: 50% reduction (see text Section 9-7a)	(700)	700
Total		$5,600

EXAMPLE 28

Assume the same facts as in Example 27. Robert is gone the same period of time but spends only two days (rather than three) vacationing.

Now no allocation of transportation is required. Because the pleasure portion of the trip is less than 25% of the total, all of the airfare qualifies for the travel deduction.

Record-Keeping Requirements

Distinguishing between business and personal expenses can be difficult (and very subjective). As a result, the tax law includes specific provisions that require the taxpayer to maintain specific, written, contemporaneous records for travel expenses.[21] These records, which assist the IRS and courts in reaching a fair determination of the legitimacy of the expenses, must include the amount, time (or dates), place, and business purpose behind the expenses.

LO.4

Determine the moving expense deduction.

9-5 MOVING EXPENSES

Moving expenses are deductible when the move relates to the start of work at a new principal workplace.[22] Both employees and self-employed individuals can deduct moving expenses. To be eligible for a moving expense deduction, a taxpayer must meet two basic tests: distance (see text Section 9-5a) and time (see text Section 9-5b).

9-5a Distance Test

To meet the distance test, the taxpayer's new job location must be at least 50 miles farther from the taxpayer's old residence than the old residence was from the former place of employment. The location of the new residence does not matter. This eliminates a moving deduction for taxpayers who purchase a new home in the same general area without changing their place of employment. Taxpayers who accept a new job in the same general area as the old job location are also eliminated. Taxpayers beginning their first job (e.g., a student graduating from college) will meet the distance test if the new job location is at least 50 miles from their former residence. The same is true for a taxpayer returning to full-time work after a substantial period of unemployment.

Concept Summary 9.2 illustrates the distance test.

---

[21]§ 274(d). Corroborating evidence (e.g., receipt from a hotel or an airline ticket) is also required. In general, approximations and estimates are not sufficient. If a taxpayer is unable to substantiate expenses, courts use the Cohan rule to estimate the deductible amount [*Cohan v. Commissioner*, 39 F.2d 540 (CA-2, 1930)].

[22]§ 217(a).

Concept Summary 9.2

Meeting and Not Meeting the Distance Test

Old main job location

3 miles

Former residence

58 miles

New main job location

DISTANCE TEST IS MET

The new main job location is at least 50 miles farther from the former residence than the old main job location was.

38 miles

New main job location

DISTANCE TEST IS *NOT* MET

The new main job location is *not* at least 50 miles farther from the former residence than the old main job location was.

9-5b **Time Test**

To meet the time test, an employee must be employed on a full-time basis at the new location for 39 weeks in the 12-month period following the move. If the taxpayer is self-employed, she must work in the new location for 78 weeks during the next two years (including 39 weeks in the first 12 months). The time test is ignored if the taxpayer dies, becomes disabled, is discharged from the military (other than for willful misconduct), or is transferred by the employer.

The 12-month period following the move could bridge two tax years. For example, a taxpayer-employee who moves in October 2017 would not be able to tell if she satisfied the 39-week test until sometime in 2018. As a result, the taxpayer is provided two options:

Option 1: The taxpayer can take the deduction in the year the expenses are incurred, even though the 39-week test has not been met. If the taxpayer later fails to meet the test, either (1) the income of the following year is increased by an amount equal to the deduction previously claimed for moving expenses or (2) an amended return is filed for the year of the move.

Option 2: The taxpayer can wait until the test is met and then file an amended tax return for the year of the move.

Persons who retire and move to a new location incur personal nondeductible moving expenses. If the retired person accepts a full-time job in the new location, the moving expenses are deductible.

EXAMPLE

29

At the time of his retirement from the national office of a major accounting firm, Gordon had an annual salary of $420,000. He moves from New York City to Seattle to retire.

To qualify for the moving expense deduction, Gordon accepts a full-time teaching position at a Seattle junior college at an annual salary of $15,000. If Gordon satisfies the 39-week test, his moving expenses are deductible. The disparity between the two salaries (previous and current) is of no consequence.

Gordon could also qualify for the moving expense deduction if he were to open his own consulting practice, working full-time. In this case, he would have to satisfy the 78-week test.

The distance and time tests are summarized in Concept Summary 9.3. Members of the armed forces are subject to special rules.[23]

Concept Summary 9.3

Qualifying for the Moving Expense Deduction

Start Here:

Is the new main job location at least 50 miles farther from the former residence than the old main job location was? → No → The taxpayer cannot deduct the moving expenses

↓ Yes

Is the taxpayer an employee? → No → Is the taxpayer self-employed? → No → (The taxpayer cannot deduct the moving expenses)

↓ Yes ↓ Yes

Did the taxpayer work full-time as an employee for at least 39 weeks in the first 12 months after arriving in the new area? — No

Did the taxpayer work full-time as an employee or a self-employed person for at least 78 weeks in the first 24 months (which includes 39 weeks in the first 12 months) after arriving in the new area? → No → (The taxpayer cannot deduct the moving expenses)

↓ Yes ↓ Yes

The taxpayer may be able to deduct the moving expenses

9-5c **Treatment of Moving Expenses**

What Is Included

"Qualified" moving expenses include *reasonable* expenses of:

- Moving household goods and personal effects.
- Traveling from the former residence to the new place of residence.

For this purpose, *traveling* includes lodging, but not meals, for the taxpayer and members of the household.[24] The taxpayer can elect to use actual auto expenses

---

[23]See IRS Publication 521 (*Moving Expenses*), pp. 14–15 and § 217.   [24]§ 217(b).

(no depreciation is allowed) or the automatic mileage method. In this case, moving expense mileage is limited in 2017 to 17 cents per mile for each car (down from 19 cents per mile in 2016). These expenses are also limited by the reasonableness standard. For example, if one moves from Texas to Florida via Maine and takes six weeks to do so, the transportation and lodging must be allocated between personal and moving expenses.

EXAMPLE

30

Jill is transferred by her employer from the Atlanta office to the San Francisco office. In this connection, she spends the following amounts:

Cost of moving furniture	$4,800
Transportation	700
Meals	450
Lodging	600

Jill's total qualified moving expense is $6,100 ($4,800 + $700 + $600).

The moving expense deduction is allowed regardless of whether the employee is transferred by the existing employer or is employed by a new employer. It is allowed if the employee moves to a new area and obtains employment or switches from self-employed status to employee status (and vice versa). The moving expense deduction is also allowed if an individual is unemployed before obtaining employment in a new area.

What Is Not Included

In addition to meals while en route, the moving expense deduction does *not* include the following costs:

- Loss on the sale of a residence or penalty for breaking a lease (including the loss of a security deposit).
- Pre-move house-hunting expenses.
- Temporary living expenses.

Reporting and Deducting Moving Expenses

Qualified moving expenses that are paid (or reimbursed) by the employer are not included in the gross income of the employee.[25] Moving expenses that are paid (or reimbursed) by the employer and are *not* qualified moving expenses are included in the employee's gross income and are not deductible.

The employer is responsible for allocating the reimbursement between the qualified and nonqualified moving expenses. Reimbursed qualified moving expenses are reported on the employee's Form W–2 for the year involved. If an employee receives a moving allowance (normally, a specific amount with no documentation required by the employer), this amount will be included in the employee's gross income, and the employee will then deduct any qualified moving expenses.

Qualified moving expenses that are deductible (including those of self-employed taxpayers) are deductions *for* AGI.[26] Form 3903 is used to report the details of the moving expense deduction.

The Big Picture

EXAMPLE

31

Return to the facts of *The Big Picture* on p. 9-1. Even though this is her first job, Morgan will be entitled to a moving expense deduction. This presumes that she is not reimbursed by Enrichment Child Care Center for these expenses. She should not forget that the mileage on her auto also is allowed. Her deduction is *for* AGI and can be claimed even if she chooses the standard deduction option.

---

[25]§§ 132(a)(6) and (g). [26]§ 62(a)(15).

LO.5

Differentiate between deductible and nondeductible education expenses.

9-6 EDUCATION EXPENSES

9-6a General Requirements

An employee can deduct education expenses provided the expenses are:

- To meet the specific employer requirements or legal requirements to keep his or her job, or.
- To maintain or improve existing skills required in the present job.

Education expenses are *not* deductible if the education is for either of the following purposes (except as discussed in text Section 9-6e, Deduction for Qualified Tuition and Related Expenses):

- To meet the minimum educational standards for qualification in the taxpayer's existing job.
- To qualify the taxpayer for a new trade or business.[27]

Fees incurred for professional qualification exams (the bar exam, for example) and fees for review courses (such as a CPA review course) are not deductible.[28] If the education incidentally results in a promotion or raise, the deduction still can be taken as long as the education maintained and improved existing skills and did not qualify a person for a new trade or business. A deduction is generally allowed for education related to new duties if the new duties involve the same general work. For example, the IRS has ruled that a practicing dentist's education expenses incurred to become an orthodontist are deductible.[29]

9-6b Employer or Legal Requirements to Keep a Job

Taxpayers are permitted to deduct education expenses if the education is required by the employer or by legal requirements. Many states require a minimum of a bachelor's degree and a specified number of additional courses to retain a teaching job. In addition, some public school systems require a master's degree and expect teachers to make satisfactory progress toward a master's degree to keep their job.

If, however, the required education is the minimum degree required for the job, no deduction is allowed. So a taxpayer classified as a staff accountant who went back to school to obtain a bachelor's degree in accounting was not allowed to deduct the expenses, since a bachelor's degree was the minimum requirement for his job.[30]

Education required by law for various professions also qualifies for a deduction.

EXAMPLE 32

To satisfy the State Board of Public Accountancy rules for maintaining her CPA license, Nancy takes an auditing course sponsored by a local college. The cost of the education is deductible.

9-6c Maintaining or Improving Existing Skills

The "maintaining or improving existing skills" requirement has been difficult for both taxpayers and the courts to interpret. For example, a business executive may be permitted to deduct the costs of obtaining an MBA on the grounds that the advanced management education is undertaken to maintain and improve existing management skills. The executive can also deduct the costs of specialized, nondegree management courses that maintain or improve existing skills. Expenses incurred by the executive to obtain a law degree are not deductible, however, because the education constitutes training for a

---

[27]Reg. §§ 1.162–5(b)(2) and (3).

[28]Reg. § 1.212–1(f) and Rev.Rul. 69–292, 1969–1 C.B. 84.

[29]Rev.Rul. 74–78, 1974–1 C.B. 44.

[30]Reg. § 1.162–5(b)(2)(iii) Example (2); *Collin J. Davidson*, 43 TCM 743, T.C.Memo. 1982–119. But see the subsequent discussion of § 222 (i.e., the deduction for higher education qualified tuition and related expenses).

GLOBAL TAX ISSUES   **Expatriates and the Moving Expense Deduction**

Expatriates, U.S. persons who accept work assignments overseas, enjoy several favorable tax advantages regarding foreign moves. First, the cost of storing household goods qualifies as a moving expense. This could lead to a major tax saving because expatriates do not ship most of their household effects to the foreign location. Furthermore, the cost of storage, particularly in a climate-controlled facility, is not insignificant.

The second advantage expatriates could enjoy is an exemption from the time test. Those who return to the United States to retire are absolved from the 39-week or 78-week work requirement. Thus, the return home expenses are treated as qualified moving expenses.

Source: Internal Revenue Code § 217(i).

new trade or business. The Regulations specifically deny a self-employed accountant a deduction for expenses relating to law school.[31]

The conditions required for the regular education expense deduction are summarized in Concept Summary 9.4.

Concept Summary 9.4

Condition for Deducting Regular Education Expenses

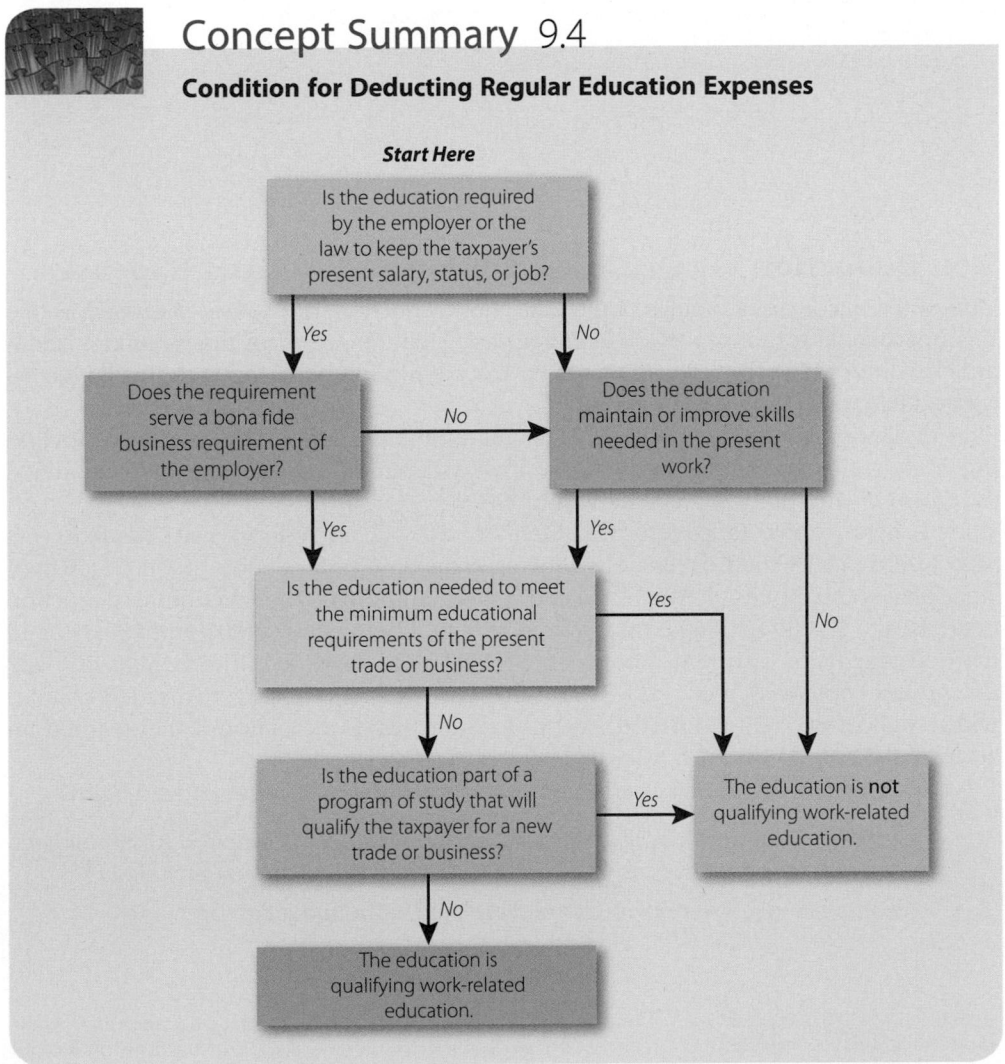

9-6d **What Expenses Are Allowed?**

Education expenses include books and supplies, tuition, and transportation (e.g., from the office to night school) and travel (e.g., meals and lodging while away from home at summer school).

Bill, who holds a bachelor of education degree, is a secondary education teacher in the Charleston school system. The school board recently raised its minimum education requirement for new teachers from four years of college training to five. A grandfather clause allows teachers with only four years of college to continue to qualify if they show satisfactory progress toward a graduate degree. Bill enrolls at the University of South Carolina and takes two graduate courses. His unreimbursed expenses for this purpose are as follows:

Books and tuition	$3,600
Lodging while in travel status (June–August)	2,150
Meals while in travel status	1,100
Laundry while in travel status	220
Transportation	900

Bill has an itemized deduction as follows:

Books and tuition	$3,600
Lodging	2,150
Meals less 50% reduction (see text Section 9-7a)	550
Laundry	220
Transportation	900
	$7,420

9-6e **Deduction for Qualified Tuition and Related Expenses**

One of the major shortcomings of the education deduction, previously discussed, is that it is unavailable for taxpayers obtaining a basic skill (i.e., to meet the minimum standards required for a job). This shortcoming has been partly resolved with the **deduction for qualified tuition and related expenses**.

A deduction *for* AGI is allowed for qualified tuition and related expenses involving higher education. The deduction allowed depends on the taxpayer's modified AGI (MAGI) and filing status (see Exhibit 9.1).[32]

In general, single taxpayers with MAGI of $65,000 or less, or married taxpayers with MAGI of $130,000 or less, are allowed a maximum deduction of $4,000. A two-step phaseout applies if MAGI exceeds these amounts. The maximum deduction decreases to $2,000 for single taxpayers with MAGI between $65,001 and $80,000 and married taxpayers with MAGI between $130,001 and $160,000. The benefit of § 222 *disappears completely* with the second step. Thus, a single taxpayer (married couple) with MAGI of $80,000 ($160,000) would lose the entire deduction if they earned an additional $1.[33]

Various aspects of the higher education tuition deduction are summarized below:

- *Qualified tuition and related expenses* include whatever is required for enrollment. Usually, student activity fees, books, and room and board are not included.[34]

- The expense need not be employment related, although it can be.

---

[32]MAGI is modified adjusted gross income as defined in § 222(b)(2)(C). Examples of some of these modifications include the adding back to regular AGI of the foreign earned income exclusion and the domestic production activities deduction. See IRS Publication 970 (*Tax Benefits for Education*).

[33]Section 222 expires on December 31, 2016, but might be extended by Congress. The various § 222 dollar amounts are not adjusted for inflation.

[34]Section 222(d) refers to § 25A(f), which deals with the American Opportunity and lifetime learning credits (see Chapter 13). Student activity fees and prescribed course-related books may be allowed if they are a condition for enrollment.

EXHIBIT 9.1	Limitations for Qualified Tuition Deduction	

Filing Status	Modified AGI	Maximum Deduction Allowed
Single	$65,000 or less	$4,000
	More than $65,000 and less than or equal to $80,000	$2,000
	More than $80,000	None
Married	$130,000 or less	$4,000
	More than $130,000 and less than or equal to $160,000	$2,000
	More than $160,000	None

- The deduction is available for a taxpayer's spouse or dependent, but is not available for married persons who file separate returns.
- To avoid a "double benefit," the deduction must be coordinated with other education provisions (e.g., American Opportunity and lifetime learning credits). No deduction is allowed for a taxpayer who qualifies as another's dependent.[35]
- The deduction *for* AGI classification avoids the 2%-of-AGI floor on miscellaneous itemized deductions. As noted later in the chapter, other education-related employee expenses are subject to this limitation.

The deduction for qualified tuition and related expenses is claimed by completing Form 8917 (Tuition and Fees Deduction) and filing it with a Form 1040 (or Form 1040–A). The taxpayer must have received a Form 1098–T (Tuition Statement) from a higher education institution in order to claim a deduction.

The Big Picture

EXAMPLE

34

Return to the facts of *The Big Picture* on p. 9-1. After starting her new job, Morgan enrolls in the evening master's degree program in child development of a local university and begins attending classes.

Although Morgan believes that the master's degree would be useful, it is not a requirement of ECCC and it is not needed to maintain or improve existing skills in her current job. As a result, except for the deduction allowed by § 222, none of her education expenses are deductible.[36]

9-6f Other Provisions Dealing with Education

Although this chapter deals with employment-related expenses, a wide variety of tax provisions deal with education. Because the encouragement of education is a desirable social goal, Congress continues to enact laws that provide tax incentives. The incentives come in the form of income exclusions, deductions (both *for* AGI and *from* AGI), and various credits.

Concept Summary 9.5 reviews the tax consequences of the various provisions dealing with education and indicates where they are discussed in the text.

---

[35]§ 222(c).

[36]*Steven Galligan*, 83 TCM 1859, T.C.Memo. 2002–150.

Concept Summary 9.5

Tax Consequences of Provisions Dealing with Education

Provision	Tax Effect	Income Phaseout[a]	Reference Code	Reference Text
Educational savings bonds	*Exclusion* for interest on U.S. Series EE bonds used for higher education	Yes	§ 135	Ch. 5, p. 5-24
Qualified tuition program	No deduction; *exclusion* for distributions	No	§ 529	Ch. 5, p. 5-25
Educational assistance plans	*Exclusion* of up to $5,250 for employer-provided assistance	No[b]	§ 127	Ch. 5, p. 5-15
Scholarships	*Exclusion* allowed for education costs (excluding room and board)	No	§ 117	Ch. 5, p. 5-7
Qualified tuition reduction plan	*Exclusion* as to tuition waivers for employees (and dependents) of nonprofit educational institutions	No[b]	§ 117(d)	Ch. 5, p. 5-7
Coverdell Education Savings Account (CESA)	No deduction ($2,000 maximum annual contribution); *exclusion* for distributions	Yes[c]	§ 530	Ch. 5, p. 5-25
Premature distributions from IRAs	If used for qualified higher education, income recognized but penalty waived	—	§ 72(t)	Ch. 19, p. 19-22
Qualified tuition and related expenses	*Deduction for* AGI; up to $4,000	Yes	§ 222	Ch. 9, p. 9-20
Educator expenses	*Deduction for* AGI; up to $250	No	§ 62(a)(2)(D)	Ch. 9, p. 9-31
Interest on student loans	*Deduction for* AGI; up to $2,500 per year	Yes	§ 221	Ch. 10, p. 10-13
Job-related education expenses	*Deduction from* AGI for an *employee* and subject to 2%-of-AGI floor; *deduction for* AGI for *self-employed*	No	§ 162	Ch. 9, p. 9-18
American Opportunity credit	Formerly the HOPE credit; extended to four years of postsecondary education; up to $2,500 per year	Yes	§ 25A(i)	Ch. 13, p. 13-18
Lifetime learning credit	20% of qualifying expenses (not to exceed $10,000 per year)	Yes	§ 25(A)(c)	Ch. 13, p. 13-18

[a]The phaseout of benefits occurs when income reaches a certain level. The phaseout amounts vary widely, depend on filing status (i.e., single or married filing jointly), and are based on MAGI (modified AGI).
[b]The availability of the benefit cannot be discriminatory (i.e., cannot favor higher-income taxpayers).
[c]The phaseout begins once AGI reaches $190,000 (married taxpayers) or $95,000 (unmarried taxpayers).

9-7 ENTERTAINMENT AND MEAL EXPENSES

LO.6

Explain how entertainment and meal expenses are treated.

Many taxpayers attempt to deduct personal entertainment expenses as business expenses. For this reason, the tax law provides an overall limit on the deductibility of **entertainment expenses** and meals, restricts certain types of these expenses, and contains strict record-keeping requirements to support these deductions.

9-7a Overall Limit (The 50 Percent Rule)

Since entertainment and business meals contain an element of personal enjoyment, only 50 percent of these expenses are allowed as a deduction.[37] The limitation applies to both employees and self-employed taxpayers. Although the 50 percent reduction can apply to either the employer or the employee, it will not apply twice. The reduction applies to the one who actually pays (economically) for the meals or entertainment.

EXAMPLE 35

Jane, an employee of Pato Corporation, entertains one of her clients. If Pato Corporation does not reimburse Jane, she is subject to the 50% reduction. If, however, Pato Corporation reimburses Jane (or pays for the entertainment directly), Pato's deduction is reduced by 50%.

---

[37]§ 274(n).

What Is Covered

In addition to entertainment and meals, the 50 percent limit also applies to taxes and tips relating to entertainment and meals. Cover charges, parking fees at an entertainment location, and room rental fees for a meal or cocktail party are also subject to the 50 percent rule. Transportation expenses are not subject to the 50 percent limitation.

Joe pays a $40 cab fare to meet his client for dinner. The meal costs $150, and Joe leaves a $30 tip. His deduction is $130 [($150 + $30) × 50% + $40 cab fare].

Exceptions to the 50 Percent Rule

The 50 percent rule has a number of exceptions.[38] One exception covers the case where the full value of the meals or entertainment is included in the compensation of the employee (or independent contractor).

Myrtle wins an all-expense-paid trip to Europe for selling the most insurance for her company during the year. Her employer treats this trip as additional compensation to Myrtle. The 50 percent rule does not apply to the employer.

Another exception applies if the taxpayer's hours of service are regulated by the U.S. government and away-from-home meals are frequent and necessary (e.g., airline pilots, truck and bus drivers, and train crews). Here, 80 percent of the meals are allowed as a deduction (rather than 50 percent).

Jason is a commercial airline pilot who works for a charter service out of Chicago. His employer provides a flat daily allowance for meals during Jason's out-of-town trips. During the year, Jason pays $6,000 for his meals (with receipts); his employer provided an allowance of $4,200 for these meals. Jason can deduct $1,440 of his excess meal cost [($6,000 − $4,200) × 80%].

Additional exceptions apply to meals and entertainment in a subsidized eating facility or where the *de minimis* fringe benefit rule is met (see Chapter 5).

Exceptions to the 50 Percent Limit

General Hospital has an employee cafeteria on the premises for its doctors, nurses, and other employees. The cafeteria operates at cost. The 50 percent rule does not apply to General Hospital.

Canary Corporation gives a ham, a fruitcake, and a bottle of wine to each employee at year-end. Because the *de minimis* fringe benefit exclusion applies to business gifts of packaged foods and beverages, their *full* cost is deductible by Canary.

A similar exception applies to employer-paid recreational activities for employees (e.g., the annual holiday party or spring picnic).[39]

9-7b **Types of Entertainment Expenses**

Entertainment expenses must be either *directly related* to business or *associated with* business.[40] Directly related expenses are related to an actual business meeting or discussion. It is not necessary to show that actual benefit resulted from the entertainment as

---

[38]§ 274(n).

[39]§ 274(e)(4).

[40]§ 274(a)(1)(A).

long as there was a reasonable expectation of benefit. To qualify as *directly related*, the expense should be incurred in a clear business setting (e.g., hosting a hospitality room at a conference). If there is little possibility of engaging in the active conduct of a trade or business due to the nature of entertainment (e.g., a symphony concert or a sporting event), it is difficult to qualify the expenditure as directly related to business.

Associated with business entertainment must serve a specific business purpose, such as obtaining new business or maintaining existing business. These expenditures qualify only if the expenses directly precede or follow a bona fide business discussion (e.g., taking a client to a sporting event after a business meeting). Entertainment occurring on the same day as the business discussion meets the test.

9-7c Restrictions on Deductibility

Business Meals

A business meal is deductible only if all of the following are true:[41]

- The meal is directly related to or associated with the active conduct of a business.
- The expense is reasonable (i.e., not lavish or extravagant).
- The taxpayer (or an employee) is present at the meal.

Business Meals

EXAMPLE 41

Lance Smith has submitted a proposed consulting contract to a local business. He invites the two business owners to dinner to discuss the contract and pays for the meal, during which Lance answers questions about the proposed contract. Lance can deduct 50% of this qualified business meal.

EXAMPLE 42

Assume the same facts as Example 41, except that Lance buys dinner for the two business owners but does not attend the dinner. No deduction is allowed.

A business meal with a business associate or customer is not deductible unless business is discussed before, during, or after the meal. If, however, the taxpayer is in travel status, his or her meal can be deducted, subject to the 50 percent rule.

EXAMPLE 43

Lacy travels to San Francisco for a business convention. She pays for dinner with three colleagues and is not reimbursed by her employer. They do not discuss business. She can deduct 50% of the cost of her meal. However, she cannot deduct the cost of her colleagues' meals.

ETHICS & EQUITY **Your Turn or Mine?**

Natalie (a CPA), Mathew (an attorney), Jacob (a banker), and Avery (an insurance agent) all live and work in the same community. They have been friends since college. Every Friday, they have lunch together and make it a point to discuss some business matters. They take turns paying for the group's lunches, and each deducts the amount he or she paid for the lunch as an entertainment expense. Presuming that one of the four is audited, do you anticipate any difficulty with the IRS? Explain.

Club Dues

In general, club dues are not deductible.[42] However, the IRS allows a deduction for dues to clubs whose primary purpose is public service and community volunteerism (e.g., Kiwanis, Lions, and Rotary).

Even though dues are not deductible, actual entertainment at a club may qualify.

---

[41]§ 274(k).

[42]§ 274(a)(3).

During the current year, Vincent spent $1,400 on business lunches at the Lakeside Country Club. The annual membership fee was $6,000, and Vincent used the facility 60% of the time for business. Presuming that the lunches meet the business meal test, Vincent may claim $700 (50% × $1,400) as a deduction. None of the club dues are deductible.

Ticket Purchases for Entertainment

A deduction for the cost of a ticket for an entertainment activity is limited to the face value of the ticket (including any taxes).[43] This amount is then limited by the 50 percent rule. As a result, any payment in excess of this amount to a ticket broker (e.g., StubHub) is not deductible.

Expenses for renting or using a luxury skybox at a sports arena for entertainment are also limited. Here, the deduction is limited to the face value of nonluxury box seats in the arena, after which the 50 percent rule is applied. All seats in the luxury skybox are counted, even when some seats are unoccupied. Food and beverage expenses in the skybox are also allowed, subject to the 50 percent rule.

Castillo Company pays $12,000 to rent a 10-seat skybox at City Stadium for three football games. Nonluxury box seats at each event range from $55 to $120 a seat. In September, a Castillo representative and eight clients use the skybox for the first game. The entertainment follows a bona fide business discussion, and Castillo spends $490 for food and beverages during the game. The deduction for the first sports event is as follows:

Food and beverages	$ 490
Deduction for seats ($120 × 10 seats)	1,200
Total entertainment expense	$1,690
50% limitation	× 50%
Deduction	$ 845

Business Gifts

Although not subject to the 50 percent limit on meals and entertainment, business gifts are deductible only to the extent of $25 per donee per year.[44] Incidental costs such as engraving, gift-wrapping, mailing, and delivery are also allowed (in addition to the $25 maximum). Gifts costing $4 or less (e.g., pens with the employee's or company's name on them) or promotional materials are not subject to the $25 limit. Records must be maintained to substantiate business gifts.

Business Gifts

EXAMPLE 46

In December, Prism Associates purchases framed prints from a local artist and mails one to each of its clients. Each print costs $70; packaging and shipping costs are $10 per print. Prism may deduct $35 for each print sent ($25 gift maximum plus $10 for packaging and shipping).

EXAMPLE 47

Assume the same facts as Example 46. In addition to the framed prints, Prism also encloses a coffee mug imprinted with its name and logo. Each mug costs $3.

The coffee mug would be considered a promotional item, and its cost would also be allowed as a deduction.

---

[43]§ 274(l).

[44]§ 274(b)(1). Multiple gifts to members of the same customer's family are consolidated (so there will be only one $25 deduction allowed). Gifts to an employer (or an employee's superior) are not deductible.

Record-Keeping/Documentation Requirements

Proper documentation of entertainment and meal expenses is essential because of the strict record-keeping requirements and the restrictive tests that must be met. For example, documentation that consists solely of credit card receipts and canceled checks may be inadequate to substantiate the business purpose and business relationship.[45] Taxpayers should maintain detailed records of amounts, time, place, business purpose, and business relationships. A credit card receipt details the place, date, and amount of the expense. A notation made on the receipt of the names of the person(s) attending, the business relationship, and the topic of discussion should be sufficient.

Associated with or goodwill entertainment is not deductible unless a business discussion is conducted immediately before or after the entertainment. And a business purpose must exist for the entertainment. Taxpayers should document both the business discussion and the business purpose, such as obtaining business from a prospective customer, in order to ensure the deduction.

9-8 OTHER EMPLOYEE EXPENSES

LO.7

Identify other employee expenses.

9-8a Office in the Home

Most expenses for personal use assets are not deductible. Except for certain expenses (primarily, interest and taxes), this is the case with a personal residence. However, employees and self-employed individuals are allowed a deduction for office in the home expenses if a portion of the residence is used *exclusively* on a *regular basis* as either:

- The principal place of business for any trade or business of the taxpayer, or
- A place of business used by clients, patients, or customers.

Employees must meet an additional test: The use must be for the *convenience of the employer* rather than merely being "appropriate and helpful."[46]

The term *principal place of business* includes a place of business that satisfies the following requirements:[47]

- The office is used by the taxpayer to conduct administrative or management activities of a trade or business, and
- There is no other fixed location of the trade or business where the taxpayer conducts these activities.

EXAMPLE 48

Dr. Smith is a self-employed anesthesiologist. During the year, he spends 30 to 35 hours per week administering anesthesia and postoperative care to patients in three hospitals, none of which provides him with an office. He also spends two or three hours per day in a room in his home that he uses exclusively as an office. He does not meet patients there, but he performs a variety of tasks related to his medical practice (e.g., contacting surgeons, doing bookkeeping, and reading medical journals).

A deduction will be allowed because Dr. Smith uses the office in the home to conduct administrative or management activities of his trade or business and there is no other fixed location where these activities can be carried out.

The exclusive use requirement means that part of the home must be used *solely* for business purposes. An exception allows mixed use (both business and personal) of the home if a licensed day-care business is involved.

Exclusive Use Requirement

EXAMPLE 49

Troy is self-employed and maintains an office in his home for business purposes. The office is also used by his wife to pay the family bills and by his children to do homework assignments. Troy does not satisfy the exclusive use requirement, and no office in the home deduction is allowed.

---

[45]*Kenneth W. Guenther*, 54 TCM 382, T.C.Memo. 1987–440.

[46]§ 280A(c)(1).

[47]§ 280A(c)(1) as modified by the Tax Reform Act of 1997.

Exclusive Use Requirement

EXAMPLE 50

Muriel operates a licensed day-care center in her home. The children use the living room as a play area during the day, and Muriel and her family use it for personal purposes in the evening and on weekends. The mixed use of the living room does not disqualify Muriel from an office in the home deduction.

The office in the home deduction can be determined in either of two ways: the Regular (actual expense) Method or the Simplified (safe harbor) Method.

Regular Method

When using the Regular Method, relevant expenses must be categorized as direct or indirect. Direct expenses benefit only the business part of the home (e.g., repainting the office) and are deducted in full. Indirect expenses are for maintaining and operating the home (e.g., utilities and insurance). Because indirect expenses benefit both business and personal use, an allocation between the two is necessary. The allocation is made based on the floor space involved, dividing the business area by the total home area to arrive at the business percentage.

The allowable home office expenses cannot exceed the gross income from the business less all other business expenses (i.e., this deduction cannot create a loss). And the home office expenses that are allowed as itemized deductions anyway (e.g., mortgage interest and real estate taxes) must be deducted first.

The home office expenses of an employee are miscellaneous itemized deductions, except those (such as interest and taxes) that qualify as other personal itemized deductions. Home office expenses of a self-employed individual are trade or business expenses and are deductible *for* AGI.

Any disallowed home office expenses are *carried forward* and used in future years subject to the same limitations.

EXAMPLE 51

Rick is a certified public accountant employed by a regional CPA firm as a tax manager. He operates a separate furniture refinishing business that he operates out of his home. For this business, he uses two rooms in the basement exclusively and regularly. The floor space of the two rooms is 240 square feet, which is 10% of the total floor space of his 2,400-square-foot residence. Gross income from the business totals $8,000. Expenses of the business (other than home office expenses) are $6,500. Rick incurs the following home office expenses:

Real property taxes on residence	$ 4,000
Interest expense on residence	7,500
Operating expenses of residence (including homeowners insurance)	2,000
MACRS cost recovery on residence (based on 10% business use)	350

Rick's deductions are determined as follows:

Business income		$ 8,000
Less: Other business expenses		(6,500)
Net income from the business (before the office in the home deduction)		$ 1,500
Less: Allocable taxes ($4,000 × 10%)	$400	
Allocable interest ($7,500 × 10%)	750	(1,150)
		$ 350
Allocable operating expenses of the residence ($2,000 × 10%)		(200)
		$ 150
Allocable MACRS cost recovery ($350, limited to remaining income)		(150)
		$ –0–

Rick has a carryover of $200 (the unused excess MACRS cost recovery). Because he is self-employed, the allocable taxes and interest ($1,150), the other deductible office expenses ($200 + $150), and $6,500 of other business expenses are deductible *for* AGI.

As noted in Example 51, the office in the home deduction includes an allocable portion of the cost recovery on the personal residence. To arrive at this cost recovery, taxpayers use the MACRS percentage for 39-year nonresidential real property. Except for the first and last years (i.e., 1 and 40), the applicable percentage is 2.564 percent—see Exhibit 8.8 in Chapter 8. Cost recovery for office equipment and furnishings is computed using the MACRS rules for personal property discussed in Chapter 8—see Exhibits 8.1 and 8.3. These assets can also be expensed under § 179.

An office in the home deduction is also available to those who rent (rather than own) their home. If the taxpayer does not own the property, the applicable percentage of business use is applied to the rent being paid.

If the Regular Method is used, the office in the home deduction is claimed using Form 8829 (Expenses for Business Use of Your Home).

Simplified Method

Because of the complexity involved in using the Regular Method and, in particular, the difficulty in working with Form 8829, the IRS established an optional Simplified Method for the office in the home deduction.[48] If the Simplified Method is used, Form 8829 is not required. Taxpayers using the Simplified Method are allowed a deduction of $5 per square foot of space devoted to the office. However, as no more than 300 square feet can be counted, the maximum deduction is limited to $1,500.

The various rules governing the use of the Simplified Method are summarized below.

- No depreciation on the residence can be claimed.

- Actual expenses of maintaining and operating the home (e.g., qualified residence interest, property taxes, homeowners insurance, utilities) are ignored. Expenses that are deductible elsewhere on the tax return (e.g., qualified residence interest, property taxes) can be claimed in full without any reduction due to a home office deduction being claimed.

- Office in the home deductions in excess of the net income from the business *cannot* be carried over to a future year. An unused Regular Method deduction from a prior year *cannot* be carried to a Simplified Method year.

Taxpayers can choose between the Regular Method and the Simplified Method each year. However, once a choice is made, that choice cannot be changed. Care should be taken in making the choice because the Simplified Method may yield a smaller deduction.

EXAMPLE 52

Assume the same facts as in Example 51, except that Rick chooses the Simplified Method. This choice results in the following deduction:

Net income from the business (before the office in the home deduction)	$1,500
Simplified Method office in the home deduction ($5 × 240 square feet)	1,200
Net income from the business	$ 300

In comparing the results of Examples 51 and 52, note that the use of the Simplified Method left Rick with $500 less in deductions (counting the $200 unused carryover). However, Rick can now use the property taxes ($400) and interest ($750) allocated to the office in the home deduction under the Regular Method as itemized deductions on Schedule A.

---

[48]Rev.Proc. 2013–13, 2013–6 I.R.B. 478.

Which Method to Use

The availability of the Simplified Method presents an annual decision for the taxpayer. In choosing which method to use, here are some factors to consider:

- The Simplified Method requires fewer calculations and less record keeping.
- Because no depreciation is allowed, the Simplified Method will avoid the 25 percent tax on real estate gains (see Chapter 17).
- Even though the Simplified Method frees up certain home-related expenses (e.g., qualified residence interest, property taxes, homeowners insurance, utilities), are these expenses otherwise deductible? Some are (property taxes), and some are not (homeowners insurance). But even the expenses that are deductible (property taxes) may be subject to other itemized deduction limitations (see Chapter 10).
- With a maximum deduction of $1,500, the Simplified Method, in most cases, will result in a smaller deduction than the Regular Method.
- Under the Simplified Method, a taxpayer is not allowed to carry over unused deductions.
- Once a taxpayer has made a choice for a year, the choice cannot be changed.

EXAMPLE 53

Tyler, a calendar year taxpayer, prepared and filed his own tax return for 2016. Being in a hurry, he decided to use the Simplified Method of computing his home office deduction. In March 2018, Tyler seeks tax advice and learns how much he could have saved by using the Regular Method. Tyler cannot file an amended return for 2016, but he can switch to the Regular Method for 2017.

The Big Picture

EXAMPLE 54

Return to the facts of *The Big Picture* on p. 9-1. Morgan is using her apartment's second bedroom as a home office. Her apartment has 1,200 square feet; the second bedroom has 200 square feet. Her home office is, therefore, one-sixth of her apartment (200 square feet ÷ 1,200 square feet). During 2017, her apartment expenses include:

Rent ($1,250 per month)	$15,000
Utilities	2,600
Renter's insurance	1,100
Total	$18,700

In addition, she purchases various supplies and software for her tutoring ($700) and freelance driving ($75), as well as office furniture ($100 for a file cabinet to store her business records, $400 for a table, $250 for chairs, and $50 for a lamp; $800 total). The office furniture, which she can expense immediately under § 179, will be allocated to her freelance businesses based on total revenues.

Income from her tutoring amounts to $6,795, and she earned $8,305 from her freelance driving. She also has documented her business mileage for the year (630 for tutoring and 5,400 for freelance driving) and has receipts for freeway tolls of $175 (all related to her freelance driving). As indicated in Example 13, Morgan will use the automatic mileage method for her business miles.

Using the Simplified Method, Morgan's home office deduction would be $1,000 (200 square feet × $5 per square foot). Morgan will be better off using the Actual Cost Method, where her deduction will be $3,117 ($18,700 total apartment expenses × 1/6). This deduction will be allocated to her freelance businesses (tutoring and freelance driving), based on total revenues.

continued

	Tutoring	Freelance Driving	Total
Revenues	$ 6,795	$ 8,305	$15,100
Expenses:			
– Business mileage:			
630 × $0.535/mile	(337)		(337)
5,400 × $0.535/mile		(2,889)	(2,889)
– Business tolls		(175)	(175)
– Supplies/Software	(700)	(75)	(775)
– Office furniture ($800)	(360)	(440)	(800)
– Home office	(1,403)	(1,714)	(3,117)
Net income	$ 3,995	$ 3,012	$ 7,007

This example assumes that Morgan meets the "exclusive use" requirement for her home office (see text Section 9-8a and Examples 48, 49, and 50). As discussed there, the "exclusive use" requirement is a significant constraint. What would happen if on *one day* during the year Morgan went into the home office, opened her laptop computer, and spent *one hour* responding to her personal e-mails? Answer: the "exclusive use" test would not be met, and Morgan would lose the home office deduction. Further, proving a negative is difficult (how does one document that the home office was *never* used for personal purposes?). But Morgan needs to understand the standard and ensure that she complies with it. In our example, that means that when she wants to use her laptop for personal purposes, she uses it somewhere other than the office.

9-8b Miscellaneous Employee Expenses

Miscellaneous employee expenses include costs that are job-related, not reimbursed by the employer, and not covered elsewhere in the tax law. Expenses related to maintaining job status make up a significant category of miscellaneous expenses. They include such costs as union dues, membership dues to professional organizations, subscriptions to trade publications and professional journals, and various license fees paid to government agencies and other regulatory bodies.

Special Clothing

To be deductible, special clothing must be both specifically required as a condition of employment and not adaptable for regular wear. For example, a police officer's uniform must be worn when "on duty" but is not suitable for "off-duty" activities. Its cost, therefore, is deductible. When special clothing qualifies for deductibility, so does the cost of its maintenance (i.e., alterations, laundry, and dry cleaning).

The cost of clothing possessing *safety* features to prevent workplace injuries also qualifies. This includes such items as safety glasses, steel-toed shoes, special gloves, lab coats, and hard hats. These items are also not suitable for personal use.

Job Hunting

Job hunting expenses are deductible under certain conditions. However, no deduction is allowed for the costs of obtaining the first job. To qualify, the search must involve the same business as the taxpayer's current position, and it does not matter whether the search is successful. Costs that qualify include job counseling, résumé printing, compilation and distribution of biographical data (such as work history), and unreimbursed travel for job interviews.

The Big Picture

EXAMPLE

55

Return to the facts of *The Big Picture* on p. 9-1. Recall that Morgan conducted an extensive job search before obtaining her position with ECCC. Because this is her first job, the expenses she incurred in the search are not deductible.

Educator Expenses

Many teachers pay for professional development courses or purchase school supplies for classroom use and are not reimbursed by their employer. These expenses are miscellaneous itemized deductions (i.e., *from* AGI deductions) and are subject to a 2%-of-AGI floor (see text Section 9-11a). Thus, these restrictions can reduce or eliminate any tax benefit available to the teacher.

Modest relief is provided for elementary and secondary school educators, allowing them to claim up to $250 of these expenses as a deduction *for* AGI.[49] Eligible educators must work at least 900 hours during a school year as a teacher, an instructor, a counselor, a principal, or an aide. Covered costs include unreimbursed expenses for professional development courses, books, supplies, computer and other equipment, and supplementary materials used in the classroom.

Connie is a full-time teacher at Hoover Elementary. During the year, she spends $1,200 for school supplies for her fourth-grade class. Under an accountable plan (see later in the chapter), Hoover reimburses her for $400 of these supplies. As to the $800 balance, Connie may claim $250 as a deduction *for* AGI and $550 as a miscellaneous itemized deduction (subject to the 2%-of-AGI floor). **EXAMPLE 56**

9-9 CONTRIBUTIONS TO RETIREMENT ACCOUNTS

LO.8

Compare various deductions for contributions to retirement accounts.

Retirement planning is critical for employees. As noted in Chapter 1, using the tax law to provide retirement security for employees can be justified on both economic and social grounds. Although Social Security provides some retirement income, it is not sufficient for most recipients. As a result, the private sector must fill the need. Congress has enacted a variety of laws that provide significant tax advantages for retirement plans. These plans fall into two major classifications: those available to employees and those available to self-employed persons. As Chapter 19 provides significant coverage of deferred compensation and retirement planning, only a brief discussion occurs here.

9-9a Employee IRAs

Pension plans covering employees follow one of two income tax approaches. Most plans allow an *exclusion* for the contributions the employee makes to the plan. The employee's income tax return shows nothing regarding the contribution—no income, exclusion, or deduction. This is the case even if the contribution is funded entirely (or partially) by means of a salary reduction.[50]

The other income tax approach is followed by the **traditional IRA**. Here, the contributing employee is allowed a deduction *for* AGI. The amount, a maximum of $5,500 in 2017 and 2016 or $6,500 in 2017 and 2016 for those age 50 and older, is reported as a deduction on Form 1040.[51] As with the exclusion variety of pension plan, nothing is taxed to the employee-participant until distributions from the traditional IRA occur. Consequently, all of these types of retirement plans carry the advantage of deferring the taxation of income. As described in Chapter 19, all retirement plans are subject to various rules regarding coverage requirements, degree of vesting, excessive contributions, and premature distributions. Generally, these rules are less stringent for traditional IRAs.

The traditional IRA is to be distinguished from the **Roth IRA**, which takes a radically different tax approach. No tax benefit (i.e., exclusion or deduction) results from the initial contribution to a Roth IRA. Instead, later distributions (including postcontribution earnings) are recovered tax-free.[52]

---

[49]§ 62(a)(2)(D).

[50]See, for example, §§ 401(k), 403(b), and 457.

[51]§§ 219 and 408.

[52]§ 408A.

9-9b **Self-Employed Keogh (H.R. 10) Plans**

Self-employed taxpayers can also participate in retirement plans with tax-favored benefits. Known as Keogh (or H.R. 10) plans, these arrangements follow the deduction approach of traditional IRAs.[53] The amount contributed under a plan is a deduction *for* AGI and is reported as a deduction on Form 1040. The plan established by a self-employed taxpayer who has employees must meet stringent requirements to ensure that it provides similar retirement benefits for the group. The law is structured to ensure that employees share an owner-employer's ability to defer taxes.

Retirement plans for self-employed taxpayers and other small businesses are not restricted to H.R. 10 plans. Other options include solo or individual § 401(k) plans, simplified employee pension (SEP) plans, and savings incentive match plans for employees (SIMPLEs).[54] The operational rules governing all of these plans are covered in Chapter 19.

9-10 **CLASSIFICATION OF EMPLOYEE EXPENSES**

Demonstrate the difference between accountable and nonaccountable employee plans.

The classification of employee expenses depends on whether the expenses are reimbursed by the employer under an accountable plan. If so, neither the reimbursement nor the expense is reported by the employee. In effect, therefore, this result is equivalent to treating the expenses as deductions *for* AGI. If the expenses are reimbursed under a nonaccountable plan or are not reimbursed at all, then they are classified as deductions *from* AGI and can be claimed only if the employee-taxpayer itemizes. An exception is made for moving expenses and the employment-related expenses of a qualified performing artist.[55] Here, a deduction *for* AGI classification is allowed.

For classification purposes, therefore, the difference between accountable and nonaccountable plans is significant.

9-10a **Accountable Plans**

An **accountable plan** requires the employee to satisfy these two requirements:

- Substantiate the expenses. An employee provides an *adequate accounting* by submitting a record (e.g., completing an employer-provided travel expense reimbursement form), with receipts and other substantiation, to the employer.[56]
- Return any excess reimbursement or allowance. An "excess reimbursement or allowance" is any amount the employee does not adequately account for as an ordinary and necessary business expense.

Substantiation

No deduction is allowed for any travel, entertainment, business gift, or listed property (e.g., automobiles and computers) expenses unless properly substantiated by adequate records. The records should contain the following information:[57]

- The amount of the expense.
- The time and place of travel or entertainment (or date of gift).
- The business purpose of the expense.
- The business relationship of the taxpayer to the person entertained (or receiving the gift).

As a result, the taxpayer must keep records (e.g., in a calendar or by other means) to document these expenses. Documentary evidence, such as itemized receipts, is required to support any lodging expenses while traveling away from home and for any other

---

[53]§ 401(c).

[54]The relevant Code Sections are § 408(k) for SEPs and § 408(p) for SIMPLEs.

[55]As defined in § 62(b).

[56]Reg. § 1.162–17(b)(4).

[57]§ 274(d).

expenditure of $75 or more. If a taxpayer fails to keep adequate records, a written or oral statement of the exact details of the expense will be required, along with other corroborating evidence.[58]

Inadequate Substantiation

Ben has travel expenses substantiated only by canceled checks. The checks establish the date, place, and amount of the expenditure. Because neither the business relationship nor the business purpose is established, the deduction is disallowed.[59]

EXAMPLE 57

Justin has travel and entertainment expenses substantiated by a digital diary showing the time, place, and amount of the expenditure. He is able to provide information about the business relationship and business purpose orally. However, because he has no receipts, any expenditures of $75 or more are disallowed.[60]

EXAMPLE 58

Deemed Substantiation

In lieu of reimbursing actual expenses for travel away from home, many employers reduce their paperwork by adopting a policy of reimbursing employees with a *per diem* allowance, a flat dollar amount per day of business travel. Of the substantiation requirements listed previously, the *amount* of the expense is proved, or *deemed substantiated*, by using such a per diem allowance or reimbursement procedure. The amount of expenses that is deemed substantiated is equal to the lesser of the per diem allowance or the amount of the Federal per diem rate.

The regular Federal per diem rate is the highest amount the Federal government will pay to its employees for lodging, meals, and incidental expenses[61] while traveling. The rates are different for different locations.[62]

The use of the standard Federal per diem rates for meals and incidental expenses also constitutes an adequate accounting. Employees and self-employed persons can use these standard allowances instead of deducting the actual cost of daily meals and incidental expenses, even if not reimbursed. There is no standard lodging allowance, however.

Only the amount of the expense is considered substantiated under the deemed substantiated method. Records must be maintained for the other items: place, date, business purpose of the expense, and the business relationship of the parties involved.

9-10b Nonaccountable Plans

A nonaccountable plan is a plan in which an adequate accounting or return of excess amounts, or both, is not required. All expense reimbursements are included as wages on the employee's Form W–2. Any allowable expenses are deductible in the same manner as unreimbursed expenses.

Unreimbursed Employee Expenses

Unreimbursed employee business expenses are treated as miscellaneous itemized deductions subject to the 2%-of-AGI floor (see text Section 9-11). Meals and entertainment expenses are subject to the 50 percent limit. If the employee could have received, but did not seek, reimbursement for whatever reason, none of the employment-related expenses are deductible.

---

[58]Reg. § 1.274–5T(c)(3).

[59]*William T. Whitaker*, 56 TCM 47, T.C.Memo. 1988–418.

[60]*W. David Tyler*, 43 TCM 927, T.C.Memo. 1982–160.

[61]For this purpose, incidental expenses include tips and fees to porters, bellhops, hotel maids, etc. These expenses are expected to be relatively small and typically paid out in cash.

[62]*Per Diem Rates* (IRS Publication 1542) contains the list and amounts for the year. This publication is available only on the internet at **www.irs.gov**. Links to per diem rates can also be found at **www.gsa.gov**.

Failure to Comply with Accountable Plan Requirements

An employer may have an accountable plan and require employees to return excess reimbursements or allowances, but an employee may fail to follow the rules of the plan. In that case, the expenses and reimbursements are subject to nonaccountable plan treatment.

9-10c Reporting Procedures

When a reimbursement under an accountable plan is paid in separate amounts relating to designated expenses such as meals or entertainment, no reporting problem occurs. If the reimbursement is made in a single amount, an allocation must be made to determine the appropriate portion of the reimbursement that applies to meals and entertainment and to other employee expenses.

Sophia, who is employed by Garnet Company, had AGI of $60,000 during the year. She incurred employment-related expenses as follows: $4,000 (transportation), $3,000 (lodging), $2,000 (meals), and $1,000 (entertainment). Under an accountable plan, Sophia received partial reimbursement from Garnet of $6,000. Because Sophia was not fully reimbursed, she must make an allocation to determine the portion attributable to the expenses subject to the 50 percent reduction for meals and entertainment.

$$\frac{\$2,000 \text{ (meals)} + \$1,000 \text{ (entertainment)}}{\$10,000 \text{ (total expenses)}} = 30\%$$

Thus, 30% of the reimbursement, or $1,800, relates to meals and entertainment, while the balance of $4,200 applies to transportation and lodging. Further computations follow to account for the reimbursement (treated, in effect, as a deduction *for* AGI), apply the 50 percent reduction, and deduct the 2% floor.

	No Adjustment	50% Reduction
Transportation and lodging ($4,000 + $3,000)	$ 7,000	
Meals and entertainment ($2,000 + $1,000)		$ 3,000
Less reimbursement		
(70% × $6,000)	(4,200)	
(30% × $6,000)		(1,800)
	$ 2,800	$ 1,200
50% reduction (50% × $1,200)		(600)
Unreimbursed portion	$ 2,800	$ 600

The unreimbursed portion of $3,400 ($2,800 + $600) is reported on Schedule A and is reduced by 2% of AGI. Thus, $3,400 − $1,200 [2% × $60,000 (AGI)] yields a deduction *from* AGI of $2,200. Sophia does not have to report any of the $6,000 reimbursement.

9-10d Improving the Tax Position of Employees

For an employee with job-related expenses who receives reimbursement from the employer, the ideal tax position results from the following arrangement:

- Render an adequate accounting to the employer.
- Be fully reimbursed.
- Return any excess reimbursement.

If these conditions exist, the employee will avoid the 50 percent reduction for meals and entertainment and will completely eliminate the 2 percent floor on employee expenses. As all of the employee expenses are shifted to the employer, the employee may even be able to claim the standard deduction rather than itemize.

Even if the reimbursement of expenses is partial (not full), some planning is possible. Consider what happens in Example 59 if Garnet's reimbursement states that it specifically covers the $2,000 meals and $1,000 entertainment expenditures. Now the 50 percent meal and entertainment reduction does not apply to Sophia, and her deduction is increased.

9-11 LIMITATIONS ON ITEMIZED DEDUCTIONS

LO.10

Apply the limitations on miscellaneous itemized deductions.

Many itemized deductions (*from* AGI deductions) are subject to limitations based on a taxpayer's AGI. For example, only those medical expenses in excess of 10 percent of AGI are deductible (this is often called a "floor") and most charitable contributions are limited to a maximum of 50 percent of a taxpayer's AGI (this is often called a "ceiling"). These limitations are discussed in Chapter 10. Miscellaneous itemized deductions (including employee business expenses) are also subject to an AGI floor.

9-11a Miscellaneous Itemized Deductions Subject to the 2 Percent Floor

Certain miscellaneous itemized deductions, including most *unreimbursed employee business expenses*, are aggregated and then reduced by 2 percent of AGI.[63] Expenses subject to the 2 percent floor include:

- All § 212 expenses, except expenses of producing rent and royalty income (see Chapter 6).
- All unreimbursed employee business expenses, after the 50 percent limit for entertainment and meals, if applicable (except moving expenses).
- Professional dues and subscriptions.
- Union dues and work uniforms.
- Employment-related education expenses (except § 222 qualified tuition and related expenses).
- Expenses of job hunting (including employment agency fees and résumé-writing expenses).
- Home office expenses of an employee or outside salesperson.
- Legal, accounting, and tax return preparation fees.
- Hobby expenses, up to hobby income (see Chapter 6).
- Investment expenses, including investment counsel fees, subscriptions, and safe deposit box rental.
- Custodial fees relating to income-producing property or a traditional IRA or a Keogh plan.
- Appraisal fees paid to determine a casualty loss or charitable contribution.

9-11b Miscellaneous Itemized Deductions Not Subject to the 2 Percent Floor

Certain miscellaneous itemized deductions, including the following, are not subject to the 2 percent floor:

- Impairment-related work expenses of individuals with a disability.
- Amortizable premium on taxable bonds.
- Losses from Ponzi-type investment schemes.
- Gambling losses to the extent of gambling winnings.
- Unrecovered investment in an annuity.

---
[63]§ 67.

EXAMPLE

60

Ted, who has AGI of $40,000, has the following miscellaneous itemized deductions:

Gambling losses (to extent of gains)	$2,200
Tax return preparation fees	500
Unreimbursed employee transportation	600
Professional dues and subscriptions	360
Safe deposit box rental	90

Ted's itemized deductions are as follows:

Deduction not subject to 2% floor (gambling losses)		$2,200
Deductions subject to 2% floor ($500 + $600 + $360 + $90)	$1,550	
Less 2% of AGI	(800)	750
Total miscellaneous itemized deductions		$2,950

What if Ted's AGI is $80,000? Now the 2%-of-AGI floor is $1,600 (2% of $80,000); in this case, he can only deduct the gambling losses of $2,200 because his miscellaneous itemized deductions subject to the 2% floor do not exceed $1,600.

9-12 TAX PLANNING

LO.11

List and evaluate tax planning ideas related to employee business expenses.

9-12a Employment Status

When considering the merits of employee or independent contractor status, much depends on which party is involved. Earlier in the chapter, we discussed some of the employer implications of this choice. If it is the worker, being self-employed carries the obvious advantage of a deduction *for* AGI category of work-related expenses and the avoidance of the 2%-of-AGI floor related to any unreimbursed expenses.

However, a self-employed individual may have other costs, such as local gross receipts taxes, license fees, franchise fees, personal property taxes, and occupation taxes. In addition, the record-keeping and filing requirements can be quite burdensome.

One of the most expensive considerations is the Social Security tax versus the self-employment tax. For an employee in 2017, for example, the Social Security tax applies at a rate of 6.2 percent on a base amount of wages of $127,200 ($118,500 in 2016) and the Medicare tax applies at a rate of 1.45 percent with no limit on the base amount. Further, a .9 percent additional Medicare tax applies to certain high earners. For self-employed persons, the Social Security and Medicare tax rates *double* (to 12.4 percent and 2.9 percent, respectively). Even though a deduction *for* AGI is allowed for part of the self-employment tax paid, an employee and a self-employed individual are not in the same tax position on equal amounts of earnings. The self-employment tax is explained in Chapter 13. For the applicability of these taxes to employees, see Chapter 1.

9-12b Implications of Misclassifying Workers

The Patient Protection and Affordable Care Act, also known as the Affordable Care Act (ACA) or ObamaCare, places specific compliance burdens (both financial and reporting) on employers regarding the provision of health care coverage for their employees. The rules are complex and vary according to the size of the employer (large or small) and the status of the employee (full- or part-time).[64] Because the ACA does not apply to independent contractors and part-time employees, employers may be more likely to misclassify workers. To discourage this from happening, penalties are levied on those employers who wrongfully categorize workers as independent contractors.

---

[64]Large employers are those with 50 or more full-time or full-time equivalent employees. Part-time employees work less than 30 hours per week.

There are many reasons to favor classifying workers as independent contractors rather than as employees. Besides avoiding payroll taxes and income tax withholdings, the employer circumvents a myriad of state and local laws. Examples include vacation pay obligations, unemployment tax and workers' compensation requirements, and overtime and minimum wage restrictions. Because complying with these rules is costly and burdensome, many employers are motivated to misclassify their workers as independent contractors.

In the event of misclassification, two remedies are available regarding Federal employment taxes—one legislative and one administrative. The legislative option, known as Section 530 relief, absolves the employer of the employment taxes that should have been paid.[65] To obtain Section 530 relief, *all* three of the following requirements must be met:

- The employer has a reasonable basis for *not* treating the workers as employees. Reasonable basis means reliance on any of the following:
  - ➤ A court case, a published IRS ruling, or IRS technical advice.
  - ➤ A past IRS audit that resulted in no employment tax assessment.
  - ➤ A long-standing practice of independent contractor status in the same industry.
- The employer has consistently treated the workers as independent contractors.
- The employer filed a Form 1099–MISC (Miscellaneous Income) for each worker (when required).

A Federal administrative remedy for employers who are misclassifying workers is the Voluntary Classification Settlement Program (VCSP).[66] A type of amnesty arrangement, the VCSP allows the applicant to be absolved from all employment taxes that should have been paid plus any interest and penalties that would be due. To be accepted, Form 8952 [Application for Voluntary Classification Settlement Program (VCSP)] must be filed with the IRS and certain conditions met.[67] A major condition is the payment of 10 percent of the employment taxes that are usually due when workers are reclassified.

9-12c **Transportation and Travel Expenses**

Adequate detailed records of all transportation and travel expenses should be kept. Because the automatic (standard) mileage method applies to all automobiles in the same manner, a new, expensive automobile used primarily for business may generate a higher deduction using the actual cost method. Once a method is chosen, a later change may be possible. Switching from the automatic mileage method to the actual cost method is allowed if a basis adjustment is made for depreciation deemed taken (see Example 11). Switching from the actual cost method to the automatic mileage method is possible only if the taxpayer has not used the MACRS statutory percentage method and has not claimed § 179 limited expensing.

If an automobile has mixed use (i.e., both personal and business), maintaining a record of business miles driven is critical. Further, the business use portion should be realistic under the circumstances. Although a 95 percent business use allocation for a one-car family living in the suburbs is possible, the IRS might question this allocation (i.e., does the 5 percent allocated to personal use reasonably account for commuting to work, trips to the grocery store and mall, soccer practice, and dance lessons?).

If a taxpayer wants to sightsee or vacation on a business trip, scheduling business on both the Friday and Monday surrounding the weekend turns the weekend into business days for allocation purposes. It is especially crucial to schedule appropriate business days when foreign travel is involved.

---

[65]This safe harbor for withholding purposes originated in Section 530 of the Revenue Act of 1978. See IRS *Headliner*, vol. 152 (March 27, 2006). Section 530 relief does not absolve an employer of any Affordable Care Act (ObamaCare) penalties.

[66]Announcement 2011–64, 2011–4 I.R.B. 503.

[67]The conditions to be met are identified in the instructions for Form 8952. Many of these conditions are the same as those required for Section 530 relief.

9-12d **Education Expenses**

Education expenses are treated as nondeductible personal items unless the individual is employed or is engaged in a trade or business. A temporary leave of absence for further education is one way to reasonably ensure that the taxpayer is still qualified, even if a full-time student. An individual was permitted to deduct education expenses even though he resigned from his job, returned to school full-time for two years, and accepted another job in the same field upon graduation. The court held that the student had merely suspended active participation in his field.[68]

If the time away from the field is too long, educational expense deductions will be disallowed. For example, a teacher who left the field for four years to raise her child and curtailed her employment searches and writing activities was denied a deduction. She was not actively engaged in the trade or business of being an educator.[69]

The deduction for qualified tuition and related expenses (§ 222) provides some relief from the current restrictions on the deduction of education expenses by employees. First, the education expense does not have to be work-related. Second, it is a deduction *for* (not *from*) AGI. Unfortunately, the annual amount allowed as a deduction not only is quite modest (a maximum of $4,000) but also may be unavailable to certain taxpayers. It is not available, for example, to those whose income exceeds a modified AGI ceiling ($80,000 for singles; $160,000 for marrieds) or to someone who can be claimed as a dependent.

Before selecting this deduction, however, taxpayers should consider the American Opportunity credit or the lifetime learning credit under § 25A.[70] As credits provide a dollar-for-dollar reduction of tax liability, these credits could yield a greater tax benefit than deductions *for* AGI. But these credits also have limits that apply to higher-income taxpayers.

REFOCUS ON THE BIG PICTURE

THE FIRST JOB

The first issue that might arise as a result of Morgan's new job is the dependency exemption possibility. If Morgan was living at home and accepted the job late in the year, she could qualify as a dependent of her parents. If so, they might also be able to claim the qualified tuition deduction (or the lifetime learning credit). If, however, her employment began early in the year, she could not be a qualifying child (due to the self-supporting limitation) or a qualifying relative (due to the gross income limitation)—see Chapter 3.

Although Morgan's "extensive search" for employment indicates that she may have incurred job hunting expenses, such expenses are not deductible in a *first job* setting (see Example 55). Her qualified moving expenses, however, are deductible. Moving expenses are deductions *for* AGI (see Example 31).

Morgan can claim an office in the home deduction because she is using her second bedroom exclusively for her tutoring and freelance driving businesses. She can use either the Regular (actual expense) Method or the Simplified (safe harbor) Method. Under the Regular Method, the deduction would include a portion of the rent, utilities, and insurance paid. The Simplified Method would allow Morgan $5 per square foot for business space, but not more than 300 square feet, or $1,500. As her second bedroom is 200 square feet, the Simplified Method produces a

continued

---

[68]*Stephen G. Sherman*, 36 TCM 1191, T.C.Memo. 1977–301.

[69]*Brian C. Mulherin*, 42 TCM 834, T.C.Memo. 1981–454; *George A. Baist*, 56 TCM 778, T.C.Memo. 1988–554.

[70]These credits are briefly mentioned on p. 9-21 and are discussed at greater length in Chapter 13.

ISTOCKPHOTO.COM/SVETIKD

$1,000 deduction (see Example 54). Under either method, she would also be allowed to deduct other business expenses including her software, supplies, and depreciation (or expensing) of office equipment and furnishings (e.g., computer, copier, desk, file cabinet). She must be careful, however, not to violate the "exclusive use" restriction (see Examples 49, 51, and 52) regardless of which method she uses. Morgan will use the Regular Method, as it results in a larger deduction ($3,117; see Example 54).

In addition to commuting between her apartment and her job at ECCC, Morgan will also use her car for her freelance businesses (see Example 9). Normally, she would need to make a choice between the automatic mileage method and the actual cost method. However, because she is using a car given to her by her parents (see Example 13), she will use the automatic mileage method.

In addition to her automobile expenses, Morgan should document any meal expenses she incurs while driving for Uber and other companies. However, any meals are subject to the 50 percent limitation. These expenses will be *for* AGI deductions.

Any expenses she incurs related to her job with Enrichment Child Care Center will be classified as employee business expenses. The total of all employment-related expenses is an itemized deduction (a *from* AGI deduction) subject to the 2%-of-AGI floor.

Morgan must maintain adequate records regarding all of these transactions. Detailed records are particularly important in arriving at her office in the home deduction (if the Regular Method is used) and the business use of her car (for her freelancing jobs).

Key Terms

Accountable plan, 9-32	Independent contractor, 9-2	Statutory employees, 9-5
Automatic mileage method, 9-7	Moving expenses, 9-14	Traditional IRA, 9-31
Deduction for qualified tuition and related expenses, 9-20	Nonaccountable plan, 9-33	Transportation expenses, 9-5
	Office in the home expenses, 9-26	Travel expenses, 9-10
Education expenses, 9-18	Roth IRA, 9-31	
Entertainment expenses, 9-22		

Discussion Questions

1. **LO.1, 9** Sophia and Jacob are married and file a joint return. Their 2016 tax return included a Form 2106 for each of them. Their 2017 tax return, however, included a Form 2106 and a Schedule C. In terms of employment status, what could have changed?   Issue ID

2. **LO.1** Mason performs services for Isabella. In determining whether Mason is an employee or an independent contractor, comment on the relevance of each of the factors listed below.
   a. Mason performs services only for Isabella and does not work for anyone else.
   b. Mason sets his own work schedule.
   c. Mason reports his job-related expenses on a Schedule C.
   d. Mason obtained his job skills from Isabella's training program.
   e. Mason performs the services at Isabella's business location.
   f. Mason is paid based on time worked rather than on task performed.

Issue ID   3.   **LO.2** Milton is a resident of Mobile (AL) and is employed by Scaup Corporation. Because Scaup closed its Mobile office, Milton no longer has any nondeductible commuting expenses although he continues to work for Scaup. Explain why.

Issue ID   4.   **LO.2** In 2015, Emma purchased an automobile, which she uses for both business and personal purposes. Although Emma does not keep records as to operating expenses (e.g., gas, oil, and repairs), she can prove the percentage of business use and the miles driven each year. In March 2017, Emma seeks your advice as to what income tax benefit, if any, she can derive from the use of her automobile. What would you suggest?

Issue ID   5.   **LO.3** Dr. Werner is a full-time professor of accounting at Pelican University. During the year, he teaches continuing education programs for CPA groups in several cities. He also serves as an expert witness in numerous lawsuits involving accounting fraud. Comment on the possible tax treatment of Dr. Werner's job-related expenses.

6.   **LO.4** To qualify for the moving expense deduction, a taxpayer must satisfy a time test.
   a.   What is the time test?
   b.   When might the taxpayer be excused from satisfying the time test?
   c.   What reporting procedure should be followed when the taxpayer has to file a return *after* the moving expenses have been incurred but *before* the time test requirement is met?
   d.   Create a brief PowerPoint presentation (two or three slides) summarizing your solution, and e-mail it to your instructor.

7.   **LO.4** Emma, who lives and works in Wisconsin, is planning to retire and move to Costa Rica. She has heard that when you retire and move to a foreign country, all moving expenses are deductible. Does Emma have a correct grasp of the rules involved? Explain.

8.   **LO.5, 10** Jamie has an undergraduate degree in finance and is employed full-time by a bank. She is taking courses at a local university leading to an MBA degree.
   a.   Is the full cost of this education deductible to her?
   b.   If so, what limitations are imposed on the deduction?

9.   **LO.5, 10** In connection with § 222 (deduction for qualified tuition and related expenses), comment on the relevance of the following:
   a.   The standard deduction is claimed.
   b.   Enrollment at a college does not require the payment of a student activity fee.
   c.   Miscellaneous itemized deductions are less than 2% of AGI.
   d.   The taxpayer is married and files a separate return.
   e.   A father pays the tuition on behalf of a daughter who does not qualify as his dependent.
   f.   The taxpayer is single and has MAGI of $80,001.
   g.   The lifetime learning credit is claimed.
   h.   The taxpayer, a CPA, pays for tuition and course materials to attend law school.

10.   **LO.6** In each of the following situations, indicate whether the 50% reduction for meals and entertainment expenses applies.
   a.   Each year, the employer awards its top salesperson an all-expense-paid trip to Jamaica.
   b.   The employer has a cafeteria for its employees where meals are furnished at cost.
   c.   The employer sponsors an annual Labor Day picnic for its employees.
   d.   Every Christmas, the employer gives each employee a fruitcake.

e. The taxpayer, an airline pilot, pays for meals and lodging during a layover between flights.

f. The taxpayer pays a cover charge to take key clients to a nightclub.

g. The taxpayer gives business gifts to her clients at Christmas.

h. The taxpayer purchases tickets to take clients to an athletic event.

11. **LO.7** In connection with the office in the home deduction, comment on the following:

a. The exclusive use requirement.

b. The distinction between *direct* and *indirect* expenses.

c. The effect of the taxpayer's work status (i.e., employed or self-employed) on the deduction.

d. The ownership status of the residence (i.e., owned or rented).

e. The tax treatment of office furnishings (e.g., desk, chairs, and file cabinets).

f. The treatment of expenses that exceed the gross income from the business.

12. **LO.7** Review the advantages and disadvantages of the Simplified Method for determining the office in the home deduction. Create a brief summary of your findings, and e-mail it to your instructor.

13. **LO.4, 7** Trent, a resident of Florida, attends Rice University. After graduation, he   Issue ID
moves to Dallas, where he begins a job search. Shortly thereafter, he accepts a position with a local TV station as a reporter. Trent's college degree is in accounting. Presuming no reimbursement, what employment-related expenses might Trent be eligible to deduct?

14. **LO.8** Regarding the tax implications of various retirement plans, comment on the following:

a. The difference between Keogh (H.R. 10) and traditional deductible IRA plans.

b. The difference between traditional IRA and Roth IRA plans.

15. **LO.9** What tax return reporting procedures must be followed by an employee under the following circumstances?

a. Expenses and reimbursements are equal under an accountable plan.

b. Reimbursements at the appropriate Federal per diem rate exceed expenses, and an adequate accounting is made to the employer.

c. Expenses exceed reimbursements under a nonaccountable plan.

Computational Exercises

16. **LO.2** Michael holds a full-time job with Brown Company and a part-time job with Tan Corporation. During a workday, he drives 20 miles to Brown, returns home, has a meal, and then drives 15 miles to Tan. Tan is located 12 miles from Brown. What is Michael's deductible mileage?

17. **LO.2** Lara uses the standard mileage method for determining auto expenses. During 2017, she used her car as follows: 9,000 miles for business, 2,000 miles for personal use, 2,500 miles for a move to a new job, 1,000 miles for charitable purposes, and 500 miles for medical visits. Presuming that all the mileage expenses are allowable (i.e., not subject to percentage limitations), what is Lara's deduction for:

a. Business?

b. Moving?

c. Charitable?

d. Medical?

18. **LO.3** Fred travels from Denver to Miami primarily on business. He spends five days conducting business and two days sightseeing. His expenses are $400 (airfare), $150 per day (meals), and $300 per night (lodging). What are Fred's deductible expenses?

19. **LO.3** Brenda travels from Chicago to Barcelona (Spain) on business. She is gone 10 days (including 2 days of travel) during which time she spends 5 days conducting business and 3 days sightseeing. Her expenses are $1,500 (airfare), $200 per day (meals), and $400 per night (lodging). Because Brenda stayed with relatives while sightseeing, she only paid for 5 nights of lodging. What is Brenda's deduction for:
    a. Airfare?
    b. Meals?
    c. Lodging?

20. **LO.4** After accepting his first job upon graduating from college, Christian has the following moving expenses:

Rental of moving van	$450
Meals	200
Lodging	250

    Presuming no reimbursement, what is Christian's moving expense deduction?

21. **LO.5** Samantha was recently employed by an accounting firm. During the year, she spends $2,500 for a CPA exam review course and begins working on a law degree in night school. Her law school expenses were $4,200 for tuition and $450 for books (which are not a requirement for enrollment in the course). Assuming no reimbursement, how much can Samantha deduct for the:
    a. CPA exam review course?
    b. Law school expenses?

22. **LO.6** Robert entertains four key clients and their spouses at a nightclub. Substantive business discussions occurred over dinner and prior to the entertainment beginning. Expenses were $200 (limo charge), $120 (cover charge), $700 (drinks and dinner), and $140 (tips to servers). If Robert is self-employed, how much can he deduct for this event?

23. **LO.6** The CEO of Crimson, Inc., entertains seven clients at a skybox in Memorial Stadium for an athletic event. Substantive business discussions occurred at various times during the event. The box costs $2,000 per event and seats 10 people. (The cost of a regular seat at Memorial ranges from $55 to $100.) Refreshments served during the event cost $700. How much of these costs may Crimson deduct?

24. **LO.6** Andrew sends Godiva chocolates to 10 of his key clients at Christmas. The chocolates cost $50 a box not including $4 for gift wrapping and shipping. How much can Andrew deduct?

25. **LO.7** Cindy maintains an office in her home that comprises 8% (200 square feet) of total floor space. Gross income for her business is $42,000, and her residence expenses are as follows:

Real property taxes	$2,400
Interest on mortgage	4,000
Operating expenses	2,200
Depreciation (based on 8% business use)	450

    What is Cindy's office in the home deduction based on:
    a. The Regular Method?
    b. The Simplified Method?

26. **LO.4, 7** Mason, a licensed pharmacist, has always lived and worked in Boston. When he retires from a national drugstore chain, he conducts an extensive job search for any kind of employment in Florida. He finally moves to Tampa, where he is able to obtain a position as a night manager of a motel. In connection with the relocation, he incurs job search expenses of $7,000 and qualified moving expenses of $12,000. How much can Mason deduct?

27. **LO.10** Ava has AGI of $58,000 and the following miscellaneous itemized deductions:

Home office expenses	$1,200
Union dues and work uniforms	350
Unreimbursed employee expenses	415
Gambling losses to the extent of gambling winnings	890

What is Ava's total itemized deduction (after any percentage limit)?

Problems

28. **LO.2, 3** During the year, Olivia holds two jobs. After an eight-hour day at the first job, she works three hours at the second job. On Fridays of each week, she returns home for dinner before going to the second job. On the other days (Monday through Thursday), she goes directly from the first job to the second job, stopping along the way for a meal. The mileage involved is as follows:

Home to first job	15
First job to second job	18
Home to second job	20

a. Assuming that Olivia works 48 weeks during the year, how much of her mileage is deductible?
b. Can Olivia deduct the dinners she purchased? Why or why not?

29. **LO.2, 5** William is employed by an accounting firm and uses his automobile in connection with his work. During the month of October 2017, he works at the office for 3 days and participates in the audit of a key client for 19 days. In the audit situation, William goes directly from his home to the client's office. On all other days, he drives to his employer's office. On four Saturdays in October, he drives from his home to a local university where he attends classes in a part-time MBA program. Relevant mileage is as follows:

Home to office	12
Office to audit client	13
Home to audit client	14
Home to university	10

Using the automatic mileage method, what is William's deduction for the month?

30. **LO.2** Ella is the regional sales manager for a clothing store. She starts her work day by driving from home to the regional office, works there for several hours, and then visits the three stores in her region. Relevant mileage is as follows:

Home to regional office	10
Regional office to Store 1	13
Store 1 to Store 2	11
Store 2 to Store 3	9
Store 3 to home	15

If Ella uses the automatic mileage method and works 240 days in 2017, what is her deduction for the year?

31. **LO.2** Jackson uses his automobile 90% for business and during 2017 drove a total of 14,000 business miles. Information regarding his car expenses is listed below.

Business parking	$ 140
Auto insurance	1,300
Auto club dues (includes towing service)	180
Toll road charges (business-related)	200
Oil changes and engine tune-ups	210
Repairs	160
Depreciation allowable	2,850
Fines for traffic violations (incurred during business use)	320
Gasoline purchases	2,800

What is Jackson's deduction in 2017 for the use of his car if he uses:

a. The actual cost method?

b. The automatic mileage method?

c. What records must Jackson maintain?

32. **LO.2** On July 1, 2013, Rex purchases a new automobile for $40,000. He uses the car 80% for business and drives the car as follows: 8,000 miles in 2013, 19,000 miles in 2014, 20,000 miles in 2015, and 15,000 miles in 2016. Determine Rex's basis in the business portion of the auto as of January 1, 2017, under the following assumptions:

a. Rex uses the automatic mileage method.

b. Rex uses the actual cost method. [Assume that no § 179 expensing is claimed and that 200% declining-balance cost recovery with the half-year convention is used—see Chapter 8. The recovery limitation for an auto placed in service in 2013 is as follows: $3,160 (first year), $5,100 (second year), $3,050 (third year), and $1,875 (fourth year).]

33. **LO.3** Kristen, the regional manager for a national hardware chain, is based in Atlanta. During March and April of this year, she has to replace the district manager in Jackson (Mississippi) temporarily. During this period, Kristen flies to Jackson on Sunday night, spends the week at the district office, and returns home to Atlanta on Friday afternoon. The cost of returning home is $550, while the cost of spending the weekend in Jackson would have been $490.

a. Presuming no reimbursement by her employer, how much, if any, of these weekend expenses may Kristen deduct?

b. Would your answer in part (a) change if the amounts involved were reversed (i.e., the trip home would have cost $490; staying in Jackson would have been $550)? Explain.

34. **LO.3, 6** In June of this year, Dr. and Mrs. Bret Spencer traveled to Denver to attend a three-day conference sponsored by the American Society of Implant Dentistry. Bret, a practicing oral surgeon, participated in scheduled technical sessions dealing with the latest developments in surgical procedures. On two days, Mrs. Spencer attended group meetings where various aspects of family tax planning were discussed. On the other day, she went sightseeing. Mrs. Spencer does not work for her husband, but she does their tax returns and handles the family investments. Expenses incurred in connection with the conference are summarized below.

Airfare (two tickets)	$2,000
Lodging (single and double occupancy are the same rate—$250 each day)	750
Meals ($200 × 3 days)*	600
Conference registration fee (includes $120 for Family Tax Planning sessions)	620
Car rental	300

*Split equally between Dr. and Mrs. Spencer.

How much, if any, of these expenses can the Spencers deduct?

35. **LO.1, 3, 6** Kim works for a clothing manufacturer as a dress designer. She travels to New York City to attend five days of fashion shows and then spends three days sightseeing. Her expenses are as follows:

Airfare	$1,500
Lodging (8 nights)	1,920
Meals (8 days)	1,440
Airport transportation	120

[Assume that lodging/meals are the same amount for the business and personal portion of the trip ($240 per day for lodging and $180 per day for meals).]

a. Presuming no reimbursement, how much can Kim deduct as to the trip?

b. Would the tax treatment of Kim's deduction differ if she was an independent contractor (rather than an employee)? Explain.

36. **LO.3** On Thursday, Justin flies from Baltimore (his home office) to Cadiz (Spain). He conducts business on Friday and Tuesday; vacations on Saturday, Sunday, and Monday (a legal holiday in Spain); and returns to Baltimore on Thursday. Justin was scheduled to return home on Wednesday, but all flights were canceled due to bad weather. Therefore, he spent Wednesday watching floor shows at a local casino.

a. For tax purposes, what portion of Justin's trip is regarded as being for business?

b. Suppose Monday was not a legal holiday. Would this change your answer to part (a)? Explain.

c. Under either part (a) or (b), how much of Justin's airfare qualifies as a deductible business expense?

37. **LO.3** Monica travels from her office in Boston to Lisbon, Portugal, on business. Her absence of 13 days was spent as follows:

Decision Making

Thursday	Depart for and arrive at Lisbon
Friday	Business transacted
Saturday and Sunday	Vacationing
Monday through Friday	Business transacted
Saturday and Sunday	Vacationing
Monday	Business transacted
Tuesday	Depart Lisbon and return to office in Boston

a. For tax purposes, how many days has Monica spent on business?

b. What difference does it make?

c. Could Monica have spent more time than she did vacationing on the trip without loss of existing tax benefits? Explain.

38. **LO.4** Caden Lange (Social Security number 123-45-6789), a financial planner, decides to quit his job with an investment bank in Charleston, South Carolina, and establish a private financial planning practice in Santa Fe, New Mexico. In connection with the move in 2016, he incurs the following expenses:

Moving van charge	$4,500
Lodging during move	540
Meals during move	410
Loss on sale of residence in Charleston	9,000
Mileage for personal autos	3,500 miles

a. How much of these expenses, if any, can Caden deduct?

b. Based on your answer to part (a), complete a Form 3903 for Caden.

39. **LO.4, 7** Upon losing his job as a plant manager in Quincy, Massachusetts, Anthony incurs $6,200 in job search expenses. Having no success in finding new employment in the same type of work, Anthony moves to Clearwater, Florida, in 2017 and begins a charter boat business. His expenses in connection with the move are summarized below.

Penalty for breaking lease on Quincy rented residence	$2,800
Forfeiture of membership in Quincy Country Club	2,200
Packing and moving van charges	7,100
Lodging during move (3 nights)	380
Meals during move	360
Mileage (for two automobiles)	2,400 miles

How much of these expenses may Anthony deduct?

40. **LO.4** After being downsized by his former employer in November 2016, Wayne moves from Minnesota to Alabama to accept a new job. When filing his Federal income tax return for 2016, Wayne deducts the $14,000 in moving expenses he incurred (none of which were reimbursed by either his former or new employer). On June 6, 2017, Wayne's employment terminates. What are the tax consequences if the termination occurred because:

   a. Wayne was killed by a drunk driver?

   b. Wayne was downsized by the new employer?

   c. Wayne was fired by the new employer because he assaulted a client?

   d. Wayne quit because he inherited a large amount of money and decided he did not want to work anymore?

41. **LO.5** Elijah is employed as a full-time high school teacher. The school district where he works recently instituted a policy requiring all of its teachers to start working on a master's degree. Pursuant to this new rule, Elijah spent most of the summer of 2017 taking graduate courses at an out-of-town university. His expenses are as follows:

Tuition	$6,600
Books and course materials	1,500
Lodging	1,700
Meals	2,200
Laundry and dry cleaning	200
Campus parking	300

In addition, Elijah drove his personal automobile 2,200 miles in connection with the education. He uses the automatic mileage method.

   a. How much, if any, of these expenses might qualify as deductions *for* AGI?

   b. How much, if any, of these expenses might qualify as deductions *from* AGI?

42. **LO.5** In each of the following independent situations, determine how much, if any, qualifies as a deduction *for* AGI under § 222 (qualified tuition and related expenses):

   a. Lily is single and is employed as an architect. During 2017, she spends $4,100 in tuition to attend law school at night. Her MAGI is $64,000.

   b. Liam is single and is employed as a pharmacist. During 2017, he spends $2,400 ($2,100 for tuition and $300 for books) to take a course in herbal supplements at a local university. His MAGI is $81,000.

   c. Hailey is married and is employed as a bookkeeper. She spends $5,200 for tuition and $900 for books and supplies pursuing a bachelor's degree in accounting. Her MAGI is $40,000 on the separate return she files.

   d. John spends $6,500 of his savings on tuition to attend Carmine State College. John is claimed as a dependent by his parents.

   e. How much, if any, of the above amounts *not allowed under* § 222 might otherwise qualify as a deduction *from* AGI?

43. **LO.6, 9** Eric is a licensed commercial pilot who works for Snipe Charter Jet Service. Typically, Eric, who lives near the airport, flies a charter out of Tupelo, Mississippi, to either Las Vegas or Reno, spends several nights there, and then returns home with the same group. Snipe provides Eric with a travel allowance of $1,800 per month but requires no accountability. For the current calendar year, Eric had the following job-related expenses:

Meals	$ 7,000
Lodging	10,000
Transportation (taxis, limos)	500
Uniforms	1,300
Dry cleaning of uniforms	400
Annual physical exam	1,500

The uniforms are required to be worn on the job. The Federal Aviation Administration requires the annual physical exam for the maintenance of a commercial pilot's license. How may Eric treat these expenses for Federal income tax purposes?

44. **LO.6** Stork Associates paid $60,000 for a 20-seat skybox at Veterans Stadium for eight professional football games. Regular seats to these games range from $80 to $250 each. At one game, an employee of Stork entertained 18 clients. Stork furnished food and beverages for the event at a cost of $1,300. The game was preceded by a bona fide business discussion, and all expenses are adequately substantiated.

    a.   How much may Stork deduct for this event?

    b.   What if there was no bona fide business discussion either before or after the event?

45. **LO.6** During the current year, Paul, the vice president of a bank, made gifts in the following amounts:

To Sarah (Paul's personal assistant) at Christmas	$36
To Darryl (a key client)—$3 was for gift wrapping	53
To Darryl's wife (a homemaker) on her birthday	20
To Veronica (Paul's boss) at Christmas	30

In addition, on professional assistants' day, Paul takes Sarah to lunch at a cost of $82. Presuming that Paul has adequate substantiation and is not reimbursed, how much can he deduct?

46. **LO.7** Melanie is employed full-time as an accountant for a national hardware chain. She recently started a private consulting practice, which provides tax advice and financial planning to the general public. For this purpose, she maintains an office in her home. Expenses relating to her home for 2017 are as follows:

Real property taxes	$3,600
Interest on home mortgage	3,800
Operating expenses of home	900

Melanie's residence cost $350,000 (excluding land) and has living space of 2,000 square feet, of which 20% (400 square feet) is devoted to business. The office was placed in service in February 2016, and under the Regular Method, Melanie had an unused office in the home deduction of $800 for 2016. Presuming sufficient net income from her consulting practice, what is Melanie's office in the home deduction under the:

    a.   Regular Method.

    b.   Simplified Method.

47. **LO.7** Christine is a full-time teacher of the fourth grade at Vireo Academy. During the current year, she spends $1,400 for classroom supplies. On the submission of adequate substantiation, Vireo reimburses her for $500 of these expenses—the maximum reimbursement allowed for supplies under school policy. [The

reimbursement is not shown as income (Box 1) of Form W–2 given to Christine by Vireo.] What are the income tax consequences of the $1,400 if Christine:

a.   Itemizes her deductions *from* AGI?

b.   Chooses the standard deduction?

48.   **LO.3, 6, 9** Charles has AGI of $94,000 during the year and the following expenses related to his employment:

Lodging while in travel status	$5,000
Meals during travel	4,000
Business transportation	6,000
Entertainment of clients	3,800
Professional dues and subscriptions	800

Charles is reimbursed $14,000 under his employer's accountable plan. What are his deductions *for* and *from* AGI?

Decision Making   49.   **LO.3, 6, 9** During the year, Brenda has the following expenses related to her employment:

Airfare	$8,500
Meals	4,000
Lodging	4,900
Transportation while in travel status (taxis and limos)	940
Entertainment of clients	8,000

Although Brenda renders an adequate accounting to her employer, she is reimbursed for only $12,000 of the above expenses. What are Brenda's tax consequences based on the following assumptions?

a.   The $12,000 reimbursement does not designate which expenses are covered.

b.   The reimbursement specifically covers *only* the meals and entertainment expenses.

c.   The reimbursement covers any of the expenses *other than* meals and entertainment.

d.   If Brenda has a choice of reimbursement procedures [parts (a), (b), or (c) above], which should she select? Why?

50.   **LO.6, 9, 10** Audry, age 38 and single, earns a salary of $59,000. She has interest income of $1,600 and has a $2,000 long-term capital loss from the sale of a stock investment. Audry incurs the following employment-related expenses during the year:

Transportation	$5,500
Meals	2,800
Lodging	4,200
Entertainment of clients	2,200
Professional dues and subscriptions	300

Under an accountable plan, Audry receives reimbursements of $4,500 from her employer. Calculate her AGI and itemized employee business expenses.

Decision Making   51.   **LO.6, 9, 10, 11** Ava recently graduated from college and is interviewing for a position in marketing. Gull Corporation has offered her a job as a sales representative that will require extensive travel and entertainment but provide valuable experience. Under the offer, she has two options: a salary of $53,000 and she absorbs all expenses; a salary of $39,000 and Gull reimburses for all expenses. Gull assures Ava that the $14,000 difference in the two options will be adequate to cover the expenses incurred. What issues should have an impact on Ava's choice?

52.   **LO.5, 7, 10** B. J. and Carolyn Grace are full-time employees. B. J. is an elementary school teacher, and Carolyn is a registered nurse at a hospital. During the year, they incur the following employment-related expenses:

School supplies for use in the classroom	$1,400
Emergency room uniforms	800
Union dues (teachers association)	200
Job hunting expenses (Carolyn obtained another nursing position but decided not to change jobs)	1,300
Continuing education correspondence courses (required to maintain nursing license)	380
Professional dues and subscriptions	1,100

None of these expenses are reimbursed by the employers.

For the year, the Graces file a joint return reflecting salary income of $90,000. They also have gambling income of $6,000 and gambling losses of $7,000 (fully substantiated). They pay $400 to have their tax return prepared. They have other itemized deductions (i.e., interest on home mortgage, property taxes on personal residence, state income taxes, and charitable contributions) of $14,500. Determine the total amount of itemized deductions allowed to the Graces.

53. **LO.1, 2, 4, 5, 7, 10** Complete the following table by classifying each of the independent expenditures (assume that no reimbursement takes place).

Expense Item	Deductible *for* AGI	Deductible *from* AGI	Not Deductible
a. Moving expense of an employee	_____	_____	_____
b. Tax return preparation fee incurred by an employed plumber	_____	_____	_____
c. Safety glasses purchased by an employed pipefitter	_____	_____	_____
d. Dues to auto club (e.g., AAA) for taxpayer who uses the automatic mileage method	_____	_____	_____
e. Nursing refresher course for taxpayer who retired from nursing five years ago	_____	_____	_____
f. Gambling loss *not* in excess of gambling gain by a self-employed architect	_____	_____	_____
g. Contribution to Roth IRA by a self-employed attorney	_____	_____	_____
h. Business travel expenses by a statutory employee	_____	_____	_____
i. Job hunting expense by an elementary school teacher seeking a position as an elementary school principal	_____	_____	_____
j. Cost of bar exam review course taken by a recent law school graduate	_____	_____	_____

Cumulative Problems

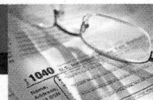

54. David R. and Ella M. Cole (ages 39 and 38, respectively) are husband and wife who live at 1820 Elk Avenue, Denver, CO 80202. David is a regional sales manager for Wren Industries, a national wholesaler of plumbing and heating supplies, and Ella is a part-time dental hygienist for a chain of dental clinics.

Tax Return Problem

Communications

TAX SOFTWARE

- David is classified by Wren as a statutory employee with compensation for 2016 (based on commissions) of $95,000. He is expected to maintain his own office and pay for all business expenses from this amount. Wren does not require him to render any accounting as to the use of these funds. It does not withhold Federal and state income taxes but does withhold and account for the payroll taxes incurred (e.g., Social Security and Medicare). The Coles are adequately covered by Wren's noncontributory medical plan but have chosen not to participate in its § 401(k) retirement plan.

David's employment-related expenses for 2016 are summarized below.

Airfare	$8,800
Lodging	5,000
Meals (during travel status)	4,800
Entertainment	3,600
Ground transportation (e.g., limos, rental cars, and taxis)	800
Business gifts	900
Office supplies (includes postage, overnight delivery, and copying)	1,500

The entertainment involved business meals for purchasing agents, store owners, and building contractors. The business gifts consisted of $50 gift certificates to a national restaurant. These were sent by David during the Christmas holidays to 18 of his major customers.

In addition, David drove his 2014 Ford Expedition 11,000 miles for business and 3,000 for personal use during 2016. He purchased the Expedition on August 15, 2013, and has always used the automatic (standard) mileage method for tax purposes. Parking and tolls relating to business use total $340 in 2016.

- When the Coles purchased their present residence in April 2013, they devoted 450 of the 3,000 square feet of living space to an office for David. The property cost $440,000 ($40,000 of which is attributable to the land) and has since appreciated in value. Expenses relating to the residence in 2016 (except for mortgage interest and property taxes; see below) are as follows:

Insurance	$2,600
Repairs and maintenance	900
Utilities	4,700
Painting office area; area rugs and plants (in the office)	1,800

In terms of depreciation, the Coles use the MACRS percentage tables applicable to 39-year nonresidential real property. As to depreciable property (e.g., office furniture), David tries to avoid capitalization and uses whatever method provides the fastest write-off for tax purposes.

- Ella works part-time as a substitute for whichever hygienist is ill or on vacation or when one of the clinics is particularly busy (e.g., prior to the beginning of the school year). Besides her transportation, she must provide and maintain her own uniforms. Her expenses for 2016 appear below.

Uniforms	$690
State and city occupational licenses	380
Professional journals and membership dues in the American Dental Hygiene Association	340
Correspondence study course (taken online) dealing with teeth whitening procedures	420

Ella's salary for the year is $42,000, and her Form W–2 for the year shows income tax withholdings of $4,000 (Federal) and $1,000 (state) and the proper amount of Social Security and Medicare taxes. Because Ella is a part-time employee, she is not included in her employer's medical or retirement plans.

- Besides the items already mentioned, the Coles had the following receipts during 2016.

Interest income—		
State of Colorado general purpose bonds	$2,500	
IBM bonds	800	
Wells Fargo Bank	1,200	$ 4,500
Federal income tax refund for year 2015		510
Life insurance proceeds paid by Eagle Assurance Corporation		200,000
Inheritance of savings account from Sarah Cole		50,000
Sales proceeds from two ATVs		9,000

For several years, the Coles' household has included David's divorced mother, Sarah, who has been claimed as their dependent. In late November 2016, Sarah unexpectedly died of coronary arrest in her sleep. Unknown to Ella and David, Sarah had a life insurance policy and a savings account (with David as the designated beneficiary of each). In 2015, the Coles purchased two ATVs for $14,000. After several near mishaps, they decided that the sport was too dangerous. In 2016, they sold the ATVs to their neighbor.

- Additional expenditures for 2016 include:

Funeral expenses for Sarah		$ 4,500
Taxes—		
Real property taxes on personal residence	$6,400	
Colorado state income tax due (paid in April 2016 for tax year 2015)	310	6,710
Mortgage interest on personal residence (Rocky Mountain Bank)		6,600
Paid church pledge		2,400
Contributions to traditional IRAs for Ella and David ($5,500 + $5,500)		11,000

In 2016, the Coles made quarterly estimated tax payments of $1,400 (Federal) and $500 (state) for a total of $5,600 (Federal) and $2,000 (state).

Part 1—Tax Computation

Using the appropriate forms and schedules, compute the Coles' Federal income tax for 2016. Disregard the alternative minimum tax (AMT) and various education credits as these items are not discussed until later in the text (Chapters 12 and 13). Relevant Social Security numbers are:

David Cole	123-45-6788
Ella Cole	123-45-6787
Sarah Cole	123-45-6799

The Coles do not want to contribute to the Presidential Election Campaign Fund. Also, they want any overpayment of tax refunded to them and *not* applied toward next year's tax liability. Suggested software: H&R BLOCK Tax Software.

Part 2—Follow-Up Advice

Ella has always wanted to pursue a career in nursing. To this end, she has earned a substantial number of college credits on a part-time basis. With Sarah no longer requiring home care, Ella believes that she can now complete her degree by attending college on a full-time basis.

David would like to know how Ella's plans will affect their income tax position. Specifically, he wants to know:

- How much Federal income tax they will save if Ella quits her job.
- Any tax benefits that might be available from the cost of the education.

Write a letter to David addressing these concerns. Note: In making your projections, assume that David's salary and expenses remain the same. Also disregard any consideration of the educational tax credits (i.e., American Opportunity and lifetime learning) as they are not discussed until Chapter 13.

Tax Computation Problem   55. Addison Parker, single and age 32, lives at 3218 Columbia Drive, Spokane, WA 99210. She is employed as regional sales manager by VITA Corporation, a manufacturer and distributor of vitamins and food supplements. Addison is paid an annual salary of $83,000 and a separate travel allowance of $24,000. As to the travel allowance, VITA does not require any accounting on the part of Addison.

- Addison participates in VITA's contributory health and § 401(k) plans. During 2017, she paid $3,500 for her share of the medical insurance and contributed $11,000 to the § 401(k) retirement plan.

- Addison uses her automobile 70% for business and 30% for personal. The automobile, a Toyota Avalon, was purchased new on June 30, 2015, for $37,000 (no trade-in was involved). Depreciation has been claimed under MACRS 200% declining balance method, and no § 179 election was made in the year of purchase. (For depreciation information, see the IRS Instructions for Form 4562, Part V). During 2017, Addison drove 15,000 miles and incurred and paid the following expenses relating to the automobile:

Gasoline	$3,100
Insurance	2,900
Auto club dues	240
Interest on car loan	1,100
Repairs and maintenance	1,200
Parking (during business use)	600
Traffic fines (during business use)	500

- Because VITA does not have an office in Spokane, the company expects Addison to maintain one in her home. Out of 1,500 square feet of living space in her apartment, Addison has set aside 300 square feet as an office. Expenses for 2017 relating to the office are listed below.

Rent	$18,000
Utilities	4,000
Insurance (renter's casualty and theft coverage)	1,600
Carpet replacement (office area only)	1,200

- Addison's employment-related expenses (except for the trip to Korea) for 2017 are summarized below.

Airfare	$4,100
Lodging	3,200
Meals	2,800
Entertainment (business lunches)	2,400
Transportation (taxis and airport limos)	300
Business gifts	540
Continuing education	400
Professional journals	140

Most of Addison's business trips involve visits to retail outlets in her region. Store managers and their key employees, as well as some suppliers, were the parties entertained. The business gifts were boxes of candy costing $30 ($25 each plus $5 for wrapping and shipping) sent to 18 store managers at Christmas. The continuing education was a noncredit course dealing with improving management skills that Addison took online.

- In July 2017, Addison traveled to Korea to investigate a new process that is being developed to convert fish parts to a solid consumable tablet form. She spent one week checking out the process and then took a one-week vacation tour of the country. The round-trip airfare was $3,600, while her expenses relating to business were $2,100 for lodging ($300 each night), $1,470 for meals, and $350 for transportation. Upon returning to the United States, Addison sent her findings about the process to her employer. VITA was so pleased with her report that it gave her an employee achievement award of $10,000. The award was sent to Addison in January 2018.

- Addison provides more than 50% of the support of her parents (Gordon and Anita Parker), who live in Seattle. In addition to modest Social Security benefits, her parents receive a small amount of interest on municipal bonds and nontaxable retirement income.

- Besides the items already mentioned, Addison had the following receipts in 2017:

Interest income—		
City of Tacoma general purpose bonds	$ 350	
Olympia State Bank	400	$ 750
Proceeds from property sales—		
City lot	$13,000	
Sailboat	18,000	31,000
Cash found at airport		5,000

Regarding the city lot (located in Vancouver), Addison purchased the property in 2002 for $16,000 and held it as an investment. Unfortunately, the neighborhood where the lot was located deteriorated, and property values declined. In 2017, Addison decided to cut her losses and sold the property for $13,000. The sailboat was used for pleasure and was purchased in 2013 for $16,500. Addison sold the boat because she purchased a new and larger model (see below). While at the Spokane airport, Addison found an unmarked envelope containing $5,000 in $50 bills. As no mention of any lost funds was noted in the media, Addison kept the money.

- Addison's expenditures for 2017 (not previously noted) are summarized below.

Medical (not covered by insurance)	$7,000
State and local general sales tax	3,300
Church pledge (2017 and 2018)	5,600
Fee paid for preparation of 2016 income tax return	500
Contribution to mayor's reelection campaign fund	200
Premiums on life insurance policy	2,100
Contribution to a Coverdell Education Savings account (on behalf of a favorite nephew)	2,000

Most of the medical expenses Addison paid were for her mother's dental implants. Addison keeps careful records regarding sales taxes. In 2017, the sales tax total was unusually high due to the purchase of a new sailboat. In 2017, Addison decided to pay her church pledge for both 2017 and 2018. The insurance premium was on a policy covering her father's life. (Addison is the designated beneficiary under the policy.)

Relevant Social Security numbers are 123-45-6785 (Addison), 123-45-6783 (Gordon), and 123-45-6784 (Anita). Addison's employer withheld $5,600 for Federal income tax purposes, and she applied her $800 overpayment for 2016 toward the 2017 tax liability.

Compute Addison's Federal income tax payable (or refund) for 2017. In making the calculation, use the Tax Rate Schedule and disregard the application of the alternative minimum tax (AMT), which is not discussed until Chapter 12.

Research Problems

THOMSON REUTERS
CHECKPOINT®
Student Edition

Note: Solutions to the Research Problems can be prepared by using the Thomson Reuters Checkpoint® Student Edition online tax research database, which accompanies this textbook. Solutions can also be prepared by using research materials found in a typical tax library.

Research Problem 1. Aaron, a resident of Minnesota, has been a driver for Green Delivery Service for the past six years. For this purpose, he leases a truck from Green, and his compensation is based on a percentage of the income resulting from his pickup and delivery services. Green allows its drivers to choose their 10-hour shifts and does not exercise any control on how these services are carried out (e.g., the route to be taken or the order in which parcels are delivered or picked up). Under Green's operating agreement with its drivers, Green can terminate the arrangement after 30 days' notice. In practice, however, Green allows its truckers to quit immediately without giving advance notice. The agreement also identifies the drivers as independent contractors. Green maintains no health or retirement plans for its drivers, and each year it reports their income by issuing Forms 1099–MISC (and not Forms W–2). Green requires its drivers to maintain a commercial driver's license and be in good standing with the state highway law enforcement division.

Citing the employment tax Regulations in §§ 31.3121(d)–1(c)(2) and 31.3306(i)–1(b), an IRS agent contends that Aaron is an independent contractor and, therefore, is subject to the self-employment tax. Based on *Peno Trucking, Inc.* (93 TCM 1027, T.C.Memo. 2007–66), Aaron disagrees and contends that he is an employee (i.e., not self-employed). Who is correct? Why?

Research Problem 2. Your client, a large construction firm organized as a C corporation, allows certain employees (including the president of the corporation) to use its company-owned airplane for nonbusiness flights. The employees include the value of the flights in their income. Your client is uncertain about how to treat the expenses related to these nonbusiness flights. In certain situations, the expenses of operating the plane are more than the income imputed to the employees, and in certain circumstances, the expenses are less. In doing some of its own research, your client found *Sutherland Lumber-Southwest, Inc.* [114 T.C. 197 (2000)], which suggests that as long as the employee imputes income, the full amount of the related expenses can be deducted. [The decision in the case was affirmed on appeal, *Sutherland Lumber-Southwest, Inc. v. Comm.*, 2001–2 USTC ¶50,503, 88 AFTR 2d 2001–5026, 255 F.3d 495 (CA–8, 2001).] Should your client follow the approach in *Sutherland?* Explain.

Communications   **Research Problem 3.** Rick Beam has been an independent sales representative for various textile manufacturers for many years. His products consist of soft goods, such as tablecloths, curtains, and drapes. Rick's customers are clothing store chains, department stores, and smaller specialty stores. The employees of these companies who are responsible for purchasing merchandise are known as buyers. These companies generally prohibit their buyers from accepting gifts from manufacturers' sales representatives.

Each year, Rick gives cash gifts (never more than $25) to most of the buyers who are his customers. Generally, he cashes a large check in November and gives the money personally to the buyers around Christmas. Rick says, "This is one of the ways I maintain my relationship with my buyers." He maintains adequate substantiation of all of the gifts.

Rick's deductions for these gifts have been disallowed by the IRS, based on § 162(c)(2). Rick is confused and comes to you, a CPA, for advice.

a. Write a letter to Rick concerning his tax position on this issue. Rick's address is 948 Octavia Street, Baton Rouge, LA 70821.

b. Prepare a memo for your files supporting the advice you have given.

Use internet tax resources to address the following questions. Look for reliable websites and blogs of the IRS and other government agencies, media outlets, businesses, tax professionals, academics, think tanks, and political outlets.

Research Problem 4. In reporting the transactions of a self-employed taxpayer, when can a Schedule C–EZ be used instead of the regular Schedule C of Form 1040?

Research Problem 5 Prepare a blog post for the "Online Tutor Match Company" to explain to its freelancers the tax implications of their work. Topics should include (1) what records to keep (both for income and expenses), (2) unique situations facing freelancers (e.g., home office deductions; self-employment status), and (3) what tax forms must be filed and (briefly) how to prepare those forms [e.g., Schedule C (Form 1040)].

Communications

Research Problem 6 Download IRS Form 1099–K and its instructions from the IRS website. What is the purpose of the form and when is it used? Go to the Square, Inc. website **(www.squareup.com)** and search for information about this form. Summarize what you discover in an e-mail to your instructor.

Communications

Research Problem 7. Download IRS Form 8919 (Uncollected Social Security and Medicare Tax on Wages) from the IRS website. According to the instructions, who should file this form?

Roger CPA Review Questions

1. The following facts pertain to Lewis Productions, a sole proprietorship owned by Lewis, in the current year:

Total cost of holiday gifts given to top 10 clients (each gift identical)	$ 550
Receivable for prior-year purchase from Egan, who declared bankruptcy in the current year	2,500
Lodging costs incurred by Lewis while traveling to client sites	3,000
Meal costs incurred by Lewis only while traveling to and from client sites	1,500
Meal costs incurred by Lewis while entertaining business clients and engaging in some business-related discussion	3,000

Considering only the above facts, what is the total amount of business expenses that Lewis can deduct on Schedule C of the current year's tax return?

a. $8,000
b. $5,500
c. $6,250
d. $8,750

2. Pinnacle Productions, Inc., holds a luxury skybox season ticket at a local sporting arena. Pinnacle uses the skybox to entertain clients while holding business meetings. The cost of Pinnacle's luxury skybox season ticket is $25,000; the cost of the most expensive non-luxury season ticket is $15,000. How much of the luxury skybox season ticket cost may Pinnacle deduct in computing its corporate taxable income?

a. $7,500
b. $20,000
c. $10,000
d. $15,000

3. Betty, a salesperson, is an employee with $52,000 AGI who maintains a home office for the convenience of her employer, Smart Systems. The office takes up 5% of Betty's home and is used exclusively for her job. Smart Systems reimburses all of

Communications

Betty's direct costs of maintaining the home office. Betty also has the following expenses associated with her home:

Expense	Amount
Real property taxes on residence	$3,500
Interest expense on residence	5,000
Operating expenses on residence	1,800
Depreciation on residence (based on 5% home office use)	150

Considering these facts, how much may Betty deduct *from* AGI on her tax return, assuming she elects to itemize deductions?

a. $0
b. $665

c. $9,410
d. $10,450

4. In 2017, Archer, a single individual, moved from Minneapolis to Phoenix to start a new job with InnoTech, which began February 1, 2017. Archer worked for Inno-Tech until November 15, 2017, when Archer accepted a job offer from InnoTech's Phoenix rival MegaTech. The following 2017 facts apply to Archer:

Income	$75,000
Expenses incurred during Minneapolis–Phoenix move:	
1,000	Moving truck rental
1,000	Packing and unloading costs paid to moving company
1,500	Loss on sale of Minneapolis home
750	Lodging
250	Meals
100	Storage costs in Phoenix prior to move-in to new home

Considering only the above facts, what is Archer's 2017 adjusted gross income?

a. $70,475
b. $70,650

c. $72,150
d. $75,000

5. Which allowable deduction can be claimed in arriving at an individual's adjusted gross income?

a. Half the cost of meals eaten while moving over 50 miles for a new job
b. Alimony paid directly to a college for education expenses, as dictated by divorce decree
c. Home mortgage loan interest, subject to certain limits
d. Medical insurance premiums paid by an employee

CHAPTER

10

Deductions and Losses: Certain Itemized Deductions

LEARNING OBJECTIVES: *After completing Chapter 10, you should be able to:*

LO.1 Distinguish between deductible and nondeductible personal expenses.

LO.2 Define medical expenses and compute the medical expense deduction.

LO.3 Contrast deductible taxes with nondeductible fees, licenses, and other charges.

LO.4 Explain the Federal income tax treatment of state and local income taxes and sales taxes.

LO.5 Distinguish between deductible and nondeductible interest and apply the appropriate limitations to deductible interest.

LO.6 Recognize charitable contributions and identify their related measurement problems and percentage limitations.

LO.7 List the business and personal expenditures that are deductible either as miscellaneous itemized deductions or as other itemized deductions.

LO.8 Recognize the limitation on certain itemized deductions applicable to high-income taxpayers.

LO.9 Identify tax planning strategies that can maximize the benefit of itemized deductions.

CHAPTER OUTLINE

ISTOCKPHOTO.COM/IZUSEK

THE BIG PICTURE

IMPACT OF ITEMIZED DEDUCTIONS ON MAJOR PURCHASES

John and Susan Williamson, a young professional couple, have been renting an apartment in Atlanta, Georgia, since they were married. Their income has grown as they've become more established in their careers, and they now believe the time has come to purchase their own home. In addition, their desire to buy a home now may be coming at a good time, because John's mother, Martha, needs to move in with them due to her declining health and their current apartment is too small to accommodate her. John and Susan's current monthly rent is $2,000, but they are willing to spend up to $2,500 per month on an after-tax basis for their first home.

After months of house hunting, they have found the perfect home, but they are concerned it may be too expensive. If they acquire a standard mortgage to finance the purchase of the home, the total cash outlay during the first year of ownership will be $43,000 ($2,000 principal payments, $37,000 interest payments, and $4,000 real estate taxes). Alternatively, if they use their retirement and taxable investments to secure the home financing, they can qualify for a lower interest rate and thereby reduce the interest charge from $37,000 to $35,000. They expect their Federal AGI to be $200,000, and their taxable income to range between $160,000 and $185,000 for the year. John and Susan have not itemized their deductions in prior years because the amount of their qualifying personal expenses has been just below the standard deduction amount. Assume that the Williamsons' marginal income tax rate under Georgia law is 6 percent.

Can John and Susan Williamson afford to pursue their dream of home ownership?

Read the chapter and formulate your response.

FRAMEWORK 1040 **Tax Formula for Individuals**

This chapter covers the boldfaced portions of the Tax Formula for Individuals that was introduced in Concept Summary 3.1 on p. 3-3. Below those portions are the sections of Form 1040 where the results are reported.

Income *(broadly defined)*	$xx,xxx
Less: Exclusions	(x,xxx)
Gross income	$xx,xxx
Less: Deductions *for* adjusted gross income	(x,xxx)

FORM 1040 (p. 1)

25	Health savings account deduction. Attach Form 8889	25	
29	Self-employed health insurance deduction	29	
33	Student loan interest deduction	33	

Adjusted gross income	$xx,xxx
Less: The greater of total **itemized deductions** *or* the standard deduction	(x,xxx)

FORM 1040 (p. 2)

40 **Itemized deductions** (from Schedule A) **or** your **standard deduction**	

Personal and dependency exemptions	(x,xxx)
Taxable income	$xx,xxx
Tax on taxable income *(see Tax Tables or Tax Rate Schedules)*	$ x,xxx
Less: Tax credits *(including income taxes withheld and prepaid)*	(xxx)
Tax due (or refund)	$ xxx

LO.1

Distinguish between deductible and nondeductible personal expenses.

As a general rule, personal expenses are not deductible (see § 262 of the Code). However, Congress has chosen to allow certain personal expenses to be deducted as itemized deductions. Personal expenses that are deductible as itemized deductions include medical expenses, certain taxes, mortgage interest, investment interest, and charitable contributions. These (and other) personal expenses allowed as itemized deductions are covered in this chapter. Although certain exceptions exist (e.g., alimony and traditional IRA contributions are deductible *for* AGI), personal expenses not specifically allowed as itemized deductions by the tax law are nondeductible.

Allowable itemized deductions are deductible *from* AGI in arriving at taxable income if the taxpayer *elects* to itemize. A taxpayer will elect to itemize when total itemized deductions exceed the standard deduction based on the taxpayer's filing status.[1]

The Big Picture

EXAMPLE 1

Return to the facts of *The Big Picture* on p. 10-1. John and Susan Williamson will discover that with the purchase of a home, they will be able to itemize their deductions for the first time instead of claiming the standard deduction. Assuming that the home mortgage interest expense and real estate taxes meet the requirements discussed in this chapter, they will be deducted *from* AGI because their total would exceed the amount of the standard deduction for a married couple filing a joint return. Further, other qualifying expenses, such as state income taxes and charitable contributions, likewise will be deductible as itemized deductions, providing an explicit tax benefit to the Williamsons.

---

[1]See §§ 63(c) and (d), respectively, for the definitions of the terms *standard deduction* and *itemized deductions*.

10-1 MEDICAL EXPENSES

LO.2

Define medical expenses and compute the medical expense deduction.

Medical expenses paid for the care of the taxpayer, spouse, and dependents are allowed as an itemized deduction to the extent the expenses are not reimbursed. The medical expense deduction is limited to the amount by which such expenses *exceed* a threshold percentage of the taxpayer's AGI. Currently, the threshold percentage is 10 percent. For taxpayers age 65 and older, however, the threshold is 7.5 percent of AGI through 2016, after which it increases to 10 percent.[2]

The threshold percentage, sometimes referred to as a "floor," is used to restrict deductions, as expenses below the floor are not deductible. Here, the floor is significant. Only medical expenses in excess of the "10%-of-AGI floor" are deductible. As a result, a medical expense deduction is rare (especially for high-income taxpayers).

The Big Picture

EXAMPLE

2

Return to the facts of *The Big Picture* on p. 10-1. Because the Williamsons' AGI for the year is $200,000, to receive a tax benefit from any unreimbursed medical expenses, they must itemize their deductions and have more than $20,000 ($200,000 × 10%) of those expenses. If they incurred $21,000 of unreimbursed medical expenses during the year and itemize their deductions, their total itemized deductions increase by $1,000 ($21,000 unreimbursed medical expenses − $20,000 AGI floor).

10-1a Medical Expenses Defined

The term *medical care* includes expenses incurred for the "diagnosis, cure, mitigation, treatment, or prevention of disease, or for the purpose of affecting any structure or function of the body."[3] A *partial* list of deductible and nondeductible medical items appears in Exhibit 10.1.

EXHIBIT 10.1	Examples of Deductible and Nondeductible Medical Expenses Paid by Taxpayer

Deductible	Nondeductible
Medical (including dental, mental, and hospital) care	Funeral, burial, or cremation expenses
Prescription drugs and insulin	Over-the-counter medicines (except insulin)
Special equipment:	Bottled water
• Wheelchairs	Toiletries, cosmetics
• Crutches	Diaper service, maternity clothes
• Artificial limbs	Programs for the *general* improvement of health:
• Eyeglasses (including contact lenses)	• Weight reduction
• Hearing aids	• Health spas
Transportation for medical care	• Social activities (e.g., dancing and swimming lessons)
Medical and hospital insurance premiums	Unnecessary cosmetic surgery
Long-term care insurance premiums (subject to limitations)	
Cost of alcohol and drug rehabilitation	
Certain costs to stop smoking	
Weight reduction programs related to obesity	

---

[2]Prior to 2013, the percentage threshold for regular income tax purposes was 7.5 percent of AGI for all taxpayers.

[3]§ 213(d)(1)(A).

A medical expense does not have to relate to a particular ailment to be deductible. Because the definition of medical care is broad enough to cover preventive measures, the cost of periodic physical and dental exams qualifies even for a taxpayer in good health.

Amounts paid for unnecessary *cosmetic surgery* are not deductible medical expenses. Cosmetic surgery is necessary—and, therefore, deductible—when it improves the effects of (1) a deformity arising from a congenital abnormality, (2) a personal injury, or (3) a disfiguring disease.[4]

EXAMPLE 3

Art, age 75, paid $21,000 to a plastic surgeon for a face-lift. Art merely wanted to improve his appearance. The $21,000 does not qualify as a medical expense because the surgery was unnecessary.

In contrast, Marge's face is disfigured as a result of a serious automobile accident. The cost of restorative cosmetic surgery is deductible as a medical expense.

The cost of care in a *nursing home or home for the aged*, including meals and lodging, is a deductible medical expense if the primary reason for being in the home is to get medical care. If the primary reason for being there is personal, any costs for medical or nursing care are deductible medical expenses, but the cost of meals and lodging must be excluded.[5]

EXAMPLE 4

Norman has a chronic heart ailment. In October, his family decides to place Norman in a nursing home equipped to provide medical and nursing care. Total nursing home expenses amount to $80,000 during the year. Of this amount, $50,000 is directly attributable to medical and nursing care.

Because Norman is in need of significant medical and nursing care and is placed in the facility primarily for this purpose, all $80,000 of the nursing home costs are deductible (subject to the AGI floor, explained earlier).

Tuition expenses of a dependent at a special school for a mentally or physically handicapped individual may be deductible as a medical expense. The deduction is allowed if a principal reason for sending the individual to the school is the school's special resources for alleviating the infirmities. In this case, the cost of meals and lodging, in addition to the tuition, is a proper medical expense deduction.[6]

EXAMPLE 5

Jason's daughter Sophia attended public school through the seventh grade. Because Sophia was a poor student, she was examined by a psychiatrist who concluded that Sophia had dyslexia. Upon the recommendation of the psychiatrist, Sophia is enrolled in a private school so she can receive individual attention. The school specializes in students with learning disabilities and has a program of study designed to help students with dyslexia (including a staff of educational and psychological professionals who have developed the specialized curriculum).

The expense related to Sophia's attendance is deductible as a medical expense. The cost of any psychiatric care also qualifies as a medical expense.[7]

10-1b Capital Expenditures for Medical Purposes

When capital expenditures are incurred for medical purposes, they must be deemed medically necessary by a physician and used primarily by the patient. In addition, its cost must be reasonable. Examples include dust elimination systems,[8] elevators,[9] and vans specially

[4] § 213(d)(9)(A).

[5] Reg. § 1.213–1(e)(1)(v). In general, medical care is required if a taxpayer is deemed to be chronically ill and under a prescribed plan of care. A taxpayer is chronically ill if he or she cannot perform at least two daily living tasks (dressing, eating, bathing, toileting, moving from one place to another, continence) for 90 days or more (§ 7702B).

[6] Reg. § 1.213–1(e)(1)(v)(a). See *Donald R. Pfeifer*, 37 TCM 816, T.C.Memo. 1978–189. Also see Rev.Rul. 78–340, 1978–2 C.B. 124. Based on recent rulings, the IRS is allowing a deduction where there is a diagnosis of a neurologically based learning disability or other handicap, leading to a recommendation of and attendance at an institution specially equipped to help the student overcome the handicap.

[7] Ltr.Rul. 200521003.

[8] Ltr.Rul. 7948029.

[9] *Riach v. Frank*, 62–1 USTC ¶9419, 9 AFTR 2d 1263, 302 F.2d 374 (CA–9, 1962).

designed for wheelchair-bound taxpayers. Other expenditures that may qualify are swimming pools (if the taxpayer does not have access to a neighborhood pool) and air conditioners if they do not become permanent improvements (e.g., window units).[10]

Both a capital expenditure for a permanent improvement and related operating and maintenance costs may qualify as medical expenses. The allowable costs are deductible in the year incurred. Although depreciation is required for most other capital expenditures, it is not required for those qualifying for medical purposes (in other words, the entire cost of a qualifying capital expenditure is immediately deductible).

A permanent capital improvement that ordinarily would not have a medical purpose qualifies as a medical expense if it is directly related to prescribed medical care (e.g., an elevator in a personal residence). Here, the cost is deductible to the extent it *exceeds* the increase in value of the related property. Appraisal costs related to capital improvements are also deductible, but not as medical expenses. These costs are classified as miscellaneous itemized deductions (expenses incurred in the determination of the taxpayer's tax liability).[11]

Fred is afflicted with heart disease. His physician advises him to install an elevator in his residence so that he will not be required to climb the stairs. The cost of installing the elevator is $10,000, and the increase in the value of the residence is determined to be only $4,000.

Therefore, $6,000 ($10,000 − $4,000) is treated as a medical expense. Additional utility costs to operate the elevator and maintenance costs are also medical expenses as long as the medical reason for the capital expenditure continues to exist.

The full cost of certain home-related capital expenditures incurred to enable a *physically handicapped* individual to live independently and productively qualifies as a medical expense. Qualifying costs include expenditures for constructing entrance and exit ramps to the residence, widening hallways and doorways to accommodate wheelchairs, installing support bars and railings in bathrooms and other rooms, and adjusting electrical outlets and fixtures.[12] These expenditures are only subject to the AGI floor; the increase in the home's value is deemed to be zero.

10-1c Medical Expenses Incurred for Spouse and Dependents

In computing the medical expense deduction, a taxpayer may include medical expenses for a spouse and for a person who was a dependent at the time the expenses were paid or incurred. Of the requirements that normally apply in determining dependency status,[13] neither the gross income nor the joint return test applies in determining dependency status for medical expense deduction purposes.

William (age 22) is married and a full-time student at a university. During the year, William incurred medical expenses that were paid by Karen (William's mother). She provided more than half of William's support for the year.

Even if William files a joint return with his wife, Karen may claim the medical expenses she paid for him. Karen would combine William's expenses with her own before applying the AGI floor.

For *divorced persons* with children, a special rule applies to the noncustodial parent. The noncustodial parent may claim any medical expenses he or she pays even though the custodial parent claims the children as dependents.

Irv and Joan were divorced last year, and Joan was awarded custody of their child, Keith. During the current year, Irv pays $2,500 of Keith's medical bills. Together, Irv and Joan provide more than half of Keith's support.

Even though Joan claims Keith as a dependent, Irv can combine the $2,500 of medical expenses that he pays for Keith with his own when calculating his medical expense deduction.

---

[10]Reg. § 1.213–1(e)(1)(iii).
[11]§ 212(3).

[12]For a complete list of the items that qualify, see Rev.Rul. 87–106, 1987–2 C.B. 67.
[13]Refer to Chapter 3 for discussion of these requirements.

10-1d Transportation, Meal, and Lodging Expenses for Medical Treatment

Payments for transportation to and from a point of treatment for medical care are deductible as medical expenses (subject to the AGI floor). These costs include bus, taxi, train, or plane fare; charges for ambulance service; and out-of-pocket expenses for the use of an automobile. A mileage allowance of 17 cents per mile for 2017 may be used instead of actual out-of-pocket automobile expenses.[14] Whether the taxpayer chooses to claim out-of-pocket automobile expenses or the 17 cents per mile automatic mileage option, related parking fees and tolls can also be deducted. Also included are transportation expenditures for someone such as a family member or nurse who must accompany the patient. The cost of meals while en route to obtain medical care is not deductible.

A deduction is allowable for lodging while away from home for medical care if the following requirements are met:[15]

- The lodging is primarily for and essential to medical care.
- Medical care is provided by a physician in a licensed hospital or a similar medical facility (e.g., a clinic).
- The lodging is not lavish or extravagant.
- There is no significant element of personal pleasure in the travel.

The deduction for lodging expenses cannot exceed $50 *per* night for *each* person. The lodging deduction is allowed not only for the patient but also for anyone who must travel with the patient.

The Big Picture

EXAMPLE 9

Return to the facts of *The Big Picture* on p. 10-1. John's mother, Martha, eventually moves in with the Williamsons because of her declining health, and she becomes their dependent. Later, John is advised by Martha's physician that she needs specialized treatment for her heart condition. Consequently, John and Martha fly to Cleveland, Ohio, where Martha receives the therapy at a heart clinic on an outpatient basis. Expenses in connection with the trip are as follows:

Round-trip airfare ($250 each)	$500
Lodging in Cleveland for two nights ($120 each per night)	480

Assuming that the Williamsons itemize their deductions (including medical expenses), the medical expense deduction for transportation is $500 and the medical expense deduction for lodging is $200 ($50 per night per person). Because of the severity of Martha's health condition, it is assumed that John's accompanying her is justified.

No deduction is allowed for the cost of meals unless they are part of the medical care and are furnished at a medical facility. If deductible, these meals are not subject to the 50 percent limit applicable to business meals (see Chapter 9).

10-1e Amounts Paid for Medical Insurance Premiums

Medical insurance premiums (including Medicare insurance costs withheld from a Social Security recipient's monthly benefits) are included with other medical expenses subject to the AGI floor. Premiums paid by the taxpayer under a group plan or an individual plan are included as medical expenses. If an employer pays all or part of the taxpayer's medical insurance premiums, the amount paid by the employer is not included in the employee's gross income (and these amounts are not deductible by the employee). However, the medical insurance premiums paid by the

---

[14]This amount is adjusted periodically. In 2016, the allowance was 19 cents per mile.

[15]§ 213(d)(2).

employer are deductible as business expenses on the employer's tax return (see Chapter 6).

If a taxpayer is *self-employed*, insurance premiums paid for medical coverage are deductible as a *business* expense (*for* AGI).[16] The deduction *for* AGI is allowed for premiums paid for the taxpayer, the taxpayer's spouse, and dependents of the taxpayer. However, this deduction is not allowed if the taxpayer (or taxpayer's spouse) is eligible to participate in an employer-provided health plan.

The Big Picture

EXAMPLE 10

Return to the facts of *The Big Picture* on p. 10-1. John Williamson is the sole practitioner in his unincorporated accounting practice. During the year, he paid health insurance premiums of $12,000 for his own coverage and $8,000 for coverage for his wife, Susan. John can deduct $20,000 as a business deduction (*for* AGI) in computing their taxable income.

Taxpayers may also include premiums paid on qualified long-term care insurance contracts in medical expenses, subject to limitations based on the age of the insured. For 2017, the per-person limits range from $410 for taxpayers age 40 and under to $5,110 for taxpayers over age 70.[17]

10-1f **Year of Deduction**

Regardless of a taxpayer's method of accounting, medical expenses are deductible only in the year *paid*. In effect, individual taxpayers are on a cash basis for the medical expense deduction. One exception, however, is allowed for deceased taxpayers. If the medical expenses are paid within one year from the day following the day of death, they can be treated as being paid at the time they were *incurred*. As a result, these expenses may be reported on the final income tax return of the decedent or on earlier returns if incurred before the year of death.

No current deduction is allowed for payment for medical care to be rendered in the future unless the taxpayer is under an obligation to make the payment. Whether an obligation to make the payment exists depends on the policy of the physician or the institution furnishing the medical care.

EXAMPLE 11

Upon the recommendation of his regular dentist, in December 2017, Gary consults Dr. Smith, a prosthodontist, who specializes in crown and bridge work. Dr. Smith tells Gary that he can do the necessary restorative work for $12,000 and that he requires all new patients to prepay 40% of the total cost of the procedure. Accordingly, Gary pays $4,800 in December 2017. The balance of $7,200 is paid when the work is completed in January 2018.

Under these circumstances, the qualifying medical expense deductions are $4,800 for 2017 and $7,200 in 2018. The result would be the same even if Gary prepaid the full $12,000 in 2017.

10-1g **Reimbursements**

If medical expenses are reimbursed in the same year as paid, no problem arises. The reimbursement merely reduces the amount that would otherwise qualify for the medical expense deduction. But what happens if the reimbursement occurs in a later year than the expenditure? In computing casualty losses, any reasonable prospect of recovery must be considered (refer to Chapter 7). For medical expenses, however, any expected reimbursement is disregarded in measuring the amount of the deduction. Instead, the reimbursement is accounted for separately in the year in which it occurs.

---

[16]§ 162(l).

[17]The amounts for 2016 were $390 for taxpayers age 40 and under and $4,870 for taxpayers over age 70. See IRS Publication 502 for details relat-

ing to requirements for deducting costs associated with qualified long-term care insurance contracts.

Under the *tax benefit rule*, a taxpayer who receives an insurance reimbursement for medical expenses deducted in a previous year must include the reimbursement in income up to the amount of the deductions that decreased taxable income in the earlier year. A taxpayer who did not itemize deductions in the year the expenses were paid did not receive a tax benefit and is *not* required to include a reimbursement in gross income.

EXAMPLE 12

Daniel had AGI of $45,000 for 2017. He was injured in a car accident and paid $4,300 for hospital expenses and $700 for doctor bills. Daniel also incurred medical expenses of $600 for his dependent child. In 2018, Daniel was reimbursed $650 by his insurance company for the medical expenses attributable to the car accident. His deduction for medical expenses in 2017 is computed as follows:

Hospitalization	$ 4,300
Bills for doctor's services	700
Medical expenses for dependent	600
Total	$ 5,600
Less: Medical expense floor (10% of $45,000)	(4,500)
Medical expense deduction (assuming that Daniel itemizes his deductions)	$ 1,100

Assume that Daniel would have elected to itemize his deductions even if he had no medical expenses in 2017. If the reimbursement for medical care had occurred in 2017, the medical expense deduction would have been only $450 [$5,600 (total medical expenses) − $650 (reimbursement) − $4,500 (floor)] and Daniel would have paid more income tax.

Because the reimbursement was made in a subsequent year, Daniel will include $650 in gross income for 2018. If Daniel had not itemized in 2017, he would *not* have included the $650 reimbursement in 2018 gross income because he would have received no tax benefit for the medical expenses in 2017.

10-1h Health Savings Accounts

Qualifying individuals may make deductible contributions to a **Health Savings Account (HSA)**.[18] A taxpayer can use an HSA in conjunction with a high-deductible medical insurance policy to help reduce the overall cost of medical coverage. Converting from a low-deductible to a high-deductible plan can generally save an individual a considerable amount in premiums. The high-deductible policy provides coverage for extraordinary medical expenses (in excess of the deductible), and expenses not covered by the policy can be paid with funds withdrawn tax-free from the HSA.

EXAMPLE 13

Sanchez, who is married and has three dependent children, carries a high-deductible medical insurance policy with a deductible of $4,400. He establishes an HSA and contributes the maximum allowable amount to the HSA in 2017.

During 2017, the Sanchez family incurs medical expenses of $7,000. The high-deductible policy covers $2,600 of the expenses ($7,000 expenses − $4,400 deductible). Sanchez may withdraw $4,400 from the HSA to pay the medical expenses not covered by the high-deductible policy.

High-Deductible Plans

High-deductible policies are less expensive than low-deductible policies, so taxpayers with low medical costs can benefit from the lower premiums and use funds from the HSA to pay costs not covered by the high-deductible policy. A plan must meet two requirements to qualify as a high-deductible plan.[19]

---

[18]§ 223. An HSA is a qualified trust or custodial account administered by a qualified HSA trustee, which can be a bank, an insurance company, or another IRS-approved trustee.

[19]§ 223(c)(2).

1. The annual deductible in 2017 is not less than $1,300 for self-only coverage ($2,600 for family coverage).
2. The annual limit in 2017 on total out-of-pocket costs (excluding premiums) under the plan does not exceed $6,550 for self-only coverage ($13,100 for family coverage).

Tax Treatment of HSA Contributions and Distributions

To establish an HSA, a taxpayer contributes funds to a custodial account.[20] As illustrated in the preceding example, funds can be withdrawn from an HSA to pay medical expenses that are not covered by the high-deductible policy. The following general tax rules apply to HSAs:

1. Contributions made by the taxpayer to an HSA are deductible from gross income to arrive at AGI (deduction *for* AGI). Thus, the taxpayer does not need to itemize to take the deduction.
2. Earnings on HSAs are not subject to taxation unless distributed, in which case taxability depends on the way the funds are used.[21]

   • Distributions from HSAs are excluded from gross income if they are used to pay for medical expenses not covered by the high-deductible policy.

   • Distributions that are not used to pay for medical expenses are included in gross income and are subject to an additional 20 percent penalty if made before age 65, death, or disability. Any distributions made by reason of death or disability and distributions made after the HSA beneficiary becomes eligible for Medicare are taxed but not penalized.

HSAs have at least two other attractive features. First, an HSA is portable. Taxpayers who switch jobs can take their HSAs with them. Second, anyone under age 65 who has a high-deductible plan and is not covered by another policy that is not a high-deductible plan can establish an HSA.

Deductible Amount

The annual deduction for contributions to an HSA is limited to an amount that depends on whether the taxpayer has self-only coverage or family coverage. The annual limit for an individual who has self-only coverage in 2017 is $3,400, while the annual limit for an individual who has family coverage in 2017 is $6,750. These amounts are subject to annual cost-of-living adjustments.[22] An eligible taxpayer who has attained age 55 by the end of the tax year may make an additional annual contribution in 2017 of up to $1,000. This additional amount is referred to as a *catch-up* contribution. A deduction is not allowed after the individual becomes eligible for Medicare coverage.

Determining the Maximum HSA Contribution Deduction

Liu (age 45), who is married and self-employed, carries a high-deductible medical insurance policy with family coverage and an annual deductible of $4,000. In addition, he has established an HSA. Liu's maximum annual deductible contribution to the HSA in 2017 is $6,750.

EXAMPLE
14

During 2017, Adam, who is self-employed, made 12 monthly payments of $1,200 for an HSA contract that provides medical insurance coverage with a $3,600 deductible. The plan covers Adam, his wife, and two children. Of the $1,200 monthly fee, $675 was for the high-deductible policy and $525 was deposited into an HSA.

EXAMPLE
15

continued

---

[20]§ 223(d).
[21]§ 223(f).

[22]§ 223(b)(2). The annual limits were $3,350 and $6,750 in 2016.

Because Adam is *self-employed*, he can deduct $8,100 of the amount paid for the high-deductible policy ($675 per month × 12 months) as a deduction *for* AGI (refer to Example 10 and related discussion). In addition, he can deduct the $6,300 ($525 × 12) paid to the HSA as a deduction *for* AGI. Note that the $6,300 HSA deduction does not exceed the $6,750 annual ceiling.

LO.3

Contrast deductible taxes with nondeductible fees, licenses, and other charges.

10-2 TAXES

A deduction is allowed for certain state and local taxes paid or accrued by a taxpayer.[23] There are multiple reasons behind allowing these deductions. The state and local income tax deduction was created to relieve the burden of multiple taxes on the same source of revenue. The deduction for real estate taxes was created to encourage home ownership. Overall, state and local taxes are viewed as affecting a taxpayer's ability to pay Federal income taxes. As a result, a Federal deduction for these taxes promotes equity.

10-2a Deductibility as a Tax

It is important to understand the difference between a tax and a fee, because fees are not deductible unless incurred as a business expense or as an expense in the production of income. Here is the IRS definition of a tax:

> A tax is an enforced contribution exacted pursuant to legislative authority in the exercise of taxing power, and imposed and collected for the purpose of raising revenue to be used for public or governmental purposes, and not as payment for some special privilege granted or service rendered. Taxes are, therefore, distinguished from various other contributions and charges imposed for particular purposes under particular powers or functions of the government. In view of such distinctions, the question whether a particular contribution or charge is to be regarded as a tax depends upon its real nature.[24]

As a result, fees for dog licenses, automobile inspections, automobile titles and registration, hunting and fishing licenses, bridge and highway tolls, driver's licenses, parking meter deposits, and postage are not deductible if personal in nature. Deductible and nondeductible taxes are summarized in Exhibit 10.2.

EXHIBIT 10.2	Deductible and Nondeductible Taxes
Deductible	**Nondeductible**
State, local, and foreign real property taxes	Federal income taxes
	FICA taxes imposed on employees
State and local personal property taxes	Employer FICA taxes paid on domestic household workers
State and local income taxes *or* sales/use taxes	Estate, inheritance, and gift taxes
Foreign income taxes	Federal, state, and local excise taxes (e.g., gasoline, tobacco, and spirits)
	Foreign income taxes if the taxpayer chooses the foreign tax credit option
	Taxes on real property to the extent such taxes are to be apportioned and treated as imposed on another taxpayer

---

[23]Most deductible taxes are listed in § 164, while nondeductible items are included in § 275.

[24]Rev.Rul. 57–345, 1957–2 C.B. 132 and Rev.Rul. 70–622, 1970–2 C.B. 41.

10-2b Property Taxes

State, local, and foreign taxes on real property are generally deductible only by the person upon whom the tax is imposed. Deductible personal property taxes must be *ad valorem* (assessed in relation to the value of the property). So a motor vehicle tax based on weight, model, year, and horsepower is not deductible. However, a tax based on value and other criteria will be partially deductible.

The Big Picture

EXAMPLE 16

Return to the facts of *The Big Picture* on p. 10-1. Assuming that the Williamsons proceed with the purchase of a home, the real estate taxes they pay will be deductible *from* AGI because they qualify to itemize their deductions. However, if they also pay a personal property tax on their automobile, the payment may be only partially deductible.

For example, assume that in their state, the government imposes a motor vehicle registration tax on 2% of the value of the vehicle plus 40 cents per hundredweight. The Williamsons own a car having a value of $20,000 and weighing 3,000 pounds. They pay an annual registration tax of $412. Of this amount, $400 (2% × $20,000 of value) is deductible as a personal property tax. The remaining $12, based on the weight of the car, is not deductible.

Assessments for Local Benefits

As a general rule, real property taxes do not include taxes assessed for local benefits because such assessments tend to increase the value of the property (e.g., special assessments for streets, sidewalks, curbing, and other similar improvements).[25] Instead of being deductible, these assessments are added to the basis of the taxpayer's property.

Apportionment of Real Property Taxes between Seller and Purchaser

Real estate taxes for the entire year are apportioned between the buyer and seller on the basis of the number of days the property was held by each during the real property tax year. This apportionment is required whether the tax is paid by the buyer or the seller or is prorated according to the purchase agreement. The apportionment determines who is entitled to deduct the real estate taxes in the year of sale. The required apportionment prevents the shifting of the deduction for real estate taxes from the buyer to the seller, or vice versa. In making the apportionment, the assessment date and the lien date are disregarded.[26]

EXAMPLE 17

A county's real property tax year runs from January 1 to December 31. Abigail, the owner on January 1 of real property located in the county, sells the real property to Bob on June 30. Bob owns the real property from June 30 through December 31. The tax for the real property tax year, January 1 through December 31, is $3,650.

Assuming that this is not a leap year, the portion of the real property tax treated as imposed upon Abigail, the seller, is $1,800 [(180/365) × $3,650, January 1 through June 29], while $1,850 of the tax [(185/365) × $3,650, June 30 through December 31] is treated as imposed upon Bob, the purchaser.

If the actual real estate taxes are not prorated between the buyer and seller as part of the purchase agreement, adjustments are required. The adjustments are necessary to determine the amount realized by the seller and the basis of the property to the buyer. If the buyer pays the entire amount of the tax, he or she has, in effect, paid the seller's portion of the real estate tax and has therefore paid more for the property than the actual purchase price. As a result, the amount of real estate tax

---

[25]Reg. § 1.164–4(a); see *Erie H. Rose*, 31 TCM 142, T.C.Memo. 1972–39, where a taxpayer was denied a deduction for the cost of a new sidewalk in front of his personal residence, even though the construction was required by the city and the sidewalk may have provided an incidental benefit to public welfare.

[26]For most years, the apportionment is based on a 365-day year. However, in a leap year (i.e., a year that is evenly divisible by 4, such as 2016), the taxes are prorated over 366 days. In making the apportionment, the date of sale counts as a day the property is owned by the buyer.

that is apportioned to the seller (for Federal income tax purposes) and paid by the buyer is added to the buyer's basis. The seller must increase the amount realized on the sale by the same amount.

EXAMPLE 18

Seth sells real estate on October 3 for $400,000. The buyer, Wilma, pays the real estate taxes of $3,650 for the calendar year, which is the real estate property tax year.

Assuming that this is not a leap year, $2,750 (for 275 days) of the real estate taxes is apportioned to and is deductible by the seller, Seth, and $900 (for 90 days) of the taxes is deductible by Wilma.

Wilma has, in effect, paid Seth's real estate taxes of $2,750 and has therefore paid $402,750 for the property. Wilma's basis is increased to $402,750, and the amount realized by Seth from the sale is increased to $402,750.

The opposite result occurs if the seller (rather than the buyer) pays the real estate taxes. In this case, the seller reduces the amount realized from the sale by the amount that has been apportioned to the buyer. The buyer is required to reduce his or her basis by a corresponding amount.

LO.4

Explain the Federal income tax treatment of state and local income taxes and sales taxes.

10-2c **State and Local Income Taxes and Sales Taxes**

The position of the IRS is that state and local income taxes imposed upon an individual are deductible only as itemized deductions, even if the taxpayer's sole source of income is from a business, rents, or royalties.

Cash basis taxpayers are entitled to deduct state income taxes in the year *payment is made*. This includes taxes withheld by the employer, amounts paid with the state income tax return when filed, and estimated state income tax payments.[27] If the taxpayer overpays state income taxes, any refund received is included in gross income in the year received to the extent the deduction reduced taxable income in the prior year.

EXAMPLE 19

Leona, a cash basis, unmarried taxpayer, had $800 of state income tax withheld during 2017. Also in 2017, Leona paid $100 that was due when she filed her 2016 state income tax return and made estimated payments of $300 toward her 2017 state income tax liability. When Leona files her 2017 Federal income tax return in April 2018, she elects to itemize deductions, which amount to $12,500, including the $1,200 of state income tax payments and withholdings, all of which reduce her taxable income.

As a result of overpaying her 2017 state income tax, Leona receives a refund of $200 early in 2018. She will include this amount in her 2018 gross income in computing her Federal income tax. It does not matter whether Leona received a check from the state for $200 or applied the $200 toward her 2018 state income tax.

Itemized Deduction for Sales Taxes Paid

Individuals can elect to deduct *either* their state and local income taxes *or* their sales/use taxes paid as an itemized deduction. This election is intended to provide equity to taxpayers living in states that do not have a state income tax (but do have sales taxes). Taxpayers making this election can either deduct actual sales/use tax payments *or* an amount from an IRS table (see Appendix A). The IRS table amount can be increased by sales tax paid on the purchase of motor vehicles, boats, and other specified items.

---

[27]Rev.Rul. 71–190, 1971–1 C.B. 70. See also Rev.Rul. 82–208, 1982–2 C.B. 58, where a deduction is not allowed when the taxpayer cannot, in good faith, reasonably determine that there is additional state income tax liability.

10-3 INTEREST

LO.5
Distinguish between deductible and nondeductible interest and apply the appropriate limitations to deductible interest.

A deduction for interest has been allowed since the income tax law was enacted in 1913. However, despite its long history, the interest deduction has been one of the most controversial areas in the tax law. Should all interest be allowed as a deduction? If not, what limits should apply? Should an interest deduction be allowed for only the taxpayer's principal residence (or all residences)? What about credit card interest? These questions (and others) continue to be raised.

Currently, personal (consumer) interest is not deductible. This includes credit card interest, interest on car loans, and other types of personal interest. However, interest on qualified student loans, qualified residence (home mortgage) interest, and investment interest continue to be deductible, subject to the limits discussed on the following pages.[28]

10-3a Allowed and Disallowed Items

The Supreme Court has defined *interest* as compensation for the use of money.[29] The general rule permits a deduction for interest paid or accrued within the taxable year on indebtedness.

Interest on Qualified Student Loans

Taxpayers who pay interest on a qualified student loan may be able to deduct the interest as a deduction *for* AGI. The deduction is allowed if the proceeds of the loan are used to pay qualified education expenses. These payments must be made to qualified educational institutions.[30]

The maximum annual deduction for qualified student loan interest is $2,500. However, in 2017, the deduction is phased out for taxpayers with modified AGI (MAGI) between $65,000 and $80,000 ($135,000 and $165,000 on joint returns). The interest expense deduction is phased out by applying the following formula:

$$\text{Education interest expense} \times \frac{\text{Modified AGI} - \text{AGI phaseout floor}}{\$15,000 \ (\$30,000 \text{ for married filing jointly})}$$

The deduction is not allowed for taxpayers who are claimed as dependents or for married taxpayers filing separately.[31]

EXAMPLE 20

In 2017, Curt and Rita, who are married and file a joint return, paid $3,000 of interest on a qualified student loan. Their MAGI was $142,500. Their maximum potential deduction for qualified student loan interest is $2,500, but it must be reduced by $625 as a result of the phaseout rules.

$$\$2,500 \text{ interest} \ \times \ \frac{\$142,500 \ (\text{MAGI}) - \$135,000 \ (\text{AGI phaseout floor})}{\$30,000 \ (\text{phaseout range})} = \$625 \text{ reduction}$$

Curt and Rita are allowed a student loan interest deduction of $1,875 ($2,500 maximum deduction − $625 reduction = $1,875 deduction *for* AGI).

Qualified Residence Interest

Qualified residence interest is interest paid or accrued during the taxable year on indebtedness (subject to limitations) *secured* by a qualified residence of the taxpayer. Qualified residence interest falls into two categories: (1) interest on acquisition indebtedness and (2) interest on home equity loans. Before each of these categories is discussed, however, the term *qualified residence* must be defined.

---

[28]As discussed in Chapter 6, interest expense paid or incurred in a trade or business is also deductible (§ 162; a *for* AGI deduction).

[29]*Old Colony Railroad Co. v. Comm.*, 3 USTC ¶880, 10 AFTR 786, 52 S.Ct. 211 (USSC, 1932).

[30]See IRS Publication 970, *Tax Benefits for Education*, for details.

[31]§ 221. See § 221(b)(2)(C) for the definition of MAGI. For 2016, the MAGI threshold amounts were $65,000 and $80,000 ($130,000 and $160,000 on joint returns).

A *qualified residence* includes the taxpayer's principal residence and one other residence of the taxpayer or spouse. The *principal residence* meets the requirement for nonrecognition of gain upon sale under § 121 (see Chapter 15). The *one other residence*, or second residence, is used as a residence if not rented or, if rented, meets the requirements for a personal residence under the rental of vacation home rules (refer to Chapter 6). A taxpayer who has more than one second residence can choose the qualified second residence each year (i.e., the taxpayer can select a different second residence each year). A residence includes a house, a cooperative apartment, a condominium, and mobile homes and boats that have living quarters (sleeping accommodations, a toilet, and cooking facilities).

Although in most cases interest paid on a home mortgage is fully deductible, there are limitations.[32] Interest paid or accrued during the tax year on aggregate **acquisition indebtedness** of $1 million or less ($500,000 for married persons filing separate returns) is deductible as qualified residence interest. *Acquisition indebtedness* refers to amounts incurred in acquiring, constructing, or substantially improving a qualified residence of the taxpayer.

The Big Picture

EXAMPLE 21

Return to the facts of *The Big Picture* on p. 10-1. Given that John and Susan Williamson will need to borrow at least a portion of the purchase price of a new home, a standard mortgage likely will qualify as acquisition indebtedness because the borrowed funds are used to acquire a principal residence. However, the interest on the acquisition indebtedness will be fully deductible only if the amount of the mortgage is $1 million or less (assuming that John and Susan file a joint return) and the mortgage is secured by the home, which is the typical case.

Recall that the Williamsons are also considering what appears to be a less expensive route of using their retirement and taxable investments to secure the debt. If they choose this alternative, the interest will not be deductible as qualified residence interest because the loan would not be acquisition indebtedness (i.e., the loan would not be secured by the home).

Qualified residence interest also includes interest on **home equity loans**. These loans utilize the personal residence of the taxpayer as security, typically in the form of a second mortgage. Because the funds from home equity loans can be used for personal purposes (e.g., auto purchases, vacations, medical expenses), what would otherwise have been nondeductible personal interest becomes deductible qualified residence interest.

However, interest is deductible only on the portion of a home equity loan that does not exceed the *lesser of*:

- The fair market value of the residence, reduced by the acquisition indebtedness, *or*
- $100,000 ($50,000 for married persons filing separate returns).

EXAMPLE 22

Larry owns a personal residence with a fair market value of $450,000 and an outstanding first mortgage of $420,000. Therefore, his equity in his home is $30,000 ($450,000 − $420,000). Larry borrows $15,000 that is secured by a second mortgage on his home to purchase a new family automobile.

All interest on the $435,000 of first and second mortgage debt is treated as qualified residence interest.

In certain situations, mortgage insurance premiums paid by the taxpayer on a qualified residence may be deducted (treated as qualified residence interest). However, the deduction begins to phase out for taxpayers with AGI in excess of $100,000 ($50,000 for married taxpayers filing separately). The deduction is fully phased out when AGI exceeds $109,000 ($54,500 for married taxpayers filing separately).[33]

---

[32]§ 163(h)(3).

[33]§§ 163(h)(3)(E)(i) and (ii). This provision expired at the end of December 2016. However, many tax professionals expect that Congress will extend this provision.

Interest Paid for Services

Mortgage loan companies commonly charge a fee, often called a loan origination fee, for finding, placing, or processing a mortgage loan. Loan origination fees are typically nondeductible amounts included in the basis of the acquired property. Other fees, sometimes called **points** and expressed as a percentage of the loan amount, are paid to reduce the interest rate charged over the term of the loan. Essentially, the payment of points is a prepayment of interest and is considered compensation to a lender for the use of money.[34]

In general, points are capitalized and are amortized and deductible ratably over the life of the loan. However, the purchaser of a principal residence can deduct qualifying points in the year of payment.[35] This exception also covers points paid to obtain funds for home improvements.

Points paid to *refinance* an existing home mortgage must be capitalized and amortized as an interest deduction over the life of the new loan.[36]

EXAMPLE

23

Sandra purchased her residence many years ago, obtaining a 30-year mortgage at an annual interest rate of 6%. In the current year, Sandra refinances the mortgage to reduce the interest rate to 4%. To obtain the refinancing, she has to pay points of $2,600.

The $2,600, which is considered prepayment of interest, must be capitalized and amortized over the life of the mortgage.

Points paid by the seller for a buyer are, in effect, treated as an adjustment to the price of the residence, and the buyer is treated as having used cash to pay the points that were paid by the seller. A buyer may deduct seller-paid points in the tax year in which they are paid if certain conditions are met.[37]

Prepayment Penalty

When a mortgage or loan is paid off in full in a lump sum before its term (early), the lending institution may require an additional payment (normally, a specific percentage of the loan balance). This is known as a prepayment penalty and is considered to be interest (e.g., personal, qualified residence, or investment) in the year paid. The general rules for deductibility of interest also apply to prepayment penalties.

Interest Paid to Related Parties

Nothing prevents the deduction of interest paid to a related party as long as the payment actually took place and the interest meets the requirements for deductibility. Recall from Chapter 6 that a special rule for related taxpayers applies when the debtor uses the accrual basis and the related creditor is on the cash basis. If this rule applies, interest that has been accrued but not paid at the end of the debtor's tax year is not deductible until payment is made and the income is reportable by the cash basis recipient.

Investment Interest

Taxpayers frequently borrow funds they use to acquire investment assets. Congress, however, has limited the deductibility of interest on funds borrowed to purchase or hold investment property. The deduction for investment interest expense is limited to the net investment income for the year. A complete discussion of investment interest occurs in Chapter 11.

Tax-Exempt Securities

No deduction is allowed for interest on debt incurred to purchase or hold tax-exempt securities.[38] Refer to Chapter 6 for a detailed discussion of this topic.

---

[34]Rev.Rul. 69–188, 1969–1 C.B. 54. To be deductible, points must be in the nature of interest and cannot be a form of service charge or payment for specific services.

[35]§ 461(g)(2).

[36]Rev.Rul. 87–22, 1987–1 C.B. 146.

[37]Refer to Revenue Procedure 94–27 for a complete list of these conditions and additional aspects of this arrangement. Rev.Proc. 94–27, 1994–1 C.B. 613.

[38]§ 265(a)(2).

10-3b **Restrictions on Deductibility and Timing Considerations**

Even if the interest expense is deductible (e.g., qualified residence interest), a current deduction still may not be available unless certain additional conditions described below are met.

Taxpayer's Obligation

Allowed interest is deductible if the related debt represents a bona fide obligation of the taxpayer.[39] For interest to be deductible, both the debtor and the creditor must intend for the loan to be repaid. Intent of the parties can be especially crucial between related parties such as a shareholder and a closely held corporation.

In addition, an individual may not deduct interest paid on behalf of another taxpayer. For example, a shareholder may not deduct interest paid by the corporation on his or her behalf.[40] Likewise, a husband may not deduct interest paid on his wife's property if he files a separate return, except in the case of qualified residence interest. If both husband and wife consent in writing, either the husband or the wife may deduct the allowed interest on the principal residence and one other residence.

Time of Deduction

Under the cash method, interest must be paid to secure a deduction. Under the accrual method, interest is deductible ratably over the life of the loan.

EXAMPLE 24

On November 1, 2017, Ramon borrows $2,000 to purchase appliances for a rental house. The loan is payable in 90 days at 6% interest. On the due date in late January 2018, Ramon pays the $2,000 note and interest amounting to $30.

Ramon can deduct the accrued portion ($2/3 \times \$30 = \$20$) of the interest in 2017 only if he is an accrual basis taxpayer. Otherwise, the entire amount of interest ($30) is deductible in 2018.

Prepaid Interest

The accrual method must be used by cash basis taxpayers for interest prepayments that extend beyond the end of the taxable year.[41] These payments must be allocated to the tax years to which the interest payments relate. This provision prevents cash basis taxpayers from *manufacturing* tax deductions before the end of the year by prepaying interest.

10-3c **Classification of Interest Expense**

Whether interest is deductible *for* AGI or as an itemized deduction (*from* AGI) depends on whether the indebtedness has a business, investment, or personal purpose. If the indebtedness is incurred in relation to a business (other than performing services as an employee) or for the production of rent or royalty income, the interest is deductible *for* AGI. Business expenses appear on Schedule C of Form 1040, and expenses related to rents or royalties are reported on Schedule E.

If the indebtedness is incurred for personal use, such as qualified residence interest, any deduction allowed is taken *from* AGI and is reported on Schedule A of Form 1040 (the taxpayer must itemize deductions to get any benefit). Recall, however, that interest on a student loan is a deduction *for* AGI. If the taxpayer is an employee who incurs debt in relation to his or her employment, the interest is considered to be personal, or consumer, interest and is not deductible.

See Concept Summary 10.1 for a summary of the interest deduction rules.

---

[39]*Arcade Realty Co.*, 35 T.C. 256 (1960).

[40]*Continental Trust Co.*, 7 B.T.A. 539 (1927).

[41]§ 461(g)(1).

Concept Summary 10.1

Deductibility of Personal, Student Loan, Mortgage, and Investment Interest

Type	Deductible	Comments
Personal (consumer) interest	No	Includes any interest that is not qualified residence interest, qualified student loan interest, investment interest, or business interest. Examples include interest on car loans and credit card debt.
Qualified student loan interest	Yes	Deduction *for* AGI; subject to limitations.
Qualified residence interest on acquisition indebtedness	Yes	Deductible as an itemized deduction; limited to indebtedness of $1 million.
Qualified residence interest on home equity indebtedness	Yes	Deductible as an itemized deduction; limited to indebtedness equal to the lesser of $100,000 or the FMV of residence minus acquisition indebtedness.
Investment interest (*not* related to rental or royalty property)	Yes	Itemized deduction; limited to net investment income for the year; disallowed interest can be carried over to future years. See Chapter 11 for a complete discussion of investment interest.
Investment interest (related to rental or royalty property)	Yes	Deduction *for* AGI; limited to net investment income for the year; disallowed interest can be carried over to future years. See Chapter 11 for a complete discussion of investment interest.

10-4 CHARITABLE CONTRIBUTIONS

LO.6

Recognize charitable contributions and identify their related measurement problems and percentage limitations.

Section 170 allows individuals and corporations to deduct contributions made to qualified *domestic* organizations. Contributions to qualified charitable organizations serve certain social welfare needs and thus relieve the government of the cost of providing these needed services to the community.

The charitable contribution provisions are among the most complex in the tax law. To determine the amount deductible as a charitable contribution, several important questions must be answered:

- What constitutes a charitable contribution?
- Was the contribution made to a qualified organization?
- When is the contribution deductible?
- What record-keeping and reporting requirements apply to charitable contributions?
- How is the value of donated property determined?
- What special rules apply to contributions of property that has increased in value?
- What percentage limitations apply to the charitable contribution deduction?
- What rules apply to amounts in excess of percentage limitations (carryovers)?

These questions are addressed in the sections that follow.

10-4a Criteria for a Gift

A *charitable contribution* is defined as a gift of property made to a qualified organization.[42] The major elements needed to qualify a contribution as a gift are a donative intent, the absence of consideration, and acceptance by the donee. Consequently, the taxpayer has the burden of establishing that the transfer was made from motives of *disinterested generosity* as established by the courts.[43] This test is quite subjective and has led to problems of interpretation (refer to the discussion of gifts in Chapter 5).

---

[42]§ 170(c). In recent years, easements have become a popular means of claiming a charitable contribution deduction (e.g., for scenic, historical, noncommercial development, or other similar purposes), and many court cases have focused on the valuation of these easements. See Chapter 14 for additional details about easements and their effect on the basis of property.

[43]*Comm. v. Duberstein*, 60–2 USTC ¶9515, 5 AFTR 2d 1626, 80 S.Ct. 1190 (USSC, 1960).

Benefit Received Rule

When a donor derives a tangible benefit from a contribution, he or she cannot deduct the value of the benefit.

> Ralph purchases a ticket at $100 for a special performance of the local symphony (a qualified charity). If the price of a ticket to a symphony concert is normally $35, Ralph is allowed only $65 as a charitable contribution. Even if Ralph does not attend the concert, the deduction is limited to $65.
>
> If, however, Ralph does *not* accept the ticket from the symphony (or returns it prior to the event), he can deduct the full $100.

An exception to this benefit rule provides for the deduction of an automatic percentage of the amount paid for the right to purchase athletic tickets from colleges and universities.[44] Under this exception, 80 percent of the amount paid to or for the benefit of the institution qualifies as a charitable contribution deduction.

> Janet donates $5,000 to State University's athletic department. The payment guarantees that she will have preferred seating on the 50-yard line at football games. Subsequently, Janet buys four $50 game tickets. Under the exception to the benefit rule, she is allowed a $4,000 (80% of $5,000) charitable contribution deduction for the taxable year.
>
> If, however, Janet's $5,000 donation includes four $50 tickets, that portion [$200 ($50 × 4)] and the remaining portion of $4,800 ($5,000 − $200) are treated as separate amounts. Thus, Janet is allowed a charitable contribution deduction of $3,840 (80% of $4,800).

Contribution of Services

No deduction is allowed for a contribution of one's services to a qualified charitable organization. However, unreimbursed expenses related to the services rendered may be deductible. For example, the cost of a uniform (without general utility) that is required to be worn while performing services may be deductible. In addition, deductions are permitted for out-of-pocket transportation costs, reasonable expenses for lodging, and the cost of meals while away from home that are incurred in performing the donated services. In lieu of these out-of-pocket costs for an automobile, a standard mileage rate of 14 cents per mile is allowed.[45] The travel expenses are not deductible if the travel involves a significant element of personal pleasure, recreation, or vacation.[46]

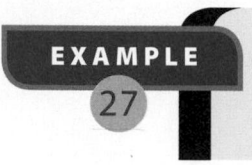

> Grace, a delegate representing her church in Miami, Florida, travels to a two-day national meeting in Denver, Colorado, in February. After the meeting, Grace spends two weeks at a nearby ski resort.
>
> Under these circumstances, none of the transportation, meals, or lodging is deductible because the travel involved a significant element of personal pleasure, recreation, or vacation.

Nondeductible Items

In addition to the benefit received rule and the restrictions placed on contributions of services, the following items may *not* be deducted as charitable contributions:

- Dues, fees, or bills paid to country clubs, lodges, fraternal orders, or similar groups.
- Cost of raffle, bingo, or lottery tickets.
- Cost of tuition.
- Value of blood given to a blood bank.
- Donations to homeowners associations.

---

[44]§ 170(l).
[45]§ 170(i).
[46]§ 170(j).

- Gifts to individuals.
- Rental value of property used by a qualified charity.

10-4b **Qualified Organizations**

To be deductible, a contribution must be made to one of the following organizations:[47]

- A state or possession of the United States (or any subdivision).
- A corporation, trust, community chest, fund, or foundation located in the United States and organized and operated exclusively for religious, charitable, scientific, literary, or educational purposes or for the prevention of cruelty to children or animals.
- A veterans' organization.
- A fraternal organization operating under the lodge system.
- A cemetery company.

It is commonly understood that contributions to a church, synagogue, or other religious organization are allowed. But for less well-known recipients, taxpayers can consult an IRS list of organizations that have applied for and received tax-exempt status under § 501 of the Code.[48]

Gifts made to needy individuals are not deductible (e.g., a needy family or a homeless individual). A deduction is allowed only if the gift is made to a qualified organization.

ETHICS & EQUITY **An Indirect Route to a Contribution Deduction**

In July, a plane crashed into a residential community in Middleboro, destroying and damaging many homes. Chloe's church, a qualified charitable organization, initiated a fund-raising drive to help the Middleboro citizens whose homes had been affected. Chloe donated $50,000 to First Middleboro Church and suggested to the pastor that $25,000 of her contribution should be given to her sister, Rebecca, whose home had suffered extensive damage. The pastor appointed a committee to award funds to needy citizens. The committee solicited applications from the community and awarded Rebecca $15,000. Discuss whether Chloe is justified in deducting $50,000 as a charitable contribution.

10-4c **Time of Deduction**

A charitable contribution generally is deducted in the year the payment is made. This rule applies to both cash and accrual basis individuals. A contribution is ordinarily deemed to have been made on the delivery of the property to the donee. For example, if a gift of common stock is made to a qualified charitable organization, the gift is considered complete on the day of delivery or mailing. However, if the donor delivers the stock certificate to his or her bank or broker or to the issuing corporation, the gift is considered complete on the date the stock is transferred on the books of the corporation.

A contribution made by check is considered delivered on the date of mailing. Thus, a check mailed on December 31, 2017, is deductible on the taxpayer's 2017 tax return. If the contribution is charged on a credit card, the date the charge is made determines the year of deduction.

---

[47]§ 170(c).

[48]Although this *Cumulative List of Organizations*, IRS Publication 78, may be helpful, qualified organizations are not required to be listed. Not all organizations that qualify are listed in this publication. The IRS maintains a searchable database at **www.irs.gov/charities-non-profits/organizations-eligible-to-receive-tax-deductible-charitable-contributions**.

10-4d **Record-Keeping and Valuation Requirements**

Recall that income tax deductions allowed by law are a matter of legislative grace, but a taxpayer still bears the burden of showing that he or she is entitled to claim the deduction. Not surprisingly, the IRS provides specific documentation requirements that must be met to claim a charitable contribution deduction.

Record-Keeping Requirements

In order to claim a charitable contribution deduction, the taxpayer must have appropriate documentation. The specific type of documentation required depends on the amount of the contribution and whether the contribution is made in cash or noncash property.[49] In addition, special rules may apply to gifts of certain types of property (e.g., used cars or boats) where Congress has noted taxpayer abuse in the past. Further, for certain gifts of noncash property, Form 8283 (Noncash Charitable Contributions) must be attached to the taxpayer's return.

The taxpayer must have the required documentation before the tax return is filed for the year the contribution is claimed (and no later than the due date, including extensions, of that tax return). Failure to comply with the reporting rules may result in disallowance of the charitable contribution deduction. In addition, substantial penalties may apply if the taxpayer significantly overvalues any contributed property.

Common documentation and substantiation requirements are summarized in Concept Summary 10.2.

Concept Summary 10.2

Documentation and Substantiation Requirements for Charitable Contributions

Cash gifts	• A deduction is allowed only if the taxpayer has a proper receipt (e.g., bank record such as a canceled check or written statement from the charity) showing the name of the charitable organization and the date and amount of the contribution.
	• A written statement from the charity is required if a payment is for more than $75 and is partly a contribution and partly for goods or services. The statement must provide an estimate of the value of the goods and services received by the donor.
Noncash gifts (e.g., household items)	• A receipt from the charity must be kept for any gift of property other than money. Clothes or other household items are deductible if they are in "good used condition or better" at the time of the gift.
	• If the items are not in good used condition or better and their value is $500 or more, a deduction is allowed if a "qualified appraisal" is included with the return.
Used cars or boats	• The deduction is generally limited to the amount the charity receives on the sale of the car or boat. The taxpayer should obtain a statement from the charity documenting the sales price.
Cash or noncash gifts of $250 or more	• Written acknowledgment from the charity (or certain payroll records in the case of gifts made by payroll deductions) is required to deduct a single cash or property contribution of $250 or more. The acknowledgment must include the amount of money and a description of any other property contributed, whether the charity provided any goods or services in return for the contribution, and a description and estimated value of the goods or services provided.
Noncash gifts of more than $500	• Additional substantiation (e.g., how the property was acquired and its basis) is required on the tax return if donated noncash property is valued at more than $500. Qualified appraisals may be required if noncash contributions exceed $5,000 in value.
Antiques, paintings, jewelry, and other "tangible personal property"	• The deduction is equal to the property's appreciated FMV only if the charity puts the property to "a use related to its tax-exempt purpose." Otherwise, the deduction is limited to the property's cost. The taxpayer should obtain a statement from the charity documenting the property's use.

---

[49]The specific documentation thresholds and requirements are provided in
§ 170(f).

GLOBAL TAX ISSUES   **Choose the Charity Wisely**

Eleonora, a U.S. citizen of Italian descent, was distressed by the damage caused by a major earthquake in central Italy. She donated $100,000 to the Earthquake Victims' Relief Fund, an Italian charitable organization that was set up to help victims of the earthquake. Stefano, also a U.S. citizen of Italian descent, donated $100,000 to help with the relief effort. However, Stefano's contribution went to his church, which sent the proceeds of a fund drive to the Earthquake Victims' Relief Fund in Italy. Eleonora's contribution is not deductible, but Stefano's is. Why? Contributions to charitable organizations are not deductible unless the organization is a U.S. charity.

Valuation Requirements

Property donated to a charity is generally valued at fair market value at the time the gift is made. The Code and Regulations give very little guidance on the measurement of the fair market value. Revenue Ruling 59–60 provides this definition:[50] "The fair market value is the price at which the property would change hands between a willing buyer and a willing seller, neither being under any compulsion to buy or sell and both having reasonable knowledge of relevant facts."

Generally, charitable organizations do not provide the fair market value of the donated property. Nevertheless, as noted in Concept Summary 10.2, the taxpayer must obtain written evidence of the donation from the charity and value the donation appropriately.

10-4e Limitations on Charitable Contribution Deduction

The charitable contribution deduction is the total of all donations made during the year, both money and property. However, the charitable contribution deduction is subject to a number of limitations (based on the taxpayer's AGI, the type of property contributed, and the charity receiving the property). In general:

- If the qualifying contributions for the year total 20 percent or less of AGI, they are fully deductible.
- If the qualifying contributions are more than 20 percent of AGI, the deductible amount may be limited to 20 percent, 30 percent, or 50 percent of AGI, depending on the type of property given and the type of organization to which the donation is made.
- In any case, the maximum charitable contribution deduction may not exceed 50 percent of AGI for the tax year.

If a taxpayer's contributions for the year exceed the limitations, the excess contributions may be carried forward and deducted during a five-year carryover period.

To understand the complex rules for computing the amount of a charitable contribution deduction, it is necessary to understand the distinction between ordinary income property and capital gain property. In addition, it is necessary to understand when the 50 percent, 30 percent, and 20 percent limitations apply. These topics are discussed in the sections that follow.

Ordinary Income Property

Ordinary income property is any property that, if sold, will result in the recognition of ordinary income. The term includes inventory for sale in the taxpayer's trade or business, a work of art created by the donor, and a manuscript prepared by the donor. It also includes, *for purposes of the charitable contribution calculation*, a capital asset held by the donor for a year or less (this is the required holding period for long-term capital gain treatment; see Chapter 16). If a business contributes depreciable property, it is ordinary income property to the extent of any depreciation recapture that would have been

---

[50]1959–1 C.B. 237.

recognized had the property been sold. Ordinary income property also includes personal use and investment assets that have declined in value (i.e., the fair market value is *less than* the taxpayer's basis). Used clothing contributed to the Salvation Army would fit this description.[51]

If ordinary income property is contributed, the deduction is equal to the fair market value of the property less the amount of ordinary income that would have been reported if the property were sold. In most instances, the deduction is limited to the basis of the property to the donor.

Tim donates stock in White Corporation to a university on May 1, 2017. Tim had purchased the stock for $2,500 on March 3, 2017, and the stock had a value of $3,600 when he made the donation. Because he had not held the property long enough to meet the long-term capital gain requirement, Tim would have recognized a short-term capital gain of $1,100 if he had sold the property.

Because short-term capital gain property is treated as ordinary income property for charitable contribution purposes, Tim's charitable contribution deduction is limited to the property's basis of $2,500 ($3,600 − $1,100).

Assume, instead, that the stock had a fair market value of $2,300 (rather than $3,600) when Tim donated it to the university. Because the fair market value now is less than the basis, the charitable contribution deduction is $2,300.

Capital Gain Property

Capital gain property is any property that would have resulted in the recognition of long-term capital gain or § 1231 gain if the property had been sold by the donor.[52] As a general rule, the deduction for a contribution of capital gain property is equal to the fair market value of the property.

Two common exceptions disallow the deductibility of the appreciation on capital gain property. The first exception relates to the contribution of *tangible personalty*. Tangible personalty is all property that is not realty (land and buildings) and does not include intangible property (such as stock or securities). If tangible personalty is contributed to a public charity (such as a museum, church, or university) and the property is put to an *unrelated use*, the charitable deduction is limited to the property's basis (rather than its fair market value). The term *unrelated use* means a use that is unrelated to the exempt purpose or function of the charitable organization. For example, artwork donated to the American Red Cross is unlikely to be put to a related use. Instead, the Red Cross would likely sell the art to generate funds that would then be used to support its mission of providing assistance to individuals who have been struck by disasters.

Knowing this, taxpayers usually specify how their contributed property will be used and target donors appropriately (i.e., giving artwork to a museum rather than the Red Cross). As a result, this reduction will not apply if the property is put to a related use or if, at the time of the contribution, it was reasonable to anticipate that the property would not be put to an unrelated use by the donee.[53]

Emma contributes a Picasso painting, for which she paid $20,000, to a local museum. She had owned the painting for four years. It had a value of $30,000 at the time of the donation. The museum displays the painting for five years and subsequently sells it for $50,000.

The charitable contribution is $30,000. It is not reduced by the unrealized appreciation because the painting is not put to an unrelated use even though it is later sold by the museum.

The second exception relates to certain private foundations. Private foundations are organizations that traditionally do not receive their funding from the general public (e.g., the Bill and Melinda Gates Foundation). Generally, foundations fall into two

---

[51]We discuss the depreciation recapture rules in Chapter 17. For a more complete discussion of the difference between ordinary income and capital gain property, see Chapter 16.

[52]See text Section 16–4 for a discussion of holding periods.

[53]§ 170(e)(1)(B)(i) and Reg. § 1.170A–4(b)(3)(ii)(b).

categories: operating and nonoperating. A private *operating* foundation spends substantially all of its income in the active conduct of its charitable purposes. Other private foundations are *nonoperating* foundations. Often, only the private foundation knows its status (operating or nonoperating) for sure, and the status can change from year to year.

If capital gain property is contributed to a private *nonoperating* foundation, the taxpayer must reduce the contribution by the long-term capital gain that would have been recognized if the property had been sold at its fair market value. The effect of this provision is to limit the deduction to the property's basis.[54]

Ten years ago, Walter purchased land for $8,000 and has held it as an investment since then. This year, when the land is worth $20,000, he donates it to a private *nonoperating* foundation. Walter's charitable contribution is $8,000 ($20,000 − $12,000), the land's basis.

If, instead, Walter had donated the land to either a public charity or a private *operating* foundation, his charitable contribution would have been $20,000, the fair market value of the land.

Fifty Percent Ceiling

Contributions made to public charities may not exceed 50 percent of an individual's AGI for the year. Given that this ceiling is quite high, most taxpayers making contributions never have their charitable contributions limited. The 50 percent ceiling on contributions applies to public charities such as churches; schools; hospitals; and Federal, state, or local governmental units. The 50 percent ceiling also applies to contributions to private operating foundations and certain private nonoperating foundations.

In the remaining discussion of charitable contributions, public charities and private foundations (both operating and nonoperating) that qualify for the 50 percent ceiling will be referred to as *50 percent organizations*.

During the year, Tom and Emma Waters contribute $8,000 to their church, donate $500 to the Salvation Army, and give used clothes to Goodwill Industries (cost of $1,000; fair market value of $200). The clothes are ordinary income property, and the charitable contribution deduction is limited to the fair market value. Their AGI for the year is $125,000.

Tom and Emma's charitable contribution deduction is $8,700 ($8,000 + $500 + $200). Their charitable contribution deduction is not limited, as $8,700 is less than 50% of their AGI ($62,500; $125,000 × 50%).

Thirty Percent Ceiling

A 30 percent ceiling applies to contributions of cash and ordinary income property to private nonoperating foundations that are not 50 percent organizations. The 30 percent ceiling also applies to contributions of appreciated capital gain property to 50 percent organizations.[55]

In the event the contributions for any one tax year involve both 50 percent and 30 percent property, the allowable deduction comes first from the 50 percent property.

During the year, Lisa makes the following donations to her church: cash of $2,000 and unimproved land worth $30,000. Lisa had purchased the land four years ago for $22,000 and held it as an investment. Therefore, it is capital gain property. Lisa's AGI for the year is $60,000. Disregarding percentage limitations, Lisa's potential deduction is $32,000 [$2,000 (cash) + $30,000 (fair market value of land)].

In applying the percentage limitations, however, the *current* deduction for the land is limited to $18,000 [30% (limitation applicable to capital gain property) × $60,000 (AGI)]. Thus, the total current deduction is $20,000 ($2,000 cash + $18,000 land). Note that the total deduction does not exceed $30,000, which is 50% of Lisa's AGI.

---

[54]§ 170(e)(1)(B)(ii).

[55]Under a special election, a taxpayer may choose to permanently forgo a deduction of the appreciation on capital gain property. Referred to as the

reduced deduction election, this enables the taxpayer to move from the 30% limitation to the 50% limitation. See § 170(b)(1)(C)(iii).

Twenty Percent Ceiling

A 20 percent ceiling applies to contributions of appreciated capital gain property to private nonoperating foundations that are not 50 percent organizations.

Concept Summary 10.3 summarizes limitations on the deductibility of charitable gifts.

Concept Summary 10.3

Determining the Deduction for Contributions of Appreciated Property by Individuals

If the Type of Property Contributed Is:	And the Property Is Contributed to:	The Contribution Is Measured by:	But the Deduction Is Limited to:
1. Capital gain property (see Example 32)	A 50% organization	Fair market value of the property	30% of AGI
2. Ordinary income property (see Example 28)	A 50% organization	The basis of the property*	50% of AGI
3. Capital gain property (and the property is tangible personal property put to an unrelated use by the donee; see Example 29)	A 50% organization	The basis of the property*	50% of AGI
4. Capital gain property (see Example 30)	A private nonoperating foundation that is not a 50% organization	The basis of the property*	The lesser of: 1. 20% of AGI 2. 50% of AGI minus other contributions to 50% organizations

*If the fair market value of the property is less than the basis (i.e., the property has declined in value instead of appreciating), the fair market value is used.

Contribution Carryovers

Contributions that exceed the percentage limitations for the current year can be carried over for five years. In the carryover process, such contributions do not lose their identity for limitation purposes. Thus, if the contribution originally involved 30 percent property, the carryover will continue to be classified as 30 percent property in the carryover year.

EXAMPLE 33

Assume the same facts as in Example 32. Because only $18,000 of the $30,000 value of the land is deducted in the current year, the balance of $12,000 may be carried over to the following year. But the carryover will still be treated as capital gain property and is subject to the 30%-of-AGI limitation in the carryover year.

In applying the percentage limitations, current charitable contributions must be claimed first before any carryovers can be considered. If carryovers involve more than one year, they are utilized in a first-in, first-out order.

LO.7

List the business and personal expenditures that are deductible either as miscellaneous itemized deductions or as other itemized deductions.

10-5 MISCELLANEOUS ITEMIZED DEDUCTIONS

In general, no deduction is allowed for personal, living, or family expenses.[56] However, a taxpayer who is an employee, for example, may incur a number of expenditures related to employment. In this situation, if the employee incurs unreimbursed business expenses, including travel and transportation, the expenses potentially are deductible as miscellaneous itemized deductions.[57] However, these and other qualifying expenses may be deductible only if, in total, they exceed 2 percent of the taxpayer's AGI (and only the amount in excess of the 2%-of-AGI floor is allowed as

---

[56]§ 262.

[57]Actors and performing artists who meet certain requirements are not subject to this rule. See § 62(a)(2)(B).

a deduction). The miscellaneous itemized deductions that are subject to the 2%-of-AGI floor include (but are not limited to) the following:

- Professional dues to membership organizations.
- Cost of uniforms or other clothing that cannot be used for normal wear.
- Fees incurred for the preparation of one's tax return or fees incurred for tax litigation before the IRS or the courts.
- Job-hunting costs.
- Fee paid for a safe deposit box used to store papers and documents relating to taxable income-producing investments.
- Investment expenses that are deductible under § 212 as discussed in Chapter 6.
- Appraisal fees to determine the amount of a casualty loss or the fair market value of donated property.
- Hobby losses up to the amount of hobby income (refer to Chapter 6).
- Unreimbursed employee expenses (refer to Chapter 9).

Certain employee business expenses that are reimbursed are not itemized deductions, but are deducted *for* AGI. Employee business expenses are discussed in depth in Chapter 9.

10-6 OTHER MISCELLANEOUS DEDUCTIONS

Certain expenses and losses do not fall into any category of itemized deductions already discussed but are nonetheless deductible. The following expenses and losses are deductible on line 28 of Schedule A as Other Miscellaneous Deductions. These are not subject to the 2%-of-AGI floor.

- Gambling losses up to the amount of gambling winnings.
- Impairment-related work expenses of a handicapped person.
- Federal estate tax on income in respect of a decedent.
- Deduction for repayment of amounts under a claim of right (but only if more than $3,000; discussed in Chapter 18).
- The unrecovered investment in an annuity contract when the annuity ceases by reason of death, discussed in Chapter 4.

10-7 COMPREHENSIVE EXAMPLE OF SCHEDULE A

Harry and Jean Brown (ages 42 and 43, respectively), married filing jointly, had the following transactions for 2016:

Medicines that required a prescription	$ 430
Doctor and dentist bills paid and not reimbursed	3,120
Medical insurance premium payments	1,200
Contact lenses	170
Transportation for medical purposes on March 1, 2016 (279 miles × 19 cents/mile + $10.00 parking)	63
State income tax withheld (This amount exceeds the sales tax from the sales tax table)	3,900
Real estate taxes	1,580
Interest paid on qualified residence mortgage	2,340
Qualifying charitable contributions paid by check	860
Transportation in performing charitable services (800 miles × 14 cents/mile + $7.00 parking and tolls)	119
Unreimbursed employee expenses (from Form 2106)	870
Tax return preparation	150
Safe deposit box (used for keeping investment documents and tax records)	170

The Browns' AGI is $40,000. Their completed 2016 Schedule A (on the following page) reports itemized deductions totaling $10,172. A 2016 example (and related illustration using a 2016 Schedule A) is used because the 2017 form is not yet available.

SCHEDULE A
(Form 1040)

Department of the Treasury
Internal Revenue Service (99)

Itemized Deductions

▶ Information about Schedule A and its separate instructions is at *www.irs.gov/schedulea.*
▶ **Attach to Form 1040.**

OMB No. 1545-0074

20**16**

Attachment
Sequence No. **07**

Name(s) shown on Form 1040

Harry and Jean Brown

Your social security number

111-11-1111

Medical and Dental Expenses	**Caution:** Do not include expenses reimbursed or paid by others.			
	1 Medical and dental expenses (see instructions)	**1**	*4,983*	
	2 Enter amount from Form 1040, line 38 **2** *40,000*			
	3 Multiply line 2 by 10% (0.10). But if either you or your spouse was born before January 2, 1952, multiply line 2 by 7.5% (0.075) instead	**3**	*4,000*	
	4 Subtract line 3 from line 1. If line 3 is more than line 1, enter -0-	**4**		*983*
Taxes You Paid	**5** State and local (**check only one box**):			
	a ☒ Income taxes, **or**	**5**	*3,900*	
	b ☐ General sales taxes			
	6 Real estate taxes (see instructions)	**6**	*1,580*	
	7 Personal property taxes	**7**		
	8 Other taxes. List type and amount ▶ _____	**8**		
	9 Add lines 5 through 8	**9**		*5,480*
Interest You Paid **Note:** Your mortgage interest deduction may be limited (see instructions).	**10** Home mortgage interest and points reported to you on Form 1098	**10**	*2,340*	
	11 Home mortgage interest not reported to you on Form 1098. If paid to the person from whom you bought the home, see instructions and show that person's name, identifying no., and address ▶ _____	**11**		
	12 Points not reported to you on Form 1098. See instructions for special rules	**12**		
	13 Mortgage insurance premiums (see instructions) . . .	**13**		
	14 Investment interest. Attach Form 4952 if required. (See instructions.)	**14**		
	15 Add lines 10 through 14	**15**		*2,340*
Gifts to Charity If you made a gift and got a benefit for it, see instructions.	**16** Gifts by cash or check. If you made any gift of $250 or more, see instructions .	**16**	*860*	
	17 Other than by cash or check. If any gift of $250 or more, see instructions. You **must** attach Form 8283 if over $500 . . .	**17**	*119*	
	18 Carryover from prior year	**18**		
	19 Add lines 16 through 18	**19**		*979*
Casualty and Theft Losses	**20** Casualty or theft loss(es). Attach Form 4684. (See instructions.)	**20**		
Job Expenses and Certain Miscellaneous Deductions	**21** Unreimbursed employee expenses—job travel, union dues, job education, etc. Attach Form 2106 or 2106-EZ if required. (See instructions.) ▶ _____	**21**	*870*	
	22 Tax preparation fees	**22**	*150*	
	23 Other expenses—investment, safe deposit box, etc. List type and amount ▶ *Safe deposit box* _____	**23**	*170*	
	24 Add lines 21 through 23	**24**	*1,190*	
	25 Enter amount from Form 1040, line 38 **25** *40,000*			
	26 Multiply line 25 by 2% (0.02)	**26**	*800*	
	27 Subtract line 26 from line 24. If line 26 is more than line 24, enter -0-	**27**		*390*
Other Miscellaneous Deductions	**28** Other—from list in instructions. List type and amount ▶ _____	**28**		
Total Itemized Deductions	**29** Is Form 1040, line 38, over $155,650?			
	☒ **No.** Your deduction is not limited. Add the amounts in the far right column for lines 4 through 28. Also, enter this amount on Form 1040, line 40.	**29**		*10,172*
	☐ **Yes.** Your deduction may be limited. See the Itemized Deductions Worksheet in the instructions to figure the amount to enter.			
	30 If you elect to itemize deductions even though they are less than your standard deduction, check here . . . . ▶ ☐			

For Paperwork Reduction Act Notice, see Form 1040 instructions.   Cat. No. 17145C   Schedule A (Form 1040) 2016

10-8 OVERALL LIMITATION ON CERTAIN ITEMIZED DEDUCTIONS

LO.8

Recognize the limitation on certain itemized deductions applicable to high-income taxpayers.

Similar in effect to the exemption phaseout described in Chapter 3, high-income taxpayers also are subject to a limitation on the tax benefits from certain itemized deductions. In 2017, the phaseout of itemized deductions (also referred to as a *cutback adjustment*) applies to married taxpayers filing jointly whose AGI exceeds $313,800 ($261,500 for single filers).[58] Phaseouts of this type are sometimes referred to as "stealth taxes," which can lead to an unpleasant and unexpectedly higher Federal income tax liability than would have been expected had the itemized deductions been fully deductible.

The limitation applies to the following frequently encountered itemized deductions:

- Taxes.
- Home mortgage interest, including points.
- Charitable contributions.
- Miscellaneous itemized deductions subject to the 2%-of-AGI floor.

The following are *not* subject to the limitation on itemized deductions:

- Medical expenses.
- Investment interest expense.
- Nonbusiness casualty and theft losses.
- Gambling losses.

In 2017, taxpayers subject to the limitation must reduce itemized deductions by the *lesser* of:

- 3 percent of the amount by which AGI exceeds $313,800 ($261,500 if single).
- 80 percent of itemized deductions that are affected by the limit.

The overall limitation is applied after applying all other limitations to those itemized deductions that are affected by the overall limitation. For example, other limitations apply to charitable contributions, certain meals and entertainment expenses, and certain miscellaneous itemized deductions.

EXAMPLE

34

Gavin, who is single, had AGI of $275,000 for 2017. He incurred the following expenses and losses during the year:

Medical expenses before 10%-of-AGI limitation	$29,500
State and local income taxes	3,200
Real estate taxes	2,800
Home mortgage interest	7,200
Charitable contributions	2,000
Casualty loss before 10% limitation (after $100 floor)	29,000
Unreimbursed employee expenses (subject to 2%-of-AGI limitation)	5,800
Gambling losses (Gavin had $3,000 of gambling income)	7,000

continued

---

[58]§ 68. The AGI thresholds are $287,650 for heads of household and $156,900 for married taxpayers filing separately. In 2016, the phaseouts applied to married taxpayers filing jointly whose AGI exceeded $311,300 ($259,400 for single taxpayers, $285,350 for heads of household, and $155,650 for married taxpayers filing separately).

Gavin's itemized deductions *before* the overall limitation are computed as follows:

Medical expenses [$29,500 − (10% × $275,000)]	$ 2,000
State and local income taxes	3,200
Real estate taxes	2,800
Home mortgage interest	7,200
Charitable contributions	2,000
Casualty loss [$29,000 − (10% × $275,000)]	1,500
Unreimbursed employee expenses [$5,800 − (2% × $275,000)]	300
Gambling losses ($7,000 loss limited to $3,000 of gambling income)	3,000
Total itemized deductions before overall limitation	$22,000

Gavin's itemized deductions subject to the overall limitation are as follows:

State and local income taxes	$ 3,200
Real estate taxes	2,800
Home mortgage interest	7,200
Charitable contributions	2,000
Unreimbursed employee expenses	300
Total	$15,500

Gavin must reduce these itemized deductions by the *lesser* of:

• 3% × ($275,000 AGI − $261,500)	$ 405
• 80% of itemized deductions subject to limitation ($15,500 × .80)	12,400

As a result, the amount of the reduction is $405, and Gavin has $21,595 of deductible itemized deductions, computed as follows:

Deductible itemized deductions subject to overall limitation ($15,500 − $405)	$15,095

Itemized deductions not subject to overall limitation:

Medical expenses	2,000
Casualty loss	1,500
Gambling losses	3,000
Deductible itemized deductions	$21,595

LO.9

Identify tax planning strategies that can maximize the benefit of itemized deductions.

10-9 TAX PLANNING

10-9a **Effective Use of Itemized Deductions**

Because an individual may use the standard deduction in one year and itemize deductions in another year, maximum benefits can be obtained by shifting itemized deductions from one year to another. For example, if a taxpayer's itemized deductions and the standard deduction are approximately the same for each year of a two-year period, the taxpayer should use the standard deduction in one year and shift itemized deductions (to the extent permitted by law) to the other year. The individual could, for example, prepay a church pledge for a particular year to shift the deduction to the current year or avoid paying end-of-the-year medical expenses to shift the deduction to the following year.

10-9b **Use of Medical Deductions**

When a taxpayer anticipates that medical expenses will be close to the percentage floor for a year, the taxpayer should consider accelerating other medical expenses into the year. Any of the following techniques can help build a deduction by the end of the year:

- Incur the obligation for needed dental work or have needed work carried out.[59]

---

[59]Prepayment of medical expenses does not generate a current deduction unless the taxpayer is under an obligation to make the payment.

- Have elective remedial surgery that may have been postponed from prior years.
- Incur the obligation for capital improvements to the taxpayer's personal residence recommended by a physician (e.g., an air filtration system to alleviate a respiratory disorder).

The use of credit cards is deemed to be payment for purposes of timing the deductibility of charitable and medical expenses.

On December 13, 2017, Marge (a calendar year taxpayer) purchases two pairs of prescription contact lenses and one pair of prescribed orthopedic shoes for a total of $850. These purchases are charged separately to Marge's credit card. On January 6, 2018, Marge receives her statement containing these charges and makes payment shortly thereafter.

The purchases are deductible as medical expenses in the year charged (2017), rather than in the year the account is settled (2018).

Recognizing which expenses qualify for the medical deduction also may be crucial to exceeding the percentage limitations.

Ethan employs Leah (an unrelated party) to care for his incapacitated and dependent mother. Leah is not a trained nurse but spends approximately one-half of the time performing nursing duties (e.g., administering injections and providing physical therapy) and the rest of the time doing household chores. An allocable portion of Leah's wages that Ethan pays (including the employer's portion of FICA taxes) qualifies as a medical expense.

10-9c Timing the Payment of Deductible Taxes

It is sometimes possible to defer or accelerate the payment of certain deductible taxes (e.g., state income tax, real property tax, or personal property tax). For instance, the final installment of estimated state income tax is generally due in mid-January (after the end of a given tax year). Accelerating the payment of the final installment to December could result in larger itemized deductions for the current year.

Jenny, who is single, expects to have itemized deductions of $6,200 in 2017 and $4,000 in 2018. She plans to pay $900 as the final installment on her 2017 estimated state income tax, which is due on January 15, 2018. The standard deduction for 2017 is $6,350 for single taxpayers. If Jenny does not pay the final installment until 2018, she will not itemize in either 2017 or 2018.

However, if she pays the final installment in December 2017, her itemized deductions will be $7,100 ($6,200 + $900) in 2017 and she will benefit from itemizing.

10-9d Protecting the Interest Deduction

Although the deductibility of prepaid interest by a cash basis taxpayer has been severely restricted, one exception allows a deduction for points paid by the buyer to obtain financing for the purchase or improvement of a principal residence in the year of payment. However, these points must actually be paid by the taxpayer obtaining the loan and must represent a charge for the use of money. It has been held that points paid from the mortgage proceeds do not satisfy the payment requirement.[60] Also, the portion of the points attributable to service charges does not represent deductible interest.[61] Taxpayers financing home purchases or improvements usually should direct their planning toward avoiding these two hurdles to immediate deductibility.

In rare instances, a taxpayer may find it desirable to forgo the immediate expensing of points in the year paid. Instead, it could prove beneficial to capitalize the points and write them off as interest expense over the life of the mortgage.

---

[60]*Alan A. Rubnitz*, 67 T.C. 621 (1977). Seller-paid points may also be deductible by the buyer under the provisions of Rev.Proc. 94–27, cited in footnote 37.

[61]*Donald L. Wilkerson*, 70 T.C. 240 (1978).

EXAMPLE 38

Alexander purchases a home on December 15, 2017, for $380,000 with $120,000 cash and a 15-year mortgage of $260,000 financed by the Greater Metropolis National Bank. Alexander pays two points in addition to interest allocated to the period from December 15 until December 31, 2017, at an annual rate of 4%.

If Alexander does not have enough itemized deductions to exceed the standard deduction for 2017, he should elect to capitalize the points and amortize them over 15 years. In this instance, Alexander would deduct $346.67 for 2018, as part of his qualified residence interest expense [$5,200 (two points) divided by 15 years], if he elects to itemize that year.

Because personal (consumer) interest is not deductible, taxpayers should consider making use of home equity loans. These loans use the personal residence of the taxpayer as security. The funds from these loans can be used for personal purposes (e.g., auto purchases and vacations). By making use of home equity loans, interest that would have been nondeductible personal interest becomes deductible qualified residence interest.

10-9e Ensuring the Charitable Contribution Deduction

For a charitable contribution deduction to be available, the recipient must be a qualified charitable organization. Sometimes the mechanics of how the contribution is carried out can determine whether a deduction results.

EXAMPLE 39

Fumiko wants to donate $5,000 to her church's mission in Kobe, Japan. In this regard, she considers three alternatives:

1. Send the money directly to the mission.
2. Give the money to her church in Charlotte with the understanding that it is to be passed on to the mission.
3. Give the money directly to the missionary in charge of the mission who is currently in the United States on a fund-raising trip.

If Fumiko wants to obtain a deduction for the contribution, she should choose alternative 2. A direct donation to the mission (alternative 1) is not deductible because the mission is a foreign charity. A direct gift to the missionary (alternative 3) does not comply because an individual cannot be a qualified charity for income tax purposes.[62]

When making noncash donations, the type of property chosen can have significant implications in determining the amount, if any, of the deduction.

EXAMPLE 40

Sam wants to give $60,000 in value to his church in some form other than cash. In this connection, he considers four alternatives:

1. Stock held for two years as an investment with a basis of $100,000 and a fair market value of $60,000.
2. Stock held for five years as an investment with a basis of $10,000 and a fair market value of $60,000.
3. The rent-free use for a year of a building that normally leases for $5,000 a month.
4. A valuable stamp collection held as an investment and owned for 10 years with a basis of $10,000 and a fair market value of $60,000. The church plans to sell the collection if and when it is donated.

Alternative 1 is ill-advised as the subject of the gift. Even though Sam would obtain a deduction of $60,000, he would forgo the potential loss of $40,000 that would be recognized if the property were sold.[63]

continued

---

[62]*Thomas E. Lesslie*, 36 TCM 495, T.C.Memo. 1977–111.   [63]*LaVar M. Withers*, 69 T.C. 900 (1978).

Alternative 2 makes good sense because the deduction still is $60,000 and none of the $50,000 of appreciation that has occurred must be recognized as income.

Alternative 3 yields no deduction at all and is not a wise choice.

Alternative 4 involves tangible personalty that the recipient does not plan to use. As a result, the amount of the deduction is limited to $10,000, the stamp collection's basis.[64]

For property transfers (particularly real estate), the ceiling limitations on the amount of the deduction allowed in any one year (50 percent, 30 percent, or 20 percent of AGI, as the case may be) could be a factor to take into account. With proper planning, donations can be controlled to stay within the limitations and avoid the need for a carryover of unused charitable contributions.

EXAMPLE 41

Andrew wants to donate to Eastern University (a qualified charitable organization) a tract of unimproved land held as an investment. The land has been held for six years and has a current fair market value of $300,000 and a basis to Andrew of $50,000. Andrew's AGI for the current year is estimated to be $200,000, and he expects much the same for the next few years. In the current year, he deeds (transfers) an undivided one-fifth interest in the real estate to the university.

What has Andrew in Example 41 accomplished for income tax purposes? In the current year, he will be allowed a charitable contribution deduction of $60,000 ($^1/_5 \times$ $300,000), which will be within the applicable AGI limitation (30% × $200,000). Presuming no other charitable contributions for the year, Andrew has avoided the possibility of a carryover. In future years, Andrew can follow the same pattern. The only difficulty with this approach is the need to revalue the real estate each year before the donation, because the amount of the deduction is based on the fair market value of the interest contributed at the time of the donation.

REFOCUS ON THE BIG PICTURE

ITEMIZED DEDUCTIONS CAN REDUCE THE AFTER-TAX COST OF MAJOR PURCHASES

Because the Federal tax law provides that qualified residence interest and real estate taxes are deductible by individual taxpayers, the after-tax cost of a home purchase will be reduced by the tax savings associated with these itemized tax deductions (see Example 1). Given the Williamsons' projected taxable income, they are in the 28 percent Federal income tax bracket and the 6 percent state income tax bracket (i.e., aggregate marginal tax bracket of 34 percent). As a result, the after-tax cost of financing the purchase of the home will be:

Nondeductible principal payments	$ 2,000
Deductible qualified residence interest and real estate taxes [($37,000 + $4,000) × (1 − .34)]	27,060
Total	$29,060
After-tax monthly cost ($29,060 ÷ 12)	$ 2,422

continued

ISTOCKPHOTO.COM/IZUSEK

---

[64]No reduction of appreciation is necessary in alternative 2 because stock is intangible property and not tangible personalty.

Because the Williamsons will be able to itemize their deductions if they purchase a new home and will be able to deduct most of their monthly house payment, the home purchase will be affordable (see Examples 16 and 21).

What If?

What if the Williamsons use the less expensive route to finance the purchase of their home by using their retirement and taxable portfolio as security for the loan? What may at first appear to be a cost-effective approach ends up being more costly when considering the impact of the tax law. With this approach, the interest expense is not deductible because it is not qualified residence interest (see Example 21); further, it is not deductible as investment interest (see Chapter 11). Therefore, the after-tax cost of financing the home using this approach makes the home more expensive, and perhaps unaffordable, for the Williamsons.

Nondeductible principal and interest payments ($2,000 + $35,000)	$37,000
Deductible real estate taxes [$4,000 × (1 − .34)]	2,640
Total	$39,640
After-tax monthly cost ($39,640 ÷ 12)	$ 3,303

Key Terms

Acquisition indebtedness, 10-14

Capital gain property, 10-22

Charitable contribution, 10-17

Health Savings Account (HSA), 10-8

Home equity loans, 10-14

Medical expense, 10-3

Miscellaneous itemized deductions, 10-24

Ordinary income property, 10-21

Points, 10-15

Qualified residence interest, 10-13

Discussion Questions

1. **LO.1, 2** Dan, a self-employed individual taxpayer, prepared his own income tax return for the past year and has asked you to check it for accuracy. Your review indicates that Dan failed to claim certain business entertainment expenses.

   a. Will the correction of this omission affect the amount of medical expenses Dan can deduct? Explain.

   b. Would it matter if Dan were employed rather than self-employed? Explain.

2. **LO.2** Joe was in an accident and required cosmetic surgery for injuries to his nose. He also had the doctor do additional surgery to reshape his chin, which had not been injured. Will the cosmetic surgery to Joe's nose qualify as a medical expense? Will the cosmetic surgery to Joe's chin qualify as a medical expense? Explain.

3. **LO.2, 9** Jerry and Ernie are comparing their tax situations. Both are paying all of the nursing home expenses of their parents. Jerry can include the expenses in computing his medical expense deduction, but Ernie cannot. What explanation can you offer for the difference?

Issue ID 4. **LO.2** Cheryl incurred $8,700 of medical expenses in November 2017. On December 5, the clinic where she was treated mailed her the insurance claim form it had prepared for her with a suggestion that she sign and return the form immediately to receive her reimbursement from the insurance company by December 31. What tax issues should Cheryl consider in deciding whether to sign and return the form in December 2017 or January 2018?

5. **LO.2** David, a sole proprietor of a bookstore, pays a $7,500 premium for medical insurance for him and his family. Joan, an employee of a small firm that doesn't provide her with medical insurance, pays medical insurance premiums of $8,000 for herself. How does the tax treatment differ for David and Joan?

6. **LO.2** Jayden, a calendar year taxpayer, paid $16,000 in medical expenses and sustained a $20,000 casualty loss in 2017. He expects $12,000 of the medical expenses and $14,000 of the casualty loss to be reimbursed by insurance companies in 2018. Before considering any limitations on these deductions, how much can Jayden include in determining his itemized deductions for 2017?

7. **LO.2** Jacob, a self-employed taxpayer, is married and has two children. He has asked you to explain the tax and nontax advantages of creating a Health Savings Account (HSA) for him and his family.

8. **LO.5, 9** Diane owns a principal residence in Georgia, a townhouse in San Francisco, and a yacht in Cape Cod. All of the properties have mortgages on which Diane pays interest. What are the limitations on Diane's mortgage interest deduction? What strategy should Diane consider to maximize her mortgage interest deduction?

Decision Making

9. **LO.5, 9** Mason Gregg's car was destroyed by a flood. Unfortunately, his insurance had lapsed two days before he incurred the loss. Mason uses his car for both business and personal use. Mason, who is self-employed, does not have adequate savings to replace the car and must borrow money to purchase a new car. He is considering taking out a home equity loan, at a 5% interest rate, to obtain funds for the purchase. Margaret, his wife, would prefer not to do so because they paid off their mortgage recently and she does not want to incur any obligations related to their home. She would prefer to sell some of their stock in Bluebird, Inc., to raise funds to purchase the new car. Mason does not want to sell the stock because it has declined in value since they purchased it and he is convinced that its price will increase in the next two years. Mason has suggested that they obtain conventional financing for the purchase from their bank, which charges 7% interest on car loans. Identify the tax issues related to each of the three alternatives Mason and Margaret are considering.

Issue ID

10. **LO.5** Commercial Bank has initiated an advertising campaign that encourages customers to take out home equity loans to pay for purchases of automobiles. Are there any tax advantages related to this type of borrowing? Explain.

11. **LO.5** Thomas purchased a personal residence from Rachel. To sell the residence, Rachel agreed to pay $5,500 in points related to Thomas's mortgage. Discuss the deductibility of the points.

12. **LO.6** The city of Lawrence recently was hit by a tornado, leaving many families in need of food, clothing, shelter, and other necessities. Betty contributed $500 to a family whose home was completely destroyed by the tornado. Jack contributed $700 to the family's church, which gave the money to the family. Discuss the deductibility of these contributions.

13. **LO.6** Mike purchased four $100 tickets to a fund-raising dinner and dance sponsored by the public library, a qualified charitable organization. In its advertising for the event, the library indicated that the cost of the tickets would be deductible for Federal income tax purposes. Comment on the library's assertion.

14. **LO.6, 9** William, a high school teacher, earns about $50,000 each year. In December 2017, he won $1 million in the state lottery. William plans to donate $100,000 to his church. He has asked you, his tax adviser, whether he should donate the $100,000 in 2017 or 2018. Identify the tax issues related to William's decision.

Issue ID

Computational Exercises

15. **LO.2** Barbara incurred the following expenses during the year: $840 dues at a health club she joined at the suggestion of her physician to improve her general physical condition, $240 for multiple vitamins and antioxidant vitamins, $500 for a smoking cessation program, $250 for nonprescription nicotine gum, $600 for insulin, and $7,200 for funeral expenses for her mother who passed away in June. Before considering the AGI limitation, what amount may Barbara include in computing her medical expense deduction?

16. **LO.3** Tabitha sells real estate on March 2 for $260,000. The buyer, Ramona, pays the real estate taxes of $5,200 for the calendar year, which is the real estate property tax year. Assume that this is not a leap year.

   a. Determine the real estate taxes apportioned to and deductible by the seller, Tabitha, and the amount of taxes deductible by Ramona.

   b. Calculate Ramona's basis in the property and the amount realized by Tabitha from the sale.

17. **LO.4** Pierre, a cash basis, unmarried taxpayer, had $1,400 of state income tax withheld during 2017. Also in 2017, Pierre paid $455 that was due when he filed his 2016 state income tax return and made estimated payments of $975 toward his 2017 state income tax liability. When Pierre files his 2017 Federal income tax return in April 2018, he elects to itemize deductions, which amount to $15,650, including the state income tax payments and withholdings, all of which reduce his taxable income.

   a. What is Pierre's 2017 state income tax deduction?

   b. As a result of overpaying his 2017 state income tax, Pierre receives a refund of $630 early in 2018. The standard deduction for single taxpayers for 2017 was $6,350. How much of the $630 will Pierre include in his 2018 gross income?

18. **LO.4** Derek, a cash basis, unmarried taxpayer, had $610 of state income tax withheld during 2017. Also in 2017, Derek paid $50 that was due when he filed his 2016 state income tax return and made estimated payments of $100 toward his 2017 state income tax liability. When Derek files his 2017 Federal income tax return in April 2018, he elects to take the standard deduction, which reduced his taxable income. As a result of overpaying his 2017 state income tax, Derek receives a refund of $435 early in 2018. How much of the $435 will Derek include in his 2018 gross income?

19. **LO.5** Miller owns a personal residence with a fair market value of $195,000 and an outstanding first mortgage of $157,500. Miller gets a second mortgage on the residence and in return borrows $10,000 to purchase new jet skis. How much of the first and second mortgage debt is treated as qualified residence indebtedness?

20. **LO.6** Donna donates stock in Chipper Corporation to the American Red Cross on September 10, 2017. She purchased the stock for $18,100 on December 28, 2016, and it had a fair market value of $27,000 when she made the donation.

   a. What is Donna's charitable contribution deduction?

   b. Assume instead that the stock had a fair market value of $15,000 (rather than $27,000) when it was donated to the American Red Cross. What is Donna's charitable contribution deduction?

21. **LO.7** Issac has AGI of $73,400 and incurred the following expenses. How much of the business and personal expenditures are deductible (after any limitation) either as miscellaneous itemized deductions or as other itemized deductions?

Cost of uniforms required by his employer	$ 535
Tax return preparation fees	600
Fee paid for a safe deposit box used to store papers and documents relating to taxable income-producing investments	65
Job-hunting costs	1,100

22. **LO.8** Pedro, who is a single taxpayer, had AGI of $328,000 for 2017. He incurred the following expenses during the year:

Medical expenses before 10%-of-AGI limitation	$12,000
State and local income taxes	8,900
Real estate taxes	1,600
Home mortgage interest	16,000
Charitable contributions	2,200
Deductible investment interest expense	1,700

Compute the amount of Pedro's itemized deductions after any applicable reductions.

23. **LO.9** The Wilmoths plan to purchase a house but want to determine the after-tax cost of financing its purchase. Given their projected taxable income, the Wilmoths are in the 28% Federal income tax bracket and the 8% state income tax bracket (i.e., an aggregate marginal tax bracket of 36%). The total cash outlay during the first year of ownership will be $23,400 ($1,200 principal payments, $22,200 qualified residence interest payments). Determine the initial year after-tax cost of financing the purchase of the home.

Problems

24. **LO.2** Emma Doyle is employed as a corporate attorney. For calendar year 2017,   Communications
she had AGI of $100,000 and paid the following medical expenses:

Medical insurance premiums	$3,700
Doctor and dentist bills for Bob and April (Emma's parents)	6,800
Doctor and dentist bills for Emma	5,200
Prescription medicines for Emma	400
Nonprescription insulin for Emma	350

Bob and April would qualify as Emma's dependents except that they file a joint return. Emma's medical insurance policy does not cover them. Emma filed a claim for reimbursement of $2,800 of her own expenses with her insurance company in December 2017 and received the reimbursement in January 2018. What is Emma's maximum allowable medical expense deduction for 2017? Prepare a memo for your firm's tax files in which you document your conclusions.

25. **LO.2** Reba, who is single, does a lot of business entertaining at home. Lawrence, Reba's 84-year-old dependent grandfather, lived with Reba until this year, when he moved to Lakeside Nursing Home because he needs medical and nursing care. During the year, Reba made the following payments on behalf of Lawrence:

Room at Lakeside	$11,000
Meals for Lawrence at Lakeside	2,200
Doctor and nurse fees at Lakeside	1,700
Cable TV service for Lawrence's room at Lakeside	380
Total	$15,280

Lakeside has medical staff in residence. Disregarding the 10%-of-AGI floor, how much, if any, of these expenses qualifies for a medical expense deduction by Reba?

26. **LO.2** Paul suffers from emphysema and severe allergies and, upon the recommendation of his physician, has a dust elimination system installed in his personal residence. In connection with the system, Paul incurs and pays the following amounts during 2017:

Doctor and hospital bills	$ 2,500
Dust elimination system	10,000
Increase in utility bills due to the system	450
Cost of certified appraisal	300

In addition, Paul pays $750 for prescribed medicines.

The system has an estimated useful life of 20 years. The appraisal was to determine the value of Paul's residence with and without the system. The appraisal states that his residence was worth $350,000 before the system was installed and $356,000 after the installation. Paul's AGI for the year was $50,000. How much of the medical expenses qualify for the medical expense deduction in 2017?

27. **LO.2** For calendar year 2017, Jean was a self-employed consultant with no employees. She had $80,000 of net profit from consulting and paid $7,000 in medical insurance premiums on her policy covering 2017. How much of these premiums may Jean deduct as a deduction *for* AGI? How much may she deduct as an itemized deduction (subject to the AGI floor)?

28. **LO.2** During 2017, Susan incurred and paid the following expenses for Beth (her daughter), Ed (her father), and herself:

Surgery for Beth	$4,500
Red River Academy charges for Beth:	
Tuition	5,100
Room, board, and other expenses	4,800
Psychiatric treatment	5,100
Doctor bills for Ed	2,200
Prescription drugs for Susan, Beth, and Ed	780
Insulin for Ed	540
Nonprescription drugs for Susan, Beth, and Ed	570
Charges at Heartland Nursing Home for Ed:	
Medical care	5,000
Lodging	2,700
Meals	2,650

Beth qualifies as Susan's dependent, and Ed would also qualify except that he receives $7,400 of taxable retirement benefits from his former employer. Beth's psychiatrist recommended Red River Academy because of its small classes and specialized psychiatric treatment program that is needed to treat Beth's illness. Ed, who is a paraplegic and diabetic, entered Heartland in October. Heartland offers the type of care that he requires.

Upon the recommendation of a physician, Susan has an air filtration system installed in her personal residence. She suffers from severe allergies. In connection with this equipment, Susan incurs and pays the following amounts during the year:

Filtration system and cost of installation	$6,500
Increase in utility bills due to the system	700
Cost of certified appraisal	360

The system has an estimated useful life of 10 years. The appraisal was to determine the value of Susan's residence with and without the system. The appraisal states that the system increased the value of Susan's residence by $2,200. Ignoring the 10%-of-AGI floor, what is the total of Susan's expenses that qualifies for the medical expense deduction?

29. **LO.2** In May, Rebecca's daughter, Isabella, sustained a serious injury that made it impossible for her to continue living alone. Isabella, who is a novelist, moved back into Rebecca's home after the accident. Isabella has begun writing a novel based on her recent experiences. To accommodate Isabella, Rebecca incurred significant remodeling expenses (widening hallways, building a separate bedroom and bathroom, and making kitchen appliances accessible to Isabella). In addition, Rebecca had an indoor swimming pool constructed so that Isabella could do rehabilitation exercises prescribed by her physician.

    Issue ID

    In September, Isabella underwent major reconstructive surgery in Denver. The surgery was performed by Dr. Rama Patel, who specializes in treating injuries of the type sustained by Isabella. Rebecca drove Isabella from Champaign, Illinois, to Denver, a total of 1,100 miles, in Isabella's specially equipped van. They left Champaign on Tuesday morning and arrived in Denver on Thursday afternoon. Rebecca incurred expenses for gasoline, highway tolls, meals, and lodging while traveling to Denver. Rebecca stayed in a motel near the clinic for eight days while Isabella was hospitalized. Identify the relevant tax issues based on this information, and prepare a list of questions you would need to ask Rebecca and Isabella to advise them as to the resolution of any issues you have identified.

30. **LO.2** In the current year, Roger pays a $3,000 premium for high-deductible medical insurance for him and his family. In addition, he contributed $2,600 to a Health Savings Account.

    a. How much may Roger deduct if he is self-employed? Is the deduction *for* AGI or *from* AGI?

    b. How much may Roger deduct if he is an employee? Is the deduction *for* AGI or *from* AGI?

31. **LO.3** Alicia sold her personal residence to Rick on June 30 for $300,000. Before the sale, Alicia paid the real estate tax of $4,380 for the calendar year. For income tax purposes, the deduction is apportioned as follows: $2,160 to Alicia and $2,220 to Rick. What is Rick's basis in the residence?

32. **LO.4** Norma, who is single and uses the cash method of accounting, lives in a state that imposes an income tax. In April 2017, she files her state income tax return for 2016 and pays an additional $1,000 in state income taxes. During 2017, her withholdings for state income tax purposes amount to $7,400, and she pays estimated state income tax of $700. In April 2018, she files her state income tax return for 2017, claiming a refund of $1,800. Norma receives the refund in August 2018.

    a. Assuming that Norma itemized deductions in 2017, how much may she claim as a deduction for state income taxes on her Federal return for calendar year 2017 (filed April 2018)?

    b. Assuming that Norma itemized deductions in 2017 (which totaled $20,000), how will the refund of $1,800 that she received in 2018 be treated for Federal income tax purposes?

    c. Assume that Norma itemized deductions in 2017 (which totaled $20,000) and that she elects to have the $1,800 refund applied toward her 2018 state income tax liability. How will the $1,800 be treated for Federal income tax purposes?

    d. Assuming that Norma did not itemize deductions in 2017, how will the refund of $1,800 received in 2018 be treated for Federal income tax purposes?

33. **LO.5** Ten years ago, Liam, who is single, purchased a personal residence for $340,000 and took out a mortgage of $200,000 on the property. In May of the current year, when the residence had a fair market value of $440,000 and Liam owed $140,000 on the mortgage, he took out a home equity loan for $220,000. He used the funds to purchase a recreational vehicle, which he uses 100% for personal use. What is the maximum amount on which Liam can deduct home equity interest?

34. **LO.5** Malcolm owns 60% and Buddy owns 40% of Magpie Corporation. On July 1, 2017, each lends the corporation $30,000 at an annual interest rate of 5%. Malcolm and Buddy are not related. Both shareholders use the cash method of accounting, and Magpie Corporation is on the accrual method. All parties use the calendar year for tax purposes. On June 30, 2018, Magpie repays the loans of $60,000 together with the specified interest of $3,000.

    a. How much of the interest can Magpie Corporation deduct in 2017? In 2018?

    b. When is the interest included in Malcolm and Buddy's gross income?

35. **LO.6** Nadia donates $4,000 to Eastern University's athletic department. The payment guarantees that Nadia will have preferred seating near the 50-yard line.

    a. Assume that Nadia subsequently buys four $100 game tickets. How much can she deduct as a charitable contribution to the university's athletic department?

    b. Assume that Nadia's $4,000 donation includes four $100 tickets. How much can she deduct as a charitable contribution to the university's athletic department?

36. **LO.6** Liz had AGI of $130,000 in 2017. She donated Bluebird Corporation stock with a basis of $10,000 to a qualified charitable organization on July 5, 2017.

    a. What is the amount of Liz's deduction assuming that she purchased the stock on December 3, 2016, and the stock had a fair market value of $17,000 when she made the donation?

    b. Assume the same facts as in part (a), except that Liz purchased the stock on July 1, 2014.

    c. Assume the same facts as in part (a), except that the stock had a fair market value of $7,500 (rather than $17,000) when Liz donated it to the charity.

37. **LO.6** During the year, Ricardo made the following contributions to a qualified public charity:

Cash	$220,000
Stock in Seagull, Inc. (a publicly traded corporation)	280,000

Ricardo acquired the stock in Seagull, Inc., as an investment five years ago at a cost of $120,000. Ricardo's AGI is $840,000. (For purposes of this problem, ignore the potential application of the overall limitation on certain itemized deductions.)

    a. What is Ricardo's charitable contribution deduction?

    b. How are excess amounts, if any, treated?

    c. Ricardo expects his taxable income to vacillate over the next several years, and his ability to claim the remaining charitable contribution deduction in those years is uncertain. Calculate the present value of the tax savings from the charitable contribution if the excess contribution deduction is taken in the *third year* following the actual contribution or is taken in the *fifth year* following the contribution. Assume that Ricardo is in the 39.6%, 25%, and 15% tax brackets in the year of contribution, the third year following the contribution, and the fifth year following the contribution, respectively. See Appendix H for the present value factors, and assume a 6% discount rate.

38. **LO.6** Ramon had AGI of $180,000 in 2017. He is considering making a charitable   Decision Making
    contribution this year to the American Heart Association, a qualified chari-
    table organization. Determine the current allowable charitable contribution deduction
    in each of the following independent situations, and indicate the treatment for any
    amount that is not deductible currently.

    a. A cash gift of $95,000.

    b. A gift of OakCo stock worth $95,000 on the contribution date. Ramon had
        acquired the stock as an investment two years ago at a cost of $84,000.

    c. A gift of a painting worth $95,000 that Ramon purchased three years ago for
        $60,000. The charity has indicated that it would sell the painting to generate
        cash to fund medical research.

    d. Ramon has decided to make his $95,000 gift to the American Heart Association
        in the form of cash. However, he is considering delaying his gift until next year
        when his AGI will increase to $300,000 and he will be in the 33% income tax
        bracket, an increase from his current-year income tax bracket of 28%. Ramon
        asks you to determine the tax savings from the tax deduction in present value
        terms if he were to make the gift this year, rather than delaying the gift until
        next year. For purposes of this analysis, ignore the potential impact of the over-
        all limitation on certain itemized deductions. See Appendix H for the present
        value factors, and assume a 6% discount rate.

39. **LO.6** On December 27, 2017, Roberta purchased four tickets to a charity ball spon-
    sored by the city of San Diego for the benefit of underprivileged children.
    Each ticket cost $200 and had a fair market value of $35. On the same day as the
    purchase, Roberta gave the tickets to the minister of her church for personal use by
    his family. At the time of the gift of the tickets, Roberta pledged $4,000 to the build-
    ing fund of her church. The pledge was satisfied by a check dated December 31,
    2017, but not mailed until January 3, 2018.

    a. Presuming that Roberta is a cash basis and calendar year taxpayer, how much
        can she deduct as a charitable contribution for 2017?

    b. Would the amount of the deduction be any different if Roberta was an accrual
        basis taxpayer? Explain.

40. **LO.6, 9** In December of each year, Eleanor Young contributes 10% of her gross   Decision Making
    income to the United Way (a 50% organization). Eleanor, who is in the
    28% marginal tax bracket, is considering the following alternatives for satisfying the   Communications
    contribution.

	Fair Market Value
(1) Cash donation	$23,000
(2) Unimproved land held for six years ($3,000 basis)	23,000
(3) Blue Corporation stock held for eight months ($3,000 basis)	23,000
(4) Gold Corporation stock held for two years ($28,000 basis)	23,000

    Eleanor has asked you to help her decide which of the potential contributions listed
    above will be most advantageous taxwise. Evaluate the four alternatives, and write a
    letter to Eleanor to communicate your advice to her. Her address is 2622 Bayshore
    Drive, Berkeley, CA 94709.

41. **LO.2, 3, 4, 5, 7, 9** Bart and Elizabeth Forrest are married and have no dependents.   Decision Making
    They have asked you to advise them whether they should file
    jointly or separately in 2017. They present you with the following information: Communications

	Bart	Elizabeth	Joint
Salary	$38,000		
Business net income		$110,000	
Interest income	400	1,200	$2,200
Deductions *for* AGI	2,400	14,000	
Medical expenses	10,427	3,358	
State income tax	800	1,800	
Real estate tax			3,800
Mortgage interest			4,200
Unreimbursed employee expenses	1,200		

If they file separately, Bart and Elizabeth will split the real estate tax and mortgage interest deductions equally.

a.   Write Bart and Elizabeth a letter in which you make and explain a recommendation on filing status for 2017. Bart and Elizabeth reside at 2003 Highland Drive, Durham, NC 27707.

b.   Complete Bart's Schedule A for 2017 (use the most current version of Schedule A available). For this purpose, assume that Bart and Elizabeth file separate returns. Bart's Social Security number is 123-45-6789.

42.   **LO.2, 3, 4, 5, 6, 7, 8**   Evan is single and has AGI of $277,300 in 2017. His potential itemized deductions before any limitations for the year total $52,300 and consist of the following:

Medical expenses (before the 10%-of-AGI limitation)	$28,000
Interest on home mortgage	8,700
State income taxes	9,500
Real estate taxes	3,600
Charitable contributions	2,500

After all necessary adjustments are made, what is the amount of itemized deductions Evan may claim?

43.   **LO.2, 3, 4, 5, 6, 7, 8**   Linda, who files as a single taxpayer, had AGI of $280,000 for 2017. She incurred the following expenses and losses during the year:

Medical expenses (before the 10%-of-AGI limitation)	$33,000
State and local income taxes	4,500
State sales tax	1,300
Real estate taxes	4,000
Home mortgage interest	5,000
Automobile loan interest	750
Credit card interest	1,000
Charitable contributions	7,000
Casualty loss (before 10% limitation but after $100 floor)	34,000
Unreimbursed employee expenses subject to the 2%-of-AGI limitation	7,600

Calculate Linda's allowable itemized deductions for the year.

44.   **LO.2, 3, 4, 5, 6, 7, 8**   For calendar year 2017, Stuart and Pamela Gibson file a joint return reflecting AGI of $350,000. Their itemized deductions are as follows:

Casualty loss after $100 floor (not covered by insurance)	$48,600
Home mortgage interest	19,000
Credit card interest	800
Property taxes on home	16,300
Charitable contributions	28,700
State income tax	18,000
Tax return preparation fees	1,200

Calculate the amount of itemized deductions the Gibsons may claim for the year.

Cumulative Problems

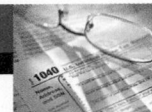

45. Alice J. and Bruce M. Byrd are married taxpayers who file a joint return. Their Social Security numbers are 123-45-6789 and 111-11-1112, respectively. Alice's birthday is September 21, 1969, and Bruce's is June 27, 1968. They live at 473 Revere Avenue, Lowell, MA 01850. Alice is the office manager for Lowell Dental Clinic, 433 Broad Street, Lowell, MA 01850 (employer identification number 98-7654321). Bruce is the manager of a Super Burgers fast-food outlet owned and operated by Plymouth Corporation, 1247 Central Avenue, Hauppauge, NY 11788 (employer identification number 11-1111111).

Tax Return Problem

Decision Making

TAX SOFTWARE

The following information is shown on their Wage and Tax Statements (Form W-2) for 2016.

Line	Description	Alice	Bruce
1	Wages, tips, other compensation	$58,000	$62,100
2	Federal income tax withheld	4,500	6,300
3	Social Security wages	58,000	62,100
4	Social Security tax withheld	3,596	3,850
5	Medicare wages and tips	58,000	62,100
6	Medicare tax withheld	841	900
15	State	Massachusetts	Massachusetts
16	State wages, tips, etc.	58,000	62,100
17	State income tax withheld	2,950	3,100

The Byrds provide over half of the support of their two children, Cynthia (born January 25, 1992, Social Security number 123-45-6788) and John (born February 7, 1996, Social Security number 123-45-6786). Both children are full-time students and live with the Byrds except when they are away at college. Cynthia earned $4,200 from a summer internship in 2016, and John earned $3,800 from a part-time job.

During 2016, the Byrds provided 60% of the total support of Bruce's widower father, Sam Byrd (born March 6, 1940, Social Security number 123-45-6787). Sam lived alone and covered the rest of his support with his Social Security benefits. Sam died in November, and Bruce, the beneficiary of a policy on Sam's life, received life insurance proceeds of $1,600,000 on December 28.

The Byrds had the following expenses relating to their personal residence during 2016:

Property taxes	$5,000
Qualified interest on home mortgage	8,700
Repairs to roof	5,750
Utilities	4,100
Fire and theft insurance	1,900

The Byrds had the following medical expenses for 2016:

Medical insurance premiums	$4,500
Doctor bill for Sam incurred in 2015 and not paid until 2016	7,600
Operation for Sam	8,500
Prescription medicines for Sam	900
Hospital expenses for Sam	3,500
Reimbursement from insurance company, received in 2016	3,600

The medical expenses for Sam represent most of the 60% that Bruce contributed toward his father's support.

Other relevant information follows:

- When they filed their 2015 state return in 2016, the Byrds paid additional state income tax of $900.
- During 2016, Alice and Bruce attended a dinner dance sponsored by the Lowell Police Disability Association (a qualified charitable organization). The Byrds paid $300 for the tickets. The cost of comparable entertainment would normally be $50.
- The Byrds contributed $5,000 to Lowell Presbyterian Church and gave used clothing (cost of $1,200 and fair market value of $350) to the Salvation Army. All donations are supported by receipts, and the clothing is in very good condition.
- Alice and Bruce made a gift to a needy family who lost their home in a fire ($100). In addition, they made several cash gifts to homeless men downtown ($35).
- In 2016, the Byrds received interest income of $2,750, which was reported on a Form 1099–INT from Second National Bank, 125 Oak Street, Lowell, MA 01850 (Employer Identification Number 98-7654322).
- The home mortgage interest was reported on Form 1098 by Lowell Commercial Bank, P.O. Box 1000, Lowell, MA 01850 (Employer Identification Number 98-7654323). The mortgage (outstanding balance of $425,000 as of January 1, 2016) was taken out by the Byrds on May 1, 2012.
- Alice's employer requires that all employees wear uniforms to work. During 2016, Alice spent $850 on new uniforms and $566 on laundry charges.
- Bruce paid $400 for an annual subscription to the *Journal of Franchise Management* and $741 for annual membership dues to his professional association.
- Neither Alice's nor Bruce's employer reimburses for employee expenses.
- The Byrds do not keep the receipts for the sales taxes they paid and had no major purchases subject to sales tax.
- All members of the Byrd family had health insurance coverage for all of 2016.
- This year the Byrds gave each of their children $2,000, which was then deposited into their Roth IRAs.
- Alice and Bruce paid no estimated Federal income tax. Neither Alice nor Bruce wants to designate $3 to the Presidential Election Campaign Fund.

Part 1—Tax Computation

Compute net tax payable or refund due for Alice and Bruce Byrd for 2016. If they have overpaid, they want the amount to be refunded to them. If you use tax forms for your computations, you will need Forms 1040 and 2106 and Schedules A and B. Suggested software: H&R BLOCK At Home.

Part 2—Tax Planning

Alice and Bruce are planning some significant changes for 2017. They have provided you with the following information and asked you to project their taxable income and tax liability for 2017.

The Byrds will invest the $1,600,000 of life insurance proceeds in short-term certificates of deposit (CDs) and use the interest for living expenses during 2017. They expect to earn total interest of $32,000 on the CDs.

Bruce has been promoted to regional manager, and his salary for 2017 will be $88,000. He estimates that state income tax withheld will increase by $4,000 and the Social Security tax withheld will be $5,456.

Alice, who has been diagnosed with a serious illness, will take a leave of absence from work during 2017, so she will not receive a salary or incur any work-related expenses during the year. The estimated cost for her medical treatment is $15,400, of which $6,400 will be reimbursed by their insurance company in 2017. Their medical insurance premiums will increase to $9,769. Property taxes on their residence are expected to increase to $5,100. The Byrds' home mortgage interest expense and charitable contributions are expected to be unchanged from 2016.

John will graduate from college in December 2016 and will take a job in New York City in January 2017. His starting salary will be $46,000.

Assume that all of the information reported in 2016 will be the same in 2017 unless other information has been presented above.

46. Paul and Donna Decker are married taxpayers, ages 44 and 42, respectively, who file a joint return for 2017. The Deckers live at 1121 College Avenue, Carmel, IN 46032. Paul is an assistant manager at Carmel Motor Inn, and Donna is a teacher at Carmel Elementary School. They present you with W–2 forms that reflect the following information: **Tax Computation Problem**

	Paul	Donna
Salary	$68,000	$56,000
Federal tax withheld	6,770	6,630
State income tax withheld	900	800
FICA (Social Security and Medicare) withheld	5,202	4,284
Social Security numbers	111-11-1112	123-45-6789

Donna is the custodial parent of two children from a previous marriage who reside with the Deckers throughout the school year. The children, Larry and Jane Parker, reside with their father, Bob, during the summer. Relevant information for the children follows:

	Larry	Jane
Age	17	18
Social Security numbers	123-45-6788	123-45-6787
Months spent with Deckers	9	9

Under the divorce decree, Bob pays child support of $150 per month per child during the nine months the children live with the Deckers. Bob says that he spends $200 per month per child during the three summer months they reside with him. Donna and Paul can document that they provide $2,000 support per child per year. The divorce decree is silent as to which parent can claim the exemptions for the children.

In August, Paul and Donna added a suite to their home to provide more comfortable accommodations for Hannah Snyder (123-45-6786), Donna's mother, who had moved in with them in February 2016 after the death of Donna's father. Not wanting to borrow money for this addition, Paul sold 300 shares of Acme Corporation stock for $50 per share on May 3, 2017, and used the proceeds of $15,000 to cover construction costs. The Deckers had purchased the stock on April 29, 2012, for $25 per share. They received dividends of $750 on the jointly owned stock a month before the sale.

Hannah, who is 66 years old, received $7,500 in Social Security benefits during the year, of which she gave the Deckers $2,000 to use toward household expenses and deposited the remainder in her personal savings account. The Deckers determine that they have spent $2,500 of their own money for food, clothing, medical expenses, and other items for Hannah. They do not know what the rental value of Hannah's suite would be, but they estimate it would be at least $300 per month.

Interest paid during the year included the following:

Home mortgage interest (paid to Carmel Federal Savings & Loan)	$7,890
Interest on an automobile loan (paid to Carmel National Bank)	1,660
Interest on Citibank Visa card	620

In July, Paul hit a submerged rock while boating. Fortunately, he was uninjured after being thrown from the boat and landing in deep water. However, the boat, which was uninsured, was destroyed. Paul had paid $25,000 for the boat in June 2016, and its value was appraised at $18,000 on the date of the accident.

The Deckers paid doctor and hospital bills of $10,700 and were reimbursed $2,000 by their insurance company. They spent $640 for prescription drugs and medicines and $5,904 for premiums on their health insurance policy. They have filed additional claims of $1,200 with their insurance company and have been told they will receive payment for that amount in January 2018. Included in the amounts paid for doctor and hospital bills were payments of $380 for Hannah and $850 for the children. All members of the Decker family had health insurance coverage for all of 2017.

Additional information of potential tax consequence follows:

Real estate taxes paid	$3,850
Sales taxes paid (per table)	1,379
Contributions to church	1,950
Appraised value of books donated to public library	740
Paul's unreimbursed employee expenses to attend hotel management convention:	
Airfare	340
Hotel	170
Meals	95
Registration fee	340
Refund of state income tax for 2016 (the Deckers itemized on their 2016 Federal tax return)	1,520

Compute net tax payable or refund due for the Deckers for 2017. Ignore the child tax credit in your computations. If the Deckers have overpaid, the amount is to be credited toward their taxes for 2018.

Research Problems

THOMSON REUTERS
CHECKPOINT®
Student Edition

Note: Solutions to the Research Problems can be prepared by using the Thomson Reuters Checkpoint® Student Edition online tax research database, which accompanies this textbook. Solutions can also be prepared by using research materials found in a typical tax library.

Research Problem 1. Jane suffers from a degenerative spinal disorder. Her physician said that swimming could help prevent the onset of permanent paralysis and recommended the installation of a swimming pool at her residence for her use. Jane's residence had a market value of approximately $500,000 before the swimming pool was installed. The swimming pool was built, and an appraiser estimated that the value of Jane's home increased by $98,000 because of the addition.

The pool cost $194,000, and Jane claimed a medical expense deduction of $96,000 ($194,000 − $98,000) on her tax return. Upon audit of the return, the IRS determined that an adequate pool should have cost $70,000 and would increase the value of her home by only $31,000. Thus, the IRS claims that Jane is entitled to a deduction of only $39,000 ($70,000 − $31,000).

a. Is there any ceiling limitation on the amount deductible as a medical expense? Explain.

b. Can capital expenditures be deductible as medical expenses? Explain.

c. What is the significance of a "minimum adequate facility"? Should aesthetic or architectural qualities be considered in the determination? Why or why not?

Research Problem 2. Ken and Mary Jane Blough, your neighbors, have asked you for advice after receiving correspondence in the mail from the IRS. You learn that the IRS is asking for documentation in support of the itemized deductions the Bloughs claimed on a recent tax return. The Bloughs tell you that their income in the year of question was $75,000. Because their record-keeping habits are poor, they felt justified in claiming itemized deductions equal to the amounts that represent the average claimed by other taxpayers in their income bracket. These averages are calculated and reported by the IRS annually based on actual returns filed in an earlier year. Accordingly, they claimed medical expenses of $7,102, taxes of $6,050, interest of $10,659, and charitable contributions of $2,693. What advice do you give the Boughs?

Partial list of research aids:
Cheryl L. de Werff, T.C. Summary Opinion, 2011–29.

Research Problem 3. Marcia, a shareholder in a corporation with stores in five states, donated stock with a basis of $10,000 to a qualified charitable organization in 2016. Although the stock of the corporation was not traded on a public stock exchange, many shares had been sold over the past several years. Based on the average selling price for the stock in 2016, Marcia deducted $95,000 on her 2016 tax return. Marcia received a notice from the IRS that the $95,000 deduction had been reduced to $10,000 because she had not obtained a qualified appraisal or attached a summary of her appraisal to her tax return. Marcia has asked you to advise her on this matter. Write a letter containing your conclusions to Ms. Marcia Meyer, 1311 Santos Court, San Bruno, CA 94066.

Communications

Partial list of research aids:
Reg. § 1.170A–13(c)(2).

Use internet tax resources to address the following questions. Look for reliable websites and blogs of the IRS and other government agencies, media outlets, businesses, tax professionals, academics, think tanks, and political outlets.

Research Problem 4. The Federal government incurs a cost for every item that is deductible in the computation of taxable income. These costs, which take the form of forgone tax revenue, are often referred to as "tax expenditures." The Joint Committee on Taxation regularly estimates the current and projected tax expenditures associated with of a long list of provisions in the tax law. Locate the Joint Committee on Taxation's most recent analysis, and identify the current tax expenditure associated with the deductions for medical expenses, interest on student loans, mortgage interest, and charitable contributions. How are these costs expected to change over the next five years? How is the concept of tax expenditures helpful to tax policy analysts?

Research Problem 5. Use the IRS's website to determine whether taxpayers who are not U.S. residents can claim itemized deductions when calculating their taxable income.

Roger CPA Review Questions

1. Kellye, a teacher, volunteers for eight hours per week at a school for high-risk children, a qualified charitable organization. Kellye's normal rate for teaching is $30 per hour. Kellye's out-of-pocket costs in 2017 were $250 for supplies, and she spent $20 each week in transportation getting to and from the school. Kellye had no cash contributions to charity in 2017. If Kellye volunteered every week in 2017, what is her charitable contributions deduction?

   a. $0
   b. $250

   c. $1,290
   d. $13,770

2. Aaron has $30,000 of adjusted gross income in 2017. His expenses are as follows:

Non-prescription medicine	$ 100
Prescription medicine	500
Doctor visits	500
Weekly meal preparation for a diet plan	2,000
Elective removal of a benign facial mole	400
Contact lenses	500
Eyeglasses	200
Dental services	300

   What is Aaron's itemized deduction for medical expenses?

   a. $0
   b. $1,500

   c. $2,000
   d. $4,500

3. Which of the following deductions for taxes paid may be taken in the same year?
   a. Real estate taxes, state income taxes, state sales taxes.
   b. Real estate taxes, property taxes, state income taxes.
   c. Property taxes, state income taxes, state sales taxes.
   d. Real estate taxes, property taxes, state income taxes, state sales taxes.

4. Zunilda is 77-year-old individual with an AGI of $25,000 in 2016. She began living in a nursing home in 2016 upon the recommendation of her primary care physician in order to receive medical care for a specific condition. She had the following unreimbursed expenses in 2016:

Expense	Amount
Nursing home health care costs	$5,000
Nursing home meal and lodging costs	8,000
Prescription drugs	1,500

   As a result of these unreimbursed expenses, how much may Zunilda deduct from AGI on her 2016 tax return? Assume Zunilda elects to itemize deductions.

   a. $12,000
   b. $4,000

   c. $12,625
   d. $4,625

CHAPTER

11

Investor Losses

LEARNING OBJECTIVES: *After completing Chapter 11, you should be able to:*

LO.1 Explain the tax shelter problem and the reasons for at-risk and passive activity loss limitations.

LO.2 Discuss the at-risk limitation.

LO.3 Describe how the passive activity loss rules limit deductions for losses and identify the taxpayers subject to these restrictions.

LO.4 Explore the elements required for an activity to be treated as passive and review the rules for identifying an activity.

LO.5 Identify the tests for material participation.

LO.6 Describe the nature of rental activities under the passive activity loss rules.

LO.7 Determine the relationship between the at-risk and passive activity loss limitations.

LO.8 Recognize the special treatment available to real estate activities.

LO.9 Determine the proper tax treatment on the disposition of a passive activity.

LO.10 Identify restrictions placed on the deductibility of other investor losses and deductions, including those that apply to investment interest.

LO.11 Suggest tax planning strategies to minimize the effect of the passive activity loss and investment interest limitations and recognize the general impact of the additional tax on net investment income.

CHAPTER OUTLINE

RIDO/SHUTTERSTOCK.COM

INVESTOR LOSS LIMITATIONS AFFECT THE VIABILITY OF CERTAIN INVESTMENT OPPORTUNITIES

Trudy and Jim Reswick are considering ways to enhance their financial security. In fact, they are willing to borrow a substantial sum so that they can make an appropriate investment.

Currently, Trudy and Jim's sole source of income is their salaries, totaling $100,000, from their full-time jobs. Their most significant asset is their personal residence (fair market value of $500,000 with a mortgage of $350,000). The Reswicks' broker suggests that they borrow $100,000 at 6 percent and use the proceeds to make *one* of the following investments:

- A high-growth, low-yield portfolio of marketable securities. The portfolio's value is expected to grow 8 percent each year.

- An interest in a limited partnership that owns and operates orange groves in Florida. The limited partnership interest is expected to generate tax losses of $25,000 in each of the next five years, after which profits are expected. The broker predicts that after taking into account the tax benefit from the losses, the Reswicks would average an annual 8 percent return over a 10-year period.

- An interest in a local limited partnership that owns and rents apartments to college students. This limited partnership interest also would generate losses of $25,000 per year for five years, after which profits would follow. These expected profits and losses would produce an average annual total return of 8 percent over a 10-year period.

Trudy and Jim want to choose the alternative that produces the best after-tax return over a 10-year planning horizon. They are aware, however, that tax restrictions may limit the advantages of some of these investment options. In this connection, evaluate each option.

Read the chapter and formulate your response.

FRAMEWORK 1040 Tax Formula for Individuals

This chapter covers the boldfaced portions of the Tax Formula for Individuals that was introduced in Concept Summary 3.1 on p. 3-3. Below those portions are the sections of Form 1040 where the results are reported.

Income *(broadly defined)*	$xx,xxx
Less: Exclusions	(x,xxx)
Gross income	$xx,xxx
Less: Deductions *for* adjusted gross income	(x,xxx)

FORM 1040 (p. 1)

12	Business income or (loss). Attach Schedule C or C-EZ	
13	Capital gain or (loss). Attach Schedule D if required. If not required, check here ▶ ☐	
14	Other gains or (losses). Attach Form 4797	
17	Rental real estate, royalties, partnerships, S corporations, trusts, etc. Attach Schedule E	

Adjusted gross income	$xx,xxx
Less: The greater of total **itemized deductions** *or* the standard deduction	(x,xxx)

FORM 1040 (p. 2)

40	**Itemized deductions** (from Schedule A) **or** your **standard deduction** . . . .

Personal and dependency exemptions	(x,xxx)
Taxable income	$xx,xxx
Tax on taxable income *(see Tax Tables or Tax Rate Schedules)*	$ x,xxx
Less: Tax credits *(including income taxes withheld and prepaid)*	(xxx)
Tax due (or refund)	$ xxx

s discussed in Chapter 6, a tax deduction for an expense or a loss is not allowed unless specifically permitted by Congress. For example, losses can be recognized and deducted in the case of certain unprofitable investments only because the Code allows them. These losses can arise from the operation of an activity or on its sale. For most individual taxpayers, deductible investor losses come within the scope of § 165(c)(2) relating to transactions entered into for profit.[1] But what happens if the investment is mostly motivated by the tax loss it generates, rather than the profits it might create? Or what if the investment generates expenses that offset ordinary income and it later is expected to produce appreciation taxed at capital gain rates? This chapter addresses these tax minimization strategies and the rules put in place to restrict their use.

11-1 THE TAX SHELTER PROBLEM

LO.1

Explain the tax shelter problem and the reasons for at-risk and passive activity loss limitations.

Before Congress passed laws to reduce their effectiveness, tax shelters provided a popular way to avoid or defer taxes, as they could generate deductions and other benefits to offset income from other sources. Because of the tax avoidance potential of many tax shelters, they were attractive to wealthy taxpayers in high income tax brackets. Many tax shelters merely provided an opportunity for "investors" to buy deductions and credits in ventures that were not expected to generate a profit, even in the long run.

---

[1]If the losses are incurred in connection with a trade or business, § 165(c)(1) applies.

Although it may seem odd that a taxpayer would intentionally invest in an activity that was designed to produce losses, there is a logical explanation. The typical tax shelter operated as a partnership and relied heavily on nonrecourse financing.[2] Accelerated depreciation and interest expense deductions generated large losses in the early years of the activity. At the very least, the tax shelter deductions deferred the recognition of any net income until the activity was sold. In the best of situations, the investor could realize additional tax savings by offsetting other income (e.g., salary, interest, dividends) with deductions flowing from the tax shelter. Ultimately, the sale of the investment would result in capital gain. The following example illustrates what was possible *before* Congress stepped in to curb tax shelter abuses.

EXAMPLE

1

Bob, who earned a salary of $400,000 as a business executive and dividend income of $15,000, invested $20,000 for a 10% interest in a cattle-breeding tax shelter. Through the use of $800,000 of nonrecourse financing and available cash of $200,000, the partnership acquired a herd of an exotic breed of cattle costing $1 million. Depreciation, interest, and other deductions related to the activity resulted in a loss of $400,000, of which Bob's share was $40,000. Bob was allowed to deduct the $40,000 loss even though he had invested and stood to lose only $20,000 if the investment became worthless.

The net effect of the $40,000 deduction from the partnership was that a portion of Bob's salary and dividend income was "sheltered" (i.e., offset or neutralized by the deduction), and as a result, he was required to calculate his tax liability on only $375,000 of income [$415,000 (salary and dividends) − $40,000 (deduction)] rather than $415,000. If this deduction were available under current law and if Bob was in a combined Federal and state income tax bracket of 40%, this deduction would generate a tax savings of $16,000 ($40,000 × 40%) in the first year alone!

A review of Example 1 shows that the taxpayer took a *two-for-one* write-off ($40,000 deduction, $20,000 amount invested). In the heyday of these types of tax shelters, promoters often promised tax deductions for the investor well in excess of the amount invested.

The first major law change aimed at tax shelters was the **at-risk limitation** . Its objective is to limit a taxpayer's deductions to the amount "at risk," which is the amount the taxpayer stands to lose if the investment becomes worthless. So, in Example 1, the at-risk rule limits Bob's loss to $20,000—the amount he invested.

The second major attack on tax shelters came with the passage of the **passive activity loss** rules. The passive activity loss rules require the taxpayer to segregate all income and losses into three categories: active, portfolio, and passive (these categories are defined in text Section 11-3). In general, the passive activity loss rules disallow the deduction of passive activity losses against *active or portfolio income* even when the taxpayer is at risk to the extent of the loss. In general, passive activity losses can only offset passive activity income.

So, in Example 1, the passive activity loss rules disallow a current deduction for any of the loss. The loss from the tax shelter is a passive activity loss because Bob does not "materially participate" in the activity (see text Section 11-3c). As a result, the $20,000 loss that is allowed under the at-risk rules is disallowed under the passive activity loss rules. Why? Because Bob does not report any passive activity income for the year—he reports only active and portfolio income. Consequently, Bob's current-year income only includes his nonpassive activity income of $415,000. As explained later in the chapter, the disallowed $20,000 passive activity loss is suspended and may be deducted in a future year under certain conditions.

The nature of the at-risk limits and the passive activity loss rules and their impact on investors are discussed in the pages that follow. Because of these rules, investors now

---

[2]Nonrecourse debt is an obligation for which the borrower is not personally liable. An example of nonrecourse debt is a liability on real estate acquired by a partnership without the partnership or any of the partners assuming any liability for the mortgage. The acquired property generally is pledged as collateral for the loan.

primarily focus on the economics of the investment instead of the tax benefits or tax avoidance possibilities that an investment may generate.

Discuss the at-risk limitation.

11-2 AT-RISK LIMITS

The at-risk rules limit the deductibility of losses from business and income-producing activities. These rules, which apply to individuals and closely held corporations, are designed to prevent taxpayers from deducting losses in excess of their actual economic investment in an activity. In the case of an S corporation or a partnership, the at-risk limits apply at the owner level. Under the at-risk rules, a taxpayer's deductible loss from an activity for any taxable year is limited to the amount the taxpayer has at risk at the end of the taxable year (the amount the taxpayer could actually lose in the activity).

While the amount at risk usually changes over time, the initial "at-risk" amount includes the following:[3]

- The amount of cash and the adjusted basis of property contributed to the activity by the taxpayer, and
- Amounts borrowed for use in the activity for which the taxpayer is personally liable or has pledged as security property not used in the activity.

This amount generally is increased each year by the taxpayer's share of income and is decreased by the taxpayer's share of deductible losses and withdrawals from the activity. In addition, because general partners are jointly and severally liable for recourse debts of the partnership, their at-risk amounts are increased when the partnership increases its debt and are decreased when the partnership reduces its debt. However, a taxpayer generally is *not* considered at risk with respect to borrowed amounts if:

- The taxpayer is not personally liable for repayment of the debt (e.g., nonrecourse debt), or
- The lender has an interest (other than as a creditor) in the activity.

An important exception provides that in the case of an activity that holds real property, a taxpayer is considered at risk for his or her share of any *qualified nonrecourse financing* that is secured by real property used in the activity.[4]

A taxpayer may deduct a loss as long as the at-risk amount is positive (but the passive activity loss rules still may apply to limit the deduction). However, once the at-risk amount is exhausted, any remaining loss cannot be deducted until a later year. Any losses disallowed for any given taxable year by the at-risk rules may be deducted when there is, and to the extent of, a positive at-risk amount.

The Big Picture

EXAMPLE 2

Return to the facts of *The Big Picture* on p. 11-1. In addition to the three investment options presented to the Reswicks, in 2017, they invest $40,000 in an oil partnership that incurs a first-year net loss, of which $60,000 is their share. Assume that the Reswicks' interest in the partnership is subject to the at-risk limits but is not subject to the passive activity loss limits.

Because the Reswicks have only $40,000 of capital at risk, they cannot deduct more than $40,000 against their other income and must reduce their at-risk amount to zero ($40,000 at-risk amount − $40,000 loss deducted). The nondeductible loss of $20,000 ($60,000 loss generated − $40,000 loss allowed) can be carried over to 2018.

[3]§ 465(b)(1).

[4]Section 465(b)(6) defines qualified nonrecourse financing.

Continue with the facts of the previous example. In 2018, the Reswicks have taxable income of $15,000 from the oil partnership and invest an additional $10,000 in the venture. Their at-risk amount is now $25,000 ($0 beginning balance + $15,000 taxable income + $10,000 additional investment). This enables them to deduct the carryover loss and requires them to reduce their at-risk amount to $5,000 ($25,000 at-risk amount − $20,000 carryover loss allowed).

EXAMPLE
3

Complicating the at-risk rule is the fact that previously allowed losses must be recaptured to the extent the at-risk amount falls below zero.[5] Under this rule, taxpayers must recognize income to bring the at-risk amount up to zero. Typically, this rule is triggered when the taxpayer receives a distribution or when the status of indebtedness changes from recourse to nonrecourse.

Calculation of at-risk amount is reviewed in Concept Summary 11.1.

Concept Summary 11.1

Calculation of At-Risk Amount

Increases to a taxpayer's at-risk amount:

- Cash and the adjusted basis of property contributed to the activity.

- Amounts borrowed for use in the activity for which the taxpayer is personally liable or has pledged as security property not used in the activity.

- Taxpayer's share of amounts borrowed for use in the activity that are qualified nonrecourse financing.

- Taxpayer's share of the activity's income.

Decreases to a taxpayer's at-risk amount:

- Withdrawals from the activity.

- Taxpayer's share of the activity's deductible loss.

- Taxpayer's share of any reductions of debt for which recourse against the taxpayer exists or any reductions of qualified nonrecourse debt.

11-3 PASSIVE ACTIVITY LOSS LIMITS

LO.3

Describe how the passive activity loss rules limit deductions for losses and identify the taxpayers subject to these restrictions.

This section identifies and explains the key issues that apply to the passive activity loss limits. Here are some key points:

- The limits apply only to passive activity losses incurred by certain types of taxpayers.

- Losses are limited under these rules only if they are generated by a passive activity.

- Special rules exist for interests in real estate activities.

- Any suspended losses are generally allowed when a passive activity is sold.

11-3a Classification and Impact of Passive Activity Income and Losses

The passive activity loss rules (§ 469) operate by requiring taxpayers to classify their income and losses into three categories. Then, the rules limit the extent to which losses in the passive category can be used to offset income in the other categories.

---

[5]§ 465(e).

Classification

The passive activity loss rules require income and losses to be classified into one of three categories: active, portfolio, or passive.

Active income includes:

- Wages, salary, commissions, bonuses, and other payments for services rendered by the taxpayer.
- Profit from a trade or business in which the taxpayer is a material participant (material participation is described later in the chapter).
- Gain on the sale or other disposition of assets used in an active trade or business.
- Income from intangible property if the taxpayer's personal efforts significantly contributed to the creation of the property.

Portfolio income includes:

- Interest, dividends, annuities, and royalties not derived in the ordinary course of a trade or business.
- Gain or loss from the disposition of property that produces portfolio income or is held for investment purposes.

Passive activity income or loss arises from activities that are treated as passive, which include:

- Any trade or business or income-producing activity in which the taxpayer does not materially participate.
- Subject to certain exceptions (discussed later in the chapter), all rental activities, whether the taxpayer materially participates or not.

General Impact

Losses or expenses generated by passive activities can be deducted only to the extent of income from the taxpayer's passive activities. Any excess passive activity loss may not be used to offset active income or portfolio income. Instead, any unused passive activity losses are suspended and carried forward to future years to offset passive activity income generated in those years. Any remaining suspended losses may be used only when a taxpayer disposes of his or her *entire interest* in an activity. When that occurs, generally all current and suspended passive activity losses related to the activity may offset active and portfolio income.

The Big Picture

EXAMPLE 4

Return to the facts of *The Big Picture* on p. 11-1. In addition to their salaries of $100,000 from full-time jobs, assume that the Reswicks receive $12,000 in dividends and interest from various portfolio investments. Further, assume that they decide to invest $100,000 in the orange grove limited partnership, which produces a $25,000 loss for the Reswicks this year.

Because their at-risk basis in the partnership is $100,000, the current $25,000 loss is not limited by the at-risk rules. However, because the loss is a passive activity loss, it is not deductible against their other income. The loss is suspended and carried over to the future.

If the Reswicks have passive activity income from this investment or from other passive activities in the future, they can offset the suspended loss against that passive activity income. If they do not have passive activity income to offset this suspended loss in the future, they will be allowed to offset the loss against other types of income when they eventually dispose of their investment in the passive activity.

Impact of Suspended Losses

When a taxpayer disposes of his or her entire interest in a passive activity, the actual economic gain or loss from the investment, including any suspended losses, can finally be determined. As a result, under the passive activity loss rules, when a fully taxable disposition occurs, any overall loss realized from the taxpayer's activity is recognized and can be offset against any income.

A *fully taxable disposition* generally involves a sale of the property to a third party at arm's length. This would imply that the sales price is equal to the property's fair market value. As presented in the following example, a gain recognized on the sale of a passive activity generally is treated as passive and is first offset by the suspended passive activity losses from that activity.

EXAMPLE
5

Rex sells an apartment building, a passive activity, with an adjusted basis of $100,000 for $180,000. In addition, he has suspended losses of $60,000 associated with the building. His total gain, $80,000, and his taxable gain, $20,000, are calculated as follows:

Net sales price	$ 180,000
Less: Adjusted basis	(100,000)
Total gain	$ 80,000
Less: Suspended losses	(60,000)
Taxable gain (passive)	$ 20,000

As highlighted in Example 5, gain recognized on the sale of a passive activity generally is treated as passive and is first offset by any suspended losses from that activity. This accomplishes the purpose of determining the true economic gain or loss from the activity.

But what happens if the suspended losses exceed the gain recognized or the sale results in a loss? In this case, the excess loss is allowed to offset other income in the following order:

1. Net passive activity income or gains (if any); and
2. Nonpassive income or gains (active or portfolio).

EXAMPLE
6

Dean sells an apartment building, a passive activity, with an adjusted basis of $100,000 for $150,000. In addition, he has current and suspended losses of $60,000 associated with the building and has no other passive activities. His total gain of $50,000 and his deductible loss of $10,000 are calculated as follows:

Net sales price	$ 150,000
Less: Adjusted basis	(100,000)
Total gain	$ 50,000
Less: Suspended losses	(60,000)
Deductible loss (not passive)	($ 10,000)

The $10,000 deductible loss is offset against Dean's active and portfolio income.

What would be the outcome if Dean sold the building for $90,000? In this case, there would be a loss on the sale of $10,000 and an overall deductible loss of $70,000. This total loss, including the suspended losses, is deductible as a nonpassive activity loss.

Carryovers of Suspended Losses

The preceding examples assumed that the taxpayer had an interest in only one passive activity; as a result, the suspended loss was related exclusively to the activity that was sold. However, taxpayers often own interests in more than one activity, in which case any suspended losses must be allocated among those passive activities that generated losses. The allocation to an activity is made by multiplying the disallowed passive activity loss from all activities using the following fraction:

$$\frac{\text{Loss from one passive activity}}{\text{Sum of losses for taxable year from all passive activities having losses}}$$

EXAMPLE 7

Diego has investments in three passive activities with the following income and losses for 2016:

Activity A	($30,000)
Activity B	(20,000)
Activity C	25,000
Net passive activity loss	($25,000)
Net passive activity loss of $25,000 allocated to:	
Activity A ($25,000 × $30,000/$50,000)	($15,000)
Activity B ($25,000 × $20,000/$50,000)	(10,000)
Total suspended losses	($25,000)

Suspended losses are carried over indefinitely and are offset in the future first against any passive activity income from the activities to which they relate and then against passive activity income from other passive activities.[6] Taxpayers subject to the passive activity loss limitation rule must maintain records to track the suspended losses and the activities to which they belong.

EXAMPLE 8

Assume that the facts are the same as in Example 7 and that in 2017, Activity A produces $10,000 of income. Diego may use $10,000 of Activity A's suspended loss of $15,000 from 2016 to offset the $10,000 income from this activity.

If Diego sells Activity A in early 2018, the remaining $5,000 suspended loss is used to offset any income from the activity reported by Diego in 2018 and to determine his final gain or loss.

Passive Activity Credits

Credits (such as the low-income housing credit and rehabilitation credit—discussed in Chapter 13) that arise from passive activities are limited in much the same way as passive activity losses. Passive activity credits can be used only against regular tax attributable to passive activity income,[7] which is calculated by comparing the tax on all income (including passive activity income) with the tax on income excluding passive activity income.

EXAMPLE 9

Sam owes $50,000 of tax, disregarding net passive activity income, and $80,000 of tax, considering both net passive activity and other taxable income (disregarding the credits in both cases). The amount of tax attributable to the passive activity income is $30,000.

In the preceding example, Sam can claim a maximum of $30,000 of passive activity credits; the excess credits are carried over. These passive activity credits can be used only against the *regular* tax attributable to passive activity income. If a taxpayer has a net loss from passive activities during a given year, no credits can be used.

Carryovers of Passive Activity Credits

Tax credits related to passive activities can be carried forward indefinitely much like suspended passive activity losses. Unlike passive activity losses, however, passive activity credits are permanently lost when the activity is disposed of in a taxable transaction where a *loss* is recognized. Credits are allowed on dispositions only when there is sufficient tax on passive activity income to absorb them.

Use of Passive Activity Credits on Disposition of an Activity

EXAMPLE 10

Alicia sells a passive activity for a gain of $10,000. The activity had suspended losses of $40,000 and suspended credits of $15,000. The $10,000 gain is offset by $10,000 of the suspended losses, and the remaining $30,000 of suspended losses is deductible against Alicia's active and portfolio income. The suspended credits are permanently lost because the sale of the activity did not generate any tax.

---

[6] § 469(b).   [7] § 469(d)(2).

Use of Passive Activity Credits on Disposition of an Activity

If Alicia in Example 10 had realized a $100,000 gain on the sale of the passive activity, the suspended credits could have been used to the extent of the regular tax related to the net passive activity income.

Gain on sale	$100,000
Less: Suspended losses	(40,000)
Taxable gain	$ 60,000

If the tax related to the taxable gain of $60,000 is $15,000 or more, the entire $15,000 of suspended credits can be used. If the tax related to the gain is less than $15,000, the excess of the suspended credits over the tax related to the gain is lost.

EXAMPLE 11

When a taxpayer has sufficient regular tax liability from passive activities to trigger the use of suspended credits, the credits lose their character as passive activity credits. They are reclassified as regular tax credits and made subject to the same limits as other credits (discussed in Chapter 13).

Passive Activity Changes to Active

If a passive activity becomes an active one, suspended losses are allowed to the extent of income from the now active business.[8] If any of the suspended loss remains, it continues to be treated as a loss from a passive activity. The excess suspended loss can be deducted from passive activity income or carried over to the next tax year and deducted to the extent of income from the now active business in the succeeding year(s). The activity must continue to be the same activity.

For several years, Rebecca has owned an interest in a passive activity that has produced losses of $80,000 during that period. Because she did not have passive activity income from other sources, she could not deduct any of the activity's passive activity losses.

In the current year, she has become a material participant in the activity (i.e., the passive activity is now an active one) and her share of the business profits total $25,000. As a result, she may use $25,000 of the suspended passive activity loss to offset the current business profits. Rebecca's remaining suspended passive activity loss from the activity is $55,000 ($80,000 − $25,000), which is carried over to future years and used to offset income from the formerly passive activity or income from other passive activities.

EXAMPLE 12

11-3b Taxpayers Subject to the Passive Activity Loss Rules

The passive activity loss rules apply to individuals, estates, trusts, personal service corporations, and closely held C corporations.[9] Passive activity income or loss from investments in partnerships or S corporations (see Chapter 20) flows through to the owners, and the passive activity loss rules are applied at the owner level.

Personal Service Corporations

Application of the passive activity loss limitations to personal service corporations is intended to prevent taxpayers from sheltering personal service income by creating personal service corporations and acquiring passive activities at the corporate level.

Two tax accountants who earn an aggregate of $200,000 a year in their individual practices agree to work together in a newly formed personal service corporation. Shortly after its formation, the corporation invests in a passive activity that produces a $200,000 loss during the year. Because the passive activity loss rules apply to personal service corporations, the corporation may not deduct the $200,000 passive activity loss against the $200,000 of active income.

EXAMPLE 13

---

[8]§ 469(f).   [9]§ 469(a).

Determination of whether a corporation is a personal service corporation is based on rather broad definitions. A personal service corporation is a regular (or C) corporation that meets *both* of the following conditions:

- The principal activity is the performance of personal services.
- Such services are substantially performed by employee-owners.

Generally, personal service corporations include those in the fields of health, law, engineering, architecture, accounting, actuarial science, performing arts, and consulting.[10] A corporation is treated as a personal service corporation if more than 10 percent of the stock (by value) is held by employee-owners.[11] An employee is treated as an employee-owner if he or she owns stock on *any day* during the taxable year.[12] For these purposes, shareholder status and employee status do not have to occur on the same day.

Closely Held C Corporations

Application of the passive activity loss rules to closely held (nonpersonal service) C corporations is also intended to prevent individuals from incorporating to avoid the passive activity loss limitations. A corporation is classified as a closely held corporation if at any time during the taxable year more than 50 percent of the value of its outstanding stock is owned, directly or indirectly, by or for five or fewer individuals. Closely held C corporations (other than personal service corporations) may use passive activity losses to offset *active* income but not portfolio income.

Silver Corporation, a closely held (nonpersonal service) C corporation, has $475,000 of passive activity losses from a rental activity, $400,000 of active income, and $100,000 of portfolio income. The corporation may offset $400,000 of the $475,000 passive activity loss against the $400,000 of active business income but may not offset the remainder against the $100,000 of portfolio income. As a result, $75,000 of the passive activity loss is suspended ($475,000 passive activity loss − $400,000 offset against active income).

Applying the passive activity loss limitations to closely held C corporations inhibits taxpayers from transferring their portfolio investments (like stocks and bonds) to these corporations.

11-3c **Rules for Determining Passive Activities**

LO.4

Explore the elements required for an activity to be treated as passive and review the rules for identifying an activity.

As noted earlier, the following types of activities are treated as passive:

- Any trade or business or income-producing activity in which the taxpayer does not materially participate.
- All rental activities, subject to certain exceptions pertaining to real estate (discussed later).

To understand the meaning of the term *passive activity* and the impact of the rules, one must address the following issues, each of which is the subject of statutory or administrative guidance:

- What constitutes an activity?
- What is meant by material participation?
- When is an activity a rental activity?

Even though guidance is available to help the taxpayer deal with these issues, their resolution is anything but simple.

---

[10]§ 448(d)(2)(A).

[11]§ 469(j)(2).

[12]§ 269A(b)(2).

Identification of an Activity

Identifying what constitutes an activity is the first step in applying the passive activity loss rules. Taxpayers who are involved in complex business operations need to determine whether a given segment of their overall business operations constitutes a separate activity or is to be treated as part of a larger activity. Proper treatment is necessary to determine whether income or loss from an activity is active or passive.

Treatment as a Component of an Activity or as a Separate Activity

Ben owns a business with two separate departments. Department A generates net income of $120,000, and Department B generates a net loss of $95,000. Ben participates 700 hours in the operations of Department A and 100 hours in Department B. If Ben is allowed to treat the departments as components of a single activity, he can offset the $95,000 loss from Department B against the $120,000 of income from Department A.

EXAMPLE 15

Assume the same facts as in the previous example. If Ben is required to treat each department as a separate activity, the tax result is not as favorable. Because he is a material participant in Department A (having devoted 700 hours to it), the $120,000 profit is active income. Assuming that Ben is not considered a material participant in Department B (100 hours), the $95,000 loss is a passive activity loss. As a result, Ben cannot offset the $95,000 passive activity loss from Department B against the $120,000 of active income from Department A. (A discussion of the material participation rules follows.)

EXAMPLE 16

On the disposition of a passive activity, a taxpayer is allowed to offset suspended losses from the activity against other types of income. As illustrated in the next example, identifying what constitutes an activity is of crucial importance for this purpose too.

Linda owns a business with two departments. Department A has a net loss of $125,000 in the current year, and Department B has a $70,000 net loss. She sells Department B at the end of the year.

Assuming that Linda is allowed to treat the two departments as separate passive activities, she can offset the passive activity loss from Department B against other types of income in the following order: gain from disposition of the passive activity, other passive activity income, and nonpassive activity income. This treatment leaves her with a suspended loss of $125,000 from Department A.

If, however, Departments A and B are treated as components of the same activity, when Department B is sold, its $70,000 net loss would be suspended along with the other $125,000 of suspended loss of the activity (from Department A).

EXAMPLE 17

Treasury Regulations have provided guidelines to be used in identifying activities subject to the passive activity loss rules.[13] These guidelines indicate, in general, that a taxpayer can treat one or more trade or business activities or rental activities as a single activity if those activities form an *appropriate economic unit* for measuring gain or loss. In making this decision, all of the relevant facts and circumstances must be considered. Taxpayers may use any reasonable method in applying the facts and circumstances. The following example, adapted from the Regulations, illustrates the application of the general rules for grouping activities.[14]

George owns a men's clothing store and a brewpub in Chicago. He also owns a men's clothing store and a brewpub in Milwaukee. Reasonable methods of applying the facts and circumstances test may result in any of the following groupings:

• All four activities may be grouped into a single activity because of common ownership and control.

EXAMPLE 18

continued

---

[13]Reg. § 1.469–4.

[14]Reg. § 1.469–4(c)(3).

- The clothing stores may be grouped into an activity, and the brewpubs may be grouped into a separate activity.

- The Chicago activities may be grouped into an activity, and the Milwaukee activities may be grouped into a separate activity.

- Each of the four activities may be treated as a separate activity.

Regrouping of Activities Taxpayers should carefully consider all tax factors when deciding how to group their activities. Once activities have been grouped, they cannot be regrouped unless the original grouping was clearly inappropriate or there has been a material change in the facts and circumstances. The Regulations allow the IRS to regroup activities when *both* of the following conditions exist:[15]

- The taxpayer's grouping fails to reflect one or more appropriate economic units.
- One of the primary purposes of the taxpayer's grouping is to avoid the passive activity loss limitations.

Special Grouping Rules for Rental Activities Two rules deal specifically with the grouping of rental activities. These rules are designed to prevent taxpayers from grouping rental activities, which are generally passive, with other businesses in a way that would result in a tax advantage.

First, a rental activity may be grouped with a trade or business activity only if one activity is insubstantial in relation to the other. That is, the rental activity must be insubstantial in relation to the trade or business activity, or the trade or business activity must be insubstantial in relation to the rental activity. The Regulations provide no clear guidelines as to the meaning of "insubstantial."[16]

EXAMPLE 19

Schemers, a firm of CPAs, owns a building in downtown Washington, D.C., in which it conducts its public accounting practice. The firm also rents space on the street level of the building to several retail establishments, which generally is considered a passive activity. Of the total revenue generated by the firm, 95% is associated with the public accounting practice and 5% is related to the rental operation.

It is likely that the rental activity would be considered insubstantial relative to the accounting practice and the two ventures could be grouped as one nonrental activity. This grouping could be advantageous to the firm, particularly if the rental operation generates a loss, as the rental loss could be used to offset any income from the public accounting practice.

Alternatively, treating the rental operation as a *separate* activity may be advantageous if this operation produces (passive activity) income. The passive activity income could then be used to absorb otherwise nondeductible passive activity losses.

Second, taxpayers generally may not treat an activity involving the rental of real property and an activity involving the rental of personal property as a single activity.

Material Participation

LO.5

Identify the tests for material participation.

If an individual taxpayer *materially participates* in a nonrental trade or business activity, any loss from that activity is treated as an active loss that can offset active or portfolio income. If a taxpayer does not materially participate, the loss is treated as a passive activity loss, which can only offset passive activity income. As a result, controlling whether a particular activity is treated as active or passive is an important part of the tax strategy of a taxpayer who owns an interest in one or more businesses. Consider the following examples.

---

[15]Reg. § 1.469–4(f).   [16]Reg. § 1.469–4(d).

Implications of Material Participation Status

EXAMPLE 20

Noah, a corporate executive, earns a salary of $600,000 per year. In addition, he owns a separate business in which he participates. The business produces a loss of $100,000 during the year. If Noah materially participates in the business, the $100,000 loss is an active loss that may offset his active income from his corporate employer.

If he does not materially participate, the loss is passive and is suspended unless he has other passive activity income. Noah may use the suspended loss in the future only when he has passive activity income or disposes of the activity.

EXAMPLE 21

Kay, an attorney, earns $350,000 a year in her law practice. In addition, she owns interests in two activities, A and B, in which she participates. Activity A, in which she does *not* materially participate, produces a loss of $50,000. Activity B produces income of $80,000. However, Kay has not yet met the material participation standard, described below, for Activity B. But Kay can meet the material participation standard if she spends an additional 50 hours in Activity B during the year. Should Kay attempt to meet the material participation standard for Activity B?

If she continues working in Activity B and becomes a material participant, the $80,000 of income from the activity is *active*, and the $50,000 passive activity loss from Activity A must be suspended. A more favorable tax strategy is for Kay *not to meet* the material participation standard for Activity B, thus making the income from that activity passive. This enables her to offset the $50,000 passive activity loss from Activity A against most of the passive activity income from Activity B.

It is possible to devise numerous scenarios in which the taxpayer could control the tax outcome by increasing or decreasing his or her participation in different activities. Examples 20 and 21 demonstrate some of the possibilities. In most analyses of this type, taxpayers will benefit by having profitable activities classified as passive so that any passive activity losses can be used to offset that passive activity income. If the activity produces a loss, however, the taxpayer will benefit if it is classified as active so that the loss is not subject to the passive activity loss limitations.

A nonrental trade or business in which a taxpayer owns an interest must be treated as a passive activity unless the taxpayer materially participates. A material participant is one who has "a significant nontax economic profit motive" for taking on activities and selects them for their economic value.[17] In contrast, a passive investor mainly seeks a return from a capital investment (including a possible reduction in taxes) as a supplement to an ongoing source of livelihood.

Even if the concept of being a material participant is clear, the precise meaning of the term material participation can be vague. As enacted, § 469 requires a taxpayer to participate on a *regular, continuous, and substantial* basis to be a material participant. In many situations, however, it is difficult or impossible to gain any assurance that this nebulous standard is met.

In response to this dilemma, Temporary Regulations[18] provide seven tests that serve to determine when material participation is achieved. Material participation is achieved by meeting any *one* of the tests. These tests are listed in Concept Summary 11.2 and can be divided into three categories:

- Tests based on current participation.
- Tests based on prior participation.
- Test based on facts and circumstances.

---

[17]*General Explanation of the Tax Reform Act of 1986* ("Blue Book"), prepared by The Staff of the Joint Committee on Taxation, May 4, 1987, H.R. 3838, 99th Cong., p. 212.

[18]Temp.Reg. § 1.469–5T(a). The Temporary Regulations are also Proposed Regulations. Temporary Regulations have the same effect as final Regulations. Refer to Chapter 2 for a discussion of the different categories of Regulations.

Concept Summary 11.2

Tests to Determine Material Participation

Tests Based on Current Participation

1. The individual participates in the activity for more than 500 hours during the year.

2. The individual's participation in the activity for the taxable year constitutes substantially all of the participation in the activity of all individuals (including nonowner employees) for the year.

3. The individual participates in the activity for more than 100 hours during the year, and this participation is not less than that participation of any other individual (including nonowner employees) for the year.

4. The activity is a significant participation activity (where the person's participation *exceeds* 100 hours during the year), and the hours for all significant participation activities during the year is more than 500 hours.

Tests Based on Prior Participation

5. The individual materially participated in the activity for any 5 taxable years during the 10 taxable years that immediately precede the current taxable year.

6. The activity is a personal service activity, and the individual materially participated in the activity for any 3 preceding taxable years.

Test Based on Facts and Circumstances

7. Based on all of the facts and circumstances, the individual participates in the activity on a regular, continuous, and substantial basis during the year.

Participation Defined Participation generally includes any work done by an individual in an activity that he or she owns. Participation does not include work if it is of a type not customarily done by owners *and* if one of its principal purposes is to avoid the disallowance of passive activity losses or credits. Also, work done in an individual's capacity as an investor (e.g., reviewing financial reports in a nonmanagerial capacity) is not counted in applying the material participation tests. However, participation by an owner's spouse counts as participation by the owner.[19]

EXAMPLE 22

Tom, who is a partner in a CPA firm, owns a computer store that operated at a loss during the year. To offset this loss against the income from his CPA practice, Tom would like to avoid having the computer business classified as a passive activity. During the year, he worked 480 hours in the business in management and selling activities and 30 hours doing janitorial chores. In addition, Tom's wife participated 40 hours as a salesperson.

It is likely that Tom's 480 hours of participation in management and selling activities will count as participation in work customarily done by owners, but the 30 hours spent doing janitorial chores will not. However, the 40 hours of participation by his wife will also count.

Assuming that none of the participation's principal purposes is to avoid the disallowance of passive activity losses or credits, Tom will qualify as a material participant under the more-than-500-hour rule (480 + 40 = 520).

Limited Partners A *limited* partner is a partner whose liability to third-party creditors of the partnership is limited to the amount the partner has invested in the partnership. Such a partnership must have at least one *general* partner who is fully liable in an individual capacity for the debts of the partnership to third parties.

Generally, a *limited partner* is not considered a material participant unless he or she qualifies under Test 1, 5, or 6 as shown in Concept Summary 11.2. However, a *general partner* may qualify as a material participant by meeting any of the seven tests. If a general partner also owns a limited interest in the same limited partnership, all interests are treated as a general interest.[20]

---

[19]§ 469(h)(5) and Temp.Reg. § 1.469–5T(f)(3).

[20]§ 469(h)(2) and Temp.Reg. § 1.469–5T(e)(3)(ii). Under Prop.Reg. § 1.469–5, however, material participation status for owners of LLCs and LLPs is dependent on the taxpayer's general involvement in the business.

Rental Activities Defined

Subject to certain exceptions, all rental activities are treated as passive activities.[21] A rental activity is defined as any activity where payments are received principally for the use of tangible (real or personal) property.[22] Importantly, an activity that is classified as a rental activity is subject to the passive activity loss rules even if the taxpayer involved is a material participant.

LO.6
Describe the nature of rental activities under the passive activity loss rules.

> Sarah owns a fleet of automobiles that are held for rent, and she spends an average of 60 hours a week in the activity. Assuming that her automobile business is classified as a rental activity, it is *automatically* subject to the passive activity rules even though Sarah spends more than 500 hours a year in its operation.

EXAMPLE 23

Certain rentals of real and personal property might be classified under the passive activity loss rules as *nonrental* activities.[23] In these situations, assuming that the activity is a trade or business, the material participation tests shown in Concept Summary 11.2 must be applied to determine whether the activity is a passive activity. Consider the following example.

> Dan owns a bicycle rental business at a nearby resort. Because the average period of customer use is seven days or less, Dan's business is not treated as a rental activity.

EXAMPLE 24

Example 24 illustrates an exception to the definition of a rental activity. This exception is based on the presumption that a person who rents property for seven days or less is generally required to provide significant services to the customer. Providing these services supports a conclusion that the person is engaged in a service business rather than a rental business. Other examples of this exception include most hotels or motels and businesses that rent tools, tuxedos, or cars.[24]

This result, however, does not mean that Dan's business is a nonpassive activity. Instead, it is treated as a trade or business activity subject to the material participation standards listed in Concept Summary 11.2. If Dan is a material participant, the business is treated as active. If he is not a material participant, it is treated as a passive activity.

11-3d Interaction of the At-Risk and Passive Activity Loss Limits

LO.7
Determine the relationship between the at-risk and passive activity loss limitations.

The determination of whether a loss is suspended under the passive activity loss rules is made *after* application of the at-risk rules, as well as other rules relating to the measurement of taxable income. A loss that is not allowed for the year because of the at-risk rules is suspended under those rules, not under the passive activity loss rules. Further, a taxpayer's at-risk basis is reduced by the losses (but not below zero) even if the deductions are not currently usable because of the passive activity loss rules. The following examples illustrate these points.

At-Risk and Passive Activity Loss Interactions

> Jack's adjusted basis in a passive activity is $10,000 at the beginning of 2016. His loss from the activity in 2016 is $4,000. Because Jack has no passive activity income, the $4,000 cannot be deducted. At year-end, Jack has an adjusted basis and an at-risk amount of $6,000 in the activity and a suspended passive activity loss of $4,000.

EXAMPLE 25

---

[21]§ 469(c)(2).

[22]§ 469(j)(8).

[23]Temp.Reg. § 1.469–1T(e)(3).

[24]For additional discussion of the rental exceptions, see IRS Publication 925 (*Passive Activity and At-Risk Rules*).

At-Risk and Passive Activity Loss Interactions

EXAMPLE
26

Jack in Example 25 has a loss of $9,000 in the activity in 2017. Because the $9,000 exceeds his at-risk amount ($6,000) by $3,000, that $3,000 loss is disallowed by the at-risk rules. If Jack has no passive activity income, the remaining $6,000 is suspended under the passive activity rules. At year-end, he has:

- A $3,000 loss suspended under the at-risk rules.
- $10,000 of suspended passive activity losses ($4,000 from 2016 and $6,000 from 2017).
- An adjusted basis and an at-risk amount in the activity of zero.

EXAMPLE
27

Jack in Example 26 realizes $1,000 of passive activity income from the activity in 2018. Because the $1,000 increases his at-risk amount, $1,000 of the $3,000 unused loss from 2017 is reclassified as a passive activity loss. If he has no other passive activity income, the $1,000 income is offset by $1,000 of suspended passive activity losses. At the end of 2018, Jack has:

- No taxable passive activity income.
- $2,000 ($3,000 − $1,000) of suspended losses under the at-risk rules.
- $10,000 of (reclassified) suspended passive activity losses ($10,000 + $1,000 of reclassified suspended at-risk losses − $1,000 of passive activity losses offset against passive activity income).
- An adjusted basis and an at-risk amount in the activity of zero.

EXAMPLE
28

In 2019, Jack has no gain or loss from the activity in Example 27. He contributes $5,000 more to the passive activity. Because the $5,000 increases his at-risk amount, the $2,000 of losses suspended under the at-risk rules is reclassified as passive. Jack gets no passive activity loss deduction in 2019. At year-end, he has:

- No suspended losses under the at-risk rules.
- $12,000 of suspended passive activity losses ($10,000 + $2,000 of reclassified suspended at-risk losses).
- An adjusted basis and an at-risk amount of $3,000 ($5,000 additional investment − $2,000 of reclassified losses).

The Big Picture

EXAMPLE
29

Return to the facts of *The Big Picture* on p. 11-1. If the Reswicks invest in the orange grove limited partnership, the at-risk rules will not limit the deductibility of the $25,000 losses until after year 4. Ample at-risk basis will exist until the close of that year (i.e., the at-risk basis is reduced from $100,000 by $25,000 over each of the first four years of the investment).

However, the passive activity loss rules prohibit deductions for the losses in the first four years of the investment (assuming that the Reswicks do not have passive activity income from other sources). Based on the facts provided, none of the suspended losses would be deductible until year 6, when the orange grove is expected to begin producing profits.

Concept Summary 11.3 illustrates the interactions of the at-risk and passive activity limits.

LO.8

Recognize the special treatment available to real estate activities.

11-3e Special Passive Activity Rules for Real Estate Activities

The passive activity loss limits contain two exceptions related to real estate activities. These exceptions allow all or part of real estate rental losses to offset active or portfolio income even though the activity otherwise is defined as a passive activity.

Concept Summary 11.3

Treatment of Losses Subject to the At-Risk and Passive Activity Loss Limitations

Material Participation in a Real Property Rental Trade or Business

The first exception provides relief to real estate professionals.[25] Under this exception, taxpayers meeting a special material participation rule will have any losses from real estate rental activities treated as *nonpassive*. To qualify for nonpassive treatment, a taxpayer must satisfy both of the following requirements:

- More than half of the personal services that the taxpayer performs in trades or businesses are performed in real property trades or businesses in which the taxpayer materially participates.
- The taxpayer performs more than 750 hours of services in these real property trades or businesses as a material participant.

Taxpayers who do not satisfy the above requirements must continue to treat income and losses from real estate rental activities as passive activity income and losses.

> **EXAMPLE 30**
>
> During the current year, Della performs personal service activities as follows: 900 hours as a personal financial planner, 550 hours in a real estate development business, and 600 hours in a real estate rental activity. Any loss Della incurs in either real estate activity will not be subject to the passive activity loss rules.
>
> - Being a nonrental business, the real estate development business is deemed active under the more-than-500-hour material participation test.
> - The real estate rental activity is active because more than 50% of her personal services are devoted to real property trades or businesses (i.e., the development and rental businesses) *and* her material participation in those real estate activities exceeds 750 hours.
> - As a result, any losses from either real estate activity can offset active and portfolio sources of income. Likewise, any income from these activities is nonpassive (active) income.

As discussed earlier, a spouse's work is taken into consideration in satisfying the material participation requirement. However, the hours worked by a spouse are *not* taken into account when evaluating whether a taxpayer has worked for more than 750 hours in real property trades or businesses during a year.[26] Services performed by an

---

[25] § 469(c)(7).

[26] § 469(c)(7)(B) and Reg. § 1.469–9. In *Frank Aragona Trust*, 142 T.C. 165 (2014), the Tax Court found that a trust also could qualify for the real estate professional rule.

employee are not treated as being related to a real estate trade or business unless the employee performing the services owns more than a 5 percent interest in the employer. In addition, a closely held C corporation may also qualify for the passive activity loss relief if more than 50 percent of its gross receipts for the year are derived from real property trades or businesses in which it materially participates.

ETHICS & EQUITY   Punching the Time Clock at Year-End

As the end of the tax year approaches, Ralph, a successful full-time real estate developer and investor, recognizes that his income tax situation for the year could be bleak. Unless he and his wife are able to generate more hours of participation in one of his real estate rental activities, they will not reach the material participation threshold. Consequently, the tax losses from the venture will not be deductible. To ensure deductibility, Ralph suggests the following plan:

- He will document the time he spends "thinking" about his rental activities.

- During the week, his wife will visit the apartment building to oversee (in a management role) the operations of the rentals.

- On weekends, he and his wife will visit the same units to further evaluate the operations.

- Also on the weekends, while they are doing their routine household shopping, they will be on the lookout for other rental properties to buy. Ralph plans to count both his and his wife's weekend hours toward the tally of total participation.

Ralph contends that the law clearly allows the efforts of one's spouse to count for purposes of the material participation tests. Likewise, nothing in the tax law requires taxpayers to be efficient in their hours of participation. How do you react?

Real Estate Rental Activities with Active Participation

The second exception to the passive activity loss limits is more significant in that it is *not* restricted to real estate professionals. This exception allows individuals to deduct up to $25,000 of losses from real estate rental activities against active and portfolio income each year.[27] The potential annual $25,000 deduction is reduced by 50 percent of the taxpayer's AGI in excess of $100,000. As a result, the entire deduction is phased out at $150,000 of AGI. If married individuals file separately, the $25,000 deduction is reduced to zero unless they lived apart for the entire year. In this case, the loss amount is $12,500 each and the phaseout begins at $50,000 of AGI.[28]

To qualify for the $25,000 exception, a taxpayer must meet both of the following requirements:[29]

- *Actively participate* in the real estate rental activity.

- Own 10 percent or more (in value) of all interests in the activity during the entire taxable year (or shorter period during which the taxpayer held an interest in the activity).

The difference between *active participation* and *material participation* is that the active participation threshold can be satisfied *without* regular, continuous, and substantial involvement in operations. The active participation standard is met if the taxpayer participates in making management decisions in a significant and bona fide sense. Approving new tenants, deciding on rental terms, and approving capital or repair expenditures meet this test.

---

[27] § 469(i).

[28] AGI for purposes of the phaseout is calculated without regard to IRA deductions, Social Security benefits, interest deductions on education loans, and net losses from passive activities.

[29] § 469(i)(6).

The Big Picture

EXAMPLE 31

Return to the facts of *The Big Picture* on p. 11-1. If the Reswicks invest in the apartment rental limited partnership, their $25,000 loss would be deductible under the real estate rental activities exception. This assumes that they actively participate and own at least a 10% interest in the partnership.

The loss will be deductible in each of the first four years of their investment before their at-risk basis has been exhausted (as explained earlier, the Reswick's original at-risk basis of $100,000 will be reduced to $0 over four years) even if they do not have passive activity income from other sources.

The $25,000 allowance is available after all active participation rental losses and gains are netted and applied to other passive activity income. If a taxpayer has a real estate rental loss in excess of the amount that can be deducted under the real estate rental exception, that excess is treated as a passive activity loss, usable in future years.

EXAMPLE 32

Brad has $90,000 of AGI before considering rental activities. Brad also has $85,000 of losses from a real estate rental activity in which he actively participates. He also actively participates in another real estate rental activity from which he has $30,000 of income. He has other passive activity income of $36,000.

Of the net rental loss of $55,000 ($30,000 − $85,000), $36,000 is absorbed by the passive activity income, leaving $19,000 that can be deducted against active or portfolio income because of the availability of the $25,000 allowance.

The $25,000 allowance is an aggregate of both deductions and the "deduction equivalent" of credits. The deduction equivalent of a passive activity credit is the amount of deductions that reduces the tax liability for the taxable year by an amount equal to the credit.[30] A taxpayer with $5,000 of credits and a tax bracket of 25 percent would have a deduction equivalent of $20,000 ($5,000 ÷ 25%).

If the total deduction and deduction equivalent exceed $25,000, the taxpayer must allocate the allowance on a pro rata basis, first among the losses (including real estate rental activity losses suspended in prior years) and then to credits in the following order: (1) credits other than rehabilitation and low-income housing credits, (2) rehabilitation credits, and (3) low-income housing credits.

Deduction Equivalent Considerations

EXAMPLE 33

Kevin is an active participant in a real estate rental activity that produces $8,000 of income, $26,000 of deductions, and $1,500 of credits. Kevin is a single taxpayer with $85,000 of AGI before considering this rental activity and is in the 25% tax bracket. As a result, he may deduct the net passive activity loss of $18,000 ($8,000 − $26,000).

After deducting the loss, he has an available deduction equivalent of $7,000 ($25,000 − $18,000 passive activity loss). Because the actual credits produce a $6,000 deduction equivalent ($1,500 ÷ 25% = $6,000) and this amount is less than $7,000, Kevin may claim the entire $1,500 credit.

EXAMPLE 34

Kelly is an active participant in three separate real estate rental activities. Kelly is a single taxpayer with $92,000 of AGI before considering these rental activities, and is in the 25% tax bracket. The relevant tax results for each activity are as follows:

- Activity A: $20,000 of losses.
- Activity B: $10,000 of losses.
- Activity C: $4,200 of credits.

continued

---

[30]§ 469(j)(5).

Kelly's deduction equivalent from the credits is $16,800 ($4,200 ÷ 25%). As a result, the total passive activity losses and deduction equivalents are $46,800 ($20,000 + $10,000 + $16,800), which exceeds the maximum allowable amount of $25,000. Consequently, Kelly must allocate the $25,000 allowance on a pro rata basis, first from among losses and then from among credits. Deductions from losses are limited as follows:

- Activity A {$25,000 × [$20,000 ÷ ($20,000 + $10,000)]} = $16,667.
- Activity B {$25,000 × [$10,000 ÷ ($20,000 + $10,000)]} = $8,333.

Because the amount of passive activity losses exceeds the $25,000 maximum, the remaining losses of $5,000 and passive activity credits of $4,200 must be carried forward. Kelly's suspended losses and credits by activity are as follows:

	Total	Activity A	Activity B	Activity C
Allocated losses	$ 30,000	$ 20,000	$10,000	$ –0–
Allocated credits	4,200	–0–	–0–	4,200
Utilized losses	(25,000)	(16,667)	(8,333)	–0–
Suspended losses	5,000	3,333	1,667	–0–
Suspended credits	4,200	–0–	–0–	4,200

LO.9

Determine the proper tax treatment on the disposition of a passive activity.

11-3f Dispositions of Passive Interests

If a taxpayer disposes of an entire interest in a passive activity, any suspended losses (and in certain cases, suspended credits) may be used when calculating the final economic gain or loss on the investment. In addition, if there is an overall loss from the disposition, that loss can offset other types of income. However, the tax consequences may be different if the activity is disposed of in transactions that are not fully taxable (e.g., a transfer at death or by gift or an installment sale). The following sections discuss these types of dispositions.

Disposition of a Passive Activity at Death

When a transfer of a taxpayer's interest occurs because of a taxpayer's death, suspended losses are allowed (to the decedent) to the extent they exceed the amount, if any, of the allowed increase (step-up) in basis.[31] Suspended losses that are equal to or less than the amount of the basis increase are, however, lost. The losses allowed generally are reported on the final return of the deceased taxpayer.

Disposition of Suspended Passive Activity Losses at Death

EXAMPLE 35

Alyson dies with passive activity property having an adjusted basis of $40,000, suspended losses of $10,000, and a fair market value at the date of her death of $75,000. The increase (step-up) in basis is $35,000 (fair market value at date of death in excess of adjusted basis).

None of the $10,000 suspended loss is deductible on Alyson's final return or by the beneficiary. The suspended losses ($10,000) are lost because they do not exceed the step-up in basis ($35,000).

EXAMPLE 36

Assume the same facts as in the previous example, except that the property's fair market value at the date of Alyson's death is $47,000.

Because the step-up in basis is only $7,000 ($47,000 − $40,000), the suspended losses allowed are limited to $3,000 ($10,000 suspended loss at time of death − $7,000 increase in basis). The $3,000 loss available to Alyson is reported on her final income tax return.

---

[31]§ 469(g)(2); the basis of inherited property is generally the fair market value on the date of death (see Chapter 14).

Disposition of a Passive Activity by Gift

If a taxpayer's interest in a passive activity is transferred by gift, the suspended losses are added to the donee's basis of the property.[32] As a result, the donor will see no benefit from any suspended losses. However, a tax *benefit* may be available to the donee. Due to the increase in the property's basis, greater depreciation deductions can result, and there will be less gain (or more loss) on a subsequent sale of the property. The benefits of increased basis do not materialize if the recipient is a charity, as such organizations generally are not subject to income taxation.

Carlton makes a gift to Emma of passive activity property having an adjusted basis of $40,000, suspended losses of $10,000, and a fair market value at the date of the gift of $100,000. Carlton cannot deduct the suspended losses in the year of the disposition. However, the suspended losses transfer with the property and are added to the adjusted basis of the property, which becomes $50,000 in Emma's hands.

Assuming that Emma is able to sell the property for $105,000 soon after she receives the gift, her taxable gain would be $55,000 ($105,000 − $50,000), which reflects the benefit from the increased basis.

Installment Sale of a Passive Activity

An installment sale of a taxpayer's entire interest in a passive activity triggers recognition of the suspended losses.[33] The losses are allowed each year as payments are received on the installment obligation in the ratio that the gain recognized in each year bears to the total gain on the sale.

Lucas sells his entire interest in a passive activity for $100,000. His adjusted basis in the property is $60,000. If he uses the installment method, his gross profit ratio is 40% ($40,000 gross profit/ $100,000 sales proceeds). If Lucas receives a $20,000 down payment, he will recognize a gain of $8,000 (40% of $20,000). If the activity has a suspended loss of $25,000, Lucas will deduct $5,000 [($8,000 ÷ $40,000) × $25,000] of the suspended loss in the first year.

This pattern will continue as Lucas receives installment payments. So, for example, if Lucas receives a $10,000 installment payment in the following year, he will recognize gain of $4,000 and can deduct $2,500 of the suspended loss in that year.

The general rules relating to passive activity losses are reviewed in Concept Summary 11.4.

11-4 INVESTMENT INTEREST LIMITATION

LO.10

Identify restrictions placed on the deductibility of other investor losses and deductions, including those that apply to investment interest.

Another way investors used the tax law to create wealth involved the use of the interest deduction. By borrowing to purchase investments that would appreciate over time, the interest on the debt was claimed as an ordinary deduction when paid. Later, when the asset was sold at a gain, only a capital gains tax was due on the appreciation. In addition to the "mismatch" of ordinary deductions leading to capital gains, the time value of money also played a role in these decisions (current deductions leading to lower taxes today; capital gains at lower rates at some point in the future).

11-4a **Limitation Imposed**

In response, Congress has limited the deductibility of investment interest, which is interest paid on debt borrowed for the purpose of purchasing or continuing to hold

---

[32]§ 469(j)(6).   [33]§ 469(g)(3).

Concept Summary 11.4

Passive Activity Loss Rules: Key Issues and Answers

What is the fundamental passive activity rule?	Passive activity losses may be deducted only against passive activity income and gains. Losses not allowed are suspended and used in future years.
Who is subject to the passive activity rules?	Individuals.
	Estates.
	Trusts.
	Personal service corporations.
	Closely held C corporations.
What is a passive activity?	Trade or business or income-producing activity in which the taxpayer does not materially participate during the year or rental activities, subject to certain exceptions, regardless of the taxpayer's level of participation.
What is an activity?	One or more trade or business or rental activities that comprise an appropriate economic unit.
How is an appropriate economic unit determined?	Based on a reasonable application of the relevant facts and circumstances.
What is material participation?	In general, the taxpayer participates on a regular, continuous, and substantial basis. More specifically, when the taxpayer meets the conditions of one of the seven tests provided in the Regulations.
What is a rental activity?	In general, an activity where payments are received for the use of tangible property. Special rules apply to rental real estate.

investment property. The deduction for investment interest allowed during the tax year is limited to the lesser of the investment interest paid or net investment income.[34]

The Big Picture

EXAMPLE 39

Return to the facts of *The Big Picture* on p. 11-1. If the Reswicks invest in the high-growth, low-yield portfolio of marketable securities, most of the investment return will consist of appreciation, which will not be taxed until the securities are sold. Relatively little of the current return will consist of currently taxable interest and dividend income.

Assume that the interest and dividend income for the year from these securities equals $500 and that all of it is treated as investment income. If the investment interest expense on the $100,000 loan is $6,000, only $500 of this interest will be deductible this year (i.e., the deduction for the investment interest is limited to the $500 of net investment income).

Investment Income and Expenses

Net investment income, which serves as the ceiling on the deductibility of investment interest, is the excess of investment income over investment expenses. **Investment income** includes gross income from interest, annuities, and royalties not derived in the ordinary course of a trade or business.[35] However, investment income does not include any income taken into account when calculating income or loss from a passive activity.

Investment expenses are those deductible expenses directly connected with the production of investment income, such as property taxes on investment holdings, brokerage charges, and investment counsel fees. Investment expenses do not include interest expense.

---

[34]§ 163(d)(1).   [35]§ 163(d)(4)(B).

11-4b **Computation of Allowable Deduction**

After net investment income is determined, the allowable deductible investment interest expense is calculated.

> **EXAMPLE 40**
>
> Ethan's financial records for the year reflect the following:
>
> | | |
> |---|---:|
> | Interest income from bank savings account | $10,000 |
> | Taxable annuity receipts | 5,500 |
> | Local ad valorem property tax on investments | 200 |
> | Investment interest expense | 17,000 |
>
> Ethan's investment income amounts to $15,500 ($10,000 + $5,500), and investment expenses total $200. As a result, his net investment income is $15,300 ($15,500 − $200). Consequently, the investment interest deduction is limited to $15,300 (the lesser of investment interest expense or net investment income).

The amount of investment interest disallowed is carried over to future years. In Example 40, the amount that is carried over to the following year is $1,700 ($17,000 investment interest expense − $15,300 deduction allowed). No limit is placed on the length of the carryover period.[36] The investment interest expense deduction is determined by completing Form 4952 (Investment Interest Deduction).

11-5 **OTHER INVESTMENT LOSSES**

The investment activities summarized below are discussed elsewhere in this text as shown in Concept Summary 11.5.

- Sales of securities held as investments for less than basis result in capital losses. These losses can offset capital gains. In the case of individual taxpayers, excess losses are applied against ordinary income up to $3,000 (§ 1211). Any remaining excess capital losses are carried over for use in future years (§ 1212).

- When an activity is classified as a hobby, any losses resulting are limited to the income from the activity [§ 183(b)(2)]. If the activity is not a hobby (i.e., a profit motive controls), however, full deduction of the losses is allowed [§§ 162 and 212(2)].

- Losses on small business stock (i.e., stock that qualifies under § 1244) are treated as ordinary losses up to a maximum of $100,000. As a result, the limitations placed on capital losses (see above) are avoided.

- Vacation homes that are rented for part of the year may generate investment losses depending on the extent of the rental period as compared to time devoted to personal use (§ 280A). If sufficient rental activity takes place, the vacation home may be treated as rental property. As a result, any losses could be subject to the passive activity loss rules.

- Securities held as an investment that become worthless produce capital losses. The losses are usually long term because they are treated as occurring on the last day of the year in which the securities become worthless [§ 165(g)(1)]. Because the securities must be completely worthless, determining the year when this takes place is often difficult.

---

[36]§ 163(d)(2).

Concept Summary 11.5

Common Investment Loss Limitation Rules

Item	Refer to Chapter	General Nature of Limitation
At-risk rules	11	Losses in excess of the at-risk basis are not deducted in the current year. Losses not deducted are suspended and used in future years when the at-risk basis increases.
Capital losses	16	Individuals may offset capital gains by capital losses realized. Up to $3,000 of realized net capital losses may offset ordinary income. Remaining excess capital losses are carried over to future years.
Hobby losses	6	Losses from hobby activities may be deducted to the extent of income from hobby activities. Excess hobby losses are carried forward to future years.
Investment interest	11	The deduction of investment interest is limited to the taxpayer's net investment income. Excess investment interest is deductible in future years.
Passive activity loss limitations	11	Generally, passive activity losses are deducted only to the extent of passive activity income. Excess passive activity losses are suspended and used in future years.
Small business (§ 1244) stock	7	Losses from the disposition of small business stock are given ordinary treatment up to a maximum of $100,000 per year.
Vacation homes	6	The deductibility of losses from vacation homes may be limited, depending on the relative number of rental use days and personal use days of the property.
Worthless securities	7	Losses arising from investment securities that become worthless are treated as occurring on the last day of the tax year.

LO.11

Suggest tax planning strategies to minimize the effect of the passive activity loss and investment interest limitations and recognize the general impact of the additional tax on net investment income.

11-6 TAX PLANNING

11-6a Using Passive Activity Losses

Perhaps the biggest challenge individuals face with the passive activity loss rules is to recognize the potential impact of the rules and then to structure their affairs to minimize this impact. Taxpayers who have passive activity losses should adopt a strategy of buying an interest in an activity that is generating passive activity income, that can be offset (or sheltered) by the existing passive activity losses. From a tax perspective, it would be foolish to buy a loss-generating passive activity unless (1) the taxpayer has other passive activity income to shelter, (2) the activity is rental real estate that can qualify for the $25,000 exception, or (3) the activity qualifies for the exception available to real estate professionals.

If a taxpayer does invest in an activity that produces losses subject to the passive activity loss rules, the following strategies may help minimize the loss of current deductions:

- If money is borrowed to finance the purchase of a passive activity, the associated interest expense is generally treated as part of any passive activity loss. Consequently, by using more available (i.e., not borrowed) cash to purchase the passive investment, the investor will need less debt and will incur less interest expense. By incurring less interest expense, a possible suspended passive activity loss deduction is reduced.

- If the investor does not have sufficient cash readily available for the larger down payment, cash can be obtained by borrowing against the equity in his or her personal residence. The interest expense on such debt will be deductible under the qualified residence interest rules (see Chapter 10) and will not be subject to the passive activity loss limitations. As a result, the taxpayer avoids the passive activity loss limitation and secures a currently deductible interest expense.

As explained earlier, unusable passive activity losses often accumulate and provide no current tax benefit because the taxpayer has no passive activity income. When the taxpayer disposes of the entire interest in a passive activity, however, any suspended losses from that activity are used to reduce the taxable gain. If any taxable gain still remains, it can be offset by losses from other passive activities. As a result, the taxpayer should carefully select the year in which to dispose of a passive activity. It is to the taxpayer's advantage to wait until sufficient passive activity losses have accumulated to offset any gain recognized on the asset's disposition.

Bill, a calendar year taxpayer, owns interests in two passive activities: Activity A, which he plans to sell in December of this year at a gain of $100,000, and Activity B, which he plans to keep indefinitely. Current and suspended losses associated with Activity B total $60,000, and Bill expects losses from the activity to be $40,000 next year.

If Bill sells Activity A this year, the $100,000 gain can be offset by the current and suspended losses of $60,000 from Activity B, producing a net taxable gain of $40,000. However, if Bill delays the sale of Activity A until January of next year, the $100,000 gain will be fully offset by the $100,000 of losses generated by Activity B ($60,000 current and prior losses + $40,000 next year's loss). Consequently, by postponing the sale by one month, he could avoid recognizing $40,000 of gain that would otherwise result.

Taxpayers with passive activity losses should consider the level of their involvement in all other trades or businesses in which they have an interest. If they do not materially participate in a profitable activity, the activity becomes a passive activity. Any income generated by the profitable business then could be sheltered by current and suspended passive activity losses. Family partnerships in which certain members do not materially participate would qualify. The silent partner in any general partnership engaged in a trade or business also would qualify.

Gail has an investment in a limited partnership that produces annual passive activity losses of approximately $25,000. She also owns a newly acquired interest in a convenience store where she works. Her share of the store's income is $35,000. If she works enough to be classified as a material participant, her $35,000 share of income is treated as active income. This results in $35,000 being subject to tax every year, while her $25,000 loss is suspended.

However, if Gail reduces her involvement at the store so that she is not a material participant, the $35,000 of income receives passive treatment. Consequently, the $35,000 of income can be offset by the $25,000 passive activity loss, resulting in only $10,000 being subject to tax. By reducing her involvement, Gail ensures that the income from the profitable trade or business receives passive treatment and can then be used to absorb passive activity losses from other passive activities.

The impact of the passive activity loss rules often extend to other seemingly unrelated Code sections. For example, because of the restrictive nature of the passive activity loss rules, it may be advantageous for a taxpayer to use a vacation home enough to convert it to a second residence. This would enable all of the qualified interest and real estate taxes to be deducted without limitation. However, this strategy would lead to the loss of other deductions, such as repairs, maintenance, and insurance. See Examples 33 and 35 and the related discussion in Chapter 6.

The passive activity loss rules can have a dramatic effect on a taxpayer's ability to claim passive activity losses currently. As a result, it is important to keep accurate records of all sources of income and losses, particularly any suspended passive activity losses and credits and the activities to which they relate, so that their potential tax benefit will not be lost.

11-6b **Planning with the Investment Interest Limitation**

The term *investment income* includes net capital gain and qualified dividend income only if the taxpayer *elects* to treat them as such. For this purpose,

- net capital gain includes gain attributable to property held for investment and
- qualified dividend income includes dividends that are taxed at the same marginal rate that is applicable to a net capital gain.

By electing to include net capital gain and qualified dividend income as components of investment income, the amount of investment interest deductible in a particular year likewise increases. Form 4952 is used to make such an election. However, the election comes with a cost and is available only if the taxpayer agrees to reduce amounts qualifying for the preferential tax rates that otherwise apply to net capital gain (see Chapter 16) and qualified dividends (refer to Chapter 4) by an equivalent amount.[37]

EXAMPLE 43

Olivia incurred $13,000 of interest expense related to her investments during the year. Her investment income included $4,000 of interest, $2,000 of qualified dividends, and a $5,000 net capital gain on the sale of investment securities.

If Olivia does not make the election to include the net capital gain and qualified dividends in investment income, her investment income for purposes of computing the investment income limitation is $4,000 (interest income). If she does make the election, her investment income is $11,000 ($4,000 interest + $2,000 qualified dividends + $5,000 net capital gain). In that case, $11,000 of her interest expense, rather than $4,000, is deductible currently.

Should Olivia in the previous example make the election to include the additional $7,000 of qualified dividends and net capital gain as investment income? By doing so, the current-year investment interest deduction increases by $7,000, and the investment interest deduction potentially carried forward to future years is reduced by the same amount. That is, the election allows for an acceleration of the investment interest deduction. As Olivia evaluates her decision, she should consider the following points:

- The election would make sense only if her marginal ordinary income tax rate exceeds the applicable capital gains rate.
- Using present value concepts, she should compare the tax cost of postponing the interest deduction to a subsequent year with the impact of losing the benefit from the preferential capital gains rate. In performing this analysis, consideration should be given to the length of the deferral of the investment interest deduction and the current and future years' tax brackets.

11-6c **Effect of the Additional Tax on Net Investment Income**

As if the passive activity loss and investment interest limitations are not complicated enough, under the Affordable Care Act (ObamaCare), individuals, estates, and trusts also are subject to an additional 3.8 percent tax on net investment income.[38] Net investment income *for this purpose* generally includes amounts such as interest, dividends, long- and short-term capital gains, royalties, rents, and income from passive activities. The tax is levied at the flat 3.8 percent rate on the lesser of the taxpayer's net investment income or the excess of modified AGI over a threshold amount. The threshold amounts for individuals are $250,000 for surviving spouses and taxpayers filing a joint return, $125,000 for married taxpayers filing separate returns, and $200,000 for all other individual taxpayers. As a consequence, this tax is aimed at higher-income taxpayers. This tax can be a surprise to taxpayers, potentially increasing the marginal capital gain tax rate to 23.8 percent (from 20 percent) and the marginal ordinary income tax rate to 43.4 percent (from 39.6 percent). See text Section 13-6c of Chapter 13 for a complete discussion of this tax.

---

[37]Reg. § 1.163(d)–1.   [38]§ 1411.

INVESTOR LOSS LIMITATIONS CAN SIGNIFICANTLY AFFECT INVESTMENT RETURNS

The objective for most investors should be to maximize after-tax wealth from among investment alternatives. This requires an understanding of the relevant tax restrictions that apply to certain expenses and losses arising from various investment choices. The after-tax returns from the three alternatives the Reswicks are considering may be affected by the at-risk, passive activity, and investment interest limitations.

The high-growth, low-yield portfolio is expected to generate very little, if any, current interest and dividend income (i.e., investment income). Nonetheless, if the broker's prediction is correct, the market value of the securities will grow by approximately 8 percent a year. However, the annual $6,000 interest expense on the debt incurred to purchase the securities is not deductible as investment interest to the extent there is no investment income. Unless investment income is generated from this or some other source, the interest will not be deductible until the securities are sold (see Example 39). In addition, to the extent that any capital gain from the portfolio's sale is treated as investment income, the gain will not be subject to preferential capital gains rates (see Example 43). As a result, the net after-tax return will be impaired because of the investment interest limitation.

The net returns from the other two investment choices will be diminished by the at-risk and passive activity loss rules in addition to the investment interest limitation. The projected 8 percent return is apparently contingent on the investors being able to use the current tax losses as they arise. These benefits will be deferred because the at-risk and passive activity loss rules delay the timing of the deductions. For example, in the case of the orange grove investment, none of the passive activity losses are deductible until year 6, when the investment is expected to produce passive activity income (see Example 29). In the real estate rental venture, however, the Reswicks could deduct the $25,000 passive activity loss under the exception for rental real estate for the first four years (see Example 31); the at-risk rules would limit any additional losses in year 5 to the at-risk amount. Consequently, because the at-risk and passive activity loss rules limit the tax losses flowing to the Reswicks, the after-tax return will not be nearly as high as their broker predicts.

What If?

If the Reswicks decide that the investment in marketable securities is their best option, could they modify their plan so that they avoid the restriction imposed by the investment interest limitation? The Reswicks' net after-tax return would improve if the interest cost of financing their investment could be deducted as incurred. They could finance their investment by borrowing up to $100,000 against the equity in their home (see Chapter 10). The interest on the home equity loan would be fully deductible; consequently, the after-tax return from their investment would increase. Furthermore, any gain recognition would be deferred until the securities are sold, and the tax on the gain would qualify for the preferential capital gains rate.

RIDO/SHUTTERSTOCK.COM

Key Terms

Active income, 11-6

At-risk limitation, 11-3

Closely held corporation, 11-10

Investment income, 11-22

Investment interest, 11-21

Material participation, 11-13

Net investment income, 11-22

Passive activity loss, 11-3

Personal service corporation, 11-10

Portfolio income, 11-6

Rental activity, 11-15

Significant participation activity, 11-14

Tax shelters, 11-2

Discussion Questions

1. **LO.1, 2, 3** Identify two rules designed to limit the tax benefits a taxpayer may obtain from a tax shelter investment. Describe how these rules reduce or defer the recognition of tax losses.

2. **LO.2** List some events that increase or decrease an investor's at-risk amount. What are some strategies that a taxpayer can employ to increase the at-risk amount to claim a higher deduction for losses?

3. **LO.2, 3** Roberto invested $18,000 in a chicken production operation. Using nonrecourse notes, the business purchases $120,000 worth of grain to feed the chickens. If Roberto's share of the expense is $26,000, how much can he deduct?

4. **LO.3** Explain the meaning of the terms *active income, portfolio income,* and *passive activity income.*

5. **LO.3** Carlos owns an interest in an activity that produces a $100,000 loss during the year. Would he prefer to have the activity classified as active or passive? Explain.

6. **LO.3** Kim owns an interest in an activity that produces $100,000 of income during the year. Would Kim prefer to have the activity classified as active or passive? Discuss.

7. **LO.3** On a taxable disposition of a passive activity, the taxpayer can use any suspended losses and credits related to that activity. Do you agree? Explain.

8. **LO.3** Discuss whether the passive activity loss rules apply to the following: individuals, closely held C corporations, S corporations, partnerships, and personal service corporations.

9. **LO.3** Bronze Corporation has $100,000 of active income, $55,000 of portfolio income, and a $55,000 passive activity loss. Under what circumstances is Bronze prohibited from deducting the loss? Allowed to deduct the loss?

10. **LO.4** Discuss what constitutes a passive activity.

11. **LO.5** What is the significance of the term *material participation*? Why is the extent of a taxpayer's participation in an activity important in determining whether a loss from the activity is deductible or nondeductible?

12. **LO.5** How many hours must a participant work in a nonrental activity to be guaranteed material participation status?

Decision Making   13. **LO.5** Suzanne owns interests in a bagel shop, a lawn and garden store, and a convenience store. Several full-time employees work at each of the enterprises. As of the end of November of the current year, Suzanne has worked 150 hours in the bagel shop, 250 hours at the lawn and garden store, and 70 hours at the convenience store. In reviewing her financial records, you learn that she has no passive investments that are generating income and that she expects these three ventures collectively to produce a loss. What recommendation would you offer Suzanne as she plans her activities for the remainder of the year?

14. **LO.5, 11** John, an engineer, operates a separate business that he acquired eight years ago. If he participates 85 hours in the business and it incurs a loss of $34,000, under what circumstances can John claim an active loss?

15. **LO.2, 3, 5** Rita retired from public accounting after a long and successful career of 45 years. As part of her retirement package, she continues to share in the profits and losses of the firm, albeit at a lower rate than when she was working full-time. Because Rita wants to stay busy during her retirement years, she has invested and works in a local hardware business, operated as a partnership. Unfortunately, the business has recently gone through a slump and has not been generating profits. Identify relevant tax issues for Rita.   Issue ID

16. **LO.5** Some types of work are counted in applying the material participation standards, and some types are not counted. Discuss and give examples of each type.

17. **LO.5** Last year Alan's accountant informed him that he could not claim any of his passive activity losses on his income tax return because of his lack of material participation. To circumvent the tax problem this year, Alan tells his wife that she may have to put in some time at the various businesses. Identify the tax issues that Alan faces.   Issue ID

18. **LO.5** Sean, a limited partner in Ivy Nursery, is informed that his portion of the entity's current loss is $18,000. As a limited partner, can Sean assume that his share of the partnership loss is a passive activity loss? Explain.

19. **LO.6** Explain why some rental activities may not be *treated* as such under the passive activity loss rules.

20. **LO.3, 4, 5, 6** How is *passive activity* defined in the Code? What aspects of the definition have been clarified by final or Temporary Regulations?

21. **LO.8** What is a *real estate professional*? Why could qualifying for this status be beneficial under the passive activity loss rules?

22. **LO.8** Caroline owns a real estate rental activity that produces a loss of $65,000 during the current year. Under what circumstances can Caroline treat the entire loss as nonpassive?

23. **LO.8** Since his college days, Charles has developed an entrepreneurial streak. After working in his family's grocery business, he starts several ventures on his own. Even though Charles is independently wealthy, he is looking forward to working in each of the ventures. He plans to "drop in" on the businesses from time to time between personal trips to Europe and the Caribbean. As of the end of the year, he has established computer software stores in Dayton (Ohio), Austin, and Seattle; bagel bakeries in Albany, Athens (Georgia), and Tallahassee; and mountain bike and ski rental shops in small towns in Vermont, West Virginia, Colorado, and California. Identify the tax issues facing Charles.   Issue ID

24. **LO.8** Brad owns a small townhouse complex that generates a loss during the year. Under what circumstances can Brad deduct a loss from the rental activity? What limitations apply?

25. **LO.8** In connection with passive activities, what is a *deduction equivalent* and how is it computed?

26. **LO.10** What is *investment interest expense*? Describe the basic rules that may limit its deductibility.

Computational Exercises

27. **LO.2** In the current year, Ed invests $30,000 in an oil partnership. He has taxable income for the current year of $2,000 from the oil partnership and withdraws $10,000. What is Ed's at-risk amount at the end of the year?

28. **LO.3** Lucy sells her partnership interest, a passive activity, with an adjusted basis of $305,000 for $330,000. In addition, she has current and suspended losses of $28,000 associated with the partnership and has no other passive activities. Calculate Lucy's total gain and her current deductible loss. Describe the type of income that the deductible loss may offset.

29. **LO.4, 5** Forrester owns a nonrental business with two separate departments. Department A generates net income of $70,000, and Department B generates a net loss of $58,000. Forrester participates 800 hours in the operations of Department A and 300 hours in the operations of Department B. If Forrester is allowed to treat the departments as components of a single activity, calculate the amount of the Department B loss that can be offset against the income from Department A in the current year.

30. **LO.7** Rhonda has an adjusted basis and an at-risk amount of $7,500 in a passive activity at the beginning of the year. She also has a suspended passive activity loss of $1,500 carried over from the prior year. During the current year, she has a loss of $12,000 from the passive activity. Rhonda has no passive activity income from other sources this year. Determine the following items relating to Rhonda's passive activity as of the end of the year.
    a. Adjusted basis and at-risk amount in the passive activity.
    b. Loss suspended under the at-risk rules.
    c. Suspended passive activity loss.

31. **LO.8** Noah, who has $62,000 of AGI before considering rental activities, has $70,000 of losses from a real estate rental activity in which he actively participates. He also actively participates in another real estate rental activity from which he has $33,000 of income. He has other passive activity income of $20,000. What amount of rental loss can Noah use to offset active or portfolio income in the current year?

32. **LO.9** Rose dies with passive activity property having an adjusted basis of $65,000, suspended losses of $13,000, and a fair market value at the date of her death of $90,000. Of the $13,000 suspended loss existing at the time of Rose's death, how much is deductible on her final return or by the beneficiary?

33. **LO.10** Troy's financial records for the year reflect the following:

Interest income from bank savings account	$ 900
Taxable annuity receipts	1,800
City ad valorem property tax on investments	125
Investment interest expense	3,200

Calculate Troy's net investment income and his current investment interest deduction. How is any potential excess investment interest deduction treated?

34. **LO.2** In 2016, Fred invested $50,000 in a general partnership. Fred's interest is not considered to be a passive activity. If his share of the partnership losses is $35,000 in 2016 and $25,000 in 2017, how much can he deduct in each year?

35. **LO.2** In the current year, Bill Parker (54 Oak Drive, St. Paul, MN 55164) is considering making an investment of $60,000 in Best Choice Partnership. The prospectus provided by Bill's broker indicates that the partnership investment is not a passive activity and that Bill's share of the entity's loss in the current year will likely be $40,000, while his share of the partnership loss next year will probably be $25,000. Write a letter to Bill in which you indicate how the losses would be treated for tax purposes in the current year and the following year.

Communications

36. **LO.2, 11** Heather wants to invest $40,000 in a relatively safe venture and has discovered two alternatives that would produce the following reportable ordinary income and loss over the next three years:

Decision Making

Year	Alternative 1 Income (Loss)	Alternative 2 Income (Loss)
1	($20,000)	($48,000)
2	(28,000)	32,000
3	72,000	40,000

She is interested in the after-tax effects of these alternatives over a three-year horizon. Assume that Heather's investment portfolio produces sufficient passive activity income to offset any potential passive activity loss that may arise from these alternatives, that her cost of capital is 6% (see Appendix H for the present value factors), that she is in the 25% tax bracket, that each investment alternative possesses equal growth potential, and that each alternative exposes her to comparable financial risk. In addition, assume that in the loss years for each alternative, there is no cash flow from or to the investment (i.e., the loss is due to depreciation), while in those years when the income is positive, cash flows to Heather equal the amount of the income. Based on these facts, compute the present value of these two investment alternatives and determine which option Heather should choose.

37. **LO.1, 3** Dorothy acquired a 100% interest in two passive activities: Activity A in January 2012 and Activity B in 2013. Through 2015, Activity A was profitable, but it produced losses of $200,000 in 2016 and $100,000 in 2017. Dorothy has passive activity income from Activity B of $20,000 in 2016 and $40,000 in 2017. After offsetting passive activity income, how much of the net losses may she deduct?

38. **LO.1, 3** A number of years ago, Kay acquired an interest in a partnership in which she is not a material participant. Kay's basis in her partnership interest at the beginning of 2016 is $40,000. Kay's share of the partnership loss is $35,000 in 2016, while her share of the partnership income is $15,000 in 2017. How much may Kay deduct in 2016 and 2017, assuming that she owns no other passive activities?

39. **LO.3** Mike, an attorney, earns $200,000 from his law practice and receives $45,000 in dividends and interest during the year. In addition, he incurs a loss of $50,000 from an investment in a passive activity acquired three years ago. What is Mike's net income for the current year after considering the passive investment?

40. **LO.3, 11** Emily has $100,000 that she wants to invest and is considering the following two options:

Decision Making

- Option A: Investment in Redbird Mutual Fund, which is expected to produce interest income of $8,000 per year.

- Option B: Investment in Cardinal Limited Partnership (buys, sells, and operates wine vineyards). Emily's share of the partnership's ordinary income and loss over the next three years would be as follows:

Year	Income (Loss)
1	($ 8,000)
2	(2,000)
3	34,000

Emily is interested in the after-tax effects of these alternatives over a three-year horizon. Assume that Emily's investment portfolio produces ample passive activity income to offset any passive activity losses that may be generated. Her cost of capital is 8% (see Appendix H for the present value factors), and she is in the 28% tax bracket. The two investment alternatives possess equal growth potential and comparable financial risk. Based on these facts, compute the present value of these two investment alternatives and determine which option Emily should choose.

41. **LO.3** Ray acquired an activity several years ago, and in the current year, it generates a loss of $50,000. Ray has AGI of $140,000 before considering the loss from the activity. If the activity is a bakery and Ray is not a material participant, what is his AGI?

Decision Making 42. **LO.3, 11** Jorge owns two passive investments, Activity A and Activity B. He plans to sell Activity A in the current year or next year. Juanita has offered to buy Activity A this year for an amount that would produce a taxable passive activity gain to Jorge of $115,000. However, if the sale, for whatever reason, is not made to Juanita, Jorge believes that he could find a buyer who would pay about $7,000 less than Juanita. Passive activity losses and gains generated (and expected to be generated) by Activity B follow:

Two years ago	($35,000)
Last year	(35,000)
This year	(8,000)
Next year	(30,000)
Future years	Minimal profits

All of Activity B's losses are suspended. Should Jorge close the sale of Activity A with Juanita this year, or should he wait until next year and sell to another buyer? Jorge is in the 28% tax bracket.

43. **LO.3** Sarah has investments in four passive activity partnerships purchased several years ago. Last year the income and losses were as follows:

Activity	Income (Loss)
A	$ 30,000
B	(30,000)
C	(15,000)
D	(5,000)

In the current year, she sold her interest in Activity D for a $10,000 gain. Activity D, which had been profitable until last year, had a current loss of $1,500. How will the sale of Activity D affect Sarah's taxable income in the current year?

44. **LO.3** Leon sells his interest in a passive activity for $100,000. Determine the tax effect of the sale based on each of the following independent facts:

a. Adjusted basis in this investment is $35,000. Losses from prior years that were not deductible due to the passive activity loss restrictions total $40,000.

b. Adjusted basis in this investment is $75,000. Losses from prior years that were not deductible due to the passive activity loss restrictions total $40,000.

c. Adjusted basis in this investment is $75,000. Losses from prior years that were not deductible due to the passive activity loss restrictions total $40,000. In addition, suspended credits total $10,000.

45. **LO.3** Ash, Inc., a closely held personal service corporation, has $100,000 of passive activity losses. In addition, Ash has $80,000 of active business income and $20,000 of portfolio income. How much of the passive activity loss may Ash use to offset the other types of income?

46. **LO.3** In the current year, White, Inc., earns $400,000 from operations and receives $36,000 of interest income from various portfolio investments. White also pays $150,000 to acquire a 20% interest in a passive activity that produces a $200,000 loss.

a. Assuming that White is a personal service corporation, how will these transactions affect its taxable income?

b. Same as part (a), except that White is closely held but not a personal service corporation.

47. **LO.2, 3, 7, 11** Kristin Graf (123 Baskerville Mill Road, Jamison, PA 18929) is trying to decide how to invest a $10,000 inheritance. One option is to make an additional investment in Rocky Road Excursions in which she has an at-risk basis of $0, suspended losses under the at-risk rules of $7,000, and suspended passive activity losses of $1,000. If Kristin makes this investment, her share of the expected profits this year will be $8,000. If her investment stays the same, her share of profits from Rocky Road Excursions will be $1,000. Another option is to invest $10,000 as a limited partner in the Ragged Mountain Winery; this investment will produce passive activity income of $9,000. Write a letter to Kristin to review the tax consequences of each alternative. Kristin is in the 28% tax bracket.

Decision Making

Communications

48. **LO.2, 3, 7, 11** The end of the year is approaching, and Maxine has begun to focus on ways of minimizing her income tax liability. Several years ago she purchased an investment in Teal Limited Partnership, which is subject to the at-risk and the passive activity loss rules. (Last year Maxine sold a different investment that was subject to these rules and that produced passive activity income.) She believes that her investment in Teal has good long-term economic prospects. However, it has been generating tax losses for several years in a row. In fact, when she was discussing last year's income tax return with her tax accountant, he said that unless "things change" with respect to her investments, she would not be able to deduct losses this year.

Decision Making

a. What was the accountant referring to in his comment?

b. You learn that Maxine's current at-risk basis in her investment is $1,000 and that her share of the current loss is expected to be $13,000. Based on these facts, how will her loss be treated?

c. After reviewing her situation, Maxine's financial adviser suggests that she invest at least an additional $12,000 in Teal to ensure a full loss deduction in the current year. How do you react to his suggestion?

d. What would you suggest Maxine consider as she attempts to maximize her current-year deductible loss?

49. **LO.2, 3, 7** A number of years ago, Lee acquired a 20% interest in the BlueSky Partnership for $60,000. The partnership was profitable through 2016, and Lee's amount at risk in the partnership interest was $120,000 at the beginning of 2017. BlueSky incurred a loss of $400,000 in 2017 and reported income of $200,000 in 2018. Assuming that Lee is not a material participant, how much of his loss from BlueSky Partnership is deductible in 2017 and 2018? Consider the at-risk and passive activity loss rules, and assume that Lee owns no other passive investments.

50. **LO.2, 3, 5, 7** Grace acquired an activity four years ago. The loss from the activity is $50,000 in the current year (at-risk basis of $40,000 as of the beginning of the year). Without considering the loss from the activity, she has gross income of $140,000. If the activity is a convenience store and Grace is a material participant, what is the effect of the activity on her taxable income?

51. **LO.2, 3, 5, 7** Jonathan, a physician, earns $200,000 from his practice. He also receives $18,000 in dividends and interest from various portfolio investments. During the year, he pays $45,000 to acquire a 20% interest in a partnership that produces a $300,000 loss. Compute Jonathan's AGI, assuming that:

a. He does not participate in the operations of the partnership.

b. He is a material participant in the operations of the partnership.

52. **LO.2, 3, 7** Five years ago Gerald invested $150,000 in a passive activity, his sole investment venture. On January 1, 2016, his amount at risk in the activity was $30,000. His shares of the income and losses were as follows:

Year	Income (Loss)
2016	($40,000)
2017	(30,000)
2018	50,000

Gerald holds no suspended at-risk or passive activity losses at the beginning of 2016. How much can Gerald deduct in 2016 and 2017? What is his taxable income from the activity in 2018? Consider the at-risk rules as well as the passive activity loss rules.

Communications 53. **LO.3, 8** Several years ago Benny Jackson (125 Hill Street, Charleston, WV 25311) acquired an apartment building that currently generates a loss of $60,000. Benny's AGI is $130,000 before considering the loss. The apartment building is in an exclusive part of the city, and Benny is an active participant. Write a letter to Benny explaining what effect the loss will have on his AGI.

54. **LO.3, 5, 8** This year Maria works 1,200 hours as a computer consultant, 320 hours in a real estate development business, and 400 hours in real estate rental activities. Juan, her husband, works 250 hours in the real estate development business and 180 hours in the real estate rental business. Maria earns $60,000 as a computer consultant, while she and Juan lost $18,000 in the real estate development business and $26,000 in the real estate rental business. How should they treat the losses?

Decision Making 55. **LO.3, 8, 11** Bonnie and Jake (ages 35 and 36, respectively) are married with no dependents and live in Montana (not a community property state). Because Jake has large medical expenses, they seek your advice about filing separately to save taxes. Their income and expenses for 2017 are as follows:

Bonnie's salary	$ 42,500
Jake's salary	26,000
Interest income (joint)	1,500
Rental loss from actively managed rental property	(23,000)
Jake's unreimbursed medical expenses	8,500
All other itemized deductions:*	
Bonnie	9,000
Jake	3,400

*None subject to limitations

Determine whether Bonnie and Jake should file jointly or separately for 2017.

Decision Making 56. **LO.3, 8, 11** Mary and Charles have owned a beach cottage on the New Jersey shore for several years and have always used it as a family retreat. When they acquired the property, they had no intentions of renting it. Because family circumstances have changed, they are considering using the cottage for only two weeks a year and renting it for the remainder of the year. Their AGI approximates $80,000 per year, and they are in the 32% tax bracket (combined Federal and state). Interest and real estate taxes total $8,000 per year and are expected to continue at this level in the foreseeable future. If Mary and Charles rent the property, their *incremental* revenue and expenses are projected to be:

Rent income	$ 22,000
Rental commissions	(4,000)
Maintenance expenses	(9,000)
Depreciation expense	(10,000)

If the cottage is converted to rental property, they plan to be actively involved in key rental and maintenance decisions. Given the tax effects of converting the property to rental use, would the cash flow from renting the property be enough to meet the $12,000 annual mortgage payment? Explain.

57. **LO.3, 8** During the current year, Gene, a CPA, performs services as follows: 1,800 hours in his tax practice and 50 hours in an apartment leasing operation in which he has a 15% interest. Because of his oversight duties, Gene is considered to be an active participant. He expects that his share of the loss realized from the apartment leasing operation will be $30,000 and that his tax practice will show a profit of approximately $80,000. Gene is single and has no other income. Discuss the character and treatment of the income and losses generated by these activities.

58. **LO.3, 8** Ida, who has AGI of $80,000 before considering rental activities, is active in three separate real estate rental activities and is in the 28% tax bracket. She has $12,000 of losses from Activity A, $18,000 of losses from Activity B, and income of $10,000 from Activity C. She also has $2,100 of tax credits from Activity A. Calculate the deductions and credits that she is allowed and the suspended losses and credits.

59. **LO.8** Ella has $105,000 of losses from a real estate rental activity in which she actively participates. She has other rental income of $25,000 and other passive activity income of $32,000. Her AGI before considering these items of income and loss is $95,000. How much rental loss can Ella deduct against active and portfolio income (ignoring the at-risk rules)? Does she have any suspended losses to carry over? Explain.

60. **LO.9** At death, Francine owns an interest in a passive activity property (adjusted basis of $160,000, suspended losses of $16,000, and fair market value of $170,000). What is deductible on Francine's final income tax return?

61. **LO.9** In the current year, Abe gives an interest in a passive activity to his daughter, Andrea. The value of the interest at the date of the gift is $25,000, and its adjusted basis to Abe is $13,000. During the time that Abe owned the investment, losses of $3,000 could not be deducted because of the passive activity loss limitations. What is the tax treatment of the suspended passive activity losses to Abe and Andrea?

62. **LO.9** Tonya sells a passive activity in the current year for $150,000. Her adjusted basis in the activity is $50,000, and she uses the installment method of reporting the gain. The activity has suspended losses of $12,000. Tonya receives $60,000 in the year of sale. What is her gain? How much of the suspended losses can she deduct?

63. **LO.10, 11** In 2017, Kathleen Tweardy incurs $30,000 of interest expense related to her investments. Her investment income includes $7,500 of interest, $6,000 of qualified dividends, and a $12,000 net capital gain on the sale of securities. Kathleen asks you to compute the amount of her deduction for investment interest, taking into consideration any options she might have. In addition, she wants your

Decision Making

Communications

suggestions as to any tax planning alternatives that are available. Write a letter to her that contains your advice. Kathleen lives at 11934 Briarpatch Drive, Midlothian, VA 23113.

64. **LO.10** Helen Derby borrowed $150,000 to acquire a parcel of land to be held for investment purposes. During the current year, she reported AGI of $90,000 and paid interest of $12,000 on the loan. Other items related to Helen's investments include the following:

Interest and annuity income	$11,000
Long-term capital gain on sale of stock	3,500
Real estate tax on the investment land	800

a. Determine Helen's investment interest deduction for the current year.

b. Discuss the treatment of the portion of Helen's investment interest that is disallowed for the current year.

c. Complete Helen's Form 4952 for the current year. For this purpose, assume that she chooses not to include the long-term capital gain as investment income. Her Social Security number is 123-45-6789.

Research Problems

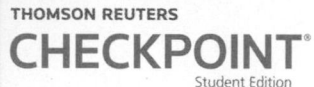

Note: Solutions to the Research Problems can be prepared by using the Thomson Reuters Checkpoint® Student Edition online tax research database, which accompanies this textbook. Solutions can also be prepared by using research materials found in a typical tax library.

Research Problem 1. Carol is a successful physician who owns 100% of her incorporated medical practice. She and her husband, Dick, are considering the purchase of a commercial office building located near the local community hospital. If they purchase the building, Carol will move her medical practice to the new location and rent space for an arm's length price. The rent income Carol and Dick receive will be available to absorb passive activity losses generated by other passive activities they own. The net effect of this arrangement is a reduction in their income tax liability. Will Carol and Dick's plan work? Why or why not?

Research Problem 2. Five years ago Bridget decided to purchase a limited partnership interest in a fast-food restaurant conveniently located near the campus of Southeast State University. The general partner of the restaurant venture promised her that the investment would prove to be a winner. During the process of capitalizing the business, $2 million was borrowed from Northside Bank; however, each of the partners was required to pledge personal assets as collateral to satisfy the bank loan in the event that the restaurant defaulted. Bridget pledged shares of publicly traded stock (worth $200,000, basis of $75,000) to satisfy the bank's requirement.

The restaurant did a good business until just recently, when flagrant health code violations were discovered and widely publicized by the media. As a result, business has declined to a point where the restaurant's continued existence is doubtful. In addition, the $2 million loan is now due for payment. Because the restaurant cannot pay, the bank has called for the collateral provided by the partners to be used to satisfy the debt. Bridget sells the pledged stock for $200,000 and forwards the proceeds to the bank. Bridget believes that her share of the restaurant's current and suspended passive activity losses can offset the $125,000 gain from the stock sale. As a result, after netting the passive activity losses against the gain, none of the gain is subject to tax.

How do you react to Bridget's position?

Research Problem 3. Ida Ross has decided to purchase a new home in a retirement community for $400,000. She has $50,000 in cash for the down payment but needs to borrow the remaining $350,000 to finance the purchase. Her financial adviser, Marc, suggests that rather than seeking a conventional mortgage, she should borrow the funds from State Bank using her portfolio of appreciated securities as collateral. Selling the securities to generate $350,000 in cash would lead to a substantial tax on the capital gain recognized. As a result, a better strategy would be to borrow against her securities and then claim a deduction for the interest paid on the loan. How do you react to the financial adviser's strategy?

Partial list of research aids:
Temp.Reg. § 1.163–8T(c).

Use internet tax resources to address the following questions. Look for reliable websites and blogs of the IRS and other government agencies, media outlets, businesses, tax professionals, academics, think tanks, and political outlets.

Research Problem 4. Investment advisers and tax professionals are continuously striving to create sophisticated transactions and investment vehicles (i.e., tax-advantaged investments) that are designed to provide economic benefits to investors by reducing their taxes. These professionals might like to patent such schemes. Identify whether patenting a tax strategy is a legal possibility.

Research Problem 5. Scan the materials offered in several newsgroups frequented by tax advisers and consultants. In what context are "tax shelters" discussed by these professionals? Do these advisers and consultants adequately take into account the rules of §§ 465 and 469?

Research Problem 6. Oil and gas ventures operating as publicly traded partnerships typically attract sophisticated investors who purchase limited partnership interests. Investments in these types of publicly traded partnerships are subject to a restrictive set of passive activity loss rules. Identify three publicly traded oil and gas partnerships that are currently marketed to investors, describe the benefits the promoters claim will result from such investments, and briefly review the basic nature of the unique passive activity loss restrictions placed on such investments.

Roger CPA Review Questions

1. Lee, a married individual, is an employee with three rental properties in which Lee does not actively participate. In 2016, Property 1 had a net loss of $10,000, Property 2 had a net gain of $25,000, and Property 3 had a net loss of $5,000. Lee's W–2 income in 2016 was $110,000. Considering only the foregoing facts, what is Lee's 2016 adjusted gross income?

   a. $120,000   c. $110,000
   b. $125,000   d. $135,000

2. Anscomb is an employee who also solely owns and actively participates in a rental activity which produced a $20,000 loss in the current year. Anscomb's W–2 income in the current year is $115,000. Considering only the foregoing facts, what should Anscomb's adjusted gross income be for the current year?

   a. $97,500   c. $107,500
   b. $115,000   d. $102,500

3. Lewis is not an active participant in three rental activities, which have turned profits in recent years. The following gain and losses apply to the current year for Lewis:

	Gain or (Loss)
Rental Activity 1	($10,000)
Rental Activity 2	12,000
Rental Activity 3	(8,000)
Total	($ 6,000)

What amount of the suspended loss should Lewis allocate to Rental Activity 3?

   a. $4,500

   b. $2,667

   c. $0

   d. Suspended losses may be allocated according to the taxpayer's preference

4. Smith bought a rental property in year 1 for $100,000. In year 1, Smith's adjusted gross income (AGI) was $125,000 and Smith sustained a $30,000 loss on the property. In year 2, Smith's AGI was $175,000 and Smith sustained a $20,000 loss on the property. In year 3, Smith sold the property for $155,000. What amount of gain or loss must Smith report on Smith's year 3 tax return as a result of the sale? Assume Smith actively participated in the rental activity in all three years, but is not considered a real estate professional for tax purposes.

   a. $17,500 gain   c. $22,500 gain

   b. $0 (no gain or loss)   d. $20,000 gain

5. Patel bought a rental property in year 1 for $150,000. In year 1, Patel's adjusted gross income (AGI) was $100,000 and Patel sustained a $15,000 loss on the property. In year 2, Patel's AGI was $140,000 and Patel sustained a $10,000 loss on the property. In year 3, Patel sold the property for $175,000. What amount of gain or loss must Patel report on Patel's year 3 tax return as a result of the sale? Assume Patel did not actively participate in the rental activity in any of the three years.

   a. $25,000   c. $5,000

   b. $0 (no income or loss)   d. $20,000

6. The following chart applies to Bettelli, an investor who owns two rental activities, Property A and Property B, and has no other involvement in passive activities:

	Property	Income (Loss)
Year 1	A	($12,000)
	B	5,000
Year 2	A	(6,000)
	B	1,000

Bettelli met the requirements for active participation in year 1 but not in year 2. Bettelli's AGI in year 1 was $140,000; in year 2, $180,000. In year 3, Bettelli sells Property A for a $15,000 gain. How much of the gain must Bettelli report on Bettelli's year 3 tax return?

   a. $0   c. $8,000

   b. $3,000   d. $13,000

7. Albert, Berry, and Collins formed ABC Partnership in the current year. Collins, a limited partner, contributed $20,000 in cash to the partnership and also pledged $10,000 of personal property as collateral to meet any partnership debts that may arise. Collins's share of the current ABC Partnership loss is $50,000. How much of the loss is deductible by Collins under the at-risk rules?

   a. $0   c. $20,000

   b. $10,000   d. $30,000

PART 4

SPECIAL TAX COMPUTATION METHODS, PAYMENT PROCEDURES, AND TAX CREDITS

CHAPTER **12**

Alternative Minimum Tax

CHAPTER **13**

Tax Credits and Payment Procedures

Part 4 presents several topics that relate to the theme of tax liability determination. The taxpayer must calculate the tax liability first using the basic tax formula, and then using the alternative minimum tax (AMT) formula. The basic tax formula was presented in Part 1, and the AMT formula is covered here. A wide variety of tax credits can be used to reduce the tax liability. However, these credits are not always available and are subject to various limitations. As part of arriving at overall tax liability, payroll taxes (including the self-employment tax) must be taken into account. Taxes (and penalties) imposed by the Affordable Care Act are also covered. Part 4 concludes with a discussion of the specific procedures related to payment of the tax liability.

CHAPTER

12

Alternative Minimum Tax

LEARNING OBJECTIVES: *After completing Chapter 12, you should be able to:*

LO.1 Explain the rationale for the alternative minimum tax (AMT).

LO.2 Present and explain the formula for computing the AMT for individuals.

LO.3 Identify the adjustments made in calculating AMTI.

LO.4 Identify the preferences that are included in calculating AMTI.

LO.5 Compute the AMT and complete Form 6251.

LO.6 Describe and illustrate the role of the AMT credit in the alternative minimum tax structure.

LO.7 Compare the individual AMT calculation with the corporate AMT calculation.

LO.8 Identify and apply tax planning opportunities to minimize the AMT.

CHAPTER OUTLINE

WAVEBREAKMEDIA/SHUTTERSTOCK.COM

THE PRESENCE OR ABSENCE OF THE AMT

Bob and Carol are unmarried individuals who have been engaged for four months. They work for the same employer and earn identical compensation. They have the same amount of gross income, including the same amount of investment income, which consists solely of interest income; they have similar investments in tax-exempt bonds that produce identical amounts of interest income. They also have the same amount of deductions.

Bob's tax return is prepared by Adam, and Carol's tax return is prepared by Ava. While discussing their tax liability one day at lunch, Carol is dismayed to learn that she paid $15,000 more in Federal income taxes than Bob did for the tax year. Carol meets with Ava that evening. Ava reviews Carol's tax return and assures her that her tax liability was properly calculated.

The above events raise a number of interesting questions for Bob and Carol that can be answered after completing this chapter. Why didn't Bob and Carol have the same tax liability? Were both tax returns properly prepared? Should Carol consider replacing her tax return preparer Ava with Adam? Is it possible and/or desirable for Carol to file an amended return? Should Bob do anything?

Read the chapter and formulate your response.

FRAMEWORK 1040   Tax Formula for Individuals

This chapter covers the boldfaced portions of the Tax Formula for Individuals that was introduced in Concept Summary 3.1 on p. 3-3. Below those portions are the sections of Form 1040 where the results are reported.

Income *(broadly defined)*	$xx,xxx
Less: Exclusions	(x,xxx)
Gross income	$xx,xxx
Less: Deductions *for* **adjusted gross income**	(x,xxx)
Adjusted gross income	$xx,xxx
Less: The greater of total **itemized deductions** *or* the standard deduction	(x,xxx)
Personal and dependency exemptions	(x,xxx)
Taxable income	$xx,xxx
Tax on taxable income *(see Tax Tables or Tax Rate Schedules)*	$ x,xxx
Less: Tax credits *(including income taxes withheld and prepaid)*	(xxx)
Tax due (or refund)	$ xxx

FORM 1040 (p. 2)

45	**Alternative minimum tax** (see instructions). Attach Form 6251	

LO.1

Explain the rationale for the alternative minimum tax (AMT).

The tax law contains many incentives that are intended to influence the economic and social behavior of taxpayers (refer to Chapter 1). Some taxpayers were able to take advantage of enough of these incentives to significantly minimize or entirely avoid any Federal income tax liability. Although these taxpayers were legally minimizing their tax liabilities, Congress became concerned about the inequity that results when taxpayers with substantial economic incomes can avoid paying income tax.[1] To attempt to alleviate this inequity, the **alternative minimum tax (AMT)** was enacted. The goal of the AMT is to ensure that all taxpayers with more than modest economic incomes pay some minimum amount of tax. In the recent past, approximately 4 million individual taxpayers indicated a positive AMT liability on their Form 1040, raising more than $25 billion in revenues for the U.S. Treasury annually.

The AMT applies to individuals, as well as C corporations, trusts, and estates. While the calculations involved are similar for all taxpayers subject to the AMT, some portions of the AMT formula are unique to specific entities.

The first part of this chapter presents a discussion of the individual AMT; the corporate AMT is discussed in the second part of the chapter. The AMT provisions for trusts and estates are not addressed in this chapter.

LO.2

Present and explain the formula for computing the AMT for individuals.

12-1 INDIVIDUAL ALTERNATIVE MINIMUM TAX

In theory, all individual taxpayers subject to the Federal income tax are subject to AMT. As will be seen in this chapter, whether a taxpayer has an AMT liability depends on a number of factors, including the taxpayer's income, geographic location, and family situation as well as the exclusions, deductions, and credits utilized in the calculation of their regular Federal income tax liability.

---

[1]Joint Committee on Taxation, *General Explanation of the Tax Reform Act of 1986 ("Blue Book")*, (JCS-10-87) May 4, 1987, pp. 432–433.

12-1a **Alternative Minimum Taxable Income (AMTI)**

The tax base used to determine AMT liability is referred to as the alternative minimum taxable income (AMTI) amount (Exhibit 12.1). The calculation of AMTI does not follow the direct approach taken in the calculation of the taxpayer's regular taxable income.[2] Rather than having taxpayers recalculate the components of the individual income tax formula using a different set of AMT rules, the calculation of AMTI *begins* with regular taxable income as shown in Exhibit 12.1. In other words, the AMT calculation requires a taxpayer to reconcile taxable income to AMTI, thus taking an indirect approach to the calculation.

Part of the reason for this indirect approach may be that many items of income and expense are treated the same way for both regular income tax and AMT purposes. For example, a taxpayer's salary is included in computing taxable income and is also included in AMTI. Alimony paid and certain itemized deductions, such as charitable contributions and gambling losses, also are allowed for both regular income tax and AMT purposes.

While many amounts are left unchanged, the tax law provides that certain income and expense items are treated differently for regular income tax and AMT purposes. In some cases, the income or expense amount is reconsidered in aggregate. For example, interest income on bonds issued by state, county, and local governments is excluded in computing taxable income. However, if such bonds are private activity bonds, the interest income earned is included in AMTI.

In other cases, the income or expense amount is included in both the regular income tax and AMT computations, but the amount differs. For example, the completed contract method can be used to report income from some long-term contracts for regular income tax purposes, but the percentage of completion method is required for AMT purposes. Thus, in the tax year, the amount of income from the contract included in taxable income will differ from the amount included in AMTI. Similarly, housing interest is deductible in calculating both taxable income and AMTI, but the deductible amount for AMT may be limited if the proceeds of the loan were not used to acquire or improve the taxpayer's residence.[3]

As shown in Exhibit 12.1, differences between regular tax and AMT income and expense amounts are categorized as either adjustments or preferences. Most adjustments relate to timing differences that arise because of different regular income tax and AMT treatments. Adjustments that are caused by timing differences will eventually reverse; positive adjustments will be offset by negative adjustments in the future and vice versa.[4]

EXHIBIT 12.1	Alternative Minimum Tax Formula for Individuals

Taxable income (increased by any standard deduction and personal or dependency exemptions)

Plus or minus: Adjustments

Plus: Preferences

Equals: Alternative minimum taxable income (AMTI)

Minus: Exemption

Equals: Alternative minimum tax (AMT) base

Multiplied by: 26% or 28% rate

Equals: Tentative minimum tax before foreign tax credit

Minus: AMT foreign tax credit

Equals: Tentative minimum tax (TMT)

Minus: Regular tax liability (less any foreign tax credit)

Equals: AMT (if TMT > regular tax liability)

---

[2] A "direct approach" means that in calculating regular taxable income, a gross income amount is reduced by deductions to arrive at the taxable income amount.

[3] § 56(b)(1)(C).

[4] § 56.

Depreciation provides a good example of a timing difference. In general, AMT depreciation methods are slower than regular tax depreciation methods. Initially then, there will be less depreciation for AMT purposes than for regular tax purposes. This difference will result in positive timing differences until AMT depreciation is larger than regular tax depreciation, when the timing difference will become negative. However, over time, the same amount of depreciation will be deducted for regular tax and AMT purposes because the basis for regular tax and AMT depreciation is the same.

In contrast, in the reconciliation of taxable income to AMTI, preference items will always serve to increase the starting point of the AMTI calculation.[5] Certain deductions and exclusions allowed to taxpayers for regular income tax purposes provide significant tax savings. AMT preferences are designed to take back all or part of the tax benefit derived as a result of the use of these deductions and exclusions. This is why preference items serve only to increase the taxable income amount that is the starting point of the AMTI calculation. The effect of adding back these preference items is to disallow them for AMT purposes. Examples of preferences include percentage depletion in excess of the property's adjusted basis and excess intangible drilling costs. Both adjustments and preferences are discussed in more detail later in the chapter.

ETHICS & EQUITY   Accelerating Expenses in an AMT Year

Kirby and Alex are married, and they reside in California. Together, they earn $145,000 from their work (Kirby as an engineer and Alex as a school principal). In 2017, they expect to be in AMT as a result of a substantial ($250,000) long-term capital gain they realized on the sale of a rental property on the California coastline.

In the past, Kirby and Alex have prepaid their state income taxes, so as to increase their itemized deductions. In other words, the couple pays the fourth-quarter state income tax installment in the current year, rather than waiting to pay the last installment until the following year's January due date. In addition to quarterly state income tax payments of $7,000, they also have a $46,000 itemized deduction for mortgage interest.

Because the couple will be subject to the AMT this year, their tax adviser has suggested that they not prepay their last quarterly state income tax installment in 2016. Their adviser reminds them that because the AMT does not provide for a beneficial capital gains tax rate, they will gain more of a tax benefit by waiting to pay their fourth-quarter installment in 2017 and prepaying their 2017 state income tax liability. In 2017, the couple will not be subject to the AMT, and as a result, they will benefit from the additional tax deductions.

The couple's 2016 and 2017 tax liability under the two scenarios is shown in the table below. Kirby and Alex would save $1,050 in Federal income taxes by not prepaying their state income taxes in 2016.

Is it appropriate for Kirby and Alex to minimize their tax liability in this way? Is it wise?

	Scenario 1 Prepayment of State Tax		Scenario 2 No State Tax Prepayment	
	2016	**2017**	**2016**	**2017**
Taxable income	$312,900	$62,900	$319,900	$55,900
Regular tax liability	44,208	8,503	46,308	7,453
TMT	83,781	3,770	83,781	3,770
AMT	39,573	–0–	37,473	–0–
Total tax	83,781	8,503	83,781	7,453
Two-year tax total	92,284		91,234	

---

[5]§ 57.

12-1b **AMT Formula: Other Components**

Calculating AMTI is the first step in the determination of whether a taxpayer will have an alternative minimum tax liability. To complete the AMT calculation, as shown in Exhibit 12.1, the exemption, rates, credit, and regular tax liability must all be considered.

Exemption Amount

After calculating AMTI, the taxpayer determines the AMT exemption amount. Tax law provides for exemption amounts in both the regular tax and AMT liability calculations. The exemption amounts for AMT are higher than the exemption amounts for regular tax liability purposes. The AMT exemption amount can be thought of as a materiality provision. Taxpayers with few or minimal positive adjustments and preferences will avoid being subject to the AMT as a result of the exemption.

The initial exemption amounts for 2017 are listed as follows.[6] The annual exemption is phased out at a rate of 25 cents on the dollar when AMTI exceeds certain amounts (see Example 1). These amounts are tied to the taxpayer's filing status. The exemption phaseout is an application of the wherewithal to pay concept. Congress believes that as a taxpayer's AMTI increases, so does the taxpayer's ability to pay income taxes.

		Phaseout	
Status	Exemption	Begins at	Ends at
Married, joint	$84,500	$160,900	$498,900
Single or head of household	54,300	120,700	337,900
Married, separate	42,250	80,450	249,450

Once AMTI equals the end of the phaseout range, a taxpayer's exemption amount will equal zero. Example 1 explains the calculation of the phaseout of the AMT exemption.

Harry, who is single, records AMTI of $192,500 for the year. His $54,300 initial exemption amount is reduced by $17,950 [($192,500 − $120,700) × 25% phaseout rate]. Harry's AMT exemption is $36,350 ($54,300 exemption − $17,950 reduction).

EXAMPLE 1

AMT Liability

After the exemption is calculated, a taxpayer's AMT liability can be determined. As shown in Exhibit 12.1, AMTI less the exemption equals the AMT tax base; then the tax is computed and credits are allowed, resulting in the tentative minimum tax (TMT).

The relationship between the regular tax liability and the TMT is key to the AMT calculation. If the regular tax liability exceeds the TMT, the taxpayer's AMT liability is zero. However, if the TMT exceeds the regular tax liability, the excess is the taxpayer's AMT liability. Technically, the AMT is a surtax; both tax law and the Form 6251 categorize any excess of TMT over the taxpayer's regular tax liability as the AMT amount.[7] For practical purposes, the taxpayer pays whichever tax liability is greater—that calculated using the regular income tax rules or that calculated using the AMT rules.

A graduated, two-tier AMT rate schedule applies to noncorporate taxpayers. A 26 percent rate applies on an AMT base up to $187,800 ($93,900 for married, filing separately), and a 28 percent rate applies to that base amount and above.[8] Any net capital gain or qualified dividend income included in the AMT base is taxed at the favorable tax rates for capital gains (0, 15, or 20 percent) rather than at the AMT statutory rates. See the discussion of the tax treatment of capital gains in text Section 16-5.

---

[6]The exemption amounts are indexed annually for inflation. § 55(d)(4)(A).

[7]§ 55(a).

[8]§§ 55(b)(1)(A) and (d)(4)(B).

EXAMPLE 2

Anna, an unmarried individual, has regular taxable income of $95,950. Anna itemizes deductions; she has positive adjustments of $40,000 and preferences of $25,000. Anna's regular tax liability for 2017 is $19,848. Her AMT in 2017 is calculated as follows.

Taxable income (prior to the personal exemption)	$100,000
Plus: Adjustments	40,000
Plus: Preferences	25,000
Equals: AMTI	$165,000
Minus: AMT exemption ($54,300 − $11,075)	43,225
Equals: AMT base	$121,775
Times: AMT rate of 26%	× .26
Equals: TMT	$ 31,662
Minus: Regular tax liability	19,848
Equals: AMT	$ 11,814

Anna will pay the IRS a total of $31,662, consisting of her regular tax liability of $19,848 plus her AMT of $11,814.

Credits against regular tax liability (see Chapter 13) are allowed to some taxpayers depending on their economic circumstances or the type of business activity in which they engage. Personal nonrefundable credits (e.g., Adoption Credit, Lifetime Learning Credit, and Saver's Credit) can offset any AMT liability as well as any regular tax liability.[9]

EXAMPLE 3

Michael has total personal nonrefundable credits of $11,000, regular tax liability of $33,000, and tentative minimum tax of $26,000. The entire $11,000 credit is available to offset Michael's $33,000 tax liability.

LO.3

Identify the adjustments made in calculating AMTI.

12-1c AMT Adjustments

As discussed previously, **adjustments** relate to timing differences that arise because of differences in how an item is treated for regular income tax and AMT purposes. As a result, it is necessary to determine not only what the amount of an adjustment is but also whether the adjustment is positive or negative.

Remember that the AMTI calculation begins with the regular taxable income amount before any standard deduction or personal exemptions taken by the taxpayer. Where the regular tax and AMT treatment of an item of expense (or deduction) differ, the direction of the adjustment is determined as follows.

Conversely, the direction of an adjustment attributable to a revenue (or income) item can be determined as follows.

The remainder of this section discusses specific AMT adjustments.

Depreciation of Post-1986 Real Property

As discussed in text Section 8-2b, for regular income tax purposes, real property is depreciated using the straight-line method. The cost of residential real property is recovered over 27.5 years, and the cost of all other real property is recovered over 39 years.[10] Whether an AMT adjustment is required for real property depreciation depends on when the property was placed in service.

For real property placed in service after 1986 (MACRS property) and before 1999, AMT depreciation is computed using the straight-line method, but the alternative depreciation system (ADS) recovery period of 40 years is used (see Exhibit 8.9 in Chapter 8). Any difference in regular tax and AMT depreciation amounts results in an AMT adjustment. Note that these adjustments will be positive during the real property's regular income tax recovery period, because the cost is written off over a shorter period for regular income tax purposes. These adjustments will become negative once the asset is fully depreciated for regular tax purposes, as additional depreciation is allowed for AMT purposes.

For real property placed in service after 1998, no AMT adjustment is required.[11] After 1998, real property depreciation is the same for both AMT and regular tax purposes. In other words, because straight-line depreciation and the same recovery period (see Exhibit 8.8 in Chapter 8) are used for both regular tax and AMT purposes, no AMT adjustment is necessary.

Depreciation of Post-1986 Personal Property

For most personal property that is MACRS property, the depreciation deduction for regular income tax purposes is calculated using the 200 percent declining-balance method with a switch to straight-line depreciation when that method produces a larger depreciation deduction. The MACRS recovery period is the general depreciation system (GDS) prescribed recovery period (see Exhibit 8.3 in Chapter 8). Similar to the real property provisions, for AMT purposes, the depreciation calculation and the resulting adjustment depend on when the property was placed in service.

For property placed in service after 1986 and before 1999, the taxpayer calculates depreciation for AMT using the 150 percent declining-balance method with a similar switch to straight-line depreciation. In addition, the recovery period is the ADS prescribed recovery period rather than the GDS recovery period.[12] (See Exhibit 8.6 in Chapter 8.) Thus, for property placed in service prior to 1999, the difference between regular income tax depreciation and AMT depreciation is caused by both longer recovery periods (GDS versus ADS) and a larger declining-balance accelerated depreciation percentage (200 percent versus 150 percent).

For property placed in service after 1998, the taxpayer continues to calculate AMT depreciation using the 150 percent declining-balance method with the switch to straight-line depreciation. However, the recovery period is the GDS recovery period for both AMT and regular tax purposes.[13] (See Exhibit 8.6 in Chapter 8.) Thus, for personal property placed in service after 1998, the difference between regular income tax depreciation and AMT depreciation is caused only by a larger accelerated depreciation percentage (200 percent versus 150 percent). Example 4 illustrates the adjustments required where a three-year asset is depreciated.

EXAMPLE

4

Sawyer placed an $8,000 breeding hog, a prime breeder sow, in service in year 1. The MACRS recovery period for breeding hogs is three years. Regular tax (using 200% declining balance) and AMT depreciation (using 150% declining balance) amounts over the recovery period of the asset are as follows.

Tax Year	Regular Income Tax Deduction	AMT Deduction	AMT Adjustment
1	$2,666	$2,000	$666
2	3,556	3,000	556
3	1,185	2,000	(815)
4	593	1,000	(407)

---

[10]The 39-year life generally applies to nonresidential real property placed in service on or after May 13, 1993.

[11]§ 56(a)(1)(A).

[12]§ 56(a)(1)(A)(i).

[13]§ 56(a)(1)(A)(ii).

As is shown in Example 4, the same conventions are used for regular tax and AMT depreciation. Thus, the asset is fully depreciated over four years for both regular tax and AMT purposes, because the same recovery period is used and the half-year convention applies for both calculations. The AMT depreciation deduction is initially smaller because of the lesser declining balance percentage used for AMT purposes. As a result, the adjustments in year 1 and year 2 are positive; taxable income is increased by these amounts to arrive at the AMT depreciation amount. In the last two years of the asset's life, the AMT adjustments are negative. Taxable income will be decreased by these amounts to arrive at the AMT depreciation amount. In total, the same amount of depreciation is taken for both regular tax and AMT purposes.

All personal property is taken into consideration in computing one net AMT depreciation adjustment, regardless of the date placed in service. Using this netting process, the AMT adjustment for a tax year is the difference between the total regular tax depreciation for all personal property and the total depreciation computed for that property for AMT purposes. The same principles that apply in Example 4 apply in aggregate.

Finally, a taxpayer may elect to use the AMT depreciation method for personal property for regular income tax purposes. If this election is made, no AMT adjustment is required because the depreciation deduction is the same for regular income tax and for the AMT. This election eliminates the necessity to maintain two sets of tax depreciation records.

Additional First-Year Depreciation

As discussed in text Section 8-3a, for regular tax purposes, an additional first-year depreciation deduction equal to 50 percent of the unadjusted depreciable basis of qualified property is available for property placed in service after 2011 and before 2018. For property to which this additional first-year depreciation deduction (also known as bonus depreciation) is elected, no depreciation adjustment for AMT purposes is required.[14] This is true both in the year the asset is placed in service and in all succeeding years in which the asset is depreciated.

Pollution Control Facilities

To encourage private industry to abate pollution, tax law provides beneficial amortization provisions for certified pollution control facilities in lieu of depreciation. For regular income tax purposes, a taxpayer may elect to amortize the cost of certified facilities over 60 months. For AMT purposes, such an election is not allowed. Instead, the cost of certified pollution control facilities is recovered through depreciation. Similar to the depreciation provisions discussed previously, the method is dictated by when the facility was placed in service.

Facilities placed in service after 1986 and before 1999 are depreciated using the alternative depreciation system (ADS) method. Thus, costs are recovered using the straight-line method over 40 years if the property is real property or over the class life if the property is personal property.[15] For facilities placed in service after 1998, depreciation for AMT purposes is calculated using the straight-line method over the recovery period that would be used for regular tax (MACRS) purposes. Irrespective of when the property was placed in service, the adjustment for AMTI is equal to the difference between the regular tax amortization deduction and the AMT depreciation amount. The adjustment may be positive or negative.

Circulation Expenditures

Circulation expenditures are expenses incurred to establish, maintain, or increase the circulation of a newspaper, a magazine, or another periodical. For regular income tax purposes, circulation expenditures, other than those the taxpayer elects to charge to a capital account, may be expensed in the year incurred.[16] For AMT purposes, circulation

---

[14]§ 168(k).
[15]§ 56(a)(5).

[16]§ 173(a).

expenditures are not deductible in the year incurred. In computing AMTI, these expenditures must be capitalized and amortized ratably over the three-year period beginning in the year the expenditures were made.[17]

The AMT adjustment for circulation expenditures is calculated by comparing the amount expensed for regular income tax purposes with the amount that can be amortized for AMT purposes. In general, in the year the circulation expenditures are incurred, the adjustment will be positive; more circulation expenditures are deducted for regular tax purposes than are allowed for AMT purposes. In the second and third years, the adjustment will be negative; a deduction is allowed for AMT purposes that was taken in the first year for regular tax purposes.

> **EXAMPLE 5**
>
> In year 1, Lindsay's sole proprietorship incurred $30,000 of circulation expenditures. These expenditures were deducted in full for regular tax purposes but amortized over three years for AMT purposes. Thus, in year 2, Lindsay will not have a regular tax deduction for circulation expenditures, but will be allowed to deduct $10,000 of circulation expenditures for AMT purposes. As a result, a negative AMT adjustment is required in year 2.
>
> | | | |
> |---|---:|---:|
> | Year 2 taxable income (prior to standard deduction and personal exemption) | | $ 95,000 |
> | Plus or minus: AMT adjustments | | |
> | Circulation expenditures deducted for regular income tax purposes | $ –0– | |
> | Circulation expenditures allowed for AMT purposes | (10,000) | |
> | Negative adjustment | | (10,000) |
> | Plus: AMT preferences | | –0– |
> | AMTI | | $ 85,000 |

In Example 5, the allowable AMT deduction is $10,000 more than the allowable regular income tax deduction. Therefore, AMTI is $10,000 less than taxable income. This result is obtained by making a negative AMT adjustment of $10,000.

A taxpayer can avoid an AMT adjustment for circulation expenditures by electing to write off the expenditures over a three-year period for regular income tax purposes.[18]

Expenditures Requiring 10-Year Write-Off for AMT Purposes

Certain expenditures that may be deducted in the year incurred for regular income tax purposes must be written off over a 10-year period for AMT purposes. These rules apply to (1) mine exploration and development costs and (2) research and experimental expenditures.

In computing taxable income, taxpayers are allowed to deduct expenditures paid or incurred during the taxable year for exploration (ascertaining the existence, location, extent, or quality of a deposit or mineral) and for development of a mine or other natural deposit, other than an oil or gas well.[19] Mine development expenditures are expenses paid or incurred after the existence of ores and minerals in commercially marketable quantities has been discovered.

For AMT purposes, however, mine exploration and development costs must be capitalized and amortized ratably over a 10-year period.[20] Although circulation expenditures are recoverable over a three-year period for AMT purposes, the calculation of the adjustment for mine exploration and development costs is similar in spirit to that for circulation expenditures. The AMT adjustment is calculated by comparing the amount of mine exploration and development costs expensed (if any) for regular tax purposes with the amount amortized for AMT purposes. In general, the adjustment will be positive in the year these expenses are incurred and negative thereafter.

---

[17]§ 56(b)(2)(A)(i).

[18]§ 59(e)(2)(A).

[19]§§ 617(a) and 616(a).

[20]§ 56(a)(2).

EXAMPLE 6

This year, Audrey incurs $150,000 of mine exploration expenditures and deducts this amount for regular income tax purposes. For AMT purposes, these mine exploration expenditures must be amortized over a 10-year period. Audrey makes a positive adjustment for AMTI of $135,000 ($150,000 allowed for regular income tax − $15,000 for AMT) for this year (i.e., the year in which the expenses were incurred). For AMT purposes, in each of the next nine years, Audrey makes a negative adjustment of $15,000 ($0 allowed for regular income tax − $15,000 for AMT).

To avoid the AMT adjustments for mine exploration and development costs, a taxpayer may elect to write off the expenditures over a 10-year period for regular income tax purposes.[21]

Similarly, for regular tax purposes, rather than capitalize the costs of research and experimentation, a taxpayer can choose to deduct those costs in the year incurred. For AMT purposes, such costs must be amortized over a 10-year period. As a result, the calculation of the adjustment for research and experimental expenditures is similar to the mine development and exploration costs adjustment and similar in spirit to the adjustment for circulation expenditures.

Completed Contract Method of Accounting

For a long-term contract, taxpayers are required to use the percentage of completion method for AMT purposes.[22] However, in limited circumstances, taxpayers can use the completed contract method for regular income tax purposes.[23] Thus, where the percentage of completion method is not used for regular tax purposes, a taxpayer recognizes a different amount of income for regular income tax purposes than for AMT purposes. The resulting AMT adjustment is equal to the difference between income reported under the percentage of completion method and the amount reported using the completed contract method. The adjustment can be either positive or negative, depending on the amount of income recognized under the different methods.

Similar to many of the other adjustments discussed previously, a taxpayer can avoid an AMT adjustment on long-term contracts by using the percentage of completion method for regular income tax purposes rather than the completed contract method.

Incentive Stock Options

Like other compensatory options, **incentive stock options (ISOs)** are granted by employers to motivate employees to work harder to increase the value of the company. In return, employees should benefit from the increased compensation that a higher stock price brings.

At the time an ISO is granted, the option typically has a zero value. As a result, no gross income is recognized at the date of grant for regular tax purposes, and no adjustment is required for AMT purposes. If the value of the stock increases during the option period, the employee can obtain shares at a favorable price by exercising the option. For regular tax purposes, the exercise of an ISO does not increase taxable income.[24] However, for AMT purposes, the excess of the fair market value of the stock over the exercise price (the *spread* or the *bargain element*) is treated as an adjustment in the taxable year in which the option is exercised.[25]

EXAMPLE 7

In January 2017, Manuel exercised an ISO that had been granted by his employer, Gold Corporation, in March 2013. Manuel acquired 1,000 shares of Gold stock for the exercise price of $20 per share. The fair market value of the stock at the date of exercise was $50 per share. The transaction does not affect regular taxable income in either 2013 or 2017. For AMT purposes, Manuel records a positive adjustment of $30,000 ($50,000 fair market value − $20,000 exercise price) for 2017.

---

[21]§§ 59(e)(2)(D) and (E).

[22]§ 56(a)(3).

[23]See text Section 18-3e for a detailed discussion of the completed contract and percentage of completion methods of accounting.

[24]§ 421(a).

[25]§ 56(b)(3).

As a result of this adjustment, the regular income tax basis of the stock acquired through the exercise of ISOs is different from the AMT basis. The regular income tax basis of the stock is equal to its cost, the exercise price of the option, whereas the AMT basis is equal to the fair market value of the stock on the date the option is exercised. Consequently, the amount of any gain or loss upon disposition of the stock will likely differ for regular income tax and AMT purposes.

Assume the same facts as in the previous example, and assume that Manuel sells the stock acquired with the option for $60,000 in December 2018. His gain for regular income tax purposes is $40,000 ($60,000 amount realized − $20,000 regular income tax basis). For AMT purposes, the gain is $10,000 ($60,000 amount realized − $50,000 AMT basis). Therefore, Manuel will make a negative $30,000 adjustment in computing AMT in 2018. Because the gain on sale was larger for regular tax purposes, the gain reflected in taxable income is decreased by $30,000 ($40,000 regular income tax gain − $10,000 AMT gain) to reflect the $10,000 AMT gain. Note that this $30,000 negative adjustment upon disposition in 2018 offsets the $30,000 positive adjustment made in the year of exercise.

An employee may be restricted as to when he or she can dispose of stock acquired with an ISO. In other words, the stock acquired with the option may not be freely transferable until some specified period has passed (see text Section 19-6a for further discussion of ISOs). If there were some restriction, then the employee would not make the AMT adjustment until the stock was freely transferable.

In January 2016, Manuel exercised an ISO that had been granted by his employer, Gold Corporation, in March 2013. Manuel acquired 1,000 shares of Gold stock for the exercise price of $20 per share, when the fair market value of the stock was $50 per share. The stock became freely transferable in February 2017, when the fair market value was $55 per share. For AMT purposes, Manuel will make a positive adjustment of $30,000 ($50,000 fair market value − $20,000 exercise price) in 2017. The option contract does not affect regular taxable income in any tax year.

Finally, if the taxpayer exercises the ISO and disposes of the stock in the same tax year, otherwise known as a disqualifying disposition, compensation income is reported for regular tax purposes, which means that an AMT adjustment is not required for that option exercise.

Adjusted Gain or Loss

When property is sold or disposed of during the year, gain or loss reported for regular income tax may differ from gain or loss determined for AMT purposes. This difference occurs because the adjusted basis of the property for AMT purposes must reflect any current and prior AMT adjustments for the following.[26]

- Depreciation.
- Circulation expenditures.
- Research and experimental expenditures.
- Mine exploration and development costs.
- Certified pollution control facility amortization.

Remember that the AMT calculation begins with regular taxable income. Thus, any gain or loss adjustment should reflect the difference between the regular tax and AMT gain or loss amount. A negative gain or loss adjustment is required if:

- Any gain for AMT purposes is less than the gain for regular income tax purposes,
- Any loss for AMT purposes is more than the loss for regular income tax purposes, or
- A loss is computed for AMT purposes and a gain is computed for regular income tax purposes.

Where the relationship between the regular tax and the AMT amount is reversed, the AMT gain or loss adjustment is positive.

---

[26]§ 56(a)(6).

EXAMPLE 10

Sawyer sells the breeding hog he placed in service in year 1 (Example 4) on September 1 of year 3, for $12,500. When Sawyer sells the animal, two AMT adjustments result: the depreciation adjustment for year 3 and any gain (or loss) adjustment resulting from the sale.

The regular income tax depreciation for year 3 is $593 [$8,000 cost × 14.81% (Chapter 8, Exhibit 8.8) × .5]. AMT depreciation for that year is $1,000 [$8,000 × 25% (Chapter 8, Exhibit 8.9) × .5]. Sawyer's negative AMT adjustment for year 3, reflecting the additional depreciation for AMT purposes, is $407 ($593 regular income tax depreciation − $1,000 AMT depreciation).

In computing gain (or loss) as a result of the sale, the adjusted basis in the animal is different for regular income tax and AMT purposes because of depreciation. The adjusted basis for each purpose is determined as follows.

	Regular Income Tax	AMT
Cost	$ 8,000	$ 8,000
Less: Depreciation for prior tax years (see Example 4)	(6,222)	(5,000)
Depreciation for year 3 (see prior paragraph)	(593)	(1,000)
Adjusted basis	$ 1,185	$ 2,000

Having determined the adjusted basis, the recognized gain for regular tax and AMT purposes is calculated as follows.

	Regular Income Tax	AMT
Amount realized	$12,500	$12,500
Adjusted basis	(1,185)	(2,000)
Recognized gain	$11,315	$10,500

Because the regular income tax gain is greater than the AMT gain on the sale of the animal, Sawyer incurs a negative AMT adjustment of $815 ($11,315 regular income tax gain − $10,500 AMT gain). Note that this negative adjustment offsets the prior and current year adjustments for depreciation.

Passive Activity Losses

Losses on passive activities are not deductible in computing either regular taxable income or AMTI. However, the rules for computing taxable income differ from the rules for computing AMTI. It follows, then, that the rules for computing such a loss for regular income tax purposes differ from the AMT rules for computing such a loss. For example, where a passive activity involves depreciable assets, if the amount of depreciation differs for regular tax and AMT purposes, the amount of loss disallowed for AMT purposes will be larger or smaller than the loss disallowed for regular tax purposes. Therefore, any *passive activity loss* computed for regular income tax purposes may differ from the passive activity loss computed for AMT purposes.[27]

EXAMPLE 11

Matt acquired two passive activities this year. He received net passive income of $10,000 from Activity A and had no AMT adjustments or preferences in connection with the activity. Activity B produced gross income of $27,000 and operating expenses (not affected by AMT adjustments or preferences) of $19,000. Matt claimed MACRS depreciation of $20,000 for Activity B; AMT depreciation totaled $15,000. In addition, Matt deducted $10,000 of percentage depletion in excess of basis (an AMT preference). The following comparison illustrates the differences in the computation of the passive activity loss for regular income tax and AMT purposes for Activity B.

continued

---

[27]See text Section 11-3.

	Regular Income Tax	AMT
Gross income	$27,000	$27,000
Deductions		
Operating expenses	(19,000)	(19,000)
Depreciation	(20,000)	(15,000)
Depletion	(10,000)	–0–
Passive activity loss	($22,000)	($ 7,000)

Because of the $5,000 adjustment for depreciation and the preference for depletion (see the discussion of AMT preferences later in the chapter), the regular income tax passive activity loss of $22,000 for Activity B is reduced, resulting in a passive activity loss of $7,000 for AMT purposes.

For regular income tax purposes, Matt would offset the $10,000 of net passive income from Activity A with $10,000 of the passive loss from Activity B. For AMT purposes, he would offset the $10,000 of net passive income from Activity A with the $7,000 passive loss allowed from Activity B, resulting in passive activity income of $3,000. Thus, in computing AMTI, Matt makes a positive passive activity loss adjustment of $3,000 [$10,000 (passive activity loss allowed for regular income tax) − $7,000 (passive activity loss allowed for the AMT)].

To avoid duplication, the AMT adjustment for depreciation and the AMT preference for depletion are *not* reported separately. They are accounted for in determining the passive activity loss adjustment. Also note that differences in regular tax and AMT passive activity loss amounts in the current year will affect the amount of suspended passive activity losses carried forward to future tax years.

Assume the same facts as in the previous example. For regular income tax purposes, Matt reports a suspended passive activity loss of $12,000 [$22,000 (amount of loss) − $10,000 (used this year)]. This suspended passive activity loss can offset passive activity income in the future, or it can offset active or portfolio income when Matt disposes of the loss activity (see text Section 11-3f). For AMT purposes, Matt's suspended passive activity loss is $0 [$7,000 (amount of loss) − $7,000 (amount used this year)].

Alternative Tax Net Operating Loss Deduction

In computing taxable income, taxpayers can deduct net operating loss (NOL) carryovers and carrybacks (see text Section 7-6). While the NOL deduction is allowed for AMT purposes, the regular income tax NOL must be modified to compute AMTI correctly.

The starting point in computing the **alternative tax NOL deduction (ATNOLD)** is the NOL computed for regular income tax purposes. The regular income tax NOL is modified for AMT adjustments and tax preferences to arrive at the ATNOLD. Preferences and adjustment items that have benefited the taxpayer in computing the regular income tax NOL (in other words, the adjustments and preferences that have increased the regular tax NOL) are added back, thereby reducing or eliminating the NOL for AMT purposes.[28]

In 2017, Max incurred an NOL of $400,000. Max owns an item of MACRS five-year property, placed in service on March 15, 2017, at a cost of $1,000,000. Regular tax depreciation is $200,000 ($1,000,000 × .20), and AMT depreciation is $150,000 ($1,000,000 × .15). Max's deductions also include tax preferences of $80,000. His ATNOLD carryback to 2015 is $270,000 [$400,000 regular income tax NOL − $80,000 tax preferences deducted in computing the NOL − ($200,000 regular tax depreciation − $150,000 AMT depreciation)].

---

[28]§ 56(a)(4).

In Example 13, if the regular income tax NOL was allowed in full for AMT purposes, the $80,000 in tax preference items and the excess regular tax depreciation would have the effect of reducing AMTI in the year (or years) the 2017 NOL was utilized. Given that these amounts were disallowed in the calculation of AMTI, such an outcome is contradictory to the purpose of the AMT.

Finally, in keeping with the goal of ensuring that taxpayers with economic income pay some minimum amount of tax, a ceiling exists on the amount of the ATNOLD that can be deducted in the carryback or carryforward year. The deduction is limited to 90 percent of AMTI (before the ATNOLD) for the carryback or carryforward year.[29]

Assume the same facts as in the previous example, except that Max's AMTI (before the ATNOLD) in 2015 is $190,000. Therefore, of the $270,000 ATNOLD carried back to 2015 from 2017, only $171,000 ($190,000 × 90%) can be used in recalculating the 2015 AMT. The unused $99,000 of 2017 ATNOLD is next carried to 2016 for use in recalculating that year's AMT.

A taxpayer who has an ATNOLD that is carried back or over to another year must use the ATNOLD against AMTI in the carryback or carryforward year, even if the taxpayer is not subject to the AMT. This can result in the loss of an ATNOLD, even when the taxpayer does not have an AMT liability.

Emily's ATNOLD for 2017 (carried over from 2016) is $10,000. AMTI in 2017, before considering the ATNOLD, is $25,000. If Emily's regular income tax liability exceeds her TMT, the AMT does not apply. Nevertheless, Emily's ATNOLD of $10,000 is "used up" in 2017 and is not available for carryover to a later year.

For regular income tax purposes, the NOL generally can be carried back 2 years and forward 20 years. However, the taxpayer may elect to forgo the 2-year carryback. These rules generally apply to the ATNOLD as well, except that the election to forgo the 2-year carryback is available for the ATNOLD only if the taxpayer made the election for the regular income tax NOL.

Itemized Deductions

Most of the itemized deductions that are allowed for regular income tax purposes are allowed for AMT purposes. As discussed below, for AMT purposes, the itemized deduction for certain taxes, miscellaneous itemized deductions, and interest expense requires adjustment. The itemized deduction phaseout also triggers an AMT adjustment.

Taxes and Miscellaneous Itemized Deductions State, local, and foreign income taxes, sales taxes, and property taxes are not allowed as a deduction in computing AMTI.[30] Miscellaneous itemized deductions that are subject to the 2%-of-AGI floor also are not allowed in computing AMTI.[31] A positive AMT adjustment equal to the total amount of the regular income tax deduction for each is required.

Also remember that under the tax benefit rule, a tax refund is included in regular taxable income to the extent the taxpayer obtained a tax benefit by deducting the tax in a prior year. If the taxpayer's gross income includes the recovery of any tax deducted as an itemized deduction for regular income tax purposes, a negative AMT adjustment in the amount of the recovery is allowed for AMTI purposes.[32] For example, state income taxes can be deducted for regular income tax purposes but cannot be deducted in computing AMTI. Because of this, any refund of such taxes from a prior year that would be included in the calculation of regular taxable income is not included in AMTI.

---

[29]§ 56(d)(1)(A)(i)(II).
[30]§ 56(b)(1)(A).

[31]§ 56(b)(1)(A).
[32]§ 56(b)(1)(D).

Joann, age 35, is a resident of Minnesota. In 2016, her Federal taxable income included an itemized deduction of $4,200 for Minnesota income taxes. In February 2017, Joann received a Federal income tax refund of $5,800 and a Minnesota income tax refund of $600.

In 2017, Joann makes a negative AMT adjustment of ($600) for the state tax refund. The $600 refund is included in 2017 regular taxable income because the deduction for state taxes reduced her prior year Federal income tax liability. However, the $600 refund is excluded from her 2017 AMTI because the deduction for state taxes is not allowed for AMT purposes.

Joann's Federal income tax refund does not create an AMT adjustment, as Federal income taxes are not deducted in the calculation of regular taxable income or AMTI.

Medical Expenses For regular tax purposes, from 2013–2016 for taxpayers aged 65 and older, medical expenses were deductible to the extent they exceeded 7.5 percent of AGI. During these same years, for AMT purposes, medical expenses for such taxpayers were deductible to the extent they exceeded 10 percent of AGI. However, for tax years beginning after 2016, medical expenses in excess of 10 percent of AGI are deductible for both regular tax and AMT purposes. Thus, no adjustment for medical expenses is required for taxpayers of any age.[33]

Interest in General The AMT itemized deduction allowed for interest expense includes only qualified housing interest[34] and investment interest[35] to the extent of net investment income that is included in the calculation of AMTI. Any interest that is deducted in calculating regular taxable income that is not permitted in calculating AMTI is treated as a positive adjustment.

In computing regular taxable income, taxpayers who itemize can deduct the following types of interest (refer to text Section 10-3).

- Qualified residence interest.
- Investment interest, subject to the investment interest limitations (discussed under Investment Interest, which follows).

Housing Interest Under current regular income tax rules, taxpayers who itemize can deduct *qualified residence interest* on up to two residences. The deduction is limited to interest on acquisition indebtedness up to $1 million and home equity indebtedness up to $100,000. Acquisition indebtedness is debt that is incurred in acquiring, constructing, or substantially improving a qualified residence of the taxpayer and is secured by the residence. Home equity indebtedness is indebtedness secured by a qualified residence of the taxpayer, but does not include acquisition indebtedness.

The mortgage interest deduction for AMT purposes is limited to *qualified housing interest*, rather than *qualified residence interest*. Qualified housing interest includes only interest incurred to acquire, construct, or substantially improve the taxpayer's principal residence and such interest on one other qualified dwelling used for personal purposes. Thus, interest on a home equity loan is deductible for AMT purposes only if the home equity loan meets the definition of qualified housing interest, which is not always the case.

When additional mortgage interest is incurred (e.g., a mortgage refinancing), interest paid is deductible as qualified housing interest for AMT purposes only if:

- The proceeds are used to acquire or substantially improve a qualified residence,
- Interest on the prior loan was qualified housing interest, and
- The amount of the loan was not increased.

A positive AMT adjustment is required in the amount of the difference between qualified *residence* interest allowed as an itemized deduction for regular income tax purposes and qualified *housing* interest allowed in the determination of AMTI.

---

[33]§ 56(b)(1)(B) and § 213(f).
[34]§ 56(b)(1)(C)(i).

[35]§ 56(b)(1)(C)(iii).

Investment Interest Investment interest is deductible for regular income tax purposes and for AMT purposes to the extent of qualified net investment income.

However, because the categorization of interest as investment interest may differ for regular tax and AMT purposes, an adjustment is required if the amount of investment interest deductible for regular income tax purposes differs from the amount deductible for AMT purposes. For example, an adjustment will arise if proceeds from a home equity loan are used to purchase investments. Interest on a home equity loan is deductible as qualified residence interest for regular income tax purposes, but is not deductible for AMT purposes unless the proceeds are used to acquire or substantially improve a qualified residence. For AMT purposes, however, interest on a home equity loan is deductible as investment interest expense if proceeds from the loan are used for investment purposes.

To determine the AMT adjustment for investment interest expense, it is necessary to compute the investment interest expense deduction for both regular income tax and AMT purposes.

EXAMPLE 17

Tom had $20,000 interest income from corporate bonds and $5,000 dividends from preferred stock. He reported the following amounts of investment income for regular income tax and AMT purposes.

	Regular Income Tax	AMT
Corporate bond interest	$20,000	$20,000
Preferred stock dividends	5,000	5,000
Net investment income	$25,000	$25,000

Tom incurred investment interest expense of $10,000 related to the corporate bonds. He also incurred $4,000 interest on a home equity loan, the proceeds of which were used to purchase preferred stock. For regular income tax purposes, this $4,000 is deductible as qualified residence interest. His *investment* interest expense for regular income tax and AMT purposes is computed below.

	Regular Income Tax	AMT
To carry corporate bonds	$10,000	$10,000
On home equity loan to carry preferred stock	–0–	4,000
Total investment interest expense	$10,000	$14,000

Investment interest expense is deductible to the extent of net investment income. Because the amount deductible for regular income tax purposes ($10,000) differs from the amount deductible for AMT purposes ($14,000), an AMT adjustment is required. The adjustment is computed as follows.[36]

AMT deduction for investment interest expense	$ 14,000
Regular income tax deduction for investment interest expense	(10,000)
Negative AMT adjustment	$ 4,000

As discussed subsequently under AMT Preferences, the interest on private activity bonds usually is a tax preference for AMT purposes. Such interest can also affect the calculation of the AMT investment interest deduction in that it is included in the calculation of net investment income.

Cutback Adjustment The 3 percent/80 percent cutback adjustment that applies to regular income tax itemized deductions of certain high-income taxpayers (see text

---

[36]For regular tax purposes, investment interest expense does not include qualified residence interest. However, a positive $4,000 adjustment will be required in calculating the amount of deductible housing interest allowed for AMT purposes because the home equity loan proceeds were not used to acquire or improve a qualified residence.

Section 10-8) serves to disallow a portion of the taxpayer's itemized deductions for regular income tax purposes. This cutback does not apply in computing AMTI.[37] As a result, a negative adjustment is made for the amount of the cutback taken into consideration in the regular taxable income calculation.

Computations and Elections Unlike many other AMT adjustments, a taxpayer cannot mitigate the effect of the itemized deduction adjustments by electing to treat the amounts in the same way for regular income tax and AMT purposes. Also note that a taxpayer who elects the standard deduction for regular tax purposes cannot claim itemized deductions for AMT purposes.[38]

Other Adjustments

Neither the standard deduction nor the personal and dependency exemption is allowed in the calculation of AMTI. Thus, these amounts also give rise to AMT adjustments.[39] However, these adjustments enter the AMTI calculation indirectly by adjusting the taxable income amount that begins the AMTI calculation. If a taxpayer itemizes deductions, then the starting point for the AMTI calculation is adjusted gross income (AGI) less itemized deductions. If, instead, a taxpayer takes the standard deduction, the starting point for the AMTI calculation is AGI. Thus, any standard deduction or exemption amount taken in the calculation of regular taxable income is accounted for by adjusting the starting point of the AMTI calculation. As discussed later in the chapter, a separate exemption (see Exemption Amount) is allowed for AMT purposes.

EXAMPLE

18

Michael is single and has no dependents. He earned a salary of $110,000 in 2017, and his itemized deductions totaled $18,000. Based on this information, Michael's taxable income for 2017 is $87,950 ($110,000 − $18,000 itemized deductions − $4,050 exemption). However, Michael's taxable income starting point for the AMTI calculation would be $92,000, as the adjustment for the personal exemption is made to the taxable income amount that starts the AMTI calculation. Any remaining adjustments related to itemized deductions are made in the AMTI calculation.

Concept Summary 12.1 summarizes the key points related to AMT adjustments.

Concept Summary 12.1

Summary of AMT Adjustment Provisions

1. Adjustments that reflect *timing differences* can be either positive or negative.

2. Apart from adjustments related to itemized deductions, many adjustments *can be avoided* if the taxpayer adopts the same tax treatment for regular tax purposes as is required for AMT purposes.

3. *Not all* itemized deductions trigger adjustments.

4. When bonus depreciation is claimed, *no depreciation adjustment* is required for the asset either in the year placed in service or in subsequent years in which depreciation is claimed.

5. Adjustments for the standard deduction and personal and dependency exemptions *enter the AMT calculation indirectly* by adjusting the taxable income amount that begins the AMTI computation.

12-1d **AMT Preferences**

Unlike adjustments, which can be positive or negative, AMT preferences always are positive. In other words, preferences are added back to taxable income in the calculation of AMTI. The following section discusses AMT preferences for individual taxpayers.

LO.4

Identify the preferences that are included in calculating AMTI.

---

[37]§ 56(b)(1)(F).

[38]CCA 200103073.

[39]§ 56(b)(1)(E).

Percentage Depletion

Congress enacted the percentage depletion rules to provide taxpayers with incentives to invest in the development of certain natural resources. Percentage depletion is computed by multiplying a rate specified in the Code by the gross income from the property (see text Section 8-6b).[40] The rate is based on the type of mineral involved. Generally, the basis of the property is reduced by the amount of depletion taken until the basis reaches zero. However, because percentage depletion is based on gross income, rather than the investment in the property, taxpayers are allowed to continue taking percentage depletion deductions even after the basis of the property reaches zero. Thus, over the life of the property, depletion deductions may greatly exceed the cost of the property.

The percentage depletion preference is equal to the excess of the regular income tax deduction for percentage depletion over the adjusted basis of the property at the end of the taxable year.[41] Note that the end-of-year basis is determined without regard to the depletion deduction for the taxable year. This preference is calculated separately for each mineral property owned by the taxpayer.[42] As a result, a taxpayer cannot use basis in one property to reduce the preference for excess depletion on another property.

EXAMPLE 19

Kim owns a mineral property that qualifies for a 22% depletion rate. The basis of the property at the beginning of the year, prior to any current year depletion deduction, is $10,000. Gross income from the property for the year is $100,000. For regular income tax purposes, Kim's percentage depletion deduction (assume that it is not limited by taxable income from the property) is $22,000. For AMT purposes, Kim has a tax preference of $12,000 ($22,000 − $10,000).

Intangible Drilling Costs

In computing regular taxable income, taxpayers can deduct certain intangible drilling and development costs in the year incurred, although such costs are normally capital in nature (see text Section 8-6a). The deduction is allowed for costs incurred in connection with oil and gas wells and geothermal wells.

For AMT purposes, excess intangible drilling costs (IDC) for the year are treated as a preference.[43] The excess IDC preference is computed as follows.

IDC expensed in the year incurred
Minus: Deduction if IDC were capitalized and amortized over 10 years
Equals: Excess of IDC expense over amortization
Minus: 65% of net oil and gas or geothermal income
Equals: Tax preference amount

The IDC preference is computed separately for oil and gas wells and geothermal wells.

EXAMPLE 20

Ben, who incurred IDC of $50,000 during the year, elected to expense that amount. His net oil and gas income for the year was $60,000. Currently, Ben has no income from geothermal wells. Ben's preference for IDC is $6,000 [($50,000 IDC − $5,000 amortization) − (65% × $60,000 income)].

A taxpayer can avoid the preference for IDC by electing to write off the expenditures over a 10-year period for regular income tax purposes.

Interest on Private Activity Bonds

Like interest income earned on other municipal bonds, income from private activity bonds is not included in taxable income, and expenses related to carrying such bonds

---

[40]§ 613(a).

[41]§ 57(a)(1). The preference does not include percentage depletion on oil and gas wells of independent producers or royalty owners, as defined in § 613A(c).

[42]§ 614(a).

[43]§ 57(a)(2).

are not deductible for regular income tax purposes. However, interest on private activity bonds is considered a preference in computing AMTI. As a result, expenses incurred in carrying the bonds are offset against the interest income in computing the preference amount.[44] Due to legislation to encourage the economic recovery, interest on private activity bonds issued after 2008 and before 2011 is not treated as a preference.

In general, private activity bonds are bonds issued by states or municipalities where more than 10 percent of the proceeds are used for private business use.[45] For example, a bond issued by a city whose proceeds are used to construct a factory that is leased to a private business at a favorable rate is a private activity bond.

The vast majority of tax-exempt bonds issued by states and municipalities are not classified as private activity bonds. Therefore, the interest income from such bonds does not regularly create a preference for AMT purposes for most individuals.

The Big Picture

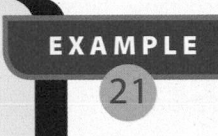

Return to the facts of *The Big Picture* on p. 12-1. Bob and Carol both have invested substantial amounts in private activity bonds. All of the private activity bonds that each of them owns were issued in 2010. Consequently, a tax preference does not result for either Carol or Bob.

In the current year, Lindsay earned $8,300 of interest income, comprised of the following amounts.

10-year Treasury bond (issued in 2012)	$4,000
10-year municipal bond (issued in 2009)	2,500
10-year private activity bond (issued in 2015)	1,800

All of the bonds were purchased on their issuance date. Lindsay's preference for interest is $1,800, the interest on the private activity bond. Treasury bond interest is included in both regular taxable income and AMTI; the interest from the non-private activity municipal bond is not included in either regular taxable income or AMTI.

Depreciation

For real property and leased personal property placed in service before 1987, there is an AMT preference for the excess of accelerated depreciation over straight-line depreciation.[46] However, examination of the cost recovery tables for pre-1987 real property reveals that from the eighth year on, accelerated depreciation will not exceed straight-line depreciation. Consequently, taxpayers no longer have preferences attributable to pre-1987 real property.

Exclusion for Certain Small Business Stock

Gain on the sale of certain small business stock is excluded from gross income for regular income tax purposes if that stock was acquired after September 28, 2010.[47]

For AMT purposes, for years in which the 100 percent exclusion applies for regular tax purposes, the exclusion does not create an AMT preference.[48]

---

[44]§ 57(a)(5).

[45]§ 141.

[46]§ 57(a)(6).

[47]§ 1202(a)(4). Different percentages for the excluded gain applied prior to this date.

[48]§§ 57(a)(7) and 1202(a)(4)(C).

ETHICS & EQUITY   Large Families and the AMT

The taxpayer claimed 12 personal and dependency exemptions (taxpayer, spouse, and 10 children) on their Federal income tax return. The taxpayers' itemized deductions included medical and dental expenses and state and local income and property taxes.

Under the regular income tax calculation, the taxpayers' taxable income was a negative amount. However, applying the AMT adjustments for personal and dependency exemptions, medical and dental expenses, and state and local income and property taxes resulted in the taxpayers being subject to the AMT.

The taxpayers are members of a religious denomination that encourages large families. The tax return they filed showed a $0 Federal income tax liability and did not include a Form 6251. According to the taxpayers, the AMT should not apply to them for the following reasons.

- Congress did not intend for a large family in itself to be a causative factor producing an AMT.
- They had no tax preferences.
- The AMT burdened the taxpayers' free exercise of religion.
- The AMT violated their equal protection and due process rights.

Both the Tax Court and the Third Circuit Court of Appeals rejected these arguments and held that the taxpayers were subject to the AMT.

Should taxpayers who have large families and no tax preferences be subject to the AMT? Was this the intended objective of the AMT?

Source: Based on *Klaassen v. Comm.*, 99–1 USTC ¶50,418, 83 AFTR 2d 99–1750, 182 F.3d 932 (CA–3, 1999), *aff'g* 76 TCM 20, T.C.Memo. 1998–241.

LO.5

Compute the AMT and complete Form 6251.

12-1e Illustration of the AMT Computation

The computation of the AMT is illustrated in the following example. Because the 2017 Form 6251 was not available at the time of printing, the 2016 AMT exemption amounts and tax brackets are used in the following example.

EXAMPLE

23

Molly Seims, who is single and age 56, had taxable income for 2016 as follows.

Salary		$ 92,000
Interest		8,000
Adjusted gross income		$100,000
Less itemized deductions:		
Medical expenses ($17,500 − 10% of $100,000 AGI)	$ 7,500*	
State income taxes	4,000	
Interest[a]		
Home mortgage (for qualified housing)	20,000*	
Investment interest	3,300*	
Charitable contributions (cash)	5,000*	
Casualty losses ($14,000 − 10% of $100,000 AGI)	4,000*	(43,800)
		$ 56,200
Less personal exemption		(4,050)
Taxable income		$ 52,150

[a]In this illustration, all interest is deductible in computing AMTI. Qualified housing interest is deductible without adjustment. Investment interest ($3,300) is deductible to the extent of net investment income included in AMTI. For this purpose, the $8,000 of interest income is treated as net investment income.

Deductions marked with an asterisk are allowed for AMT purposes. Thus, an adjustment is required for state income taxes; no adjustment is required for medical expenses as Molly is not older than 65.

In addition, Molly earned $40,000 of interest income on private activity bonds issued in 2013. She also exercised ISOs in 2016. The option spread (the difference between the exercise price and

continued

the fair market value on the date of exercise) was $35,000. Molly's regular tax liability in 2016 is $8,809. AMTI is computed as follows.

Taxable income[b]	$ 56,200
Plus: Adjustments	
State income taxes	4,000
Incentive stock options	35,000
Plus: Preference (interest on private activity bonds)	40,000
Equals: AMTI	$135,200
Minus: AMT exemption[c]	(50,025)
Equals: Minimum tax base	$ 85,175
Multiplied by: AMT tax rate	× 26%
Equals: Tentative minimum tax (TMT)	$ 22,146
Minus: Regular tax liability	(8,809)
Equals: AMT	$ 13,337

[b] Note that although the personal exemption is technically an adjustment, the Form 6251 adds the personal exemption to the taxable income amount that begins the AMTI calculation, rather than include the personal exemption with the other adjustments.

[c] Because Molly's AMTI exceeds the $119,700 exemption phaseout amount, she is not entitled to the maximum 2016 exemption amount of $53,900. Her exemption amount is $50,025 [$53,900 − .25($135,200 − $119,700)].

The solution to Example 23 is also presented on Form 6251 on the following page.

12-1f **AMT Credit**

LO.6

Describe and illustrate the role of the AMT credit in the alternative minimum tax structure.

As was illustrated in several of the examples in this chapter, timing differences that give rise to AMT adjustments eventually reverse. To provide equity for taxpayers, a tax credit is created in a year in which a taxpayer pays AMT as a result of these timing differences.[49]

This credit, known as the alternative minimum tax credit , is created only by the AMT liability that results from timing differences.[50] A credit is not created or increased by AMT exclusions, which create permanent differences between the regular income tax liability and the AMT. These AMT exclusions include the following amounts.

- The standard deduction.
- Personal and dependency exemptions.
- Itemized deductions not allowable for AMT purposes, including miscellaneous itemized deductions, taxes, and interest expense.
- Excess percentage depletion.
- Tax-exempt interest on private activity bonds.

Patrick, who is single, has zero taxable income for 2017. He also has positive timing adjustments of $300,000 and AMT exclusions of $100,000. Because of the amount of his AMTI, the exemption is phased out completely and his AMT base is $400,000. Patrick's TMT is $108,244 [($187,800 × 26% AMT rate) + ($212,200 × 28% AMT rate)].

EXAMPLE 24

To determine the amount of AMT credit to carry over, the AMT must be recomputed to reflect only the effect of timing differences, as shown in Example 25.

Assume the same facts as in the previous example. If there had been no positive timing adjustments for the year, Patrick's TMT would have been $11,882 [($100,000 AMT exclusions − $54,300 exemption) × 26% AMT rate]. Patrick may carry over an AMT credit of $96,362 ($108,244 AMT − $11,882 related to AMT exclusions) to 2018 and subsequent years.

EXAMPLE 25

---

[49] § 53. [50] S. Rep. No. 99–313 (PL 99–514) p. 536.

Form **6251**

Department of the Treasury
Internal Revenue Service (99)

Alternative Minimum Tax—Individuals

► Information about Form 6251 and its separate instructions is at *www.irs.gov/form6251.*
► Attach to Form 1040 or Form 1040NR.

OMB No. 1545-0074

2016

Attachment
Sequence No. **32**

Name(s) shown on Form 1040 or Form 1040NR
Molly Seims

Your social security number
111-11-1111

Part I   Alternative Minimum Taxable Income (See instructions for how to complete each line.)

1	If filing Schedule A (Form 1040), enter the amount from Form 1040, line 41, and go to line 2. Otherwise, enter the amount from Form 1040, line 38, and go to line 7. (If less than zero, enter as a negative amount.)	**1**	*56,200*
2	Medical and dental. If you or your spouse was 65 or older, enter the **smaller** of Schedule A (Form 1040), line 4, **or** 2.5% (0.025) of Form 1040, line 38. If zero or less, enter -0-	**2**	
3	Taxes from Schedule A (Form 1040), line 9	**3**	*4,000*
4	Enter the home mortgage interest adjustment, if any, from line 6 of the worksheet in the instructions for this line	**4**	
5	Miscellaneous deductions from Schedule A (Form 1040), line 27.	**5**	
6	If Form 1040, line 38, is $155,650 or less, enter -0-. Otherwise, see instructions	**6**	( )
7	Tax refund from Form 1040, line 10 or line 21	**7**	( )
8	Investment interest expense (difference between regular tax and AMT).	**8**	
9	Depletion (difference between regular tax and AMT)	**9**	
10	Net operating loss deduction from Form 1040, line 21. Enter as a positive amount	**10**	
11	Alternative tax net operating loss deduction	**11**	( )
12	Interest from specified private activity bonds exempt from the regular tax	**12**	*40,000*
13	Qualified small business stock, see instructions	**13**	
14	Exercise of incentive stock options (excess of AMT income over regular tax income)	**14**	*35,000*
15	Estates and trusts (amount from Schedule K-1 (Form 1041), box 12, code A)	**15**	
16	Electing large partnerships (amount from Schedule K-1 (Form 1065-B), box 6)	**16**	
17	Disposition of property (difference between AMT and regular tax gain or loss)	**17**	
18	Depreciation on assets placed in service after 1986 (difference between regular tax and AMT)	**18**	
19	Passive activities (difference between AMT and regular tax income or loss)	**19**	
20	Loss limitations (difference between AMT and regular tax income or loss)	**20**	
21	Circulation costs (difference between regular tax and AMT)	**21**	
22	Long-term contracts (difference between AMT and regular tax income)	**22**	
23	Mining costs (difference between regular tax and AMT)	**23**	
24	Research and experimental costs (difference between regular tax and AMT)	**24**	
25	Income from certain installment sales before January 1, 1987	**25**	( )
26	Intangible drilling costs preference	**26**	
27	Other adjustments, including income-based related adjustments	**27**	
28	**Alternative minimum taxable income.** Combine lines 1 through 27. (If married filing separately and line 28 is more than $247,450, see instructions.)	**28**	*135,200*

Part II   Alternative Minimum Tax (AMT)

29 Exemption. (If you were under age 24 at the end of 2016, see instructions.)

IF your filing status is . . .	**AND line 28 is not over . . .**	**THEN enter on line 29 . . .**
Single or head of household	$119,700	$53,900
Married filing jointly or qualifying widow(er)	159,700	83,800
Married filing separately.	79,850	41,900

If line 28 is **over** the amount shown above for your filing status, see instructions.

29	*50,025*

30	Subtract line 29 from line 28. If more than zero, go to line 31. If zero or less, enter -0- here and on lines 31, 33, and 35, and go to line 34	**30**	*85,175*
31	• If you are filing Form 2555 or 2555-EZ, see instructions for the amount to enter. • If you reported capital gain distributions directly on Form 1040, line 13; you reported qualified dividends on Form 1040, line 9b; **or** you had a gain on both lines 15 and 16 of Schedule D (Form 1040) (as refigured for the AMT, if necessary), complete Part III on the back and enter the amount from line 64 here. • **All others:** If line 30 is $186,300 or less ($93,150 or less if married filing separately), multiply line 30 by 26% (0.26). Otherwise, multiply line 30 by 28% (0.28) and subtract $3,726 ($1,863 if married filing separately) from the result.	**31**	*22,146*
32	Alternative minimum tax foreign tax credit (see instructions)	**32**	
33	Tentative minimum tax. Subtract line 32 from line 31	**33**	*22,146*
34	Add Form 1040, line 44 (minus any tax from Form 4972), and Form 1040, line 46. Subtract from the result any foreign tax credit from Form 1040, line 48. If you used Schedule J to figure your tax on Form 1040, line 44, refigure that tax without using Schedule J before completing this line (see instructions)	**34**	*8,809*
35	**AMT.** Subtract line 34 from line 33. If zero or less, enter -0-. Enter here and on Form 1040, line 45	**35**	*13,337*

For Paperwork Reduction Act Notice, see your tax return instructions.   Cat. No. 13600G   Form **6251** (2016)

Where a taxpayer has an AMT credit, the credit can be utilized only in a year in which the taxpayer is not subject to the AMT. In addition, as demonstrated in the following example, the amount of the credit that can be used is equal to the excess of the taxpayer's regular tax liability over their tentative minimum tax liability. Finally, while the AMT credit cannot be carried back, the credit can be carried forward indefinitely.

EXAMPLE 26

Amber holds a $5,800 AMT credit from 2013. In 2017, prior to consideration of the AMT credit, Amber's regular tax liability is $30,000 and her tentative minimum tax is $27,000. In this situation, Amber can use $3,000 of the AMT credit from 2013 to reduce her 2017 regular tax liability. Thus, Amber's tax liability in 2017 is $27,000. The remaining $2,800 AMT credit is carried forward to future tax years.

Key points related to AMT preferences are summarized in Concept Summary 12.2. A broader summary of AMT adjustments and preferences for individual taxpayers is included in Concept Summary 12.3.

Concept Summary 12.2

Summary of AMT Preference Provisions

1. Preferences are *always* positive in amount. A preference reflects a permanent difference between the regular tax and the AMT treatment of an amount.

2. With the exception of the IDC preference, preferences *cannot be avoided* by adopting the same tax treatment for regular tax and AMT purposes. In general, preferences

can be avoided by not engaging in the activity that causes the preference, which may not be economically rational.

3. On occasion, Congress changes the tax code to stimulate economic activity. To the extent that an AMT preference could hinder this economic goal, the *preference may also be modified* (e.g., private activity bond interest, small business stock gain).

Concept Summary 12.3

AMT Adjustments and Preferences for Individuals

Adjustments	Positive	Negative	Both*
Adjusted gain or loss on property dispositions			X
Alternative tax NOL deduction (ATNOLD)			X
Circulation expenditures			X
Completed contract method			X
Depreciation of post-1986 personal property			X
Depreciation of post-1986 real property			X
Incentive stock options	X**		
Itemized deductions:			
Medical expenses (2013–2016)	X		
Miscellaneous itemized deductions	X		
Private activity bond interest that is AMT investment interest		X	
Property tax on personalty	X		
Property tax on realty	X		
Qualified residence interest that is AMT investment interest		X	
Qualified residence interest that is not qualified housing interest	X		
State income taxes	X		
Tax benefit rule for state income tax refund		X	

continued

Adjustments	Positive	Negative	Both
Mine exploration and development costs			X
Passive activity losses			X
Personal and dependency exemptions	X		
Pollution control facilities			X
Research and experimental expenditures			X
Standard deduction	X		
Preferences			
Depreciation on pre-1987 leased personal property	X		
Intangible drilling costs	X		
Percentage depletion in excess of adjusted basis	X		
Private activity bond interest income	X***		

*Timing differences.

**While the adjustment is positive, the AMT basis for the stock acquired is increased by the amount of the positive adjustment.

***Interest on private activity bonds issued after 2008 and before 2011 is not treated as a tax preference.

Compare the individual AMT calculation with the corporate AMT calculation.

12-2 CORPORATE ALTERNATIVE MINIMUM TAX

The AMT calculation for C corporations is similar to that for individual taxpayers. However, there are several important differences.

- The corporate AMT rate is 20 percent, instead of the 26 and 28 percent rates that are used by individuals.[51]

- The AMT exemption for corporations is $40,000 reduced by 25 percent of the amount by which AMTI exceeds $150,000 and is not indexed to inflation.[52]

- With the exception of the ACE adjustment, many of the adjustments and preferences applicable to individual taxpayers also are applicable to corporate taxpayers.

Although there are computational differences, the corporate AMT and the individual AMT have the identical objective: to try to ensure that taxpayers who have economic income pay some income tax. The formula for determining the corporate AMT appears in Exhibit 12.2.

12-2a Small Corporations and the AMT

Two provisions exist that allow small corporations to avoid the AMT. For these provisions, a corporation is classified as a small corporation based on the amount of its annual gross receipts.

In its first tax year of existence, a corporation will automatically be classified as a small corporation, which means that a corporation is not subject to AMT in its first year of existence.[53]

For each succeeding tax year, the prior year's average annual gross receipts must be less than a certain threshold for the corporation to continue to be exempt from AMT. In its second year of operations, if a corporation's annual average gross receipts in the prior year were less than $5 million, the corporation is not subject to AMT. For each succeeding year of operations (i.e., the third year and after), if the corporation's average annual gross receipts for the three-year period ending before the current tax year do not exceed $7.5 million, the corporation continues to be exempt from AMT.

---

[51]§ 55(b)(1)(B).

[52]§§ 55(d)(2) and (3).

[53]§ 55(e)(1)(C).

EXHIBIT 12.2	**AMT Formula for Corporations**

Taxable income prior to any regular tax NOL deduction

Plus or minus: Adjustments

Plus: Preferences

Equals: Pre-ACE alternative minimum taxable income (AMTI)

Plus or minus: ACE adjustment

Equals: AMTI before ATNOLD

Minus: ATNOLD (limited to 90% of AMTI before ATNOLD)

Equals: AMTI

Minus: Exemption

Equals: Alternative minimum tax (AMT) base

Multiplied by: 20%

Equals: Tentative minimum tax before AMT foreign tax credit

Minus: AMT foreign tax credit

Equals: Tentative minimum tax (TMT)

Minus: Regular tax liability (less any foreign tax credit)

Equals: AMT (if TMT > regular tax liability)

However, if a corporation ever fails the gross receipts test, it is ineligible for small corporation classification in any future tax year.[54]

12-2b **AMT Adjustments**

AMT adjustments for both individuals and C corporations arise because the provisions in the regular tax law for a particular item differ from the AMT tax law provisions. The following adjustments that were discussed in connection with the individual AMT also apply to the corporate AMT calculation.

- Excess of MACRS over AMT depreciation on real and personal property placed in service after 1986.

- Pollution control facilities placed in service after 1986.

- Mine and exploration expenditures.

- Income from long-term contracts.

- Adjusted gain or loss on the dispositions of assets.

While the NOL deduction must be recalculated for AMT purposes, the deduction is allowed in the corporate AMT calculation. In addition, the corporate ATNOLD cannot exceed 90 percent of AMTI before the deduction for the ATNOLD.[55]

EXAMPLE
27

Bluebird Corporation acquired used office furniture costing $20,000 on March 15, 2015. The furniture was sold on December 31, 2017, for $15,000. Depreciation, basis, and gain amounts for regular tax and AMT purposes are computed as follows.

	Depreciation				
	2015	**2016**	**2017**	**Basis**	**Gain on Sale**
Regular tax	$2,858	$4,898	$1,749	$10,495	$4,505
AMT	2,142	3,826	1,503	12,529	2,471

continued

[54]§§ 55(e)(1)(A) and (B). In a corporation's third year of operations, the average annual gross receipts are calculated for the prior two-year period; the corporation does not yet have three years of gross receipts.

[55]§ 56(d).

Two AMT adjustments related to the office furniture are required in 2017. A positive $246 adjustment for depreciation is required, as regular tax depreciation is greater than AMT depreciation by this amount in 2017. This means that $246 *less* depreciation is allowed for AMT than was taken for regular tax purposes.

A negative $2,034 adjustment is required for the gain on sale. The gain for regular tax purposes exceeds the gain for AMT purposes, which means that *less* gain is recognized for AMT purposes than for regular tax purposes. The AMT gain adjustment offsets the AMT adjustments made for depreciation in prior years.

Adjustment for C Corporations

The adjusted current earnings (ACE) adjustment is required only of C corporations.[56] The **ACE adjustment** differs from those discussed previously because the ACE amount is intended to approximate a corporation's economic income and, as a result, the entity's true tax-paying ability. In other words, the ACE adjustment is intended to limit the benefits of certain tax provisions that the other adjustments, by their nature, cannot limit.

The details of the ACE calculation and adjustment are not discussed in this chapter. The instructions for Form 4626 illustrate the ACE adjustment and provide a worksheet for its computation.

12-2c AMT Preferences

As is shown in Exhibit 12.2, the corporate AMTI calculation also includes preferences. The preference items discussed in the individual AMTI calculation also apply to corporations.

EXAMPLE 28

In the current year, Brown Corporation, a calendar year taxpayer, reports taxable income of $4,000,000. The following expenses also were incurred.

Mine exploration costs	$ 500,000
Percentage depletion claimed (the property has a zero adjusted basis)	2,600,000

Brown is not a small corporation for AMT purposes. Brown's AMTI is determined as follows.

Taxable income	$4,000,000
Plus or minus: Adjustment:	
Excess mine exploration costs [$500,000 (amount expensed) − $50,000 (amount allowed over a 10-year amortization period)]	450,000
Plus: Preference:	
Excess depletion	2,600,000
AMTI	$7,050,000

12-2d Exemption Amount

The corporate tentative minimum tax (TMT) is calculated at a rate of 20 percent of AMTI that exceeds the corporation's exemption amount. The exemption amount for a corporation is $40,000 reduced by a phaseout of 25 percent of the amount by which AMTI exceeds $150,000. Neither the exemption amount nor the exemption phaseout threshold is indexed to inflation.

EXAMPLE 29

Blue Corporation has AMTI of $180,000. The exemption amount is reduced by $7,500 [25% × ($180,000 − $150,000)], and the amount remaining is $32,500 ($40,000 − $7,500). Thus, Blue Corporation's AMT base (refer to Exhibit 12.2) is $147,500 ($180,000 − $32,500).

---

[56]§ 56(c).

The exemption amount phases out entirely when AMTI reaches $310,000, which is why many C corporations realize no benefit from the exemption in the calculation of AMT.

12-2e Other Aspects of the Corporate AMT

In a year in which the corporation is subject to the AMT, the AMT amount creates a minimum tax credit available for carryover to future years. Unlike the individual minimum tax credit calculation, the entire AMT amount is available for a corporation to carry over (no adjustment to the amount is required).

EXAMPLE 30

As calculated in Example 28, Brown Corporation's AMTI is $7,050,000. As a result, Brown's TMT is $1,410,000 (20% of $7,050,000). If the corporation's regular income tax liability is $1,360,000, the AMT liability is $50,000 ($1,410,000 − $1,360,000). Brown's minimum tax credit is $50,000, available in future years to offset any excess of regular corporate income tax liability over TMT.

The only credit available to offset a corporate taxpayer's TMT is the foreign tax credit. Unlike the individual AMT calculation, no other credits can reduce a corporate taxpayer's TMT. In addition, to the extent the C corporation is allowed other credits, those are allowed only to offset the excess of any regular tax liability (after the foreign tax credit) over the TMT (after the foreign tax credit).

Form 4626 (Alternative Minimum Tax—Corporations) is the form corporations use to report AMT amounts to the IRS. Any AMT calculated is carried to Schedule J of Form 1120 (U.S. Corporation Income Tax Return).

12-3 TAX PLANNING

LO.8
Identify and apply tax planning opportunities to minimize the AMT.

12-3a Avoiding Preferences and Adjustments

One strategic approach to managing AMT liabilities is to avoid preference and adjustment amounts where possible.

- A taxpayer who expects to be subject to the AMT should not invest in private activity bonds unless doing so makes good investment sense. Any AMT triggered by interest on private activity bonds reduces the yield on an investment in such bonds.

- A taxpayer could be better off taking itemized deductions even when those deductions are less than the standard deduction if the itemized deductions do not require AMT adjustments. For example, a taxpayer with itemized deductions comprised of charitable contributions (that were less than the standard deduction) would not make an AMT adjustment for such contributions, but would be required to make an adjustment for the standard deduction, which could potentially put the taxpayer into AMT.

- Neither property taxes nor real estate taxes are deductible for AMT if they are categorized as itemized deductions. However, taxes deductible as a part of business operations or rental activities are allowed for AMT purposes. Therefore, a taxpayer who could qualify for a home-office deduction would be able to deduct a portion of his or her home's real estate taxes as business expenses rather than as an itemized deduction.

- A taxpayer who expects to be subject to the AMT will not realize a tax benefit from using a home equity loan to buy a car. Although the interest may be deductible for regular tax purposes, an AMT adjustment will be required. A lower interest rate may be obtained from a regular car loan. In addition, if the car is used in the taxpayer's business, some of the interest on the car loan may be deductible as a trade or business expense.

12-3b Controlling the Timing of Preferences and Adjustments

If preference and adjustment amounts cannot be avoided, the timing of these amounts may help to mitigate AMT liabilities.

- The AMT exemption often keeps items of tax preference from being subject to the AMT. To use the AMT exemption effectively, taxpayers should attempt to control the timing of such preference items when possible.

- In a year that a taxpayer expects to be subject to the AMT, real estate or fourth-quarter estimated state tax payments should not be made in December. Any benefit received from the regular income tax deduction for these amounts will be offset by the AMT adjustment made.

12-3c Other AMT Tax Planning Strategies

A potential AMT liability can be reduced by decreasing adjusted gross income (AGI). Certain contributions to qualified retirement savings plans are excluded from gross income, which would result in a decreased AGI amount. Where a taxpayer participates in a § 401(k), § 457(b) plan, or SIMPLE IRA plan (see text Sections 19-1e and 19-4b), the maximum allowable salary deferral contributions to such a plan would reduce AGI, which is beneficial for both regular tax and AMT purposes as well as for retirement planning.

While the lower tax rates for long-term capital gains apply for both regular tax and AMT purposes, such long-term capital gains increase AGI and AMTI, and these income items could reduce the amount of the AMT exemption available to a taxpayer. In a year for which a taxpayer expects to be subject to the AMT, the taxpayer should evaluate how the recognition of long-term capital gains affects AMTI and consider, where possible, whether those gains should be deferred to a future year.

REFOCUS ON THE BIG PICTURE

THE PRESENCE OR ABSENCE OF THE AMT

Bob contacts Adam, his tax return preparer, and explains that he believes he underpaid his Federal income tax liability for the year by $15,000. He is worried about the negative effects of any underpayment if it is discovered during an IRS audit, including the effect on his future marriage to Carol. Adam reviews Bob's tax return and assures him that it was properly prepared. Bob indicates that Carol has provided him with a copy of her tax return. He asks Adam to compare the returns and then explain the tax liability difference to him. He e-mails a copy of Carol's return to Adam.

Adam examines the two tax returns and discovers that the difference relates to the treatment of the interest earned on the tax-exempt bonds. Both Bob and Carol own tax-exempt bonds, including private activity bonds that usually are subject to the AMT. However, Carol's accountant, Ava, apparently overlooked the fact that interest on private activity bonds is not a tax preference for such bonds issued in 2010. So the $15,000 AMT that was reported on Carol's Form 6251 is in error. Bob texts Carol the good news that she is eligible for a Federal income tax refund.

WAVEBREAKMEDIA/SHUTTERSTOCK.COM

Key Terms

ACE adjustment, 12-26

Adjustments, 12-6

Alternative minimum tax (AMT), 12-2

Alternative minimum tax credit, 12-21

Alternative tax NOL deduction (ATNOLD), 12-13

Exemption amount, 12-5

Incentive stock options (ISOs), 12-10

Preferences, 12-17

Private activity bonds, 12-19

Discussion Questions

1. **LO.1** Kelly was recently promoted and received a substantial raise. She talks to her tax adviser about potential tax ramifications. After making some projections, her adviser welcomes her to the AMT club. Kelly believes that it is unfair that she must pay more than the regular income tax, as she does not feel wealthy and has substantial college-related debts. Explain to Kelly the purpose of the AMT and why it applies to her.

2. **LO.2** How could the AMT be calculated without using regular taxable income as a starting point?

3. **LO.3** How might a taxpayer who cannot avoid engaging in activities that generate AMT adjustments minimize or eliminate such adjustments?

4. **LO.2** Explain the AMT calculation presented in Exhibit 12.1 using the figure as a guide for your explanation.

5. **LO.2** AMT liability results if the tentative minimum tax (TMT) exceeds the regular income tax liability. What happens if the regular income tax liability exceeds the TMT? Does this create a negative AMT amount that can be carried to other years? Explain.

6. **LO.2** Alfred is single, and his AMTI of $350,000 consists of the following.

Ordinary income	$250,000
Long-term capital gains	70,000
Qualified dividends	30,000

What tax rates are applicable in calculating Alfred's TMT?

7. **LO.2** Can any nonrefundable credits, other than the foreign tax credit, reduce the regular income tax liability below the amount of the TMT? Explain.

8. **LO.3** Tad, who owns and operates a business, acquired machinery and placed it in service in June 2008. The machinery is 10-year property. Does Tad need to make an AMT adjustment in 2008 or 2017 for the depreciation on the machinery? Explain.

9. **LO.3** Evaluate the validity of the following statement: In a year in which depreciable personal property is sold, the amount of the AMT gain adjustment will equal the amount of the current year's AMT depreciation adjustment.

10. **LO.3** Evaluate the validity of the following statements: If the stock received under an incentive stock option (ISO) is sold in the year of exercise, there is no AMT adjustment. If the stock is sold in a later year, there will be an AMT adjustment.

11. **LO.3** In 1998, Douglas purchased an office building for $500,000 to be used in his business. He sells the building in the current tax year. Explain why his recognized gain or loss for regular income tax purposes will be different from his recognized gain or loss for AMT purposes.

12. **LO.3, 8** Celine is going to be subject to the AMT in 2017. She owns an investment   Issue ID
building and is considering disposing of it and investing in other realty. Based on an appraisal of the building's value, the realized gain would be $85,000. Ed has offered to purchase the building from Celine with the closing date being December 29, 2017. Ed wants to close the transaction in 2017 because certain beneficial tax consequences will result only if the transaction is closed prior to the beginning of 2018.

Abby has offered to purchase the building with the closing date being January 2, 2018. The building has a $95,000 greater AMT adjusted basis than regular tax basis. For regular income tax purposes, Celine expects to be in the 25% tax bracket in 2017 and the 28% tax bracket in 2018. What are the relevant tax issues that Celine faces in making her decision?

13. **LO.3** Paola exercised an incentive stock option on March 1, 2017. She acquired 2,000 shares of stock at an exercise price of $3 per share when the fair market value of the stock was $15 per share. However, Paola was concerned that the stock was overvalued, so she sold all of the stock acquired with the option on December 21, 2017, for $17 per share.

Will Paola incur an AMT adjustment in 2017 as a result of the exercise of the option or the sale of the shares? Explain.

14. **LO.5** How is it possible that a taxpayer could have an AMT NOL larger than his or her alternative minimum taxable income (AMTI), yet still have a positive tentative minimum tax (TMT) amount?

Issue ID   15. **LO.3, 4, 8** Matt, who is single, always has elected to itemize deductions rather than take the standard deduction. In prior years, his itemized deductions always exceeded the standard deduction by a substantial amount. As a result of paying off the mortgage on his residence, he projects that his itemized deductions for 2017 will exceed the standard deduction by only $500. Matt anticipates that the amount of his itemized deductions will remain about the same in the foreseeable future.

Matt's AGI is $150,000. He is investing the amount of his former mortgage payment each month in tax-exempt bonds that were issued in 2013. A friend recommends that Matt buy a beach house to increase his itemized deductions with the mortgage interest deduction. What are the relevant tax issues for Matt?

16. **LO.3** A friend tells you that she does not have to worry about AMT because she does not itemize deductions and, as a result, she does not have many AMT adjustments. Evaluate the validity of your friend's assertion.

17. **LO.3** In the calculation of AMTI, where is the adjustment for personal and dependency exemptions made and what is the reason for the adjustment?

Decision Making   18. **LO.4** During the year, Rachel earned $18,000 of interest income on private activity bonds that she had purchased in 2008. She also incurred interest expense of $7,000 in connection with amounts borrowed to purchase the bonds. What is the effect on Rachel's taxable income? Could there be a related beneficial effect in calculating AMTI? Explain.

19. **LO.7** Comment on the validity of the following statement: Because the regular tax NOL deduction must be added back to the taxable income starting point of the corporate AMTI calculation, an NOL deduction is not allowed for corporate AMT purposes.

Issue ID   20. **LO.7** Dart Corporation (a calendar year C corporation) would like to invest some of its excess earnings from retail operations in real estate. Dart is considering a purchase of 10 acres of land in a city whose economic prospects are good and whose population is growing. The company believes that the land will be attractive to a developer in the next five years. Does the AMT adjustment for real estate taxes make this a less attractive investment for Dart? Explain.

Computational Exercises

21. **LO.2** Compute the 2017 AMT exemption for the following taxpayers.

    a. Bristol, who is single, reports AMTI of $149,500.

    b. Marley and Naila are married and file a joint tax return. Their AMTI is $498,000.

22. **LO.3** In March 2017, Serengeti exercised an ISO that had been granted by his employer, Thunder Corporation, in December 2014. Serengeti acquired 5,000 shares of Thunder stock for the exercise price of $65 per share. The fair market value of the stock at the date of exercise was $90 per share.

    What is Serengeti's 2014 AMT adjustment related to the ISO? What is the 2017 adjustment?

23. **LO.3** Brennen sold a machine used in his business for $180,000. The machine was purchased eight years ago for $340,000. Depreciation up to the date of the sale for regular income tax purposes was $210,000 and $190,000 for AMT purposes.

    What, if any, AMT adjustment arises as a result of the sale of the machine?

24. **LO.4** Dimitri owns a gold mine that qualifies for a 15% percentage depletion rate. The basis of the property at the beginning of the year, prior to any current year depletion deduction, is $21,000. Gross income from the property for the year is $200,000, and taxable income before depletion is $65,000.

    What is Dimitri's AMT depletion preference?

25. **LO.4** Kiki, who incurred intangible drilling costs (IDC) of $94,000 during the year, deducted that amount for regular tax purposes. Her net oil and gas income for the year was $110,000. Currently, Kiki has no income from geothermal wells.

    Kiki has calculated her current-year IDC preference to be $9,400. Is this the correct preference amount?

26. **LO.5** Yanni, who is single, provides you with the following information for 2017.

Salary	$80,000
State income taxes	6,800
Mortgage interest expense	6,200
Charitable contributions	1,500
Interest income	1,300
Personal exemption	4,050

    a. What is Yanni's 2017 taxable income?

    b. What is Yanni's 2017 AMTI?

    c. What is Yanni's 2017 TMT?

27. **LO.6** Elijah is single. He holds a $12,000 AMT credit from 2016. In 2017, his regular tax liability is $28,000 and his tentative minimum tax is $24,000.

    Does Elijah owe AMT in 2017? How much (if any) of the AMT credit can Elijah use in 2017?

28. **LO.7** Siga, Inc., a calendar year C corporation, records the following gross receipts and taxable income amounts.

Tax Year	Gross Receipts	Taxable Income
1	$4,200,000	$ 900,000
2	7,000,000	1,600,000
3	7,700,000	1,900,000

    Is Siga exempt from AMT in any of its first three tax years? Explain.

Problems

29. **LO.2** Use the following data to calculate Chiara's AMT base in 2017.

Taxable income	$148,000
Positive AMT adjustments	73,000
Negative AMT adjustments	55,000
Preferences	30,000

Chiara will itemize deductions and will file as a single taxpayer. Taxable income is computed before the personal exemption amount, which is not included in the positive AMT adjustments amount above.

Communications 30. **LO.2** Arthur Wesson, an unmarried individual who is age 68, reports taxable income of $160,000 in 2017. He records positive AMT adjustments of $40,000 and preferences of $35,000. Arthur itemizes his deductions, and his regular tax liability in 2017 is $37,050.

a. What is Arthur's AMT?

b. What is the total amount of Arthur's tax liability?

c. Draft a letter to Arthur explaining why he must pay more than the regular income tax liability. Arthur's address is 100 Colonel's Way, Conway, SC 29526.

31. **LO.3, 4** In the current year, Dylan earned taxable and tax-exempt interest from the following investments.

Investment	Interest Income
10-year municipal bond (issued in 2009)	$1,300
10-year private activity bond (issued in 2010)	1,600
10-year Treasury bond (issued in 2013)	2,000
10-year private activity bond (issued in 2015)	900
Savings account	1,100

Dylan purchased all of the bonds on their issuance date. In addition, Dylan borrowed funds with which to purchase the 2010 private activity bond and incurred interest expense of $350 on that loan in the current year.

a. How much interest income will Dylan recognize for regular tax purposes in the current year?

b. What is her current-year AMT preference or adjustment for interest?

32. **LO.2, 3** Calculate the exemption amount for the following cases in 2017 for a married taxpayer filing jointly and for a married taxpayer filing separately. In addition, in an Excel formula, express your solution for Case 2 for the taxpayer who is married filing jointly. Place any parameter that could change annually in a separate cell, and incorporate the cell references into the formula.

Case	AMTI
1	$150,000
2	300,000
3	800,000

33. **LO.2** Lisa records nonrefundable Federal income tax credits of $65,000 for the year. Her regular income tax liability before credits is $190,000, and her TMT is $150,000.

a. What is Lisa's AMT?

b. What is Lisa's regular income tax liability after credits?

34. **LO.2,3,8** Angela, who is single, incurs circulation expenditures of $153,000 during **Decision Making** 2017. She is deciding whether to deduct the entire $153,000 or to capitalize it and elect to deduct it over a three-year period.

    Angela knows that she will be subject to the AMT for 2017 at both the 26% and 28% rates. Angela is in the 28% bracket for regular income tax purposes this year; she reports regular taxable income of $153,000 before considering the circulation expenses. Angela expects to be in the 28% regular tax bracket in 2018 and 2019. Advise Angela on how to treat the expenditures in 2017. Take the time value of money into consideration when calculating the tax savings of one alternative over another. Use the tables in Appendix H for this purpose, and assume that the pertinent discount rate is 4%.

35. **LO.3** Archie runs a small mineral exploration business (as a sole proprietorship). In 2015, he purchased land (for $68,000) where he suspected a magnesium deposit was located. He incurred $18,000 of exploration costs related to the development of the magnesium mine in 2015, and an additional $22,000 of exploration costs in 2016. Archie elected to deduct these expenditures for regular tax purposes in both 2015 and 2016.

    In 2017, given a decline in magnesium prices, Archie chose to sell the property for $66,000, rather than bring the mine to production.

    What AMT adjustments are required in 2017 related to mine exploration expenditures and the sale of the land?

36. **LO.3** Lonzo owns two apartment buildings. He acquired Forsythia Acres on February 21, 1998, for $300,000 ($90,000 allocated to the land) and Square One on November 12, 2017, for $800,000 ($100,000 allocated to the land). Neither apartment complex qualifies as low-income housing. If Lonzo elects to deduct the cost of each building as quickly as possible, what is the effect of depreciation (cost recovery) on his AMTI for:

    a. 1998?

    b. 2017?

37. **LO.3,8** In March 2017, Helen Carlon acquired used equipment for her business at **Decision Making** a cost of $300,000. The equipment is five-year property for depreciation **Communications** purposes.

    a. If Helen depreciates the equipment using the method that will produce the greatest deduction for 2017 for regular income tax purposes, what is the amount of the AMT adjustment? Helen does not elect § 179 expensing.

    b. How can Helen reduce the AMT adjustment to $0? What circumstances would motivate her to do so?

    c. Draft a letter to Helen regarding the choice of depreciation methods. Helen's address is 500 Monticello Avenue, Glendale, AZ 85306.

38. **LO.3,8** In 2017, Geoff incurred $900,000 of mine and exploration expenditures. He **Decision Making** elects to deduct the expenditures as quickly as the tax law allows for regular income tax purposes.

    a. How will Geoff's treatment of mine and exploration expenditures affect his regular income tax and AMT computations for 2017?

    b. How can Geoff avoid having AMT adjustments related to the mine and exploration expenditures?

    c. What factors should Geoff consider in deciding whether to deduct the expenditures in the year incurred?

39. **LO.3** Rust Company is a real estate construction business with average annual gross receipts of $3 million. Rust uses the completed contract method on a particular contract that requires 16 months to complete. The contract is for $500,000, with estimated costs of $300,000. At the end of 2016, $180,000 of costs had been incurred. The contract is completed in 2017, with the total cost being $295,000. Determine the amount of adjustments for AMT purposes for 2016 and 2017.

40. **LO.3** Burt, the CFO of Amber, Inc., was granted incentive stock options in 2012. Burt exercised the stock options in February 2016 when the exercise price was $75,000 and the fair market value of the stock was $90,000. He sold the stock in September 2017 for $150,000. What are the regular income tax consequences and the AMT consequences for Burt in:

    a.   2012?

    b.   2016?

    c.   2017?

41. **LO.3** In 2017, Liza exercised an incentive stock option that had been granted to her in 2014 by her employer, White Corporation. Liza acquired 100 shares of White stock for the option price of $190 per share. The fair market value of the stock at the date of exercise was $250 per share. Liza sells the stock for $340 per share in 2019.

    a.   What is the amount of Liza's AMT adjustment in 2017? What is her recognized gain on the sale for regular income tax and for AMT purposes in 2019?

    b.   How would your answers in part (a) change if Liza had sold the stock in 2017 rather than 2019?

42. **LO.3, 4** Valentina, who is single, itemizes deductions and has no dependents. In the current year, she earned $6,000 of municipal bond interest income and paid state income taxes of $5,600, mortgage interest of $8,000, and $3,900 of interest on a home equity loan. Her regular taxable income is $95,000.

    a.   What is Valentina's AMTI if she uses the proceeds of the home equity loan to remodel her existing home?

    b.   What is Valentina's AMTI if she uses the proceeds of the home equity loan to purchase a new boat?

43. **LO.4** Christopher regularly invests in internet company stocks, hoping to become wealthy by making an early investment in the next high-tech phenomenon. In 2011, Christopher purchased 3,000 shares of FlicksNet, a film rental company, for $15 per share shortly after the company went public. Because Christopher purchased the shares in their initial offering, the shares are qualified small business stock.

    In 2018, Christopher sold 800 of the shares (at $325 per share) so that he could purchase a reservation for a seat on Elon Musk's first human mission to Mars. What regular income tax consequences and AMT consequences arise for Christopher as a result of the sale of these shares?

44. **LO.3** Sammy and Monica, both age 67, incur and pay medical expenses in excess of insurance reimbursements during the year as follows.

For Sammy	$16,000
For Monica (spouse)	4,000
For Chuck (son)	2,500
For Carter (Monica's father)	5,000

Sammy and Monica's 2017 AGI is $130,000. They file a joint return. Chuck and Carter are Sammy and Monica's dependents.

    a.   What is Sammy and Monica's medical expense deduction for regular income tax purposes?

    b.   What is Sammy and Monica's AMT adjustment for medical expenses?

45. **LO.3** Wolfgang, who is age 33, records AGI of $125,000. He incurs the following itemized deductions for 2017.

Medical expenses [$15,000 − (10% × $125,000)]	$ 2,500
State income taxes	4,200
Charitable contributions	5,000
Home mortgage interest on his personal residence	6,000
Casualty loss (after $100 and 10% reductions)	1,800
Miscellaneous itemized deductions [$3,500 − 2%($125,000)]	1,000
	$20,500

a. Calculate Wolfgang's itemized deductions for AMT purposes.

b. What is the total amount of his AMT adjustments from these items?

c. Use the solution to part (b) to complete Part I of Form 6251, the AMT form for individuals.

46. **LO.3** Walter, who is single, owns a personal residence in the city. He also owns a cabin near a ski resort in the mountains. He uses the cabin as a vacation home. In the current year, he borrowed $60,000 on a home equity loan and used the proceeds to reduce credit card obligations and other debt. During the year, he paid the following amounts of interest.

On his personal residence	$16,000
On the cabin	7,000
On the home equity loan	2,500
On credit card obligations	1,500
On the purchase of an SUV	1,350

What amount, if any, must Walter recognize as an AMT adjustment?

47. **LO.3, 4** During the current year, Yoon earned $10,000 in interest on corporate bonds and incurred $13,000 of investment interest expense related to the bond holdings. Yoon also earned $5,000 interest on private activity bonds that were issued in 2013 and incurred interest expense of $3,500 in connection with the bonds.

a. How much investment interest expense can Yoon deduct for regular income tax purposes for the year?

b. What AMT adjustments and preferences arise as a result of the private activity bond interest income and expense?

48. **LO.3, 4** Gabriel, age 40, and Emma, age 33, are married with two dependents. They had AGI of $110,000 in 2017 that included net investment income of $3,000 and gambling winnings of $2,500.

They incurred the following expenses during the year (all of which resulted in itemized deductions for regular income tax purposes).

Medical expenses (before 10%-of-AGI floor)	$8,000
State income taxes	2,800
Personal property tax	1,200
Real estate tax	9,100
Interest on personal residence	8,600
Interest on home equity loan (proceeds were used to remodel the couple's kitchen)	1,800
Investment interest expense	4,500
Charitable contribution (cash)	4,200
Unreimbursed employee expenses (before 2%-of-AGI floor)	3,800

a. What is Gabriel and Emma's AMT adjustment for itemized deductions in 2017? Is it positive or negative?

b. Gabriel and Emma also earned interest of $5,000 on private activity bonds that were issued in 2013. They borrowed money to buy these bonds and paid interest of $3,900 on the loan. Determine the effect on AMTI.

49. **LO.3** Chance and Lindsay, both 37, are married and file a joint return in 2017. Their AGI is $580,000. They report $39,000 of itemized deductions, consisting of the following amounts.

Home mortgage interest	$25,000
Charitable contributions	14,000

Given that the couple's AGI exceeds the applicable amount ($313,800 in 2017), their itemized deductions are subject to a potential 3%/80% cutback.

a. What is the amount of Chance and Lindsay's itemized deductions for regular tax purposes for 2017?

b. What is the couple's AMT adjustment for itemized deductions in 2017?

50. **LO.2, 3** Chuck is single, has no dependents, and does not itemize deductions. In 2017, he claims a personal exemption of $4,050 and reports taxable income of $120,000. His tax preferences total $51,000. What is Chuck's AMTI for 2017?

51. **LO.3, 4** Emily owns a coal mine (basis of $12,000 at the beginning of the year) that qualifies for a 15% depletion rate. Gross income from the property was $140,000, and net income before the percentage depletion deduction was $60,000.

a. What is Emily's tax preference for excess depletion?

b. Use the solution to part (a) to complete the depletion preference entry on Form 6251, the AMT form for individuals.

52. **LO.4** Amos incurred and expensed intangible drilling costs (IDC) of $70,000. His net oil and gas income was $60,000. What is the amount of Amos's preference for IDC?

53. **LO.2, 3, 4** Jane and Robert Brown are married and have eight children, all of whom are eligible to be claimed as the couple's dependents. Robert earns $94,000 working as an accountant, and Jane earns $38,000 as a teaching aide. Given their large family, they live in a frugal manner. The Browns maintain a large garden and some fruit trees from which they get most of their produce, and the children take family and consumer science classes so that they can help make the family's clothing.

The Browns record no gross income other than their salaries (all of their investment income is earned from qualified retirement savings), and their itemized deductions are less than the standard deduction. In addition, they incur no additional adjustments or preferences for AMT purposes.

a. What is the couple's 2017 regular tax liability?

b. What is the couple's 2017 AMT?

c. Express the calculation of the couple's AMT for 2017 as an Excel formula. Place any parameter that could change annually in a separate cell, and incorporate the cell references into the formula.

54. **LO.2, 3, 4** Pat, who is age 66 and single with no dependents, received a salary of $90,000 in 2017. She earned interest income of $1,000, dividend income of $5,000, gambling winnings of $4,000, and interest income from private activity bonds (issued in 2014) of $40,000. The dividends are not qualified dividends. The following additional information is relevant.

Medical expenses (before 10%-of-AGI floor)	$12,000
State income taxes	4,100
Real estate taxes	2,800
Mortgage interest on residence	3,100
Investment interest expense	1,800
Gambling losses	5,100

Compute Pat's tentative minimum tax for 2017.

55. **LO.2, 5** Renee and Sanjeev Patel, who are married, reported taxable income of $273,000 for 2017. They incurred positive AMT adjustments of $38,000, negative AMT adjustments of $14,000, and tax preference items of $67,500. The couple itemizes their deductions.
    a. Compute the Patels' AMTI for 2017.
    b. Compute their tentative minimum tax for 2017.

56. **LO.2, 3, 4, 5** Farr is single, has no dependents and does not itemize her deductions. She reports the following items on her 2017 tax return.

Bargain element from the exercise of an ISO (no restrictions apply to the stock)	$ 45,000
MACRS depreciation on shopping mall building acquired in 2013	49,000
Percentage depletion in excess of property's adjusted basis	50,000
Taxable income for regular income tax purposes	121,000
Regular tax liability	26,862

    a. Determine Farr's AMT adjustments and preferences for 2017.
    b. Calculate Farr's AMT for 2017.

57. **LO.2, 3, 4, 5** Lynn, age 45, is single and has no dependents. Her income and expenses for 2017 are reported as follows.

Income—	
Salary	$33,000
Taxable interest on corporate bonds	3,700
Business income	64,000
Expenditures—	
Medical expenses	12,000
State income taxes	6,000
Real estate taxes	8,500
Mortgage (qualified housing) interest	9,200
Investment interest	5,500
Cash contributions to various charities	2,900

The $64,000 business income is from Apex Office Supplies Company, a sole proprietorship that Lynn owns and operates. Apex claimed MACRS depreciation of $3,175 on real and personal property used in the business. AMT depreciation on the property would have been $2,500. Lynn received interest of $30,000 on City of Pensacola private activity bonds that were issued in 2011.
    Based on the information presented above, compute Lynn's AMT for 2017.

58. **LO.5, 6** Bonnie, who is single, reports a zero taxable income for 2017. Bonnie itemizes deductions and takes the personal exemption. She incurs positive timing adjustments of $200,000 and AMT exclusion items of $100,000 for the year. What is Bonnie's AMT credit carryover to 2018?

59. **LO.7** Aqua, Inc., a calendar year corporation, records the following gross receipts and taxable income amounts.

Tax Year	Gross Receipts	Taxable Income
1	$6,000,000	$1,400,000
2	7,000,000	1,312,000
3	7,500,000	985,000
4	7,200,000	1,002,000

Is Aqua exempt from AMT in any of its first four tax years? Explain.

60. **LO.7** In the current year, Redland Corporation's regular tax liability was $28,000, and its AMTI was $232,000. Redland is not a small corporation, and this is not its first year of operations.

   a.   Compute Redland's current-year AMT.

   b.   How would your answer to part (a) change if Redland's regular tax liability was $88,000 in the current year?

61. **LO.7** Brown Corporation (a calendar year taxpayer) provides you with the following information.

Taxable income	$2,600,000
Depreciation for regular income tax purposes on realty placed in service in 2008	550,000
Excess amortization of certified pollution control facilities	450,000
Tax-exempt interest on private activity bonds (issued in 2013)	1,030,000
Percentage depletion in excess of the property's adjusted basis	60,000

   a.   Calculate Brown's regular income tax liability.

   b.   Calculate Brown's TMT. Assume that the corporation is not a small corporation, this is not its first year of operations, and it does not record an ACE adjustment.

   c.   Calculate Brown's AMT.

Cumulative Problems

Tax Return Problem

H&R BLOCK

TAX SOFTWARE

62. Robert A. Kliesh, age 41, is single and has no dependents. Robert's Social Security number is 111-11-1112. His address is 201 Front Street, Missoula, MT 59812. He does not contribute to the Presidential Election Campaign fund through the Form 1040.

   Robert is independently wealthy as a result of having inherited sizable holdings in real estate and corporate stocks and bonds. Robert is a minister at First Presbyterian Church, but he accepts no salary from the church. However, he does reside in the church's parsonage free of charge. The fair rental value of the parsonage is $3,000 a month. The church also provides him with a cash grocery allowance of $200 a week. Examination of Robert's financial records provides the following information for 2016.

   a. On January 16, 2016, Robert sold 1,000 shares of stock for a loss of $12,000. The stock was acquired 14 months ago for $17,000 and sold for $5,000. On February 15, 2016, he sold 400 shares of stock for a gain of $13,100. That stock was acquired in 2009 for $6,000 and sold for $19,100.

   b. He received $30,000 of interest on private activity bonds that he had purchased in 2013. He also received $40,000 of interest on tax-exempt bonds that are not private activity bonds.

   c. Robert received gross rent income of $190,000 from an apartment complex he owns. He qualifies as an active participant in the activity.

   d. Expenses related to the apartment complex, which he acquired in 2008, were $225,000.

   e. Robert's interest income (on CDs) totaled $23,000. Because he invests only in growth stocks, he has no dividend income.

   f. He won $60,000 in the Montana lottery.

   g. Robert was the beneficiary of an $800,000 life insurance policy on the life of his uncle Jake. He received the proceeds in October.

   h. Robert contributed $5,500 to his traditional IRA.

   i. Robert incurred the following potential itemized deductions.

   • $5,200 fair market value of stock contributed to Presbyterian Church (basis of stock was $3,000). He had owned the stock for two years.

   • $4,200 interest on consumer purchases.

- $3,900 state and local income tax.
- $15,000 of medical expenses that he paid on behalf of a parishioner who died.
- $300 for a safe deposit box that is used to store investments and related legal documents.
- $5,000 paid for lottery tickets associated with playing the state lottery. Robert contributed $5,000 of his winnings to the church.
- Because Robert lived in Montana, he paid no sales tax.
- $750 contribution to the campaign of the Democratic candidate for governor.

j. Robert made estimated Federal tax payments of $7,500.
k. Robert was covered by health insurance for the entire tax year.

Use Forms 1040 and 6251 and Schedules A, B, D, and E to compute the tax liability (including AMT) for Robert A. Kliesh for 2016. Omit Forms 8283, 8582, and 8949. Suggested software: H&R BLOCK Tax Software.

63. Jacob, age 42, and Jane Brewster, age 37, are married and file a joint return in 2017. **Tax Computation Problem** The Brewsters have two dependent children, Ellen and Sean, 10-year-old twins.

Jacob is a factory supervisor; he earned $95,000 in 2017. Jane is a computer systems analyst; she earned $103,000 in 2017. In addition to their salaries, the Brewsters reported the following income items in 2017.

Interest income (Carmel Sanitation District Bonds)	$22,000 (a)
Interest income (Carmel National Bank)	8,500
Qualified dividend income (Able Computer Corporation)	12,000
Gambling winnings	6,500
Gift from Uncle Raymond to Jacob	27,000
"Citizen of the Year" award (Jane)	7,500 (b)
Gain on land sale	14,000 (c)

a. The Carmel Sanitation District Bonds are private activity bonds that were originally issued in April 2013.
b. Jane was selected "Citizen of the Year" by the Carmel City Council. She used the award proceeds to pay down the family's credit card debt.
c. Jacob sold 5 acres of land to a real estate developer on October 12, 2017, for $100,000. He had acquired the land on May 15, 2009, for $86,000.

On April 1, 2017, Jacob exercised an incentive stock option granted by his employer. At the date of exercise, the fair market value of the stock was $18 per share and the exercise price was $10 per share. Jacob purchased 500 shares with the ISO exercise. As of December 31, 2017, the stock's fair market value had declined to $13 per share.
The Brewsters incurred the following expenses during 2017.

Medical expenses (doctor and hospital bills)	$28,000
Charitable contributions (cash)	9,500 (d)
Real property tax on personal residence	8,100
Mortgage interest—personal residence (reported on Form 1098)	8,600
Mortgage interest—home equity loan	1,800 (e)
Investment interest expense	3,500
Gambling losses	6,800

d. In addition to their cash charitable contributions, the Brewsters contributed stock in Ace Corporation, which they acquired on February 9, 2006, at a cost of $6,500, to the Carmel Salvation Army, a qualifying charity. The fair market value of the stock was $11,000 on November 1, 2017, the date of the contribution.
e. The home equity loan was used to purchase the family's new minivan.

Taking into consideration the above amounts, the Brewsters' 2017 AGI is $246,500; their taxable income is $177,950.

The following table presents a first draft of the Brewsters' 2017 AMTI calculation.

Regular taxable income	$177,950
Adjustments and preferences	
"Citizen of the Year" award	(7,500)
Reduction in medical expenses (10% of AGI for AMT)	6,163
Real property taxes	(8,100)
Mortgage interest	10,400
Charitable contribution of stock (difference between basis and FMV)	4,500
Incentive stock option exercise	1,000
Gambling loss disallowed for regular tax purposes	(300)
AMTI	$184,113
Exemption amount	(84,500)
AMTI base	$ 99,613

Review the AMTI calculation, and prepare a list, including explanations, of any errors in the calculation. An error could include a missing amount or an amount that should not have been included, an amount that enters the calculation in the wrong direction, or a figure that enters the calculation in the wrong amount. You can presume that the Brewsters' AGI and taxable income amounts for the year are calculated correctly.

Research Problems

Note: Solutions to the Research Problems can be prepared by using the Thomson Reuters Checkpoint® Student Edition online tax research database, which accompanies this textbook. Solutions can also be prepared by using research materials found in a typical tax library.

Research Problem 1. Samuel had worked for Pearl, Inc., for 35 years when he was discharged and his position filled by a much younger person. He filed and pursued a suit for age discrimination and received an award of $1.5 million. Under the contingent fee arrangement with his attorney, one-third of the award was paid directly to the attorney with the balance going to Samuel. Of the $1.5 million received, Samuel included $1 million on his income tax return but did not include the $500,000 paid to the attorney.

The IRS audited Samuel's return and included the $500,000 contingency fee in his gross income. In addition, Samuel was allowed a miscellaneous itemized deduction (subject to the 2% floor) for the fee paid to the attorney. The IRS adjustment caused a tax deficiency to be assessed for both the regular income tax and the AMT.

Evaluate the result reached.

Research Problem 2. Jolene receives tax-exempt interest of $33,000 on bonds that are classified as private activity bonds. She properly excludes the $33,000 from her gross income for regular income tax purposes [under §§ 103(a) and (b)(1)]. Jolene asks your advice on the treatment of the interest for AMT purposes. Locate the Code Section that covers this matter, and advise Jolene accordingly.

Research Problem 3. On his 2016 Federal income tax return, Walter deducted state income taxes of $8,000 for amounts withheld and estimated tax payments made in 2016. When he filed his 2016 state income tax return in April 2017, he discovered that he had overpaid his state income taxes by $1,500. Rather than having the $1,500 refunded to him, he treated it as a 2017 estimated tax payment. The year 2016 was not an AMT year for Walter.

In preparing his 2017 Federal income tax return, Walter is confused about how he should treat the $1,500. He knows that under the tax benefit rule, he should include the $1,500 in gross income in calculating his regular taxable income. However, because he will be subject to the AMT, he is uncertain as to how he should treat the $1,500 in calculating AMT. He thinks that the amount could be treated as a negative adjustment in converting taxable income to AMTI if 2016 had been an AMT year for him. Because it was not, Walter is unsure of the treatment.

Advise Walter on the appropriate treatment of the $1,500 in calculating his 2017 Federal income tax liability.

Research Problem 4. Thirty years ago, Jason found a painting at a yard sale that he thought would look great in his college dorm room. He bought the painting for $5. After the painting had been hanging in his dorm room for a few months, his room-mate, an art history major, realized that the painter was a relatively famous artist. Over Christmas break, Jason took the painting home and had it appraised. Since that time, because of its substantial value, the painting has been secured in storage.

Jason is now nearing retirement and is considering what to do with the painting. One alternative is to sell the painting. Another alternative is to donate the painting and take a charitable contribution deduction. He has been approached by the museum that houses a significant collection of the painter's work, and it would like to acquire the painting that Jason owns. Jason is considering that option, because he hasn't had much in the way of tax deductions since he paid off his mortgage a few years ago.

Jason knows that for regular tax purposes, the full fair market value of the painting will be allowed as a charitable deduction (subject to AGI limitations), because the painting is a long-term capital gain asset and the museum will display the painting as a part of its collection. However, he is concerned that the difference between his basis in the painting and the painting's fair market value will create a preference for AMT purposes, which would substantially reduce the tax benefit of the deduction.

Advise Jason on the appropriate treatment of charitable contributions of appreciated property for AMT purposes.

Use internet tax resources to address the following questions. Look for reliable websites and blogs of the IRS and other government agencies, media outlets, businesses, tax professionals, academics, think tanks, and political outlets.

Research Problem 5. In May 2015, Senator Ron Wyden (D-OR) proposed legislation that would create a new type of municipal bond. Determine what the proposed legislation named the new type of bond and what the intended uses were for the proceeds of these bond issuances. Determine whether the interest income earned on the bonds would have created a preference for AMT purposes. Has the legislation been adopted?

Research Problem 6. Find some planning opportunities suggested by tax professionals to minimize or reduce potential AMT exposure. In an e-mail to your instructor, outline an AMT planning opportunity not mentioned in the chapter. In the e-mail, discuss the feasibility of the suggested planning opportunity.

Communications

Research Problem 7. The precursor to the Alternative Minimum Tax enacted by the Tax Reform Act of 1986 was the minimum tax, which was originally enacted in 1969. Find a website that discusses the rationale for the 1969 minimum tax. Describe the taxpayer profile that persuaded Congress to enact the original minimum tax. Summarize your findings in no more than five PowerPoint slides to present to your school's accounting club.

Communications

Roger CPA Review Questions

1. Mary, age 60, reported adjusted gross income of $150,000 for the year. Mary also incurred $20,000 in medical expenses. In computing Mary's alternative minimum tax, what is the adjustment for Mary's medical expenses?

    a. $0
    b. $3,750
    c. $5,000
    d. $8,750

2. When an entity is responsible for paying the alternative minimum tax (AMT) due to adjustments related to the timing of income recognition, such as including the excess of fair market value over option price upon the exercise of qualified stock options for AMT purposes but not until the shares are sold for regular tax purposes, how might that excess tax be recovered?

    a.   File a claim for a refund in the year paid.
    b.   Carry forward to offset against a future AMT liability *only*.
    c.   Carry forward to offset against future AMT *or* regular tax liabilities.
    d.   Carry forward to offset against a future regular tax liability *only*.

3. Which of the following will increase a taxpayer's alternative minimum taxable income (AMTI)?

	Personal Exemption	Property Taxes	Medical Expenses over 10% of AGI
a.	Yes	Yes	Yes
b.	Yes	Yes	No
c.	No	Yes	Yes
d.	Yes	No	Yes

4. Corbin reported adjusted gross income of $170,000. Other information is as follows.

Standard deduction	$ 6,350
Personal exemption	4,050
Property and local taxes paid	5,000
Business expenses subject to the 2% AGI threshold	10,000

    What amount is added back to taxable income as an adjustment in the calculation of Corbin's alternative minimum taxable income?

    a. $22,000
    b. $25,400
    c. $15,400
    d. $17,950

Tax Credits and Payment Procedures

LEARNING OBJECTIVES: *After completing Chapter 13, you should be able to:*

LO.1 Explain how tax credits are used as a tool of Federal tax policy.

LO.2 Distinguish between refundable and nonrefundable credits and understand the order in which they can be used by taxpayers.

LO.3 Describe various business-related tax credits.

LO.4 Describe various tax credits that are available primarily to individual taxpayers.

LO.5 Describe the tax withholding and payment procedures applicable to employers.

LO.6 Explain and illustrate the payment procedures applicable to self-employed persons.

LO.7 Explain some of the key tax provisions of the Affordable Care Act.

LO.8 Identify tax planning opportunities related to tax credits and payment procedures.

CHAPTER OUTLINE

YELLOW DOG PRODUCTIONS/GETTY IMAGES

EDUCATION TAX CREDITS

Tom and Jennifer Snyder have two children in college. Lora is a freshman, and her tuition and required fees in 2017 total $14,000. Lora has a partial scholarship amounting to $6,500, and the Snyders paid the balance of her tuition ($7,500), plus room and board of $8,500. Sam is a junior, and the Snyders paid $8,100 for his tuition, plus $7,200 for his room and board. Both students qualify as Tom and Jennifer's dependents.

The Snyders have AGI of $158,000. They would like to know what tax options are available to them related to these educational expenses. They have heard about education tax credits, but they believe that their income is too high for them to get any benefit. Are they correct?

Read the chapter and formulate your response.

FRAMEWORK 1040 **Tax Formula for Individuals**

This chapter covers the boldfaced portions of the Tax Formula for Individuals that was introduced in Concept Summary 3.1 on p. 3-3. Below those portions are the sections of Form 1040 where the results are reported.

Income *(broadly defined)*	$xx,xxx
Less: Exclusions	(x,xxx)
Gross income	$xx,xxx
Less: Deductions *for* **adjusted gross income**	(x,xxx)
Adjusted gross income	$xx,xxx
Less: The greater of total **itemized deductions** *or* the standard deduction	(x,xxx)
Personal and dependency exemptions	(x,xxx)
Taxable income	$xx,xxx
Tax on taxable income *(see Tax Tables or Tax Rate Schedules)*	$ x,xxx
Less: **Tax credits** *(including income taxes withheld and prepaid)*	(xxx)

FORM 1040 (p. 2)

48	Foreign tax credit. Attach Form 1116 if required	48	
49	Credit for child and dependent care expenses. Attach Form 2441	49	
50	Education credits from Form 8863, line 19	50	
51	Retirement savings contributions credit. Attach Form 8880	51	
52	Child tax credit. Attach Schedule 8812, if required . . .	52	
53	Residential energy credits. Attach Form 5695	53	
54	Other credits from Form: **a** ☐ 3800 **b** ☐ 8801 **c** ☐ ____	54	
55	Add lines 48 through 54. These are your **total credits**		

Tax due (or refund)	$ xxx

A s explained in Chapter 1, Federal tax law often serves purposes besides merely raising revenue for the government. Evidence of equity, social, and economic considerations is found throughout the tax law, including in the area of **tax credits**. Consider the following examples.

EXAMPLE 1

Paul and Peggy, husband and wife, are both employed outside the home. Their combined salaries are $50,000. However, after paying for child care expenses of $2,000 on behalf of their daughter, Polly, the net economic benefit from both spouses working is $48,000. The child care expenses are, in a sense, business-related because they would not have been incurred if both spouses did not work outside the home. If no tax benefits are associated with the child care expenditures, $50,000 is subject to tax.

Another couple, Alicia and Diego, also have a child, John. Diego stays home to care for John (the value of those services is $2,000) while Alicia earns a $48,000 salary. Because the value of Diego's services rendered is not subject to tax, only Alicia's earnings of $48,000 are subject to tax.

The *credit for child and dependent care expenses* mitigates the inequity felt by working taxpayers who must pay for child care services to work outside the home.

EXAMPLE 2

Consider two taxpayers, Graham and Olga, both of whom incur the same economic income in 2017.

Graham, age 66, is a retired taxpayer who receives $17,000 of Social Security benefits as his only source of income. His Social Security benefits are excluded from gross income. Therefore, Graham's income tax is $0.

continued

Olga, a single taxpayer 66 years of age, has, as her sole source of income, $17,000 from a pension plan funded by her former employer. Assuming that Olga has no itemized deductions or deductions *for* AGI, her income tax (before credits) is computed as follows.

Pension plan benefits	$17,000
Less: Basic standard deduction	(6,350)
Additional standard deduction	(1,550)
Personal exemption	(4,050)
Taxable income	$ 5,050
Income tax (at 10%)	$ 505

The *tax credit for elderly or disabled taxpayers* was enacted to mitigate the perceived inequity of taxpayers with equal incomes paying different amounts of Federal income tax.

EXAMPLE

3

Jane is a single parent who depends on the government's "safety net" for survival—she receives benefits under the Temporary Assistance to Needy Families program in the amount of $15,000 per year. However, she very much wants to work. Jane has located a job that will pay $15,500 per year and has found an individual to care for her child at no cost. But with the $1,185.75 ($15,500 × 7.65% tax rate) withholding for Social Security and Medicare taxes, the economic benefit from working is less than remaining reliant on the government ($14,314.25 versus $15,000).

The *earned income credit* helps offset the effect of Social Security and Medicare taxes on wages of the working poor and to provide an incentive to work. In addition, the earned income credit helps to offset the regressive nature of certain Federal taxes, such as the Social Security and Medicare taxes, which may impose a relatively larger burden on low-income taxpayers than on more affluent taxpayers.

The tax credits available to individuals and other types of taxpayers are a major focus of this chapter. Tax credits are categorized as being either refundable or nonrefundable. The distinction between refundable and nonrefundable credits is important because it may affect the taxpayer's ability to enjoy a tax benefit from a particular credit. The chapter continues with a discussion of the credits available to businesses and to individual taxpayers and the ways in which credits enter into the calculation of the tax liability.

The Federal income tax system largely is based on the pay-as-you-go concept. That is, taxpayers or their employers are required to make deposits with the Federal government during the year related to the annual tax liability. These deposits are, in effect, refundable credits. The chapter concludes with a brief discussion of employer withholding procedures; special rules encountered by self-employed persons; penalties imposed on underpayments; and an overview of the tax provisions that are part of the Affordable Care Act, including the additional Medicare taxes on high-income individuals.

13-1 **TAX POLICY CONSIDERATIONS**

LO.1

Explain how tax credits are used as a tool of Federal tax policy.

Congress generally has used tax credits to achieve social or economic objectives or to promote equity among different types of taxpayers. For example, the disabled access credit was enacted to accomplish a social objective: to encourage taxpayers to renovate older buildings so that they would be in compliance with the Americans with Disabilities Act. The foreign tax credit, which has been a part of the law for decades, has as its purpose the economic and equity objectives of mitigating the burden of multiple taxation on a single stream of income that is generated in more than one country. The use of tax credits as a tax policy tool continues to evolve as economic and political circumstances change.

A tax credit is much different from an income tax deduction. Income tax deductions reduce a taxpayer's tax base; tax credits reduce a taxpayer's tax liability. As a result, the tax benefit received from a tax deduction depends on the tax rate; a tax credit is not affected by the tax rate of the taxpayer.

EXAMPLE 4

Assume that Congress wants to encourage a certain type of expenditure. One way to accomplish this objective is to allow a tax credit of 25% for these expenditures. Another way is to allow an itemized deduction for the expenditures. Assume that Abby's tax rate is 15% and Bill's tax rate is 35% and that each itemizes deductions. In addition, assume that Carmen does not incur enough qualifying expenditures to itemize deductions. The following tax benefits are available to each taxpayer for a $1,000 expenditure.

	Abby	Bill	Carmen
Tax benefit if a 25% credit is allowed	$250	$250	$250
Tax benefit if an itemized deduction is allowed	150	350	–0–

As these results indicate, tax credits provide benefits on a more equitable basis than do tax deductions—all three taxpayers reduce their tax liabilities by the same amount. Equally apparent is that the deduction approach in this case benefits only taxpayers who itemize deductions, while the credit approach benefits all taxpayers who make the specified expenditure.

LO.2

Distinguish between refundable and nonrefundable credits and understand the order in which they can be used by taxpayers.

13-2 OVERVIEW AND PRIORITY OF CREDITS

13-2a Refundable versus Nonrefundable Credits

As illustrated in Exhibit 13.1, certain credits are refundable while others are non-refundable. Refundable credits are paid to the taxpayer even if the amount of the credit (or credits) exceeds the taxpayer's tax liability.

EXHIBIT 13.1	Partial Listing of Refundable and Nonrefundable Credits

Refundable Credits

Taxes withheld on wages

Earned income credit

Affordable Care Act premium tax credit

Nonrefundable Credits

General business credit, which includes:
- Tax credit for rehabilitation expenditures
- Work opportunity tax credit
- Research activities credit
- Low-income housing credit
- Disabled access credit
- Credit for small employer pension plan startup costs
- Credit for employer-provided child care

Credit for elderly and disabled

Foreign tax credit

Adoption expenses credit

Child tax credit*

Credit for child and dependent care expenses

Education tax credits**

Energy credits

Credit for certain retirement plan contributions

Small employer health insurance credit

---

*The credit is refundable to the extent of 15% of the taxpayer's earned income in excess of $3,000. Parents with three or more qualifying children compute the refundable portion using an alternative method.

**Forty percent of the American Opportunity credit is refundable.

Ted, who is single, had taxable income of $21,000 in 2017. His income tax from the 2017 Tax Rate Schedule is $2,684. During 2017, Ted's employer withheld income tax of $3,200. Ted is entitled to a refund of $516, because the credit for tax withheld on wages is a refundable credit.

Nonrefundable credits are not paid if they exceed the taxpayer's tax liability.

Tina is single, age 67, and retired. Her taxable income for 2017 is $1,320, and the tax on this amount is $132. Tina's tax credit for the elderly is $225. This credit can be used to reduce her net tax liability to zero, but it will not result in a refund, even though the credit ($225) exceeds Tina's tax liability ($132). This result occurs because the tax credit for the elderly is a nonrefundable credit.

Some nonrefundable credits, like the foreign tax credit, can be "carried over" to other tax years if they exceed the credit allowed in a given year. Other nonrefundable credits, like the tax credit for the elderly, simply are lost if they exceed the limitations. Because some credits are refundable and others are not and because some credits are subject to carryover provisions while others are not, the order in which credits are offset against the tax liability can be important.

13-2b General Business Credit

The **general business credit** is composed of a number of other credits, each of which is computed separately under its own set of rules.[1] The general business credit combines these credits into one amount to limit the amount of business credits that can be used to offset a taxpayer's income tax liability.

Two special rules apply to the general business credit. First, any unused credit must be carried back 1 year, then forward 20 years. Second, for any tax year, the general business credit is limited to the taxpayer's *net income tax* reduced by the greater of:[2]

- The *tentative minimum tax*.
- 25 percent of *net regular tax liability* that exceeds $25,000.[3]

Net regular tax liability is the regular tax liability reduced by certain nonrefundable credits (e.g., credit for child and dependent care expenses and foreign tax credit).

Floyd's general business credit for the current year is $70,000. His net income tax is $150,000, tentative minimum tax is $130,000, and net regular tax liability is $150,000. He has no other tax credits. Floyd's general business credit allowed for the tax year is computed as follows.

Net income tax	$ 150,000
Less: The greater of	
$130,000 (tentative minimum tax)	
$31,250 [25% × ($150,000 − $25,000)]	(130,000)
Amount of general business credit allowed for tax year	$ 20,000

Floyd then has $50,000 ($70,000 − $20,000) of unused general business credits that may be carried back or forward as discussed below.

13-2c Treatment of Unused General Business Credits

Unused general business credits are initially carried back one year and are applied to reduce the tax liability during that year. Thus, the taxpayer may receive a tax refund as a result of the carryback. Any remaining unused credits are then carried forward 20 years.[4]

---

[1]The separate credits are listed in § 38(b).
[2]§ 38(c).

[3]This amount is $12,500 for married taxpayers filing separately unless one of the spouses is not entitled to the general business credit.
[4]§ 39(a)(1).

A FIFO method is applied to the carrybacks, carryovers, and utilization of credits earned during a particular year. By using the oldest credits first, the FIFO method minimizes the potential for loss of a general business credit benefit due to the expiration of credit carryovers.

EXAMPLE 8

This example illustrates the use of general business credit carryovers.

General business credit carryovers		
2014	$ 4,000	
2015	6,000	
2016	2,000	
Total carryovers	$12,000	
2017 general business credit		$ 40,000
Total credit allowed in 2017 (based on tax liability)	$50,000	
Less: Utilization of carryovers		
2014	(4,000)	
2015	(6,000)	
2016	(2,000)	
Remaining credit allowed in 2017	$38,000	
Applied against		
2017 general business credit		(38,000)
2017 unused amount carried forward to 2018		$ 2,000

LO.3

Describe various business-related tax credits.

13-3 SPECIFIC BUSINESS-RELATED TAX CREDITS

Each component of the general business credit is determined separately under its own set of rules. Some of the more important credits that make up the general business credit are explained here in the order listed in Exhibit 13.1.

13-3a Tax Credit for Rehabilitation Expenditures

The **rehabilitation expenditures credit** is intended to discourage businesses from moving from older, economically distressed areas (e.g., inner cities) to newer locations and to encourage the preservation of historic structures. Here is a summary of the credit.[5]

Rate of the Credit for Rehabilitation Expenses	Nature of the Property
10%	Nonresidential buildings and residential rental property, other than certified historic structures, originally placed in service before 1936
20%	Nonresidential and residential certified historic structures

When taking the credit, the basis of a rehabilitated building must be reduced by the full rehabilitation credit allowed.[6]

EXAMPLE 9

Juan spent $60,000 to rehabilitate a building (adjusted basis of $40,000) that had originally been placed in service in 1932. He is allowed a $6,000 (10% × $60,000) credit for rehabilitation expenditures. Juan then increases the basis of the building by $54,000 [$60,000 (rehabilitation expenditures) − $6,000 (credit allowed)].

If the building were a historic structure, the credit allowed would be $12,000 (20% × $60,000) and the building's depreciable basis would increase by $48,000 [$60,000 (rehabilitation expenditures) −$12,000 (credit allowed)].

[5]§ 47.   [6]§ 50(c).

To qualify for the credit, buildings must be substantially rehabilitated. A building has been *substantially rehabilitated* if qualified rehabilitation expenditures exceed the greater of:

- The adjusted basis of the property before the rehabilitation expenditures, or
- $5,000.

Qualified rehabilitation expenditures do not include the cost of acquiring a building, the cost of facilities related to a building (such as a parking lot), and the cost of enlarging an existing building.

Recapture of Tax Credit for Rehabilitation Expenditures

The rehabilitation credit taken must be recaptured if the rehabilitated property is disposed of prematurely or if it ceases to be qualifying property. The **rehabilitation expenditures credit recapture** is based on a holding period requirement of five years and is added to the taxpayer's regular tax liability in the recapture year. Exhibit 13.2 provides the recapture percentages, which are based on how long the taxpayer held the property. Any amount recaptured is *added* to the adjusted basis of the rehabilitation expenditures for purposes of determining the amount of gain or loss realized on the property's disposition.

EXAMPLE 10

On March 15, 2014, Rashad placed in service $30,000 of rehabilitation expenditures on a building qualifying for the 10% credit. A credit of $3,000 ($30,000 × 10%) was allowed, and the basis of the building was increased by $27,000 ($30,000 − $3,000). The building was sold on December 15, 2017.

Rashad must recapture a portion of the rehabilitation credit based on the schedule in Exhibit 13.2. Because he held the rehabilitated property for more than three years but less than four, 40% of the credit, or $1,200, is added to his 2017 tax liability. In addition, the adjusted basis of the rehabilitation expenditures is increased by the $1,200 recapture amount.

13-3b Work Opportunity Tax Credit

The **work opportunity tax credit** was enacted to encourage employers to hire individuals from one or more of a number of targeted and economically disadvantaged groups.[7] Examples include long-term unemployed individuals (those unemployed for at least 27 weeks), qualified ex-felons, high-risk youths, food stamp recipients, veterans, summer youth employees, and long-term family assistance recipients.

EXHIBIT 13.2	Recapture Calculation for Rehabilitation Expenditures Credit

If the Property Is Held for	The Recapture Percentage Is
Less than 1 year	100
One year or more but less than 2 years	80
Two years or more but less than 3 years	60
Three years or more but less than 4 years	40
Four years or more but less than 5 years	20
Five years or more	0

---

[7]§ 51. The credit is available for qualifying employees who start work before 2020.

Computation of the Work Opportunity Tax Credit: General

The credit is generally equal to 40 percent of the first $6,000 of wages (per eligible employee) for the first 12 months of employment. In general, the credit is not available for any wages paid to an employee after the *first year* of employment. If the employee's first year overlaps two of the employer's tax years, however, the employer may take the credit over two tax years. If the credit is taken, the employer's tax deduction for wages is reduced by the amount of the credit.

For an employer to qualify for the 40 percent credit, the employee must (1) be certified by a designated local agency as being a member of one of the targeted groups and (2) have completed at least 400 hours of service to the employer. If an employee meets the first condition but not the second, the credit rate is reduced to 25 percent provided the employee has completed a minimum of 120 hours of service to the employer.

Work Opportunity Credit Calculation

EXAMPLE 11

In January 2017, Green Company hires four individuals who are certified to be members of a qualifying targeted group. Each employee works 800 hours and is paid wages of $8,000 during the year. Green Company's work opportunity credit is $9,600 [($6,000 × 40%) × 4 employees].

If the tax credit is taken, Green must reduce its deduction for wages paid by $9,600. No credit is available for wages paid to these employees after their first year of employment.

EXAMPLE 12

On June 1, 2017, Maria, a calendar year taxpayer, hires Joe, a certified member of a targeted group. During the last seven months of 2017, Joe is paid $3,500 for 500 hours of work. Maria is allowed a credit of $1,400 ($3,500 × 40%) for 2017. Joe continues to work for Maria in 2018 and is paid $7,000 through May 31, 2018.

Because up to $6,000 of first-year wages are eligible for the credit, Maria is allowed a 40% credit on $2,500 [$6,000 − $3,500 (wages paid in 2017)] of wages paid in 2018. The credit is $1,000 ($2,500 × 40%). None of Joe's wages paid after May 31, 2018, the end of the first year of Joe's employment, are eligible for the credit.

13-3c   Research Activities Credit

To encourage business-related research and experimentation, also termed research and development (R&D), a credit is allowed for certain qualifying expenditures paid or incurred by a taxpayer. The **research activities credit** is the *sum* of three components: an incremental research activities credit, a basic research credit, and an energy research credit.[8]

Incremental Research Activities Credit

The incremental research activities credit is equal to 20 percent of the *excess* of qualified research expenses for the taxable year over the base amount.[9]

In general, *research expenditures* qualify if the research relates to discovering technological information that is intended for use in the development of a new or improved business component of the taxpayer. If the research is performed in-house (by the taxpayer or employees), all of the expenses qualify. If the research is contracted to others outside the taxpayer's business, only 65 percent of the amount paid qualifies for the credit.[10]

---

[8]§ 41. An eligible small business ($50 million or less in gross receipts) can use the credit to reduce its alternative minimum tax (AMT) liability. In addition, a qualified startup company (less than $5 million in gross receipts) can offset the credit against its payroll tax liability.

[9]In lieu of determining the incremental research credit as described here, a taxpayer may elect to calculate the credit using an alternative simplified credit procedure. See §§ 41(c)(4) and (5).

[10]In the case of payments to a qualified research consortium, § 41(b)(3)(A) provides that 75% of the amount paid qualifies for the credit. In contrast, for amounts paid to an energy research consortium, § 41(b)(3)(D) allows the full amount to qualify for the credit.

George incurs the following research expenditures.

EXAMPLE

13

| In-house wages, supplies, computer time | $50,000 |
| Paid to Cutting Edge Scientific (a contractor) | 30,000 |

George's qualified research expenditures are $69,500 [$50,000 + ($30,000 × 65%)].

The incremental research credit is *not* allowed for:[11]

- Research conducted once commercial production begins.
- Surveys and studies such as market research, testing, or routine data collection.
- Research conducted *outside* the United States, Puerto Rico, or U.S. possessions.
- Research in the social sciences, arts, or humanities.

Determining the *base amount* involves a relatively complex series of computations meant to approximate recent historical levels of research activity by the taxpayer. Thus, the credit is allowed only for increases in research expenses.

Jack, a calendar year taxpayer, incurs qualifying research expenditures of $200,000 at the beginning of the year. Assuming that the base amount is $100,000, the incremental research activities credit is $20,000 [($200,000 − $100,000) × 20%].

EXAMPLE

14

In addition to qualifying for the research credit, research expenditures also can be *deducted* in the year incurred.[12] One of three options must be chosen by the taxpayer.[13]

1. Use the full credit and reduce the expense deduction for research expenses by 100 percent of the credit,
2. Retain the full expense deduction and reduce the credit by the product of the full credit times the maximum corporate tax rate (35 percent), or
3. Use the full credit, *capitalize* the research expenses, and *amortize* them over 60 months or more.[14]

Assume the same facts as in Example 14, which shows that the potential incremental research activities credit is $20,000. In the current year, the expense that the taxpayer can deduct and the credit amount under each of the three choices are as follows.

EXAMPLE

15

	Credit Amount	Deduction Amount
Full credit and reduced deduction		
$20,000 − $0	$20,000	
$200,000 − $20,000		$180,000
Reduced credit and full deduction		
$20,000 − [(100% × $20,000) × 35%]	13,000	
$200,000 − $0		200,000
Full credit and capitalize and elect to amortize costs over 60 months		
$20,000 − $0	20,000	
($200,000/60) × 12		40,000

---

[11]§ 41(d). See also Reg. §§ 1.41–1 through 1.41–7.

[12]§ 174. Also refer to the discussion of rules for deducting research and experimental expenditures in text Section 7-4.

[13]§ 280C(c).

[14]In this case, the amount capitalized and subject to amortization is reduced by the full amount of the credit *only* if the credit exceeds the amount allowable as a deduction.

Basic Research Credit

Corporations (other than S corporations or personal service corporations) are allowed an additional 20 percent credit for basic research payments made in *excess* of a base amount. *Basic research* is defined generally as any original investigation for the advancement of scientific knowledge not having a specific commercial objective. Basic research conducted outside the United States and in the social sciences, arts, or humanities does not qualify. This reflects the intent of Congress to use the credit to encourage domestic high-tech research.

The basic research credit calculation is complex and is based on expenditures in excess of a specially defined base amount. The portion of the basic research expenditures not in excess of the base amount qualifies for the incremental research activities credit.

Orange Corporation pays $75,000 to a university for basic research. Orange's base amount for the basic research credit is $50,000. The basic research activities credit allowed is $5,000 [($75,000 − $50,000) × 20%]. The $50,000 of basic research expenditures that equal the base amount also can be treated as research expenses for purposes of the regular incremental research activities credit.

Energy Research Credit

This component of the research credit encourages taxpayers to support a specific type of exempt organization conducting energy research (called an energy research consortium). The credit is equal to 20 percent of payments made to these organizations.

13-3d Low-Income Housing Credit

To encourage building owners to make affordable housing available for low-income individuals, a credit is available to owners of qualified low-income housing projects.[15]

More than any other, the `low-income housing credit` is influenced by nontax factors. For example, these credits are distributed nationally to various state and local agencies. So the property must be approved by the appropriate agency authorized to provide low-income housing credits.

The credit is based on the number of units rented to low-income tenants. Tenants are low-income tenants if their income does not exceed a specified percentage of the area median gross income. The amount of the credit is determined by multiplying the qualified basis by a credit rate.[16]

Generally, first-year credits are prorated based on the date the project is placed in service. A full year's credit is taken in each of the next nine years, and any remaining first-year credit is claimed in the eleventh year. The credit is claimed over a 10-year period if the property continues to meet the required conditions.

Sarah spends $1 million to build a qualified low-income housing project that is completed on January 1 of the current year. The entire project is rented to low-income families. Assume that the credit rate for property placed in service during January is 7.48%. Sarah may claim a credit of $74,800 ($1,000,000 × 7.48%) in the current year and in each of the following nine years.

If Sarah only made 75% of the project's units available to low-income families, her credit would be $56,100 [($1,000,000 × 75%) × 7.48%]

Recapture of a portion of the credit may be required if certain events occur (e.g., if the number of low-income tenant units falls below a minimum threshold or if the taxpayer sells the property).

---

[15]§ 42.

[16]The qualified basis is the property's cost times the percentage of units made available to low-income tenants; the rate is subject to adjustment every month by the IRS.

13-3e **Disabled Access Credit**

The disabled access credit is designed to encourage eligible small businesses to make their facilities more accessible to disabled individuals. The credit, created as part of the Americans with Disabilities Act of 1990, is 50 percent of the eligible expenditures that exceed $250 but do not exceed $10,250. As a result, the maximum credit is $5,000 ($10,000 × 50%).[17]

An *eligible small business* is a business that during the previous year either had gross receipts of $1 million or less or had no more than 30 full-time employees. An eligible business can include a sole proprietorship, a partnership, a regular corporation, or an S corporation.

Eligible expenditures include reasonable and necessary amounts that are paid or incurred to make older buildings accessible (only buildings first placed in service before November 6, 1990, qualify). Qualifying projects include installing ramps, widening doorways, and adding raised markings on elevator control buttons. Costs to assist hearing- or visually-impaired employees or customers who interact with the business also qualify. These costs can include both personnel (e.g., an interpreter) or equipment (e.g, audio or visual equipment or modifications to existing equipment).

The property's tax basis is reduced by the amount of the credit.

EXAMPLE 18

This year, Red, Inc., an eligible small business, makes $11,000 of capital improvements to a building that had been placed in service in June 1990. The improvements make Red's business more accessible to the disabled and are eligible expenditures for purposes of the disabled access credit.

The amount of the credit is $5,000 [($10,250 − $250) × 50%]. Although $11,000 of eligible expenditures are incurred, only $10,000 qualifies for the credit. The capital improvements have a depreciable basis of $6,000 [$11,000 (cost) − $5,000 (amount of the credit)].

13-3f **Credit for Small Employer Pension Plan Startup Costs**

Small businesses are entitled to a nonrefundable credit for administrative costs associated with establishing and maintaining certain qualified retirement plans.[18] While these costs (e.g., payroll system changes, retirement-related education programs, and consulting fees)[19] are deductible as ordinary and necessary business expenses, the credit lowers the after-tax cost of establishing a qualified retirement program and encourages eligible employers to offer retirement plans for their employees.

The credit for small employer pension plan startup costs is 50 percent of qualified startup costs. An eligible employer is one with fewer than 100 employees who have earned at least $5,000 of compensation. The maximum credit is $500 (based on a maximum $1,000 of qualifying expenses), and the deduction for the startup costs incurred is reduced by the amount of the credit. The credit can be claimed for qualifying costs incurred in each of the three years beginning with the tax year in which the retirement plan becomes effective (maximum total credit over three years of $1,500).

EXAMPLE 19

Maple Company decides to establish a qualified retirement plan for its employees. In the process, it pays consulting fees of $1,200 to a firm that will provide educational seminars to Maple's employees and will assist the payroll department in making necessary changes to the payroll system.

Maple may claim a credit for the pension plan startup costs of $500 ($1,200 of qualifying costs, limited to $1,000 × 50%), and its deduction for these expenses is reduced to $700 ($1,200 − $500).

---

[17]§ 44.
[18]§ 45E.

[19]§§ 45E(c)(1) and (d)(1).

13-3g **Credit for Employer-Provided Child Care**

An employer's expenses to provide for the care of employee children is a deductible business expense. Alternatively, employers may claim a credit for providing child care facilities to their employees during normal working hours.[20]

The credit for employer-provided child care, limited annually to $150,000, is composed of the aggregate of two components: 25 percent of qualified child care expenses and 10 percent of qualified child care resource and referral services. *Qualified child care expenses* include the costs of acquiring, constructing, rehabilitating, expanding, and operating a child care facility. *Child care resource and referral services* include amounts paid or incurred under a contract to provide child care resource and referral services to an employee.

Any qualifying expenses otherwise deductible by the taxpayer are reduced by the amount of the credit. In addition, the taxpayer's basis for any property acquired or constructed and used for qualifying purposes is reduced by the amount of the credit. If within 10 years of being placed in service a child care facility ceases to be used for a qualified use, the taxpayer will be required to recapture a portion of the credit previously claimed.[21]

EXAMPLE 20

During the year, Tan Company constructed a child care facility for $400,000. The facility will be used by Tan employees who have preschool-aged children in need of child care services while their parents are at work. In addition, Tan incurred salaries for child care workers and other administrative costs associated with the facility of $100,000.

As a result, Tan's credit for employer-provided child care is $125,000 [($400,000 + $100,000) × 25%]. Correspondingly, the basis of the facility is reduced to $300,000 ($400,000 − $100,000), and the deduction for salaries and administrative costs is reduced to $75,000 ($100,000 − $25,000).

13-4 **OTHER TAX CREDITS**

13-4a **Earned Income Credit**

LO.4

Describe various tax credits that are available primarily to individual taxpayers.

The earned income credit provides income tax equity to the working poor. In addition, the credit helps to offset other Federal taxes, such as the gasoline tax, that impose a relatively larger burden on low-income taxpayers. Further, the credit encourages economically disadvantaged individuals to become contributing members of the workforce.

The earned income credit is determined by multiplying a maximum amount of earned income by the appropriate credit percentage (see Exhibit 13.3). Generally, earned income includes employee compensation and net earnings from self-employment; it excludes items such as interest, dividends, pension benefits, nontaxable employee compensation, and alimony.[22] If a taxpayer has children, the credit percentage used in the calculation depends on the number of qualifying children.

In 2017, the maximum earned income credit for a taxpayer with one qualifying child is $3,400 ($10,000 × 34%), $5,616 ($14,040 × 40%) for a taxpayer with two qualifying children, and $6,318 ($14,040 × 45%) for a taxpayer with three or more qualifying children. However, the maximum earned income credit is phased out completely if the taxpayer's earned income or AGI exceeds certain thresholds, as shown in Exhibit 13.3.[23]

To the extent that the greater of earned income or AGI exceeds $23,930 in 2017 for married taxpayers filing a joint return ($18,340 for other taxpayers), the difference, multiplied by the appropriate phaseout percentage, is subtracted from the maximum earned income credit.

---

[20]§ 45F.

[21]§ 45F(d).

[22]§ 32. The earned income credit is not available if the taxpayer's unearned income (e.g., interest and dividends) exceeds $3,450 in 2017 ($3,400 in 2016). See § 32(i).

[23]§ 32(a)(2)(B).

EXHIBIT 13.3	Earned Income Credit and Phaseout Percentages						
Tax Year	Number of Qualifying Children	Earned Income Base Amount	Credit Percentage	Maximum Credit	Phaseout Base	Phaseout Percentage	Phaseout Ends at Income of
2017	*Married, Filing Jointly*						
	No children	$ 6,670	7.65	$ 510	$13,930	7.65	$20,600
	One child	10,000	34.00	3,400	23,930	15.98	45,207
	Two children	14,040	40.00	5,616	23,930	21.06	50,597
	Three or more children	14,040	45.00	6,318	23,930	21.06	53,930
	Other Taxpayers						
	No children	$ 6,670	7.65	$ 510	$ 8,340	7.65	$15,010
	One child	10,000	34.00	3,400	18,340	15.98	39,617
	Two children	14,040	40.00	5,616	18,340	21.06	45,007
	Three or more children	14,040	45.00	6,318	18,340	21.06	48,340
2016	*Married, Filing Jointly*						
	No children	$ 6,610	7.65	$ 506	$13,820	7.65	$20,430
	One child	9,920	34.00	3,373	23,740	15.98	44,846
	Two children	13,930	40.00	5,572	23,740	21.06	50,198
	Three or more children	13,930	45.00	6,269	23,740	21.06	53,505
	Other Taxpayers						
	No children	$ 6,610	7.65	$ 506	$ 8,270	7.65	$14,880
	One child	9,920	34.00	3,373	18,190	15.98	39,296
	Two children	13,930	40.00	5,572	18,190	21.06	44,648
	Three or more children	13,930	45.00	6,269	18,190	21.06	47,955

EXAMPLE 21

In 2017, Grace Brown, who is married, files a joint return and otherwise qualifies for the earned income credit. Grace receives wages of $26,000, and she and her husband earn no other income. The Browns have one qualifying child. The current earned income credit is $3,400 ($10,000 × 34%) reduced by $331 [($26,000 − $23,930) × 15.98%]. As a result, the earned income credit is $3,069.

If, instead, the Browns have three or more qualifying children, the calculation produces a credit of $6,318 ($14,040 × 45%) reduced by $436 [($26,000 − $23,930) × 21.06%]. As a result, the Browns' earned income credit is $5,882.

Earned Income Credit Table

It is not necessary to compute the credit as shown in Example 21. To simplify the compliance process, the IRS issues an Earned Income Credit Table for the determination of the appropriate amount of the credit. This table and a worksheet are included in the instructions available to individual taxpayers.

Eligibility Requirements

Eligibility for the credit depends not only on the taxpayer meeting the earned income and AGI thresholds but also on whether he or she has a qualifying child. The term *qualifying child* generally has the same meaning here as it does for purposes of determining who qualifies as a dependent (see text Section 3-4a).

In addition to being available for taxpayers with qualifying children, the earned income credit is also available to certain *workers without children*. It is available only to taxpayers ages 25 through 64 who cannot be claimed as a dependent on another taxpayer's return. As shown in Exhibit 13.3, the credit for 2017 is calculated on a maximum earned income of $6,670 times 7.65 percent and reduced by 7.65 percent of earned income over $13,930 for married taxpayers filing a joint return ($8,340 for other taxpayers).

EXAMPLE 22

Walt, who is single, is 28 years of age, and is not claimed as a dependent on anyone else's return, earns $8,500 during 2017. Even though he does not have any qualifying children, he qualifies for the earned income credit. His credit is $510 ($6,670 × 7.65%) reduced by $12 [($8,500 − $8,340) × 7.65%]. As a result, Walt's earned income credit is $498.

If, instead, Walt's earned income is $8,000, his earned income credit is $510. Here, there is no phaseout of the maximum credit because his earned income does not exceed $8,340..

13-4b **Tax Credit for Elderly or Disabled Taxpayers**

The credit for the elderly provides tax relief to individuals who are not receiving substantial benefits from tax-free Social Security payments.[24] The **tax credit for the elderly or disabled** is available to:

- Taxpayers age 65 or older, or
- Taxpayers under age 65 who are retired with a **permanent and total disability** and who have disability income from a public or private employer on account of the disability.

The *maximum* allowable credit is 15 percent of qualifying retirement income (in general, $5,000 for single taxpayers or married taxpayers where one spouse qualifies; $7,500 for married taxpayers filing jointly where both spouses qualify). This qualifying income amount is *reduced* by (1) Social Security, Railroad Retirement, and certain excluded pension benefits and (2) one-half of the taxpayer's AGI in excess of a threshold amount based on filing status (in general, $10,000 for married filing jointly, $7,500 for single or head of household, and $5,000 for married filing separately). Given the AGI thresholds, very few taxpayers qualify for this credit.

13-4c **Foreign Tax Credit**

Individual taxpayers and corporations may claim a tax credit for foreign income tax paid on income earned and subject to income tax in another country or a U.S. possession.[25] Alternatively, a taxpayer can claim a deduction instead of a credit.[26] In most instances, the **foreign tax credit (FTC)** is advantageous because it provides a direct offset against the tax liability.

The FTC is designed to mitigate double taxation because income earned in a foreign country is subject to both U.S. and foreign income taxes. However, the FTC is subject to an overall limitation. This limitation may result in some form of double taxation on income where the applicable U.S. tax rates are *lower* than those of the countries in which the income is earned.

Computation

The FTC allowed is the *lesser* of the foreign taxes paid or incurred, or the *overall limitation* computed as follows.[27]

$$\frac{\text{Foreign-source taxable income}}{\text{Worldwide taxable income}} \quad \times \quad \text{U.S. tax before FTC}$$

For individual taxpayers, worldwide taxable income is determined *before* personal and dependency exemptions are deducted.

---

[24]§ 22. This credit is not subject to indexation.

[25]Section 27 provides for the credit, but the qualifications and calculation procedure for the credit are contained in §§ 901–908.

[26]§ 164.

[27]§ 904.

In 2017, Ian, a calendar year taxpayer, records $10,000 of income from Country Y, which imposes a 15% tax, and $20,000 from Country Z, which imposes a 50% tax. He reports taxable income of $53,800 from within the United States, is married filing a joint return, and claims two dependency exemptions. Thus, although Ian's taxable income for purposes of determining U.S. tax is $83,800, taxable income amounts used in the limitation formula are not reduced by personal and dependency exemptions. For this purpose, taxable income is $100,000 [$83,800 + (4 × $4,050)]. Assume that Ian's U.S. tax before the credit is $12,428. The overall limitation is computed as follows.

$$\frac{\text{Foreign-source taxable income}}{\text{Worldwide taxable income}} \times \frac{\$30,000}{\$100,000} \times \$12,428 = \$3,728$$

In this case, $3,728 is allowed as the FTC because this amount is less than the $11,500 of foreign taxes imposed [$1,500 (Country Y) + $10,000 (Country Z)].

Thus, the overall limitation may result in some of the foreign income being subjected to double taxation. Unused FTCs [e.g., the $7,772 ($11,500 − $3,728) from Example 23] can be carried back 1 year and forward 10 years.[28]

Only income taxes, war profits taxes, and excess profits taxes (or taxes paid in lieu of such taxes) qualify for the credit.[29] Value added taxes (VAT), severance taxes, property taxes, and sales taxes do not qualify for the FTC because they are not taxes on income.

13-4d **Adoption Expenses Credit**

The **adoption expenses credit** assists taxpayers who incur nonrecurring costs directly associated with the adoption process, such as adoption fees, attorney fees, court costs, social service review costs, and transportation costs.[30]

In 2017, up to $13,570 of costs incurred to adopt an eligible child qualify for the credit.[31] An eligible child is either:

- Under 18 years of age at the time of the adoption, or
- Physically or mentally incapable of taking care of himself or herself.

In general, taxpayers claim the credit in the year the adoption is completed. If the adoption is not completed, the credit can be claimed in a following year. A married couple must file a joint return to claim the credit.

In late 2016, Sam and Martha pay $4,000 in legal fees, adoption fees, and other expenses directly related to the adoption of an infant daughter, Susan. In 2017, the year in which the adoption is completed, they pay an additional $10,000. Sam and Martha are eligible for a $13,570 credit in 2017 (for expenses of $14,000, paid in 2016 and 2017, limited by the $13,570 ceiling in 2017).

The credit is phased out for taxpayers whose AGI (modified for this purpose) exceeds $203,540 in 2017, and the credit is completely eliminated when AGI reaches $243,540. The resulting credit is calculated by reducing the allowable credit (determined without this reduction) by the allowable credit multiplied by the ratio of the excess of the taxpayer's AGI over $203,540 to $40,000.[32]

Assume the same facts as in the previous example, except that Sam and Martha's AGI is $228,540 in 2017. As a result, their available credit in 2017 is reduced from $13,570 to $5,089 {$13,570 − [$13,570 × ($25,000/$40,000)]}.

The adoption credit is nonrefundable. However, any unused adoption expenses credit may be carried forward for up to five years, being utilized on a first-in, first-out basis.

---

[28]§ 904(c) and Reg. § 1.904–2(g), Example 1.

[29]Reg. § 1.901–1(a)(3)(i).

[30]§ 23.

[31]§ 23(b)(1). In 2016, the maximum amount of eligible costs was $13,460. Unique rules are used in calculating the credit when adopting "a child with special needs." See § 23(d)(3).

[32]§ 23(b)(2). The AGI threshold amount is indexed for inflation. In 2016, the phaseout of the credit began when AGI exceeded $201,920.

13-4e **Child Tax Credit**

A child tax credit is provided to individual taxpayers based on the *number* of their qualifying children. This credit is one of several "family-friendly" provisions in the Federal income tax law. To be eligible for the credit, the child must be under age 17, must be a U.S. citizen, and must be claimed as a dependent on the taxpayer's return.

Maximum Credit and Phaseouts

The credit available is $1,000 per child.[33] The available credit is phased out when AGI reaches $110,000 for joint filers ($55,000 for married taxpayers filing separately) and $75,000 for single taxpayers. The credit is phased out by $50 for each $1,000 (or part thereof) of AGI above the $110,000 (or $55,000) amounts.[34] Because the maximum credit amount depends on the number of qualifying children, the income level at which the credit is phased out completely also depends on the number of qualifying children.[35]

EXAMPLE 26

Juanita and Alberto are married and file a joint tax return claiming their two children, ages 6 and 8, as dependents. Their AGI is $122,400. Juanita and Alberto's maximum child tax credit is $2,000 ($1,000 × 2 children).

Because Juanita and Alberto's AGI is in excess of the $110,000 threshold, the maximum credit must be reduced by $50 for every $1,000 (or part thereof) above the threshold amount {$50 × [($122,400 − $110,000)/$1,000]}. Thus, the credit reduction equals $650 [$50 × 13 (rounded up from 12.4)]. Therefore, Juanita and Alberto's child tax credit is $1,350 ($2,000 − $650).

13-4f **Credit for Child and Dependent Care Expenses**

The credit for child and dependent care expenses mitigates the inequity felt by working taxpayers who must pay for child care services to work outside the home.[36] The credit is a specified percentage of child and dependent care expenses. The credit percentage varies based on the taxpayer's AGI, and expenses are capped at a maximum of $6,000.

Eligibility

To be eligible for the credit, an individual must have either:

- A dependent under age 13, or
- A dependent or spouse who is physically or mentally incapacitated and who lives with the taxpayer for more than one-half of the year.

Generally, married taxpayers must file a joint return to obtain the credit.

Eligible Employment-Related Expenses

Eligible expenses include amounts paid for household services and care of a qualifying individual that are incurred to enable the taxpayer to be employed. The care can be provided in the home (e.g., by a nanny) or outside the home (e.g., at a day care center).

Out-of-the-home expenses incurred for an older dependent or spouse who is physically or mentally incapacitated qualify for the credit if that person regularly spends at least eight hours each day in the taxpayer's household. This makes the credit available to taxpayers who keep handicapped older children and elderly relatives in the home instead of institutionalizing them.

Child care payments to a relative are eligible for the credit unless the relative is a child (under age 19) of the taxpayer.

---

[33]§ 24.

[34]AGI is modified for purposes of this calculation. The threshold amounts are *not* indexed for inflation. See §§ 24(a) and (b).

[35]The child tax credit generally is refundable to the extent of 15% of the taxpayer's earned income in excess of $3,000.

[36]§ 21.

Wilma is an employed mother of an 8-year-old child. She pays her mother, Rita, $1,500 per year to care for the child after school. Wilma pays her daughter Eleanor, age 17, $900 for the child's care during the summer. Of these amounts, only the $1,500 paid to Rita qualifies as employment-related child care expenses.

EXAMPLE
27

Earned Income Ceiling

Qualifying employment-related expenses are limited to an individual's earned income. For married taxpayers, this limitation applies to the spouse with the *lesser* amount of earned income. Special rules are provided for taxpayers with nonworking spouses who are disabled or are full-time students. Here, the nonworking spouse is *deemed* to have earned income of $250 per month if there is one qualifying individual in the household or $500 per month if there are two or more qualifying individuals in the household. In the case of a student-spouse, only months when the student is enrolled on a full-time basis are counted.[37]

Calculation of the Credit

In general, the credit is equal to a percentage of *unreimbursed* employment-related expenses up to $3,000 for one qualifying individual and $6,000 for two or more individuals. The credit rate varies between 20 percent and 35 percent, depending on the taxpayer's AGI (see Exhibit 13.4).

Nancy, who has two children under age 13, worked full-time while her spouse, Ron, was attending college for 10 months during the year. Nancy earned $22,000 and incurred $6,200 of child care expenses. Ron is deemed to have earned $500 for each of the 10 months (or a total of $5,000).

Because Nancy and Ron report AGI of $22,000, they are allowed a credit rate of 31%. Nancy and Ron are limited to $5,000 in qualified child care expenses ($6,000 maximum expenses, limited to Ron's deemed earned income of $5,000). Therefore, they are entitled to a tax credit of $1,550 (31% × $5,000).

EXAMPLE
28

EXHIBIT 13.4	Child and Dependent Care Credit Computations	
Adjusted Gross Income		
Over	**But Not Over**	**Applicable Rate of Credit**
$ 0	$15,000	35%
15,000	17,000	34%
17,000	19,000	33%
19,000	21,000	32%
21,000	23,000	31%
23,000	25,000	30%
25,000	27,000	29%
27,000	29,000	28%
29,000	31,000	27%
31,000	33,000	26%
33,000	35,000	25%
35,000	37,000	24%
37,000	39,000	23%
39,000	41,000	22%
41,000	43,000	21%
43,000	No limit	20%

[37]§ 21(d).

ETHICS & EQUITY Is This the Right Way to Use the Credit for Child and Dependent Care Expenses?

Your friends, Tim and Susan, have hired a child care provider (Rebecca) to come into their home while they are at work to care for their two children. Rebecca charges $4,500 for her services for the year. Tim and Susan have discovered that up to $6,000 of qualifying expenditures will generate a credit for child and dependent care expenses and that qualifying expenditures can include payments for housecleaning services.

As a result, they ask Rebecca whether she would be interested in working several hours more per week, after Tim returns from work, for the sole purpose of cleaning the house.

Tim and Susan offer to pay Rebecca $1,500 for the additional work. For Tim and Susan, the net cost of the additional services would be $1,200 [$1,500 − ($1,500 × 20%)] due to the availability of the credit for child and dependent care expenses.

You learn of Tim and Susan's opportunity but think it is unfair. If you hired someone to perform similar housecleaning services at the same price, your net cost would be $1,500, not $1,200, because you do not qualify for the credit. You are troubled by this inequity. Is your intuition correct?

Dependent Care Assistance Program

A taxpayer is allowed an exclusion from gross income for a limited amount of employer-reimbursed child or dependent care expenses. If this occurs, the $3,000 and $6,000 ceilings for allowable child and dependent care expenses are reduced dollar for dollar by the amount of reimbursement.[38]

EXAMPLE 29

Assume the same facts as in Example 28, except that of the $6,200 paid for child care, Nancy was reimbursed $2,500 by her employer under a qualified dependent care assistance program. Under the employer's plan, the reimbursement reduces Nancy's taxable wages. As a result, Nancy and Ron have AGI of $19,500 ($22,000 − $2,500).

In this case, the child care ceiling of $6,000 is reduced by the $2,500 reimbursement, resulting in a tax credit of $1,120 [32% × ($6,000 − $2,500)].

13-4g Education Tax Credits

The **American Opportunity credit** and the **lifetime learning credit**[39] are available to help qualifying low- and middle-income individuals defray the cost of higher education. The credits are available for qualifying tuition and related expenses incurred by students pursuing undergraduate or graduate degrees or vocational training. Books and other course materials are eligible for the American Opportunity credit (but not the lifetime learning credit).[40] Room and board are ineligible for both credits.

Maximum Credit

The American Opportunity credit permits a maximum credit of $2,500 per year (100 percent of the first $2,000 of tuition expenses plus 25 percent of the next $2,000 of tuition expenses) for the *first four years* of postsecondary education. The lifetime learning credit permits a credit of 20 percent of qualifying expenses (up to $10,000 per year) incurred in a year in which the American Opportunity credit is not claimed. Generally, the lifetime learning credit is used for individuals who are beyond the first four years of postsecondary education.

Eligible Individuals

Both education credits are available for qualified expenses incurred by a taxpayer, taxpayer's spouse, or taxpayer's dependent. The American Opportunity credit is available per eligible student, while the lifetime learning credit is calculated per taxpayer. To be eligible for the American Opportunity credit, a student must take at least one-half the full-time course load for at least one academic term at a qualifying educational institution. No comparable requirement exists for the lifetime learning credit. So taxpayers who are seeking new job skills or maintaining existing skills through graduate training

---

[38]§ 21(c).

[39]§ 25A.

[40]§ 25A(i)(3).

or continuing education are eligible for the lifetime learning credit. Taxpayers who are married must file a joint return to claim either education credit.

Income Limitations and Refundability

Both education credits are subject to income limitations, which differ by credit. Forty percent of the American Opportunity credit is refundable, and it can offset a taxpayer's alternative minimum tax (AMT) liability (the lifetime learning credit is neither refundable nor an AMT liability offset).[41]

The American Opportunity credit amount is phased out beginning when the taxpayer's AGI (modified for this purpose) reaches $80,000 ($160,000 for married taxpayers filing jointly).[42] The credit is phased out proportionally over a $10,000 ($20,000 for married taxpayers filing jointly) phaseout range. As a result, the credit is eliminated when modified AGI reaches $90,000 ($180,000 for married taxpayers filing jointly).

For 2017, the lifetime learning credit amount is phased out beginning when the taxpayer's AGI (modified for this purpose) reaches $56,000 ($112,000 for married taxpayers filing jointly).[43] The credit is phased out proportionally over a $10,000 ($20,000 for married taxpayers filing jointly) range. As a result, the credit is eliminated when AGI reaches $66,000 ($132,000 for married taxpayers filing jointly).

The Big Picture

EXAMPLE 30

Return to the facts of *The Big Picture* on p. 13-1. Recall that Tom and Jennifer Snyder are married; file a joint tax return; have modified AGI of $158,000; and have two children, Lora and Sam. The Snyders paid $7,500 of tuition and $8,500 for room and board for Lora (a freshman) and $8,100 of tuition plus $7,200 for room and board for Sam (a junior). Both Lora and Sam are full-time students and are Tom and Jennifer's dependents.

Lora's tuition and Sam's tuition are qualified expenses for the American Opportunity credit. For 2017, Tom and Jennifer may claim a $2,500 American Opportunity credit for both Lora's and Sam's expenses [(100% × $2,000) + (25% × $2,000)]; in total, they qualify for a $5,000 American Opportunity credit.

The Big Picture

EXAMPLE 31

Return to the facts of *The Big Picture* on p. 13-1. Now assume that Tom and Jennifer's 2017 modified AGI is $172,000 instead of $158,000. In this case, Tom and Jennifer can claim a $2,000 American Opportunity credit for 2017 (rather than a $5,000 credit).

The credit is reduced because the taxpayers' modified AGI exceeds the $160,000 limit for married taxpayers. The reduction is the amount by which modified AGI exceeds the limit, expressed as a percentage of the phaseout range. In this case, the reduction is 60%, computed as [($172,000 − $160,000)/$20,000]. Therefore, the maximum available credit for 2017 is $2,000 ($5,000 × 40% allowable portion).

The Big Picture

EXAMPLE 32

Return to the facts of *The Big Picture* on p. 13-1. Now assume that Tom and Jennifer's modified AGI is $126,000. In addition, assume that Tom is going to school on a part-time basis to complete a graduate degree and pays qualifying tuition and fees of $4,000 during 2017.

As Tom and Jennifer's modified AGI is below $160,000, a $5,000 American Opportunity credit is available to them ($2,500 for both Lora and Sam).

In addition, Tom's qualifying expenses are eligible for the lifetime learning credit. The potential lifetime learning credit of $800 ($4,000 × 20%) is reduced because the Snyders' modified AGI exceeds the $112,000 limit for married taxpayers. As modified AGI exceeds the $112,000 limit by $14,000 and the phaseout range is $20,000, the couple's lifetime learning credit is reduced by 70%.

Therefore, the lifetime learning credit for 2017 is $240 ($800 × 30%), and total education credits amount to $5,240 ($5,000 American Opportunity credit and $240 lifetime learning credit).

---

[41]If the credit is claimed for a taxpayer subject to § 1(g) (the "kiddie tax"), the credit is not refundable.

[42]These amounts are not adjusted for inflation.

[43]§ 25A(d). For 2016, the AGI bases were $55,000 and $111,000. § 25A(h)(2)(A).

Restrictions on Double Tax Benefit

Taxpayers who claim an education credit may not deduct the expenses, nor may they claim the credit for amounts that are otherwise excluded from gross income (e.g., scholarships and employer-paid educational assistance).

13-4h **Energy Credits**

The Internal Revenue Code contains a variety of credits for businesses and individuals to encourage the conservation of natural resources and the development of energy sources other than oil and gas. The energy tax credits include incentives to:

- Install energy-efficient windows, insulation, and heating and cooling equipment;
- Purchase solar and other energy-efficient water heaters; and
- Install equipment in a business to produce electricity using solar, wind, or geothermal sources.

Credit amounts and expiration dates differ for the various provisions.

13-4i **Credit for Certain Retirement Plan Contributions**

Taxpayers may claim a nonrefundable credit for certain retirement plan contributions based on eligible contributions of up to $2,000 to certain qualified retirement plans, like traditional and Roth IRAs and § 401(k) plans.[44] This credit, sometimes referred to as the "saver's credit," encourages lower- and middle-income taxpayers to contribute to qualified retirement plans. If a taxpayer (and/or spouse) contributes to and receives distributions from a qualifying plan, these amounts must be netted. Distributions in the tax year, in the two prior tax years, and during the period prior to the due date of the return are used in this netting process.

The credit rate applied to the eligible contributions depends on the taxpayer's AGI[45] and filing status as shown in Exhibit 13.5. However, the maximum credit allowed to an individual is $1,000 ($2,000 × 50%). Once AGI exceeds the upper end of the applicable range, no credit is available. To qualify for the credit, the taxpayer must be at least 18 years of age and cannot be a dependent of another taxpayer or a full-time student.

EXAMPLE 33

Earl and Josephine, married taxpayers, each contribute $2,500 to § 401(k) plans offered through their employers. AGI reported on their joint return is $45,000. The eligible retirement plan contributions for purposes of the credit are limited to $2,000 for Earl and $2,000 for Josephine.

As a result, Earl and Josephine may claim a $400 retirement plan contributions credit [($2,000 × 2) × 10%]. They would not qualify for the credit if their AGI had exceeded $62,000.

Concept Summary 13.1 provides an overview of the tax credits discussed in this chapter.

EXHIBIT 13.5	"Saver's" Credit Rate and AGI Thresholds, 2017						
Joint Return		**Head of Household**		**All Other Cases**		**Applicable Percentage**
Over	**Not Over**	**Over**	**Not Over**	**Over**	**Not Over**	
$ 0	$37,000	$ 0	$27,750	$ 0	$18,500	50%
37,000	40,000	27,750	30,000	18,500	20,000	20%
40,000	62,000	30,000	46,500	20,000	31,000	10%
62,000		46,500		31,000		0%

---

[44]§ 25B.

[45]The AGI thresholds are indexed annually for inflation. For purposes of this credit, the AGI thresholds are modified to include certain excluded income items. See § 25B(e).

Concept Summary 13.1

Tax Credits

Credit	Computation	Comments
Tax withheld on wages (§ 31)	Amount is reported to employee on Form W–2.	Refundable credit.
Earned income (§ 32)	Amount is determined by reference to Earned Income Credit Table published by IRS. Computations of underlying amounts in Earned Income Credit Table are illustrated in Example 21.	Refundable credit. A form of negative income tax to assist low-income taxpayers. Earned income and AGI must be less than certain threshold amounts. Generally, one or more qualifying children must reside with the taxpayer.
Child and dependent care (§ 21)	Rate ranges from 20% to 35% depending on AGI. Maximum base for credit is $3,000 for one qualifying individual, $6,000 for two or more.	Nonrefundable personal credit. No carryback or carryforward. Benefits taxpayers who incur employment-related child or dependent care expenses in order to work or seek employment. Eligible taxpayers must have a dependent under age 13 or a dependent (any age) or spouse who is physically or mentally incapacitated.
Elderly or disabled (§ 22)	15% of sum of base amount minus reductions for (1) Social Security and other nontaxable benefits and (2) excess AGI. Base amount is fixed by law (e.g., $5,000 for a single taxpayer).	Nonrefundable personal credit. No carryback or carryforward. Provides relief for taxpayers not receiving substantial tax-free retirement benefits.
Adoption expenses (§ 23)	Up to $13,570 of costs incurred to adopt an eligible child qualify for the credit. Taxpayer claims the credit in the year qualified expenses were paid or incurred if they were paid or incurred during or after year in which adoption was finalized. For expenses paid or incurred in a year prior to when adoption was finalized, credit must be claimed in tax year following the tax year during which the expenses are paid or incurred.	Nonrefundable credit. Unused credit may be carried forward five years. Purpose is to assist taxpayers who incur nonrecurring costs associated with the adoption process.
Child (§ 24)	Credit is based on *number* of qualifying children under age 17. Maximum credit is $1,000 per child. Credit is phased out for higher-income taxpayers.	Generally a nonrefundable credit. Refundable in certain cases. Purpose is to provide tax relief for low- to moderate-income families with children.
Education (§ 25A)	American Opportunity credit is available for qualifying education expenses of students in first four years of postsecondary education. Maximum credit is $2,500 per year per eligible student. Credit is phased out for higher-income taxpayers.	Credit is partially refundable. Credit is designed to help defray costs of first four years of higher education for low- to middle-income families.
	Lifetime learning credit permits a credit of 20% of qualifying expenses (up to $10,000 per year) provided American Opportunity credit is not claimed with respect to those expenses. Credit is calculated per taxpayer, not per student, and is phased out for higher-income taxpayers.	Nonrefundable credit. Credit is designed to help defray costs of higher education beyond first four years and of costs incurred in maintaining or improving existing job skills for low- to middle-income taxpayers.
Credit for certain retirement plan contributions (§ 25B)	Calculation is based on amount of contribution multiplied by a percentage that depends on the taxpayer's filing status and AGI.	Nonrefundable credit. Purpose is to encourage contributions to qualified retirement plans by low- and middle-income taxpayers.
Foreign tax (§ 27)	Foreign taxable income/total worldwide taxable income × U.S. tax = Overall limitation. Lesser of foreign taxes imposed or overall limitation.	Nonrefundable credit. Unused credits may be carried back 1 year and forward 10 years. Purpose is to prevent double taxation of foreign-source income.

continued

Tax Credits—(Continued)

Credit	Computation	Comments
General business (§ 38)	May not exceed net income tax minus the greater of tentative minimum tax or 25% of net regular tax liability that exceeds $25,000.	Nonrefundable credit. Components include tax credit for rehabilitation expenditures, work opportunity tax credit, research activities credit, low-income housing credit, disabled access credit, credit for small employer pension plan startup costs, and credit for employer-provided child care. Unused credit may be carried back 1 year and forward 20 years. FIFO method applies to carrybacks, carryovers, and credits earned during current year.
Rehabilitation expenditures (§ 47)	Qualifying investment times rehabilitation percentage, depending on type of property. Regular rehabilitation rate is 10%; rate for certified historic structures is 20%.	Nonrefundable credit. Part of general business credit and therefore subject to same carryback, carryover, and FIFO rules. Purpose is to discourage businesses from moving from economically distressed areas to newer locations.
Research activities (§ 41)	Incremental credit is 20% of excess of computation year expenditures over the base amount. Basic research credit is allowed to certain corporations for 20% of cash payments to qualified organizations that exceed a specially calculated base amount. Energy research credit also available.	Nonrefundable credit. Part of general business credit and therefore subject to same carryback, carryover, and FIFO rules. Purpose is to encourage high-tech and energy research in the United States.
Low-income housing (§ 42)	Appropriate rate times eligible basis (portion of project attributable to low-income units). Credit is available each year for 10 years. Recapture may apply.	Nonrefundable credit. Part of general business credit and therefore subject to same carryback, carryover, and FIFO rules. Purpose is to encourage construction of housing for low-income individuals.
Disabled access (§ 44)	Credit is 50% of eligible access expenditures that exceed $250 but do not exceed $10,250. Maximum credit is $5,000. Available only to eligible small businesses.	Nonrefundable credit. Part of general business credit and therefore subject to same carryback, carryover, and FIFO rules. Purpose is to encourage small businesses to become more accessible to disabled individuals.
Credit for small employer pension plan startup costs (§ 45E)	Credit equals 50% of qualified startup costs incurred by eligible employers. Maximum annual credit is $500. Deduction for related expenses is reduced by the amount of the credit.	Nonrefundable credit. Part of general business credit and therefore subject to same carryback, carryover, and FIFO rules. Purpose is to encourage small employers to establish qualified retirement plans for their employees.
Credit for employer-provided child care (§ 45F)	Credit is equal to 25% of qualified child care expenses plus 10% of qualified expenses for child care resource and referral services. Maximum credit is $150,000. Deduction for related expenses or basis must be reduced by the amount of the credit.	Nonrefundable credit. Part of general business credit and therefore subject to same carryback, carryover, and FIFO rules. Purpose is to encourage employers to provide child care for their employees' children during normal working hours.
Work opportunity (§ 51)	Credit is limited to 40% of the first $6,000 of wages paid to each eligible employee.	Nonrefundable credit. Part of the general business credit and therefore subject to the same carryback, carryover, and FIFO rules. Purpose is to encourage employment of individuals in specified groups.

13-5 **PAYMENT PROCEDURES**

LO.5

Describe the tax withholding and payment procedures applicable to employers.

The tax law contains elaborate "pay-as-you-go" rules that require the prepayment of various Federal taxes. In addition, these rules carry penalties for any lack of compliance.[46] Prepayment procedures fall into two major categories: those applicable to employers and those applicable to self-employed persons. For employers, both payroll taxes (FICA and FUTA) and income taxes may be involved. With self-employed taxpayers, the focus is on the income tax and the self-employment tax.

13-5a **Employers**

Employment taxes include FICA (Federal Insurance Contributions Act; commonly known as Social Security) and FUTA (Federal Unemployment Tax Act). The employer usually is responsible for withholding the employee's share of FICA and appropriate amounts for income taxes. In addition, the employer must match the FICA portion withheld and fully absorb the cost of FUTA. Employers are required to pay these amounts to the IRS on a regular basis (usually weekly or monthly).

The key to employer compliance in this area involves the following.

- Identifying which employees and wages are covered by employment taxes and are subject to withholding for income taxes.
- Determining at the amount to be paid and / or withheld.
- Reporting and paying employment taxes and income taxes withheld to the IRS on a timely basis through the use of proper forms and procedures.

IRS Publication 15, *Employer's Tax Guide* (Circular E), is a key resource for employers.

Amount of FICA Taxes

The FICA tax has two components: Social Security tax (old age, survivors, and disability insurance) *and* Medicare tax (hospital insurance). The tax rates and wage base under FICA have increased substantially over the years. The base amount is adjusted each year for inflation. Exhibit 13.6 shows the base amounts for both the Social Security and Medicare taxes and the related employee tax rates. The employer must match the employee's portion, so the total Social Security tax rate is 12.4 percent and the total Medicare tax rate is 2.9 percent.

Employee withholdings continue until the maximum base amount is reached. In 2017, for example, FICA withholding for the Social Security portion (6.2 percent) ends once the employee has earned $127,200 of wages. However, the employer will continue to withhold Medicare taxes on wages above $127,200 as there is no limit on this portion of the FICA tax.

EXHIBIT 13.6	**FICA Rates and Base**

	Social Security Tax			**Medicare Tax**			
	Percent	×	**Base Amount**	+ **Percent**	×	**Base Amount**	= **Maximum Tax**
2013	6.20%	×	113,700	+ 1.45%**	×	Unlimited	= Unlimited
2014	6.20%	×	117,000	+ 1.45%**	×	Unlimited	= Unlimited
2015	6.20%	×	118,500	+ 1.45%**	×	Unlimited	= Unlimited
2016	6.20%	×	118,500	+ 1.45%**	×	Unlimited	= Unlimited
2017	6.20%	×	127,200	+ 1.45%	×	Unlimited	= Unlimited
2018 on	6.20%	×	*	+ 1.45%**	×	Unlimited	= Unlimited

*Not yet determined.
**Does not include the additional Medicare taxes on high-income individuals.

---

[46]See, for example, § 3403 (employer liable for any taxes withheld and not paid over to the IRS), § 6656 (penalty on amounts withheld and not paid over), and § 6654 (penalty for failure by an individual to pay estimated income taxes).

In 2017, Keshia earned a salary of $140,000 from her employer. Therefore, FICA taxes withheld from her salary are $7,886.40 ($127,200 × 6.2%) plus $2,030.00 ($140,000 × 1.45%) for a total of $9,916.40. In addition to paying the amount withheld from Keshia's salary to the Federal government, her employer also must pay $9,916.40.

In at least two situations, changing jobs during the year or having multiple jobs at the same time, it is possible for an employee to have paid excess FICA taxes during a tax year.

Excess FICA Taxes Withheld

During 2017, Kevin changed employers in the middle of the year and earned $67,500 (all of which was subject to FICA) from each job. As a result, each employer withheld $5,163.75 [(6.2% × $67,500) + (1.45% × $67,500)] for a total of $10,327.50.

Although each employer acted properly, Kevin's total FICA tax liability for the year is only $9,843.90 [(6.2% × $127,200) + (1.45% × $135,000)]. Thus, Kevin has overpaid his share of FICA taxes by $483.60 [$10,327.50 (amount paid) − $9,843.90 (amount of correct liability)]. Kevin can claim this amount as a tax credit when filing his 2017 income tax return.

During 2017, Lori earned $106,000 from her regular job and $29,000 from a part-time job (all of which was subject to FICA). As a result, one employer withheld $8,109 [(6.2% × $106,000) + (1.45% × $106,000)] while the other employer withheld $2,218.50 [(6.2% × $29,000) + (1.45% × $29,000)], for a total withheld for Lori of $10,327.50.

Lori's total FICA tax liability for the year is only $9,843.90 [(6.2% × $127,200) + (1.45% × $135,000)]. Thus, Lori has overpaid her share of FICA taxes by $483.60 [$10,327.50 (amount paid) − $9,843.90 (amount of correct liability)]. Lori can claim this amount as a tax credit when filing her 2017 income tax return.

The FICA tax must be paid for an individual employed by his or her spouse. No tax is collected for children under the age of 18 who are employed in a parent's trade or business.

Amount of Income Tax Withholding

Three steps are used to determine the employee's income tax withholdings.

1. Have the employee complete Form W–4, Employee's Withholding Allowance Certificate.
2. Determine the employee's payroll period.
3. Compute the amount to be withheld, usually using either the wage-bracket tables or the percentage method.[47]

Form W–4 reflects the employee's marital status and **withholding allowances**. Generally, this form need not be filed with the IRS and is retained by the employer as part of its payroll records.

On the Form W–4, an employee may claim *withholding allowances* equal to the number of personal and dependency exemptions claimed on the tax return. Additional withholding allowances are allowed in the situations specified on Form W–4 (e.g., if the taxpayer expects to claim a child and dependent care credit). An employee who plans to itemize deductions or claim adjustments to income (e.g., alimony and deductible IRA contributions) can use the worksheet provided on page 2 of Form W–4 to determine the correct number of additional allowances.

---

[47]The withholding provisions are contained in §§ 3401 and 3402. IRS Publication 15, *Employer's Tax Guide* (Circular E), contains detailed information about the income tax withholding process along with examples illustrating the wage-bracket and percentage withholding methods, which are beyond the scope of this text.

To avoid having too little tax withheld, some employees may find it necessary to reduce the number of withholding allowances. This might be the case for an employee who has more than one job or who has other sources of income that are not subject to adequate withholding.

If both spouses of a married couple are employed, they may allocate their total allowances between themselves as they see fit. The same allocation procedure is used if a taxpayer has more than one job. An employee can direct the employer to withhold a certain dollar amount in addition to the required amount.

Carl G. and Carol D. Simmons live at 4886 Sycamore Lane, Elmhurst, IL 60126. Carl earns $90,000 as a software engineer, and Carol earns $60,000 as a marketing manager. They have three dependent children and will claim the standard deduction. Assume that they do not qualify to claim the child tax credit. Together they should be entitled to five allowances [2 (for personal exemptions) + 3 (for dependency exemptions)]. The special withholding allowance is not available because both spouses earn more than $1,500. If Carl is the spouse first employed and his Form W–4 reflects five allowances, Carol's Form W–4 should claim zero allowances. The couple could, however, reallocate their allowances between them as long as the total claimed does not exceed five.

A Form W–4 has been completed for Carl (see p. 13-26), assuming that he claims all three dependents and Carol claims herself on her Form W–4.

Reporting and Payment Procedures

Employers devote a significant amount of time and expense in complying with the various employment tax and income tax withholding rules. Among the Federal forms that must be filed are the following.

Tax Form	Title
W–2	Wage and Tax Statement
940 or 940 EZ	Employer's Annual Federal Unemployment (FUTA) Tax Return
941	Employer's Quarterly Federal Tax Return

Form W–2 furnishes essential information to employees concerning wages paid, FICA, and income tax withholdings. This form (reporting information for the previous calendar year) must be furnished to an employee not later than January 31 (see Exhibit 13.7). Employees then report the relevant amounts on the appropriate lines of their Form 1040. For example, the amount in box 1 (Wages, tips, other compensation) is reported on Form 1040, page 1, line 7; the amount in box 2 (Federal income tax withheld) is included on page 2, line 64 of the Form 1040. If the taxpayer itemizes deductions, amounts reported in boxes 17 and 19 (state and local income taxes, respectively) can be included on line 5 of Schedule A (Form 1040). These amounts also typically are used on the state and/or local tax return.

Form 940 (or Form 940 EZ) is the employer's annual accounting of its FUTA liability. Generally, it is due one month after the end of the calendar year (i.e., no later than January 31, 2018, for the 2017 calendar year) and must include any remaining FUTA due.

Employers make deposits of employment taxes, usually weekly or monthly,[48] and they pay any outstanding amounts at the end of every quarter, using Form 941.

Backup Withholding

Some payments made to individuals by banks or businesses are subject to backup withholding. Backup withholding is designed to ensure that income tax is collected on interest income and other payments reported on a Form 1099. Backup withholding is required if the taxpayer does not give his or her Social Security number to the business or bank when required.[49] If backup withholding applies, the payor withholds 28 percent of the gross amount.

---

[48]Deposit requirements are specified in IRS Publication 15, *Employer's Tax Guide* (Circular E).

[49]§ 3406(a). The backup withholding rate is equal to the fourth lowest tax rate for single filers.

Form W-4 (2017)

Purpose. Complete Form W-4 so that your employer can withhold the correct federal income tax from your pay. Consider completing a new Form W-4 each year and when your personal or financial situation changes.

Exemption from withholding. If you are exempt, complete **only** lines 1, 2, 3, 4, and 7 and sign the form to validate it. Your exemption for 2017 expires February 15, 2018. See Pub. 505, Tax Withholding and Estimated Tax.

Note: If another person can claim you as a dependent on his or her tax return, you can't claim exemption from withholding if your total income exceeds $1,050 and includes more than $350 of unearned income (for example, interest and dividends).

Exceptions. An employee may be able to claim exemption from withholding even if the employee is a dependent, if the employee:

- Is age 65 or older,
- Is blind, or
- Will claim adjustments to income; tax credits; or itemized deductions, on his or her tax return.

The exceptions don't apply to supplemental wages greater than $1,000,000.

Basic instructions. If you aren't exempt, complete the **Personal Allowances Worksheet** below. The worksheets on page 2 further adjust your withholding allowances based on itemized deductions, certain credits, adjustments to income, or two-earners/multiple jobs situations.

Complete all worksheets that apply. However, you may claim fewer (or zero) allowances. For regular wages, withholding must be based on allowances you claimed and may not be a flat amount or percentage of wages.

Head of household. Generally, you can claim head of household filing status on your tax return only if you are unmarried and pay more than 50% of the costs of keeping up a home for yourself and your dependent(s) or other qualifying individuals. See Pub. 501, Exemptions, Standard Deduction, and Filing Information, for information.

Tax credits. You can take projected tax credits into account in figuring your allowable number of withholding allowances. Credits for child or dependent care expenses and the child tax credit may be claimed using the **Personal Allowances Worksheet** below. See Pub. 505 for information on converting your other credits into withholding allowances.

Nonwage income. If you have a large amount of nonwage income, such as interest or dividends, consider making estimated tax payments using Form 1040-ES, Estimated Tax for Individuals. Otherwise, you may owe additional tax. If you have pension or annuity income, see Pub. 505 to find out if you should adjust your withholding on Form W-4 or W-4P.

Two earners or multiple jobs. If you have a working spouse or more than one job, figure the total number of allowances you are entitled to claim on all jobs using worksheets from only one Form W-4. Your withholding usually will be most accurate when all allowances are claimed on the Form W-4 for the highest paying job and zero allowances are claimed on the others. See Pub. 505 for details.

Nonresident alien. If you are a nonresident alien, see Notice 1392, Supplemental Form W-4 Instructions for Nonresident Aliens, before completing this form.

Check your withholding. After your Form W-4 takes effect, use Pub. 505 to see how the amount you are having withheld compares to your projected total tax for 2017. See Pub. 505, especially if your earnings exceed $130,000 (Single) or $180,000 (Married).

Future developments. Information about any future developments affecting Form W-4 (such as legislation enacted after we release it) will be posted at *www.irs.gov/w4*.

Personal Allowances Worksheet (Keep for your records.)

A	Enter "1" for **yourself** if no one else can claim you as a dependent	**A**	*1*
B	Enter "1" if: { • You're single and have only one job; or • You're married, have only one job, and your spouse doesn't work; or • Your wages from a second job or your spouse's wages (or the total of both) are $1,500 or less. } . . .	**B**	
C	Enter "1" for your **spouse**. But, you may choose to enter "-0-" if you are married and have either a working spouse or more than one job. (Entering "-0-" may help you avoid having too little tax withheld.)	**C**	
D	Enter number of **dependents** (other than your spouse or yourself) you will claim on your tax return	**D**	*3*
E	Enter "1" if you will file as **head of household** on your tax return (see conditions under **Head of household** above) . .	**E**	
F	Enter "1" if you have at least $2,000 of **child or dependent care expenses** for which you plan to claim a credit . . .	**F**	
	(**Note:** Do **not** include child support payments. See Pub. 503, Child and Dependent Care Expenses, for details.)		
G	**Child Tax Credit** (including additional child tax credit). See Pub. 972, Child Tax Credit, for more information.		
	• If your total income will be less than $70,000 ($100,000 if married), enter "2" for each eligible child; then **less** "1" if you have two to four eligible children or **less** "2" if you have five or more eligible children.		
	• If your total income will be between $70,000 and $84,000 ($100,000 and $119,000 if married), enter "1" for each eligible child.	**G**	
H	Add lines A through G and enter total here. (**Note:** This may be different from the number of exemptions you claim on your tax return.) ▶	**H**	*4*

For accuracy, **complete all worksheets that apply.**	• If you plan to **itemize** or **claim adjustments to income** and want to reduce your withholding, see the **Deductions and Adjustments Worksheet** on page 2. • If you are **single and have more than one job** or are **married and you and your spouse both work** and the combined earnings from all jobs exceed $50,000 ($20,000 if married), see the **Two-Earners/Multiple Jobs Worksheet** on page 2 to avoid having too little tax withheld. • If **neither** of the above situations applies, **stop here** and enter the number from line H on line 5 of Form W-4 below.	

---------------------------- **Separate here and give Form W-4 to your employer. Keep the top part for your records.** ----------------------------

Form W-4

Department of the Treasury
Internal Revenue Service

Employee's Withholding Allowance Certificate

▶ Whether you are entitled to claim a certain number of allowances or exemption from withholding is subject to review by the IRS. Your employer may be required to send a copy of this form to the IRS.

OMB No. 1545-0074

2017

1 Your first name and middle initial	Last name	2 Your social security number
Carl G.	*Simmons*	*123-45-6789*

Home address (number and street or rural route)	3 ☐ Single ☑ Married ☐ Married, but withhold at higher Single rate.
4886 Sycamore Lane	**Note:** If married, but legally separated, or spouse is a nonresident alien, check the "Single" box.

City or town, state, and ZIP code	4 If your last name differs from that shown on your social security card, check here. You must call 1-800-772-1213 for a replacement card. ▶ ☐
Elmhurst, IL 60126	

5	Total number of allowances you are claiming (from line **H** above **or** from the applicable worksheet on page 2)	**5**	*4*
6	Additional amount, if any, you want withheld from each paycheck	**6**	$
7	I claim exemption from withholding for 2017, and I certify that I meet **both** of the following conditions for exemption. • Last year I had a right to a refund of **all** federal income tax withheld because I had **no** tax liability, **and** • This year I expect a refund of **all** federal income tax withheld because I expect to have **no** tax liability. If you meet both conditions, write "Exempt" here . . . . ▶	**7**	

Under penalties of perjury, I declare that I have examined this certificate and, to the best of my knowledge and belief, it is true, correct, and complete.

Employee's signature
(This form is not valid unless you sign it.) ▶   **Date** ▶

8 Employer's name and address (Employer: Complete lines 8 and 10 only if sending to the IRS.)	9 Office code (optional)	10 Employer identification number (EIN)

For Privacy Act and Paperwork Reduction Act Notice, see page 2.   Cat. No. 10220Q   Form **W-4** (2017)

EXHIBIT 13.7 **Form W–2**

a Employee's social security number		
b Employer identification number (EIN)	**1** Wages, tips, other compensation	**2** Federal income tax withheld
c Employer's name, address, and ZIP code	**3** Social security wages	**4** Social security tax withheld
	5 Medicare wages and tips	**6** Medicare tax withheld
	7 Social security tips	**8** Allocated tips
d Control number	**9** Verification code	**10** Dependent care benefits
e Employee's first name and initial Last name Suff.	**11** Nonqualified plans	**12a** See instructions for box 12
	13 Statutory employee Retirement plan Third-party sick pay	**12b**
	14 Other	**12c**
		12d
f Employee's address and ZIP code		

OMB No. 1545-0008

Safe, accurate, FAST! Use **IRS e-file**

Visit the IRS website at www.irs.gov/efile

15 State	Employer's state ID number	16 State wages, tips, etc.	17 State income tax	18 Local wages, tips, etc.	19 Local income tax	20 Locality name

Form **W-2** **Wage and Tax Statement** **2017**

Department of the Treasury—Internal Revenue Service

Copy B—To Be Filed With Employee's FEDERAL Tax Return.
This information is being furnished to the Internal Revenue Service.

13-5b Self-Employed Taxpayers

Although the following discussion largely centers on self-employed taxpayers, employed taxpayers may be required to pay estimated tax if they have income other than wages that is not subject to withholding (e.g., investment income, or a second trade or business in a self-employment capacity).

LO.6

Explain and illustrate the payment procedures applicable to self-employed persons.

Estimated Tax for Individuals

Estimated tax is the amount of tax (including AMT and self-employment tax) an individual expects to owe for the year after subtracting tax credits and income tax withheld. Any individual who has estimated tax of $1,000 or more *and* whose withholding does not equal or exceed the required annual payment (discussed below) must make quarterly payments.[50] If these payments are not made, a penalty may be assessed. No quarterly payments are required (and no penalty will apply) if the taxpayer's estimated tax is under $1,000. In addition, no penalty will apply if the taxpayer had a zero tax liability for the prior tax year, provided the prior tax year was 12 months (i.e., not a short year) *and* the taxpayer was a citizen or resident for that entire year.

The required annual payment must be computed first. This is the *smaller* of the following amounts.

- Ninety percent of the tax shown on the current year's return.
- One hundred percent of the tax shown on the preceding year's return (the return must cover the full 12 months of the preceding year). If the AGI on the preceding year's return exceeds $150,000 ($75,000 if married filing separately), the 100 percent requirement is increased to 110 percent.

---

[50]§§ 6654(c)(1) and 6654(e)(1).

In general, one-fourth of this required annual payment is due on April 15, June 15, and September 15 of the tax year and January 15 of the following year.

An equal part of withholding is deemed paid on each due date. So if $10,000 has been withheld during the year, $2,500 is applied to each quarter. If the quarterly estimates are determined to be $3,000, then $500 ($3,000 − $2,500) must be paid each quarter. Payments are submitted with the payment voucher for the appropriate quarter from Form 1040–ES.

Penalty on Underpayments

A nondeductible penalty is imposed on any estimated tax underpayment. The penalty rate is adjusted quarterly to reflect changes in the average prime rate.

An *underpayment* occurs when any installment (the sum of estimated tax paid and income tax withheld) is less than 25 percent of the required annual payment. The penalty is applied to the amount of the underpayment for the period of the underpayment.[51]

EXAMPLE 38

Marta made the following payments of estimated Federal income tax for 2017. Marta had no Federal income tax withheld.

April 18, 2017	$1,400
June 15, 2017	2,300
September 15, 2017	1,500
January 16, 2018	1,800

Marta's actual tax for 2017 is $8,000, and her tax in 2016 was $10,000. As a result, each installment should have been at least $1,800 [($8,000 × 90%) × 25%]. Of the payment on June 15, $400 will be credited to the unpaid balance of the first quarterly installment due on April 18,[52] effectively stopping the underpayment penalty for the first quarter. Of the remaining $1,900 payment on June 15, $100 is credited to the September 15 payment, resulting in this third quarterly payment being $200 short.

Then $200 of the January 16 payment is credited to the September 15 shortfall, ending the underpayment period for that amount. The January 16, 2018 installment is now underpaid by $200, and a penalty will apply from January 16, 2018, to April 17, 2018 (unless some tax is paid sooner). Marta's underpayments for the periods of underpayment are as follows.

1st installment due	$400 from April 18 to June 15, 2017
2nd installment due	Paid in full
3rd installment due	$200 from September 15, 2017, to January 16, 2018
4th installment due	$200 from January 16, 2018, to April 17, 2018

If a possible underpayment of estimated tax is indicated, Form 2210 is filed to compute the penalty due or to justify that no penalty applies.

Self-Employment Tax

The tax on self-employment income is levied to provide Social Security and Medicare benefits (old age, survivors, and disability insurance and hospital insurance) for self-employed individuals. Individuals with net earnings of $400 or more from self-employment are subject to the **self-employment tax**.[53] For 2017, the self-employment tax is 15.3 percent of self-employment income up to $127,200 and 2.9 percent of self-employment income in excess of $127,200 (see Exhibit 13.8).

Net earnings from self-employment includes gross income from a trade or business less allowable trade or business deductions, the distributive share of any partnership income or loss derived from a trade or business activity, and net income from rendering personal services as an independent contractor. This amount includes profits from sales of inventory.

Self-employed taxpayers are allowed a deduction from net earnings from self-employment, at one-half of the self-employment rate, for purposes of determining self-employment tax[54] *and* an income tax deduction (normally, one-half of the self-employment tax liability).[55]

---

[51]§ 6654(b)(2).

[52]Payments are credited to unpaid installments in the order in which the installments are required to be paid. § 6654(b)(3).

[53]§ 6017.

[54]§ 1402(a)(12).

[55]§ 164(f).

EXHIBIT 13.8	Self-Employment Tax: Social Security and Medicare Portions		
Year		**Tax Rate**	**Ceiling Amount**
2017	Social Security portion	12.4%	$127,200
	Medicare portion	2.9%	Unlimited
	Aggregate rate	15.3%	
2016	Social Security portion	12.4%	$118,500
	Medicare portion	2.9%	Unlimited
	Aggregate rate	15.3%	

Determining the amount of self-employment tax to be paid for 2017 involves completing the steps in Exhibit 13.9. The result of step 3 or 4 is the amount of self-employment tax to be paid. For *income tax purposes*, the amount to be reported is net earnings from self-employment before the deduction for the self-employment tax. Then the taxpayer is allowed a deduction *for* AGI of the appropriate amount of the self-employment tax.

EXHIBIT 13.9	2017 Self-Employment Tax Worksheet

1. Net earnings from self-employment. _____
2. Multiply line 1 by 92.35%. _____
3. If the amount on line 2 is $127,200 or less, multiply the line 2 amount by 15.3%. This is the self-employment tax. _____
4. If the amount on line 2 is more than $127,200, multiply the excess of line 2 over $127,200 by 2.9% and add $19,461.60. This is the self-employment tax. _____

In 2017, Ned and Terry report net earnings from self-employment of $55,000 and $145,000, respectively. Using the format in Exhibit 13.9, determine their self-employment tax.

EXAMPLE 39

Ned's Self-Employment Tax Worksheet

1. Net earnings from self-employment. $55,000.00
2. Multiply line 1 by 92.35%. $50,792.50
3. If the amount on line 2 is $127,200 or less, multiply the line 2 amount by 15.3%. This is the self-employment tax. $ 7,771.25
4. If the amount on line 2 is more than $127,200, multiply the excess of line 2 over $127,200 by 2.9% and add $19,461.60. This is the self-employment tax. _____

Terry's Self-Employment Tax Worksheet

1. Net earnings from self-employment. $145,000.00
2. Multiply line 1 by 92.35%. $133,907.50
3. If the amount on line 2 is $127,200 or less, multiply the line 2 amount by 15.3%. This is the self-employment tax. _____
4. If the amount on line 2 is more than $127,200, multiply the excess of line 2 over $127,200 by 2.9% and add $19,461.60. This is the self-employment tax. $ 19,656.12

For income tax purposes, Ned has net earnings from self-employment of $55,000 and a deduction *for* AGI of $3,885.63 ($7,771.25 × 50%). Terry has net earnings from self-employment of $145,000 and a deduction *for* AGI of $9,828.06 ($19,656.12 × 50%). Both taxpayers benefit from the self-employment tax deduction.

If an individual also receives wages subject to the FICA tax, the ceiling amount of the Social Security portion on which the self-employment tax is computed is reduced. However, a combination of FICA wages and self-employment earnings will not reduce the Medicare component of the self-employment tax, as there is no ceiling on this component of the tax.

EXAMPLE 40

In 2017, Kelly reported $86,000 of net earnings from a data imaging services business she owns. During the year, she also received wages of $54,000 as an employee of a small accounting firm. The amount of Kelly's self-employment income subject to the Social Security portion (12.4%) is $73,200 ($127,200 − $54,000), producing a tax of $9,076.80 ($73,200 × 12.4%); note that $73,200 is less than $79,421 of net self-employment income.

	Social Security Portion
Ceiling amount	$127,200
Less: FICA wages	(54,000)
Net ceiling	$ 73,200
Net self-employment income ($86,000 × 92.35%)	$ 79,421
Lesser of net ceiling or net self-employment income	$ 73,200

Although there is a limit on Social Security taxes ($127,200 maximum base in 2017), no such limit exists for the Medicare portion of the self-employment tax. Therefore, all of Kelly's net self-employment income ($86,000 × .9235 = $79,421) is subject to the 2.9% Medicare portion of the self-employment tax. The self-employment tax on this portion is $2,303.21 ($79,421 × 2.9%).

If Kelly's wages were only $30,000, then the net ceiling in the table above would be $97,200. Because her net self-employment income ($79,421) is less than this amount, she would compute her self-employment tax using the format in Exhibit 13.9.

For 2016, the self-employment tax computations are different from those for 2017, as the tax base was lower (see Exhibit 13.10).

EXHIBIT 13.10	**2016 Self-Employment Tax Worksheet**

1. Net earnings from self-employment. _____
2. Multiply line 1 by 92.35%. _____
3. If the amount on line 2 is $118,500 or less, multiply the line 2 amount by 13.3%. This is the self-employment tax. _____
4. If the amount on line 2 is more than $118,500, multiply the excess of line 2 over $118,500 by 2.9% and add $18,130.50. This is the self-employment tax. _____

LO.7

Explain some of the key tax provisions of the Affordable Care Act.

13-6 AFFORDABLE CARE ACT PROVISIONS

Some of the most sweeping new legislation in the last decade is known as the Affordable Care Act (ACA) or "ObamaCare." The Affordable Care Act was enacted to increase the quality and affordability of health insurance, reduce the number of uninsured individuals in the United States by expanding public and private insurance coverage, and lower health care costs for individuals and the government.

To assist in achieving these goals, the ACA enacted a number of individual tax provisions, including the individual shared responsibility payment, a premium tax credit, and additional Medicare taxes on the net investment income and the wages of certain high-income taxpayers. Each of these tax provisions is discussed briefly below.

13-6a **Individual Shared Responsibility Payment**

The ACA's "individual mandate"—which has been deemed a "tax" by the U.S. Supreme Court[56]—requires all individuals not covered by an employer-sponsored health plan, Medicare, Medicaid, or other public insurance programs to secure a private insurance policy or pay a penalty for each month they do not have health coverage. The penalty is called the individual shared responsibility payment (ISRP).[57]

Under this provision, individuals without coverage in 2017 will pay an ISRP of the greater of a flat amount of $695 per adult and $347.50 per child up to a maximum of $2,085 per family (three times the flat dollar amount), or 2.5 percent of household income (these amounts were the same for 2016). In general, household income is adjusted gross income increased by any nontaxable Social Security benefits, tax-exempt interest, and tax-exempt foreign income. These flat amounts will be increased annually by a cost-of-living adjustment. The ISRP cannot be greater than the national average cost of a bronze-level health plan.[58]

Exemptions are granted for financial hardship, religious objections, Native Americans, individuals without coverage for less than three months, undocumented immigrants, incarcerated individuals, individuals for whom the lowest cost plan option exceeds a specified percentage of household income, and those with incomes below the tax filing threshold (in 2017, the percentage is 8.16 percent and the income threshold for taxpayers under age 65 is $10,400 for singles and $20,800 for couples).[59]

13-6b **Premium Tax Credit**

Individuals and families whose household incomes are at least 100 percent but no more than 400 percent of the federal poverty level (also called the federal poverty line, or FPL) may be eligible to receive a federal subsidy (the premium tax credit, or PTC) if they purchase insurance via the Health Insurance Marketplace (the Marketplace).[60] Individuals whose income exceeds 400% of the FPL are not eligible for a PTC. For 2017 tax returns, the FPL for claiming a PTC is $11,880 for a single person (an additional $4,140 is added to that amount for each person in the household).[61]

Individuals can choose to receive their PTC in advance, and the Marketplace will send the money directly to the insurer to reduce the monthly insurance payments. Alternatively, individuals can receive the PTC as a refundable credit when they file their tax return for the year. Most individuals choose to receive their PTC in advance. In either case, however, taxpayers will be required to complete Form 8962 (Premium Tax Credit) when their tax return is filed.[62]

Taxpayers who enrolled in health care coverage via the Marketplace will receive information necessary to complete Form 8962 by the end of January each year.[63] Taxpayers who received the credit in advance must reconcile the credit based on actual income that year with the amounts that were subsidized through the Marketplace. They will receive a refund (if the advance credit was too low) or owe an additional tax obligation (if the advance credit was too large).[64]

---

[56]*National Federation of Independent Business v. Sebelius*, 132 S.Ct. 2566 (2012).

[57]§ 5000A.

[58]$223 per month per individual for 2016 (Rev.Proc. 2016–43, 2016–36 I.R.B. 316); 2017 information was not available at press date.

[59]Rev.Proc. 2016–24, 2016–18 I.R.B. 677. Individuals eligible for an exemption must file Form 8695 (Health Coverage Exemptions); this form also includes worksheets for calculating any ISRP owed.

[60]§ 36B. Also see Rev.Proc. 2014–37, 2014–33 I.R.B. 363.

[61]80 FR 3236. Different amounts apply for Alaska and Hawaii.

[62]Taxpayers who claim the premium tax credit cannot use Form 1040EZ (they must use either Form 1040A or Form 1040).

[63]This information is reported on Form 1095–A (Health Insurance Marketplace Statement). Included in this information statement are monthly health insurance premium payments and any premium tax credit received in advance. This information also is reported to the IRS.

[64]At the end of the year, taxpayers might discover that their household income unexpectedly exceeds 400% of the FPL. Rather than repaying their PTC, the taxpayer might be able to make a deductible contribution to an Individual Retirement Account, which would reduce household income and preserve the PTC.

13-6c **Additional Medicare Taxes on High-Income Individuals**

Two provisions result in increased Medicare taxes for high-income individuals: (1) an additional .9 percent tax on *wages* received in excess of specified amounts and (2) an additional 3.8 percent tax on *unearned income*.

Additional Tax on Wages

An additional .9 percent Medicare tax is imposed on wages received in excess of $250,000 for married taxpayers filing a joint return ($125,000 if married filing separately) and $200,000 for all other taxpayers.[65] Unlike the general 1.45 percent Medicare tax on wages, the additional tax on a joint return is based on the *combined* wages of the employee and the employee's spouse. As a result, the Medicare tax rate is:

1. 1.45 percent on the first $200,000 of wages ($125,000 on a married filing separate return; $250,000 of combined wages on a married filing joint return), and
2. 2.35 percent (1.45% + .9%) on wages in excess of $200,000 ($125,000 on a married filing separate return; $250,000 of combined wages on a married filing joint return).

Additional Medicare Tax on Wages

EXAMPLE 41

Jenna, who is single, earns wages of $500,000 in 2017. Jenna will pay $2,900 of Medicare taxes on the first $200,000 of her wages ($200,000 × 1.45%) and $7,050 of Medicare taxes on her wages in excess of $200,000 ($300,000 × 2.35%). In total, her Medicare tax is $9,950, of which $2,700 ($300,000 × .9%) represents Jenna's additional Medicare tax.

EXAMPLE 42

Patrick and Paula file a joint return in 2017. During the year, Patrick earns wages of $125,000, and Paula earns wages of $175,000—so their total wages are $300,000. Patrick and Paula will pay total Medicare taxes of $4,800 ($250,000 × 1.45% plus $50,000 × 2.35%), of which $450 ($50,000 × .9%) represents Patrick and Paula's additional Medicare tax.

Employers must withhold the additional .9 percent Medicare tax on wages paid in excess of $200,000.[66] An employer is not responsible for determining wages earned by an employee's spouse (and the implications of those wages on the total Medicare tax to be paid).

EXAMPLE 43

Return to the facts of Example 42. In 2017, neither Patrick's nor Paula's employer will withhold the additional Medicare tax as both wage amounts are less than $200,000. Therefore, Paula will have $2,537.50 of Medicare tax withheld ($175,000 × 1.45%), and Patrick will have $1,812.50 of Medicare tax withheld ($125,000 × 1.45%). Total Medicare tax withheld is $4,350.00 ($2,537.50 + $1,812.50). Patrick and Paula pay an additional $450.00 of Medicare taxes when they file their return.[67]

The additional Medicare tax also applies to self-employed individuals—with net earnings from self-employment being used for the threshold computations. As a result, the tax rate for the Medicare tax on self-employment income will be:

1. 2.9 percent on the first $200,000 of net earnings from self-employment ($125,000 on a married filing separate return; $250,000 on a married filing joint return), and
2. 3.8 percent (2.9% + .9%) on net earnings from self-employment in excess of $200,000 ($125,000 on a married filing separate return; $250,000 on a married filing joint return).

For married taxpayers, one of whom has wages and one of whom has self-employment income, the thresholds are reduced (but not below zero) by the amount of

---

[65]§ 3101(b)(2). The base amounts are not indexed for inflation.
[66]§ 3102(f).

[67]Couples in this situation might need to make estimated tax payments to cover the additional Medicare taxes.

wages taken into account in determining the additional .9 percent Medicare tax on wages.[68] Although self-employed individuals are allowed an income tax deduction for part of the self-employment tax, this additional .9 percent Medicare tax will *not* create a deduction (i.e., the deduction is determined without regard to this additional tax).[69]

Additional Tax on Unearned Income (Net Investment Income Tax)

An additional 3.8 percent Medicare tax is imposed on the unearned income of individuals, estates, and trusts.[70] Also known as the net investment income tax, the tax is 3.8 percent of the lesser of:[71]

1. Net investment income or
2. The excess of modified adjusted gross income over $250,000 for married taxpayers filing a joint return ($125,000 if married filing separately) and $200,000 for all other taxpayers.[72]

In general, "net investment income" includes interest, dividends, annuities, royalties, rents, income from passive activities, and net gains from the sale of investment property less deductions allowed in generating that income.[73] Modified adjusted gross income (MAGI) is adjusted gross income (AGI) increased by any foreign earned income exclusion.[74] Thus, for individuals who don't incur any excluded foreign earned income, MAGI is the same as AGI.

Additional Medicare Tax on Unearned Income

In 2017, Jill earns net investment income of $50,000 and MAGI of $180,000 and files as a single taxpayer. As Jill's MAGI does not exceed $200,000, she need not pay the additional Medicare tax on unearned income.

EXAMPLE 44

Assume the same facts as in Example 44, except that Jill reports net investment income of $85,000 and MAGI of $220,000.
   In this case, she pays a Medicare tax on the lesser of (1) $85,000 (her net investment income) or (2) $20,000 (the amount by which her MAGI exceeds the $200,000 threshold). As a result, Jill's additional Medicare tax on unearned income is $760 ($20,000 × 3.8%).

EXAMPLE 45

Assume the same facts as Example 45, except that Jill's MAGI is $290,000.
   Because her MAGI exceeds the threshold amount by $90,000, she pays a Medicare tax on the entire $85,000 of net investment income. As a result, Jill's additional Medicare tax on unearned income is $3,230 ($85,000 × 3.8%).

EXAMPLE 46

The 3.8 percent additional Medicare tax on unearned income is *in addition to* the additional .9 percent Medicare tax on wages or self-employment income. Taxpayers who have both high wages (or self-employment income) *and* high investment income may be subject to both taxes.

Assume the same facts as Example 46, except that Jill reports MAGI of $325,000 (including $240,000 of wages and $85,000 of net investment income).
   In this case, in addition to her $3,230 additional Medicare tax on unearned income, Jill also is subject to an additional Medicare tax on wages of $360 ($40,000 × .9%, her wages in excess of $200,000).

EXAMPLE 47

---

[68]§ 1401(b)(2)(B).
[69]§ 164(f).
[70]§ 1411.
[71]§ 1411(a)(1).
[72]§ 1411(b). The base amounts are not indexed for inflation.

[73]§ 1411(c). Certain types of income, including qualified retirement plan distributions, tax-exempt income, and any untaxed gain from the sale of a principal residence, are excluded from this definition.
[74]§ 1411(d).

LO.8

Identify tax planning opportunities related to tax credits and payment procedures.

13-7 TAX PLANNING

13-7a Foreign Tax Credit

A U.S. citizen or resident working abroad (commonly referred to as an *expatriate*) may elect to take either a foreign tax credit or the foreign earned income exclusion (see text Section 5-9). In cases where the income tax of a foreign country is higher than the U.S. income tax, the credit choice usually is preferable. If the reverse is true, electing the foreign earned income exclusion probably reduces the overall tax burden.

Unfortunately, the choice between the credit and the earned income exclusion is not without some limitations. The election of the foreign earned income exclusion, once made, can be revoked for a later year. However, once revoked, the earned income exclusion will not be available for a period of five years unless the IRS consents to an earlier date. This will create a dilemma for expatriates whose job assignments over several years shift between low- and high-bracket countries.

In 2016, Ira, a calendar year taxpayer, is sent by his employer to Saudi Arabia (a low-tax country). For 2016, therefore, Ira elects the foreign earned income exclusion. In 2017, Ira's employer transfers him to France (a high-tax country). Accordingly, he revokes the foreign earned income exclusion election for 2017 and chooses instead to use the foreign tax credit.

If Ira is transferred back to Saudi Arabia (or any other low-tax country) within five years, he may not utilize the foreign earned income exclusion.

13-7b Credit for Child and Dependent Care Expenses

A taxpayer may incur employment-related expenses that also qualify as medical expenses (e.g., a nurse is hired to provide in-home care for an incapacitated dependent parent). These expenses may be either deducted as medical expenses (generally subject to the 10 percent of AGI limitation) or used in determining the child and dependent care credit. If the child and dependent care credit is chosen and the employment-related expenses exceed the limitation ($3,000, $6,000, or earned income, as the case may be), the excess will qualify as a medical expense. If, however, the taxpayer chooses to deduct qualified employment-related expenses as medical expenses, any portion that is not deductible because of the percentage limitation may not be used in computing the credit for child and dependent care expenses.

Alicia reports the following information for the current year.

Adjusted gross income		$30,000
Potential itemized deductions *from* AGI—		
Other than medical expenses	$3,500	
Medical expenses	6,600	$10,100

All of Alicia's medical expenses were incurred to provide nursing care for her disabled father while she was working. Alicia's father lives with her and qualifies as her dependent.

What should Alicia do in this situation? One approach would be to use $3,000 of the nursing care expenses to obtain the maximum child and dependent care credit allowed of $810 (27% × $3,000). The remaining expenses should be claimed as medical expenses. After a reduction of 10 percent of AGI, this would produce a medical expense deduction of $600 [$3,600 (remaining medical expenses) − (10% × $30,000)].

Another approach would be to claim the full $6,600 as a medical expense and forgo the child and dependent care credit. After applying the 10%-of-AGI floor of $3,000 (10% × $30,000), a deduction of $3,600 remains.

The choice, then, is between a credit of $810 plus a deduction of $600 or a credit of $0 plus a deduction of $3,600. Which is better, of course, depends on the relative tax savings involved, which in turn are dependent on the taxpayer's marginal tax rate.

One of the traditional goals of *family tax planning* is to minimize the present value of the total tax burden of the family unit. With proper planning and implementation, the child and dependent care credit can be used to help achieve this goal. For example, payments to certain relatives for the care of qualifying dependents and children qualify for the credit if the care provider is *not* a child (under age 19) of the taxpayer. So if the care provider is in a lower tax bracket than the taxpayer, the following benefits result.

- Income is shifted to a lower-bracket family member.
- The taxpayer qualifies for the credit for child and dependent care expenses.

In addition, the goal of minimizing the family income tax liability can be enhanced in some other situations, but only if the credit's limitations are recognized and avoided. For example, tax savings may be enjoyed even if the qualifying expenditures incurred by a cash basis taxpayer have reached the annual ceiling ($3,000 or $6,000). To the extent that any additional payments can be shifted into future tax years, the benefit from the credit may be preserved on these excess expenditures.

Andre, a calendar year and cash basis taxpayer, has spent $3,000 by December 1 on qualifying child care expenditures for his dependent 11-year-old son. The $250 that is due the care provider for child care services rendered in December does not generate a tax credit benefit if the amount is paid in the current year because the $3,000 ceiling has been reached. However, if the payment can be delayed until the next year, the total credit over the two-year period for which Andre is eligible may be increased.

EXAMPLE 50

A similar shifting of expenses to the next year may be wise if the potential credit would be limited by the tax liability.

13-7c Adjustments to Increase Withholding

The penalty for underpayment of estimated tax by individuals is computed for each quarter of the tax year. A taxpayer can play *catch-up* to a certain extent. Each quarterly payment is credited to the unpaid portion of any previous required installment. Thus, the penalty stops on that portion of the underpayment for the previous quarter. However, because income tax withheld is assumed to have been paid evenly throughout the year and is allocated equally among the four installments in computing any penalty, a taxpayer who otherwise would be subject to a penalty for underpayment should increase withholdings late in the year. This can be done by changing the number of allowances claimed on Form W–4 or by making a special arrangement with the employer to increase the amount withheld.

A similar way to avoid (or reduce) a penalty for underpayment is to have the employer continue Social Security withholding beyond the base amount.

Rose, a calendar year taxpayer, earns $140,200 from her job. In late October 2017, she realizes that she will be subject to a penalty for underpayment of estimated tax due to income from outside sources. As a result, she instructs her employer to continue FICA withholdings for the rest of 2017.

If this is done, an extra $13,000 [$140,200 (annual salary) − $127,200 (base amount of the Social Security portion for 2017)] is subject to the 6.2% Social Security portion of the FICA tax [7.65% (total FICA rate) − 1.45% (Medicare portion of the FICA rate)]. Thus, Rose generates an additional $806 (6.2% × $13,000) that will be deemed withheld ratably during 2017.

EXAMPLE 51

13-7d Adjustments to Avoid Overwithholding

Publication 505, *Tax Withholding and Estimated Tax*, contains worksheets that taxpayers may use to take advantage of special provisions for avoiding overwithholding. Extra exemptions for withholding purposes are allowed if the taxpayer has unusually large itemized deductions, deductions *for* AGI, or tax credits. Net losses from Schedules C, D, E, and F may be considered in computing the number of extra withholding exemptions. Net operating loss carryovers may also be considered in the computation. A taxpayer who is entitled to extra withholding exemptions for any of these reasons should file a new Form W–4, Employee's Withholding Allowance Certificate, with his or her employer.

REFOCUS ON THE BIG PICTURE

EDUCATION TAX CREDITS

YELLOW DOG PRODUCTIONS/GETTY IMAGES

The American Opportunity tax credit provides some relief for Tom and Jennifer Snyder.

Both Lora and Sam qualify for the American Opportunity credit in 2017 as they are both in their first four years of postsecondary education. Lora and Sam both qualify for a $2,500 credit (100 percent of the first $2,000 and 25 percent of the next $2,000 of qualified expenses).

These credits phase out over a range of $20,000 once married taxpayers' AGI exceeds $160,000. As the Snyders' AGI ($158,000) is less than this amount, the total education credits available to them amount to $5,000, and they may claim this amount as a credit on their 2017 income tax return (see Example 30). Further, this credit may be used to offset any AMT liability, and 40 percent ($2,000) is refundable to the Snyders.

What If?

What if the Snyders' AGI is $188,000? In 2017, the Snyders would not qualify for any education credits (their income exceeds the limits for both the American Opportunity and the lifetime learning credits). Although a deduction *for* AGI is allowed for qualified tuition and related expenses involving higher education, their AGI exceeds the $160,000 maximum allowed for a deduction (see text Section 9-6e for additional details).

Key Terms

Discussion Questions

1. **LO.1** Would an individual taxpayer receive greater benefit from deducting an expenditure or from taking a credit equal to 25% of the expenditure? How would your response change if the item would only be deductible *from* AGI?

2. **LO.2** Clint, a self-employed engineering consultant, is contemplating purchasing an old building for renovation. After the work is completed, Clint plans to rent out two-thirds of the floor space to businesses and to live and work in the remaining portion. Identify the relevant tax issues for Clint.

   Issue ID

3. **LO.3** Sonja is considering the purchase and renovation of an old building. She has heard about the tax credit for rehabilitation expenditures but does not know the specific rules applicable to the credit. Explain the most important and relevant provisions for her.

   Issue ID

4. **LO.3** Explain the purpose of the disabled access credit, and identify several examples of the type of structural changes to a building that qualify for the credit.

5. **LO.4** Is the earned income credit a form of negative income tax? Why or why not?

6. **LO.4** Individuals who receive substantial Social Security benefits are usually not eligible for the tax credit for the elderly or disabled because these benefits effectively eliminate the base upon which the credit is computed. Explain.

7. **LO.4, 8** Tim was recently called into the partner's office and offered a two-year assignment in his public accounting firm's Shanghai office. Realizing that Tim will face incremental expenses while in Shanghai, such as foreign income taxes and rent, the firm will try to make him "whole" from a financial perspective by increasing his salary to help offset the expenses he will incur while living overseas. If Tim takes the assignment, he will likely rent his personal residence and sell several major tangible assets such as his personal automobile. Identify the relevant tax issues.

   Issue ID

8. **LO.4** Mark and Lisa are approaching an exciting time in their lives as their oldest son, Austin, graduates from high school and moves on to college. What are some of the tax issues Mark and Lisa should consider as they think about paying for Austin's college education?

   Issue ID

9. **LO.5** Elaborate rules exist that require employers to prepay various types of Federal taxes. Summarize the major issues that an employer must resolve if it is to comply with the requirements.

   Issue ID

10. **LO.5** Kathy, a sole proprietor, owns and operates a grocery store. Kathy's husband and her 16-year-old daughter work in the business and are paid wages. Will the husband and daughter be subject to FICA? Explain.

11. **LO.6** Describe the exposure (i.e., wage base and tax rate) that a self-employed individual has to the self-employment tax for 2017.

12. **LO.7** Describe the two additional Medicare taxes that are assessed on high-income taxpayers.

Computational Exercises

13. **LO.2** Carlson's general business credit for the current year is $84,000. His net income tax is $190,000, tentative minimum tax is $175,000, and net regular tax liability is $185,000. He has no other Federal income tax credits. Determine Carlson's general business credit for the year.

14. **LO.3** Emily spent $135,000 to rehabilitate a building (adjusted basis of $90,000) that originally had been placed in service in 1935.

    a. What is Emily's rehabilitation expenditures tax credit?

    b. What would be your answer if the building was a historic structure?

15. **LO.3** During 2017, Lincoln Company hires seven individuals who are certified to be members of a qualifying targeted group. Each employee works in excess of 600 hours and is paid wages of $7,500 during the year. Determine the amount of Lincoln's work opportunity credit.

16. **LO.3** Dora incurs the following research expenditures.

In-house wages	$60,000
In-house supplies	5,000
Payment to ABC, Inc., for research	80,000

    a. Determine the amount of qualified research expenditures.

    b. Assuming that the base amount is $50,000, determine Dora's incremental research activities credit.

17. **LO.4** Samuel and Annamaria are married, file a joint return, and have three qualifying children. In 2017, they earn wages of $34,000 and no other income. Determine the amount of their earned income credit for 2017.

18. **LO.4** In 2017, Henri, a U.S. citizen and calendar year taxpayer, reports $30,000 of income from France, which imposes a 10% income tax, and $50,000 from Italy, which imposes a 40% tax. In addition, Henri reports taxable income of $69,750 from within the United States.

    Henri is married filing a joint return, and he claims three dependency exemptions. Henri's U.S. tax before the foreign tax credit is $28,915. Determine the amount of Henri's foreign tax credit.

19. **LO.4** In late 2016, Randy and Rachel Erwin paid $7,000 in legal fees, adoption fees, and other expenses directly related to the adoption of an infant son, Jameson. In 2017, the year in which the adoption becomes final, they pay an additional $8,000. Their AGI in 2017 is $135,000.

    a. Determine the amount of the Erwins' adoption tax credit in 2017.

    b. Instead assume that the Erwins' 2017 AGI is $210,000. Determine the amount of the Erwins' adoption tax credit in 2017.

20. **LO.4** Santiago and Amy are married and file a joint tax return claiming their three children, ages 12, 14, and 18, as dependents. Their AGI is $140,000. Determine the amount of the couple's child tax credit.

21. **LO.4** Ivanna, who has three children under age 13, worked full-time while her spouse, Sergio, was attending college for nine months during the year. Ivanna earned $28,000 and incurred $9,100 of child care expenses. Determine Ivanna and Sergio's child and dependent care credit.

Decision Making 22. **LO.4, 8** Polly and her husband, Leo, file a joint return and expect to report AGI of $75,000 in 2017. Polly's employer offers a child and dependent care reimbursement plan that allows up to $5,000 of qualifying expenses to be reimbursed in exchange for a $5,000 reduction in the employee's salary. Because Polly and Leo have two minor children requiring child care that costs $5,800 each year, Polly is wondering if she should sign up for the program instead of taking advantage of the credit for child and dependent care expenses.

    Assuming that Polly and Leo are in the 25% tax bracket, analyze the effect of the two alternatives. How would your answer differ if Polly and Leo's AGI was $25,000 instead of $75,000? Assume in this case that their marginal tax rate is 10%.

23. **LO.4** Paola and Isidora are married; file a joint tax return; report modified AGI of $148,000; and have one dependent child, Dante. The couple paid $12,000 of tuition and $10,000 for room and board for Dante (a freshman). Dante is a full-time student. Determine the amount of the American Opportunity credit for the year.

24. **LO.4** Rafael and Lucy, married taxpayers, each contribute $2,900 to their respective § 401(k) plans offered through their employers. The AGI reported on the couple's joint return is $38,000. Determine their credit for retirement plan contributions (the Saver's Credit).

25. **LO.5** In 2017, Bianca earned a salary of $164,000 from her employer. Determine the amount of FICA taxes and Medicare taxes withheld from her salary.

26. **LO.6** In 2017, Miranda records net earnings from self-employment of $146,000. She has no other income. Determine the amount of Miranda's self-employment tax and her *for* AGI income tax deduction.

27. **LO.7** Determine the additional Medicare taxes for these individuals.
    a. Mario, who is single, earns wages of $440,000 in 2017.
    b. George and Shirley are married and file a joint return in 2017. During the year, George earns wages of $138,000, and Shirley earns wages of $210,000.
    c. Simon has net investment income of $38,000 and MAGI of $223,000 and files as a single taxpayer.

Problems

28. **LO.2** Adelyn has a tentative general business credit of $42,000 for the current year. Adelyn's net regular tax liability before the general business credit is $107,000, and her tentative minimum tax is $88,000. Compute Adelyn's allowable general business credit for the year.

29. **LO.2** Oak Corporation has the following general business credit carryovers.

2013	$ 5,000
2014	15,000
2015	6,000
2016	19,000
Total carryovers	$45,000

If the general business credit generated by activities during 2017 equals $36,000 and the total credit allowed during the current year is $60,000 (based on tax liability), what amounts of the current general business credit and carryovers are utilized against the 2017 income tax liability? What is the amount of unused credit carried forward to 2018?

30. **LO.3, 8** In the current year, Paul Chaing (4522 Fargo Street, Geneva, IL 60134) acquires a qualifying historic structure for $350,000 (excluding the cost of the land) and plans to substantially rehabilitate the structure. He is planning to spend either $320,000 or $380,000 on rehabilitation expenditures.

    Write a letter to Paul and a memo for the tax files explaining, for the two alternative expenditures, (1) the computation that determines the rehabilitation expenditures tax credit available to Paul, (2) the impact of the credit on Paul's adjusted basis in the property, and (3) the cash-flow differences as a result of the tax consequences related to his expenditure choice.

Decision Making

Communications

31. **LO.3** Green Corporation hires six individuals on January 4, 2017, all of whom qualify for the work opportunity credit. Three of these individuals receive wages of $8,500 during 2017, and each works more than 400 hours during the year. The other three individuals work 300 hours and receive wages of $5,000 during the year.

a. Calculate the amount of Green's work opportunity credit for 2017.

b. If Green pays total wages of $140,000 to its employees during the year, how much of this amount is deductible in 2017 assuming that the work opportunity credit is taken?

Decision Making 32. **LO.3, 8** Tom, a calendar year taxpayer, informs you that during the year, he incurs expenditures of $40,000 that qualify for the incremental research activities credit. In addition, it is determined that his base amount for the year is $32,800.

a. Determine Tom's incremental research activities credit for the year.

b. Tom is in the 25% tax bracket. Determine which approach to the research expenditures and the research activities credit (other than capitalization and subsequent amortization) would provide the greater tax benefit to Tom.

Communications 33. **LO.3** Ahmed Zinna (16 Southside Drive, Charlotte, NC 28204), one of your clients, owns two retail establishments in downtown Charlotte and has come to you seeking advice concerning the tax consequences of complying with the Americans with Disabilities Act. He understands that he needs to install various features at his stores (e.g., ramps, doorways, and restrooms that are handicap-accessible) to make them more accessible to disabled individuals. He asks whether any tax credits will be available to help offset the cost of the necessary changes. He estimates the cost of the planned changes to his facilities as follows.

Location	Projected Cost
Calvin Street	$22,000
Stowe Avenue	8,500

He reminds you that the Calvin Street store was constructed in 2004, while the Stowe Avenue store is in a building that was constructed in 1947. Ahmed operates his business as a sole proprietorship and has approximately eight employees at each location. Write a letter to Ahmed in which you summarize your conclusions concerning the tax consequences of his proposed capital improvements.

34. **LO.4** Which of the following individuals qualify for the earned income credit for 2017?

a. Thomas is single, is 21 years of age, and has no qualifying children. His income consists of $9,000 in wages.

b. Shannon, who is 27 years old, maintains a household for a dependent 11-year-old son and is eligible for head-of-household tax rates. Her income consists of $16,050 of salary and $50 of taxable interest (Shannon's AGI is $16,100).

c. Keith and Susan, both age 30, are married and file a joint return. Keith and Susan have no dependents. Their combined income consists of $28,500 of salary and $100 of taxable interest (their AGI is $28,600).

d. Colin is a 26-year-old self-supporting, single taxpayer. He has no qualifying children and generates earnings of $9,000.

35. **LO.4** Jason, a single parent, lives in an apartment with his three minor children, whom he supports. Jason earned $27,400 during 2017, paid $800 in qualified moving expenses during the year, and uses the standard deduction. Calculate the amount, if any, of Jason's earned income credit.

Decision Making 36. **LO.4, 8** Joyce, a widow, lives in an apartment with her two minor children (ages 8 and 10), whom she supports. Joyce earns $33,000 during 2017. She uses the standard deduction.

a. Calculate the amount, if any, of Joyce's earned income credit.

b. During the year, Joyce is offered a new job that has greater future potential than her current job. If she accepts the job offer, her earnings for the year will be $39,000; however, she is afraid she will not qualify for the earned income credit. Using after-tax cash-flow calculations, determine whether Joyce should accept the new job offer.

37. **LO.4, 8** Kim, a U.S. citizen and resident, owns and operates a novelty goods busi-   **Decision Making**
    ness. During 2017, Kim reports taxable income of $100,000: $50,000 from
    foreign sources and $50,000 from U.S. sources. In calculating taxable income, the
    standard deduction is used. The income from foreign sources is subject to foreign
    income taxes of $26,000. For 2017, Kim files a joint return claiming his three children
    as dependents.

    a. Assuming that Kim chooses to claim the foreign taxes as an income tax credit,
       what is his income tax liability for 2017?

    b. Recently, Kim has become disenchanted with the location of his business and is
       considering moving his foreign operation to a different country. Based on his
       research, if he moved his business to his country of choice, all relevant revenues
       and costs would remain approximately the same, except that the income taxes
       payable to that country would be only $8,000. Given that all of the foreign
       income taxes paid are available to offset the U.S. tax liability (whether he oper-
       ates in a high-tax or low-tax foreign jurisdiction), what effect will this have on his
       decision regarding the potential move?

38. **LO.4** Blue Sky, Inc., a U.S. corporation, is a manufacturing concern that sells most
    of its products in the United States. It also conducts some business in the
    European Union through various branches. During the current year, Blue Sky
    reports taxable income of $700,000, of which $500,000 is U.S.-sourced and $200,000
    is foreign-sourced. Foreign income taxes paid amounted to $45,000. Blue Sky's U.S.
    income tax liability is $238,000. What is its U.S. income tax liability net of the allow-
    able foreign tax credit?

39. **LO.4** Ann and Bill were on the list of a local adoption agency for several years,
    seeking to adopt a child. Finally, in 2016, good news comes their way, and an
    adoption seems imminent. They pay qualified adoption expenses of $5,000 in 2016
    and $11,000 in 2017. Assume that the adoption becomes final in 2017. Ann and Bill
    always file a joint income tax return.

    a. Determine the amount of the adoption expenses credit available to Ann and
       Bill, assuming that their combined annual income is $120,000. What year(s) will
       they benefit from the credit?

    b. Assuming that Ann and Bill's modified AGI in 2016 and 2017 is $220,000, calcu-
       late the amount of the adoption expenses credit.

40. **LO.4** Durell and Earline are married; file a joint return; and claim dependency
    exemptions for their two children, ages 5 years and 6 months. They also claim
    Earline's son from a previous marriage, age 18, as a dependent. Durell and Earline's
    combined AGI is $68,000.

    a. Compute Durell and Earline's child tax credit.

    b. Assume the same facts, except that Durell and Earline's combined AGI is
       $122,000. Compute their child tax credit.

41. **LO.4** Paul and Karen Kent are married, and both are employed (Paul earns $44,000
    and Karen earns $9,000 during 2017). Paul and Karen have two dependent
    children, both under the age of 13 (Samuel and Joy). So that they can work, Paul
    and Karen pay $3,800 ($1,900 for each child) to Sunnyside Day Care Center (422
    Sycamore Road, Ft. Worth, TX 76028; Employer Identification Number: 11-2345678)
    to care for their children while they are working.

    a. Assuming that Paul and Karen file a joint return, what, if any, is their tax credit
       for child and dependent care expenses?

    b. Complete Form 2441 for Paul and Karen; their AGI is $53,750, and their tax liability
       before any available child care credit is $2,825. Relevant Social Security numbers
       are as follows: Paul (123-45-6789); Sam (123-45-6788); Joy (123-45-6787). Neither
       Paul nor Karen received any child care benefits from their employers.

42. **LO.4** Jim and Mary Jean are married and have two dependent children under the age of 13. Both parents are gainfully employed and during 2017 earn salaries as follows: $16,000 (Jim) and $5,200 (Mary Jean). To care for their children while they work, they pay Eleanor (Jim's mother) $5,600. Eleanor does not qualify as a dependent of Jim and Mary Jean. Assuming that Jim and Mary Jean file a joint tax return, what, if any, is their credit for child and dependent care expenses?

Communications 43. **LO.4, 8** Bernadette, a longtime client of yours, is an architect and the president of the local Rotary chapter. To keep up to date with the latest developments in her profession, she attends continuing education seminars offered by the architecture school at State University. During 2017, Bernadette spends $2,000 on course tuition to attend such seminars. She also spends another $400 on architecture books during the year.

Bernadette's son, Pablo, is a senior majoring in engineering at the University of the Midwest. During the 2017 calendar year, Pablo incurs the following expenses: $8,200 for tuition ($4,100 per semester) and $750 for books and course materials. Pablo, who Bernadette claims as a dependent, lives at home while attending school full-time. Bernadette is married, files a joint return, and reports a combined AGI with her husband of $114,000.

a. Calculate Bernadette's education tax credit for 2017.

b. In her capacity as president of the local Rotary chapter, Bernadette has asked you to make a 30- to 45-minute speech outlining the different ways the tax law helps defray (1) the cost of higher education and (2) the cost of continuing education once someone is in the workforce. Prepare an outline of possible topics for presentation. A tentative title for your presentation is "How Can the Tax Law Help Pay for College and Continuing Professional Education?"

44. **LO.4** Kathleen and Glenn decide that this is the year to begin getting serious about saving for their retirement by participating in their employers' § 401(k) plans. As a result, they each have $3,000 of their salary set aside in their qualified plans.

a. Calculate the credit for certain retirement plan contributions available to Kathleen and Glenn if the AGI on their joint return is $35,000.

b. Kathleen and Glenn persuade their dependent 15-year-old son, Joel, to put $500 of his part-time earnings into a Roth IRA during the year. What is the credit for certain retirement plan contributions available to Joel? His AGI is $7,000.

45. **LO.5** In each of the following independent situations, determine the amount of FICA that should be withheld from the employee's 2017 salary by the employer.

a. Harry earns a $50,000 salary, files a joint return, and claims four withholding allowances.

b. Hazel earns a $115,000 salary, files a joint return, and claims four withholding allowances.

c. Tracy earns a $190,000 salary, files a joint return, and claims four withholding allowances.

d. Alicia's 17-year-old son, Carlos, earns $10,000 at the family sole proprietorship.

Communications 46. **LO.5** During 2017, Greg Cruz (1401 Orangedale Road, Troy, MI 48084) works for Maple Corporation and Gray Company. He earns $90,000 at Maple Corporation, where he is a full-time employee. Greg also works part-time for Gray Company for wages of $50,000.

a. Did Greg experience an overwithholding of FICA taxes? Write a letter to Greg and a memo for the tax files in which you explain your conclusion.

b. Did Maple Corporation and Gray Company overpay the employer's portion of FICA? Explain.

47. **LO.5** In each of the following independent situations, determine the maximum withholding allowances that Eli (an employee) is permitted on Form W–4.

    a. Eli is single with no dependents.

    b. Eli is married to a nonemployed spouse, and they have no dependents.

    c. Eli is married to Vera, an employed spouse who earns $25,000, and they have three dependent children. Eli and Vera do not qualify for the child tax credit. On the Form W–4 that she filed with the employer, Vera claimed zero allowances.

    d. Assume the same facts as in part (c), except that Eli and Vera fully support Eli's mother, who lives with them. The mother (age 70 and blind) qualifies as their dependent. (Refer to text Section 3-4b.)

    e. Eli is single with no dependents but works for two employers, one on a full-time basis and the other on a part-time basis. The Form W–4 filed with the first employer (the full-time job) reflects two withholding exemptions. The wages from each job exceed $1,500.

    f. Assume the same facts as in part (e), except that Eli is married to a nonemployed spouse.

48. **LO.5** Jane, who is expecting to finish college in May 2017, is fortunate to have   Decision Making
    already arranged full-time employment after graduation. She will begin work on July 1, 2017, as a staff accountant at a nearby professional services firm with a starting salary of $48,600 per year. Jane is married to Craig, who plans to be a full-time student throughout the year. They anticipate generating no income for the year other than the salary from her new position.

    a. How many withholding allowances would you expect Jane to claim on her Form W–4?

    b. Assuming that Jane and Craig use the standard deduction, calculate the Federal income tax liability on their projected taxable income for 2017. What advice would you give to Jane?

    c. What further changes should she make to her W–4 at the beginning of 2018?

49. **LO.6** Julie, being self-employed, is required to make estimated payments of her tax liability for the year. Her tax liability for 2016 was $25,000, and her AGI was less than $150,000. For 2017, Julie ultimately determines that her income tax liability is $18,000. During the year, however, she made the following payments, totaling $13,000.

April 18, 2017	$ 4,500
June 15, 2017	2,800
September 15, 2017	4,100
January 16, 2018	1,600
Total paid	$13,000

    Because Julie prepaid so little of her ultimate income tax liability, she now realizes that she may be subject to the penalty for underpayment of estimated tax.

    a. Determine Julie's exposure to the penalty for underpayment of estimated tax.

    b. The same as part (a), except that Julie's tax liability for 2016 was $15,960.

50. **LO.6** In 2017, Maria records self-employed earnings of $135,000. Using the format illustrated in the text, compute Maria's self-employment tax liability and the allowable income tax deduction for the self-employment tax paid.

Cumulative Problems

Tax Return Problem

TAX SOFTWARE

51. Beth R. Jordan lives at 2322 Skyview Road, Mesa, AZ 85201. She is a tax accountant with Mesa Manufacturing Company, 1203 Western Avenue, Mesa, AZ 85201 (employer identification number 11-1111111). She also writes computer software programs for tax practitioners and has a part-time tax practice. Beth is single and has no dependents. Beth's birthday is July 4, 1972, and her Social Security number is 123-45-6789. She wants to contribute $3 to the Presidential Election Campaign Fund.

The following information is shown on Beth's Wage and Tax Statement (Form W–2) for 2016.

Line	Description	Amount
1	Wages, tips, other compensation	$65,000.00
2	Federal income tax withheld	10,500.00
3	Social Security wages	65,000.00
4	Social Security tax withheld	4,030.00
5	Medicare wages and tips	65,000.00
6	Medicare tax withheld	942.50
15	State	Arizona
16	State wages, tips, etc.	65,000.00
17	State income tax withheld	1,954.00

During the year, Beth received interest of $1,300 from Arizona Federal Savings and Loan and $400 from Arizona State Bank. Each financial institution reported the interest income on a Form 1099–INT. She received qualified dividends of $800 from Blue Corporation, $750 from Green Corporation, and $650 from Orange Corporation. Each corporation reported Beth's dividend payments on a Form 1099–DIV.

Beth received a $1,100 income tax refund from the state of Arizona on April 29, 2016. On her 2015 Federal income tax return, she reported total itemized deductions of $8,200, which included $2,200 of state income tax withheld by her employer.

Fees earned from her part-time tax practice in 2016 totaled $3,800. She paid $600 to have the tax returns processed by a computerized tax return service.

On February 8, 2016, Beth bought 500 shares of Gray Corporation common stock for $17.60 a share. On September 12, 2016, Beth sold the stock for $14 a share.

Beth bought a used sport utility vehicle for $6,000 on June 5, 2016. She purchased the vehicle from her brother-in-law, who was unemployed and was in need of cash. On November 2, 2016, she sold the vehicle to a friend for $6,500.

On January 2, 2016, Beth acquired 100 shares of Blue Corporation common stock for $30 a share. She sold the stock on December 19, 2016, for $55 a share.

During the year, Beth records revenues of $16,000 from the sale of a software program she developed. Beth incurred the following expenditures in connection with her software development business.

Cost of personal computer	$7,000
Cost of printer	2,000
Furniture	3,000
Supplies	650
Fee paid to computer consultant	3,500

Beth elected to expense the maximum portion of the cost of the computer, printer, and furniture allowed under the provisions of § 179. These items were placed in service on January 15, 2016, and used 100% in her business.

Although her employer suggested that Beth attend a convention on current developments in corporate taxation, Beth was not reimbursed for the travel expenses of $1,420 she incurred in attending the convention. The $1,420 included $200 for the cost of meals.

During the year, Beth paid $300 for prescription medicines and $2,875 for doctor bills and hospital bills. Medical insurance premiums were paid for her by her employer. Beth paid real property taxes of $1,766 on her home. Interest on her home mortgage (Valley National Bank) was $3,845, and interest to credit card companies was $320. Beth contributed $2,080 to various qualifying charities during the year. Professional dues and subscriptions totaled $350.

Beth paid estimated taxes of $1,000.

Part 1—Tax Computation

Compute the net tax payable or refund due for Beth R. Jordan for 2016. If you use tax forms for your solution, you will need Forms 1040, 2106–EZ, and 4562 and Schedules A, B, C, D, and SE. Suggested software: H&R BLOCK Tax Software.

Part 2—Tax Planning

Beth is anticipating significant changes in her life in 2017, and she has asked you to estimate her taxable income and tax liability for 2017. She just received word that she has been qualified to adopt a 2-year-old daughter. Beth expects that the adoption will be finalized in 2017 and that she will incur approximately $2,000 of adoption expenses. In addition, she expects to incur approximately $3,500 of child and dependent care expenses relating to the care of her new daughter, which will enable her to keep her job at Mesa Manufacturing Company. However, with the additional demands on her time because of her daughter, she has decided to discontinue her two part-time jobs (i.e., the part-time tax practice and her software business), and she will cease making estimated income tax payments. In your computations, assume that all other income and expenditures will remain at approximately the same levels as in 2016.

52. Tim and Sarah Lawrence are married and file a joint return. Tim's Social Security number is 123-45-6789, and Sarah's Social Security number is 111-11-1111. They reside at 100 Olive Lane, Covington, LA 70434. They have two dependent children, Sean and Debra, ages 12 and 16, respectively. Sean's Social Security number is 123-45-6788, and Debra's Social Security number is 123-45-6787. Tim is a self-employed businessperson (sole proprietor of an unincorporated business), and Sarah is a corporate executive. Tim has the following income and expenses from his business.

Tax Computation Problem

Gross income	$325,000
Business expenses	201,000

Records related to Sarah's employment provide the following information.

Salary	$145,000
Unreimbursed travel expenses (including $200 of meals)	1,100
Unreimbursed entertainment expenses	500

Other pertinent information for the tax year includes the following.

Proceeds from sale of stock acquired on July 15, 2017 (cost of $12,000), and sold on August 1, 2017	$ 9,800
Proceeds from sale of stock acquired on September 18, 2016 (cost of $5,000), and sold on October 5, 2017	3,800
Wages paid to full-time domestic worker for housekeeping and child supervision	10,000
Interest income received	7,000
Total itemized deductions (not including any potential deductions above)	27,900
Federal income tax withheld	31,850
Estimated payments of Federal income tax	34,000

Compute the net tax payable or refund due for Tim and Sarah Lawrence for 2017.

Research Problems

THOMSON REUTERS

Student Edition

Note: Solutions to the Research Problems can be prepared by using the Thomson Reuters Checkpoint® Student Edition online tax research database, which accompanies this textbook. Solutions can also be prepared by using research materials found in a typical tax library.

Research Problem 1. Ashby and Curtis, married professionals, have a 2-year-old son, Jason. Curtis works full-time as an electrical engineer, but Ashby has not worked outside the home since Jason was born. As Jason is getting older, Ashby thinks that Jason would benefit from attending nursery school several times a week, which would give her an opportunity to reinvigorate her love of painting at a nearby art studio. Ashby thinks that if she is lucky, the proceeds from the sale of her paintings will pay for the nursery school tuition. But in addition, she is planning to claim the credit for child and dependent care expenses, because the care provided Jason at the nursery school is required for her to pursue her art career. Can Ashby and Curtis claim the credit for child and dependent care expenses for the nursery school expenditure? Why or why not?

Communications   **Research Problem 2.** Your ophthalmologist, Dr. Hunter Francis (55 Wheatland Drive, Hampton, CT 06247), has been very pleased with the growth of his practice in the 15 years he has been in business. This growth has resulted, at least in part, because Hunter has marketed his services aggressively, and he has tried to accommodate clients with various needs.

This year Dr. Francis purchased a sophisticated piece of equipment that enables him to diagnose persons with mental handicaps, hearing impairments, and physical disabilities without having to go through a series of questions. In addition, he can treat his patients who are not disabled more accurately and efficiently by using this equipment. Since purchasing the machine this year for $9,500, Hunter has used it on many occasions. Unfortunately, he has not been able to attract any disabled patients, even though previously he referred such people to other ophthalmologists who owned the necessary equipment. Therefore, the primary purpose for acquiring the equipment (i.e., to attract disabled patients) has not been realized, but he has put it to good use in treating other patients. Write a letter to Dr. Francis explaining whether he may claim the disabled access credit for this acquisition.

Research Problem 3. During a recent Sunday afternoon excursion, Miriam, an admirer of early twentieth-century architecture, discovers a 1920s-era house in the countryside outside Mobile, Alabama. She wants not only to purchase and renovate this particular house but also to move the structure into Mobile so that her community can enjoy its architectural features. Being aware of the availability of the tax credit for rehabilitation expenditures, she wants to maximize her use of the provision, if it is available in this case, once the renovation work begins in Mobile. Miriam also informs you that she will pursue the purchase, relocation, and renovation of the house only if the tax credit is available. Comment on Miriam's decision and on whether any renovation expenditures incurred will qualify for the tax credit for rehabilitation expenditures.

Partial list of research aids:
George S. Nalle III v. Comm., 93–2 USTC ¶50,468, 72 AFTR 2d 93–5705, 997 F.2d 1134 (CA–5, 1993).

Use internet tax resources to address the following questions. Look for reliable websites and blogs of the IRS and other government agencies, media outlets, businesses, tax professionals, academics, think tanks, and political outlets.

Research Problem 4. Taxpayers who purchase health insurance coverage through the Health Insurance Marketplace may be eligible for the premium tax credit under § 36B. Use the IRS's website (**www.irs.gov**) to read about this provision and determine which taxpayers are eligible for the credit.

Research Problem 5. The IRS provides a web-based tool to help taxpayers determine whether they are eligible for the earned income tax credit. Locate this tool at the IRS website. Then apply the facts related to a hypothetical taxpayer, and determine whether the earned income credit is available.

Roger CPA Review Questions

ROGER
CPA Review

1. The following facts apply to Brooke, a self-employed individual.

Income	$50,000
Student loan interest	1,000
Alimony received	6,000
Child support received	12,000

   The FICA/Medicare tax rate is 15.3%. Considering only the above, what is Brooke's adjusted gross income?

   a. $47,350
   b. $51,175
   c. $53,350
   d. $57,175

2. Kellye is a calendar year taxpayer who makes and sells custom dog collars. This year, her cash receipts were $10,000, and her cost to make the collars was $2,000. Additionally, Kellye contributed $2,000 to a retirement plan. What amount will be the basis for Kellye's self-employment tax?

   a. $10,000
   b. $8,000
   c. $7,000
   d. $6,000

3. Which of the following is correct regarding the deduction for self-employment taxes?

   a. Self-employment taxes are deductible in full to arrive at adjusted gross income
   b. Self-employment taxes are deductible on Schedule A, subject to a 10% AGI limitation
   c. 50% of self-employment taxes are deductible on Schedule A
   d. 50% of self-employment taxes are deductible to arrive at adjusted gross income

4. Ruth paid $5,000 in self-employment taxes throughout the year. What is Ruth's deduction for self-employment taxes to arrive at adjusted gross income?

   a. $5,000
   b. $2,500
   c. $1,530
   d. $0

5. Which of the following is correct regarding self-employment taxes?

   I. For purposes of the portion of self-employment tax that is equivalent to Social Security tax, taxable self-employment income is limited to a prescribed maximum amount reduced by other wages earned by the taxpayer that are subject to FICA and Medicare taxes.

   II. For purposes of the portion of self-employment tax that is equivalent to the Medicare tax, taxable self-employment income is limited to a prescribed maximum amount reduced by other wages earned by the taxpayer that are subject to FICA and Medicare taxes.

   a. I only
   b. II only
   c. I and II
   d. Neither I or II

6. What are the due dates for estimated tax payments for a calendar year taxpayer who is self-employed?

   a. April, June, and September 15 of the current year, and January 15 of the subsequent year

   b. March, June, September, and December 15 of the current year

   c. January, April, July, and October 15 of the current year

   d. April, July, and October 15 of the current year, and January 15 of the subsequent year

7. Which of the following credits is **not** refundable?

   a. Child Tax Credit
   b. Child and Dependent Care Credit
   c. American Opportunity Tax Credit
   d. Earned Income Credit

8. Which of the following credits is refundable?

   a. Child Tax Credit
   b. Child and Dependent Care Credit
   c. Lifetime Learning Credit
   d. Foreign Tax Credit

9. Which of the following education-related expenses can be used to claim an education credit?

	Tuition	Fees	Room and Board	Meals
a.	Yes	Yes	Yes	Yes
b.	Yes	Yes	Yes	No
c.	Yes	Yes	No	Yes
d.	Yes	Yes	No	No

10. Michael and Kathy have one dependent, Dustin, who is in his third year of college. Michael is taking classes in the evening toward an MBA. What credits can Michael and Kathy claim as to these amounts?

    I. American Opportunity Tax Credit
    II. Lifetime Learning Credit

    a. I only
    b. II only
    c. I and II
    d. I or II

11. Which of the following best describes the effect of a tax credit?

    a. It reduces a person's gross income

    b. It reduces a person's adjusted gross income

    c. It reduces a person's taxable income

    d. It reduces a person's tax liability

PART 5

PROPERTY TRANSACTIONS

Part 5 presents the tax treatment of sales, exchanges, and other dispositions of property. Included here are the rules used to determine the realized gain or loss and recognized gain or loss, along with the classification of any recognized gain or loss as capital or ordinary. The topic of basis is evaluated both in terms of its effect on the calculation of the gain or loss and in terms of the determination of the basis of any property acquired as part of the transaction.

Property Transactions: Determination of Gain or Loss and Basis Considerations

LEARNING OBJECTIVES: *After completing Chapter 14, you should be able to:*

LO.1 State and explain the computation of realized gain or loss on property dispositions.

LO.2 Distinguish between realized and recognized gain or loss.

LO.3 Review and illustrate how basis is determined for various methods of asset acquisition.

LO.4 Describe various loss disallowance provisions.

LO.5 Identify tax planning opportunities related to selected property transactions.

CHAPTER OUTLINE

ISTOCKPHOTO.COM/MICHAEL COURTNEY

PROPOSED SALE OF A HOUSE AND OTHER PROPERTY TRANSACTIONS

Alice owns a house that she received from her mother, Paula, seven months ago. Paula, paid $275,000 for the house. Alice is considering selling the house to her favorite nephew, Dan, for $275,000. Alice anticipates that she will have no gain or loss on the transaction. She comes to you for advice.

As Alice's tax adviser, you need answers to the following questions:

- You are aware that Paula died around the time Alice received the house from her mother. Did Alice receive the house by gift prior to her mother's death or did she inherit it after her mother's death? What was Paula's adjusted basis for the house, and when did she buy it? What was the fair market value of the house on the date of Paula's death? Answers to these questions will help you determine Alice's basis in the house.

- Is the house Alice's principal residence? If so, when did it become her principal residence (before or after she received it from Paula)?

- To help determine the tax consequences of Alice's potential sale of the house to Dan, you need answers to these questions: What is the current fair market value of the house? Does Alice intend for the transaction with Dan to be a sale or part sale and part gift? What does Alice intend to do with the sale proceeds?

Alice would also like to know the tax consequences of selling her boat, which she purchased for $22,000 four months ago. She has been using it exclusively for personal use but is disappointed with its layout and capacity. Because it is a new model, there is significant demand for the boat, and based on listings in her area, she anticipates that she can sell it for $20,000 to $23,000.

While you are talking, Alice mentions that earlier this year, she sold some stock in Green Corporation at a realized loss. A few days later, after hearing Green Corporation's quarterly earnings report, she decided to buy back the shares. You ask her to provide additional information so that you can determine the tax effects of these transactions.

Once you have more information, you can provide the advice Alice needs.

Read the chapter and formulate your response.

FRAMEWORK 1040 **Tax Formula for Individuals**

This chapter covers the boldfaced portions of the Tax Formula for Individuals that was introduced in Concept Summary 3.1 on p. 3-3. Below those portions are the sections of Form 1040 where the results are reported.

Income *(broadly defined)*	$ xx,xxx
Less: Exclusions	(x,xxx)
Gross income	$xx,xxx

FORM 1040 (p. 1)

12	Business income or (loss). Attach Schedule C or C-EZ	.
13	Capital gain or (loss). Attach Schedule D if required. If not required, check here ▶	☐
14	Other gains or (losses). Attach Form 4797	.

Less: **Deductions** *for* **adjusted gross income**	(x,xxx)
Adjusted gross income...	$ xx,xxx
Less: The greater of total **itemized deductions** *or* the standard deduction	(x,xxx)
Personal and dependency exemptions	(x,xxx)
Taxable income	$ xx,xxx
Tax on taxable income *(see Tax Tables or Tax Rate Schedules)*...............................	$ x,xxx
Less: Tax credits *(including income taxes withheld and prepaid)*	(xxx)
Tax due (or refund)	$ xxx

This chapter and the following three chapters explain the income tax consequences of property transactions (the sale or other disposition of property). These chapters explore the key tax issues related to property transactions:

- Is there a realized gain or loss?
- If so, is the gain or loss recognized?
- If the gain or loss is recognized, is it ordinary or capital?
- What is the basis of any replacement property that is acquired?

Chapters 14 and 15 discuss the determination of realized and recognized gain or loss and the basis of property. Chapters 16 and 17 cover the classification of the recognized gain or loss as ordinary or capital.

LO.1

State and explain the computation of realized gain or loss on property dispositions.

14-1 DETERMINATION OF GAIN OR LOSS

Gains and losses result from "realization events" such as a sales, exchanges, or other dispositions of property. Very few gains and losses are recognized without first being realized. Realization events involve a significant change in ownership rights, and once a realization event has occurred, a realized gain or loss can be determined. Many, but not all, realized gains and losses are also recognized (included in the determination of taxable income) at the time of the realization event.

14-1a **Realized Gain or Loss**

Sale or Other Disposition

The term *sale or other disposition* is defined broadly in the tax law and includes virtually any disposition of property. Transactions such as trade-ins, casualties, condemnations, thefts, and bond retirements are all treated as property dispositions. Sales or exchanges are the most common dispositions of property. Identifying a specific economic event (e.g., a sale) is a key factor in determining whether a disposition has occurred.[1] A change in the value of the property is not sufficient.[2]

Lori owns Tan Corporation stock that she bought for $3,000. The stock has appreciated in value and is now worth $5,000. Lori has no realized gain because a change in value is not an identifiable event for tax purposes. Here, Lori has an *unrealized gain* of $2,000.

The same is true if the stock had declined in value to $1,000. As there was no identifiable event, there is no realized loss. Here, Lori would have an *unrealized loss* of $2,000.

Computation of Realized Gains and Losses

Realized gain or loss is the difference between the amount realized from the sale or other disposition of property and the property's adjusted basis on the disposition date. If the amount realized exceeds the property's adjusted basis, the result is a realized gain. On the other hand, if the property's adjusted basis exceeds the amount realized, the result is a realized loss.[3]

Carl sells Swan Corporation stock with an adjusted basis of $3,000 for $5,000. Carl's realized gain is $2,000. If Carl had sold the stock for $2,000, he would have had a realized loss of $1,000.

Concept Summary 14.1 summarizes this calculation. The various terms that are part of Concept Summary 14.1 are discussed on the following pages.

Concept Summary 14.1

Realized Gain or Loss

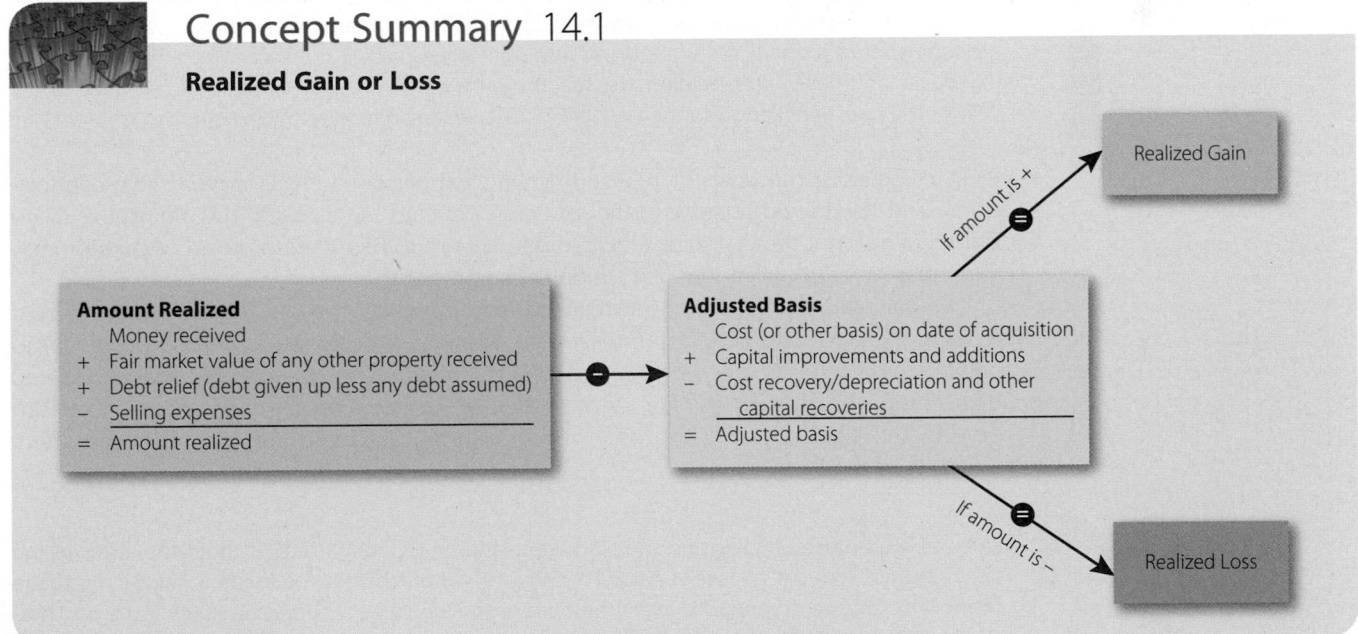

Amount Realized

The amount realized from a sale or other disposition of property is a measure of the economic value received for property given up. In general, it is the sum of any money received (which includes any debt relief) plus the fair market value of other property received.[4]

---

[1]Reg. § 1.1001–1(c)(1).

[2]*Lynch v. Turrish*, 1 USTC ¶18, 3 AFTR 2986, 38 S.Ct. 537 (USSC, 1918).

[3]§ 1001(a) and Reg. § 1.1001–1(a).

[4]§ 1001(b) and Reg. § 1.1001–1(b). The amount realized also includes any real property taxes treated as imposed on the seller that are actually paid by the buyer. The reason for including these taxes in the amount realized is that by paying the taxes, the purchaser is, in effect, paying an additional amount to the seller of the property. Refer to Chapter 10 (and Examples 17 and 18 in that chapter) for a discussion of this subject.

Debt relief includes any liability (like a mortgage) assumed by the buyer when the property is sold. Debt relief also occurs if property is sold subject to the mortgage. In addition, debt relief is not limited by the fair market value of the property.[5]

Amount Realized

Juan sells a machine used in his landscaping business to Peter for $20,000 cash plus four acres of property that Peter owns in a nearby town with a fair market value of $36,000. Juan's amount realized on this sale is $56,000 ($20,000 + $36,000).

Barry owns property on which there is a mortgage of $20,000. He sells the property to Cole for $50,000 cash and Cole's agreement to assume the mortgage. Barry's amount realized from the sale is $70,000 ($50,000 cash + $20,000 debt relief).

In a property transaction, the **fair market value** of property received is the price determined by a willing seller and a willing buyer when neither is compelled to sell or buy.[6] All of the relevant factors must be considered,[7] and if the fair market value of the property received cannot be determined, the value of the property given up by the taxpayer may be used.[8]

Return to the facts of Example 3. There are several ways one can determine the fair market value of the land Juan is receiving. Although a cost is involved, an appraiser can be asked to provide an appraisal of the land. City or county property tax assessment information may also be helpful; the city or county assessor is tasked with the responsibility of determining the fair market value of property so that property taxes are levied appropriately. Finally, if the exchange is between a willing buyer and seller, determining the fair market value of Juan's landscaping machine could answer the question (i.e., given the facts of the case, it should be worth $56,000).

In calculating the amount realized, selling expenses (such as advertising, commissions, and legal fees) relating to the sale are deducted. As a result, the amount realized is the net amount the taxpayer received directly or indirectly, in the form of cash or anything else of value, from the disposition of the property.

The calculation of the amount realized may appear to be one of the least complex areas associated with property transactions. However, because numerous positive and negative adjustments may be required, this calculation can be complex and confusing. In addition, determining the fair market value of the items received by the taxpayer can be difficult. The following example provides insight into various items that can affect the amount realized.

Ridge sells an office building and the associated land on October 1, 2017. Under the terms of the sales contract, Ridge is to receive $600,000 in cash. The purchaser is to assume Ridge's mortgage of $300,000 on the property. To assist the purchaser, Ridge agrees to pay $15,000 of the purchaser's closing costs (a "closing cost credit"). The broker's commission on the sale is $45,000. The amount realized by Ridge is determined as follows:

continued

---

[5]*Crane v. Comm.*, 47–1 USTC ¶9217, 35 AFTR 776, 67 S.Ct. 1047 (USSC, 1947) and *Comm. v. Tufts*, 83–1 USTC ¶9328, 51 AFTR 2d 83–1132, 103 S.Ct. 1826 (USSC, 1983). Although a legal distinction exists between the direct assumption of a mortgage and the taking of property subject to a mortgage, the tax consequences in calculating the amount realized are the same.

[6]*Comm. v. Marshman*, 60–2 USTC ¶9484, 5 AFTR 2d 1528, 279 F.2d 27 (CA–6, 1960).

[7]*O'Malley v. Ames*, 52–1 USTC ¶9361, 42 AFTR 19, 197 F.2d 256 (CA–8, 1952).

[8]*U.S. v. Davis*, 62–2 USTC ¶9509, 9 AFTR 2d 1625, 82 S.Ct. 1190 (USSC, 1962).

Selling price:		
Cash	$600,000	
Mortgage assumed by purchaser	300,000	
		$900,000
Less:		
Broker's commission	$ 45,000	
Closing cost credit provided by Ridge	15,000	(60,000)
Amount realized		$840,000

Adjusted Basis

The **adjusted basis** of property disposed of is the property's original basis adjusted to the date of disposition.[9] Original basis is the cost or other basis of the property on the date acquired by the taxpayer. Many assets are acquired without purchasing them (e.g., via gift or inheritance). We'll discuss how to determine basis for these acquisitions later in the chapter. *Capital additions* increase and *capital recoveries* decrease the original basis.[10] As a result, adjusted basis is determined as follows:

> Cost (or other adjusted basis) on date of acquisition
> + Capital additions
> − Capital recoveries
> = Adjusted basis on date of disposition

Capital Additions

Capital additions include the cost of capital improvements and betterments made to the property by the taxpayer. These costs are different from repair and maintenance expenses, which are neither capitalized nor added to the original basis (refer to Chapter 6). Repair and maintenance expenses are deductible in the current taxable year if they are related to business or income-producing property. Any liability on property that is assumed by the buyer is also included in the buyer's original basis of the property. The same rule applies if property is acquired subject to a liability. Amortization of the discount on bonds increases the adjusted basis of the bonds.[11]

Capital Recoveries

Capital recoveries decrease the adjusted basis of property. The prominent types of capital recoveries are discussed below.

Depreciation and Cost Recovery The original basis of depreciable property is reduced by any cost recovery or depreciation allowed while the property is held by the taxpayer. The amount subtracted annually from the original basis is the greater of the *allowed* or *allowable* cost recovery or depreciation.[12]

> **EXAMPLE 7**
>
> Refer back to Example 3. The machine Juan sold was acquired four years ago for $100,000. It was 7-year MACRS property, and Juan did not take either an immediate expense deduction (§179) or bonus depreciation on the property. Juan's adjusted basis is $37,485, computed as follows:
>
> *continued*

---

[9]§ 1011(a) and Reg. § 1.1011–1.

[10]§ 1016(a) and Reg. § 1.1016–1.

[11]See Chapter 16 for a discussion of bond discount and the related amortization.

[12]§ 1016(a)(2) and Reg. § 1.1016–3(a)(1)(i). In most cases, these amounts are the same (refer to Chapter 8).

Original cost		$100,000
Cost recovery:		
Year 1 ($100,000 × .1429)	$14,290	
Year 2 ($100,000 × .2449)	24,490	
Year 3 ($100,000 × .1749)	17,490	
Year 4 ($100,000 × .1249 × 1/2)	6,245	
Total cost recovery		(62,515)
Adjusted basis		$ 37,485

As Juan's amount realized on the sale was $56,000, his realized gain is $18,515, computed as follows:

Amount realized	$ 56,000
− Adjusted basis	(37,485)
Realized gain (loss)	$ 18,515

Casualties and Thefts A casualty or theft may result in the reduction of the adjusted basis of property.[13] The adjusted basis is reduced by the amount of the deductible loss. In addition, the adjusted basis is reduced by the amount of insurance proceeds received. However, the receipt of insurance proceeds may result in a recognized gain rather than a deductible loss. The gain increases the adjusted basis of the property.[14]

Capital Recoveries: Casualties and Thefts

EXAMPLE 8

An insured truck that Marvin used in his trade or business is destroyed in an accident. At the time of the accident, the adjusted basis was $8,000, and the fair market value was $6,500. Marvin receives insurance proceeds of $6,500.

The amount of the casualty loss is $1,500 ($6,500 insurance proceeds − $8,000 adjusted basis). The truck's adjusted basis is reduced by the $1,500 casualty loss and the $6,500 of insurance proceeds received ($8,000 basis before casualty − $1,500 casualty loss − $6,500 insurance proceeds = $0 adjusted basis).

EXAMPLE 9

How would your answer to Example 8 change if the basis of the truck was $6,000, its fair market value was $9,000, and Marvin received a $9,000 insurance settlement? Now Marvin has a casualty gain of $3,000 ($9,000 insurance proceeds − $6,000 adjusted basis). The truck's adjusted basis is increased by the $3,000 casualty gain and is reduced by the $9,000 of insurance proceeds received ($6,000 basis before casualty + $3,000 casualty gain − $9,000 insurance proceeds = $0 adjusted basis).

Certain Corporate Distributions A nontaxable corporate distribution is treated as a return of capital, and it reduces the shareholder's stock basis.[15] Corporations normally disclose this information to shareholders. Once the basis of the stock is reduced to zero, the amount of any subsequent distributions is a capital gain if the stock is a capital asset. These rules are illustrated in Example 33 of Chapter 20.

Amortizable Bond Premium The basis in a bond purchased at a premium is reduced by the amortizable portion of the bond premium.[16] Investors in taxable bonds may *elect* to amortize the bond premium, with an interest deduction allowed for the amount of the amortized premium.[17] So the election enables the taxpayer to take an annual interest deduction to offset ordinary income in exchange for a larger capital gain or smaller capital loss on the disposition of the bond. The amortization deduction is allowed for taxable bonds because the premium is viewed as a cost of earning the taxable interest from the bonds.

---

[13]Refer to Chapter 7 for the discussion of casualties and thefts.
[14]Reg. § 1.1016–6(a).
[15]§ 1016(a)(4) and Reg. § 1.1016–5(a).

[16]§ 1016(a)(5) and Reg. § 1.1016–5(b). The accounting treatment of bond premium amortization is the same as for tax purposes. The amortization results in a decrease in the bond investment account.
[17]§ 171(c).

Unlike taxable bonds, the premium on tax-exempt bonds *must be* amortized (and the basis is reduced even though the amortization is not allowed as a deduction). No amortization deduction is permitted on tax-exempt bonds because the interest income is exempt from tax and the amortization of the bond premium merely represents an adjustment of the tax-exempt income earned on the bond.

Antonio purchases Eagle Corporation taxable bonds with a face value of $100,000 for $110,000, thus paying a premium of $10,000. The annual interest rate is 7%, and the bonds mature 10 years from the date of purchase. The annual interest income is $7,000 (7% × $100,000).

If Antonio elects to amortize the bond premium, the $10,000 premium is deducted over the 10-year period. Antonio's basis for the bonds is reduced each year by the amount of the amortization deduction.

If the bonds were tax-exempt, amortization of the bond premium and the basis adjustment would be mandatory. However, no deduction would be allowed for the amortization.

Easements An easement is the legal right to use another's land for a special purpose. Historically, easements have been used to obtain rights-of-way for utility lines, roads, and pipelines. In recent years, grants of conservation easements have become a popular means of obtaining charitable contribution deductions and reducing the value of real estate for transfer tax (i.e., estate and gift) purposes. For example, a conservation easement on property containing a rare wildlife habitat might prohibit any development, while one on a farm might allow continued farming and the building of additional agricultural structures but no other development. Although a conservation easement can be sold, typically it is donated to a charitable organization (like the Nature Conservancy). If donated, the difference between the value of the land with and without the easement would be a charitable contribution. Likewise, scenic easements (granted to protect open spaces or scenic views) are used to reduce the value of land as assessed for property tax purposes.

The amount received for granting an easement is subtracted from the basis of the property. If the taxpayer does not retain any right to the use of the land, all of the basis is assigned to the easement. However, if the use of the land is only partially restricted, an allocation of some of the basis to the easement is appropriate. If, however, it is impossible or impractical to separate the basis of the part of the property on which the easement is granted, the basis of the whole property is reduced by the amount received. If the amount received for the easement exceeds the basis, a taxable gain results.[18]

Additional Complexities

Three types of issues tend to complicate the determination of adjusted basis. First, the applicable tax provisions for calculating the adjusted basis depend on how the property was acquired (e.g., purchase, taxable exchange, nontaxable exchange, gift, or inheritance). These complications are discussed in text Section 14-2. Second, if the asset is subject to depreciation, cost recovery, amortization, or depletion, adjustments must be made to the basis during the time period the asset is held by the taxpayer. When the asset is sold, the taxpayer's records for both acquisition basis and adjustments to basis may not be complete. For example, the donee may not know the amount of the donor's basis. Third, the complex positive and negative adjustments encountered in calculating the amount realized are also involved in calculating the adjusted basis.

Jane purchased a personal residence in 2008. The purchase price and the related closing costs were as follows:

Purchase price	$325,000
Recording costs	140
Title fees and title insurance	815
Survey costs	225
Attorney's fees	750
Appraisal fee	250

continued

---

[18]See Rev.Rul. 68–291, 1968–1 C.B. 351 and Rev.Rul. 77–414, 1977–2 C.B. 299.

Other relevant tax information for the house during the time Jane owned it is as follows:

- Constructed a swimming pool for medical reasons. The cost was $20,000, of which $5,000 was deducted as a medical expense.

- Added a solar heating system. The cost was $18,000.

- Deducted home office expenses of $6,000. Of this amount, $5,200 was for depreciation.

The adjusted basis of the house is $354,980, calculated as follows:

Purchase price	$325,000
Recording costs	140
Title fees and title insurance	815
Survey costs	225
Attorney's fees	750
Appraisal fee	250
Swimming pool ($20,000 − $5,000)	15,000
Solar heating system	18,000
	$360,180
Less: Depreciation deducted on home office	(5,200)
Adjusted basis	$354,980

Distinguish between realized and recognized gain or loss.

14-1b **Recognized Gain or Loss**

Recognized gain is the amount of the realized gain that is included in the taxpayer's gross income.[19] A **recognized loss**, on the other hand, is the amount of a realized loss that is deductible for tax purposes.[20] As a general rule, the entire amount of a realized gain or loss is recognized.[21]

Concept Summary 14.2 summarizes the realized gain or loss and recognized gain or loss concepts.

Concept Summary 14.2

Realized and Recognized Gain or Loss

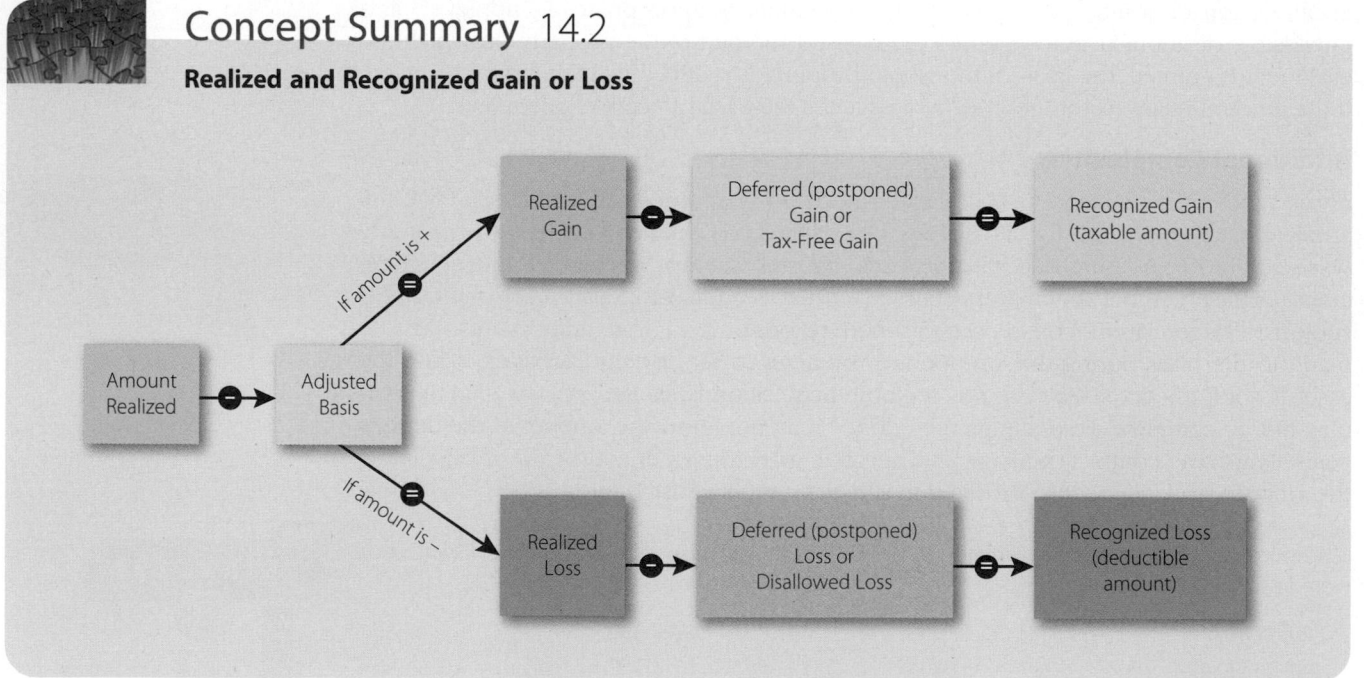

---

[19]§ 61(a)(3) and Reg. § 1.61–6(a).

[20]§ 165(a) and Reg. § 1.165–1(a).

[21]§ 1001(c) and Reg. § 1.1002–1(a).

14-1c Nonrecognition of Gain or Loss

In certain cases, a realized gain or loss on a property disposition is not recognized. Non-taxable exchanges, which are covered in Chapter 15, are one example. Others include losses realized on the sale, exchange, or condemnation of personal use assets (as opposed to business or income-producing property) and gains realized on the sale of a residence (see Chapter 15). In addition, realized losses from the sale or exchange of business or income-producing property between certain related parties are not recognized.[22]

Sale, Exchange, or Condemnation of Personal Use Assets

A realized loss from the sale, exchange, or condemnation of personal use assets (e.g., a personal residence or an automobile used only for personal purposes) is not recognized for tax purposes. An exception exists for casualty or theft losses from personal use assets (see Chapter 7). On the other hand, any gain realized from the sale or other disposition of personal use assets is, generally, fully taxable.

The Big Picture

EXAMPLE 12

Return to the facts of *The Big Picture* on p. 14-1. Assume that Alice sells the boat, which she has held exclusively for personal use, for $23,000. Recall that her adjusted basis of the boat is $22,000. Alice has a realized and recognized gain of $1,000.

The Big Picture

EXAMPLE 13

Assume that Alice sells the boat in Example 12 for $20,000. She has a realized loss of $2,000, but the loss is not recognized because the boat is a personal use asset.

14-2 BASIS CONSIDERATIONS

LO.3

Review and illustrate how basis is determined for various methods of asset acquisition.

A key element in calculating gain or loss from a property transaction is the asset's basis at the time of the transaction. Various methods for determining basis apply, depending on how the asset was acquired.

14-2a Determination of Cost Basis

As noted earlier, the basis of property is generally the property's cost. Cost is the amount paid for the property in cash or other property.[23]

A *bargain purchase* of property is an exception to the general rule for determining basis. A bargain purchase results when an employer transfers property to an employee at less than the property's fair market value (as compensation) or when a corporation transfers property to a shareholder at less than the property's fair market value (a dividend). The amount included in income as either compensation for services or dividend income is the difference between the bargain purchase price and the property's fair market value. The basis of property acquired in a bargain purchase is the property's fair market value.[24] If the basis of the property were not increased by the bargain amount, the taxpayer would be taxed on this amount again at disposition.

---

[22]§ 267(a)(1).

[23]§ 1012 and Reg. § 1.1012–1(a).

[24]Reg. §§ 1.61–2(d)(2)(i) and 1.301–1(j). See the discussion in Chapter 5 of the circumstances under which what appears to be a taxable bargain purchase is an excludible qualified employee discount.

Wade buys land from his employer for $10,000 on December 30. The fair market value of the land is $15,000.

    Wade must include the $5,000 difference between the cost and the fair market value of the land in gross income for the taxable year. The bargain element represents additional compensation to Wade. His basis for the land is $15,000, the land's fair market value.

Identification Problems

Cost identification problems are frequently encountered in securities transactions. For example, the Regulations require that the taxpayer adequately identify the particular stock that has been sold (specific identification).[25] A problem arises when the taxpayer has purchased separate lots of stock on different dates or at different prices and cannot adequately identify the lot from which a particular sale takes place. In this case, the stock is presumed to come from the first lot or lots purchased (a FIFO presumption).[26] Brokers are now required to provide investors with an annual report on the cost basis of stock sold during the year (to be included on Form 1099–B and reported to the IRS).

Polly purchases 100 shares of Olive Corporation stock on July 1, 2015, for $5,000 ($50 a share) and another 100 shares of Olive stock on July 1, 2016, for $6,000 ($60 a share). She sells 50 shares of the stock on January 2, 2017.

    The cost of the stock sold, assuming that Polly cannot adequately identify the shares, is $50 a share, or $2,500. This is the cost Polly will compare with the amount realized in determining the gain or loss from the sale.

Allocation Problems

When a taxpayer acquires *multiple assets in a lump-sum purchase*, the total cost must be allocated among the individual assets.[27] Allocation is necessary for several reasons:

- Some of the assets acquired may be depreciable (e.g., buildings), while others are not (e.g., land).

- If one of the assets acquired is sold, its basis must be known in order to compute realized gain or loss.

- Some of the assets may be capital or § 1231 assets that receive special tax treatment when sold in the future.

    The lump-sum cost is allocated on the basis of the fair market values of the individual assets acquired.

Harry purchases a building and land for $800,000. Because of the depressed nature of the industry in which the seller was operating, Harry was able to negotiate a very favorable purchase price. Appraisals of the individual assets indicate that the fair market value of the building is $600,000 and that of the land is $400,000.

    Harry's basis for the building is $480,000 [($600,000/$1,000,000) × $800,000], and his basis for the land is $320,000 [($400,000/$1,000,000) × $800,000].

    If a business is purchased and goodwill is involved, a special allocation rule applies. Initially, the purchase price is allocated among the assets acquired, other than goodwill, based on their fair market value. Goodwill is then assigned the residual amount of the purchase price. This allocation applies to both the buyer and the seller.[28]

---

[25]Reg. § 1.1012–1(c)(1).

[26]*Kluger Associates, Inc.*, 69 T.C. 925 (1978).

[27]Reg. § 1.61–6(a).

[28]§ 1060. The classification of the seller's recognized gain associated with the goodwill is discussed in Chapter 16.

Rocky sells his business to Paul. An independent appraisal indicates that the fair market value of the business assets, other than goodwill, are as follows:

Inventory	$ 50,000
Building	500,000
Land	200,000

After negotiations, Rocky and Paul agree on a sales price of $1 million. Applying the residual method with respect to goodwill results in the following allocation of the $1 million purchase price:

Inventory	$ 50,000
Building	500,000
Land	200,000
Goodwill	250,000

The residual method requires that all of the excess of the purchase price over the fair market value of the assets other than goodwill ($1,000,000 − $750,000 = $250,000) be allocated to goodwill.

EXAMPLE 17

In the case of *nontaxable stock dividends*, the allocation depends on whether the dividend is a common stock dividend on common stock or a preferred stock dividend on common stock. If the stock dividend is common on common, the cost of the original common shares is allocated to the total shares owned after the dividend.[29]

Susan owns 100 shares of Sparrow Corporation common stock for which she paid $1,100. She receives a 10% common stock dividend, giving her a new total of 110 shares. Before the stock dividend, Susan's basis was $11 per share ($1,100 ÷ 100 shares). The basis of each share after the stock dividend is $10 ($1,100 ÷ 110 shares).

EXAMPLE 18

If the nontaxable stock dividend is preferred stock on common, the cost of the original common shares is allocated between the common and preferred shares on the basis of their relative fair market values on the date of distribution.[30]

Fran owns 100 shares of Cardinal Corporation common stock for which she paid $1,000. She receives a nontaxable stock dividend of 50 shares of preferred stock on her common stock. The fair market values on the date of distribution of the preferred stock dividend are $30 a share for common stock and $40 a share for preferred stock.

Fair market value of common ($30 × 100 shares)	$3,000
Fair market value of preferred ($40 × 50 shares)	2,000
	$5,000

Basis of common: 3/5 × $1,000	$ 600
Basis of preferred: 2/5 × $1,000	$ 400

The basis per share for the common stock is $6 ($600/100 shares). The basis per share for the preferred stock is $8 ($400/50 shares).

EXAMPLE 19

The holding period for a nontaxable stock dividend, whether received in the form of common stock or preferred stock, includes the holding period of the original shares.[31] The significance of the holding period for capital assets is discussed in Chapter 16.

---

[29]§§ 305(a) and 307(a).

[30]Reg. § 1.307–1(a).

[31]§ 1223(5) and Reg. § 1.1223–1(e).

14-2b **Gift Basis**

When a taxpayer receives property as a gift, there is no cost to the donee (recipient). Thus, under the cost basis provision, the donee's basis would be zero. However, this would violate the statutory intent that gifts not be subject to the income tax.[32] With a zero basis, if the donee sold the property, all of the amount realized would be treated as realized gain. Therefore, a basis is assigned to the property received depending on the following:

- The date of the gift.
- The basis of the property to the donor.
- The amount of the gift tax paid.
- The fair market value of the property.

Gift Basis Rules, in General

The basis rules for gifts of property are as follows:

- If the fair market value of the property on the date of the gift exceeds (or is equal to) the donor's basis, then the recipient's (donee's) basis is the same as the donor's (i.e., a carryover basis).[33]

EXAMPLE 20

Melissa purchased stock in 2016 for $10,000. She gave the stock to her son, Joe, in 2017, when the fair market value was $15,000. Joe subsequently sells the property for $18,000. Joe's basis is $10,000, and he has a realized gain of $8,000.

If Joe sold the stock for $12,000, he would have a realized gain of $2,000 (his basis is $10,000). If Joe sold the stock for $7,000, he would have a realized loss of $3,000 ($7,000 − $10,000).

- If the fair market value of the property on the date of the gift is less than the donor's basis, then special *dual basis* rules apply. Here, the donee has one basis for measuring a gain and a different basis for measuring a loss. This special rule is in place to prevent the shifting of losses (typically among family members) to the individual who would receive the greatest benefit. Under this rule, the donee's gain basis is the donor's adjusted basis; the donee's loss basis is the fair market value of the property.

EXAMPLE 21

Burt purchased stock in 2016 for $10,000. He gave the stock to his son, Cliff, in 2017, when the fair market value was $7,000. Cliff later sells the stock for $6,000.

Cliff's basis is $7,000 (fair market value is less than donor's adjusted basis of $10,000), and the realized loss from the sale is $1,000 ($6,000 amount realized − $7,000 basis).

The amount of the loss basis will *differ* from the amount of the gain basis only if, at the date of the gift, the adjusted basis of the property exceeds the property's fair market value. Note that the loss basis rule prevents the donee from receiving a tax benefit from a decline in value that occurred while the donor held the property.

Therefore, in Example 21, Cliff has a loss of only $1,000 rather than a loss of $4,000 ($6,000 − $10,000). The $3,000 difference represents the decline in value that occurred while Burt held the property. Ironically, however, the donee may be subject to income tax on the appreciation that occurred while the donor held the property, as illustrated in Example 20.

If the amount realized from a sale is *between* the donee's loss basis and gain basis, no gain or loss is realized.

---

[32]§ 102(a).

[33]§ 1015(a) and Reg. § 1.1015–1(a)(1). See Reg. § 1.1015–1(a)(3) for cases in which the facts necessary to determine the donor's adjusted basis are unknown. Refer to Example 23 for the effect of depreciation deductions by the donee.

Assume the same facts as in Example 21, except that Cliff sells the stock for $8,000. Application of the gain basis rule produces a loss of $2,000 ($8,000 − $10,000). Application of the loss basis rule produces a gain of $1,000 ($8,000 − $7,000).

Because the amount realized is between the gain basis and the loss basis, Cliff recognizes neither a gain nor a loss.

Adjustment for Gift Tax

Because of the size of the unified estate and gift tax exemption ($5.49 million in 2017), basis adjustments for gift taxes paid are rare. If, however, gift taxes are paid by the donor, the portion of the gift tax paid that is related to any appreciation is taken into account in determining the donee's gain basis.[34]

For *gifts made before 1977*, the full amount of the gift tax paid is added to the donor's basis, with basis capped at the donor's fair market value at the date of the gift.

Holding Period

The holding period for property acquired by gift begins on the date the donor acquired the property if the gain basis rule applies.[35] The holding period starts on the date of the gift if the loss basis rule applies.[36] The significance of the holding period for capital assets is discussed in Chapter 16.

Basis for Depreciation

The basis for depreciation on depreciable gift property is the donee's gain basis.[37] This rule is applicable even if the donee later sells the property at a loss and uses the loss basis rule in calculating the amount of the realized loss.

Vito gave a machine (a MACRS 5-year asset) to Tina in 2017. At that time, the adjusted basis was $32,000 (cost of $40,000 − accumulated depreciation of $8,000), and the fair market value was $26,000. No gift tax was paid. Tina's gain basis at the date of the gift is $32,000, and her loss basis is $26,000. During 2017, Tina deducts depreciation (cost recovery) of $6,400 ($32,000 × 20%). At the end of 2017, Tina's gain basis and loss basis are calculated as follows:

	Gain Basis	Loss Basis
Donor's basis or fair market value	$32,000	$26,000
Depreciation	(6,400)	(6,400)
	$25,600	$19,600

14-2c **Inherited Property**

Special basis rules apply for inherited property (property acquired from a decedent). Typically, these rules are favorable to the taxpayer receiving this property.

General Rules

The basis of inherited property is generally the property's fair market value at the date of death (referred to as the *primary valuation amount*).[38] The property's basis is the fair market value six months after the date of death if the executor or administrator of the estate *elects* the alternate valuation date for estate tax purposes. This amount is referred to as the *alternate valuation amount*.

---

[34]§ 1015(d)(6) and Reg. § 1.1015–5(c)(2). Examples illustrating these rules can be found in Reg. § 1.1015–5(c)(5) and IRS Publication 551 (*Basis of Assets*), p. 9.

[35]§ 1223(2) and Reg. § 1.1223–1(b).

[36]Rev.Rul. 59–86, 1959–1 C.B. 209.

[37]§ 1011 and Reg. §§ 1.1011–1 and 1.167(g)–1.

[38]§§ 1014(a) and 1022. See *South-Western Federal Taxation: Corporations, Partnerships, Estates & Trusts*, Chapter 18, for additional information.

The Big Picture

EXAMPLE 24

Return to the facts of *The Big Picture* on p. 14-1. Alice and various other family members inherited property from Paula, who died in 2016. At the date of death, Paula's basis for the property Alice inherited—Paula's house—was $275,000. The house's fair market value at the date of death was $475,000. The alternate valuation date was not elected.

Alice's basis for income tax purposes is $475,000. This is commonly referred to as a *stepped-up basis.*

The Big Picture

EXAMPLE 25

Assume the same facts as in Example 24, except that the house's fair market value at the date of Paula's death was $260,000.

Alice's basis for income tax purposes is $260,000. This is commonly referred to as a *stepped-down basis.*

The alternate valuation date and amount are only available to estates for which an estate tax return must be filed [generally, estates with a valuation in excess of $5.49 million in 2017 ($5.45 million in 2016)]. Even if an estate tax return is filed and the executor elects the alternate valuation date, the six months after death date is available only for property that the executor has not distributed before this date.[39]

The alternate valuation date can be elected *only if,* as a result of the election, both the value of the gross estate and the estate tax liability are lower than they would have been if the primary valuation date had been used.[40]

Income in Respect of a Decedent

Income in respect of a decedent (IRD) usually exists when a cash basis taxpayer dies and, on the date of death, is entitled to some form of income (e.g., compensation, interest, or dividends) but has yet to receive it. IRD is most frequently applicable to decedents using the cash basis of accounting. IRD also occurs, for example, when a taxpayer at the time of death held installment notes receivable on which the gain has been deferred. For both cash and accrual taxpayers, IRD includes most post-death distributions from retirement plans, including traditional IRAs and § 401(k) plans. With the exception of Roth IRAs, distributions from retirement plans invariably contain an income component that has not yet been subject to income tax.

IRD is included in the gross estate at its fair market value (on the appropriate valuation date). Because IRD is not subject to the step-up or step-down rules applicable to property passed by death, the income tax basis of the decedent transfers to the estate or heirs.[41] Furthermore, the recipient of IRD must classify it in the same manner (e.g., ordinary income or capital gain) as the decedent would have.[42]

EXAMPLE 26

George, age 58, was entitled to a salary payment of $18,000 and a bonus of $20,000 at the time of his death. In addition, George had been contributing to a traditional IRA for over 20 years. The IRA has a basis of $83,000 (due to some nondeductible contributions over the years) and a current value of $560,000. George's estate collects the salary and bonus payments, and George's wife (his only beneficiary) cashes in the IRA.

continued

---

[39]§ 2032(a)(1) and Rev.Rul. 56–60, 1956–1 C.B. 443. For any property distributed by the executor during the six-month period preceding the alternate valuation date, the adjusted basis to the beneficiary will equal the fair market value on the date of distribution.

[40]§ 2032(c); this provision prevents the alternate valuation election from being used to increase the basis of the property to the beneficiary for

income tax purposes without simultaneously increasing the estate tax liability (because of estate tax deductions or credits).

[41]§ 1014(c).

[42]§ 691(a)(3).

Both the estate and George's wife have income in respect of a decedent (IRD) and must include ordinary income in their computation of taxable income for the year. The estate has IRD of $38,000 (salary of $18,000 + bonus of $20,000), and George's wife has IRD of $477,000 ($560,000 proceeds − $83,000 basis). A better outcome might be achieved for George's wife if she rolled over the inherited IRA into an IRA in her name and deferred receiving distributions until required. (Note: Only a surviving spouse can roll over an inherited IRA without tax consequences.[43])

Survivor's Share of Property

Both the decedent's share and the survivor's share of *community property* have a basis equal to the fair market value on the date of the decedent's death.[44] This occurs because the decedent's share of the community property is included in the estate and assumes a fair market value basis, while the surviving spouse's share is treated as if it were received from the decedent at its fair market value.

EXAMPLE 27

Floyd and Vera are married and reside in a community property state. They own, as community property, 200 shares of Biltmore Company stock acquired in 1991 for $100,000. Floyd dies in 2017, when the securities are valued at $300,000. One-half of the Biltmore stock is included in Floyd's estate. If Vera inherits Floyd's share of the community property, the basis for gain or loss is $300,000, determined as follows:

Vera's one-half of the community property (stepped up from $50,000 to $150,000 due to Floyd's death)	$150,000
Floyd's one-half of the community property (stepped up from $50,000 to $150,000 due to inclusion in his gross estate)	150,000
Vera's new basis	$300,000

In a *common law* state, only one-half of jointly held property of spouses (tenants by the entirety or joint tenants with rights of survivorship) is included in the estate.[45] In such a case, no adjustment of the basis is permitted for the excluded property interest (the surviving spouse's share).

EXAMPLE 28

Assume the same facts as in Example 27, except that the property is jointly held by Floyd and Vera who reside in a common law state. Floyd purchased the property and made a gift of one-half of the property to Vera when the stock was acquired. No gift tax was paid. Only one-half of the Biltmore stock is included in Floyd's estate. Vera's basis for determining gain or loss in the excluded half is not adjusted upward for the increase in value to date of death. Therefore, Vera's basis is $200,000, determined as follows:

Vera's one-half of the jointly held property (carryover basis of $50,000)	$ 50,000
Floyd's one-half of the jointly held property (stepped up from $50,000 to $150,000 due to inclusion in his gross estate)	150,000
Vera's new basis	$200,000

Holding Period of Inherited Property

The holding period of inherited property is *deemed to be long term* (held for the required long-term holding period). This rule applies regardless of whether the property is disposed of at a gain or at a loss.[46]

14-2d Disallowed Losses

LO.4

Describe various loss disallowance provisions.

In certain situations, realized losses that normally would be recognized are disallowed. Transactions between related parties and wash sales are two of these situations.

---

[43]See *South-Western Federal Taxation: Corporations, Partnerships, Estates & Trusts*, Chapter 19, for additional information.

[44]§ 1014(b)(6). See the listing of community property states in Chapter 4.

[45]§ 2040(b).

[46]§ 1223(11).

Related Taxpayers

Section 267 provides that realized losses from sales or exchanges of property, directly or indirectly, between certain related parties are not recognized. This loss disallowance rule applies to several types of related-party transactions. The most common involve (1) members of a family and (2) an individual and a corporation (where the individual owns, directly or indirectly, more than 50 percent in value of the corporation's outstanding stock.)[47] The loss disallowance rules (1) prevent a taxpayer from directly transferring an unrealized loss to a related taxpayer in a higher tax bracket who could receive a greater tax benefit from recognition of the loss and (2) eliminate a substantial administrative burden on the Internal Revenue Service as to the appropriateness of the selling price (i.e., fair market value). The rules governing the relationships covered by § 267 were discussed in Chapter 6.

If income-producing or business property is transferred to a related taxpayer and a loss is disallowed, the related-party buyer's basis is equal to the amount paid (i.e., its cost). However, if the related-party buyer later sells the property and realizes a gain, the gain is reduced by the loss that was previously disallowed.[48] This *right of offset* is not applicable if the original sale involved the sale of a personal use asset (e.g., the sale of a personal residence between related taxpayers). Furthermore, the right of offset is available only to the original transferee (the related-party buyer).[49]

EXAMPLE 29

Pedro sells business property with an adjusted basis of $50,000 to his daughter, Josefina, for its fair market value of $40,000. Pedro's realized loss of $10,000 is not recognized.

- How much gain does Josefina recognize if she sells the property for $52,000? Josefina recognizes a $2,000 gain. Her realized gain is $12,000 ($52,000 less her basis of $40,000), but she can offset Pedro's $10,000 loss against the gain.

- How much gain does Josefina recognize if she sells the property for $48,000? Josefina recognizes no gain or loss. Her realized gain is $8,000 ($48,000 less her basis of $40,000), but she can offset $8,000 of Pedro's $10,000 loss against the gain. The balance of Pedro's disallowed loss ($2,000) disappears and cannot be used. Note that Pedro's loss can only offset Josefina's gain. It cannot create a loss for Josefina.

- How much loss does Josefina recognize if she sells the property for $38,000? Josefina recognizes a $2,000 loss, the same as her realized loss ($38,000 less $40,000 basis). Pedro's loss does not increase Josefina's loss. His loss can be offset only against a gain. Because Josefina has no realized gain, Pedro's loss cannot be used and is never recognized. Note that if the property was a personal use asset (not business), her $2,000 loss would be personal and would not be recognized.

The holding period of the buyer for the property is not affected by the holding period of the seller. That is, the buyer's *holding period* includes only the period of time he or she has held the property.[50]

Wash Sales

The wash sale rules (§ 1091) are designed to eliminate the opportunity to sell stock at a loss, recognize the loss for tax purposes, but replace the stock sold by buying identical shares shortly before or after the sale. If § 1091 applies, a realized loss on the sale or exchange of stock or securities is not recognized. Recognition of the loss is disallowed because the taxpayer is considered to be in substantially the same economic position after the sale and repurchase as before the sale and repurchase. The wash sale rule applies if a taxpayer sells or exchanges stock or securities at a loss and within 30 days

---

[47]§ 707 provides a similar disallowance provision where the related parties are a partner and a partnership in which the partner owns, directly or indirectly, more than 50 percent of the capital interests or profits interests in the partnership. See Chapter 15 for a discussion of the special rules under § 1041 for property transfers between spouses or incident to divorce.

[48]§ 267(d) and Reg. § 1.267(d)–1(a).

[49]The loss disallowance rules are applicable even where the selling price is equal to the fair market value and can be validated (e.g., listed stocks).

[50]§§ 267(d) and 1223(2) and Reg. § 1.267(d)–1(c)(3).

before *or* after the date of the sale or exchange acquires substantially identical stock or securities.[51] An option to purchase substantially identical securities is treated the same as actually buying the stock. Corporate bonds and preferred stock normally are not considered substantially identical to the corporation's common stock.[52] Attempts to avoid the application of the wash sales rules by having a related taxpayer repurchase the securities have been unsuccessful.[53] The wash sales provisions do *not* apply to gains. Concept Summary 14.3 provides an overview of the wash sale rules.

Concept Summary 14.3

Wash Sale Rules

Realized loss that is not recognized is added to the *basis* of the substantially identical stock or securities whose acquisition resulted in the nonrecognition of loss.[54] In other words, the basis of the replacement stock or securities is increased by the amount of the unrecognized loss. If the loss were not added to the basis of the newly acquired stock or securities, the taxpayer would never recover the entire basis of the old stock or securities.

The basis of the new stock or securities includes the unrecovered portion of the basis of the formerly held stock or securities. Therefore, the *holding period* of the new stock or securities begins on the date of acquisition of the old stock or securities.[55]

---

[51]§ 1091(a) and Reg. §§ 1.1091–1(a) and (f).

[52]Rev.Rul. 56–406, 1956–2 C.B. 523. However, if the bonds and preferred stock are convertible into common stock, they may be considered substantially identical under certain circumstances.

[53]*McWilliams v. Comm.*, 47–1 USTC ¶9289, 35 AFTR 1184, 67 S.Ct. 1477 (USSC, 1947).

[54]§ 1091(d) and Reg. § 1.1091–2(a).

[55]§ 1223(4) and Reg. § 1.1223–1(d).

The Big Picture

EXAMPLE 30

Return to the facts of *The Big Picture* on p. 14-1. Alice owned 100 shares of Green Corporation stock (basis of $20,000). She sold 50 shares for $8,000. Ten days later, she purchased 50 shares of the same stock for $7,000.

Alice's realized loss of $2,000 ($8,000 amount realized − $10,000 basis of 50 shares) is not recognized because it resulted from a wash sale. Alice's basis in the newly acquired stock is $9,000 ($7,000 purchase price + $2,000 unrecognized loss from the wash sale).

A taxpayer may acquire fewer shares than the number sold in a wash sale. In this case, the loss from the sale is prorated between recognized and unrecognized loss on the basis of the ratio of the number of shares acquired to the number of shares sold.[56] The wash sale rules do not apply to taxpayers engaged in the business of buying and selling securities.[57]

14-2e Conversion of Property from Personal Use to Business or Income-Producing Use

As discussed previously, losses from the sale of personal use assets are not recognized for tax purposes, but losses from the sale of business and income-producing assets are deductible. Can a taxpayer convert a personal use asset that has declined in value to business or income-producing use and then sell the asset to recognize a business or income-producing loss?

The tax law prevents this practice by specifying that the *original basis for loss* on personal use assets converted to business or income-producing use is the *lower* of the property's adjusted basis or fair market value on the date of conversion.[58] The *gain basis* for converted property is the property's adjusted basis on the date of conversion. The tax law is not concerned with gains on converted property because gains are recognized regardless of whether property is business, income-producing, or personal use.

EXAMPLE 31

Diane's personal residence has an adjusted basis of $175,000 and a fair market value of $160,000. Diane converts the personal residence to rental property. Her basis for loss is $160,000 (lower of $175,000 adjusted basis and fair market value of $160,000). The $15,000 decline in value is a personal loss and can never be recognized for tax purposes. Diane's basis for gain is $175,000.

The basis for loss is also the *basis for depreciating* the converted property.[59] This is an exception to the general rule that the basis for depreciation is the gain basis (e.g., property received by gift). This exception prevents the taxpayer from recovering a personal loss indirectly through depreciation of the higher original basis. After the property is converted, both its basis for loss and its basis for gain are adjusted for depreciation deductions from the date of conversion to the date of disposition. These rules apply only if a conversion from personal to business or income-producing use has actually occurred.

EXAMPLE 32

At a time when his personal residence (adjusted basis of $140,000) is worth $150,000, Keith converts one-half of it to rental use. For simplicity, assume that the property is not covered by MACRS, will be depreciated using the straight-line method, has an estimated useful life of 20 years, and has no salvage value. As a result, annual depreciation will be $3,500 ($70,000 ÷ 20 years).

After renting the converted portion for five years, Keith sells the property for $144,000. All amounts relate only to the building; assume that the land has been accounted for separately. Keith has a $2,000 realized gain from the sale of the personal use portion of the residence and a $19,500 realized gain from the sale of the rental portion. These gains are computed as follows:

continued

---

[56]§ 1091(b) and Reg. § 1.1091–1(c).
[57]Reg. § 1.1091–1(a).

[58]Reg. § 1.165–9(b)(2).
[59]Reg. § 1.167(g)–1.

	Personal Use	Rental
Original basis for gain and loss—adjusted basis on date of conversion (fair market value is greater than the adjusted basis)	$70,000	$ 70,000
Depreciation—five years	(–0–)	(17,500)
Adjusted basis—date of sale	$70,000	$ 52,500
Amount realized	72,000	72,000
Realized gain	$ 2,000	$ 19,500

As discussed in Chapter 15, Keith may be able to exclude the $2,000 realized gain from the sale of the personal use portion of the residence (see text Section 15-4). If the exclusion applies, only $17,500 (equal to the depreciation deducted) of the $19,500 realized gain from the rental portion is recognized.

EXAMPLE
33

Assume the same facts as in Example 32, except that the fair market value on the date of conversion is $130,000 and the sales proceeds are $90,000. Keith has a $25,000 realized loss from the sale of the personal use portion of the residence and a $3,750 realized loss from the sale of the rental portion. These losses are computed as follows:

	Personal Use	Rental
Original basis for loss—fair market value on date of conversion (fair market value is less than the adjusted basis)	*	$ 65,000
Depreciation—five years	(–0–)	(16,250)**
Adjusted basis—date of sale	$70,000	$ 48,750
Amount realized	45,000	45,000
Realized loss	($25,000)	($ 3,750)

*Not applicable.
**($65,000 ÷ 20) × 5.

The $25,000 loss from the sale of the personal use portion of the residence is not recognized. The $3,750 loss from the rental portion is recognized.

14-2f **Summary of Basis Adjustments**

Some of the more common items that either increase or decrease the basis of an asset appear in Concept Summary 14.4.

There are a number of techniques for determining basis for tax purposes, with the method dependent on the manner in which the asset was acquired. In summary, the basis of an asset can be determined by:

- Reference to the asset's cost.
- Reference to the basis of another asset.
- Reference to the asset's fair market value.
- Reference to the basis of the asset to another taxpayer.

Concept Summary 14.4

Adjustments to Basis

Item	Effect	Refer to Chapter	Explanation
Amortization of bond discount	Increase	16	Amortization is mandatory for certain taxable bonds and elective for tax-exempt bonds.
Amortization of bond premium	Decrease	14	Amortization is mandatory for tax-exempt bonds and elective for taxable bonds.
Amortization of covenant not to compete	Decrease	8	Covenant must be for a definite and limited time period. The amortization period is a statutory period of 15 years.
Amortization of intangibles	Decrease	8	Intangibles are amortized over a 15-year period.
Assessment for local benefits	Increase	10	To the extent not deductible as taxes (e.g., assessment for streets and sidewalks that increase the value of the property versus one for maintenance or repair or for meeting interest charges).
Bad debts	Decrease	7	Only the specific charge-off method is permitted.
Capital additions	Increase	14	Certain items, at the taxpayer's election, can be capitalized or deducted (e.g., selected medical expenses).
Casualty	Decrease	7	For a casualty loss, the amount of the adjustment is the sum of the deductible loss and the insurance proceeds received. For a casualty gain, the amount of the adjustment is the insurance proceeds received reduced by the recognized gain.
Condemnation	Decrease	15	See casualty explanation.
Cost recovery	Decrease	8	§ 168 is applicable to tangible assets placed in service after 1980 whose useful life is expressed in terms of years.
Depletion	Decrease	8	Use the greater of cost or percentage depletion. Percentage depletion can still be deducted when the basis is zero.
Depreciation	Decrease	8	§ 167 is applicable to tangible assets placed in service before 1981 and to tangible assets not depreciated in terms of years.
Easement	Decrease	14	If the taxpayer does not retain any use of the land, all of the basis is allocable to the easement transaction. However, if only part of the land is affected by the easement, only part of the basis is allocable to the easement transaction.
Improvements by lessee to lessor's property	Increase	5	Adjustment occurs only if the lessor is required to include the fair market value of the improvements in gross income under § 109.
Imputed interest	Decrease	18	Amount deducted is not part of the cost of the asset.
Inventory: lower of cost or market	Decrease	18	Not available if the LIFO method is used.
Limited expensing under § 179	Decrease	8	Occurs only if the taxpayer elects § 179 treatment.
Medical capital expenditure permitted as a medical expense	Decrease	10	Adjustment is the amount of the deduction (the effect on basis is to increase it by the amount of the capital expenditure net of the deduction).
Real estate taxes: apportionment between the buyer and seller	Increase or decrease	10	To the extent the buyer pays the seller's pro rata share, the buyer's basis is increased. To the extent the seller pays the buyer's pro rata share, the buyer's basis is decreased.
Rebate from manufacturer	Decrease		Because the rebate is treated as an adjustment to the purchase price, it is not included in the buyer's gross income.
Stock dividend	Decrease	5	Adjustment occurs only if the stock dividend is nontaxable. While the basis per share decreases, the total stock basis does not change.
Stock rights	Decrease	14	Adjustment to stock basis occurs only for nontaxable stock rights and only if the fair market value of the rights is at least 15% of the fair market value of the stock or, if less than 15%, the taxpayer elects to allocate the basis between the stock and the rights.
Theft	Decrease	7	See casualty explanation.

14-3 TAX PLANNING

LO.5

Identify tax planning opportunities related to selected property transactions.

14-3a Cost Identification and Documentation Considerations

When multiple assets are acquired in a single transaction, the contract price must be allocated for several reasons. First, some of the assets may be depreciable, while others are not. Here, the buyer and the seller may have different tax perspectives that will need to be reconciled. The seller will likely prefer a high allocation for nondepreciable assets (see Chapters 16 and 17), while the purchaser will likely prefer a high allocation for depreciable assets (so that costs can be recovered via MACRS). Second, the seller must be able to characterize gains and losses appropriately as capital or ordinary. Allocating the price among the assets sold allows this to happen. For example, an allocation to goodwill or to a covenant not to compete (see Chapters 8, 16, and 17) produces different tax consequences to the seller. Third, the buyer must be able to identify the adjusted basis of each asset to be able to determine cost recovery, amortization, or depletion (if available) and to calculate the realized gain or loss if an asset is sold.

14-3b Selection of Property for Making Gifts

A donor can achieve several tax advantages by making gifts of appreciated property. The donor avoids income tax on the unrealized gain that would have occurred had the property been sold. And if the donee is in a lower tax bracket than the donor, there will be tax savings if the property is sold. Any increase in value after the gift will also be taxed at a lower rate. Such gifts of appreciated property can be an effective tool in family tax planning.

Taxpayers should generally not make gifts of depreciated property (property that, if sold, would produce a realized loss) because the donor does not receive an income tax deduction for the unrealized loss element. In addition, the donee receives no benefit from this unrealized loss upon the subsequent sale of the property because of the loss basis rule. If the donor anticipates that the donee will sell the property upon receiving it, the donor should sell the property and take the loss deduction, assuming that the loss is deductible. The donor can then give the proceeds from the sale to the donee.

14-3c Selection of Property for Inheritances

A taxpayer should generally distribute appreciated property via his or her will. Doing so enables both the decedent and the heir to avoid income tax on the unrealized gain because the recipient takes the fair market value as his or her basis.

Taxpayers generally should not distribute depreciated property (property that, if sold, would produce a realized loss) via his or her will because the decedent does not receive an income tax deduction for the unrealized loss element. In addition, the heir will receive no benefit from this unrealized loss upon the subsequent sale of the property.

EXAMPLE 34

On the date of her death in 2017, Marta owned land held for investment purposes. The land had an adjusted basis of $130,000 and a fair market value of $100,000. If Marta had sold the property before her death, the recognized loss would have been $30,000.

If Roger inherits the property and later sells it for $90,000, the recognized loss is $10,000 (the decline in value since Marta's death). In addition, regardless of the period of time Roger holds the property, the holding period is long term (see Chapter 16).

From an income tax perspective, it is better to transfer appreciated property as an inheritance rather than as a gift. Why? Because inherited property receives a step-up in basis, while property received by gift has a carryover basis to the donee. However, in making this decision, the estate tax consequences of the inheritance should also be weighed against the gift tax consequences of the gift.

14-3d **Disallowed Losses**

Section 267 Disallowed Losses

Taxpayers should avoid transactions that activate the related-party loss disallowance rules. Even with the ability of the related-party buyer to offset his or her realized gain by the related-party seller's disallowed loss, several inequities exist. First, any tax benefit associated with the disallowed loss is shifted to the related-party buyer (the related-party seller receives no tax benefit). Second, the tax benefit of this offset is delayed until the related-party buyer sells the property. Third, if the property does not appreciate during the time period the related-party buyer holds it, part or all of the disallowed loss is permanently lost. Fourth, the right of offset is available only to the original transferee (the related-party buyer). As a result, the disallowed loss will be permanently lost if the original transferee transfers the property by gift or inheritance.

EXAMPLE 35

Tim sells property with an adjusted basis of $35,000 to Wes, his brother, for $25,000, the fair market value of the property. The $10,000 realized loss to Tim is disallowed by § 267.

If Wes subsequently sells the property to an unrelated party for $37,000, he has a recognized gain of $2,000 (realized gain of $12,000 reduced by disallowed loss of $10,000). Therefore, from the perspective of the family unit, the original $10,000 realized loss ultimately is recognized.

However, if Wes sells the property for $29,000, he has a recognized gain of $0 (realized gain of $4,000 reduced by disallowed loss of $4,000 necessary to offset the realized gain). From the perspective of the family unit, $6,000 of the realized loss of $10,000 is permanently lost ($10,000 realized loss − $4,000 offset permitted).

Wash Sales

The wash sale rules can be avoided if the security that was sold is replaced with a similar rather than a substantially identical security. For example, a sale of AT&T common stock accompanied by a purchase of Verizon common stock is not treated as a wash sale. This can enable the taxpayer to use an otherwise unrealized capital loss to offset any capital gains recognized during the year. The taxpayer can sell the security before the end of the taxable year, offset the recognized capital loss against the capital gain, and invest the sales proceeds in a similar security.

The wash sale rules do not apply to gains. As a result, taxpayers with capital losses (or capital loss carryovers from prior years) can use a wash sale gain to offset these losses. Because the basis of the replacement stock will be the purchase price, the taxpayer gets an increased basis for the stock while using the capital gain to offset otherwise nondeductible capital losses.

ETHICS & EQUITY   **Washing a Loss Using an IRA**

Sam owns 1,500 shares of Eagle, Inc. stock that he purchased over 10 years ago for $80,000. Although the stock has a current market value of $52,000, Sam still views the stock as a solid long-term investment. He has sold other stock during the year with overall gains of $30,000, so he would like to sell the Eagle stock and offset the $28,000 loss against these gains—but somehow keep his Eagle investment. He has devised a plan to keep his Eagle investment by using funds in his traditional IRA to purchase 1,500 Eagle shares immediately after selling the shares he currently owns. Evaluate Sam's treatment of these stock transactions. Can his plan work?

PROPOSED SALE OF A HOUSE AND OTHER PROPERTY TRANSACTIONS

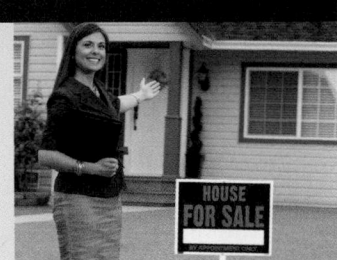

Alice's tax adviser asked a number of questions to advise her on her proposed transaction for the house. Alice provided the following answers (refer to Example 24):

- Alice inherited the house from her mother, Paula. The fair market value of the house at the date of Paula's death, based on the estate tax return, was $475,000. Based on an appraisal, the house currently is worth $485,000. Paula lived in the house for 38 years. According to Paula's attorney, her adjusted basis for the house was $275,000.

- As a child, Alice lived in the house for 10 years. She has not lived there during the 25 years she has been married.

- The house has been vacant during the seven months Alice has owned it. She has been trying to decide whether she should sell it for its fair market value or sell it to her nephew for $275,000. Alice has suggested a $275,000 price for the sale to Dan because she believes this is the amount at which she will have no gain or loss.

- Alice intends to invest the $275,000 in stock.

You advise Alice that her adjusted basis for the house is the $475,000 fair market value on the date of her Paula's death. If Alice sells the house for $485,000 (assuming no selling expenses), she would have a recognized gain of $10,000 ($485,000 amount realized − $475,000 adjusted basis). The house is a capital asset, and Alice's holding period is long term because she inherited the house. Thus, the gain would be classified as a long-term capital gain. If, instead, Alice sells the house to her nephew for $275,000, she will have a part sale and part gift. The realized gain on the sale of $5,670 is recognized.

Amount realized	$ 275,000
Less: Adjusted basis	(269,330)*
Realized gain	$ 5,670
Recognized gain	$ 5,670

*[($275,000/$485,000) × $475,000] = $269,330.

The gain is classified as a long-term capital gain. Alice is then deemed to have made a gift to Dan of $210,000 ($485,000 − $275,000). With this information, Alice can make an informed selection between the two options.

See Examples 12 and 13 for the tax consequences associated with Alice's questions regarding selling the boat. See Example 30 for the tax consequences associated with Alice's questions regarding the wash sale of the stock.

ISTOCKPHOTO.COM/MICHAEL COURTNEY

Key Terms

Discussion Questions

1.   **LO.1** Upon the sale or other disposition of property, what four questions should be considered for income tax purposes?

Decision Making   2.   **LO.1** Ivan invests in land, and Grace invests in taxable bonds. The land appreciates by $8,000 each year, and the bonds earn interest of $8,000 each year. After holding the land and bonds for five years, Ivan and Grace sell them. There is a $40,000 realized gain on the sale of the land and no realized gain or loss on the sale of the bonds. Are the tax consequences to Ivan and Grace the same for each of the five years? Explain.

3.   **LO.1** Carol and Dave each purchase 100 shares of stock of Burgundy, Inc., a publicly owned corporation, in July for $10,000 each. Carol sells her stock on December 31 for $8,000. Because Burgundy's stock is listed on a national exchange, Dave is able to ascertain that his shares are worth $8,000 on December 31. Does the tax law treat the decline in value of the stock differently for Carol and Dave? Explain.

4.   **LO.1** If a taxpayer sells property for cash, the amount realized consists of the net proceeds from the sale. For each of the following, indicate the effect on the amount realized:
   a.   The property is sold on credit.
   b.   A mortgage on the property is assumed by the buyer.
   c.   A mortgage on the property is assumed by the seller.
   d.   The buyer acquires the property subject to a mortgage of the seller.
   e.   Stock that has a basis to the purchaser of $6,000 and a fair market value of $10,000 is received by the seller as part of the consideration.

Decision Making   5.   **LO.1** Taylor is negotiating to buy some land. Under the first option, Taylor will give Ella $150,000 and assume her mortgage on the land for $100,000. Under the second option, Taylor will give Ella $250,000, and she will immediately pay off the mortgage. Taylor wants his basis for the land to be as high as possible. Given this objective, which option should Taylor select?

6.   **LO.1** Marge owns land and a building (held for investment) with an adjusted basis of $75,000 and a fair market value of $250,000. The property is subject to a mortgage of $400,000. Because Marge is in arrears on the mortgage payments, the creditor is willing to accept the property in return for canceling the amount of the mortgage.
   a.   How can the adjusted basis of the property be less than the amount of the mortgage?
   b.   If the creditor's offer is accepted, what are the effects on the amount realized, the adjusted basis, and the realized gain or loss for Marge?

7.   **LO.1** On July 16, 2017, Logan acquires land and a building for $500,000 to use in his sole proprietorship. Of the purchase price, $400,000 is allocated to the building, and $100,000 is allocated to the land. Cost recovery of $4,708 is deducted in 2017 for the building (nonresidential real estate).
   a.   What is the adjusted basis for the land and the building at the acquisition date?
   b.   What is the adjusted basis for the land and the building at the end of 2017?

8.   **LO.1** Auralia owns stock in Orange Corporation and Blue Corporation. She receives a $10,000 distribution from both corporations. The instructions from Orange state that the $10,000 is a dividend. The instructions from Blue state that the $10,000 is not a dividend. What could cause the instructions to differ as to the tax consequences?

9. **LO.2** Wanda is considering selling two personal use assets that she owns. One has appreciated in value by $20,000, and the other has declined in value by $17,000. Wanda believes that she should sell both assets in the same tax year so that the loss of $17,000 can offset the gain of $20,000.

    a. Advise Wanda regarding the tax consequences of her plan.

    b. Could Wanda achieve better tax results by selling the assets in different tax years? Explain.

Decision Making

10. **LO.2** Ron sold his sailboat for a $5,000 loss in the current year because he was diagnosed with skin cancer. His spouse wants him to sell his Harley-Davidson motorcycle because her brother broke his leg while riding his motorcycle. Because Ron no longer has anyone to ride with, he is seriously considering accepting his wife's advice. Because the motorcycle is a classic, Ron has received two offers. Each offer would result in a $5,000 gain. Joe would like to purchase the motorcycle before Christmas, and Jeff would like to purchase it after New Year's. Identify the relevant tax issues Ron faces in making his decision.

Issue ID

11. **LO.1, 2, 3, 5** Simon owns stock that has declined in value since acquired. He has decided either to give the stock to his nephew, Fred, or to sell it and give Fred the proceeds. If Fred receives the stock, he will sell it to obtain the proceeds. Simon is in the 15% tax bracket, while Fred's bracket is 25%. In either case, the holding period for the stock will be short term. Identify the tax issues relevant to Simon in deciding whether to give the stock or the sale proceeds to Fred.

Issue ID

12. **LO.3** Robin inherits 1,000 shares of Wal-Mart stock from her aunt in 2017. According to the information received from the executor of her aunt's estate, Robin's adjusted basis for the stock is $55,000. Albert, Robin's fiancé, receives 1,000 shares of Wal-Mart stock from his uncle as a gift in 2017. His uncle tells Albert that his adjusted basis for the Wal-Mart stock is $7,000. What could cause the substantial difference in the adjusted basis for Robin's and Albert's respective 1,000 shares of Wal-Mart stock?

13. **LO.3** Thelma inherited land from Sadie on June 7, 2017. The land appreciated in value by 100% during the six months it was owned by Sadie. The value has remained stable during the three months Thelma has owned it, and she expects it to continue to do so in the near future. Although she would like to sell the land now, Thelma has decided to postpone the sale for another three months. The delay is to enable the recognized gain to qualify for long-term capital gain treatment. Evaluate Thelma's understanding of the tax law.

14. **LO.4** Marilyn owns land that she acquired three years ago as an investment for $250,000. Because the land has not appreciated in value as she anticipated, she sells it to her brother, Amos, for its fair market value of $180,000. Amos sells the land two years later for $240,000.

    a. Explain why Marilyn's realized loss of $70,000 ($180,000 amount realized − $250,000 adjusted basis) is disallowed at the time of the sale to her brother.

    b. Explain why Amos has neither a recognized gain nor a recognized loss on his sale of the land.

    c. How does the related-party disallowance rule affect the total gain or loss recognized by the family unit?

    d. Which party wins, and which party loses?

    e. How could Marilyn have avoided the loss disallowance on her sale of the land?

Decision Making

15. **LO.4, 5** Comment on the following transactions:

    a. Mort owns 500 shares of Pear, Inc. stock with an adjusted basis of $22,000. On July 28, 2017, he sells 100 shares for $3,000. On August 16, 2017, he purchases another 100 shares for $3,400. Mort's realized loss of $1,400 ($3,000 − $4,400)

Decision Making

on the July 28 sale is not recognized, and his adjusted basis for the 100 shares purchased on August 16 is $4,800. Explain.

b.   How would your answer in part (a) change if Mort purchased the 100 shares on December 27, 2017, rather than on August 16, 2017?

Computational Exercises

16. **LO.1** Sally owns real property for which the annual property taxes are $9,000. She sells the property to Kate on March 9, 2017, for $550,000. Kate pays the real property taxes for the entire year on October 1, 2017.

a.   How much of the property taxes can be deducted by Sally and how much by Kate?

b.   What effect does the property tax apportionment have on Kate's adjusted basis in the property?

c.   What effect does the apportionment have on Sally's amount realized from the sale?

d.   How would the answers in parts (b) and (c) differ if the taxes were paid by Sally?

17. **LO.1** Melba purchases land from Adrian. Melba gives Adrian $225,000 in cash and agrees to pay Adrian an additional $400,000 one year later plus interest at 5%.

a.   What is Melba's adjusted basis for the land at the acquisition date?

b.   What is Melba's adjusted basis for the land one year later?

18. **LO.1** On July 1, 2017, Katrina purchased tax-exempt bonds (face value of $75,000) for $82,000. The bonds mature in five years, and the annual interest rate is 6%. The market rate of interest is 2%.

a.   How much interest income and/or interest expense must Katrina report in 2017, assuming straight-line amortization is appropriate?

b.   What is Katrina's adjusted basis for the bonds on January 1, 2018?

19. **LO.3** Luciana, a nonshareholder, purchases a condominium from her employer for $85,000. The fair market value of the condominium is $120,000. What is Luciana's basis in the condominium and the amount of any income as a result of this purchase?

20. **LO.3** Sebastian purchases two pieces of equipment for $100,000. Appraisals of the equipment indicate that the fair market value of the first piece of equipment is $72,000 and that of the second piece of equipment is $108,000. What is Sebastian's basis in these two assets?

21. **LO.3** Heather owns 400 shares of Diego Corporation common stock for which she paid $4,000. She receives a nontaxable stock dividend of 20 shares of preferred stock on her common stock. The fair market values on the date of distribution of the preferred stock dividend are $20 a share for common stock and $100 a share for preferred stock. What is Heather's basis in the common and preferred shares?

22. **LO.3** Juliana purchased land three years ago for $50,000. She gave the land to Tom, her brother, in the current year, when the fair market value was $70,000. No gift tax is paid on the transfer. Tom subsequently sells the property for $63,000.

a.   What is Tom's basis in the land, and what is his realized gain or loss on the sale?

b.   Assume, instead, that the land has a fair market value of $45,000 and that Tom sold the land for $43,000. Now what is Tom's basis in the land, and what is his realized gain or loss on the sale?

23. **LO.3** Ashley inherited all of the property of her aunt, who died in 2017. Her aunt's adjusted basis for the property at the date of death was $1,200,000. The property's fair market value was $4,500,000 at the date of death and $4,800,000 six months after the date of death. What is Ashley's adjusted basis of the property for income tax purposes?

24. **LO.4** Lisa sells business property with an adjusted basis of $130,000 to her son, Alfred, for its fair market value of $100,000.
    a. What is Lisa's realized and recognized gain or loss?
    b. What is Alfred's recognized gain or loss if he subsequently sells the property for $138,000? For $80,000?

25. **LO.4** Juan owned 200 shares of Circle Corporation stock (adjusted basis of $30,000). He sold 100 shares for $12,000. Twenty days later he purchased 100 shares of the same stock for $8,500. What is Juan's realized and recognized loss? What is his basis in the newly acquired shares?

26. **LO.4** Arianna's personal residence has an adjusted basis of $230,000 and a fair market value of $210,000. Arianna converts the personal residence to rental property. What is Arianna's gain basis? What is her loss basis?

27. **LO.4** Peyton sells an office building and the associated land on May 1 of the current year. Under the terms of the sales contract, Peyton is to receive $1,600,000 in cash. The purchaser is to assume Peyton's mortgage of $950,000 on the property. To enable the purchaser to obtain adequate financing, Peyton is to pay the $9,000 in points charged by the lender. The broker's commission on the sale is $75,000. What is Peyton's amount realized?

Problems

28. **LO.1** Anne sold her home for $290,000 in 2017. Selling expenses were $17,400. She purchased it in 2011 for $200,000. During the period of ownership, Anne did the following:

    - Deducted $50,500 office-in-home expenses, which included $4,500 in depreciation. (Refer to Chapter 9.)
    - Deducted a casualty loss in 2013 for residential trees destroyed by a hurricane. The total loss was $19,000 (after the $100 floor and the 10%-of-AGI floor), and Anne's insurance company reimbursed her for $13,500. (Refer to Chapter 7.)
    - Paid street paving assessment of $7,000 and added sidewalks for $8,000.
    - Installed an elevator for medical reasons. The total cost was $20,000, and Anne deducted $13,000 as medical expenses. (Refer to Chapter 10.)

    What is Anne's realized gain?

29. **LO.1** Kareem bought a rental house in March 2012 for $300,000, of which $50,000 is allocated to the land and $250,000 to the building. Early in 2014, he had a tennis court built in the backyard at a cost of $7,500. Kareem has deducted $30,900 for depreciation on the house and $1,300 for depreciation on the court. In January 2017, he sells the house and tennis court for $330,000 cash.
    a. What is Kareem's realized gain or loss?
    b. If an original mortgage of $80,000 is still outstanding and the buyer assumes the mortgage in addition to the cash payment, what is Kareem's realized gain or loss?
    c. If the buyer takes the property subject to the $80,000 mortgage, rather than assuming it, what is Kareem's realized gain or loss?

30. **LO.1** Norm is negotiating the sale of a tract of his land to Pat. Use the following classification scheme to classify each of the items contained in the proposed sales contract:

Legend		
DARN	=	Decreases amount realized by Norm
IARN	=	Increases amount realized by Norm
DABN	=	Decreases adjusted basis to Norm
IABN	=	Increases adjusted basis to Norm
DABP	=	Decreases adjusted basis to Pat
IABP	=	Increases adjusted basis to Pat

   a. Norm is to receive cash of $50,000.
   b. Norm is to receive Pat's note payable for $25,000, payable in three years.
   c. Pat assumes Norm's mortgage of $5,000 on the land.
   d. Pat agrees to pay the realtor's sales commission of $8,000.
   e. Pat agrees to pay the property taxes on the land for the entire year. If each party paid his or her respective share, Norm's share would be $1,000 and Pat's share would be $3,000.
   f. Pat pays legal fees of $500.
   g. Norm pays legal fees of $750.

31. **LO.1** Nissa owns a building (adjusted basis of $600,000 on January 1, 2017) that she rents to Len, who operates a restaurant in the building. The municipal health department closed the restaurant for three months during 2017 because of health code violations. Under MACRS, the cost recovery deduction for 2017 would be $20,500. However, Nissa deducted cost recovery only for the nine months the restaurant was open because she waived the rent income during the three-month period the restaurant was closed.
   a. What is the amount of the cost recovery deduction Nissa should report on her 2017 income tax return?
   b. Calculate the adjusted basis of the building at the end of 2017.

32. **LO.1, 2** Pam owns a personal use boat that has a fair market value of $35,000 and an adjusted basis of $45,000. Pam's AGI is $100,000. Calculate the realized and recognized gain or loss if:
   a. Pam sells the boat for $35,000.
   b. Pam exchanges the boat for another boat worth $35,000.
   c. The boat is stolen and Pam receives insurance proceeds of $35,000.
   d. Would your answer in part (a) change if the fair market value and the selling price of the boat were $48,000?

33. **LO.1** Ricky owns stock in Dove Corporation. His adjusted basis for the stock is $90,000. During the year, he receives a distribution from the corporation of $75,000 that is labeled a return of capital (i.e., Dove has no earnings and profits).
   a. Determine the tax consequences to Ricky.
   b. Assume instead that the amount of the distribution is $150,000. Determine the tax consequences to Ricky.
   c. Assume instead in part (a) that the $75,000 distribution is labeled a taxable dividend (i.e., Dove has earnings and profits of at least $75,000).

34. **LO.1, 2** Chee purchases Tan, Inc. bonds for $108,000 on January 2, 2017. The face value of the bonds is $100,000; the maturity date is December 31, 2021; and the annual interest rate is 5%. Chee will amortize the premium only if he is required to do so. Chee sells the bonds on July 1, 2019, for $106,000.

a. Determine the interest income Chee should report for 2017.

b. Calculate Chee's recognized gain or loss on the sale of the bonds in 2019.

35. **LO.1, 2** Which of the following results in a recognized gain or loss?
    a. Kay sells her vacation cabin (adjusted basis of $100,000) for $150,000.
    b. Adam sells his personal residence (adjusted basis of $150,000) for $100,000.
    c. Carl's personal residence (adjusted basis of $65,000) is condemned by the city. He receives condemnation proceeds of $55,000.
    d. Olga's land is worth $40,000 at the end of the year. She had purchased the land six months earlier for $25,000.
    e. Vera's personal vehicle (adjusted basis of $22,000) is stolen. She receives $23,000 from the insurance company and does not plan to replace the automobile.
    f. Jerry sells used clothing (adjusted basis of $500) to a thrift store for $50.

36. **LO.1, 2** Yancy's personal residence is condemned as part of an urban renewal project. His adjusted basis for the residence is $480,000. He receives condemnation proceeds of $460,000 and invests the proceeds in stocks and bonds.
    a. Calculate Yancy's realized and recognized gain or loss.
    b. If the condemnation proceeds are $505,000, what are Yancy's realized and recognized gain or loss?
    c. What are Yancy's realized and recognized gain or loss in part (a) if the house was rental property?

37. **LO.3** Buddy Morgan is a real estate agent for Coastal Estates, a residential real   Communications
    estate development. Because of his outstanding sales performance, Buddy is permitted to buy a lot for $300,000 that normally would sell for $500,000. Buddy is the only real estate agent for Coastal Estates who is permitted to do so.
    a. Does Buddy have gross income from the transaction? Explain.
    b. What is Buddy's adjusted basis for the land?
    c. Write a letter to Buddy informing him of the tax consequences of his acquisition of the lot. His address is 100 Tower Road, San Diego, CA 92182.

38. **LO.1, 2, 3** Karen Samuels (Social Security number 123-45-6789) makes the following purchases and sales of stock:

Transaction	Date	Number of Shares	Company	Price per Share
Purchase	1-1-2015	300	MDG	$ 75
Purchase	6-1-2015	150	GRU	300
Purchase	11-1-2015	60	MDG	70
Sale	12-3-2015	200	MDG	80
Purchase	3-1-2016	120	GRU	375
Sale	8-1-2016	90	GRU	330
Sale	1-1-2017	150	MDG	90
Sale	2-1-2017	75	GRU	500

Assuming that Karen is unable to identify the particular lots that are sold with the original purchase, determine the recognized gain or loss on each type of stock:
    a. As of July 1, 2015.
    b. As of December 31, 2015.
    c. As of December 31, 2016.
    d. As of July 1, 2017.
    e. Form 8949 and Schedule D (Form 1040) are used to report sales of capital assets (which include stock sales). Go to the IRS website, and download the 2016 Form 8949 and Schedule D (Form 1040). Then complete the forms for part (c) of this problem, assuming that the brokerage firm did not report Karen's basis to the IRS [complete Schedule D (Form 1040) through line 16].

39. **LO.1, 2, 3** Kevin purchases 1,000 shares of Bluebird Corporation stock on October 3, 2017, for $300,000. On December 12, 2017, Kevin purchases an additional 750 shares of Bluebird stock for $210,000. According to market quotations, Bluebird stock is selling for $285 per share on December 31, 2017. Kevin sells 500 shares of Bluebird stock on March 1, 2018, for $162,500.

    a. What is the adjusted basis of Kevin's Bluebird stock on December 31, 2017?

    b. What is Kevin's recognized gain or loss from the sale of Bluebird stock on March 1, 2018, assuming that the shares sold are from the shares purchased on December 12, 2017?

    c. What is Kevin's recognized gain or loss from the sale of Bluebird stock on March 1, 2018, assuming that Kevin cannot adequately identify the shares sold?

Communications   40. **LO.3** Rod Clooney purchases Agnes Mitchell's sole proprietorship for $990,000 on August 15, 2017. The assets of the business are as follows:

Asset	Agnes's Adjusted Basis	FMV
Accounts receivable	$ 70,000	$ 70,000
Inventory	90,000	100,000
Equipment	150,000	160,000
Furniture and fixtures	95,000	130,000
Building	190,000	250,000
Land	25,000	75,000
Total	$620,000	$785,000

    a. Calculate Agnes's realized and recognized gain.

    b. Determine Rod's basis for each of the assets.

    c. Write a letter to Rod informing him of the tax consequences of the purchase. His address is 300 Riverview Drive, Delaware, OH 43015.

41. **LO.3** Donna owns 800 shares of common stock in Macaw Corporation (adjusted basis of $40,000). She receives a 5% stock dividend when the stock is selling for $60 per share.

    a. How much gross income must Donna recognize because of the stock dividend?

    b. What is Donna's basis for her 840 shares of stock?

42. **LO.1, 2, 3** Roberto has received various gifts over the years. He has decided to dispose of the following assets he received as gifts:

    a. In 1951, he received land worth $32,000. The donor's adjusted basis was $35,000. Roberto sells the land for $95,000 in 2017.

    b. In 1956, he received stock in Gold Company. The donor's adjusted basis was $19,000. The fair market value on the date of the gift was $34,000. Roberto sells the stock for $40,000 in 2017.

    c. In 1962, he received land worth $15,000. The donor's adjusted basis was $20,000. Roberto sells the land for $9,000 in 2017.

    d. In 2003, he received stock worth $30,000. The donor's adjusted basis was $42,000. Roberto sells the stock for $38,000 in 2017.

    What is the recognized gain or loss from each of the preceding transactions? Assume for each of the gift transactions that no gift tax was paid.

43. **LO.1, 2, 3** Nicky receives a car from Sam as a gift. Sam paid $48,000 for the car. He had used it for business purposes and had deducted $10,000 for depreciation up to the time he gave the car to Nicky. The fair market value of the car is $33,000.

    a. Assuming that Nicky uses the car for business purposes, what is her basis for depreciation?

b. Assume that Nicky deducts depreciation of $6,500 and then sells the car for $32,500. What is her recognized gain or loss?

c. Assume that Nicky deducts depreciation of $6,500 and then sells the car for $20,000. What is her recognized gain or loss?

44. **LO.3** Margo receives a gift of real estate with an adjusted basis of $175,000 and a fair market value of $100,000. The donor paid gift tax of $15,000 on the transfer. If Margo later sells the property for $110,000, what is her recognized gain or loss?

45. **LO.3** On September 18, 2017, Gerald received land and a building from Frank as a gift. Frank's adjusted basis and the fair market value at the date of the gift are as follows:

Asset	Adjusted Basis	FMV
Land	$100,000	$212,000
Building	80,000	100,000

No gift tax was paid on the transfer.

a. Determine Gerald's adjusted basis for the land and building.

b. Assume instead that the fair market value of the land was $87,000 and that of the building was $65,000. Determine Gerald's adjusted basis for the land and building.

46. **LO.1, 2, 3, 5** Ira Cook is planning to make a charitable contribution to the Boy Scouts of Crystal, Inc. stock worth $20,000. The stock has an adjusted basis of $15,000. A friend has suggested that Ira sell the stock and contribute the $20,000 in proceeds rather than contribute the stock.

Decision Making

Communications

a. Should Ira follow the friend's advice? Why or why not?

b. Assume that the fair market value is only $13,000. In this case, should Ira follow the friend's advice? Why or why not?

c. Rather than make a charitable contribution to the Boy Scouts, Ira is going to make a gift to Nancy, his niece. Advise Ira regarding parts (a) and (b).

d. Write a letter to Ira regarding whether in part (a) he should sell the stock and contribute the cash or contribute the stock. He has informed you that he purchased the stock six years ago. Ira's address is 500 Ireland Avenue, DeKalb, IL 60115.

47. **LO.3** As sole heir, Dazie receives all of Mary's property (adjusted basis of $1,400,000 and fair market value of $3,820,000). Six months after Mary's death in 2017, the fair market value is $3,835,000.

a. Can the executor of Mary's estate elect the alternate valuation date and amount? Explain.

b. What is Dazie's basis for the property?

c. Assume instead that the fair market value six months after Mary's death is $3,800,000. Respond to parts (a) and (b).

48. **LO.3** Dan bought a hotel for $2,600,000 in January 2013. In May 2017, he died and left the hotel to Ed. While Dan owned the hotel, he deducted $289,000 of cost recovery. The fair market value in May 2017 was $2,800,000. The fair market value six months later was $2,850,000.

a. What is the basis of the property to Ed?

b. What is the basis of the property to Ed if the fair market value six months later was $2,500,000 (not $2,850,000) and the objective of the executor was to minimize the estate tax liability?

49. **LO.3** Helene and Pauline are twin sisters who live in Louisiana and Mississippi, respectively. Helene is married to Frank, and Pauline is married to Richard. Frank and Richard are killed in an auto accident in 2017 while returning from a sporting event.

    Helene and Frank jointly owned some farmland in Louisiana, a community property state (value of $940,000, cost of $450,000). Pauline and Richard jointly owned some farmland in Mississippi, a common law state (value of $940,000, cost of $450,000). Assume that all of Frank's and Richard's property passes to their surviving wives.

    a. Calculate Helene's basis in the land.
    b. Calculate Pauline's basis in the land.
    c. What causes the difference?

50. **LO.3, 4** Sheila sells land to Elane, her sister, for the fair market value of $40,000. Six months later when the land is worth $45,000, Elane gives it to Jacob, her son. (No gift tax resulted.) Shortly thereafter, Jacob sells the land for $48,000.

    a. Assuming that Sheila's adjusted basis for the land is $24,000, what are Sheila's and Jacob's recognized gain or loss on the sales?
    b. Assuming that Sheila's adjusted basis for the land is $60,000, what are Sheila's and Jacob's recognized gain or loss on the sales?

51. **LO.1, 2, 3, 4** Louis owns three pieces of land with an adjusted basis as follows: parcel A, $75,000; parcel B, $125,000; and parcel C, $175,000. Louis sells parcel A to his uncle for $50,000, parcel B to his partner for $120,000, and parcel C to his mother for $150,000.

    a. What is the recognized gain or loss from the sale of each parcel?
    b. If Louis's uncle eventually sells his land for $90,000, what is his recognized gain or loss?
    c. If Louis's partner eventually sells his land for $130,000, what is his recognized gain or loss?
    d. If Louis's mother eventually sells her land for $165,000, what is her recognized gain or loss?

Decision Making   52. **LO.1, 2, 3, 4** Tyneka inherited 1,000 shares of Aqua, Inc. stock from Joe. Joe's basis was $35,000, and the fair market value on July 1, 2017 (the date of death) was $45,000. The shares were distributed to Tyneka on July 15, 2017. Tyneka sold the stock on July 30, 2018, for $33,000. After giving the matter more thought, she decides that Aqua is a good investment and purchases 1,000 shares for $30,000 on August 20, 2018.

    a. What is Tyneka's basis for the 1,000 shares purchased on August 20, 2018?
    b. Could Tyneka have obtained different tax consequences in part (a) if she had sold the 1,000 shares on December 27, 2017, and purchased the 1,000 shares on January 5, 2018? Explain.

Decision Making   53. **LO.1, 2, 4** On December 28, 2017, Kramer sells 150 shares of Lavender, Inc. stock for $77,000. On January 10, 2018, he purchases 100 shares of the same stock for $82,000.

    a. Assuming that Kramer's adjusted basis for the stock sold is $65,000, what is his recognized gain or loss? What is his basis for the new shares?
    b. Assuming that Kramer's adjusted basis for the stock sold is $89,000, what is his recognized gain or loss? What is his basis for the new shares?
    c. Advise Kramer on how he can avoid any negative tax consequences encountered in part (b).

54. **LO.1, 2, 4** Abby's home had a basis of $360,000 ($160,000 attributable to the land) and a fair market value of $340,000 ($155,000 attributable to the land)

when she converted 70% of it to business use by opening a bed-and-breakfast. Four years after the conversion, Abby sells the home for $500,000 ($165,000 attributable to the land).

a. Calculate Abby's basis for gain, loss, and cost recovery for the portion of her personal residence that was converted to business use.

b. Calculate the cost recovery deducted by Abby during the four-year period of business use, assuming that the bed-and-breakfast is opened on January 1 of year 1 and the house is sold on December 31 of year 4.

c. What is Abby's recognized gain or loss on the sale of the business use portion?

55. **LO.4, 5** Surendra's personal residence originally cost $340,000 (ignore land). After living in the house for five years, he converts it to rental property. At the date of conversion, the fair market value of the house is $320,000. As to the rental property, calculate Surendra's basis for: Decision Making

a. Loss.

b. Depreciation.

c. Gain.

d. Could Surendra have obtained better tax results if he had sold his personal residence for $320,000 and then purchased another house for $320,000 to hold as rental property? Explain.

56. **LO.3, 5** Hun, age 93, has accumulated substantial assets during his life. Among his many assets are the following, which he is considering giving to Koji, his grandson.   Decision Making

Asset	Adjusted Basis	Fair Market Value
Silver Corporation stock	$900,000	$700,000
Red Corporation stock	70,000	71,000
Emerald Corporation stock	200,000	500,000

Hun has been in ill health for the past five years. His physician has informed him that he probably will not live for more than six months. Advise Hun on which of the stocks should be transferred as gifts and which as inheritances.

Cumulative Problems

57. Alton Newman, age 67, is married and files a joint return with his wife, Clair, age 65. Alton and Clair are both retired, and during 2016, they received Social Security benefits of $10,000. Both Alton and Clair are covered by Medicare. Alton's Social Security number is 111-11-1112, and Clair's is 123-45-6789. They reside at 210 College Drive, Columbia, SC 29201.   Tax Return Problem

Alton, who retired on January 1, 2016, receives benefits from a qualified pension plan of $2,750 a month for life. His total contributions to the plan (none of which were deductible) were $168,250. In January 2016, he received a bonus of $2,000 from his former employer for service performed in 2015. No income taxes were withheld on this bonus by his former employer (Amalgamated Industries, Inc.; EIN 12-3456789; 114 Main Street, Columbia, SC 29201). Although Amalgamated Industries, Inc. accrued the bonus in 2015, it was not paid until 2016.

Clair, who retired on December 31, 2015, started receiving benefits of $1,400 a month on January 1, 2016. Her contributions to the qualified pension plan (none of which were deductible) were $74,100.

On September 27, 2016, Alton and Clair received a pro rata 10% stock dividend on 600 shares of stock they owned. They had bought the stock on March 5, 2009, for $20 a share. On December 16, 2016, they sold the 60 dividend shares for $55 a share.

On October 10, 2016, Clair sold the car she had used in commuting to and from work for $17,000. She had paid $31,000 for the car in 2010.

On July 14, 2008, Alton and Clair received a gift of 1,000 shares of stock from their son, Thomas. Thomas's basis in the stock was $35 a share (fair market value at the date of gift was $25). No gift tax was paid on the transfer. Alton and Clair sold the stock on October 8, 2016, for $24 a share.

On May 1, 2016, Clair's mother died, and Clair inherited her personal residence. In February 2016, her mother had paid the property taxes for 2016 of $2,100. The residence had a fair market value of $235,000 and an adjusted basis to the mother of $160,000 on the date of her death. Clair listed the house with a real estate agent, who estimated it was worth $240,000 as of December 31, 2016.

Clair received rent income of $6,000 on a beach house she inherited three years ago from her uncle Charles. She had rented the property for one week during the July 4 holiday and one week during the Thanksgiving holiday. Charles's adjusted basis in the beach house was $150,000, and its fair market value on the date of his death was $240,000. Clair and Alton used the beach house for personal purposes for 56 days during the year. Expenses associated with the house were $3,700 for utilities, maintenance, and repairs; $2,200 for property taxes; and $800 for insurance. There are no mortgages on the property.

Clair and Alton paid estimated Federal income tax of $3,100 and had itemized deductions of $6,800 (excluding any itemized deductions associated with the beach house). If they have overpaid their Federal income tax, they want the amount refunded. Both Clair and Alton want $3 to go to the Presidential Election Campaign Fund.

Compute their net tax payable or refund due for 2016. If you use tax forms for your computations, you will need at a minimum Form 1040 and Schedule D. Suggested software: H&R BLOCK Tax Software.

Tax Computation Problem

Decision Making

Communications

58. John Benson, age 40, is single. His Social Security number is 111-11-1111, and he resides at 150 Highway 51, Tangipahoa, LA 70465.

John has a 5-year-old child, Kendra, who lives with her mother, Katy. John pays alimony of $6,000 per year to Katy and child support of $12,000. The $12,000 of child support covers 65% of Katy's costs of rearing Kendra. Kendra's Social Security number is 123-45-6789, and Katy's is 123-45-6788.

John's mother, Sally, lived with him until her death in early September 2017. He incurred and paid medical expenses for her of $12,900 and other support payments of $11,000. Sally's only sources of income were $5,500 of interest income on certificates of deposit and $5,600 of Social Security benefits, which she spent on her medical expenses and on maintenance of John's household. Sally's Social Security number was 123-45-6787.

John is employed by the Highway Department of the State of Louisiana in an executive position. His salary is $95,000. The appropriate amounts of Social Security tax and Medicare tax were withheld. In addition, $9,500 was withheld for Federal income taxes, and $4,000 was withheld for state income taxes.

In addition to his salary, John's employer provides him with the following fringe benefits:

- Group term life insurance with a maturity value of $95,000. The cost of the premiums for the employer was $295.
- Group health insurance plan. John's employer paid premiums of $5,800 for his coverage. The plan paid $2,600 for John's medical expenses during the year.

Upon the death of his aunt Josie in December 2016, John, her only recognized heir, inherited the following assets:

Asset	Josie's Adjusted Basis	FMV at Date of Death
Car	$35,000	$ 19,000
Land—300 acres	90,000	175,000
IBM stock	15,000	40,000
Cash	10,000	10,000

Three months prior to her death, Josie gave John a mountain cabin. Her adjusted basis for the mountain cabin was $120,000, and the fair market value was $195,000. No gift taxes were paid.

During the year, John had the following transactions:

- On February 1, 2017, he sold for $45,000 Microsoft stock that he inherited from his father four years ago. His father's adjusted basis was $49,000, and the fair market value at the date of the father's death was $41,000.

- The car John inherited from Josie was destroyed in a wreck on October 1, 2017. He had loaned the car to Katy to use for a two-week period while the engine in her car was being replaced. Fortunately, neither Katy nor Kendra was injured. John received insurance proceeds of $16,000, the fair market value of the car on October 1, 2017.

- On December 28, 2017, John sold the 300 acres of land to his brother, James, for its fair market value of $160,000. James planned on using the land for his dairy farm.

Other sources of income for John were as follows:

Dividend income (qualified dividends)	$ 3,500
Interest income:	
Guaranty Bank	1,000
City of Kentwood water bonds	2,000
Award from state of Louisiana for outstanding	
suggestion for highway beautification	10,000

Potential itemized deductions for John, in addition to items already mentioned, were as follows:

Property taxes paid on his residence and cabin	$7,000
Property taxes paid on personalty	3,500
Estimated Federal income taxes paid	3,000
Charitable contributions	4,500
Mortgage interest on his residence	7,200
Orthodontic expenses for Kendra	4,000

Part 1—Tax Computation
Compute John's net tax payable or refund due for 2017.

Part 2—Tax Planning
Assume that rather than selling the land to James, John is considering leasing it to him for $12,000 annually with the lease beginning on October 1, 2017. James would prepay the lease payments through December 31, 2017. Thereafter, he would make monthly lease payments at the beginning of each month. What effect would this have on John's 2017 tax liability? What potential problem might John encounter? Write a letter to John in which you advise him of the tax consequences of leasing versus selling. Also prepare a memo for the tax files.

Research Problems

Note: Solutions to the Research Problems can be prepared by using the Thomson Reuters Checkpoint® Student Edition online tax research database, which accompanies this textbook. Solutions can also be prepared by using research materials found in a typical tax library.

THOMSON REUTERS
CHECKPOINT®
Student Edition

Research Problem 1. Terry owns real estate with an adjusted basis of $600,000 and a fair market value of $1.1 million. The amount of the nonrecourse mortgage on the property is $2.5 million. Because of substantial past and projected future losses associated with the real estate development (occupancy rate of only 37% after three years), Terry deeds the property to the creditor.

a. What are the tax consequences to Terry?

b. Assume that the data are the same, except that the fair market value of the property is $2,525,000. Therefore, when Terry deeds the property to the creditor, she also receives $25,000 from the creditor. What are the tax consequences to Terry?

Research Problem 2. Your client, Jacob, turned 66 years old this year. Jacob has no heirs and has decided that he would like to sell a life insurance policy to fund a trip to Africa that he has wanted to take.

Jacob knew that he could surrender the policy (a whole-life policy) back to the insurance company, but a friend told him he could get more for the policy if he sold it to a life settlement company. A life settlement company buys life insurance policies from policyholders who are not ill and who generally have a life expectancy of between 2 and 15 years. In return, the seller of the policy receives a lump-sum payment. The life settlement company either holds the policy to maturity or resells the policy to an investor.

The lump sum received depends on factors such as age, health, and the terms and conditions of the policy, but is generally more than the policy's cash surrender value (which would be received from the life insurance company upon surrender of the policy).

In November 2017, Jacob (who was not terminally or chronically ill) sold his policy to a life settlement company for $160,000. During the time he owned the policy, Jacob did not borrow against the policy or receive any distributions. Jacob also had paid premiums totaling $122,000 (of which $32,000 was paid for the provision of insurance before the sale of the policy).

How should Jacob calculate his basis in the life insurance policy to determine whether he has a realized gain or loss on the surrender of the policy?

Communications   **Research Problem 3.** Ruth Ames died on January 10, 2017. In filing the estate tax return, her executor, Melvin Sims, elects the primary valuation date and amount (fair market value on the date of death). On March 12, 2017, Melvin invests $30,000 of cash that Ruth had in her money market account in acquiring 1,000 shares of Orange, Inc. ($30 per share). On January 10, 2017, Orange was selling for $29 per share. The stock is distributed to a beneficiary, Annette Rust, on June 1, 2017, when it is selling for $33 per share. Melvin wants you to determine the amount at which the Orange shares should appear on the estate tax return and the amount of Annette's adjusted basis for the stock. Write a letter to Melvin in which you respond to his inquiry, and prepare a memo for the tax files. His address is 100 Center Lane, Miami, FL 33124.

Communications   **Research Problem 4.** How are transactions using Bitcoin (virtual currency) treated under U.S. tax law? Some background on Bitcoin can be found at **https://bitcoin .org/en/faq**. Locate the IRS guidance on this question, and provide a one-page written summary for your instructor.

Use internet tax resources to address the following questions. Look for reliable websites and blogs of the IRS and other government agencies, media outlets, businesses, tax professionals, academics, think tanks, and political outlets.

Research Problem 5. Many see the "step-up in basis at death" rule of § 1014 as an expensive tax loophole enjoyed by the wealthy. Find the latest estimates of the revenue loss to the Treasury that is attributable to this rule.

a. How does Canada's tax law determine the basis of property acquired from a decedent?

b. Send an e-mail to a member of the House Ways and Means Committee expressing a preference for the preservation of the current § 1014 rule or the modifications made to it by the Tax Relief Reconciliation Act of 2001 and the Tax Relief Act of 2010.

Research Problem 6. The specific identification method is important when one invests in mutual funds. When taxpayers sell part of their holdings, the basis of the surrendered shares can be difficult to compute. Go to the site of an investment adviser or a mutual fund to find instructions on how to compute the basis of the shares sold. What options are available to the taxpayer according to this information? Illustrate each of the alternatives.

Roger CPA Review Questions

1. Stephen purchased a video game console five years ago for $500. In order to raise money for the "latest and greatest" console, Stephen sold his console for $100. Because of advances in technology, Stephen can purchase the new console for $400. What is the tax treatment of Stephen's sale of his console?

   a. Stephen recognizes a $400 loss.

   b. Stephen does not report the sale.

   c. Stephen recognizes a $300 loss.

   d. Stephen recognizes a $100 gain.

2. Uncle Ubb gave his nephew, Leroy Lamprey, a gift of stock worth $10,000. Uncle Ubb's basis in the stock was $15,000. Leroy sold the stock to an unrelated party for $11,000. What amount of gain or loss should Leroy report as a result of this sale?

   a. $0   c. $200 gain

   b. $4,000 loss   d. $1,000 gain

3. On June 1, 2016, Heloise gave Henrietta a gift of stock worth $10,000. Heloise had purchased the stock on January 1, 2016 for $13,000. Henrietta sold the stock to an unrelated party on January 1, 2017 for $13,500. What is the amount and character of Henrietta's gain or loss upon the sale?

   a. $500 short-term capital gain   c. $500 long-term capital gain

   b. $3,500 short-term capital gain   d. $3,500 long-term capital gain

4. On July 1, 2017, Penelope gave Peter a gift of stock worth $9,000. Penelope had purchased the stock for $10,000 in 2014. On November 1, 2017, Peter sold the stock to an unrelated party for $8,500. What is the amount and character of Peter's gain or loss upon the sale?

   a. $500 short-term capital loss   c. $500 long-term capital loss

   b. $1,500 long-term capital loss   d. $1,500 short-term capital loss

5. On June 1, 2017, Gary gave Gertrude a gift of stock worth $10,000, paying no gift tax on the transaction. Gary had purchased the stock for $7,500 in 2013. On October 1, 2017, Gertrude sold the stock to an unrelated party for $11,000. What is the amount and character of Gertrude's gain upon the sale?

   a. $1,000 short-term capital gain   c. $1,000 long-term capital gain

   b. $3,500 long-term capital gain   d. $3,500 short-term capital gain

6. Shomit purchases 100 shares of stock in Classy Corporation for $500 in year 1. On December 20 of year 2, he purchases an additional 100 shares in the company for $400. On December 27 of year 2, Shomit sells the 100 shares acquired in year 1 for $410. What is Shomit's resulting basis in the shares acquired on December 20 of year 2?

   a. $400   c. $490

   b. $500   d. $410

7. Helmut purchases 100 shares of stock in Caisson Corporation for $1,000 in year 1. On December 1 of year 2, he purchases an additional 100 shares in the company for $1,500. On December 28 of year 2, Helmut sells the 100 shares acquired in year 1 for $1,200. What is Helmut's recognized gain or loss from the December 28 sale, and what is his resulting basis in the stock purchased on December 1 of year 2?

	Recognized Gain or Loss on Sale	Resulting Basis in December 1 Purchase
a.	$0	$1,800
b.	$0	1,500
c.	$300 loss	1,200
d.	$200 gain	1,500

8. Sengupta died on February 1, 2017, and bequeathed two different assets to a beneficiary, Roberts. Asset One was distributed to Roberts on April 24, 2017; Asset Two was distributed to Roberts on October 25, 2017. The executor of Sengupta's estate makes a qualified alternate valuation date election. The basis of each bequeathed asset will thus be the fair market value on which date?

	Asset One	Asset Two
a.	August 1, 2017	August 1, 2017
b.	April 24, 2017	August 1, 2017
c.	April 24, 2017	October 25, 2017
d.	August 1, 2017	October 25, 2017

9. Which of the following answer choices best describes income in respect of a decedent?

   a. Income earned or received by the decedent up to 30 days after the date of death

   b. Income pledged by others to charitable causes out of respect toward a recent decedent's wishes

   c. Income paid to an estate that was earned by the decedent prior to death

   d. Estate income earmarked for the provision of a respectful funeral ceremony for the decedent

CHAPTER

15

Property Transactions: Nontaxable Exchanges

LEARNING OBJECTIVES: *After completing Chapter 15, you should be able to:*

LO.1 State and explain the rationale for nonrecognition (postponement) of gain or loss in certain property transactions.

LO.2 Apply the nonrecognition provisions and basis determination rules for like-kind exchanges.

LO.3 Explain the nonrecognition provisions available on the involuntary conversion of property.

LO.4 Describe the provision for the permanent exclusion of gain on the sale of a personal residence.

LO.5 Review and apply various tax planning opportunities related to the nonrecognition provisions discussed in the chapter.

IAIN MASTERTON/ALAMY STOCK PHOTO

THE BIG PICTURE

ALTERNATIVE USES OF PROPERTY

Recall the situation introduced in *The Big Picture* in Chapter 14. After 11 months, Alice has changed her mind about selling the house to her nephew for $275,000. As a result of a recent groundbreaking for an upscale real estate development nearby, the appraised value of the house has increased to $600,000. Alice has decided that she needs to do something with the house other than let it remain vacant. She is considering the following options and has come to you for advice.

- Sell the house for approximately $600,000 using the services of a real estate agent. The real estate commission rate is 5 percent, and her inherited basis is $475,000.

- Convert the house to a vacation home (100 percent personal use by Alice and her family); then sell it in two years.

- Convert the house to a vacation home (projected 40 percent rental use and 60 percent personal use); then sell it in two years.

- Sell her current home and move into the inherited house. She has owned and lived in the current home for 15 years, and her gain on the sale would be about $200,000. Because she is nearing retirement, she would live in the inherited house for only the required two-year minimum period and then sell it.

Alice expects the inherited house to continue to appreciate in value by about 5 percent per year. She plans on retiring from her job in two years and moving to a warmer climate. Until then, she is neutral as to which house she lives in. What advice can you offer Alice?

Read the chapter and formulate your response.

FRAMEWORK 1040 Tax Formula for Individuals

This chapter covers the boldfaced portions of the Tax Formula for Individuals that was introduced in Concept Summary 3.1 on p. 3-3. Below those portions are the sections of Form 1040 where the results are reported.

Income *(broadly defined)*	$xx,xxx
Less: Exclusions	(x,xxx)
Gross income	$xx,xxx

FORM 1040 (p. 1)

12	Business income or (loss). Attach Schedule C or C-EZ	
13	Capital gain or (loss). Attach Schedule D if required. If not required, check here ▶	☐
14	Other gains or (losses). Attach Form 4797	

Less: Deductions *for* adjusted gross income	(x,xxx)
Adjusted gross income	$xx,xxx
Less: The greater of total **itemized deductions** *or* the standard deduction	(x,xxx)
Personal and dependency exemptions	(x,xxx)
Taxable income	$xx,xxx
Tax on taxable income *(see Tax Tables or Tax Rate Schedules)*	$ x,xxx
Less: Tax credits *(including income taxes withheld and prepaid)*	(xxx)
Tax due (or refund)	$ xxx

Chapter 14 was the first of a four-chapter sequence in Part 5 dealing with property transactions. In Chapter 14, we explained the sale or exchange concept along with how basis is determined. As we noted in Concept Summary 14.2, the intermediate result is realized gain or loss. What happens to the realized gain or loss depends on the nature of the sale or exchange. Some or all of the gain or loss may be recognized, deferred, or even avoided. Chapter 15 concentrates on several types of sales or exchanges where the usual result is deferral or avoidance of recognizing realized gain or loss.

LO.1

State and explain the rationale for nonrecognition (postponement) of gain or loss in certain property transactions.

15-1 GENERAL CONCEPT OF A NONTAXABLE EXCHANGE

A taxpayer who is going to replace a business asset (e.g., machinery) may decide to sell the old asset and purchase a new asset. In this case, any realized gain or loss on the asset sold is recognized, and the basis of the new asset is its cost. Alternatively, the taxpayer may be able to trade the old asset for the new asset. This exchange of assets might qualify for nontaxable exchange treatment.

The tax law recognizes that nontaxable exchanges result in a change in the *form* but not in the *substance* of the taxpayer's relative economic position. Effectively, the replacement property received in the exchange is viewed as a continuation of the old investment.[1] In addition, a nontaxable exchange often does not provide the taxpayer with the *wherewithal to pay* the tax on any realized gain that would be recognized (i.e., the taxpayer does not have the cash that would have been received in a sale).

In a nontaxable exchange, realized gains or losses are not recognized. Instead, the recognition of gain or loss is *postponed* (deferred) until the property received in the nontaxable exchange is subsequently sold in a taxable transaction. This "deferral" is accomplished by assigning a carryover basis to the replacement property.

---

[1]Reg. § 1.1002–1(c).

> **EXAMPLE 1**
>
> Debra completes a *nontaxable exchange* of property with an adjusted basis of $10,000 and a fair market value of $12,000 for property with a fair market value of $12,000.
>
> Debra has a realized gain of $2,000 ($12,000 amount realized − $10,000 adjusted basis). Her recognized gain is $0. Her basis in the replacement property is a carryover basis of $10,000.
>
> Assume that the replacement property is nondepreciable and that Debra subsequently sells it for $12,000. Her realized and recognized gain will be the $2,000 gain that was postponed (deferred) in the nontaxable transaction. If the replacement property is depreciable, the carryover basis of $10,000 is used in calculating depreciation.

In some nontaxable exchanges, only part of the property involved in the transaction qualifies for nonrecognition treatment. If the taxpayer receives cash or other nonqualifying property, part or all of the realized gain from the exchange is recognized, since the taxpayer has the wherewithal to pay tax. Here, the basis of the replacement property is adjusted to reflect any deferred gain (gain realized but not recognized).

It is important to distinguish between a nontaxable disposition, as the term is used in the statute, and a tax-free transaction. The term *nontaxable* refers to postponement of recognition via a carryover basis. In a *tax-free* transaction, the nonrecognition is permanent. Here, the basis of any property acquired does not depend on the basis of the property sold by the taxpayer. In this chapter, we discuss two nontaxable transactions (like-kind exchanges and involuntary conversions) and one tax-free transaction (sale of a personal residence).

15-2 LIKE-KIND EXCHANGES—§ 1031

LO.2

Apply the nonrecognition provisions and basis determination rules for like-kind exchanges.

Section 1031 requires nontaxable exchange treatment if the following requirements are satisfied:[2]

- The property is like-kind property.
- The form of the transaction is an exchange.
- Both the property given up and the property received are either "used in a trade or business" *or* "held for investment."

Like-kind exchanges only apply to business and investment property. Property held for personal use, inventory, domestic property exchanged for foreign property, and partnership interests (both limited and general) do not qualify under the like-kind exchange provisions. The same is true for financial instruments (like stock, bonds, or a note), even though they are held for investment.

If a taxpayer exchanges like-kind property solely for like-kind property, gain or loss realized is not recognized (it is deferred) and the basis and holding period from the old property attaches (or carries over) to the new property.

> **EXAMPLE 2**
>
> During the current year, Andy exchanged 40 acres of unimproved land in Illinois (fair market value $200,000; basis $70,000) for 10 acres of unimproved land in California (fair market value $200,000).
>
> Although Andy has a realized gain of $130,000 on this transaction ($200,000 amount realized − $70,000 basis), none of the gain is recognized since the transaction qualifies as a like-kind exchange. Andy's basis in the new property is $70,000. This carryover basis reflects the realized gain that is deferred ($200,000 California property fair market value − $130,000 gain deferred).
>
> If Andy were to sell the California property, he would have a realized and recognized gain of $130,000. The like-kind exchange rules also acknowledge that Andy—after the exchange—would not have the wherewithal to pay tax if the realized gain were recognized.

Subject to certain exceptions, related parties can engage in tax-free like-kind exchanges, but a two-year holding period applies to both the relinquished property and the replacement property.[3]

The nonrecognition provision for like-kind exchanges is *mandatory* rather than elective. A taxpayer who wants to recognize a realized gain or loss will have to structure the

---

[2]§ 1031(a) and Reg. § 1.1031(a)–1(a). [3]§ 1031(f).

transaction in a way that fails the like-kind exchange requirements. For example, a taxpayer may want to avoid like-kind treatment so that a realized loss can be recognized. Or a taxpayer might want to recognize a gain so that capital loss carryovers can be used. We discuss this more in the Tax Planning section of the chapter.

EXAMPLE 3

During the current year, Stephanie exchanged her rental condo in Vail, worth $250,000 (basis of $325,000), plus $80,000 of cash for a rental condo in Malibu worth $330,000. Although Stephanie has a realized loss of $75,000 on this transaction ($250,000 amount realized − $325,000 basis), none of the loss is recognized since the transaction qualifies as a like-kind exchange.

Stephanie would likely be better off by selling her Vail condo (and recognizing the loss) and then buying the Malibu property.

One final point: the like-kind exchange rules are applied independently to each taxpayer in the exchange; one taxpayer may qualify for like-kind treatment, and the other may not.

15-2a Like-Kind Property

"The words 'like-kind' refer to the nature or character of the property and not to its grade or quality. One kind or class of property may not … be exchanged for property of a different kind or class."[4]

According to the Regulations, the term *like-kind* is intended to be interpreted very broadly. The key phrase, however, is "kind or class of property." For the like-kind exchange rules to apply, real estate can be exchanged only for other real estate, and personalty can be exchanged only for other personalty.[5] For example, the exchange of a machine (personalty) for an office building (realty) is not a like-kind exchange.

Real property (or realty) includes principally rental buildings, office and store buildings, manufacturing plants, warehouses, and land. It is immaterial whether realty is improved or unimproved. Thus, unimproved land can be exchanged for an apartment house. *Personalty* includes principally machines, equipment, trucks, automobiles, furniture, and fixtures.

EXAMPLE 4

Wade made the following exchanges during the taxable year:

(a) Inventory for a machine used in business.
(b) Land held for investment for a building used in business.
(c) Shares of stock held for investment for equipment used in business.
(d) A light-duty business truck for a light-duty business truck.
(e) An automobile used for personal transportation for an automobile used in business.
(f) Land held for investment in New York for land held for investment in London.

Exchanges (b), investment real property for business real property, and (d), business personalty for business personalty, qualify as exchanges of like-kind property.

The other exchanges do not qualify because they involve (a), inventory; (c), financial instruments; (e), personal use automobile (not held for business or investment purposes); and (f), U.S. and foreign real property.

The like-kind exchange regulations also indicate that if the exchange transaction involves multiple assets of a business (e.g., a television station for another television station), the determination of whether the assets qualify as like-kind property are not made at the business level.[6] Instead, the underlying assets must be evaluated.

Special Rule for Depreciable Tangible Personal Property

The Regulations provide more detail in determining whether depreciable tangible personal property is "like-kind." In order to qualify as "like-kind," the exchanged property

---

[4]Reg. § 1.1031(a)–1(b).

[5]Livestock of different genders are also not "like-kind." § 1031(e).

[6]Reg. § 1.1031(j)–1.

must be in the same *general business asset class* (detailed by the IRS in Revenue Procedure 87–57).[7] The following are examples of general business asset classes:

- Office furniture, fixtures, and equipment.
- Information systems (computers and peripheral equipment).
- Airplanes.
- Automobiles and taxis.
- Buses.
- Light general-purpose trucks.
- Heavy general-purpose trucks.

In general, for personal property to qualify as "like-kind," it must have the same general use to the taxpayer. As a result, the Regulations make it more difficult for depreciable tangible personal property to qualify for like-kind exchange treatment. For example, the exchange of office equipment for a computer does not qualify as an exchange of like-kind property. Even though both assets are depreciable tangible personal property, they are not like-kind property because they are in different general business asset classes.

15-2b Exchange Requirement

The transaction must involve a direct exchange of property to qualify as a like-kind exchange. The sale of old property and the purchase of new property, even though like kind, is generally not an exchange. However, if the two transactions are mutually dependent, the IRS may treat them as a like-kind exchange. For example, if the taxpayer sells an old business machine to a dealer and purchases a new one from the same dealer, like-kind exchange treatment could result.[8]

Time Limitations

Like-kind exchanges—especially those involving real estate—can be complex. Further, it can be extremely difficult to coordinate a simultaneous transaction if the properties being exchanged are located in different counties or states. As a result, delayed (non-simultaneous) exchanges are allowed, but there are time limits on its completion.

In a delayed like-kind exchange (often called a *Starker exchange*[9]), one party does not take immediate title to the new property because it has not yet been identified. The Code provides that the delayed swap—sometimes made with the assistance of a qualified intermediary—will qualify as a like-kind exchange if the following requirements are satisfied (see Concept Summary 15.1):[10]

- *Identification period.* The new property must be identified within 45 days of the date when the old property was transferred.
- *Exchange period.* The new property must be received by the earlier of the following:
  - Within 180 days of the date when the old property was transferred.
  - The due date (including extensions) for the tax return covering the year of the transfer.

EXAMPLE 5

Phil owns a store in downtown Plano. Adjacent to his store is a commercial parking lot owned by Sally (fair market value of $175,000). Phil would like to acquire the parking lot, which would allow him to expand his store, but Sally does not want to sell the lot due to the large gain she would recognize (her basis in the lot is only $3,000).

Phil agrees to purchase any "like-kind" property worth $175,000 that is acceptable to Sally if Sally agrees to immediately transfer the parking lot to Phil. Sally agrees to the plan, and the commercial lot is transferred to Phil on October 1 of the current year.

continued

[7]As noted in Chapter 8, Rev.Proc. 87–57 is used to determine an asset's MACRS class. *Product classes* (provided by the Department of Commerce) are used if a general business asset class is not provided for a particular asset.
[8]Rev.Rul. 61–119, 1961–1 C.B. 395.
[9]*T.J. Starker v. U.S.*, 79–2 USTC ¶9541, 44 AFTR2d 79–5525, 602 F.2d 1341 (CA–9, 1979). This Supreme Court case first allowed deferred like-kind exchanges.
[10]§ 1031(a)(3).

> Later that month, Sally identifies a townhouse worth $175,000 and directs Phil to buy it for her. Phil negotiates the sale, which closes on December 12, and transfers the property to Sally.
>
> This delayed exchange will qualify as a like-kind exchange since the replacement property was identified within 45 days of the parking lot being transferred to Phil and the townhouse was transferred to Sally within 180 days of the original transfer date. In effect, Sally sold the parking lot to Phil for $175,000 and then reinvested the proceeds in another piece of real estate without having to pay tax on the realized gain. Her basis in the townhouse ($3,000) reflects the realized gain that is deferred.

Concept Summary 15.1

Delayed § 1031 Exchange

Exchange Period: 180-Day Maximum

Are these time limits firm, or can they be extended due to unforeseen circumstances? In general, the IRS allows *no deviation* from either the identification period or the exchange period even when events outside the taxpayer's control preclude strict compliance.[11]

ETHICS & EQUITY   A Delayed § 1031 Like-Kind Exchange: If At First You Don't Succeed, Try Again

Randall owns an office building (adjusted basis of $250,000) that he has been renting to a group of physicians. During negotiations over a new seven-year lease, the physicians offer to purchase the building for $900,000. Randall accepts the offer with the stipulation that the sale be structured as a delayed § 1031 transaction. Consequently, the sales proceeds are paid to a qualified third-party intermediary on the closing date of September 30, 2017.

On October 2, 2017, Randall properly identifies an office building that he would like to acquire. Unfortunately, on November 10, 2017, the property Randall selected is withdrawn from the market. Working with the intermediary, on November 12, 2017, Randall identifies another office building that meets his requirements. The purchase of this property closes on December 15, 2017, and the title is transferred to Randall.

Randall treats the transaction as a § 1031 like-kind exchange. Even though the original office building identified was not acquired, Randall concludes that in substance, he has satisfied the 45-day rule. He identified the acquired office building as soon as the negotiations ceased on his first choice. Should the IRS accept Randall's attempt to comply?

---

[11]However, see Rev.Proc. 2010–14, 2010–12 I.R.B. 456, where the IRS allowed an exception where the qualified intermediary defaulted due to bankruptcy.

15-2c **Boot**

It is unusual to find like-kind transactions where the value of the property given up is equal to the value of the property received. In most situations, one party normally provides some other property (e.g., cash) to "even out" the exchange. When a taxpayer in a like-kind exchange gives or receives some property that is *not* like-kind property, gain or loss recognition may occur. Property that is not like-kind property, including cash, is referred to as boot . Although the term *boot* does not appear in the Code, tax practitioners commonly use it rather than saying "property that is not like-kind property."

The *receipt* of boot will trigger recognition of gain if there is realized gain. The amount of the recognized gain is the *lesser* of the boot received or the realized gain (realized gain serves as the ceiling on recognition). If a taxpayer recognizes gain in a like-kind exchange, the character of the gain depends on the character of the asset given up (and depreciation recapture rules can apply; see Chapter 17).

Implications of Boot Received

EXAMPLE 6

Emily and Fran exchange machinery, and the exchange qualifies as like kind under § 1031. Because Emily's machinery (adjusted basis of $20,000) is worth $24,000 and Fran's machine has a fair market value of $19,000, Fran also gives Emily cash of $5,000.

Emily's recognized gain is $4,000, the lesser of the realized gain ($24,000 amount realized − $20,000 adjusted basis = $4,000) or the fair market value of the boot received ($5,000).

EXAMPLE 7

Assume the same facts as in the previous example, except that Fran's machine is worth $21,000 (not $19,000). Under these circumstances, Fran gives Emily cash of $3,000 to make up the difference.

Emily's recognized gain is $3,000, the lesser of the realized gain of $4,000 ($24,000 amount realized − $20,000 adjusted basis) or the fair market value of the boot received of $3,000.

The receipt of boot does not result in recognition if there is realized loss.

Implications of Boot Received

EXAMPLE 8

Assume the same facts as in Example 6, except that the adjusted basis of Emily's machine is $30,000.

Emily's realized loss is $6,000 ($24,000 amount realized − $30,000 adjusted basis). The receipt of the boot of $5,000 does not trigger loss recognition. Therefore, the recognized loss is $0.

The *giving* of boot usually does not trigger recognition. If the boot given is cash, no realized gain or loss is recognized.

Implications of Boot Given

EXAMPLE 9

Sarah and Gary exchange equipment in a like-kind exchange. Sarah receives equipment with a fair market value of $75,000 and transfers equipment worth $63,000 (adjusted basis of $45,000) and cash of $12,000.

Sarah's realized gain is $18,000 ($75,000 amount realized − $45,000 adjusted basis − $12,000 cash). However, none of the realized gain is recognized.

If, however, the boot given is appreciated or depreciated property, gain or loss is recognized to the extent of the difference between the adjusted basis and the fair market value of the boot. For this purpose, *appreciated or depreciated property* is defined as property whose adjusted basis is not equal to the fair market value.

Implications of Boot Given

EXAMPLE 10

Assume the same facts as in Example 9, except that Sarah transfers equipment worth $30,000 (adjusted basis of $36,000) and boot worth $45,000 (adjusted basis of $27,000). Sarah's net gain on this exchange is $12,000 [$75,000 − adjusted basis of $63,000 ($36,000 + $27,000)]. But she is transferring two pieces of property: equipment (like-kind property) with a built-in realized loss of

continued

$6,000 ($30,000 fair market value − $36,000 adjusted basis) and non-like-kind property (boot) with a built-in realized gain of $18,000 ($45,000 fair market value − $27,000 adjusted basis).

In this case, the $6,000 realized loss on the like-kind property is *deferred* (not recognized) and the $18,000 realized gain on the non-like-kind property is recognized. In other words, the realized loss on the like-kind property *cannot* be used to offset the realized gain on the boot given up as part of the transaction.

15-2d Basis and Holding Period of Property Received

If an exchange qualifies as nontaxable under § 1031, the basis of property received must be adjusted to reflect any postponed (deferred) gain or loss. The *basis of like-kind property* received in the exchange is the property's fair market value less postponed gain or plus postponed loss. The *basis* of any *boot* received is the boot's fair market value.

Basis of Like-Kind Property Received

 EXAMPLE 11

Jaime exchanges a building (used in his business) with an adjusted basis of $430,000 and a fair market value of $438,000 for land with a fair market value of $438,000. The exchange qualifies as like kind (an exchange of business real property for investment real property).

The basis of the land is $430,000 (land's fair market value of $438,000 − $8,000 postponed gain on the building). If the land is later sold for its fair market value of $438,000, the $8,000 postponed gain is recognized.

EXAMPLE 12

Assume the same facts as in the previous example, except that the building has an adjusted basis of $480,000 and a fair market value of only $380,000.

The basis in the newly acquired land is $480,000 (fair market value of $380,000 + $100,000 postponed loss on the building). If the land is later sold for its fair market value of $380,000, the $100,000 postponed loss is recognized.

The Code provides an alternative approach for determining the basis of like-kind property received:

> Adjusted basis of like-kind property surrendered
> + Adjusted basis of boot given
> + Gain recognized
> − Fair market value of boot received
> − Loss recognized
> = *Basis of like-kind property received*

This approach is logical in terms of the recovery of capital doctrine. That is, the unrecovered cost or other basis is increased by additional cost (boot given) or decreased by cost recovered (boot received). Any gain recognized is included in the basis of the new property. The taxpayer has been taxed on this amount and is now entitled to recover it tax-free. Any loss recognized is deducted from the basis of the new property. The taxpayer has received a tax benefit on that amount.

The holding period of the property surrendered in the exchange carries over and *tacks on* to the holding period of the like-kind property received.[12] The holding period for boot received in a like-kind exchange begins with the date of the exchange. See Chapter 16 for a discussion of the relevance of the holding period.

Depreciation recapture potential carries over to the property received in a like-kind exchange.[13] See Chapter 17 for a discussion of this topic.

The following comprehensive example illustrates the like-kind exchange rules.

---

[12]§ 1223(1) and Reg. § 1.1223–1(a). For this carryover holding period rule to apply to like-kind exchanges after March 1, 1954, the like-kind property surrendered must have been either a capital asset or § 1231 property.

[13]Reg. §§ 1.1245–2(a)(4) and 1.1250–2(d)(1).

Vicki exchanged the following old machines for new machines in five independent like-kind exchanges:

EXAMPLE
13

Exchange	Adjusted Basis of Old Machine	Fair Market Value of Old Machine	Fair Market Value of New Machine	Adjusted Basis of Boot Given	Fair Market Value of Boot Received
1	$4,000	$ 9,000	$9,000	$ –0–	$ –0–
2	4,000	6,000	9,000	3,000	–0–
3	4,000	3,000	9,000	6,000	–0–
4	4,000	12,000	9,000	–0–	3,000
5	4,000	3,800	3,500	–0–	300

Vicki's realized and recognized gains and losses and the basis of each of the like-kind properties received are as follows:

				New Basis Calculation			
Exchange	Realized Gain (Loss)	Recognized Gain (Loss)	Old Adj. Basis +	Boot Given +	Gain Recognized −	Boot Received =	New Basis
1	$ 5,000	$–(0)–	$4,000 +	$ –0– +	$ –0– −	$ –0– =	$ 4,000*
2	2,000	–(0)–	4,000 +	3,000 +	–0– −	–0– =	7,000*
3	(1,000)	–(0)–	4,000 +	6,000 +	–0– −	–0– =	10,000**
4	8,000	3,000	4,000 +	–0– +	3,000 −	3,000 =	4,000*
5	(200)	–(0)–	4,000 +	–0– +	–0– −	300 =	3,700**

* Basis may be determined in gain situations under the alternative method by subtracting the gain not recognized from the fair market value of the new property:
$9,000 − $5,000 = $4,000 for exchange 1.
$9,000 − $2,000 = $7,000 for exchange 2.
$9,000 − $5,000 = $4,000 for exchange 4.
** In loss situations, basis may be determined by adding the loss not recognized to the fair market value of the new property:
$9,000 + $1,000 = $10,000 for exchange 3.
$3,500 + $200 = $3,700 for exchange 5.
The basis of the boot received is the boot's fair market value.

If the taxpayer assumes a liability (or takes property subject to a liability), the amount of the liability is treated as boot given. For the taxpayer whose liability is assumed (or whose property is taken subject to the liability), the amount of the liability is treated as boot received. Example 14 illustrates the effect of such a liability. In addition, the example illustrates the tax consequences for both parties involved in the like-kind exchange.

EXAMPLE
14

Jill Saunders and Rick Thompson exchange real estate investments. Jill gives up property with an adjusted basis of $250,000 (fair market value of $420,000) that is subject to a mortgage of $80,000 (assumed by Rick). In return for this property, Jill receives property with a fair market value of $340,000 (Rick's adjusted basis in the property is $200,000). Jill's and Rick's realized and recognized gains and their basis in the like-kind property received are computed as follows:[14]

	Jill	Rick
Compute Realized Gain (Loss)		
FMV of like-kind property received	$ 340,000	$ 420,000
+ FMV of other property received		
+ Cash received		
+ Debt relief	80,000	
− Cash paid		
− Debt assumed		(80,000)
= Net Consideration Received	$ 420,000	$ 340,000
− Adjusted basis of property given	(250,000)	(200,000)
= Realized Gain (Loss)	$ 170,000	$ 140,000

continued

---

[14]Example (2) of Reg. § 1.1031(d)–2 illustrates a special situation where both the buyer and the seller transfer liabilities that are assumed by the other party (or both parties acquire property that is subject to a liability).

	Jill	Rick
Compute Boot Received		
Debt relief	$ 80,000	$ -0-
+ Cash received		
+ FMV of other property received		
= Boot Received	$ 80,000	$ -0-
Compute Recognized Gain		
Lesser of realized gain or boot received	$ 80,000	$ -0-
Compute Basis for New Property (Other Than Cash)		
Adjusted Basis of Property Given	$ 250,000	$ 200,000
+ Boot given (cash paid; debt assumed)	-0-	80,000
+ Gain recognized	80,000	-0-
− Boot received	(80,000)	-0-
= Basis of New Property	$ 250,000	$ 280,000

15-2e **Reporting Considerations**

Section 1031 transactions are reported on Form 8824 (Like-Kind Exchanges). Part III of Form 8824 has been completed based on the information provided for Jill Saunders's exchange (Example 14).

This form should be filed even though the like-kind exchange transaction results in no recognized gain or loss. It must be filed with the regular return for the tax year in which the taxpayer transfers property in a like-kind exchange.

Form 8824 (2016)   Page **2**

Name(s) shown on tax return. Do not enter name and social security number if shown on other side.	Your social security number
Jill Saunders (Example 14)	

Part III   Realized Gain or (Loss), Recognized Gain, and Basis of Like-Kind Property Received

Caution: *If you transferred* **and** *received* **(a)** *more than one group of like-kind properties or* **(b)** *cash or other (not like-kind) property, see* **Reporting of multi-asset exchanges** *in the instructions.*

Note: *Complete lines 12 through 14* **only** *if you gave up property that was not like-kind. Otherwise, go to line 15.*

12	Fair market value (FMV) of other property given up	**12**	
13	Adjusted basis of other property given up	**13**	
14	Gain or (loss) recognized on other property given up. Subtract line 13 from line 12. Report the gain or (loss) in the same manner as if the exchange had been a sale	**14**	
	Caution: *If the property given up was used previously or partly as a home, see* **Property used as home** *in the instructions.*		
15	Cash received, FMV of other property received, plus net liabilities assumed by other party, reduced (but not below zero) by any exchange expenses you incurred. See instructions . . .	**15**	80,000
16	FMV of like-kind property you received	**16**	340,000
17	Add lines 15 and 16	**17**	420,000
18	Adjusted basis of like-kind property you gave up, net amounts paid to other party, plus any exchange expenses **not** used on line 15. See instructions	**18**	250,000
19	**Realized gain or (loss).** Subtract line 18 from line 17	**19**	170,000
20	Enter the smaller of line 15 or line 19, but not less than zero	**20**	80,000
21	Ordinary income under recapture rules. Enter here and on Form 4797, line 16. See instructions	**21**	0
22	Subtract line 21 from line 20. If zero or less, enter -0-. If more than zero, enter here and on Schedule D or Form 4797, unless the installment method applies. See instructions	**22**	80,000
23	**Recognized gain.** Add lines 21 and 22	**23**	80,000
24	Deferred gain or (loss). Subtract line 23 from line 19. If a related party exchange, see instructions .	**24**	90,000
25	**Basis of like-kind property received.** Subtract line 15 from the sum of lines 18 and 23 . .	**25**	250,000

15-3 INVOLUNTARY CONVERSIONS—§ 1033

LO.3

Explain the nonrecognition provisions available on the involuntary conversion of property.

In most cases, taxpayers sell property (or exchange it) when they need to do so. There are times, however, when the taxpayer *involuntarily* (i.e., outside the taxpayer's control) disposes of property. When this happens, the taxpayer usually receives some sort of compensation, like insurance proceeds or a condemnation award. Section 1033 provides that a taxpayer who suffers an involuntary conversion of property may postpone recognition of *gain* realized from the conversion. As a result, this provision provides relief to a taxpayer who has suffered hardship and does not have the wherewithal to pay the tax on any gain realized from the conversion.

Realized gain is postponed to the extent that the taxpayer *reinvests* the amount realized (e.g., insurance proceeds) in replacement property. The rules for nonrecognition of gain are as follows:

- If the amount reinvested in replacement property *equals or exceeds* the amount realized, realized gain is *not recognized*.

- If the amount reinvested in replacement property is *less than* the amount realized, realized gain *is recognized* to the extent of the deficiency.

Involuntary Conversions: General Rules

EXAMPLE 15

Jason operates a charter fishing business in Port St. Lucie, Florida, taking customers out in the Atlantic Ocean on daylong fishing trips. Unfortunately, his boat was completely destroyed when Hurricane Matthew hit the Florida coast. His boat had a basis of $78,000 ($120,000 cost − $42,000 of accumulated depreciation). Fortunately, Jason had insurance (which included a replacement cost rider). He filed an insurance claim the week after he lost his boat and received $175,000 in insurance proceeds three weeks later.

Jason has a realized gain of $97,000, computed as follows:

Amount realized (insurance proceeds)	$175,000
Less: Adjusted basis	(78,000)
Realized gain	$ 97,000

Jason can defer the entire gain provided he uses all of the insurance proceeds to purchase a new boat.

EXAMPLE 16

Refer to the facts of Example 15, and assume that Jason buys a new boat for $180,000. He uses the entire insurance settlement as part of the purchase.

In this case, Jason's $97,000 realized gain is deferred, and the basis of his new boat must reflect that deferral. As a result, his new boat's basis is $83,000 ($180,000 cost − $97,000 deferred gain).

EXAMPLE 17

Continuing with the facts of Example 15, assume that Jason is able to negotiate an excellent price for his new boat. In fact, he is able to replace his old boat for only $168,000 and uses the $7,000 remaining from the insurance settlement to pay for other business expenses. What is the outcome?

In this case, Jason must recognize a gain of $7,000, the difference between the $175,000 insurance settlement and the amount he paid for the new boat (the amount of the insurance proceeds he reinvested in replacement property).

The balance of the realized gain is deferred, and the basis of his new boat must reflect that deferral. As a result, his new boat's basis is $78,000 ($168,000 cost − $90,000 deferred gain).

If an involuntary conversion results in a *loss*, § 1033 does not change the normal loss recognition rules. In other words, if a realized loss would otherwise be recognized, § 1033 does not change the result.

Refer to the facts of Example 15, but assume that Jason had only partial coverage on his boat, and his insurance settlement is only $50,000. In this case, Jason has a loss of $28,000, computed as follows:

Amount realized (insurance proceeds)	$50,000
Less: Adjusted basis	(78,000)
Realized loss	($28,000)

In this case, § 1033 will not apply to the transaction, and Jason's realized loss of $28,000 is recognized.

With this background, we will now explore the various terms (and related definitions) that are part of § 1033, the reinvestment timing required to secure gain deferral, and the related reporting requirements.

15-3a Involuntary Conversion Defined

An involuntary conversion results from the destruction (complete or partial), theft, seizure, condemnation, or sale or exchange under threat of condemnation (e.g., a city seizing property under its right of eminent domain) of the taxpayer's property.[15] A voluntary act, such as a taxpayer destroying the property by arson, is not an involuntary conversion.[16]

Government seizures are unique events (and as a result, a unique set of rules have developed under § 1033). In general, for § 1033 to apply, the government entity must have made a decision to acquire the property for public use, and the taxpayer must have reasonable grounds to believe the property will be taken.[17]

15-3b Computing the Amount Realized

The amount realized from an involuntary conversion is normally any insurance proceeds received. In the case of the condemnation of property, the amount realized usually includes only the amount received as compensation for the property.[18]

Any amount received that is designated as severance damages by both the government and the taxpayer is not included in the amount realized. *Severance awards* usually occur when only a portion of the property is condemned (e.g., a strip of land is taken to build a highway). Severance damages are awarded because the value of the taxpayer's remaining property has declined as a result of the condemnation. In general, severance damages are a tax-free recovery of capital and reduce the basis of the property.

§ 1033 and Severance Damages

The government condemns a portion of Ron's farmland to build part of an interstate highway. Because the highway denies his cattle access to a pond and some grazing land, Ron receives severance damages in addition to the condemnation proceeds for the land taken.

Ron must reduce the basis of the property by the amount of the severance damages. If the amount of the severance damages received exceeds the adjusted basis, Ron recognizes gain.

15-3c Replacement Property

The requirements for replacement property generally are more restrictive than those for like-kind property under § 1031. The basic requirement is that the replacement property be *similar or related in service or use* to the involuntarily converted property.[19]

Different interpretations of the phrase *similar or related in service or use* apply depending on whether the involuntarily converted property is held by an *owner-user* (e.g., in a business or by an individual) or by an *owner-investor* (e.g., lessor). For an

---

[15]§ 1033(a) and Reg. §§ 1.1033(a)–1(a) and –2(a).

[16]Rev.Rul. 82–74, 1982–1 C.B. 110.

[17]Rev.Rul. 63–221, 1963–2 C.B. 332 and *Joseph P. Balistrieri*, 38 TCM 526, T.C.Memo. 1979–115.

[18]*Pioneer Real Estate Co.*, 47 B.T.A. 886 (1942), *acq.* 1943 C.B. 18.

[19]§ 1033(a) and Reg. § 1.1033(a)–1.

owner-investor, the *taxpayer use* test applies, and for an owner-user, the *functional use test* applies. As you might guess, the functional use test is more restrictive than the taxpayer use test. Furthermore, a special test applies in the case of involuntary conversions that result from condemnations.

Taxpayer Use Test

The taxpayer use test for owner-investors provides much more flexibility in terms of what qualifies as replacement property. Essentially, the properties must be used by the owner-investor in similar endeavors. For example, rental property held by an owner-investor qualifies if replaced with other rental property, regardless of the type of rental property involved. For example, the test is met if the owner-investor of a building being rented to a business to house light manufacturing replaces the manufacturing facility with a building rented to a business as a grocery warehouse.[20] The replacement of a rental residence with a personal residence does not meet the test.[21]

Functional Use Test

The functional use test applies to owner-users (e.g., a manufacturer whose manufacturing plant is destroyed by fire is required to replace the plant with another facility of similar functional use). Under this test, the taxpayer's use of the replacement property and of the involuntarily converted property must be the same. Replacing a manufacturing plant with an office building (both used in the same business) does not meet this test. The manufacturing plant would have to be replaced with another manufacturing plant. Replacing a rental residence with a personal residence also does not pass the test.

Special Rule for Condemnations

If business real property or investment real property is *condemned*, the broader replacement rules for like-kind exchanges can be used instead of the narrower involuntary conversion replacement rules. This gives the taxpayer substantially more flexibility in selecting replacement property. For example, improved real property can be replaced with unimproved real property.

The rules concerning the nature of replacement property are illustrated in Concept Summary 15.2.

Concept Summary 15.2

Involuntary Conversions: Replacement Property Tests

Type of Property and User	Taxpayer Use Test	Functional Use Test	Special Rule for Condemnations*
An investor's rented shopping mall is destroyed by fire; the mall may be replaced with other rental properties (e.g., an apartment building).	X		
A manufacturing plant is destroyed by fire; replacement property must consist of another manufacturing plant that is functionally the same as the property converted.		X	
Personal residence of a taxpayer is condemned by a local government authority; replacement property must consist of another personal residence.		X	
Land used by a manufacturing company is condemned by a local government authority.			X
Apartment and land held by an investor are sold due to the threat or imminence of condemnation.			X

*Applies the same test as in the case of like-kind exchanges.

---

[20]*Loco Realty Co. v. Comm.*, 62–2 USTC ¶9657, 10 AFTR 2d 5359, 306 F.2d 207 (CA–8, 1962).

[21]Rev.Rul. 70–466, 1970–2 C.B. 165.

15-3d **Time Limitation on Replacement**

In general, the taxpayer must acquire replacement property within a two-year period after the close of the taxable year in which gain is realized.[22] Typically, gain is realized when insurance proceeds or damages are received.

EXAMPLE 20

Megan's building is destroyed by fire on December 16, 2016. The adjusted basis is $325,000. Megan receives $400,000 from the insurance company on February 2, 2017. She is a calendar year and cash method taxpayer.

The latest date for replacement is December 31, 2019 (the end of the taxable year in which realized gain occurred plus two years). The critical date is not the date the involuntary conversion occurred, but rather the date of gain realization.

In the case of a condemnation of real property used in a trade or business or held for investment, a three-year period is substituted for the normal two-year period.

EXAMPLE 21

Assume the same facts as in the previous example, except that Megan's building is condemned. Megan receives notification of the future condemnation on November 1, 2016. The condemnation occurs on December 16, 2016, with the condemnation proceeds being received on February 2, 2017.

The latest date for replacement is December 31, 2020 (the end of the taxable year in which realized gain occurred plus three years).

The *earliest date* for replacement typically is the date the involuntary conversion occurs. However, if the property is condemned, it is possible to replace the condemned property before this date. In this case, the earliest date is the date of the threat of condemnation of the property. This rule allows the taxpayer to make an orderly replacement of the condemned property.

EXAMPLE 22

Assume the same facts as in Example 21. The earliest date that Megan can replace the building is November 1, 2016, which is the date of the condemnation of the building.

15-3e **Nonrecognition of Gain**

Nonrecognition of gain can be either mandatory or elective, depending on whether the conversion is direct (into replacement property) or indirect (into money).

Direct Conversion

If the conversion is directly into replacement property rather than into money, nonrecognition of realized gain is *mandatory*. In this case, the basis of the replacement property is the same as the adjusted basis of the converted property. Direct conversion is rare in practice and usually involves condemnations.

EXAMPLE 23

Lupe's property, with an adjusted basis of $20,000, is condemned by the state. Lupe receives property with a fair market value of $50,000 as compensation for the property taken.

Because the nonrecognition of realized gain is mandatory for direct conversions, Lupe's realized gain of $30,000 is not recognized and the basis of the replacement property is $20,000 (adjusted basis of the condemned property).

Conversion into Money

If the conversion is into money, the realized gain is recognized only to the extent the amount realized from the involuntary conversion exceeds the cost of the qualifying

---

[22]§§ 1033(a)(2)(B) and (g)(4) and Reg. § 1.1033(a)–2(c)(3). The two-year period is extended to a four-year period if the property is located in a Presidentially-declared disaster area. The taxpayer can apply for an extension of this time period anytime before its expiration [Reg. § 1.1033(a)–2(c)(3)]. Also, the period for filing the application for extension can be extended if the taxpayer shows reasonable cause.

replacement property.[23] This is the usual case, and nonrecognition (postponement) is *elective*. If the election is not made, the realized gain is recognized.

The basis of the replacement property is the property's cost less any postponed (deferred) gain.[24] If the election to postpone gain is made, the holding period of the replacement property includes the holding period of the converted property.

Section 1033 applies *only to gains* and *not to losses*. Losses from involuntary conversions are recognized if the property is held for business or income-producing purposes. Personal casualty losses are recognized, but condemnation losses related to personal use assets (e.g., a personal residence) are neither recognized nor postponed.

Involuntary Conversion Gain or Loss

EXAMPLE 24

Walt's building (used in his trade or business), with an adjusted basis of $50,000, is destroyed by fire on October 5, 2017. Walt is a calendar year taxpayer. On November 17, 2017, he receives an insurance reimbursement of $100,000 for the loss. Walt invests $80,000 in a new building and uses the other $20,000 of insurance proceeds to pay off credit card debt.

- Walt has until December 31, 2019, to make the new investment and qualify for the non-recognition election.

- Walt's realized gain is $50,000 ($100,000 insurance proceeds received − $50,000 adjusted basis of old building).

- Assuming that the replacement property qualifies as similar or related in service or use, Walt's recognized gain is $20,000. Because he reinvested $20,000 less than the insurance proceeds received ($100,000 proceeds − $80,000 reinvested), his realized gain is recognized to that extent.

- Walt's basis in the new building is $50,000. This is the building's cost of $80,000 less the postponed gain of $30,000 (realized gain of $50,000 − recognized gain of $20,000).

EXAMPLE 25

Assume the same facts as in the previous example, except that Walt receives only $45,000 of insurance proceeds. He has a realized and recognized loss of $5,000. The basis of the new building is the building's cost of $80,000.

If the destroyed building in Example 25 had been held for personal use, the recognized loss would have been subject to the casualty loss limitations.[25] The loss of $5,000 would have been limited to the decline in fair market value of the property, and the amount of the loss would have been reduced first by $100 and then by 10 percent of adjusted gross income (refer to Chapter 7).

15-3f **Reporting Considerations**

Involuntary conversions from casualty and theft are reported first on Form 4684, Casualties and Thefts. Casualty and theft losses on personal use property for the individual taxpayer are carried from Form 4684 to Schedule A of Form 1040. For other casualty and theft items, the Form 4684 amounts are generally reported on Form 4797, Sales of Business Property, unless Form 4797 is not required. In the latter case, the amounts are reported directly on the tax return involved.

Except for personal use property, recognized gains and losses from involuntary conversions other than by casualty and theft are reported on Form 4797. If the property involved in the involuntary conversion (other than by casualty and theft) is personal use property, any realized loss is not recognized. Any realized gain is treated as gain on a voluntary sale.

What if the taxpayer intends to acquire qualifying replacement property but has not done so by the time the tax return is filed? The taxpayer should elect § 1033 and report

---

[23]§ 1033(a)(2)(A) and Reg. § 1.1033(a)–2(c)(1).

[24]§ 1033(b).

[25]§ 165(c)(3) and Reg. § 1.165–7.

all of the details of the transaction on a statement attached to the return. When the qualifying replacement property is acquired, the taxpayer should attach a statement to the tax return that contains relevant information on the replacement property.

An amended return must be filed if qualified replacement property is not acquired during the replacement time period. An amended return also is required if the cost of the replacement property is less than the amount realized from the involuntary conversion. In this case, the return would recognize the portion of the realized gain that can no longer be deferred.

Describe the provision for the permanent exclusion of gain on the sale of a personal residence.

15-4 SALE OF A RESIDENCE—§ 121

A taxpayer's **personal residence** is a personal use asset. Therefore, a realized loss from the sale of a personal residence is not recognized.[26]

A realized gain from the sale of a personal residence is taxable. However, taxpayers meeting the **§ 121 exclusion** requirements are allowed to exclude up to $250,000 of realized gain on the sale of a principal residence.[27] Any gain in excess of this amount normally qualifies as a long-term capital gain (with preferential tax rates).

EXAMPLE 26

Tom and Eileen Atwood bought their home in 2008 for $525,000 and have used it as their principal residence since that time. In July 2017, they sell their home for $670,000. The Atwoods have a realized gain of $145,000 on the sale ($670,000 − $525,000), and the entire gain is excluded as a result of § 121.

What if the Atwoods sold their home for $500,000? In this case, since their home is a personal use asset, they would have a $25,000 realized loss that would not be recognized.

15-4a Principal Residence

Whether property is the taxpayer's principal residence "depends upon all of the facts and circumstances in each case." According to the Regulations, the most important factor is where the taxpayer spends most of his or her time.[28] A residence does not have to be a house. For example, a houseboat, a house trailer, or a motor home can qualify.[29] The principal residence includes the land on which a home sits (so any gain on the land also qualifies for exclusion). An adjacent lot can qualify if it is regularly used by the owner as part of the residential property.

EXAMPLE 27

Mitch graduates from college and moves to Boston, where he is employed. He decides to rent an apartment in Boston because of its proximity to his place of employment. He purchases a beach condo in the Cape Cod area that he occupies most weekends. Mitch does not intend to live at the beach condo except on weekends. The apartment in Boston is his principal residence.

15-4b Requirements for Exclusion Treatment

To qualify for exclusion treatment, at the date of the sale, the residence must have been *owned* and *used* by the taxpayer as the principal residence for at least two years during the five-year period ending on the date of the sale.[30]

EXAMPLE 28

Melissa sells her principal residence on September 18, 2017. She had purchased it on July 5, 2015, and lived in it since then. The sale of Melissa's residence qualifies for the § 121 exclusion.

---

[26]§ 165(c).

[27]§ 121(b).

[28]Other factors include the address listed on a driver's license and/or voter registration card, the location of the taxpayer's employer, and the mailing address used for bills and correspondence. Regulation § 1.121–1(b)(2) includes the complete list of factors to be considered.

[29]Reg. § 1.121–1(b)(1); Reg. § 1.1034–1(c)(3)(i).

[30]§ 121(a). However, § 121(d)(10) provides that exclusion treatment does not apply if the residence was acquired in a like-kind exchange within the prior five years of the sale of the residence.

The ownership and use requirements are *two separate tests*. Although in most situations ownership and use overlap (as in Example 28), there is no requirement that they do for purposes of § 121. Further, the law does not require that the two-year periods be continuous.[31]

Ownership and Use Tests

Sarah purchased a home in San Diego in May 2002 and lived in it until she took a new job in Los Angeles on January 1, 2013. From January 2013 until she sold the house on July 31, 2017, she only used the home occasionally, as she lived in an apartment near her job in downtown Los Angeles. As the house was sold on July 31, 2017, the five-year window runs from August 1, 2012, to the date of sale.

In determining whether the § 121 exclusion is available, Sarah has met the ownership test because she owned the house for two of the five years prior to its sale. However, she fails the use test because she did not use the home as her principal residence for two of the five years before its sale (during the five-year window, she used the house as her principal residence from August 1, 2012, to December 31, 2012—only five months).

EXAMPLE 29

Charles lives in a townhouse that he rents from 2010 through January 17, 2014. On January 18, 2014, he purchases the townhouse. On February 1, 2015, due to a decline in health, Charles moves into his daughter's home. On May 25, 2017, while still living in his daughter's home, Charles sells his townhouse.

The § 121 exclusion will apply because Charles owned the townhouse for at least two years out of the five years preceding the sale (from January 19, 2014, until May 25, 2017)[32] and he used the townhouse as his principal residence for at least two years during the five-year period preceding the sale [from May 25, 2012 (the beginning of the five-year window) until February 1, 2015].

EXAMPLE 30

In applying the use test, short absences (i.e., vacation or other seasonal absence) are counted as periods of use. In addition, short-term rental of the property is ignored.[33]

Aaron has owned and used his house as his principal residence since 2001. On January 31, 2014, Aaron moves to another state. Aaron rents his house to tenants from that date until April 18, 2016, when he sells it.

Aaron is eligible for the § 121 exclusion because he has owned and used the house as his principal residence for at least two of the five years preceding the sale.

EXAMPLE 31

The five-year window enables the taxpayer to qualify for the § 121 exclusion even though the property is not his or her principal residence at the date of the sale.

Benjamin sells his former principal residence on August 16, 2017. He had purchased it on April 1, 2009, and lived in it until July 1, 2016, when he converted it to rental property.

Even though the property is rental property on August 16, 2017, rather than Benjamin's principal residence, the sale qualifies for the § 121 exclusion.[34] During the five-year period from August 16, 2012, to August 16, 2017, Benjamin owned and used the property as his principal residence for at least two years.

EXAMPLE 32

In addition to the ownership and use requirements, the tax law allows § 121 to be used only once every two years.[35] This provision restricts taxpayers who might be tempted to make liberal use of the § 121 exclusion as a means of speculating when the price of residential housing is rising. Without any time restriction on its use, § 121 would permit the exclusion of realized gain on multiple sales of principal residences.

---

[31]According to Reg. § 1.121–1(c)(1), taxpayers must document 730 days (365 × 2) of ownership and use during the five-year period that ends on the sale date.

[32]As discussed in Chapter 16, holding period begins the day after acquisition date and includes the disposition date.

[33]Reg. § 1.121–1(c)(2)(i).

[34]However, any realized gain on the sale that is attributable to depreciation is not eligible for the § 121 exclusion. See Example 46.

[35]§ 121(b)(3) denies the application of the § 121 exclusion to sales occurring within two years of its last use.

EXAMPLE 33

Mike sells his principal residence (the first residence) in June 2016 for $150,000 (realized gain of $60,000). He then buys and sells the following (all of which qualify as principal residences):

	Date of Purchase	Date of Sale	Amount Involved
Second residence	July 2016		$160,000
Second residence		April 2017	180,000
Third residence	May 2017		200,000

Because multiple sales have taken place within a period of two years, § 121 does not apply to the sale of the second residence. Thus, the realized gain of $20,000 [$180,000 (selling price) − $160,000 (purchase price)] must be recognized.

15-4c Calculation of the Exclusion Amount

General Rule

The amount of the available § 121 exclusion on the sale of a principal residence is $250,000.[36] If the realized gain does not exceed $250,000, there is no recognized gain.

Realized gain is calculated in the normal manner. The *amount realized* is the selling price less any selling expenses (e.g., real estate broker commissions, advertising expenses, and legal fees). Repairs and maintenance costs to aid in selling the property are personal expenses and not deductible (and they do not increase the home's basis).

The Big Picture

EXAMPLE 34

Return to the facts of *The Big Picture* on p. 15-1. Recall that one of Alice's options is to sell her current house and move into the inherited house. Assume that Alice, who is single, sells her current personal residence (adjusted basis of $130,000) for $348,000. She has owned and lived in the house for 15 years. Her selling expenses are $18,000. Three weeks prior to the sale, Alice pays a carpenter and a painter $1,000 to make some repairs and paint the two bathrooms. Her recognized gain would be calculated as follows:

Amount realized ($348,000 − $18,000)	$ 330,000
Adjusted basis	(130,000)
Realized gain	$ 200,000
§ 121 exclusion	(200,000)
Recognized gain	$ −0−

Since the available § 121 exclusion of $250,000 exceeds Alice's realized gain of $200,000, her recognized gain is $0.

The Big Picture

EXAMPLE 35

Continue with *The Big Picture* and the facts of Example 34, but assume that the selling price is $490,000.

Amount realized ($490,000 − $18,000)	$ 472,000
Adjusted basis	(130,000)
Realized gain	$ 342,000
§ 121 exclusion	(250,000)
Recognized gain	$ 92,000

Since the realized gain of $342,000 exceeds the § 121 exclusion amount of $250,000, Alice's recognized gain is $92,000.

---

[36]§ 121(b)(1).

Married Couples

If a married couple files a joint return, the $250,000 amount is increased to $500,000 if the following requirements are met:[37]

- Either spouse meets the at-least-two-years *ownership* requirement.
- Both spouses meet the at-least-two-years *use* requirement.
- Neither spouse sold a principal residence within the prior two years and used the § 121 exclusion.

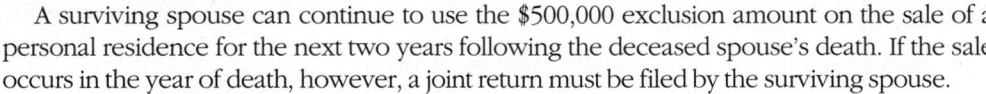

Margaret sells her personal residence (adjusted basis of $150,000) for $650,000. She has owned and lived in the residence for six years. Her selling expenses are $40,000. Margaret is married to Ted, and they file a joint return. Ted has lived in the residence since they were married two and one-half years ago.

Amount realized ($650,000 − $40,000)	$ 610,000
Adjusted basis	(150,000)
Realized gain	$ 460,000
§ 121 exclusion	(460,000)
Recognized gain	$ –0–

Because the realized gain of $460,000 is less than the available § 121 exclusion amount of $500,000, no gain is recognized.

EXAMPLE 36

A surviving spouse can continue to use the $500,000 exclusion amount on the sale of a personal residence for the next two years following the deceased spouse's death. If the sale occurs in the year of death, however, a joint return must be filed by the surviving spouse.

15-4d Exceptions to the Two-Year Rules

The two-year ownership and use requirements and the "only once every two years" rule could create a hardship for taxpayers in certain situations that are beyond their control. As a result, under the following special circumstances, the requirements are waived:[38]

- Change in place of employment.
- Health.
- Unforeseen circumstances (as identified in Treasury Department Regulations).

Guidance on these three exceptions has been provided by Treasury Department Regulations and are discussed in the sections that follow.[39] Each of these exceptions provides a *partial* exclusion. The calculation of the partial exclusion is discussed later in this section.

Change in Place of Employment

For this exception to apply, the distance requirements related to the moving expense deduction must be met (see Chapter 9). As a result, the location of the taxpayer's new employment must be at least 50 miles further from the old residence than the old residence was from the old job. In addition, the house being sold must be used as the principal residence of the taxpayer when the employment change happens. The exception applies whether the taxpayer takes a job with a new employer, is transferred by the current employer, or, if self-employed, moves the proprietorship to a new location.

Assume the same facts as in Example 33, except that in March 2017, Mike's employer transfers him to a job in another state that is 400 miles away.

As a result, the sale of the second residence and the purchase of the third residence were due to relocation of employment. Consequently, the § 121 exclusion is partially available on the sale of the second residence.

EXAMPLE 37

---

[37]§ 121(b)(2).
[38]§ 121(c)(2)(B).

[39]See Reg. § 1.121–3 and IRS Publication 523 (*Selling Your Home*) for further details and illustrations.

Health

The health exception can be satisfied using either a general facts and circumstances approach or a safe harbor established in the Regulations. If a physician recommends a change of location due to health issues (or to obtain specialized care), the safe harbor should be met. A sale that is merely beneficial to the general health or well-being of the individual will not qualify.

Unforeseen Circumstances

For the unforeseen circumstances exception to apply, the primary reason for the sale or exchange of the residence must be an event the taxpayer did not anticipate before purchasing and occupying the residence. The Regulations provide a safe harbor that applies in any of the following instances:

- Involuntary conversion of the residence.
- Natural or human-made disasters or acts of war or terrorism resulting in a casualty to the residence.
- Death of a qualified individual.
- Cessation of employment that results in eligibility for unemployment compensation.
- Change in employment or self-employment that results in the taxpayer being unable to pay housing costs and reasonable basic living expenses for the taxpayer's household.
- Divorce or legal separation.
- Multiple births resulting from the same pregnancy.

If none of the safe harbor instances apply, the taxpayer can use a general facts and circumstances approach to justify the exception.

EXAMPLE 38

Debra and Roy are engaged and buy a house (sharing the mortgage payments) and live in it as their personal residence. Eighteen months after the purchase, they cancel their wedding plans, and Roy moves out of the house. Because Debra cannot afford to make the payments alone, they sell the house.

While the sale does not fit under the safe harbor, the broken engagement is an unforeseen event and the sale will qualify under the unforeseen circumstances exception.[40]

Partial § 121 Exclusion

A partial § 121 exclusion is available when one of the exceptions applies. In this case, the § 121 exclusion amount ($250,000 or $500,000) is multiplied by a fraction, the numerator of which is the number of qualifying months and the denominator of which is 24 months. The resulting amount is the excluded gain.[41]

EXAMPLE 39

On October 1, 2016, Rich and Audrey, who file a joint return and live in Chicago, sell their personal residence, which they have owned and lived in for eight years. The realized gain of $325,000 is excluded under § 121. They purchase another personal residence for $525,000 on October 2, 2016. Audrey's employer transfers her to the Denver office in August 2017. Rich and Audrey sell their Chicago residence on August 2, 2017, and they purchase a residence in Denver shortly thereafter. The realized gain on the sale is $300,000.

The $325,000 gain on the first Chicago residence is excluded under § 121. The sale of the second Chicago residence is within the two-year window of the prior sale, but because it resulted from a change in employment, Rich and Audrey can qualify for partial § 121 exclusion treatment as follows:

Realized gain	$ 300,000
§ 121 exclusion:	
$\dfrac{10 \text{ months}}{24 \text{ months}} \times \$500,000$	(208,333)
Recognized gain	$ 91,667

---

[40]Reg. § 1.121–3(e)(4), Example (6).   [41]§ 121(c)(1).

Basis of New Residence

Because § 121 is an exclusion provision rather than a postponement of gain provision, the basis of a new residence is its cost.[42]

15-4e Involuntary Conversion and Using §§ 121 and 1033

A taxpayer can use both the § 121 exclusion of gain provision and the § 1033 postponement of gain provision.[43] The taxpayer initially can elect to exclude realized gain under § 121 to the extent of the statutory amount. Then a qualified replacement of the residence under § 1033 can be used to postpone the remainder of the realized gain. In applying § 1033, the amount of the required reinvestment is reduced by the amount of the § 121 exclusion.

EXAMPLE 40

Angel's principal residence is destroyed by a tornado. Her adjusted basis for the residence is $140,000. She receives insurance proceeds of $480,000.

If Angel does not elect to use the § 121 exclusion, her realized gain on the involuntary conversion of her principal residence is $340,000 ($480,000 amount realized − $140,000 adjusted basis). Thus, to postpone the $340,000 realized gain under § 1033, she would need to acquire qualifying property costing at least $480,000.

Using the § 121 exclusion enables Angel to reduce the amount of the required reinvestment for § 1033 purposes from $480,000 to $230,000. That is, by using § 121 in conjunction with § 1033, the amount realized, for § 1033 purposes, is reduced to $230,000 ($480,000 insurance proceeds − $250,000 § 121 exclusion).

Note that if Angel does not acquire qualifying replacement property for § 1033 purposes, her recognized gain is $90,000 ($480,000 insurance proceeds − $140,000 adjusted basis − $250,000 § 121 exclusion).

15-5 TAX PLANNING

LO.5

Review and apply various tax planning opportunities related to the nonrecognition provisions discussed in the chapter.

15-5a Like-Kind Exchanges

Because the like-kind exchange provisions are mandatory rather than elective, in certain instances, it may be preferable to avoid qualifying for § 1031 nonrecognition. If so, the taxpayer can structure the transaction so that at least one of the § 1031 like-kind exchange requirements is failed. If the like-kind exchange provisions do not apply, the end result may be the recognition of capital gain and a higher basis in the newly acquired asset. The immediate recognition of gain may be preferable when the taxpayer has:

- Unused net operating loss carryovers.
- Unused general business credit carryovers.
- Suspended or current passive activity losses.

EXAMPLE 41

Alicia disposes of a machine (used in her business) with an adjusted basis of $3,000 for $4,000. She also acquires a new business machine for $9,000.

If § 1031 applies, the $1,000 realized gain is not recognized and the basis of the new machine is reduced by $1,000 (from $9,000 to $8,000).

If § 1031 does not apply, a $1,000 gain is recognized and may receive favorable capital gain treatment to the extent the gain is not recognized as ordinary income due to the depreciation recapture provisions (see Chapter 17). In addition, the basis for depreciation on the new machine is $9,000 rather than $8,000 because there is no unrecognized gain.

The like-kind exchange rules should also be avoided when a realized loss exists (adjusted basis exceeds the fair market value).

---

[42]§ 1012. [43]§ 121(d)(5).

EXAMPLE 42

Assume the same facts as in the previous example, except that the fair market value of the machine is $2,500. If § 1031 applies, the $500 realized loss is not recognized.

To recognize the loss, Alicia should sell the old machine and purchase the new one. The purchase and sale transactions should be with different taxpayers.

The like-kind exchange procedure can also be used to control the amount of recognized gain.

EXAMPLE 43

Rex has property with an adjusted basis of $40,000 and a fair market value of $100,000. Sandra wants to buy Rex's property, but Rex wants to limit the amount of recognized gain on the proposed transaction. Sandra acquires other like-kind property (from an outside party) for $80,000. She then exchanges this property and $20,000 of cash for Rex's property.

Rex has a realized gain of $60,000 ($100,000 amount realized − $40,000 adjusted basis). His recognized gain is only $20,000, the lower of the $20,000 boot received or the $60,000 realized gain. Rex's basis for the like-kind property is $40,000 ($40,000 adjusted basis + $20,000 gain recognized − $20,000 boot received). Further, it is permissible for Rex to identify the like-kind property that he wants Sandra to purchase.[44]

If Rex had sold the property to Sandra for its fair market value of $100,000, the result would have been a $60,000 recognized gain ($100,000 amount realized − $40,000 adjusted basis).

One final point: the beneficial result of tax deferral of realized gain could be more than offset by future tax rate increases. Taxpayers may prefer to pay no more than 20 percent today (the current maximum tax rate on long-term capital gains) if they believe that tax rates will go up in the future. Although turning down a tax deferral may sound like a strange strategy, it fits the notion of "pay a tax today to avoid a higher tax tomorrow."

15-5b **Involuntary Conversions**

In certain cases, a taxpayer may prefer to recognize gain from an involuntary conversion. Keep in mind that § 1033, unlike § 1031 (dealing with like-kind exchanges), generally is an elective provision.

EXAMPLE 44

Ahmad has a $40,000 realized gain from the involuntary conversion of an office building. He reinvests the entire proceeds of $450,000 in a new office building. He does not elect to postpone gain under § 1033, however, because of an expiring net operating loss carryover that is offset against the gain.

As a result, none of the realized gain of $40,000 is postponed. Because Ahmad did not elect § 1033 postponement, his basis in the replacement property is the property's cost of $450,000 rather than $410,000 ($450,000 reduced by the $40,000 realized gain).

15-5c **Sale of a Principal Residence**

Election to Forgo

The § 121 exclusion automatically applies if the taxpayer is eligible (i.e., the taxpayer need not make an election). However, a taxpayer can elect to waive the § 121 exclusion.[45]

EXAMPLE 45

George owns two personal residences that satisfy the two-year ownership and use test with respect to the five-year window. The Elm Street residence has appreciated by $25,000, and the Maple Street residence has appreciated by $230,000. He intends to sell both of them and move into rental property. He sells the Elm Street residence in December 2017 and expects to sell the Maple Street residence early next year.

Unless George elects not to apply the § 121 exclusion to the sale of the Elm Street residence, he will exclude the $25,000 realized gain on that residence in 2017. In 2018, however, he will have a recognized gain of $230,000 on the sale of the Maple Street residence.

continued

---

[44]*Franklin B. Biggs*, 69 T.C. 905 (1978); Rev.Rul. 73–476, 1973–2 C.B. 300; and *Starker v. U.S.*, 79–2 USTC ¶9541, 44 AFTR 2d 79–5525, 602 F.2d 1341 (CA–9, 1979).

[45]§ 121(f).

If George makes the election to forgo, he will report a recognized gain of $25,000 on the sale of the Elm Street residence in 2017. But by using the § 121 exclusion in 2018, he will eliminate the recognized gain of $230,000 on the sale of the Maple Street residence.

Negative Effect of Renting or Using as a Home Office

The residence does not have to be the taxpayer's principal residence at the date of sale to qualify for the § 121 exclusion. During part of the five-year window, it could have been rental property (e.g., either a vacation home or entirely rental property). Or the taxpayer might have used part of the principal residence as a qualifying home office. In either of these circumstances, the taxpayer may claim deductions for the expenses attributable to the rental or business use. But what effect, if any, do such deductions have on a later sale of the residence? Will the sales proceeds still qualify for nonrecognition of gain treatment under § 121?

As long as the various § 121 requirements are met, an income exclusion will be available. However, if the taxpayer deducted depreciation, any realized gain on the sale that is attributable to depreciation claimed after May 5, 1997, is not eligible for the § 121 exclusion.[46]

EXAMPLE

46

On December 5, 2017, Amanda sells her principal residence, which qualifies for the § 121 exclusion. Her realized gain is $190,000. From January through November 2016, she was temporarily out of town on a job assignment in another city and rented the residence to a college student. For this period, she deducted MACRS cost recovery of $7,000.

Without the depreciation provision, Amanda could exclude the $190,000 realized gain. However, the depreciation taken requires her to recognize $7,000 of the realized gain.

Qualification for § 121 Exclusion

The key requirement for the § 121 exclusion is that the taxpayer must have *owned* and *used* the property as a principal residence for at least two years during the five-year window. As taxpayers advance in age, they quite frequently make decisions related to their personal residence(s):

- Sell the principal residence and buy a smaller residence or rent the principal residence.
- Sell vacation homes they own.
- Sell homes they are holding as rental property.

These properties may have experienced substantial appreciation while owned by the taxpayers. Proper planning can make it possible for multiple properties to qualify for the exclusion. Although this strategy may require taxpayers to be flexible about where they live, it can result in substantial tax savings.

EXAMPLE

47

Thelma and David, residents of Virginia, are approaching retirement. They have substantial appreciation on their principal residence (in Richmond) and on a house they own in Virginia Beach (about two hours away). After retirement, they plan to move to Florida. They have owned and lived in the principal residence for 28 years and have owned the beach house for 9 years.

If they sell their principal residence, it qualifies for the § 121 exclusion. At retirement, they could move into their beach house for two years and make it eligible for the exclusion before they relocate to Florida.

If the beach house were close enough, they could sell the principal residence now and move into the beach house to start the running of the two-year use period. As noted above, any realized gain on the beach house attributable to depreciation is not eligible for the § 121 exclusion. In addition, a reduction in the § 121 exclusion for prior use as a vacation home is required.[47]

---

[46]§ 121(d)(6).

[47]Additional information and examples can be found on pp. 3–6 of IRS Publication 523 (*Selling Your Home*).

IAIN MASTERTON/ALAMY STOCK PHOTO

REFOCUS ON THE BIG PICTURE

ALTERNATIVE USES OF PROPERTY

Alice needs to be aware of the different tax consequences of her proposals and whether there are any limits to these consequences.

- *Sale of the inherited house.* This is by far the simplest transaction for Alice. Based on the facts, her recognized gain would be:

Amount realized ($600,000 − $30,000)	$ 570,000
Adjusted basis	(475,000)
Recognized gain	$ 95,000

Because the sale of the house is not eligible for the § 121 exclusion, the tax liability is $14,250 ($95,000 × 15%). So Alice's net cash flow would be $555,750 ($570,000 − $14,250).

- *Conversion into a vacation home with only personal use.* With this alternative, the only tax benefit Alice would receive is the deduction for property taxes as an itemized deduction. She would continue to incur upkeep costs (e.g., repairs, utilities, and insurance). At the end of the two-year period, the sales results are similar to those of a current sale. The sale of the house would not be eligible for the § 121 exclusion.

- *Conversion into a vacation home with partial personal use and partial rental use.* In this case, Alice would be able to deduct 40 percent of costs such as property taxes, the agent's management fee, depreciation, maintenance and repairs, utilities, and insurance. However, this amount cannot exceed the rent income generated. The remaining 60 percent of the property taxes can be claimed as an itemized deduction.

  At the end of the two-year period, the sales results would be similar to those of a current sale. In determining recognized gain, adjusted basis must be reduced by the amount of the depreciation claimed. The sale of the house would not be eligible for the § 121 exclusion.

- *Current sale of present home with sale of inherited home in two years.* The present sale of her current principal residence and the future sale of her inherited residence would enable Alice to qualify for the § 121 exclusion as to each sale (see Example 34). She would satisfy the two-year ownership requirement, the two-year use requirement, and the allowance of the § 121 exclusion only once every two years. Alice must be careful to occupy the inherited residence for at least two years. Also, the period between the sales of the first and second houses must be greater than two years. Qualifying for the § 121 exclusion of up to $250,000 would allow Alice to avoid any Federal income tax liability.

With this information, Alice can make an informed choice. In all likelihood, she probably will select the strategy of selling her current house now and the inherited house in the future. A noneconomic benefit of this option is that she will have to sell only one house at the time of her retirement.

Key Terms

Discussion Questions

1. **LO.1** In most nontaxable exchanges, is the nonrecognition of the realized gain or loss temporary or permanent? Explain.

2. **LO.1** Distinguish between a loss that is not recognized on a nontaxable exchange and a loss that is not recognized on the sale or exchange of a personal use asset.

3. **LO.2** Karla exchanges personal use property for property to be held for productive use in her business. Can this transaction qualify for like-kind exchange treatment? Explain.

4. **LO.2** Which of the following qualify as like-kind exchanges under § 1031?
   a. Improved for unimproved real estate.
   b. Vending machine (used in business) for inventory.
   c. Rental house for personal residence.
   d. Business equipment for securities.
   e. Warehouse for office building (both used for business).
   f. Truck for computer (both used in business).
   g. Rental house for land (both held for investment).
   h. Ten shares of stock in Blue Corporation for 10 shares of stock in Red Corporation.
   i. Office furniture for office equipment (both used in business).
   j. Unimproved land in Jackson, Mississippi, for unimproved land in Toledo, Spain.
   k. General partnership interest for a general partnership interest.

5. **LO.2** Melissa owns a residential lot in Spring Creek, Louisiana, that has appreciated substantially in value. She holds the lot for investment. She is considering exchanging the lot for a residential lot located in Paris, France, that she also will hold for investment. Identify the relevant tax issues for Melissa.   Issue ID

6. **LO.2** Ross would like to dispose of some land he acquired five years ago because he believes that it will not continue to appreciate. Its value has increased by $50,000 over the five-year period. He also intends to sell stock that has declined in value by $50,000 during the eight-month period he has owned it. Ross has four offers to acquire the stock and land: Issue ID

   Buyer 1:   Exchange land.
   Buyer 2:   Purchase land for cash.
   Buyer 3:   Exchange stock.
   Buyer 4:   Purchase stock for cash.

   Identify the tax issues relevant to Ross in disposing of this land and stock.

7. **LO.2** Edith exchanges a machine used in her business for another machine and stock of Teal, Inc. If Edith had sold her machine, she would have had a realized gain. Explain why the new machine will have a different holding period than the stock.

8. **LO.2** Mortgaged real estate may be received in a like-kind exchange. If the taxpayer's mortgage is assumed, what effect does the mortgage have on the recognition of realized gain? On the basis of the real estate received?

9. **LO.3** Sheila's appreciated property is involuntarily converted. She receives insurance proceeds equal to the fair market value of the property. What is the minimum amount Sheila must reinvest in qualifying property to defer recognition of realized gain?

10. **LO.3** Ed receives severance damages from the state government for a public road built across his property. What are the tax implications of the severance damages?

11. **LO.3** Vera owns an office building that she leases to tenants. If the building is destroyed by a tornado, is the functional use test or the taxpayer use test applied as to replacement property? Explain the differences between the two tests.

12. **LO.3** Reba, a calendar year taxpayer, owns an office building that she uses in her business. The building is involuntarily converted on November 15, 2017. On January 5, 2018, Reba receives enough proceeds to produce a realized gain. What is the latest date she can replace the building and qualify for § 1033 postponement treatment if the conversion event is:

   a.   A flood?

   b.   A condemnation?

   c.   A tornado?

13. **LO.3** Bob is notified by the city public housing authority on May 3, 2017, that his apartment building is going to be condemned as part of an urban renewal project. On June 1, 2017, Carol offers to buy the building from Bob. Bob sells the building to Carol on June 30, 2017. Condemnation occurs on September 1, 2017, and Carol receives the condemnation proceeds from the city. Assume that both Bob and Carol are calendar year taxpayers.

   a.   What is the earliest date on which Bob can dispose of the building and qualify for § 1033 postponement treatment?

   b.   Does the sale to Carol qualify as a § 1033 involuntary conversion? Why or why not?

   c.   What is the latest date on which Carol can acquire qualifying replacement property and qualify for postponement of the realized gain?

   d.   What type of property will be qualifying replacement property?

Issue ID   14. **LO.3** A warehouse owned by Martha and used in her business (i.e., to store inventory) is being condemned by the city to provide a right-of-way for a highway. The warehouse has appreciated by $180,000 based on Martha's estimate of its fair market value. In the negotiations, the city is offering $35,000 less than what Martha believes the property is worth. Alan, a real estate broker, has offered to purchase Martha's property for $20,000 more than the city's offer. Martha plans to invest the proceeds she will receive in an office building she will lease to various tenants.

   a.   Identify the relevant tax issues for Martha.

   b.   Would the answer in part (a) change if Martha's warehouse was property being held for investment rather than being used in her business? Explain.

15. **LO.4** To qualify for exclusion treatment on the sale of a principal residence, the residence must have been owned and used by the taxpayer for at least two years during the five-year period ending on the date of the sale. Are there any exceptions to this provision? Explain.

Computational Exercises

16. **LO.2, 5** Andrew owns a lathe (adjusted basis of $40,000) that he uses in his business. He exchanges the lathe and $20,000 in cash for a new lathe worth $50,000. May Andrew avoid like-kind exchange treatment to recognize his realized loss of $10,000? Explain.

17. **LO.2** Sue exchanges a sport-utility vehicle (adjusted basis of $16,000; fair market value of $19,500) for cash of $2,000 and a pickup truck (fair market value of $17,500). Both vehicles are for business use. Sue believes that her basis for the truck is $17,500. In calculating her basis, what has Sue failed to consider?

18. **LO.2** Logan and Johnathan exchange land, and the exchange qualifies as like kind under § 1031. Because Logan's land (adjusted basis of $85,000) is worth $100,000 and Johnathan's land has a fair market value of $80,000, Johnathan also gives Logan cash of $20,000.

    a. What is Logan's recognized gain?

    b. Assume instead that Johnathan's land is worth $90,000 and he gives Logan $10,000 cash. Now what is Logan's recognized gain?

19. **LO.2** Mandy and Timothy exchange equipment in a like-kind exchange. Mandy receives equipment with a fair market value of $28,000 and transfers equipment worth $20,000 (adjusted basis of $14,000) and cash of $8,000. What is Mandy's realized and recognized gain?

20. **LO.3** On June 5, 2017, Brown, Inc., a calendar year taxpayer, receives cash of $750,000 from the county upon condemnation of its warehouse building (adjusted basis of $500,000 and fair market value of $750,000).

    a. What must Brown do to qualify for § 1033 postponement of gain treatment?

    b. How would your advice to Brown differ if the adjusted basis was $795,000?

21. **LO.3** Camilo's property, with an adjusted basis of $155,000, is condemned by the state. Camilo receives property with a fair market value of $180,000 as compensation for the property taken.

    a. What is Camilo's realized and recognized gain?

    b. What is the basis of the replacement property?

22. **LO.3** On February 24, 2017, Allison's building, with an adjusted basis of $1.3 million (and used in her trade or business), is destroyed by fire. On March 31, 2017, she receives an insurance reimbursement of $1.65 million for the loss. Allison invests $1.55 million in a new building and buys stock with the balance of insurance proceeds. Allison is a calendar year taxpayer.

    a. By what date must Allison make the new investment to qualify for the non-recognition election?

    b. Assuming that the replacement property qualifies as similar or related in service or use, what are Allison's realized gain, recognized gain, and basis in the replacement building?

23. **LO.4** Gary, who is single, sells his principal residence (owned and occupied by him for seven years) in November 2017 for a realized gain of $148,000. He had purchased a more expensive new residence eight months prior to the sale. He anticipates that he will occupy this new house as his principal residence for only about 18 additional months. He expects it to appreciate substantially while he owns it. Gary would like to recognize the realized gain on the 2017 sale to offset a large investment loss from the sale of stock. Can he recognize the realized gain of $148,000 on the sale of his principal residence in 2017? Explain.

24. **LO.4** Arnold, who is single, sold his principal residence on April 10, 2017, and excluded the realized gain under § 121 (exclusion on the sale of a principal residence). On April 12, 2017, he purchased another principal residence, which he sells on January 12, 2018, for a realized gain of $80,000. Can Arnold exclude the $80,000 realized gain on the January 2018 sale if his reason for selling was:

    a. His noisy neighbors? Explain.

    b. A job transfer to another city? Explain.

25. **LO.4** Constanza, who is single, sells her current personal residence (adjusted basis of $165,000) for $450,000. She has owned and lived in the house for 30 years. Her selling expenses are $22,500. What is Constanza's realized and recognized gain?

26. **LO.4** On August 31, 2016, Harvey and Margaret, who file a joint return and live in Charleston, South Carolina, sell their personal residence, which they have owned and lived in for 10 years. The realized gain of $292,000 was excluded under § 121. They purchased another personal residence in Charleston for $480,000 on September 1, 2016. However, in 2017, Harvey's employer transfers him to Houston, Texas. They sell their Charleston home on February 28, 2017, and purchase a new home in Houston. The realized gain on the second sale is $180,000. What is Harvey and Margaret's recognized gain on the second sale?

Problems

27. **LO.2** Katrina owns undeveloped land with an adjusted basis of $300,000. She exchanges it for undeveloped land worth $750,000.
    a. What are Katrina's realized and recognized gain or loss?
    b. What is Katrina's basis in the undeveloped land she receives?
    c. Would the answers in parts (a) and (b) change if Katrina exchanged the undeveloped land for land and a building? Explain.

28. **LO.2** Kareem owns a pickup truck that he uses exclusively in his business. The adjusted basis is $22,000, and the fair market value is $14,000. Kareem exchanges the truck for another truck that he will use exclusively in his business.
    a. What are Kareem's realized and recognized gain or loss?
    b. What is his basis in the new truck?
    c. What are the tax consequences to Kareem in parts (a) and (b) if he used the old truck and will use the new truck exclusively for personal purposes?

Decision Making

Communications

29. **LO.2** Tanya Fletcher owns undeveloped land (adjusted basis of $80,000 and fair market value of $92,000) on the East Coast. On January 4, 2017, she exchanges it with Lisa Martin (an unrelated party) for undeveloped land on the West Coast and $3,000 cash. Lisa has an adjusted basis of $72,000 for her land, and its fair market value is $89,000. As the real estate market on the East Coast is thriving, on September 1, 2018, Lisa sells the land she acquired for $120,000.
    a. What are Tanya's recognized gain or loss and adjusted basis for the West Coast land on January 4, 2017?
    b. What are Lisa's recognized gain or loss and adjusted basis for the East Coast land on January 4, 2017?
    c. What is Lisa's recognized gain or loss from the September 1, 2018 sale?
    d. What effect does Lisa's 2018 sale have on Tanya?
    e. Write a letter to Tanya advising her of the tax consequences of this exchange. Her address is The Corral, El Paso, TX 79968.

30. **LO.2** Sarah exchanges a yellow bus (used in her business) for Tyler's gray bus and some garage equipment (used in his business). The assets have the following characteristics:

	Adjusted Basis	Fair Market Value
Yellow bus	$6,000	$15,000
Gray bus	3,000	11,000
Equipment	2,000	4,000

    a. What are Sarah's recognized gain or loss and basis for the gray bus and garage equipment?
    b. What are Tyler's recognized gain or loss and basis for the yellow bus?

31. **LO.2, 5** In two unrelated transactions, Laura exchanges property that qualifies for like-kind exchange treatment. In the first exchange, Laura gives up office equipment purchased in May 2015 (adjusted basis of $20,000; fair market value of $17,000) in exchange for new office equipment (fair market value of $15,000) and $2,000 cash. In the second exchange, Laura receives a parking garage (to be used in her business) with a fair market value of $50,000 in exchange for a plot of land she had held for investment. The land was purchased in April 2009 for $12,000 and has a current fair market value of $48,000. In addition to transferring the land, Laura pays an additional $2,000 to the other party.

    a. What is Laura's adjusted basis for the new office equipment?
    b. When does the holding period begin?
    c. What is Laura's adjusted basis for the parking garage?
    d. When does the holding period begin?
    e. How could Laura structure either of the transactions differently to produce better tax consequences?

32. **LO.2** Susan owns a car that she uses exclusively for personal purposes. Its original cost was $26,000, and the fair market value is $12,000. She exchanges the car and $18,000 cash for a new car.

    a. Calculate Susan's realized and recognized gain or loss.
    b. Calculate Susan's basis for the new car.
    c. Determine when Susan's holding period for the new car begins.

33. **LO.2** Stephanie owns a machine (adjusted basis of $90,000; fair market value of $125,000) that she uses in her business. She exchanges it for another machine (worth $100,000) and stock (worth $25,000). Determine Stephanie's:

    a. Realized and recognized gain or loss on the exchange.
    b. Basis in the new machine.
    c. Basis in the stock she received.

34. **LO.2** Ed owns investment land with an adjusted basis of $35,000. Polly has offered to purchase the land from Ed for $175,000 for use in a real estate development. The amount offered by Polly is $10,000 in excess of what Ed perceives as the fair market value of the land. Ed would like to dispose of the land to Polly but does not want to incur the tax liability that would result. He identifies an office building with a fair market value of $175,000 that he would like to acquire. Polly purchases the office building and then exchanges the office building for Ed's land.

    a. Calculate Ed's realized and recognized gain on the exchange and his basis for the office building.
    b. Calculate Polly's realized and recognized gain on the exchange and her basis in the land.

35. **LO.2** What is the basis of the new property in each of the following exchanges?

    a. Apartment building held for investment (adjusted basis of $145,000) for office building to be held for investment (fair market value of $225,000).
    b. Land and building used as a barbershop (adjusted basis of $190,000) for land and building used as a grocery store (fair market value of $350,000).
    c. Office building (adjusted basis of $45,000) for bulldozer (fair market value of $42,000), both held for business use.
    d. IBM common stock (adjusted basis of $20,000) for ExxonMobil common stock (fair market value of $28,000).
    e. Rental house (adjusted basis of $90,000) for mountain cabin to be held for rental use (fair market value of $225,000).
    f. General partnership interest (adjusted basis of $400,000) for a limited partnership interest (fair market value of $580,000).

36. **LO.2** Steve owns Machine A (adjusted basis of $12,000 and fair market value of $15,000), which he uses in his business. Steve sells Machine A for $15,000 to Aubry (a dealer) and then purchases Machine B for $15,000 from Joan (also a dealer). Machine B would normally qualify as like-kind property.
    a. What are Steve's realized and recognized gain on the sale of Machine A?
    b. What is Steve's basis for Machine B?
    c. What factors would motivate Steve to sell Machine A and purchase Machine B rather than exchange one machine for the other?
    d. Assume that the adjusted basis of Machine A is $15,000 and the fair market value of both machines is $12,000. Respond to parts (a) through (c).

37. **LO.2** Tab exchanges real estate used in his business along with stock for real estate to be held for investment. The stock transferred has an adjusted basis of $45,000 and a fair market value of $50,000. The real estate transferred has an adjusted basis of $85,000 and a fair market value of $190,000. The real estate acquired has a fair market value of $240,000.
    a. What is Tab's realized gain or loss?
    b. His recognized gain or loss?
    c. The basis of the newly acquired real estate?

Decision Making 38. **LO.2, 5** Tom Howard and Frank Peters are good friends (and former college roommates). Each owns investment property in the other's hometown (Tom lives in Kalamazoo, MI; Frank lives in Austin, TX). To make their lives easier, they decide to exchange the investment properties. Under the terms of the exchange, Frank will transfer realty (20 acres of unimproved land; adjusted basis of $52,000; fair market value of $80,000) and Tom will exchange realty (25 acres of unimproved land; adjusted basis of $60,000; fair market value of $92,000). Tom's property is subject to a mortgage of $12,000 that will be assumed by Frank.
    a. What are Frank's and Tom's recognized gains?
    b. What are their adjusted bases?
    c. As an alternative, Frank has proposed that rather than assuming the mortgage, he will transfer cash of $12,000 to Tom. Tom would use the cash to pay off the mortgage. Advise Tom on whether this alternative would be beneficial to him from a tax perspective.
    d. Assuming that Tom and Frank proceed with the original exchange (rather than the alternative), complete Form 8824 (Parts I and III) for Tom. Assume that the exchange occurs on September 19, 2016 (Tom acquired his 25-acre parcel on February 15, 2008). Tom's Social Security number is 123-45-6789.

39. **LO.2** Determine the realized, recognized, and postponed gain or loss and the new basis for each of the following like-kind exchanges:

	Adjusted Basis of Old Machine	Boot Given	Fair Market Value of New Asset	Boot Received
a.	$ 7,000	$ –0–	$12,000	$4,000
b.	14,000	2,000	15,000	–0–
c.	3,000	7,000	8,000	500
d.	15,000	–0–	29,000	–0–
e.	10,000	–0–	11,000	1,000
f.	17,000	–0–	14,000	–0–

40. **LO.2** Shontelle owns an apartment house that has an adjusted basis of $760,000 but is subject to a mortgage of $192,000. She transfers the apartment house to Dave and receives from him $120,000 in cash and an office building with a fair market value of $780,000 at the time of the exchange. Dave assumes the $192,000 mortgage on the apartment house.

a. What is Shontelle's realized gain or loss?
b. What is her recognized gain or loss?
c. What is the basis of the newly acquired office building?

41. **LO.3** Howard's roadside vegetable stand (adjusted basis of $275,000) is destroyed by a tractor-trailer accident. He receives insurance proceeds of $240,000 ($300,000 fair market value − $60,000 coinsurance). Howard immediately uses the proceeds plus additional cash of $45,000 to build another roadside vegetable stand at the same location. What are the tax consequences to Howard?

42. **LO.3** Albert owns 100 acres of land on which he grows spruce Christmas trees. His adjusted basis for the land is $100,000. He receives condemnation proceeds of $10,000 when the city's new beltway takes 5 acres along the eastern boundary of his property. He also receives a severance award of $6,000 associated with the possible harmful effects of exhaust fumes on his Christmas trees. Albert invests the $16,000 in a growth mutual fund. Determine the tax consequences to Albert of the:

a. Condemnation proceeds.
b. Severance award.

43. **LO.3** For each of the following involuntary conversions, indicate whether the property acquired qualifies as replacement property, the recognized gain, and the basis for the property acquired:

a. Frank owns a warehouse that is destroyed by a tornado. The space in the warehouse was rented to various tenants. The adjusted basis was $470,000. Frank uses all of the insurance proceeds of $700,000 to build a shopping mall in a neighboring community where no property has been damaged by tornadoes. The shopping mall is rented to various tenants.

b. Ivan owns a warehouse that he uses in his business. The adjusted basis is $300,000. The warehouse is destroyed by fire. Because of economic conditions in the area, Ivan decides not to rebuild the warehouse. Instead, he uses all of the insurance proceeds of $400,000 to build a warehouse to be used in his business in another state.

c. Ridge's personal residence is condemned as part of a local government project to widen the highway from two lanes to four lanes. The adjusted basis is $170,000. Ridge uses all of the condemnation proceeds of $200,000 to purchase another personal residence.

d. Juanita owns a building that she uses in her retail business. The adjusted basis is $250,000. The building is destroyed by a hurricane. Because of an economic downturn in the area caused by the closing of a military base, Juanita decides to rent space for her retail outlet rather than replace the building. She uses all of the insurance proceeds of $300,000 to buy a four-unit apartment building in another city. A real estate agent in that city will handle the rental of the apartments for her.

e. Susan and Rick's personal residence is destroyed by a tornado. They had owned it for 15 months. The adjusted basis was $170,000. Because they would like to travel, they decide not to acquire a replacement residence. Instead, they invest all of the insurance proceeds of $200,000 in a duplex, which they rent to tenants.

f. Ellen and Harry's personal residence (adjusted basis of $245,000) is destroyed in a flood. They had owned it for 18 months. Of the insurance proceeds of $350,000, they reinvest $342,000 in a replacement residence four months later.

44. **LO.3** Mitchell, a calendar year taxpayer, is the sole proprietor of a fast-food restaurant. His adjusted basis for the building and the related land is $450,000. On March 12, 2017, state authorities notify Mitchell that his property is going to be condemned so that the highway can be widened. On June 20, Mitchell's property is officially condemned, and he receives an award of $625,000. Because Mitchell's business was successful in the past, he would like to reopen the restaurant in a new location.

a.   What is the earliest date Mitchell can acquire a new restaurant and qualify for § 1033 postponement?

b.   On June 30, Mitchell purchases land and a building for $610,000. Assuming that he elects postponement of gain under § 1033, what is his recognized gain?

c.   What is Mitchell's adjusted basis for the new land and building?

d.   If he does not elect § 1033, what are Mitchell's recognized gain and adjusted basis?

e.   Suppose he invests the $625,000 condemnation proceeds in the stock market on June 30. What is Mitchell's recognized gain?

45. **LO.3** Edith's warehouse (adjusted basis of $450,000) is destroyed by a hurricane in October 2017. Edith, a calendar year taxpayer, receives insurance proceeds of $525,000 in January 2018. Calculate Edith's realized gain or loss, recognized gain or loss, and basis for the replacement property if she:

a.   Acquires a new warehouse for $550,000 in January 2018.

b.   Acquires a new warehouse for $500,000 in January 2018.

c.   Does not acquire replacement property.

Decision Making   46. **LO.3** Cabel's warehouse, which has an adjusted basis of $380,000 and a fair market value of $490,000, is condemned by an agency of the Federal government to make way for a highway interchange. The initial condemnation offer is $425,000. After substantial negotiations, the agency agrees to transfer to Cabel a surplus warehouse that he believes is worth $490,000. Cabel is a calendar year taxpayer. The condemnation and related asset transfer occur during September 2017.

a.   What are the recognized gain or loss and the basis of the replacement warehouse if Cabel's objective is to recognize as much gain as possible?

b.   Advise Cabel regarding what he needs to do by what date to achieve his objective.

47. **LO.3** What are the *maximum* postponed gain or loss and the basis for the replacement property for the following involuntary conversions?

	Property	Type of Conversion	Amount Realized	Adjusted Basis	Amount Reinvested
a.	Drugstore (business)	Casualty	$160,000	$130,000	$110,000
b.	Apartments (investment)	Condemned	100,000	125,000	175,000
c.	Grocery store (business)	Casualty	400,000	300,000	450,000
d.	Residence (personal)	Casualty	16,000	18,000	17,000
e.	Vacant lot (investment)	Condemned	240,000	160,000	220,000
f.	Residence (personal)	Casualty	20,000	18,000	19,000
g.	Residence (personal)	Condemned	18,000	20,000	26,000
h.	Apartments (investment)	Condemned	150,000	100,000	200,000

Decision Making   48. **LO.3, 5** Wanda, a calendar year taxpayer, owned a building (adjusted basis of $250,000) in which she operated a bakery that was destroyed by fire in December 2017. She receives insurance proceeds of $290,000 for the building the following March. Wanda is considering two options regarding the investment of the insurance proceeds. First, she could purchase a local building (suitable for a bakery) that is for sale for $275,000. Second, she could buy a new home for $290,000 and go back to college and finish her degree.

a.   To minimize her tax liability, which of these alternatives should Wanda choose?

b.   What is the latest date on which Wanda can replace the involuntarily converted property to qualify for § 1033?

c.   What is the latest date on which Wanda can replace the involuntarily converted property to qualify for § 1033 if the involuntary conversion is a condemnation?

49. **LO.4, 5** Karl purchased his residence on January 2, 2016, for $260,000, after hav-   Decision Making
    ing lived in it during 2015 as a tenant under a lease with an option to buy
    clause. On August 1, 2017, Karl sells the residence for $315,000. On June 13, 2017,
    Karl purchases a new residence for $367,000.

    a. What is Karl's recognized gain? His basis for the new residence?
    b. Assume instead that Karl purchased his original residence on January 2, 2015
        (rather than January 2, 2016). What is Karl's recognized gain? His basis for the
        new residence?
    c. In part (a), what could Karl do to minimize his recognized gain?

50. **LO.4** Taylor has owned and occupied her personal residence (adjusted basis of
    $190,000) for four years. In April 2017, she sells the residence for $300,000
    (selling expenses are $20,000). On the same day as the sale, Taylor purchases
    another house for $350,000. Because of noisy neighbors, she sells the new house
    after just 10 months. The selling price is $483,000 (selling expenses are $18,000).

    a. What is Taylor's recognized gain on the sale of the first residence?
    b. What is Taylor's basis for her second residence?
    c. What is Taylor's recognized gain on the sale of the second residence?
    d. Assume instead that the sale of the second residence was due to Taylor's job
        transfer to another state. What is her recognized gain on the sale of the second
        residence?

51. **LO.4** Wesley, who is single, listed his personal residence with a real estate agent
    on March 3, 2017, at a price of $390,000. He rejected several offers in the
    $350,000 range during the summer. Finally, on August 16, 2017, he and the pur-
    chaser signed a contract to sell for $363,000. The sale (i.e., closing) took place on
    September 7, 2017. The closing statement showed the following disbursements:

Real estate agent's commission	$ 21,780
Appraisal fee	600
Exterminator's certificate	300
Recording fees	800
Mortgage to First Bank	305,000
Cash to seller	34,520

    Wesley's adjusted basis for the house is $200,000. He owned and occupied the
    house for seven years. On October 1, 2017, Wesley purchases another residence for
    $325,000.

    a. Calculate Wesley's recognized gain on the sale.
    b. What is Wesley's adjusted basis for the new residence?
    c. Assume instead that the selling price is $800,000. What is Wesley's recognized
        gain? His adjusted basis for the new residence?

52. **LO.4** Pedro, age 57, is the sole owner of his principal residence, which he has
    owned and occupied for 10 years. Maria, his spouse, has also lived there 10
    years. He sells the house for a realized gain of $340,000.

    a. Can Pedro use the § 121 exclusion if he and Maria file a joint return? If so, what
        are the available amount of the exclusion and the recognized gain?
    b. Can Pedro use the § 121 exclusion if he files a separate return? If so, what are
        the available amount of the exclusion and the recognized gain?
    c. Assume instead that the realized gain is $550,000 and a joint return is filed.
    d. Assume instead that the realized gain is $550,000 and separate returns are filed.
    e. Assume instead that Maria and Pedro have been married for only 18 months
        and that she has lived in his house only since their marriage. They file a joint
        return.

Communications 53. **LO.4** Nell, Nina, and Nora Sanders, who are sisters, sell their principal residence (owned as tenants in common) in which they have lived for the past 25 years. The youngest of the sisters is age 60. The selling price is $960,000, selling expenses and legal fees are $63,000, and the adjusted basis is $120,000 (the fair market value of the residence when inherited from their parents 25 years ago; they made no capital improvements during the time they held the residence). Because the sisters are going to live in rental housing, they do not plan to acquire another residence. Nell has contacted you on behalf of the three sisters regarding the tax consequences of the sale.

  a. Write a letter to Nell advising her of the tax consequences and how taxes can be minimized. Nell's address is 100 Oak Avenue, Billings, MT 59101.

  b. Prepare a memo for the tax files.

Decision Making 54. **LO.4** Lloyd owns a beach house (four years) and a cabin in the mountains (six years). His adjusted basis is $300,000 in the beach house and $315,000 in the mountain cabin. Llyod also rents a townhouse in the city where he is employed. During the year, he occupies each of the three residences as follows:

Townhouse	135 days
Beach house	155 days
Mountain cabin	75 days

The beach house is close enough to the city that he can commute to work during the spring and summer. While this level of occupancy may vary slightly from year to year, it is representative during the time period that Lloyd has owned the two residences.

  As Lloyd plans on retiring in several years, he sells both the beach house and the mountain cabin. The mountain cabin is sold on March 3, 2017, for $540,000 (related selling expenses of $35,000). The beach house is sold on December 10, 2017, for $700,000 (related selling expenses of $42,000).

  a. Calculate Lloyd's lowest recognized gain on the sale of the two residences.

  b. Assume instead that both residences satisfy the two-year ownership and use tests as Lloyd's principal residence. Because the mountain cabin is sold first, is it possible for Lloyd to apply the § 121 exclusion to the sale of the beach house? Why or why not?

Decision Making 55. **LO.4, 5** Cisco, a calendar year taxpayer who is age 63, owns a residence in which he has lived for 21 years. The residence is destroyed by fire on August 8, 2017. The adjusted basis is $190,000, and the fair market value is $320,000. Cisco receives insurance proceeds of $320,000 for the residence on September 1, 2017. He is trying to decide whether to purchase a comparable house. He anticipates that he will retire in two years and will move to a warmer climate, where he will rent in case he decides to live in different places.

  a. Advise Cisco of the tax consequences of replacing versus not replacing the residence.

  b. Which do you recommend to him?

  c. How would your answer in part (a) change if the fair market value and insurance proceeds received were $510,000?

Decision Making 56. **LO.4, 5** Missy, age 30, has owned her principal residence (adjusted basis of $225,000) for five years. During the first three years of ownership, she occupied it as her principal residence. During the past two years, she was in graduate school and rented the residence. After graduate school, Missy returned to the same location where she previously worked. At this point, she purchased another residence for $400,000 and listed her old residence for sale at $340,000. Due to a slow real estate market, 11 months later Missy finally receives an offer of $330,000.

a. What is Missy's recognized gain if she immediately accepts the $330,000 offer (i.e., 11 months after the listing date)? Selling expenses are $20,000.

b. What is Missy's recognized gain if she rejects the $330,000 offer and accepts another offer of $340,000 three months later (i.e., 14 months after the listing date)?

c. Advise Missy on which offer she should accept (assume that she is in the 28% tax bracket).

Cumulative Problems

Tax Return Problem

H&R BLOCK
TAX SOFTWARE

57. Devon Bishop, age 45, is single. He lives at 1507 Rose Lane, Albuquerque, NM 87131. His Social Security number is 111-11-1112. Devon does not want $3 to go to the Presidential Election Campaign Fund.

Devon's wife, Ariane, passed away in 2012. Devon's son, Tom, who is age 16, resides with Devon. Tom's Social Security number is 123-45-6788.

Devon owns a sole proprietorship for which he uses the accrual method of accounting and maintains no inventory. His revenues and expenses for 2016 are as follows:

Sales revenue	$740,000
Cost of goods sold (based on purchases for the year)	405,000
Salary expense	88,000
Rent expense	30,000
Utilities	8,000
Telephone	6,500
Advertising	4,000
Bad debts	5,000
Depreciation*	21,000
Health insurance**	26,000
Accounting and legal fees	7,000
Supplies	1,000

*New office equipment ($21,000); Devon chose to use the immediate expense election.
**$18,000 for employees and $8,000 for Devon.

Other income received by Devon includes the following:

Dividend income (qualified dividends):	
Swan, Inc.	$10,000
Wren, Inc.	2,000
Interest income:	
First National Bank	11,000
Second City Bank	2,500
County of Santa Fe, NM bonds	17,000

During the year, Devon and his sole proprietorship had the following property transactions:

a. Sold Blue, Inc. stock for $45,000 on March 12, 2016. He had purchased the stock on September 5, 2013, for $50,000.

b. Received an inheritance of $300,000 from his uncle, Henry. Devon used $200,000 to purchase Green, Inc. stock on May 15, 2016, and invested $100,000 in Gold, Inc. stock on May 30, 2016.

c. Received Orange, Inc. stock worth $9,500 as a gift from his aunt, Jane, on June 17, 2016. Her adjusted basis for the stock was $5,000. No gift taxes were paid on the transfer. Jane had purchased the stock on April 1, 2010. Devon sold the stock on July 1, 2016, for $22,000.

d. On July 15, 2016, Devon sold one-half of the Green, Inc. stock for $40,000.

e. Devon was notified on August 1, 2016, that Yellow, Inc. stock he purchased from a colleague on September 1, 2015, for $52,500 had become worthless. While he perceived that the investment was risky, he did not anticipate that the corporation would declare bankruptcy.

f. On August 15, 2016, Devon received a parcel of land in Phoenix worth $220,000 in exchange for a parcel of land he owned in Tucson. Because the Tucson parcel was worth $245,000, he also received $25,000 cash. Devon's adjusted basis for the Tucson parcel was $210,000. He originally purchased it on September 18, 2013.

g. On December 1, 2016, Devon sold the condominium in which he had been living for the past 20 years (1844 Lighthouse Lane, Albuquerque, NM 87131) and moved into a rented townhouse. The sales price was $480,000, selling expenses were $28,500, and repair expenses related to the sale were $9,400. Devon purchased the condominium for $180,000.

Devon's potential itemized deductions, exclusive of the aforementioned information, are as follows:

Medical expenses (before the 10% floor)	$ 9,500
Property taxes on residence	5,800
State income taxes	4,000
Charitable contributions	10,000
Mortgage interest on residence (First National Bank)	9,900
Sales taxes paid	5,000

During the year, Devon makes estimated Federal income tax payments of $40,000.

Compute Devon's lowest net tax payable or refund due for 2016 assuming that he makes any available elections that will reduce the tax. If you use tax forms for your computations, you will need Forms 1040, 4562, 8824, and 8949 and Schedules A, B, C, D, and SE. Suggested software: H&R BLOCK Tax Software.

Tax Computation Problem
Decision Making
Communications

58. Tom and Alice Honeycutt, ages 35 and 36, respectively, live at 101 Glass Road, Delton, MI 49046. Tom is a county employee, and Alice is a self-employed accountant. Tom's Social Security number is 111-11-1111; Alice's Social Security number is 123-45-6789. The income and expenses associated with Alice's accounting practice for 2017 are as follows:

Revenues (cash receipts during 2017)	$185,000
Expenses	
Salaries	$ 45,000
Office supplies	3,200
Postage	2,900
Depreciation of equipment	42,000
Telephone	800
	$ 93,900

Because Alice is a cash method taxpayer, she does not record her receivables as revenue until she receives cash payment. At the beginning of 2017, her accounts receivable were $48,000, and the balance had decreased to $8,000 by the end of the year.

Alice used one room in their 10-room house as the office for her accounting practice (400 square feet out of a total square footage of 4,000). They paid the following expenses related to the house during 2017:

Utilities	$4,500
Insurance	2,100
Property taxes	5,200
Repairs	3,500

Tom and Alice purchased the house on September 1, 2016, for $400,000 (exclusive of land cost).

Tom and Alice have one child, Connor, age 16. Connor's Social Security number is 123-45-6788.

Tom received a salary of $50,000 during 2017. The appropriate amounts of Social Security tax and Medicare tax were withheld. In addition, $5,000 of Federal income taxes and $2,000 of state income taxes were withheld.

Alice provides part of the support of her father, age 69. Her father's Social Security number is 123-45-6787. The total support in 2017 for her father was as follows:

Social Security benefits	$5,200
From Alice	3,200
From Bob, Alice's brother	2,200
From Susan, Alice's sister	2,300

Bob and Susan have both indicated their willingness to sign a multiple support waiver form if it will benefit Alice.

Tom and Alice's allowable itemized deductions during 2017, excluding any itemized deductions related to the house, were $11,000. They made estimated tax payments of $25,000.

Part 1—Tax Computation
Compute Tom and Alice's lowest net tax payable or refund due for 2017.

Part 2—Tax Planning
Tom and Alice have 30 acres of prime farmland that they inherited from Tom's father several years ago. At that time, the fair market value of the land was $150,000 (which became their basis in the land). The Honeycutts have been holding the land as an investment. The property was recently appraised for $190,000, and there is an outstanding mortgage on the land of $28,000. They are considering trading this land for property in the mountains of southern Colorado. Ultimately, they would like to build a vacation home on the Colorado property. The Colorado property owner— who has significant land holdings in the area—has provided two options to Tom and Alice (in both cases, the Colorado property owner would assume the mortgage as part of the exchange):

1. 15 acres of property with a fair market value of $135,000 plus $27,000 of cash; or
2. 10 acres of property with a fair market value of $160,000 plus $2,000 of cash.

The Honeycutts have come to you for advice, believing either transaction to be a like-kind exchange that will allow them to defer any gain. Assume that Tom and Alice expect their marginal tax rate to remain the same for 2018. Write a letter to Tom and Alice that contains your advice on the proposed transactions. Also prepare a memo for the tax files.

Research Problems

Note: Solutions to the Research Problems can be prepared by using the Thomson Reuters Checkpoint® Student Edition online tax research database, which accompanies this textbook. Solutions can also be prepared by using research materials found in a typical tax library.

Research Problem 1. Charlene and Alton Dutro had lived in their home for two and one-half years when they decided to enlarge and remodel the house. However, their architect advised them that more stringent building and permit restrictions had been imposed since the house was built 10 years earlier. So the Dutros decided to demolish the house and rebuild on the same site. Rather than occupying the new house, however, the Dutros sold it for a realized gain in excess of $500,000.

In calculating the recognized gain on their Federal income tax return, the Dutros reduced the realized gain of more than $500,000 by the $500,000 exclusion of § 121. The IRS has issued an income tax deficiency notice on the grounds that the Dutros did not satisfy the two-out-of-five-years requirement of § 121(a).

Who is correct?

Partial list of research aids:
§ 121(a)(1).
David A. Gates, 135 T.C. 1 (2010).

Research Problem 2. Ted and Marvin Brown purchased an apartment building in 2006 as equal tenants in common. After a hectic decade of co-ownership, the brothers decided that their business association should be terminated. This led to the sale of the apartment building and a division of the proceeds.

The realized gain on the sale of the apartment building for each brother was $350,000. Ted recognized gain on his share and used the net proceeds to invest in stock. Marvin wanted to defer any recognized gain, so he worked with a realtor to identify property that would be eligible for § 1031 like-kind exchange treatment. After one prospect failed, the realtor identified a single-family home on Lake Tahoe that was currently being rented by the owner. Marvin agreed with the choice and acquired the single-family house using the proceeds from the apartment building. Because the single-family house qualified as like-kind property, Marvin deferred all of his realized gain.

After attempting to rent the property for eight months without success, Marvin concluded that he could not continue to make the mortgage payments on his primary residence and this rental property. To ease his financial liquidity problem, Marvin sold his principal residence for a realized gain of $190,000 and moved into the Lake Tahoe house. He reported no recognized gain on the sale of his principal residence as the sale qualified for § 121 exclusion treatment.

The IRS issued a deficiency notice to Marvin associated with the sale of the apartment building. The position of the IRS was that Marvin did not hold the single-family residence for investment purposes as required by § 1031. Instead, his intention was personal—to use it as a replacement for his current residence that he planned on selling.

Who should prevail?

Research Problem 3. Taylor owns a 150-unit motel that was constructed in the late 1960s. It is located on 10 acres on the main highway leading into the city. Taylor renovated the motel three years ago.

Taylor's motel is condemned by the city, which is going to use 2 of the 10 acres for a small park. The other 8 acres are to be sold to a time-share developer who intends to build 400 units on the property. The developer has already secured approval from the city planning commission.

Taylor's attorney advises him not to contest the condemnation of the 2 acres for the park. Under the eminent domain provision, the city does have the right to take "private property for public use." However, the attorney advises Taylor to contest the condemnation of the remaining property. According to the attorney, the city does not have the right to take "private property for private use."

The city's position is that the condemnation will result in a substantial number of new jobs and additional tax revenue for the city.

Will Taylor be successful if he follows his attorney's advice? Explain.

Use internet tax resources to address the following questions. Look for reliable websites and blogs of the IRS and other government agencies, media outlets, businesses, tax professionals, academics, think tanks, and political outlets.

Research Problem 4. Find two newspaper stories about transactions to which you believe the involuntary conversion rules could apply. Do not limit your search to individual taxpayers.

Research Problem 5. In general, the 45-day identification period and the 180-day exchange period for like-kind exchanges cannot be extended. Does this rule change if the like-kind property or the taxpayer involved in the exchange is located in a Presidentially declared disaster area? Use the IRS's website (**www.irs.gov**) to find the answer.

Roger CPA Review Questions

1. Kellye purchased her home in 2012 for $140,000. After living in it for five years, she sold it in 2017 for $170,000, its market value. What is the tax treatment of the sale of Kellye's home?

    a. A $30,000 gain is recognized but not reported.

    b. A $30,000 gain is recognized and reported.

    c. A $30,000 gain is carried forward.

    d. The transaction is not reported.

2. Ike, a single taxpayer, is reassigned for his job and must move to a new state. While searching for a place to live, he encounters a person who is selling her home in order to move to Ike's current city. The two agree to trade their properties to each other without any further consideration. Ike's house has a fair market value of $200,000 and basis of $130,000. He has lived in the house for one year. The house he is acquiring in the trade has a fair market value of $300,000. What gain will Ike recognize for Federal tax purposes?

    a. $50,000   c. $0

    b. $100,000   d. $300,000

3. Kathryn has lived in her house for one year. Her company recently relocated to a city 100 miles away, forcing her to move. She purchased her house a year ago for $400,000 and sold it for $525,000, its current fair market value. What amount of gain will Kathryn recognize for Federal tax purposes?

    a. $0   c. $125,000

    b. $62,500   d. $250,000

4. An office building owned by Milo was destroyed by Hurricane Mel on September 25, 2016. On October 2, 2016, the President of the United States declared the area where the office building was located a federal disaster area. Milo received settlement of his insurance claim for the destruction of his building on January 2, 2017. In order to qualify for nonrecognition of gain on this involuntary conversion, what is the last date for Milo to acquire qualified replacement property?

    a. December 31, 2020   c. December 31, 2021

    b. October 2, 2020   d. January 2, 2021

5. Mikhail owns real estate with a basis of $400,000 and a fair market value of $650,000. He exchanges it for other real estate with a fair market value of $480,000. In addition, Mikhail is relieved of a mortgage on the old property of $200,000, assumes a mortgage on the new property of $100,000, and receives $70,000 in cash. Under Code Section 1031, what is Mikhail's recognized gain on the exchange?

    a. $170,000   c. $70,000

    b. $270,000   d. $350,000

CHAPTER

16

Property Transactions: Capital Gains and Losses

LEARNING OBJECTIVES: *After completing Chapter 16, you should be able to:*

LO.1 Explain the general scheme of taxation for capital gains and losses.

LO.2 Distinguish capital assets from ordinary assets.

LO.3 State and explain the relevance of a sale or exchange to classification as a capital gain or loss and apply the special rules for the capital gain or loss treatment of the retirement of corporate obligations, options, patents, franchises, and lease cancellation payments.

LO.4 Determine whether the holding period for a capital asset is long term or short term.

LO.5 Describe the beneficial tax treatment for capital gains and the detrimental tax treatment for capital losses for noncorporate taxpayers.

LO.6 Describe the tax treatment for capital gains and the detrimental tax treatment for capital losses for corporate taxpayers.

LO.7 Identify tax planning opportunities arising from the sale or exchange of capital assets.

CHAPTER OUTLINE

AUREMAR/SHUTTERSTOCK.COM

MANAGING CAPITAL ASSET TRANSACTIONS

Maurice has come to you for tax advice regarding his investments. He inherited $500,000 from his uncle, Joe. A financial adviser suggested that he make the following investments, which he did nine months ago.

- $5,000 for 100 shares of Eagle Company stock.

- $50,000 for a 50 percent interest in a patent that Kevin, a college roommate who is an unemployed inventor, obtained for a special battery he developed to power green cars. To date, Kevin has been unable to market the battery to an auto manufacturer or supplier, but he has high hopes of doing so in the future.

- $95,000 to purchase a franchise from Orange, Inc.

- $200,000 in the stock of Purple, a publicly held bank that follows a policy of occasionally paying dividends. At one time, the stock appreciated to $300,000, but now it is worth only $210,000. Maurice is considering unloading this stock.

- $50,000 in tax-exempt bonds. The interest rate on the bonds is only 3 percent. Maurice is considering moving this money into taxable bonds that pay 3.5 percent.

- $100,000 for a 10 percent ownership interest as a limited partner in a real estate development. Lots in the development are selling well.

Maurice read an article that talked about the beneficial tax rates for capital assets and dividends. He really liked the part about "costless" capital gains, although he did not understand it.

Maurice has retained his job as a toll booth supervisor at the municipal airport. His annual compensation is $35,000. He likes the job and has met some interesting people there.

Respond to Maurice's request for tax advice.

Read the chapter and formulate your response.

FRAMEWORK 1040 **Tax Formula for Individuals**

This chapter covers the boldfaced portions of the Tax Formula for Individuals that was introduced in Concept Summary 3.1 on p. 3-3. Below those portions are the sections of Form 1040 where the results are reported.

Income *(broadly defined)* .... $ xx,xxx

Less: Exclusions .... (x,xxx)

Gross income .... $ xx,xxx

Less: Deductions *for* adjusted gross income .... (x,xxx)

FORM 1040 (p. 1)

12	Business income or (loss). Attach Schedule C or C-EZ . . . .
13	Capital gain or (loss). Attach Schedule D if required. If not required, check here ▶ ☐
14	Other gains or (losses). Attach Form 4797 . . . .

Adjusted gross income .... $ xx,xxx

Less: The greater of total **itemized deductions** *or* the standard deduction .... (x,xxx)

Personal and dependency exemptions .... (x,xxx)

Taxable income .... $ xx,xxx

Tax on taxable income *(see Tax Tables or Tax Rate Schedules)* .... $ x,xxx

FORM 1040 (p. 2)

| 44 | **Tax** (see instructions). Check if any from: **a** ☐ Form(s) 8814   **b** ☐ Form 4972   **c** ☐ _____ |

Less: Tax credits *(including income taxes withheld and prepaid)* .... (xxx)

Tax due (or refund) .... $ xxx

Fourteen years ago, a taxpayer purchased 100 shares of IBM stock for $17 a share. This year, the taxpayer sells the shares for $150 a share. Should the $133 per-share gain receive any special tax treatment? The $133 gain has built up over 14 years, so it may not be fair to tax it the same as income that was all earned this year.

What if the stock had been purchased for $150 per share and sold for $17 a share? Should the $133 loss be fully deductible? The tax law has an intricate approach to answering these investment activity-related questions.

Property transactions involve the *disposition* of *assets*. The sale of the IBM stock was the disposition of an investment-related asset. As you study this chapter, keep in mind that how investment-related gains and losses are taxed can dramatically affect whether taxpayers make investments, and which investments are made. Except for a brief discussion in Chapter 3, earlier chapters dwelt on how to determine the amount of gain or loss from a property disposition, but did not discuss the classification of gains and losses. This chapter will focus on that topic.

The tax law requires capital gains and capital losses to be separated from other types of gains and losses. There are two reasons for this treatment. First, long-term capital gains may be taxed at a lower rate than ordinary gains. Second, a net capital loss is subject to deduction limitations. For noncorporate taxpayers, a net capital loss is only deductible up to $3,000 per year. Any excess loss over the annual limit carries over and may be deductible in a future tax year.

For these reasons, capital gains and losses must be distinguished from other types of gains and losses. This chapter and the next chapter describe:

- The intricate rules needed to determine what *type* of gains and losses the taxpayer has;

- How those gains and losses are intermingled among themselves;
- How the result of that intermingling then is integrated with the other items on the taxpayer's tax return; and
- How those gains and losses are taxed as part of the taxpayer's taxable income.

As a result of the need to distinguish and separately match capital gains and losses, the individual tax forms include very extensive reporting requirements for capital gains and losses. This chapter explains the rules underlying the forms and illustrates them with an example at the end of the chapter.

16-1 GENERAL SCHEME OF TAXATION

LO.1
Explain the general scheme of taxation for capital gains and losses.

Recognized gains and losses must be properly *classified*. Proper classification depends on three characteristics:

- The tax *status* of the property (capital, § 1231, or ordinary).
- The manner of the property's *disposition* (sale, exchange, casualty, theft, or condemnation).
- The *holding period* of the property (*short-term*: one year or less; *long-term*: more than one year).

The major focus of this chapter is capital gains and losses. Chapter 17 discusses § 1231 assets. Both chapters discuss ordinary gains and losses.

16-2 CAPITAL ASSETS

LO.2
Distinguish capital assets from ordinary assets.

Personal use assets and investment assets are the most common capital assets owned by individual taxpayers. Personal use assets usually include things like a residence, furniture, clothing, recreational equipment, and automobiles. Investment assets usually include stocks, bonds, and mutual funds. Remember, however, that losses from the sale or exchange of personal use assets are not recognized.

The crux of capital asset determination hinges on whether the asset is held for personal use (capital asset), investment (capital asset), or business (ordinary asset). How a taxpayer uses the property typically answers this question.

EXAMPLE
1

David buys an expensive painting.

- If David purchased the painting for personal use (as a decoration in his home) and it is not of investment quality, it is a capital asset; however, any loss on its sale is not usable, whereas gain from its sale is taxable. Investment quality generally means that the painting is expected to appreciate in value.

- If the painting is used to decorate David's business office and is of investment quality, the painting is not depreciable and, therefore, is a capital asset.

- If David's business is buying and selling paintings, the painting is inventory and, therefore, an ordinary asset.

- If the painting is not of investment quality and the business did not purchase it for investment, the painting is an ordinary asset and it is depreciable even though it serves a decorative purpose in David's office. If David depreciates the painting, that is evidence that the painting is held for use in his business (and *not* being held for investment or as inventory). As a result, it is not a capital asset.

Since capital assets are provided preferential tax treatment, taxpayers prefer capital gains rather than ordinary gains. So the definition of a capital asset is critically important. As discussed next, this definition has been the subject of many court cases and rulings.

16-2a **Definition of a Capital Asset (§ 1221)**

Capital assets are not directly defined in the Code. Instead, § 1221(a) defines what is *not* a capital asset. In general, a capital asset is property *other than* inventory, accounts and notes receivable, supplies, and most fixed assets of a business.

Specifically, the Code defines a capital asset as property held by the taxpayer (when it is connected with the taxpayer's business) that is *not* any of the following:

- Inventory or property held primarily for sale to customers in the ordinary course of a business.[1]
- Accounts and notes receivable generated from the sale of goods or services in a business.
- Depreciable property or real estate used in a business.
- Certain copyrights; literary, musical, or artistic compositions; or letters, memoranda, or similar property created by or for the taxpayer.[2]
- Certain U.S. government publications.
- Supplies used in a a business.

Often, the only business asset that is a capital asset is "self-generated" goodwill (purchased goodwill is a § 1231 asset). The following discussion provides further detail on each part of the capital asset definition.

Inventory

What constitutes inventory is determined by the taxpayer's business.

Inventory Determination

EXAMPLE 2

Green Company buys and sells used cars. Its cars are inventory. Its gains from the sale of the cars are ordinary income.

EXAMPLE 3

Soong sells her personal use automobile at a $500 gain. The automobile is a personal use asset and, therefore, a capital asset. The gain is a capital gain.

No asset is inherently capital or ordinary. If Soong (Example 3) sells her "capital asset" automobile to Green Company (Example 2), that same automobile loses its capital asset status, because it is inventory to Green Company. Whether an asset is capital or ordinary, therefore, depends entirely on the relationship of the asset to the taxpayer who sold it. This classification dilemma is but one feature of capital asset treatment that makes this area so confusing and complicated.

Accounts and Notes Receivable

Accounts and notes receivable are often created as part of a business transaction. These assets may be collected by the creditor, be sold by the creditor, or become completely or partially worthless. Also, the creditor may be on the accrual or cash basis of accounting.

Collection of an *accrual basis* account or note receivable does not result in a gain or loss because the amount collected equals the receivable's basis. If sold, an ordinary gain or loss is generated if the receivable is sold for more or less than its basis (the receivable

---

[1]The Supreme Court, in *Malat v. Riddell*, defined *primarily* as meaning "of first importance or principally" [66–1 USTC ¶9317, 17 AFTR 2d 604, 86 S.Ct. 1030 (USSC, 1966)].

[2]§ 1221(b)(3).

is an ordinary asset). If the receivable is partially or wholly worthless, the creditor has a "bad debt," which may result in an ordinary deduction (see text Section 7-1).

Collection of a *cash basis* account or note receivable does not result in a gain or loss because the amount collected is ordinary income. In addition, a cash basis receivable has a zero basis since no revenue is recorded until the receivable is collected. If sold, an ordinary gain is generated (the receivable is an ordinary asset). There is no bad debt deduction for cash basis receivables because they have no basis. See text Section 16-3 for more details on "sale or exchange."

Oriole Company has accounts receivable of $100,000. Because Oriole needs working capital, it sells the receivables for $83,000 to a financial institution.

If Oriole is an *accrual basis taxpayer*, it has a $17,000 ordinary loss. Revenue of $100,000 would have been recorded, and a $100,000 basis would have been established when the receivable was created.

If Oriole is a *cash basis taxpayer*, it has $83,000 of ordinary income because it would not have recorded any revenue earlier; thus, the receivable has no tax basis.

Business Fixed Assets

Depreciable personal property and real estate (both depreciable and nondepreciable) used by a business are *not* capital assets. The tax law related to this property is very complex; most of these rules are discussed in Chapter 17. Although business fixed assets are not capital assets, a long-term capital gain can sometimes result from their sale. Chapter 17 discusses the potential capital gain treatment for business fixed assets under § 1231. Another rule—real property subdivided for sale (§ 1237)—is discussed in text Section 16-2c.

Copyrights and Creative Works

Generally, the person whose efforts led to the copyright or creative work has an ordinary asset, not a capital asset. *Creative works* include the works of authors, composers, and artists. Also, the person for whom a letter, a memorandum, or another similar property was created has an ordinary asset. Finally, a person receiving a copyright, creative work, a letter, a memorandum, or similar property by gift from the creator or the person for whom the work was created has an ordinary asset. A taxpayer may elect to treat the sale or exchange of a musical composition or a copyright of a musical work as the disposition of a capital asset. Patents are subject to special rules discussed later in text Section 16-3d.

Creative Works

Wanda is a part-time music composer. A music publisher purchases one of her songs for $5,000.

Wanda has a $5,000 ordinary gain from the sale of an ordinary asset unless she elects to treat the gain as a capital gain.

Ed received a letter from the President of the United States in 1982. In the current year, Ed sells the letter to a collector for $300.

Ed has a $300 ordinary gain from the sale of an ordinary asset (because the letter was created for Ed).

Isabella gives her son a song she composed. The son sells the song to a music publisher for $5,000.

The son has a $5,000 ordinary gain from the sale of an ordinary asset unless he elects to treat the gain as a capital gain.

If the son inherits the song from Isabella, his basis for the song is its fair market value at Isabella's death. In this situation, the song is a capital asset because the son's basis is not related to Isabella's basis for the song.

ETHICS & EQUITY **Sculpture as a Capital Asset**

Cynthia is a successful sculptor who created a work that is now worth $400,000 and has no tax basis. Cynthia forms a corporation and contributes the sculpture to it in exchange for the corporation's shares. Fourteen months later, she sells all the stock for $400,000. She wants to treat the sale of the stock as a long-term capital gain. Evaluate the propriety of Cynthia's actions.

U.S. Government Publications

U.S. government publications received from the U.S. government (or its agencies) for a reduced price are *not* capital assets. This prevents a taxpayer from later donating the publications to charity and claiming a charitable contribution deduction equal to the fair market value of the publications. A charitable contribution of an ordinary asset generally is equal to the asset's basis. If the taxpayer received it at no cost, its basis is equal to zero. If this property is given to someone else, it retains its ordinary asset status (see text Section 10-4e for more about property contributions).

16-2b **Effect of Judicial Action**

Because the Code only lists categories of what are *not* capital assets, judicial interpretation is sometimes required to determine whether a specific item fits into one of those categories. The Supreme Court follows a literal interpretation of the categories. For instance, because corporate stock is not mentioned in § 1221, it is *usually* a capital asset. However, what if corporate stock is purchased for resale to customers? Then it is *inventory* and not a capital asset because inventory is one of the categories in § 1221.

Intent also matters. What happens when a taxpayer who normally does not acquire stock for resale to customers acquires stock with the intention of resale? The Supreme Court decided that because the stock was not acquired primarily for sale to customers (the taxpayer did not sell the stock to its regular customers), the stock was a capital asset.[3]

Because of the uncertainty associated with capital asset status, Congress has enacted several Code Sections to clarify its definition. These clarifications are discussed next.

16-2c **Statutory Expansions**

In several instances, Congress has clarified its general definition of what is *not* a capital asset.

Dealers in Securities

As a general rule, securities (stocks, bonds, and other financial instruments) held by a dealer are considered to be inventory and are, therefore, not subject to capital gain or loss treatment. A *dealer in securities* is a merchant (e.g., a brokerage firm) that regularly engages in the purchase and resale of securities to customers. The dealer must identify any securities being held for investment. Generally, if a dealer clearly identifies certain securities as held for investment purposes by the close of business on the acquisition date, gain from the securities' sale will be capital gain. However, the gain will not be capital gain if the dealer ceases to hold the securities for investment prior to the sale. Losses are capital losses if at any time the securities have been clearly identified by the dealer as held for investment.

---

[3]*Arkansas Best v. Comm.*, 88–1 USTC ¶9210, 61 AFTR 2d 88–655, 108 S.Ct. 971 (USSC, 1988).

Tracy is a securities dealer. She purchases 100 shares of Swan stock. If Tracy takes no further action, the stock is inventory and an ordinary asset. If she designates in her records that the stock is held for investment, the stock is a capital asset. Tracy must designate the investment purpose by the close of business on the acquisition date. If Tracy maintains her investment purpose and later sells the stock, the gain or loss is capital gain or loss. If Tracy redesignates the stock as held for resale (inventory) and then sells it, any gain is ordinary, but any loss is capital loss.

Real Property Subdivided for Sale (§ 1237)

Substantial real property development activities may result in the owner being considered a dealer for tax purposes. If so, ordinary income will result from any lots sold. However, § 1237 allows real estate investors capital gain treatment if they engage *only* in *limited* development activities. To be eligible for § 1237 treatment, the following requirements must be met:

- The taxpayer may not be a corporation.
- The taxpayer may not be a real estate dealer.
- No substantial improvements may be made to the lots sold. *Substantial* generally means more than a 10 percent increase in the value of a lot. Shopping centers and other commercial or residential buildings are considered substantial, while filling, draining, leveling, and clearing operations are not.
- The taxpayer must have held the lots sold for at least 5 years, except for inherited property. The substantial improvements test is less stringent if the property is held at least 10 years.

If these requirements are met, all gain is capital gain until the tax year in which the *sixth* lot is sold. Sales of contiguous lots to a single buyer in the same transaction count as the sale of one lot. Beginning with the tax year the *sixth* lot is sold, 5 percent of the revenue from lot sales is potential ordinary income. That potential ordinary income is offset by any selling expenses from the lot sales. As sales commissions often are at least 5 percent of the sales price, typically none of the gain is treated as ordinary income.

Section 1237 does not apply to losses. A loss from the sale of subdivided real property is an ordinary loss unless the property qualifies as a capital asset under § 1221. The following example illustrates the application of § 1237.

EXAMPLE
9

Jack owns a large tract of land and subdivides it for sale. Assume that Jack meets all of the requirements of § 1237 and during the tax year sells the first 10 lots to 10 different buyers for $10,000 each. Jack's basis in each lot sold is $3,000, and he incurs total selling expenses of $4,000 ($400 for each lot) on the sales. Jack's gain is computed as follows:

Selling price (10 × $10,000)	$100,000	
Less: Selling expenses (10 × $400)	(4,000)	
Amount realized		$ 96,000
Basis (10 × $3,000)		(30,000)
Realized and recognized gain		$ 66,000
Classification of recognized gain:		
Ordinary income		
Five percent of selling price (5% × $100,000)	$ 5,000	
Less: Selling expenses	(4,000)	
Ordinary gain		1,000
Capital gain		$ 65,000

A portion of the gain is given ordinary treatment because the *sixth* lot is sold in the current year.

Nonbusiness Bad Debts

A loan not made in the ordinary course of business is classified as a nonbusiness receivable. In the year the receivable becomes completely worthless, it is a *nonbusiness bad debt*, and the bad debt is treated as a short-term capital loss. Even if the receivable was outstanding for more than one year, the loss is still a short-term capital loss. Chapter 7 discusses nonbusiness bad debts more thoroughly (see text Section 7-1b).

LO.3

State and explain the relevance of a sale or exchange to classification as a capital gain or loss and apply the special rules for the capital gain or loss treatment of the retirement of corporate obligations, options, patents, franchises, and lease cancellation payments.

16-3 **SALE OR EXCHANGE**

Recognition of capital gain or loss usually requires a sale or exchange of a capital asset. The Code uses the term sale or exchange , but does not define it. Generally, a property *sale* involves the receipt of money by the seller and/or the assumption by the purchaser of the seller's liabilities. An *exchange* involves the transfer of property for other property. Thus, an involuntary conversion (casualty, theft, or condemnation) is not a sale or exchange.

In several situations, Congress has created rules that specifically provide for sale or exchange treatment. For example, assume that the expiration of a right to personal property (other than stock) that would be a capital asset in the hands of the taxpayer results in a recognized gain or loss. This is a capital gain or loss.[4] Several of these special rules are discussed below, including worthless securities, the retirement of corporate obligations, options, patents, franchises, and lease cancellation payments.

16-3a **Worthless Securities and § 1244 Stock**

Occasionally, securities such as stock and, especially, bonds may become worthless due to the insolvency of their issuer. If such a security is a capital asset, the loss is deemed to have occurred as the result of a sale or exchange on the *last day* of the tax year.[5] This last-day rule may have the effect of converting what otherwise would have been a short-term capital loss into a long-term capital loss. Section 1244 allows an ordinary deduction on disposition of stock at a loss. The stock must be that of a small business corporation, and the ordinary deduction is limited to $50,000 ($100,000 for married taxpayers filing jointly) per year. See Chapter 7 (and text Sections 7-2a and 7-2b) for a more complete discussion of these rules.

16-3b **Special Rule—Retirement of Corporate Obligations**

A debt obligation (e.g., a bond or note payable) may have a tax basis in excess of or less than its redemption value because it may have been acquired at a premium or discount. Consequently, the collection of the redemption value may result in a loss or gain. Generally, the collection of a debt obligation is *treated* as a sale or exchange.[6] Therefore, any loss or gain can be a capital loss or capital gain because a sale or exchange has taken place.

EXAMPLE 10

Fran acquires $1,000 of Osprey Corporation bonds for $980 in the open market. If the bonds are held to maturity, the $20 difference between Fran's collection of the $1,000 redemption value and her cost of $980 is treated as capital gain.

Original Issue Discount (§§ 1272–1288)

The benefit of the sale or exchange exception that allows a capital gain from the collection of certain obligations is reduced when the obligation has original issue discount. Original issue discount (OID) arises when the issue price of a debt obligation is

---

[4]§ 1234A.
[5]§ 165(g)(1).

[6]§ 1271.

less than the maturity value of the obligation. OID must generally be amortized over the life of the debt obligation using the effective interest method. The OID amortization increases the basis of the bond.

Most new publicly traded bond issues do not carry OID because the stated interest rate is set to make the market price on issue the same as the bond's face amount. In addition, even if the issue price is less than the face amount, the difference is not considered to be OID if the difference is less than one-fourth of 1 percent of the redemption price at maturity multiplied by the number of years to maturity.[7]

In the case where OID does exist, it may or may not have to be amortized, depending upon the date the obligation was issued. When OID is amortized, the amount of gain upon collection, sale, or exchange of the obligation is correspondingly reduced. The obligations covered by the OID amortization rules and the method of amortization are presented in §§ 1272–1275. Similar rules for other obligations can be found in §§ 1276–1288.

Jerry purchases $10,000 of newly issued White Corporation bonds for $6,000. The bonds have OID of $4,000. Jerry must amortize the discount over the life of the bonds. The OID amortization *increases* his interest income. (The bonds were selling at a discount because the market rate of interest was greater than the bonds' stated interest rate.) After Jerry has amortized $1,800 of OID, he sells the bonds for $8,000. Jerry has a capital gain of $200 [$8,000 − ($6,000 cost + $1,800 OID amortization)].

The OID amortization rules prevent him from converting ordinary interest income into capital gain. Without the OID amortization, Jerry would have capital gain of $2,000 ($8,000 − $6,000 cost).

16-3c **Options**

Frequently, a potential buyer of property wants some time to make the purchase decision, but wants to control the sale and/or the sale price in the meantime. **Options** are used to achieve these objectives. The potential purchaser (grantee) pays the property owner (grantor) for an option on the property. The grantee then becomes the option holder. The option, which usually sets a price at which the grantee can buy the property, expires after a specified period of time.

Sale of an Option

A grantee may sell or exchange the option rather than exercising it or letting it expire. Generally, the grantee's sale or exchange of the option results in capital gain or loss if the option property is (or would be) a capital asset to the grantee.[8]

Rosa wants to buy some vacant land for investment purposes. However, she cannot afford the full purchase price at the present time. Instead, Rosa (grantee) pays the landowner (grantor) $3,000 to obtain an option to buy the land for $100,000 anytime in the next two years. The option is a capital asset for Rosa because if she actually purchased the land, the land would be a capital asset.

Three months after purchasing the option, Rosa sells it for $7,000. She has a $4,000 ($7,000 − $3,000) short-term capital gain on this sale because she held the option for one year or less.

Failure to Exercise Options

If an option holder (grantee) fails to exercise the option, the lapse of the option is considered a sale or exchange on the option expiration date. Thus, the loss is a capital loss if the property subject to the option is (or would be) a capital asset in the hands of the grantee.

---

[7]§ 1273(a)(3).

[8]§ 1234(a) and Reg. § 1.1234–1(a)(1). Stock options are discussed in Chapter 19.

The grantor of an option on *stocks, securities, commodities, or commodity futures* receives short-term capital gain treatment upon the expiration of the option. Options on property *other than* stocks, securities, commodities, or commodity futures (for instance, vacant land) result in ordinary income to the grantor when the option expires.

For example, an individual investor who owns certain stock (a capital asset) may sell a call option, entitling the buyer of the option to acquire the stock at a specified price higher than the value at the date the option is granted. The writer of the call receives a premium (e.g., 10 percent) for writing the option. If the price of the stock does not increase during the option period, the option will expire unexercised. Upon the expiration of the option, the grantor must recognize short-term capital gain (whereas the grantee recognizes a loss, the character of which depends on the underlying asset). These provisions do not apply to options held for sale to customers (the inventory of a securities dealer).

Exercise of Options by Grantee

If the option is exercised, the amount paid for the option is added to the optioned property's selling price. This increases the gain (or reduces the loss) to the grantor resulting from the sale of the property. The grantor's gain or loss is capital or ordinary depending on the tax status of the property. The grantee adds the cost of the option to the basis of the property purchased.

The Big Picture

EXAMPLE 13

Return to the facts of *The Big Picture* on p. 16-1. On February 1, 2017, Maurice purchases 100 shares of Eagle Company stock for $5,000. On April 1, 2017, he writes a call option on the stock, giving the grantee the right to buy the stock for $6,000 during the following six-month period. Maurice (the grantor) receives a call premium of $500 for writing the call.

- If the call is exercised by the grantee on August 1, 2017, Maurice has $1,500 ($6,000 + $500 − $5,000) of short-term capital gain from the sale of the stock. The grantee has a $6,500 ($500 option premium + $6,000 purchase price) basis for the stock.

- Investors sometimes get nervous and want to "lock in" gains or losses.
  - Assume that Maurice, prior to exercise of the grantee's call, decides to sell his stock for $6,000 and enters into a closing transaction by purchasing a call on 100 shares of Eagle Company stock for $5,000.
  - Because the Eagle stock is selling for $6,000, Maurice must pay a call premium of $1,000.
  - He recognizes a $500 short-term capital loss [$500 (call premium received) − $1,000 (call premium paid)] on the closing transaction.
  - On the actual sale of the Eagle stock, Maurice has a short-term capital gain of $1,000 [$6,000 (selling price) − $5,000 (cost)].
  - The original grantee is not affected by Maurice's closing transaction. The original option is still in existence, and the grantee's tax consequences depend on what action the grantee takes—exercising the option, letting the option expire, or selling the option.

- Assume that the original option expired unexercised. Maurice has a $500 short-term capital gain equal to the call premium received for writing the option. This gain is not recognized until the option expires. The grantee has a loss from expiration of the option. The nature of the loss will depend upon whether the option was a capital asset or an ordinary asset.

Concept Summary 16.1 summarizes the consequences of various transactions involving options, to both the grantor and grantee.

Concept Summary 16.1

Options: Consequences to the Grantor and Grantee

Event	Effect on	
	Grantor	**Grantee**
Option is granted.	Receives value and has a contract obligation (a liability).	Pays value and has a contract right (an asset).
Option expires.	Has a short-term capital gain if the option property is stocks, securities, commodities, or commodity futures. Otherwise, gain is ordinary income.	Has a loss (capital loss if option property would have been a capital asset for the grantee).
Option is exercised.	Amount received for option increases proceeds from sale of the option property.	Amount paid for option becomes part of the basis of the option property purchased.
Option is sold or exchanged by grantee.	Result depends upon whether option later expires or is exercised (see above).	Could have gain or loss (capital gain or loss if option property would have been a capital asset for the grantee).

16-3d Patents

Transfer of a patent is treated as the sale or exchange of a long-term capital asset when *all substantial rights* to the patent are transferred by a *holder*.[9] The transferor/holder may receive payment in virtually any form, including contingent payments based on the transferee/purchaser's productivity, use, or disposition of the patent. If the transfer meets these requirements, any gain or loss is *automatically a long-term* capital gain or loss. Whether the asset was a capital asset for the transferor, whether a sale or exchange occurred, and how long the transferor held the patent are not relevant.

Substantial Rights

To receive favorable capital gain treatment, *all substantial rights* to the patent must be transferred. All substantial rights have not been transferred when the transfer is limited geographically within the issuing country or when the transfer is for a period less than the remaining life of the patent. All the facts and circumstances of the transaction, not just the language of the transfer document, are examined when making this determination.[10]

Example 14 illustrates the special treatment for patents.

The Big Picture

EXAMPLE 14

Return to the facts of *The Big Picture* on p. 16-1. Kevin transfers his remaining 50% share of the rights in the patent to the Green Battery Company, Inc., in exchange for a $1 million lump-sum payment plus $.50 for each battery sold. Assuming that Kevin has transferred all substantial rights, the question of whether the transfer is a sale or exchange of a capital asset is not relevant. Kevin automatically has a long-term capital gain from both the $1 million lump-sum payment and the $.50 per battery royalty to the extent those proceeds exceed his basis for the patent.

Kevin also had an automatic long-term capital gain when he sold the other 50% of his rights in the patent to Maurice, because Kevin transferred an undivided interest that included all substantial rights in the patent.

Whether Maurice gets long-term capital gain treatment depends upon whether Maurice is a holder. See the following discussion and Example 15.

Holder Defined

The *holder* of a patent must be an *individual* (normally the invention's creator or an individual who purchases the patent rights from the creator before the patented invention is reduced to practice). So if the creator's employer has all rights to an employee's inventions,

---

[9]§ 1235. [10]Reg. § 1.1235–2(b)(1).

the employer is *not* eligible for long-term capital gain treatment. The employer will normally have an ordinary asset because the patent was developed as part of its business.

The Big Picture

EXAMPLE 15

Return to the facts of *The Big Picture* on p. 16-1. Continuing with the facts of Example 14, Kevin is clearly a holder of the patent because he is the inventor and was not an employee when he invented the battery. When Maurice purchased a 50% interest in the patent nine months ago, he became a holder if the patent had not yet been reduced to practice. Because the patent apparently was not being utilized in the manufacturing process at the time of the purchase, it had not been reduced to practice.

Consequently, Maurice is also a holder, and he has an automatic long-term capital gain or loss if he transfers all substantial rights in his 50% interest to the Green Battery Company. Maurice's basis for his share of the patent is $50,000, and his proceeds equal $1 million plus $.50 for each battery sold. Thus, Maurice has a long-term capital gain even though he has not held his interest in the patent for more than one year.

16-3e Franchises, Trademarks, and Trade Names (§ 1253)

A mode of operation, a widely recognized brand name (trade name), and a widely known business symbol (trademark) are all valuable assets. These assets may be licensed (commonly known as franchising) by their owner for use by other businesses. Many fast-food restaurants (such as McDonald's and Taco Bell) are franchises. The franchisee usually pays the owner (franchisor) an initial fee plus a contingent fee. The contingent fee is often based upon the franchisee's sales volume.

For Federal income tax purposes, a franchise is an agreement that gives the franchisee the right to distribute, sell, or provide goods, services, or facilities within a specified area.[11] A franchise transfer includes the grant of a franchise, a transfer by one franchisee to another person, or the renewal of a franchise.

Section 1253 provides that a transfer of a franchise, trademark, or trade name is not a transfer of a capital asset when the transferor retains any significant power, right, or continuing interest in the property transferred.

Significant Power, Right, or Continuing Interest

In most franchising operations, the transferor retains some powers or rights. As a result, the transaction is *not* a capital asset transfer. *Significant powers, rights, or continuing interests* include control over franchise assignment, quality of products and services, sale or advertising of products or services, the requirement that substantially all supplies and equipment be purchased from the transferor, and the right to terminate the franchise.

In the unusual case where the transferor does not retain any significant power, right, or continuing interest, a capital gain or loss may occur. For capital gain or loss treatment to be available, the asset transferred must qualify as a capital asset.

The Big Picture

EXAMPLE 16

Return to the facts of *The Big Picture* on p. 16-1. Maurice sells for $210,000 to Mauve, Inc., the franchise purchased from Orange, Inc., nine months ago. The $210,000 received by Maurice is not contingent, and all significant powers, rights, and continuing interests are transferred.

The $115,000 gain ($210,000 proceeds − $95,000 basis) is a short-term capital gain because Maurice has held the franchise for only nine months.

Franchise Payments

In most franchise settings, when the transferor retains significant power or rights, both contingent (e.g., based on sales) and noncontingent payments occur.

Noncontingent Payments Any noncontingent payments made by the franchisee to the franchisor are ordinary income to the franchisor. The franchisee capitalizes the

---

[11]§ 1253(b)(1).

payments and amortizes them over 15 years. If the franchise is sold, the amortization is subject to recapture under § 1245.[12]

Grey Company signs a 10-year franchise agreement with DOH Donuts. Grey (the franchisee) makes payments of $3,000 per year for the first 8 years of the franchise agreement—a total of $24,000. Grey cannot deduct $3,000 per year as the payments are made. Instead, Grey may amortize the $24,000 total over 15 years. Thus, Grey may deduct $1,600 per year for each of the 15 years of the amortization period.

The same result would occur if Grey made a $24,000 lump-sum payment at the beginning of the franchise period. Assuming that DOH Donuts (the franchisor) retains significant powers, rights, or a continuing interest, it will have ordinary income when it receives the payments from Grey.

Contingent Payments Any contingent franchise payments are ordinary income for the franchisor and an ordinary deduction for the franchisee. Contingent payments must meet the following requirements:

• The payments are made at least annually throughout the term of the transfer agreement.

• The payments are substantially equal in amount or are payable under a fixed formula.

TAK, a spicy chicken franchisor, transfers an eight-year franchise to Otis. TAK retains a significant power, right, or continuing interest. Otis, the franchisee, agrees to pay TAK 15% of sales. This contingent payment is ordinary income to TAK and a business deduction for Otis as the payments are made.

Sports Franchises

Professional sports franchises (e.g., the Detroit Tigers) are subject to § 1253.[13] Player contracts are usually one of the major assets acquired with a sports franchise. These contracts last only for the time stated in the contract. By being classified as § 197 intangibles, the player contracts and other intangible assets acquired in the purchase of the sports franchise are amortized over a statutory 15-year period.[14]

Concept Summary 16.2 reviews the effects of transactions involving franchises on both the franchisor and franchisee.

Concept Summary 16.2

Franchises: Consequences to the Franchisor and Franchisee

Event	Effect on	
	Franchisor	**Franchisee**
Franchisor Retains Significant Powers and Rights		
Noncontingent payment	Ordinary income.	Capitalized and amortized over 15 years as an ordinary deduction; if franchise is sold, amortization is subject to recapture under § 1245.
Contingent payment	Ordinary income.	Ordinary deduction.
Franchisor Does *Not* Retain Significant Powers and Rights		
Noncontingent payment	Ordinary income if franchise rights are an ordinary asset; capital gain if franchise rights are a capital asset (unlikely).	Capitalized and amortized over 15 years as an ordinary deduction; if the franchise is sold, amortization is subject to recapture under § 1245.
Contingent payment	Ordinary income.	Ordinary deduction.

---

[12]See Chapter 17 for a discussion of the recapture provisions.

[13]Section 1253(e) previously exempted sports franchises from § 1253, but was repealed for franchises acquired after October 22, 2004.

[14]§ 197(a).

16-3f **Lease Cancellation Payments**

The tax treatment of payments received for canceling a lease depends on whether the recipient is the **lessor** or the **lessee** and whether the lease is a capital asset.

Lessee Treatment

Lease cancellation payments received by a lessee are treated as an exchange.[15] The treatment of these payments depends on the underlying use of the property and how long the lease has existed.[16]

- If the property was used personally (e.g., an apartment used as a residence), the payment results in a capital gain (and long term if the lease existed for more than one year).
- If the property was used for business and the lease existed for one year or less, the payment results in ordinary income.
- If the property was used for business and the lease existed for more than one year, the payment results in a § 1231 gain.

Mark owns an apartment building that he is going to convert into an office building. Vicki is one of the apartment tenants and receives $1,000 from Mark to cancel the lease.

   Vicki has a capital gain of $1,000 (which is long term or short term depending upon how long she has held the lease). Mark has an ordinary deduction of $1,000.

Lessor Treatment

Payments received by a lessor for a lease cancellation are always ordinary income because they are considered to be in lieu of rental payments.[17]

Floyd owns an apartment building near a university campus. Hui-Fen is one of the tenants. Hui-Fen is graduating early and offers Floyd $800 to cancel the apartment lease. Floyd accepts the offer.

   Floyd has ordinary income of $800. Hui-Fen has a nondeductible payment because the apartment was personal use property.

Determine whether the holding period for a capital asset is long term or short term.

16-4 **HOLDING PERIOD**

16-4a **General Rules**

Property must be held *more than one year* to qualify for long-term capital gain or loss treatment.[18] Property held for one year or less results in short-term capital gain or loss. To compute the **holding period**, start counting on the day *after* the property was acquired and include the day of disposition.

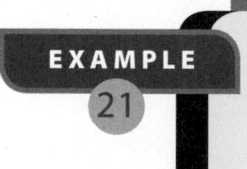

Return to the facts of *The Big Picture* on p. 16-1. Assume that Maurice purchased the Purple stock on January 15, 2017. If he sells it on January 16, 2018, Maurice's holding period is more than one year and the gain or loss is long term.

   If instead Maurice sells the stock on January 15, 2018, the holding period is exactly one year and the gain or loss is short term.

---

[15]§ 1241 and Reg. § 1.1241–1(a).

[16]Reg. § 1.1221–1(b) and PLR 200045019.

[17]Reg. § 1.61–8(b).

[18]§ 1222(3).

To be held for more than one year, a capital asset acquired on the last day of any month must not be sold until on or after the first day of the thirteenth succeeding month.[19]

Leo purchases a capital asset on February 28, 2017. If Leo sells the asset on February 28, 2018, the holding period is one year and Leo will have a short-term capital gain or loss.

If Leo sells the asset on March 1, 2018, the holding period is more than one year and he will have a long-term capital gain or loss.

16-4b **Special Holding Period Rules**

There are several special holding period rules.[20] The application of these rules depends upon the type of asset and how it was acquired.

Nontaxable Exchanges

The holding period of property received in a like-kind exchange includes the holding period of the former asset if the property that has been exchanged is a capital asset or a § 1231 asset. In these settings, the holding period of the former property is *tacked on* to the holding period of the newly acquired property.

On April 22, 2017, Vern exchanges a business truck he acquired on March 15, 2014, for another truck in a qualifying like-kind exchange.

The holding period of the replacement truck begins March 15, 2014, because the holding period of the truck given up in the exchange *tacks* to the holding period of the replacement truck.

Gifts

When a gift occurs, if the donor's basis carries over to the recipient, the donor's holding period is *tacked on* to the recipient's holding period. This will occur when the property's fair market value at the date of the gift is greater than the donor's adjusted basis. These transactions are discussed in Chapter 14.

Carryover Basis

Kareem acquires 100 shares of Robin Corporation stock for $1,000 on December 31, 2013. He transfers the shares by gift to Megan on December 31, 2016, when the stock is worth $2,000. Kareem's basis of $1,000 becomes the basis for determining gain or loss on a subsequent sale by Megan. Megan's holding period begins with the date the stock was acquired by Kareem.

Assume the same facts as in Example 24, except that the fair market value of the shares is only $800 on the date of the gift. The holding period begins on the date of the gift if Megan sells the stock for a loss. The value of the shares on the date of the gift is used in the determination of her basis for loss. If she sells the shares for $500 on April 1, 2017, Megan has a $300 recognized capital loss and the holding period is from December 31, 2016, to April 1, 2017 (thus, the loss is short term).

Certain Disallowed Loss Transactions

Under several Code provisions, realized losses are disallowed. When a loss is disallowed, there is no carryover of holding period. Losses can be disallowed under § 267 (sale or exchange between related taxpayers) and § 262 (sale or exchange of personal use assets) as well as other Code Sections. Taxpayers who acquire property in a disallowed loss transaction will have a new holding period begin and will have a basis equal to the purchase price.

---

[19]Rev.Rul. 66–7, 1966–1 C.B. 188.   [20]§ 1223.

EXAMPLE 26

Janet sells her personal automobile at a loss. She may not deduct the loss because it arises from the sale of personal use property. Janet purchases a replacement automobile for more than the selling price of her former automobile. Janet has a basis equal to the cost of the replacement automobile, and her holding period begins when she acquires the replacement automobile.

Inherited Property

The holding period for inherited property is treated as long term no matter how long the property is actually held by the heir. The holding period of the decedent or the decedent's estate is not relevant for the heir's holding period.

EXAMPLE 27

Shonda inherits Blue Company stock from her father, who died in 2017. She receives the stock on April 1, 2017, and sells it on November 1, 2017. Even though Shonda did not hold the stock more than one year, she receives long-term capital gain or loss treatment on the sale.

16-4c Special Rules for Short Sales

General

The Code provides special holding period rules for short sales.[21] A **short sale** occurs when a taxpayer sells borrowed property and repays the lender with substantially identical property either held on the date of the sale or purchased after the sale.

Short sales usually involve corporate stock. The seller's objective is to make a profit in anticipation of a decline in the stock's price. If the price declines, the seller in a short sale recognizes a profit equal to the difference between the sales price of the borrowed stock and the price paid for the replacement stock.

EXAMPLE 28

Chris does not own any shares of Brown Corporation. However, Chris sells 30 shares of Brown. The shares are borrowed from Chris's broker and must be replaced within 45 days. Chris has a short sale because he was short the shares he sold. He will *close* the short sale by purchasing Brown shares and delivering them to his broker.

If the original 30 shares were sold for $10,000 and Chris later purchases 30 shares for $8,000, he has a gain of $2,000. Chris's hunch that the price of Brown stock would decline was correct. Chris was able to profit from selling high and buying low.

If Chris had to purchase Brown shares for $13,000 to close the short sale, he would have a loss of $3,000. In this case, Chris would have sold low and bought high—not the result he wanted. Chris would be making a short sale against the box if he borrowed shares from his broker to sell and then closed the short sale by delivering other Brown shares he owned at the time he made the short sale.

Concept Summary 16.3 summarizes the short sale rules. These rules are intended to prevent the conversion of short-term capital gains into long-term capital gains and long-term capital losses into short-term capital losses.

In most settings, short sale gain or loss results in a capital gain or loss. The gain or loss is not recognized until the short sale is closed. Generally, the holding period of the short sale property is determined by how long the property used to close the short sale was held. However, when *substantially identical property* (e.g., other shares of the same stock) is held by the taxpayer, the holding period is determined as follows:

- The short sale *gain or loss* is *short term* when, on the short sale date, the substantially identical property has been held *short term* (i.e., for one year or less). (See Examples 29 and 30.)

---

[21]§ 1233.

Concept Summary 16.3

Short Sales of Securities

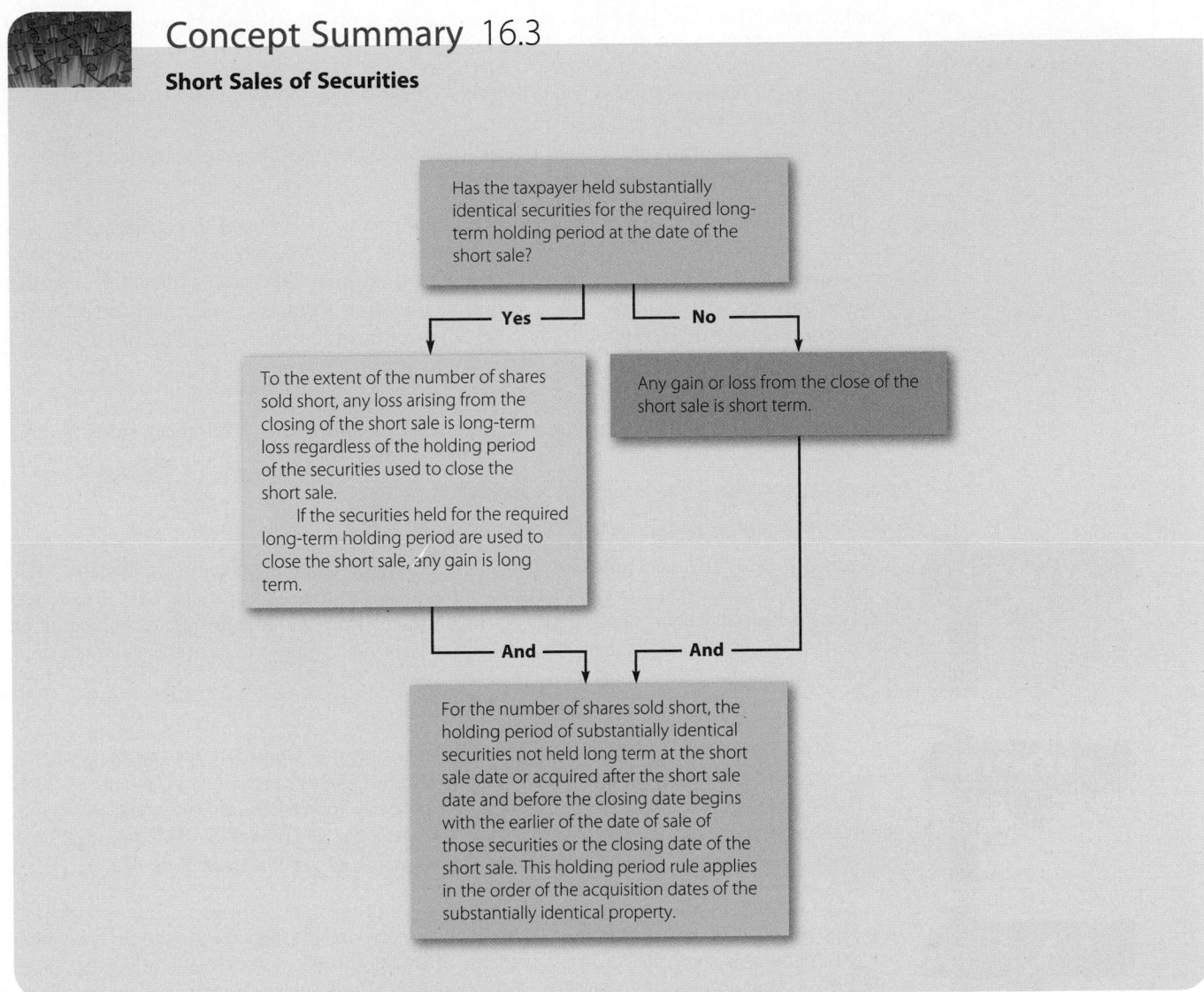

- The short sale *gain* is *long term* when, on the short sale date, the substantially identical property has been held *long term* (i.e., for more than one year) *and* is used to close the short sale. If the long-term substantially identical property is not used to close the short sale, the short sale gain is *short term*. (See Example 31.)

- The short sale *loss* is *long term* when, on the short sale date, the substantially identical property has been held *long term* (i.e., for more than one year).

- The short sale *gain or loss* is *short term* if the substantially identical property is acquired *after* the short sale date and on or before the closing date. (See Example 32.)

Disposition Rules for Short Sales against the Box

A *short sale against the box* occurs when the stock is borrowed from a broker by a seller and the seller already owns the substantially identical securities on the short sale date or acquires them before the closing date.[22] To remove the taxpayer's flexibility as to when the short sale gain must be reported, a constructive sale approach is used. If the taxpayer has not closed the short sale by delivering the short sale securities to the

---

[22]The "box" is the safe deposit box stock owners routinely used to keep stock certificates. Although stockbrokers today generally keep stock for their customers, the terminology *short sale against the box* is still used.

broker *before* January 31 of the year following the short sale, the short sale is deemed to have been closed on the *earlier* of two events:

- On the short sale date if the taxpayer owned substantially identical securities at that time.
- On the date during the year of the short sale that the taxpayer acquired substantially identical securities.[23]

The basis of the shares in the deemed transfer of shares is used to compute the gain or loss on the short sale. As Examples 31 and 32 illustrate, when shares are *actually* transferred to the broker to close the short sale, there may be a gain or loss because the shares transferred will have a basis equal to the short sale date price and the value at the *actual* short sale closing date may be different from the short sale date price.

Illustrations

The following examples illustrate the treatment of short sales and short sales against the box.

Short Sales and Short Sales Against the Box

EXAMPLE 29

On January 4, 2017, Donald purchases five shares of Osprey Corporation common stock for $100. On April 14, 2017, he engages in a short sale of five shares of the same stock for $150. On August 15, Donald closes the short sale by repaying the borrowed stock with the five shares purchased on January 4. Because his substantially identical shares were held short term as of the short sale date, Donald's $50 capital gain is short term.

EXAMPLE 30

Assume the same facts as in the previous example, except that Donald closes the short sale on January 28, 2018, by repaying the borrowed stock with five shares purchased on January 27, 2018, for $200. Because Donald's substantially identical property (purchased on January 4, 2017) was short-term property at the April 14, 2017 short sale date, his $50 capital loss ($200 cost of stock purchased on January 27, 2018, and a short sale selling price of $150) is short term.

EXAMPLE 31

On January 18, 2016, Rita purchases 200 shares of Owl Corporation stock for $1,000. On November 11, 2017, she sells short, for $1,300, 200 shares of Owl Corporation stock that she borrows from her broker. On February 10, 2018, Rita closes the short sale by delivering the 200 shares of Owl Corporation stock that she had acquired in 2016. On that date, Owl Corporation stock had a market price of $3 per share.

Because Rita owned substantially identical stock on the date of the short sale and did not close the short sale before January 31, 2018, she is *deemed* to have closed the short sale on November 11, 2017 (the date of the short sale). On her 2017 tax return, she reports a $300 long-term capital gain ($1,300 short sale price − $1,000 basis).

On February 10, 2018, Rita has a $700 short-term capital loss [$600 short sale closing date price (200 shares × $3 per share) − $1,300 basis] because the holding period of the shares used to close the short sale commences with the date of the short sale.

EXAMPLE 32

Assume the same facts as in Example 31, except that Rita did not own any Owl Corporation stock on the short sale date and acquired the 200 shares of Owl Corporation stock for $1,000 on December 12, 2017 (after the November 11, 2017 short sale date).

The *deemed* closing of the short sale is December 12, 2017, because Rita held substantially identical shares at the end of 2017 and did not close the short sale before January 31, 2018. Her 2017 short sale gain is a *short-term* gain of $300 ($1,300 short sale price − $1,000 basis), and she still has a short-term capital loss of $700 on February 10, 2018.

---

[23]§ 1259.

16-5 TAX TREATMENT OF CAPITAL GAINS AND LOSSES OF NONCORPORATE TAXPAYERS

LO.5

Describe the beneficial tax treatment for capital gains and the detrimental tax treatment for capital losses for noncorporate taxpayers.

All taxpayers net their capital gains and losses. Short-term gains and losses (if any) are netted against one another, and long-term gains and losses (if any) are netted against one another. The results will be net short-term gain or loss and net long-term gain or loss. If these two net positions are of opposite sign (one is a gain and one is a loss), they are netted against each other.

Six possibilities exist for the result after all possible netting has been completed.

1. A net long-term capital gain (NLTCG).
2. A net short-term capital gain (NSTCG).
3. Both NLTCG and NSTCG.
4. A net long-term capital loss (NLTCL).
5. A net short-term capital loss (NSTCL).
6. Both NLTCL and NSTCL.

Net long-term capital gains of noncorporate taxpayers are eligible for an alternative tax calculation that normally results in a lower tax liability. Neither NLTCLs nor NSTCLs are treated as ordinary losses. Treatment as an ordinary loss generally is preferable to capital loss treatment because ordinary losses are deductible in full while the deductibility of capital losses is subject to certain limitations. An individual taxpayer may deduct a maximum of $3,000 of net capital losses for a taxable year.[24]

16-5a Capital Gain and Loss Netting Process

Net short-term capital gain is not eligible for any special tax rate. It is taxed at the same rate as the taxpayer's other taxable income.

Net long-term capital gain is eligible for one or more of *five* alternative tax rates: 0 percent, 15 percent, 20 percent, 25 percent, and 28 percent. The 25 percent and 28 percent rates are used only in unique circumstances. The net long-term capital gain components are referred to as the *0%/15%/20% gain*, the *25% gain*, and the *28% gain*.

The *25% gain* is called the unrecaptured § 1250 gain and is related to gain from disposition of § 1231 assets (discussed in Chapter 17). Here, the discussion focuses only on how the *25% gain* is taxed and not how it is determined. The *28% gain* relates to collectibles and small business stock gain (both discussed later in this section).

The *0% gain* portion of the *0%/15%/20% gain* applies to long-term capital gains that would otherwise be taxed at the 10 percent or 15 percent ordinary tax rates. The *15% gain* portion of the *0%/15%/20% gain* applies to long-term capital gains that would otherwise be taxed at a rate higher than 15 percent but less than 39.6 percent. The *20% gain* portion of the *0%/15%/20% gain* applies to long-term capital gains that would otherwise be taxed at the 39.6 percent ordinary tax rate.

When the long-term capital gain exceeds short-term capital loss, a net capital gain (NCG) exists.[25] Net capital gain qualifies for beneficial alternative tax treatment (see the coverage later in the chapter).

Because there are both short- and long-term capital gains and losses and because the long-term capital gains may be taxed at various rates, an *ordering procedure* is required. The ordering procedure, which ensures that any long-term

---

[24]§ 1211(b).   [25]§ 1222(11).

capital gain is taxed at the lowest preferential rate possible, includes the following steps:

Step 1. Group all gains and losses into four groups: short term, and 28%, 25%, and 0%/15%/20% long term.

Step 2. Net the gains and losses within each group.

Step 3. Offset the net 28% and net 25% amounts, if they are of opposite sign.

Step 4. Offset the results after step 3 against the 0%/15%/20% amount, if they are of opposite sign. If the 0%/15%/20% amount is a loss, offset it against the *highest-taxed gain first.* After this step, there is a net long-term capital gain or loss. If there is a net long-term capital gain, it may consist of only *28% gain,* only *25% gain,* only *0%/15%/20% gain,* or some combination of all of these gains. If there is a net long-term capital loss, it is simply a net long-term capital loss.

Step 5. Offset the net short-term amount against the long-term results of step 4, if they are of opposite sign. The netting rules offset net short-term capital loss against the *highest-taxed gain first.* So a net short-term capital loss first offsets any *28% gain,* then any *25% gain,* and finally any *0%/15%/20% gain.*

If the result of step 5 is *only* a short-term capital gain, the taxpayer is not eligible for a reduced tax rate. If the result of step 5 is a loss, the taxpayer may be eligible for a *capital loss deduction* (discussed later in this chapter). If there was no offsetting in step 5 because the short-term and step 4 results were both gains *or* if the result of the offsetting is a long-term gain, a net capital gain exists and the taxpayer may be eligible for a reduced tax rate. The net capital gain may consist of *28% gain, 25% gain,* and/or *0%/15%/20% gain.*

As you might suspect, this *ordering procedure* can produce many different results. The following series of examples illustrates some of these outcomes.

Capital Gain and Loss Netting Process

EXAMPLE 33

This example shows how a *net short-term capital gain* may result from the netting process.

		Long-Term Gains and Losses			
Step	Short Term	28%	25%	0%/15%/20%	Comment
1	$13,000	$ 12,000		$ 3,000	
	(2,000)	(20,000)			
2	$11,000	($ 8,000)		$ 3,000	
3					No 28%/25% netting because no opposite sign.
4		3,000 →		(3,000)	Netted because of opposite sign.
		($ 5,000)		$ –0–	
5	(5,000) ←	5,000			The net short-term capital gain is taxed as ordinary income.
	$ 6,000	$ –0–			
	Net short-term capital gain				

Capital Gain and Loss Netting Process

This example shows how a *net long-term capital gain* may result from the netting process.

EXAMPLE 34

Step	Short Term	Long-Term Gains and Losses 28%	25%	0%/15%/20%	Comment
1	$ 3,000	$15,000	$4,000	$ 3,000	
	(5,000)	(7,000)		(8,000)	
2	($ 2,000)	$ 8,000	$4,000	($ 5,000)	
3					No 28%/25% netting because no opposite sign.
4		(5,000) ←		5,000	Netted because of opposite sign. Net 0%/15%/20% loss is netted against 28% gain first.
		$ 3,000		$ –0–	
5	2,000 →	(2,000)			The net short-term capital loss is netted against 28% gain first. The net long-term capital gain is $5,000 ($1,000 + $4,000).
	$ –0–	$ 1,000	$4,000		
		Net 28% gain	Net 25% gain		

This example shows how a *net long-term capital loss* may result from the netting process.

EXAMPLE 35

Step	Short Term	Long-Term Gains and Losses 28%	25%	0%/15%/20%	Comment
1	$ 3,000	$ 1,000		$ 3,000	
				(8,000)	
2	$ 3,000	$ 1,000		($ 5,000)	
3					No 28%/25% netting because no opposite sign.
4		(1,000) →		1,000	Netted because of opposite sign.
		$ –0–		($ 4,000)	
5	(3,000) →	→		3,000	The net short-term capital gain is netted against the net long-term capital loss, and the remaining loss is eligible for the capital loss deduction.
	$ –0–			($ 1,000)	
				Net long-term capital loss	

Use of Capital Loss Carryovers

A short-term capital loss carryover to the current year retains its character as short-term and is combined with the short-term items of the current year. A net long-term capital loss carries over as a long-term capital loss and is combined with the current-year long-term items. The long-term loss carryover is first offset with *28% gain* of the current year, then *25% gain*, and then *0%/15%/20% gain* until it is absorbed.

EXAMPLE 36

In 2017, Abigail has a $4,000 short-term capital gain, a $36,000 28% long-term capital gain, and a $13,000 0%/15%/20% long-term capital gain. She also has a $3,000 short-term capital loss carryover and a $2,000 long-term capital loss carryover from 2016.

Thus, in 2017, Abigail has a $1,000 net short-term capital gain ($4,000 − $3,000), a $34,000 net 28% long-term capital gain ($36,000 − $2,000), and a $13,000 net 0%/15%/20% long-term capital gain.

Definition of Collectibles

Capital assets that are collectibles, even though they are held long term, are not eligible for the *0%/15%/20%* alternative tax rate. Instead, a 28 percent alternative tax rate applies.

For capital gain or loss purposes, collectibles include:[26]

- Any work of art.
- Any rug or antique.
- Any metal or gem.
- Any stamp.
- Any alcoholic beverage.
- Most coins.
- Any historical objects (documents, clothes, etc.).

Small Business Stock

A special *exclusion* is available to noncorporate taxpayers who derive capital gains from the sale or exchange of qualified small business stock.[27] Any amount not excluded from income is taxed at a maximum rate of 28 percent (as noted earlier). The exclusion amount varies, depending on when the qualified small business stock was acquired:

- 100 percent of the gain is excluded for qualified stock acquired after September 27, 2010.
- 75 percent of the gain is excluded for qualified stock acquired after February 17, 2009, and before September 28, 2010.
- 50 percent of the gain is excluded for qualified stock acquired before February 18, 2009.

As a result, the maximum effective tax rate on gains from the sale of qualified small business stock is 0 percent (28% × 0%), 7 percent (28% × 25%), or 14 percent (28% × 50%).

EXAMPLE 37

In March 2017, Yolanda realized a $100,000 gain on the sale of qualified small business stock that she acquired in 2005. Yolanda is subject to the 33% marginal tax rate without considering this gain. As the stock was acquired before February 18, 2009, $50,000 of this gain (50%) is excluded from gross income, and the other $50,000 is taxed at the maximum rate of 28%. As a result, Yolanda owes Federal income tax of $14,000 on the stock sale ($50,000 × 28%), an effective tax rate of 14% on the entire $100,000 gain.

If, instead, Yolanda acquired the stock in January 2011, she would exclude 100% of the gain.

Given this very favorable treatment, Congress wanted to ensure that the gain exclusion only applied in very specific situations. As a result, they imposed the following restrictions:

- The stock must have been newly issued *after* August 10, 1993.
- The taxpayer must have held the stock *more than five years*.
- The issuing corporation must use at least 80 percent of its assets, determined by their value, in the *active conduct* of a trade or business.

---

[26]§ 408(m)(2) and Reg. § 1.408–10(b).   [27]§ 1202(a).

- When the stock was issued, the issuing corporation's assets must not have exceeded $50 million, at adjusted basis, including the proceeds of the stock issuance.

- The corporation does not engage in banking, financing, insurance, investing, leasing, farming, mineral extraction, hotel or motel operations, restaurant operations, or any business whose principal asset is the *reputation or skill* of its employees (such as accounting, architecture, health, law, engineering, or financial services).

Even if each of these requirements is met, the amount of gain eligible for the exclusion is limited to the *greater* of 10 times the taxpayer's basis in the stock or $10 million per taxpayer per company,[28] computed on an aggregate basis.

Rachel purchased $100,000 of qualified small business stock when it was first issued in October 2001. This year, she sold the stock for $4 million. Her gain is $3.9 million ($4,000,000 − $100,000). Although this amount exceeds 10 times her basis ($100,000 × 10 = $1,000,000), it is *less* than $10 million. As a result, the entire $3.9 million gain is eligible for a 50% exclusion.

Transactions that fail to satisfy *any one* of the applicable requirements are taxed as capital gains (and losses) realized by noncorporate taxpayers generally.

Gains are also eligible for *nonrecognition* treatment if the sale proceeds are invested in other qualified small business stock within 60 days.[29] To the extent that the sale proceeds are not so invested, gain is recognized, but the exclusion still applies. To be eligible for this treatment, the stock sold must have been held more than six months.

Assume the same facts as in the preceding example, except that Rachel sold her stock in January 2018 and used $3.5 million of the sale proceeds to purchase other qualified small business stock one month later. Rachel's gain is recognized to the extent that the sale proceeds were not reinvested—namely, $500,000 ($4,000,000 sale proceeds − $3,500,000 reinvested). A 50% exclusion will apply, however, to the $500,000.

16-5b Qualified Dividend Income

Dividends paid by domestic and certain foreign corporations are eligible to be taxed at the 0%/15%/20% long-term capital gain rates if they are **qualified dividend income (QDI)** (see the discussion of QDI in text Section 4-3b). Here, the discussion focuses on how the qualified dividend income is taxed.

The Big Picture

Return to the facts of *The Big Picture* on p. 16-1. After holding the Purple stock for 10 months, Maurice receives $350 of dividends. If Purple is a domestic or qualifying foreign corporation, these are qualified dividends eligible for the 0%/15%/20% tax rate.

After the net capital gain or loss has been determined, the QDI is added to the net long-term capital gain portion of the net capital gain and is taxed as *0%/15%/20% gain*. If there is a net capital loss, the net capital loss is still deductible *for* AGI up to $3,000 per year with the remainder of the loss (if any) carrying forward. In this case, the QDI is still eligible to be treated as *0%/15%/20% gain* in the alternative tax calculation (it is *not* offset by the net capital loss).

---

[28]For married persons filing separately, the limitation is $5 million.   [29]§ 1045(a).

EXAMPLE 41

Refer to Example 34, but assume that there is qualified dividend income (QDI) of $2,500 in addition to the items shown. The QDI is not netted against the capital gains and losses. Instead, the taxpayer has $1,000 of *28% gain*, $4,000 of *25% gain*, and $2,500 of QDI taxed at 0% / 15% / 20%.

Refer to Example 35, but assume that there is QDI of $2,500 in addition to the items shown. The QDI is not netted against the net capital loss. The taxpayer has a $1,000 capital loss deduction and $2,500 of QDI taxed at 0% / 15% / 20%.

16-5c Alternative Tax on Net Capital Gain and Qualified Dividend Income

Code § 1 contains the rules that enable the *net capital gain* to be taxed at special rates (0, 15, 20, 25, and 28 percent). This calculation is referred to as the **alternative tax** on net capital gain.[30] The alternative tax applies only if taxable income includes some long-term capital gain (there is net capital gain) and/or qualified dividend income (QDI). Taxable income includes *all* of the net capital gain and/or QDI unless taxable income is less than the net capital gain and/or QDI. In addition, the net capital gain and/or QDI is taxed *last*, after other taxable income (including any short-term capital gain).

EXAMPLE 42

Joan, a single taxpayer, has taxable income of $118,000, including a $10,000 net capital gain and $2,000 QDI. The last $12,000 of her $118,000 taxable income is the layer related to the net capital gain and/or QDI. The first $106,000 ($118,000 − $12,000) of her taxable income is her other taxable income and is not subject to any special tax rate, so it is taxed using the regular tax rates.

Because the net capital gain and/or QDI may be made up of various *rate layers*, it is important to know in what order those layers are taxed. (Review the five-step ordering procedure discussed in text Section 16-5a and the related examples.) For *each* of the layers, the taxpayer compares the regular tax rate on that layer of income and the alternative tax rate on that portion of the net capital gain and/or QDI.

The layers are taxed in the following order:

- Any *25% gain,*
- Any *28% gain,*
- The 0 percent portion of the *0% / 15% / 20% gain* and/or QDI,
- The 15 percent portion of the *0% / 15% / 20% gain* and/or QDI, and then
- The 20 percent portion of the *0% / 15% / 20% gain* and/or QDI.

As a result of this layering:

- The taxpayer benefits from the 0 percent portion of the net capital gain and/or QDI if the taxpayer is still in the 10 percent or 15 percent regular rate bracket after taxing other taxable income and the 25 percent and 28 percent portions of the net capital gain.

- The taxpayer benefits from the 15 percent portion of the net capital gain and/or QDI if the taxpayer is still in the 25 percent, 28 percent, 33 percent, or 35 percent regular rate bracket after taxing other taxable income and the 25 percent, 28 percent, and 0 percent portions of the net capital gain and/or QDI.

- The taxpayer benefits from the 20 percent portion of the net capital gain and/or QDI when taxable income reaches the 39.6 percent regular tax bracket.

---

[30]§ 1(h) Note: Examples 43, 44, and 45 use the 2017 Tax Rate Schedules rather than the 2017 Tax Tables (which are not yet available) to calculate the tax on the non-long-term capital gain portion of taxable income. This approach is used to better illustrate the concepts under discussion. The actual tax on the non-long-term portion of taxable income would be calculated using the Tax Tables because that income is less than $100,000.

Concept Summary 16.4 summarizes the alternative tax computation.

Concept Summary 16.4

Income Layers for Alternative Tax on Capital Gain Computation

Compute tax on:	Other taxable income (including net short-term capital gain) using the regular tax rates.
Compute tax on:	Each of the layers below using the *lower* of the alternative tax rate or the regular tax rate for that layer (or portion of a layer) of taxable income.
+	25% long-term capital gain (unrecaptured § 1250 gain) portion of taxable income
+	28% long-term capital gain
+	0% long-term capital gain (portion of *0%/15%/20% gain* and/or qualified dividend income (QDI) that is taxed at 0%; available only if other taxable income plus 25% and 28% capital gain layers do not put the taxpayer above the 15% regular tax bracket; 0% rate is no longer available once income, including the portion of the gain and/or QDI taxed at 0%, puts the taxpayer out of the 15% regular tax bracket)
+	15% long-term capital gain (portion of *0%/15%/20% gain* and/or QDI that is taxed at 15%; available only if other taxable income plus the 25%, 28%, and 0% layers put the taxpayer above the 15% regular tax bracket and only until other taxable income plus the 25%, 28%, 0%, and 15% layers put the taxpayer above the 35% regular tax bracket)
+	20% long-term capital gain (portion of *0%/15%/20% gain* and/or QDI that is taxed at 20%; available when other taxable income plus the 25%, 28%, 0%, and 15% layers put the taxpayer above the 35% regular tax bracket)
=	Alternative tax on taxable income

Alternative Tax on Net Capital Gain

EXAMPLE 43

Assume that Joan's $10,000 net capital gain in Example 42 is made up of $7,000 *25% gain* and $3,000 *0%/15%/20% gain*. In addition, she has $2,000 of QDI. Examination of the 2017 tax rates reveals that $106,000 ($118,000 − $12,000) of other taxable income for a single individual puts Joan at a marginal tax rate of 28%. Consequently, she uses the alternative tax on the $7,000 gain, the $3,000 gain, and the $2,000 QDI.

Her alternative tax liability for 2017 is $25,162:

	$22,662 (tax on $106,000 of other taxable income)
+	1,750 ($7,000 × .25; 25% rate on *25% gain*)
+	450 ($3,000 × .15; 15% rate on *0%/15%/20% gain*)
+	300 ($2,000 × .15; 15% rate on QDI)
=	$25,162 Alternative Tax Liability

Because the combination of the $106,000 other taxable income and her $7,000 *25% gain* puts her above the 15% regular tax bracket, none of the $3,000 *0%/15%/20% gain* or $2,000 QDI is taxed at 0%.

Her regular tax liability on $118,000 is $26,022. As a result, Joan saves $860 ($26,022 − $25,162) by using the alternative tax calculation. Since none of Joan's taxable income puts her in the 39.6% bracket, none of her *0%/15%/20% gain* or QDI is taxed at the 20% alternative tax rate.

EXAMPLE 44

Assume that Joan, a single taxpayer, has 2017 taxable income of $25,000. Of this amount, $11,000 is net capital gain, $1,000 is QDI, and $13,000 is other taxable income. The $11,000 net capital gain is made up of $8,300 of *25% gain* and $2,700 of *0%/15%/20% gain*.

Her alternative tax liability for 2017 is $2,729:

	$1,484 (tax on $13,000 of other taxable income)
+	1,245 (tax on $8,300 *25% gain* at 15%)
+	0 (tax on $2,700 *0%/15%/20% gain* at 0%)
+	0 (tax on $1,000 QDI at 0%)
=	$2,729 Alternative Tax Liability

continued

> Because her marginal rate is still 15% after taxing the $13,000 of other taxable income, she uses the 15% regular tax rate rather than the 25% alternative tax rate on the $8,300 *25% gain*. After taxing the $13,000 and the $8,300, a total of $21,300 of the $25,000 taxable income has been taxed. Because her marginal rate is still 15%, she uses the 0% alternative rate for the $2,700 of *0%/15%/20% gain* and $1,000 QDI.
>
> Joan's regular tax liability on $25,000 is $3,284. As a result, she saves $555 ($3,284 − $2,729) by using the alternative tax calculation.

The alternative tax computation allows the taxpayer to receive the *lower of* the regular tax or the alternative tax on *each layer* of net capital gain and/or QDI or *portion of each layer* of net capital gain and/or QDI.

EXAMPLE 45

> Assume the same facts as in Example 44, except that Joan's 2017 taxable income is $40,000, consisting of $11,000 of net capital gain, $1,000 of QDI, and $28,000 of other taxable income.
>
> Not all of the combined *0%/15%/20% gain* and QDI ($3,700; $2,700 + $1,000) is taxed at 0% because Joan's taxable income exceeds $37,950, taking her out of the 15% regular tax bracket. Consequently, the last $2,050 ($40,000 − $37,950) of the $3,700 is taxed at 15% rather than 0%.
>
> Her tax liability using the alternative tax computation is $5,287:
>
> $3,734 (tax on $28,000 of other taxable income)
> + 1,245 (tax on $8,300 *25% gain* at 15%)
> +   0 (tax on $1,650 of the $3,700 combined *0%/15%/20% gain* and QDI at 0%)
> +   308 (tax on $2,050 of the $3,700 combined *0%/15%/20% gain* and QDI at 15%)
> = $5,287 Alternative Tax Liability
>
> Joan's regular tax liability on $40,000 is $5,739. Thus, she saves $452 ($5,739 − $5,287) by using the alternative tax calculation.

16-5d Treatment of Net Capital Losses

Computation of Net Capital Loss

A net capital loss (NCL) results if capital losses exceed capital gains for the year. An NCL may be all long term, all short term, or part long and part short term.[31] The characterization of an NCL as long or short term is important in determining the capital loss deduction (discussed next).

EXAMPLE 46

> Three different individuals have the following capital gains and losses during the year:
>
> | Taxpayer | Short Term | | | Long Term | | | Combined Short Term and Long Term | Description of Result |
> |---|---|---|---|---|---|---|---|---|
> | | STCG | STCL | Net Short Term | LTCG | LTCL | Net Long Term | | |
> | Robert | $1,000 | ($ 500) | $ 500 | $1,000 | ($2,800) | ($1,800) | ($1,300) | NLTCL |
> | Carlos | 1,000 | (2,800) | (1,800) | 1,000 | (500) | 500 | (1,300) | NSTCL |
> | Troy | 500 | (1,200) | (700) | 400 | (1,200) | (800) | (1,500) | NSTCL ($700) |
> | | | | | | | | | NLTCL ($800) |
>
> Robert's NCL of $1,300 is all long term. Carlos's NCL of $1,300 is all short term. Troy's NCL is $1,500, $700 of which is short term and $800 of which is long term.

---

[31]Section 1222(10) defines a net capital loss as the net loss after the capital loss deduction. However, that definition confuses the discussion of net capital loss. Therefore, net capital loss is used here to mean the result after netting capital gains and losses and before considering the capital loss deduction. The capital loss deduction is discussed later in this section.

Capital Loss Deduction

A net capital loss is deductible *for* AGI, but limited to no more than $3,000 per tax year.[32] So although a net capital gain receives favorable tax treatment, there is *unfavorable* treatment for capital losses due to the $3,000 annual limitation. If the NCL includes both long-term and short-term capital loss, the short-term capital loss is counted first toward the $3,000 annual limitation.

Burt has an NCL of $5,500, of which $2,000 is STCL and $3,500 is LTCL. Burt has a capital loss deduction of $3,000 ($2,000 of STCL and $1,000 of LTCL). He has an LTCL carryforward of $2,500 ($3,500 − $1,000).

EXAMPLE 47

Carryovers

Taxpayers are allowed to carry over unused capital losses indefinitely. The short-term capital loss (STCL) retains its character as STCL. Likewise, the long-term capital loss retains its character as LTCL.

In 2017, Mark incurred $1,000 of STCL and $11,000 of LTCL. In 2018, Mark has a $400 LTCG.

- Mark's NCL for 2017 is $12,000. Mark deducts $3,000 ($1,000 STCL and $2,000 LTCL). He has $9,000 of LTCL carried forward to 2018.

- Mark combines the $9,000 LTCL carryforward with the $400 LTCG for 2018. He has an $8,600 NLTCL for 2018. Mark deducts $3,000 of LTCL in 2018 and carries forward $5,600 of LTCL to 2019.

EXAMPLE 48

Concept Summary 16.5 summarizes the rules for noncorporate taxpayers' treatment of capital gains and losses.

Concept Summary 16.5

Final Results of the Capital Gain and Loss Netting Process and How They Are Taxed

Result	Maximum Tax Rate	Comments
Net short-term capital loss	—	Eligible for capital loss deduction ($3,000 maximum per year).
Net long-term capital loss	—	Eligible for capital loss deduction ($3,000 maximum per year).
Net short-term capital loss *and* net long-term capital loss	—	Eligible for capital loss deduction ($3,000 maximum per year). Short-term capital losses are counted first toward the deduction.
Net short-term capital gain	10%–39.6%	Taxed as ordinary income.
Net long-term capital gain	0%–28%	The net long-term capital gain may have as many as five tax rate components: 25%, 28%, and 0%/15%/20%.
• The net long-term capital gain is the *last* portion of taxable income.		The components are taxed in the following order: 25%, 28%, 0%, 15%, 20%. They are taxed *after* the non-long-term capital gain portion of taxable income has been taxed. The 0%/15%/20% component may include qualified dividend income.
• Each net long-term capital gain component of taxable income is taxed at the *lower* of the regular tax on that component or the alternative tax.		The alternative tax on net long-term capital gain can never increase the tax on taxable income, but it can reduce the tax on taxable income.
Net short-term capital gain *and* net long-term capital gain	10%–39.6% on net short-term capital gain; 0%–28% on net long-term capital gain	The net short-term capital gain is taxed as ordinary income; the net long-term capital gain is taxed as discussed above for just net long-term capital gain.

[32]§ 1211(b)(1). Married taxpayers filing separate returns are limited to a $1,500 deduction per tax year. When a taxpayer has both a capital loss deduction and negative taxable income, a special computation of the capital loss carryover is required. See § 1212(b).

16-5e **Reporting Procedures**

The following example is used to discuss and illustrate the tax forms used for reporting (2016 forms are used because the 2017 tax forms are not yet available).

During 2016, Joan Rapson (Social Security number 123-45-6789) had the following sales of capital assets. In addition, she has $300 of qualified dividend income and $65,700 of other taxable income. Joan is single and has no dependents.

Description	Acquired On	Date Sold	Sales Price	Tax Basis	Gain or Loss	Character
100 shares Blue stock	1/21/16	11/11/16	$11,000	$17,000	($ 6,000)	STCL
100 shares Yellow stock	9/12/11	10/12/16	36,000	20,000	16,000	LTCG
100 shares Purple stock	3/14/14	10/12/16	14,000	12,000	2,000	LTCG

Joan has a net capital gain of $12,000 ($16,000 *0%/15%/20% gain* + $2,000 *0%/15%/20% gain* − $6,000 short-term capital loss). Consequently, all of the net capital gain is composed of *0%/15%/20% gain*. Joan's $78,000 taxable income includes $65,700 of other taxable income, a $12,000 net capital gain, and $300 qualified dividend income.

Joan's stockbroker reported total stock sales to her on Form 1099–B, which showed the sales proceeds and adjusted basis for each of her transactions. Following a discussion of the reporting rules, Joan's completed forms and a related worksheet are presented.

Capital gains and losses are reported on Schedule D of Form 1040 (Capital Gains and Losses). Part I of Schedule D is used to report short-term capital gains and losses. Part II of Schedule D is used to report long-term capital gains and losses. The information shown in Parts I and II comes from Form 8949 (Sales and Other Dispositions of Assets). Form 8949 is used to accumulate gains and losses from three sources:

- Capital gain and loss transactions for which a Form 1099–B (Proceeds from Broker and Barter Exchange Transactions) has been received and the provider of the form had information on the sales proceeds *and* the tax basis of the assets disposed of.

- Capital gain and loss transactions for which a Form 1099–B has been received and the provider of the form had information on the sales proceeds *but did not* have information on the tax basis of the assets disposed of.

- Capital gain and loss transactions for which a Form 1099–B was not received.

Part III of Form 1040 Schedule D summarizes the results of Parts I and II and indicates whether the taxpayer has a net capital gain or a net capital loss. Part III then helps determine which alternative tax worksheet is used to calculate the alternative tax on long-term capital gains and qualified dividends.

- If the taxpayer has a net long-term capital gain that does *not* include any 28% or 25% long-term capital gain, then the alternative tax is calculated using the Qualified Dividends and Capital Gain Worksheet from the Form 1040 instructions.

- If the taxpayer has a net long-term capital gain that includes either 28% or 25% long-term capital gain, then the alternative tax is calculated using the Schedule D Tax Worksheet from the Schedule D instructions.

These worksheets do not have to be filed with the tax return, but are kept for the taxpayer's records.

**SCHEDULE D
(Form 1040)**

Department of the Treasury
Internal Revenue Service (99)

Capital Gains and Losses

▶ Attach to Form 1040 or Form 1040NR.
▶ Information about Schedule D and its separate instructions is at *www.irs.gov/scheduled*.
▶ Use Form 8949 to list your transactions for lines 1b, 2, 3, 8b, 9, and 10.

OMB No. 1545-0074

2016

Attachment
Sequence No. **12**

Name(s) shown on return
Joan Rapson

Your social security number
123-45-6789

Part I   Short-Term Capital Gains and Losses—Assets Held One Year or Less

See instructions for how to figure the amounts to enter on the lines below. This form may be easier to complete if you round off cents to whole dollars.	(d) Proceeds (sales price)	(e) Cost (or other basis)	(g) Adjustments to gain or loss from Form(s) 8949, Part I, line 2, column (g)	(h) Gain or (loss) Subtract column (e) from column (d) and combine the result with column (g)
1a Totals for all short-term transactions reported on Form 1099-B for which basis was reported to the IRS and for which you have no adjustments (see instructions). However, if you choose to report all these transactions on Form 8949, leave this line blank and go to line 1b .				
1b Totals for all transactions reported on Form(s) 8949 with **Box A** checked	*11,000*	*17,000*		*(6,000)*
2 Totals for all transactions reported on Form(s) 8949 with **Box B** checked				
3 Totals for all transactions reported on Form(s) 8949 with **Box C** checked				

4 Short-term gain from Form 6252 and short-term gain or (loss) from Forms 4684, 6781, and 8824 .	**4**	
5 Net short-term gain or (loss) from partnerships, S corporations, estates, and trusts from Schedule(s) K-1	**5**	
6 Short-term capital loss carryover. Enter the amount, if any, from line 8 of your **Capital Loss Carryover Worksheet** in the instructions	**6** ( )
7 **Net short-term capital gain or (loss).** Combine lines 1a through 6 in column (h). If you have any long-term capital gains or losses, go to Part II below. Otherwise, go to Part III on the back	**7**	*(6,000)*

Part II   Long-Term Capital Gains and Losses—Assets Held More Than One Year

See instructions for how to figure the amounts to enter on the lines below. This form may be easier to complete if you round off cents to whole dollars.	(d) Proceeds (sales price)	(e) Cost (or other basis)	(g) Adjustments to gain or loss from Form(s) 8949, Part II, line 2, column (g)	(h) Gain or (loss) Subtract column (e) from column (d) and combine the result with column (g)
8a Totals for all long-term transactions reported on Form 1099-B for which basis was reported to the IRS and for which you have no adjustments (see instructions). However, if you choose to report all these transactions on Form 8949, leave this line blank and go to line 8b .				
8b Totals for all transactions reported on Form(s) 8949 with **Box D** checked	*50,000*	*32,000*		*18,000*
9 Totals for all transactions reported on Form(s) 8949 with **Box E** checked				
10 Totals for all transactions reported on Form(s) 8949 with **Box F** checked.				

11 Gain from Form 4797, Part I; long-term gain from Forms 2439 and 6252; and long-term gain or (loss) from Forms 4684, 6781, and 8824	**11**	
12 Net long-term gain or (loss) from partnerships, S corporations, estates, and trusts from Schedule(s) K-1	**12**	
13 Capital gain distributions. See the instructions	**13**	
14 Long-term capital loss carryover. Enter the amount, if any, from line 13 of your **Capital Loss Carryover Worksheet** in the instructions	**14** ( )
15 **Net long-term capital gain or (loss).** Combine lines 8a through 14 in column (h). Then go to Part III on the back	**15**	*18,000*

For Paperwork Reduction Act Notice, see your tax return instructions.   Cat. No. 11338H   Schedule D (Form 1040) 2016

Schedule D (Form 1040) 2016   Page **2**

Part III	**Summary**

16 Combine lines 7 and 15 and enter the result   . . . . | **16** | *12,000* |

- If line 16 is a **gain,** enter the amount from line 16 on Form 1040, line 13, or Form 1040NR, line 14. Then go to line 17 below.
- If line 16 is a **loss,** skip lines 17 through 20 below. Then go to line 21. Also be sure to complete line 22.
- If line 16 is **zero,** skip lines 17 through 21 below and enter -0- on Form 1040, line 13, or Form 1040NR, line 14. Then go to line 22.

17 Are lines 15 and 16 **both** gains?
☒ **Yes.** Go to line 18.
☐ **No.** Skip lines 18 through 21, and go to line 22.

18 Enter the amount, if any, from line 7 of the **28% Rate Gain Worksheet** in the instructions   . . ▶ | **18** | *0* |

19 Enter the amount, if any, from line 18 of the **Unrecaptured Section 1250 Gain Worksheet** in the instructions   . . . . ▶ | **19** | *0* |

20 Are lines 18 and 19 **both** zero or blank?
☒ **Yes.** Complete the **Qualified Dividends and Capital Gain Tax Worksheet** in the instructions for Form 1040, line 44 (or in the instructions for Form 1040NR, line 42). **Don't** complete lines 21 and 22 below.

☐ **No.** Complete the **Schedule D Tax Worksheet** in the instructions. **Don't** complete lines 21 and 22 below.

21 If line 16 is a loss, enter here and on Form 1040, line 13, or Form 1040NR, line 14, the **smaller** of:

- The loss on line 16 or
- ($3,000), or if married filing separately, ($1,500)   } . . . . | **21** | ( ) |

Note: When figuring which amount is smaller, treat both amounts as positive numbers.

22 Do you have qualified dividends on Form 1040, line 9b, or Form 1040NR, line 10b?

☐ **Yes.** Complete the **Qualified Dividends and Capital Gain Tax Worksheet** in the instructions for Form 1040, line 44 (or in the instructions for Form 1040NR, line 42).

☐ **No.** Complete the rest of Form 1040 or Form 1040NR.

Schedule D (Form 1040) 2016

Form **8949**	**Sales and Other Dispositions of Capital Assets**	OMB No. 1545-0074
Department of the Treasury Internal Revenue Service	▶ Information about Form 8949 and its separate instructions is at *www.irs.gov/form8949*. ▶ File with your Schedule D to list your transactions for lines 1b, 2, 3, 8b, 9, and 10 of Schedule D.	20**16** Attachment Sequence No. **12A**

Name(s) shown on return

Joan Rapson

Social security number or taxpayer identification number

123-45-6789

Before you check Box A, B, or C below, see whether you received any Form(s) 1099-B or substitute statement(s) from your broker. A substitute statement will have the same information as Form 1099-B. Either will show whether your basis (usually your cost) was reported to the IRS by your broker and may even tell you which box to check.

Part I **Short-Term.** Transactions involving capital assets you held 1 year or less are short term. For long-term transactions, see page 2.

Note: You may aggregate all short-term transactions reported on Form(s) 1099-B showing basis was reported to the IRS and for which no adjustments or codes are required. Enter the totals directly on Schedule D, line 1a; you aren't required to report these transactions on Form 8949 (see instructions).

You *must* check Box A, B, *or* C below. **Check only one box.** If more than one box applies for your short-term transactions, complete a separate Form 8949, page 1, for each applicable box. If you have more short-term transactions than will fit on this page for one or more of the boxes, complete as many forms with the same box checked as you need.

☒ **(A)** Short-term transactions reported on Form(s) 1099-B showing basis was reported to the IRS (see **Note** above)

☐ **(B)** Short-term transactions reported on Form(s) 1099-B showing basis **wasn't** reported to the IRS

☐ **(C)** Short-term transactions not reported to you on Form 1099-B

1 (a) Description of property (Example: 100 sh. XYZ Co.)	(b) Date acquired (Mo., day, yr.)	(c) Date sold or disposed of (Mo., day, yr.)	(d) Proceeds (sales price) (see instructions)	(e) Cost or other basis. See the **Note** below and see *Column (e)* in the separate instructions	Adjustment, if any, to gain or loss. If you enter an amount in column (g), enter a code in column (f). See the separate instructions. (f) Code(s) from instructions	(g) Amount of adjustment	(h) Gain or (loss). Subtract column (e) from column (d) and combine the result with column (g)
100 Shares Blue Stock	*01/21/16*	*11/11/16*	*11,000*	*17,000*			*(6,000)*
2 Totals. Add the amounts in columns (d), (e), (g), and (h) (subtract negative amounts). Enter each total here and include on your Schedule D, **line 1b** (if **Box A** above is checked), **line 2** (if **Box B** above is checked), or **line 3** (if **Box C** above is checked) ▶			*11,000*	*17,000*			*(6,000)*

Note: If you checked Box A above but the basis reported to the IRS was incorrect, enter in column (e) the basis as reported to the IRS, and enter an adjustment in column (g) to correct the basis. See *Column (g)* in the separate instructions for how to figure the amount of the adjustment.

For Paperwork Reduction Act Notice, see your tax return instructions. Cat. No. 37768Z Form **8949** (2016)

Form 8949 (2016)   Attachment Sequence No. **12A**   Page **2**

Name(s) shown on return. Name and SSN or taxpayer identification no. not required if shown on other side	Social security number or taxpayer identification number

Before you check Box D, E, or F below, see whether you received any Form(s) 1099-B or substitute statement(s) from your broker. A substitute statement will have the same information as Form 1099-B. Either will show whether your basis (usually your cost) was reported to the IRS by your broker and may even tell you which box to check.

Part II   **Long-Term.** Transactions involving capital assets you held more than 1 year are long term. For short-term transactions, see page 1.

Note: You may aggregate all long-term transactions reported on Form(s) 1099-B showing basis was reported to the IRS and for which no adjustments or codes are required. Enter the totals directly on Schedule D, line 8a; you aren't required to report these transactions on Form 8949 (see instructions).

You must check Box D, E, or F below. Check only one box. If more than one box applies for your long-term transactions, complete a separate Form 8949, page 2, for each applicable box. If you have more long-term transactions than will fit on this page for one or more of the boxes, complete as many forms with the same box checked as you need.

☒ **(D)** Long-term transactions reported on Form(s) 1099-B showing basis was reported to the IRS (see **Note** above)

☐ **(E)** Long-term transactions reported on Form(s) 1099-B showing basis **wasn't** reported to the IRS

☐ **(F)** Long-term transactions not reported to you on Form 1099-B

1 (a) Description of property (Example: 100 sh. XYZ Co.)	(b) Date acquired (Mo., day, yr.)	(c) Date sold or disposed of (Mo., day, yr.)	(d) Proceeds (sales price) (see instructions)	(e) Cost or other basis. See the **Note** below and see *Column (e)* in the separate instructions	Adjustment, if any, to gain or loss. If you enter an amount in column (g), enter a code in column (f). See the separate instructions.		(h) Gain or (loss). Subtract column (e) from column (d) and combine the result with column (g)
					(f) Code(s) from instructions	(g) Amount of adjustment	
100 Shares Yellow Stock	*09/12/11*	*10/12/16*	*36,000*	*20,000*			*16,000*
100 Shares Purple Stock	*03/14/14*	*10/12/16*	*14,000*	*12,000*			*2,000*
2 Totals. Add the amounts in columns (d), (e), (g), and (h) (subtract negative amounts). Enter each total here and include on your Schedule D, **line 8b** (if **Box D** above is checked), **line 9** (if **Box E** above is checked), or **line 10** (if **Box F** above is checked) ▶			*50,000*	*32,000*			*18,000*

Note: If you checked Box D above but the basis reported to the IRS was incorrect, enter in column (e) the basis as reported to the IRS, and enter an adjustment in column (g) to correct the basis. See *Column (g)* in the separate instructions for how to figure the amount of the adjustment.

Form **8949** (2016)

Qualified Dividends and Capital Gain Tax Worksheet—Line 44

Keep for Your Records

Before you begin:	✓ See the earlier instructions for line 44 to see if you can use this worksheet to figure your tax.
	✓ Before completing this worksheet, complete Form 1040 through line 43.
	✓ If you do not have to file Schedule D and you received capital gain distributions, be sure you checked the box on line 13 of Form 1040.

1. Enter the amount from Form 1040, line 43. However, if you are filing Form 2555 or 2555-EZ (relating to foreign earned income), enter the amount from line 3 of the Foreign Earned Income Tax Worksheet . . . . **1.**   _78,000_

2. Enter the amount from Form 1040, line 9b* . . . .   **2.**   _300_

3. Are you filing Schedule D?*
   ☒ **Yes.** Enter the **smaller** of line 15 or 16 of Schedule D. If either line 15 or line 16 is blank or a loss, enter -0-.   **3.**   _12,000_
   ☐ **No.** Enter the amount from Form 1040, line 13.

4. Add lines 2 and 3 . . . .   **4.**   _12,300_

5. If filing Form 4952 (used to figure investment interest expense deduction), enter any amount from line 4g of that form. Otherwise, enter -0- . . . .   **5.**

6. Subtract line 5 from line 4. If zero or less, enter -0- . . . .   **6.**   _12,300_

7. Subtract line 6 from line 1. If zero or less, enter -0- . . . .   **7.**   _65,700_

8. Enter:
   $37,650 if single or married filing separately,
   $75,300 if married filing jointly or qualifying widow(er),
   $50,400 if head of household.   **8.**   _37,650_

9. Enter the smaller of line 1 or line 8 . . . .   **9.**   _37,650_

10. Enter the smaller of line 7 or line 9 . . . .   **10.**   _37,650_

11. Subtract line 10 from line 9. This amount is taxed at 0% . . . .   **11.**   _0_

12. Enter the smaller of line 1 or line 6 . . . .   **12.**   _12,300_

13. Enter the amount from line 11 . . . .   **13.**   _0_

14. Subtract line 13 from line 12 . . . .   **14.**   _12,300_

15. Enter:
    $415,050 if single,
    $233,475 if married filing separately,
    $466,950 if married filing jointly or qualifying widow(er),
    $441,000 if head of household.   **15.**   _415,050_

16. Enter the smaller of line 1 or line 15 . . . .   **16.**   _78,000_

17. Add lines 7 and 11 . . . .   **17.**   _65,700_

18. Subtract line 17 from line 16. If zero or less, enter -0- . . . .   **18.**   _12,300_

19. Enter the smaller of line 14 or line 18 . . . .   **19.**   _12,300_

20. Multiply line 19 by 15% (0.15) . . . .   **20.**   _1,845_

21. Add lines 11 and 19 . . . .   **21.**   _12,300_

22. Subtract line 21 from line 12 . . . .   **22.**   _0_

23. Multiply line 22 by 20% (0.20) . . . .   **23.**   _0_

24. Figure the tax on the amount on line 7. If the amount on line 7 is less than $100,000, use the Tax Table to figure the tax. If the amount on line 7 is $100,000 or more, use the Tax Computation Worksheet . . . .   **24.**   _12,203_

25. Add lines 20, 23, and 24 . . . .   **25.**   _14,048_

26. Figure the tax on the amount on line 1. If the amount on line 1 is less than $100,000, use the Tax Table to figure the tax. If the amount on line 1 is $100,000 or more, use the Tax Computation Worksheet . . . .   **26.**   _15,278_

27. **Tax on all taxable income.** Enter the **smaller** of line 25 or line 26. Also include this amount on Form 1040, line 44. If you are filing Form 2555 or 2555-EZ, do not enter this amount on Form 1040, line 44. Instead, enter it on line 4 of the Foreign Earned Income Tax Worksheet . . . .   **27.**   _14,048_

If you are filing Form 2555 or 2555EZ, see the footnote in the Foreign Earned Income Tax Worksheet before completing this line.

LO.6

Describe the tax treatment for capital gains and the detrimental tax treatment for capital losses for corporate taxpayers.

16-6 TAX TREATMENT OF CAPITAL GAINS AND LOSSES OF CORPORATE TAXPAYERS

The treatment of a corporation's net capital gain or loss differs from the rules for individuals. Briefly, the differences are as follows:

- There is an NCG alternative tax rate of 35 percent.[33] However, because the maximum corporate tax rate is 35 percent, the alternative tax is not beneficial.
- Capital losses offset only capital gains. No deduction of capital losses is permitted against other taxable income (whereas a $3,000 deduction is allowed to individuals).[34]
- Corporations may carry back net capital losses (whether long-term or short-term) as short-term capital losses for three years; if losses still remain after the carryback, the remaining losses may be carried forward five years.[35] Individuals may carry forward unused capital losses indefinitely, but there is no carryback.

EXAMPLE 50

Sparrow Corporation has a $15,000 NLTCL for the current year and $57,000 of other taxable income. Sparrow may not offset the $15,000 NLTCL against its other income by taking a capital loss deduction.

The $15,000 NLTCL becomes a $15,000 STCL for carryback and carryover purposes. This amount may be offset against capital gains in the three-year carryback period or, if not absorbed there, offset capital gains in the five-year carryforward period. Any amount remaining after this carryforward period expires is permanently lost.

The rules applicable to corporations are discussed in greater detail in Chapter 20.

LO.7

Identify tax planning opportunities arising from the sale or exchange of capital assets.

16-7 TAX PLANNING

16-7a Importance of Capital Asset Status

Why is capital asset status important? Because of the alternative tax on net capital gain. Individuals who receive income in the form of long-term capital gains or qualified dividend income have an advantage over taxpayers who cannot receive income in these forms.

If a net capital loss results, the maximum deduction is $3,000 per year. Consequently, capital gains and losses must be segregated from other types of gains and losses and must be reported separately on Schedule D of Form 1040.

16-7b Planning for Capital Asset Status

Capital asset status often is a question of objective evidence. Property that is not a capital asset to one person may qualify as a capital asset to another person.

EXAMPLE 51

Diane, a real estate dealer, transfers by gift a tract of land to Jeff, her son. The land was recorded as part of Diane's inventory (it was held for resale) and was therefore not a capital asset to her. Jeff, however, treats the land as an investment. The land is a capital asset in Jeff's hands, and any later taxable disposition of the property by him will yield a capital gain or loss.

With proper tax planning, even a dealer may obtain long-term capital gain treatment on the sale of property normally held for resale.

---

[33]§ 1201.
[34]§ 1211(a).

[35]§ 1212(a)(1).

GLOBAL TAX ISSUES **Capital Gain Treatment in the United States and Other Countries**

The United States currently requires a very complex tax calculation when taxable income includes net long-term capital gain. However, the alternative tax on net long-term capital gain can generate tax savings even when the taxpayer is in the lowest regular tax bracket (10 percent) because there is an alternative tax rate of 0 percent. Many other countries also have an alternative tax rate on long-term capital gains. Consequently, even though the U.S. system is complex, it may be preferable because of the lower tax rates and because the lower rates are available to taxpayers in all tax brackets.

Jim, a real estate dealer, segregates Tract A from the real estate he regularly holds for resale and designates the property as being held for investment purposes. The property is not advertised for sale and is disposed of several years later. The negotiations for the subsequent sale were initiated by the purchaser and not by Jim. Under these circumstances, it would appear that any gain or loss from the sale of Tract A should be a capital gain or loss.[36]

EXAMPLE 52

When a business is being sold, one of the major decisions usually concerns whether a portion of the sales price is for goodwill. For the seller, goodwill generally represents the disposition of a capital asset. Goodwill has no basis and represents a residual portion of the selling price that cannot be allocated reasonably to the known assets. The amount of goodwill thus represents capital gain.

From a legal perspective, the buyer may prefer that the residual portion of the purchase price be allocated to a covenant not to compete (a promise that the seller will not compete against the buyer by conducting a business similar to the one the buyer has purchased). Both purchased goodwill and a covenant not to compete are § 197 intangibles. Thus, both must be capitalized and can be amortized over a 15-year statutory period.

To the seller, a covenant produces ordinary income. Thus, the seller would prefer that the residual portion of the selling price be allocated to goodwill—a capital asset. If the buyer does not need the legal protection provided by a covenant, the buyer is neutral regarding whether the residual amount be allocated to a covenant or to goodwill. Because the seller would receive a tax advantage from labeling the residual amount as goodwill, the buyer should factor this into the negotiation of the purchase price.

Marcia is buying Jack's dry cleaning proprietorship. An appraisal of the assets indicates that a reasonable purchase price would exceed the value of the known assets by $30,000. If the purchase contract does not specify the nature of the $30,000, the amount will be for goodwill and Jack will have a long-term capital gain of $30,000. Marcia will have a 15-year amortizable $30,000 asset.

If Marcia is paying the extra $30,000 to prevent Jack from conducting another dry cleaning business in the area (a covenant not to compete), Jack will have $30,000 of ordinary income. Marcia will have a $30,000 deduction over the statutory 15-year amortization period rather than over the actual life of the covenant (e.g., 5 years).

EXAMPLE 53

16-7c **Effect of Capital Asset Status in Transactions Other Than Sales**

The nature of an asset (capital or ordinary) is important in determining the tax consequences that result when a sale or exchange occurs. It may, however, be just as significant in circumstances other than a taxable sale or exchange. When a capital asset is

---

[36]*Toledo, Peoria & Western Railroad Co.*, 35 TCM 1663, T.C.Memo. 1976–366.

disposed of, the result is not always a capital gain or loss. Rather, in general, the disposition must be a sale or exchange. Collection of a debt instrument having a basis less than the face value results in a capital gain if the debt instrument is a capital asset. The collection is a sale or exchange. Sale of the debt shortly before the due date for collection will produce a capital gain.[37] If selling the debt in such circumstances could produce a capital gain but collecting could not, the consistency of what constitutes a capital gain or loss would be undermined. Another illustration of the sale or exchange principle involves a donation of certain appreciated property to a qualified charity. Recall that in certain circumstances, the measure of the charitable contribution is fair market value when the property, if sold, would have yielded a long-term capital gain (refer to the discussion of contributions of capital gain property in Chapter 10).

EXAMPLE 54

Sharon wants to donate a tract of unimproved land (basis of $40,000 and fair market value of $200,000) held for the required long-term holding period to State University (a qualified charitable organization). However, Sharon currently is under audit by the IRS for capital gains she reported on certain real estate transactions during an earlier tax year. Although Sharon is not a licensed real estate broker, the IRS agent conducting the audit is contending that she has achieved dealer status by virtue of the number and frequency of the real estate transactions she has conducted.

Under these circumstances, Sharon would be well advised to postpone the donation to State University until her status is clarified. If she has achieved dealer status, the unimproved land may be inventory (refer to Example 52 for another possible result) and Sharon's charitable contribution deduction would be limited to $40,000. If not and if the land is held as an investment, Sharon's deduction is $200,000 (the fair market value of the property).

16-7d **Stock Sales**

The following rules apply in determining the date of a stock sale:

- The date the sale is executed is the date of the sale. The execution date is the date the broker completes the transaction on the stock exchange.
- The settlement date is the date the cash or other property is paid to the seller of the stock. This date is *not* relevant in determining the date of sale.

EXAMPLE 55

Lupe, a cash basis taxpayer, sells stock that results in a gain. The sale was executed on December 29, 2016. The settlement date is January 2, 2017. The date of sale is December 29, 2016 (the execution date). The holding period for the stock sold ends with the execution date.

16-7e **Maximizing Benefits**

Ordinary losses generally are preferable to capital losses because of the limitations imposed on the deductibility of net capital losses and the requirement that capital losses be used to offset capital gains. The taxpayer may be able to convert what would otherwise have been capital loss to ordinary loss. For example, business (but not nonbusiness) bad debts, losses from the sale or exchange of small business investment company stock, and losses from the sale or exchange of small business corporation stock all result in ordinary losses.[38]

Although capital losses can be carried over indefinitely, *indefinite* becomes definite when a taxpayer dies. Any loss carryovers not used by the taxpayer are permanently lost. That is, no tax benefit can be derived from the carryovers subsequent to death.[39] Therefore, the potential benefit of carrying over capital losses diminishes when dealing with older taxpayers.

It is usually beneficial to spread gains over more than one taxable year. In some cases, this can be accomplished through the installment sales method of accounting.

---

[37]§ 1271(b).

[38]§§ 166(d), 1242, and 1244. Refer to the discussion in Chapter 7.

[39]Rev.Rul. 74–175, 1974–1 C.B. 52.

16-7f **Year-End Planning**

The following general rules can be applied for timing the recognition of capital gains and losses near the end of a taxable year:

- If the taxpayer already has recognized more than $3,000 of capital loss, sell assets to generate capital gain equal to the excess of the capital loss over $3,000.

EXAMPLE

56

Kevin has already incurred a $7,000 STCL. Kevin should generate $4,000 of capital gain. The gain will offset $4,000 of the loss. The remaining loss of $3,000 can be deducted against ordinary income.

- If the taxpayer already has recognized capital gain, sell assets to generate capital loss equal to the capital gain. The gain will not be taxed, and the loss will be fully *deductible* against the gain.
- Generally, if the taxpayer has a choice between recognizing short-term capital gain or long-term capital gain, long-term capital gain should be recognized because it is subject to a lower tax rate.

REFOCUS ON THE BIG PICTURE

MANAGING CAPITAL ASSET TRANSACTIONS

You explain to Maurice that your area of expertise is tax, so you are providing tax advice and not investment advice. From an overall perspective, he is correct that certain capital gains and dividends are eligible for either a 0 percent, a 15 percent, or a 20 percent tax rate rather than the regular income tax rates that go as high as 39.6 percent. You then discuss the potential tax consequences of each of his investments.

- *Purple stock and Eagle stock.* To qualify for the beneficial tax rate, the holding period for the stock must be longer than one year. From a tax perspective, Maurice should retain his stock investments for at least an additional three months and a day. To be eligible for the "costless" capital gains (i.e., capital gains taxed at 0%), his taxable income should not exceed $37,950 for 2017. The dividends received on the Purple stock are "qualified dividends" eligible for the *0%/15%/20%* alternative tax rate.
- *Patent.* Because he is a "holder" of the patent, it will qualify for the beneficial capital gain rate regardless of the holding period if the patent should produce income in excess of his $50,000 investment. However, if he loses money on the investment, he will be able to deduct only $3,000 of the loss per year against his ordinary income (assuming that there are no offsetting capital gains).
- *Tax-exempt bonds.* The after-tax return on the taxable bonds would be less than the 3 percent on the tax-exempt bonds. In addition, the interest on the taxable bonds would increase his taxable income, possibly moving it out of the desired 15 percent marginal tax rate into the 25 percent marginal tax rate.
- *Franchise rights.* The franchise rights purchased from Orange, Inc., probably require the payment of a franchise fee based upon the sales in the franchise business. Maurice should either start such a business or sell the franchise rights.
- *Partnership interest.* Whether Maurice receives capital or ordinary treatment associated with his partnership interest depends on whether he is reporting his share of profits or losses (ordinary income or ordinary loss) or is reporting recognized gain or loss from the sale of his partnership interest (capital gain or capital loss).

You conclude your tax advice to Maurice by telling him that whatever he does regarding his investments should make economic sense. There are no 100 percent tax rates. For example, disposing of the bank stock in the current market could be the wise thing to do.

AUREMAR/SHUTTERSTOCK.COM

Key Terms

Discussion Questions

Issue ID   1.   **LO.2, 4, 5** Sheila inherited 300 shares of stock, 100 shares of Magenta and 200 shares of Purple. She has a stockbroker sell the shares for her, uses the proceeds for personal expenses, and thinks nothing further about the transactions. What issues does she face when she prepares her Federal income tax return?

Issue ID   2.   **LO.2** An individual taxpayer sells some used assets at a garage sale. Why are none of the proceeds taxable in most situations?

Issue ID   3.   **LO.2, 4** Alison owns a painting that she received as a gift from her aunt 10 years ago. The aunt created the painting. Alison has displayed the painting in her home and has never attempted to sell it. Recently, a visitor noticed the painting and offered Alison $5,000 for it. If Alison decides to sell the painting, what tax issues does she face?

4.   **LO.2** Is a note receivable that arose in the ordinary course of the taxpayer's retail business a capital asset? Why or why not?

5.   **LO.2** Anwar owns vacant land that he purchased many years ago as an investment. After getting approval to subdivide it into 35 lots, he made minimal improvements and then sold the entire property to a real estate developer. Anwar's recognized gain on the sale was $1.2 million. Is this transaction eligible for the "real property subdivided for sale" provisions? Why or why not?

Issue ID   6.   **LO.3** Hubert purchases all of the rights in a patent from the inventor who developed the patented product. After holding the patent for two years, Hubert sells all of the rights in the patent for a substantial gain. What issues does Hubert face if he wants to treat the gain as a long-term capital gain?

7.   **LO.3** Blue Corporation and Fuchsia Corporation are engaged in a contract negotiation over the use of Blue's trademarked name, DateSiteForSeniors. For a one-time payment of $45,000, Blue licensed Fuchsia to use the name DateSiteForSeniors, and the license requires that Fuchsia pay Blue a royalty every time a new customer signs up on Fuchsia's website. Blue is a developer of "website ideas" that it then licenses to other companies such as Fuchsia. Did Fuchsia purchase a franchise right from Blue, or did Fuchsia purchase the name DateSiteForSeniors from Blue?

8.   **LO.4** At the date of a short sale, Sylvia has held substantially identical securities for more than 12 months. What is the nature of any gain or loss from the close of her short sale?

9.   **LO.5** After netting all of her short-term and long-term capital gains and losses, Misty has a net short-term capital loss and a net long-term capital loss. Can she net these against each other? Why or why not?

10. **LO.2, 5** Charlie sells his antique farm tractor collection at a loss. He had acquired all of the tractors for his personal pleasure and sold all of them for less than

he paid for them. What is the tax status of the tractors? Is his loss a 28% collectibles loss? Explain.

11. **LO.2, 5, 7** Near the end of 2017, Byron realizes that he has a net short-term capital   Issue ID
loss of $13,000 for the year. Byron has taxable income (not including the loss) of $123,000 and is single. He owns numerous stocks that could be sold for a long-term capital gain. What should he do before the end of 2017?

Computational Exercises

12. **LO.2** Dexter owns a large tract of land and subdivides it for sale. Assume that Dexter meets all of the requirements of § 1237 and during the tax year sells the first eight lots to eight different buyers for $22,000 each. Dexter's basis in each lot sold is $15,000, and he incurs total selling expenses of $900 on each sale. What is the amount of Dexter's capital gain and ordinary income? Formulate your answer by constructing a spreadsheet using a format similar to that found in Example 9.

13. **LO.3** Shelia purchases $50,000 of newly issued Gingo Corporation bonds for $45,000. The bonds have original issue discount (OID) of $5,000. After Sheila amortized $2,300 of OID and held the bonds for four years, she sold the bonds for $48,000. What is the amount and character of her gain or loss?

14. **LO.3** Olivia wants to buy some vacant land for investment purposes. She cannot afford the full purchase price. Instead, Olivia pays the landowner $8,000 to obtain an option to buy the land for $175,000 anytime in the next four years. Fourteen months after purchasing the option, Olivia sells the option for $10,000. What is the amount and character of Olivia's gain or loss?

15. **LO.3** On May 9, 2017, Glenna purchases 500 shares of Ignaz Company stock for $7,500. On June 30, 2017, she writes a call option on the stock, giving the grantee the right to buy the stock for $9,000 during the following 12-month period. Glenna receives a call premium of $750 for writing the call. The call is exercised by the grantee on December 15, 2017.
   a.   What is the amount and character of Glenna's gain or loss?
   b.   Assume that the original option expired unexercised. What is the amount and character of Glenna's gain or loss?

16. **LO.4** Shen purchased corporate stock for $20,000 on April 10, 2015. On July 14, 2017, when the stock was worth $12,000, Shen died and his son, Mijo, inherited the stock. Mijo sold the stock for $14,200 on November 12, 2017. What is the amount and character of Mijo's gain or loss?

17. **LO.5** Coline has the following capital gain and loss transactions for 2017.

Short-term capital gain	$ 5,000
Short-term capital loss	(2,100)
Long-term capital gain (28%)	6,000
Long-term capital gain (15%)	2,000
Long-term capital loss (28%)	(10,500)

After the capital gain and loss netting process, what is the amount and character of Coline's gain or loss?

18. **LO.5** Elliott has the following capital gain and loss transactions for 2017.

Short-term capital gain	$ 1,500
Short-term capital loss	(3,600)
Long-term capital gain (28%)	12,000
Long-term capital gain (25%)	4,800

Long-term capital gain (15%)	$ 6,000
Long-term capital loss (28%)	(4,500)
Long-term capital loss (15%)	(9,000)

After the capital gain and loss netting process, what is the amount and character of Elliott's gain or loss?

Problems

19. **LO.2** During the year, Eugene had the four property transactions summarized below. Eugene is a collector of antique glassware and occasionally sells a piece to get funds to buy another. What are the amount and nature of the gain or loss from each of these transactions?

Property	Date Acquired	Date Sold	Adjusted Basis	Sales Price
Antique vase	06/18/06	05/23/17	$37,000	$42,000
Blue Growth Fund (100 shares)	12/23/08	11/22/17	22,000	38,000
Orange bonds	02/12/09	04/11/17	34,000	42,000*
Green stock (100 shares)	02/14/17	11/23/17	11,000	13,000

*The sales price included $750 of accrued interest.

Decision Making 20. **LO.2, 5** Rennie owns a video game arcade. He buys vintage video games from estates, often at much less than the retail value of the property. He usually installs the vintage video games in a special section of his video game arcade that appeals to players of "classic" video games. Recently, Rennie sold a classic video game that a customer "just had to have." Rennie paid $11,250 for it, owned it for 14 months, and sold it for $18,000. Rennie had suspected that this particular classic video game would be of interest to collectors; so he had it refurbished, put it on display in his video arcade, and listed it for sale on the internet. No customers in the arcade had played it other than those testing it before considering it for purchase. Rennie would like the gain on the sale of the classic video game to be a long-term capital gain. Did he achieve that objective? Why or why not?

21. **LO.2** George is the owner of numerous classic automobiles. His intention is to hold the automobiles until they increase in value and then sell them. He rents the automobiles for use in various events (e.g., antique automobile shows) while he is holding them. In 2017, he sold a classic automobile for $1.5 million. He had held the automobile for five years, and it had a tax basis of $750,000.

a. Was the automobile a capital asset? Why or why not?

b. Assuming a rate of return of 7%, how much would he have had to invest five years ago (instead of putting $750,000 into the car) to have had $1.5 million this year? See Appendix H for the present value factors.

22. **LO.2, 4** Barbella purchased a wedding ring for $15 at a yard sale in May. She thought the ring was costume jewelry, but it turned out to be a real diamond ring. She is not in the business of buying and selling anything. She researched the ring on the internet and discovered that it was worth at least $1,000. She sold it on an internet auction site for $1,100 in July. Was the ring a capital asset? What were the amount and nature of the gain or loss from its sale by Barbella?

23. **LO.2** Puce is a corporation that buys and sells financial assets. It purchases notes receivable from manufacturers that need cash immediately and cannot wait to collect the notes. Puce pays about 88% of the face value of the receivables and

then collects them. Because of the quality of the notes, Puce collected less than it paid for some of the notes. Does Puce have a capital loss when it collects the receivables for less than it paid for them? Explain.

24. **LO.2** Faith Godwin is a dealer in securities. She has spotted a fast-rising company and would like to buy and hold its stock for investment. The stock is currently selling for $2 per share, and Faith thinks it will climb to $40 a share within two years. Faith's coworkers have told her that there is "no way" she can get long-term capital gain treatment when she purchases stock because she is a securities dealer. Faith has asked you to calculate her potential gain and tell her whether her coworkers are right. Draft a letter to Faith responding to her request. Her address is 200 Catamon Drive, Great Falls, MT 59406.

Communications

25. **LO.2** Maria meets all of the requirements of § 1237 (subdivided realty). In 2017, she begins selling lots and sells four separate lots to four different purchasers. She also sells two contiguous lots to another purchaser. The sales price of each lot is $30,000. Maria's basis for each lot is $15,000. Selling expenses are $500 per lot.

   a.   What are the realized and recognized gain?

   b.   Explain the nature of the gain (i.e., ordinary income or capital gain).

   c.   Would your answers change if, instead, the lots sold to the fifth purchaser were not contiguous? If so, how?

26. **LO.2, 3, 5** Melaney has had a bad year with her investments. She lent a friend $8,000; the friend did not repay the loan when it was due and then declared bankruptcy. The loan is totally uncollectible. Melaney also was notified by her broker that the Oak corporate bonds she owned became worthless on October 13, 2017. She had purchased the bonds for $22,000 on November 10, 2016. Melaney also had a $60,000 loss on the disposition of § 1244 corporate stock that she purchased several years ago. Melaney is single.

Decision Making

   a.   What are the nature and amount of Melaney's losses?

   b.   What is Melaney's AGI for 2017 assuming that she has $65,000 of ordinary gross income from sources other than those discussed?

   c.   What are the nature and amount of Melaney's loss carryforwards?

27. **LO.2, 3** Benny purchased $400,000 of Peach Corporation face value bonds for $320,000 on November 13, 2016. The bonds had been issued with $80,000 of original issue discount because Peach was in financial difficulty in 2016. On December 3, 2017, Benny sold the bonds for $283,000 after amortizing $1,000 of the original issue discount. What are the nature and amount of Benny's gain or loss?

28. **LO.3** Fred is an investor in vacant land. When he thinks he has identified property that would be a good investment, he approaches the landowner, pays the landowner for a "right of first refusal" to purchase the land, records this right in the property records, and then waits to see if the land increases in value. The right of first refusal is valid for four years. Fourteen months ago, Fred paid a landowner $9,000 for a right of first refusal. The land was selected as the site of a new shopping center, and the landowner was offered $1 million for the land. In its title search on the land, the buyer discovered Fred's right of first refusal and involved him in the purchase negotiations. Ultimately, the landowner paid Fred $220,000 to give up his right of first refusal; the landowner then sold the land to the buyer for $4,220,000. Fred has a marginal tax rate of 39.6%.

Decision Making

   a.   What difference does it make whether Fred treats the right of first refusal as an option to purchase the land?

   b.   What difference does it make whether Fred is a "dealer" in land?

29. **LO.3** Carla was the owner of vacant land that she was holding for investment. She paid $2 million for the land in 2015. Raymond was an investor in vacant land.

He thought Carla's land might be the site of an exit ramp from a new freeway. Raymond gave Carla $836,000 for an option on her land in 2016. The option was good for two years and gave Raymond the ability to purchase Carla's land for $4,765,000. The freeway was not approved by the government, and Raymond's option expired in 2017. Does Carla have $836,000 of long-term capital gain upon the expiration of the option? Explain.

30. **LO.3** Hilde purchased all of the rights to a patent on a new garden tool developed by a friend of hers who was an amateur inventor. The inventor had obtained the patent rights, set up a manufacturing company to produce and sell the garden tool, and produced substantial quantities of the tool, but he then became discouraged when no large garden company would agree to distribute the tool for him. Hilde purchased the patent rights (but not the manufacturing company) for $120,000 on October 24, 2016. Hilde had never engaged in such a transaction before, but she is a salesperson in the garden industry and thought she could succeed where her friend had failed. On June 27, 2017, she sold all of the patent rights to Garden Tool Company for $1,233,000. Garden Tool will manufacture the tool in its own factory and sell it to its customers. What is the nature of Hilde's gain from this transaction?

Decision Making   31. **LO.3, 4, 7** Mac, an inventor, obtained a patent on a chemical process to clean old aluminum siding so that it can be easily repainted. Mac has a $50,000 tax basis in the patent. Mac does not have the capital to begin manufacturing and selling this product, so he has done nothing with the patent since obtaining it two years ago. Now a group of individuals has approached him and offered two alternatives. Under one alternative, they will pay Mac $600,000 (payable evenly over the next 15 years) for the exclusive right to manufacture and sell the product. Under the other, they will form a business and contribute capital to it to begin manufacturing and selling the product; Mac will receive 20% of the company's shares of stock in exchange for all of his patent rights. Discuss which alternative is better for Mac.

32. **LO.3** Freys, Inc., sells a 12-year "stuffed potato" franchise to Reynaldo. The franchise contains many restrictions on how Reynaldo may operate his store. For instance, Reynaldo cannot use less than Grade 10 Idaho potatoes; must bake the potatoes at a constant 410 degrees; must dress store personnel in Freys-approved uniforms; and must have a Freys sign that meets detailed specifications on size, color, and construction. When the franchise contract is signed, Reynaldo makes a noncontingent $160,000 payment to Freys. During the same year, Reynaldo pays Freys $300,000—14% of Reynaldo's sales. How does Freys treat each of these payments? How does Reynaldo treat each of the payments?

Issue ID   33. **LO.3** Angie owns numerous strip malls. A major tenant of one of the strip malls wanted to cancel its lease because it was moving to another city. After lengthy negotiations, the tenant paid Angie $60,000 to cancel its obligations under the lease. If the tenant had fulfilled the lease terms, Angie would have received rent of $700,000. What factors should Angie consider to determine the amount and character of her income from these circumstances?

34. **LO.3** Consuela was a tenant in a campus apartment. She is a student at State University. Her lease began on August 1, 2017, and was due to expire on July 31, 2018. However, her landlord sold the building, and the new owner wanted to demolish it to build a retail building. Consuela's landlord paid her $1,000 to cancel the lease. Consuela received the $1,000 on November 30, 2017; moved out; and rented another apartment. How should Consuela treat the $1,000?

35. **LO.4** Maria held vacant land that qualified as an investment asset. She purchased the vacant land on April 10, 2013. She exchanged the vacant land for a rental house in a qualifying like-kind exchange on January 22, 2017. Maria was going to hold the house for several years and then sell it. However, she got an "offer she

could not refuse" and sold it on November 22, 2017, for a substantial gain. What was Maria's holding period for the house?

36. **LO.4** Roger inherited 100 shares of Periwinkle stock when his mother, Emily, died. Emily had acquired the stock for a total of $60,000 on November 15, 2013. She died on August 10, 2017, and the shares were worth a total of $55,000 at that time. Roger sold the shares for $36,000 on December 22, 2017. How much gain or loss does Roger recognize? What is the nature of that gain or loss?

37. **LO.4** Sarah received a gift of farmland from her father. The land was worth $4 million at the date of the gift, had been farmed by her father for 40 years, and had a tax basis for her father of $30,000. Sarah never farmed the land and sold it eight months after receiving it from her father for $4.2 million. What is Sarah's holding period for the farmland? What is the nature of the gain from its disposition?

38. **LO.4** Dennis sells short 100 shares of ARC stock at $20 per share on January 15, 2017. He buys 200 shares of ARC stock on April 1, 2017, at $25 per share. On May 2, 2017, he closes the short sale by delivering 100 of the shares purchased on April 1.

    a. What are the amount and nature of Dennis's loss upon closing the short sale?

    b. When does the holding period for the remaining 100 shares begin?

    c. If Dennis sells (at $27 per share) the remaining 100 shares on January 20, 2018, what will be the nature of his gain or loss?

39. **LO.5** Elaine Case (single with no dependents) has the following transactions in 2017:

AGI (exclusive of capital gains and losses)	$240,000
Long-term capital gain	22,000
Long-term capital loss	(8,000)
Short-term capital gain	19,000
Short-term capital loss	(23,000)

    What is Elaine's net capital gain or loss? Draft a letter to Elaine describing how the net capital gain or loss will be treated on her tax return. Assume that Elaine's income from other sources puts her in the 39.6% bracket. Elaine's address is 300 Ireland Avenue, Shepherdstown, WV 25443.

    Communications

40. **LO.3, 5** In 2017, Bertha Jarow had a $28,000 loss from the sale of a personal residence. She also purchased a patent on a rubber bonding process from an individual inventor for $7,000 (and resold it in two months for $18,000). The patent had not yet been reduced to practice. Bertha purchased the patent as an investment. In addition, she had the following capital gains and losses from stock transactions:

Long-term capital loss	($ 6,000)
Long-term capital loss carryover from 2016	(12,000)
Short-term capital gain	21,000
Short-term capital loss	(7,000)

    What is Bertha's net capital gain or loss? Draft a letter to Bertha explaining the tax treatment of the sale of her personal residence. Assume that Bertha's income from other sources puts her in the 28% bracket. Bertha's address is 1120 West Street, Ashland, OR 97520.

    Communications

41. **LO.2, 4, 5** Bridgette is known as the "doll lady." She started collecting dolls as a child, always received one or more dolls as gifts on her birthday, never sold any dolls, and eventually owned 600 dolls. She is retiring and moving to a small apartment and has decided to sell her collection. She lists the dolls on an internet auction site and, to her great surprise, receives an offer from another doll collector of $45,000 for

    Issue ID

the entire collection. Bridgette sells the entire collection, except for five dolls she purchased during the last year. She had owned all of the dolls sold for more than a year. What tax factors should Bridgette consider in deciding how to report the sale?

42. **LO.5** Phil and Susan Hammond are married taxpayers filing a joint return. The couple have two dependent children. Susan has wages of $34,000 in 2016. Phil does not work due to a disability, but he is a buyer and seller of stocks. He generally buys and holds for long-term gain, but occasionally gets in and out of a stock quickly. The couple's 2016 stock transactions are detailed below. In addition, they have $2,300 of qualifying dividends.

    a. What is Phil and Susan's AGI?

Item	Date Acquired	Date Sold	Cost	Sales Price
Blue stock (10 shares)	11/10/15	03/12/16	$ 3,000	$ 6,000
Purple stock (100 shares)	12/13/14	05/23/16	36,000	32,000
Beige stock (50 shares)	12/14/11	07/14/16	13,000	14,500
Red stock (100 shares)	06/29/15	05/18/16	26,000	27,000
Black stock (100 shares)	05/15/15	10/18/16	67,000	67,800
Gray stock (100 shares)	04/23/14	10/18/16	89,000	88,200

    b. Complete a Form 8949 for the Hammonds (Phil's Social Security number is 123-45-6789). Assume that the stock sale information was reported to the Hammonds on a Form 1099–B and that basis information was provided to the IRS.

43. **LO.5** Paul has the following long-term capital gains and losses for 2017: $62,000 28% gain, $21,000 28% loss, $18,000 25% gain, and $64,000 0%/15%/20% gain. He also has a $53,000 short-term loss and a $5,000 short-term gain. What is Paul's AGI from these transactions? If he has a net long-term capital gain, what is its makeup in terms of the alternative tax rates?

44. **LO.5** Helena has the following long-term capital gains and losses for 2017: $65,000 28% gain, $53,000 28% loss, $28,000 25% gain, and $24,000 0%/15%/20% loss. She also has a $33,000 short-term loss and a $65,000 short-term gain. What is Helena's AGI from these transactions? If she has a net long-term capital gain, what is its makeup in terms of the alternative tax rates?

45. **LO.5** For 2017, Ashley has gross income of $38,350 and a $5,000 long-term capital loss. She claims the standard deduction. Ashley is 35 years old and unmarried with two dependent children. How much of Ashley's $5,000 capital loss carries over to 2018?

46. **LO.5** Jane and Blair are married taxpayers filing jointly and have 2017 taxable income of $97,000. The taxable income includes $5,000 of gain from a capital asset held five years, $2,100 of gain from a capital asset held seven months, and $13,000 of gain from a capital asset held four years. All of the capital assets were stock in publicly traded corporations. Jane and Blair also have qualified dividend income of $3,000. What is the couple's tax on taxable income?

47. **LO.5** For 2017, Wilma has properly determined taxable income of $36,000, including $3,000 of unrecaptured § 1250 gain and $8,200 of 0%/15%/20% gain. Wilma qualifies for head-of-household filing status. Compute Wilma's tax liability and the tax savings from the alternative tax on net capital gain.

48. **LO.5** Asok's AGI for 2017 is $133,050. Included in this AGI is a $45,000 25% long-term capital gain and a $13,000 0%/15%/20% long-term capital gain. Asok is single, uses the standard deduction, and has only his personal exemption. Compute his taxable income, the tax liability, and the tax savings from the alternative tax on net capital gain.

49. **LO.6** Gray, Inc., a C corporation, has taxable income from operations of $1,452,000 for 2017. It also has a net long-term capital loss of $355,000 from the sale of a subsidiary's stock. The year 2017 is the first year in the last 10 years that Gray has not had at least $500,000 per year of net long-term capital gains. What is Gray's 2017 taxable income? What, if anything, can it do with any unused capital losses?

50. **LO.2, 3, 7** Harriet, who is single, is the owner of a sole proprietorship. Two years ago, Harriet developed a process for preserving doughnuts that gives the doughnut a much longer shelf life. The process is not patented or copyrighted, and only Harriet knows how it works. Harriet has been approached by a company that would like to buy the process. Harriet insists that she receive a long-term employment contract with the acquiring company as well as be paid for the rights to the process. The acquiring company offers Harriet a choice of two options: (1) $650,000 in cash for the process and a 10-year covenant not to compete at $65,000 per year or (2) $650,000 in cash for a 10-year covenant not to compete and $65,000 per year for 10 years in payment for the process. Which option should Harriet accept? What is the tax effect on the acquiring company of each approach?

Decision Making

Cumulative Problems

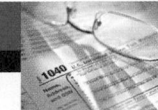

51. Ashley Panda lives at 1310 Meadow Lane, Wayne, OH 43466, and her Social Security number is 123-45-6789. Ashley is single and has a 20-year-old son, Bill. His Social Security number is 111-11-1112. Bill lives with Ashley, and she fully supports him. Bill spent 2016 traveling in Europe and was not a college student. He had gross income of $4,655 in 2016. Bill paid $4,000 of lodging expenses that Ashley reimbursed after they were fully documented. Ashley paid the $4,000 to Bill using a check from her sole proprietorship. That amount is not included in the items listed below.

Tax Return Problem

TAX SOFTWARE

Ashley owns Panda Enterprises, LLC sole proprietorship, a data processing service (98-7654321), which is located at 456 Hill Street, Wayne, OH 43466. The business activity code is 514210. Her 2016 Form 1040, Schedule C for Panda Enterprises shows revenues of $315,000, office expenses of $66,759, employee salary of $63,000, employee payroll taxes of $4,820, meals and entertainment expenses (before the 50% reduction) of $22,000, and rent expense of $34,000. The rent expense includes payments related to renting an office ($30,000) and payments related to renting various equipment ($4,000). There is no depreciation because all depreciable equipment owned has been fully depreciated in previous years. No fringe benefits are provided to the employee. Ashley personally purchases health insurance on herself and Bill. The premiums are $23,000 per year.

Ashley has an extensive stock portfolio and has prepared the following analysis:

Stock	Number of Shares	Date Purchased	Date Sold	Per-Share Cost	Per-Share Selling Price	Total Dividends
Beige	10	10/18/15	10/11/16	$80	$ 74	$30
Garland	30	10/11/09	10/11/16	43	157	70
Puce	15	3/10/16	8/11/16	62	33	45

NOTE: Ashley received a Form 1099–B from her stockbroker that included the adjusted basis and sales proceeds for each of her stock transactions. The per-share cost includes commissions, and the per-share selling price is net of commissions. Also, the dividends are the actual dividends received in 2016, and these are both ordinary dividends and qualified dividends.

Ashley had $800 of interest income from State of Ohio bonds and $600 of interest income on her Wayne Savings Bank account. She paid $25,000 of alimony to her former husband. His Social Security number is 123-45-6788.

Ashley itemizes her deductions and had the following items, which may be relevant to her return:

Item	Amount	Comment
Unreimbursed medical expenses for Ashley (all for visits to doctors)	$1,786	Does not include health insurance premiums.
State income taxes paid	1,830	
Real property taxes on personal residence	3,230	
Interest paid on home mortgage (Form 1098)	8,137	The loan is secured by the residence and was incurred when the home was purchased.
Charitable contributions	1,399	$940 cash payments to Ashley's church and $459 cash payments made to homeless persons for whom she felt sorry. She can document all the expenditures.
Sales taxes	619	Amount per sales tax table.

Ashley made a $30,000 estimated Federal income tax payment, does not want any of her taxes to finance presidential elections, has no foreign bank accounts or trusts, and wants any refund to be applied against her 2017 taxes.

Compute Ashley's net tax payable or refund due for 2016. If you use tax forms for your computations, you will need Form 1040 and its Schedules A, C, D, and SE and Form 8949. Suggested software: H&R BLOCK Tax Software.

Tax Computation Problem
Communications

52. Paul Barrone is a graduate student at State University. His 10-year-old son, Jamie, lives with him, and Paul is Jamie's sole support. Paul's wife died in 2016, and Paul has not remarried. Paul received $320,000 of life insurance proceeds (related to his wife's death) in early 2017 and immediately invested the entire amount as shown below:

Item	Date Acquired	Cost	Date Sold	Selling Price	Dividends/ Interest
1,000 shares Blue	01/23/17	$ 14,000	12/03/17	$ 3,500	None
400 shares Magenta	01/23/17	23,000			$750
600 shares Orange	01/23/17	230,000			$2,300
100 shares Brown	06/23/11	2,800	01/23/17	14,000	None
Green bonds	01/23/17	23,000			$1,200
Gold money market account	01/23/17	30,000			$600

Paul had $42,000 of taxable graduate assistant earnings from State University and received a $10,000 scholarship. He used $8,000 of the scholarship to pay his tuition and fees for the year and $2,000 for Jamie's day care. Jamie attended Little Kids Daycare Center, a state-certified child care facility. Paul received a statement related to the Green bonds saying that there was $45 of original issue discount amortization during 2017. Paul maintains the receipts for the sales taxes he paid of $735.

Paul lives at 1610 Cherry Lane, Bradenton, FL 34212, and his Social Security number is 111-11-1111. Jamie's Social Security number is 123-45-6789. The university withheld $3,000 of Federal income tax from Paul's salary. Paul is not itemizing his deductions.

Part 1—Tax Computation
Compute Paul's lowest tax liability for 2017.

Part 2—Tax Planning
Paul is concerned because the Green bonds were worth only $18,000 at the end of 2017, $5,000 less than he paid for them. He is an inexperienced investor and wants to know if this $5,000 is deductible. The bonds had original issue discount of $2,000 when he purchased them, and he is curious about how that affects his investment in the bonds. The bonds had 20 years left to maturity when he purchased them. Draft a brief letter to Paul explaining how to handle these items. Also prepare a memo for Paul's tax file.

Research Problems

Note: Solutions to the Research Problems can be prepared by using the Thomson Reuters Checkpoint® Student Edition online tax research database, which accompanies this textbook. Solutions can also be prepared by using research materials found in a typical tax library.

Research Problem 1. Ali owns 100 shares of Brown Corporation stock. He purchased the stock at five different times and at five different prices per share as indicated:

Share Block	Number of Shares	Per-Share Price	Purchase Date
A	10	$60	10/10/99
B	20	20	8/11/00
C	15	15	10/24/01
D	35	30	4/23/02
E	20	25	7/28/02

On April 28, 2017, Ali will sell 40 shares of Brown stock for $40 per share. All of Ali's shares are held by his stockbroker. The broker's records track when the shares were purchased. May Ali designate the shares he sells? If so, which shares should he sell? Assume that Ali wants to maximize his gain because he has a capital loss carryforward.

Research Problem 2. Clyde had worked for many years as the chief executive of Red Industries, Inc., and had been a major shareholder. Clyde and the company had a falling out, and Clyde was terminated. Clyde and Red executed a document under which Clyde's stock in Red would be redeemed and Clyde would agree not to compete against Red in its geographic service area. After extensive negotiations between the parties, Clyde agreed to surrender his Red stock in exchange for $600,000. Clyde's basis in his shares was $143,000, and he had held the shares for 17 years. The agreement made no explicit allocation of any of the $600,000 to Clyde's agreement not to compete against Red. How should Clyde treat the $600,000 payment on his 2017 tax return?

Research Problem 3. Siva Nathaniel owns various plots of land in Fulton County, Georgia. He acquired the land at various times during the last 20 years. About every fourth year, Siva subdivides into lots one of the properties he owns. He then has water, sewer, natural gas, and electricity hookups put in each lot and paves new streets. Siva has always treated his sales of such lots as sales of capital assets. His previous tax returns were prepared by an accountant whose practice you recently purchased. Has the proper tax treatment been used on the prior tax returns? Explain

Partial list of research aids:
§§ 1221 and 1237 and *Jesse W. and Betty J. English*, 65 TCM 2160, T.C.Memo. 1993–111.

Use internet tax resources to address the following questions. Look for reliable websites and blogs of the IRS and other government agencies, media outlets, businesses, tax professionals, academics, think tanks, and political outlets.

Research Problem 4. Perform a Google search to find information about capital gains tax rates worldwide (and across U.S. states). Try searching for "capital gains rate by country (state)." What jurisdiction has the highest capital gains tax rate? What U.S. states have high capital gains tax rates?

Research Problem 5. Find a website, other than the IRS website, that discusses the taxation of short sales of securities.

Roger CPA Review Questions

1. Identify which of the following is a capital asset:

   I.   A canvas painting of a portrait client, in the painter's hands
   II. Depreciable fixtures in a business parking lot
   III. Office supplies held by a business
   a.   II only
   b.   II and III only
   c.   III only
   d.   None of the above

2. On January 15 of the current year, Kreutzer, an individual, received as an inheritance from Gladstone's estate shares of stock worth $25,000. Gladstone had purchased the shares in June of the previous year for $20,000, and the shares were worth $25,000 at Gladstone's date of death in November of the previous year. The executor of Gladstone's estate did not elect to use the alternate valuation date. In March of the current year, Kreutzer sold the shares for $27,000. As a result of the sale, what is the amount and type of gain reported by Kreutzer?
   a. $7,000 long-term capital gain
   b. $2,000 short-term capital gain
   c. $7,000 short-term capital gain
   d. $2,000 long-term capital gain

3. The following facts apply to Collins, an individual:

   In February of the current year, Hodge, who had owed a $5,000 personal debt to Collins for the past three years, declared bankruptcy.

   Collins sold land held for investment for a $10,000 gain. The land had been purchased by Collins five years prior.

   In July of the current year, Collins received shares of stock as a gift from Bellamy. The stock was worth more than Bellamy paid for it when it was gifted to Collins. Bellamy had purchased the shares in January of the current year. In November, Collins sold the stock for a gain of $3,000.

   Considering only the above facts, what will Collins report on the current year tax return?
   a. $2,000 long-term capital gain
   b. $8,000 long-term capital gain
   c. $10,000 ordinary income and $2,000 short-term capital loss
   d. $10,000 long-term capital gain and $3,000 short-term capital gain

4. In 2017 Colossus Corporation incurred a net capital loss in the amount of $25,000. Colossus had the following net capital gains in the previous five years:

   2016: $7,000
   2015: $2,000
   2014: $5,000
   2013: $4,000
   2012: $3,000

   How much of the 2017 net capital loss may Colossus carry over to 2018?
   a. $0
   b. $25,000
   c. $11,000
   d. $4,000

5. The following facts apply to Eliot, an individual, in the current year:

    April 2: Sold shares of stock, purchased on April 1 of the previous year, for a $2,000 gain.

    May 15: Sold equipment used in Eliot's business, which had been purchased in July of the previous year, for a $2,000 gain.

    July 12: Sold shares of stock, purchased in February of the previous year, for a $7,000 gain.

    November 3: Sold equipment used in Eliot's business, which had been purchased in January of the current year, for a $1,000 loss.

    December 9: Sold shares of stock, purchased on February 22 of the current year, for a $3,000 loss.

    Considering only the above facts, what is Eliot's net capital gain for the current year?

    a. $7,000 long-term capital gain
    b. $9,000 long-term capital gain
    c. $5,000 long-term capital gain
    d. $6,000 long-term capital gain

Property Transactions: § 1231 and Recapture Provisions

LEARNING OBJECTIVES: *After completing Chapter 17, you should be able to:*

LO.1 State the rationale for and the nature and treatment of gains and losses from the disposition of business assets.

LO.2 Distinguish § 1231 assets from ordinary assets and capital assets and calculate the § 1231 gain or loss.

LO.3 Determine when § 1245 recapture applies and how it is computed.

LO.4 Determine when § 1250 recapture applies.

LO.5 Identify considerations common to §§ 1245 and 1250.

LO.6 Recognize special recapture provisions that are part of the tax law.

LO.7 Describe and apply the reporting procedures for §§ 1231, 1245, and 1250.

LO.8 Identify tax planning opportunities associated with §§ 1231, 1245, and 1250.

CHAPTER OUTLINE

RL PRODUCTIONS/GETTY IMAGES

THE BIG PICTURE

DEPRECIATION RECAPTURE

Hazel Brown (a sole proprietor filing a Form 1040 Schedule C) owns and operates a retail arts and crafts store. She has some 15-year-old snow removal equipment with a $1,000 tax basis. Next to her store is a small lot that she bought several years ago for $15,000 to expand the store's parking lot. In 2014, she remodeled the store and replaced the store's equipment (counters, display racks, etc.), at a cost of $450,000, with used equipment that she bought from a competitor. The equipment is 7-year MACRS property. That year she claimed $250,000 of § 179 expense on it and depreciated the balance. She did not expense the entire $450,000 (the maximum § 179 deduction in 2014 was $500,000) because she expected to be in a higher tax bracket in later years and wanted to "save" some of the depreciation. As of June 30, 2017, the equipment has an adjusted basis of $74,960 ($450,000 cost − $250,000 § 179 expense − $125,040 of regular MACRS depreciation). Now Hazel is again planning to replace the store's equipment, and she has determined that she can sell all of the existing equipment for $128,000.

If Hazel completes this transaction, what will be the impact on her 2017 tax return?

Read the chapter and formulate your response.

FRAMEWORK 1040 **Tax Formula for Individuals**

This chapter covers the boldfaced portions of the Tax Formula for Individuals that was introduced in Concept Summary 3.1 on p. 3-3. Below those portions are the sections of Form 1040 where the results are reported.

Income *(broadly defined)* .... $ xx,xxx
Less: Exclusions .... (x,xxx)
Gross income .... $ xx,xxx
Less: Deductions *for* adjusted gross income .... (x,xxx)

FORM 1040 (p. 1)		
12	Business income or (loss). Attach Schedule C or C-EZ	
13	Capital gain or (loss). Attach Schedule D if required. If not required, check here ▶ ☐	
14	Other gains or (losses). Attach Form 4797	

Adjusted gross income .... $ xx,xxx
Less: The greater of total itemized deductions *or* the standard deduction .... (x,xxx)
        Personal and dependency exemptions .... (x,xxx)
Taxable income .... $ xx,xxx
Tax on taxable income *(see Tax Tables or Tax Rate Schedules)* .... $ x,xxx

FORM 1040 (p. 2)		
44	**Tax** (see instructions). Check if any from: **a** ☐ Form(s) 8814 **b** ☐ Form 4972 **c** ☐ _____	

Less: Tax credits *(including income taxes withheld and prepaid)* .... (xxx)
Tax due (or refund) .... $ xxx

G eneric Manufacturing LLC (a limited liability company) sold machinery, office furniture, and unneeded production plants for $100 million last year. The company's disposition of these assets resulted in $60 million of gains and $13 million of losses. How are these gains and losses treated for tax purposes? Do any special tax rules apply? Could any of the gains and losses receive capital gain or loss treatment?

This chapter answers these questions by explaining how to *classify* gains and losses from the disposition of assets that are used in the business rather than held for resale. Chapter 8 discussed how to *depreciate* such assets. Chapters 14 and 15 discussed how to determine the *adjusted basis* and the *amount* of gain or loss from their disposition.

A long-term capital gain was defined in Chapter 16 as the recognized gain from the sale or exchange of a capital asset held for the required long-term holding period.[1] Long-term capital assets are capital assets held more than one year.

This chapter is concerned with classification under § 1231, a very complex Code section, but one that impacts many transactions involving business assets. Taxpayers that are affected by § 1231 are those involved in a business (sole proprietors, partnerships, corporations, and some trusts) and taxpayers owning rental property. In general, § 1231 applies to the sale or exchange of business properties and to certain involuntary conversions. These properties are *not* capital assets because they are depreciable and/or real property used in business or for the production of income.[2] Nonetheless, these business properties may be held for long periods of time and may be sold at a gain.

Congress decided many years ago that § 1231 assets deserved *limited* capital gain-type treatment, which sometimes gives too much tax advantage when assets are eligible for depreciation (or cost recovery). As a result, depreciation recapture rules

---

[1] § 1222(3).   [2] § 1221(a)(2).

were created to prevent capital gain treatment when gains are realized on § 1231 assets. This chapter covers the recapture rules that treat a portion (or all) of the gain as ordinary income (even though the gain might otherwise qualify for long-term capital gain treatment).

17-1 SECTION 1231 ASSETS

LO.1

State the rationale for and the nature and treatment of gains and losses from the disposition of business assets.

17-1a Relationship to Capital Assets

Because depreciable property and real property used in business are not capital assets, the recognized gains from the disposition of this property would appear to be ordinary income rather than capital gain. Due to § 1231, however, *net gain* from the disposition of this property is sometimes *treated* as *long-term capital gain*. In order for this to occur:

- A long-term holding period requirement must be met (held for *more than* a year);
- The disposition must generally be from a sale, exchange, or involuntary conversion; and
- Certain recapture provisions must be satisfied.

Section 1231 may also apply to involuntary conversions of capital assets even though such a disposition, which is not a sale or exchange, normally would not result in a capital gain.

If the disposition of depreciable property and real property used in business results in a *net loss*, § 1231 *treats* the *loss* as an *ordinary loss* rather than as a capital loss. Ordinary losses are fully deductible *for* adjusted gross income (AGI). Capital losses are offset by capital gains, and if any loss remains, the loss is deductible to the extent of $3,000 per year for individuals and currently is not deductible at all by regular corporations. In general, § 1231 provides the *best* of both potential results: net gain may be treated as long-term capital gain, and net loss is treated as ordinary loss.

The Big Picture

EXAMPLE 1

Return to the facts of *The Big Picture* on p. 17-1. If Hazel sells the parking lot for $18,000, she will have disposed of a § 1231 asset because it was property used in a trade or business and held for the long-term holding period (more than one year).

Hazel's gain will be $3,000 ($18,000 selling price − $15,000 adjusted basis). Because the asset is a § 1231 asset, all of the gain is § 1231 gain, and it *may* be treated as long-term capital gain (depending on its netting with any other § 1231 gains or losses during the year).

The Big Picture

EXAMPLE 2

Return to the facts of *The Big Picture* on p. 17-1. Assume that Hazel sells the snow removal equipment for $100, generating a $900 loss, and the parking lot for $15,700, generating a $700 gain.

Both properties were held for use in her business for the long-term holding period and, therefore, are § 1231 assets. Hazel's net § 1231 loss is $200, and that net loss is an ordinary loss.

The rules regarding § 1231 treatment do *not* apply to *all* business property. Important in this regard are the holding period requirements and the fact that the property must be either depreciable property or real estate used in business. Nor is § 1231 necessarily limited to business property. Transactions involving certain capital assets may fall into the § 1231 category. Thus, § 1231 singles out only some types of business property.

As discussed in Chapter 16, long-term capital gains receive beneficial tax treatment. Section 1231 requires netting of § 1231 gains and losses . If the result is a gain, it may be treated as a long-term capital gain. The net gain is added to the "real" long-term capital gains (if any) and netted with capital losses (if any). As a result, the net § 1231 gain may eventually be eligible for beneficial capital gain treatment or help avoid the deduction limitations that apply to a net capital loss. If the § 1231 gain and loss netting results in a loss, it is an ordinary loss. Finally, § 1231 assets are treated the same as capital assets for purposes of the appreciated property charitable contribution provisions (refer to Chapter 10).

LO.2

Distinguish § 1231 assets from ordinary assets and capital assets and calculate the § 1231 gain or loss.

17-1b **Property Included**

Section 1231 property generally includes the following assets if they are held for more than one year:

- Depreciable or real property used in business or for the production of income (principally machinery and equipment, buildings, and land).
- Timber, coal, or domestic iron ore to which § 631 applies.
- Livestock held for draft, breeding, dairy, or sporting purposes.
- Unharvested crops on land used in business.
- Certain *purchased* intangible assets (such as patents and goodwill) that are eligible for amortization.

These assets are ordinary assets until they have been held for more than one year. Only then do they become § 1231 assets.

17-1c **Property Excluded**

Section 1231 property generally does *not* include the following:

- Property not held for the long-term holding period.[3]
- Nonpersonal use property where casualty losses exceed casualty gains for the taxable year. If a taxpayer has a net casualty loss, the individual casualty gains and losses are treated as ordinary gains and losses.
- Inventory and property held primarily for sale to customers.
- Copyrights; literary, musical, or artistic compositions; and certain U.S. government publications.
- Accounts receivable and notes receivable arising in the ordinary course of the trade or business.

17-1d **Special Rules for Certain § 1231 Assets**

A rather diverse group of assets is included under § 1231. The following discussion summarizes the special rules for some of those assets.

Timber

In order to encourage reforestation of timberlands, Congress has provided preferential treatment relative to the natural growth value of timber, which takes a relatively long time to mature. If timber is held for investment, the timber is a capital asset. If timber is used in a business, it will be a § 1231 asset if held for more than a year. But if the timber is inventory, an ordinary gain or loss will normally result. If the timber is inventory, the taxpayer can *elect* to treat the cutting of timber as a sale or exchange and, if the election is made, to treat the sale as the disposition of a § 1231 asset.[4]

The recognized § 1231 gain or loss is determined at the time the timber is cut and is equal to the difference between the timber's fair market value as of the *first day* of the

---

[3]Because the benefit of § 1231 is long-term capital gain treatment, the holding period must correspond to the more-than-one-year holding period that applies to capital assets. Livestock must be held at least 12 months (24 months in some cases). Unharvested crops do not have to be held for the required long-term holding period, but the land must be held for the long-term holding period.

[4]§ 631(a) and Reg. § 1.631–1. To receive § 631 treatment, the holding period for the timber must be greater than one year.

taxable year and the adjusted basis for depletion. If a taxpayer sells the timber for more or less than the fair market value as of the first day of the taxable year in which it is cut, the difference is ordinary income or loss.

Several years ago Tom, a timber dealer, purchased a tract of land with a substantial stand of trees on it. The land cost $40,000, and the timber cost $100,000. On the first day of 2017, the timber was appraised at $250,000. In August 2017, Tom cut the timber and sold it for $265,000. Tom elects to treat the cutting as a sale or exchange under § 1231. He has a $150,000 § 1231 gain ($250,000 − $100,000) and a $15,000 ordinary gain ($265,000 − $250,000).

What if the timber had been sold for $235,000? Tom would still have a $150,000 § 1231 gain, but he would also have a $15,000 ordinary loss. The price for computing § 1231 gain is the price at the beginning of the tax year. Any difference between that price and the sales price is ordinary gain or loss. Here, because the price declined by $15,000, Tom has an ordinary loss in that amount.

EXAMPLE
3

Livestock

Cattle and horses must be held 24 months or more and other livestock must be held 12 months or more to qualify under § 1231.[5] Poultry is *not* livestock for purposes of § 1231.

Section 1231 Assets Disposed of by Casualty or Theft

When § 1231 assets are disposed of by casualty or theft, a special netting rule is applied. For simplicity, the term *casualty* is used to mean both casualty and theft dispositions. First, the casualty gains and losses from § 1231 assets *and* the casualty gains and losses from long-term nonpersonal use capital assets are determined.[6] A nonpersonal use capital asset might be art held as an investment or a baseball card collection held by a nondealer.

Next, the § 1231 asset casualty gains and losses and the nonpersonal use capital asset casualty gains and losses are netted together (see Concept Summary 17.1 later in the chapter).

- If the result is a *net loss*, the § 1231 casualty gains and the nonpersonal use capital asset casualty gains are treated as ordinary gains, the § 1231 casualty losses are deductible *for* AGI, and the nonpersonal use capital asset casualty losses are deductible *from* AGI subject to the 2%-of-AGI limitation.

- If the result of the netting is a *net gain*, the net gain is treated as a § 1231 gain.

As a result, a § 1231 asset disposed of by casualty may or may not get § 1231 treatment, depending on whether the netting process results in a gain or a loss. Also, a nonpersonal use capital asset disposed of by casualty may get § 1231 treatment or ordinary treatment, but it will not get capital gain or loss treatment.

Casualties, thefts, and condemnations are *involuntary conversions*. Involuntary conversion gains may be deferred if conversion proceeds are reinvested; involuntary conversion losses are recognized currently (refer to Chapter 15) regardless of whether the conversion proceeds are reinvested. Thus, the special netting process discussed previously for casualties and thefts would not include gains that are not currently recognizable because the insurance proceeds are reinvested.

The special netting process for casualties and thefts also does not include condemnation gains and losses. Consequently, a § 1231 asset disposed of by condemnation will receive § 1231 treatment. This variation between recognized casualty and condemnation

---

[5]Note that the holding period is "12 months or more" and not "more than 12 months." Congress enacted this rule due to considerable litigation over whether the livestock was inventory or a § 1231 asset.

[6]*Personal use property casualty* gains and losses are not subject to the § 1231 rules. If the result of netting these gains and losses is a gain, the net gain is a capital gain. If the netting results in a loss, the net loss is a deduction *from* AGI to the extent it exceeds 10 percent of AGI.

gains and losses sheds considerable light on what § 1231 is all about. Section 1231 has no effect on whether *realized* gain or loss is recognized. Instead, § 1231 merely dictates how such *recognized* gain or loss is *classified* (ordinary, capital, or § 1231) under certain conditions.[7]

17-1e General Procedure for § 1231 Computation

Most of the time, § 1231 gains and losses result from the sale of business assets. However, as we have already discussed, disposition by casualty and/or theft can also be part of the § 1231 discussion. Consequently, the tax treatment of § 1231 gains and losses depends on the results of a complex *netting* procedure. When there are no casualties and/or thefts (the usual case), step 1 below can be skipped and the procedure is much simpler. Here are the steps that need to be followed:

Step 1: Casualty Netting

Net all recognized long-term gains and losses from casualties of § 1231 assets and non-personal use capital assets. Casualty gains result when insurance proceeds exceed the adjusted basis of the property. These are gains remaining after any *depreciation recapture* (discussed later in text Sections 17-2 and 17-3). This casualty netting is beneficial because if there is a net gain, the gain may receive long-term capital gain treatment. If there is a net loss, it receives ordinary loss treatment.

a. If the casualty gains exceed the casualty losses, add the excess to the other § 1231 gains for the taxable year.
b. If the casualty losses exceed the casualty gains, exclude all casualty losses and gains from further § 1231 computation. If this is the case, all casualty gains are ordinary income. Section 1231 asset casualty losses are deductible *for* AGI. Other casualty losses are deductible *from* AGI.

Step 2: § 1231 Netting

After adding any net casualty gain from step 1a to the other § 1231 gains and losses (including recognized § 1231 asset condemnation gains and losses), net all § 1231 gains [gains remaining after any *depreciation recapture* (discussed later in text Sections 17-2 and 17-3)] and losses.

a. If the gains exceed the losses, the net gain is offset by the "lookback" nonrecaptured § 1231 losses (see step 3).
b. If the losses exceed the gains, all gains are ordinary income. Section 1231 asset losses are deductible *for* AGI. Other casualty losses are deductible *from* AGI.

Step 3: § 1231 Lookback Provision

The net § 1231 gain from step 2a is offset by the nonrecaptured net § 1231 losses for the five preceding taxable years (the § 1231 lookback provision). For transactions in 2017, the lookback years are 2012, 2013, 2014, 2015, and 2016.

a. To the extent of the nonrecaptured net § 1231 loss, the current-year net § 1231 gain is ordinary income. The *nonrecaptured* net § 1231 losses are losses that have not already been used to offset net § 1231 gains.
b. Only the net § 1231 gain exceeding this net § 1231 loss carryforward is given long-term capital gain treatment.

Concept Summary 17.1 summarizes the § 1231 computation procedure. Examples 4 through 7 illustrate its application without the § 1231 lookback provision. Examples 6 and 7 illustrate its application with the § 1231 lookback provision.

---

[7]*Personal use property condemnation* gains and losses are not subject to the § 1231 rules. The gains are capital gains (because personal use property is a capital asset), and the losses are nondeductible because they arise from the disposition of personal use property.

Concept Summary 17.1

Section 1231 Netting Procedure

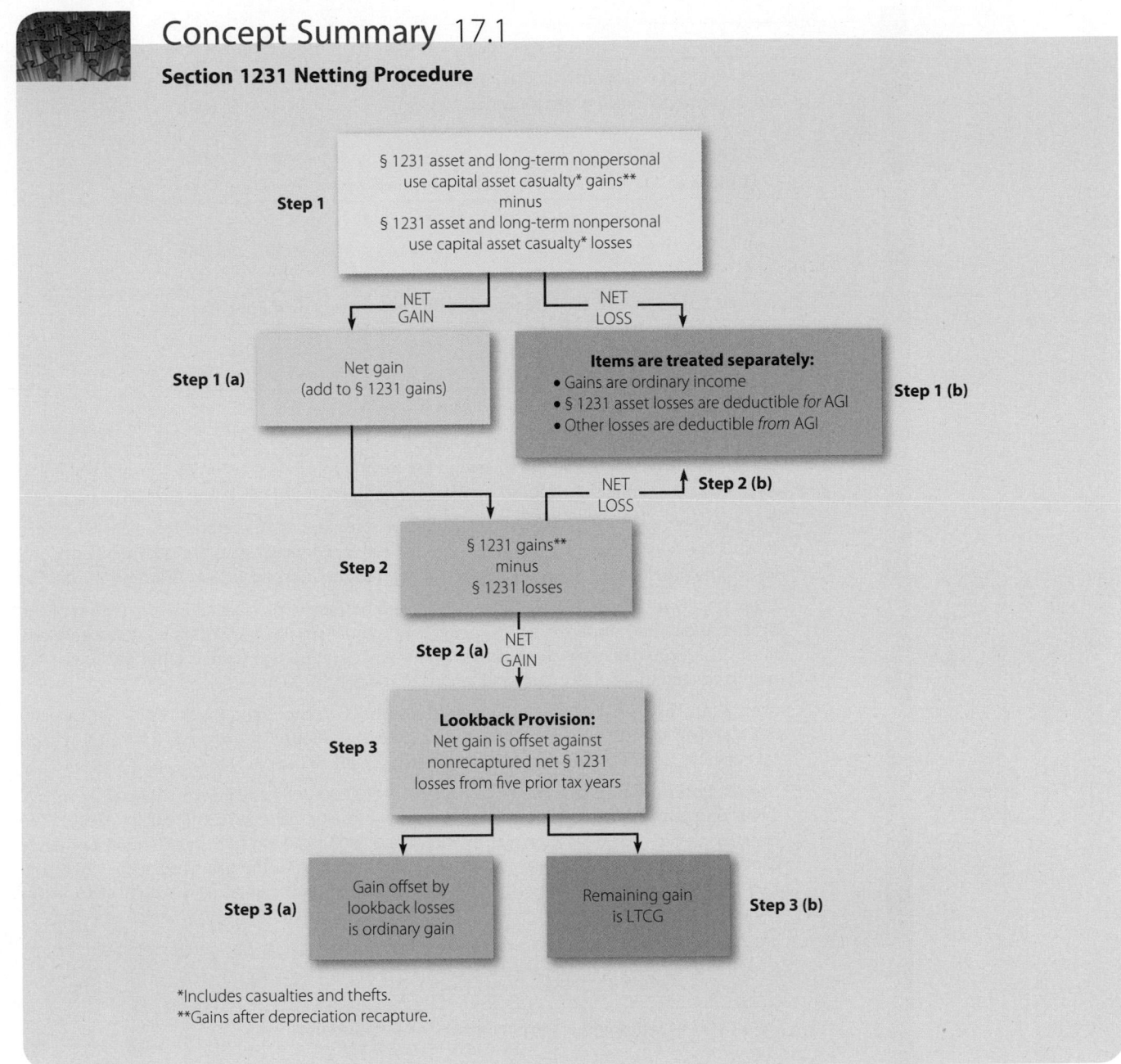

Step 1

§ 1231 asset and long-term nonpersonal use capital asset casualty* gains**
minus
§ 1231 asset and long-term nonpersonal use capital asset casualty* losses

NET GAIN

NET LOSS

Step 1 (a)

Net gain
(add to § 1231 gains)

Items are treated separately:
- Gains are ordinary income
- § 1231 asset losses are deductible *for* AGI
- Other losses are deductible *from* AGI

Step 1 (b)

NET LOSS   **Step 2 (b)**

Step 2

§ 1231 gains**
minus
§ 1231 losses

Step 2 (a)   NET GAIN

Step 3

Lookback Provision:
Net gain is offset against nonrecaptured net § 1231 losses from five prior tax years

Step 3 (a)

Gain offset by lookback losses is ordinary gain

Remaining gain is LTCG

Step 3 (b)

*Includes casualties and thefts.
**Gains after depreciation recapture.

Section 1231 Computations

During 2017, Ross had $125,000 of AGI before considering the following recognized gains and losses:

Capital Gains and Losses

Long-term capital gain	$3,000
Long-term capital loss	(400)
Short-term capital gain	1,000
Short-term capital loss	(200)

continued

EXAMPLE

4

Casualties

Theft of diamond ring (owned four months)	($800)*
Fire damage to personal residence (owned 10 years)	(400)*
Gain from insurance recovery on fire loss to business building (owned two years)	200

§ 1231 Gains and Losses from Depreciable Business Assets Held Long Term

Asset A	$ 300
Asset B	1,100
Asset C	(500)

Gains and Losses from Sale of Depreciable Business Assets Held Short Term

Asset D	$ 200
Asset E	(300)

*As adjusted for the $100 floor on personal casualty losses.

Ross had no net § 1231 losses in tax years before 2017.

Ross's gains and losses receive the following tax treatment. [The gains on the business building and Assets A and B are *after* any depreciation recapture (discussed later in the chapter)].

- The diamond ring and the residence are personal use assets. Therefore, these casualties are not § 1231 transactions. The $800 (ring) plus $400 (residence) losses are potentially deductible *from* AGI. However, the total loss of $1,200 does not exceed 10% of AGI.

- **Step 1:** Only the business building (a § 1231 asset) casualty gain remains. The netting of the § 1231 asset and nonpersonal use capital asset casualty gains and losses contains only one item—the $200 gain from the business building. Consequently, there is a net gain, and that gain is treated as a § 1231 gain (and added to the § 1231 gains).

- **Step 1 (a):** The gains from § 1231 transactions (Assets A and B and the § 1231 asset casualty gain) exceed the losses (Asset C) by $1,100 ($1,600 − $500). This excess is a long-term capital gain and is added to Ross's other long-term capital gains.

- **Step 2:** Ross's net long-term capital gain is $3,700 ($3,000 + $1,100 from § 1231 transactions − $400 long-term capital loss). Ross's net short-term capital gain is $800 ($1,000 − $200). The result is capital gain net income of $4,500. The $3,700 net long-term capital gain portion is eligible for beneficial capital gain treatment [assume that all of the gain is *0%/15%/20% gain* (see the discussion in Chapter 16)]. The $800 net short-term capital gain is subject to tax as ordinary income.[8]

- Ross treats the gain and loss from Assets D and E (depreciable business assets held for less than the long-term holding period) as ordinary gain and loss.

Results of the Gains and Losses on Ross's Tax Computation

NLTCG	$ 3,700
NSTCG	800
Ordinary gain from sale of Asset D	200
Ordinary loss from sale of Asset E	(300)
AGI from other sources	125,000
AGI	$129,400

- Ross will have personal use property casualty losses of $1,200 [$800 (diamond ring) + $400 (personal residence)]. A personal use property casualty loss is deductible only to the extent it exceeds 10% of AGI. Thus, none of the $1,200 is deductible ($129,400 × 10% = $12,940).

---

[8]Ross's taxable income (unless his itemized deductions and the personal and dependency exemptions are extremely large) will put him in at least the 28% bracket. Thus, the alternative tax computation will yield a lower tax. See Example 43 in Chapter 16.

Section 1231 Computations

EXAMPLE 5

Assume the same facts as in Example 4, except that the loss from Asset C was $1,700 instead of $500.

- The treatment of the casualty losses is the same as in Example 4.
- **Step 1 (b):** The losses from § 1231 transactions now exceed the gains by $100 ($1,700 − $1,600). As a result, the gains from Assets A and B and the § 1231 asset casualty gain are ordinary income, and the loss from Asset C is a deduction *for* AGI (a business loss). The same result can be achieved by simply treating the $100 net loss as a deduction *for* AGI.
- Capital gain net income is $3,400 ($2,600 long term + $800 short term). The $2,600 net long-term capital gain portion is eligible for beneficial capital gain treatment, and the $800 net short-term capital gain is subject to tax as ordinary income.

Results of the Gains and Losses on Ross's Tax Computation	
NLTCG	$ 2,600
NSTCG	800
Net ordinary loss on Assets A, B, and C and § 1231 casualty gain	(100)
Ordinary gain from sale of Asset D	200
Ordinary loss from sale of Asset E	(300)
AGI from other sources	125,000
AGI	$128,200

- None of the personal use property casualty losses will be deductible because $1,200 does not exceed 10% of $128,200.

EXAMPLE 6

Assume the same facts as in Example 4, except that Ross has a $700 nonrecaptured net § 1231 loss from 2016.

- The treatment of the casualty losses is the same as in Example 4.
- **Step 3 (a):** The 2017 net § 1231 gain of $1,100 is treated as ordinary income to the extent of the 2016 nonrecaptured § 1231 loss of $700.
- **Step 3 (b):** The remaining $400 net § 1231 gain is a long-term capital gain and is added to Ross's other long-term capital gains.
- Ross's net long-term capital gain is $3,000 ($3,000 + $400 from § 1231 transactions − $400 long-term capital loss). Ross's net short-term capital gain is still $800 ($1,000 − $200). The result is capital gain net income of $3,800. The $3,000 net long-term capital gain portion is eligible for beneficial capital gain treatment, and the $800 net short-term capital gain is subject to tax as ordinary income.

Results of the Gains and Losses on Ross's Tax Computation	
NLTCG	$ 3,000
NSTCG	800
Ordinary gain from recapture of § 1231 losses	700
Ordinary gain from sale of Asset D	200
Ordinary loss from sale of Asset E	(300)
AGI from other sources	125,000
AGI	$129,400

- None of the personal use property casualty losses will be deductible because $1,200 does not exceed 10% of $129,400.

Section 1231 Computations

EXAMPLE

7

Assume the same facts as in Example 4, except that Ross had a net § 1231 loss of $2,700 in 2015 and a net § 1231 gain of $300 in 2016.

- The treatment of the casualty losses is the same as in Example 4.

- **Step 3 (a):** The 2015 net § 1231 loss of $2,700 will have carried over to 2016 and been offset against the 2016 net § 1231 gain of $300. Thus, the $300 gain will have been classified as ordinary income, and $2,400 of nonrecaptured 2015 net § 1231 loss will carry over to 2017. The 2017 net § 1231 gain of $1,100 will be offset against this loss, resulting in $1,100 of ordinary income. The nonrecaptured net § 1231 loss of $1,300 ($2,400 − $1,100) carries over to 2018.

- Capital gain net income is $3,400 ($2,600 net long-term capital gain + $800 net short-term capital gain). The $2,600 net long-term capital gain portion is eligible for beneficial capital gain treatment, and the $800 net short-term capital gain is subject to tax as ordinary income.

Results of the Gains and Losses on Ross's Tax Computation

NLTCG	$ 2,600
NSTCG	800
Ordinary gain from recapture of § 1231 losses	1,100
Ordinary gain from sale of Asset D	200
Ordinary loss from sale of Asset E	(300)
AGI from other sources	125,000
AGI	$129,400

- None of the personal use property casualty losses will be deductible because $1,200 does not exceed 10% of $129,400.

LO.3

Determine when § 1245 recapture applies and how it is computed.

17-2 SECTION 1245 RECAPTURE

Now that the basic rules of § 1231 have been introduced, it is time to add some complications. The Code contains two major *recapture* provisions—§§ 1245 and 1250.[9] These provisions cause *gain* to be treated *initially* as ordinary gain. Thus, what may appear to be a § 1231 gain is ordinary gain instead. This recapture phenomenon applies exclusively to § 1231 gains; § 1231 assets generating losses are unaffected by these recapture provisions.

These recapture provisions may also cause a gain in a nonpersonal use casualty to be *initially* ordinary gain rather than casualty gain. Classifying gains (and losses) properly is important; improper initial classification may lead to incorrect mixing and matching of gains and losses. We begin by discussing the § 1245 recapture rules; the § 1250 recapture rules are discussed in text Section 17-3.

Section 1245 requires taxpayers to treat all gain as ordinary gain unless the property is disposed of for more than its original cost. This result is accomplished by requiring that all gain be treated as ordinary gain to the extent of the depreciation taken on the property disposed of. The excess of the sales price over the original cost is § 1231 gain. Section 1245 applies *primarily* to non-real-estate property like machinery, trucks, and office furniture. Section 1245 does not apply if property is disposed of at a loss. Generally, the loss will be a § 1231 loss unless the form of the disposition is a casualty.

The Big Picture

EXAMPLE

8

Refer to the facts of *The Big Picture* on p. 17-1. Hazel purchased the equipment for $450,000 and has deducted $375,040 of depreciation ($250,000 § 179 expense + $125,040 regular MACRS depreciation). As a result, the equipment's adjusted basis is $74,960.

continued

---

[9]Due to the passage of time, § 1250 is largely ineffective, but is still important in certain situations.

If Hazel sells the equipment for $128,000, she will have a gain of $53,040 ($128,000 − $74,960). If it were not for § 1245, the $53,040 gain would be § 1231 gain. Section 1245 prevents this potentially favorable result by treating as ordinary income (not as § 1231 gain) any gain to the extent of depreciation taken. In this example, the entire $53,040 gain would be ordinary income.

If, instead, Hazel sold the equipment for $485,000, she would have a gain of $410,040 ($485,000 − $74,960 adjusted basis). The § 1245 gain would be $375,040 (equal to the depreciation taken), and the § 1231 gain would be $35,000 (equal to the excess of the sales price over the $450,000 original cost).

Section 1245 recapture provides, in general, that the portion of recognized gain from the sale or other disposition of § 1245 property that represents depreciation is *recaptured* as ordinary income.[10] As a result, in Example 8, $53,040 of the $375,040 depreciation taken is recaptured as ordinary income when the business equipment is sold for $128,000. Only $53,040 is recaptured rather than $375,040 because Hazel is only required to recognize § 1245 recapture ordinary gain equal to the *lower* of the depreciation taken or the gain recognized.

The method of depreciation (e.g., accelerated or straight-line) does not matter. All depreciation taken is potentially subject to recapture. For this reason, § 1245 recapture is often referred to as *full recapture*. Any remaining gain after subtracting the amount recaptured as ordinary income will usually be § 1231 gain.

If the property is disposed of in a casualty event, however, the remaining gain will be casualty gain. If the business equipment in Example 8 had been disposed of by casualty and the $128,000 received had been an insurance recovery, Hazel would still have a gain of $53,040 and the gain would still be recaptured by § 1245 as ordinary gain. The § 1245 recapture rules apply before there is any casualty gain. Because all of the $53,040 gain is recaptured, no casualty gain arises from the casualty.

The following examples illustrate the general application of § 1245.

Section 1245 Recapture Computations

In the current year, Gary sold for $13,000 a machine acquired several years ago for $12,000. He had taken $10,000 of depreciation on the machine.

- The recognized gain from the sale is $11,000. This is the amount realized of $13,000 less the adjusted basis of $2,000 ($12,000 cost − $10,000 depreciation taken).

- Depreciation taken is $10,000. Therefore, because § 1245 recapture gain is the lower of depreciation taken or gain recognized, $10,000 of the $11,000 recognized gain is ordinary income, and the remaining $1,000 gain is § 1231 gain.

- The § 1231 gain of $1,000 is also equal to the excess of the sales price over the original cost of the property ($13,000 − $12,000 = $1,000 § 1231 gain).

Assume the same facts as in the previous example, except that the asset is sold for $9,000 instead of $13,000.

- The recognized gain from the sale is $7,000. This is the amount realized of $9,000 less the adjusted basis of $2,000.

- Depreciation taken is $10,000. Therefore, because the $10,000 depreciation taken exceeds the recognized gain of $7,000, the entire $7,000 recognized gain is ordinary income.

- The § 1231 gain is zero. There is no § 1231 gain because the selling price ($9,000) does not exceed the original purchase price ($12,000).

---

[10]The term *depreciation* includes § 167 depreciation, § 168 cost recovery, § 179 immediate expensing, § 168(k) additional first-year depreciation, and § 197 amortization.

Section 1245 Recapture Computations

EXAMPLE 11

Assume the same facts as in Example 9, except that the asset is sold for $1,500 instead of $13,000.

- The recognized loss from the sale is $500. This is the amount realized of $1,500 less the adjusted basis of $2,000.

- Because there is a loss, there is no depreciation recapture. All of the loss is § 1231 loss.

If § 1245 property is disposed of in a transaction other than a sale, exchange, or involuntary conversion, the maximum amount recaptured is the excess of the property's fair market value over its adjusted basis. See the discussion under Considerations Common to §§ 1245 and 1250 in text Section 17-4.

17-2a **Section 1245 Property**

Generally, **§ 1245 property** includes all depreciable personal property (e.g., machinery and equipment), including livestock. Buildings and their structural components generally are not § 1245 property. The following property is *also* subject to § 1245 treatment:

- Amortizable personal property such as goodwill, patents, copyrights, and leaseholds of § 1245 property.
- Professional baseball and football player contracts.
- Certain depreciable tangible real property (other than buildings and their structural components) employed as an integral part of certain activities such as manufacturing and production. For example, a natural gas storage tank where the gas is used in the manufacturing process is § 1245 property.
- Pollution control facilities, railroad grading and tunnel bores, on-the-job training, and child care facilities.
- Single-purpose agricultural and horticultural structures and petroleum storage facilities (e.g., a greenhouse or silo).
- Fifteen-year, 18-year, and 19-year nonresidential real estate for which accelerated cost recovery is used. This property, known as ACRS property, would have been placed in service after 1980 and before 1987.

EXAMPLE 12

Steve acquired nonresidential real estate on December 1, 1986, for $100,000. He used the required ACRS accelerated method to compute the cost recovery. He sells the asset on January 15, 2017, for $120,000. The amount and nature of Steve's gain are computed as follows:

Amount realized		$120,000
Adjusted basis		
Cost	$ 100,000	
Less cost recovery: 1986–2005	(100,000)	
2006–2017	(–0–)	
January 15, 2017 adjusted basis		(–0–)
Gain realized and recognized		$120,000

The gain of $120,000 is treated as ordinary income to the extent of *all* depreciation taken because the property is 19-year nonresidential real estate for which accelerated depreciation was used. Thus, Steve reports ordinary income of $100,000 and § 1231 gain of $20,000 ($120,000 − $100,000).

17-2b **Observations on § 1245**

- In most instances, the total depreciation taken will exceed the recognized gain. Therefore, the disposition of § 1245 property usually results in ordinary income rather than § 1231 gain. No § 1231 gain will occur unless the § 1245 property is disposed of for more than its original cost. Refer to Examples 9 and 10.

- Recapture applies to the total amount of depreciation allowed or allowable regardless of the depreciation method used.

- Recapture applies regardless of the holding period of the property. If the property is held for less than the long-term holding period, the entire recognized gain is ordinary income because § 1231 does not apply.

- Section 1245 does not apply to losses, which receive § 1231 treatment.

- Gains from the disposition of § 1245 assets may also be treated as passive activity gains (see Chapter 11).

17-3 SECTION 1250 RECAPTURE

LO.4

Determine when § 1250 recapture applies.

Generally, § 1250 property is depreciable real property (principally buildings and their structural components) that is not subject to § 1245.[11] Intangible real property, such as leaseholds of § 1250 property, is also included.

Section 1250 recapture rarely applies because only the amount of *additional depreciation* (depreciation *in excess* of straight-line depreciation) is subject to recapture. Straight-line depreciation is not recaptured (except for property held one year or less). Because the straight-line depreciation method is required for depreciable real property placed in service after 1986, there will usually be *no § 1250 depreciation recapture* on such property. Finally, § 1250 does not apply if the real property is sold at a loss.

Although there is no depreciation recapture on § 1250 property, the gain from this property may be subject to a special 25 percent tax rate. See the discussion of Unrecaptured § 1250 Gain (Real Estate 25% Gain) in text Section 17-3b.

EXAMPLE

13

Sanjay acquires a residential rental building on January 1, 2016, for $300,000. He receives an offer of $450,000 for the building in 2017 and sells it on December 23, 2017.

- Sanjay takes $20,909 {($300,000 × .03485) + [$300,000 × .03636 × (11.5/12)] = $20,909} of total depreciation for 2016 and 2017, and the adjusted basis of the property is $279,091 ($300,000 − $20,909).

- Sanjay's recognized gain is $170,909 ($450,000 − $279,091).

- All of the gain is § 1231 gain.

17-3a Section 1250 Recapture Situations

In addition to residential real estate acquired before 1987 and nonresidential real estate acquired before 1981, accelerated depreciation may be taken on other types of real property. The § 1250 recapture rules apply to the following property for which accelerated depreciation was used:

- Any immediate expense deduction (§ 179) and/or additional first-year depreciation [§ 168(k)] exceeding straight-line depreciation taken on leasehold improvements and qualified improvement property.

- Real property used predominantly outside the United States.

- Certain government-financed or low-income housing.[12]

Concept Summary 17.2 compares and contrasts the § 1245 and § 1250 depreciation recapture rules.

---

[11]As noted above, in one limited circumstance, § 1245 does apply to nonresidential real estate. If the nonresidential real estate was placed in service after 1980 and before 1987 and accelerated depreciation was used, the § 1245 recapture rules would apply (rather than the § 1250 recapture rules).

[12]Described in § 1250(a)(1)(B).

Concept Summary 17.2

Comparison of § 1245 and § 1250 Depreciation Recapture

	§ 1245	§ 1250
Property affected	All depreciable personal property, but also nonresidential real property acquired after December 31, 1980, and before January 1, 1987, for which accelerated cost recovery was used. Also includes miscellaneous items such as § 179 expense and § 197 amortization of intangibles such as goodwill, patents, and copyrights.	Nonresidential real property acquired after December 31, 1969, and before January 1, 1981, on which accelerated depreciation was taken. Residential rental real property acquired after December 31, 1975, and before January 1, 1987, on which accelerated depreciation was taken.
Depreciation recaptured	Potentially all depreciation taken. If the selling price is greater than or equal to the original cost, all depreciation is recaptured. If the selling price is between the adjusted basis and the original cost, only some depreciation is recaptured.	Normally, there is no depreciation recapture, but in the special situations listed above, there can be § 1250 depreciation recapture of additional depreciation (the excess of accelerated cost recovery over straight-line cost recovery or the excess of accelerated depreciation over straight-line depreciation).
Limit on recapture	Lower of depreciation taken or gain recognized.	Lower of additional depreciation or gain recognized.
Treatment of gain exceeding recapture gain	Usually § 1231 gain.	Usually § 1231 gain.
Treatment of loss	No depreciation recapture; loss is usually § 1231 loss.	No depreciation recapture; loss is usually § 1231 loss.

17-3b Unrecaptured § 1250 Gain (Real Estate 25% Gain)

Any **unrecaptured § 1250 gain** is subject to a 25 percent tax rate. This gain, which relates to the sale of depreciable real estate, is used in the alternative tax computation for net capital gain discussed in Chapter 16. Unrecaptured § 1250 gain (*25% gain*) is some or all of the § 1231 gain that is treated as long-term capital gain.

The maximum amount of this *25% gain* is the depreciation taken on real property sold at a recognized gain. That maximum amount is computed in one or more of the following ways:

- The recognized gain from disposition is more than the depreciation taken. The *25% gain* is equal to the depreciation taken. Refer to Example 13. The depreciation taken was $20,909, but the recognized gain was $170,909. Consequently, *some* of the recognized gain is potential *25% § 1231 gain.*

- The recognized gain from disposition is less than or equal to the depreciation taken. In this case, the *25% gain* is all of the recognized gain. Refer to Example 13, but assume that the building sales price is $285,000. The recognized gain is $5,909 ($285,000 − $279,091), all of this gain is a § 1231 gain, and it is entirely a *25% § 1231 gain.*

- There is § 1245 depreciation recapture because the property is nonresidential real estate acquired in 1981–1986 on which accelerated depreciation was taken. No *25% § 1231 gain* will be left because § 1245 will recapture all of the depreciation or the recognized gain, whichever is less. Refer to Example 12. Depreciation of $100,000 was taken, but all of it was recaptured as ordinary income by § 1245. Thus, there is no remaining potential *25% § 1231 gain.* The entire $20,000 § 1231 gain in Example 12 is potential *0%/15%/20% gain.*

- Section 1231 loss from disposition of other § 1231 assets held long term reduces the gain from real estate.

- Section 1231 lookback losses convert some or all of the potential *25% § 1231 gain* to ordinary income.

Special 25% Gain Netting Rules

Where there is a § 1231 gain from real estate and that gain includes both potential *25% gain* and potential *0%/15%/20% gain*, any § 1231 loss from disposition of other § 1231 assets *first offsets* the *0%/15%/20%* portion of the § 1231 gain and then offsets the *25% gain* portion of the § 1231 gain. Also, any § 1231 lookback loss *first recharacterizes* the *25% gain* portion of the § 1231 gain and then recharacterizes the *0%/15%/20%* portion of the § 1231 gain as ordinary income.

Net § 1231 Gain Limitation

The amount of unrecaptured § 1250 gain may not exceed the net § 1231 gain that is eligible to be treated as long-term capital gain. The unrecaptured § 1250 gain is the *lesser of* the unrecaptured § 1250 gain or the net § 1231 gain that is treated as capital gain. Thus, if there is a net § 1231 gain but it is all converted to ordinary income by the five-year § 1231 lookback loss provision, there is no surviving § 1231 gain or unrecaptured § 1250 gain.

Refer to Example 6. There was $200 of § 1231 gain from the building fire that would also be potential *25% gain* if at least $200 of depreciation was taken. The net § 1231 gain was $1,100 including the $200 building gain. (The $500 loss from Asset C would offset the potential *0%/15%/20%* § 1231 gain and not the potential *25% gain*, so all of the potential *25% gain* of $200 is in the $1,100 net § 1231 gain.) However, the $700 of § 1231 lookback losses would *first* absorb the $200 building gain, so the $400 of § 1231 gain that is treated as long-term capital gain includes no *25% gain*.

Section 1250 Property for Purposes of the Unrecaptured § 1250 Gain

Section 1250 property includes any real property (other than § 1245 property) that is or has been depreciable. Land is *not* § 1250 property because it is not depreciable.

EXAMPLE

14

Bill is a single taxpayer with 2017 taxable income of $120,000 composed of:

- $100,000 ordinary taxable income,
- $3,000 short-term capital loss,
- $15,000 long-term capital gain from sale of stock, and
- $8,000 § 1231 gain that is all unrecaptured § 1250 gain (the actual unrecaptured gain was $11,000, but net § 1231 gain is only $8,000).

Bill's net capital gain is $20,000 ($15,000 long-term capital gain + $8,000 unrecaptured § 1250 gain/net § 1231 gain − $3,000 short-term capital loss). The $3,000 short-term capital loss is offset against the $8,000 unrecaptured § 1250 gain, reducing that gain to $5,000 (see the discussion in Chapter 16 concerning netting of capital losses). Bill's adjusted net capital gain is $15,000 ($20,000 net capital gain − $5,000 unrecaptured § 1250 gain).

Bill's total tax (using the alternative tax calculation discussed in Chapter 16) is $24,482 [$20,982 (tax on $100,000 other taxable income) + $1,250 ($5,000 unrecaptured § 1250 gain × 25%) + $2,250 ($15,000 adjusted net capital gain × 15%)].

ETHICS & EQUITY The Sale of a "Cost-Segregated" Building

Many taxpayers have "cost-segregated" their buildings. This means that an engineering study is done to determine whether some of a building's cost can be segregated into tangible personal property (generally a 5-year or 7-year MACRS life with accelerated depreciation) rather than real property (a 27.5-year or 39-year MACRS life with straight-line depreciation). The faster depreciation for the tangible personal property yields significant tax savings. A CPA is determining the gain or loss from disposition of an office building. A sale document details the selling price of the land and building. However, the building was cost-segregated and the CPA finds records of cost and related depreciation for the tangible personal property that was part of the cost segregation. No mention of this tangible personal property was made in the sale agreement, but the building and all of its contents were sold. What should the CPA do?

LO.5

Identify considerations
common to §§ 1245
and 1250.

17-4 CONSIDERATIONS COMMON TO §§ 1245 AND 1250

17-4a Exceptions

Gifts

Depreciation recapture potential carries over to the donee.[13]

EXAMPLE 15

Wade gives his daughter, Helen, § 1245 property with an adjusted basis of $1,000. The amount of recapture potential is $700. Helen uses the property in her business and claims further depreciation of $100 before selling it for $1,900.

Helen's recognized gain is $1,000 ($1,900 amount realized − $900 adjusted basis), of which $800 is recaptured as ordinary income ($100 depreciation taken by Helen + $700 recapture potential carried over from Wade). The remaining gain of $200 is § 1231 gain. Even if Helen used the property for personal purposes, the $700 recapture potential would still be carried over.

Death

Although not a very attractive tax planning approach, death eliminates all recapture potential.[14] Any depreciation recapture potential is eliminated when property passes from a decedent to an estate or heir.

EXAMPLE 16

Assume the same facts as in Example 15, except that Helen receives the property as a result of Wade's death. The $700 recapture potential from Wade is extinguished. Helen has a basis for the property equal to the property's fair market value at Wade's death (assume that the FMV is $1,700).

Helen will have a $300 gain when the property is sold because the selling price ($1,900) exceeds the property's adjusted basis of $1,600 ($1,700 original basis to Helen − $100 depreciation) by $300. Because of § 1245, $100 is ordinary income. The remaining gain of $200 is § 1231 gain.

Charitable Transfers

Depreciation recapture potential reduces the amount of the charitable contribution deduction.[15]

The Big Picture

EXAMPLE 17

Return to the facts of *The Big Picture* on p. 17-1. If instead of selling the old equipment Hazel gives it to a charity, her charitable contribution will be zero.

The potential § 1245 recapture on the equipment is $375,040 (the depreciation taken). When that amount is subtracted from the equipment's $128,000 fair market value, the result is zero because the charitable contribution cannot be less than zero.

Certain Nontaxable Transactions

In certain transactions, the transferor's adjusted basis of property carries over to the transferee.[16] If this is the case, any depreciation recapture potential also carries over to the transferee.[17] Included in this category are the following transfers of property:

- Nontaxable incorporations under § 351.
- Certain subsidiary liquidations under § 332.

---

[13]§§ 1245(b)(1) and 1250(d)(1) and Reg. §§ 1.1245–4(a)(1) and 1.1250–3(a)(1).

[14]§§ 1245(b)(2) and 1250(d)(2).

[15]§ 170(e)(1)(A) and Reg. § 1.170A–4(b)(1). In certain circumstances, § 1231 gain also reduces the amount of the charitable contribution. See § 170(e)(1)(B).

[16]§§ 1245(b)(3) and 1250(d)(3) and Reg. §§ 1.1245–4(c) and 1.1250–3(c).

[17]Reg. §§ 1.1245–2(a)(4) and −2(c)(2) and 1.1250–2(d)(1) and (3) and −3(c)(3).

- Nontaxable contributions to a partnership under § 721.
- Nontaxable reorganizations.

Gain may be recognized in these transactions if boot is received. If gain is recognized, it is treated as ordinary income to the extent of the recapture potential or recognized gain, whichever is lower.[18]

Like-Kind Exchanges (§ 1031) and Involuntary Conversions (§ 1033)

Realized gain is recognized to the extent of boot received in a like-kind exchange. Realized gain also will be recognized to the extent the proceeds from an involuntary conversion are not reinvested in similar property. Any recognized gain is subject to recapture as ordinary income under §§ 1245 and 1250. The remaining recapture potential, if any, carries over to the property received in the exchange. Realized losses are not recognized in like-kind exchanges, but are recognized in involuntary conversions (see Chapter 15).

The Big Picture

EXAMPLE 18

Refer to the facts of *The Big Picture* on p. 17-1. Rather than sell the equipment, Hazel could exchange it. If the equipment received in the exchange is worth $150,000, Hazel would have to pay $22,000 ($150,000 − the $128,000 fair market value of the equipment given up in the exchange) and would have a § 1031 like-kind exchange.

Her realized gain is $53,040 ($128,000 fair market value of the equipment given up − $74,960 adjusted basis of the equipment given up), but the gain is not recognized because boot was given (the $22,000 cash) and not received. The $375,040 of depreciation taken on the equipment given up carries over to the replacement equipment as potential § 1245 depreciation recapture.

17-4b Other Applications

The §§ 1245 and 1250 recapture rules *override* all other Code sections.[19] Special applications include installment sales and property dividends.

Installment Sales

Recapture gain is recognized in the year of the sale regardless of whether gain is otherwise recognized under the installment method.[20] All gain is ordinary income until the recapture potential is fully absorbed. Nonrecapture (§ 1231) gain is recognized under the installment method as cash is received.

Gain is also recognized on installment sales in the year of the sale in an amount equal to the § 179 (immediate expensing) deduction taken with respect to the property sold.

The Big Picture

EXAMPLE 19

Return to the facts of *The Big Picture* on p. 17-1. Assume that Hazel could sell the used equipment for $28,000 down, with the $100,000 balance received in five yearly installments of $20,000 plus interest.

Helen would have to recognize her entire $53,040 gain ($128,000 sales price − $74,960 adjusted basis) in 2017. All of the gain is § 1245 depreciation recapture gain because the $375,040 depreciation taken exceeds the $53,040 recognized gain.

---

[18]§§ 1245(b)(3) and 1250(d)(3) and Reg. §§ 1.1245–4(c) and 1.1250–3(c). Some of these special corporate problems are discussed in Chapter 20. Partnership contributions are also discussed in Chapter 20.

[19]§§ 1245(d) and 1250(i).

[20]§ 453(i). The installment method of reporting gains on the sale of property is discussed in Chapter 18.

Property Dividends

A corporation generally recognizes gain if it distributes appreciated property as a dividend. Recapture under §§ 1245 and 1250 applies to the extent of the *lower* of the recapture potential or the excess of the property's fair market value over the adjusted basis.[21]

Emerald Corporation distributes § 1245 property as a dividend to its shareholders. The amount of the recapture potential is $300, and the excess of the property's fair market value over the adjusted basis is $800. Emerald recognizes $300 of ordinary income and $500 of § 1231 gain.

Concept Summary 17.3 integrates the depreciation recapture rules with the § 1231 netting process. It is an expanded version of Concept Summary 17.1.

Concept Summary 17.3

Depreciation Recapture and § 1231 Netting Procedure

```
§ 1231 asset and            § 1231 asset and long-term           § 1231 asset and
long-term                   nonpersonal use capital              long-term
nonpersonal      Remaining  asset casualty* gains                nonpersonal
use capital asset   Gain     minus                               use capital asset
casualty gains         →    § 1231 asset and long-term   ←       casualty losses
                            nonpersonal use capital
   │                        asset casualty* losses
   │ Depreciation
   │ Recapture                   │ NET              │ NET
   ↓                             │ GAIN             │ LOSS
                                 ↓                  ↓
Ordinary                    Net gain           Items are treated separately:
income                      (add to § 1231 gains)  • Gains are ordinary income
                                                    • § 1231 asset losses are deductible for AGI
   ↑                             │                  • Other losses are deductible from AGI
   │ Depreciation                │
   │ Recapture                   │ NET              │ NET
   │                             │ GAIN             │ LOSS
§ 1231 assets    Remaining   § 1231 gains       ←   § 1231 assets
sold at a gain      Gain      minus                 sold at a loss
                     →        § 1231 losses

                             │ NET
                             │ GAIN
                             ↓
                        Lookback Provision:
                        Net gain is offset against
                        nonrecaptured net § 1231
                        losses from five prior tax years

                    ↓                        ↓
             Gain offset by            Remaining gain
             lookback losses            is LTCG
             is ordinary gain
```

*Includes casualties and thefts.

---

[21]§ 311(b) and Reg. §§ 1.1245–1(c) and –6(b) and 1.1250–1(a)(4), –1(b)(4), and –1(c)(2).

GLOBAL TAX ISSUES   **Depreciation Recapture in Other Countries**

The rules for dispositions of depreciated property are more complex in the United States than in any other country. Most countries treat the gain or loss from the disposition of business depreciable assets as ordinary income or loss. Consequently, although the U.S. rules are more complex, they can be more beneficial than those of other countries because at least some gains from the disposition of depreciable business property may be taxed at the lower capital gain rates.

17-5 SPECIAL RECAPTURE PROVISIONS

LO.6
Recognize special recapture provisions that are part of the tax law.

17-5a Special Recapture for Corporations

Corporations selling depreciable real estate may have ordinary income in addition to that required by § 1250.[22] Under this provision, corporations selling depreciable real property are required to recapture as ordinary income the smaller of two amounts: (1) 20 percent of the recognized gain or (2) 20 percent of the depreciation taken. See the discussion of this topic in Chapter 20.

17-5b Gain from Sale of Depreciable Property between Certain Related Parties

If related parties sell or exchange property that is depreciable in the hands of the *transferee* (principally machinery, equipment, and buildings, but not land), any gain recognized by the *transferor* is ordinary income.[23] This rule applies to both direct and indirect sales or exchanges. A related party is defined as an individual and his or her controlled corporation or partnership or a taxpayer and any trust in which the taxpayer (or the taxpayer's spouse) is a beneficiary.

EXAMPLE 21

Isabella sells a personal use automobile (therefore nondepreciable) to her controlled corporation. The automobile, which was purchased two years ago, originally cost $5,000 and is sold for $7,000. The automobile is to be used in the corporation's business.

If the related-party provision did not exist, Isabella would realize a $2,000 long-term capital gain. The income tax consequences would be favorable because Isabella's controlled corporation is entitled to depreciate the automobile based on the purchase price of $7,000. Under the related-party provision, Isabella's $2,000 gain is ordinary income.

17-5c Intangible Drilling Costs

Taxpayers may elect to either *expense or capitalize* intangible drilling and development costs for oil, gas, or geothermal properties.[24] Intangible drilling and development costs (IDCs) include operator (one who holds a working or operating interest in any tract or parcel of land) expenditures for wages, fuel, repairs, hauling, and supplies. These expenditures must be incident to and necessary for the drilling of wells and preparation of wells for production. In most instances, taxpayers elect to expense IDCs to maximize tax deductions during drilling.

Intangible drilling and development costs are subject to § 1254 recapture when the property is sold. Any gain realized on the disposition is recognized as ordinary income to the extent of IDCs expensed (but limited to the realized gain).

---

[22]§ 291(a)(1).

[23]§ 1239.

[24]§ 263(c).

Describe and apply the reporting procedures for §§ 1231, 1245, and 1250.

17-6 **REPORTING PROCEDURES**

Noncapital gains and losses are reported on Form 4797 (Sales of Business Property). However, before Form 4797 is filled out, Part B of Form 4684 (Casualties and Thefts) must be completed to determine whether any casualties will enter into the § 1231 computation procedure. Recall that recognized gains from § 1231 asset casualties may be recaptured by § 1245 or § 1250. These gains will not appear on Form 4684. The § 1231 gains and nonpersonal use long-term capital gains are netted against § 1231 losses and nonpersonal use long-term capital losses on Form 4684 to determine if there is a net gain to transfer to Form 4797, Part I.

Because 2017 tax forms are not yet available, 2016 tax forms are used for the remainder of the discussion.

Form 4797 is divided into four parts; each part's function is summarized below.

Part	Function
I	To report regular § 1231 gains and losses [including recognized gains and losses from certain involuntary conversions (condemnations)].
II	To report ordinary gains and losses.
III	To determine the portion of the gain that is subject to recapture (e.g., §§ 1245 and 1250 gain).
IV	Computation of recapture amounts under §§ 179 and 280F when business use of depreciable property drops to 50% or less.

Generally, the best approach to completing Form 4797 is to start with Part III. Once the recapture amount has been determined, it is transferred to Part II. Any gain remaining after the recapture has been accounted for is transferred from Part III to Part I. Also transferred to Part I is any net gain from certain casualties and thefts as reported on Form 4684, Part B (refer to the beginning of this section and Chapter 15). If the netting process in Form 4797, Part I, results in a gain, it is reduced by the nonrecaptured net § 1231 losses from prior years (line 8 of Part I). Any remaining gain is shifted to Schedule D (Capital Gains and Losses) of Form 1040. If the netting process in Part I of Form 4797 results in a loss, the loss moves to Part II to be treated as an ordinary loss.

The complex rules for the alternative tax on net capital gain for individuals, estates, and trusts affect the reporting of gains and losses from the disposition of business and rental assets. For example, a partnership or an S corporation that uses Form 4797 must provide information to its partners or shareholders related to the gain surviving Form 4797, Part I (the gain that goes to Schedule D). As part of its reporting, it must identify what portion of this gain is *28% gain*, *25% gain*, or *0%/15%/20% gain*.

The process followed in Example 22 is based on an analysis of Form 1040, Schedule D, and Form 4797 and their instructions. Here are some key points:

- All gains and losses treated as ordinary gains and losses (those that end up in Part II of Form 4797) are not eligible for any of the special tax rates for net capital gain.

- The net § 1231 gain goes from Part I of Form 4797 to line 11 of Schedule D (as a long-term capital gain).

- The *25% gain* (if any) from Form 4797 is part of the Schedule D, line 11, gain. *Nothing on the face of Form 4797 or Schedule D identifies this gain.* Only when the alternative tax on net capital gain is computed is the *25% gain* portion of the Form 4797 net gain specifically mentioned (see Schedule D, line 19).

- Section 1231 assets are assets held more than one year. Therefore, no gain or loss is reportable on Form 4797, Part I or Part III, unless that holding period requirement is satisfied.

For 2016, Troy Williams, a single taxpayer (Social Security Number: 111-11-1111), has taxable income of $133,000 *including* the following recognized gains and losses (assume that Troy has no nonrecaptured § 1231 losses from prior years):

Sale of Depreciable Business Assets Held Long Term

Asset A (Note 1)	$36,500
Asset B (Note 2)	20,126
Asset C (Note 3)	(880)

Sale of Depreciable Business Assets Held Short Term

Asset D (Note 4)	($ 600)

Capital Assets

Long-term gain (Note 5)	$3,000
Short-term loss (Note 6)	(200)

Note 1. Asset A was acquired on June 23, 2013, for $50,000. It was 5-year MACRS property, and four years' cost recovery totaled $38,480. The property was sold for $48,020 on August 31, 2016.

Note 2. Asset B was purchased on May 10, 2006, for $37,000. It was 27.5-year residential rental real estate, and straight-line depreciation totaled $14,126. Asset B was sold for $43,000 on November 10, 2016.

Note 3. Asset C was purchased on December 9, 2013, for $16,000. It was 5-year MACRS property, and four years' cost recovery totaled $12,314. The property was sold for $2,806 on December 30, 2016.

Note 4. Asset D was purchased for $7,000 on July 27, 2016. It was 5-year MACRS property but proved unsuitable to Troy's business. Troy sold it for $6,400 on November 3, 2016.

Note 5. The LTCG resulted from the sale of 100 shares of Orange Corporation stock purchased for $10,000 on April 5, 2014. The shares were sold on October 21, 2016, for $13,223. Expenses of sale were $223.

Note 6. The STCL resulted from the sale of 50 shares of Blue Corporation stock purchased for $350 on March 14, 2016. The shares were sold for $170 on August 20, 2016. Expenses of sale were $20.

Reporting Consequences

Form 4797

Part III. The sales of Assets A and B are reported here because both generated gains.

- **Asset A (§ 1245 Recapture Potential).** The sale of Asset A results in the recapture of cost recovery (depreciation) deductions. Here, the depreciation recapture potential ($38,480) is greater than the realized gain. So all of the gain will be treated as depreciation recaptured under § 1245 (and ordinary income). That recapture is shown on line 25b and is carried to line 31.

- **Asset B (§ 1250 Recapture Potential).** As straight-line cost recovery was used on Asset B, there is no § 1250 recapture. The $20,126 gain from the sale of Asset B is included on lines 30 and 32 and then is carried from line 32 to Part I, line 6.

Part I. Gains and losses from § 1231 assets not appearing in Part III are reported here. In addition, the § 1231 netting process occurs here (on lines 7 to 9).

- **Asset C.** The loss from Asset C is reported on line 2.

- **§ 1231 Netting.** The § 1231 gains and losses are netted and appear on line 7. Given that Troy has no nonrecaptured net § 1231 losses from prior years (these would be reported on line 8), the net gain on line 7 is transferred to Schedule D, line 11.

Part II. Any ordinary gains and losses are accumulated here.

- **Asset D.** The loss from Asset D is reported on line 10.

- The depreciation recapture from Part III, line 31 appears on line 13.

- The net gain on line 18 is ordinary income and is transferred to Form 1040, line 14.

continued

Schedule D (Form 1040)

Part I. Short-Term Capital Gains and Losses.

- **Blue Corporation Stock.** The short-term capital loss from the Blue Corporation stock is reported on line 1a. It is assumed that the sale of the Blue Corporation stock was reported to Troy on a Form 1099–B that showed the adjusted basis and selling price of the stock. If not, a Form 8949 would be required.

Part II. Long-Term Capital Gains and Losses.

- **Orange Corporation Stock.** The long-term capital gain from the Orange Corporation stock is reported on line 8a. It is assumed that the sale of the Orange Corporation stock was reported to Troy on a Form 1099–B that showed the adjusted basis and selling price of the stock. If not, a Form 8949 would be required.

- **Net § 1231 Gain.** The net § 1231 gain transferred from Form 4797 appears on line 11.

Part III. Summary.

- The combination of short-term and long-term capital gains and losses appears on line 16. In this case, the amount is a *net capital gain*. The net capital gain is then carried to line 13 of Form 1040.

Tax Computation

- In 2016, five alternative tax rates applied: 25%, 28%, and 0%/15%/20%.

- On Form 4797, Part III, the $20,126 § 1231 gain from Asset B is made up of $14,126 of potential *25% gain* (equal to the depreciation taken) and $6,000 of potential *0%/15%/20% gain*.

   ➤ The $880 § 1231 loss from Form 4797, Part I, line 2 offsets the potential *0%/15%/20%* portion of the $20,126 § 1231 gain on Form 4797, Part I, line 6.

   ➤ Consequently, the $19,246 § 1231 gain that goes from Form 4797, Part I, line 7 to Schedule D, line 11 is made up of (1) $14,126 *25% gain* and (2) $5,120 *0%/15%/20% gain*.

- Schedule D, Part III, line 19 shows an unrecaptured § 1250 gain of $13,926. A worksheet in the Form 1040 Schedule D instructions must be used to determine this amount. This gain results from the $14,126 *25% gain* being reduced by the $200 short-term capital loss from Schedule D, line 7.

- Troy's 2016 tax liability is $28,804, computed as follows:

$24,104	Tax on other taxable income of $110,954
	($133,000 taxable income − $22,046 net long-term capital gain)
+ 3,482	Tax on the *25% gain* ($13,926 × .25)
+ 1,218	Tax on the *0%/15%/20% gain* ($8,120 × .15)
$28,804	

The 2016 tax form solution for Example 22 appears on the following pages.

ETHICS & EQUITY   Incorrect Depreciation and Recognized Gain

A staff accountant for a large international company is calculating the tax gain from a disposition of business equipment. The equipment was 7-year MACRS property and has been fully depreciated for tax purposes. The staff accountant notices that the equipment was used in Germany, not the United States, although it is listed as an asset of the U.S. company for which the staff accountant works. Because the property was used outside the United States, it should have been depreciated using straight-line over a nine-year life. Consequently, the tax depreciation has been overstated, and the tax basis should be greater than zero, causing a smaller gain. What should the staff accountant do?

Form **4797**

Department of the Treasury
Internal Revenue Service

Sales of Business Property
(Also Involuntary Conversions and Recapture Amounts Under Sections 179 and 280F(b)(2))
▶ **Attach to your tax return.**
▶ **Information about Form 4797 and its separate instructions is at** *www.irs.gov/form4797.*

OMB No. 1545-0184

2016

Attachment
Sequence No. **27**

Name(s) shown on return

Troy Williams

Identifying number

111 - 11 - 1111

1 Enter the gross proceeds from sales or exchanges reported to you for 2016 on Form(s) 1099-B or 1099-S (or substitute statement) that you are including on line 2, 10, or 20. See instructions . . . . | **1** |

Part I **Sales or Exchanges of Property Used in a Trade or Business and Involuntary Conversions From Other Than Casualty or Theft—Most Property Held More Than 1 Year** (see instructions)

2	(a) Description of property	(b) Date acquired (mo., day, yr.)	(c) Date sold (mo., day, yr.)	(d) Gross sales price	(e) Depreciation allowed or allowable since acquisition	(f) Cost or other basis, plus improvements and expense of sale	(g) Gain or (loss) Subtract (f) from the sum of (d) and (e)
	Asset C	*12/09/13*	*12/30/16*	*2,806*	*12,314*	*16,000*	*(880)*

3	Gain, if any, from Form 4684, line 39	**3**	
4	Section 1231 gain from installment sales from Form 6252, line 26 or 37	**4**	
5	Section 1231 gain or (loss) from like-kind exchanges from Form 8824	**5**	
6	Gain, if any, from line 32, from other than casualty or theft	**6**	*20,126*
7	Combine lines 2 through 6. Enter the gain or (loss) here and on the appropriate line as follows:	**7**	*19,246*

Partnerships (except electing large partnerships) and S corporations. Report the gain or (loss) following the instructions for Form 1065, Schedule K, line 10, or Form 1120S, Schedule K, line 9. Skip lines 8, 9, 11, and 12 below.

Individuals, partners, S corporation shareholders, and all others. If line 7 is zero or a loss, enter the amount from line 7 on line 11 below and skip lines 8 and 9. If line 7 is a gain and you didn't have any prior year section 1231 losses, or they were recaptured in an earlier year, enter the gain from line 7 as a long-term capital gain on the Schedule D filed with your return and skip lines 8, 9, 11, and 12 below.

8	Nonrecaptured net section 1231 losses from prior years. See instructions	**8**	
9	Subtract line 8 from line 7. If zero or less, enter -0-. If line 9 is zero, enter the gain from line 7 on line 12 below. If line 9 is more than zero, enter the amount from line 8 on line 12 below and enter the gain from line 9 as a long-term capital gain on the Schedule D filed with your return. See instructions	**9**	

Part II **Ordinary Gains and Losses** (see instructions)

10 Ordinary gains and losses not included on lines 11 through 16 (include property held 1 year or less):

	Asset D	*07/27/16*	*11/03/16*	*6,400*	*0*	*7,000*	*(600)*

11	Loss, if any, from line 7	**11** ( )
12	Gain, if any, from line 7 or amount from line 8, if applicable	**12**	
13	Gain, if any, from line 31	**13**	*36,500*
14	Net gain or (loss) from Form 4684, lines 31 and 38a	**14**	
15	Ordinary gain from installment sales from Form 6252, line 25 or 36	**15**	
16	Ordinary gain or (loss) from like-kind exchanges from Form 8824.	**16**	
17	Combine lines 10 through 16	**17**	*35,900*

18 For all except individual returns, enter the amount from line 17 on the appropriate line of your return and skip lines a and b below. For individual returns, complete lines a and b below:

a If the loss on line 11 includes a loss from Form 4684, line 35, column (b)(ii), enter that part of the loss here. Enter the part of the loss from income-producing property on Schedule A (Form 1040), line 28, and the part of the loss from property used as an employee on Schedule A (Form 1040), line 23. Identify as from "Form 4797, line 18a." See instructions . . | **18a** |

b Redetermine the gain or (loss) on line 17 excluding the loss, if any, on line 18a. Enter here and on Form 1040, line 14 | **18b** | *35,900* |

For Paperwork Reduction Act Notice, see separate instructions.   Cat. No. 13086I   Form **4797** (2016)

Form 4797 (2016)   Page **2**

Part III Gain From Disposition of Property Under Sections 1245, 1250, 1252, 1254, and 1255
(see instructions)

19	(a) Description of section 1245, 1250, 1252, 1254, or 1255 property:		(b) Date acquired (mo., day, yr.)	(c) Date sold (mo., day, yr.)
A	*Asset A*		*06/23/13*	*08/31/16*
B	*Asset B*		*05/10/06*	*11/10/16*
C				
D				

	These columns relate to the properties on lines 19A through 19D. ▶		**Property A**	**Property B**	**Property C**	**Property D**
20	Gross sales price (**Note:** *See line 1 before completing.*) .	20	*48,020*	*43,000*		
21	Cost or other basis plus expense of sale	21	*50,000*	*37,000*		
22	Depreciation (or depletion) allowed or allowable. . .	22	*38,480*	*14,126*		
23	Adjusted basis. Subtract line 22 from line 21	23	*11,520*	*22,874*		
24	Total gain. Subtract line 23 from line 20	24	*36,500*	*20,126*		
25	**If section 1245 property:**					
a	Depreciation allowed or allowable from line 22 . . .	25a	*38,480*			
b	Enter the **smaller** of line 24 or 25a	25b	*36,500*			
26	**If section 1250 property:** If straight line depreciation was used, enter -0- on line 26g, except for a corporation subject to section 291.					
a	Additional depreciation after 1975. See instructions .	26a				
b	Applicable percentage multiplied by the **smaller** of line 24 or line 26a. See instructions	26b				
c	Subtract line 26a from line 24. If residential rental property **or** line 24 isn't more than line 26a, skip lines 26d and 26e	26c				
d	Additional depreciation after 1969 and before 1976. .	26d				
e	Enter the **smaller** of line 26c or 26d	26e				
f	Section 291 amount (corporations only)	26f				
g	Add lines 26b, 26e, and 26f.	26g		*0*		
27	**If section 1252 property:** Skip this section if you didn't dispose of farmland or if this form is being completed for a partnership (other than an electing large partnership).					
a	Soil, water, and land clearing expenses	27a				
b	Line 27a multiplied by applicable percentage. See instructions	27b				
c	Enter the **smaller** of line 24 or 27b	27c				
28	**If section 1254 property:**					
a	Intangible drilling and development costs, expenditures for development of mines and other natural deposits, mining exploration costs, and depletion. See instructions	28a				
b	Enter the **smaller** of line 24 or 28a	28b				
29	**If section 1255 property:**					
a	Applicable percentage of payments excluded from income under section 126. See instructions	29a				
b	Enter the **smaller** of line 24 or 29a. See instructions .	29b				

Summary of Part III Gains. Complete property columns A through D through line 29b before going to line 30.

30	Total gains for all properties. Add property columns A through D, line 24	30	*56,626*
31	Add property columns A through D, lines 25b, 26g, 27c, 28b, and 29b. Enter here and on line 13	31	*36,500*
32	Subtract line 31 from line 30. Enter the portion from casualty or theft on Form 4684, line 33. Enter the portion from other than casualty or theft on Form 4797, line 6	32	*20,126*

Part IV Recapture Amounts Under Sections 179 and 280F(b)(2) When Business Use Drops to 50% or Less
(see instructions)

			(a) Section 179	(b) Section 280F(b)(2)
33	Section 179 expense deduction or depreciation allowable in prior years.	33		
34	Recomputed depreciation. See instructions	34		
35	Recapture amount. Subtract line 34 from line 33. See the instructions for where to report . .	35		

Form **4797** (2016)

SCHEDULE D
(Form 1040)

Department of the Treasury
Internal Revenue Service (99)

Capital Gains and Losses

▶ Attach to Form 1040 or Form 1040NR.
▶ Information about Schedule D and its separate instructions is at *www.irs.gov/scheduled.*
▶ Use Form 8949 to list your transactions for lines 1b, 2, 3, 8b, 9, and 10.

OMB No. 1545-0074

20**16**

Attachment
Sequence No. **12**

Name(s) shown on return	Your social security number
Troy Williams	*111-11-1111*

Part I   Short-Term Capital Gains and Losses—Assets Held One Year or Less

See instructions for how to figure the amounts to enter on the lines below. This form may be easier to complete if you round off cents to whole dollars.	**(d)** Proceeds (sales price)	**(e)** Cost (or other basis)	**(g)** Adjustments to gain or loss from Form(s) 8949, Part I, line 2, column (g)	**(h) Gain or (loss)** Subtract column (e) from column (d) and combine the result with column (g)
1a Totals for all short-term transactions reported on Form 1099-B for which basis was reported to the IRS and for which you have no adjustments (see instructions). However, if you choose to report all these transactions on Form 8949, leave this line blank and go to line 1b .	*170*	*370*		*(200)*
1b Totals for all transactions reported on Form(s) 8949 with **Box A** checked				
2 Totals for all transactions reported on Form(s) 8949 with **Box B** checked				
3 Totals for all transactions reported on Form(s) 8949 with **Box C** checked				

4 Short-term gain from Form 6252 and short-term gain or (loss) from Forms 4684, 6781, and 8824 .	**4**	
5 Net short-term gain or (loss) from partnerships, S corporations, estates, and trusts from Schedule(s) K-1	**5**	
6 Short-term capital loss carryover. Enter the amount, if any, from line 8 of your **Capital Loss Carryover Worksheet** in the instructions	**6** ( )	
7 **Net short-term capital gain or (loss).** Combine lines 1a through 6 in column (h). If you have any long-term capital gains or losses, go to Part II below. Otherwise, go to Part III on the back	**7**	*(200)*

Part II   Long-Term Capital Gains and Losses—Assets Held More Than One Year

See instructions for how to figure the amounts to enter on the lines below. This form may be easier to complete if you round off cents to whole dollars.	**(d)** Proceeds (sales price)	**(e)** Cost (or other basis)	**(g)** Adjustments to gain or loss from Form(s) 8949, Part II, line 2, column (g)	**(h) Gain or (loss)** Subtract column (e) from column (d) and combine the result with column (g)
8a Totals for all long-term transactions reported on Form 1099-B for which basis was reported to the IRS and for which you have no adjustments (see instructions). However, if you choose to report all these transactions on Form 8949, leave this line blank and go to line 8b .	*13,223*	*10,223*		*3,000*
8b Totals for all transactions reported on Form(s) 8949 with **Box D** checked				
9 Totals for all transactions reported on Form(s) 8949 with **Box E** checked				
10 Totals for all transactions reported on Form(s) 8949 with **Box F** checked				

11 Gain from Form 4797, Part I; long-term gain from Forms 2439 and 6252; and long-term gain or (loss) from Forms 4684, 6781, and 8824	**11**	*19,246*
12 Net long-term gain or (loss) from partnerships, S corporations, estates, and trusts from Schedule(s) K-1	**12**	
13 Capital gain distributions. See the instructions	**13**	
14 Long-term capital loss carryover. Enter the amount, if any, from line 13 of your **Capital Loss Carryover Worksheet** in the instructions	**14** ( )	
15 **Net long-term capital gain or (loss).** Combine lines 8a through 14 in column (h). Then go to Part III on the back	**15**	*22,246*

For Paperwork Reduction Act Notice, see your tax return instructions.   Cat. No. 11338H   Schedule D (Form 1040) 2016

Schedule D (Form 1040) 2016   Page **2**

Part III   Summary

16   Combine lines 7 and 15 and enter the result . . . . | **16** | *22,046* |

    • If line 16 is a **gain,** enter the amount from line 16 on Form 1040, line 13, or Form 1040NR, line 14. Then go to line 17 below.

    • If line 16 is a **loss,** skip lines 17 through 20 below. Then go to line 21. Also be sure to complete line 22.

    • If line 16 is **zero,** skip lines 17 through 21 below and enter -0- on Form 1040, line 13, or Form 1040NR, line 14. Then go to line 22.

17   Are lines 15 and 16 **both** gains?
    ☒ **Yes.** Go to line 18.
    ☐ **No.** Skip lines 18 through 21, and go to line 22.

18   Enter the amount, if any, from line 7 of the **28% Rate Gain Worksheet** in the instructions . . ▶ | **18** | *0* |

19   Enter the amount, if any, from line 18 of the **Unrecaptured Section 1250 Gain Worksheet** in the instructions . . . . ▶ | **19** | *13,926* |

20   Are lines 18 and 19 **both** zero or blank?
    ☐ **Yes.** Complete the **Qualified Dividends and Capital Gain Tax Worksheet** in the instructions for Form 1040, line 44 (or in the instructions for Form 1040NR, line 42). **Don't** complete lines 21 and 22 below.

    ☒ **No.** Complete the **Schedule D Tax Worksheet** in the instructions. **Don't** complete lines 21 and 22 below.

21   If line 16 is a loss, enter here and on Form 1040, line 13, or Form 1040NR, line 14, the **smaller** of:

    • The loss on line 16 or
    • ($3,000), or if married filing separately, ($1,500)   } . . . . | **21** | (   ) |

Note: When figuring which amount is smaller, treat both amounts as positive numbers.

22   Do you have qualified dividends on Form 1040, line 9b, or Form 1040NR, line 10b?

    ☐ **Yes.** Complete the **Qualified Dividends and Capital Gain Tax Worksheet** in the instructions for Form 1040, line 44 (or in the instructions for Form 1040NR, line 42).

    ☐ **No.** Complete the rest of Form 1040 or Form 1040NR.

Schedule D (Form 1040) 2016

17-7 TAX PLANNING

17-7a Timing of § 1231 Gain

Although § 1245 recaptures much of the gain from the disposition of business property, sometimes § 1231 gain is still substantial. For instance, land held as a business asset will generate either § 1231 gain or § 1231 loss. If the taxpayer already has a capital loss for the year, the sale of land at a gain should be postponed so that the net § 1231 gain is not netted against the capital loss. The capital loss deduction will therefore be maximized for the current tax year, and the capital loss carryforward (if any) may be offset against the gain when the land is sold. If the taxpayer already has a § 1231 loss, § 1231 gains might be postponed to maximize the ordinary loss deduction this year. However, the carryforward of unrecaptured § 1231 losses will make some or all of the § 1231 gain next year an ordinary gain.

In the examples below, the 2017 and 2018 long-term capital gain rates are assumed to be the same.

LO.8

Identify tax planning opportunities associated with §§ 1231, 1245, and 1250.

Section 1231 Planning

EXAMPLE 23

Mark has a $2,000 net STCL for 2017. He could sell business land held 27 months for a $3,000 § 1231 gain. He will have no other capital gains and losses or § 1231 gains and losses in 2017 or 2018. He has no nonrecaptured § 1231 losses from prior years. Mark is in the 28% tax bracket in 2017 and will be in the 25% bracket in 2018. If he sells the land in 2017, he will have a $1,000 net LTCG ($3,000 § 1231 gain − $2,000 STCL) and will pay a tax of $150 ($1,000 × 15%).

If Mark sells the land in 2018, he will have a 2017 tax savings of $560 ($2,000 capital loss deduction × 28% tax rate on ordinary income). In 2018, he will pay tax of $450 ($3,000 × 15%).

By postponing the sale by a year, Mark gets the use of $710 ($560 + $150) of tax savings until he has to pay $450 in 2018, for a net savings of $260 between the two years without considering the time value of money and other factors.

EXAMPLE 24

Beth has a $15,000 § 1231 loss in 2017. She could sell business equipment held 30 months for a $20,000 § 1231 gain and a $12,000 § 1245 gain. Beth is in the 28% tax bracket in 2017 and will be in the 25% bracket in 2018. She has no nonrecaptured § 1231 losses from prior years. If she sold the equipment in 2017, she would have a $5,000 net § 1231 gain and $12,000 of ordinary gain. Her tax would be $4,110 [($5,000 § 1231 gain × 15%) + ($12,000 ordinary gain × 28%)].

If Beth postponed the equipment sale until 2018, she would have a 2017 ordinary loss of $15,000 and tax savings of $4,200 ($15,000 × 28%). In 2018, she would have $5,000 of § 1231 gain (the 2017 § 1231 loss carries over and recaptures $15,000 of the 2018 § 1231 gain as ordinary income) and $27,000 of ordinary gain. Her tax would be $7,500 [($5,000 § 1231 gain × 15%) + ($27,000 ordinary gain × 25%)].

By postponing the sale of the § 1231 property until 2018, Beth gets the use of $8,310 ($4,200 + $4,110) of tax savings until she has to pay $7,500 in 2018, for a net savings of $810 between the two years without considering the time value of money and other factors.

17-7b Timing of Recapture

Because recapture is usually not triggered until the property is sold or disposed of, it may be possible to plan for recapture in low tax bracket or loss years. If a taxpayer has net operating loss (NOL) carryovers that are about to expire, the recognition of ordinary income from recapture may be advisable to absorb the loss carryovers.

EXAMPLE 25

Ahmad has a $15,000 NOL carryover that will expire this year. He owns a machine that he plans to sell in the early part of next year. The expected gain of $17,000 from the sale of the machine will be recaptured as ordinary income under § 1245. Ahmad sells the machine before the end of this year and uses the $15,000 NOL carryover to offset $15,000 of the ordinary income.

17-7c **Postponing and Shifting Recapture**

It is also possible to postpone recapture or to shift the burden of recapture to others. For example, recapture is avoided upon the disposition of a § 1231 asset if the taxpayer replaces the property by entering into a like-kind exchange. In this instance, recapture potential is merely carried over to the newly acquired property (refer to Example 18).

Recapture can be shifted to others through the gratuitous transfer of § 1245 or § 1250 property to family members. A subsequent sale of such property by the donee will trigger recapture to the donee rather than the donor (refer to Example 15). This procedure would be advisable only if the donee was in a lower income tax bracket compared with the donor.

17-7d **Avoiding Recapture**

The immediate expensing election (§ 179) is subject to § 1245 recapture. If the election is not made, the § 1245 recapture potential will accumulate more slowly (refer to Chapter 8). Because using the immediate expense deduction complicates depreciation and book accounting for the affected asset, not taking the deduction may make sense even though the time value of money might indicate that it should be taken.

REFOCUS ON THE BIG PICTURE

DEPRECIATION RECAPTURE

RL PRODUCTIONS/GETTY IMAGES

Even though Hazel did not maximize her depreciation deductions when she acquired the store equipment in 2014, she still has ordinary income when she sells the equipment in 2017. She has a basis lower than the store equipment's value due to the § 179 immediate expense deduction she took and the rapid 7-year MACRS depreciation. Section 1245 "recaptures" this gain as ordinary income.

One way Hazel could avoid currently recognizing the $53,040 gain ($128,000 sales price − $74,960 adjusted basis) would be to do a like-kind exchange of the equipment acquired in 2014 for the replacement equipment to be acquired in 2017 (see Example 18). She would likely have to give up the 2014 equipment plus cash to acquire the replacement equipment. As a result, there would be no "boot received" and, therefore, no current gain recognized. However, the depreciation recapture potential on the 2014 equipment would carry over to the replacement equipment.

Key Terms

Discussion Questions

1. **LO.1, 2** Harriet, an organic farmer, has owned depreciable farm equipment for several years. Is the equipment a capital asset? Why or why not?   Issue ID

2. **LO.1** If there is a net loss from the sale of depreciable business property held long term, what is the character of the loss? How is it deducted (*for* or *from* AGI)?

3. **LO.1, 2** Bernice, a sole proprietor, sold two business assets during the year. As a result, she has an ordinary loss and a § 1231 gain. The loss asset was office furniture that was held for eight months, and the gain asset is land that was held for five years. Why doesn't the ordinary loss offset the § 1231 gain?   Issue ID

4. **LO.1, 2** Hakim's rental building was not insured when it was destroyed by a hurricane. His adjusted basis for the building was substantial, but was less than he had paid for the building in 2013. The building was Hakim's only asset that was damaged by the hurricane. How should Hakim handle this situation?   Issue ID

5. **LO.2** An individual taxpayer had a net § 1231 loss in 2017. Could any of this loss be treated as a long-term capital loss? Why or why not?

6. **LO.2** Steven established a sole proprietorship in 2012. He sold § 1231 assets at a loss in 2015 and 2016. He had only sold § 1231 assets at a gain before 2015. In 2017, he could sell a § 1231 asset at a gain and would like to have the gain taxed as a long-term capital gain. What issue is Steven facing?   Issue ID

7. **LO.2** Review Examples 4 and 6 in the text. In both examples, the taxpayer's AGI is $129,400 even though in Example 6 there is $700 of nonrecaptured § 1231 loss from 2016. Explain why the two AGI amounts are the same.

8. **LO.3** A depreciable business dump truck has been owned for four years and is no longer useful to the taxpayer. What would have to be true for the disposition of the dump truck to generate at least some § 1231 loss?

9. **LO.1, 3** If depreciable equipment used in a business is sold at a recognized gain on July 10, 2017, and it was purchased on August 21, 2016, does § 1245 depreciation recapture apply to the asset? Explain.

10. **LO.3** A professional football player's contract is sold at a gain after it has been held for two years. What issues should the team consider in determining the nature of this gain?   Issue ID

11. **LO.3** A retailer's store is destroyed by a tornado but is insured for its replacement cost. Consequently, the retailer has a $40,000 gain after receiving the insurance proceeds. The store is not replaced because the retailer spends the insurance proceeds on additional inventory. What is the nature of the gain if the building originally cost $100,000 three years ago and had an adjusted basis of $82,000 at the time of its destruction?

12. **LO.4** In the current year, an individual taxpayer has net long-term capital gain from disposition of capital assets and has unrecaptured § 1250 gain. What would the circumstances have to be for the unrecaptured § 1250 gain to be taxed at 25%?

13. **LO.3, 5** Mary receives tangible personal property as a gift. The property was depreciated by the donor, and Mary will also depreciate it. At the date of the gift, the property was worth more than the donor's adjusted basis. What is the impact of these facts on Mary when she sells the property at a gain several years after she acquired it?

14. **LO.3, 5** Thomas receives tangible personal property as an inheritance from a decedent who died in 2017. The property was depreciated by the deceased, and Thomas will also depreciate it. At the date of the deceased's death, the property was worth more than the deceased's adjusted basis. What is the impact of these facts on Thomas when he sells the property at a gain several years after he acquired it?

15. **LO.3, 5** Dino contributes to charity some tangible personal property that he had used in his business and depreciated. At the date of the donation, the property has a fair market value greater than its adjusted basis, but less than the original cost. What is the impact of these facts on Dino's charitable contribution?

16. **LO.3, 5** A corporation distributes a truck it has owned for three years to its sole shareholder. The shareholder will use the truck for personal use activity. The truck's fair market value at the time of the distribution is greater than its adjusted basis but less than its original cost. Does the corporation recognize a gain? If so, what is the character of the gain?

17. **LO.6** A corporation distributes a truck it has owned for three years to its sole shareholder. The shareholder will use the truck for business activity. The truck's fair market value at the time of the distribution is greater than its adjusted basis but less than its original cost. Does the corporation recognize a gain? If so, what is the character of the gain?

18. **LO.6** Complete the following statements regarding special recapture provisions.
    a.   Corporations selling depreciable real property are required to recapture as ordinary income the _____ of two amounts: (1) _____% of the recognized gain or (2) _____% of the depreciation taken.
    b.   When the sale or exchange of property, which in the hands of the transferee is depreciable property, is between certain related parties, _____ recognized is ordinary income.
    c.   Intangible drilling and development costs are subject to _____ recapture when the property is disposed of.

19. **LO.7** Refer to Form 4797 near the end of this chapter. Where would a § 1231 loss be entered on the form?

20. **LO.7** Refer to Form 4797 near the end of this chapter. Where would a § 1231 gain on the disposition of business land be entered on the form?

Computational Exercises

21. **LO.1** Lena is a sole proprietor. In April of this year, she sold equipment purchased four years ago for $26,000 with an adjusted basis of $15,500 for $17,000. Later in the year, Lena sold another piece of equipment purchased two years ago with an adjusted basis of $8,200 for $5,500. What is the amount and character of Lena's gain or loss?

22. **LO.2** Several years ago Nicolas, a timber dealer, purchased a tract of land with a substantial stand of trees on it. The land cost $8,000, and the timber cost $250,000. On the first day of 2017, the timber was appraised at $325,000. In August 2017, Nicolas cut the timber and sold it for $360,000. Nicolas elects to treat the cutting as a sale or exchange under § 1231. What is the amount and character of Nicolas's gain or loss?

23. **LO.3** Renata Corporation purchased equipment in 2015 for $180,000 and has taken $83,000 of regular MACRS depreciation. Renata Corporation sells the equipment in 2017 for $110,000. What is the amount and character of Renata's gain or loss?

24. **LO.3** Jacob purchased business equipment for $56,000 in 2014 and has taken $35,000 of regular MACRS depreciation. Jacob sells the equipment in 2017 for $26,000. What is the amount and character of Jacob's gain or loss?

25. **LO.1, 2, 3** Sissie owns two items of business equipment. Both were purchased in 2013 for $100,000, both have a 7-year MACRS recovery period, and both have an adjusted basis of $37,490. Sissie is considering selling these assets in 2017. One of them is worth $60,000, and the other is worth $23,000. Because both items were used in her business, Sissie simply assumes that the loss on one will be offset against the gain from the other and that the net gain or loss will increase or reduce her business income. What is the amount and character of Sissie's gain or loss?

26. **LO.4** An apartment building was acquired in 2008. The depreciation taken on the building was $123,000, and the building was sold for a $34,000 gain. What is the maximum amount of *25% gain*?

27. **LO.4** An individual taxpayer has $25,000 of § 1231 gain from the disposition of non-residential real estate. Straight-line depreciation of $43,000 was deducted on the real estate. The taxpayer also has a § 1231 loss of $56,000 from the sale of equipment. How much of the § 1231 gain is taxed as unrecaptured § 1250 gain?

28. **LO.4** Enzo is a single taxpayer with the following gains and losses for 2017:

- $2,100 short-term capital loss.
- $24,000 long-term capital gain from sale of stock.
- $14,000 § 1231 gain that is all unrecaptured § 1250 gain.

What is the amount and character of Enzo's gain or loss?

29. **LO.5** In a § 1031 like-kind exchange, Rafael exchanges a piece of equipment that originally cost $200,000. On the date of the exchange, the equipment given up has an adjusted basis of $85,000 and a fair market value of $110,000. Rafael pays $15,000 and receives equipment with a fair market value of $125,000. What is the amount and character of Rafael's gain or loss?

30. **LO.5** Gaston Corporation distributes § 1245 property as a dividend to its shareholders. The property's fair market value is $580,000, and the adjusted basis is $560,000. In addition, the amount of the recapture potential is $55,000. What is the amount and character of Gaston's gain or loss?

Problems

31. **LO.1, 2** Jenny purchased timber on a 100-acre tract of land in South Dakota in March 2015 for $100,000. On January 1, 2017, the timber had a fair market value of $145,000. Because of careless cutting in November 2017, when the fair market value was $158,000, the wood was sold on January 30, 2018, for $98,000.
    a. What gain (loss) was recognized in 2016, 2017, and 2018 if Jenny elected to treat the cutting as a sale?
    b. What was the nature of the gains (losses) in part (a)?
    c. Does the answer change if the timber was sold in December 2017? Why or why not?
    d. If the timber was worth only $58,000 on January 1, 2017, was cut in November when it was worth $33,000, and was sold in December for $59,000, how would the answers to parts (a) and (b) change?

32. **LO.2** Bob owns a farming sole proprietorship. During the year, Bob sold a milk cow that he had owned for 15 months and a workhorse that he had owned for 66 months. The cow had an adjusted basis of $38,000 and was sold for $55,000. The horse had an adjusted basis of $750 and was sold for $4,000. Bob also has a $200 long-term capital loss from the sale of corporate stock. He has $55,000 of other AGI (not associated with the items above) for the year. He has $4,000 non-recaptured § 1231 losses from the previous five years. What is the nature of the gains or losses from the disposition of the farm animals? What is Bob's AGI for the year?

Communications   33. **LO.2** A sculpture that Korliss Kane held for investment was destroyed in a flood. The sculpture was insured, and Korliss had a $60,000 gain from this casualty. He also had a $17,000 loss from an uninsured antique vase that was destroyed by the flood. The vase was also held for investment. Korliss had no other property transactions during the year and has no nonrecaptured § 1231 losses from prior years. Both the sculpture and the vase had been held more than one year when the flood occurred. Compute Korliss's net gain or loss, and identify how it would be treated. Also write a letter to Korliss, explaining the nature of the gain or loss. Korliss's address is 2367 Meridian Road, Hannibal, MO 63401.

34. **LO.2** Keshara has the following net § 1231 results for each of the years shown. What would be the nature of the net gains in 2016 and 2017?

Tax Year	Net § 1231 Loss	Net § 1231 Gain
2012	$18,000	
2013	33,000	
2014	42,000	
2015		$41,000
2016		30,000
2017		41,000

Decision Making   35. **LO.2, 8** Jinjie owns two parcels of business land (§ 1231 assets). One parcel can be sold at a loss of $60,000, and the other parcel can be sold at a gain of $70,000. Jinjie has no nonrecaptured § 1231 losses from prior years. The parcels could be sold at any time because potential purchasers are abundant. Jinjie has a $35,000 short-term capital loss carryover from a prior tax year and no capital assets that could be sold to generate long-term capital gains. Both land parcels have been held more than one year. What should Jinjie do based upon these facts? (Assume that tax rates are constant, and ignore the present value of future cash flow.)

36. **LO.1, 2, 3** Siena Industries (a sole proprietorship) sold three § 1231 assets during 2017. Data on these property dispositions are as follows:

Asset	Cost	Acquired	Depreciation	Sold for	Sold on
Rack	$100,000	10/10/13	$62,000	$85,000	10/10/17
Forklift	35,000	10/16/14	23,000	5,000	10/10/17
Bin	87,000	03/12/16	34,000	60,000	10/10/17

a. Determine the amount and the character of the recognized gain or loss from the disposition of each asset.

b. Assuming that Siena has no nonrecaptured net § 1231 losses from prior years, how much of the 2017 recognized gains is treated as capital gains?

37. **LO.2, 3** Amber Industries (a sole proprietorship) sold three § 1231 assets during 2017. Data on these property dispositions are as follows:

Asset	Cost	Acquired	Depreciation	Sold for	Sold on
Rack	$100,000	10/10/13	$100,000	$145,000	10/10/17
Forklift	35,000	10/16/14	23,000	3,000	10/10/17
Bin	87,000	03/12/16	31,000	60,000	10/10/17

a. Determine the amount and the character of the recognized gain or loss from the disposition of each asset.

b. Assuming that Amber has $5,000 nonrecaptured net § 1231 losses from the five prior years, how much of the 2017 recognized gains is treated as capital gains?

38. **LO.2, 3** Copper Industries (a sole proprietorship) sold three § 1231 assets during 2017. Data on these property dispositions are as follows:

Asset	Cost	Acquired	Depreciation	Sold for	Sold on
Rack	$110,000	10/10/14	$70,000	$55,000	10/10/17
Forklift	45,000	10/16/13	21,000	15,000	10/10/17
Bin	97,000	03/12/16	31,000	60,000	10/10/17

   a. Determine the amount and the character of the recognized gain or loss from the disposition of each asset.

   b. Assuming that Copper has $6,000 nonrecaptured net § 1231 losses from prior years, how much of the 2017 recognized gains is treated as capital gains?

39. **LO.2, 3** On December 1, 2015, Lavender Manufacturing Company (a corporation) purchased another company's assets, including a patent. The patent was used in Lavender's manufacturing operations; $49,500 was allocated to the patent, and it was amortized at the rate of $275 per month. On July 30, 2017, Lavender sold the patent for $95,000. Twenty months of amortization had been taken on the patent. What are the amount and nature of the gain Lavender recognizes on the disposition of the patent? Prepare your solution using Excel (or a similar program). Write a letter to Lavender, discussing the treatment of the gain. Lavender's address is 6734 Grover Street, Boothbay Harbor, ME 04538. The letter should be addressed to Bill Cubit, Controller. *Communications*

40. **LO.2, 4** On June 1, 2013, Skylark Enterprises (not a corporation) acquired a retail store building for $500,000 (with $100,000 being allocated to the land). The store building was 39-year real property, and the straight-line cost recovery method was used. The property was sold on June 21, 2017, for $385,000.

   a. Compute the cost recovery and adjusted basis for the building using Exhibit 8.8 from Chapter 8.

   b. What are the amount and nature of Skylark's gain or loss from disposition of the building? What amount, if any, of the gain is unrecaptured § 1250 gain?

41. **LO.2, 3, 4** On May 2, 1987, Hannah Weather (Social Security Number: 111-22-3333) acquired residential rental real estate for $450,000. Of the cost, $100,000 was allocated to the land and $350,000 to the building. On August 20, 2016, the building, which then had an adjusted basis of $0, was sold for $545,000 and the land for $200,000.

   a. Determine the amount and character of the recognized gain from the sale of the building.

   b. Determine the amount and character of the recognized gain from the sale of the land.

   c. Complete a Form 4797 for these transactions. Assume that there are no § 1231 lookback losses.

42. **LO.2, 3, 4** Larry is the sole proprietor of a trampoline shop. During 2017, the following transactions occurred:

   • Unimproved land adjacent to the store was condemned by the city on February 1. The condemnation proceeds were $15,000. The land, acquired in 1985, had an allocable basis of $40,000. Larry has additional parking across the street and plans to use the condemnation proceeds to build his inventory.

   • A truck used to deliver trampolines was sold on January 2 for $3,500. The truck was purchased on January 2, 2013, for $6,000. On the date of sale, the adjusted basis was zero.

   • Larry sold an antique rowing machine at an auction. Net proceeds were $4,900. The rowing machine was purchased as used equipment 17 years ago for $5,200 and is fully depreciated.

- Larry sold an apartment building for $300,000 on September 1. The rental property was purchased on September 1, 2014, for $150,000 and was being depreciated over a 27.5-year life using the straight-line method. At the date of sale, the adjusted basis was $124,783.
- Larry's personal yacht was stolen on September 5. The yacht had been purchased in August at a cost of $25,000. The fair market value immediately preceding the theft was $19,600. Larry was insured for 50% of the original cost, and he received $12,500 on December 1.
- Larry sold a Buick on May 1 for $9,600. The vehicle had been used exclusively for personal purposes. It was purchased on September 1, 2013, for $20,800.
- Larry's trampoline stretching machine (owned two years) was stolen on May 5, but the business's insurance company will not pay any of the machine's value because Larry failed to pay the insurance premium. The machine had a fair market value of $8,000 and an adjusted basis of $6,000 at the time of theft.
- Larry had AGI of $102,000 from sources other than those described above.
- Larry has no nonrecaptured § 1231 lookback losses.

a. For each transaction, what are the amount and nature of recognized gain or loss?

b. What is Larry's 2017 AGI?

Communications   43. **LO.2, 4** On January 1, 2008, Stephanie Bridges acquired depreciable real property for $50,000. She used straight-line depreciation to compute the asset's cost recovery. The asset was sold for $96,000 on January 3, 2017, when its adjusted basis was $38,000.

a. What are the amount and nature of the gain if the real property was residential?

b. Stephanie is curious about how the recapture rules differ for tangible personal property and for residential rental real estate acquired in 1987 and thereafter. Write a letter to Stephanie, explaining the differences. Her address is 2345 Westridge Street #23, Edna, KS 67342.

Decision Making   44. **LO.2, 3, 5, 8** Joanne is in the 28% tax bracket and owns depreciable business equipment that she purchased several years ago for $135,000. She has taken $100,000 of depreciation on the equipment, and it is worth $55,000. Joanne's niece, Susan, is starting a new business and is short of cash. Susan has asked Joanne to gift the equipment to her so that Susan can use it in her business. Joanne no longer needs the equipment. Identify the alternatives available to Joanne if she wants to help Susan and the tax effects of those alternatives. (Assume that all alternatives involve the business equipment in one way or another, and ignore the gift tax.)

45. **LO.2, 3, 5** Anna received tangible personal property with a fair market value of $65,000 as a gift in 2015. The donor had purchased the property for $77,000 and had taken $77,000 of depreciation. Anna used the property in her business. Anna sells the property for $23,000 in 2017. What are the tax status of the property and the nature of the recognized gain when she sells the property?

46. **LO.2, 3, 5** Miguel receives tangible personal property as an inheritance in 2015. The property was depreciated by the deceased (Miguel's father), and Miguel will also depreciate it. At the date of the deceased's death, the property was worth $532,000. The deceased had purchased it for $900,000 and had taken $523,000 of depreciation on the property. Miguel takes $223,000 of depreciation on the property before selling it for $482,000 in 2017. What are the tax status of the property and the nature of the recognized gain when Miguel sells the property?

47. **LO.5** David contributes to charity some tangible personal property that he had used in his business and depreciated. At the date of the donation, the property has a fair market value of $233,000 and an adjusted basis of zero; it was originally acquired for $400,000. What is the amount of David's charitable contribution?

48. **LO.2, 3, 5** Dedriea contributes to her wholly owned corporation some tangible personal property she had used in her sole proprietorship business and depreciated. She had acquired the property for $566,000 and had taken $431,000 of depreciation on it before contributing it to the corporation. At the date of the contribution, the property had a fair market value of $289,000. The corporation took $100,000 of depreciation on the property and then sold it for $88,000 in 2017. What are the tax status of the property to the corporation and the nature of the recognized gain or loss when the corporation sells the property?

49. **LO.2, 3, 6** Tan Corporation purchased depreciable tangible personal property for $100,000 in 2015 and immediately expensed the entire cost under § 179. In 2017, when the property was worth $80,000, Tan distributed it as a dividend to the corporation's sole shareholder. What was the tax status of this property for Tan? What is the nature of the recognized gain or loss from the distribution of the property?

50. **LO.5** Jasmine owned rental real estate that she sold to her tenant in an installment sale. Jasmine acquired the property in 2005 for $400,000; took $178,000 of depreciation on it; and sold it for $210,000, receiving $25,000 immediately and the balance (plus interest at a market rate) in equal payments of $18,500 for 10 years.

    a. What is the nature of the recognized gain or loss from this transaction?

    b. Assuming that the interest rate on the installment contract is 5%, what is the present value of the installment payments? See Appendix H for present value factors.

51. **LO.4, 7** Sasha and Tara are married, filing jointly. Their correctly determined 2017 taxable income is $127,000. This taxable income includes a $5,000 § 1231 gain from the sale of business land that was included in their $22,000 of net long-term capital gain. None of the net long-term capital gain was from collectibles.

    a. In addition to their Form 1040, what tax forms related to their property transactions would the couple include in their income tax return?

    b. Calculate the couple's tax on taxable income using the alternative tax on net capital gain method.

52. **LO.7** On August 10, 2015, Jasper purchased business equipment for $40,000. On his 2015 tax return, $40,000 of § 179 immediate expense was taken on the equipment. On July 14, 2016, Jasper sold the equipment for $12,000. What is the nature of disposition gain or loss? Where is it reported on the 2016 Form 4797?

53. **LO.7** Adrian has a 2016 Form 4797, line 9 gain of $56,000. He also has one transaction on his 2016 Form 1040 Schedule D, Part I—a loss of $58,000. What is Adrian's AGI from these events?

54. **LO.7** Theresa has a 2016 Form 1040 Schedule D, line 16 gain of $45,000. There is also a $45,000 gain on the form's line 19. What is the nature of the gain? What alternative tax rate applies to it?

55. **LO.3, 8** Jay sold three items of business equipment for a total of $300,000. None of the equipment was appraised to determine its value. Jay's cost and adjusted basis for the assets are as follows:

    Decision Making

Asset	Cost	Adjusted Basis
Skidder	$230,000	$ 40,000
Driller	120,000	60,000
Platform	620,000	–0–
Total	$970,000	$100,000

Jay has been unable to establish the fair market values of the three assets. All he can determine is that combined they were worth $300,000 to the buyer in this arm's length transaction. How should Jay allocate the sales price and figure the gain or loss on the sale of the three assets?

Cumulative Problems

Tax Return Problem

TAX SOFTWARE

56. Justin Stone was an employee of DataCare Services, Inc. His salary was $45,000 through November 10, 2016, when he was laid off. DataCare Services provided medical insurance for Justin and his family during his employment and agreed to continue this coverage through the end of 2016. He received $7,000 of unemployment compensation from November 11, 2016, through December 31, 2016. FICA withholdings were as follows: Social Security of $2,790 ($45,000 × 6.2%) and Medicare of $653 ($45,000 × 1.45%). Justin lives at 112 Green Road, Crown City, OH 45623. His Social Security number is 111-11-1112. Justin owned an apartment building until November 22, 2016, when he sold it for $200,000 (the apartment building's address is 4826 Orange Street, Crown City, OH 45623). For 2016, he had rent revenue of $33,000. He incurred and paid expenses as follows: $4,568 of repairs, $12,000 of mortgage interest, $10,000 of real estate taxes, and $1,000 of miscellaneous expenses. He purchased the building on January 2, 2010, for $125,000. The building generated an operating profit each year that Justin owned it. Justin received $13,000 in cash as a gift from his mother to help "tide him over" while he was unemployed. He also withdrew $10,000 from his checking account. He "invested" $300 in lottery tickets during the year but had no winnings.

Other information follows:

- On November 22, 2016, Justin sold for $3,500 equipment that had been used for repairing various items in the apartments. The equipment was purchased for $25,000 on July 10, 2009, and was fully depreciated prior to 2016.

- Justin has $3,000 of unrecaptured § 1231 losses from prior years.

- Justin is age 38; is single; is divorced; and has custody of his 9-year-old son, Flint. Justin provides more than 50% of Flint's support. Flint's Social Security number is 123-45-6789.

- Justin had $1,000 interest income from Blue Corporation bonds.

- Justin had $1,500 interest income from a State Bank certificate of deposit.

- Justin had a $2,000 *0%/15%/20%* long-term capital gain distribution from the Brown Stock Investment Fund.

- Justin had the following itemized deductions: $4,600 real estate taxes on his home; $8,900 mortgage interest on his home; $4,760 charitable contributions (all in cash, all properly documented, and no single contribution exceeding $25); $4,300 state income tax withholding during 2016; $2,000 state estimated income tax payments during 2016; $2,600 sales taxes paid.

- Justin does not want to donate to the Presidential Election Campaign Fund.

- He had $12,000 of Federal income tax withholding during 2016 and made total Federal estimated income tax payments of $14,000 during 2016.

Compute Justin's 2016 net tax payable or refund due. If you use tax forms for your computations, you will need Form 1040 and Schedules A, B, D, and E. You will also need Form 4797. Suggested software: H&R BLOCK Tax Software.

Tax Computation Problem

Communications

57. Glen and Diane Okumura (both age 48) are married, file a joint return, and live at 39 Kaloa Street, Honolulu, HI 96815. Glen's Social Security number is 111-11-1111, and Diane's is 123-45-6789. The Okumuras have two dependent children, Amy (age 15) and John (age 9). Amy's Social Security number is 123-45-6788, and John's Social Security number is 123-45-6787. Glen works for the Hawaii Public Works Department, and Diane works in a retail dress shop. Glen's employer provided medical insurance to Glen and his family during 2017. The Okumuras had the following transactions during 2017:

a. Glen earned $57,000 in wages and had Federal income tax withholding of $2,000.

b. Diane earned $38,000 in wages from the dress shop and had Federal income tax withholding of $1,000.

c. The Okumuras sold a small apartment building for $89,980 on November 15, 2017. The building was acquired in October 2011 for $200,000; cost recovery was $66,820.

d. The Okumuras received $3,000 in qualified dividends on various domestic corporation stocks they own.

e. The Okumuras sold stock on November 5 for a $23,000 long-term capital gain and other stock on December 10 at a $2,000 short-term capital loss.

f. The Okumuras had the following itemized deductions: $12,895 unreimbursed medical expenses, $10,500 personal use real property taxes, $7,000 qualified residence interest, $1,500 of Glen's unreimbursed employee business expenses, $535 of investment-related expenses, $2,700 of state income taxes paid, and $1,061 of sales taxes from the sales tax table.

g. The Okumuras spent $3,000 on qualifying child care expenses during the year.

Compute the Okumuras' 2017 net tax payable or refund due. Also write a letter to the Okumuras, describing how the sale of the apartment building affects their return.

Research Problems

Note: Solutions to the Research Problems can be prepared by using the Thomson Reuters Checkpoint® Student Edition online tax research database, which accompanies this textbook. Solutions can also be prepared by using research materials found in a typical tax library.

Research Problem 1. Walter is both a real estate developer and the owner and manager of residential rental real estate. Walter is retiring and is going to sell both the land he is holding for future development and the rental properties he owns. Straight-line depreciation was used to depreciate the rental real estate. The rental properties will be sold at a substantial loss, and the development property will be sold at a substantial gain. What is the nature of these gains and losses?

Partial list of research aids:
§§ 1221 and 1231.
Zane R. Tollis, 65 TCM 1951, T.C.Memo. 1993–63.

Research Problem 2. Your client, Alternate Fuel, Inc. (a regular corporation), owns three sandwich shops in the Philadelphia area. In 2014, the year Alternate Fuel incorporated, it acquired land on the outskirts of Philadelphia with the hope of someday farming the land to cultivate humanely harvested meat and grow organic fruits and vegetables to use in its sandwich shops. In 2016, Alternate Fuel drew up plans for the farm and began consulting with agricultural experts about the best locations for crops and the number of animals that could be sustained on the acreage. After reviewing those plans, Alternate Fuel's CEO decided that the plans are not currently financially feasible and would like to sell the land in 2017. The land has appreciated substantially in value, and the company could use the cash infusion. Given that the land has not been used in the business, will any gain realized be categorized as a § 1231 gain or as a long-term capital gain? Explain.

Use internet tax resources to address the following questions. Look for reliable websites and blogs of the IRS and other government agencies, media outlets, businesses, tax professionals, academics, think tanks, and political outlets.

Research Problem 3. Search for the phrase "mortgage and real estate fraud" on the IRS's website (**www.irs.gov**). Read the articles you find, and explain why this type of fraud is often unearthed by the IRS.

Research Problem 4. Find a state website that has tax forms and instructions for the state. Call that state "X." Find a discussion in those sources that reveals whether state X taxes gains from the sale of real estate that is located in state Y when the taxpayer is an individual and is a full-time resident of state X.

Roger CPA Review Questions

1. Joe purchased a van for $30,000 on February 1, 2015, for use with his business, Crew Airport Transport. Joe elected to take the § 179 deduction for the entire cost. On January 1, 2017, Joe sold the van for $20,000. What were the tax effects of this transaction?

   a. $10,000 loss

   b. $20,000 capital gain

   c. $20,000 ordinary gain

   d. $10,000 capital gain, $10,000 ordinary gain

2. In year 1, Gardner used funds earmarked for use in Gardner's business to make a personal loan to Carson. In year 3, Carson declared bankruptcy, having paid off only $500 of the loan at that time. In year 1, Gardner purchased equipment for use in Gardner's business. In year 3, Gardner sold the equipment at a $5,000 loss. In January of year 3, Gardner received shares of stock as a gift from Smith; the shares had been purchased by Smith in year 1. In November of year 3, Gardner sold the shares of stock for a $5,000 gain.

   Which of the above transactions will Gardner report as long-term capital gains or losses for year 3?

   I.   The bad debt write-off
   II. The sale of equipment
   III. The sale of shares

   a. II and III only   c. III only

   b. I only   d. None of the above

3. On March 1 of the current year, Reiter, an individual, sold an office building for $300,000 that had an adjusted basis of $220,000, resulting in a gain of $80,000. Reiter had purchased the building for $260,000 on April 1 of the previous year, and $30,000 of the total depreciation taken took advantage of a special tax incentive program Reiter qualified for. How should Reiter report this gain on the current year tax return?

   a. $80,000 ordinary gain

   b. $30,000 ordinary gain and $50,000 long-term capital gain

   c. $50,000 ordinary gain and $30,000 long-term capital gain

   d. $40,000 ordinary gain and $40,000 short-term capital gain

4. In year 3, Daniels, an individual, sold depreciable equipment for $21,000 that had an adjusted basis of $12,000, resulting in a $9,000 gain. The property had cost Daniels $20,000 when purchased in year 1, and $8,000 of MACRS depreciation had been taken. How should Daniels report the gain on Daniels' year 3 tax return?

   a. As a long-term capital gain of $9,000

   b. As an ordinary gain of $1,800 and a § 1231 gain of $7,200

   c. As an ordinary gain of $8,000 and a § 1231 gain of $1,000

   d. As an ordinary gain of $7,200 and a § 1231 gain of $1,800

5. Cowabunga Corp. had a highly profitable year 4, during which it purchased $1,000,000 in tangible personal property and elected to claim the highest depreciation expense allowed for tax purposes under Code § 179. In year 6 Cowabunga sells the tangible personal property, which now has an adjusted basis of $200,000 as a result of the heavy depreciation taken in years 4 and 5. Had only MACRS depreciation been taken on the property, its adjusted basis at the time of sale would have been $800,000. At a sales price of $930,000, how much of the $730,000 realized gain must be reported as ordinary gain for tax purposes?

   a. $720,000   c. $0

   b. $600,000   d. $730,000

PART 6

ACCOUNTING PERIODS, ACCOUNTING METHODS, AND DEFERRED COMPENSATION

CHAPTER **18**
Accounting Periods and Methods

CHAPTER **19**
Deferred Compensation

Part 6 provides a comprehensive examination of the accounting periods and accounting methods that were introduced in Part 2. A discussion of special accounting methods is also included. Part 6 concludes with an analysis of the tax consequences of deferred compensation.

CHAPTER

18

Accounting Periods and Methods

LEARNING OBJECTIVES: *After completing Chapter 18, you should be able to:*

LO.1 Explain the relevance of the accounting period concept, the different types of accounting periods, and the limitations on their use.

LO.2 Apply the cash method, accrual method, and hybrid method of accounting.

LO.3 Utilize the procedure for changing accounting methods.

LO.4 Determine when the installment method of accounting applies and its effect on taxable income.

LO.5 Review and illustrate the alternative methods of accounting for long-term contracts (the completed contract method and the percentage of completion method), including the limitations on the use of the completed contract method.

LO.6 Recognize when accounting for inventories must occur, be aware of the types of costs that must be included in inventories, and apply the LIFO method.

LO.7 Identify tax planning opportunities related to accounting periods and accounting methods.

CHAPTER OUTLINE

ACCOUNTING PERIOD AND METHOD

Pearl, Inc. (a C corporation), Tweety, Inc. (an S corporation), and Belinda (an individual) are going to form a partnership (Silver Partnership). The ownership interests and tax years of the partners are as follows:

Partner	Partnership Interest	Tax Year Ends
Belinda	25%	December 31
Pearl, Inc.	35%	November 30
Tweety, Inc.	40%	June 30

The partnership expects to begin business on April 1, 2017. The partners have several issues they would like you to address.

- A potential conflict exists among the partners regarding when the tax year should end for Silver. Belinda and Pearl would like a year-end close to their own year-ends, while Tweety would like to have a June 30 year-end. Is this a decision Tweety can make because it owns more of the partnership than either of the other two partners? Is this a decision Belinda and Pearl can make because collectively they own more of the partnership than Tweety owns?

- Because Silver will begin business on April 1, 2017, will the first tax year be a "short" tax year or a "long" tax year? Will annualization of the net income of the partnership be required?

- How will the partners know when their share of Silver's net income or net loss should be reported on their respective income tax returns?

- Belinda is a cash basis taxpayer, and the other partners use the accrual method to report their incomes. What accounting method must be used to compute Belinda's share of the partnership income?

Read the chapter and formulate your response.

FRAMEWORK 1040   **Tax Formula for Individuals**

This chapter covers the boldfaced portions of the Tax Formula for Individuals that was introduced in Concept Summary 3.1 on p. 3-3. Below those portions are the sections of Form 1040 where the results are reported.

Income *(broadly defined)*	$ xx,xxx
Less: Exclusions	(x,xxx)
Gross income..	$ xx,xxx

FORM 1040 (p. 1)

12	Business income or (loss). Attach Schedule C or C-EZ	

Less: Deductions *for* adjusted gross income..	(x,xxx)
Adjusted gross income..	$ xx,xxx
Less: The greater of total itemized deductions *or* the standard deduction...........................	(x,xxx)
Personal and dependency exemptions	(x,xxx)
Taxable income	$ xx,xxx
Tax on taxable income *(see Tax Tables or Tax Rate Schedules)*............................	$ x,xxx
Less: Tax credits *(including income taxes withheld and prepaid)*	(xxx)
Tax due (or refund)	$ xxx

Tax practitioners must deal with the issue of *when* particular items of income and expense are recognized as well as the basic issue of *whether* the items are includible in taxable income. Earlier chapters discussed the types of income subject to tax (gross income and exclusions) and allowable deductions (the *whether* issue).[1] This chapter focuses on the related issue of the periods in which income and deductions are reported (the *when* issue). Generally, a taxpayer's income and deductions must be assigned to particular 12-month periods—calendar years or fiscal years.

Income and deductions are placed within particular years through the use of tax accounting methods. The basic accounting methods are the cash method, accrual method, and hybrid method. Other special purpose methods, such as the installment method and the methods used for long-term construction contracts, are available for specific circumstances or types of transactions.

Over the long run, the accounting period used by a taxpayer will not affect the aggregate amount of reported taxable income. However, taxable income for any particular year may vary significantly due to the use of a particular reporting period. Also, through the choice of accounting methods or accounting periods, it is possible to postpone the recognition of taxable income and to enjoy the benefits from deferring the related tax. This chapter discusses the taxpayer's alternatives for accounting periods and accounting methods.

LO.1

Explain the relevance of the accounting period concept, the different types of accounting periods, and the limitations on their use.

18-1 **ACCOUNTING PERIODS**

Generally, an individual or a corporation that keeps adequate books and records may be permitted to elect a `fiscal year`, a 12-month period ending on the *last day* of a month other than December, for the `accounting period`. Otherwise, a *calendar year* must be used.[2] Frequently, corporations can satisfy the record-keeping requirements and elect to

---

[1]See Chapters 4, 5, and 6.   [2]§ 441(c) and Reg. § 1.441–1(b)(1)(ii).

use a fiscal year.[3] Often the fiscal year conforms to a natural business year (e.g., a summer resort's fiscal year may end on September 30, after the close of the season). Individuals seldom use a fiscal year because they do not maintain the necessary books and records and because complications can arise as a result of changes in the tax law (e.g., often the transition rules and effective dates differ for fiscal year taxpayers).

Generally, a taxable year may not exceed 12 calendar months. However, if certain requirements are met, a taxpayer may elect to use an annual period that varies from 52 to 53 weeks.[4] In that case, the year-end must be on the same day of the week (e.g., the Tuesday falling closest to September 30 or the last Tuesday in September). The day of the week selected for ending the year will depend upon business considerations. For example, a retail business that is not open on Sundays may end its tax year on a Sunday so that it can take an inventory without interrupting business operations.

EXAMPLE 1

Wade, Inc., is in the business of selling farm supplies. Its natural business year terminates at the end of October with the completion of harvesting. At the end of the fiscal year, Wade must take an inventory, which is most easily accomplished on a Wednesday. Therefore, Wade could adopt a 52- to 53-week tax year ending on the Wednesday closest to October 31. If the company selects this method, the year-end date may fall in the following month if that Wednesday is closer to October 31. The tax year ending in 2017 will contain 52 weeks beginning on Thursday, November 3, 2016, and ending on Wednesday, November 1, 2017. The tax year ending in 2018 will have 52 weeks beginning on Thursday, November 2, 2017, and ending on Wednesday, October 31, 2018.

18-1a Specific Provisions for Partnerships, S Corporations, and Personal Service Corporations

When a partner's tax year and the partnership's tax year differ, the partner will enjoy a deferral of income. This results because the partner reports his or her share of the partnership's income and deductions for the partnership's tax year ending within or with the partner's tax year.[5] For example, if the tax year of the partnership ends on January 31, a calendar year partner will not report partnership profits for the first 11 months of the partnership tax year until the following year. Therefore, partnerships are subject to special tax year requirements.

In general, the partnership tax year must be the same as the tax year of the majority interest partners. The **majority interest partners** are the partners who together own a greater-than-50-percent interest in the partnership capital and profits. If there are no majority interest partners, the partnership must adopt the same tax year as its principal partners. A **principal partner** is a partner with a 5 percent or more interest in the partnership capital or profits.[6]

EXAMPLE 2

The RST Partnership is owned equally by Rose Corporation, Steve Corporation, and Tom. The partners have the following tax years:

	Partner's Tax Year Ending
Rose Corporation	June 30
Steve Corporation	June 30
Tom	December 31

The partnership's tax year must end on June 30 because Rose Corporation and Steve Corporation together have a greater-than-50% interest in the partnership. If Steve Corporation's as well as Tom's year ended on December 31, the partnership would be required to adopt a calendar year.

---

[3]Reg. § 1.441–1(e)(2).
[4]§ 441(f).

[5]Reg. § 1.706–1(a).
[6]§§ 706(b)(1)(B) and 706(b)(3).

If the principal partners do not all have the same tax year and no majority of partners have the same tax year, the partnership must use a year that results in the *least aggregate deferral* of income.[7] Under the least aggregate deferral method , the different tax years of the principal partners are tested to determine which produces the least aggregate deferral. This is calculated by first multiplying the combined percentages of the principal partners with the same tax year by the months of deferral for the test year. Once this is done for each set of principal partners with the same tax year, the resulting products are summed to produce the aggregate deferral. After the aggregate deferral is calculated for each of the test years, the test year with the smallest summation (the least aggregate deferral) is the tax year for the partnership.

The Big Picture

EXAMPLE

3

Return to the facts of *The Big Picture* on p. 18-1. The Code and Regulations eliminate the need for the Silver partners to bargain among themselves over the tax year-end. The partnership's tax year must end on November 30 because using that year-end results in the least aggregate deferral of partnership income as demonstrated below.

Test for Tax Year Ending December 31

	Partner's Year-End	1 Profit Percentage	2 Months Income Deferred	1 × 2 Aggregate Months of Deferral
Belinda	12/31	25%	0	0
Pearl, Inc.	11/30	35%	11	3.85
Tweety, Inc.	6/30	40%	6	2.40
				6.25

Test for Tax Year Ending November 30

	Partner's Year-End	Profit Percentage	Months Income Deferred	Aggregate Months of Deferral
Belinda	12/31	25%	1	0.25
Pearl, Inc.	11/30	35%	0	0
Tweety, Inc.	6/30	40%	7	2.80
				3.05

Test for Tax Year Ending June 30

	Partner's Year-End	Profit Percentage	Months Income Deferred	Aggregate Months of Deferral
Belinda	12/31	25%	6	1.50
Pearl, Inc.	11/30	35%	5	1.75
Tweety, Inc.	6/30	40%	0	0
				3.25

---

[7]Reg. § 1.706–1(b)(3).

Generally, S corporations must adopt a calendar year.[8] However, partnerships and S corporations may *elect* an otherwise *impermissible year* under any of the following conditions:

- A business purpose for the year can be demonstrated.[9]
- The partnership or S corporation makes a timely election to use a taxable year that results in a deferral of not more than three months' income, and the entity agrees to make required tax payments.[10]

Business Purpose

The only business purpose for a fiscal year the IRS has acknowledged is the need to conform the tax year to the natural business year of a company.[11] Generally, only seasonal businesses have a natural business year. For example, the natural business year for a department store may end on January 31, after Christmas returns have been processed and clearance sales have been completed.

Required Tax Payments

Under the required payments system, tax payments are due from a fiscal year partnership or S corporation by May 15 of each tax year.[12] The amount due is computed by applying the highest individual tax rate plus 1 percentage point to an estimate of the deferral period income. The deferral period runs from the close of the fiscal year to the end of the required year. Estimated income for this period is based on the average monthly earnings for the previous fiscal year. The amount due is reduced by the amount of required tax payments for the previous year.[13]

EXAMPLE 4

Brown, Inc., an S corporation, timely elected a fiscal year ending September 30. Bob is the only shareholder and is a calendar year taxpayer. The "required" tax year ends on December 31, 2017, the major shareholder's year-end, and the deferral period is the maximum of three months. For the fiscal year ending September 30, 2017, Brown earned $100,000. The required tax payment for the previous year was $5,000. The corporation must pay $5,150 by May 15, 2018, calculated as follows:

$$(\$100,000 \times {}^{3}/_{12} \times 40.6\%^{*}) - \$5,000 = \$5,150$$

*Maximum individual tax rate of 39.6% + 1%.

ETHICS & EQUITY **Who Benefits from the Change in Tax Year?**

A public accounting sole practitioner has reached a breaking point. All of his clients use the calendar year to report income. Many of the clients are S corporations and partnerships. His workload the first four months of the year is so heavy that it is putting the quality of his work at risk. He is considering telling his clients that any new partnership or S corporation that is formed must timely elect under § 444 to use a fiscal year ending September 30 (assuming that the required year would otherwise be a calendar year). Although the shareholders and partners would be subject to the "required tax payments" rules, the accountant will sell the plan by promising better service. Evaluate the plan proposed by the accountant.

---

[8]§§ 1378(a) and (b).

[9]§§ 706(b)(1)(C) and 1378(b)(2).

[10]§ 444. See Form 8716.

[11]Rev.Proc. 2006–46, 2006–2 C.B. 859.

[12]§ 444(c) and Reg. § 1.7519–2T(a)(4)(ii). No payment is required if the calculated amount is $500 or less. See Form 8752.

[13]§ 7519(b).

Personal Service Corporations

A personal service corporation (PSC) is a corporation whose shareholder-employees provide personal services (e.g., medical, dental, legal, accounting, engineering, actuarial, consulting, or performing arts). Generally, a PSC must use a calendar year.[14] However, a PSC can *elect* a fiscal year under any of the following conditions:

- A business purpose for the year can be demonstrated.
- The PSC year results in a deferral of not more than three months' income, the corporation pays the shareholder-employee's salary during the portion of the calendar year after the close of the fiscal year, and the salary for that period is at least proportionate to the shareholder-employee's salary received for the preceding fiscal year.[15]

Nancy's corporation paid Nancy a salary of $120,000 during its fiscal year ending September 30, 2017. The corporation cannot satisfy the business purpose test for a fiscal year. The corporation can continue to use its fiscal year without any negative tax effects, provided Nancy receives at least $30,000 [(3 months/12 months) × $120,000] as salary during the period October 1 through December 31, 2017.

If the salary test is not satisfied, the PSC can retain the fiscal year, but the corporation's deduction for salary for its next fiscal year is limited to the following:

$$A + A(F/N)$$

Where A = Amount paid after the close of the fiscal year.

F = Number of months in the fiscal year minus number of months from the end of the fiscal year to the end of the ongoing calendar year.

N = Number of months from the end of the fiscal year to the end of the ongoing calendar year.

Assume that the corporation in the previous example paid Nancy $10,000 of salary during the period October 1 through December 31, 2017. The deduction for Nancy's salary for the corporation's fiscal year ending September 30, 2018, is thus limited to $40,000 calculated as follows:

$$\$10,000 + \left[\$10,000\left(\frac{12-3}{3}\right)\right] = \$10,000 + \$30,000 = \$40,000$$

Salary payments in excess of the limitation are not allowed as a deduction of the corporation for the year of the payment, but may be carried to a subsequent year and are subject to the limitation on deductions in the later year.

18-1b Selecting the Tax Year

A taxpayer elects to use a calendar year or, if eligible, a fiscal year by the timely filing of his or her initial tax return. For all subsequent tax years, the taxpayer must use this same period unless approval for change is obtained from the IRS.[16]

18-1c Changes in the Accounting Period

A taxpayer must obtain consent from the IRS before changing its tax year.[17] This power to approve or not to approve a change is significant in that it permits the IRS to issue authoritative administrative guidelines that must be met by taxpayers who want to change their accounting period. An application for permission to change

---

[14]§ 441(i).

[15]§§ 444 and 280H.

[16]Reg. §§ 1.441–1(b)(3) and 1.441–1(b)(4).

[17]§ 442. Under certain conditions, corporations are allowed to change tax years without obtaining IRS approval. See Reg. § 1.442–1(c)(1); Rev.Proc. 2006–45, 2006 C.B. 851, modified by Rev.Proc. 2007–64, 2007–2 C.B. 818.

tax years must be made on Form 1128, Application for Change in Accounting Period. Generally, the application must be filed by the due date (including extensions) for the short taxable period that results from the change.[18]

EXAMPLE 7

Beginning in 2017, Gold Corporation, a calendar year taxpayer, would like to switch to a fiscal year ending March 31. This change results in a short-period return encompassing January 1 to March 31, 2017. The extended due date for this short period return is January 15, 2018, which is also the due date for the Form 1128.

IRS Requirements

The IRS will not grant permission for the change unless the taxpayer can establish a substantial business purpose for the request. One substantial business purpose is to change to a tax year that coincides with the *natural business year* (the completion of an annual business cycle). The IRS applies an objective gross receipts test to determine whether the entity has a natural business year. At least 25 percent of the entity's gross receipts for the 12-month period must be realized in the final two months of the 12-month period for three consecutive years.[19]

EXAMPLE 8

A Virginia Beach motel had gross receipts as follows:

	2015	2016	2017
July–August receipts	$ 300,000	$250,000	$ 325,000
September 1–August 31 receipts	1,000,000	900,000	1,250,000
Receipts for final 2 months divided by receipts for 12 months	30.0%	27.8%	26.0%

Because it satisfies the natural business year test, the motel will be allowed to use a fiscal year ending August 31.

The IRS usually establishes certain conditions that the taxpayer must accept if the approval for change is to be granted. In particular, if the taxpayer has a net operating loss (NOL) for the short period, the IRS may require that the loss only be carried forward.[20] Recall that NOLs are ordinarily carried back for 2 years and forward for 20 years (see text Section 7-6a). Denying a carryback is intended to prevent abuse of the change in tax year rules.

EXAMPLE 9

Parrot Corporation, a manufacturer that is not an S corporation, changed from a calendar year to a fiscal year ending September 30. The short-period return for the nine months ending September 30, 2017, reflected a $60,000 NOL. The corporation had taxable income for 2015 and 2016. As a condition for granting approval, the IRS requires Parrot to carry the loss forward rather than carry the loss back to the two preceding years (the usual order for applying an NOL).

18-1d **Taxable Periods of Less Than One Year**

A short taxable year (or short period) is a period of less than 12 calendar months. A taxpayer may have a short year for (1) the first income tax return, (2) the final income tax return, or (3) a change in the tax year. If the short period results from a change in the taxpayer's annual accounting period, the taxable income for the period must be annualized. Due to the progressive tax rate structure, taxpayers could reap benefits

---

[18]Reg. § 1.442–1(b)(1), Rev.Proc. 2006–45, 2006–2 C.B. 851, and Form 1128 instructions.

[19]Rev.Proc. 2006–46, 2006–2 C.B. 859; Rev.Rul. 87–57, 1987–2 C.B. 117; and Rev.Proc. 2002–39, 2002–1 C.B. 1046.

[20]Rev.Proc. 2002–39, 2002–1 C.B. 1046, modified by Rev.Proc. 2003–34, 2003–1 C.B. 856.

from a short-period return if some adjustments were not required. Thus, the taxpayer is required to do the following:

1. Annualize the short-period income.

2. Compute the tax on the annualized income.
3. Convert the tax on the annualized income to a short-period tax.

EXAMPLE
10

Gray Corporation, a retailer that is not an S corporation, obtained permission to change from a calendar year to a fiscal year ending September 30, beginning in 2017. For the short period January 1 through September 30, 2017, the corporation's taxable income was $48,000. The relevant tax rates and the resulting short-period tax are as follows:

Amount of Taxable Income	Tax Rates
$1–$50,000	15% of taxable income
$50,001–$75,000	$7,500 plus 25% of taxable income in excess of $50,000

Calculation of Short-Period Tax

Annualized income
$$\$48,000 \times {}^{12}/_9 = \underline{\$64,000}$$

Tax on annualized income
$$\$7,500 + .25(\$64,000 - \$50,000) = \underline{\$11,000}$$

Short-period tax
$$\$11,000 \times {}^{9}/_{12} = \underline{\$8,250}$$

Annualizing the income increased the tax by $1,050:

Tax with annualizing	$ 8,250
Tax without annualizing (.15 × $48,000)	(7,200)
	$ 1,050

Rather than annualize the short-period income, the taxpayer can (1) elect to calculate the tax for a 12-month period beginning on the first day of the short period and (2) convert the tax in (1) to a short-period tax as follows:[21]

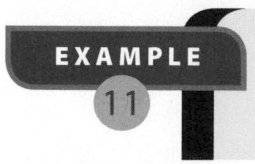

EXAMPLE
11

Assume that Gray Corporation's taxable income for the calendar year 2017 was $60,000. The tax on the full 12 months of income would have been $10,000 [$7,500 + .25($60,000 − $50,000)]. The short-period tax would be $8,000 [($48,000/$60,000) × $10,000]. Thus, if the corporation utilized this option, the tax for the short period would be $8,000 (rather than $8,250, as calculated in Example 10).

The short year counts as a full year for purposes of the net operating loss carryback and carryforward rules.[22]

---

[21]§§ 443(b)(1) and (2).   [22]Reg. § 1.172–4(a)(2).

18-1e **Mitigation of the Annual Accounting Period Concept**

Several provisions in the Code are designed to give the taxpayer relief from the seemingly harsh results that may be produced by the combined effects of an arbitrary accounting period and a progressive rate structure. For example, except for the change in accounting period restriction explained earlier, under the NOL carryback and carryover rules, a loss in one year can be carried back and offset against taxable income for the preceding two years. Unused NOLs are then carried over for 20 years.[23] In addition, the Code provides special relief provisions for casualty losses pursuant to a disaster and for the reporting of insurance proceeds from destruction of crops.[24]

Farm Relief

Farmers and fishermen are often subject to wide fluctuations in income between years, some of which are due to the weather. Congress has provided these taxpayers with a special method of computing their tax on income from farming or fishing. In the high-income years, these taxpayers can elect to compute their tax on income from farming or fishing as though it were earned equally in the three previous years.[25] Thus, the tax on the farming or fishing income for the year is the sum of the additional tax that would have been due in the three previous years if one-third of the income had been earned in each of those years. This averaging system enables the taxpayer to avoid the higher marginal tax rates associated with a large amount of income received in one year.

The income pattern for farmers can also be disrupted by natural disasters that are covered by insurance. The disaster may occur and the crop insurance proceeds may be received in a year before the income from the crop would have been realized. Under these circumstances, the farmer can defer reporting the income until the year following the disaster. Similar relief is available when livestock must be sold on account of drought or other weather-related conditions.[26]

Restoration of Amounts Received under a Claim of Right

The court-made claim of right doctrine applies when the taxpayer receives property as income and treats it as his or her own but a dispute arises over the taxpayer's rights to the income.[27] According to the doctrine, the taxpayer must include the amount as income in the year of receipt. The rationale for the doctrine is that the Federal government cannot await the resolution of all disputes before exacting a tax. As a corollary to the doctrine, if the taxpayer is later required to repay the funds, generally, a deduction is allowed in the year of repayment.[28]

> In 2017, Pedro received a $5,000 bonus computed as a percentage of profits. In 2018, Pedro's employer determined that the 2017 profits had been incorrectly computed, and Pedro had to refund the $5,000 in 2018. Pedro was required to include the $5,000 in his 2017 gross income, but he can claim a $5,000 deduction in 2018.

EXAMPLE 12

In Example 12, the transactions were a wash; that is, the income and deduction were the same ($5,000). Suppose, however, that Pedro was in the 35 percent tax bracket in 2017 but in the 15 percent bracket in 2018. Without some relief provision, the mistake would be costly to Pedro. He paid a $1,750 tax in 2017 (.35 × $5,000), but the deduction reduced his tax liability in 2018 by only $750 (.15 × $5,000). The Code does provide the needed relief in such cases. Under § 1341, when income that has been taxed under the claim of right doctrine must later be repaid, in effect, the taxpayer gets to apply to the deduction the tax rate of the year that will produce the greatest tax benefit. Thus, in Example 12, the repayment in 2018 would reduce Pedro's 2018 tax liability

---

[23]§ 172. Refer to Chapter 7.

[24]§§ 165(i) and 451(d).

[25]§ 1301. The tax is calculated on Schedule J.

[26]§§ 451(d) and (e).

[27]*North American Consolidated Oil Co. v. Burnet*, 3 USTC ¶943, 11 AFTR 16, 52 S.Ct. 613 (USSC, 1932).

[28]*U.S. v. Lewis*, 51–1 USTC ¶9211, 40 AFTR 258, 71 S.Ct. 522 (USSC, 1951).

by the higher 2017 rate (.35) applied to the $5,000. However, relief is provided only in cases where the tax is significantly different; that is, when deduction for the amount previously included in income exceeds $3,000.

ETHICS & EQUITY **Special Tax Relief**

A taxpayer who is required to report income in one year but must repay the income in a subsequent year is granted special tax relief. If the taxpayer is in a lower marginal tax bracket in the year the income is repaid than in the year it was received, the deduction reduces the tax for the year of repayment by using the higher tax rate that applied to the income when it was received.

In contrast, if a taxpayer takes a deduction in one year and receives a refund of the amount giving rise to

the deduction in a subsequent year, the refund is taxed at the marginal tax rate in the year of refund. This is true even though the taxpayer's marginal tax rate in the year of receipt is higher than that in the year of the deduction.

Should both adjustments to income and adjustments to deductions receive the same tax relief? Or should neither situation be granted special relief?

LO.2

Apply the cash method, accrual method, and hybrid method of accounting.

18-2 ACCOUNTING METHODS

Accounting methods include overall methods such as cash or accrual. They also include special accounting methods, such as those used by farmers or for prepaid income. These topics are explained in this section.

18-2a **Permissible Methods**

Section 446 requires the taxpayer to compute taxable income using the method of accounting regularly employed in keeping his or her books, provided the method clearly reflects income. The Code recognizes the following as generally permissible accounting methods :

- The cash receipts and disbursements method.
- The accrual method.
- A hybrid method (a combination of cash and accrual).

The Regulations refer to these alternatives as *overall methods* and add that the term *method of accounting* includes not only the taxpayer's overall method of accounting but also the accounting treatment of any item.[29]

Generally, any of the three methods of accounting may be used if the method is consistently employed and clearly reflects income. However, in most cases, the taxpayer is required to use the accrual method for sales and cost of goods sold if inventories are an income-producing factor to the business.[30] Other situations in which the accrual method is required are discussed later. Special methods are also permitted for installment sales, long-term construction contracts, and farmers.

A taxpayer who has more than one trade or business may use a different method of accounting for each trade or business activity. Furthermore, a taxpayer may use one method of accounting to determine income from a trade or business and use another method to compute nonbusiness items of income and deductions.[31]

---

[29]Reg. § 1.446–1(a)(1).

[30]Reg. § 1.446–1(a)(4)(i). As discussed in text Section 18-2b, as a matter of administrative convenience, the IRS will permit taxpayers to use the cash method even though inventory is a material income-producing factor if

average annual gross receipts are not more than $1 million for the most recent three-year period.

[31]§ 446(d) and Reg. § 1.446–1(c)(1)(iv)(b).

Linda operates a grocery store and owns stocks and bonds. The sales and cost of goods sold from the grocery store must be computed by the accrual method because inventories are material. However, Linda can report her dividends and interest from the stocks and bonds under the cash method.

EXAMPLE 13

The Code grants the IRS broad powers to determine whether the taxpayer's accounting method *clearly reflects income*. Thus, if the method employed does not clearly reflect income, the IRS has the power to prescribe the method to be used by the taxpayer.[32]

18-2b Cash Receipts and Disbursements Method—Cash Basis

Most individuals and many businesses use the cash basis to report income and deductions. The popularity of this method can largely be attributed to its simplicity and flexibility.

Under the cash method, income is not recognized until the taxpayer actually receives, or constructively receives, cash or its equivalent (e.g., the receipt of accounts receivable does not trigger income until collected). Cash is constructively received if it is available to the taxpayer.[33] Generally, a cash equivalent is anything with a fair market value, including any goods or services received in a barter transaction and a note receivable from a customer.

The Big Picture

Return to the facts of *The Big Picture* on p. 4-1 in Chapter 4. Recall that Dr. Cliff Payne has opened a dental practice as a sole proprietorship and does not accept credit cards. In the second year of his business, he adopts a new policy of requiring that his patients either pay cash at the time the services are performed or give him a note receivable with interest at the market rate. Generally, the notes can be sold to the local banks for 95% of their face amount.

At the end of the second year, Dr. Payne has $60,000 in notes receivable from patients. The notes receivable are a cash equivalent and have a fair market value of $57,000 ($60,000 × 95%). Therefore, Dr. Payne must include $57,000 in his gross income for this year.

EXAMPLE 14

Deductions are generally permitted in the year of payment. Thus, year-end accounts payable and accrued expenses are not deducted in the determination of taxable income.

In many cases, a taxpayer using the cash method can choose the year in which a deduction is claimed simply by postponing or accelerating the payment of expenses. For fixed assets, however, the cash basis taxpayer claims deductions through depreciation or amortization, the same as an accrual basis taxpayer. In addition, prepaid expenses must be capitalized and amortized if the life of the asset extends substantially beyond the end of the tax year.[34]

The Regulations have established a one-year rule for prepaid expenses that permits the taxpayer to deduct expenditures for rights that do not extend beyond the earlier of (1) 12 months after the first date on which the taxpayer realizes the right or (2) the end of the tax year following the year of payment. Both cash basis and accrual basis taxpayers are permitted to use the one-year rule.[35]

Restrictions on Use of the Cash Method

The cash method can distort income from a merchandising or manufacturing operation because the cost of goods sold is a function of when payments for the goods were

---

[32]§ 446(b).

[33]Reg. § 1.451–1(a). Refer to Chapter 4 for a discussion of constructive receipt.

[34]Reg. § 1.461–1(a)(1).

[35]Reg. § 1.263(a)–4(f). Refer to Chapter 6 for further discussion of the one-year rule.

made rather than when they were sold. Thus, the Regulations require the accrual method to measure sales and cost of goods sold if inventories are material to the business. This prohibition on the use of the cash method is intended to ensure that annual income is clearly reflected.[36]

In addition, the following three types of taxpayers may not use the cash method (and must use the accrual method) for Federal income tax purposes regardless of whether inventories are material: (1) a corporation (other than an S corporation), (2) a partnership with a corporate partner (that is not an S corporation), and (3) a tax shelter. This accrual method requirement has three exceptions:[37]

- A farming business (other than certain corporations).
- A qualified personal service corporation (a corporation that performs services in health, law, engineering, architecture, accounting, actuarial science, performing arts, or consulting and whose employees own substantially all of the stock), regardless of gross receipts level.
- A corporation, or a partnership with a corporate partner, that is not a tax shelter, whose average annual gross receipts for all prior three-year periods are $5 million or less.

As a matter of administrative convenience, the IRS allows any entity with average annual gross receipts of $1 million or less for the most recent three-year period to use a modified form of the cash method even if the taxpayer is buying and selling inventory. Sales can be reported on the cash method, but the cost of the inventory is deductible only in the year of sale or in the year the taxpayer actually pays for the inventoriable items, whichever is later.

The IRS allows another exception to the required use of the accrual method. Companies whose principal business activity (the activity producing the largest percentage of gross receipts) does not involve sales of goods, manufacturing, mining, and certain publishing activities and whose average annual gross receipts are greater than $1 million but are not more than $10 million for the most recent three-year period may use the cash method. However, under this exception, inventory on hand at the end of the tax year cannot be deducted until it is sold. C corporations, as well as partnerships with a C corporation partner, must use the accrual method and, therefore, are not eligible for this exception if their average annual gross receipts for prior three-year periods exceed $5 million. In addition, tax shelters must always use the accrual method. The major beneficiaries of the $10 million exception are small construction companies and small service businesses that sell some goods in conjunction with the services provided.[38]

Special Rules for Small Farmers

The general tax accounting rules contain several exceptions specifically addressed to farmers. Although inventories are material to farming operations and the accrual method would appear to be required, an exception to the general rule allows small farmers to use the cash method of accounting.[39] The purpose of the exception is to relieve the small farmer from the bookkeeping burden of accrual accounting. Generally, this exception applies to unincorporated farms and certain closely held farming corporations with gross receipts for the year of $25 million or less.[40]

Nevertheless, cash method farmers must capitalize their costs of raising trees that have a preproduction period of more than two years.[41] For example, an apple farmer generally must capitalize the costs of raising the trees until they produce apples in merchantable quantities. However, to simplify the farmer's tax accounting, the cash method farmer is given an option: the preproduction cost of the trees can be expensed if the taxpayer elects to use the alternative depreciation system (refer to Chapter 8) for all of the farming assets.

---

[36]Reg. § 1.446–1(a)(4)(i).

[37]§§ 448(a) and 448(b). For this purpose, the hybrid method of accounting is considered the same as the cash method. Also see § 447.

[38]Rev.Proc. 2001–10, 2001–1 C.B. 272, and Rev.Proc. 2002–28, 2002–1 C.B. 815.

[39]Reg. § 1.61–4.

[40]See §§ 447(c) and 464.

[41]§ 263A(d).

GLOBAL TAX ISSUES **Tax Accounting Methods as Well as Tax Rates in Foreign Countries Are Important Considerations**

When considering whether to conduct business in a foreign country, corporations must consider the accounting methods used to compute taxable income. Some countries have more generous depreciation and inventory valuation methods than do others. Also, many countries permit expensing of start-up costs, whereas other countries require capitalization and amortization (such as in the United States).

Farmers who produce crops that take more than a year from planting to harvesting (e.g., pineapples) can elect to use the crop method to report the income. Under the **crop method**, the costs of raising the crop are capitalized as those costs are incurred and then deducted in the year the income from the crop is realized.[42] This method is analogous to the completed contract method used by contractors (discussed later in this chapter).

Generally, a cash basis farmer must capitalize the purchase price of an animal, whether it is acquired for sale or for breeding. However, the cost of raising the animal can be expensed.[43]

18-2c **Accrual Method**

The tax rules governing when an accrual method taxpayer reports income or claims deductions include an "all events test." The timing rules for deductions also include an "economic performance" requirement. These timing rules for income and deductions of accrual method taxpayers are explained below.

All Events Test for Income

Under the **accrual method**, an item is generally included in gross income for the year in which it is earned, regardless of when the income is collected. An item of income is earned when (1) all of the events have occurred to fix the taxpayer's right to receive the income and (2) the amount of income (the amount the taxpayer has a right to receive) can be determined with reasonable accuracy.[44]

Andre Corporation, a calendar year taxpayer that uses the accrual basis of accounting, was to receive a bonus equal to 6% of Blue Corporation's net income for its fiscal year ending each June 30. For the fiscal year ending June 30, 2017, Blue Corporation had net income of $240,000, and for the six months ending December 31, 2017, the corporation's net income was $150,000.

Andre Corporation will report $14,400 (.06 × $240,000) for 2017 because its right to the amount became fixed when Blue Corporation's year closed. However, Andre Corporation would not accrue income based on Blue Corporation's profits for the last six months of 2017 because its right to the income does not accrue until the close of Blue's tax year.

EXAMPLE 15

An accrual basis taxpayer's amount of income and the tax year the income is recognized are based on its right to receive the income. Thus, unlike the case of a cash basis taxpayer, the fair market value of a receivable is irrelevant.

Marcey Corporation, an accrual basis taxpayer, has provided services to clients and has the right to receive $60,000. The clients have signed notes receivable to Marcey that have a fair market value of $57,000. The corporation must include $60,000, the amount it has the right to receive, in its gross income, rather than the fair market value of the notes of $57,000.

EXAMPLE 16

If an accrual basis taxpayer receives advance payments for services, goods, or licensing of software, it should consider adopting the special deferral method of Revenue

---

[42]Reg. §§ 1.61–4 and 1.162–12(a).
[43]Reg. § 1.162–12(a).

[44]Reg. § 1.451–1(a). Refer to Chapter 4 for further discussion of the accrual method.

Procedure 2004–34. Under this special accounting method, in the year the advance payment is received, the taxpayer reports on its tax return the same amount reported on its financial statement. In the subsequent year, the balance of the advance payment is reported on the tax return regardless of how much is reported on the financial statement for that year. (See text Section 4-2d.)

Troy Corporation is an accrual method taxpayer that has properly adopted the deferral method of Revenue Procedure 2004–34. Troy sells computers and two-year service contracts on the computers. On November 1, 2017, Troy Corporation sold a 24-month service contract and received $240. For financial reporting, Troy reports $20 of gross income for 2017, $120 for 2018, and $100 for 2019. For tax purposes, Troy reports $20 of income for 2017 (same as for financial reporting) and $220 for 2018 (the balance of the advance payment).

Prepaid rental income and prepaid interest income must be recognized in the year of receipt and may not be deferred.[45]

In a situation where the accrual method taxpayer's right to income is being contested and the income has not yet been collected, generally, no income is recognized until the dispute has been settled.[46] Before the settlement, "all of the events have not occurred that fix the right to receive the income."

All Events and Economic Performance Tests for Deductions

A three-part test is applied to determine when an accrual method taxpayer considers an event as either an expense or a capital expenditure. The three parts are (1) **all events test**, (2) amount determinable with reasonable accuracy, and (3) **economic performance test**.[47]

As to when economic performance is met, that depends on the nature of the liability. For example, if an accrual method taxpayer owes money to another company that provided services to it, economic performance is met as the services are provided. Concept Summary 18.1 lists common types of liabilities covered by the economic performance Regulations (Reg. § 1.461–4) and when economic performance is met for each liability.

Concept Summary 18.1

Accruals Under the Economic Performance Test

Event	Example	When Economic Performance Is Satisfied
The taxpayer's use of the owner's property	Rent	Ratably over the period used
Specific property provided to the taxpayer	A company's office supplies are purchased	When the taxpayer receives the supplies
Specific services provided to the taxpayer	The taxpayer contracts for repairs to be made to its equipment	When the repairs are made
Services to be provided for a specific time period	The taxpayer purchases a service contract, such as for cleaning services	Ratably over the contract period
Property or services provided by the taxpayer	A manufacturer contracts to customize a customer's van	When the manufacturer incurs costs under the contract
Rebates	Manufacturer rebates based on quantity of purchases	When the rebate is paid
Tort claims	Customers are awarded claims for harm caused by the taxpayer's product	When payment is made to the injured party; not eligible for the recurring item exception
State income tax	Taxes due when filing the return	When payment is made

---

[45]Rev.Proc. 2004–34, 2004–1 C.B. 991.

[46]*Burnet v. Sanford & Brooks Co.*, 2 USTC ¶636, 9 AFTR 603, 51 S.Ct. 150 (USSC, 1931).

[47]§ 461(h)(4).

One common liability illustrated in Example 18 is where a taxpayer has a liability because another party provided services.

An accrual basis calendar year taxpayer, JAB, Inc., promoted a boxing match held in the company's arena on December 31, 2017. CLN, Inc., had contracted to clean the arena for $5,000, but did not actually perform the work until January 1, 2018. JAB, Inc., did not pay the $5,000 until 2019. Although financial accounting rules would require JAB, Inc., to accrue the $5,000 cleaning expense in 2017 to match the revenues from the fight, the economic performance test was not satisfied until 2018, when CLN, Inc., performed the service. Thus, JAB, Inc., must deduct the expense in 2018.

EXAMPLE 18

If the taxpayer is obligated to provide property or services, economic performance occurs in the year the taxpayer incurs costs in satisfying its obligation to provide the property or services, as illustrated in Example 19.

Agmax Corporation farms land owned by an individual. Agmax's contract to use the land is for three years, and at the end of three years, Agmax agreed to apply lime to the farmland. The contract term expired in 2017, and Agmax applied the lime in 2018. The all events test was satisfied at the end of 2017. However, Agmax did not provide the lime until 2018. Agmax was obligated to provide property (lime) and services. The deduction is not permitted until 2018, when Agmax incurs costs in fulfilling its obligation.[48]

EXAMPLE 19

The economic performance requirement is accelerated, and thus, year-end accruals can be deducted, if all of the following conditions are met (known as the *recurring item exception*):

- The obligation exists, and the amount of the liability can be reasonably estimated.
- Economic performance occurs on or before the earlier of the date the taxpayer files the return (including extension) or $8\frac{1}{2}$ months after the close of the taxable year.
- The item is recurring in nature and is treated consistently by the taxpayer.
- Either the accrued item is not material or accruing it results in a better matching of revenues and expenses.

Green Corporation often sells goods that are on hand but cannot be shipped for another week. The all events test for the sale are satisfied; therefore, the revenue is recognized although the goods have not been shipped at year-end. Green Corporation is obligated to pay shipping costs. Although the company's obligation for shipping costs can be determined with reasonable accuracy, economic performance is not satisfied until Green (or its agent) actually delivers the goods. However, accruing shipping costs on sold items will better match expenses with revenues for the period. Therefore, the company should be allowed to accrue the shipping costs on items sold but not shipped at year-end.

EXAMPLE 20

The economic performance test as set forth in the Code does not address all possible accrued expenses. That is, in some cases, the taxpayer incurs cost even though no property or services were received. In these instances, according to the Regulations, economic performance generally is not satisfied until the liability is paid. The following liabilities are cases in which payment is the only means of satisfying economic performance:[49]

1. Workers' compensation.
2. Torts.
3. Breach of contract.
4. Violation of law.
5. Rebates and refunds.
6. Awards, prizes, and jackpots.
7. Insurance, warranty, and service contracts.[50]
8. Taxes.

---

[48]Reg. § 1.461–4.

[49]Reg. §§ 1.461–4(g)(2)–(6) and 1.461–5(c).

[50]This item applies to contracts the taxpayer enters into for his or her own protection, rather than the taxpayer's liability as insurer, warrantor, or service provider.

FINANCIAL DISCLOSURE INSIGHTS **Tax Deferrals from Reserves**

The tax law generally applies the all events and economic performance tests in determining when an expense is deductible. Accordingly, the use of reserves for financial accounting purposes does not carry over to the tax return. When a business creates a reserve, for example, to account for warranty obligations to customers or vacation pay for employees, book expenses are allowed, but the corresponding tax deduction usually is delayed until an expenditure is actually incurred. The temporary book-tax difference typically creates or adds to a deferred tax asset on the entity's balance sheet.

Deferred tax assets and liabilities are classified as *current* or *noncurrent* for balance sheet purposes. This classification is determined by the following:

- The nature of the underlying asset (e.g., deferral of a bad debt relates to an account receivable, typically a current asset).

- Any knowledge by the entity as to when the required expenditure will occur (e.g., as to the timing and amounts of a legal settlement or award).

For instance, suppose a software developer sells a program to a customer and agrees to provide free annual updates for the next three years. If the revenue from the sale is included in gross income in the year of sale, for financial accounting purposes, a reserve for the anticipated costs of the updates should be deducted and a reserve should be created in the year of the sale. In the simplest case, one-third of the costs associated with the contract are deductible in the year the contract is sold and used by the customer. Of the remaining warranty costs, one-half generates a current deferred tax asset (the costs will actually be incurred within the next tax year), and one-half generates a noncurrent deferred tax asset (for the third contract year).

Current versions of the related IFRS provisions eliminate the classification of deferred tax assets as current or noncurrent. Under IAS 1, all deferred tax assets are deemed to be noncurrent.

EXAMPLE 21

Yellow Corporation sold defective merchandise that injured a customer. Yellow admitted liability in 2017, but did not pay the claim until January 2018. The customer's tort claim cannot be deducted until it is paid.

However, items (5) through (8) above are eligible for the recurring item exception.

EXAMPLE 22

Pelican Corporation filed its 2017 state income tax return in March 2018 and its Federal return on September 15, 2018. At the time the state return was filed, Pelican was required to pay an additional $5,000. The state taxes are eligible for the recurring item exception. Thus, the $5,000 of state income taxes can be deducted on the corporation's 2017 Federal tax return. The deduction is allowed because all of the events had occurred to fix the liability as of the end of 2017, the payment was made by the earlier of the return filing date or $8\frac{1}{2}$ months after the end of the tax year, the item is recurring in nature, and allowing the deduction in 2017 results in a better matching of revenues and expenses.

Reserves

Generally, the all events and economic performance tests will prevent the use of reserves (e.g., for product warranty expense) frequently used in financial accounting to match expenses with revenues. However, small banks are allowed to use a bad debt reserve.[51] Furthermore, an accrual basis taxpayer in a service business is permitted not to accrue revenue that appears uncollectible based on experience. In effect, this approach indirectly allows a reserve.[52]

18-2d **Hybrid Method**

A hybrid method of accounting involves the use of more than one method. For example, a taxpayer who uses the accrual basis to report sales and cost of goods sold but uses the cash basis to report other items of income and expense is employing a hybrid

---

[51]§ 585.   [52]§ 448(d)(5).

method. The Code permits the use of a hybrid method provided the taxpayer's income is clearly reflected.[53] A taxpayer who uses the accrual method for business expenses must also use the accrual method for business income.

EXAMPLE

23

The Loyal Pet Clinic boards animals, provides veterinarian services, and sells pet supplies and medicines. The clinic's gross receipts are approximately $4 million per year, and 40% of the receipts are from sales of pet supplies. Under a hybrid method of accounting, the clinic would use the accrual method for the sales of supplies because inventories are an income-producing factor. However, the services income may be reported using the cash method.

18-2e **Change of Method**

LO.3

Utilize the procedure for changing accounting methods.

The taxpayer, in effect, makes an election to use a particular accounting method when an initial tax return is filed using that method. If a subsequent change in method is desired, the taxpayer must obtain the permission of the IRS. The request for change is made on Form 3115, Application for Change in Accounting Method. Generally, the form must be filed within the taxable year of the desired change.[54]

As previously mentioned, the term *accounting method* encompasses not only the overall accounting method used by the taxpayer (the cash or accrual method) but also the treatment of any material item of income or deduction.[55] Thus, a change in the method of deducting property taxes from a cash basis to an accrual basis that results in a deduction for taxes in a different year constitutes a change in an accounting method. Another example of an accounting method change is a change involving the method or basis used in the valuation of inventories. However, a change in treatment resulting from a change in the underlying facts does not constitute a change in the taxpayer's method of accounting.[56] For example, a change in employment contracts so that an employee accrues one day of vacation pay for each month of service rather than 12 days of vacation pay for a full year of service is a change in the underlying facts and is therefore not an accounting method change.

Correction of an Error

A change in accounting method should be distinguished from the *correction of an error*. The taxpayer can correct an error (by filing amended returns) without permission, and the IRS can simply adjust the taxpayer's liability if an error is discovered on audit of the return. Some examples of errors are incorrect postings, errors in the calculation of tax liability or tax credits, deductions of business expense items that are actually personal, and omissions of income and deductions.[57] Unless the taxpayer or the IRS corrects the error within the statute of limitations, the taxpayer's total lifetime taxable income will be overstated or understated by the amount of the error.

Change from an Incorrect Method

An *incorrect accounting method* is the consistent (for at least two years) use of an incorrect rule to report an item of income or expense. The incorrect accounting method generally will not affect the taxpayer's total lifetime income (unlike the error). That is, an incorrect method has a self-balancing mechanism. For example, deducting freight on inventory in the year the goods are purchased, rather than when the inventory is sold, is an incorrect accounting method. The total cost of goods sold over the life of the business is not affected, but the year-to-year income is incorrect.[58]

If a taxpayer is employing an incorrect method of accounting, permission must be obtained from the IRS to change to a correct method. An incorrect method is not treated as a mechanical error that can be corrected by merely filing an amended tax return.

---

[53]§ 446(c).

[54]See Rev.Proc. 2015–13, 2015–5 I.R.B. 419, for the method change procedures and Rev.Proc. 2015–14, 2015–5 I.R.B. 450, for the list of automatic method changes. Generally, for an automatic method change, the Form 3115 is due when the tax return for the year of change is filed.

[55]Reg. § 1.446–1(a)(1).

[56]Reg. § 1.446–1(e)(2)(ii).

[57]Reg. § 1.446–1(e)(2)(ii)(b).

[58]But see *Korn Industries v. U.S.*, 76–1 USTC ¶9354, 37 AFTR 2d 76–1228, 532 F.2d 1352 (Ct.Cls., 1976).

The tax return preparer as well as the taxpayer will be subject to penalties if the tax return is prepared using an incorrect method of accounting and permission for a change to a correct method has not been requested.[59]

Net Adjustments Due to Change in Accounting Method

In the year of a change in accounting method, an adjustment is generally required in order to prevent the omission or duplication of income or expense items.

In all years prior to 2017, White Corporation used the cash method of accounting for sales and cost of goods sold, even though it was required to use the accrual method. In 2017, the corporation, with consent from the IRS, switched from the cash to the accrual method for reporting sales and cost of goods sold. The corporation's accrual basis gross profit for the year was computed as follows:

Sales		$100,000
Beginning inventory	$ 15,000	
Purchases	60,000	
Less: Ending inventory	(10,000)	
Cost of goods sold		(65,000)
Gross profit		$ 35,000

At the end of the previous year, White Corporation had accounts receivable of $25,000 and accounts payable for merchandise of $34,000. The accounts receivable from the previous year in the amount of $25,000 were never included in gross income because White was on the cash basis and did not recognize the uncollected receivables. In the current year, the $25,000 was not included in the accrual basis sales because the sales are from a prior year. Therefore, a $25,000 adjustment to income is required to prevent the receivables from being omitted from income.

The corollary of the failure to recognize a prior year's receivables is the failure to recognize a prior year's accounts payable. The beginning of the year's accounts payable were not included in the current or prior year's purchases. Thus, a deduction for the $34,000 was not taken in either year and is therefore included as an adjustment to income for the period of change.

An adjustment is also required to reflect the $15,000 beginning inventory that White deducted (due to the use of a cash method of accounting) in the previous year. In this instance, the cost of goods sold during the year of change was increased by the beginning inventory and resulted in a double deduction.

The net adjustment due to the change in accounting method is computed as follows:

Beginning inventory (deducted in prior and current year)	$ 15,000
Beginning accounts receivable (omitted from income)	25,000
Beginning accounts payable (omitted from deductions)	(34,000)
Net increase in taxable income	$ 6,000

This adjustment (the $6,000 increase in taxable income) is referred to as a "net § 481 adjustment" because it is required under § 481. These adjustments are either "positive" (increasing taxable income) or "negative" (decreasing taxable income).

Disposition of the Net § 481(a) Adjustment

Required changes in accounting methods can result from an IRS examination. The IRS usually will examine all years that are open under the statute of limitations. Generally, this means that the three preceding years are examined. Generally, if the IRS auditor finds that a taxpayer is using an incorrect method of accounting, the auditor will impose a change, but on less favorable terms than if the taxpayer had corrected the erroneous method on his or her own. For example, the IRS may require the taxpayer to correct the method for the earliest year open under the statute of limitations and pick up any positive § 481 adjustment all in that year (rather than over four years allowed for a voluntary change in method). Additional tax and interest will be due. However, if the adjustment is greater than $3,000, the taxpayer can elect to calculate the tax by spreading the adjustment over one or more

---

[59]§ 446(f). See *South-Western Federal Taxation: Corporations, Partnerships, Estates & Trusts*, Chapter 17.

previous years.[60] The election is beneficial if the taxpayer's marginal tax rate for the prior years is lower than the marginal tax rate for the year of the change.

To encourage taxpayers to *voluntarily* change (rather than wait for an IRS audit resulting in a required change) from incorrect methods and to facilitate changes from one correct method to another, the IRS generally allows the taxpayer to spread a positive adjustment into future years. One-fourth of the adjustment is applied to the year of the change, and one-fourth of the adjustment is applied to each of the next three taxable years. A negative adjustment must be deducted in the year of the change.[61]

White Corporation in Example 24 voluntarily changed from an incorrect method (the cash basis was incorrect because inventories were material to the business) to a correct method. The company must add $1,500 (¼ × $6,000 positive adjustment) to its 2017, 2018, 2019, and 2020 income.

EXAMPLE 25

ETHICS & EQUITY   Change in Accounting Method

The IRS faces a difficult choice when it deals with taxpayers who use incorrect accounting methods. On the one hand, the taxpayer who has used an incorrect accounting method may be just as culpable as a person who has omitted income or taken an improper deduction. On the other hand, it is often difficult to discover that a taxpayer is using an incorrect accounting method. Therefore, the IRS relies to some extent on self-reporting by taxpayers. The Service encourages voluntary changes in incorrect accounting methods by waiving penalties for underpayment of prior years' taxes and permitting the taxpayer, in effect, to pay the related taxes over a four-year period. Is this equitable treatment?

18-3 SPECIAL ACCOUNTING METHODS

LO.4
Determine when the installment method of accounting applies and its effect on taxable income.

Generally, accrual basis taxpayers recognize income when goods are sold. Cash basis taxpayers generally recognize income from a sale on the collection of cash from the customer. The tax law provides special accounting methods for certain installment sales and long-term contracts. These special methods were enacted, in part, to ensure that the tax will be due when the taxpayer is best able to pay the tax.

18-3a Installment Method

Under the general rule for computing the gain or loss from the sale of property, the taxpayer recognizes the entire amount of gain or loss upon the sale or other disposition of the property.

Mark sells property to Fran for $10,000 cash plus Fran's note (fair market value and face amount of $90,000). Mark's basis for the property was $15,000. Gain or loss is computed under either the cash or accrual basis as follows:

EXAMPLE 26

Selling price	
Cash down payment	$ 10,000
Note receivable	90,000
	$100,000
Basis in the property	(15,000)
Realized gain	$ 85,000

---

[60]§ 481(b). Guidance on IRS-initiated method changes can be found in Rev.Proc. 2002–18, 2002–1 C.B. 678.

[61]Rev.Proc. 2015–13, 2015–5 I.R.B. 419.

In Example 26, the general rule for recognizing gain or loss requires Mark to pay a substantial amount of tax on the gain in the year of sale even though he received only $10,000 cash. Congress enacted the installment sales provisions to prevent this sort of hardship by allowing the taxpayer to spread the gain from installment sales over the collection period, when the taxpayer is best able to pay the tax. The installment method is an important planning tool because of the tax deferral possibilities.

Eligibility and Calculations

The `installment method` applies to *gains* (but not losses) from the sale of property by a taxpayer who will receive at least one payment *after* the year of sale. However, the installment method cannot be used for the following:[62]

- Gains on property held for sale in the ordinary course of business.
- Depreciation recapture under § 1245 or § 1250.
- Gains on stocks or securities traded on an established market.

As an exception to the first item, the installment method may be used to report gains from sales of the following:[63]

- Time-share units (e.g., the right to use real property for two weeks each year).
- Residential lots (if the seller is not to make any improvements).
- Any property used or produced in the trade or business of farming.

The Nonelective Aspect

As a general rule, eligible sales *must* be reported by the installment method.[64] A special election is required to report the gain by any other method of accounting (see the relevant discussion in text Section 18-3d).

Computing the Gain for Each Year Payments Are Received

The gain reported on each sale is computed using the following formula:

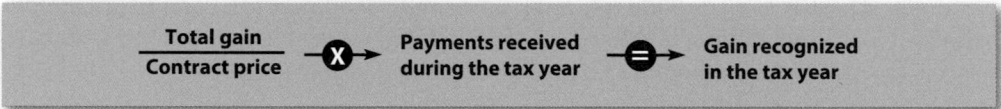

$$\frac{\text{Total gain}}{\text{Contract price}} \quad \boxed{X} \rightarrow \quad \text{Payments received during the tax year} \quad \boxed{=} \rightarrow \quad \text{Gain recognized in the tax year}$$

The taxpayer must compute each variable as follows:

1. *Total gain* is the selling price reduced by selling expenses and the adjusted basis of the property. The selling price is the total consideration received by the seller, including notes receivable from the buyer and the seller's liabilities assumed by the buyer.
2. *Contract price* is the selling price less the seller's liabilities that are assumed by the buyer. Generally, the contract price is the amount, other than interest, the seller will receive from the purchaser.
3. *Payments received* are the collections on the contract price received in each tax year. This generally is equal to the cash received less the interest income collected for the period. If the buyer pays any of the seller's expenses, the seller regards the amount paid as a payment received.[65]

---

[62]§§ 453(b), (i), and (l).
[63]§ 453(l)(2).

[64]§ 453(a).
[65]The gain is reported on Form 6252.

The seller is not a dealer, and the facts are as follows:

Sales price		
Cash down payment	$ 1,000	
Seller's mortgage assumed by the buyer	3,000	
Notes payable to the seller	13,000	$ 17,000
Selling expenses		(500)
Seller's basis		(10,000)
Total gain		$ 6,500

The contract price is $14,000 ($17,000 − $3,000). Assuming that the $1,000 is the only payment in the year of sale, the recognized gain in that year is computed as follows:

$$\frac{\$6{,}500 \text{ (total gain)}}{\$14{,}000 \text{ (contract price)}} \times \$1{,}000 = \$464 \text{ (gain recognized in year of sale)}$$

If the sum of the seller's basis and selling expenses is less than the liabilities assumed by the buyer, the difference must be added to the contract price and to the payments (treated as *deemed payments*) received in the year of sale.[66] This adjustment to the contract price is required so that the ratio of total gain to contract price will not be greater than one. The adjustment also accelerates the reporting of income from the deemed payments.

Assume the same facts as in Example 27, except that the seller's basis in the property is only $2,000. The total gain, therefore, is $14,500 [$17,000 − ($2,000 + $500)]. Payments in the year of sale are $1,500 and are calculated as follows:

Down payment	$1,000
Excess of mortgage assumed over seller's basis and selling expenses ($3,000 − $2,000 − $500)	500
Total payments	$1,500

The contract price is $14,500 [$17,000 (selling price) − $3,000 (seller's mortgage assumed) + $500 (excess of mortgage assumed over seller's basis and selling expenses)]. The gain recognized in the year of sale is computed as follows:

$$\frac{\$14{,}500 \text{ (total gain)}}{\$14{,}500 \text{ (contract price)}} \times \$1{,}500 \text{ total payments received} =$$

$$\$1{,}500 \text{ (gain recognized in year of sale)}$$

In subsequent years, all amounts the seller collects on the note principal ($13,000) will be recognized gain ($13,000 × 100%).

As previously discussed, gains attributable to ordinary income recapture under §§ 1245 and 1250 are *ineligible* for installment reporting. Therefore, the § 1245 or § 1250 gain realized must be recognized in the year of sale, and the installment sale gain is the remaining gain.

---

[66]Reg. § 15a.453–1(b)(3)(i).

Olaf sold an apartment building for $50,000 cash and a $75,000 note due in two years. Olaf's cost of the property was $90,000, and he had deducted depreciation of $65,000, $40,000 of which was in excess of what the straight-line amount would have been. Thus, the basis in the property was $25,000 ($90,000 − $65,000), and he recaptured $40,000 ordinary income under § 1250.

Olaf's realized gain is $100,000 ($125,000 − $25,000), and the $40,000 recapture must be recognized in the year of sale. Of the $60,000 remaining § 1231 gain, $24,000 must be recognized in the year of sale:

$$\frac{\text{§ 1231 gain}}{\text{Contract price}} \times \text{Payment received} = \frac{\$125,000 - \$25,000 - \$40,000}{\$125,000} \times \$50,000$$

$$= \frac{\$60,000}{\$125,000} \times \$50,000 = \$24,000$$

The remaining realized gain of $36,000 ($60,000 − $24,000) will be recognized as the $75,000 note is collected.

Character of the Gain on Depreciable Real Estate

As discussed in Chapter 17, an individual's recognized gain from the sale of depreciable real estate may be subject to a 25 percent tax rate. The gain to the extent of straight-line depreciation taken is subject to the special rate and is referred to as "unrecaptured § 1250 gain." The recognized gain in excess of the depreciation is a § 1231 gain eligible for the 15%/20% rate. Under the installment sale rules, when the sale results in both 25% gain and 15%/20% gain, the 25% gain is reported first and then the 15%/20% gain.

Continuing with the facts in Example 29, the realized gain was $100,000, of which $40,000 was § 1250 ordinary income. The straight-line depreciation would have been $25,000 (total depreciation of $65,000 less excess depreciation of $40,000). Therefore, the unrecaptured § 1250 gain is $25,000. The recognized installment gain in the year of sale of $24,000 was less than the unrecaptured § 1250 gain of $25,000. Therefore, the $24,000 recognized gain in the year of sale is subject to the 25% tax rate.

Imputed Interest

If a deferred payment contract for the sale of property with a selling price greater than $3,000 does not contain a reasonable interest rate, a reasonable rate is imputed.[67] The imputing of interest effectively restates the selling price of the property to equal the sum of the payments at the date of the sale and the discounted present value of the future payments. The difference between the present value of a future payment and the payment's face amount is taxed as interest income, as discussed in the following paragraphs. Thus, the **imputed interest** rules prevent sellers of capital assets from increasing the selling price to reflect the equivalent of unstated interest on deferred payments and thereby converting ordinary (interest) income into long-term capital gains. In addition, the imputed interest rules are important because they affect the timing of income recognition.

Generally, if the contract does not charge at least the Federal rate, interest will be imputed at the Federal rate. The Federal rate is the interest rate the Federal government pays on new borrowing and is published monthly by the IRS.[68]

---

[67]§§ 483 and 1274.

[68]§ 1274(d)(1). There are three Federal rates: short-term (not over three years), midterm (over three years but not over nine years), and long-term (over nine years).

As a general rule, the buyer and seller must account for interest on the accrual basis with semiannual compounding.[69] Requiring the use of the accrual basis ensures that the seller's interest income and the buyer's interest expense are reported in the same tax year. The following example illustrates the calculation and amortization of imputed interest.

EXAMPLE

31

Peggy, a cash basis taxpayer, sold land on January 1, 2017, for $200,000 cash and $6 million due on December 31, 2018, with 2% interest payable December 31, 2017, and December 31, 2018. At the time of the sale, the Federal rate was 4% (compounded semiannually). Because Peggy did not charge interest at least equal to the Federal rate, interest will be imputed at 4% (compounded semiannually).

Date	Payment	Present Value (at 4%) on 1/1/2017	Imputed Interest
12/31/2017	$ 120,000	$ 115,384	$ 4,616
12/31/2018	6,120,000	5,658,284	461,716
	$6,240,000	$5,773,668	$466,332

Thus, the selling price will be restated to $5,973,668 ($200,000 + $5,773,668) rather than $6,200,000 ($200,000 + $6,000,000), and Peggy will recognize interest income in accordance with the following amortization schedule:

	Beginning Balance	Interest (at 4%)*	Received	Ending Balance
2017	$5,773,668	$230,947	$ 120,000	$5,884,615
2018	5,884,615	235,385	6,120,000	–0–

*Compounded semiannually.

Congress has created several exceptions regarding the rate at which interest is imputed and the method of accounting for the interest income and expense. The general rules and exceptions are summarized in Concept Summary 18.2.

Related-Party Sales of Nondepreciable Property

If the Code did not contain special rules, a taxpayer could make an installment sale of property to a related party (e.g., a family member) who would obtain a basis in the property equal to the purchase price (the fair market value of the property). Then the purchasing family member could immediately sell the property to an unrelated party for cash with no recognized gain or loss (the amount realized would equal the basis). The related-party purchaser would not pay the installment note to the selling family member until a later year or years. The net result would be that the family has the cash, but no taxable gain is recognized until the intrafamily transfer of the cash (when the purchasing family member makes payments on the installment note).

Under special rules designed to combat the scheme described above, the proceeds from the subsequent sale (the second sale) by the purchasing family member are treated as though they were used to pay the installment note due the selling family member (the first sale). As a result, the recognition of gain from the original sale between the related parties is accelerated.[70]

[69]§§ 1274(a), 1273(a), and 1272(a). [70]§ 453(e).

Concept Summary 18.2

Interest on Installment Sales

	Imputed Interest Rate
General rule	Federal rate
Exceptions:	
• Principal amount not over $2.8 million.[1]	Lesser of Federal rate or 9%
• Sale of land (with a calendar year ceiling of $500,000) between family members (the seller's spouse, brothers, sisters, ancestors, or lineal descendants).[2]	Lesser of Federal rate or 6%

	Method of Accounting for Interest	
	Seller's Interest Income	Buyer's Interest Expense
General rule[3]	Accrual	Accrual
Exceptions:		
• Total payments under the contract are $250,000 or less.[4]	Taxpayer's overall method	Taxpayer's overall method
• Sale of a farm (sales price of $1 million or less).[5]	Taxpayer's overall method	Taxpayer's overall method
• Sale of a principal residence.[6]	Taxpayer's overall method	Taxpayer's overall method
• Sale for a note with a principal amount of not over $2 million, the seller is on the cash basis, the property sold is not inventory, and the buyer agrees to report expense by the cash method.[7]	Cash	Cash

[1]§ 1274A(b). This amount is adjusted annually for inflation (see Rev.Rul. 2016–30, 2016–52 I.R.B. 876). For 2017, the amount is $5,717,400.
[2]§§ 1274(c)(3)(F) and 483(e).
[3]§§ 1274(a) and 1272(a)(3).
[4]§§ 1274(c)(3)(C) and 483.
[5]§§ 1274(c)(3)(A) and 483.
[6]§§ 1274(c)(3)(B) and 483.
[7]§ 1274A(c). This amount is adjusted annually for inflation (see Rev.Rul. 2016–30, 2016–52 I.R.B. 876). For 2017, the amount is $4,083,800.

However, even with these special rules, Congress did not eliminate the benefits of all related-party installment sales.

- Related parties include the first seller's brothers, sisters, ancestors, lineal descendants, controlled corporations, and partnerships, trusts, and estates in which the seller has an interest.[71]

- There is no acceleration if the second disposition occurs more than two years after the first sale.[72]

Thus, if the taxpayer can sell the property to an unrelated party (not a related party) or a patient family member, the intrafamily installment sale is still a powerful tax planning tool. Other exceptions also can be applied in some circumstances.[73]

Related-Party Sales of Depreciable Property

The installment method cannot be used to report a gain on the sale of depreciable property to a controlled entity. The purpose of this rule is to prevent the seller from deferring

---

[71]§ 453(f)(1), cross-referencing §§ 267(b) and 318(a). Although spouses are related parties, the exemption of gain between spouses (§ 1041) makes the second-disposition rules inapplicable when the first sale was between spouses.

[72]§ 453(e)(2). But see § 453(e)(2)(B) for extensions of the two-year period.
[73]See §§ 453(e)(6) and (7).

gain (until collections are received) while the related purchaser is enjoying a stepped-up basis for depreciation purposes.[74]

The prohibition on the use of the installment method applies to sales between the taxpayer and a partnership or corporation in which the taxpayer holds a more-than-50-percent interest. Constructive ownership rules are used in applying the ownership test (e.g., the taxpayer is considered to own stock owned by a spouse and certain other family members).[75] However, if the taxpayer can establish that tax avoidance was not a principal purpose of the transaction, the installment method can be used to report the gain.

Alan purchased an apartment building from his controlled corporation, Emerald Corporation. Alan was short of cash at the time of the purchase (December 2017), but was to collect a large cash payment in January 2018. The agreement required Alan to pay the entire arm's length price in January 2018. Alan had good business reasons for acquiring the building.

Emerald Corporation should be able to convince the IRS that tax avoidance was not a principal purpose for the installment sale because the tax benefits are not overwhelming. The corporation will report all of the gain in the year following the year of sale, and the building must be depreciated over 27.5 years (the cost recovery period).

18-3b Disposition of Installment Obligations

Generally, a taxpayer must recognize the deferred profit from an installment sale when the obligation is transferred to another party or otherwise relinquished. The rationale for accelerating the gain is that the deferral should continue for no longer than the taxpayer owns the installment obligation.[76]

The gift or cancellation of an installment note is treated as a taxable disposition by the donor. This discourages attempts to shift income among family members. The amount realized from the cancellation is the face amount of the note if the parties (obligor and obligee) are related to each other.[77]

Liz cancels a note issued by Tina (Liz's daughter) that arose in connection with the sale of property. At the time of the cancellation, the note had a basis to Liz of $10,000, a face amount of $25,000, and a fair market value of $20,000. Presuming that the initial sale by Liz qualified as an installment sale, the cancellation results in gain of $15,000 ($25,000 − $10,000) to Liz.

Certain exceptions to the recognition of gain provisions are provided for transfers of installment obligations to the transferor's 80 percent controlled corporation, contributions of capital to a partnership, certain corporate liquidations, transfers due to the taxpayer's death, and transfers between spouses or incident to divorce.[78] In such situations, the deferred profit is merely shifted to the transferee, who is responsible for the payment of tax on the subsequent collections of the installment obligations. The exception to this rule is that in the case of a transfer of installment obligations to a partnership by a partner, the transferor partner is taxed on the income when the partnership collects on the installment receivables.

The Big Picture

Return to the facts of *The Big Picture* on p. 18-1. Assume that Belinda's capital contribution to the partnership in 2017 was an installment obligation with a basis of $40,000 and a face amount of $100,000. In 2018, the partnership collected the $100,000. The transfer in 2017 was not a taxable disposition, but in 2018 when the receivable is collected, Belinda is required to recognize a gain of $60,000.

---

[74]§ 453(g).
[75]§§ 1239(b) and (c).
[76]§ 453B(a).

[77]§ 453B(f)(2).
[78]§§ 453B(c), (d), and (g). See Chapter 20 for a discussion of some of these subjects.

18-3c **Interest on Deferred Taxes**

With the installment method, the seller earns interest on the receivable. The receivable includes the deferred gain. Thus, one could argue that the seller is earning interest on the deferred taxes. Some commentators reason that the government is, in effect, making interest-free loans to taxpayers who report gains by the installment method. Following the argument that the amount of the deferred taxes is a loan, the taxpayer is required to pay interest on the deferred taxes in some situations.[79]

The taxpayer is required to pay interest on the deferred taxes only if *both* of the following requirements are met:

- The installment obligation arises from the sale of property (other than farming property) for more than $150,000.

- The taxpayer's total installment obligations outstanding at the close of the tax year exceed $5 million.

Interest on the deferred taxes is payable only for the portion of the taxes that relates to the installment obligations in *excess* of $5 million. The interest is calculated using the underpayment rate in § 6621.

18-3d **Electing Out of the Installment Method**

A taxpayer can *elect not to use* the installment method. The election is made by reporting on a timely filed return the gain computed by the taxpayer's usual method of accounting (cash or accrual).[80] However, the Regulations provide that the amount realized by a cash basis taxpayer cannot be less than the fair market value of the property sold. This rule differs from the usual cash basis accounting rules (discussed earlier),[81] which measure the amount realized in terms of the fair market value of the property received. The net effect of the Regulations is to allow the cash basis taxpayer to report his or her gain as an accrual basis taxpayer. The election is frequently applied to year-end sales by taxpayers who expect to be in a higher tax bracket in the following year.

EXAMPLE 35

On December 31, 2017, Kurt sold investment land to Jodie for $20,000 (fair market value). He had owned the land for seven years. The cash was to be paid on January 4, 2018. Kurt is a cash basis taxpayer, and his basis in the land is $8,000. Kurt has a large casualty loss that, when combined with his other income in 2017, puts him at a marginal tax rate of 15% in 2017. He expects his tax rate to increase to 35% in 2018.

The transaction constitutes an installment sale because a payment will be received in a tax year after the tax year of disposition. Jodie's promise to pay Kurt is an installment obligation, and under the Regulations, the value of the installment obligation is equal to the value of the property sold ($20,000). If Kurt elects out of the installment method, he will shift $12,000 of gain ($20,000 − $8,000) from the expected higher rate in 2018 of 15% to the 0% rate for long-term capital gains in 2017. The expected tax savings based on the rate differential may exceed the benefit of the tax deferral available with the installment method.

Permission of the IRS is required to revoke an election not to use the installment method.[82]

---

[79]§ 453A.

[80]§ 453(d) and Reg. § 15a.453–1(d).

[81]Refer to Chapter 4, Example 6.

[82]§ 453(d)(3) and Reg. § 15a.453–1(d)(4).

18-3e **Long-Term Contracts**

A long-term contract is a building, installation, construction, or manufacturing contract that is entered into but not completed within the same tax year. However, a *manufacturing* contract is long term *only* if the contract is to manufacture (1) a unique item not normally carried in finished goods inventory or (2) items that normally require more than 12 calendar months to complete.[83] An item is *unique* if it is designed to meet the customer's particular needs and is not suitable for use by others. A contract to perform services (e.g., auditing or legal services) is not considered a contract for this purpose and thus cannot qualify as a long-term contract.

LO.5

Review and illustrate the alternative methods of accounting for long-term contracts (the completed contract method and the percentage of completion method), including the limitations on the use of the completed contract method.

EXAMPLE

36

Rocky, a calendar year taxpayer, entered into two contracts during the year. One contract was to construct a building foundation. Work was to begin in October 2017 and was to be completed by June 2018. The contract is long term because it will not be entered into and completed in the same tax year. The fact that the contract requires less than 12 calendar months to complete is not relevant because the contract is not for manufacturing. The second contract was for architectural services to be performed over two years. These services will not qualify for long-term contract treatment because the taxpayer will not build, install, construct, or manufacture a product.

Generally, the taxpayer must accumulate all of the direct and indirect costs incurred under a contract. This means that the production costs must be accumulated and allocated to individual contracts. Furthermore, mixed services costs, costs that benefit contracts as well as the general administrative operations of the business, must be allocated to production. Exhibit 18.1 lists the types of costs that must be accumulated and allocated to contracts. The taxpayer must develop reasonable bases for cost allocations.[84]

EXAMPLE

37

Falcon, Inc., uses detailed cost accumulation records to assign labor and materials to its contracts in progress. The total cost of fringe benefits is allocated to a contract on the following basis:

$$\frac{\text{Labor on the contract}}{\text{Total salaries and labor}} \times \text{Total cost of fringe benefits}$$

Similarly, storage and handling costs for materials are allocated to contracts on the following basis:

$$\frac{\text{Contract materials}}{\text{Material purchases}} \times \text{Storage and handling costs}$$

The cost of the personnel operations, a mixed services cost, is allocated between production and general administration based on the number of employees in each function. The personnel cost allocated to production is allocated to individual contracts on the basis of the formula used to allocate fringe benefits.

The accumulated costs are deducted when the revenue from the contract is recognized. Generally, two methods of accounting are used in varying circumstances to determine when the revenue from a contract is recognized:[85]

- The completed contract method.
- The percentage of completion method.

---

[83]§ 460(f) and Reg. § 1.460–2(a).

[84]Reg. §§ 1.460–5(b) and 1.263A–1(e).

[85]§ 460.

EXHIBIT 18.1	Contract Costs, Mixed Services Costs, and Current Expense Items for Contracts

	Contracts Eligible for the Completed Contract Method	Other Contracts
Contract costs:		
Direct materials (a part of the finished product).	Capitalize	Capitalize
Indirect materials [consumed in production but not in the finished product (e.g., grease and oil for equipment)].	Capitalize	Capitalize
Storage, handling, and insurance on materials.	Expense	Capitalize
Direct labor (worked on the product).	Capitalize	Capitalize
Indirect labor [worked in the production process but not directly on the product (e.g., a construction supervisor)].	Capitalize	Capitalize
Fringe benefits for direct and indirect labor (e.g., vacation, sick pay, unemployment, and other insurance).	Capitalize	Capitalize
Pension costs for direct and indirect labor:		
Current cost.	Expense	Capitalize
Past service costs.	Expense	Capitalize
Depreciation on production facilities:		
For financial statements.	Capitalize	Capitalize
Tax depreciation in excess of financial statements.	Expense	Capitalize
Depreciation on idle facilities.	Expense	Expense
Property taxes, insurance, rent, and maintenance on production facilities.	Capitalize	Capitalize
Bidding expenses—successful.	Expense	Capitalize
Bidding expenses—unsuccessful.	Expense	Expense
Interest to finance real estate construction.	Capitalize	Capitalize
Interest to finance personal property:		
Production period of one year or less.	Expense	Expense
Production period exceeds one year and costs exceed $1 million.	Capitalize	Capitalize
Production period exceeds two years.	Capitalize	Capitalize
Mixed services costs:		
Personnel operations.	Expense	Allocate
Data processing.	Expense	Allocate
Purchasing.	Expense	Allocate
Selling, general, and administrative expenses (including an allocated share of mixed services).	Expense	Expense
Losses.	Expense	Expense

The *completed contract method may be used* for (1) home construction contracts (contracts in which at least 80 percent of the estimated costs are for dwelling units in buildings with four or fewer units) and (2) certain other real estate construction contracts. Other real estate contracts can qualify for the completed contract method if the following requirements are satisfied:

- The contract is expected to be completed within the two-year period beginning on the commencement date of the contract.
- The contract is performed by a taxpayer whose average annual gross receipts for the three taxable years preceding the taxable year in which the contract is entered into do not exceed $10 million.

All other contractors must use the percentage of completion method.

Completed Contract Method

Under the completed contract method , no revenue from the contract is recognized until the contract is completed and accepted. Generally, the contract is completed when it is accepted by the customer or the customer begins using the subject matter of the contract.[86]

In some situations, the original contract price may be disputed, or the buyer may want additional work to be done on a long-term contract. If the disputed amount is substantial (it is not possible to determine whether a profit or loss will ultimately be realized on the contract), the Regulations provide that no amount of income or loss is recognized until the dispute is resolved. In all other cases, the profit or loss (reduced by the amount in dispute) is recognized in the current period upon completion of the contract. However, additional work may need to be performed with respect to the disputed contract. When the amount in dispute is less than the net profit on the contract before the estimated additional cost, the taxpayer must report in the year of completion the profit as reduced by the estimated additional cost.[87]

EXAMPLE 38

Ted, a calendar year taxpayer utilizing the completed contract method of accounting, constructed a building for Brad under a long-term contract. The gross contract price was $500,000. Ted finished construction in 2017 at a cost of $475,000. When Brad examined the building, he insisted that the building be repainted or the contract price be reduced. The estimated cost of repainting is $10,000. Because under the terms of the contract Ted is assured a profit of at least $15,000 ($500,000 − $475,000 − $10,000) even if the dispute is ultimately resolved in Brad's favor, Ted must include $490,000 ($500,000 − $10,000) in gross income and is allowed deductions of $475,000 for 2017.

In 2018, Ted and Brad resolve the dispute, and Ted repaints certain portions of the building at a cost of $6,000. Ted must include $10,000 in 2017 gross income and may deduct the $6,000 expense in that year.

If the net profit less the estimated additional cost results in a loss, the loss is deferred until the dispute is resolved.

EXAMPLE 39

Assume the same facts as in the previous example, except that the estimated cost of repainting the building is $50,000. Because the resolution of the dispute completely in Brad's favor would mean a net loss on the contract for Ted ($500,000 − $475,000 − $50,000 = $25,000 loss), Ted does not recognize any income or loss until the year the dispute is resolved.

Frequently, a contractor receives payment at various stages of completion. For example, when the contract is 50 percent complete, the contractor may receive 50 percent of the contract price less a retainage. The taxation of these payments is generally governed by Regulation § 1.451–5, "advance payments for goods and long-term contracts" (discussed in Chapter 4). Generally, contractors are permitted to defer the advance payments until the payments are recognized as income under the taxpayer's method of accounting.

Percentage of Completion Method

Under the percentage of completion method , a portion of the gross contract price is included in income during each period as the work progresses. The revenue accrued each period (except for the final period) is computed as follows:[88]

$$\frac{C}{T} \times P$$

Where $C =$ Contract costs incurred during the period
$T =$ Estimated total cost of the contract
$P =$ Contract price

---

[86]Reg. § 1.460–1(c)(3).

[87]Reg. §§ 1.451–3(d)(2)(ii)–(vii), Example 2.

[88]§ 460(b)(1)(A).

All of the costs allocated to the contract during the period are deductible from the accrued revenue.[89] The revenue reported in the final period is simply the unreported revenue from the contract. Because T in this formula is an estimate that frequently differs from total actual costs, which are not known until the contract has been completed, the profit on a contract for a particular period may be overstated or understated.

Tan, Inc., entered into a contract that was to take two years to complete, with an estimated cost of $2,250,000. The contract price was $3,000,000. Costs of the contract for 2016, the first year, totaled $1,350,000. The gross profit reported by the percentage of completion method for 2016 was $450,000 [($1,350,000/$2,250,000 × $3,000,000) − $1,350,000].

The contract was completed at the end of 2017 at a total cost of $2,700,000. In retrospect, 2016 profit should have been $150,000 [($1,350,000/$2,700,000 × $3,000,000) − $1,350,000]. Thus, taxes were overpaid for 2016.

A *de minimis* rule enables the contractor to delay the recognition of income for a particular contract under the percentage of completion method. If less than 10 percent of the estimated contract costs have been incurred by the end of the taxable year, the taxpayer can elect to defer the recognition of income and the related costs until the taxable year in which cumulative contract costs are at least 10 percent of the estimated contract costs.[90]

Lookback Provisions

In the year a contract is completed, a *lookback* provision requires the recalculation of annual profits reported on the contract under the percentage of completion method. Interest is paid to the taxpayer if taxes were overpaid, and interest is payable by the taxpayer if there was an underpayment.[91] For a corporate taxpayer, the lookback interest paid by the taxpayer is deductible, but for an individual taxpayer, it is nondeductible personal interest associated with a tax liability.

Assume that Tan, Inc., in Example 40, was in the 35% tax bracket in both years and the relevant interest rate was 5%. For 2016, the company paid excess taxes of $105,000 [($450,000 − $150,000) × .35]. When the contract is completed at the end of 2017, Tan, Inc., should receive interest of $5,250 for one year on the tax overpayment ($105,000 × .05).

 LO.6

Recognize when accounting for inventories must occur, be aware of the types of costs that must be included in inventories, and apply the LIFO method.

18-4 INVENTORIES

The use of inventories is necessary to clearly reflect income of any business engaged in the production, purchase, or sale of merchandise.[92] Generally, tax accounting and financial accounting for inventories are much the same:

- The use of inventories is necessary to clearly reflect the income of any business engaged in the production and sale or purchase and sale of goods.[93]
- The inventories should include all finished goods, goods in process, and raw materials and supplies that will become part of the product (including containers).

---

[89]Reg. § 1.451–3(c)(3).

[90]§ 460(b)(5).

[91]§§ 460(b)(2) and (6). The taxpayer can elect not to apply the lookback method in situations where the cumulative taxable income as of the close of each prior year is within 10% of the correct income for each prior year.

[92]Reg. § 1.471–1.

[93]§ 471(a) and Reg. §§ 1.471–1 and −2.

- Inventory rules must give effect to the *best* accounting practice of a particular trade or business, and the taxpayer's method should be consistently followed from year to year.

- All items included in inventory should be valued at either (1) cost or (2) the lower of cost or market value.

The following are *not* acceptable methods or practices in valuing inventories:

- A deduction for a reserve for anticipated price changes.

- The use of a constant price or nominal value for a so-called normal quantity of materials or goods in stock (e.g., the base stock method).

- The inclusion in inventory of stock in transit to which title is not vested in the taxpayer.

- The direct costing approach (excluding fixed indirect production costs from inventory).

- The prime costing approach (excluding all indirect production costs from inventory).

The reason for the similarities between tax and financial accounting for inventories is that § 471 sets forth what appears to be a two-prong test. Under this provision, "inventories shall be taken … on such basis … as conforming as nearly as may be to the *best accounting practice* in the trade or business and as most *clearly reflecting the income*." The best accounting practice is synonymous with generally accepted accounting principles (GAAP). However, the IRS determines whether an inventory method clearly reflects income.

In *Thor Power Tool Co. v. Comm.*, there was a conflict between the two tests.[94] The taxpayer's method of valuing obsolete parts was in conformity with GAAP. The IRS, however, successfully argued that the clear reflection of income test was not satisfied because the taxpayer's procedures for valuing its inventories were contrary to the Regulations. Under the taxpayer's method, inventories for parts in excess of estimated future sales were written off (expensed), although the parts were kept on hand and their asking prices were not reduced. [Under Regulation § 1.471–4(b), inventories cannot be written down unless the selling prices also are reduced.] The taxpayer contended that conformity to GAAP creates a presumption that the method clearly reflects income. The Supreme Court disagreed, concluding that the clear reflection of income test was *paramount*. Moreover, it is the opinion of the IRS that controls in determining whether the method of inventory clearly reflects income. Thus, the best accounting practice test was rendered practically meaningless. It follows that the taxpayer's method of inventory must strictly conform to the Regulations regardless of what GAAP may require.

18-4a Determining Inventory Cost

For merchandise purchased, cost is the invoice price less trade discounts plus freight and other handling charges.[95] Cash discounts approximating a fair interest rate can be deducted or capitalized at the taxpayer's option, provided that the method used is consistently applied.

Uniform Capitalization (UNICAP)

Section 263A provides that for inventory and property produced by the taxpayer, "(A) the direct cost of such property, and (B) such property's share of those indirect costs (including taxes) part or all of which are allocable to such property" must be capitalized. The Committee Reports observe that Congress is attempting to achieve a set of capitalization rules that will apply to all types of businesses: contractors, manufacturers,

---

[94]79–1 USTC ¶9139, 43 AFTR 2d 79–362, 99 S.Ct. 773 (USSC, 1979). See Chapter 4, text Section 4-1d for the Supreme Court's discussion of the differences between tax and financial accounting.

[95]Reg. § 1.471–3(b).

GLOBAL TAX ISSUES   **Inventory Acquired from a Foreign Subsidiary**

Generally, a parent corporation and its foreign subsidiaries are treated as separate corporations. If a foreign subsidiary is producing goods in a country whose tax rates are lower than the U.S. tax rates, tax savings can accrue to the group if the foreign subsidiary's prices to the U.S. parent are as high as permissible. This will increase the income in the foreign country, but will reduce taxable income subject to the higher U.S. rates. Section 482 is the IRS's weapon against such income shifting. Under § 482, the prices charged on transactions between related parties must be equal to an "arm's length price."

farmers, wholesalers, and retailers.[96] Congress has labeled the system the **uniform capitalization (UNICAP) rules**, and practitioners refer to the rules as a *super-full absorption costing system*.

To value inventory under the UNICAP rules, a *producer* must apply the following steps:[97]

- Classify all costs into three categories: (1) production, (2) general administrative expense, and (3) mixed services.

- Allocate mixed services costs to production and general administrative expenses.[98]

- Allocate the production costs between the cost of goods sold and the ending inventory.

Exhibit 18.1 (see the "Other Contracts" column) lists typical items that are included in the three classes of costs. The mixed services costs should be allocated to production on a rational basis. For example, the costs of operating the personnel department may be allocated between production and general administration based on the number of applications processed or the number of employees. In lieu of allocating each mixed services cost, the taxpayer can elect a *simplified method* whereby the total of all mixed services costs is allocated to production as follows:[99]

$$MSP = \frac{TP}{TC} \times TMS$$

Where MSP = Mixed services costs allocated to production
    TP = Total production costs, other than interest and mixed services
    TC = Total costs, other than interest; state, local, or foreign income taxes; and mixed services costs
    TMS = Total mixed services costs

The usual cost accounting techniques (e.g., average cost per equivalent unit) can be used to allocate the costs between the cost of goods sold and the ending inventory.

Alternatively, the producer can elect to allocate mixed services costs to production on the basis of labor charges only (production labor as a percentage of total labor costs).

The costs included in the inventory of *wholesalers and retailers* are comparable to those of the producer. However, many of these costs are captured in the price these taxpayers pay for the goods. The following additional costs must be capitalized by these taxpayers:

- All storage costs for wholesalers.

- Off-site storage costs for retailers.

- Purchasing costs (e.g., buyers' wages or salaries).

- Handling, processing, assembly, and repackaging.

- The portion of mixed services costs allocable to these functions.

---

[96]H. Rep. 99–841, 99th Cong., 2nd Sess., 1986, pp. 302–309. See also Reg. § 1.263A–1(a).

[97]Reg. § 1.263A–1(c).

[98]Producers with mixed services costs of less than $200,000 for the year are not required to allocate mixed services costs if the simplified method is used to allocate their production costs. Reg. § 1.263A–1(b)(12).

[99]Reg. § 1.263A–1(h)(5).

Mixed services costs must be allocated to off-site storage, purchasing, and packaging on the basis of direct labor costs of these departments as a percentage of total payroll. Thus, the storage, purchasing, and packaging costs allocated to ending inventory include some mixed services costs.

The UNICAP rules may result in some costs being capitalized for tax purposes but not for financial accounting purposes. For example, a wholesaler's or a manufacturer's storage costs are generally expensed for financial reporting purposes but are capitalized for tax purposes. Also, the taxpayer may capitalize straight-line depreciation of production equipment for financial accounting purposes, but the total tax depreciation must be capitalized under uniform capitalization.

Exemption from UNICAP

Taxpayers with average annual gross receipts of $10 million or less (calculated over the previous three years) are not required to apply the UNICAP rules to their inventories of merchandise purchased and held for resale. If the small business engages in production as well as reselling, UNICAP must be applied to the goods the taxpayer produces, with limited exceptions.[100]

A farmer who is permitted to use the cash method is not required to apply the UNICAP rules to (1) any animals or (2) any plants with a preproduction period of two years or less that the farmer produces. In exchange for this concession, the farmer is required to use the alternative depreciation system (see Chapter 8) for property used in the farming business.[101]

Lower of Cost or Market

Except for those taxpayers who use the LIFO method, inventories may be valued at the **lower of cost or market (replacement cost)**.[102] Taxpayers using LIFO must value inventory at cost. However, the write-down of damaged or shopworn merchandise and goods that are otherwise unsalable at normal prices is not considered to be an application of the lower of cost or market method. Such items should be valued at bona fide selling price less direct cost of disposal.[103]

In the case of excess inventories (as in *Thor Power Tool Co.*, discussed previously), the goods can be written down only to the taxpayer's offering price. If the offering price on the goods is not reduced, the goods must be valued at cost.

The Cardinal Publishing Company invested $50,000 in printing 10,000 copies of a book. Although only 7,000 copies were sold in the first 3 years and none in the next 5 years, management is convinced that the book will become a classic in 20 years. Cardinal leaves the price the same as it was when the book was first distributed ($15 per copy). The remaining 3,000 books must be valued at cost ($15,000). Note that the tax law provides an incentive for the taxpayer to destroy or abandon its excess inventory and obtain an immediate deduction rather than wait for the event of future sales.

EXAMPLE 42

In applying the lower of cost or market method, *each* item included in the inventory must be valued at the lower of its cost or market value.[104]

EXAMPLE 43

The taxpayer's ending inventory is valued as follows:

Item	Cost	Market	Lower of Cost or Market
A	$5,000	$ 4,000	$4,000
B	3,000	2,000	2,000
C	1,500	6,000	1,500
	$9,500	$12,000	$7,500

Under the lower of cost or market method, the taxpayer's inventory is valued at $7,500 rather than $9,500.

---

[100]§ 263A(b)(2), Reg. § 1.263A–1(b) and Reg. 1.263A–3(a)(2).
[101]§§ 263A(d) and (e)(3).
[102]Reg. § 1.472–4.

[103]Reg. § 1.471–2(c).
[104]Reg. § 1.471–4(c).

Inventory Shrinkage

The difference between the inventory per physical count and according to the company's records is referred to as *inventory shrinkage*. Inventory shrinkage is the result of accidents, theft, and errors in recording. Many companies take physical inventories at times other than the last day of the tax year and adjust their inventory per books to agree with the physical count. The inventory of the last day of the tax year, which is used to compute cost of goods sold, is based on the perpetual records. Such companies often adjust the ending inventory for the estimated shrinkage that has occurred between the date of the physical inventory and the last day of the tax year. The adjustment is often based on the historical relationship between inventory shrinkage and sales.[105]

Determining Cost—Specific Identification, FIFO, and LIFO

In some cases, it is feasible to determine the cost of the particular item sold. For example, an automobile dealer can easily determine the specific cost of each automobile that has been sold. However, in most businesses, it is necessary to resort to a flow of goods assumption such as *first in, first out (FIFO)*, *last in, first out (LIFO)*, or an *average cost* method. A taxpayer may use any of these methods, provided the method selected is consistently applied from year to year.

During a period of rising prices, LIFO will generally produce a lower ending inventory valuation and will result in a greater cost of goods sold than would be obtained under the FIFO method. The following example illustrates how LIFO and FIFO affect the computation of the cost of goods sold.

EXAMPLE 44

On January 1, 2017, the taxpayer opened a retail store to sell refrigerators. At least 10 refrigerators must be carried in inventory to satisfy customer demands. The initial investment in the 10 refrigerators is $5,000. During the year, 10 refrigerators were sold at $750 each and were replaced at a cost of $6,000 ($600 each). Gross profit under the LIFO and FIFO methods is computed as follows:

		FIFO		LIFO
Sales (10 × $750)		$ 7,500		$ 7,500
Beginning inventory	$ 5,000		$ 5,000	
Purchases	6,000		6,000	
	$11,000		$11,000	
Ending inventory				
10 × $600	(6,000)			
10 × $500			(5,000)	
Cost of goods sold		(5,000)		(6,000)
Gross profit		$ 2,500		$ 1,500

Dollar-Value LIFO

In the previous example, the taxpayer was buying and selling a single product, a particular model of a refrigerator. The taxpayer employed the specific goods LIFO technique. Under the specific goods approach, if the identical items are not on hand at the end of the period, the LIFO inventory is depleted and all of the deferred profit must be recaptured. Thus, taxpayers who frequently change the items carried in inventory would realize little benefit from LIFO. However, the dollar-value LIFO technique avoids the LIFO depletion problem associated with the specific goods technique.

Under dollar-value LIFO, each inventory item is assigned to a pool. A *pool* is a collection of similar items and is treated as a separate inventory. Determining whether items are similar involves considerable judgment. In general, however, the taxpayer would prefer

---

[105]§ 471(b).

broad pools so that when a particular item is sold out, it can be replaced with increases in other items in the same pool. Generally, all products manufactured at a particular plant can be treated as a pool.[106] A department store may have a separate pool for each department. An automobile dealer may have separate pools for new cars, lightweight trucks, heavy-duty trucks, and car and truck parts.

At the end of the period, the ending inventory must be valued at the current-year prices and then at the LIFO base period (the year LIFO was adopted). The ratio of the ending inventory at current prices to the ending inventory at base period prices is the *LIFO index*. If the total current inventory at base period prices is greater than the base period inventory at base period prices, a LIFO layer must be added. The LIFO index is applied to the LIFO layer to convert it to current prices.

EXAMPLE 45

Black Company adopted LIFO effective January 1, 2017. The base LIFO inventory (from December 31, 2016) was $1,000,000. On December 31, 2017, the inventory was $1,320,000 at end-of-2017 prices and $1,200,000 at end-of-2016 (the base period) prices. Thus, Black added a 2017 layer of $200,000 ($1,200,000 − $1,000,000) at base period prices. The layer must be converted to 2017 prices as follows:

$$\text{LIFO index} = \$1,320,000/\$1,200,000 = 1.10$$
$$2016 \text{ layer} \times \text{LIFO index} = \$200,000 \times 1.10 = \$220,000$$

Therefore, the 2017 ending inventory is $1,000,000 + $220,000 = $1,220,000.

The inventory on December 31, 2018, is $1,325,000 using 2018 prices and $1,250,000 using base period prices. Thus, the LIFO index for 2018 is $1,325,000/$1,250,000 = 1.06. The LIFO inventory is $1,273,000, computed as follows:

BLACK COMPANY
LIFO Inventory
December 31, 2018

	Base Period Cost	LIFO Index	LIFO Layers
Base inventory	$1,000,000	1.00	$1,000,000
2017 layer	200,000	1.10	220,000
2018 layer	50,000	1.06	53,000
	$1,250,000		$1,273,000

ETHICS & EQUITY Preserving the LIFO Reserve

Blanch Corporation has been using the dollar-value LIFO inventory method for 20 years. The company maintains one inventory pool that includes raw materials, goods in process, and finished goods. The LIFO deferral is several million dollars. At the end of the current year, the corporation's inventory of finished goods was almost depleted because the company's major competitor had to recall a substantial portion of its products. Blanch's management is aware that if the inventory is not replenished, the corporation will be required to recognize income that has been deferred for the past 20 years. The controller has suggested that the company buy sufficient raw materials to substitute for the depleted finished goods.

This will require having on hand at the end of the year the raw materials required for the next 18 months, when ordinarily the company has only a three-month supply on hand. The controller argues that the cost of carrying the additional inventory is much less than the additional taxes that will be due if the inventories are allowed to decrease.

The operations manager has suggested that the company buy the raw materials before the end of the year and have the supplier store the materials. Furthermore, the supplier would act as Blanch's agent to sell the excess materials. This would minimize the actual investment in inventory. Do you think the corporation should follow either proposal?

---

[106]See, generally, Reg. § 1.472–8.

18-4b **The LIFO Election**

A taxpayer may adopt LIFO by merely using the method in the tax return for the year of the change and by attaching Form 970 (Application to Use LIFO Inventory Method) to the tax return. Thus, a taxpayer does not have to request approval for the change. Once the election is made, it cannot be revoked. However, a prospective change from LIFO to any other inventory method can be made only if the consent of the IRS is obtained.[107]

The beginning inventory valuation for the first year LIFO is used is computed by the costing method employed in the preceding year. Thus, the beginning LIFO inventory is generally the same as the closing inventory for the preceding year. Because lower of cost or market cannot be used in conjunction with LIFO, previous write-downs to market for items included in the beginning inventory must be restored to income. The amount the inventories are written up is an adjustment due to a change in accounting method.[108] The taxpayer is allowed to spread the adjustment ratably over the year of the change and the two succeeding years.[109]

EXAMPLE 46

In 2016, Paul used the lower of cost or market FIFO inventory method. The FIFO cost of his ending inventory was $30,000, and the market value of the inventory was $24,000. Therefore, the ending inventory for 2016 was $24,000. Paul switched to LIFO in 2017 and was required to write up the beginning inventory to $30,000. Paul must add $2,000 ($6,000 ÷ 3) to his income for each of the years 2017, 2018, and 2019.

Congress added this provision to the Code to overrule the previous IRS policy of requiring the taxpayer to include the entire adjustment in income for the year preceding the change to LIFO.[110]

Once the LIFO election is made for tax purposes, the taxpayer's financial reports to owners and creditors must also be prepared on the basis of LIFO.[111] The original reason for the conformity requirement was to make the taxpayers stand by their argument that LIFO was necessary to clearly reflect income. The *conformity* of financial reports to tax reporting is specifically required by the Code and is strictly enforced by the IRS. However, the Regulations permit the taxpayer to make a footnote disclosure of the net income computed by another method of inventory valuation (e.g., FIFO).[112]

18-4c **Special Inventory Methods Relating to Farming and Ranching**

Farmers who do not use the cash method and therefore account for inventories may elect to use the **farm price method** or the **unit-livestock-price method** rather than one of the inventory methods discussed previously. Under the farm price method, the inventory is valued at its market price less disposition costs (e.g., transportation and selling expenses).[113] If the taxpayer uses the unit-livestock-price method, the animals are valued at a standard cost, which is based on the average cost of raising an animal with the characteristics of the animals included in the ending inventory.[114] The farmer can also elect to use the lower of cost or market inventory method.

LO.7

Identify tax planning opportunities related to accounting periods and accounting methods.

18-5 **TAX PLANNING**

The tax accounting period and method rules sometimes present opportunities for tax planning.

---

[107]Reg. §§ 1.472–3(a) and 1.472–5.

[108]Reg. § 1.472–2(c). In Rev.Rul. 76–282, 1976–2 C.B. 137, the IRS required the restoration of write-downs for damaged and shopworn goods when the taxpayer switched to LIFO.

[109]§ 472(d).

[110]§ 472(d).

[111]§ 472(c).

[112]Reg. § 1.472–2(e).

[113]Reg. § 1.471–6(d).

[114]Reg. § 1.471–6(e). See also IRS Pub. 225 (*Farmers Tax Guide*), p. 7.

18-5a **Taxable Year**

Under the general rules for tax years, partnerships and S corporations frequently will be required to use a calendar year. However, if the partnership or S corporation can demonstrate a business purpose for a fiscal year, the IRS will allow the entity to use the requested year. The advantage to a fiscal year is that the calendar year partners and S corporation shareholders may be able to defer from tax the income earned from the close of the fiscal year until the end of the calendar year. Tax advisers for these entities should apply the IRS's gross receipts test described in Revenue Procedure 2006–46 to determine whether permission for the fiscal year will be granted.[115]

18-5b **Cash Method of Accounting**

The cash method of accounting gives the taxpayer considerable control over the recognition of expenses and some control over the recognition of income. This method can be used by proprietorships, partnerships, S corporations, and small C corporations (gross receipts of $5 million or less) that provide services (inventories are not material to the service business). Farmers (except certain farming corporations), as well as small taxpayers with inventory ($1 million or less of gross receipts), can also use the cash method.

18-5c **Installment Method**

Unlike the cash and accrual methods, the installment method often results in an interest-free loan (of deferred taxes) from the government. The installment method is not available for the sale of inventory and certain other property (e.g., equipment subject to depreciation recapture). But when eligible property is sold, the installment method is an important tax planning technique. That is, the seller may defer gain and attain a higher interest rate than from alternative investments. These benefits must be weighed against the risks of nonpayment by the buyer. If, on the other hand, the taxpayer expects to be in a higher tax bracket when the payments will be received, he or she can elect not to use the installment method.

Related Parties

Intrafamily installment sales can still be a useful family tax planning tool. If the related party holds the property more than two years, a subsequent sale will not accelerate the gain from the first disposition. Patience and forethought are rewarded.

Disposition of Installment Obligations

A disposition of an installment obligation is also a serious matter. Gifts of the obligations will accelerate income to the seller. The list of taxable and nontaxable dispositions of installment obligations should not be trusted to memory. In each instance where transfers of installment obligations are contemplated, the practitioner should conduct research to make sure he or she knows the consequences.

18-5d **Completed Contract Method**

Small contractors (average annual gross receipts do not exceed $10 million) working on contracts that are completed within a two-year period can elect to use the completed contract method and defer profit until the year in which the contract is completed.

18-5e **Inventories**

A $1 reduction in ending inventory valuation decreases taxable income for the year by $1. The ending inventory valuation can be minimized and thus taxable income reduced by using elective accounting methods: (1) purchase prices can be stated net of cash

---

[115]Rev.Proc. 2006–46, 2006–2 C.B. 859.

discounts, (2) the lower of cost or market method may be applied, and (3) the LIFO method can be adopted during rising prices.

REFOCUS ON THE BIG PICTURE

ACCOUNTING PERIOD AND METHOD

Selection of a Tax Year

An entity's tax form will govern the rules for determining the entity's tax year. Because Silver is a partnership, the Code's provisions for partnerships are applicable.

In this case, Tweety's 40 percent ownership interest in Silver is not sufficient to enable it to control the selection of the partnership's tax year. Likewise, Belinda and Pearl's collective controlling interest will not allow them to control the selection of the tax year for the partnership.

The Code and related Regulations have a very precise set of rules regarding the selection of a tax year for a partnership. The partnership applies these rules in the following sequence:

- *Majority interest tax year.* The tax year of the partners who have a common year-end and collectively own a greater-than-50-percent interest in the partnership capital and profits.

- *Principal partners' tax year.* The tax year if all of the principal partners (5 percent or greater interest in capital or profits) have the same tax year.

- *Least aggregate deferral tax year.* The tax year of the principal partners (grouped by a common year-end) that produces the least aggregate deferral of income.

Alternatively, the partnership can select its tax year based on a business purpose for the tax year selected. However, this requires the approval of the IRS, which is unlikely to be granted. The only business purpose the IRS has acknowledged is the need to conform the tax year to the entity's natural business year.

Therefore, from the data provided, it appears that Silver will determine its tax year by using the least aggregate deferral method. Based on this method, Silver's tax year will end on November 30 (see the calculations in Example 3).

Short Tax Year

Silver will have a short tax year that begins on April 1, 2017, and ends on November 30, 2017, as determined by the least aggregate deferral method. Silver will not have to annualize the income reported on its first income tax return. Note, however, that annualization will be required if Silver ever changes its tax year.

Partner's Reporting of Share of Net Income

Each of the partners will receive a Schedule K–1 that reports the partner's share of net income. From a timing perspective, the partner will include the Schedule K–1 items on the partner's income tax return only if a partnership tax year ends within or with the partner's tax year.

Partnership's Accounting Method

If Silver Partnership's average annual gross receipts exceed $5 million, it must use the accrual method to compute its income. Even though Belinda is a cash basis taxpayer, her share of the partnership income would be computed using the accrual method.

TETRA IMAGES/GETTY IMAGES

Key Terms

Accounting methods, 18-10

Accounting period, 18-2

Accrual method, 18-13

All events test, 18-14

Cash method, 18-11

Claim of right doctrine, 18-9

Completed contract method, 18-29

Crop insurance proceeds, 18-9

Crop method, 18-13

Dollar-value LIFO, 18-34

Economic performance test, 18-14

Farm price method, 18-36

Fiscal year, 18-2

Hybrid method, 18-16

Imputed interest, 18-22

Installment method, 18-20

Least aggregate deferral method, 18-4

Long-term contract, 18-27

Lower of cost or market (replacement cost), 18-33

Majority interest partners, 18-3

One-year rule for prepaid expenses, 18-11

Percentage of completion method, 18-29

Personal service corporation (PSC), 18-6

Principal partner, 18-3

Short period, 18-7

Short taxable year, 18-7

Uniform capitalization (UNICAP) rules, 18-32

Unit-livestock-price method, 18-36

Discussion Questions

1. **LO.1** Would a tax year ending December 31 be appropriate for a ski lodge? Why or why not?

2. **LO.1** Assume that a partnership is profitable and that its tax year ends on December 31 but one of the partners' tax year ends on September 30. Does the partner enjoy a tax benefit or detriment from the partnership's use of a December 31 tax year-end? Explain.

3. **LO.1** A law practice was incorporated on January 1, 2017, and expects to earn $25,000 per month before deducting the lawyer's salary. The lawyer owns 100% of the stock. The corporation and the lawyer both use the cash method of accounting. The corporation does not need to retain any of the earnings in the business; thus, the salary of the lawyer (a calendar year taxpayer) will equal the corporation's net income before salary expense. If the corporation could choose any tax year and pay the lawyer's salary at the time that would be most tax efficient (but at least once every 12 months), what tax year should the corporation choose? When should the salary be paid each year?

   Decision Making

4. **LO.1** Art Funkel started his incorporated medical practice on June 1, 2017. He immediately made an S election for the corporation. Art would like the corporation to adopt a tax year ending May 31 so that a full 12 months of income would be included in the first tax year. Can the corporation elect a fiscal year ending May 31? Explain.

5. **LO.1** Fred, a cash basis taxpayer, received a $15,000 bonus from his employer in 2017. The bonus was based on the company's profits for 2016. In 2018, the company discovered that its 2016 profits were computed incorrectly. As a result, Fred received an additional $10,000 with respect to 2016 profits. Fred's marginal tax rate in 2017 was 15%, and it was 35% in 2018. Sue, also a cash basis taxpayer, received a $35,000 bonus in 2018 that was based on 2017 profits. In 2018, the company discovered that it had overstated its profits in 2017. As a result, Sue was required to repay $10,000 of her bonus in 2018. Sue was in the 35% marginal tax bracket in 2017 and in the 15% marginal bracket in 2018. What special tax treatment is available to Fred and Sue as a result of their employer's errors?

   Issue ID

6. **LO.2** Under what conditions would the cash method of accounting be advantageous as compared with the accrual basis?

7. **LO.2** In December 2017, Nell, Inc., an accrual basis taxpayer, paid $12,000 for insurance premiums for her business for the 2018 calendar year. How much of the premiums can Nell, Inc., deduct in 2017?

8. **LO.2** In 2016, the taxpayer became ineligible to use the cash method of accounting. At the beginning of the year, accounts receivable totaled $240,000, accounts payable for merchandise totaled $80,000, and the inventory on hand totaled $320,000. What is the amount of the adjustment due to the change in accounting method?

9. **LO.2** Osprey Corporation, an accrual basis taxpayer, had taxable income for 2017 and paid $40,000 on its estimated state income tax for the year. During 2017, the company received a $4,000 refund upon filing its 2016 state income tax return. The company filed its 2017 state income tax return in August 2018 and paid the $7,000 state income tax due for 2017. In December 2017, the company received a notice from the state tax commission that an additional $6,000 of income tax was due for 2015 because of an error on the return. The company acknowledged the error in December 2017 and paid the additional $6,000 in tax in February 2018. What is Osprey's 2017 Federal income tax deduction for state income taxes?

10. **LO.2** Compare the cash and accrual methods of accounting for the following events:
    a. Purchased new equipment, paying $50,000 cash and giving a note payable for $30,000 due next year.
    b. Paid $3,600 for a three-year service contract on the new equipment.
    c. Collected $1,800 for services to be provided over the current and following years.
    d. Received a $3,000 note from a customer for services provided in the current year. The market value of the note was only $2,400.

Decision Making   11. **LO.2** Edgar uses the cash method to report the income from his software consulting business. A large publicly held corporation has offered to invest in Edgar's business as a limited partner. What tax accounting complications would be created if Edgar and the corporation became partners?

12. **LO.2** Samantha, an accrual basis taxpayer, subscribes to a service that updates a database used in her business. In December 2017, Samantha paid the $120,000 subscription for the period January 2017 through December 2018. What is Samantha's deduction for 2017?

13. **LO.2** Emerald Motors is an automobile dealer. The controller consults with you about the type of accounting used for a special offer to its new car customers. Emerald has offered to provide at no charge to the customer the first four recommended service visits (i.e., at 3,000, 6,000, 9,000, and 12,000 miles). It is a virtual certainty that all customers will exercise their rights to the service, and the cost of the services can be accurately estimated. The controller reasons that the estimated cost should be accrued when the sale of an automobile is made so that all of the costs of the sale can be matched with the revenue. How would you respond to the controller?

Decision Making   14. **LO.4, 7** Irene has made Sara an offer on the purchase of a capital asset. Irene will pay (1) $200,000 cash or (2) $50,000 cash and a 6% installment note for $150,000 guaranteed by City Bank of New York. If Sara sells for $200,000 cash, she will invest the after-tax proceeds in certificates of deposit yielding 6% interest. Sara's cost of the asset is $25,000. Why would Sara prefer the installment sale?

15. **LO.4** Arnold gave land to his son, Bruce. Arnold's basis in the land was $100,000, and its fair market value at the date of the gift was $150,000. Bruce borrowed

$130,000 from a bank that he used to improve the property. He sold the property to Della for $360,000. Della paid Bruce $90,000 in cash, assumed his $120,000 mortgage, and agreed to pay $150,000 in two years. Bruce's selling expenses were $10,000. Della is going to pay adequate interest. What is Bruce's installment sale gain in the year of sale?

16. **LO.4** A seller and a buyer agree that the sales/purchase price for land is $1,500,000 down and two annual payments of $1,500,000 each to be made over the next two years. The buyer intends to construct a building on the land that will be used as the buyer's warehouse. It will be built over the next two years. The seller proposes that the contract should read that the total selling price is $4,300,000 and that the two deferred payments of $1,500,000 each include interest at 4%, which is the current Federal intermediate-term rate but is less than the interest rate on commercial real estate. The land is a capital asset to the seller, and the holding period is four years. Why should the seller and not the buyer be more concerned about the stated interest rate?

17. **LO.4, 7** On June 1, 2015, Father sold land to Son for $300,000. Father reported the gain by the installment method, with the gain to be spread over five years. In May 2017, Son received an offer of $400,000 for the land, to be paid over three years. What would be the tax consequences of Son's sale? How could the tax consequences be improved? — Decision Making

18. **LO.4, 7** In December 2017, Carl Corporation sold land it held as an investment. The corporation received $50,000 in 2017 and a note payable (with adequate interest) for $150,000 to be paid in 2019. Carl Corporation's cost of the land was $80,000. The corporation has a $90,000 net capital loss carryover that will expire in 2017. Should Carl Corporation report the sale in 2017 or use the installment method to report the income as payments are received? — Decision Making

19. **LO.2, 5** What are the similarities between the crop method used for farming and the completed contract method used for long-term construction?

20. **LO.5** Nathan uses the percentage of completion method to report income from his real estate construction contracts. A contract was begun in 2017 and completed in 2018. In 2017, Nathan reported gross income from the partial completion of the contract. In 2018, however, costs had increased above the original estimate. The contract was completed with the actual profit on the contract being less than the income from the contract reported in 2017. What mechanism should be used to correct for the overpayment of tax in 2017?

21. **LO.5** Neal uses the percentage of completion method to report his gross income from long-term contracts that were to begin in 2017. In 2018, he completes a contract for more than the estimate of total costs that was used in the prior year. What are the tax accounting implications of the incorrect estimate?

22. **LO.5** The Hawk Corporation builds yachts. The vessels it currently produces are practically identical and are completed in approximately 8 months. A customer has approached Hawk about constructing a larger yacht that would take approximately 15 months to complete. What are the tax implications of accepting the contract proposal?

23. **LO.6** Largo Company is an engineering consulting business that uses the accrual method of accounting for its services. Mango Company is a manufacturer of nuts and bolts that also uses the accrual method to account for its sales. Each company has a personnel department. How should the cost of personnel operations be treated by each of the two companies? — Issue ID

24. **LO.6** Amber Auto Parts adopted the dollar-value LIFO inventory method. The company has consistently used a retail price index when it should have used a — Issue ID

producer's. As a result, its LIFO layers have been consistently undervalued. Why is the company's error exacerbated by the fact that the company uses the LIFO method instead of the FIFO method?

Issue ID   25. **LO.6** Opal, Inc., is about to make its first attempt to borrow from a local bank. The company uses LIFO for tax purposes, solely to defer taxes, and believes that income computed using the FIFO method would better reflect its income. The company also uses the double-declining balance method of depreciation for tax, although the straight-line method better reflects the actual depreciation. The company would like to present its financial position in the most favorable light. Therefore, Opal's CEO intends to provide the bank with an income statement prepared using the FIFO inventory method and straight-line depreciation. What types of problems will presenting the income statement to the bank in this fashion cause for Opal?

Issue ID   26. **LO.6** Blue is a retailer that uses the FIFO inventory method. Blue has consistently taken its physical inventory at the end of the day on the last day of its tax year, December 31. This practice is very unpopular with its employees, who do not like working on New Year's Eve. The company is considering taking the inventory at the end of November and adjusting for sales and purchases in the last month of the year. However, the CFO has raised the issue that by taking the inventory at the end of November, loss from theft and breakage in December will not be taken into account until the physical inventory is taken in the following year. Is the CFO's concern valid? Explain.

Computational Exercises

27. **LO.1** Delaine is a 90% shareholder in a personal service corporation (PSC). The corporation paid Delaine a salary of $265,000 during its fiscal year ending September 30, 2017.

   a. Assume that the corporation cannot satisfy the business purpose test for a fiscal year. How much salary must Delaine receive during the period October 1 through December 31, 2017, in order for the corporation to continue to use its fiscal year?

   b. Assume that the corporation cannot satisfy the business purpose test or salary test for a fiscal year. The corporation pays Delaine a salary of $50,000 for October 1 through December 31, 2017, and salary of $300,000 from January 1, 2018, through September 30, 2018. How much must the corporation limit its deduction for salary for its fiscal year ending September 30, 2018, in order to retain the fiscal year?

28. **LO.1** Gaffey Corporation obtained permission to change from a calendar year to a fiscal year ending May 31, beginning in 2017. For the short period January 1 through May 31, 2017, the corporation's taxable income was $140,000. For computing the tax, assume a tax rate of 25%.

   a. What is Gaffey Corporation's annualized short period income?

   b. What is Gaffey Corporation's tax for the short period?

29. **LO.1** In 2017, Aurora received a $25,000 bonus computed as a percentage of profits. In 2018, Aurora's employer determined that the 2017 profits had been incorrectly computed, and Aurora had to refund the $8,000 in 2018. Assume that Aurora was in the 35% tax bracket in 2017 but in the 15% bracket in 2018.

   a. In 2017, how much is Aurora required to include in income?

   b. In 2018, what is the amount of the deduction Aurora can claim? What is the reduction in taxes for 2018 as a result of the deduction?

30. **LO.2** In 2017, Chaya Corporation, an accrual basis, calendar year taxpayer, provided services to clients and earned $25,000. The clients signed notes receivable to Chaya that have a fair market value of $22,000 at year-end. In addition, Chaya sold a 36-month service contract on June 1, 2017, and received payment in full of $12,000. How much income does Chaya report from these transactions in 2017?

31. **LO.3** For 2017, Essence Company, a calendar year taxpayer, will change from using the cash method for tax purposes to the accrual method. At the end of 2016, Essence had the following items:

Accounts receivable	$200,000
Accounts payable	135,000
Bank loan	100,000

What is the § 481(a) adjustment for this change in accounting method? Be sure to state whether it is positive or negative.

32. **LO.4** On December 30, 2017, Whitney sold a piece of property for $85,000. Her basis in the property was $40,000, and she incurred $1,200 in selling expenses. The buyer paid $5,000 down with the balance payable in $10,000 installments over the next eight years. In addition, the buyer assumed a $15,000 mortgage on the property. Round any division to four decimal places, and use in subsequent computations. Under the installment sales method, what is the total contract price, the total gain on the sale, and the amount of gain reported in 2017?

33. **LO.4** In 2017, Skylar sold an apartment building for $20,000 cash and a $300,000 note due in two years. Skylar's cost of the property was $250,000, and he had deducted depreciation of $150,000, $60,000 of which was in excess of what the straight-line amount would have been.
    a. Under the installment sales method, what is Skylar's total realized gain?
    b. In 2017, how much § 1250 gain does Skylar recognize? How much § 1231 gain does he recognize?

34. **LO.4** Mason canceled a note issued by Emma (Mason's niece) that arose in connection with the sale of property. At the time of the cancellation, the note had a basis to Mason of $30,000, a face amount of $55,000, and a fair market value of $42,000. Presuming that the initial sale by Mason qualified as an installment sale, how much gain does the cancellation result in for Mason?

35. **LO.5** Jebali Corporation, a calendar year taxpayer utilizing the completed contract method of accounting, constructed a building for Samson, Inc., under a long-term contract. The gross contract price was $2,300,000. Jebali finished construction in 2017 at a cost of $2,100,000. However, Samson insisted that Jebali redo the doorway; otherwise, the contract price would be reduced. The estimated cost of redoing the doorway is $80,000. In 2018, the dispute is settled and Jebali fixed the doorway at a cost of $65,000.
    a. How much must Jebali include in gross income? What amount of deductions is Jebali allowed for 2017?
    b. In 2018, how much must Jebali include in gross income? What amount of expenses can Jebali deduct in that year?

36. **LO.5** Shumpert, Inc., entered into a contract that was to take two years to complete, with an estimated cost of $900,000. The contract price was $1,300,000. Costs of the contract for 2016, the first year, totaled $675,000.
    a. What was the gross profit reported by the percentage of completion method for 2016?
    b. After the contract was completed at the end of 2017 at a total cost of $950,000, what was the gross profit reported by the percentage of completion method for 2017?

37. **LO.6** The taxpayer's ending inventory is valued as follows:

Item	Cost	Market
Rakes	$8,100	$7,900
Shovels	$3,800	$4,300
Hoes	$6,000	$6,250

Under the lower of cost or market method, what is the value of the taxpayer's inventory?

38. **LO.6** Shondee Corporation uses the lower of cost or market and FIFO inventory methods. At the end of 2016, the FIFO cost of the ending inventory was $181,000, and the market value of the inventory was $160,000. The corporation switched to LIFO in 2017. As a result, how much must Shondee Corporation add to income for each of the years 2017, 2018, and 2019?

Problems

39. **LO.1** Red, White, and Blue are unrelated corporations engaged in real estate development. The three corporations formed a joint venture (treated as a partnership) to develop a tract of land. Assuming that the venture does not have a natural business year, what tax year must the joint venture adopt under the following circumstances?

		Tax Year Ending	Interest in Joint Venture
a.	Red	March 31	60%
	Blue	June 30	20%
	White	October 31	20%
b.	Red	October 31	30%
	White	September 30	40%
	Blue	January 31	30%

Decision Making   40. **LO.1, 7** The Cardinal Wholesale Company is an S corporation that began business on March 1, 2017. Robert, a calendar year taxpayer, owns 100% of the Cardinal stock. He has $400,000 taxable income from other sources each year. Robert will work approximately 30 hours a week for the corporation. Cardinal sells swimming pool supplies, and its natural business year ends in September. Approximately 80% of Cardinal's gross receipts occur in June through September.

   a. What tax year should Cardinal elect, assuming that Robert anticipates the company will produce a net profit for all years?

   b. What tax year should Cardinal elect, assuming that it will lose $10,000 a month for the first 12 months and an average of $5,000 a month for the next 12 months? In the third year, the corporation will earn taxable income.

Decision Making   41. **LO.1** Zorn conducted his professional practice through Zorn, Inc. The corporation uses a fiscal year ending September 30 even though the business purpose test for a fiscal year cannot be satisfied. For the year ending September 30, 2017, the corporation paid Zorn a salary of $180,000, and during the period January through September 2017, the corporation paid him a salary of $150,000.

   a. How much salary should Zorn receive during the period October 1 through December 31, 2017?

   b. Assume that Zorn received only $24,000 salary during the period October 1 through December 31, 2017. What would be the consequences to Zorn, Inc.?

42. **LO.1** Mauve Corporation began operations as a farm supplies business and used a fiscal year ending October 31. The company gradually went out of the farm supplies business and into the mail-order Christmas gifts business. The company has received permission from the IRS to change to a fiscal year ending January 31, effective for the year ending January 31, 2018. For the short period November 1, 2017, through January 31, 2018, Mauve earned $20,000. Calculate Mauve's tax liability for the short period November 1, 2017, through January 31, 2018.

43. **LO.1** In 2016, Juan entered into a contract to write a book. The publisher advanced Juan $50,000, which was to be repaid out of future royalties. If the book was not completed by the end of 2017, however, Juan would be required to repay the publisher for the advance. Juan did not complete the book in 2017, and in accordance with the agreement, he repaid the $50,000 to the publisher in 2018. Juan is a cash basis taxpayer. What are the tax consequences to Juan of the repayment under the following assumptions?
    a. Juan's marginal tax rate was 15% in 2016 and 35% in 2018.
    b. Juan's marginal tax rate was 35% in 2016 and 15% in 2018.

44. **LO.2** Gold, Inc., is an accrual basis taxpayer. In 2017, an employee accidentally spilled hazardous chemicals on leased property. The chemicals destroyed trees on neighboring property, resulting in $30,000 of damages. In 2017, the owner of the property sued Gold, Inc., for the $30,000. Gold's attorney believes that it is liable and that the only issue is whether the neighbor will also seek punitive damages that could be as much as three times the actual damages. In addition, as a result of the spill, Gold was in violation of its lease and was therefore required to pay the landlord $15,000. However, the amount due for the lease violation is not payable until the termination of the lease in 2020. None of these costs were covered by insurance. Jeff Stuart, the president of Gold, Inc., is generally familiar with the accrual basis tax accounting rules and is concerned about when the company will be allowed to deduct the amounts the company is required to pay as a result of this environmental disaster. Write Mr. Stuart a letter explaining these issues. Gold's address is 200 Elm Avenue, San Jose, CA 95192.

    Communications

45. **LO.2** Compute Mary's income or deductions for 2017 using (1) the cash basis and (2) the accrual basis for each of the following:
    a. In May 2017, Mary paid a license fee of $1,200 for the period June 1, 2017, through May 31, 2018.
    b. In December 2017, Mary collected $10,000 for January 2018 rents. In January 2018, Mary collected $2,000 for December 2017 rents.
    c. In June 2017, Mary paid $7,200 for an office equipment service contract for the period July 1, 2017, through December 31, 2018.
    d. In June 2017, Mary purchased office furniture for $273,000. She paid $131,000 in cash and gave a $142,000 interest-bearing note for the balance. The office furniture has an MACRS cost recovery period of seven years. Mary did not make the § 179 election and elected not to take additional first-year depreciation.

46. **LO.2, 5** What accounting method (cash or accrual) would you recommend for the following businesses?
    a. A gift shop with average annual gross receipts of $900,000.
    b. An accounting partnership with annual gross receipts of $12 million.
    c. A drywall subcontractor who works on residences and has annual gross receipts of $3 million.
    d. An incorporated insurance agency with annual gross receipts of $6 million.

Decision Making   47. **LO.2** Blue Company, an architectural firm, has a bookkeeper who maintains a cash receipts and disbursements journal. At the end of the year (2017), the company hires you to convert the cash receipts and disbursements into accrual basis revenues and expenses. The total cash receipts are summarized as follows:

Cash sales	$150,000
Collections on accounts receivable	350,000
Bank loan	90,000
Total cash receipts	$590,000

The accounts receivable from customers at the end of the year are $120,000. You note that the accounts receivable at the beginning of the year were $190,000. The cash sales included $30,000 of prepayments for services to be provided over the period January 1, 2017, through December 31, 2019.

a.   Compute the company's accrual basis gross income for 2017.

b.   Would you recommend that Blue use the cash method or the accrual method? Why?

c.   The company does not maintain an allowance for uncollectible accounts. Would you recommend that such an allowance be established for tax purposes? Explain.

48. **LO.2** How do the all events and economic performance requirements apply to the following transactions by an accrual basis taxpayer?

a.   The company guarantees its products for six months. At the end of 2017, customers had made valid claims for $600,000 that were not paid until 2018. Also, the company estimates that another $400,000 in claims from 2017 sales will be filed and paid in 2018.

b.   The accrual basis taxpayer reported $200,000 in corporate taxable income for 2017. The state income tax rate was 6%. The corporation paid $7,000 in estimated state income taxes in 2017 and paid $2,000 on 2016 state income taxes when it filed its 2016 state income tax return in March 2017. The company filed its 2017 state income tax return in March 2018 and paid the remaining $5,000 of its 2017 state income tax liability.

c.   An employee was involved in an accident while making a sales call. The company paid the injured victim $15,000 in 2017 and agreed to pay the victim $15,000 a year for the next nine years.

49. **LO.3** Ross Company is a corporation providing medical diagnostic services. Ross has used the cash method since inception because its gross receipts did not exceed $5,000,000. This year its average annual gross receipts for the prior three years crossed the $5,000,000 mark, requiring Ross to change from the cash method to the accrual method (per § 448). At the end of its prior year, Ross had accounts receivable of $850,000 and accounts payable of $540,000.

a.   Compute and explain the adjustment to taxable income that Ross must make due to the change in accounting method.

b.   When must Ross include this adjustment in its income?

Decision Making   50. **LO.2, 3** Raven Finance Company experiences bad debts of about 3% of its outstanding loans. At the end of the year, the company had outstanding receivables of $18 million. This balance included $2 million of accrued interest receivable. Raven's loan loss reserve for the year was computed as follows:

Balance, January 1, 2017	$500,000
Accounts written off as uncollectible	
Loans made in 2017	(20,000)
Loans made in prior years	(40,000)
Collections on loans previously written off	15,000
Adjustment to required balance	85,000
Balance, December 31, 2017	$540,000

a. Determine the effects of the above on Raven's taxable income for 2017.

b. Assume that Raven has used the reserve method to compute its taxable income for the 10 years the company has been in existence. In 2017, you begin preparing Raven's tax return. What should be done with regard to the reserve?

51. **LO.2, 3, 6** Jeffrey Boyd, the president of Eagle Furniture Company (average annual gross receipts of $4 million), has prepared the company's financial statements and income tax returns for the past 15 years. In July 2018, however, he hires you to prepare the 2017 corporate income tax return because he has not studied taxes for over 20 years and suspects that the rules may have changed. Eagle uses the accrual method of accounting. Based on an initial examination of Eagle's trial balance and some account analyses, you have determined that the following items may require adjustments:

Communications

*   The company uses the FIFO inventory method, as valued at cost. However, all freight expenses on incoming merchandise have been expensed for the 15 years the company has been in business.
*   The company experiences inventory shrinkage (due to breakage and theft) of about 1% of sales each year. The shrinkage is not taken into account until the company takes a physical inventory each October, but the corporation's fiscal year ends January 31.
*   The company has used an allowance for uncollectible accounts, which has a balance of $60,000. In the past, the company has been able to accurately predict its actual bad debt expense.
*   The company sells a three-year service contract on its appliances. The company treats $1/36$ of the contract price as earned each month. At the beginning of the year, the company had $120,000 in its account for unearned revenues from the service contracts.
*   The company deducts its state income tax in the year paid. Thus, the 2017 state income tax expense includes the estimated taxes paid in 2017 and the additional amount paid in 2017 on 2016 taxes.

Write a letter to Mr. Boyd, explaining what adjustments will be required and how they will be implemented. The address of Eagle Furniture Company is 1000 East Maryland Street, Evansville, IL 47722.

52. **LO.4, 7** Floyd, a cash basis taxpayer, has received an offer to purchase his land. The cash basis buyer will pay him either $100,000 at closing or $50,000 at closing and $56,000 two years after the date of closing. If Floyd recognizes the entire gain in the current year, his marginal tax rate will be 25% (combined Federal and state rates). However, if he spreads the gain over the two years, his marginal tax rate on the gain will be only 20%. Floyd does not consider the buyer a credit risk, and he understands that shifting the gain to next year with an installment sale will save taxes. But he realizes that the deferred payment will, in effect, earn only $6,000 for waiting two years for the other $50,000. Floyd believes he can earn a 10% before-tax rate of return on his after-tax cash. Floyd's adjusted basis for the land is $25,000, the buyer is also a cash basis taxpayer, and the

Decision Making

short-term Federal rate is 4%. Floyd has asked you to evaluate the two alternatives on an after-tax basis.

Decision Making 53. **LO.4, 7** Ted purchased equipment and used materials to develop a patent. The development costs were deducted on prior returns. The bases and fair market values of the assets are presented below.

Assets	Fair Market Value		Basis
Equipment	$350,000	Cost	$ 350,000
		Less: Depreciation	(250,000)
Patent	250,000		–0–
	$600,000		$ 100,000

Sarah has made an offer to purchase the assets. Under one plan, she would pay $200,000 now and $400,000 plus interest at 5% (the Federal rate) in one year. Alternatively, Ted would incorporate the assets and then sell the stock to Sarah. Incorporating the assets would not be a taxable event to Ted, and his basis in the stock would equal his basis in the assets of $100,000. The corporation's basis in the assets would also be $100,000, the same as Ted's basis for the stock. Because the corporation would have a basis in the assets of less than the fair market value (and therefore, there would be less depreciation and amortization than with an asset sale by Ted), Sarah would pay $200,000 in the current year but only $350,000, plus interest at 5%, in one year. Assume that Ted's marginal tax rate is 35%.

a. What is Ted's gain in the year of sale from the installment sale of his assets?

b. Assuming that Ted's time value of money is 5%, would he prefer the sale of the assets or the sale of the stock? Why?

54. **LO.4** Kay, who is not a dealer, sold an apartment house to Polly during the current year (2017). The closing statement for the sale is as follows:

Total selling price		$ 190,000
Add: Polly's share of property taxes (six months) paid by Kay		3,000
Less: Kay's 8% mortgage assumed by Polly	$55,000	
Polly's refundable binder ("earnest money") paid in 2016	1,000	
Polly's 8% installment note given to Kay	99,000	
Kay's real estate commissions and attorney's fees	8,000	(163,000)
Cash paid to Kay at closing		$ 30,000
Cash due from Polly = $30,000 + $8,000 expenses		$ 38,000

During 2017, Kay collected $9,000 in principal on the installment note and $2,000 of interest. Kay's basis in the property was $110,000 [$125,000 − $15,000 (depreciation)]. The Federal rate is 6%.

a. Compute the following:
1. Total gain.
2. Contract price.
3. Payments received in the year of sale.
4. Recognized gain in the year of sale and the character of such gain.

(*Hint:* Think carefully about the manner in which the property taxes are handled before you begin your computations.)

b. Same as parts (a)(2) and (3), except that Kay's basis in the property was $35,000.

Decision Making 55. **LO.4** On June 30, 2017, Kelly sold property for $240,000 cash and a $960,000 note due on September 30, 2018. The note will also pay 6% interest, which is slightly higher than the Federal rate. Kelly's cost of the property was $400,000. She is concerned that Congress may increase the tax rate that will apply when the note is collected. Kelly's after-tax rate of return on investments is 6%.

a. What can Kelly do to avoid the expected higher tax rate?

b. Assuming that Kelly's marginal combined Federal and state tax rate is 25% in 2017, how much would the tax rates need to increase to make the option identified in part (a) advisable?

56. **LO.4** On December 30, 2016, Maud sold land to her son, Charles, for $50,000 cash and a 7% installment note for $350,000, payable over 10 years. Maud's cost of the land was $150,000. In October 2018, after Charles had paid $60,000 on the principal of the note, he received an offer to sell the land for $500,000 cash. What advice can you provide Charles that will minimize the present value of the tax liability for Maud and him?

Decision Making

57. **LO.4** George sold land to an unrelated party in 2016. His basis in the land was $45,000, and the selling price was $120,000—$30,000 payable at closing and $30,000 (plus 10% interest) due January 1, 2017, 2018, and 2019. What would be the tax consequences of the following? [Treat each part independently, and assume that (1) George did not elect out of the installment method and (2) the installment obligations have values equal to their face amounts. Ignore interest in your calculations.]

a. In 2017, George borrowed $40,000 from the bank. The loan was partially secured by the installment notes, but George was personally liable for the loan.

b. In 2017, George gave to his daughter the right to collect all future payments on the installment obligations.

c. On December 31, 2017, George received the payment due on January 1, 2018. On December 15, 2018, George died, and the remaining installment obligation was transferred to his estate. The estate collected the amount due on January 1, 2019.

58. **LO.5** The Wren Construction Company reports its income by the completed contract method. At the end of 2017, the company completed a contract to construct a building at a total cost of $800,000. The contract price was $1.2 million, and the customer paid Wren $900,000. However, the customer refused to accept the work and would not pay anything else on the contract because he claimed that the roof did not meet specifications. Wren's engineers estimated that it would cost $140,000 to bring the roof up to the customer's standards. In 2018, the dispute was settled in the customer's favor; the roof was improved at a cost of $150,000, and the customer accepted the building and paid the remaining $300,000.

a. What would be the effects of the above on Wren's taxable income for 2017 and 2018?

b. Same as part (a), except that Wren had $1,100,000 of accumulated costs under the contract at the end of 2017.

59. **LO.5** Rust Company is a real estate construction company with average annual gross receipts of $4 million. Rust uses the completed contract method, and the contracts require 18 months to complete.

Communications

a. Which of the following costs would be allocated to construction in progress by Rust?
   1. The payroll taxes on direct labor.
   2. The current services pension costs for employees whose wages are included in direct labor.
   3. Accelerated depreciation on equipment used on contracts.
   4. Freight charges on materials assigned to contracts.
   5. The past service costs for employees whose wages are included in direct labor.
   6. Bidding expenses for contracts awarded.

b. Assume that Rust generally builds commercial buildings under contracts with the owners and reports the income using the completed contract method. The company is considering building a series of similar stores for a retail chain. The gross profit margin would be a low percentage, but the company's gross receipts would triple. Write a letter to your client, Rust Company, explaining the tax accounting implications of entering into these contracts. Rust's mailing address is PO Box 1000, Harrisonburg, VA 22807.

60. **LO.5** On March 31, 2015, Big Boats Company entered into a contract with Vacations Unlimited to produce a state-of-the-art cruise ship, to be completed within three years. Big Boats estimated the total cost of building the ship at $300 million. The contract price was $400 million. The ship was completed on February 15, 2018.

a. What tax accounting method must Big Boats use for the contract? Why?

b. Using the financial data provided relating to the contract's performance, complete the following schedule:

Date	Total Costs Incurred to Date	Total Percentage of Contract Completed	Current-Year Revenue Accrued	Current-Year Costs Deductible
12/31/15	$ 90 million	————	————	————
12/31/16	150 million	————	————	————
12/31/17	270 million	————	————	————
12/31/18	360 million	N/A	————	————

c. What are the consequences of the total cost of $360 million exceeding the estimated total cost of $300 million?

61. **LO.5** Ostrich Company makes gasoline storage tanks. Everything produced is under contract (that is, the company does not produce until it gets a contract for a product). Ostrich makes three basic models. However, the tanks must be adapted to each individual customer's location and needs (e.g., the location of the valves and the quality of the materials and insulation). Discuss the following issues relative to Ostrich's operations:

a. An examining IRS agent contends that each of the company's contracts is to produce a "unique product." What difference does it make whether the product is unique or a "shelf item"?

b. Producing one of the tanks takes over one year from start to completion, and the total cost is in excess of $1 million. What costs must be capitalized for this contract that are not subject to capitalization for a contract with a shorter duration and lower cost?

c. What must Ostrich do with the costs of bidding on contracts?

d. Ostrich frequently makes several cost estimates for a contract, using various estimates of materials costs. These costs fluctuate almost daily. Assuming that Ostrich must use the percentage of completion method to report the income from the contract, what will be the consequence if the company uses the highest estimate of a contract's cost and the actual cost is closer to the lowest estimated cost?

Communications 62. **LO.5, 7** Swallow Company is a large real estate construction company that has made a Subchapter S election. The company reports its income using the percentage of completion method. In 2018, the company completed a contract at a total cost of $4.8 million. The contract price was $7.2 million. At the end of 2017, the year the contract was begun, Swallow estimated that the total cost of the contract would be $5.4 million. Total accumulated cost on the contract at the end of 2017 was $1.8 million. The relevant tax rate is 35%, and the relevant Federal interest rate is 5%. Assume that all income tax returns were filed and taxes were paid on March 15 following the end of the calendar tax year.

a. Compute the gross profit on the contract for 2017 and 2018.

b. Compute the lookback interest due or receivable with the 2018 tax return.

c. Before bidding on a contract, Swallow generally makes three estimates of total contract costs: (1) optimistic, (2) pessimistic, and (3) most likely (based on a blending of optimistic and pessimistic assumptions). The company has asked you to write a letter explaining which of these estimates should be used for percentage of completion purposes. In writing your letter, you should consider the fact that Swallow is incorporated and has made an S corporation election. Therefore, the income and deductions flow through to the shareholders who are all individuals in the 35% marginal tax bracket. The relevant Federal interest rate is 8%. Swallow's mailing address is 400 Front Avenue, Ashland, OR 97520.

63. **LO.6** Grouse Company is a furniture retailer whose average annual gross receipts for the three preceding years exceeded $10 million. In the current tax year, the company purchased merchandise with an invoice price of $15 million, less a 2% discount for early payment. However, the company had to borrow on a bank line of credit and paid $150,000 interest to take advantage of the discount for early payment. Freight on the merchandise purchased totaled $360,000. For September, Grouse agreed to pay the customer's freight on goods sold. The total cost of this freight-out was $70,000. The company has three stores and operates a warehouse where it stores goods. The cost of operating the warehouse was $240,000. The $240,000 includes labor, depreciation, taxes, and insurance on the building. The cost of the purchasing operations totaled $420,000. The jurisdiction where the company operates imposes a tax on inventories on hand as of January 1. The inventory tax for this year is $24,000. The invoice cost of goods on hand at the end of the year is $3 million. Compute Grouse's ending inventory using the FIFO method.

64. **LO.6, 7** Lavender Manufacturing Company began business in the current year. The company uses the simplified method to allocate mixed services costs to production. The company's costs and expenses for the year were as follows:

Decision Making

Direct labor	$ 3,000,000
Direct materials	4,000,000
Factory supervision	800,000
Property tax on factory	100,000
Personnel department	400,000
Computer operations	250,000
General administration	550,000
Marketing	800,000
State income tax	200,000
	$10,100,000

a. Determine Lavender's total production costs for the year.

b. Assume that the hourly pay for direct labor is much lower than the hourly pay for employees in general administration and that the employee turnover is much higher for production employees than for general administration employees. How should these facts affect the company's decision to use the simplified mixed services method to allocate mixed services costs to production?

65. **LO.6** Silver Creek Ranch LLC is a small, family-owned cattle ranch that began operations in the current year. The ranch grows hay that will be fed to its purebred cattle. It will take approximately three years to build up the herd and to begin producing a positive cash flow. The owners' other income will equal their deductions, so they will not be able to utilize farm losses for the first three years.

Issue ID

The owners have asked you to discuss the tax accounting issues related to their cattle business.

66. **LO.3, 6** In 2017, Gail changed from the lower of cost or market FIFO method to the LIFO inventory method. The ending inventory for 2016 was computed as follows:

Item	FIFO Cost	Replacement Cost	Lower of Cost or Market
A	$26,000	$15,000	$15,000
B	52,000	55,000	52,000
C	30,000	7,000	7,000
			$74,000

Item C was damaged goods, and the replacement cost used was actually the estimated selling price of the goods. The actual cost to replace item C was $32,000.

   a. What is the correct beginning inventory for 2017 under the LIFO method?
   b. What immediate tax consequences (if any) will result from the switch to LIFO?

Communications   67. **LO.6** At the end of 2018, Magenta Manufacturing Company discovered that construction cost had been capitalized as a cost of the factory building in 2013 when it should have been treated as a cost of production equipment installation costs. As a result of the misclassification, the depreciation through 2016 was understated by $110,000, and depreciation for 2017 was understated by $90,000. What would be the consequences of correcting for the misclassification of the property cost?

   a. The taxpayer uses the FIFO inventory method, and 25% of goods produced during the period were included in the ending inventory.
   b. The taxpayer uses the LIFO inventory method, and no new LIFO layer was added during 2017.

68. **LO.6** Amber Company has used the dollar-value LIFO technique for the past three years. The company has only one inventory pool. Its beginning inventory for the current year was computed as follows:

	Base Period Cost	LIFO Index	LIFO Layer
Base period inventory			
	$1,200,000	1.00	$1,200,000
Year 1 layer	300,000	1.04	312,000
Year 2 layer	400,000	1.06	424,000
	$1,900,000		$1,936,000

   a. The current-year ending inventory (end of year 3) at current prices is $2,124,000, and the LIFO index is 1.06. Determine the company's LIFO inventory as of the end of the current year.
   b. Assume that the current-year ending inventory at current prices is $1,850,000. What is the end-of-the-current-year LIFO inventory value?

69. **LO.4, 7** Your client, Bob Young, is negotiating a sale of investment real estate for $12 million. Bob believes that the buyer would pay cash of $8 million and a note for $4 million or $3 million cash and a note for $9 million. The notes will pay interest at slightly above the market rate. Bob realizes that the second option involves more risks of collection, but he is willing to accept that risk if the tax benefits of the installment sale are substantial. Write a letter to Bob advising him of the tax consequences of choosing the lower down payment and larger note option,

assuming that he has no other installment receivables. Bob's address is 200 Jerdone, Gettysburg, PA 17325.

70. **LO.2, 4** Ven Company is a retailer. In 2017, its before-tax net income for financial reporting purposes was $600,000. This included a $150,000 gain from the sale of land held for several years as a possible plant site. The cost of the land was $100,000, the contract price for the sale was $250,000, and the company collected $120,000 in the year of sale. The income per books also included $90,000 from a 24-month service contract entered into in July 2016 (the customer paid $180,000 in advance for this contract). The addition to the allowance for uncollectible accounts for the year was $70,000, and the actual accounts written off totaled $40,000.

Make the necessary adjustments to the before taxable income per books to compute the taxable income for the year.

 Research Problems

Note: Solutions to the Research Problems can be prepared by using the Thomson Reuters Checkpoint® Student Edition online tax research database, which accompanies this textbook. Solutions can also be prepared by using research materials found in a typical tax library.

THOMSON REUTERS
CHECKPOINT®
Student Edition

Research Problem 1. Your client is not permitted to deduct a year-end accrual for vacation pay earned but not paid. This result occurs because the tax law considers this to be deferred compensation that is ineligible for the recurring item exception, unless it is paid by March 15 of the year following the accrual [see §§ 404(a)(5) and (6)]. Your client has asked whether the related accrued Social Security taxes on the vacation pay can be accrued under the general recurring item exception because these taxes will be paid by the fifteenth day of the ninth month after the close of the tax year.

Research Problem 2. You recently obtained a new client that operates a chain of convenience stores that sell food and vehicle fuel. You notice that the company has a customer card program whereby customer purchases of fuel are entered on the card. For each gallon purchased, the customer is allowed a $.05 discount per gallon purchased within the next three months. The client treats the $.05 discount as "earned" by the customer (and deductible by the store) when the purchase is made, which gives the customer the right to the discount. The client justifies this as clearly reflecting the company's income because an obligation arises when the gasoline is purchased and the right to the future discount is earned. Is the client's accounting method correct? Explain.

Research Problem 3. Your client supplies water to a housing development. The company requires new customers to pay for the extension of the water lines to their homes. The water lines are the company's property. The company has consistently treated the amounts received from its customers as a nontaxable contribution to capital and used the amounts received as a reduction in the cost of the water lines for tax purposes. In recent decisions, the courts have consistently ruled that the payments received from the utility customers in similar circumstances should be treated as income from services, rather than as a contribution to capital. Your client has concluded that it is only a matter of time before the IRS applies the recent court decisions to the company. The client would like you to explain the tax consequences of the IRS's likely adjustments based on these decisions.

Research Problem 4. Your client is a manufacturer. For several years, the company buried empty paint cans on its property. The paint was used in the production process. Recently, a state environmental agency informed the company that it was required to dig up the paint cans and decontaminate the land. The company spent a substantial amount for this environmental cleanup in the current year. An IRS agent contends that the cost must be added to the basis in the land because the cleanup improved the land. The company's CFO has asked you to determine whether any authority exists that would support a current deduction for these costs.

Research Problem 5. In 2017, your client, Clear Corporation, changed from the cash to the accrual method of accounting for its radio station. The company had a positive § 481 adjustment of $2.4 million as a result of the change and began amortizing the adjustment in 2017. In 2018, Clear received an offer to purchase the assets of the radio station business (this would be considered a sale of a trade or business under § 1060). If the offer is accepted, Clear plans to purchase a satellite television business. Clear has asked you to explain the consequences of the sale of the radio station on the amortization of the § 481 adjustment.

Use internet tax resources to address the following questions. Look for reliable websites and blogs of the IRS and other government agencies, media outlets, businesses, tax professionals, academics, think tanks, and political outlets.

Research Problem 6. Why did the AICPA object to former Congressman Dave Camp's tax reform proposal introduced in February 2014 (later officially introduced as H.R. 1 of the 113rd Congress) regarding the use of the cash method of accounting?

Research Problem 7. President Obama and others have called for repeal of the LIFO method for tax purposes. Conduct an internet search to find arguments for and against this proposal. Prepare a summary of these arguments.

Roger CPA Review Questions

1. Abbott (an S Corporation), Bell, Costello, and Dilbertson form Best Partnership, an equally shared partnership. Each partner but Abbott has a December 31 tax year-end; Abbott's is June 30. The partners would like to choose a partnership tax year other than one ending December 31, but do not have a valid business purpose for doing so. Which of the following is an acceptable tax year-end they may choose for Best Partnership?

   I.   December 31
   II. September 30
   III. June 30

   a.   I and II only   c.   I, II, or III
   b.   I only   d.   I and III only

2. LaJoie, Bhatti, and Jenkins are going to form LBJ Partnership. The ownership interests and tax years of the partners are as follows:

Partner	Partnership Interest	Tax Year-Ends
LaJoie	20%	January 31
Bhatti	40%	June 30
Jenkins	40%	December 31

   According to Reg. § 1.706–1(b) (3), what is LBJ Partnership's required tax year-end? Assume no business purpose for a different taxable year.

   a.   January 31   c.   December 31
   b.   July 31   d.   June 30

3. Slater Slopes is a newly formed ski resort partnership with a natural business year ending May 31. The ownership and tax years of its three partners are as follows:

Partner	Partnership Interest	Tax Year-Ends
A. Slater	20%	December 31
Excelsior Enterprises	40%	November 30
Pinnacle Productions	40%	November 30

Which of the following is an acceptable year-end for Slater Slopes? Consider both § 706 and § 444.

I.   May 31
II. November 30
III. September 30

a.   II only
b.   I and II only

c.   I only
d.   I, II, and III

4. The cash method of accounting may be used for tax reporting purposes by which of the following taxpayers?

a.   A partnership with a C corporation—one with annual revenue exceeding $5 million—as a partner

b.   A C corporation with annual revenue of $2.5 million which has physical inventory levels that are material in amount

c.   A farming corporation

d.   A partnership with a personal service C corporation—one with annual revenue below $5 million—as a partner

Deferred Compensation

LEARNING OBJECTIVES: *After completing Chapter 19, you should be able to:*

LO.1 Distinguish between qualified (defined contribution and defined benefit) and nonqualified compensation arrangements.

LO.2 Identify qualification requirements for qualified plans.

LO.3 Discuss tax consequences of qualified plans.

LO.4 Calculate limitations on contributions to and benefits from qualified plans.

LO.5 State and explain the qualified plan (Keogh plan) available to a self-employed person.

LO.6 Describe benefits of the different types of Individual Retirement Accounts (IRAs).

LO.7 Review the rationale for nonqualified deferred compensation plans and the related tax treatment.

LO.8 Explain the value of restricted property plans.

LO.9 Differentiate the tax treatment of qualified and nonqualified stock options.

LO.10 Identify tax planning opportunities available with deferred compensation.

CHAPTER OUTLINE

BILL ARON/PHOTOEDIT

THE BIG PICTURE

A TAXPAYER WHO SAVES

Joyce is a junior finance major at State University. Recently, Dr. Sanchez, the professor in her finance class, delivered a lecture on retirement savings that emphasized the need for a long-term savings horizon and multiple retirement plans. Near the end of the lecture, Dr. Sanchez mentioned that she has four different retirement plans. Joyce was surprised to hear this because she knows that her father has only a single retirement plan that is provided by his employer (an automobile manufacturer).

Joyce drops in on the professor during office hours. Her goal is to find out more about how a person can have multiple retirement plans. What are some facts that would be helpful for Joyce?

Read the chapter and formulate your response.

Compensation is important in any type of organization. If you have not chosen a career, consider becoming a boxer, a baseball player, a basketball player, a racer, or a soccer player. Forbes's latest list of the top–50 World's Top-Earning Athletes included 6 soccer players, 6 baseball players, 12 basketball players, 5 tennis players, and 3 motorsports drivers. In order, the 5 top-earning world athletes were as follows:[1]

Rank	Athlete	Sport	Age	Earnings
1	Cristiano Ronaldo	Soccer	31	$88 million
2	Lionel Messi	Soccer	29	$81.4 million
3	LeBron James	Basketball	31	$77.2 million
4	Roger Federer	Tennis	35	$67.8 million
5	Kevin Durant	Basketball	28	$56.2 million

Before you decide to give up your future career in accounting, education, or the military and jump into major league sports, also consider the tax consequences. Depending on the sport, level of skill, and injury experience, a professional athlete's lifetime sports income is compressed into about 10 years. Yet income averaging is not allowed for Federal income tax purposes. As a result, the athlete will lose a larger portion of lifetime earned income in the form of taxes than someone with a comparable amount of earned income over a typical work/life cycle of 40 or more years. The athlete and others have a method, in the form of deferred compensation, available to reduce the Federal income tax liability.

This chapter discusses the various types of deferred compensation arrangements available to employees and self-employed individuals. With **deferred compensation**, an employee receives compensation for services in a later period than that in which the services were performed—quite often during retirement years. The tax law encourages employers to offer deferred compensation plans to their employees to supplement the Federal Social Security retirement system.

Qualified deferred compensation plans receive particularly favorable tax treatment. The amounts that may be deferred under these plans are limited, so they might not be perfect for highly paid athletes. For employers and more traditional employees, however, they provide helpful tax advantages. For example, contributors to qualified pension, profit sharing, or stock bonus plans receive four major tax advantages:

1. Contributions are immediately deductible by the employer.
2. Employees are not taxed until these funds are distributed to them.
3. Income earned by the plan trust, which has received the contributions, is not subject to tax until made available to the employees and thus grows at a tax-free rate.
4. Employer contributions to and benefits payable under qualified plans generally are not subject to FICA and FUTA taxes.

Compared with nonqualified plans, though, qualified plans have some disadvantages, including the following:

- The employer must make contributions for most employees on a nondiscriminatory basis.

- There are a number of limits on contributions to defined contribution plans and on benefits that may be paid under defined benefit plans.

- Qualified plans have higher startup and administrative costs.

---

[1]"The World's Highest-Paid Athletes," *Forbes*, 2016, **www.forbes.com/athletes/ #1039ecf6e349**.

A variety of deferred compensation arrangements are offered to employees, including the following:

- Qualified pension plans.
- Qualified profit sharing plans.
- Cash or deferred arrangement plans.
- SIMPLE IRAs and § 401(k) plans.
- Tax-deferred annuities.
- Incentive stock option plans.
- Nonqualified deferred compensation plans.
- Restricted property plans.
- Cafeteria benefit plans.
- Employee stock purchase plans.

19-1 QUALIFIED PENSION, PROFIT SHARING, STOCK BONUS, AND CASH BALANCE PLANS

LO.1

Distinguish between qualified (defined contribution and defined benefit) and nonqualified compensation arrangements.

To ensure that retired people will not be dependent solely on government programs, the Federal government encourages private pension and profit sharing plans. The Federal tax law provides substantial tax benefits for plans that meet certain requirements (qualified plans). The major requirement for qualification is that a plan not discriminate in favor of highly compensated employees.

19-1a Types of Plans

Qualified plans can be conveniently divided into four groups: pension, profit sharing, stock bonus, and cash balance plans.

Pension Plans

A **pension plan** is a deferred compensation arrangement that provides for systematic payments of definitely determinable retirement benefits to employees who meet the requirements set forth in the plan. Employer contributions under a qualified pension plan must *not* depend on profits. A pension plan normally must pay out benefits as lifetime annuities to provide retirement income to retired employees.

There are basically two types of qualified pension plans: defined benefit plans and defined contribution plans.

A **defined benefit plan** includes a formula that defines the benefits employees are to receive.[2] Benefits are generally measured by and based on such factors as years of service and employee compensation. Under such a plan, an employer must make annual contributions based upon actuarial computations that will be sufficient to fund the retirement benefits. If a plan document permits, employees may make contributions to the pension fund. A separate account is not maintained for each participant. A defined benefit plan provides some sense of security for employees because the benefits may be expressed in fixed dollar amounts. In a defined benefit plan, the employer (not the employee) assumes the market risk because the employer promises to pay fixed benefits. Because an expense is not deductible for tax purposes until paid, there often will be a book-tax difference because the employer accounts for the expense on an accrual basis for accounting purposes.

A **defined contribution pension plan** (or money purchase plan) defines the amount the employer is required to contribute (e.g., a flat dollar amount, an amount based on a special formula, or an amount equal to a certain percentage of compensation). A separate account must be maintained for each participant. Benefits are based solely on (1) the amount contributed and (2) income from the fund that accrues to the participant's account.[3] Consequently, actuarial calculations are not required to determine the

---

[2]§ 414(j).

[3]§ 414(i).

employer's annual contribution. Upon retirement, an employee's pension amount depends on the value of his or her account. Although it is not mandatory, a plan may require or permit employee contributions to the pension fund. Because employers record the expense for both tax and accounting purposes when funding an employee's account, book-tax differences do not often occur.

The qualified pension plan of Rose Company calls for both the employer and the employee to contribute annually to the pension trust an amount equal to 5% of the employee's compensation. Because the employer's rate of contribution is fixed, this pension plan is a defined contribution plan. If the plan called for contributions sufficient to provide retirement benefits equal to 30% of the employee's average salary for the last five years of employment, it would be a defined benefit plan.

Concept Summary 19.1 compares and contrasts a defined benefit plan and a defined contribution plan.

Concept Summary 19.1

Defined Benefit Plan and Defined Contribution Plan Compared

Defined Benefit Plan	Defined Contribution Plan
Includes a pension plan.	Includes profit sharing, stock bonus, money purchase, target benefit, qualified cash or deferred compensation, employee stock ownership plans, and some pension plans.
Determinable benefits based upon years of service and average compensation. Benefits calculated by a formula.	An account for each participant. Ultimate benefits depend upon contributions and investment performance.
Maximum annual *benefits* payable may not exceed the smaller of (1) $215,000 (in 2017)* or (2) 100% of the participant's average earnings in the three highest years of employment.	Maximum annual *contribution* to an account may not exceed the smaller of (1) $54,000** (in 2017) or (2) 100% of the participant's compensation (25% for a profit sharing plan, money purchase plan, or stock bonus plan).
Employer bears the investment risk and reward.	Employee bears the investment risk and reward.
Forfeitures must reduce subsequent funding costs and cannot increase the benefits any participant can receive under the plan.	Forfeitures may be allocated to the accounts of remaining participants.
Subject to minimum funding requirement to avoid penalties.	Exempt from funding requirements.
Greater administrative and actuarial costs and greater reporting requirements.	Costs and reporting requirements less burdensome.
Subject to Pension Benefit Guaranty Corporation (PBGC) plan termination insurance rules.	Not subject to PBGC plan termination insurance rules.
More favorable to employees who are older when plan is adopted because it is possible to fund higher benefits over a shorter period.	More favorable to younger employees because over a longer period, higher benefits may result.

*This amount is subject to indexing annually in $5,000 increments.
**This amount is subject to indexing annually in $1,000 increments.

Profit Sharing Plans

A profit sharing plan is a deferred compensation arrangement established and maintained by an employer to provide for employee participation in the company's profits. Contributions are paid from the employer to a trustee and are commingled in a single trust fund. Despite the name, an employer does not have to have current or accumulated profits to make a contribution. The contribution formula can be based on compensation, earnings, gross sales, or any other measurement chosen by the employer.

In a profit sharing plan, a separate account is maintained for each participant. The plan must provide a definite, predetermined formula for allocating the contributions made to the trustee among the participants. Likewise, it must include a definite, predetermined formula for distributing the accumulated funds after a fixed number of years; on the attainment of a stated age; or on the occurrence of certain events such as illness, layoff, retirement, or termination of the plan. A company is not required to contribute a definite, predetermined amount to the plan every year, although substantial and recurring contributions must be made to meet the permanency requirement. Forfeitures arising under this plan may be used to increase the individual accounts of the remaining participants as long as these increases do not result in prohibited discrimination.[4] Benefits to employees may normally be distributed through lump-sum payouts in a profit sharing plan. A § 401(k) cash or deferred arrangement plan, explained later in this chapter, is the most common type of profit sharing plan.

Stock Bonus Plans

A stock bonus plan is another form of deferred compensation. The employer establishes and maintains the plan to contribute shares of its stock. The contributions need not be dependent on the employer's profits. A stock bonus plan is subject to the same requirements as a profit sharing plan for purposes of allocating and distributing the stock among the employees.[5] Also, as with profit sharing plans, benefits are paid out of each separate account, and participants bear the investment risks and rewards. Any benefits of the plan normally are distributable in the form of stock of the employer company, except that distributable fractional shares may be paid in cash. Employee stock ownership plans (ESOPs) may be either profit sharing or stock bonus plans.

Cash Balance Plans

A cash balance plan is a controversial hybrid form of pension plan that is similar in many aspects to a defined benefit plan. These plans are funded by the employer, and the employer bears the investment risks and rewards. Thus, the employer bears the mortality risk if an employee elects to receive benefits in the form of a lifetime annuity and lives beyond normal life expectancy. But like defined contribution plans, a cash balance plan accrues benefits to individual accounts. The benefits for an employee depend on how much builds up over time in the employee's account and not on a formula based on years of service and preretirement pay. Cash balance plans are better for younger, mobile employees, and the companies save money by reducing pension payouts for older and longer-service employees.

ETHICS & EQUITY Uneven Compensation Playing Field

The top five executives of publicly traded corporations are subject to a $1 million limit each on the corporate deductibility of compensation paid to them. Many other highly paid individuals are not subject to this $1 million cap on deductibility.

In closely held, private corporations, an employee's salary must be reasonable. If part of an employee's salary is unreasonable, an IRS agent can disallow that portion and treat it as a distribution (usually classified as a dividend to the shareholder). Any deduction for compensation by the corporation must reflect a reasonable allowance for salaries or other compensation for personal services, reflecting what would ordinarily be paid for like services by like enterprises under like circumstances. Frequently,

the permitted deduction to the corporation exceeds $1 million.

Among those to whom the cap does not apply are highly paid entertainers receiving royalties or other compensation (other than as an executive of a company). Three entertainers on *The Big Bang Theory*—Jim Parsons, Kaley Cuoco, and Johnny Galecki—get $1 million per episode. Judge Judy (Judy Sheindlin) earns about $47 million each year, and Matt Lauer receives $22 to $25 million.

Discuss the fairness of tax policy that subjects the compensation of certain business executives to a limitation on deductibility by their corporate employers while allowing compensation paid to noncovered executives, entertainers, sport stars, and others to be exempted from this limitation.

---

[4]Reg. §§ 1.401–1(b) and 1.401–4(a)(1)(iii).

[5]Reg. § 1.401–1(b)(1)(iii).

LO.2

Identify qualification requirements for qualified plans.

19-1b **Qualification Requirements**

To be *qualified*, and thereby to receive favorable tax treatment, a plan generally must satisfy the following requirements:

- Nondiscrimination requirements.
- Participation and coverage requirements.
- Vesting requirements.
- Distribution requirements.
- Minimum funding requirements.

Qualification rules are highly technical and numerous, so the IRS maintains a staggered determination letter request process that allows plan sponsors to file a plan document with the IRS for approval. A favorable determination letter indicates that the form of the plan meets the qualification requirements and that the form of the plan's trust meets the requirements for exemption. However, the ultimate qualification of the plan depends upon its actual administration and operations. Therefore, the operations of the plan should be reviewed periodically. Favorable determination letters have an expiration date with individually designed plans on a five-year schedule and preapproved plans on a six-year schedule.

Nondiscrimination Requirements

Contributions and benefits under a plan must *not discriminate* in favor of highly compensated employees. A plan is not considered discriminatory merely because contributions and benefits are proportional to compensation.[6] For example, a pension plan that provides for the allocation of employer contributions based upon a flat 3 percent of each employee's compensation would not be discriminatory solely because highly paid employees receive greater benefits.

Participation and Coverage Requirements

A qualified plan must provide, at a minimum, that all employees in the covered group who are 21 years of age be eligible to participate after completing one year of service. A year of service is generally defined as the completion of 1,000 hours of service within a measuring period of 12 consecutive months. As an alternative, where the plan provides that 100 percent of an employee's accrued benefits will be vested upon entering the plan, the employee's participation may be postponed until the later of age 21 or two years from the date of employment. Once the age and service requirements are met, an employee must begin participating no later than the *earlier* of the following:

- The first day of the first plan year beginning after the date on which the requirements were satisfied.
- Six months after the date on which the requirements were satisfied.[7]

EXAMPLE 2

Coffee Corporation has a calendar year retirement plan covering its employees. The corporation adopts the most restrictive eligibility rules permitted. Wilma, age 21, is hired on January 31, 2016, and meets the service requirement over the next 12 months (completes at least 1,000 hours by January 31, 2017). Wilma must be included in this plan no later than July 31, 2017, because the six-month limitation would be applicable. If the company had adopted the two-year participation rule, Wilma must be included in the plan no later than July 31, 2018.

Because a qualified plan must be primarily for the benefit of employees and be non-discriminatory, the plan has to cover a reasonable percentage of the company employees. A plan will be qualified only if it satisfies one of the following tests:[8]

- The plan benefits a percentage of non-highly compensated employees equal to at least 70 percent of the percentage of highly compensated employees benefiting

---

[6]§§ 401(a)(4) and (5).

[7]§§ 410(a)(1)(A) and (B) and 410(a)(4).

[8]§ 410(b).

under the plan (the *ratio percentage test*). In other words, the plan must benefit a percentage of the non-highly paid employees, which is at least 70 percent of the highly paid employees who benefit under the same plan.

- The plan meets the *average benefits test*, described below.

If a company has no highly compensated employees, the retirement plan will automatically satisfy the coverage rules.

Suppose a company has 2 highly paid employees (HPEs) and 20 non-highly paid employees (NHPEs). If this plan covers both of the HPEs, for the NHPEs to qualify, the plan must cover at least 14 of them (70% × 20). If the plan covers only one of the HPEs, the plan must cover 7 of the NHPEs (70% × 50% = 35% × 20).

To satisfy the *average benefits test*, the nondiscriminatory plan must benefit any employees who qualify under a classification set up by the employer. In addition, the average benefit percentage for non-highly compensated employees must be at least 70 percent of the average benefit percentage for highly compensated employees. The *average benefit percentage* means, with respect to any group of employees, the average of the benefit percentages calculated separately for each employee in the group. The term *benefit percentage* means the employer-provided contributions (including forfeitures) or benefits of an employee under all qualified plans of the employer, expressed as a percentage of that employee's compensation.

An employee is a ▆highly compensated employee▆ if, at any time during the year or the preceding year, the employee satisfies *either* of the following:[9]

- Was a 5 percent owner of the company.
- Received more than $120,000 (in 2017) in annual compensation from the employer *and* was a member of the top-paid group of the employer.[10] The top-paid group clause is applicable only if the employer elects to have it apply. An employee whose compensation is in the top 20 percent of all of the employees is a member of the top-paid group.

An additional *minimum participation test* must also be met for some plans. A plan must cover at least 40 percent of all employees or, if fewer, at least 50 employees on one representative day of the plan year. In determining all employees, nonresident aliens, certain union members, and employees not fulfilling the minimum age or years-of-service requirement of the plan may be excluded.[11]

Assume that Rust Corporation's retirement plan automatically meets the 70% test (the ratio percentage test) because 70% of all non-highly compensated employees benefit. The company has 100 employees, but only 38 of these employees are covered by the plan. Therefore, this retirement plan does not meet the minimum participation requirement.

Vesting Requirements

The ▆vesting requirements▆ protect an employee who has worked a reasonable period of time for an employer from losing employer contributions because of being fired or changing jobs. An employee's right to accrued benefits derived from his or her own contributions to a defined benefit plan must be nonforfeitable from the date of contribution. The accrued benefits derived from employer contributions must be nonforfeitable in accordance with one of *two alternative minimum vesting schedules* or an even more generous vesting schedule.

---

[9]§§ 401(a)(4) and 414(q).

[10]The $120,000 amount is indexed annually in $5,000 increments.

[11]§§ 401(a)(26) and 410(b)(3) and (4).

To satisfy the *first alternative*, a participant must have a nonforfeitable right to 100 percent of his or her accrued benefits derived from employer contributions upon completion of not more than five years of service (five-year or cliff vesting). The *second alternative* is satisfied if a participant has a nonforfeitable right at least equal to a percentage of the accrued benefits derived from employer contributions as depicted in Exhibit 19.1 (graded vesting). Of the two alternatives, cliff vesting minimizes administrative expenses for a company and provides more vesting for a long-term employee.

Mitch has six years of service completed as of February 2, 2017, his employment anniversary date. If his defined benefit plan has a five-year (cliff) vesting schedule, 100% of Mitch's accrued benefits are vested. If the plan uses the graded vesting rule, Mitch's nonforfeitable percentage is 80%.

Defined contribution plans also must satisfy one of the following minimum vesting schedules: two- to six-year graded vesting as shown in Exhibit 19.2, three-year cliff vesting, or an even more generous vesting schedule.

Millie has five years of service completed as of February 2, 2017, her employment anniversary date. If her defined contribution plan uses three-year cliff vesting, Millie must be 100% vested. Under a two- to six-year vesting plan, Millie must be 80% vested.

Distribution Requirements

Uniform *minimum distribution rules* exist for all qualified defined benefit and defined contribution plans, traditional Individual Retirement Accounts (IRAs) and annuities, unfunded deferred compensation plans of state and local governments and tax-exempt employers, and tax-sheltered custodial accounts and annuities. Distributions to a participant must begin by April 1 of the calendar year *following the later* of (1) the calendar year in which the employee attains age $70\frac{1}{2}$ or (2) the calendar year in which the employee retires. Thus, an employee can delay receiving distributions until retirement. However, distributions to a 5 percent owner or a

EXHIBIT 19.1	Three- to Seven-Year Vesting for Defined Benefit Plans
Years of Service	**Nonforfeitable Percentage**
3	20%
4	40%
5	60%
6	80%
7 or more	100%

EXHIBIT 19.2	Two- to Six-Year Vesting for Defined Contribution Plans
Years of Service	**Nonforfeitable Percentage**
2	20%
3	40%
4	60%
5	80%
6 or more	100%

traditional IRA holder must begin no later than April 1 of the calendar year *following* the year in which the 5 percent owner or the IRA holder reaches age 70½.[12]

Minimum annual distributions must be made over the life of the participant or the lives of the participant and a designated individual beneficiary. The amount of the required minimum distribution for a particular year is determined by dividing the account balance as of December 31 of the prior year by the applicable life expectancy. The life expectancy of the owner and his or her beneficiary is based upon the expected return multiples in the Regulations, using ages attained within the calendar year the participant reaches age 70½.[13]

EXAMPLE

7

Beth reaches age 70½ in 2017, and she will also be age 71 in 2017. Her retirement account has a balance of $120,000 on December 31, 2016. If Beth is retired, a 5% owner, or the holder of a traditional IRA, she must withdraw $7,843 ($120,000 ÷ 15.3) for the 2017 calendar year, assuming that her multiple is 15.3. This distribution need not be made until April 1, 2018, but a second distribution must be made by December 31, 2018.

Failure to make a minimum required distribution to a particular participant results in a *50 percent nondeductible excise tax* on the excess in any taxable year of the amount that should have been distributed over the amount that actually was distributed. This tax is imposed on the individual required to take the distribution (the payee).[14] The Secretary of the Treasury is authorized to waive the tax for a given taxpayer year if the taxpayer is able to establish that the shortfall is due to reasonable error and that reasonable steps are being taken to remedy the shortfall.

If a taxpayer receives an *early distribution* from a qualified retirement plan, a 10 percent additional tax is levied on the full amount of any distribution includible in gross income.[15] The term *qualified retirement plan* includes a qualified defined benefit plan or defined contribution plan, a tax-sheltered annuity or custodial account, or a traditional IRA. The following distributions, however, are *not* treated as early distributions:

- Distributions made on or after the date the employee attains age 59½.

- Distributions made to a beneficiary (or the estate of an employee) on or after the death of the employee.

- Distributions attributable to the employee's being disabled.

- Distributions made as part of a scheduled series of substantially equal periodic payments (made not less frequently than annually) for the life of the participant (or the joint lives of the participant and the participant's beneficiary).

- Distributions made to an employee after separation from service because of early retirement under the plan after attaining age 55. This exception to early distribution treatment does not apply to a traditional IRA.

- Distributions used to pay medical expenses to the extent the expenses are deductible under § 213 (determined regardless of whether the taxpayer itemizes deductions).

- IRA distributions that are used to pay qualified higher education expenses of the taxpayer, the spouse, or any child or grandchild of the taxpayer or the taxpayer's spouse.

- IRA distributions up to $10,000 that are used to pay expenses incurred by qualified first-time homebuyers.

Minimum Funding Requirements

Minimum funding requirements apply to defined benefit plans, money purchase plans, and target benefit plans to regulate the amount that an employer must contribute to

---

[12]§ 401(a)(9). These distribution requirements do not apply to Roth IRAs.

[13]Reg. § 1.72–9. Refer to Chapter 4.

[14]§ 4974(a).

[15]§ 72(t). See Ltr.Rul. 8837071.

ensure that the plan is properly funded. The amount of contributions required for a plan year is the amount needed to fund benefits earned during a plan year (e.g., normal costs) plus the portion of other liabilities that are amortized over a period of years (e.g., investment losses). A special account called a funding standard account is required, and contribution amounts are determined under one of several acceptable actuarial cost methods. A tax equal to 10 percent of the aggregate unpaid required contribution is imposed on a single-employer plan (5 percent for a multiemployer plan). If an accumulated funding deficit is not corrected, a 100 percent tax is imposed.[16]

Discuss tax consequences of qualified plans.

19-1c Tax Consequences to the Employee and Employer

Although employer contributions to qualified plans are generally deductible immediately (subject to contribution and deductibility rules), these amounts are not subject to taxation until distributed to employees.[17] If benefits are paid to a creditor of the employee, a child of the employee, etc., the benefits paid are treated as if paid to the employee. When benefits are distributed to employees or paid with respect to an employee, the employer does not receive another deduction.

The tax benefit to the employee amounts to a substantial tax deferral and may be viewed as an interest-free loan from the government to the trust fund. Another advantage of a qualified plan is that any income earned by the trust is not taxable to the trust.[18] Employees, in effect, are taxed on such earnings when they receive the retirement benefits.

The taxation of amounts received by employees in periodic or installment payments is generally subject to the annuity rules in § 72 (refer to Chapter 4). In any situation where employee contributions have been subject to tax previously, they are included in the employee's investment in the contract. Two other alternative options generally are available for benefit distributions. A taxpayer may (1) receive the distribution in a lump-sum payment or (2) roll over the benefits into an IRA or another qualified employer retirement plan.

Lump-Sum Distributions from Qualified Plans

A lump-sum distribution occurs when an employee receives his or her entire payout from a qualified plan in a single payment rather than receiving the amount in installments. The annuity rules do not apply to a lump-sum distribution. All such payments are thrown into one year. Because lump-sum payments have been accumulated over a number of years, bunching retirement benefits into one taxable year may impose a high tax burden because of progressive rates.

Rollover Treatment

A taxpayer who receives a distribution can avoid current taxation by rolling the distribution into another qualified employer retirement plan or into an IRA.[19] The taxation of the distribution is deferred until distributions are made from the recipient's qualified employer retirement plan or IRA. A rollover can be *direct* with the balance in the account going directly from a qualified employer retirement plan to another qualified employer retirement plan or an IRA (sometimes called a conversion). The rollover can be *indirect* with the proceeds going to the taxpayer who has 60 days to transfer the proceeds into another qualified employer retirement plan or an IRA. One can use an indirect rollover to borrow from an IRA, but the "loan" must be fully reinvested in another retirement plan or IRA within the 60-day window so that the amount will not be taxable. A benefit of the direct rollover is that it is not subject to the 20 percent withholding applicable to indirect rollovers.[20]

---

[16]§ 412.

[17]§ 402(a)(1).

[18]§ 501(a).

[19]§ 402(c).

[20]§ 3405(c).

19-1d **Limitations on Contributions to and Benefits from Qualified Plans**

LO.4

Calculate limitations on contributions to and benefits from qualified plans.

The annual limitations on contributions to and benefits from qualified plans appearing in § 415 must be written into a qualified plan. Section 404 sets the limits on deductibility applicable to the employer. These limits may have an impact on the amount the employer is willing to contribute. In fact, a defined benefit plan or defined contribution plan is not allowed a deduction for the amount that exceeds the § 415 limitations.[21]

Defined Contribution Plans

Under a *defined contribution plan*, the annual addition to an employee's account cannot exceed the smaller of $54,000 (in 2017) or 100 percent of the employee's compensation.[22] However, this individual percentage limitation of 100 percent normally is not attainable for small plans because the employer's deduction limit cannot exceed 25 percent of eligible compensation for all participants. The $54,000 amount is indexed (in $1,000 increments).[23]

Defined Benefit Plans

Under a *defined benefit plan*, the annual benefit payable to an employee is limited to the smaller of $215,000 (in 2017)[24] or 100 percent of the employee's average compensation for the highest three years of employment. This benefit limit is subject to a $10,000 *de minimis* floor. The $215,000 limitation is reduced actuarially if the benefits begin before the Social Security normal retirement age (currently age 65 and 10 months) and is increased actuarially if the benefits begin after the Social Security normal retirement age. The dollar limit on annual benefits ($215,000) is reduced by one-tenth for each year of *participation* under 10 years by the employee. Furthermore, the 100 percent of compensation limitation and the $10,000 *de minimis* floor are reduced proportionately for a participant who has less than 10 years of *service* with the employer.[25]

The Big Picture

EXAMPLE 8

Return to the facts of *The Big Picture* on p. 19-1. The university has offered Joyce's professor, Dr. Sanchez, a choice between a defined benefit pension plan and a defined contribution plan. Dr. Sanchez expects to work at a number of universities during her career. A colleague has recommended that Dr. Sanchez choose the defined contribution plan because of its mobility (i.e., she can take the plan with her). So she needs to decide if this mobility factor is significant in making her choice and how much she can contribute annually to a defined contribution plan.

Defined Benefit Limitations

EXAMPLE 9

Adam's average compensation for the highest three years of employment is $87,000. The defined benefit plan would not qualify if the plan provides for benefits in excess of the smaller of (1) $87,000 or (2) $215,000 for Adam in 2017 (assuming normal retirement age).

EXAMPLE 10

Peggy has participated for four years in a defined benefit plan and has six years of service with her employer. Her average compensation for the three highest years is $60,000. Her four years of participation reduce her dollar limitation to $86,000 ($215,000 × 4/10). Her six years of service reduce her 100% of compensation limitation to 60%. Therefore, her limit on annual benefits is $36,000 ($60,000 × 60%).

---

[21]§ 404(j).

[22]§§ 415(c) and (d).

[23]§ 415(d)(4).

[24]This amount is indexed annually in $5,000 increments.

[25]§ 415(b).

When calculating the average of the three highest years of compensation, the amount of compensation that may be taken into account under any plan is limited to $270,000 (in 2017).[26] Thus, the benefits that highly compensated individuals receive may be smaller as a percentage of their pay than those received by non-highly compensated employees.

Swan Corporation has a defined contribution plan with a 10% contribution formula. An employee earning less than $270,000 in 2017 would not be affected by this includible compensation limitation. However, an employee earning $540,000 in 2017 would have only 5% of compensation allocated to his or her account because of the $270,000 limit on includible compensation (5% × $540,000 = $27,000).

The maximum deduction an employer is permitted for contributions to pension plans may be determined by either of two methods. First, an aggregate cost method allows an actuarially determined deduction based on a level amount, or a level percentage, of compensation over the remaining future service of covered participants. Second, the employer is permitted to deduct the so-called normal cost plus no more than 10 percent of the past service costs. The *normal cost* represents the estimated contribution required associated with work performed by employees in the current year. *Past service costs* are costs that relate to the inception of the plan and costs that result from changes in the retirement plan.

While its contributions are deductible in the tax year such amounts are allocated or credited to the pension trust, the employer may defer the actual payment of the contributions until its Federal income tax return filing date, including extensions.[27] In effect, the employer is allowed a deduction to the extent it is compelled to make such contributions to satisfy the funding requirement. If an amount in excess of the allowable amount is contributed in any tax year, the excess may be carried forward indefinitely and deducted in succeeding tax years (to the extent the carryover plus the succeeding year's contribution does not exceed the deductible limitation for that year).[28]

Limitations on Qualified Plans

During 2017, Green Corporation contributes $18,000 to its qualified pension plan. Normal cost for this year is $7,200, and the amount necessary to pay retirement benefits on behalf of employee services before 2017 is $82,000 (past service costs). The corporation's maximum deduction is $15,400. This amount consists of the $7,200 normal cost plus 10% ($8,200) of the past service costs. The corporation has a $2,100 [$17,500 (contribution) − $15,400 (deduction)] contribution carryover.

Assume in the previous example that Green Corporation has normal cost of $7,200 in 2018 and contributes $10,000 to the pension trust. The corporation's maximum deduction would be $15,400. Green Corporation may deduct $12,100, composed of this year's contribution ($10,000) plus the $2,100 contribution carryover.

A 10 percent excise tax is imposed on nondeductible contributions. The tax is levied on the employer making the contribution. The tax applies to nondeductible contributions for the current year and any nondeductible contributions for the preceding year that have not been eliminated by the end of the current year (as a carryover or by being returned to the employer in the current year).[29]

---

[26]§§ 401(a)(17) and 404(l). This amount is indexed in $5,000 increments.
[27]§§ 404(a)(1) and (6).

[28]§ 404(a)(1)(D).
[29]§ 4972.

Profit Sharing and Stock Bonus Plan Limitations

Limits on the amounts an employer may deduct in a tax year for contributions to a profit sharing or stock bonus plan may create a temporary nondeductible excess, which may be carried forward indefinitely and deducted in subsequent years. The maximum deduction in any succeeding year is 25 percent of all compensation paid or accrued in the aggregate during that taxable year.[30]

19-1e Section 401(k) Plans

A § 401(k) plan allows participants to elect either to receive up to $18,000 (in 2017)[31] in cash (taxed currently) or to have a contribution made on their behalf to a profit sharing or stock bonus plan. The plan may also be in the form of a salary-reduction agreement under which a contribution will be made only if the participant elects to reduce his or her compensation or to forgo an increase in compensation.

Any employee-elected plan contributions are pretax amounts that are excluded from gross income in the year of the deferral and are 100 percent vested. Like employer plan contributions, employee contributions are tax-deferred until distributed, as are earnings on those contributions.

EXAMPLE

14

Sam participates in a § 401(k) plan of his employer. The plan permits the participants to choose between a full salary or a reduced salary where the reduction becomes a before-tax contribution to a retirement plan. Sam elects to contribute 10% of his annual compensation of $40,000 to the plan. Income taxes are paid on only $36,000. No income taxes are paid on the $4,000—or on any earnings—until it is distributed from the plan to Sam. The main benefit of a § 401(k) plan is that Sam can shift a portion of his income to a later taxable year.

The maximum annual elective contribution to a § 401(k) plan is reduced dollar for dollar by other salary-reduction contributions to tax-sheltered annuities, simplified employee pension plans, and § 401(k) plans. Annual elective contributions are also limited by complicated nondiscrimination requirements designed to encourage participation by non-highly compensated employees and by the general defined contribution plan limitations.

A person who has attained age 50 by the end of 2017 can make catch-up contributions of $6,000.[32]

The Big Picture

EXAMPLE

15

Return to the facts of *The Big Picture* on p. 19-1. Although Dr. Sanchez is not eligible to participate in a § 401(k) plan, she does participate in a § 403(b) tax-deferred annuity plan for employees of § 501(c)(3) not-for-profit organizations [similar in many respects to a § 401(k) plan]. Dr. Sanchez indicates that because she is age 51, she is eligible to make catch-up contributions to her § 403(b) annuity.

Elective contributions in excess of the maximum limitation are taxable in the year of deferral. These amounts may be refunded from the plan tax-free before April 15 of the following year. Excess amounts not timely distributed will be double-taxed because they will be taxable in the year of distribution, even though they were included in income in the year of deferral. A 10 percent excise tax is imposed on the employer for excess elective deferral contributions not withdrawn from the plan within $2\frac{1}{2}$ months after the close of the plan year. The plan may lose its qualified status if these excess contributions (and any related income) are not withdrawn by the end of the plan year following the plan year in which the excess contributions were made.[33]

---

[30]§§ 404(a)(3)(A) and (a)(7).

[31]§§ 402(g)(1) and (4).

[32]The $5,000 amount is indexed in $500 increments in 2007 and thereafter. For 2007 and 2008, the amount remained at $5,000. For 2009–2014, the catch-up amount was $5,500, and for 2015 and 2016, the amount was $6,000.

[33]§ 4979(a).

EXAMPLE 16

Carmen, age 36, is an employee of a manufacturing corporation. She defers $20,000 in a § 401(k) plan in 2017. The $2,000 excess over the $18,000 limit, along with the appropriate earnings, must be returned to Carmen by April 17, 2018. This $2,000 excess amount plus related income is taxable to her in 2017 and will be taxed again upon distribution (if made after April 17, 2018). There will be a 10% tax on Carmen's employer on any excess contributions not returned within $2\frac{1}{2}$ months after the close of the plan year.

A qualified automatic enrollment arrangement (QAEA) allows companies to automatically enroll employees in a § 401(k) plan with a prescribed percentage (not to exceed 10 percent) of the employee's pay automatically withdrawn from each paycheck (unless the employee elects otherwise). This stated percentage must be applied uniformly to all eligible employees.

If certain requirements are met, the plan administrator may choose the investments for the participants and be protected from liability involving investment choices. A § 401(k) plan consisting solely of contributions made under a QAEA also is exempt from the top-heavy rules.[34] Small employers may establish a combined defined benefit/§ 401(k) plan (a DB/K plan); the § 401(k) component of the DB/K plan must have automatic enrollment, with an employee being treated as having elected to make deferrals of 3 percent of pay, and must provide a minimum match of 50 percent of elective deferrals up to 3 percent of pay.[35]

SIMPLE Plans

Employers with 100 or fewer employees who do not maintain another qualified retirement plan may establish a *savings incentive match plan for employees* (SIMPLE plan).[36] The plan can be in the form of a § 401(k) plan or an IRA. A SIMPLE § 401(k) plan is not subject to the nondiscrimination rules that are normally applicable to § 401(k) plans.

All employees who received at least $5,000 in compensation from the employer during any two preceding years and who reasonably expect to receive at least $5,000 in compensation during the current year must be eligible to participate in the plan. The decision to participate is up to the employee. A self-employed individual also may participate in the plan.

The contributions made by the employee (a salary-reduction approach) must be expressed as a percentage of compensation rather than as a fixed dollar amount. The SIMPLE plan must not permit the SIMPLE elective employee contribution for the year to exceed $12,500 (in 2017).[37] The SIMPLE elective deferral limit is increased under the catch-up provision for employees age 50 and over. The amount is $3,000 (in 2017) and is indexed annually for inflation in $500 increments.

Generally, the employer must either match elective employee contributions up to 3 percent of the employee's compensation or provide nonmatching contributions of 2 percent of compensation for each eligible employee. Thus, the maximum amount that may be contributed to the plan for an employee under age 50 for 2017 is $20,600 [$12,500 employee contributions + $8,100 ($270,000 compensation ceiling × 3%) employer match].

No other contributions may be made to the plan other than the employee elective contribution and the required employer matching contribution (or nonmatching contribution under the 2 percent rule). All contributions are fully vested. An employer is required to make the required matching or nonmatching contributions to a SIMPLE § 401(k) plan once it is established, whereas an employer's contributions to a traditional § 401(k) plan generally may be discretionary.

An employer's deduction for contributions to a SIMPLE § 401(k) plan is limited to the greater of 25 percent of the compensation paid or accrued or the amount the employer is required to contribute to the plan. Thus, an employer may deduct contributions to a SIMPLE § 401(k) plan in excess of 25 percent of the $270,000 salary cap. A traditional

---

[34]§§ 401(a)(3)(G), 401(k)(8)(E), 401(k)(13), 401(m)(6)(A), 401(m)(12), and 414(w).

[35]§ 414(x) and ERISA § 210(e).

[36]§ 408(p).

[37]§ 408(p)(2)(E)(i).

§ 401(k) plan is limited to 25 percent of the total compensation of plan participants for the year (excluding age 50 catch-ups).

An employer is allowed a deduction for matching contributions only if the contributions are made by the due date (including extensions) for the employer's tax return. Contributions to a SIMPLE plan are excludible from the employee's gross income, and the SIMPLE plan is tax-exempt.

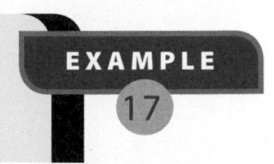

The Mauve Company has a SIMPLE plan for its employees under which it provides nonmatching contributions of 2% of compensation for each eligible employee. The maximum amount that can be added to each participant's account in 2017 is $17,900, composed of the $12,500 employee salary reduction plus an employer contribution of $5,400 ($270,000 × 2%).

Distributions from a SIMPLE plan are taxed under the IRA rules. Tax-free rollovers can be made from one SIMPLE account to another. A SIMPLE account can be rolled over to an IRA tax-free after the expiration of a two-year period since the individual first participated in the plan. Rollovers of distributions from employer-sponsored retirement plans and traditional IRAs (that are not SIMPLE IRAs) may be rolled over into a SIMPLE IRA after the expiration of the two-year period. Withdrawals of contributions during the two-year period beginning on the date an employee first participates in the SIMPLE plan are subject to a 25 percent early withdrawal tax rather than the 10 percent early withdrawal tax that otherwise would apply.

Designated Roth Contributions

Section 401(k) plans and § 403(b) plans may be amended to permit employees to irrevocably designate some or all of their future salary deferral contributions as Roth § 401(k) or Roth § 403(b) contributions.[38] These designated amounts are currently includible in the employee's gross income and are maintained in a separate plan account. The earnings on these elective contributions build up in the plan on a tax-free basis. Future qualified distributions made from designated contributions are excludible from gross income. The adjusted gross income (AGI) limitation (discussed later in the chapter) does not apply to these designated contributions, so a Roth § 401(k) should be attractive to highly paid officers and employees.

Roth § 401(k)s must comply with the nondiscrimination requirements. The contributions are treated like regular § 401(k) contributions for other purposes and may not exceed the annual limitation ($18,000 in 2017) without regard to any catch-up contributions. A person should be able to roll a designated Roth contributions (DRCs) account into another designated Roth account or into a Roth IRA (explained later in the chapter) to preserve the tax-free nature of the account after age 70½ and to avoid the minimum distribution requirements. A "qualified distribution" from a designated Roth account is a distribution that is made after the person has participated for five years and that occurs on or after the date the person attains age 59½, dies, or becomes disabled. If a distribution is not a qualified distribution, such a distribution is taxable to the participant (or a beneficiary) to the extent it consists of earnings (in a pro rata manner).

A designated Roth account has $18,800 of DRCs and $1,200 of earnings (total balance of $20,000). If a qualified distribution of $10,000 is made to the participant, the entire amount is excluded from gross income. However, if the distribution is not a qualified distribution, $9,400 is a return of capital (excluded from gross income), but a pro rata amount of $600 is included in gross income [($10,000 ÷ $20,000) × $1,200].

---

[38]§ 402A.

LO.5

State and explain the qualified plan (Keogh plan) available to a self-employed person.

19-2 RETIREMENT PLANS FOR SELF-EMPLOYED INDIVIDUALS AND THEIR EMPLOYEES

Self-employed individuals (e.g., partners and sole proprietors) and their employees are eligible to receive qualified retirement benefits under the SIMPLE plans described previously or under what are known as H.R. 10 (Keogh) plans . Because of contribution limitations and other restrictions, self-employed plans previously were less attractive than corporate plans. Contributions and benefits of a self-employed person now are subject to the general corporate provisions, putting self-employed persons on a parity with corporate employees. Consequently, Keogh plans can provide a self-employed person with an adequate retirement base.

A variety of funding vehicles can be used for Keogh investments, such as mutual funds, annuities, real estate shares, certificates of deposit, debt instruments, commodities, securities, and personal properties. Investment in most collectibles is not allowed in a self-directed plan. When an individual decides to make all investment decisions, a self-directed retirement plan is established. However, the individual may prefer to invest the funds with a financial institution such as a broker, a bank, or a savings and loan institution.

19-2a Coverage Requirements

Generally, the corporate coverage rules apply to Keogh plans. Thus, the ratio percentage and average benefits tests previously discussed also apply to self-employed plans.[39] An individual covered under a qualified corporate plan as an employee may also establish a Keogh plan for earnings from self-employment.

19-2b Contribution Limitations

A self-employed individual may annually contribute the smaller of $54,000 (in 2017) or 100 percent of earned income to a *defined contribution* Keogh plan.[40] However, if the defined contribution plan is a profit sharing plan or stock bonus plan, a 25 percent deduction limit applies. Under a *defined benefit* Keogh plan, the annual benefit payable to an employee is limited to the smaller of $215,000 (in 2017) or 100 percent of the employee's average compensation for the three highest years of employment.[41] An employee includes a self-employed person.

A defined *benefit* Keogh plan requires an actuary to calculate the amount to contribute each year. Thus, the annual actuarial fees and the required IRS reports can be expensive.

The Big Picture

EXAMPLE 19

Return to the facts of *The Big Picture* on p. 19-1. Joyce's professor, Dr. Sanchez, has a forensic consulting practice in addition to her position at the university. Also, she receives book royalties from a textbook. Therefore, because she is self-employed (she will report her earnings on a Schedule C), she is able to establish a Keogh plan.

Earned income refers to net earnings from self-employment as defined in § 1402(a).[42] Net earnings from self-employment means the gross income derived by an individual from any trade or business carried on by that individual, less appropriate deductions, plus the distributive share of income or loss from a partnership.[43] Earned income is reduced by contributions to a Keogh plan on the individual's behalf and by 50 percent of any self-employment tax.[44]

EXAMPLE 20

Pat, a partner, has earned income of $150,000 in 2017 (after the deduction for one-half of self-employment tax). The maximum contribution Pat may make to a defined contribution Keogh plan is $54,000, the lesser of $150,000 or $54,000.

---

[39]§ 401(d).
[40]§ 415(c)(1).
[41]§ 415(b)(1). This amount is indexed annually.

[42]§ 401(c)(2).
[43]§ 1402(a).
[44]§§ 401(c)(2)(A)(v) and 164(f).

For discrimination purposes, the 25 percent limitation on the employee contribution to a profit sharing plan or stock bonus plan is computed on the first $270,000 (in 2017) of earned income. Thus, the maximum contribution in 2017 is $54,000 ($270,000 − .25X = X; X = $216,000). Therefore, $270,000 − $216,000 = $54,000. Alternatively, this can be calculated by multiplying $270,000 by 20 percent.

Terry, a self-employed accountant, has a profit sharing plan with a contribution rate of 15% of compensation. Terry's earned income after the deduction of one-half of self-employment tax, but before the Keogh contribution, is $270,000. Terry's contribution is limited to $35,217 ($270,000 − .15X = X), because X = $234,783 and .15 × $234,783 = $35,217.

Although a Keogh plan must be established before the end of the year in question, contributions may be made up to the normal filing date for that year.

19-3 INDIVIDUAL RETIREMENT ACCOUNTS (IRAS)

LO.6

Describe benefits of the different types of Individual Retirement Accounts (IRAs).

Individual Retirement Accounts, or IRAs, are a fairly well-known type of retirement plan. They can be simple to create and maintain. There are several tax rules to be aware of that govern deductible contributions, taxable distributions, age requirements, and possible penalties for early withdrawals or excess contributions. Several of these rules are covered in this section.

19-3a **General Rules**

An individual can contribute to a traditional Individual Retirement Account (IRA), assuming that the person (or spouse) has earned income and is under 70½. These contributions may be deductible, depending upon income level and access to another work-related retirement plan. For 2017, the contribution ceiling is the smaller of $5,500 (or $11,000 for spousal IRAs) or 100 percent of compensation.[45] The contribution ceiling applies to all types of IRAs (traditional deductible, traditional nondeductible, and Roth). An individual who attains the age of 50 by the end of the tax year can make additional catch-up IRA contributions of up to $1,000 in 2017. The maximum contribution limit is increased by $1,000 each year.

The amount accumulated in an IRA can be substantial. For example, if a husband and wife each contribute only $4,000 annually to an IRA from age 25 to age 65 (and earn 6 percent annually), their account balances together would be approximately $1.4 million at retirement. If the taxpayer is an *active participant* in a qualified plan, the traditional IRA deduction limitation is phased out *proportionately* between certain AGI ranges, as shown in Exhibit 19.3.[46] If AGI is above the phaseout range, no IRA deduction is allowed.

AGI is calculated taking into account any § 469 passive activity losses and § 86 taxable Social Security benefits and ignoring any § 911 foreign income exclusion, § 135 savings bonds interest exclusion, and the IRA deduction. There is a $200 floor on the IRA deduction limitation for individuals whose AGI is not above the phaseout range.

EXHIBIT 19.3	Phaseout of IRA Deduction of an Active Participant in 2017	
AGI Filing Status	**Phaseout Begins***	**Phaseout Ends**
Single and head of household	$62,000	$ 72,000
Married, filing joint return	99,000	119,000
Married, filing separate return	–0–	10,000

*These amounts are indexed annually for inflation.

---

[45]§§ 219(b)(1) and (c)(2). The limit is adjusted annually for inflation in $500 increments.

[46]§ 219(g).

An individual is not considered an active participant in a qualified plan merely because the individual's spouse is an active participant in such a plan for any part of a plan year. Thus, even when filing jointly, the nonparticipating individual may take a full $5,500 deduction regardless of the participation status of his or her spouse, unless the couple has AGI above $186,000. If their AGI is above $186,000, the phaseout of the deduction begins at $186,000 and ends at $196,000 (phaseout over the $10,000 range) rather than beginning and ending at the phaseout amounts in Exhibit 19.3.[47]

To the extent an individual is ineligible to make a deductible contribution to an IRA, *nondeductible contributions* can be made to separate accounts.[48] The nondeductible contributions are subject to the same dollar limits as deductible contributions ($5,500 of earned income, $11,000 for a spousal IRA). Income in the account accumulates tax-free until distributed. Only the account earnings are taxed upon distribution because the account basis equals the contributions made by the taxpayer. A taxpayer may elect to treat deductible IRA contributions as nondeductible. If an individual has no taxable income for the year after taking into account other deductions, the election will be beneficial. The election is made on the individual's tax return for the taxable year to which the designation relates. A taxpayer may be entitled to a nonrefundable credit for contributions to an IRA or elective deferrals for a § 401(k) plan (see Chapter 13).

For distributions made after 2005, an exclusion is available for traditional IRA distributions made to charity if the owner is age 70½ or older.[49] The amount of the distribution that is eligible for this beneficial exclusion treatment is limited to $100,000 each year. These distributions are referred to as qualified charitable distributions. The rules for charitable contributions, including documentation, must be followed (see Chapter 10).

EXAMPLE 22

Amber has a traditional deductible IRA, so her basis is $0 (see the later discussion under Taxation of Benefits). Therefore, in 2017, she can have an IRA distribution of $100,000 made to a charity and exclude the $100,000 from her gross income. Assume instead that Amber has a traditional nondeductible IRA with a basis of $75,000. If she has a $100,000 IRA distribution made to a charity, she can exclude $25,000 ($100,000 − $75,000) from her gross income.

Roth IRAs

A **Roth IRA** is a *nondeductible* alternative to the traditional deductible IRA to encourage individual savings. Earnings inside a Roth IRA are not taxable, and all qualified distributions from a Roth IRA are tax-free.[50] The maximum allowable annual contribution to a Roth IRA for 2017 is the smaller of $5,500 ($11,000 for spousal IRAs) or 100 percent of the individual's compensation for the year. Contributions to a Roth IRA must be made by the due date (excluding extensions) of the taxpayer's tax return. Roth IRAs are not subject to the minimum distribution rules that apply to traditional IRAs. Contributions to a Roth IRA (unlike a traditional IRA) may continue beyond age 70½ so long as the person generates compensation income and is not barred by the AGI limits.

A taxpayer can make tax-free withdrawals from a Roth IRA after an initial five-year holding period if any of the following requirements is satisfied:

- The distribution is made on or after the date on which the participant attains age 59½.

- The distribution is made to a beneficiary (or the participant's estate) on or after the participant's death.

- The participant becomes disabled.

- The distribution is used to pay for qualified first-time homebuyer's expenses (statutory ceiling of $10,000).

---

[47]§ 219(g)(7). However, a special rule in § 219(g)(4) allows a married person filing a separate return to avoid the phaseout rules even though the spouse is an active participant. The individual must live apart from the spouse at all times during the taxable year and must not be an active participant in another qualified plan.

[48]§ 408(o).

[49]§ 408(d)(8); Notice 2007–7, 2007–1 C.B. 395, § IX; and IRS Publication 590–B.

[50]§ 408A.

Edith establishes a Roth IRA at age 42 and contributes $5,000 per year for 20 years. The account is now worth $149,400, consisting of $100,000 of nondeductible contributions and $49,400 in accumulated earnings that have not been taxed. Edith may withdraw the $149,400 tax-free from the Roth IRA because she is over age 59½ and has met the five-year holding period requirement.

If the taxpayer receives a distribution from a Roth IRA and does not satisfy the aforementioned requirements, the distribution may be taxable. If the distribution represents a return of capital, it is not taxable. Conversely, if the distribution represents a payout of earnings, it is taxable. Under the ordering rules for Roth IRA distributions, distributions are treated as first made from contributions (return of capital).

Assume the same facts as in the previous example, except that Edith is only age 50 and receives a distribution of $55,000. Because her adjusted basis for the Roth IRA is $100,000 (contributions made), the distribution is tax-free and her adjusted basis is reduced to $45,000 ($100,000 − $55,000).

Roth IRAs are subject to income limits. In 2017, the maximum annual contribution of $5,500 is phased out beginning at AGI of $118,000 for single taxpayers and $186,000 for married couples who file a joint return. The phaseout range is $10,000 for married filing jointly and $15,000 for single taxpayers. For a married taxpayer filing separately, the phaseout begins with AGI of $0 and is phased out over a $10,000 range.[51]

Bev, who is single, would like to contribute $5,500 to her Roth IRA. However, her AGI is $128,000, so her contribution is limited to $1,833 ($5,500 − $3,667) calculated as follows:

$$\frac{\$10,000}{\$15,000} \times \$5,500 = \$3,667 \text{ reduction}$$

The Big Picture

Return to the facts of *The Big Picture* on p. 19-1. Joyce's professor, Dr. Sanchez, also contributes annually to a traditional IRA. She would prefer a Roth IRA, but her AGI exceeds the phaseout limit.

As with a traditional IRA, an exclusion from gross income is available for Roth IRA distributions made to charity.[52] This exclusion treatment is beneficial for Roth IRA distributions that otherwise are not eligible for Roth IRA exclusion treatment.

A new retirement savings account—myRA—is offered under a Roth IRA that is backed by the U.S. government. No fees are charged for the Roth-type account, and the myRA is portable, meaning it is not tied to a single employer. The contributions are not deductible, but principal and earnings come out tax-free. A person can have up to a maximum of $15,000 or a lower balance up to 30 years. When either of these limits are reached, the savings can be transferred or rolled over to a private-sector Roth IRA. Employers do not administer the accounts, contribute to them, or match employee contributions.

Simplified Employee Pension Plans

An employer may contribute to an IRA covering an employee an amount equal to the lesser of $54,000 (in 2017) or 25 percent of the employee's earned income. In such a plan, the employer must make contributions for *each* employee who has reached age 21, has performed service for the employer during the calendar year and at least three

---

[51]The income limits for Roth IRA contributions are indexed for tax years after 2006.

[52]§ 408(d)(8)(A).

of the five preceding calendar years, and has received at least $550 (in 2017) in compensation from the employer for the year.[53] Known as simplified employee pension (SEP) plans , these plans are subject to many of the same restrictions applicable to qualified plans (e.g., age and period-of-service requirements and nondiscrimination limitations). Concept Summary 19.2 compares a SEP with a Keogh plan.

Concept Summary 19.2

Keogh Plan and SEP Compared

	Keogh	SEP
Form	Trust.	IRA.
Establishment	By end of year.	By extension due date of employer.
Type of plan	Qualified.	Qualified.
Contributions to plan	By extension due date.	By extension due date of employer.
Vesting rules	Qualified plan rules.	100% immediately.
Participants' rules	Flexible.	Stricter.
Lump-sum distributions and averaging	Yes, favorable 10-year forward averaging.	No, ordinary income.
Deduction limitation	Varies.*	Smaller of $54,000 (in 2017) or 25% of earned income.**
Self as trustee	Yes.	No.

*For a defined contribution pension plan, the limit is the smaller of $54,000 (in 2017) or 100% of self-employment income (after one-half of self-employment tax is deducted). A defined contribution profit sharing plan has a 25% deduction limit. A defined benefit Keogh plan's limit is the smaller of $215,000 (in 2017) or 100% of the employee's average compensation for the highest three years of employment.

**Only $270,000 of income can be taken into consideration.

EXAMPLE 27

In 2017, Ryan's compensation before his employer's contribution to a SEP is $30,000. Ryan's employer may contribute and deduct up to $7,500 ($30,000 × 25%) for 2017.

The amounts contributed to a SEP by an employer on behalf of an employee and the elective deferrals of an employee under a SEP are excludible from the employee's gross income. Elective deferrals under a SEP are subject to a statutory ceiling of $18,000 (in 2017),[54] which is increased under the catch-up provision for employees at least 50 years of age by the end of the tax year. Only $270,000 (in 2017) in compensation may be taken into account in making the SEP computation. An employer is permitted to elect to use its taxable year rather than the calendar year for purposes of determining contributions to a SEP.[55]

Simple IRA

A SIMPLE plan can be in the form of an IRA. See the earlier discussion under SIMPLE Plans.

Spousal IRA

For a married couple, each spouse may establish an IRA individually and deduct contributions of up to $5,500 if the combined compensation of both spouses is at least equal

---

[53]§§ 408(j) and (k)(2). This amount is indexed annually.

[54]Elective deferrals by an employee were repealed by the Small Business Job Protection Act of 1996 effective after December 31, 1996. However, if the employer plan was established before January 1, 1997, contributions can continue to be made under the pre-repeal provisions.

[55]§ 404(h)(1)(A). The $18,000 and $270,000 amounts are indexed annually. The elective deferral amount was increased in $1,000 annual increments until it reached $15,000 and then became subject to indexing.

to the total contributed amount. Thus, if only one spouse is employed or if both are employed but one has compensation of less than $5,500, each of them may contribute a maximum of $5,500 if their combined compensation is at least $11,000. For the spousal IRA provision to apply, a joint return must be filed.[56] The spousal IRA deduction is also proportionately reduced for active participants whose AGI exceeds the above target ranges.

Tony, who is married, is eligible to establish an IRA. He received $30,000 in compensation in 2017, and his spouse does not work outside the home. Tony can contribute up to $11,000 to two IRAs, to be divided in any manner between the two spouses, except that no more than $5,500 can be allocated to either spouse.

Assume the same facts as in the previous example, except that Tony's wife has compensation income of $2,200. Without the spousal IRA provision, Tony could contribute $5,500 to his IRA, and his spouse could contribute only $2,200 to her IRA. With the spousal IRA provision, they both can contribute $5,500 to their IRAs.

Alimony is considered to be earned income for purposes of IRA contributions. Thus, a person whose only income is alimony can contribute to an IRA.

Timing of Contributions

Contributions (both deductible and nondeductible) can be made to an IRA anytime before the due date of the individual's tax return.[57] For example, an individual can establish and contribute to an IRA through April 17, 2018 (the due date for 2017 individual returns because April 15, 2018, falls on a weekend and April 16 is a holiday in the District of Columbia), and deduct this amount on his or her tax return for 2017. IRA contributions that are made during a tax return extension period do not satisfy the requirement of being made by the return due date. An employer can make contributions up until the time of the due date for filing the return (including extensions) and treat those amounts as a deduction for the prior year.[58] As noted earlier, a similar rule applies to Keogh plans. However, the Keogh plan must be established before the end of the tax year. Contributions to the Keogh plan may then be made anytime before the due date of the individual's tax return.

19-3b **Penalty Taxes for Excess Contributions**

A cumulative, nondeductible 6 percent excise penalty tax is imposed on the smaller of (1) any excess contributions or (2) the market value of the plan assets determined as of the close of the tax year. *Excess contributions* are any contributions that exceed the maximum limitation and contributions that are made to a traditional IRA during or after the tax year in which the individual reaches age $70\frac{1}{2}$.[59] Contributions can be made to a Roth IRA during or after the tax year in which the individual reaches age $70\frac{1}{2}$. A taxpayer is not allowed a deduction for excess contributions. If the excess is corrected by contributing less than the deductible amount for a later year, a deduction then is allowable in the later year as a *makeup* deduction.

An excess contribution is taxable annually until returned to the taxpayer or reduced by the underutilization of the maximum contribution limitation in a subsequent year. The 6 percent penalty tax can be avoided if the excess amounts are returned.[60]

---

[56]§ 219(c).

[57]§ 219(f)(3).

[58]§ 404(h)(1)(B).

[59]§§ 4973(a)(1) and (b).

[60]§§ 408(d)(4) and 4973(b)(2).

Nancy, age 45, establishes a traditional IRA in 2017 and contributes $5,800 in cash to the plan. She has earned income of $22,000. Nancy is allowed a $5,500 deduction *for* AGI for 2017. Assuming that the market value of the plan assets is at least $300, there is a nondeductible 6% excise penalty tax of $18 ($300 × 6%). The $300 may be subject to an additional penalty tax in future years if it is not returned to Nancy or reduced by underutilization of the $5,500 maximum contribution limitation (ignoring any catch-up contributions).

19-3c **Taxation of Benefits**

A participant has a zero basis in the *deductible* contributions of a traditional IRA because the contributions were deducted.[61] Therefore, all withdrawals from a deductible IRA are taxed as ordinary income in the year of receipt. They are not eligible for the 10-year averaging allowed for certain lump-sum distributions.

A participant has a basis equal to the contributions made for a *nondeductible* traditional IRA, and only the earnings component of withdrawals is included in gross income. Such amounts are taxed as ordinary income in the year of receipt and are not eligible for the 10-year averaging allowed for certain lump-sum distributions.

In addition to being included in gross income, payments from IRAs made to a participant before age 59½ are subject to a nondeductible 10 percent penalty tax on such actual, or constructive, payments.[62] However, an individual may make penalty-free withdrawals to pay for medical expenses in excess of 10 percent of AGI, to pay for qualified higher education expenses, and to pay for qualified first-time homebuyer expenses (up to $10,000). Note that a qualified first-time homebuyer is defined as an individual (and spouse) who has not owned a principal residence in the two-year period preceding the date of acquisition of a principal residence. Further, an individual who has received unemployment compensation for at least 12 consecutive weeks may use IRA withdrawals to pay for health insurance for himself or herself, the spouse, and dependents without incurring the 10 percent penalty tax.[63]

All traditional IRAs of an individual are treated as one contract, and all distributions during a taxable year are treated as one distribution. If an individual who previously made both deductible and nondeductible IRA contributions makes a withdrawal from a traditional IRA during a taxable year, the excludible amount must be calculated. The amount excludible from gross income for the taxable year is calculated by multiplying the amount withdrawn by a percentage. The percentage is calculated by dividing the individual's aggregate nondeductible IRA contributions by the aggregate balance of all of his or her traditional IRAs (including rollover IRAs and SEPs).[64]

Carl, age 59, has a $12,000 deductible traditional IRA and a $2,000 nondeductible traditional IRA (without any earnings). Carl withdraws $1,000 from the nondeductible IRA. The excludible portion is $143 [($2,000/$14,000) × $1,000], and the includible portion is $857 [($12,000/$14,000) × $1,000]. Carl must also pay a 10% penalty tax on the prorated portion considered withdrawn from the deductible IRA and earnings in either type of IRA. Thus, the 10% penalty tax is $85.70 (10% × $857).

Rollovers: General Provisions

An IRA may be the recipient of a rollover from another qualified plan, including another IRA. Such a distribution from a qualified plan is not included in gross income if it is transferred within 60 days of receipt to an IRA or another qualified plan. For a series of distributions that constitute a lump-sum distribution, the 60-day period does not begin until the last distribution. Amounts received from IRAs may be rolled over tax-free only once in a 12-month period. Starting in 2015, taxpayers are only allowed one traditional IRA rollover per 12-month period regardless of how many IRAs they have. A person can

---

[61] § 408(d)(1).

[62] § 72(t). There are limited exceptions to the penalty on early distributions.

[63] §§ 72(t)(2)(B), (D), (E), and (F). For purposes of the unemployment provision, a self-employed individual who otherwise would have been eligible for unemployment compensation will qualify.

[64] § 408(d)(2).

still make unlimited direct trustee-to-trustee rollovers. Rollovers from traditional to Roth IRAs (so-called conversions) are not limited.[65]

EXAMPLE 32

Frank has both traditional IRAs and Roth IRAs. A rollover between his traditional IRA to a Roth IRA (a conversion) is not subject to the one-per-year rule. However, a rollover between his Roth IRAs will preclude a separate rollover within the one-year period between his traditional IRAs (including SEP and SIMPLE IRAs) and vice versa. The aggregation rule (which takes into account all distributions and rollovers among Frank's individual IRAs) applies to distributions from different IRAs if each of the distributions occurs after 2014.

A tax-free rollover for distributions from qualified plans is an alternative to the taxable 10-year forward averaging technique. Any rollover amount in a traditional IRA may later be rolled over into another qualified plan if the IRA consists of only the amounts from the original plan and the receiving plan permits it. The amount of nondeductible employee contributions included in a distribution may not be rolled over, but that amount is tax-free because the contributions were made with after-tax dollars. Partial rollovers are allowed, but the maximum amount that may be rolled over may not exceed the portion of the distribution that is otherwise includible in gross income. Rollovers are not available for required distributions under the minimum distribution rules once age $70\frac{1}{2}$ is reached.

The Big Picture

EXAMPLE 33

Return to the facts of *The Big Picture* on p. 19-1. Dr. Sanchez withdraws $15,000 from her traditional IRA on May 2, 2017, but she redeposits it in the same IRA on June 28, 2017. Although the withdrawal and redeposit was a partial rollover and Dr. Sanchez may have used the funds for a limited time, this process is a tax-free rollover.[66]

A rollover is different from a direct transfer of funds from a qualified plan to an IRA or another qualified plan by a trustee or an issuer. A direct transfer is not subject to the one-year waiting period and the withholding rules.[67]

Concept Summary 19.3 compares the two types of IRAs and a Roth IRA.

Concept Summary 19.3

Comparison of IRAs

	Traditional		Roth IRA
	Deductible IRA	**Nondeductible IRA**	**Roth IRA**
Maximum contribution (per year)	$5,500*	$5,500*	$5,500*
Tax-deductible contribution	Yes	No	No
Tax-free growth of income	Yes	Yes	Yes
Beginning of AGI phaseout for active participant (2017)	$62,000 single, $99,000 joint	N/A	$118,000 single, $186,000 joint
Income tax on distributions	Yes, for entire distribution	Yes, for the earnings portion	No, if satisfy 5-year holding period**
50% excise tax: age $70\frac{1}{2}$ insufficient distributions	Yes	Yes	No
10% early withdrawal penalty (before age $59\frac{1}{2}$)	Yes, with exceptions†	Yes, with exceptions†	Yes, with exceptions†

*The total of deductible, nondeductible, and Roth IRA contributions may not exceed $5,500 per year.

**In addition, the distribution must satisfy one of the following: made after age $59\frac{1}{2}$, used for qualified first-time homebuyer expenses, made to participant who is disabled, or made to a beneficiary on or after the participant's death.

†Qualified education and first-time homebuyer costs (up to $10,000) avoid the 10% penalty. See § 72(t)(2).

---

[65]Alvan L. Bobrow, *et ux*, 107 TCM 110, T.C.Memo. 2014–21; Announcement 2014–15 and 2014–16 I.R.B. 973; Announcement 2014–32, 2014–48 I.R.B. 907.

[66]Ltr.Rul. 9010007.

[67]Reg. § 35.3405–1.

An employer must withhold 20 percent of any lump-sum distributions unless the transfer is a direct transfer to an IRA or another qualified plan.[68]

EXAMPLE 34

Kay receives a distribution from a qualified retirement plan. The amount of the distribution would have been $20,000, but Kay receives only $16,000 ($20,000 − $4,000) as a result of the 20% withholding provision. After several weeks, Kay decides to contribute $20,000 (the gross amount of the distribution) to her traditional IRA. Because she received only $16,000, she will need to contribute $4,000 from another source to make a $20,000 contribution. When she files her tax return for the year, Kay will be able to claim a refund for the $4,000 that was withheld.

Distributions from a traditional IRA are generally not eligible for 10-year averaging or capital gain treatment. An exception applies in the case of a *conduit IRA*, where the sole assets of a qualified plan are rolled over into an IRA and the assets are then rolled into a qualified plan. With a conduit IRA, the lump-sum distribution from the original plan is still eligible for the special tax treatments.

Rollovers and Conversions: Roth IRAs

A Roth IRA may be rolled over tax-free into another Roth IRA. A traditional IRA may be rolled over or converted to a Roth IRA. A conversion occurs when the taxpayer notifies the IRA trustee that the IRA is now a Roth IRA.

Unlike a traditional IRA, which requires withdrawals at age $70\frac{1}{2}$, there are no required withdrawals from a Roth IRA. Thus, money can be accumulated over the taxpayer's lifetime and then passed to heirs without tax penalties.[69]

When a traditional IRA is rolled over or converted to a Roth IRA, the tax consequences depend on whether the traditional IRA was deductible or nondeductible. If deductible, the basis for the IRA is zero. Thus, the entire amount of the rollover or conversion is included in gross income. If nondeductible, the basis for the IRA is equal to the sum of the contributions. Thus, only the IRA earnings included in the rollover or conversion are included in gross income. The 10 percent penalty tax will not apply in either case.[70] Distributions from qualified retirement plans, § 403(b) annuities, and governmental § 457 plans also can be rolled over into a Roth IRA.[71]

Whether to convert a traditional IRA to a Roth IRA is a tax planning consideration. It can be considered for purposes of planning for current-year tax consequences, retirement planning, estate planning, and general asset planning. When a traditional IRA is converted, the increase in gross income (and modified AGI) may cause the individual to be subject to the additional Medicare tax and the Net Investment Income Tax (NIIT), which must be considered in overall tax planning.

LO.7

Review the rationale for nonqualified deferred compensation plans and the related tax treatment.

19-4 NONQUALIFIED DEFERRED COMPENSATION PLANS

It should come as no surprise that if there are "qualified" plans, there are also "nonqualified" plans. Special rules relevant to employers and employees for these types of arrangements are discussed in this section.

19-4a Underlying Rationale for Tax Treatment

Nonqualified deferred compensation (NQDC) plans provide a flexible way for taxpayers, particularly those in the 35 percent tax bracket (39.6 percent for certain high-income taxpayers), to defer income taxes on income payments until a potentially lower tax bracket year. When the deferred compensation is credited with annual earnings until payment, the entire deferred compensation, not just the after-tax amount, is generating investment income. Also, most NQDC plans do not have to meet the discrimination, funding, coverage, and other requirements of qualified plans. In addition to these advantages for the

---

[68]§ 3405(c).

[69]Additional details on traditional and Roth IRAs can be found in IRS Publication 590, *Individual Retirement Accounts (IRAs)*.

[70]§ 408A(d)(3)(A)(ii).

[71]§ 402(c)(8)(B).

employee, the employer may not have a current cash outflow. The IRS will issue rulings on deferred compensation plans.

19-4b Tax Treatment to the Employer and Employee

Special rules apply to nonqualified arrangements that defer the receipt of compensation income to a year later than that in which it is earned. During a taxable year in which an NQDC plan does not meet certain conditions in § 409A or is not operating in accordance with these conditions, all amounts deferred under the arrangement will be included in the participant's gross income to the extent they are not subject to a substantial risk of forfeiture. In addition, a 20 percent penalty tax is imposed on such income along with interest at the underpayment rate plus 1 percent.[72]

A three-pronged analysis determines whether a plan to defer compensation faces these punitive actions. First, does the deferred compensation fall within the NQDC provisions under § 409A? Second, are the benefits subject to a substantial risk of forfeiture (SRF)? SRF is discussed later in this chapter under Restricted Property Plans, but the definition of SRF for NQDCs differs from the normal definition. For example, a covenant not to compete can never be an SRF under § 409A, nor will conditions under the discretionary control of the employee be an SRF under § 409A. Also, an elective extension of a forfeiture period is generally disregarded as an SRF unless there are substantial additional considerations for such an extension. Third, at the time the arrangement is not covered by an SRF, has the plan suffered a "plan failure"?

Compensation arrangements that do not fall within § 409A include a qualified employer plan, any bona fide vacation leave, sick leave, educational benefits, legal settlements, indemnification arrangements, compensatory time, disability pay, and a death benefit plan.[73] Excluded qualified employer plans include tax-qualified pension, profit sharing, or § 401(k) plans; a § 403(b) tax-deferred annuity; a simplified employee pension plan; or an eligible § 457(b) plan for state, government, or tax-exempt employees.

In general, a § 409A deferral occurs where an employee has a legally binding right to compensation that has been deferred to the future. The section casts a wide net and may even cover nonqualified stock options and stock appreciation rights (SARs). These rules do not cover restricted property under § 83, as well as nondiscounted stock options, nondiscounted SARs, and statutory stock options. Discounted stock options, discounted SARs, phantom stock, and restricted stock units are covered.

Generally, funded NQDC plans must be forfeitable to keep the compensation payments from being taxable immediately. In most instances, employees prefer to have some assurance that they will ultimately receive benefits from the NQDC (that the plan provides for nonforfeitable benefits). In such instances, the plan will have to be unfunded to prevent immediate taxation to the employee. Most funded NQDC plans are subject to many of the provisions that apply to qualified plans, including the nondiscrimination requirements, and are impractical as a result.

To be effective, an unfunded deferred compensation plan must meet and comply with the following requirements under § 409A.[74]

- The NQDC plan may not distribute the deferred compensation to the employee except in these six situations: separation of service, disability, death, specified time or fixed schedule, change in employer control, or unforeseeable emergency.

- The plan must not permit any participant to accelerate the time or scheduled date of distributions (subject to some exceptions).

- A participant must elect to postpone the compensation for the current year no later than the close of the preceding tax year (initial deferral election).

- The employee must decide on the form and time of the benefits (e.g., installment payments or lump sum) when the deferral election is made if the plan permits an

---

[72]§ 409A(a)(1).

[73]§ 409A(d)(1).

[74]§ 409A(a)(2), (3), and (4).

election between alternatives, or the NQDC plan must specify the form and time of distribution when the deferral election is made.

- A participant must not change the time or form of benefits unless the employee does so at least 12 months before the scheduled distribution date and postpones the scheduled distribution date by at least five years.

- The plan should specify the amount payable (or the terms of the formula determining the amount), along with the payment schedule or triggering events that result in payment.

- Publicly held companies must provide for a six-month delay requirement for the top 50 officers with incomes of at least $130,000 (along with certain owner-employees).

Eagle Corporation and Bill, a cash basis employee, enter into an employment agreement that provides an annual salary of $120,000 to Bill. Of this amount, $100,000 is paid in current monthly installments, and $20,000 is to be paid in 10 annual installments beginning at Bill's retirement or death. Although Eagle Corporation maintains a separate account for Bill, that account is not funded. Bill is merely an unsecured creditor of the corporation. The $20,000 is not considered constructively received and is deferred. Compensation of $100,000 is currently taxable to Bill and deductible to Eagle. The other $20,000 will be taxable and deductible when paid in future years.

A deferred compensation arrangement occurs when an employee receives compensation after the 2½-month period following the end of an employer's corporate tax year in which such services were performed.[75] An employer's deduction of NQDC must be delayed to match the employee's recognition of income regardless of the employer's method of accounting.[76]

Beige, Inc., a calendar year employer, has an accrued NQDC liability of $300,000 on December 31, 2016. During 2017, the company accrues another $60,000 of NQDC. On February 13, 2018, the company pays the entire $360,000 to the employee. Because the $60,000 was paid within 2½ months after the end of 2017, only $300,000 ever met the requirement for deferred compensation. The entire $360,000 may be deducted by the company only in the year ending December 31, 2018, when the employee receives the cash and recognizes the income.

When to Use an NQDC Arrangement

As a general rule, NQDC plans are more appropriate for executives in financially secure companies. Because of the need for currently disposable income, such plans are usually not appropriate for young employees.

An NQDC plan can reduce an employee's overall tax payments by deferring the taxation of income to later years (possibly when the employee is in a lower tax bracket). In effect, these plans may produce a form of income averaging. Further, unfunded NQDC plans may discriminate in favor of shareholders, officers, specific highly compensated key employees, or a single individual.

Certain disadvantages should be noted, however. As mentioned earlier, nonqualified plans are usually required to be unfunded, which means that an employee has no assurance that funds ultimately will be available to pay the benefits. In other words, the deferred amounts are recorded as a liability on the company's books, and the employee will be an unsecured creditor in the event of the firm's bankruptcy.

Golden Parachute Arrangements

Golden parachute arrangements promise monetary benefits to key employees if they lose their jobs as a result of a change in ownership of the corporation. In essence, these are unfunded NQDC plans that do not vest until the change in ownership. These payments may

---

[75]Reg. § 1.409A–1(b)(4).   [76]§ 404(a)(5); Reg. § 1.404(a)–12(b)(1).

be unreasonable or not really for services rendered. The term golden parachute payments, as used in the Code, means *excess severance pay*.

These excessive severance payments to employees are penalized. The Code denies a deduction to an employer who makes a payment of cash or property to an employee or independent contractor that satisfies both of the following conditions:

- The payment is contingent on a change of ownership of a corporation through a stock or asset acquisition.

- The aggregate present value of the payment equals or exceeds three times the employee's (or independent contractor's) average annual compensation.[77]

The disallowed amount is the excess of the payment over a statutory base amount (a five-year average of taxable compensation if the taxpayer was an employee for the entire five-year period). Further, a 20 percent excise tax is imposed on the recipient upon the receipt of these parachute payments; the tax is withheld at the time of payment.[78]

EXAMPLE 37

Irene, an executive, receives a golden parachute payment of $380,000 from her employer. Her average annual compensation for the most recent five tax years is $120,000. The corporation will be denied a deduction for $260,000 ($380,000 payment − $120,000 base amount). Irene's excise tax is $52,000 ($260,000 × 20%).

Golden parachute payments do not include payments to or from qualified pension, profit sharing, stock bonus, annuity, or simplified employee pension plans. Also excluded is the amount of the payment that, in fact, represents reasonable compensation for personal services actually rendered or to be rendered. Such excluded payments are not taken into account when determining whether the threshold (the aggregate present value calculation) is exceeded.

S corporations are not subject to the golden parachute rules. Generally, corporations that do not have stock that is readily tradable on an established securities market or elsewhere are also exempt.

Publicly Held Companies' Compensation Limitation

For purposes of both the regular income tax and the alternative minimum tax, the deductible compensation for the top five executives of publicly traded companies is limited to $1 million for each executive. A company is publicly held if the corporation has common stock listed on a national securities exchange.[79] This $1 million deduction limitation is decreased by any nondeductible golden parachute payments made to the employee during the same year.

This deduction limitation applies when the compensation deduction would otherwise be taken. For example, in the case of a nonqualified stock option (NQSO), which is discussed later in this chapter, the deduction is normally taken in the year the NQSO is exercised, even though the option was granted with respect to services performed in a prior year.

Certain types of compensation are *not* subject to this deduction limit and are not taken into account in determining whether other compensation exceeds $1 million:

- Compensation payable on a commission basis.

- Compensation payable solely on account of the attainment of one or more performance goals when certain requirements involving the approval of outside directors and shareholders are met.

- Payments to a tax-qualified retirement plan (including salary-reduction contributions).

- Amounts that are excludible from an executive's gross income (such as employer-provided health benefits and miscellaneous fringe benefits).

---

[77]§ 280G.
[78]§ 4999.

[79]§ 162(m).

ETHICS & EQUITY   **The "Jock Tax" Is Spreading**

The so-called "jock tax" was first levied against athletes by cities or states when the athletes earned money in those jurisdictions. With better data-mining tools, more states are going after other mobile workers. For example, Senator Al

Franken, actor and comedian, had speaking engagements in 19 states and apparently failed to pay the "jock tax" in all of the states. Discuss the fairness of tax policy that subjects athletes and others to taxation in various states.

The most important exception is performance-based compensation. Compensation qualifies for this exception only if the following conditions are satisfied:

- The compensation is paid solely on account of the attainment of one or more performance goals.
- The performance goals are established by a compensation committee consisting solely of two or more outside directors.
- The material terms under which the compensation is to be paid (including the performance goals) are disclosed to and approved by the shareholders in a separate vote prior to payment.
- Prior to payment, the compensation committee certifies that the performance goals and any other material terms were in fact satisfied.

Disallowance of the compensation deduction can occur even where the employee's contract contains performance-based criteria if the employee also can receive compensation for employment that is terminated without cause or for voluntary retirement.

Compensation (other than stock options or other stock appreciation rights) is not treated as paid solely on account of the attainment of one or more performance goals unless the compensation is paid to the particular executive under a preestablished objective performance formula or standard that precludes discretion. In essence, a third party with knowledge of the relevant performance results could calculate the amount to be paid to the particular executive. A performance goal is broadly defined and includes, for example, any objective performance standard that is applied to the individual executive, a business unit (e.g., a division or a line of business), or the corporation as a whole. Performance standards could include increases in stock price, market share, sales, or earnings per share.

As part of the Affordable Care Act provisions enacted in 2010, a new compensation limit at § 162(m)(5) started in 2013 for certain compensation payments in excess of $500,000 made by a covered health insurance provider.

19-5 **RESTRICTED PROPERTY PLANS**

LO.8

Explain the value of restricted property plans.

A restricted property plan is an arrangement whereby an employer transfers property (e.g., stock of the employer-corporation) to an employee or another provider of services at no cost or at a bargain price. The usual purpose of a restricted stock plan is to retain the services of key employees who might otherwise leave. The employer hopes that such compensation arrangements will encourage company growth and attainment of performance objectives. Section 83 was enacted in 1969 to provide rules for the taxation of incentive compensation arrangements, which previously were governed by judicial and administrative interpretations. Although the following discussion refers to an employee as the provider of the services, the services may be performed by an independent contractor.

As a general rule, if an employee performs services and receives property (e.g., stock), the fair market value of that property in excess of any amount paid by the employee is includible in his or her gross income. The time for inclusion is the earlier of (1) the time the property is no longer subject to a substantial risk of forfeiture or (2) the time the property is transferable by the employee. The fair market value of the property is determined without regard to any restriction, except a restriction that by its terms will never lapse.[80] Because the amount of the compensation is determined at the date the restrictions lapse or when the property is transferable, the opportunity to generate capital gain treatment on the property is denied during a period when the ordinary income element is being deferred.

EXAMPLE 38

On October 1, 2013, Blue Corporation sold 100 shares of its stock to Ahmad, an employee, for $10 per share. At the time of the sale, the fair market value of the stock was $100 per share. Under the terms of the sale, each share of stock was nontransferable and subject to a substantial risk of forfeiture (which was not to lapse until October 1, 2017). Evidence of these restrictions was stamped on the face of the stock certificates. On October 1, 2017, the fair market value of the stock was $250 per share. Because the stock was nontransferable and was subject to a substantial risk of forfeiture, Ahmad did not include any compensation in gross income during 2013 (assuming that no special election was made). Instead, Ahmad was required to include $24,000 of compensation in gross income [100 shares × ($250 − $10 per share)] during 2017. If for some reason the forfeiture had occurred (e.g., the plan required Ahmad to surrender the stock to the corporation if he voluntarily terminated his employment with the company before October 1, 2017) and Ahmad never received the stock certificates, he would have been allowed a capital loss of $1,000 (the extent of his investment).

19-5a Substantial Risk of Forfeiture

A **substantial risk of forfeiture (SRF)** exists if a person's rights to full enjoyment of property are conditioned upon the future performance, or the refraining from the performance, of substantial services by that individual.[81] For example, if an employee must return the property (receiving only his or her original cost, if any) should there be a failure to complete a substantial period of service (for any reason), the property is subject to an SRF. Another such situation exists when an employer can compel an employee to return the property due to a breach of a substantial covenant not to compete. Any SRF should be stated on the face of the stock certificates. Assuming that an SRF does not exist, the property received is valued at its fair market value, ignoring any restrictions, except for one instance dealing with closely held stock.

19-5b Special Election Available

An employee may elect within 30 days after the receipt of restricted property to recognize immediately as ordinary income the fair market value in excess of the amount paid for the property. Any appreciation in the value of the property after receipt is classified as capital gain instead of ordinary income. No deduction is allowed to the employee for taxes paid on the original amount included in income if the property is subsequently forfeited.[82] The employee is permitted to take a capital loss for any amounts that were actually paid for the property. Furthermore, in such a case, the employer must repay taxes saved by any compensation deduction taken in the earlier year.[83]

Any increase in value between the time the property is received and the time it becomes either nonforfeitable or transferable is taxed as ordinary income if the employee does not make this special election. However, if the employee elects to be taxed immediately on the difference between the cost and fair market value on the date of issue, any future appreciation is treated as capital gain. In determining whether the gain is long-term or short-term, the holding period starts when the employee is taxed on the ordinary income.[84]

---

[80] § 83(a)(1); *Miriam Sakol*, 67 T.C. 986 (1977); *T. M. Horwith*, 71 T.C. 932 (1979).

[81] § 83(c). Regulation § 1.83–3(c)(2) includes several examples of restricted property arrangements.

[82] § 83(b).

[83] Reg. §§ 1.83–6(c) and 2(a).

[84] § 1223(6).

Restricted Stock Special Election

EXAMPLE 39

On July 1, 2007, Sparrow Company sold 100 shares of its preferred stock, worth $15 per share, to Diane (an employee) for $5 per share. The sale was subject to Diane's agreement to resell the preferred shares to the company for $5 per share if she terminated her employment during the following 10 years. The stock had a value of $25 per share on July 1, 2017, and Diane sold the stock for $30 per share on October 10, 2017. Diane made the special election to include the original spread (between the value of $15 in 2007 and the amount paid of $5) in income for 2007. Diane was required to recognize $1,000 of compensation income in 2007 ($15 − $5 = $10 × 100 shares), at which time her holding period in her stock began. Diane's tax basis in the stock was $1,500 ($1,000 + $500). When the preferred stock was sold in 2017, Diane recognized a $1,500 long-term capital gain ($30 × 100 shares − $1,500).

EXAMPLE 40

Assume the same facts as in the previous example, except that Diane sells the stock in 2018 (rather than 2017). She would not recognize any gain in 2017 when the SRF lapses. Instead, Diane would recognize the $1,500 long-term capital gain in 2018.

This "gambler's choice" special provision is usually not elected because it results in an immediate recognition of income and adverse tax consequences result from a subsequent forfeiture. However, the special election may be attractive in the following situations:

- The bargain element is relatively small.
- Substantial appreciation is expected in the future.
- A high probability exists that the restrictions will be met.

19-5c Employer Deductions

At the time the employee is required to include the compensation in income, the employer is allowed a tax deduction for the same amount. The employer must withhold on this amount in accordance with § 3402. In the no-election situation, the deduction is limited to the fair market value of the restricted property (without regard to the restrictions) at the time the restrictions lapse, reduced by the amount originally paid for the property by the employee.[85] When the employee elects to be taxed immediately, the corporate deduction also is accelerated and deductible in like amount. In cases of deferred income recognition, the employer can receive a sizable deduction if the property has appreciated.

Employer Deduction

EXAMPLE 41

On March 14, 2015, Gold Corporation sold to Harry, an employee, 10 shares of Gold common stock for $100 per share. Both the corporation and Harry were calendar year taxpayers. The common stock was subject to an SRF and was nontransferable; both conditions were to lapse on March 14, 2017. At the time of the sale, the fair market value of the common stock (without considering the restrictions) was $1,000 per share. On March 14, 2017, when the fair market value of the stock is $2,000 per share, the restrictions lapse. Harry did not make the special election. In 2017, Harry realizes ordinary income of $19,000 (10 shares at $2,000 per share less the $100 per share he had paid). Likewise, Gold Corporation is allowed a $19,000 compensation deduction in 2017.

EXAMPLE 42

In the previous example, assume that Harry made the special election. Because he was taxed on $9,000 in 2015, the corporation was allowed to deduct a like amount in 2015. No deduction would be available in 2017.

---

[85]Reg. § 1.83–6(a).

19-6 STOCK OPTIONS

LO.9

Differentiate the tax treatment of qualified and nonqualified stock options.

Various equity types of stock option programs are available for an employee's compensation package. Some authorities believe that some form of *equity kicker* is needed to attract new management, convert key officers into *partners* by giving them a share of the business, and retain the services of executives who might otherwise leave. Encouraging the managers of a business to have a proprietary interest in its successful operation should provide executives with a key motive to expand the company and improve its profits. In addition, under certain conditions, stock options may fall outside the $1 million limitation on the salaries of the top five executives of publicly traded companies. Sometimes an executive's stock option income may far exceed cash salaries and bonuses.

A stock option gives an individual the right to purchase a stated number of shares of stock from a corporation at a certain price within a specified period of time. The optionee must be under no obligation to purchase the stock, and the option may be revocable by the corporation. The option must be in writing, and its terms must be clearly expressed.[86]

19-6a Incentive Stock Options

An equity type of stock option called an *incentive stock option (ISO)* is available. An incentive stock option (ISO) is an option to purchase stock of a corporation granted to an individual for any reason connected with his or her employment that meets specific qualification requirements.[87] The option is granted by the employer-corporation or by a parent or subsidiary corporation of the employer-corporation.

There are no tax consequences for either the issuing corporation or the recipient when the option is granted. However, the *spread* (the excess of the fair market value of the share at the date of exercise over the option price)[88] is a positive tax preference item to the recipient for purposes of the alternative minimum tax. The determination of fair market value is made without regard to any lapse restrictions (restrictions that will expire after a period of time). After the option is exercised and when the stock is sold, any gain from the sale is taxed as a long-term capital gain if certain holding period requirements are met. For a gain to qualify as a long-term capital gain, the employee must not dispose of the stock within two years after the option is granted or within one year after the stock is acquired.[89] If the employee meets the holding period requirements, none of these transactions generate any business deduction for the employer.[90] If the employee pays anything for the option and does not exercise the option, any amount paid is recognized as a capital loss.

The Big Picture

EXAMPLE

43

Return to the facts of *The Big Picture* on p. 19-1. Dr. Sanchez is on the board of directors of a medium-sized company, Wren Corporation. Wren Corporation granted an ISO for 100 shares of its stock to Dr. Sanchez on March 18, 2016, for service rendered. The option price was $100 and the fair market value was $100 on the date of the grant. Dr. Sanchez exercised the option on April 1, 2016, when the fair market value of the stock was $200 per share. She sells the stock on April 6, 2017, for $300 per share. Dr. Sanchez did not recognize any ordinary income on the date of the grant or the exercise date because the option qualified as an ISO. Wren received no compensation deduction. Dr. Sanchez has a $10,000 tax preference item on the exercise date. She has a long-term capital gain of $20,000 [($300 − $100) × 100] on the sale of the stock in 2017, because the one-year holding period and other requirements have been met.

---

[86]Reg. §§ 1.421–1(a)(1) and −7(a)(1).

[87]§ 422(b).

[88]§§ 422(a), 421(a)(1), 57(a)(3), and 1234(a)(1) and (2).

[89]§ 422(a)(1).

[90]§ 421(a)(2).

As a further requirement for ISO treatment, the option holder must be an employee of the issuing corporation from the date the option is granted until 3 months (12 months if disabled) before the date of exercise. The holding period and the employee-status rules just described (the one-year, two-year, and three-month requirements) are waived in the case of the death of an employee.[91]

The Big Picture

EXAMPLE 44

Return to the facts in Example 43, except that Dr. Sanchez was not a service provider (or employee) of Wren Corporation for six months before the date she exercised the options. Dr. Sanchez must recognize $10,000 [($200 − $100) × 100] of ordinary income on the exercise date, to the extent of the spread, because she was not an employee of Wren Corporation at all times during the period beginning on the grant date and ending three months before the exercise date. Wren is allowed a deduction at the same time Dr. Sanchez reports the ordinary income.

If the holding period requirements are not satisfied but all other conditions are met, the tax is still deferred to the point of the sale. However, the difference between the option price and the value of the stock at the date the option was exercised is treated as ordinary income. The difference between the amount realized for the stock and the value of the stock at the date of exercise is short-term or long-term capital gain, depending on the holding period of the stock itself. The employer is allowed a deduction equal to the amount recognized by the employee as ordinary income. The employee does not have a tax preference for alternative minimum tax purposes.

The Big Picture

EXAMPLE 45

Assume the same facts as in Example 43, except that Dr. Sanchez sells the stock on March 22, 2017, for $290 per share. Because Dr. Sanchez did not hold the stock for more than one year, $10,000 of the gain is treated as ordinary income in 2017 and Wren Corporation is allowed a $10,000 compensation deduction in 2017. The remaining $9,000 is short-term capital gain ($29,000 − $20,000).

Qualification Requirements for Incentive Stock Option Plans

An ISO plan may permit an employee to use company stock to pay for the exercise of the option without disqualifying the ISO plan.

For an option to qualify as an ISO, the terms of the option must identify it as an ISO and meet the following conditions:

- The option must be granted under a plan specifying the number of shares of stock to be issued and the employees or class of employees eligible to receive the options. The plan must be approved by the shareholders of the corporation within 12 months before or after the plan is adopted.

- The option must be granted within 10 years of the date the plan is adopted or of the date the plan is approved by the shareholders, whichever date is earlier.

- The option must by its terms be exercisable only within 10 years of the date it is granted.

- The option price must equal or exceed the fair market value of the stock at the time the option is granted. This requirement is deemed satisfied if there has been a good-faith attempt to value the stock accurately, even if the option price is less than the stock value.

---

[91]§§ 422(a)(2) and (c)(3). Exceptions are made for parent and subsidiary situations, corporate reorganizations, and liquidations. Also, in certain situations involving an insolvent employee, the holding period rules are modified.

The crash of the financial sector of the U.S. economy shed light on the high levels of bonuses, commissions, health care coverage, and other compensation devices that some firms use to attract and retain managerial talent. Payments to qualified retirement plans are limited in amount and timing, but other "IOUs" are made available to managers, typically as unfunded but enforceable promises to make large payments or stock transfers, for example, after the executive retires or works for the firm for a certain number of years. These arrangements embarrassed some of the employers who provided them while receiving bailouts from the Federal government, but the high levels of executive pay and deferred compensation live on today.

Bonus and retirement arrangements like these create a book-tax difference, as they represent compensation expenses for GAAP purposes, but no tax deduction is allowed until the compensation is paid or becomes fully funded and vested, for example, through a trust or an escrow account. Some firms do fund the deferred payments—no book-tax difference or deferred tax asset

amount would result in that case. Usually, the employer also includes in this book-tax difference the amount by which current compensation paid to employees exceeds the tax law maximum deduction amount of § 162(m).

Some financial statements revealed the following amounts in the deferred tax asset accounts of the employer, using "deferred compensation" or "employee benefits and pay" as the line item in the tax footnote.

Employer	Deferred Tax Asset for Executive Compensation ($000)
Goldman Sachs	11,800
JPMorgan Chase	8,200
Citigroup	5,000
Bank of America	1,300
Cisco	1,200
Eli Lilly	1,150

- The option by its terms must be nontransferable other than at death and must be exercisable during the employee's lifetime only by the employee.

- The employee must not, immediately before the option is granted, own stock representing more than 10 percent of the voting power or value of all classes of stock in the employer-corporation or its parent or subsidiary. (Here, the attribution rules of § 267 are applied in modified form.) However, the stock ownership limitation will be waived if the option price is at least 110 percent of the fair market value (at the time the option is granted) of the stock subject to the option and the option by its terms is not exercisable more than five years from the date it is granted.[92]

An overall limitation is imposed on the amount of ISOs that can be first exercisable in one year by an employee. This limit is set at $100,000 per year based on the value of the stock determined at the time the option is granted. For example, an ISO plan may permit acquisition of up to $600,000 worth of stock if it provides that the options are exercisable in six installments, each of which becomes exercisable in a different year and does not exceed $100,000.

Because of these regulatory conditions and the fact that a company may never receive a tax deduction, employers may view ISOs less favorably than nonqualified stock options.

19-6b Nonqualified Stock Options

A **nonqualified stock option (NQSO)** does not satisfy the statutory requirements for ISOs. In addition, a stock option that otherwise would qualify as an ISO will be treated as an NQSO if the terms of the stock option provide that it is not an ISO. If the NQSO has a readily ascertainable fair market value (e.g., the option is traded on an established exchange), the value of the option must be included in the employee's income at the date

---

[92]§ 422(c)(5).

of grant. Thereafter, capital gain or loss is recognized only upon the disposal of the optioned stock. The employee's basis is the amount paid for the stock plus any amount reported as ordinary income. The employer obtains a corresponding tax deduction at the same time and to the extent that ordinary income is recognized by the employee.[93]

If an NQSO does not have a readily ascertainable fair market value, an employee does not recognize income at the grant date. However, as a general rule, ordinary income must then be reported in the year of exercise (the difference between the fair market value of the stock at the exercise date and the option price).[94] The amount paid by the employee for the stock plus the amount reported as ordinary income becomes the basis. Any appreciation above that basis is taxed as a long-term capital gain upon disposition (assuming that the stock is held for the required long-term holding period after exercise). The corporation receives a corresponding tax deduction at the same time and to the extent that ordinary income is recognized by the employee.

EXAMPLE 46

On February 3, 2015, Maria was granted an NQSO for 100 shares of common stock at $10 per share. On the date of the grant, there was no readily ascertainable fair market value for the option. Maria exercised the options on January 3, 2016, when the stock was selling for $15 per share. She sold one-half of the shares on April 15, 2016, and the other half on September 17, 2017. The sale price on both dates was $21 per share. Maria would not recognize any income on the grant date (February 3, 2015) but would recognize $500 ($1,500 − $1,000) of ordinary income on the exercise date (January 3, 2016). She would recognize a short-term capital gain of $300 on the sale of the first half in 2016 and a $300 long-term capital gain on the sale of the second batch of stock in 2017 [1/2($2,100 − $1,500)].

The major *advantages* of NQSOs can be summarized as follows:

- A tax deduction is available to the corporation without a cash outlay.
- The employee receives capital gain treatment on any appreciation in the stock starting either at the exercise date if the option does not have a readily ascertainable fair market value or at the date of grant if the option has a readily ascertainable fair market value.
- Options can be issued at more flexible terms than under ISO plans (e.g., longer exercise period and granted to nonemployees).

A major *disadvantage* is that the employee must recognize ordinary income on the exercise of the option or at the date of grant without receiving cash to pay the tax. Another negative factor is that the exercise price for NQSOs must not be lower than the underlying stock's fair market value on the grant date because of § 409A restrictions.

19-7 TAX PLANNING

LO.10

Identify tax planning opportunities available with deferred compensation.

A number of tax planning ideas are helpful for employers and employees.

19-7a Deferred Compensation

With the individual tax rate being as high as 35 percent (39.6 percent for certain high-income taxpayers), taxpayers are motivated to try to lower their tax burden by participating in more deferred compensation arrangements. The $1 million annual limit on the compensation deduction for the top five executives of publicly traded companies may cause a shift into § 401(k) plans, qualified retirement plans, and especially nonqualified deferred compensation arrangements. However, only $270,000 of compensation can be taken into consideration for purposes of calculating contributions or benefits under a qualified pension or profit sharing plan. The $5,500 allowed for traditional IRAs and Roth IRAs should encourage more participation in retirement vehicles. The spousal IRA option should expand retirement coverage even further.

---

[93]Reg. §§ 1.421–6(c), (d), (e), and (f); Reg. § 1.83–7.   [94]Reg. § 1.83–7(a); Reg. § 1.421–6(d).

19-7b **Qualified Plans**

Qualified plans provide maximum tax benefits for employers, because the employer receives an immediate tax deduction for contributions to a plan's trust and the income that is earned on the contributions is not taxable to the employer. The employer's contributions and the trust earnings are not taxed to the employees until those funds are made available to them.

Qualified plans are most appropriate where it is desirable to provide benefits for a cross section of employees. In some closely held corporations, the primary objective is to provide benefits for the officer-shareholder group and other highly paid personnel. The nondiscrimination requirements that must be met in a qualified plan may prevent such companies from attaining these objectives. Thus, a nonqualified arrangement may be needed as a supplement to, or used in lieu of, the qualified plan.

Cash balance plans are better for younger, mobile employees, and the converting company saves money by reducing pension payouts for older and longer-service employees. If a participant moves or retires, he or she can roll over the lump-sum payment into an IRA or another qualified plan.

Although defined benefit plans are being eliminated by larger companies, many small-business owners with few or no employees (or a young, low-paid, transient staff) are adopting them.

19-7c **Self-Employed Retirement Plans**

A Keogh or traditional deductible IRA participant may make a deductible contribution for a tax year up to the time prescribed for filing the individual's tax return. A Keogh plan must have been established by the end of the tax year (e.g., December 31) to obtain a current deduction for the contribution made in the subsequent year. An individual can establish an IRA after the end of the tax year and still receive a current deduction for the contribution made in the subsequent year. However, because the deductibility of contributions to IRAs has been restricted for many middle-income and upper-income taxpayers, Keogh plans are likely to become more important.

19-7d **Individual Retirement Accounts**

Unlike a traditional IRA, which defers taxes on the entire account, a Roth IRA allows the earnings to accumulate completely tax-free. All ordinary income and capital gains earned inside a Roth IRA are never taxed (assuming that the five-year holding period provision is satisfied). Thus, a Roth IRA runs contrary to the general principle that it is usually better for a taxpayer to postpone the payment of any tax. In many situations, a retirement plan participant will earn more wealth with a Roth IRA than with a traditional IRA. This potential for tax-free growth is so advantageous that taxpayers who have substantial traditional IRA balances and are eligible should evaluate converting at least some of their traditional IRA balances into a Roth IRA. A taxpayer does have to be careful because there can be a "big hit" in the year of conversion. Thus, timing is important.

19-7e **Comparison of § 401(k) Plan with IRA**

Most employees will find a § 401(k) plan more attractive than an IRA. Probably the biggest limitation of an IRA is the $5,500 maximum shelter in 2017 (ignoring the catch-up provision). Under § 401(k), employees are permitted to shelter compensation up to $18,000 (in 2017). The restrictions on deducting contributions to IRAs for many middle-income and upper-income taxpayers may cause many employees to utilize § 401(k) plans more frequently.

Another difference between § 401(k) plans and IRAs is the manner in which the money is treated. Money placed in an IRA may be tax-deductible, whereas dollars placed in a § 401(k) plan are considered to be deferred compensation. Thus, a § 401(k) reduction may reduce profit sharing payments, group life insurance, and Social Security benefits. Finally, many employers "match or partially match" employee elective deferrals with employer money. Concept Summary 19.4 compares a § 401(k) plan with an IRA.

Concept Summary 19.4

Section 401(k) Plan and IRA Compared

	§ 401(k) Plan	IRA
Contribution limitation	Smaller of $18,000 (in 2017) or approximately 100% of total earnings. Limited by antidiscrimination requirements of § 401(k)(3).	$5,500 or 100% of compensation.
Distributions	Early withdrawal possible to take early retirement (55 or over) or to pay medical expenses.	10% penalty for early withdrawals, except for withdrawals to pay for certain medical expenses and health insurance, qualified education expenses, and qualified first-time homebuyer expenses.
Effect on gross earnings	Gross salary reduction, which may reduce profit sharing contributions, Social Security benefits, and group life insurance.	No effect.
Employer involvement	Must keep records; monitor for compliance with antidiscrimination test.	Minimal.
Lump-sum distributions	Favorable 10-year forward averaging under limited circumstances.	Ordinary income.
Timing of contribution	Within 30 days of plan year-end or due date of employer's return.*	Grace period up to due date of tax return (not including extensions).
Loans from plan	Yes.	No.

* Elective contributions must be made to the plan no later than 30 days after the end of the plan year and nonelective contributions no later than the due date of the tax return (including extensions).

19-7f Nonqualified Deferred Compensation (NQDC) Plans

Nonqualified deferred compensation arrangements, such as restricted property plans, can be useful to attract executive talent or to provide substantial retirement benefits for executives. A restricted property plan may be used to retain a key employee of a closely held company when management continuity problems are anticipated. Without such employees, the untimely death or disability of one of the owners might cause a disruption of the business with an attendant loss in value for his or her heirs. Such plans may discriminate in favor of officers and other highly paid employees. The employer, however, does not receive a tax deduction until the employee is required to include the deferred compensation in income (upon the lapse of the restrictions).

The principal advantage of NQDC plans over current compensation is that the employee can defer the recognition of income to future periods when his or her income tax bracket may be lower (e.g., during retirement years). The time value benefits from the deferral of income should also be considered. If the current tax rates continue, an executive with a deferred compensation arrangement entered into in a prior year might want to continue to delay the income into future years. However, if future rates are projected to rise, a different decision would be appropriate.

The principal disadvantage of NQDC plans could be the bunching effect that takes place on the expiration of the period of deferral. In some cases, planning can alleviate this result.

EXAMPLE 47

During 2017, Kelly, an executive, enters into an agreement to postpone a portion of her payment for current services until retirement. The deferred amount is not segregated from the company's general assets and is subject to normal business risk. The entire payment, not the after-tax amount, is invested in securities and variable annuity contracts. Kelly is not taxed on the payment in 2017, and the company receives no deduction in 2017. If Kelly receives the deferred payment in a lump sum when she retires, the tax rates might be higher and more progressive than in 2017. Thus, Kelly may want to arrange for a number of payments to be made to her or a designated beneficiary over a number of years.

19-7g **Stock Options**

Rather than paying compensation in the form of corporate stock, a corporation may issue options to purchase stock at a specific price to an employee. Stock option plans are used more frequently by publicly traded companies than by closely held companies. This difference is due to the problems of determining the value of the stock of a company that is not publicly held, which is a practical requirement now to avoid negative treatment under § 409A.

Nonqualified stock options (NQSOs) are more flexible and less restrictive than incentive stock options (ISOs). For example, the holding period for an NQSO is not as long as that for an ISO. However, the option price of an NQSO cannot be less than the fair market value of the stock at the time the option is granted because of § 409A. An NQSO creates an employer deduction that lowers the cost of the NQSO to the employer. The employer may pass along this tax savings to the employee in the form of a cash payment. Both the employer and the employee may be better off by combining NQSOs with additional cash payments rather than using ISOs. Most stock options are nonqualified stock options. See Concept Summary 19.5.

Concept Summary 19.5

Incentive Stock Options and Nonqualified Stock Options Compared

	ISO	NQSO
Granted at any price	No	Yes
May have any duration	No	Yes
Governing Code Section	§ 422	§ 83
Spread subject to alternative minimum tax	Yes	No
Deduction to employer for spread	No	Yes
Type of gain/loss on disposal	Capital	Capital
Statutory amount ($100,000) limitation	Yes	No

For tax purposes, most companies are able to deduct the expense of options and thereby reduce their taxes. Generally, options carry an exercise price (strike price) equal to the fair market value on the date the options are approved by the board of directors. The Financial Accounting Standards Board (FASB) now requires stock options to be expensed, which lowers a company's earnings. Companies must measure the economic value of the options on the grant date and then amortize this cost equally over the vesting period of the options. Also, § 409A effectively forces stock options to be granted with an exercise price equal to the stock's fair market value.

Stock options are an effective compensation device as long as share prices are rising. When stock prices fall, the options become unexercisable and possibly worthless. In an upmarket, options are great. But during a downturn in the market, these underwater options can be ugly.

Stock options are likely to be a less dominant form of executive compensation in the future. The backdating scandals and the required expensing of stock options for financial statement purposes are causing businesses to turn to other forms of compensation. Performance-based bonuses and § 401(k) plans probably will become more popular.

19-7h **Flexible Benefit Plans**

Employees may be permitted to choose from a package of employer-provided fringe benefits.[95] In these so-called cafeteria benefit plans, some of the benefits chosen by an employee may be taxable, and some may be statutory nontaxable benefits (e.g., health and accident insurance and group term life insurance).

---

[95]§ 125.

Under general tax rules, providing a choice to employees would result in all benefits (both taxable and nontaxable) under the cafeteria benefit plan to be taxable. However, if the cafeteria plan rules are met, a special provision applies to prevent this tax result from occurring.

Employer contributions made to a flexible plan are included in an employee's gross income only to the extent the employee actually elects the taxable benefits. Certain nondiscrimination standards with respect to coverage, eligibility for participation, contributions, and benefits must be met. Thus, such a plan must cover a fair cross section of employees. Also, a flexible plan cannot include an election to defer compensation, and a key employee is not exempt from taxation on the taxable benefits made available where more than 25 percent of the statutory nontaxable benefits are provided to key employees.

19-7i **Liquidating Retirement Assets**

If a person has funds from sources other than retirement assets, which retirement assets should an individual spend first? The most tax-efficient result is to postpone the income tax obligation for as long as possible. Generally, retirement assets should be taken from assets or accounts in the following order so that the tax-deferred growth continues:

1. Taxable accounts.
2. Section 457 accounts of government employees because no penalties apply once the employee is separated from employment.
3. Section 401(k) and nonprofit § 403(b) plans because the age 55 separation rule may apply.
4. Traditional IRAs because a taxpayer must be at least age 59½ to obtain penalty-free withdrawals.
5. Roth IRAs because no required minimum distribution rules apply.[96]

REFOCUS ON THE BIG PICTURE

A TAXPAYER WHO SAVES

From her discussion with Dr. Sanchez, Joyce learns that her professor has the following retirement plans:

- *Defined contribution plan.* The university offered its faculty members a choice between a defined benefit pension plan and a defined contribution plan. Dr. Sanchez expects to work at a number of universities during her career, so she chose the defined contribution plan because of its mobility (i.e., she can take the plan with her). The maximum annual contribution the university could make to the plan is $54,000 for 2017. Because the university contribution rate is 15 percent, the actual contribution is $22,500 ($150,000 × 15%).

- *§ 403 (b) annuity.* Dr. Sanchez makes contributions to a § 403(b) annuity [i.e., the equivalent of a § 401(k) plan, but available to educators]. The maximum annual contribution she can make in 2017 is $18,000, and Dr. Sanchez has the university deduct this total amount from her salary paychecks. In addition, because she is at least age 50 (i.e., she is age 51), she has the university deduct an additional $6,000 as a catch-up contribution.

continued

---

[96]David M. Maloney and James E. Smith, "Distribution Options for Defined Contribution Plans, Part II," *The Tax Adviser*, June 2007, pp. 340 and 341.

BILL ARON/PHOTOEDIT

- *Keogh (H.R. 10) plan.* In addition to her position at the university, Dr. Sanchez has a forensic consulting practice. Because she is self-employed, she is able to establish a Keogh defined contribution plan. She contributes 20 percent of her net earnings from the consulting practice, about $8,000 per year ($40,000 × 20%), to the plan.

- *IRA.* Dr. Sanchez also contributes annually to a traditional IRA. She would prefer a Roth IRA, but her AGI exceeds the $133,000 phaseout limit. Likewise, she cannot deduct her contribution of $5,500 (the maximum) because of the amount of her AGI. Because she cannot deduct her contributions, her basis in the IRA is the summation of her contributions. The $15,000 that Dr. Sanchez withdrew from her traditional IRA is not subject to current taxation and does not reduce her basis for the IRA. This result occurs because Dr. Sanchez successfully completed a tax-free rollover (i.e., recontributed the $15,000 to her IRA within 60 days).

Dr. Sanchez explains that she wants to travel after retirement, so her goal is to retire by age 62 while she is still in good health. She anticipates that these plans will enable her to do so.

Key Terms

Cafeteria benefit plans, 19-37	Individual Retirement Account (IRA), 19-17	Section 401(k) plan, 19-13
Cash balance plan, 19-5	Lump-sum distribution, 19-10	Simplified employee pension (SEP) plans, 19-20
Deferred compensation, 19-2	Nonqualified deferred compensation (NQDC), 19-24	
Defined benefit plan, 19-3		Stock bonus plan, 19-5
Defined contribution pension plan, 19-3	Nonqualified stock option (NQSO), 19-33	Stock option, 19-31
Golden parachute payments, 19-27	Pension plan, 19-3	Substantial risk of forfeiture (SRF), 19-29
H.R. 10 (Keogh) plans, 19-16	Profit sharing plan, 19-4	Vesting requirements, 19-7
Highly compensated employee, 19-7	Restricted property plan, 19-28	
Incentive stock option (ISO), 19-31	Roth IRA, 19-18	

Discussion Questions

1. **LO.1** Determine whether each of the following independent statements best applies to a defined contribution plan *(DCP)*, a defined benefit plan *(DBP)*, both *(B)*, or neither *(N)*:

   a. The amount to be received at retirement depends on actuarial calculations.

   b. Forfeitures can be allocated to the remaining participants' accounts.

   c. Requires greater reporting requirements and more actuarial and administrative costs.

   d. Forfeitures can revert to the employer.

   e. More favorable to employees who are older at the time the plan is adopted.

   f. Employee forfeitures can be used to reduce future contributions by the employer.

   g. May exclude employees who begin employment within five years of normal retirement age.

h. Annual addition to each employee's account may not exceed the smaller of 54,000 or 100% of the employee's salary.

i. The final benefit to a participant depends upon investment performance.

j. To avoid penalties, the amount of annual contributions must meet minimum funding requirements.

2. **LO.1** Indicate whether the following statements apply to a pension plan *(P)*, a profit sharing plan *(PS)*, both *(B)*, or neither *(N)*:

a. Forfeited amounts can be used to reduce future contributions by the employer.

b. Allocation of forfeitures may discriminate in favor of the prohibited group (highly compensated employees).

c. Forfeitures can revert to the employer.

d. Forfeitures can be allocated to participants and increase plan benefits.

e. An annual benefit of $60,000 could be payable on behalf of a participant.

f. More favorable to employees who are older at the time the qualified plan is adopted.

Issue ID   3. **LO.2, 3, 6** Penny plans to retire in 2017 at age 70. Identify any issues that Penny faces with respect to distributions from her qualified retirement plan.

Issue ID   4. **LO.3, 6** Harvey Pehrson, who is age 71, is going to receive a lump-sum distribution
Communications   from a qualified plan in 2017. He has asked you to provide him with a description of the alternatives available to him for taxing the lump-sum distribution. Draft a letter to Harvey in which you respond. He resides at 3000 East Glenn, Tulsa, OK 74104.

5. **LO.3** Which of the following would be considered a tax benefit or advantage of a qualified retirement plan?

a. Certain lump-sum distributions may be subject to capital gain treatment.

b. Employer contributions are deductible by the employer in the year of contribution.

c. Employee contributions are deductible by the employee in the year of contribution.

d. The qualified trust is tax-deferred as to all income (other than unrelated business income).

Decision Making   6. **LO.3, 6** Donna is retiring and wants you to explain her alternatives for receiving payments from her qualified retirement plan.

Decision Making   7. **LO.6, 10** Should a 31-year-old self-employed single woman establish a traditional deductible IRA, a traditional nondeductible IRA, or a Roth IRA? She has two children, ages 10 and 8.

8. **LO.6** Joey, who is single, is not covered by another qualified plan and earns $120,000 at his job in 2017. How much can he contribute to a traditional IRA or to a Roth IRA in 2017?

Communications   9. **LO.4** Scott Henry calls you and asks about a savings incentive match plan for employees (SIMPLE). Prepare a memo for the tax files about your response.

10. **LO.6** Suppose an individual is 55 years old. How much of an additional catch-up IRA contribution can the person make?

Issue ID   11. **LO.7, 10** During his senior year in college, Sandy is drafted by the Los Angeles Dodgers. When he graduates, he expects to sign a five-year contract in the range of $1.7 million per year. Sandy plans to marry his girlfriend before he reports to the Dodger farm team in California. Identify the relevant tax issues facing this left-handed pitcher.

12. **LO.7** What conditions cause the golden parachute arrangement to be penalized?

13. **LO.8** What is the spread with respect to an incentive stock option? How is it treated under the tax law?

Computational Exercises

14. **LO.2** Determine the percentage of vesting for the following employees. See Exhibits 19.1 and 19.2.

    a. Glenda has five years of service completed as of September 23, 2017, her employment anniversary date. If her *defined benefit plan* has a five-year cliff vesting schedule, what percent of Glenda's accrued benefits are vested? If the plan uses the graded vesting rule, what is Glenda's nonforfeitable percentage?

    b. Cybil has four years of service completed as of July 5, 2017, her employment anniversary date. If her *defined contribution plan* uses a two- to six-year vesting plan, what is her nonforfeitable percentage?

15. **LO.4** Sergio has participated for eight years in a defined benefit plan and has nine years of service with his employer. His average compensation for the three highest years is $160,000. What is Sergio's dollar limit on annual benefits?

16. **LO.4** During 2017, Learphart Corporation contributes $35,000 to its qualified pension plan. Normal cost for this year is $15,000, and the amount necessary to pay retirement benefits on behalf of employee services before 2017 is $110,000 (past service costs).

    a. What is the corporation's maximum deduction?

    b. What is the amount of the company's carryover contribution?

17. **LO.4** Joanna, age 44, defers $23,000 in a qualified § 401(k) plan in 2017.

    a. What amount must be returned to Joanna and by what date?

    b. In what year will the amount be taxed?

    c. What percent of the tax will be imposed on the employer if excess contributions are not returned by what date?

18. **LO.5** Zack, a sole proprietor, has earned income of $85,000 in 2017 (after the deduction for one-half of self-employment tax). What is the maximum contribution Zack may make to a *defined contribution* Keogh plan?

19. **LO.5** Jadeveon, a self-employed attorney, has a profit sharing plan with a contribution rate of 15% of compensation. Jadeveon's earned income after the deduction of one-half of self-employment tax, but before the Keogh contribution, is $304,750. What is the limit of Jadeveon's contribution?

20. **LO.6** Myers, who is single, has compensation income of $69,000 in 2017. He is an active participant in his employer's qualified retirement plan. Myers contributes $5,500 to a traditional IRA. Of the $5,500 contribution, how much can Myers deduct? See Exhibit 19.3, Phaseout of IRA Deduction of an Active Participant in 2017.

21. **LO.6** Meredith, who is single, would like to contribute $5,500 to her Roth IRA. However, her AGI is $119,000. What is the maximum amount that Meredith can contribute?

22. **LO.6** In 2017, Cao's compensation before his employer's contribution to a SEP is $66,000. Up to what amount can Cao's employer contribute and deduct in 2017?

23. **LO.7** Robin, an executive, receives a golden parachute payment of $600,000 from his employer. His average annual compensation for the most recent five tax years is $150,000.

    a. For what amount will the corporation be denied a deduction?

    b. What is Robin's excise tax?

24. **LO.8** On May 31, 2012, Andro Corporation sold 500 shares of its stock to Nombeko, an employee, for $100 per share. No special election is made. At the time of the sale, the fair market value of the stock was $200 per share. Under the terms of the sale, each share of stock was nontransferable and subject to a

substantial risk of forfeiture (which was not to lapse until May 31, 2017). Evidence of these restrictions was stamped on the face of the stock certificates. On May 31, 2017, the fair market value of the stock was $400 per share.

a. What amount is Nombeko required to include as income in 2017?

b. What compensation deduction is Andro Corporation allowed?

25. **LO.9** Zaire Corporation granted an ISO for 250 shares of its stock to Bruno on July 20, 2016, for service rendered. The option price was $130 and the fair market value was $130 on the date of the grant. Bruno exercised the option on September 1, 2016, when the fair market value of the stock was $225 per share. He sells the stock on November 30, 2017, for $350 per share.

a. What is the amount of the tax preference item that Bruno has on the exercise date?

b. What is Bruno's long-term capital gain on the sale of the stock in 2017?

26. **LO.9** On April 5, 2015, Gustavo was granted an NQSO for 200 shares of common stock at $50 per share. On the date of the grant, there was no readily ascertainable fair market value for the option. Gustavo exercised the options on March 31, 2016, when the stock was selling for $60 per share. He sold the shares on December 1, 2017, for $75 per share.

a. What amount and type of income, if any, will Gustavo have on the exercise date?

b. What amount and type of income, if any, will Gustavo have on the date of the sale?

Problems

27. **LO.2** Blonde Corporation has a calendar year retirement plan covering its participants. William, age 21, is hired on January 31, 2016, and he meets the service requirement over the next 12 months (completes at least 1,000 hours by January 31, 2017).

a. If the company adopts the most restrictive eligibility rules, William must be included in the plan by no later than what date?

b. If the company adopts the two-year participation rule, William must be included in the plan by no later than what date?

28. **LO.2** Ben is a 4% owner of a title company. In the following situations, is he a highly compensated employee? Why or why not?

a. Ben receives a total salary of $110,000 and is a member of the top-paid group in the company.

b. Ben receives a total salary of $192,000, and his salary is in the top 30% of the employees.

c. Ben receives a total salary of $113,500, which puts him in the top 15% of the employees.

d. Ben receives a salary of $153,000, which puts him in the 25%–30% range of employees.

29. **LO.2** Sparrow, Inc., uses a three- to seven-year graded vesting approach in its retirement plan. Calculate the nonforfeitable percentage for each of the following participants based upon the years of service completed:

Participant	Years of Service
Mary	2
Sam	4
Peter	6
Heather	7

30. **LO.2** Mauve, Inc., uses a two- to six-year graded vesting approach in its retirement plan. Calculate the nonforfeitable percentage for each of the following participants based upon the years of service completed:

Participant	Years of Service
Caleb	3
Daniel	4
Sloane	5
Ryan	7

31. **LO.1, 4** Concept, Inc., has a profit sharing plan with some participants earning $265,000 or more. The company can maximize its participants' annual additions by using what percentage of profit sharing contribution?

32. **LO.2** Sue has worked for Yellow Corporation for four and one-half years, but she has an offer to move to Red Corporation for a moderate increase in salary. Her average salary for Yellow has been $210,000, and she receives a 2% benefit for each year of service in her retirement plan. The company uses a five-year vesting schedule. Advise Sue as to this possible switch in jobs.

Decision Making

33. **LO.4** Heather has been an active participant in a defined benefit plan for 19 years. During her last 6 years of employment, Heather earned $42,000, $48,000, $56,000, $80,000, $89,000, and $108,000, respectively (representing her highest-income years).
    a. Calculate Heather's maximum allowable benefits from her qualified plan (assume that there are fewer than 100 participants).
    b. Assume that Heather's average compensation for her three highest years is $199,700. Calculate her maximum allowable benefits.

34. **LO.4** Determine the maximum annual benefits payable to a participant from a defined benefit plan in the following independent situations:
    a. Frank, age 66, has been a participant for 17 years, and his highest average compensation for 3 years is $127,300.
    b. Ellen, age 65, has been a participant for 9 years (11 years of service), and her highest average compensation for 3 years is $102,600.

35. **LO.4** In 2017, Magenta Corporation paid compensation of $45,300 to the participants in a profit sharing plan. During 2017, Magenta Corporation contributed $13,200 to the plan.
    a. Calculate Magenta's deductible amount for 2017.
    b. Calculate the amount of any contribution carryover from 2017.

36. **LO.4, 10** Amber's employer, Lavender, Inc., has a § 401(k) plan that permits salary deferral elections by its employees. Amber's salary is $99,000, her marginal tax rate is 25%, and she is 42 years old.

Decision Making

    a. What is the maximum amount Amber can elect for salary deferral treatment for 2017?
    b. If Amber elects salary deferral treatment for the amount in part (a), how much can she save in taxes?
    c. What amount would you recommend that Amber elect for salary deferral treatment for 2017?

37. **LO.4** Shyam is a participant in a SIMPLE § 401(k) plan. He elects to contribute 4% of his $40,000 compensation to the account, while his employer contributes 3%. What amount will not vest immediately, if any?

38. **LO.2, 4, 5, 6** In 2016, Susan's sole proprietorship earns $300,000 of self-employment net income (after the deduction for one-half of self-employment tax).
    a. Calculate the maximum amount that Susan can deduct for contributions to a defined contribution Keogh plan.

b. Suppose Susan contributes more than the allowable amount to the Keogh plan. What are the consequences to her?

c. Can Susan retire and begin receiving Keogh payments at age 58 without incurring a penalty? Explain.

39. **LO.4, 5** Harvey is a self-employed accountant with earned income from the business of $120,000 (after the deduction for one-half of his self-employment tax). He has a profit sharing plan (e.g., defined contribution Keogh plan). What is the maximum amount Harvey can contribute to his retirement plan in 2017?

40. **LO.4, 6** Janet, age 29, is unmarried and is an active participant in a qualified retirement plan. Her modified AGI is $64,000 in 2017.

a. Calculate the amount Janet can contribute to a traditional IRA and the amount she can deduct.

b. Assume instead that Janet is a participant in a SIMPLE IRA and that she elects to contribute 4% of her compensation to the account, while her employer contributes 3%. What amount will be contributed for 2017? What amount will be vested?

41. **LO.4, 6** Answer the following independent questions with respect to a deductible IRA and § 401(k) contributions for 2017:

a. Govind, age 31, earns a salary of $26,000 and is not an active participant in any other qualified plan. His wife has $600 of compensation income. What is the maximum total deductible contribution to their IRAs?

b. Danos is a participant in a SIMPLE § 401(k) plan. He contributes 6% of his salary of $42,000, and his employer contributes 3%. What amount will be contributed for the year? What amount will be vested?

42. **LO.6** Answer the following independent questions with respect to traditional IRA contributions for 2017:

a. Juan, age 41, earns a salary of $28,000 and is not an active participant in any other qualified plan. His wife, Agnes, has no earned income. What is the maximum total deductible contribution to their IRAs? Juan wants to contribute as much as possible to his own IRA.

b. Abby, age 29, has earned income of $25,000, and her husband, Sam, has earned income of $2,600. They are not active participants in any other qualified plan. What is the maximum contribution to their IRAs?

c. Leo's employer makes a contribution of $3,500 to Leo's simplified employee pension plan. If Leo is single, has earned income of $32,000, and has AGI of $29,000, what amount, if any, can he contribute to an IRA?

43. **LO.6** Jimmy establishes a Roth IRA at age 47 and contributes a total of $89,600 over 18 years. The account is now worth $112,000. How much of these funds may Jimmy withdraw tax-free?

44. **LO.6** Dana, age 54, has a traditional deductible IRA with an account balance of $107,600, of which $77,300 represents contributions and $30,300 represents earnings. In 2017, she converts her traditional IRA into a Roth IRA. What amount must Dana include in her gross income for 2017?

45. **LO.6** Carri and Dane, ages 34 and 32, respectively, have been married for 11 years, and both are active participants in employer qualified retirement plans. Their total AGI in 2017 is $189,000, and they earn salaries of $87,000 and $95,000, respectively. What amount may Carri and Dane:

a. Contribute to regular IRAs?

b. Deduct for their contributions in part (a)?

c. Contribute to Roth IRAs?

d. Deduct for their contributions in part (c)?

46. **LO.4, 6** Louis is a participant in a SIMPLE IRA of his employer Brown, Inc. During 2017, he contributes 8% of his salary of $63,000, and his employer contributes 3%. What is the total amount that will be vested in his account at the end of 2017?

47. **LO.6** Gene, age 34, and Beth, age 32, have been married for nine years. Gene, who is a college student, works part-time and earns $1,500. Beth is a high school teacher and earns a salary of $34,000. Their AGI is $37,000.

    a. What is the maximum amount Gene can contribute to an IRA in 2017?

    b. What is the maximum amount Beth can contribute to an IRA in 2017?

48. **LO.6** Samuel, age 32, loses his job in a corporate downsizing. As a result of his ter-   Decision Making
    mination, he receives a distribution of the balance in his § 401(k) account of $20,000 ($25,000 − $5,000 withholding) on May 1, 2017. Samuel's marginal tax rate is 28%.

    a. What effect will the distribution have on Samuel's gross income and tax liability if he invests the $20,000 received in a mutual fund?

    b. Same as part (a) except that Samuel invests the $20,000 received in a traditional IRA within 60 days of the distribution.

    c. Same as part (a) except that Samuel invests the $20,000 received in a Roth IRA within 60 days of the distribution.

    d. How could Samuel have received better tax consequences in part (b)?

49. **LO.7** Dan, a professional basketball player, is to receive a bonus of $2 million for signing an employment contract. An NQDC plan is established to postpone the income beyond Dan's peak income years. In 2017, his employer transfers the bonus to an escrow agent, who then invests the funds in mutual funds. The funds are subject to the claims of the employer's creditors. The bonus is deferred for 10 years and becomes payable gradually in years 11 through 15. When is the bonus taxable to Dan and deductible by the employer?

50. **LO.7** Grace is an officer of a local bank that merges with a national bank, resulting in a change of ownership. She loses her job as a result of the merger, but she receives a cash settlement of $590,000 from her employer under her golden parachute. Her average annual compensation for the past five tax years was $200,000.

    a. What are the tax consequences to Grace and the bank of the $590,000 payment?

    b. Assume instead that Grace's five-year average annual compensation was $110,000 and that she receives $390,000 in the settlement. What are the tax consequences to Grace and the bank?

51. **LO.8** On February 20, 2012, Tom (an executive of Hawk Corporation) purchased 100   Decision Making
    shares of Hawk stock (selling at $20 a share) for $10. A condition of the transaction was that Tom must resell the stock to Hawk at cost if he voluntarily leaves the company within five years of receiving the stock (assume that this represents a substantial risk of forfeiture).

    a. Assuming that no special election is made under § 83(b), what amount, if any, is taxable to Tom in 2012?

    b. Five years later when the stock is selling for $40 a share, Tom is still employed by Hawk. What amount of ordinary income, if any, is taxable to Tom?

    c. Five years later, what amount, if any, is deductible by Hawk as compensation expense?

    d. Should Tom make the § 83(b) special election in 2012? Why or why not? What amount would be taxable in 2012 if he made the special election?

    e. In part (d), what amount would be deductible by Hawk five years later?

    f. Under part (d), assume that Tom sold all of the stock six years later for $65 per share. How much capital gain is included in his gross income?

g.   In part (d), what loss is available to Tom if he voluntarily resigns in 2016 before the five-year period and does not sell the stock back to the corporation?

h.   In part (g), in the year Tom resigns, what amount, if any, would be taxable to Hawk Corporation?

52. **LO.8** On July 2, 2014, Black Corporation sold 1,000 of its common shares (worth $14 per share) to Earl, an employee, for $5 per share. The sale was subject to Earl's agreement to resell the shares to the corporation for $5 per share if his employment is terminated within the following four years. The shares had a value of $24 per share on July 2, 2018. Earl sells the shares for $31 per share on September 16, 2018. No special election under § 83(b) is made.

a.   What amount, if any, is taxed to Earl on July 2, 2014?

b.   On July 2, 2018?

c.   On September 16, 2018?

d.   What deduction, if any, will Black Corporation obtain? When?

e.   Assume the same facts, except that Earl makes an election under § 83(b). What amount, if any, will be taxed to Earl on July 2, 2014, July 2, 2018, and September 16, 2018?

f.   Will the assumption made in part (e) have any effect on any deduction Black Corporation receives? Explain.

53. **LO.9** Rosa exercises ISOs for 100 shares of Copper Corporation common stock at the option price of $100 per share on May 21, 2017, when the fair market value is $120 per share. She sells the 100 shares of common stock three and one-half years later for $140.

a.   Calculate the long-term capital gain and the ordinary income on the sale.

b.   Assume that Rosa holds the stock only seven months and sells the shares for $140 per share. Calculate the capital gain and ordinary income on the sale.

c.   In part (b), what amount can Copper Corporation deduct? When?

d.   Assume instead that Rosa holds the stock for two years and sells the shares for $115 per share. Calculate any capital gain and ordinary income on this transaction.

e.   In part (a), assume that the options are nonqualified stock options with a nonascertainable fair market value on the date of the grant. Calculate the long-term capital gain and ordinary income on the date of the sale.

f.   In part (e), assume that each option has an ascertainable fair market value of $10 on the date of the grant and that no substantial risk of forfeiture exists. Calculate the long-term capital gain and the ordinary income on the date of the sale.

54. **LO.9** On November 19, 2015, Rex is granted a nonqualified stock option to purchase 100 shares of Tan Company. On that date, the stock is selling for $8 per share, and the option price is $9 per share. Rex exercises the option on August 21, 2016, when the stock is selling for $10 per share. Five months later, Rex sells the shares for $11.50 per share.

a.   What amount is taxable to Rex in 2015?

b.   What amount is taxable to Rex in 2016?

c.   What amount and type of gain are taxable to Rex in 2017?

d.   What amount, if any, is deductible by Tan Company in 2016?

e.   What amount, if any, is recognized in 2016 if the stock is sold for $9.50 per share?

Decision Making
Communications

55. **LO.4, 5, 6, 10** Sara Reid, age 35, is the owner of a small business. She is trying to decide whether to go with a § 401(k) plan or a simplified employee pension plan. She is not interested in a SIMPLE § 401(k) plan. Her salary will be approximately $45,000, and she will have no employees. She asks you to provide her with information on the advantages and disadvantages of both types of plans

and to give your recommendation. Draft a letter to Sara that contains your response. Her address is 1414 Canal Street, New Orleans, LA 70148.

56. **LO.10** Lou's employer provides a qualified cafeteria plan under which he can choose cash of $9,000 or health and accident insurance premiums worth approximately $7,000. Assuming that Lou is in the 35% tax bracket, advise him of his tax alternatives.

Decision Making

57. **LO.10** Zariat has the retirement assets listed below. She plans to retire and start withdrawing amounts on which to live. Rank the accounts in the order from which she should make withdrawals so that tax deferral is maximized.

Roth IRA	$923,408
Traditional IRA	118,120
§ 401(k) plan	837,010
§ 457 account	334,090

Research Problems

Note: Solutions to the Research Problems can be prepared by using the Thomson Reuters Checkpoint® Student Edition online tax research database, which accompanies this textbook. Solutions can also be prepared by using research materials found in a typical tax library.

THOMSON REUTERS
CHECKPOINT®
Student Edition

Research Problem 1. Your client, Casey Farber, is the CEO of a publicly traded corporation. This year, her compensation consisted of $600,000 in cash and $600,000 of stock. The stock received was part of a restricted stock grant. Casey was granted the restricted stock in 2013, when the stock's fair market value was $300,000. Casey did not make a Section 83(b) election. The restrictions on the stock lifted in the current year. The $600,000 was the stock's fair market value on the date the restrictions lifted, and Casey still owns the stock.

With respect to the compensation received by Casey this year, what will be the corporation's compensation expense deduction?

Partial list of research aids:
Regulation § 1.162–27.
Rev.Rul. 2012–19, 2012–28 I.R.B. 16.

Research Problem 2. John Curran and his wife own a construction company, and they want to set up two new corporations that will be owned by their Roth IRAs. The two Roth-owned corporations will then enter into contracts to provide services to their construction company. They believe that the Roth-owned businesses can benefit from the payments and then pay out dividends to each Roth up to $50,000 per year. The couple will continue to do all of the work for the construction company. Advise Mr. and Mrs. Curran about this strategy.

Research Problem 3. Jim Raby transfers one-half of his compensatory stock options (ISOs and nonqualified stock options) to his ex-wife as part of a divorce settlement. Discuss the tax aspects of this transfer.

Partial list of research aids:
FSA 200005006.
§§ 424(c)(4)(A) and (B).

Research Problem 4. Before Lemon Corporation was taken private in a transaction engineered by its largest stockholder, some of Lemon's employees had unexercised options to purchase stock of Lemon. Under an employee agreement, Lemon canceled the unexercised stock options by paying the employees the difference between the option price and the current fair market value of Lemon's stock. These employees reported this as ordinary income. Can Lemon Corporation deduct these payments to the employees, or are these termination payments treated as capital expenditures?

Use internet tax resources to address the following questions. Look for reliable websites and blogs of the IRS and other government agencies, media outlets, businesses, tax professionals, academics, think tanks, and political outlets.

Research Problem 5. In July 2016, the IRS issued regulations on longevity annuities that can help people prolong their retirement savings, easing their concern of outliving their savings. Conduct research on this topic, including a review of information provided by the IRS and Treasury Department. In a short article suitable for a CPA firm's newsletter that is distributed to individual clients, explain how a longevity annuity can help someone prolong his or her IRA savings.

Research Problem 6. Some corporations offer their employees restricted stock, whereas other corporations offer restricted stock units. Search the internet to find the differences between these two types of restricted stock offerings.

Research Problem 7. Jacob Patterson is limited from making a fully deductible $5,500 IRA contribution because of his income limitation. Instead, he makes a $3,500 nondeductible IRA contribution to his traditional IRA. Find out how Jacob reports this on his return, and complete the appropriate tax form he should attach to his Form 1040.

Research Problem 8. Using newspapers, magazine articles, and other resources, prepare a report on stock appreciation rights to present to your class.

Roger CPA Review Questions

1. The following facts apply to Newton, a single individual, for 2017:

W–2 income	$110,000
Traditional IRA contribution	5,000
Coverdell Education Savings Account contribution	2,000
State Qualified Tuition plan (529 plan) contribution	3,000
Qualifying medical expenses	12,000

   Newton does not participate in any pension or profit sharing plan other than the traditional IRA. Considering only the foregoing facts, what should Newton's adjusted gross income be for 2017?

   a. $104,000   c. $102,000
   b. $103,000   d. $105,000

2. Chatterjee is an executive with XYZ Corp. In 2016, XYZ gave Chatterjee 1,000 nonqualified stock options, each with an option price of $60, when the price of XYZ stock was $80. In 2017 Chatterjee exercised 500 of the stock options, at a time when the price of XYZ stock was $90. As a result of the above, what amount should Chatterjee include in 2017 gross income?

   a. $0   c. $10,000
   b. $15,000   d. $ 5,000

3. Which of the following is excluded from gross income on an individual's 2017 tax return?

   a. 2017 settlement from an employment discrimination lawsuit
   b. Seller of the Year award, in the form of a 2017 all-expenses-paid vacation
   c. Qualified stock options awarded in 2014, exercised in 2017
   d. Income from the 2017 sale of illegal drugs

4. On February 15 of the current year, Young received a $10,000 lump-sum payment from a qualified profit sharing plan, the full amount of which Young rolled over into an IRA 46 days later. How much of this lump-sum payment may Young exclude from current-year gross income?

   a. $0

   b. $10,000

   c. Depends on contribution limit

   d. $8,000

5. Claire is a self-employed individual who owns and runs Claire's Creations LLC. In 2017, she had $225,000 in net self-employment earnings, including a deduction for 50% of self-employment tax, prior to any Keogh deduction. Claire has a defined contribution, stock bonus Keogh plan. What is the highest deductible Keogh contribution Claire can make for the 2017 tax year? Assume no excess contribution carryover from prior years.

   a. $56,250

   b. $225,000

   c. $52,000

   d. $45,000

PART 7

CORPORATIONS AND PARTNERSHIPS

CHAPTER **20**

Corporations and Partnerships

This text is primarily focused on basic tax concepts and the individual taxpayer. Although many of these tax concepts also apply to corporations and partnerships, other tax provisions apply specifically to corporations or partnerships. An overview of these provisions is presented in Part 7. Comprehensive coverage of these topics appears in *South-Western Federal Taxation: Corporations, Partnerships, Estates & Trusts*.

CHAPTER

20

Corporations and Partnerships

LEARNING OBJECTIVES: *After completing Chapter 20, you should be able to:*

LO.1 Describe the non-tax characteristics that are important for entity choice.

LO.2 Identify entities treated as corporations for Federal income tax purposes.

LO.3 Contrast the income tax treatment of individuals with that applicable to corporations.

LO.4 Recognize and calculate the tax deductions available only to corporations.

LO.5 Calculate corporate tax liability and comply with various procedural and reporting requirements.

LO.6 Describe the tax rules governing the formation of corporations.

LO.7 Explain the tax rules governing the operation of corporations.

LO.8 Assess the utility and effect of the Subchapter S election.

LO.9 Review the tax consequences of forming and operating a partnership.

LO.10 Identify the advantages and disadvantages of the various forms used for conducting a business.

GARY WOODS/ALAMY STOCK PHOTO

THE BIG PICTURE

Choice of Business Entity

The Todd sisters have decided to begin a catering business to handle private parties, weddings, anniversaries, and other large social events. As their parents previously owned several restaurants, the sisters are familiar with food service operations. All sisters will participate in the operation of the business and will provide the funds for capital acquisitions (e.g., delivery trucks, kitchen equipment, and food preparation facilities) and working capital needs. Due to the cost of the premiums, the sisters plan on minimal liability insurance coverage.

In the first few years of operation, the sisters anticipate losses. When and if the business becomes profitable, however, they would consider expansion. Any such expansion would require obtaining additional capital from outside sources.

In what type of entity should the Todd sisters conduct the business?

Read the chapter and formulate your response.

Until now, this text has concentrated on the Federal income taxation of individual taxpayers. In terms of conducting a business, an individual will often operate as a sole proprietorship. Although simple and straightforward—a mere Schedule C is involved—this may not be the best choice. Other forms of business organization are available and should be considered. Besides the sole proprietorship, the choices include:

- C corporation.
- S corporation.
- Limited liability company (LLC).
- Partnership.
- Qualified joint venture.

To make an informed choice on what type of entity to select, familiarity with operational rules, nontax characteristics, and the tax consequences of each is necessary. This chapter starts with an overview of the considerations involved when making entity choice and then considers each of the above types of entity choices.

20-1 CHOICE OF ENTITY

LO.1

Describe the nontax characteristics that are important for entity choice.

The decision as to what type of entity to use for a business is referred to as a "choice of entity" question. This question arises when a business is first formed. In addition, it can arise again as a business grows or ownership changes. For example, an individual may start a business as a sole proprietorship and then convert it to a corporation if it grows and the owner seeks additional capital. In addition to tax matters, a careful consideration of legal and nontax factors such as responsibility for liabilities, the ability to raise capital through equity and debt, treatment under state law, and the relative rights and responsibilities of owners are all issues that should be analyzed prior to making the entity choice.

20-1a Nontax Considerations

The decision of which entity to use in conducting a trade or business must be weighed carefully. Of significant importance are nontax considerations, including the legal attributes of the business entity chosen. For the corporate form, those commonly include limited liability, continuity of life, free transferability of interests, and centralized management. Many, if not all, of these attributes can also be obtained through the use of a limited liability company. When nontax considerations are evaluated, close attention must be paid to applicable state law. Many states, for example, place severe restrictions on the use of corporations to practice certain professions (e.g., medicine and law). Likewise, the legal attributes of an LLC may vary from one state to another and may not be identical to those of corporations.

In most states, the form of entity is driven by the type of legal entity under state law. For example, most states require organizational documentation to be filed with the state for a corporation (e.g., articles of incorporation), generally filed with the state's Secretary of State's office. Corporations also require other corporate formalities, such as the appointment of a board of directors, adoption of bylaws, issuance of shares, minutes of board meetings, and corporate resolutions. Partnerships often do not require such legal formalities (although many partnerships have similar documents, such as a partnership agreement, to document the terms of the partnership for the partners).

One key consideration for many owners is the shelter of limited personal liability due to their involvement with a business. For years, this was a primary advantage bestowed upon the corporate form of entity. A corporation is able to take on liabilities separate from the shareholders, thus insulating shareholders from whatever debts might befall the business. However, if there is no real separation between the corporation and its owners, the courts may "pierce the corporate veil" and look through to the owners to pay liabilities ordinarily left at the corporate level.

Annette operates her business under the corporate form; however, after filing the initial articles of incorporation with the state, Annette failed to follow any of the corporate formalities required under state law (annual meetings, bylaws, issuance of shares). In addition, Annette paid personal expenses out of the corporate entity and paid corporate expenditures from her personal account. Finally, when Annette established the corporation, she did not capitalize (invest in the equity of the corporation) at the level that would be reasonable given the expected liabilities and activities of the corporation; thus, it was never likely that the corporation could stand on its own. As a result, the courts would piece the corporate veil and hold Annette personally responsible for the actions and liabilities of the corporation.

EXAMPLE 1

When the limited liability company (LLC) was introduced by a number of states, the dominion of limited liability by the corporate form was suddenly broken. The owners (or "members") of an LLC are also generally shielded from the liabilities of the business. Similar to corporations, states often require more formal paperwork to establish an LLC.

Sole proprietorships and partnerships, on the other hand, expose owners to personal liability in situations where the business cannot cover its liabilities. A sole proprietorship is not an entity separate from its owner. Thus, the individual owner is fully liable for business liabilities. Partners in a partnership are fully liable for partnership liabilities that cannot be satisfied by the partnership. Even for a limited partnership, at least one partner must be responsible for partnership liabilities (the general partner). The limited partners are typically liable only to the extent of their capital investment in the partnership.

Another important nontax aspect of entity choice relates to how the owners' rights can differ among entities. Under corporate law, the corporation functions under the state-required corporate formalities described previously. The rigidity of the corporate structure does not permit much flexibility with regard to how owners share their rights of ownership of the property and earnings of the business. The transactions that occur between the corporate entity and the shareholders, between shareholders themselves, and between the corporation and external parties are afforded little flexibility. Partnerships and LLCs, however, are afforded a great deal of flexibility through the partnership or LLC agreements that are drawn up as more of a contract between the owners wherein terms such as the sharing of income and losses, the sharing of debts, and the distribution of property can be negotiated as part of the agreement between the owners. The opportunity for flexibility has caused the tax law to include complex partnership tax rules in an effort to prevent taxpayers from taking advantage of the distribution of taxable income and losses among owners to shift tax liabilities or harm government revenue.

Finally, for the thriving entrepreneur, the corporate form is the most likely form when the business is preparing to enter into its initial public offering (IPO). Corporations operate under a centralized management beholden to the board of directors and not directly to the shareholders. The IPO can help raise the necessary capital to expand the business; however, the limited management rights of owners under the corporate form makes that entity choice the optimal one for preventing wayward shareholders from interfering with the day-to-day operations of the business as shareholder involvement is generally limited to voting for board members and other corporate resolutions. In addition, corporate form often lends itself to free transferability of ownership, allowing shareholders to set their stake in the business with lower transaction costs (e.g., on a stock exchange).

An S corporation is a corporation formed under state law that has made an "S" election under the Federal tax law. As such, most of the nontax characteristics of an S corporation are the same as for a regular corporation. A corporation that has not made an S election is referred to as a **C corporation**. When a corporation elects to be an S corporation, the tax law prescribes some requirements that impact the nontax characteristics of an S corporation. For example, an S corporation may not have more than 100 owners, may not have a foreign owner, and is not permitted to have different classes of stock. In spite of being treated like a partnership for Federal tax purposes, the same corporate formalities such as articles of incorporation, bylaws, and director meetings must be followed by an S corporation.

Other types of entities are not within the scope of this textbook, such as limited partnerships, limited liability partnerships, publicly traded partnerships, professional corporations, professional associations, master limited partnerships, and others. For further details on most of these types of entities, visit the website of the Secretary of State for your state.

A summary of the nontax characteristics is presented in Concept Summary 20.1

Concept Summary 20.1

	Sole Proprietor	C Corporation	S Corporation	General Partnership	LLC
Organization documents required to be filed with state	No	Yes	Yes	No	Yes
Corporate formalities required	No	Yes	Yes	No	No
Govern and control	Individual owner	Board of directors	Board of directors	Partners	Manager
Liabilities	Owner	Entity	Entity	Owners	Entity
Ability to arrange ownership rights and responsibilities	n/a	Inflexible	Inflexible	Flexible	Flexible
Type of owners	Individual owner	Flexible	Some restrictions	Flexible	Flexible
Management	Individual owner	Centralized	Centralized	Decentralized	Centralized or decentralized

20-1b **General Tax Consequences of Different Forms of Business Entities**

A business operation may be conducted as a sole proprietorship, a partnership, an LLC, a corporation, or a qualified joint venture.

- Sole proprietorships are not separate taxable entities. The owner of the business reports all business transactions on his or her individual income tax return.

EXAMPLE 2

Fred operates a bookstore selling rare books. The business is operated as a sole proprietorship. His bookstore generates income of $45,000 during the year. Fred will prepare a Schedule C to report his bookstore's gross income and expenses, a Schedule SE to report his self-employment tax, and any other schedules or forms required to support deductions on his Schedule C (such as a Form 4562 to report depreciation). The net earnings from Fred's bookstore business reported on Schedule C are included on his individual income tax Form 1040.

- Partnerships are not subject to the income tax. Under the conduit concept, the various tax attributes of the partnership's operations flow through to the partners to be reported on their income tax returns.

EXAMPLE 3

Chuck and Dave are brothers who operate an auto repair shop. Because they initially wanted to go into business together, the brothers formed a partnership to operate the business. Chuck and Dave share all of the income and expenses of the business equally according to the partnership agreement they both entered into. Although the partnership will prepare a tax return for informational purposes (Form 1065), each brother's share of income or losses is reported on his individual income tax forms. Thus, tax on the business income is paid by the partners.

- The tax treatment of limited liability companies (LLCs) usually follows that applicable to partnerships.
- The C corporation form of doing business carries with it the imposition of the corporate income tax. The corporation is recognized as a separate taxpaying entity apart from its shareholders. Income is taxed to the corporation as earned and taxed again to the shareholders when distributed as dividends.

Sarah operates a construction equipment rental business. Because of the risks associated with this type of business, Sarah wants limited liability and structures her business as a corporation under state law. As a separate entity, the corporation prepares its own tax return. Sarah will only include the earnings of the corporation on her individual tax return when the corporation makes a taxable distribution to her.

- A C corporation may elect to be taxed as an S corporation if certain requirements are met. This special treatment follows the conduit concept and is similar (although not identical) to the partnership rules. Income tax is generally avoided at the corporate level, and shareholders are taxed currently on the earnings of the S corporation.

Mary starts a new business with her four brothers. They want limited liability for themselves. They expect to operate at a loss for the first few years. To provide an opportunity to allow the losses to flow into the other income of the siblings, they agree to make an S corporation election. The S corporation is required to complete an informational tax return (Form 1120S), and the losses flow through to the owner's individual tax returns. Mary and her brothers also could have considered a limited liability company to achieve the same income tax results.

Because they follow the conduit concept as to the treatment of their tax attributes, partnerships, LLCs, and S corporations are often referred to as **pass-through entities**.

The Big Picture

Return to the facts of *The Big Picture* on p. 20-1. It appears that the Todd sisters should consider a C or S corporation to obtain limited liability for their catering business. (An LLC also would provide this result.) On the other hand, the conduit effect of an S corporation or a partnership is needed to enable the sisters to take advantage of the initial losses anticipated for the business. Under the conduit concept, such losses could be deducted on their individual income tax returns.

20-1c **Check-the-Box Election**

For years, the primary forms of business entity were a corporation and a general partnership. Over time, the needs of business owners provided the impetus for new types of entities. Legal entities with some characteristics of a corporation and some of a partnership were created in some states, blurring the lines between the traditional corporate and partnership forms of business. In late 1996, the IRS issued its so-called **Check-the-box Regulations**.[1] Effective beginning in 1997, these Regulations enable taxpayers to classify a business entity for tax purposes without regard to its corporate (or noncorporate) characteristics. These rules have simplified tax administration considerably and eliminated the litigation that arose with regard to association (corporation) status.

Under the rules, an entity with more than one owner can elect to be classified as either a partnership or a corporation. An entity with only one owner can elect to be classified as a corporation or a sole proprietorship. In the event of default (no election is made), unincorporated entities with multiple owners are classified as partnerships and single-person businesses as sole proprietorships.

---

[1] Reg. §§ 301.7701–1 through –4 and –7.

The election is not available to entities that are actually incorporated under state law or to entities that are required to be corporations under Federal law (e.g., certain publicly traded partnerships). LLCs not incorporated under state law can elect either corporation or partnership status for Federal tax purposes. Eligible entities make the election as to tax status by filing Form 8832 (Entity Classification Election). New elections are permitted, but only after a 60-month waiting period. Joint ventures are normally taxed as partnerships.[2] However, at the election of the taxpayers, certain joint ventures between spouses can avoid partnership classification. Known as a **qualified joint venture**, the spouses report their share of the business activities from the venture as sole proprietors (using two Schedule C forms).[3]

LO.2

Identify entities treated as corporations for Federal income tax purposes.

20-2 CORPORATIONS

Some income tax rules apply differently for corporations versus other forms of business. This section provides some examples of both similarities and differences.

20-2a Corporate Legal Concerns

As described in text Section 20-1, corporations must comply with the specific requirements for corporate status under state law. For example, it is necessary to draft articles of incorporation and file them with the state regulatory agency (usually the Secretary of State), be granted a charter, and issue stock to shareholders.

Compliance with state law, although important, is not the only requirement that must be met to qualify for corporate tax status. For example, a corporation qualifying under state law may be disregarded as a taxable entity if it is a mere sham lacking in economic substance.[4] The key consideration is the degree of business activity conducted at the corporate level.

Corporate Activities

EXAMPLE 7

Gene and Mike are joint owners of a tract of unimproved real estate they want to protect from future creditors. Gene and Mike form Falcon Corporation and transfer the land to it in return for all of the corporation's stock. The corporation merely holds title to the land and conducts no other activities. In all respects, Falcon Corporation meets the legal requirements of a corporation under applicable state law. Nevertheless, Falcon might not be recognized as a separate entity for corporate tax purposes under these facts.

EXAMPLE 8

Assume the same facts as in Example 7. In addition to holding title to the land, Falcon Corporation leases the property, collects rents, and pays the property taxes. Falcon probably would be treated as a corporation for Federal income tax purposes because of the scope of its activities.

In some instances, the IRS has attempted to disregard (or collapse) a corporation to make the income taxable directly to the shareholders.[5] In other cases, the IRS has asserted that the corporation is a separate taxable entity so as to assess tax at the corporate level and to tax corporate distributions to shareholders as dividend income (double taxation).[6]

Can an organization not qualifying as a corporation under state law still be treated as such for Federal income tax purposes? Yes. The tax law defines a corporation as including "associations, joint stock companies, and insurance companies."[7] As the Code contains no definition of an "association," the issue was the subject of frequent litigation prior to the issuance of the Check-the-box Regulations.[8]

---

[2]§ 7701(a)(2).

[3]§ 761(f). For further information, see **www.irs.gov/Businesses/ Small-Businesses-&-Self-Employed/Election-for-Husband-and-Wife-Unincorporated-Businesses**.

[4]See *Paymer v. Comm.*, 45–2 USTC 9353, 33 AFTR 1536, 150 F.2d 334 (CA–2, 1945).

[5]*Floyd Patterson*, 25 TCM 1230, T.C.Memo. 1966–239, *aff'd* in 68–2 USTC 9471, 22 AFTR 2d 5810 (CA–2, 1968).

[6]*Elot H. Raffety Farms Inc. v. U.S.*, 75–1 USTC 9271, 35 AFTR 2d 75–811, 511 F.2d 1234 (CA–8, 1975).

[7]§ 7701(a)(3).

[8]See, for example, *U.S. v. Kintner*, 54–2 USTC 9626, 46 AFTR 995, 216 F.2d 418 (CA–5, 1954).

20-2b **Individuals and Corporations Compared—An Overview**

Similarities between Corporate and Individual Tax Rules

LO.3

Contrast the income tax treatment of individuals with that applicable to corporations.

The gross income of a corporation is determined in much the same manner as for individuals. Both individuals and corporations are entitled to exclusions from gross income, such as interest on municipal bonds. Gains and losses from property transactions are also treated similarly. For example, whether a gain or loss is capital or ordinary depends on the nature and use of the asset rather than the type of taxpayer. Upon the sale or other taxable disposition of depreciable personalty, the recapture rules of § 1245 make no distinction between corporate and noncorporate taxpayers. In the case of the recapture of depreciation on real property (§ 1250), however, corporate taxpayers experience more severe tax consequences. As illustrated later, corporations must recognize as additional ordinary income 20 percent of the excess of the amount that would be recaptured under § 1245 over the amount recaptured under § 1250.[9]

In cases involving nontaxable exchanges and certain transactions allowing the deferral of gain recognition, many of the rules are the same. Thus, both individuals and corporations can utilize the like-kind exchange provisions of § 1031 and the deferral allowed by § 1033 for involuntary conversions. In contrast, the § 121 exclusion for gain from the sale of a principal residence is a relief measure available only to individual taxpayers.

The business deductions of corporations parallel those available to individuals. Corporate deductions are allowed for all ordinary and necessary expenses paid or incurred in carrying on a trade or business. Corporations may also deduct interest, certain taxes, losses, bad debts, depreciation, cost recovery, charitable contributions subject to corporate limitation rules, net operating losses, research and experimental expenditures, and other less common deductions.

Many of the tax credits available to individuals, such as the foreign tax credit, can be claimed by corporations. Not available to corporations are certain credits that are personal in nature. Examples of credits not available to corporations include the credit for child and dependent care expenses, the credit for the elderly or disabled, and the earned income credit.

Most C corporations enjoy greater flexibility in the selection of a tax year than do other business entity types. For example, C corporations usually can have different tax years from those of their shareholders. Also, a newly formed corporation generally has a free choice of any permissible accounting period without having to obtain the consent of the IRS. However, personal service corporations and S corporations are subject to severe restrictions on the use of a fiscal year.

In terms of methods of accounting, generally, any business entity type that maintains inventory for sale to customers must use the *accrual* method in determining cost of goods sold.[10]

C corporations and partnerships with a partner that is a C corporation are generally required to use the accrual method of accounting (per the required accrual method rule).[11] However, there are exceptions to this rule:

- Corporations or partnerships with average annual gross receipts in prior three-year periods that do not exceed $5 million

- Certain farming businesses

- A C corporation that is a qualified personal service corporation (QPSC)[12]

The excepted businesses (as well as S corporations because they are not subject to the required accrual method rule) are generally allowed to use either the cash or accrual

---

[9]§ 291.

[10]See Chapters 4 and 18 for a discussion of the cash and accrual methods of accounting.

[11]§ 448(a)

[12]See § 448(d)(2). The definition of a QPSC includes that substantially all of its activities involve services in the fields of health, law, engineering, architecture, accounting, actuarial science, performing arts, or consulting.

(or hybrid) method of accounting. However, businesses with inventory must use the accrual method for inventory[13] unless they meet a different set of exceptions:

- The small taxpayer exception for taxpayers with average annual gross receipts in the past three years of $1 million or less.[14]
- The qualifying small business exception for service-related businesses with average annual gross receipts in the past three years of $10 million or less unless not permitted under the required accrual method rule (C corporations or partnerships with a C corporation partner).[15]

Gross Receipts Test

EXAMPLE 9

Sheila's Plumbing, a plumbing contractor not organized as a corporation, has gross receipts of $12 million. Sheila's plumbing is not a qualifying small business under the inventory exception rules because gross receipts exceed $10 million.

EXAMPLE 10

Howe Plumbing Inc. (a C corporation), a plumbing contractor, has gross receipts of $9 million. As a C corporation, Howe is not eligible for the $10 million qualifying small business exception to using the accrual method for inventory. Because Howe's gross receipts exceed $5 million, it is subject to the required accrual method rule.

EXAMPLE 11

Blue Corporation is treated as an S corporation. It has gross receipts of $11 million. If Blue has no inventory, then it will not be required to use the accrual method of accounting. If inventory is an income-producing factor for Blue, then it will be required to use the accrual method for inventory as it does not meet either inventory exception.

The IRS has provided a helpful flowchart to assist in the determination of the overall accounting method for a business entity with inventory (reproduced in Exhibit 20.1).

Dissimilarities

Both noncorporate and corporate taxpayers are subject to progressive income tax rates. For individuals, the rates are 10, 15, 25, 28, 33, 35, and 39.6 percent. For corporations, the rates are 15, 25, 34, and 35 percent as presented in Exhibit 20.2 on p. 20-17. Corporate taxpayers lose the benefits of the lower brackets (using a phaseout approach) once taxable income reaches certain levels. Noncorporate taxpayers, however, continue to enjoy the benefits of the lower brackets even though they have reached the higher taxable income levels.

As discussed in Chapter 16, qualified dividends received by individual shareholders are subject to preferential tax rates. For those shareholders in the top tax bracket, the maximum rate of 20 percent applies (to income otherwise taxed at the 39.6 percent rate); for the next four tax brackets (25, 28, 33, and 35 percent), the rate is 15 percent; for those in the bottom two brackets (10 and 15 percent), the rate is 0 percent. Corporate taxpayers do not benefit from such preferential rates, but as discussed later, corporate shareholders enjoy the alternative of the dividends received deduction.

Many corporate and all noncorporate taxpayers are subject to the alternative minimum tax (AMT). For AMT purposes, many adjustments and tax preference items are the same for both, but other adjustments and tax preferences apply only to corporations or only to individuals. The AMT is discussed in Chapter 12.

All allowable corporate deductions are treated as business expenses. The determination of adjusted gross income, so essential for individuals, has no relevance to corporations. Corporations need not be concerned with classifying deductions into *deduction for* and *deduction from* categories.

---

[13]§ 471 and Reg. § 1.446–1(c)(2)(i).
[14]Rev.Proc. 2001–10, 2001–1 C.B. 272.

[15]Rev.Proc. 2002–28, 2002–1 C.B. 815.

EXHIBIT 20.1 **Cash Method for Inventory Exceptions Flowchart**[16]

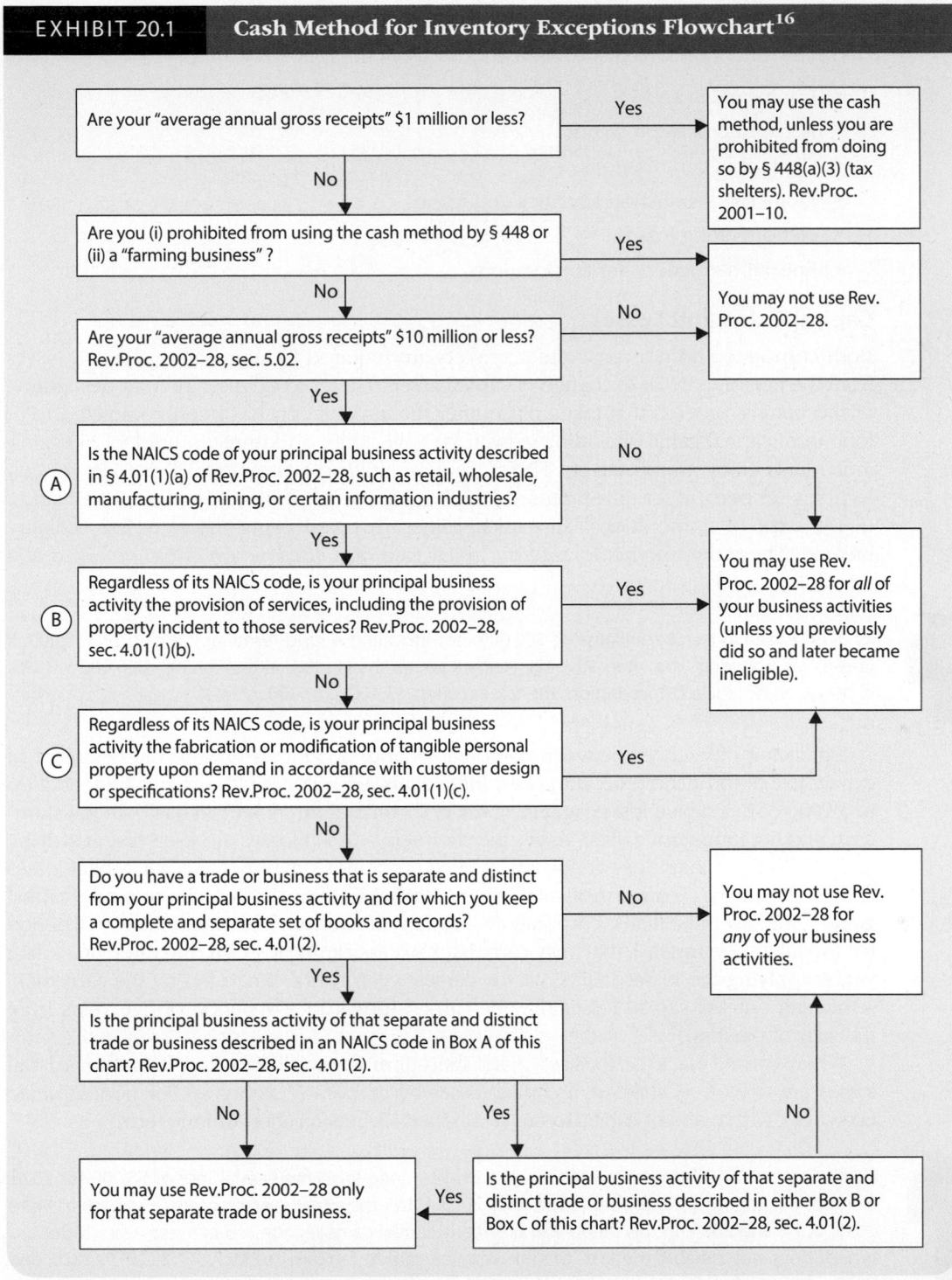

The similarities and dissimilarities between individuals and C corporations as to tax attributes are outlined in Concept Summary 20.2 on p. 20-19.

[16]The flowchart is from Rev.Proc. 2002–28, 2002–1 C.B. 815. The reference to NAICS code in the flowchart refers to the North American Industry Classification System used by the Federal government for statistical purposes. See **www.census.gov/eos/www/naics/**.

20-2c **Specific Provisions Compared**

Corporate and individual tax rules also can vary in the following areas:

- Capital gains and losses.
- Recapture of depreciation.
- Charitable contributions.
- Domestic production activities deduction.
- Net operating losses.
- Special deductions for corporations.

Capital Gains and Losses

Both corporate and noncorporate taxpayers are required to aggregate gains and losses from the taxable sale or exchange of capital assets. (Refer to Chapter 16 for a description of the netting process that takes place after the aggregation has been completed.) For long-term capital gains (including gains from collectibles and unrecaptured § 1250 gain), individuals enjoy an advantage. The maximum applicable tax rate is 28 percent for collectibles, 25 percent for unrecaptured § 1250 gain, and 20 percent for other capital gains. In the case of corporations, all capital gains are taxed using the rates for ordinary income. Therefore, the net long-term capital gain of a corporation could be taxed at a rate as high as 35 percent.

In 2017, Rose has taxable income of $80,000, not including a long-term capital gain of $10,000. If Rose is an individual, the alternative tax yields a tax on the capital gain of $1,500 ($10,000 × 15%). If, however, Rose is a C corporation, the tax becomes $3,400 ($10,000 × 34%).

Significant differences between corporations and individuals exist in the treatment of capital losses for income tax purposes. Individuals, for example, can annually deduct up to $3,000 of net capital losses against ordinary income. If an individual has both net short-term and net long-term capital losses, the short-term capital losses are used first in arriving at the $3,000 ordinary loss deduction. While corporations may not use net capital losses to offset ordinary income, they may use net capital losses to offset past or future capital gains.[17] Unlike individuals, corporations are not allowed an unlimited carryover period for capital losses. Instead, they may carry back excess capital losses to the three preceding years, applying the losses initially to the earliest year. If not exhausted by the carryback, remaining unused capital losses may be carried forward for a period of five years from the year of the loss.[18]

When carried back or forward, *both* short-term capital losses and long-term capital losses are treated as short-term capital losses by corporate taxpayers. For noncorporate taxpayers, carryovers of capital losses retain their identity as short or long term.

Hawk Corporation, a calendar year taxpayer, incurs a long-term net capital loss of $5,000 for 2016. None of the capital loss may be deducted in 2016. Hawk may, however, carry the loss back to years 2013, 2014, and 2015 (in this order) and offset any capital gains recognized in these years. If the carryback does not exhaust the loss, the loss may be carried forward to 2017, 2018, 2019, 2020, and 2021 (in this order). Such capital loss carrybacks or carryovers are treated as short-term capital losses.

Recapture of Depreciation

Corporations selling depreciable real estate may have ordinary income in addition to that required by § 1250. Under § 291, the additional ordinary income element is 20 percent of the excess of the § 1245 recapture potential over the § 1250 recapture. As a result, the § 1231 gain is correspondingly decreased by the additional recapture.

---

[17]§§ 1211(a) and (b).   [18]§ 1212(a).

Under § 1250, the excess of accelerated depreciation over straight-line depreciation is recaptured as ordinary income as to real property. Because all real property purchased since 1986 is depreciated using only the straight-line method, after 2005, the § 1250 amount is zero because the depreciation period (19 years in 1986) has expired and such buildings are fully depreciated.

EXAMPLE 14

Condor Corporation purchases residential real property on November 3, 2003, for $300,000. Straight-line cost recovery is taken in the amount of $143,624 (see Exhibit 8.8 in Chapter 8) before the property is sold on January 6, 2017, for $250,000. (Neither the purchase nor selling price includes any amount attributable to the land.)

First, determine the recognized gain:

Sales price		$ 250,000
Less adjusted basis:		
Cost of property	$ 300,000	
Less cost recovery	(143,624)	(156,376)
Recognized gain		$ 93,624

Second, determine the § 1245 recapture potential. This is the lesser of $93,624 (recognized gain) or $143,624 (cost recovery claimed).

Third, determine the § 1250 recapture amount:

Cost recovery taken	$ 143,624
Less straight-line cost recovery	(143,624)
§ 1250 ordinary income	$ –0–

Fourth, because the taxpayer is a corporation, determine the additional § 291 amount:

§ 1245 recapture potential	$ 93,624
Less § 1250 recapture amount	(–0–)
Excess § 1245 recapture potential	$ 93,624
Apply § 291 percentage	× 20%
Additional ordinary income under § 291	$ 18,725

Condor Corporation's recognized gain of $93,624 is accounted for as follows:

Ordinary income under § 1250	$ –0–
Ordinary income under § 291	18,725
§ 1231 gain	74,899
Total recognized gain	$93,624

Charitable Contributions

Generally, a charitable contribution deduction is allowed only for the tax year in which the payment is made. However, an important exception is made for accrual basis corporations. The deduction may be claimed in the tax year *preceding* payment if the following conditions are satisfied:

- The contribution is authorized by the board of directors by the end of that tax year *and*

- The contribution is paid on or before the fifteenth day of the fourth month of the next tax year.[19]

EXAMPLE 15

On December 26, 2017, the board of directors of Dove Corporation, a calendar year, accrual basis taxpayer, authorizes a $20,000 donation to a qualified charity. The donation is paid on April 15, 2018. Dove Corporation may claim all or a portion of the $20,000 donation as a deduction for 2017. As an alternative, Dove may claim the deduction in 2018 (the year of payment).

---

[19]§ 170(a)(2).

Like individuals, corporations are not permitted an unlimited charitable contribution deduction. In any one year, a corporate taxpayer is limited to 10 percent of taxable income. For this purpose, taxable income is computed without regard to the charitable contribution deduction, any net operating loss carryback or capital loss carryback, or the dividends received deduction (discussed later in this chapter).[20] Any contributions in excess of the 10 percent limitation are carried forward to the five succeeding tax years. Any carryover must be added to subsequent contributions and is subject to the 10 percent limitation. In applying the limitation, the most recent contributions must be deducted first.[21]

Carryover Situations

EXAMPLE 16

During 2017, Eagle Corporation (a calendar year taxpayer) had the following income and expenses:

Income from operations	$140,000
Expenses from operations	110,000
Dividends received	10,000
Charitable contributions made in 2017	5,000

For purposes of the 10% limitation only, Eagle's taxable income is $40,000 ($140,000 − $110,000 + $10,000). Consequently, the allowable charitable contribution deduction for 2017 is $4,000 (10% × $40,000). The $1,000 unused portion of the contribution is carried forward to 2018, 2019, 2020, 2021, and 2022 (in that order) until exhausted.

EXAMPLE 17

Assume the same facts as in Example 16. In 2018, Eagle Corporation has taxable income (after adjustments) of $50,000 and makes a charitable contribution of $4,800. The maximum deduction allowed for 2018 is $5,000 (10% × $50,000). The first $4,800 of the allowed deduction must be allocated to the 2018 contribution, and the $200 excess is allocated to the carryover from 2017. The remaining $800 of the 2017 contribution is carried over to 2019, etc.

As noted in Chapter 10, the deduction for charitable contributions of ordinary income property is limited to the lesser of the fair market value or the adjusted basis of the property. A special rule provides an exception that permits a corporation to contribute inventory (ordinary income property) to certain charitable organizations and receive a deduction equal to the adjusted basis plus one-half of the difference between the fair market value and the adjusted basis of the property. In no event, however, may the deduction exceed twice the adjusted basis of the property. To qualify for this exception, the inventory must be used by the charity in its exempt purpose for the care of *children*, the *ill*, or the *needy*.[22]

EXAMPLE 18

In the current year, Robin Company (a retail clothier) donates sweaters and overcoats to Sheltering Arms (a qualified charity caring for the homeless). The clothing is inventory and has a basis of $10,000 and a fair market value of $14,000. If Robin is a corporation, the charitable contribution that results is $12,000 [$10,000 (basis) + $2,000 (50% of the appreciation of $4,000)]. In contrast, if Robin is not a corporation, the charitable contribution is limited to $10,000 (basis).

Domestic Production Activities Deduction

As noted in Chapter 7, § 199 was designed to replace various export tax benefits that our world trading partners deemed discriminatory. Known as the domestic production activities deduction (DPAD), the provision is equally applicable to C corporations. In the case of C corporations, however, the limitation is based on taxable

---

[20]§ 170(b)(2).
[21]§ 170(d)(2).

[22]The inventory exception is prescribed by § 170(e)(3).

income, rather than AGI (both computed without considering the deduction). Thus, the DPAD is 9 percent of the *lesser* of qualified production activities income (QPAI) or taxable income. As with individual taxpayers, the DPAD cannot exceed 50 percent of the W–2 wages involved (those subject to withholding plus certain elective deferrals). Domestic gross receipts from manufacturing activities are a major source of QPAI. These gross receipts are adjusted by cost of goods sold and other assignable expenses to arrive at QPAI.

For corporations that are members of an affiliated group (based on 50 percent common control), the deduction is determined by treating the group as a single taxpayer. In effect, therefore, each member of the group is treated as being engaged in the activities of every other member. The deduction is then allocated among the members in proportion to each member's respective amount of QPAI.[23]

Affiliated Exception

Mallard and Pintail Corporations are members of an affiliated group but do not file a consolidated return. Mallard manufactures a machine at a cost of $3,000 and sells it to Pintail for $5,000. Pintail incurs additional cost of $2,000 for marketing and then sells the machine to an unrelated customer for $9,000. The QPAI deduction is based on $4,000 ($9,000 − $3,000 − $2,000) even though the seller (Pintail) did not perform any manufacturing.[24] Note that this is the same result that would have been reached if Pintail had not been involved and Mallard had conducted its own marketing function.

EXAMPLE 19

Assume the same facts as in Example 19, except that the parties are not related. Under these circumstances, Mallard has QPAI of $2,000 ($5,000 − $3,000) and Pintail has none. Pintail's activities, when considered alone, are not QPAI because they involve marketing and not manufacturing.

EXAMPLE 20

In the case of pass-through entities (e.g., partnerships, S corporations, and LLCs), special rules apply for handling the DPAD.[25] Because the deduction is determined at the owner level, each partner or shareholder must make the computation separately. Thus, the entity allocates to each owner his or her share of QPAI. The QPAI that is passed through is then combined with any qualifying activities that the owner has from other sources (e.g., a partner also conducts a manufacturing activity on his or her own).

The DPAD can be claimed in computing the alternative minimum tax (including adjusted current earnings). The deduction allowed is the lesser of QPAI or alternative minimum taxable income (AMTI). In the case of an individual taxpayer, AGI is substituted for AMTI in determining the limitation on the amount allowed as a deduction.[26]

Net Operating Losses

The computation of a net operating loss (NOL) for individuals was discussed in Chapter 7. Corporations are not subject to the complex adjustments required for individuals because a corporation's loss more clearly approximates a true economic loss. Artificial deductions (e.g., personal and dependency exemptions) that merely generate paper losses are not permitted for corporations.

In computing the NOL of a corporation, the dividends received deduction (discussed below) can be claimed in determining the amount of the loss. Generally, NOLs may be carried back 2 years and forward 20 years (or taxpayers may elect to forgo the carryback period) to offset taxable income for those years.[27]

[23]§ 199(d)(4).
[24]Reg. § 1.199–7(c).
[25]§ 199(d)(1).
[26]§ 199(d)(6).
[27]§ 172(b).

Carryover Situations

EXAMPLE 21

In 2017, Wren Corporation has gross income of $200,000 and deductions of $300,000, excluding the dividends received deduction. Wren received taxable dividends of $100,000 from ExxonMobil stock. Wren has an NOL of $170,000, computed as follows:

Gross income (including ExxonMobil dividends)		$ 200,000
Less: Business deductions	$300,000	
Dividends received deduction (70% × $100,000)	70,000	(370,000)
Taxable income (loss)		($ 170,000)

EXAMPLE 22

Assume the same facts as in Example 21, and assume that Wren Corporation had taxable income of $40,000 in 2015. The NOL of $170,000 is carried back to 2015 (unless Wren elects not to carry back the loss to that year). The carryover to 2016 is $130,000, computed as follows:

Taxable income for 2015	$ 40,000
Less: NOL carryback from 2017	(170,000)
Carryover of unabsorbed 2017 loss	($ 130,000)

In Example 22, the carryback to 2015 might have been ill-advised if Wren Corporation had little, if any, taxable income in 2015 and 2016 and if it anticipated large amounts of taxable income in the immediate future. In that case, the *election to forgo* the carryback might generate greater tax savings. In this regard, three points should be considered. First, the time value of the tax refund that is lost by not using the carryback procedure must be considered. Second, the election to forgo an NOL carryback is irrevocable. Thus, it cannot be changed later if the future high profits do not materialize. Third, future increases or decreases in corporate income tax rates that can reasonably be anticipated should be considered.

LO.4

Recognize and calculate the tax deductions available only to corporations.

20-2d Deductions Available Only to Corporations

Dividends Received Deduction

The purpose of the **dividends received deduction** is to prevent triple taxation. Without the deduction, income paid to a corporation in the form of a dividend would be subject to taxation for a second time (after being taxed first to the distributing corporation) with no corresponding deduction to the distributing corporation. A third level of tax would be assessed on the shareholders when the recipient corporation distributed the income to its shareholders. Because the dividends received deduction may be less than 100 percent, the law may provide only partial relief.

The amount of the dividends received deduction depends upon the percentage of ownership the recipient corporate shareholder holds in the corporation making the dividend distribution.[28] For dividends received or accrued, the *deduction percentage* is summarized as follows:

Percentage of Ownership by Corporate Shareholder	Deduction Percentage
Less than 20%	70%
20% or more (but less than 80%)	80%
80% or more	100%

The dividends received deduction may be limited to a percentage of the taxable income of a corporation computed without regard to the NOL deduction, the dividends received deduction, the DPAD, or any capital loss carryback. The percentage of taxable

---

[28]§ 243(a).

income limitation corresponds to the deduction percentage. Thus, if a corporate shareholder owns less than 20 percent of the stock in the distributing corporation, the dividends received deduction is limited to 70 percent of taxable income (as previously defined). However, this limitation does not apply if the DRD creates an NOL for the current taxable year.[29] In addition, the DRD applies to dividends received from domestic corporations.[30]

In working with these myriad rules, the following steps need to be taken:

1. Multiply the dividends received by the deduction percentage.
2. Multiply the taxable income (as previously defined) by the deduction percentage.
3. The deduction is limited to the lesser of step 1 or step 2, unless subtracting the amount derived from step 1 from taxable income (as previously defined) generates a negative number. If so, the amount derived in step 1 should be used.

EXAMPLE 23

Crane, Osprey, and Gull Corporations, three unrelated calendar year corporations, have the following transactions for 2017:

	Crane Corporation	Osprey Corporation	Gull Corporation
Gross income from operations	$ 400,000	$ 320,000	$ 260,000
Expenses from operations	(340,000)	(340,000)	(340,000)
Dividends received from domestic corporations (less than 20% ownership)	200,000	200,000	200,000
Taxable income before the dividends received deduction	$ 260,000	$ 180,000	$ 120,000

In determining the dividends received deduction, use the step procedure just described:

	Crane Corporation	Osprey Corporation	Gull Corporation
Step 1: (70% × $200,000)	$140,000	$140,000	$140,000
Step 2:			
70% × $260,000 (taxable income)	$182,000		
70% × $180,000 (taxable income)		$126,000	
70% × $120,000 (taxable income)			$ 84,000
Step 3:			
Lesser of step 1 or step 2	$140,000	$126,000	
Generates an NOL			$140,000

Osprey Corporation is subject to the 70 percent of taxable income limitation. It does not qualify for the loss rule treatment because subtracting $140,000 (step 1) from $180,000 does not yield a loss. Gull Corporation qualifies for the loss rule treatment because subtracting $140,000 (step 1) from $120,000 does yield a loss. In summary, each corporation has the following dividends received deduction for 2017: $140,000 for Crane, $126,000 for Osprey, and $140,000 for Gull. If a corporation already has an NOL before any dividends received deduction is claimed, the full dividends received deduction (as calculated in step 1) is allowed.

Deduction of Organizational Expenditures

A corporation may choose to amortize organizational expenses over a period of 15 years starting in the taxable year in which the corporation begins business. A special exception, similar to the expensing of startup expenditures discussed in Chapter 6, which can also apply to a corporation, allows the corporation to immediately expense the first $5,000 of

---

[29]§ 246(b).

[30]In certain circumstances, foreign corporations can also be eligible for the DRD under § 243(e) and § 245.

these costs in addition to the first year's amortization amount.[31] The exception, however, is phased out on a dollar-for-dollar basis when these expenses exceed $50,000.

Kingbird Corporation, a calendar year taxpayer, is formed on June 1, 2017 and begins business that year. In connection with its formation, it incurs organizational expenditures of $52,000. If Kingbird wants to claim as much of these expenses as soon as possible, its deduction for 2017 is as follows:

$$\text{Expense: } \$5,000 - (\$52,000 - \$50,000) = \$3,000$$

$$\text{Amortization: } \frac{\$52,000 - \$3,000}{180 \text{ months}} \times 7 \text{ (months)} = \$1,906$$

Kingbird deducts a total of $4,906 ($3,000 + $1,906) for 2017.

The election to amortize is deemed made unless the corporation clearly indicates on its first tax return that it chooses to capitalize all such expenses.[32] If the choice not to amortize is made, the expenditures cannot be deducted until the corporation ceases to conduct business and liquidates. The election covers all qualifying expenses. **Organizational expenditures** include the following:

- Legal services incident to organization (e.g., drafting the corporate charter, bylaws, minutes of organizational meetings, and terms of original stock certificates).
- Necessary accounting services.
- Expenses of temporary directors and of organizational meetings of directors and shareholders.
- Fees paid to the state of incorporation.

Expenditures connected with issuing or selling shares of stock or other securities (e.g., commissions, professional fees, printing costs) or with transferring assets to a corporation do not qualify. These expenditures are generally added to the capital account and are not subject to amortization.

20-2e Determination of Corporate Tax Liability

LO.5

Calculate corporate tax liability and comply with various procedural and reporting requirements.

Income Tax Rates

The income tax rates for corporations are reproduced in Exhibit 20.2.[33] Note that the income tax rates begin by being progressive—compare the marginal tax rate applicable to the first $50,000 (taxed at 15 percent) with that on taxable income over $50,000 (taxed at 25 percent). But the phaseout of these lower rates starts with the $100,001 to $335,000 bracket (taxed at 39 percent) and continues with the $15,000,001 to $18,333,333 bracket (taxed at 38 percent). Once taxable income reaches $18,333,334, the progression disappears (i.e., the lower brackets have been phased out) and the marginal rate on every dollar becomes 35 percent. Thus, the tax on $20 million is $7 million (35% × $20,000,000).

A calendar year corporation has taxable income of $90,000 for the current year. The income tax liability is $18,850, determined as $13,750 + ($90,000 − $75,000) × 34% or in the expanded form: $7,500 (15% × $50,000) + $6,250 (25% × $25,000) + $5,100 (34% × $15,000).

Qualified personal service corporations are taxed at a flat 35 percent rate on all taxable income. They do not enjoy the tax savings of the lower brackets. For this purpose, a *qualified* **personal service corporation** is a corporation that is substantially employee-owned and engages in one of the following activities: health, law, engineering, architecture, accounting, actuarial science, performing arts, or consulting.[34]

---

[31]§ 248.

[32]Reg. § 1.248–1(c).

[33]§ 11(b).

[34]Qualified personal service corporations were mentioned earlier in this chapter in connection with method of accounting.

EXHIBIT 20.2	**Income Tax Rates—Corporations**

Taxable income is:			
Over	**But not over**	**Tax is:**	**Of the amount over**
$ 0	$ 50,000	15%	$ 0
50,000	75,000	$ 7,500 + 25%	50,000
75,000	100,000	13,750 + 34%	75,000
100,000	335,000	22,250 + 39%*	100,000
335,000	10,000,000	113,900 + 34%	335,000
10,000,000	15,000,000	3,400,000 + 35%	10,000,000
15,000,000	18,333,333	5,150,000 + 38%**	15,000,000
18,333,333	–	35%	–

*Five percent of this rate represents a phaseout of the benefits of the lower tax rates on the first $75,000 of taxable income.

**Three percent of this rate represents a phaseout of the benefits of the lower tax rate (34% rather than 35%) on the first $10 million of taxable income.

Alternative Minimum Tax

Corporations are subject to an alternative minimum tax (AMT) that has the same objective and is structured in the same manner as that applicable to individuals. The AMT defines a more expansive tax base than for the regular tax. Like individuals, corporations are required to apply a minimum tax rate to the expanded base and pay the difference between the tentative AMT liability and the regular tax. Although many of the adjustments and tax preference items necessary to arrive at alternative minimum taxable income (AMTI) are the same for individuals and corporations, the rate and exemptions are different. As noted in Chapter 12, certain small business corporations are effectively exempt from the corporate AMT.

20-2f **Corporate Filing Requirements**

A corporation must file a return whether or not it has taxable income.[35] A corporation that was not in existence throughout an entire annual accounting period is required to file a return for the fraction of the year during which it was in existence. In addition, the corporation must file a return even though it has ceased to do business if it has valuable claims for which it will bring suit. It is relieved of filing returns once it ceases business and dissolves.

The corporate return is filed on Form 1120. Corporations making the S corporation election (discussed later in the chapter) file on Form 1120S.

Corporations with less than $250,000 of gross receipts and less than $250,000 in assets do not have to complete Schedule L (balance sheet) and Schedules M–1 and M–2 (see the next section) of Form 1120. Similar omissions are allowed for Form 1120S. These rules are intended to ease the compliance burden on small business.

In the past, a Form 1120 had to be filed on or before the fifteenth day of the third month following the close of the corporation's tax year. A 2015 tax law changed the due date to the *fourth* month following the close of the corporation's tax year.[36] Corporations can receive an automatic extension of six months for filing the corporate return by filing Form 7004 by the due date of the return.[37] However, the IRS

---

[35]§ 6012(a)(2).

[36]Due dates were changed by P.L. 114–41 (7/31/15) and generally apply to tax years beginning after December 31, 2015. Special rules apply for the normal due date of C corporations with a June 30 year-end.

[37]The due date change made by P.L. 114–41 (7/31/15) resulted in calendar year corporations having only a five-month extension for tax years 2016 through 2025. However, the IRS changed this to allow calendar year corporations a

six-month extension starting with the 2016 returns (October 15). A possible rationale for this change by the IRS is that there is no tax effect because any tax due must be paid by the unextended due date of the return. A corporation with a June 30 year-end has a due date of September 15 but an extended due date of April 15 (seven months). However, after 2025, the normal due date will be October 15, making the extended due date of April 15 a six-month extension.

may terminate an extension by mailing a 10-day notice to the taxpayer corporation.[38]

A corporation must make payments of estimated tax unless its tax liability can reasonably be expected to be less than $500. The payments must equal the lesser of 100 percent of the corporation's final tax or 100 percent of the last year's tax. These payments may be made in four installments due on or before the fifteenth day of the fourth, sixth, ninth, and twelfth months of the corporate taxable year.[39] The full amount of the unpaid tax is due on the date of the return. Failure to make the required estimated tax prepayments will result in assessment of a nondeductible penalty on the corporation. The penalty can be avoided, however, if any of various exceptions apply.[40]

20-2g Reconciliation of Corporate Taxable Income and Accounting Income

Taxable income and accounting net income are seldom the same amount. For example, a difference may arise if the corporation uses accelerated depreciation for tax purposes and straight-line depreciation for accounting purposes.

Many items of income for accounting purposes, such as proceeds from a life insurance policy on the death of a corporate officer and interest on municipal bonds, may not be includible in calculating taxable income. Some expense items for accounting purposes, such as expenses to produce tax-exempt income, estimated warranty reserves, a net capital loss, and Federal income taxes, are not deductible for tax purposes.

Schedule M–1 on the last page of Form 1120 is used to reconcile accounting net income (net income after Federal income taxes) with taxable income (as computed on the corporate tax return before the deduction for an NOL and the dividends received deduction). In the left-hand column of Schedule M–1, net income per books is added to the following: the Federal income tax liability for the year, the excess of capital losses over capital gains (which cannot be deducted in the current year), income for tax purposes that is not income in the current year for accounting purposes, and expenses recorded on the books that are not deductible on the tax return. In the right-hand column, income recorded on the books that is not currently taxable or is tax-exempt and deductions for tax purposes that are not expenses for accounting purposes are totaled and subtracted from the left-hand column total to arrive at taxable income (before the NOL or dividends received deductions).

EXAMPLE 26

During the current year, Crow Corporation had the following transactions:

Net income per books (after tax)	$92,400
Taxable income	50,000
Federal income tax liability (15% × $50,000)	7,500
Interest income from tax-exempt bonds	5,000
Interest paid on loan, the proceeds of which were used to purchase the tax-exempt bonds	500
Life insurance proceeds received as a result of the death of a key employee	50,000
Premiums paid on key employee life insurance policy	2,600
Excess of capital losses over capital gains	2,000

continued

---

[38]§ 6081.

[39]§ 6655(f). Corporations must use electronic funds transfers to make all Federal tax deposits, including estimated tax, through either the Electronic Federal Tax Payment System (EFTPS) or third-party providers.

[40]See § 6655 for the penalty involved and the various exceptions.

For book and tax purposes, Crow determines depreciation under the straight-line method. Crow's Schedule M–1 for the current year follows:

Schedule M-1	Reconciliation of Income (Loss) per Books With Income per Return				
	Note: The corporation may be required to file Schedule M-3. See instructions.				
1	Net income (loss) per books	92,400	7	Income recorded on books this year not included on this return (itemize):	
2	Federal income tax per books	7,500			
3	Excess of capital losses over capital gains .	2,000		Tax-exempt interest $ _5,000_	
4	Income subject to tax not recorded on books this year (itemize):_____			_Life insurance proceeds on key_ _employee $50,000_	55,000
			8	Deductions on this return not charged against book income this year (itemize):	
5	Expenses recorded on books this year not deducted on this return (itemize):		a	Depreciation . . . $ _____	
a	Depreciation . . . . $ _____		b	Charitable contributions $ _____	
b	Charitable contributions . $ _____			_____	
c	Travel and entertainment . $ _____			_____	
	Prem.–life ins. $2,600; Int.–exempt bonds $500	3,100	9	Add lines 7 and 8	55,000
6	Add lines 1 through 5	105,000	10	Income (page 1, line 28)—line 6 less line 9	50,000

Schedule M–2 reconciles unappropriated retained earnings at the beginning of the year with unappropriated retained earnings at year-end. Beginning balance plus net income per books, as entered on line 1 of Schedule M–1, less dividend distributions during the year equals ending retained earnings. Other sources of increases or decreases in retained earnings are also listed on Schedule M–2.

EXAMPLE 27

Assume the same facts as in Example 26. Crow Corporation's beginning balance in unappropriated retained earnings is $125,000, and Crow distributed a cash dividend of $30,000 to its shareholders during the year. Based on these further assumptions, Crow has the following Schedule M–2 for the current year:

Schedule M-2	Analysis of Unappropriated Retained Earnings per Books (Line 25, Schedule L)				
1	Balance at beginning of year	125,000	5	Distributions: a Cash	30,000
2	Net income (loss) per books	92,400		b Stock	
3	Other increases (itemize): _____			c Property . . .	
	_____		6	Other decreases (itemize):_____	
	_____		7	Add lines 5 and 6	30,000
4	Add lines 1, 2, and 3	217,400	8	Balance at end of year (line 4 less line 7)	187,400

Certain corporations must file **Schedule M–3**.[41] This schedule, designated "Net Income (Loss) Reconciliation for Corporations With Total Assets of $10 Million or More," is in lieu of Schedule M–1. It must be filed when the assets reported on Schedule L of Form 1120 total or exceed $10 million.[42] Because it reveals significant differences between book and taxable income, Schedule M–3 enables the IRS to more quickly identify potential audit areas and possible abusive transactions (e.g., use of tax shelter schemes).

Concept Summary 20.2

Summary of Income Tax Consequences

	Individuals	Corporations
Computation of gross income	§ 61.	§ 61.
Computation of taxable income	§§ 62, 63(b) through (h).	§ 63(a). Concept of AGI has no relevance.

continued

---

[41]Rev.Proc. 2004–45, 2004–2 C.B. 140. Schedule M–3 satisfies some of the disclosure requirements set forth in Reg. § 1.6011–4 when significant book-tax differences occur.

[42]For tax years ending December 31, 2014, and later, corporations and partnerships with more than $10 million of assets but less than $50 million of assets do not need to complete all parts of Schedule M–3. See the IRS website regarding Schedule M–3.

Summary of Income Tax Consequences—(Continued)

	Individuals	Corporations
Deductions	Trade or business (§ 162); nonbusiness (§ 212); some personal and employee expenses (generally deductible as itemized deductions).	Trade or business (§ 162).
Charitable contributions	Limited in any tax year to 50% of AGI; 30% for long-term capital gain property unless election is made to reduce fair market value of gift; 20% for long-term capital gain property contributed to private nonoperating foundations.	Limited in any tax year to 10% of taxable income computed without regard to the charitable contribution deduction, net operating loss or capital loss carryback, and dividends received deduction.
	Time of deduction—year in which payment is made.	Time of deduction—year in which payment is made unless accrual basis taxpayer. Accrual basis corporation may take deduction in year preceding payment if contribution was authorized by board of directors by end of that year and contribution is paid by fifteenth day of fourth month of following year.
	Contribution of ordinary income property is limited to the lesser of adjusted basis or fair market value.	Contribution of certain ordinary income property can include one-half of any appreciation on the property.
	Excess charitable contributions can be carried over for a period of up to five years.	Excess charitable contributions can be carried over for a period of up to five years.
Casualty losses	$100 floor on nonbusiness casualty and theft losses; nonbusiness casualty and theft losses deductible only to extent losses exceed 10% of AGI.	Deductible in full.
Depreciation recapture for § 1250 property	Recaptured to extent accelerated depreciation exceeds straight-line.	20% of excess of amount that would be recaptured under § 1245 over amount recaptured under § 1250 is additional ordinary income under § 291.
Domestic production activities deduction	9% of the lesser of QPAI or AGI.	9% of the lesser of QPAI or taxable income.
Net operating loss	Adjusted for nonbusiness deductions over nonbusiness income and for personal and dependency exemptions.	Generally no adjustments.
Dividends received	Qualified dividends are taxed at the same rate applicable to net long-term capital gains.	Deduction allowed (70%, 80%, or 100%) as to dividends received.
Long-term capital gains	Generally taxed at a rate no higher than 15% (20% if taxpayer is in the 39.6% bracket and 0% if taxpayer is in the 15% or lower tax bracket).	Taxed using regular corporate rates.
Capital losses	Only $3,000 of capital loss can offset ordinary income; loss is carried forward indefinitely to offset capital gains or ordinary income up to $3,000; carryovers of short-term losses remain short term; long-term losses carry over as long term.	Can offset only capital gains; carried back three years and forward five years; carrybacks and carryovers are treated as short-term losses.
Passive activity losses	Generally deductible only against income from passive activities.	For regular corporations, no limitation on deductibility. Personal service corporations and certain closely held corporations, however, are subject to same limitations as imposed on individuals. A closely held corporation is a corporation where five or fewer individuals own more than 50% of the stock either directly or indirectly.

continued

Summary of Income Tax Consequences—(Continued)

	Individuals	Corporations
Alternative minimum tax	Applied at a graduated rate schedule of 26% and 28% to AMT base (taxable income as modified by certain adjustments plus preference items minus exemption amount); exemption allowed depending on filing status; exemption phaseout begins when AMTI reaches a certain amount (e.g., $159,700 for 2016 for married filing jointly).	Applied at a 20% rate to AMT base (taxable income as modified by certain adjustments plus preference items minus exemption amount); $40,000 exemption allowed but phaseout begins once AMTI reaches $150,000; adjustments and tax preference items similar to those applicable to individuals but also include 75% of adjusted current earnings (ACE) over AMTI. Certain small business corporations are exempt from the AMT.
Tax rates	Progressive with seven rates of 10%, 15%, 25%, 28%, 33%, 35%, and 39.6%; lower brackets do not phase out.	Progressive with four rates of 15%, 25%, 34%, and 35%; lower brackets phased out at higher levels.
Filing due dates	Fifteenth day of the *fourth* month following the close of the individual's tax year.	Generally, same as for individuals.[43]
Medicare Contribution Surtax on Net Investment Income (§1411)	Applies to high-income individuals with net investment income (see Chapter 11).	Does not apply to corporations.

20-3 FORMING THE CORPORATION

LO.6

Describe the tax rules governing the formation of corporations.

20-3a Transfers to Controlled Corporations

Without special provisions in the Code, a transfer of property to a corporation in exchange for its stock would be a sale or exchange of property and would constitute a taxable transaction to the transferring shareholder. Section 351 provides for the nonrecognition of gain or loss upon such transfers of property if the transferors are in control of the corporation immediately after the transfer. Gain or loss is merely postponed in a manner similar to a like-kind exchange (see Chapter 15). The following requirements must be met to qualify under § 351:

- The transferors must be in control of the corporation immediately after the exchange. *Control* is defined as ownership of at least 80 percent of the total combined voting power of all classes of stock entitled to vote and at least 80 percent of the total number of shares of all other classes of stock.[44]

- Realized gain (but not loss) is recognized to the extent that the transferors receive property other than stock. Such nonqualifying property is commonly referred to as *boot*.

If the requirements of § 351 are satisfied and no boot is involved, nonrecognition of gain or loss is *mandatory*.

Basis Considerations and Computation of Gain

The nonrecognition of gain or loss is accompanied by a carryover of basis. The basis of stock received in a § 351 transfer is determined as follows:

- Start with the adjusted basis of the property transferred by the shareholder.
- Add any gain recognized by the shareholder as a result of the transfer.
- Subtract the fair market value of any boot received by the shareholder from the corporation.[45]

---

[43]See footnotes 36 and 37 for exceptions.

[44]§ 368(c).

[45]§ 358(a).

Shareholders who receive noncash boot have a basis in the property equal to the fair market value.

The basis of properties received by the corporation is the basis in the hands of the transferor increased by the amount of any gain recognized to the transferring shareholder.[46]

Basis Determination

EXAMPLE 28

Ann and Lori form Bluejay Corporation. Ann transfers property with an adjusted basis of $30,000 and a fair market value of $60,000 for 50% of the stock. Lori transfers property with an adjusted basis of $40,000 and a fair market value of $60,000 for the remaining 50% of the stock. The realized gain ($30,000 for Ann and $20,000 for Lori) is not recognized on the transfer because the transfer qualifies under § 351. The basis of the stock to Ann is $30,000, and the basis of the stock to Lori is $40,000. Bluejay Corporation has a basis of $30,000 in the property transferred by Ann and a basis of $40,000 in the property transferred by Lori.

EXAMPLE 29

Mike and John form Condor Corporation with the following investments: Mike transfers property (adjusted basis of $30,000 and fair market value of $70,000), and John transfers cash of $60,000. Each receives 50 shares of the Condor stock, but Mike also receives $10,000 in cash. Assume that each share of the Condor stock is worth $1,200. Mike's realized gain is $40,000, determined as follows:

Value of the Condor stock received	
[50 (shares) × $1,200 (value per share)]	$ 60,000
Cash received	10,000
Amount realized	$ 70,000
Less basis of property transferred	(30,000)
Realized gain	$ 40,000

Mike's recognized gain is $10,000, the lesser of the realized gain ($40,000) or the fair market value of the boot received ($10,000). Mike's basis in the Condor stock is $30,000, computed as follows:

Basis in the property transferred	$ 30,000
Plus recognized gain	10,000
	$ 40,000
Less boot received	(10,000)
Basis to Mike of the Condor stock	$ 30,000

Condor Corporation's basis in the property transferred by Mike is $40,000 [$30,000 (basis of the property to Mike) + $10,000 (gain recognized by Mike)]. John neither realizes nor recognizes gain or loss and will have a basis of $60,000 in the Condor stock.

The receipt of stock for the performance of *services* always results in ordinary income to the transferring shareholder. An example might be an attorney who does not charge a fee for incorporating a business but instead receives the value equivalent in stock of the newly formed corporation. The basis of stock received for the performance of services is equal to the fair market value of the services.

20-3b **Capital Contributions**

The receipt of money or property in exchange for capital stock produces neither recognized gain nor loss to the recipient corporation.[47] Gross income of a corporation does not include shareholders' contributions of money or property to the capital of the corporation.[48] Contributions by nonshareholders are also excluded from the gross income of

---

[46]§ 362(a).
[47]§ 1032.

[48]§ 118.

a corporation.[49] The basis of the property transferred by nonshareholders to the corporation is zero.

A city donates land worth $900,000 to Cardinal Corporation as an inducement for it to locate in the city. The receipt of the land does not represent gross income. The land's basis to the corporation is zero.

EXAMPLE 30

Thin Capitalization

The advantages of capitalizing a corporation with debt may be substantial. Interest on debt is deductible by the corporation, while dividend payments are not. Further, the shareholders are not taxed on loan repayments unless the payments exceed basis.

In certain instances, the IRS will claim **thin capitalization** by holding that debt is really an equity interest and will deny the shareholders the tax advantages of debt financing. If the debt instrument has too many similarities to stock, it may be treated as a form of stock, with principal and interest payments treated as dividends.[50]

Minimum Capitalization

With many small corporations, particularly nonmanufacturing personal service corporations, the capitalization is minimal. The corporation is formed with whatever investment in stock is required under applicable state law.

The Big Picture

Return to the facts of *The Big Picture* on p. 20-1. Suppose the Todd sisters decide to conduct their catering business in the corporate form—either a C or S corporation. In forming the corporation, they should probably limit their capital investment to whatever state law requires. The sisters should consider acquiring the capital assets needed to operate the business (e.g., delivery trucks, kitchen equipment, location for food preparation) on their own and leasing them to the corporation. This would allow the sisters to claim the appropriate depreciation and would provide the corporation with a deduction for the rent paid. Although this strategy would force the sisters to recognize rent income rather than preferentially taxed dividends, no dividends will be forthcoming in the early loss years of the business.

EXAMPLE 31

ETHICS & EQUITY   **Selective Incorporation**

Miguel, a cash basis taxpayer, owns and operates a home renovation business that he decides to incorporate. In forming the corporation, he transfers *most* of the business, which includes unrealized receivables and inventory items. However, he retains the land and building and the trade accounts payable.

For tax purposes, what is Miguel trying to accomplish by being selective in terms of what he transfers to the corporation? Will it work? Why or why not?

20-4 OPERATING THE CORPORATION

LO.7

Explain the tax rules governing the operation of corporations.

20-4a Dividend Distributions

Corporate distributions of cash or property to shareholders are treated as dividend income to the extent the corporation has accumulated *and/or* current earnings and

---

[49]*Edwards v. Cuba Railroad Co.*, 1 USTC ¶139, 5 AFTR 5398, 45 S.Ct. 614 (USSC, 1925).

[50]§ 385 lists several factors that might be used to determine whether a debtor-creditor relationship or a shareholder-corporation relationship exists.

GLOBAL TAX ISSUES   **Transferring Assets to Foreign Corporations—Forget § 351?**

Tax-deferred transfers to controlled corporations under § 351 may generate current taxation when those transfers cross national borders. When a U.S. person transfers appreciated assets to a foreign corporation, the United States may lose its ability to tax the deferred gain on those assets (as well as the future income generated by the assets). To protect the U.S. taxing jurisdiction, § 367 provides that transfers of assets outside the United States are generally taxable, in spite of the provisions of § 351.

EXAMPLE 32

As of January 1, 2017, Teal Corporation has a deficit in accumulated E & P of $300,000. For tax year 2017, it has current E & P of $100,000. In 2017, the corporation distributes $50,000 to its shareholders. The $50,000 distribution is treated as a dividend because it is deemed to have been made from current E & P. This is the case even though Teal still has a deficit in its accumulated E & P at the end of 2017.

profits (E & P).[51] In determining the source of the distribution, a dividend is deemed to have been made initially from current E & P.

Qualified dividend income is taxed like net long-term capital gain.[52] Consequently, the tax rate on such income cannot exceed 20 percent (0 percent for individual shareholders in the 15 percent or lower tax bracket).[53]

If a corporate distribution is not covered by E & P (either current or past), it is treated as a return of capital (refer to the discussion of the recovery of capital doctrine in Chapter 4). Because this treatment allows the shareholder to apply the amount of the distribution against the basis of the stock investment, the distribution represents a nontaxable return of capital. Any amount received in excess of the stock basis is classified as a capital gain (if the stock is a capital asset in the hands of the shareholder).

EXAMPLE 33

When Mallard Corporation has no E & P (either current or accumulated), it distributes cash of $300,000 to its sole shareholder, Helen. The basis of Helen's stock investment is $200,000. Based on these facts, the $300,000 distribution Helen receives is accounted for as follows:

Return of capital (nontaxable)	$200,000
Capital gain	100,000
Total amount of distribution	$300,000

After the distribution, Helen has a basis of zero in her stock investment.

Concept of Earnings and Profits

The term **earnings and profits** is not defined in the Code, but § 312 does include certain transactions that affect E & P. Although E & P and the accounting concept of retained earnings have certain similarities, they differ in numerous respects. For example, a nontaxable stock dividend is treated as a capitalization of retained earnings for accounting purposes, yet it does not decrease E & P for tax purposes. Taxable dividends do reduce E & P but cannot yield a deficit. Referring to Example 33, after the distribution, Mallard Corporation's E & P remains zero rather than being a negative amount.

Accumulated E & P is the sum of the corporation's prior current E & P that has not been distributed as dividends. A more detailed discussion of the concept of E & P is beyond the scope of this chapter.

---

[51]§ 316. E & P is defined in the next section.

[52]Qualified dividend income is defined in § 1(h)(11)(B), and taxation is discussed in Chapter 16.

[53]§ 1(h)(1). See the discussion in Chapter 3.

Property Dividends

A distribution of property to a shareholder is measured by the fair market value of the property on the date of distribution. The fair market value is also the shareholder's basis in the property.[54]

Drake Corporation has E & P of $60,000. It distributes land with a fair market value of $50,000 (adjusted basis of $30,000) to its sole shareholder, Art. Art has a taxable dividend of $50,000 and a basis in the land of $50,000.

A corporation that distributes appreciated property to its shareholders as a dividend must recognize the amount of the appreciation as gain.[55]

Assume the same facts as in Example 34. Drake Corporation must recognize a gain of $20,000 on the distribution it made to Art.

However, if the property distributed has a basis in excess of its fair market value, the distributing corporation cannot recognize any loss.

Constructive Dividends

In a closely held corporation, a shareholder may direct the corporation to make certain payments to a shareholder that are not intended to be classified as a dividend (e.g., rent or salary). Depending on the reasonableness of the payment and the corporation's dividend history, the IRS may reclassify the payment as a constructive dividend, thus converting the payment into a dividend for tax purposes. The following are examples of constructive dividends:

- Salaries paid to shareholder-employees that are not reasonable (refer to Example 7 in Chapter 6).

- Interest on debt owed by the corporation to shareholders that is reclassified as equity because the corporation is thinly capitalized (refer to the earlier discussion in this chapter).

- Excessive rent paid by a corporation for the use of shareholder property. The arm's length standard is used to test whether the rent is excessive (refer to Example 27 in Chapter 1).

- Advances to shareholders that are not bona fide loans.

- Interest-free (or below-market) loans to shareholders. In this situation, the dividend component is the difference between the interest provided for, if any, and that calculated using the market rate.

- Shareholder use of corporate property for less than an arm's length rate.

- Absorption by the corporation of a shareholder's personal expenses.

- Bargain purchase of corporate property by shareholders.

Like regular dividends, constructive dividends must be covered by E & P to carry dividend income consequences to the shareholders. As noted previously, however, constructive dividends need not be available to all shareholders on a pro rata basis.

---

[54]§ 301.

[55]The tax consequences to a corporation of nonliquidating distributions to shareholders are covered in § 311.

EXAMPLE
36

Return to the facts of *The Big Picture* on p. 20-1. Also recall the suggestions made in Example 31. If they choose the corporate form, the Todd sisters will need to take the following into account:

- Any salaries the sisters pay themselves should satisfy the reasonableness test.
- Rent charged to the corporation for the use of assets owned by the sisters should meet the arm's length standard.
- Loans made to the corporation for working capital purposes should provide for a market rate of interest to be charged.

Although the constructive dividend issue will not arise until the corporation becomes profitable (and has E & P), these procedures should be structured at the outset so that the parties will be prepared for a possible future challenge by the IRS.

20-4b Other Corporate Considerations

Complex tax provisions involving stock redemptions and corporate liquidations are beyond the scope of this text and are discussed in depth in *South-Western Federal Taxation: Corporations, Partnerships, Estates & Trusts*.

LO.8

Assess the utility and effect of the Subchapter S election.

20-5 THE S ELECTION

Numerous nontax reasons exist for operating a business in the corporate form (e.g., limited liability). Consequently, the existence of income tax disadvantages (e.g., double taxation of corporate income and shareholder dividends) should not deter business-people from using the corporate form. To prevent tax considerations from interfering with the exercise of sound business judgment, Congress enacted Subchapter S of the Code. The Subchapter S election enables certain taxpayers to use the corporate form for conducting a business without being taxed as a corporation.

20-5a Qualification for S Status

To achieve S corporation status, the corporation must meet certain requirements and make an effective election.

Qualifying for the Election

To qualify for S corporation status, the corporation must be a small business corporation. This includes any corporation that has the following characteristics:

- It is a domestic corporation.
- There are no more than 100 shareholders.
- Its shareholders are only individuals, estates, and certain trusts.
- No shareholder is a nonresident alien.
- It has only one class of stock outstanding.

These characteristics must continue to exist if an electing S corporation is to maintain S status.

The members of a family who own stock are treated as a single shareholder. Members of a family include all lineal descendants (e.g., children, grandchildren) of a shareholder and spouse (or ex-spouse) and the spouses (or ex-spouses) of such lineal descendants.[56]

EXAMPLE
37

Harry, a shareholder in an S corporation dies, and under his will, his stock is distributed among three children and eight grandchildren. The 11 new shareholders are treated as one shareholder for purposes of the 100-shareholder limitation.

---

[56]§ 1361(c)(1).

Making the Election

The election is made by filing Form 2553, and *all* shareholders must consent. It is important to determine who needs to sign the form. For example, if a married couple owns the stock as community property, both spouses must sign the consent, even though they count as a single shareholder.

To be effective for the current year, the election must be filed anytime during the preceding taxable year or on or before the fifteenth day of the third month of the current year.[57]

Heron, a calendar year taxpayer, is a regular corporation that wants to elect S status for 2017. If the election is filed anytime from January 1, 2016, up to and including March 15, 2017, it will be effective for 2017.

EXAMPLE 38

The IRS has the authority to waive invalid S elections (e.g., inadvertent failure to obtain all necessary shareholder consents to the original election) and to treat late elections as timely.[58]

Loss of the Election

The S election may be terminated *voluntarily* (a majority of the shareholders file to revoke the election) or *involuntarily*. An involuntary termination may occur in *either* of the following ways:

- The corporation ceases to qualify as a small business corporation (e.g., the number of shareholders exceeds 100 or a partnership becomes a shareholder).

- The corporation has passive investment income (e.g., interest and dividends) in excess of 25 percent of gross receipts for a period of three consecutive years. This possibility applies only if the corporation was previously a regular corporation and has E & P from that period.

If the holders of a *majority* of the shares consent to a voluntary revocation of S status, the election to revoke must be made on or before the fifteenth day of the third month of the tax year to be effective for that year.

The shareholders of Stork Corporation, a calendar year S corporation, elect to revoke the election on January 4, 2017. Assuming that the election is duly executed and timely filed, Stork will become a regular corporation for calendar year 2017. If the election to revoke is not made until June 2017, Stork will not become a regular corporation until calendar year 2018.

EXAMPLE 39

Suppose the shareholders in Example 39 file the election to revoke on January 4, 2017, but do not want the revocation to take place until 2018. If the election so specifies, Stork Corporation will cease to have S status as of January 1, 2018.

In the case where S status is lost because of a disqualifying act (involuntarily), the loss of the election takes effect as of the date on which the event occurs.

Crow Corporation has been a calendar year S corporation for several years. On August 12, 2017, one of its shareholders sells her stock to Kite Corporation. Because Crow Corporation no longer satisfies the definition of a small business corporation (it has another corporation as a shareholder), the election has been involuntarily terminated. For calendar year 2017, therefore, Crow will be an S corporation through August 11 and a regular corporation from August 12 through December 31, 2017.

EXAMPLE 40

Barring certain exceptions, the loss of the election places the corporation in a five-year holding period before S status can be reelected.

---

[57]§ 1362.

[58]See Rev. Proc. 2013–30, 2013–36 I.R.B. 173, and §1362(b)(5).

20-5b **Operational Rules**

The S corporation is primarily a tax-reporting rather than a taxpaying entity. In this respect, the entity is taxed much like a partnership.[59] Under the conduit concept, the taxable income and losses of an S corporation flow through to the shareholders who report them on their personal income tax returns.

To ascertain the annual tax consequences to each shareholder, it is necessary to carry out two steps at the S corporation level. First, all corporate transactions that will flow through to the shareholders on an *as is* basis under the conduit approach must be set aside. Second, what remains is aggregated as the taxable income of the S corporation and is allocated to each shareholder on a per-share and per-day of stock ownership basis.[60]

Separately Stated Items

Following are some of the items that do not lose their identity as they pass through the S corporation and are therefore picked up by each shareholder on an *as is* basis:

- Tax-exempt income.
- Long-term and short-term capital gains and losses.
- Section 1231 gains and losses.
- Charitable contributions.
- Domestic production activities deduction (DPAD).
- Qualified dividend income.
- Foreign tax credits.
- Depletion.
- Nonbusiness income or loss under § 212.
- Intangible drilling costs.
- Investment interest, income, and expenses covered under § 163(d).
- Certain portfolio income.
- Passive activity gains, losses, and credits under § 469.
- AMT adjustments and tax preference items.

In the case of the DPAD, the individual components needed to determine the deduction at the shareholder level must be broken out. These components include each shareholder's pro rata portion of QPAI and the W–2 wages paid by the corporation. This information is listed on Schedule K–1 (Form 1120S) and is picked up by the shareholder on lines 7 and 17 of his or her Form 8903 (Domestic Production Activities Deduction).

In the preceding list, the items are stated separately because each may lead to a different tax result when combined with a particular shareholder's other transactions.

EXAMPLE 41

Arnold and Jean are equal shareholders in Lark Corporation (an S corporation). For calendar year 2017, each must account for one-half of a corporate short-term capital gain of $6,000. Arnold has no other capital asset transactions, and Jean has a short-term capital loss of $3,000 from the sale of stock in IBM Corporation. In terms of overall effect, the difference between the two taxpayers is significant. Although both must report the short-term capital gain passed through to them from the S corporation, Jean will neutralize its inclusion in gross income by offsetting it with the $3,000 short-term capital loss from the sale of the IBM stock. For Arnold, the short-term capital gain results in a $3,000 increase in his taxable income.

---

[59]This is not to imply that an S corporation is always free from the income tax. For example, a tax may be imposed on certain built-in gains or certain excessive passive investment income.

[60]§ 1366.

Taxable Income

After the separately stated items have been removed, the balance represents the taxable income of the S corporation. In arriving at taxable income, the dividends received deduction, the DPAD, and the NOL deduction are not allowed. An S corporation does come under the regular corporate rules, however, for purposes of amortization of organizational expenditures.

Once taxable income has been determined, it passes through to each shareholder as of the last day of the S corporation's tax year.

Computing S Corporation Income

Harrier Corporation, a calendar year S corporation, had the following transactions during the current year:

Sales		$ 400,000
Cost of goods sold		(230,000)
Other income		
*Tax-exempt interest	$ 3,000	
*Long-term capital gain	5,000	8,000
Other expenses		
*Charitable contributions	$ 4,000	
Advertising expense	15,000	
Other operating expenses	20,000	
*Short-term capital loss	1,500	(40,500)
Net income per books		$ 137,500

When the items that are to be separately stated [those preceded by an asterisk (*)] and shown *as is* by each shareholder are withdrawn, Harrier has the following taxable income:

Sales		$ 400,000
Cost of goods sold		(230,000)
Other expenses		
Advertising expense	$15,000	
Other operating expenses	20,000	(35,000)
Taxable income		$ 135,000

If Oscar owned 10% of the stock in Harrier Corporation (refer to Example 42) during all of the current year, he must account for the following:

Separately stated items	
Tax-exempt interest	$ 300
Long-term capital gain	500
Charitable contributions	400
Short-term capital loss	150
Taxable income (10% of $135,000)	13,500

Some of the separately stated items (e.g., the tax-exempt interest) must be reported on Oscar's individual income tax return but may not lead to tax consequences. Oscar picks up his share of Harrier's taxable income ($13,500) as ordinary income.

Treatment of Losses

As previously noted, separately stated loss items (e.g., capital losses and § 1231 losses) flow through to the shareholders on an *as is* basis. Their treatment by a shareholder depends on the shareholder's individual income tax position. If the S corporation's taxable income determination results in an operating loss, it also passes through to the shareholders. As is the case with separately stated items, the amount of the loss each shareholder receives depends upon the stock ownership during the year.

EXAMPLE 44

In 2017, Oriole Corporation (a calendar year S corporation) incurred an operating loss of $365,000. During 2017, Jason's ownership in Oriole was 20% for 200 days and 30% for 165 days. Jason's share of the loss is determined as follows:

[$365,000 × (200/365)] × 20% = $40,000
[$365,000 × (165/365)] × 30% = 49,500
Total loss for Jason $89,500

Presuming that the basis limitation does not come into play (see the following discussion), Jason deducts $89,500 in arriving at adjusted gross income.

The Big Picture

EXAMPLE 45

Return to the facts of *The Big Picture* on p. 20-1. Recall that the Todd sisters anticipate losses in the early years of their catering business. If they form a C corporation, such losses will be of no benefit to the new corporation—no carryback will be available, and there will be only a potential for a delayed carryover. With an S election, however, losses pass through currently. Thus, the sisters will secure limited liability for their business and the immediate tax benefit of any losses [assuming that they materially participate in the S corporation activity (see Chapter 11)].

Basis Determination

A shareholder's *basis* in the stock of an S corporation, like that of a regular corporation, is the original investment plus additional capital contributions less return of capital distributions. At this point, however, the symmetry disappears. Generally, basis is increased by the income items passed through (including those separately stated) and decreased by the loss items passed through (including those separately stated).[61]

EXAMPLE 46

In 2017, Warbler Corporation is formed with an investment of $500,000, of which Janice contributed $100,000 for a 20% stock interest. A timely S election is made, and for 2017, Warbler earns taxable income of $50,000. Janice's basis in her stock investment now becomes $110,000 [$100,000 (original capital contribution) + $10,000 (the 20% share of the corporation's taxable income assigned to Janice)].

Distributions by an S corporation reduce the basis of a shareholder's stock investment. However, if the amount of the distribution exceeds basis, the excess normally receives capital gain treatment.

As previously noted, operating losses of an S corporation pass through to the shareholders and reduce the basis in their stock investment. Because the basis of the stock cannot fall below zero, an excess loss is then applied against the basis of any loans the shareholder may have made to the corporation.

EXAMPLE 47

Flamingo Corporation, a calendar year S corporation, has an operating loss of $60,000 for 2017. Norman, a 50% shareholder, has an adjusted basis of $25,000 in his stock investment and has made loans to the corporation of $5,000. Based on these facts, Norman may take full advantage of the $30,000 loss (50% of $60,000) on his 2017 individual income tax return. Norman's basis in the stock and the loans must be reduced accordingly, and both will be zero after the pass-through.

In the event the basis limitation precludes an operating loss from being absorbed, the loss can be carried forward and deducted when and if it is covered by basis.

---
[61]§ 1367.

EXAMPLE 48

Assume the same facts as in Example 47, except that Norman had not made any loans to Flamingo Corporation. Further assume that Flamingo has taxable income of $15,000 in the following year (2018). Norman's tax situation for 2017 and 2018 is summarized as follows:

Ordinary loss for 2017 (limited to basis of investment)	$25,000
Income to be reported in 2018 (50% of $15,000)	7,500
Restoration of stock basis in 2018 (50% of $15,000)	7,500
Loss allowed for 2018 carried over from 2017 ($30,000 − $25,000)	5,000
Basis in stock account after 2018 ($7,500 − $5,000)	2,500

Thus, Norman's unabsorbed loss of $5,000 from 2017 carries over to 2018 and is applied against the $7,500 of ordinary income for that year.

ETHICS & EQUITY **Income Tax Basis That Does Not Change?**

In 2001, Howard purchased stock in Green, a C corporation, for $100,000. In 2007, Green made a valid election under Subchapter S. In 2017, Howard sells his stock in Green for $120,000. Because he paid $100,000 for the stock, Howard plans to recognize a long-term capital gain of $20,000 as a result of the sale. Do you agree with Howard's proposed reporting?

Distributions

Because the income and losses of an S corporation are passed through to the owners, distributions to shareholders from an S corporation are generally excluded from gross income to the extent of the shareholder's stock basis. If the distribution is greater than the shareholder's basis, then the amount in excess of basis is treated as a capital gain. However, should the S corporation have been converted from an earlier C corporation that had earnings and profits at the time of the conversion, a different set of complex rules apply, making it more likely that the shareholders will not escape dividend taxation by converting to an S corporation.

A comparison of the various tax attributes of C and S corporations appears in Concept Summary 20.3.

20-6 PARTNERSHIPS

LO.9
Review the tax consequences of forming and operating a partnership.

Another choice of business entity to consider is a partnership. A partnership must have more than one owner. It has some similarities with corporations, particularly S corporations.

20-6a Nature of Partnership Taxation

Unlike corporations, partnerships are not considered separate taxable entities. Each member of a partnership is subject to income tax on the partner's distributive share of the partnership's income, even if an actual distribution is not made. The tax return (Form 1065) required of a partnership serves only to provide information necessary in determining the character and amount of each partner's distributive share of the partnership's income and expense. Because a partnership acts as a conduit, items that pass through to the partners do not lose their identity. For example, tax-exempt income earned by a partnership is picked up by the partners as tax-exempt income. In this regard, partnerships function in much the same fashion as S corporations, which also serve as conduits.

A partnership is considered a separate taxable entity for purposes of making various elections and selecting its taxable year, method of depreciation, and accounting method. A partnership is also treated as a separate legal entity under civil law with the right to own property in its own name and to transact business free from the personal debts of its partners.

Concept Summary 20.3

A Comparison of Some of the Attributes of S and C Corporations

Attribute	S Corporations	C Corporations
Number of shareholders	Limited to 100 with spouses counted as one. Can elect to count certain related shareholders as one.	Generally, no limit.
Types of shareholders	Cannot have as shareholders most trusts and corporations, partnerships, and nonresident aliens.	No restriction.
Tax year	Restricted to calendar year unless IRS approves a different year for business purposes or other exceptions apply.	Unrestricted selection allowed at time of filing first tax return, except for personal service corporations.
Due date of return	Fifteenth day of the *third* month following the close of the corporation's tax year.	Usually, the fifteenth day of the *fourth* month following the close of the corporation's tax year.
Treatment of gains:		
Tax incidence.	Generally, not taxed to entity but passed through to shareholders.	Subject to the corporate income tax.
Nature of gain.	Items such as capital gains and tax-exempt income do not lose their identity.	Identity lost. When later passed through to shareholders, treated as dividend income.
Timing of taxation to shareholders.	Taxed to shareholders as of the last day of the corporation's tax year.	Not taxed to shareholders until distributed as dividends.
Treatment of losses:		
Tax incidence.	Not deductible to the entity but passed through to shareholders.	Deductible by the corporation.
Nature of loss.	Items such as capital losses do not lose their identity.	Capital losses are deducted only to extent of capital gains.
Timing of taxation to shareholders.	Passed through to shareholders as of last day of the corporation's tax year. Deduction limited to shareholder's stock basis plus any loans made to corporation.	Not passed through to shareholders.
Shareholder's basis in stock investment	Original stock investment *plus* gains passed through *less* losses passed through *and* distributions from corporation.	Original stock investment *plus* additional capital contributions *less* return of capital distributions.

20-6b Partnership Formation and Basis

Recognition of Gain or Loss

The general rule is that no gain or loss is recognized by a partnership or any of its partners on the contribution of property in exchange for a capital interest in the partnership.[62] This rule also applies to all subsequent contributions of property.

There are certain exceptions to the nonrecognition of gain or loss rule, including the following:

- If a partner transfers property to the partnership and receives money or other consideration (boot) as a result, the transaction will be treated as a sale or exchange rather than as a contribution of capital. Realized gain is recognized to the extent of the fair market value of the boot received.

---

[62]§ 721.

- If a partnership interest is received in exchange for services rendered or to be rendered by the partner to the partnership, the fair market value of the transferred capital interest is regarded as compensation for services rendered. In such cases, the recipient of the capital interest must recognize the amount as ordinary income in the year actually or constructively received.

- If property that is subject to a liability in excess of its basis is contributed to a partnership, the contributing partner may recognize gain.

Basis of a Partnership Interest

The contributing *partner's basis* in the partnership interest received is the sum of money contributed plus the adjusted basis of any other property transferred to the partnership.[63]

In return for the contribution of property (with a basis of $50,000 and a fair market value of $80,000) and cash of $10,000 to the Brown Partnership, Marcia receives a 10% capital interest worth $90,000. Although Marcia has a realized gain of $30,000 ($90,000 − $60,000) on the transfer, none of the gain is recognized. The basis of her interest in the Brown Partnership is $60,000 [$50,000 (basis of property contributed) + $10,000 (cash contribution)].

A partner's basis in the partnership interest is determined without regard to any amount reflected on the partnership's books as capital, equity, or a similar account.

Marge and Clyde form the equal Blue Partnership with a cash contribution of $300,000 from Marge and a property contribution (adjusted basis of $180,000 and fair market value of $300,000) from Clyde. Although the books of the Blue Partnership may reflect a credit of $300,000 to each partner's capital account, only Marge has a tax basis of $300,000 in her partnership interest. Clyde's tax basis in his partnership interest is $180,000, the amount of his tax basis in the property contributed to the partnership.

After its initial determination, the basis of a partnership interest is subject to continuous fluctuations. A partner's basis is increased by additional contributions and the sum of his or her current and prior years' distributive share of the following:

- Taxable income of the partnership, including capital gains.

- Tax-exempt income of the partnership.

- The excess of the deductions for depletion over the basis of the partnership's property subject to depletion.[64]

Similarly, the basis of a partner's interest is decreased, but not below zero, by distributions of partnership property (including cash) and by the sum of the current and prior years' distributive share of the following:

- Partnership losses, including capital losses.

- Partnership expenditures that are not deductible in computing taxable income or loss and that are not capital expenditures.

Changes in the liabilities (including trade accounts payable and bank loans) of a partnership also affect the basis of a partnership interest. A partner's basis is increased by his or her assumption of partnership liabilities and by his or her pro rata share of liabilities incurred by the partnership. Likewise, the partner's basis is decreased by the amount of any personal liabilities assumed by the partnership and by the pro rata share of any decreases in the liabilities of the partnership.

---

[63]§ 722.   [64]§ 705(a).

Effect of Liability on Basis

EXAMPLE 51

Tony, Martha, and Carolyn form the Orange Partnership with the following contributions: cash of $100,000 from Tony for a 50% interest in capital and profits, cash of $50,000 from Martha for a 25% interest, and property valued at $66,000 from Carolyn for a 25% interest. The property contributed by Carolyn has an adjusted basis of $30,000 and is subject to a mortgage of $16,000, which is assumed by the partnership. Carolyn's basis in her interest in the Orange Partnership is $18,000, determined as follows:

Adjusted basis of Carolyn's contributed property	$ 30,000
Less portion of mortgage assumed by Tony and Martha and treated as a distribution of money to Carolyn (75% of $16,000)	(12,000)
Basis of Carolyn's interest in Orange Partnership	$ 18,000

EXAMPLE 52

Assuming the same facts as in Example 51, Tony and Martha have a basis in their partnership interests of $108,000 and $54,000, respectively.

	Tony	Martha
Cash contribution	$100,000	$50,000
Plus portion of mortgage assumed and treated as an additional cash contribution:		
(50% of $16,000)	8,000	
(25% of $16,000)		4,000
Basis of interest in Orange Partnership	$108,000	$54,000

Partnership's Basis in Contributed Property

The *basis of property* contributed to a partnership by a partner is the adjusted basis of the property to the contributing partner at the time of the contribution.[65] In addition, the holding period of the property for the partnership includes the period during which the property was held by the contributing partner. This is logical because the partnership's basis in the property is the same basis the property had in the hands of the partner.[66]

EXAMPLE 53

In 2017, Roger contributed equipment with an adjusted basis of $100,000 and fair market value of $300,000 to the Red Partnership in exchange for a one-third interest in the partnership. No gain or loss is recognized by Roger. The Red Partnership's basis in the equipment is $100,000. If Roger had acquired the equipment in 2011, the partnership's holding period would include the period from 2011 through 2017.

20-6c Partnership Operation

Measuring and Reporting Partnership Income

Although a partnership is not subject to Federal income taxation, it is required to determine its taxable income and file an income tax return for information purposes.[67] The tax return, Form 1065, is due on the fifteenth day of the *third* month following the close of the taxable year of the partnership. (For tax returns covering years before 2016, the due date fell on the fifteenth day of the *fourth* month.)

---

[65] § 723.

[66] § 1223(2).

[67] § 6031.

In measuring and reporting partnership income, certain transactions must be segregated and reported separately on the partnership return. Items such as charitable contributions, the domestic production activities deduction, capital gains and losses, qualified dividend income, and foreign taxes are excluded from partnership taxable income and are allocated separately to the partners.[68] These items must be segregated and allocated separately because they affect the computation of various exclusions, deductions, and credits at the individual partner level.

Similar to the procedure for an S corporation, the individual components needed to determine the DPAD at the partner level must be separated. These components include each partner's pro rata portion of QPAI and the W–2 wages paid by the partnership. This information is listed on Schedule K–1 (Form 1065) and is picked up by the partner on lines 7 and 17 of his or her Form 8903 (Domestic Production Activities Deduction).

The separate stating of certain attributes of the partnership is essential as they may result in differing tax consequences when passed through to the various partners.[69]

EXAMPLE 54

Alyssa, Madison, and Brad are equal partners in the Yellow Partnership. All parties use the calendar year for tax purposes. Among other transactions, Yellow had the following separately stated items for 2017: $30,000 in QPAI, $15,000 in long-term capital gains, and $6,000 in charitable contributions. The pass-through of these items generates the following results: Alyssa cannot use all of her $10,000 share of QPAI because of the AGI limitation; Madison's $5,000 long-term capital gain is not subject to tax (i.e., she is in a 15% or lower tax bracket); and Brad cannot benefit from his $2,000 share of the charitable contribution as he chooses not to itemize (i.e., claims the standard deduction). Thus, the pass-through of these separately stated items caused different tax consequences to the partners.

A second step in the measurement and reporting process is the computation of the partnership's ordinary income or loss. The taxable income of a partnership is computed in the same manner as the taxable income of an individual taxpayer. However, a partnership is not allowed the following deductions:[70]

- The deduction for personal and dependency exemptions.
- The deduction for taxes paid to foreign countries or possessions of the United States.
- The deduction for charitable contributions.
- The deduction for net operating losses.
- The additional itemized deductions allowed individuals in §§ 211 through 219.

The partnership's ordinary income or loss and each of the items requiring separate treatment are reported in the partnership's information return and allocated to the partners in accordance with their distributive shares.

Limitation on Partner's Share of Losses

A partner's deduction of the distributive share of partnership losses (including capital losses) could be limited. The limitation is the adjusted basis of the partnership interest at the end of the partnership year in which the losses were incurred.

The limitation for partnership loss deductions is similar to that applicable to losses of S corporations. Like S corporation losses, partnership losses may be carried forward by the partner and utilized against future increases in the basis of the partnership interest. Such increases might result from additional capital contributions to the partnership, from additional partnership liabilities, or from future partnership income. Unlike S corporations, however, loans to the entity cannot be utilized by a partner to absorb the pass-through of losses.

---

[68]§ 702(a).

[69]Review Schedule K–1 (Form 1065) to see what tax attributes are reported separately.

[70]§ 703(a).

Loss Limitation and Utilization

EXAMPLE 55

Florence and Donald do business as the Green Partnership, sharing profits and losses equally. All parties use the calendar year for tax purposes. As of January 1, 2017, Florence's basis in her partnership interest is $25,000. The partnership sustained an operating loss of $80,000 in 2017 and earned a profit of $70,000 in 2018. For the calendar year 2017, Florence may claim only $25,000 of her $40,000 distributive share of the partnership loss (one-half of the $80,000 loss). As a result, the basis in her partnership interest is reduced to zero as of January 1, 2018, and she must carry forward the remaining $15,000 of partnership losses.

EXAMPLE 56

Assuming the same facts as in Example 55, what are the income tax consequences for Florence in 2018? Because the partnership earned a profit of $70,000 for the calendar year 2018, Florence reports income from the partnership of $20,000 ($35,000 distributive share of income for 2018 less the $15,000 loss not allowed for 2017). The adjusted basis of her partnership interest now becomes $20,000.

Guaranteed Payments

Payments made by a partnership to one of its partners for services rendered or for the use of capital, to the extent they are determined without regard to the income of the partnership, are treated by the partnership in the same manner as payments made to a person who is not a partner. Referred to as **guaranteed payments**, these are generally deductible by the partnership as a business expense.[71] The payments must be reported as ordinary income by the receiving partner and do not affect the partner's basis in the partnership interest. Their deductibility distinguishes guaranteed payments from a partner's distributive share of income that is not deductible by the partnership.

EXAMPLE 57

Under the terms of the Silver Partnership agreement, Kim is entitled to a fixed annual salary of $60,000 without regard to the income of the partnership. He is also to share in the profits and losses of the partnership as a one-third partner. After deducting the guaranteed payment, the partnership has $300,000 of ordinary income. Kim must include $160,000 as ordinary income on his income tax return for his tax year with or within which the partnership tax year ends ($60,000 guaranteed payment + $100,000 one-third distributive share of partnership income).

Limited Liability Companies

Limited liability companies (LLCs) are generally treated as a partnership for tax purposes (although refer to text Section 20-1 in the chapter for Check-the-box options). An LLC differs from a partnership in a few significant ways. Generally, a partnership can be formed without any formal paperwork, whereas an LLC is required to file articles of organization with the state. Another significant difference is that unlike general partners in a partnership, LLC members (LLC owners) are not personally responsible for the debts of the LLC. Another significant difference is that an LLC can be formed with only one member. A so-called single-member LLC is treated as a disregarded entity for tax purposes. As a result, the operations of a single-member LLC are treated like a sole proprietorship for tax purposes. The way in which debt is allocated to owners can also differ between LLCs and partnerships. For a complete description of LLCs, see *South-Western Federal Taxation: Corporations, Partnerships, Estates & Trusts*.

Qualified Joint Ventures

For Federal tax purposes, an unincorporated business operated by spouses is considered a partnership. As a result, a business co-run by spouses is generally required to comply with filing and recordkeeping requirements for partnerships and partners.

---

[71]§ 707(c).

Married co-owners wanting to avoid the burden of partnership documentation can form a qualified joint venture. The election to do so is made by simply reporting each spouse's share of income, losses, gains, and deductions on a Schedule C (along with other related forms) regarding each spouse's interest in the joint venture. To qualify for joint venture treatment, the only members of the joint venture can be spouses filing a joint return, both spouses must materially participate, and both spouses must elect not to be treated as a partnership. The business must be operated by the spouses as co-owners and not through a separate entity under state law.

Other Partnership Considerations

Complex tax provisions involving liquidating and nonliquidating distributions and the sale of a partnership interest are beyond the scope of this text and are discussed in depth in *South-Western Federal Taxation: Corporations, Partnerships, Estates & Trusts.*

20-7 TAX PLANNING

LO.10

Identify the advantages and disadvantages of the various forms used for conducting a business.

As with individuals, tax planning is important for corporations and partnerships to ensure proper application of the tax law and to avoid paying more tax than legally required.

20-7a Corporate versus Noncorporate Forms of Business Organization

The applicable income tax rates will affect the choice of the form of doing business. Because of the wide range of possibilities (currently 10 to 39.6 percent for individuals and 15 to 35 percent for corporations), this factor must be evaluated on a case-by-case basis. For example, the corporate form is very appealing if the anticipated taxable income falls within the 25 percent corporate bracket and the shareholder's individual bracket is 39.6 percent. Here, the time value of the taxes saved could make operating a business as a corporation advantageous. Do not, moreover, overlook the potential impact of state and local income taxes applicable to individuals and corporations. Also, in those states that do not have an income tax, a franchise tax can pose an added tax burden on corporations (see Chapter 1).

Unless an election is made under Subchapter S, operating as a corporation yields a potential double tax result. Corporate-source income will be taxed twice—once as earned by the corporation and again when distributed to the shareholders. The payment of a dividend does not result in a deduction to the corporation, and the receipt of a dividend generally results in income to a shareholder. In the case of closely held corporations, therefore, a strong incentive exists to avoid the payment of dividends. Instead, a premium is put on distributing profits in some manner that is deductible by the corporation. This can be accomplished by categorizing the distributions as salaries, interest, or rent—all of which are deductible by the corporation. If not properly structured, however, these devices can generate a multitude of problems. Excessive debt, for example, can lead to its reclassification as equity (under the thin capitalization approach) with a resulting disallowance of any interest deduction. Large salaries could fail the reasonableness test, and rent payments must meet an arm's length standard to avoid treatment as a constructive dividend.

Changes in the tax treatment of qualified dividends have interjected an additional variable that must be taken into account when structuring corporation-shareholder dealings. Prior to 2003, it made little tax difference to an individual shareholder whether a corporate distribution was classified as a dividend, interest, salary, or rent—all were fully taxed as ordinary income. After 2002, however, qualified dividends are taxed at the same rate as for net long-term capital gain.[72] Thus, the maximum rate

---

[72]§ 1(h)(3)(B).

cannot exceed 20 percent (0 percent in some cases). In light of this preferential treatment of qualified dividends, effective planning becomes a matter of deciding who most needs the tax benefit. If it is the corporation, try to pay out profits in a deductible form (i.e., interest, salaries, and rents). If it is the shareholder, distribute the profits as qualified dividends.[73]

Other tax considerations having a bearing on the choice of the corporate form to operate a business are summarized below:

- Corporate-source income loses its identity as it passes through the corporation to the shareholders. Thus, items possessing preferential tax treatment (e.g., interest on municipal bonds) are not taxed as such to the shareholders.

- As noted earlier, it may be difficult for shareholders to recover some or all of their investment in the corporation without a dividend income result. Recall that most corporate distributions are treated as dividends to the extent of the corporation's E & P. Structuring the capital of the corporation to include debt is a partial solution to this problem. Thus, the shareholder-creditor could recoup part of his or her investment through the tax-free payment of principal. Too much debt, however, may lead to the debt being reclassified as equity.

- Corporate losses cannot be passed through to the shareholders.

- The domestic production activities deduction generated by the corporation is not available to its shareholders.

- The liquidation of a corporation may generate tax consequences to both the corporation and its shareholders. Even when the corporation being liquidated does not sell its assets but distributes them in kind (i.e., "as is") to the shareholders, gain (or loss) is not avoided. The corporation must treat the distribution as a sale and recognize gain or loss measured by the fair market value of the assets involved.

- The corporate form provides the shareholders with the opportunity to be treated as employees for tax purposes if they render services to the corporation. This status makes a number of attractive tax-sheltered fringe benefits available (e.g., group term life insurance). These benefits are not available to partners and sole proprietors.

20-7b **Regular Corporation versus S Status**

Due to the pass-through concept, the use of S status generally avoids the income tax at the corporate level, bringing the individual income tax into play. As noted in the previous section, the differential between the rates applicable to noncorporate and corporate taxpayers makes this a factor to be considered. The S election enables a business to operate in the corporate form; avoid the corporate income tax; and, depending on taxable income, possibly take advantage of the lower rates usually applicable to individuals. Also, losses incurred at the corporate level pass through to the shareholders, who will utilize them on their individual returns.

Electing S status can present several problems, however. First, the election is available only to small business corporations. Consequently, many corporations will not qualify for the election. Second, S corporations are subject to the rules governing regular corporations unless otherwise specified in the Code. For example, § 351 applies on the formation of an S corporation. Likewise, if the S corporation later carries out a stock redemption or is liquidated, the rules governing regular corporations apply. Third, a few states do not recognize S status for purposes of state and local taxation or recognize them but subject them to tax at both the entity and shareholder levels. Therefore, an S corporation might be subject to a state franchise tax or a state or local income tax.

---

[73]The 20% rate is applicable only to those in the 39.6% tax bracket. Most middle-income taxpayers will be subject to a 15% rate.

20-7c **Use of an Entity to Reduce the Family Income Tax Burden**

One objective of tax planning is to keep the income from a business within the family unit but to disperse the income in such a manner as to minimize the overall tax burden. To the extent feasible, therefore, income should be shifted from higher-bracket to lower-bracket family members.

A legislative change, however, has raised major obstacles to shifting income to children. The kiddie tax applies to all children under age 19 *and* to those who are full-time students under age 24.[74] As a result, shifting investment income (or capital gains) to a child provides no benefit to the extent the income is taxed at the parents' tax rate.

Unfortunately, the income from property (a business) cannot be shifted to another without also transferring an interest in the property. If, for example, a father wants to assign income from his sole proprietorship to his children, he must form a partnership or incorporate the business. In either case, the transfer of the interest may be subject to the Federal gift tax. But any potential gift tax can be eliminated or controlled through judicious use of the annual exclusion, the election to split gifts (for married donors), and the unified tax credit (refer to the discussion of the Federal gift tax in Chapter 1).

Consequently, the first problem to be resolved becomes which form of business organization will best fit the objective of income shifting. For the partnership form, one major obstacle arises. Family partnership rules preclude the assignment of income to a family member unless capital is a material income-producing factor.[75] If not, the family member must contribute substantial or vital services. Ordinarily, capital is not a material income-producing factor if the income of the business consists principally of compensation for personal services performed by members or employees of the partnership. Conversely, capital is a material income-producing factor if the operation of the business entails a substantial investment in physical assets (e.g., inventory, plant, machinery, or equipment).

Income shifting through the use of a partnership, therefore, may be ineffectual if a personal service business is involved. In fact, it could be hopeless if the assignees are minors. The use of the corporate form usually involves no such impediment. Regardless of the nature of the business, a gift of stock carries with it the attributes of ownership. Thus, dividends paid on stock are taxed to the owner of the stock.

But what if the corporate form is utilized and the S election is made? A new hurdle arises. The Code authorizes the IRS to make adjustments in situations where shareholders are not being adequately compensated for the value of their services or capital provided to an S corporation in a family setting.[76] Thus, an S corporation suffers from the same vulnerability that exists with family partnerships.

A further factor that favors the corporate form (either a regular or S corporation) as a device for income splitting is the ease with which it can be carried out. Presuming the entity already exists, the transfer of stock merely requires an entry in the corporation's stock ledger account. In contrast, a gift of a partnership interest probably requires an amendment to the partnership agreement.

Regardless of the form of organization used for the business, income shifting will not take place unless the transfer is complete.[77] If the donor continues to exercise control over the interest transferred and does not recognize and protect the ownership rights of the donee, the IRS may argue that the transfer is ineffective for tax purposes. In that case, the income from the transferred interest continues to be taxed to the donor.

---

[74]The kiddie tax is restricted to *unearned* income (e.g., interest, dividends) and does not apply to *earned* income (e.g., wages, salaries). See the discussion of § 1(g) in Chapter 3.

[75]§ 704(e).

[76]§ 1366(e).

[77]*Ginsberg v. Comm.*, 74–2 USTC ¶9660, 34 AFTR 2d 74–5760, 502 F.2d 965 (CA–6, 1974), and *Michael F. Beirne*, 61 T.C. 268 (1973).

REFOCUS ON THE BIG PICTURE

CHOICE OF BUSINESS ENTITY

A principal concern of the Todd sisters is limited liability. A food preparation business involves a high risk in terms of potential liability (e.g., litigation resulting from food poisoning). This hazard is further magnified by the sisters' intention to carry minimal liability insurance coverage. To obtain limited liability, therefore, the choice of entity cannot be a regular partnership—it must be a C or S corporation or a limited liability company (LLC). (Example 1)

The next concern is the pass-through of losses to the sisters in the early years of the business. This cannot be achieved with a C corporation and is only available with an S corporation or an LLC. (Examples 1 and 45)

In making the choice between a corporation and an LLC, the future must be considered. If the business is successful, the sisters could expand. This is more easily accomplished with a corporation than an LLC. A corporation can raise additional capital for expansion by issuing more stock—even going public if necessary. Issuing additional stock may cause the S corporation election to be lost, but by then, S status will have served its purpose (i.e., pass-through of losses).

When forming the corporation, the sisters should take the following into account:

- Key assets (e.g., food preparation facilities) might better be purchased by the sisters and leased to the corporation. This approach leads to a rent deduction for the corporation. (Example 31)

- A viable salary structure should be established for the services the sisters perform. This generates a salary deduction for the corporation. (Example 36)

- Interest should be charged for the funds the sisters loan to the corporation. This yields an interest deduction for the corporation. (Example 36)

If the S corporation becomes a C corporation, these rent, salary, and interest deductions will reduce the taxable income of the corporation and thereby lower any corporate income tax imposed.

GARY WOODS/ALAMY STOCK PHOTO

Key Terms

C corporation, 20-3	Limited liability company (LLC), 20-2	Schedule M–1, 20-18
Check-the-box Regulations, 20-5	Organizational expenditures, 20-16	Schedule M–3, 20-19
Constructive dividends, 20-25	Pass-through entity, 20-5	Small business corporation, 20-26
Dividends received deduction, 20-14	Personal service corporation, 20-16	Thin capitalization, 20-23
Earnings and profits, 20-24	Qualified joint venture, 20-6	
Guaranteed payments, 20-36	S corporation, 20-26	

Discussion Questions

1. **LO.1** Describe a situation in which a corporation will not be treated as such under state law.

2. **LO.1** Sylvia and Trang want to enter into business together and are unsure what type of entity to form (if any). They are concerned about the complexity of the paperwork required, the protection of personal assets from business creditors, and flexibility of sharing income and losses. Explain to Sylvia and Trang how a corporation, a partnership, or no entity at all may differ with respect to their areas of concern.

3. **LO.1** Explain why partnerships and S corporations are considered "pass-through" entities, and present an example of how the pass-through works.

4. **LO.1** What purpose is served by the check-the-box Regulations?

5. **LO.1, 10** Why are limited liability companies advantageous?

6. **LO.1** The Owen brothers have obtained financing to start a new venture. The business will be high-risk as to potential liability and is expected to incur losses before becoming profitable. What type of entity might the Owens consider using?

7. **LO.3, 4, 5** Contrast the income taxation of individuals and C corporations as to each of the following:
   a. Alternative minimum tax.
   b. Dividend income.
   c. Use of the cash method of accounting.
   d. Accounting period used for tax purposes.
   e. Applicable tax rates.
   f. Due date of the tax return.

8. **LO.3, 8, 9** The taxpayer has excess capital losses (both short-term and long-term) for the current year. Discuss the income tax ramifications of the losses if the taxpayer is:
   a. An individual.
   b. A C corporation.
   c. An S corporation.
   d. A partnership.

9. **LO.3** In late December 2017, Gray Corporation (a calendar year C corporation) pledges a $50,000 donation to a local relief agency formed to fight AIDS in Africa. Although Gray's board of directors authorized the donation in 2017, the payment is not made until April 2018. What issues are involved?

10. **LO.3** If a C corporation donates ordinary income property to a qualified charity, the measure of the amount of the deduction is the adjusted basis of the property. Do you agree with this statement? Explain.

11. **LO.3** In connection with the domestic production activities deduction, what is the difference between individual and C corporation taxpayers?

12. **LO.3** Kite, a calendar year C corporation, incurs a net operating loss for 2017. What factors should be considered before Kite Corporation chooses to carry back the loss?

13. **LO.4** The dividends received deduction does not always completely eliminate the effect of taxation of dividend income at the corporate shareholder level. Explain this statement. Issue ID

Issue ID   14. **LO.4** Two small C corporations have invested in the stock of IBM Corporation. Although they own the same number and type of shares, one corporation is able to claim a larger dividends received deduction than the other. Explain why this could be possible.

Issue ID   15. **LO.4** Mallard Corporation was formed in December 2017 and plans to use the cash basis of accounting. Mallard incurred one-half of its organizational expenses in December 2017 and one-half in January 2018. The payment of these expenses also occurred in these two months. Do you recognize any income tax problem? Explain.

Issue ID   16. **LO.5** Beige Corporation has lower taxable income than Drab Corporation. Yet, Beige's marginal income tax rate is 39%, while Drab's marginal rate is 35%. Explain how this variance can occur.

17. **LO.6** Small, closely held corporations are often formed with a minimum of capital investment. Key assets used in the business are then leased to the corporation by the shareholders. What are the advantages of this approach?

Decision Making   18. **LO.6** Cynthia and some associates want to form a corporation to develop and operate an industrial park. Cynthia is to contribute the land, which has significantly appreciated in value. She would like to recognize *some* of this gain to offset losses from other sources. In view of the rules governing the application of § 351, what do you suggest?

19. **LO.7** When a corporation distributes property as a dividend, what are the tax effects on the corporation and its shareholders under the following assumptions?
   a. The property has declined in value.
   b. The property has appreciated in value.

20. **LO.8** A calendar year corporation has an election under Subchapter S. What will be the effect, if any, of the following events on its S status?
   a. The board of directors of the corporation revokes its S election in March of the current year.
   b. A shareholder who is a citizen of Mexico and works in San Antonio retires and moves back to Mexico.
   c. The corporation acquires an interest in a partnership.
   d. Because of the death of a shareholder, the total number of shareholders increases from 98 to 101.
   e. A shareholder transfers her stock to a newly formed LLC.

Issue ID   21. **LO.8** Roadrunner Corporation receives a dividend on its stock investment in General Electric Corporation. If Roadrunner is an S corporation, it cannot claim a dividends received deduction on the GE dividend. Therefore, the GE dividend will be subject to triple taxation. Comment on the accuracy of this last statement.

Issue ID   22. **LO.8** Cynthia and Doug are equal shareholders in Penguin, a calendar year S corporation. At the end of 2017, Penguin has an operating loss. Although Cynthia and Doug have the same basis in their Penguin stock, Cynthia can deduct all of her share of the corporation's loss, while Doug cannot. How can this result take place?

23. **LO.9** Indicate whether each of the following will increase (+), decrease (−), or have no effect (*NE*) on a partner's basis in a partnership interest:
   a. Operating loss of the partnership.
   b. Capital gains of the partnership.
   c. Tax-exempt income of the partnership.
   d. Partnership expenditures that are not deductible in computing taxable income.
   e. Bank loans made to the partnership.
   f. The partnership pays off a mortgage on property it owns.
   g. Withdrawals by a partner that *are not* guaranteed payments.
   h. Withdrawals by a partner that *are* guaranteed payments.

24. **LO.9** Blaine, Cassie, and Kirstin are equal partners in the Maize Partnership. During   Issue ID
the year, Maize has qualified dividends, charitable contributions, and a
domestic production activities deduction. Explain the following results:

    a. Blaine pays less tax than Cassie and Kirstin on his share of the qualified dividends.

    b. Cassie cannot deduct any of her share of the charitable contributions.

    c. Kirstin has a larger domestic production activities deduction than either Blaine
    or Cassie.

25. **LO.9** What are guaranteed payments? When might such payments be used?

Computational Exercises

26. **LO.3** Green Corporation, a calendar year taxpayer, has ordinary income of $10,000
and a long-term capital loss of $12,000 in 2017. For past years, it had a long-
term capital gain of $2,500 in 2014 and a long-term capital gain of $5,000 in 2016.

    a. How much of the long-term capital loss can be deducted in 2017?

    b. Carried back to prior years?

    c. Carried forward to future years?

    d. What is the nature (long- or short-term) of any carrybacks or carryforwards?

27. **LO.3** Purple Corporation purchases residential rental property for $1,000,000 (disre-
garding any allocation to the land) on March 9, 2014. Straight-line cost recovery
of $130,295 is taken before the property is sold on October 23, 2017, for $1,000,000.

    a. What is Purple's recognized gain?

    b. How much of this gain is taxed under § 1250.

    c. Section 291?

    d. Section 1231?

28. **LO.3** Crimson Corporation and Tan Corporation do not file a consolidated return
but are members of an affiliated group. During the current year, Crimson
manufactures a product at a cost of $11,000 and sells it to Tan for $16,000. Tan
incurs marketing costs of $4,500 and sells the product for $23,000.

    a. What is the QPAI for these corporations?

    b. Suppose they were not members of an affiliated group?

29. **LO.4** Gold and Silver are two unrelated calendar year corporations. For the current
year, each had the following transactions:

	Gold	Silver
Income from operations	$220,000	$260,000
Expenses from operations	225,000	310,000
Dividends received from domestic corporations (15% ownership)	100,000	130,000
Taxable income before dividends received deduction	$ 95,000	$ 80,000

What is the dividends received deduction for:

    a. Gold Corporation?

    b. Silver Corporation?

30. **LO.4** Maize Corporation (a calendar year taxpayer) was formed on April 1, 2017.
Calculate the maximum deduction for organizational expenses for 2017 if
these costs were:

    a. $4,000.

    b. $24,000.

    c. $54,000.

    d. $64,000.

31. **LO.5** Maroon Corporation is a calendar year taxpayer. Determine Maroon's Federal income tax liability if its taxable income is:
    a. $68,000.
    b. $235,000.
    c. $4,000,000.
    d. $17,500,000.
    e. $21,000,000.
    f. $68,000 but Maroon is a qualified personal service corporation.

32. **LO.6** Noah and Olivia form the Gray corporation with the following investment:

	FMV
Noah—	
Cash	$180,000
Olivia—	
Property (basis of $140,000)	200,000

Each receives 1,000 shares of Gray stock, but Olivia also receives cash of $20,000. (Each share of stock is worth $180.)
    a. What is Olivia's recognized gain?
    b. Her basis in the Gray stock?
    c. What is Gray's basis in the property?

33. **LO.7** In 2017, Emily receives a distribution of $125,000 from her wholly owned calendar year corporation. As of January 1, 2017, the corporation has accumulated E & P of $15,000 and for 2017 has current E & P of $65,000. Emily's basis in her stock is $35,000. What are Emily's tax consequences?

34. **LO.8** At a time when Emerald Corporation has E & P of $200,000, it distributes land (adjusted basis of $95,000 and fair market value of $180,000) to its sole shareholder, Bill.
    a. What is Bill's dividend income?
    b. Basis in the land?
    c. What are Emerald's tax consequences?

35. **LO.8** Drab Corporation, a calendar year S corporation, had the following transactions during 2017:

Sales	$1,500,000
Cost of Goods Sold	700,000
Long-term capital gain	10,000
Short-term capital loss	5,000
Political lobbying expenditures	5,000
Amortization of organizational expenditures	2,000
Salary expense	100,000
Rent expense	140,000
Tax-exempt interest	10,000
Dividends paid to shareholders	45,000

What is Drab's taxable income for 2017?

36. **LO.8** Kim is a 40% shareholder in Taupe Corporation, a calendar year S corporation. During 2017, Taupe had an operating loss of $200,000. If Kim has a basis of $50,000 in his stock and has made a loan to Taupe of $20,000, how much of the loss can he deduct for 2017?

37. **LO.9** Christian and Mia form the CM Partnership, each receiving a 50% capital interest. Christian contributed property worth $200,000 (adjusted basis of $230,000), while Mia contributed property worth $210,000 (subject to a mortgage of $20,000 that is assumed by CM) with an adjusted basis of $150,000.

    a. How much gain (or loss) do the parties recognize?

    b. What is Mia's basis in her partnership interest?

Problems

38. **LO.3, 4, 5** Using the legend provided below, classify each statement.

Legend
I = Applies *only* to the income taxation of individuals
C = Applies *only* to the income taxation of C corporations
B = Applies to the income taxation of *both* individuals and C corporations
N = Applies to the income taxation of *neither* individuals nor C corporations

    a. A foreign tax credit is available.

    b. The deduction of charitable contributions is subject to percentage limitation(s).

    c. Excess charitable contributions can be carried forward for five years.

    d. On the contribution of inventory to charity, the full amount of any appreciation can be claimed as a deduction.

    e. Excess capital losses can be carried forward indefinitely.

    f. Excess capital losses cannot be carried back.

    g. A net short-term capital gain is subject to the same tax rate as ordinary income.

    h. A domestic production activities deduction may be available.

    i. A dividends received deduction is available.

    j. The like-kind provisions of § 1031 are available.

    k. In 2017, a taxpayer with a fiscal year of May 1–April 30 has a due date for filing a Federal income tax return of July 15.

    l. Estimated Federal income tax payments may be required.

39. **LO.3** Garnet has the following capital asset transactions during 2017:

Long-term capital gain	$8,000
Short-term capital gain	3,000

    Further, Garnet has an excess capital loss carryforward of $6,000 from 2016.

    a. What are the tax consequences of these transactions if the $6,000 loss is long-term and Garnet is an individual? Garnet is a C corporation?

    b. What are the tax consequences of these transactions if the $6,000 loss is short-term and Garnet is an individual? Garnet is a C corporation?

40. **LO.3, 8** Citron, a calendar year taxpayer, began business in January 2016. It had a long-term capital gain of $5,000 in 2016 and a long-term capital loss of $10,000 in 2017. For both years, Citron had an operating profit in excess of $100,000. How are these capital gain and loss transactions handled for income tax purposes if Citron is:

    a. An individual?

    b. A C corporation?

    c. An S corporation?

41. **LO.3** Taupe, a calendar year taxpayer, has the following capital transactions for 2017: long-term capital loss of $4,000 and a short-term capital loss of $4,000. How are these items handled for tax purposes if Taupe is:

    a.   An individual?

    b.   A C corporation?

42. **LO.3, 8** Robin had the following capital transactions in 2017:

LTCG	$10,000
LTCL	8,000
STCG	2,000
STCL	–0–

    Robin also had a net long-term capital loss in 2016 of $2,000, which it could not use, and ordinary income of $13,000. What are the tax consequences in 2017 if:

    a.   Robin is an individual.

    b.   Robin is a C corporation.

    c.   Robin is an S corporation.

43. **LO.3** On December 6, 2017, Kestrel Company (a calendar year taxpayer) authorizes a cash donation of $50,000 to the Memphis Public Library. The pledge is carried out as follows: $15,000 on December 12, 2017; $25,000 on February 13, 2018; and $10,000 on May 10, 2018. What are the alternatives for the year of the charitable contribution deduction if Kestrel is:

    a.   An accrual basis partnership?

    b.   An accrual basis C corporation?

    c.   What is the result under parts (a) and (b) if Kestrel is a cash basis taxpayer?

44. **LO.3** During 2017, Siskin Corporation (a C corporation) had the following transactions:

Income from operations	$500,000
Expenses from operations	425,000
Dividends from domestic corporations (less than 20% ownership)	45,000
Dividends received deduction (70% × $45,000)	31,500
Unused short-term capital loss from 2015 (there are no capital gains in 2016 and 2017)	2,500
NOL carryover from 2016	40,000

    In June 2017, Siskin made a contribution to a qualified charitable organization of $10,500 in cash (not included in any of the items listed above).

    a.   How much, if any, of the contribution can be claimed as a deduction for 2017?

    b.   What happens to any portion not deductible for 2017?

45. **LO.3** Auburn Company manufactures and sells furnishings for hospitals (e.g., special needs bathroom fixtures). In the current year, it donates some of its inventory to a newly constructed hospice. The hospice is adjacent to a cancer treatment center and is intended to care for indigent and terminal patients. The property donated has an adjusted basis of $40,000 and a fair market value of $90,000. What is the amount of the charitable contribution deduction if Auburn is a:

    a.   Sole proprietorship?

    b.   C corporation?

    c.   Would your answer to part (b) change if the fair market value of the property was $121,000 (not $90,000)?

46. **LO.3** Tern Corporation manufactures a motor scooter at a cost of $5,000 and sells it to Snipe Corporation for $7,000. Snipe spends $2,000 marketing the scooter and sells it to the general public for $12,000. Presuming that the taxable income and

W–2 wage limitations do not apply, what is the domestic production activities deduction (DPAD) if:

a. Tern Corporation and Snipe Corporation are not members of the same affiliated group?

b. Are members of the same affiliated group?

47. **LO.4** Determine the dividends received deduction for each of the following independent situations. Assume that the percentage of stock owned in the corporation paying the dividend is 30% for Green Corporation and less than 20% for Red Corporation and Blue Corporation.

	Red Corporation	Blue Corporation	Green Corporation
Income from operations	$3,000,000	$4,500,000	$8,000,000
Expenses of operations	2,700,000	4,800,000	8,400,000
Qualified dividends received	600,000	150,000	2,000,000

48. **LO.4** Puffin Corporation was formed on July 1, 2017, and incurred qualifying organizational expenditures. It uses a calendar year and wants to accelerate any deductions that are available. Based on this assumption, what is Puffin Corporation's deduction for 2017 if its organizational expenditures are:

a. $3,000?

b. $46,000?

c. $52,000?

d. $77,000?

49. **LO.5** In each of the following independent situations, determine the C corporation's Federal income tax liability for calendar year 2017.

Corporation	Taxable Income
Sparrow	$ 45,000*
Warbler	68,000**
Scaup	80,000
Ibis	126,000
Heron	390,000
Finch (a personal service corporation)	120,000

*Does not include a net short-term capital gain of $3,000.
**Does not include a net long-term capital loss of $4,000.

50. **LO.5** Puce, a calendar year C corporation, had the following Schedule M–1 transactions on its Form 1120 for 2017:

Taxable income	$100,000
Federal income tax	22,250
Excess capital losses over capital gains	4,000
Life insurance proceeds received on the death of Puce's vice president	100,000
Premiums paid on life insurance policy	1,000
Interest on tax-exempt bonds	10,000

What is Puce Corporation's net income per books for 2017?

51. **LO.6, 10** Doris, Walt, and Pat form Swan Corporation with the following investments:

	Basis to Transferor	Fair Market Value	Number of Shares Issued
From Doris—cash	$200,000	$200,000	200
From Walt—equipment	400,000	300,000	300
From Pat—land	550,000	600,000	500

In addition to the 500 shares of stock, Pat receives $100,000 in cash from Swan Corporation. Assume that each share of Swan stock is worth $1,000.

a. How much loss does Walt realize? Recognize?

b. What is Walt's basis in the Swan stock?

c. What is Swan Corporation's basis in the equipment?

d. How much gain does Pat realize? Recognize?

e. What is Pat's basis in the Swan stock?

f. What is Swan's basis in the land?

g. In terms of the answers to parts (a) through (f), does it matter whether Swan is formed as a C corporation or as an S corporation? Explain.

52. **LO.6** Elton, Neil, Courtney, and Zelma form Ecru Corporation with the following investments:

	Basis to Transferor	Fair Market Value	Number of Shares Issued
From Elton—cash	$ 200,000	$ 200,000	200
From Neil—inventory	230,000	270,000	260
From Courtney—machinery and equipment	400,000	370,000	350
From Zelma—land and building	1,270,000	1,300,000	1,200

In addition to its stock, Ecru distributes cash as follows: $10,000 to Neil, $20,000 to Courtney, and $100,000 to Zelma. Assume that each share of Ecru stock is worth $1,000. Regarding these transactions, provide the following information:

a. Neil's realized and recognized gain (or loss).

b. Neil's basis in the Ecru stock.

c. Ecru's basis in the inventory.

d. Courtney's realized and recognized gain (or loss).

e. Courtney's basis in the Ecru stock.

f. Ecru's basis in the machinery and equipment.

g. Zelma's realized and recognized gain (or loss).

h. Zelma's basis in the Ecru stock.

i. Ecru's basis in the land and building.

53. **LO.7** Lily is the sole shareholder of Crimson Corporation (a C corporation). At a time when Crimson has a deficit in accumulated E & P of $90,000 and current E & P of $65,000, it distributes a cash dividend of $85,000. If Lily's basis in her stock is $15,000, what are the tax consequences of the distribution to:

a. Lily?

b. Crimson Corporation?

Issue ID 54. **LO.7** Harold, Marcia, and Richard are equal shareholders in Pelican Corporation, a calendar year C corporation. During the current year, Pelican makes a $150,000 distribution to its three shareholders. Of the $50,000 that each shareholder receives, the tax result is as follows:

• $10,000 of dividend income to Harold.

• $10,000 of dividend income and $20,000 capital gain to Marcia.

• $10,000 dividend income and $40,000 capital gain to Richard.

Explain the variations in these tax consequences.

Decision Making 55. **LO.7, 10** The stock of Emerald Corporation is held equally by Barney and Faye.
Communications The shareholders would like to receive, as a dividend, value of $800,000 each. The corporation has the following assets that it can spare:

Asset	Adjusted Basis to Emerald Corporation	Fair Market Value
Unimproved land	$1,040,000	$800,000
Chevron stock	480,000	800,000

Both assets are held as investments. Emerald Corporation has a capital loss carry-over from the previous year of $80,000 and has accumulated E & P in excess of $2 million.

Barney and Faye have come to you for advice. Suggest an attractive tax plan to carry out what the parties want. Write a letter (addressed to Emerald Corporation at PO Box 940, Rochester, NY 14692) describing your plan and its tax consequences.

56. **LO.8** During 2017, Thrasher (a calendar year, accrual basis S corporation) has the following transactions:

Sales	$1,500,000
Cost of goods sold	900,000
Long-term capital gain	11,000
Short-term capital gain	5,000
Salaries	210,000
Qualified dividends from stock investments	30,000
Rent expense	170,000
Advertising expense	20,000
Interest expense on business loan	15,000
§ 1231 gain	25,000
Organizational expenditures	3,000
Charitable contributions	5,000
Bad debt (trade account receivable deemed to be uncollectible)	10,000
Cash dividend distributed to shareholders	120,000

a. Determine Thrasher Corporation's separately stated items for 2017.

b. Determine Thrasher's taxable income for 2017.

57. **LO.8** Assume the same facts as in Problem 56. Kirby Turner is a 20% shareholder in Thrasher Corporation. She is aware of the tax consequences of the various items listed on the Schedule K–1 (Form 1120S) she received but does not understand their effect on basis. She is considering selling her stock and wants to estimate the gain or loss that will result. In response to Kirby's request for assistance, write a letter to her (1120 Garden Way, Elizabeth, NJ 07207), summarizing the changes to stock basis that the 2017 transactions caused.

Communications

58. **LO.8, 10** Jim Olsen owns all of the stock in Drake, a calendar year S corporation. For calendar year 2017, Drake anticipates an operating loss of $160,000 and could, if deemed worthwhile, sell a stock investment that would generate a $10,000 long-term capital loss. Jim has an adjusted basis of $100,000 in the Drake stock. For the year, he has already realized a short-term capital gain of $7,000. He anticipates no other capital asset transactions and expects to be in the 33% tax bracket in 2017.

Write a letter to Jim (470 Bay Avenue, Bedford, MA 01730), suggesting a course of action that could save him some income taxes.

Decision Making

Communications

59. **LO.8** Ida owns 30% of the stock in Mockingbird, a calendar year S corporation. Her basis in the stock as of January 1, 2017, is $130,000. Mockingbird has an operating loss of $500,000 in 2017 and an operating profit of $600,000 in 2018. Ida withdraws $70,000 in cash from the corporation in 2018.

a. What are Ida's tax consequences in 2017?

b. 2018?

c. What is Ida's basis in her Mockingbird stock as of January 1, 2018?

d. January 1, 2019?

60. **LO.9** Guy, Alma, and Kara form the Ivory Partnership. In exchange for a 30% capital interest, Guy transfers property (basis of $200,000; fair market value of $400,000) subject to a liability of $100,000. The liability is assumed by the partnership. Alma transfers property (basis of $350,000; fair market value of $300,000) for a 30% capital interest. Kara invests cash of $400,000 for the remaining 40% capital interest. Concerning these transactions, provide the following information:

a. Guy's recognized gain.

b. Guy's basis in the partnership interest.

c. Alma's recognized loss.

d. Alma's basis in the partnership interest.

e. Kara's basis in the partnership interest.

f. Ivory Partnership's basis in the property transferred by Guy and Alma.

61. **LO.9** The Pheasant Partnership had the following transactions in the current year:

Operating income		$700,000
Cost of goods sold		400,000
Capital gains—		
Long-term	$20,000	
Short-term	10,000	30,000
Salaries		60,000
Guaranteed payments to Partner A		20,000
Tax-exempt interest income		2,000
Rent		24,000
Dividend from IBM stock investment		3,000
Utilities		8,000
Donation to American Red Cross		1,000
Contribution to governor's reelection campaign		500

a. What is Pheasant's ordinary income (or loss)?

b. What are Pheasant's separately stated items?

62. **LO.9** Aiden has a 35% capital interest in the Oro Partnership and is entitled to a yearly guaranteed payment of $40,000. As of January 1, 2017, Aiden's basis in the partnership interest is $87,000. During tax year 2017, Oro had the following transactions:

Operating profit (after consideration of guaranteed payment)	$410,000
Interest income on City of Seattle bonds	20,000
Short-term capital loss	5,000
Long-term capital gain	7,000
Funds borrowed from bank to provide working capital	30,000

During 2017, Aiden withdrew cash of $70,000 from Oro to help cover his living expenses. What is Aiden's basis in his partnership interest as of January 1, 2018?

Decision Making 63. **LO.9, 10** As of January 1, 2016, Norman has a basis of $85,000 in his 30% capital interest in the Plata Partnership. He and the partnership use the calendar year for tax purposes. The partnership incurs an operating loss of $440,000 for 2016 and a profit of $285,000 for 2017.

a. How much, if any, loss may Norman recognize for 2016?

b. How much income must Norman recognize for 2017?

c. What basis will Norman have in his partnership interest as of January 1, 2017?

d. What basis will Norman have in his partnership interest as of January 1, 2018?

e. What year-end tax planning would you suggest to ensure that a partner could deduct all of his or her share of any partnership losses?

Research Problems

THOMSON REUTERS
CHECKPOINT®
Student Edition

Note: Solutions to the Research Problems can be prepared by using the Thomson Reuters Checkpoint® Student Edition online tax research database, which accompanies this textbook. Solutions can also be prepared by using research materials found in a typical tax library.

Research Problem 1. Tyler and Travis Best are brothers and are equal shareholders in Maize Corporation, a calendar year C corporation. In 2017, they incurred travel and entertainment expenses on behalf of Maize Corporation. Because Maize was in a precarious financial condition, the brothers decided not to seek reimbursement for these expenditures. Instead, each brother deducted on his individual return (Form 1040) what he had spent on travel and entertainment expenses on behalf of the corporation. Upon audit of the returns filed by Tyler and Travis, the IRS disallowed these expenditures. Write a letter to Travis (140 Ridgeland Drive, Waynesburg, PA 15370), indicating whether he should challenge the IRS action. Explain your conclusions using nontechnical language.

Communications

Research Problem 2. During 2017, Jayden Steele received a distribution of $24,000 on stock he owns in Razorbill Corporation. He had planned to report this amount as dividend income until he talked to his father-in-law, Jim. According to Jim, who had examined Razorbill's financial statements, the company suffered an operating loss for the year. Consequently, Jim thinks that the distribution is a nontaxable return of capital. Because Jim is an accountant, Jayden is confused and seeks a second opinion from you. Write a letter to Jayden (1260 Pike Street, Eagle, ID 83616), explaining the possibilities involved.

Communications

Partial list of research aids:
Jason Michael Juha, 103 TCM 1338, T.C.Memo. 2012–68.

Research Problem 3. Scott and Brooke are the sole shareholders of Tanager Company, a calendar year Subchapter S corporation. After several loss years, in December 2017, Tanager is forced to borrow $300,000 for working capital purposes. Robin State Bank makes the loan to Tanager but only after Scott and Brooke personally guarantee the debt.

Scott and Brooke deduct Tanager's $200,000 operating loss for 2017 on their individual income tax returns. Although they have a zero basis in their stock investment, they consider the guarantee of the bank loan to be debt within the meaning of § 1366(d)(1)(B).

Are Scott and Brooke correct in their reasoning? Explain.

Partial list of research aids:
Milton T. Raynor, 50 T.C. 762 (1968).
William H. Maloof, 89 TCM 1022, T.C.Memo. 2005–75.

Use internet tax resources to address the following questions. Look for reliable websites and blogs of the IRS and other government agencies, media outlets, businesses, tax professionals, academics, think tanks, and political outlets.

Research Problem 4. Some C corporations are exempt from the application of the AMT. Review the Instructions to Form 4626 (Alternative Minimum Tax—Corporations), and be prepared to explain and illustrate the small corporation exemption.

Research Problem 5. Does your state impose income tax on an S corporation in addition to imposing tax on the shareholders? Explain.

Research Problem 6. To report its transactions for the year, a partnership must file a Form 1065 with the IRS.

a. When is this return due if the tax year is after 2015?

b. As is the case with individuals and corporations, can a partnership obtain an automatic extension for filing the Form 1065?

c. Does a partnership need to include a Schedule M–3 with its Form 1065? Explain.

Roger CPA Review Questions

1. In year 5, Naxos Inc., a C corporation, sold Section 1250 property for $400,000 that had an adjusted basis of $250,000, resulting in a gain of $150,000. The original cost of the property, which Naxos had purchased in year 1, was $350,000 and $100,000 of total depreciation had been taken on the property. Had straight-line depreciation been used, depreciation would have been $60,000. How should Naxos report the gain on its year 5 tax return?

   a. $40,000 ordinary gain and $110,000 long-term capital gain

   b. $52,000 ordinary gain and $98,000 long-term capital gain

   c. $150,000 ordinary gain

   d. $48,000 ordinary gain and $102,000 long-term capital gain

2. Kudzu, Clemmons, and Clancy form KCC Partnership with the following contributions:

Partner	Contribution	Adjusted Basis	Fair Market Value
Kudzu	Land	$52,000	$50,000
Kudzu	Services	N/A	5,000
Clemmons	Property	30,000	40,000
Clancy	Property	25,000	30,000

   What amount of taxable income to Kudzu results from the formation of KCC?

   a. $5,000   c. $7,000

   b. $0   d. $2,000

3. Identify the correct statement below regarding similarities and differences of corporate and individual taxation.

   a. If long-term capital losses exceed their allowable yearly offset to ordinary income, both individuals and corporations may carry forward the losses and claim them as long-term capital losses in future years, subject to certain limitations for corporations.

   b. Both individuals and corporations can utilize the like-kind exchange provisions of Code Section 1031.

   c. Both individuals and corporations must distinguish between deductions *for* and deductions *from* in calculating taxable income.

   d. Corporations can claim the Domestic Production Activities Deduction (DPAD), but individuals cannot.

4. Harold gives one share of stock in Harold Corp., an S Corp, to each the following individuals:

   - His nephew
   - His son
   - His adopted step-daughter
   - His grandson
   - His cousin

What is the minimum number of additional S-Corp shareholders under Code Section 1361 that will result from this distribution of stock?

a. Three

b. Four

c. Two

d. Five

5. Identify which of the following would be a separately stated item on Schedule K–1 of an S Corporation's Form 1120S:

I.   Salaries paid to employees who are not shareholders.

II. Salaries paid to officers who are shareholders.

III. Collectibles gain or loss.

a. III only

b. None of the above

c. II and III only

d. All of the above

Appendix A

Tax Rate Schedules and Tables

(The 2017 Tax Tables and 2017 Sales Tax Tables can be accessed at the IRS website when released: **www.irs.gov**)

2016 Tax Rate Schedules

Single—Schedule X

If taxable income is: Over—	But not over—	The tax is:	of the amount over—
$ 0	$ 9,275	.........10%	$ 0
9,275	37,650	$ 927.50 + 15%	9,275
37,650	91,150	5,183.75 + 25%	37,650
91,150	190,150	18,558.75 + 28%	91,150
190,150	413,350	46,278.75 + 33%	190,150
413,350	415,050	119,934.75 + 35%	413,350
415,050	....	120,529.75 + 39.6%	415,050

Head of household—Schedule Z

If taxable income is: Over—	But not over—	The tax is:	of the amount over—
$ 0	$ 13,250	.........10%	$ 0
13,250	50,400	$ 1,325.00 + 15%	13,250
50,400	130,150	6,897.50 + 25%	50,400
130,150	210,800	26,835.00 + 28%	130,150
210,800	413,350	49,417.00 + 33%	210,800
413,350	441,000	116,258.50 + 35%	413,350
441,000	....	125,936.00 + 39.6%	441,000

Married filing jointly or Qualifying widow(er)—Schedule Y–1

If taxable income is: Over—	But not over—	The tax is:	of the amount over—
$ 0	$ 18,550	.........10%	$ 0
18,550	75,300	$ 1,855.00 + 15%	18,550
75,300	151,900	10,367.50 + 25%	75,300
151,900	231,450	29,517.50 + 28%	151,900
231,450	413,350	51,791.50 + 33%	231,450
413,350	466,950	111,818.50 + 35%	413,350
466,950	....	130,578.50 + 39.6%	466,950

Married filing separately—Schedule Y–2

If taxable income is: Over—	But not over—	The tax is:	of the amount over—
$ 0	$ 9,275	.........10%	$ 0
9,275	37,650	$ 927.50 + 15%	9,275
37,650	75,950	5,183.75 + 25%	37,650
75,950	115,725	14,758.75 + 28%	75,950
115,725	206,675	25,895.75 + 33%	115,725
206,675	233,475	55,909.25 + 35%	206,675
233,475	....	65,289.25 + 39.6%	233,475

2017 Tax Rate Schedules

Single—Schedule X

If taxable income is: Over—	But not over—	The tax is:	of the amount over—
$ 0	$ 9,325	.........10%	$ 0
9,325	37,950	$ 932.50 + 15%	9,325
37,950	91,900	5,226.25 + 25%	37,950
91,900	191,650	18,713.75 + 28%	91,900
191,650	416,700	46,643.75 + 33%	191,650
416,700	418,400	120,910.25 + 35%	416,700
418,400	....	121,505.25 + 39.6%	418,400

Head of household—Schedule Z

If taxable income is: Over—	But not over—	The tax is:	of the amount over—
$ 0	$ 13,350	.........10%	$ 0
13,350	50,800	$ 1,335.00 + 15%	13,350
50,800	131,200	6,952.50 + 25%	50,800
131,200	212,500	27,052.50 + 28%	131,200
212,500	416,700	49,816.50 + 33%	212,500
416,700	444,550	117,202.50 + 35%	416,700
444,550	....	126,950.00 + 39.6%	444,550

Married filing jointly or Qualifying widow(er)—Schedule Y–1

If taxable income is: Over—	But not over—	The tax is:	of the amount over—
$ 0	$ 18,650	.........10%	$ 0
18,650	75,900	$ 1,865.00 + 15%	18,650
75,900	153,100	10,452.50 + 25%	75,900
153,100	233,350	29,752.50 + 28%	153,100
233,350	416,700	52,222.50 + 33%	233,350
416,700	470,700	112,728.00 + 35%	416,700
470,700	....	131,628.00 + 39.6%	470,700

Married filing separately—Schedule Y–2

If taxable income is: Over—	But not over—	The tax is:	of the amount over—
$ 0	$ 9,325	.........10%	$ 0
9,325	37,950	$ 932.50 + 15%	9,325
37,950	76,550	5,226.25 + 25%	37,950
76,550	116,675	14,876.25 + 28%	76,550
116,675	208,350	26,111.25 + 33%	116,675
208,350	235,350	56,364.00 + 35%	208,350
235,350	....	65,814.00 + 39.6%	235,350

2016 Tax Table

See the instructions for line 44 to see if you must use the Tax Table below to figure your tax.

Example. Mr. and Mrs. Brown are filing a joint return. Their taxable income on Form 1040, line 43, is $25,300. First, they find the $25,300-25,350 taxable income line. Next, they find the column for married filing jointly and read down the column. The amount shown where the taxable income line and filing status column meet is $2,871. This is the tax amount they should enter on Form 1040, line 44.

Sample Table

At Least	But Less Than	Single	Married filing jointly*	Married filing sepa-rately	Head of a house-hold
			Your tax is—		
25,200	25,250	3,320	2,856	3,320	3,121
25,250	25,300	3,328	2,864	3,328	3,129
25,300	25,350	3,335	(2,871)	3,335	3,136
25,350	25,400	3,343	2,879	3,343	3,144

If line 43 (taxable income) is— At least	But less than	Single	Married filing jointly *	Married filing sepa-rately	Head of a house-hold
			Your tax is—		
0	5	0	0	0	0
5	15	1	1	1	1
15	25	2	2	2	2
25	50	4	4	4	4
50	75	6	6	6	6
75	100	9	9	9	9
100	125	11	11	11	11
125	150	14	14	14	14
150	175	16	16	16	16
175	200	19	19	19	19
200	225	21	21	21	21
225	250	24	24	24	24
250	275	26	26	26	26
275	300	29	29	29	29
300	325	31	31	31	31
325	350	34	34	34	34
350	375	36	36	36	36
375	400	39	39	39	39
400	425	41	41	41	41
425	450	44	44	44	44
450	475	46	46	46	46
475	500	49	49	49	49
500	525	51	51	51	51
525	550	54	54	54	54
550	575	56	56	56	56
575	600	59	59	59	59
600	625	61	61	61	61
625	650	64	64	64	64
650	675	66	66	66	66
675	700	69	69	69	69
700	725	71	71	71	71
725	750	74	74	74	74
750	775	76	76	76	76
775	800	79	79	79	79
800	825	81	81	81	81
825	850	84	84	84	84
850	875	86	86	86	86
875	900	89	89	89	89
900	925	91	91	91	91
925	950	94	94	94	94
950	975	96	96	96	96
975	1,000	99	99	99	99

1,000

If line 43 (taxable income) is— At least	But less than	Single	Married filing jointly *	Married filing sepa-rately	Head of a house-hold
			Your tax is—		
1,000	1,025	101	101	101	101
1,025	1,050	104	104	104	104
1,050	1,075	106	106	106	106
1,075	1,100	109	109	109	109
1,100	1,125	111	111	111	111
1,125	1,150	114	114	114	114
1,150	1,175	116	116	116	116
1,175	1,200	119	119	119	119
1,200	1,225	121	121	121	121
1,225	1,250	124	124	124	124
1,250	1,275	126	126	126	126
1,275	1,300	129	129	129	129
1,300	1,325	131	131	131	131
1,325	1,350	134	134	134	134
1,350	1,375	136	136	136	136
1,375	1,400	139	139	139	139
1,400	1,425	141	141	141	141
1,425	1,450	144	144	144	144
1,450	1,475	146	146	146	146
1,475	1,500	149	149	149	149
1,500	1,525	151	151	151	151
1,525	1,550	154	154	154	154
1,550	1,575	156	156	156	156
1,575	1,600	159	159	159	159
1,600	1,625	161	161	161	161
1,625	1,650	164	164	164	164
1,650	1,675	166	166	166	166
1,675	1,700	169	169	169	169
1,700	1,725	171	171	171	171
1,725	1,750	174	174	174	174
1,750	1,775	176	176	176	176
1,775	1,800	179	179	179	179
1,800	1,825	181	181	181	181
1,825	1,850	184	184	184	184
1,850	1,875	186	186	186	186
1,875	1,900	189	189	189	189
1,900	1,925	191	191	191	191
1,925	1,950	194	194	194	194
1,950	1,975	196	196	196	196
1,975	2,000	199	199	199	199

2,000

If line 43 (taxable income) is— At least	But less than	Single	Married filing jointly *	Married filing sepa-rately	Head of a house-hold
			Your tax is—		
2,000	2,025	201	201	201	201
2,025	2,050	204	204	204	204
2,050	2,075	206	206	206	206
2,075	2,100	209	209	209	209
2,100	2,125	211	211	211	211
2,125	2,150	214	214	214	214
2,150	2,175	216	216	216	216
2,175	2,200	219	219	219	219
2,200	2,225	221	221	221	221
2,225	2,250	224	224	224	224
2,250	2,275	226	226	226	226
2,275	2,300	229	229	229	229
2,300	2,325	231	231	231	231
2,325	2,350	234	234	234	234
2,350	2,375	236	236	236	236
2,375	2,400	239	239	239	239
2,400	2,425	241	241	241	241
2,425	2,450	244	244	244	244
2,450	2,475	246	246	246	246
2,475	2,500	249	249	249	249
2,500	2,525	251	251	251	251
2,525	2,550	254	254	254	254
2,550	2,575	256	256	256	256
2,575	2,600	259	259	259	259
2,600	2,625	261	261	261	261
2,625	2,650	264	264	264	264
2,650	2,675	266	266	266	266
2,675	2,700	269	269	269	269
2,700	2,725	271	271	271	271
2,725	2,750	274	274	274	274
2,750	2,775	276	276	276	276
2,775	2,800	279	279	279	279
2,800	2,825	281	281	281	281
2,825	2,850	284	284	284	284
2,850	2,875	286	286	286	286
2,875	2,900	289	289	289	289
2,900	2,925	291	291	291	291
2,925	2,950	294	294	294	294
2,950	2,975	296	296	296	296
2,975	3,000	299	299	299	299

* This column must also be used by a qualifying widow(er).

(Continued)

2016 Tax Table—*Continued*

3,000

At least	But less than	Single	Married filing jointly *	Married filing separately	Head of a household
3,000	3,050	303	303	303	303
3,050	3,100	308	308	308	308
3,100	3,150	313	313	313	313
3,150	3,200	318	318	318	318
3,200	3,250	323	323	323	323
3,250	3,300	328	328	328	328
3,300	3,350	333	333	333	333
3,350	3,400	338	338	338	338
3,400	3,450	343	343	343	343
3,450	3,500	348	348	348	348
3,500	3,550	353	353	353	353
3,550	3,600	358	358	358	358
3,600	3,650	363	363	363	363
3,650	3,700	368	368	368	368
3,700	3,750	373	373	373	373
3,750	3,800	378	378	378	378
3,800	3,850	383	383	383	383
3,850	3,900	388	388	388	388
3,900	3,950	393	393	393	393
3,950	4,000	398	398	398	398

4,000

At least	But less than	Single	Married filing jointly *	Married filing separately	Head of a household
4,000	4,050	403	403	403	403
4,050	4,100	408	408	408	408
4,100	4,150	413	413	413	413
4,150	4,200	418	418	418	418
4,200	4,250	423	423	423	423
4,250	4,300	428	428	428	428
4,300	4,350	433	433	433	433
4,350	4,400	438	438	438	438
4,400	4,450	443	443	443	443
4,450	4,500	448	448	448	448
4,500	4,550	453	453	453	453
4,550	4,600	458	458	458	458
4,600	4,650	463	463	463	463
4,650	4,700	468	468	468	468
4,700	4,750	473	473	473	473
4,750	4,800	478	478	478	478
4,800	4,850	483	483	483	483
4,850	4,900	488	488	488	488
4,900	4,950	493	493	493	493
4,950	5,000	498	498	498	498

5,000

At least	But less than	Single	Married filing jointly *	Married filing separately	Head of a household
5,000	5,050	503	503	503	503
5,050	5,100	508	508	508	508
5,100	5,150	513	513	513	513
5,150	5,200	518	518	518	518
5,200	5,250	523	523	523	523
5,250	5,300	528	528	528	528
5,300	5,350	533	533	533	533
5,350	5,400	538	538	538	538
5,400	5,450	543	543	543	543
5,450	5,500	548	548	548	548
5,500	5,550	553	553	553	553
5,550	5,600	558	558	558	558
5,600	5,650	563	563	563	563
5,650	5,700	568	568	568	568
5,700	5,750	573	573	573	573
5,750	5,800	578	578	578	578
5,800	5,850	583	583	583	583
5,850	5,900	588	588	588	588
5,900	5,950	593	593	593	593
5,950	6,000	598	598	598	598

6,000

At least	But less than	Single	Married filing jointly *	Married filing separately	Head of a household
6,000	6,050	603	603	603	603
6,050	6,100	608	608	608	608
6,100	6,150	613	613	613	613
6,150	6,200	618	618	618	618
6,200	6,250	623	623	623	623
6,250	6,300	628	628	628	628
6,300	6,350	633	633	633	633
6,350	6,400	638	638	638	638
6,400	6,450	643	643	643	643
6,450	6,500	648	648	648	648
6,500	6,550	653	653	653	653
6,550	6,600	658	658	658	658
6,600	6,650	663	663	663	663
6,650	6,700	668	668	668	668
6,700	6,750	673	673	673	673
6,750	6,800	678	678	678	678
6,800	6,850	683	683	683	683
6,850	6,900	688	688	688	688
6,900	6,950	693	693	693	693
6,950	7,000	698	698	698	698

7,000

At least	But less than	Single	Married filing jointly *	Married filing separately	Head of a household
7,000	7,050	703	703	703	703
7,050	7,100	708	708	708	708
7,100	7,150	713	713	713	713
7,150	7,200	718	718	718	718
7,200	7,250	723	723	723	723
7,250	7,300	728	728	728	728
7,300	7,350	733	733	733	733
7,350	7,400	738	738	738	738
7,400	7,450	743	743	743	743
7,450	7,500	748	748	748	748
7,500	7,550	753	753	753	753
7,550	7,600	758	758	758	758
7,600	7,650	763	763	763	763
7,650	7,700	768	768	768	768
7,700	7,750	773	773	773	773
7,750	7,800	778	778	778	778
7,800	7,850	783	783	783	783
7,850	7,900	788	788	788	788
7,900	7,950	793	793	793	793
7,950	8,000	798	798	798	798

8,000

At least	But less than	Single	Married filing jointly *	Married filing separately	Head of a household
8,000	8,050	803	803	803	803
8,050	8,100	808	808	808	808
8,100	8,150	813	813	813	813
8,150	8,200	818	818	818	818
8,200	8,250	823	823	823	823
8,250	8,300	828	828	828	828
8,300	8,350	833	833	833	833
8,350	8,400	838	838	838	838
8,400	8,450	843	843	843	843
8,450	8,500	848	848	848	848
8,500	8,550	853	853	853	853
8,550	8,600	858	858	858	858
8,600	8,650	863	863	863	863
8,650	8,700	868	868	868	868
8,700	8,750	873	873	873	873
8,750	8,800	878	878	878	878
8,800	8,850	883	883	883	883
8,850	8,900	888	888	888	888
8,900	8,950	893	893	893	893
8,950	9,000	898	898	898	898

9,000

At least	But less than	Single	Married filing jointly *	Married filing separately	Head of a household
9,000	9,050	903	903	903	903
9,050	9,100	908	908	908	908
9,100	9,150	913	913	913	913
9,150	9,200	918	918	918	918
9,200	9,250	923	923	923	923
9,250	9,300	928	928	928	928
9,300	9,350	935	933	935	933
9,350	9,400	943	938	943	938
9,400	9,450	950	943	950	943
9,450	9,500	958	948	958	948
9,500	9,550	965	953	965	953
9,550	9,600	973	958	973	958
9,600	9,650	980	963	980	963
9,650	9,700	988	968	988	968
9,700	9,750	995	973	995	973
9,750	9,800	1,003	978	1,003	978
9,800	9,850	1,010	983	1,010	983
9,850	9,900	1,018	988	1,018	988
9,900	9,950	1,025	993	1,025	993
9,950	10,000	1,033	998	1,033	998

10,000

At least	But less than	Single	Married filing jointly *	Married filing separately	Head of a household
10,000	10,050	1,040	1,003	1,040	1,003
10,050	10,100	1,048	1,008	1,048	1,008
10,100	10,150	1,055	1,013	1,055	1,013
10,150	10,200	1,063	1,018	1,063	1,018
10,200	10,250	1,070	1,023	1,070	1,023
10,250	10,300	1,078	1,028	1,078	1,028
10,300	10,350	1,085	1,033	1,085	1,033
10,350	10,400	1,093	1,038	1,093	1,038
10,400	10,450	1,100	1,043	1,100	1,043
10,450	10,500	1,108	1,048	1,108	1,048
10,500	10,550	1,115	1,053	1,115	1,053
10,550	10,600	1,123	1,058	1,123	1,058
10,600	10,650	1,130	1,063	1,130	1,063
10,650	10,700	1,138	1,068	1,138	1,068
10,700	10,750	1,145	1,073	1,145	1,073
10,750	10,800	1,153	1,078	1,153	1,078
10,800	10,850	1,160	1,083	1,160	1,083
10,850	10,900	1,168	1,088	1,168	1,088
10,900	10,950	1,175	1,093	1,175	1,093
10,950	11,000	1,183	1,098	1,183	1,098

11,000

At least	But less than	Single	Married filing jointly *	Married filing separately	Head of a household
11,000	11,050	1,190	1,103	1,190	1,103
11,050	11,100	1,198	1,108	1,198	1,108
11,100	11,150	1,205	1,113	1,205	1,113
11,150	11,200	1,213	1,118	1,213	1,118
11,200	11,250	1,220	1,123	1,220	1,123
11,250	11,300	1,228	1,128	1,228	1,128
11,300	11,350	1,235	1,133	1,235	1,133
11,350	11,400	1,243	1,138	1,243	1,138
11,400	11,450	1,250	1,143	1,250	1,143
11,450	11,500	1,258	1,148	1,258	1,148
11,500	11,550	1,265	1,153	1,265	1,153
11,550	11,600	1,273	1,158	1,273	1,158
11,600	11,650	1,280	1,163	1,280	1,163
11,650	11,700	1,288	1,168	1,288	1,168
11,700	11,750	1,295	1,173	1,295	1,173
11,750	11,800	1,303	1,178	1,303	1,178
11,800	11,850	1,310	1,183	1,310	1,183
11,850	11,900	1,318	1,188	1,318	1,188
11,900	11,950	1,325	1,193	1,325	1,193
11,950	12,000	1,333	1,198	1,333	1,198

* This column must also be used by a qualifying widow(er).

(Continued)

2016 Tax Table—*Continued*

12,000

At least	But less than	Single	Married filing jointly *	Married filing separately	Head of a household
			Your tax is—		
12,000	12,050	1,340	1,203	1,340	1,203
12,050	12,100	1,348	1,208	1,348	1,208
12,100	12,150	1,355	1,213	1,355	1,213
12,150	12,200	1,363	1,218	1,363	1,218
12,200	12,250	1,370	1,223	1,370	1,223
12,250	12,300	1,378	1,228	1,378	1,228
12,300	12,350	1,385	1,233	1,385	1,233
12,350	12,400	1,393	1,238	1,393	1,238
12,400	12,450	1,400	1,243	1,400	1,243
12,450	12,500	1,408	1,248	1,408	1,248
12,500	12,550	1,415	1,253	1,415	1,253
12,550	12,600	1,423	1,258	1,423	1,258
12,600	12,650	1,430	1,263	1,430	1,263
12,650	12,700	1,438	1,268	1,438	1,268
12,700	12,750	1,445	1,273	1,445	1,273
12,750	12,800	1,453	1,278	1,453	1,278
12,800	12,850	1,460	1,283	1,460	1,283
12,850	12,900	1,468	1,288	1,468	1,288
12,900	12,950	1,475	1,293	1,475	1,293
12,950	13,000	1,483	1,298	1,483	1,298

13,000

At least	But less than	Single	Married filing jointly *	Married filing separately	Head of a household
13,000	13,050	1,490	1,303	1,490	1,303
13,050	13,100	1,498	1,308	1,498	1,308
13,100	13,150	1,505	1,313	1,505	1,313
13,150	13,200	1,513	1,318	1,513	1,318
13,200	13,250	1,520	1,323	1,520	1,323
13,250	13,300	1,528	1,328	1,528	1,329
13,300	13,350	1,535	1,333	1,535	1,336
13,350	13,400	1,543	1,338	1,543	1,344
13,400	13,450	1,550	1,343	1,550	1,351
13,450	13,500	1,558	1,348	1,558	1,359
13,500	13,550	1,565	1,353	1,565	1,366
13,550	13,600	1,573	1,358	1,573	1,374
13,600	13,650	1,580	1,363	1,580	1,381
13,650	13,700	1,588	1,368	1,588	1,389
13,700	13,750	1,595	1,373	1,595	1,396
13,750	13,800	1,603	1,378	1,603	1,404
13,800	13,850	1,610	1,383	1,610	1,411
13,850	13,900	1,618	1,388	1,618	1,419
13,900	13,950	1,625	1,393	1,625	1,426
13,950	14,000	1,633	1,398	1,633	1,434

14,000

At least	But less than	Single	Married filing jointly *	Married filing separately	Head of a household
14,000	14,050	1,640	1,403	1,640	1,441
14,050	14,100	1,648	1,408	1,648	1,449
14,100	14,150	1,655	1,413	1,655	1,456
14,150	14,200	1,663	1,418	1,663	1,464
14,200	14,250	1,670	1,423	1,670	1,471
14,250	14,300	1,678	1,428	1,678	1,479
14,300	14,350	1,685	1,433	1,685	1,486
14,350	14,400	1,693	1,438	1,693	1,494
14,400	14,450	1,700	1,443	1,700	1,501
14,450	14,500	1,708	1,448	1,708	1,509
14,500	14,550	1,715	1,453	1,715	1,516
14,550	14,600	1,723	1,458	1,723	1,524
14,600	14,650	1,730	1,463	1,730	1,531
14,650	14,700	1,738	1,468	1,738	1,539
14,700	14,750	1,745	1,473	1,745	1,546
14,750	14,800	1,753	1,478	1,753	1,554
14,800	14,850	1,760	1,483	1,760	1,561
14,850	14,900	1,768	1,488	1,768	1,569
14,900	14,950	1,775	1,493	1,775	1,576
14,950	15,000	1,783	1,498	1,783	1,584

15,000

At least	But less than	Single	Married filing jointly *	Married filing separately	Head of a household
15,000	15,050	1,790	1,503	1,790	1,591
15,050	15,100	1,798	1,508	1,798	1,599
15,100	15,150	1,805	1,513	1,805	1,606
15,150	15,200	1,813	1,518	1,813	1,614
15,200	15,250	1,820	1,523	1,820	1,621
15,250	15,300	1,828	1,528	1,828	1,629
15,300	15,350	1,835	1,533	1,835	1,636
15,350	15,400	1,843	1,538	1,843	1,644
15,400	15,450	1,850	1,543	1,850	1,651
15,450	15,500	1,858	1,548	1,858	1,659
15,500	15,550	1,865	1,553	1,865	1,666
15,550	15,600	1,873	1,558	1,873	1,674
15,600	15,650	1,880	1,563	1,880	1,681
15,650	15,700	1,888	1,568	1,888	1,689
15,700	15,750	1,895	1,573	1,895	1,696
15,750	15,800	1,903	1,578	1,903	1,704
15,800	15,850	1,910	1,583	1,910	1,711
15,850	15,900	1,918	1,588	1,918	1,719
15,900	15,950	1,925	1,593	1,925	1,726
15,950	16,000	1,933	1,598	1,933	1,734

16,000

At least	But less than	Single	Married filing jointly *	Married filing separately	Head of a household
16,000	16,050	1,940	1,603	1,940	1,741
16,050	16,100	1,948	1,608	1,948	1,749
16,100	16,150	1,955	1,613	1,955	1,756
16,150	16,200	1,963	1,618	1,963	1,764
16,200	16,250	1,970	1,623	1,970	1,771
16,250	16,300	1,978	1,628	1,978	1,779
16,300	16,350	1,985	1,633	1,985	1,786
16,350	16,400	1,993	1,638	1,993	1,794
16,400	16,450	2,000	1,643	2,000	1,801
16,450	16,500	2,008	1,648	2,008	1,809
16,500	16,550	2,015	1,653	2,015	1,816
16,550	16,600	2,023	1,658	2,023	1,824
16,600	16,650	2,030	1,663	2,030	1,831
16,650	16,700	2,038	1,668	2,038	1,839
16,700	16,750	2,045	1,673	2,045	1,846
16,750	16,800	2,053	1,678	2,053	1,854
16,800	16,850	2,060	1,683	2,060	1,861
16,850	16,900	2,068	1,688	2,068	1,869
16,900	16,950	2,075	1,693	2,075	1,876
16,950	17,000	2,083	1,698	2,083	1,884

17,000

At least	But less than	Single	Married filing jointly *	Married filing separately	Head of a household
17,000	17,050	2,090	1,703	2,090	1,891
17,050	17,100	2,098	1,708	2,098	1,899
17,100	17,150	2,105	1,713	2,105	1,906
17,150	17,200	2,113	1,718	2,113	1,914
17,200	17,250	2,120	1,723	2,120	1,921
17,250	17,300	2,128	1,728	2,128	1,929
17,300	17,350	2,135	1,733	2,135	1,936
17,350	17,400	2,143	1,738	2,143	1,944
17,400	17,450	2,150	1,743	2,150	1,951
17,450	17,500	2,158	1,748	2,158	1,959
17,500	17,550	2,165	1,753	2,165	1,966
17,550	17,600	2,173	1,758	2,173	1,974
17,600	17,650	2,180	1,763	2,180	1,981
17,650	17,700	2,188	1,768	2,188	1,989
17,700	17,750	2,195	1,773	2,195	1,996
17,750	17,800	2,203	1,778	2,203	2,004
17,800	17,850	2,210	1,783	2,210	2,011
17,850	17,900	2,218	1,788	2,218	2,019
17,900	17,950	2,225	1,793	2,225	2,026
17,950	18,000	2,233	1,798	2,233	2,034

18,000

At least	But less than	Single	Married filing jointly *	Married filing separately	Head of a household
18,000	18,050	2,240	1,803	2,240	2,041
18,050	18,100	2,248	1,808	2,248	2,049
18,100	18,150	2,255	1,813	2,255	2,056
18,150	18,200	2,263	1,818	2,263	2,064
18,200	18,250	2,270	1,823	2,270	2,071
18,250	18,300	2,278	1,828	2,278	2,079
18,300	18,350	2,285	1,833	2,285	2,086
18,350	18,400	2,293	1,838	2,293	2,094
18,400	18,450	2,300	1,843	2,300	2,101
18,450	18,500	2,308	1,848	2,308	2,109
18,500	18,550	2,315	1,853	2,315	2,116
18,550	18,600	2,323	1,859	2,323	2,124
18,600	18,650	2,330	1,866	2,330	2,131
18,650	18,700	2,338	1,874	2,338	2,139
18,700	18,750	2,345	1,881	2,345	2,146
18,750	18,800	2,353	1,889	2,353	2,154
18,800	18,850	2,360	1,896	2,360	2,161
18,850	18,900	2,368	1,904	2,368	2,169
18,900	18,950	2,375	1,911	2,375	2,176
18,950	19,000	2,383	1,919	2,383	2,184

19,000

At least	But less than	Single	Married filing jointly *	Married filing separately	Head of a household
19,000	19,050	2,390	1,926	2,390	2,191
19,050	19,100	2,398	1,934	2,398	2,199
19,100	19,150	2,405	1,941	2,405	2,206
19,150	19,200	2,413	1,949	2,413	2,214
19,200	19,250	2,420	1,956	2,420	2,221
19,250	19,300	2,428	1,964	2,428	2,229
19,300	19,350	2,435	1,971	2,435	2,236
19,350	19,400	2,443	1,979	2,443	2,244
19,400	19,450	2,450	1,986	2,450	2,251
19,450	19,500	2,458	1,994	2,458	2,259
19,500	19,550	2,465	2,001	2,465	2,266
19,550	19,600	2,473	2,009	2,473	2,274
19,600	19,650	2,480	2,016	2,480	2,281
19,650	19,700	2,488	2,024	2,488	2,289
19,700	19,750	2,495	2,031	2,495	2,296
19,750	19,800	2,503	2,039	2,503	2,304
19,800	19,850	2,510	2,046	2,510	2,311
19,850	19,900	2,518	2,054	2,518	2,319
19,900	19,950	2,525	2,061	2,525	2,326
19,950	20,000	2,533	2,069	2,533	2,334

20,000

At least	But less than	Single	Married filing jointly *	Married filing separately	Head of a household
20,000	20,050	2,540	2,076	2,540	2,341
20,050	20,100	2,548	2,084	2,548	2,349
20,100	20,150	2,555	2,091	2,555	2,356
20,150	20,200	2,563	2,099	2,563	2,364
20,200	20,250	2,570	2,106	2,570	2,371
20,250	20,300	2,578	2,114	2,578	2,379
20,300	20,350	2,585	2,121	2,585	2,386
20,350	20,400	2,593	2,129	2,593	2,394
20,400	20,450	2,600	2,136	2,600	2,401
20,450	20,500	2,608	2,144	2,608	2,409
20,500	20,550	2,615	2,151	2,615	2,416
20,550	20,600	2,623	2,159	2,623	2,424
20,600	20,650	2,630	2,166	2,630	2,431
20,650	20,700	2,638	2,174	2,638	2,439
20,700	20,750	2,645	2,181	2,645	2,446
20,750	20,800	2,653	2,189	2,653	2,454
20,800	20,850	2,660	2,196	2,660	2,461
20,850	20,900	2,668	2,204	2,668	2,469
20,900	20,950	2,675	2,211	2,675	2,476
20,950	21,000	2,683	2,219	2,683	2,484

* This column must also be used by a qualifying widow(er).

(Continued)

2016 Tax Table—*Continued*

If line 43 (taxable income) is—		And you are—			
At least	But less than	Single	Married filing jointly *	Married filing separately	Head of a household
		Your tax is—			

21,000

At least	But less than	Single	MFJ *	MFS	HoH
21,000	21,050	2,690	2,226	2,690	2,491
21,050	21,100	2,698	2,234	2,698	2,499
21,100	21,150	2,705	2,241	2,705	2,506
21,150	21,200	2,713	2,249	2,713	2,514
21,200	21,250	2,720	2,256	2,720	2,521
21,250	21,300	2,728	2,264	2,728	2,529
21,300	21,350	2,735	2,271	2,735	2,536
21,350	21,400	2,743	2,279	2,743	2,544
21,400	21,450	2,750	2,286	2,750	2,551
21,450	21,500	2,758	2,294	2,758	2,559
21,500	21,550	2,765	2,301	2,765	2,566
21,550	21,600	2,773	2,309	2,773	2,574
21,600	21,650	2,780	2,316	2,780	2,581
21,650	21,700	2,788	2,324	2,788	2,589
21,700	21,750	2,795	2,331	2,795	2,596
21,750	21,800	2,803	2,339	2,803	2,604
21,800	21,850	2,810	2,346	2,810	2,611
21,850	21,900	2,818	2,354	2,818	2,619
21,900	21,950	2,825	2,361	2,825	2,626
21,950	22,000	2,833	2,369	2,833	2,634

22,000

At least	But less than	Single	MFJ *	MFS	HoH
22,000	22,050	2,840	2,376	2,840	2,641
22,050	22,100	2,848	2,384	2,848	2,649
22,100	22,150	2,855	2,391	2,855	2,656
22,150	22,200	2,863	2,399	2,863	2,664
22,200	22,250	2,870	2,406	2,870	2,671
22,250	22,300	2,878	2,414	2,878	2,679
22,300	22,350	2,885	2,421	2,885	2,686
22,350	22,400	2,893	2,429	2,893	2,694
22,400	22,450	2,900	2,436	2,900	2,701
22,450	22,500	2,908	2,444	2,908	2,709
22,500	22,550	2,915	2,451	2,915	2,716
22,550	22,600	2,923	2,459	2,923	2,724
22,600	22,650	2,930	2,466	2,930	2,731
22,650	22,700	2,938	2,474	2,938	2,739
22,700	22,750	2,945	2,481	2,945	2,746
22,750	22,800	2,953	2,489	2,953	2,754
22,800	22,850	2,960	2,496	2,960	2,761
22,850	22,900	2,968	2,504	2,968	2,769
22,900	22,950	2,975	2,511	2,975	2,776
22,950	23,000	2,983	2,519	2,983	2,784

23,000

At least	But less than	Single	MFJ *	MFS	HoH
23,000	23,050	2,990	2,526	2,990	2,791
23,050	23,100	2,998	2,534	2,998	2,799
23,100	23,150	3,005	2,541	3,005	2,806
23,150	23,200	3,013	2,549	3,013	2,814
23,200	23,250	3,020	2,556	3,020	2,821
23,250	23,300	3,028	2,564	3,028	2,829
23,300	23,350	3,035	2,571	3,035	2,836
23,350	23,400	3,043	2,579	3,043	2,844
23,400	23,450	3,050	2,586	3,050	2,851
23,450	23,500	3,058	2,594	3,058	2,859
23,500	23,550	3,065	2,601	3,065	2,866
23,550	23,600	3,073	2,609	3,073	2,874
23,600	23,650	3,080	2,616	3,080	2,881
23,650	23,700	3,088	2,624	3,088	2,889
23,700	23,750	3,095	2,631	3,095	2,896
23,750	23,800	3,103	2,639	3,103	2,904
23,800	23,850	3,110	2,646	3,110	2,911
23,850	23,900	3,118	2,654	3,118	2,919
23,900	23,950	3,125	2,661	3,125	2,926
23,950	24,000	3,133	2,669	3,133	2,934

24,000

At least	But less than	Single	MFJ *	MFS	HoH
24,000	24,050	3,140	2,676	3,140	2,941
24,050	24,100	3,148	2,684	3,148	2,949
24,100	24,150	3,155	2,691	3,155	2,956
24,150	24,200	3,163	2,699	3,163	2,964
24,200	24,250	3,170	2,706	3,170	2,971
24,250	24,300	3,178	2,714	3,178	2,979
24,300	24,350	3,185	2,721	3,185	2,986
24,350	24,400	3,193	2,729	3,193	2,994
24,400	24,450	3,200	2,736	3,200	3,001
24,450	24,500	3,208	2,744	3,208	3,009
24,500	24,550	3,215	2,751	3,215	3,016
24,550	24,600	3,223	2,759	3,223	3,024
24,600	24,650	3,230	2,766	3,230	3,031
24,650	24,700	3,238	2,774	3,238	3,039
24,700	24,750	3,245	2,781	3,245	3,046
24,750	24,800	3,253	2,789	3,253	3,054
24,800	24,850	3,260	2,796	3,260	3,061
24,850	24,900	3,268	2,804	3,268	3,069
24,900	24,950	3,275	2,811	3,275	3,076
24,950	25,000	3,283	2,819	3,283	3,084

25,000

At least	But less than	Single	MFJ *	MFS	HoH
25,000	25,050	3,290	2,826	3,290	3,091
25,050	25,100	3,298	2,834	3,298	3,099
25,100	25,150	3,305	2,841	3,305	3,106
25,150	25,200	3,313	2,849	3,313	3,114
25,200	25,250	3,320	2,856	3,320	3,121
25,250	25,300	3,328	2,864	3,328	3,129
25,300	25,350	3,335	2,871	3,335	3,136
25,350	25,400	3,343	2,879	3,343	3,144
25,400	25,450	3,350	2,886	3,350	3,151
25,450	25,500	3,358	2,894	3,358	3,159
25,500	25,550	3,365	2,901	3,365	3,166
25,550	25,600	3,373	2,909	3,373	3,174
25,600	25,650	3,380	2,916	3,380	3,181
25,650	25,700	3,388	2,924	3,388	3,189
25,700	25,750	3,395	2,931	3,395	3,196
25,750	25,800	3,403	2,939	3,403	3,204
25,800	25,850	3,410	2,946	3,410	3,211
25,850	25,900	3,418	2,954	3,418	3,219
25,900	25,950	3,425	2,961	3,425	3,226
25,950	26,000	3,433	2,969	3,433	3,234

26,000

At least	But less than	Single	MFJ *	MFS	HoH
26,000	26,050	3,440	2,976	3,440	3,241
26,050	26,100	3,448	2,984	3,448	3,249
26,100	26,150	3,455	2,991	3,455	3,256
26,150	26,200	3,463	2,999	3,463	3,264
26,200	26,250	3,470	3,006	3,470	3,271
26,250	26,300	3,478	3,014	3,478	3,279
26,300	26,350	3,485	3,021	3,485	3,286
26,350	26,400	3,493	3,029	3,493	3,294
26,400	26,450	3,500	3,036	3,500	3,301
26,450	26,500	3,508	3,044	3,508	3,309
26,500	26,550	3,515	3,051	3,515	3,316
26,550	26,600	3,523	3,059	3,523	3,324
26,600	26,650	3,530	3,066	3,530	3,331
26,650	26,700	3,538	3,074	3,538	3,339
26,700	26,750	3,545	3,081	3,545	3,346
26,750	26,800	3,553	3,089	3,553	3,354
26,800	26,850	3,560	3,096	3,560	3,361
26,850	26,900	3,568	3,104	3,568	3,369
26,900	26,950	3,575	3,111	3,575	3,376
26,950	27,000	3,583	3,119	3,583	3,384

27,000

At least	But less than	Single	MFJ *	MFS	HoH
27,000	27,050	3,590	3,126	3,590	3,391
27,050	27,100	3,598	3,134	3,598	3,399
27,100	27,150	3,605	3,141	3,605	3,406
27,150	27,200	3,613	3,149	3,613	3,414
27,200	27,250	3,620	3,156	3,620	3,421
27,250	27,300	3,628	3,164	3,628	3,429
27,300	27,350	3,635	3,171	3,635	3,436
27,350	27,400	3,643	3,179	3,643	3,444
27,400	27,450	3,650	3,186	3,650	3,451
27,450	27,500	3,658	3,194	3,658	3,459
27,500	27,550	3,665	3,201	3,665	3,466
27,550	27,600	3,673	3,209	3,673	3,474
27,600	27,650	3,680	3,216	3,680	3,481
27,650	27,700	3,688	3,224	3,688	3,489
27,700	27,750	3,695	3,231	3,695	3,496
27,750	27,800	3,703	3,239	3,703	3,504
27,800	27,850	3,710	3,246	3,710	3,511
27,850	27,900	3,718	3,254	3,718	3,519
27,900	27,950	3,725	3,261	3,725	3,526
27,950	28,000	3,733	3,269	3,733	3,534

28,000

At least	But less than	Single	MFJ *	MFS	HoH
28,000	28,050	3,740	3,276	3,740	3,541
28,050	28,100	3,748	3,284	3,748	3,549
28,100	28,150	3,755	3,291	3,755	3,556
28,150	28,200	3,763	3,299	3,763	3,564
28,200	28,250	3,770	3,306	3,770	3,571
28,250	28,300	3,778	3,314	3,778	3,579
28,300	28,350	3,785	3,321	3,785	3,586
28,350	28,400	3,793	3,329	3,793	3,594
28,400	28,450	3,800	3,336	3,800	3,601
28,450	28,500	3,808	3,344	3,808	3,609
28,500	28,550	3,815	3,351	3,815	3,616
28,550	28,600	3,823	3,359	3,823	3,624
28,600	28,650	3,830	3,366	3,830	3,631
28,650	28,700	3,838	3,374	3,838	3,639
28,700	28,750	3,845	3,381	3,845	3,646
28,750	28,800	3,853	3,389	3,853	3,654
28,800	28,850	3,860	3,396	3,860	3,661
28,850	28,900	3,868	3,404	3,868	3,669
28,900	28,950	3,875	3,411	3,875	3,676
28,950	29,000	3,883	3,419	3,883	3,684

29,000

At least	But less than	Single	MFJ *	MFS	HoH
29,000	29,050	3,890	3,426	3,890	3,691
29,050	29,100	3,898	3,434	3,898	3,699
29,100	29,150	3,905	3,441	3,905	3,706
29,150	29,200	3,913	3,449	3,913	3,714
29,200	29,250	3,920	3,456	3,920	3,721
29,250	29,300	3,928	3,464	3,928	3,729
29,300	29,350	3,935	3,471	3,935	3,736
29,350	29,400	3,943	3,479	3,943	3,744
29,400	29,450	3,950	3,486	3,950	3,751
29,450	29,500	3,958	3,494	3,958	3,759
29,500	29,550	3,965	3,501	3,965	3,766
29,550	29,600	3,973	3,509	3,973	3,774
29,600	29,650	3,980	3,516	3,980	3,781
29,650	29,700	3,988	3,524	3,988	3,789
29,700	29,750	3,995	3,531	3,995	3,796
29,750	29,800	4,003	3,539	4,003	3,804
29,800	29,850	4,010	3,546	4,010	3,811
29,850	29,900	4,018	3,554	4,018	3,819
29,900	29,950	4,025	3,561	4,025	3,826
29,950	30,000	4,033	3,569	4,033	3,834

* This column must also be used by a qualifying widow(er).

(Continued)

2016 Tax Table—*Continued*

If line 43 (taxable income) is—		And you are—			
At least	But less than	Single	Married filing jointly *	Married filing sepa-rately	Head of a house-hold
			Your tax is—		

30,000

At least	But less than	Single	Married filing jointly *	Married filing separately	Head of a household
30,000	30,050	4,040	3,576	4,040	3,841
30,050	30,100	4,048	3,584	4,048	3,849
30,100	30,150	4,055	3,591	4,055	3,856
30,150	30,200	4,063	3,599	4,063	3,864
30,200	30,250	4,070	3,606	4,070	3,871
30,250	30,300	4,078	3,614	4,078	3,879
30,300	30,350	4,085	3,621	4,085	3,886
30,350	30,400	4,093	3,629	4,093	3,894
30,400	30,450	4,100	3,636	4,100	3,901
30,450	30,500	4,108	3,644	4,108	3,909
30,500	30,550	4,115	3,651	4,115	3,916
30,550	30,600	4,123	3,659	4,123	3,924
30,600	30,650	4,130	3,666	4,130	3,931
30,650	30,700	4,138	3,674	4,138	3,939
30,700	30,750	4,145	3,681	4,145	3,946
30,750	30,800	4,153	3,689	4,153	3,954
30,800	30,850	4,160	3,696	4,160	3,961
30,850	30,900	4,168	3,704	4,168	3,969
30,900	30,950	4,175	3,711	4,175	3,976
30,950	31,000	4,183	3,719	4,183	3,984

31,000

At least	But less than	Single	Married filing jointly *	Married filing separately	Head of a household
31,000	31,050	4,190	3,726	4,190	3,991
31,050	31,100	4,198	3,734	4,198	3,999
31,100	31,150	4,205	3,741	4,205	4,006
31,150	31,200	4,213	3,749	4,213	4,014
31,200	31,250	4,220	3,756	4,220	4,021
31,250	31,300	4,228	3,764	4,228	4,029
31,300	31,350	4,235	3,771	4,235	4,036
31,350	31,400	4,243	3,779	4,243	4,044
31,400	31,450	4,250	3,786	4,250	4,051
31,450	31,500	4,258	3,794	4,258	4,059
31,500	31,550	4,265	3,801	4,265	4,066
31,550	31,600	4,273	3,809	4,273	4,074
31,600	31,650	4,280	3,816	4,280	4,081
31,650	31,700	4,288	3,824	4,288	4,089
31,700	31,750	4,295	3,831	4,295	4,096
31,750	31,800	4,303	3,839	4,303	4,104
31,800	31,850	4,310	3,846	4,310	4,111
31,850	31,900	4,318	3,854	4,318	4,119
31,900	31,950	4,325	3,861	4,325	4,126
31,950	32,000	4,333	3,869	4,333	4,134

32,000

At least	But less than	Single	Married filing jointly *	Married filing separately	Head of a household
32,000	32,050	4,340	3,876	4,340	4,141
32,050	32,100	4,348	3,884	4,348	4,149
32,100	32,150	4,355	3,891	4,355	4,156
32,150	32,200	4,363	3,899	4,363	4,164
32,200	32,250	4,370	3,906	4,370	4,171
32,250	32,300	4,378	3,914	4,378	4,179
32,300	32,350	4,385	3,921	4,385	4,186
32,350	32,400	4,393	3,929	4,393	4,194
32,400	32,450	4,400	3,936	4,400	4,201
32,450	32,500	4,408	3,944	4,408	4,209
32,500	32,550	4,415	3,951	4,415	4,216
32,550	32,600	4,423	3,959	4,423	4,224
32,600	32,650	4,430	3,966	4,430	4,231
32,650	32,700	4,438	3,974	4,438	4,239
32,700	32,750	4,445	3,981	4,445	4,246
32,750	32,800	4,453	3,989	4,453	4,254
32,800	32,850	4,460	3,996	4,460	4,261
32,850	32,900	4,468	4,004	4,468	4,269
32,900	32,950	4,475	4,011	4,475	4,276
32,950	33,000	4,483	4,019	4,483	4,284

33,000

At least	But less than	Single	Married filing jointly *	Married filing separately	Head of a household
33,000	33,050	4,490	4,026	4,490	4,291
33,050	33,100	4,498	4,034	4,498	4,299
33,100	33,150	4,505	4,041	4,505	4,306
33,150	33,200	4,513	4,049	4,513	4,314
33,200	33,250	4,520	4,056	4,520	4,321
33,250	33,300	4,528	4,064	4,528	4,329
33,300	33,350	4,535	4,071	4,535	4,336
33,350	33,400	4,543	4,079	4,543	4,344
33,400	33,450	4,550	4,086	4,550	4,351
33,450	33,500	4,558	4,094	4,558	4,359
33,500	33,550	4,565	4,101	4,565	4,366
33,550	33,600	4,573	4,109	4,573	4,374
33,600	33,650	4,580	4,116	4,580	4,381
33,650	33,700	4,588	4,124	4,588	4,389
33,700	33,750	4,595	4,131	4,595	4,396
33,750	33,800	4,603	4,139	4,603	4,404
33,800	33,850	4,610	4,146	4,610	4,411
33,850	33,900	4,618	4,154	4,618	4,419
33,900	33,950	4,625	4,161	4,625	4,426
33,950	34,000	4,633	4,169	4,633	4,434

34,000

At least	But less than	Single	Married filing jointly *	Married filing separately	Head of a household
34,000	34,050	4,640	4,176	4,640	4,441
34,050	34,100	4,648	4,184	4,648	4,449
34,100	34,150	4,655	4,191	4,655	4,456
34,150	34,200	4,663	4,199	4,663	4,464
34,200	34,250	4,670	4,206	4,670	4,471
34,250	34,300	4,678	4,214	4,678	4,479
34,300	34,350	4,685	4,221	4,685	4,486
34,350	34,400	4,693	4,229	4,693	4,494
34,400	34,450	4,700	4,236	4,700	4,501
34,450	34,500	4,708	4,244	4,708	4,509
34,500	34,550	4,715	4,251	4,715	4,516
34,550	34,600	4,723	4,259	4,723	4,524
34,600	34,650	4,730	4,266	4,730	4,531
34,650	34,700	4,738	4,274	4,738	4,539
34,700	34,750	4,745	4,281	4,745	4,546
34,750	34,800	4,753	4,289	4,753	4,554
34,800	34,850	4,760	4,296	4,760	4,561
34,850	34,900	4,768	4,304	4,768	4,569
34,900	34,950	4,775	4,311	4,775	4,576
34,950	35,000	4,783	4,319	4,783	4,584

35,000

At least	But less than	Single	Married filing jointly *	Married filing separately	Head of a household
35,000	35,050	4,790	4,326	4,790	4,591
35,050	35,100	4,798	4,334	4,798	4,599
35,100	35,150	4,805	4,341	4,805	4,606
35,150	35,200	4,813	4,349	4,813	4,614
35,200	35,250	4,820	4,356	4,820	4,621
35,250	35,300	4,828	4,364	4,828	4,629
35,300	35,350	4,835	4,371	4,835	4,636
35,350	35,400	4,843	4,379	4,843	4,644
35,400	35,450	4,850	4,386	4,850	4,651
35,450	35,500	4,858	4,394	4,858	4,659
35,500	35,550	4,865	4,401	4,865	4,666
35,550	35,600	4,873	4,409	4,873	4,674
35,600	35,650	4,880	4,416	4,880	4,681
35,650	35,700	4,888	4,424	4,888	4,689
35,700	35,750	4,895	4,431	4,895	4,696
35,750	35,800	4,903	4,439	4,903	4,704
35,800	35,850	4,910	4,446	4,910	4,711
35,850	35,900	4,918	4,454	4,918	4,719
35,900	35,950	4,925	4,461	4,925	4,726
35,950	36,000	4,933	4,469	4,933	4,734

36,000

At least	But less than	Single	Married filing jointly *	Married filing separately	Head of a household
36,000	36,050	4,940	4,476	4,940	4,741
36,050	36,100	4,948	4,484	4,948	4,749
36,100	36,150	4,955	4,491	4,955	4,756
36,150	36,200	4,963	4,499	4,963	4,764
36,200	36,250	4,970	4,506	4,970	4,771
36,250	36,300	4,978	4,514	4,978	4,779
36,300	36,350	4,985	4,521	4,985	4,786
36,350	36,400	4,993	4,529	4,993	4,794
36,400	36,450	5,000	4,536	5,000	4,801
36,450	36,500	5,008	4,544	5,008	4,809
36,500	36,550	5,015	4,551	5,015	4,816
36,550	36,600	5,023	4,559	5,023	4,824
36,600	36,650	5,030	4,566	5,030	4,831
36,650	36,700	5,038	4,574	5,038	4,839
36,700	36,750	5,045	4,581	5,045	4,846
36,750	36,800	5,053	4,589	5,053	4,854
36,800	36,850	5,060	4,596	5,060	4,861
36,850	36,900	5,068	4,604	5,068	4,869
36,900	36,950	5,075	4,611	5,075	4,876
36,950	37,000	5,083	4,619	5,083	4,884

37,000

At least	But less than	Single	Married filing jointly *	Married filing separately	Head of a household
37,000	37,050	5,090	4,626	5,090	4,891
37,050	37,100	5,098	4,634	5,098	4,899
37,100	37,150	5,105	4,641	5,105	4,906
37,150	37,200	5,113	4,649	5,113	4,914
37,200	37,250	5,120	4,656	5,120	4,921
37,250	37,300	5,128	4,664	5,128	4,929
37,300	37,350	5,135	4,671	5,135	4,936
37,350	37,400	5,143	4,679	5,143	4,944
37,400	37,450	5,150	4,686	5,150	4,951
37,450	37,500	5,158	4,694	5,158	4,959
37,500	37,550	5,165	4,701	5,165	4,966
37,550	37,600	5,173	4,709	5,173	4,974
37,600	37,650	5,180	4,716	5,180	4,981
37,650	37,700	5,190	4,724	5,190	4,989
37,700	37,750	5,203	4,731	5,203	4,996
37,750	37,800	5,215	4,739	5,215	5,004
37,800	37,850	5,228	4,746	5,228	5,011
37,850	37,900	5,240	4,754	5,240	5,019
37,900	37,950	5,253	4,761	5,253	5,026
37,950	38,000	5,265	4,769	5,265	5,034

38,000

At least	But less than	Single	Married filing jointly *	Married filing separately	Head of a household
38,000	38,050	5,278	4,776	5,278	5,041
38,050	38,100	5,290	4,784	5,290	5,049
38,100	38,150	5,303	4,791	5,303	5,056
38,150	38,200	5,315	4,799	5,315	5,064
38,200	38,250	5,328	4,806	5,328	5,071
38,250	38,300	5,340	4,814	5,340	5,079
38,300	38,350	5,353	4,821	5,353	5,086
38,350	38,400	5,365	4,829	5,365	5,094
38,400	38,450	5,378	4,836	5,378	5,101
38,450	38,500	5,390	4,844	5,390	5,109
38,500	38,550	5,403	4,851	5,403	5,116
38,550	38,600	5,415	4,859	5,415	5,124
38,600	38,650	5,428	4,866	5,428	5,131
38,650	38,700	5,440	4,874	5,440	5,139
38,700	38,750	5,453	4,881	5,453	5,146
38,750	38,800	5,465	4,889	5,465	5,154
38,800	38,850	5,478	4,896	5,478	5,161
38,850	38,900	5,490	4,904	5,490	5,169
38,900	38,950	5,503	4,911	5,503	5,176
38,950	39,000	5,515	4,919	5,515	5,184

* This column must also be used by a qualifying widow(er).

(Continued)

2016 Tax Table—Continued

If line 43 (taxable income) is—		And you are—				If line 43 (taxable income) is—		And you are—				If line 43 (taxable income) is—		And you are—			
At least	But less than	Single	Married filing jointly *	Married filing separately	Head of a household	At least	But less than	Single	Married filing jointly *	Married filing separately	Head of a household	At least	But less than	Single	Married filing jointly *	Married filing separately	Head of a household
		Your tax is—						Your tax is—						Your tax is—			
39,000						**42,000**						**45,000**					
39,000	39,050	5,528	4,926	5,528	5,191	42,000	42,050	6,278	5,376	6,278	5,641	45,000	45,050	7,028	5,826	7,028	6,091
39,050	39,100	5,540	4,934	5,540	5,199	42,050	42,100	6,290	5,384	6,290	5,649	45,050	45,100	7,040	5,834	7,040	6,099
39,100	39,150	5,553	4,941	5,553	5,206	42,100	42,150	6,303	5,391	6,303	5,656	45,100	45,150	7,053	5,841	7,053	6,106
39,150	39,200	5,565	4,949	5,565	5,214	42,150	42,200	6,315	5,399	6,315	5,664	45,150	45,200	7,065	5,849	7,065	6,114
39,200	39,250	5,578	4,956	5,578	5,221	42,200	42,250	6,328	5,406	6,328	5,671	45,200	45,250	7,078	5,856	7,078	6,121
39,250	39,300	5,590	4,964	5,590	5,229	42,250	42,300	6,340	5,414	6,340	5,679	45,250	45,300	7,090	5,864	7,090	6,129
39,300	39,350	5,603	4,971	5,603	5,236	42,300	42,350	6,353	5,421	6,353	5,686	45,300	45,350	7,103	5,871	7,103	6,136
39,350	39,400	5,615	4,979	5,615	5,244	42,350	42,400	6,365	5,429	6,365	5,694	45,350	45,400	7,115	5,879	7,115	6,144
39,400	39,450	5,628	4,986	5,628	5,251	42,400	42,450	6,378	5,436	6,378	5,701	45,400	45,450	7,128	5,886	7,128	6,151
39,450	39,500	5,640	4,994	5,640	5,259	42,450	42,500	6,390	5,444	6,390	5,709	45,450	45,500	7,140	5,894	7,140	6,159
39,500	39,550	5,653	5,001	5,653	5,266	42,500	42,550	6,403	5,451	6,403	5,716	45,500	45,550	7,153	5,901	7,153	6,166
39,550	39,600	5,665	5,009	5,665	5,274	42,550	42,600	6,415	5,459	6,415	5,724	45,550	45,600	7,165	5,909	7,165	6,174
39,600	39,650	5,678	5,016	5,678	5,281	42,600	42,650	6,428	5,466	6,428	5,731	45,600	45,650	7,178	5,916	7,178	6,181
39,650	39,700	5,690	5,024	5,690	5,289	42,650	42,700	6,440	5,474	6,440	5,739	45,650	45,700	7,190	5,924	7,190	6,189
39,700	39,750	5,703	5,031	5,703	5,296	42,700	42,750	6,453	5,481	6,453	5,746	45,700	45,750	7,203	5,931	7,203	6,196
39,750	39,800	5,715	5,039	5,715	5,304	42,750	42,800	6,465	5,489	6,465	5,754	45,750	45,800	7,215	5,939	7,215	6,204
39,800	39,850	5,728	5,046	5,728	5,311	42,800	42,850	6,478	5,496	6,478	5,761	45,800	45,850	7,228	5,946	7,228	6,211
39,850	39,900	5,740	5,054	5,740	5,319	42,850	42,900	6,490	5,504	6,490	5,769	45,850	45,900	7,240	5,954	7,240	6,219
39,900	39,950	5,753	5,061	5,753	5,326	42,900	42,950	6,503	5,511	6,503	5,776	45,900	45,950	7,253	5,961	7,253	6,226
39,950	40,000	5,765	5,069	5,765	5,334	42,950	43,000	6,515	5,519	6,515	5,784	45,950	46,000	7,265	5,969	7,265	6,234
40,000						**43,000**						**46,000**					
40,000	40,050	5,778	5,076	5,778	5,341	43,000	43,050	6,528	5,526	6,528	5,791	46,000	46,050	7,278	5,976	7,278	6,241
40,050	40,100	5,790	5,084	5,790	5,349	43,050	43,100	6,540	5,534	6,540	5,799	46,050	46,100	7,290	5,984	7,290	6,249
40,100	40,150	5,803	5,091	5,803	5,356	43,100	43,150	6,553	5,541	6,553	5,806	46,100	46,150	7,303	5,991	7,303	6,256
40,150	40,200	5,815	5,099	5,815	5,364	43,150	43,200	6,565	5,549	6,565	5,814	46,150	46,200	7,315	5,999	7,315	6,264
40,200	40,250	5,828	5,106	5,828	5,371	43,200	43,250	6,578	5,556	6,578	5,821	46,200	46,250	7,328	6,006	7,328	6,271
40,250	40,300	5,840	5,114	5,840	5,379	43,250	43,300	6,590	5,564	6,590	5,829	46,250	46,300	7,340	6,014	7,340	6,279
40,300	40,350	5,853	5,121	5,853	5,386	43,300	43,350	6,603	5,571	6,603	5,836	46,300	46,350	7,353	6,021	7,353	6,286
40,350	40,400	5,865	5,129	5,865	5,394	43,350	43,400	6,615	5,579	6,615	5,844	46,350	46,400	7,365	6,029	7,365	6,294
40,400	40,450	5,878	5,136	5,878	5,401	43,400	43,450	6,628	5,586	6,628	5,851	46,400	46,450	7,378	6,036	7,378	6,301
40,450	40,500	5,890	5,144	5,890	5,409	43,450	43,500	6,640	5,594	6,640	5,859	46,450	46,500	7,390	6,044	7,390	6,309
40,500	40,550	5,903	5,151	5,903	5,416	43,500	43,550	6,653	5,601	6,653	5,866	46,500	46,550	7,403	6,051	7,403	6,316
40,550	40,600	5,915	5,159	5,915	5,424	43,550	43,600	6,665	5,609	6,665	5,874	46,550	46,600	7,415	6,059	7,415	6,324
40,600	40,650	5,928	5,166	5,928	5,431	43,600	43,650	6,678	5,616	6,678	5,881	46,600	46,650	7,428	6,066	7,428	6,331
40,650	40,700	5,940	5,174	5,940	5,439	43,650	43,700	6,690	5,624	6,690	5,889	46,650	46,700	7,440	6,074	7,440	6,339
40,700	40,750	5,953	5,181	5,953	5,446	43,700	43,750	6,703	5,631	6,703	5,896	46,700	46,750	7,453	6,081	7,453	6,346
40,750	40,800	5,965	5,189	5,965	5,454	43,750	43,800	6,715	5,639	6,715	5,904	46,750	46,800	7,465	6,089	7,465	6,354
40,800	40,850	5,978	5,196	5,978	5,461	43,800	43,850	6,728	5,646	6,728	5,911	46,800	46,850	7,478	6,096	7,478	6,361
40,850	40,900	5,990	5,204	5,990	5,469	43,850	43,900	6,740	5,654	6,740	5,919	46,850	46,900	7,490	6,104	7,490	6,369
40,900	40,950	6,003	5,211	6,003	5,476	43,900	43,950	6,753	5,661	6,753	5,926	46,900	46,950	7,503	6,111	7,503	6,376
40,950	41,000	6,015	5,219	6,015	5,484	43,950	44,000	6,765	5,669	6,765	5,934	46,950	47,000	7,515	6,119	7,515	6,384
41,000						**44,000**						**47,000**					
41,000	41,050	6,028	5,226	6,028	5,491	44,000	44,050	6,778	5,676	6,778	5,941	47,000	47,050	7,528	6,126	7,528	6,391
41,050	41,100	6,040	5,234	6,040	5,499	44,050	44,100	6,790	5,684	6,790	5,949	47,050	47,100	7,540	6,134	7,540	6,399
41,100	41,150	6,053	5,241	6,053	5,506	44,100	44,150	6,803	5,691	6,803	5,956	47,100	47,150	7,553	6,141	7,553	6,406
41,150	41,200	6,065	5,249	6,065	5,514	44,150	44,200	6,815	5,699	6,815	5,964	47,150	47,200	7,565	6,149	7,565	6,414
41,200	41,250	6,078	5,256	6,078	5,521	44,200	44,250	6,828	5,706	6,828	5,971	47,200	47,250	7,578	6,156	7,578	6,421
41,250	41,300	6,090	5,264	6,090	5,529	44,250	44,300	6,840	5,714	6,840	5,979	47,250	47,300	7,590	6,164	7,590	6,429
41,300	41,350	6,103	5,271	6,103	5,536	44,300	44,350	6,853	5,721	6,853	5,986	47,300	47,350	7,603	6,171	7,603	6,436
41,350	41,400	6,115	5,279	6,115	5,544	44,350	44,400	6,865	5,729	6,865	5,994	47,350	47,400	7,615	6,179	7,615	6,444
41,400	41,450	6,128	5,286	6,128	5,551	44,400	44,450	6,878	5,736	6,878	6,001	47,400	47,450	7,628	6,186	7,628	6,451
41,450	41,500	6,140	5,294	6,140	5,559	44,450	44,500	6,890	5,744	6,890	6,009	47,450	47,500	7,640	6,194	7,640	6,459
41,500	41,550	6,153	5,301	6,153	5,566	44,500	44,550	6,903	5,751	6,903	6,016	47,500	47,550	7,653	6,201	7,653	6,466
41,550	41,600	6,165	5,309	6,165	5,574	44,550	44,600	6,915	5,759	6,915	6,024	47,550	47,600	7,665	6,209	7,665	6,474
41,600	41,650	6,178	5,316	6,178	5,581	44,600	44,650	6,928	5,766	6,928	6,031	47,600	47,650	7,678	6,216	7,678	6,481
41,650	41,700	6,190	5,324	6,190	5,589	44,650	44,700	6,940	5,774	6,940	6,039	47,650	47,700	7,690	6,224	7,690	6,489
41,700	41,750	6,203	5,331	6,203	5,596	44,700	44,750	6,953	5,781	6,953	6,046	47,700	47,750	7,703	6,231	7,703	6,496
41,750	41,800	6,215	5,339	6,215	5,604	44,750	44,800	6,965	5,789	6,965	6,054	47,750	47,800	7,715	6,239	7,715	6,504
41,800	41,850	6,228	5,346	6,228	5,611	44,800	44,850	6,978	5,796	6,978	6,061	47,800	47,850	7,728	6,246	7,728	6,511
41,850	41,900	6,240	5,354	6,240	5,619	44,850	44,900	6,990	5,804	6,990	6,069	47,850	47,900	7,740	6,254	7,740	6,519
41,900	41,950	6,253	5,361	6,253	5,626	44,900	44,950	7,003	5,811	7,003	6,076	47,900	47,950	7,753	6,261	7,753	6,526
41,950	42,000	6,265	5,369	6,265	5,634	44,950	45,000	7,015	5,819	7,015	6,084	47,950	48,000	7,765	6,269	7,765	6,534

* This column must also be used by a qualifying widow(er).

(Continued)

2016 Tax Table—*Continued*

If line 43 (taxable income) is—		And you are—			
At least	But less than	Single	Married filing jointly *	Married filing separately	Head of a household
			Your tax is—		

48,000

At least	But less than	Single	MFJ *	MFS	HoH
48,000	48,050	7,778	6,276	7,778	6,541
48,050	48,100	7,790	6,284	7,790	6,549
48,100	48,150	7,803	6,291	7,803	6,556
48,150	48,200	7,815	6,299	7,815	6,564
48,200	48,250	7,828	6,306	7,828	6,571
48,250	48,300	7,840	6,314	7,840	6,579
48,300	48,350	7,853	6,321	7,853	6,586
48,350	48,400	7,865	6,329	7,865	6,594
48,400	48,450	7,878	6,336	7,878	6,601
48,450	48,500	7,890	6,344	7,890	6,609
48,500	48,550	7,903	6,351	7,903	6,616
48,550	48,600	7,915	6,359	7,915	6,624
48,600	48,650	7,928	6,366	7,928	6,631
48,650	48,700	7,940	6,374	7,940	6,639
48,700	48,750	7,953	6,381	7,953	6,646
48,750	48,800	7,965	6,389	7,965	6,654
48,800	48,850	7,978	6,396	7,978	6,661
48,850	48,900	7,990	6,404	7,990	6,669
48,900	48,950	8,003	6,411	8,003	6,676
48,950	49,000	8,015	6,419	8,015	6,684

49,000

At least	But less than	Single	MFJ *	MFS	HoH
49,000	49,050	8,028	6,426	8,028	6,691
49,050	49,100	8,040	6,434	8,040	6,699
49,100	49,150	8,053	6,441	8,053	6,706
49,150	49,200	8,065	6,449	8,065	6,714
49,200	49,250	8,078	6,456	8,078	6,721
49,250	49,300	8,090	6,464	8,090	6,729
49,300	49,350	8,103	6,471	8,103	6,736
49,350	49,400	8,115	6,479	8,115	6,744
49,400	49,450	8,128	6,486	8,128	6,751
49,450	49,500	8,140	6,494	8,140	6,759
49,500	49,550	8,153	6,501	8,153	6,766
49,550	49,600	8,165	6,509	8,165	6,774
49,600	49,650	8,178	6,516	8,178	6,781
49,650	49,700	8,190	6,524	8,190	6,789
49,700	49,750	8,203	6,531	8,203	6,796
49,750	49,800	8,215	6,539	8,215	6,804
49,800	49,850	8,228	6,546	8,228	6,811
49,850	49,900	8,240	6,554	8,240	6,819
49,900	49,950	8,253	6,561	8,253	6,826
49,950	50,000	8,265	6,569	8,265	6,834

50,000

At least	But less than	Single	MFJ *	MFS	HoH
50,000	50,050	8,278	6,576	8,278	6,841
50,050	50,100	8,290	6,584	8,290	6,849
50,100	50,150	8,303	6,591	8,303	6,856
50,150	50,200	8,315	6,599	8,315	6,864
50,200	50,250	8,328	6,606	8,328	6,871
50,250	50,300	8,340	6,614	8,340	6,879
50,300	50,350	8,353	6,621	8,353	6,886
50,350	50,400	8,365	6,629	8,365	6,894
50,400	50,450	8,378	6,636	8,378	6,904
50,450	50,500	8,390	6,644	8,390	6,916
50,500	50,550	8,403	6,651	8,403	6,929
50,550	50,600	8,415	6,659	8,415	6,941
50,600	50,650	8,428	6,666	8,428	6,954
50,650	50,700	8,440	6,674	8,440	6,966
50,700	50,750	8,453	6,681	8,453	6,979
50,750	50,800	8,465	6,689	8,465	6,991
50,800	50,850	8,478	6,696	8,478	7,004
50,850	50,900	8,490	6,704	8,490	7,016
50,900	50,950	8,503	6,711	8,503	7,029
50,950	51,000	8,515	6,719	8,515	7,041

51,000

At least	But less than	Single	MFJ *	MFS	HoH
51,000	51,050	8,528	6,726	8,528	7,054
51,050	51,100	8,540	6,734	8,540	7,066
51,100	51,150	8,553	6,741	8,553	7,079
51,150	51,200	8,565	6,749	8,565	7,091
51,200	51,250	8,578	6,756	8,578	7,104
51,250	51,300	8,590	6,764	8,590	7,116
51,300	51,350	8,603	6,771	8,603	7,129
51,350	51,400	8,615	6,779	8,615	7,141
51,400	51,450	8,628	6,786	8,628	7,154
51,450	51,500	8,640	6,794	8,640	7,166
51,500	51,550	8,653	6,801	8,653	7,179
51,550	51,600	8,665	6,809	8,665	7,191
51,600	51,650	8,678	6,816	8,678	7,204
51,650	51,700	8,690	6,824	8,690	7,216
51,700	51,750	8,703	6,831	8,703	7,229
51,750	51,800	8,715	6,839	8,715	7,241
51,800	51,850	8,728	6,846	8,728	7,254
51,850	51,900	8,740	6,854	8,740	7,266
51,900	51,950	8,753	6,861	8,753	7,279
51,950	52,000	8,765	6,869	8,765	7,291

52,000

At least	But less than	Single	MFJ *	MFS	HoH
52,000	52,050	8,778	6,876	8,778	7,304
52,050	52,100	8,790	6,884	8,790	7,316
52,100	52,150	8,803	6,891	8,803	7,329
52,150	52,200	8,815	6,899	8,815	7,341
52,200	52,250	8,828	6,906	8,828	7,354
52,250	52,300	8,840	6,914	8,840	7,366
52,300	52,350	8,853	6,921	8,853	7,379
52,350	52,400	8,865	6,929	8,865	7,391
52,400	52,450	8,878	6,936	8,878	7,404
52,450	52,500	8,890	6,944	8,890	7,416
52,500	52,550	8,903	6,951	8,903	7,429
52,550	52,600	8,915	6,959	8,915	7,441
52,600	52,650	8,928	6,966	8,928	7,454
52,650	52,700	8,940	6,974	8,940	7,466
52,700	52,750	8,953	6,981	8,953	7,479
52,750	52,800	8,965	6,989	8,965	7,491
52,800	52,850	8,978	6,996	8,978	7,504
52,850	52,900	8,990	7,004	8,990	7,516
52,900	52,950	9,003	7,011	9,003	7,529
52,950	53,000	9,015	7,019	9,015	7,541

53,000

At least	But less than	Single	MFJ *	MFS	HoH
53,000	53,050	9,028	7,026	9,028	7,554
53,050	53,100	9,040	7,034	9,040	7,566
53,100	53,150	9,053	7,041	9,053	7,579
53,150	53,200	9,065	7,049	9,065	7,591
53,200	53,250	9,078	7,056	9,078	7,604
53,250	53,300	9,090	7,064	9,090	7,616
53,300	53,350	9,103	7,071	9,103	7,629
53,350	53,400	9,115	7,079	9,115	7,641
53,400	53,450	9,128	7,086	9,128	7,654
53,450	53,500	9,140	7,094	9,140	7,666
53,500	53,550	9,153	7,101	9,153	7,679
53,550	53,600	9,165	7,109	9,165	7,691
53,600	53,650	9,178	7,116	9,178	7,704
53,650	53,700	9,190	7,124	9,190	7,716
53,700	53,750	9,203	7,131	9,203	7,729
53,750	53,800	9,215	7,139	9,215	7,741
53,800	53,850	9,228	7,146	9,228	7,754
53,850	53,900	9,240	7,154	9,240	7,766
53,900	53,950	9,253	7,161	9,253	7,779
53,950	54,000	9,265	7,169	9,265	7,791

54,000

At least	But less than	Single	MFJ *	MFS	HoH
54,000	54,050	9,278	7,176	9,278	7,804
54,050	54,100	9,290	7,184	9,290	7,816
54,100	54,150	9,303	7,191	9,303	7,829
54,150	54,200	9,315	7,199	9,315	7,841
54,200	54,250	9,328	7,206	9,328	7,854
54,250	54,300	9,340	7,214	9,340	7,866
54,300	54,350	9,353	7,221	9,353	7,879
54,350	54,400	9,365	7,229	9,365	7,891
54,400	54,450	9,378	7,236	9,378	7,904
54,450	54,500	9,390	7,244	9,390	7,916
54,500	54,550	9,403	7,251	9,403	7,929
54,550	54,600	9,415	7,259	9,415	7,941
54,600	54,650	9,428	7,266	9,428	7,954
54,650	54,700	9,440	7,274	9,440	7,966
54,700	54,750	9,453	7,281	9,453	7,979
54,750	54,800	9,465	7,289	9,465	7,991
54,800	54,850	9,478	7,296	9,478	8,004
54,850	54,900	9,490	7,304	9,490	8,016
54,900	54,950	9,503	7,311	9,503	8,029
54,950	55,000	9,515	7,319	9,515	8,041

55,000

At least	But less than	Single	MFJ *	MFS	HoH
55,000	55,050	9,528	7,326	9,528	8,054
55,050	55,100	9,540	7,334	9,540	8,066
55,100	55,150	9,553	7,341	9,553	8,079
55,150	55,200	9,565	7,349	9,565	8,091
55,200	55,250	9,578	7,356	9,578	8,104
55,250	55,300	9,590	7,364	9,590	8,116
55,300	55,350	9,603	7,371	9,603	8,129
55,350	55,400	9,615	7,379	9,615	8,141
55,400	55,450	9,628	7,386	9,628	8,154
55,450	55,500	9,640	7,394	9,640	8,166
55,500	55,550	9,653	7,401	9,653	8,179
55,550	55,600	9,665	7,409	9,665	8,191
55,600	55,650	9,678	7,416	9,678	8,204
55,650	55,700	9,690	7,424	9,690	8,216
55,700	55,750	9,703	7,431	9,703	8,229
55,750	55,800	9,715	7,439	9,715	8,241
55,800	55,850	9,728	7,446	9,728	8,254
55,850	55,900	9,740	7,454	9,740	8,266
55,900	55,950	9,753	7,461	9,753	8,279
55,950	56,000	9,765	7,469	9,765	8,291

56,000

At least	But less than	Single	MFJ *	MFS	HoH
56,000	56,050	9,778	7,476	9,778	8,304
56,050	56,100	9,790	7,484	9,790	8,316
56,100	56,150	9,803	7,491	9,803	8,329
56,150	56,200	9,815	7,499	9,815	8,341
56,200	56,250	9,828	7,506	9,828	8,354
56,250	56,300	9,840	7,514	9,840	8,366
56,300	56,350	9,853	7,521	9,853	8,379
56,350	56,400	9,865	7,529	9,865	8,391
56,400	56,450	9,878	7,536	9,878	8,404
56,450	56,500	9,890	7,544	9,890	8,416
56,500	56,550	9,903	7,551	9,903	8,429
56,550	56,600	9,915	7,559	9,915	8,441
56,600	56,650	9,928	7,566	9,928	8,454
56,650	56,700	9,940	7,574	9,940	8,466
56,700	56,750	9,953	7,581	9,953	8,479
56,750	56,800	9,965	7,589	9,965	8,491
56,800	56,850	9,978	7,596	9,978	8,504
56,850	56,900	9,990	7,604	9,990	8,516
56,900	56,950	10,003	7,611	10,003	8,529
56,950	57,000	10,015	7,619	10,015	8,541

* This column must also be used by a qualifying widow(er).

(Continued)

2016 Tax Table—*Continued*

57,000

If line 43 (taxable income) is—		And you are—			
At least	But less than	Single	Married filing jointly *	Married filing separately	Head of a household
		Your tax is—			
57,000	57,050	10,028	7,626	10,028	8,554
57,050	57,100	10,040	7,634	10,040	8,566
57,100	57,150	10,053	7,641	10,053	8,579
57,150	57,200	10,065	7,649	10,065	8,591
57,200	57,250	10,078	7,656	10,078	8,604
57,250	57,300	10,090	7,664	10,090	8,616
57,300	57,350	10,103	7,671	10,103	8,629
57,350	57,400	10,115	7,679	10,115	8,641
57,400	57,450	10,128	7,686	10,128	8,654
57,450	57,500	10,140	7,694	10,140	8,666
57,500	57,550	10,153	7,701	10,153	8,679
57,550	57,600	10,165	7,709	10,165	8,691
57,600	57,650	10,178	7,716	10,178	8,704
57,650	57,700	10,190	7,724	10,190	8,716
57,700	57,750	10,203	7,731	10,203	8,729
57,750	57,800	10,215	7,739	10,215	8,741
57,800	57,850	10,228	7,746	10,228	8,754
57,850	57,900	10,240	7,754	10,240	8,766
57,900	57,950	10,253	7,761	10,253	8,779
57,950	58,000	10,265	7,769	10,265	8,791

58,000

At least	But less than	Single	Married filing jointly *	Married filing separately	Head of a household
58,000	58,050	10,278	7,776	10,278	8,804
58,050	58,100	10,290	7,784	10,290	8,816
58,100	58,150	10,303	7,791	10,303	8,829
58,150	58,200	10,315	7,799	10,315	8,841
58,200	58,250	10,328	7,806	10,328	8,854
58,250	58,300	10,340	7,814	10,340	8,866
58,300	58,350	10,353	7,821	10,353	8,879
58,350	58,400	10,365	7,829	10,365	8,891
58,400	58,450	10,378	7,836	10,378	8,904
58,450	58,500	10,390	7,844	10,390	8,916
58,500	58,550	10,403	7,851	10,403	8,929
58,550	58,600	10,415	7,859	10,415	8,941
58,600	58,650	10,428	7,866	10,428	8,954
58,650	58,700	10,440	7,874	10,440	8,966
58,700	58,750	10,453	7,881	10,453	8,979
58,750	58,800	10,465	7,889	10,465	8,991
58,800	58,850	10,478	7,896	10,478	9,004
58,850	58,900	10,490	7,904	10,490	9,016
58,900	58,950	10,503	7,911	10,503	9,029
58,950	59,000	10,515	7,919	10,515	9,041

59,000

At least	But less than	Single	Married filing jointly *	Married filing separately	Head of a household
59,000	59,050	10,528	7,926	10,528	9,054
59,050	59,100	10,540	7,934	10,540	9,066
59,100	59,150	10,553	7,941	10,553	9,079
59,150	59,200	10,565	7,949	10,565	9,091
59,200	59,250	10,578	7,956	10,578	9,104
59,250	59,300	10,590	7,964	10,590	9,116
59,300	59,350	10,603	7,971	10,603	9,129
59,350	59,400	10,615	7,979	10,615	9,141
59,400	59,450	10,628	7,986	10,628	9,154
59,450	59,500	10,640	7,994	10,640	9,166
59,500	59,550	10,653	8,001	10,653	9,179
59,550	59,600	10,665	8,009	10,665	9,191
59,600	59,650	10,678	8,016	10,678	9,204
59,650	59,700	10,690	8,024	10,690	9,216
59,700	59,750	10,703	8,031	10,703	9,229
59,750	59,800	10,715	8,039	10,715	9,241
59,800	59,850	10,728	8,046	10,728	9,254
59,850	59,900	10,740	8,054	10,740	9,266
59,900	59,950	10,753	8,061	10,753	9,279
59,950	60,000	10,765	8,069	10,765	9,291

60,000

At least	But less than	Single	Married filing jointly *	Married filing separately	Head of a household
60,000	60,050	10,778	8,076	10,778	9,304
60,050	60,100	10,790	8,084	10,790	9,316
60,100	60,150	10,803	8,091	10,803	9,329
60,150	60,200	10,815	8,099	10,815	9,341
60,200	60,250	10,828	8,106	10,828	9,354
60,250	60,300	10,840	8,114	10,840	9,366
60,300	60,350	10,853	8,121	10,853	9,379
60,350	60,400	10,865	8,129	10,865	9,391
60,400	60,450	10,878	8,136	10,878	9,404
60,450	60,500	10,890	8,144	10,890	9,416
60,500	60,550	10,903	8,151	10,903	9,429
60,550	60,600	10,915	8,159	10,915	9,441
60,600	60,650	10,928	8,166	10,928	9,454
60,650	60,700	10,940	8,174	10,940	9,466
60,700	60,750	10,953	8,181	10,953	9,479
60,750	60,800	10,965	8,189	10,965	9,491
60,800	60,850	10,978	8,196	10,978	9,504
60,850	60,900	10,990	8,204	10,990	9,516
60,900	60,950	11,003	8,211	11,003	9,529
60,950	61,000	11,015	8,219	11,015	9,541

61,000

At least	But less than	Single	Married filing jointly *	Married filing separately	Head of a household
61,000	61,050	11,028	8,226	11,028	9,554
61,050	61,100	11,040	8,234	11,040	9,566
61,100	61,150	11,053	8,241	11,053	9,579
61,150	61,200	11,065	8,249	11,065	9,591
61,200	61,250	11,078	8,256	11,078	9,604
61,250	61,300	11,090	8,264	11,090	9,616
61,300	61,350	11,103	8,271	11,103	9,629
61,350	61,400	11,115	8,279	11,115	9,641
61,400	61,450	11,128	8,286	11,128	9,654
61,450	61,500	11,140	8,294	11,140	9,666
61,500	61,550	11,153	8,301	11,153	9,679
61,550	61,600	11,165	8,309	11,165	9,691
61,600	61,650	11,178	8,316	11,178	9,704
61,650	61,700	11,190	8,324	11,190	9,716
61,700	61,750	11,203	8,331	11,203	9,729
61,750	61,800	11,215	8,339	11,215	9,741
61,800	61,850	11,228	8,346	11,228	9,754
61,850	61,900	11,240	8,354	11,240	9,766
61,900	61,950	11,253	8,361	11,253	9,779
61,950	62,000	11,265	8,369	11,265	9,791

62,000

At least	But less than	Single	Married filing jointly *	Married filing separately	Head of a household
62,000	62,050	11,278	8,376	11,278	9,804
62,050	62,100	11,290	8,384	11,290	9,816
62,100	62,150	11,303	8,391	11,303	9,829
62,150	62,200	11,315	8,399	11,315	9,841
62,200	62,250	11,328	8,406	11,328	9,854
62,250	62,300	11,340	8,414	11,340	9,866
62,300	62,350	11,353	8,421	11,353	9,879
62,350	62,400	11,365	8,429	11,365	9,891
62,400	62,450	11,378	8,436	11,378	9,904
62,450	62,500	11,390	8,444	11,390	9,916
62,500	62,550	11,403	8,451	11,403	9,929
62,550	62,600	11,415	8,459	11,415	9,941
62,600	62,650	11,428	8,466	11,428	9,954
62,650	62,700	11,440	8,474	11,440	9,966
62,700	62,750	11,453	8,481	11,453	9,979
62,750	62,800	11,465	8,489	11,465	9,991
62,800	62,850	11,478	8,496	11,478	10,004
62,850	62,900	11,490	8,504	11,490	10,016
62,900	62,950	11,503	8,511	11,503	10,029
62,950	63,000	11,515	8,519	11,515	10,041

63,000

At least	But less than	Single	Married filing jointly *	Married filing separately	Head of a household
63,000	63,050	11,528	8,526	11,528	10,054
63,050	63,100	11,540	8,534	11,540	10,066
63,100	63,150	11,553	8,541	11,553	10,079
63,150	63,200	11,565	8,549	11,565	10,091
63,200	63,250	11,578	8,556	11,578	10,104
63,250	63,300	11,590	8,564	11,590	10,116
63,300	63,350	11,603	8,571	11,603	10,129
63,350	63,400	11,615	8,579	11,615	10,141
63,400	63,450	11,628	8,586	11,628	10,154
63,450	63,500	11,640	8,594	11,640	10,166
63,500	63,550	11,653	8,601	11,653	10,179
63,550	63,600	11,665	8,609	11,665	10,191
63,600	63,650	11,678	8,616	11,678	10,204
63,650	63,700	11,690	8,624	11,690	10,216
63,700	63,750	11,703	8,631	11,703	10,229
63,750	63,800	11,715	8,639	11,715	10,241
63,800	63,850	11,728	8,646	11,728	10,254
63,850	63,900	11,740	8,654	11,740	10,266
63,900	63,950	11,753	8,661	11,753	10,279
63,950	64,000	11,765	8,669	11,765	10,291

64,000

At least	But less than	Single	Married filing jointly *	Married filing separately	Head of a household
64,000	64,050	11,778	8,676	11,778	10,304
64,050	64,100	11,790	8,684	11,790	10,316
64,100	64,150	11,803	8,691	11,803	10,329
64,150	64,200	11,815	8,699	11,815	10,341
64,200	64,250	11,828	8,706	11,828	10,354
64,250	64,300	11,840	8,714	11,840	10,366
64,300	64,350	11,853	8,721	11,853	10,379
64,350	64,400	11,865	8,729	11,865	10,391
64,400	64,450	11,878	8,736	11,878	10,404
64,450	64,500	11,890	8,744	11,890	10,416
64,500	64,550	11,903	8,751	11,903	10,429
64,550	64,600	11,915	8,759	11,915	10,441
64,600	64,650	11,928	8,766	11,928	10,454
64,650	64,700	11,940	8,774	11,940	10,466
64,700	64,750	11,953	8,781	11,953	10,479
64,750	64,800	11,965	8,789	11,965	10,491
64,800	64,850	11,978	8,796	11,978	10,504
64,850	64,900	11,990	8,804	11,990	10,516
64,900	64,950	12,003	8,811	12,003	10,529
64,950	65,000	12,015	8,819	12,015	10,541

65,000

At least	But less than	Single	Married filing jointly *	Married filing separately	Head of a household
65,000	65,050	12,028	8,826	12,028	10,554
65,050	65,100	12,040	8,834	12,040	10,566
65,100	65,150	12,053	8,841	12,053	10,579
65,150	65,200	12,065	8,849	12,065	10,591
65,200	65,250	12,078	8,856	12,078	10,604
65,250	65,300	12,090	8,864	12,090	10,616
65,300	65,350	12,103	8,871	12,103	10,629
65,350	65,400	12,115	8,879	12,115	10,641
65,400	65,450	12,128	8,886	12,128	10,654
65,450	65,500	12,140	8,894	12,140	10,666
65,500	65,550	12,153	8,901	12,153	10,679
65,550	65,600	12,165	8,909	12,165	10,691
65,600	65,650	12,178	8,916	12,178	10,704
65,650	65,700	12,190	8,924	12,190	10,716
65,700	65,750	12,203	8,931	12,203	10,729
65,750	65,800	12,215	8,939	12,215	10,741
65,800	65,850	12,228	8,946	12,228	10,754
65,850	65,900	12,240	8,954	12,240	10,766
65,900	65,950	12,253	8,961	12,253	10,779
65,950	66,000	12,265	8,969	12,265	10,791

* This column must also be used by a qualifying widow(er).

(Continued)

2016 Tax Table—Continued

66,000

If line 43 (taxable income) is— At least	But less than	Single	Married filing jointly *	Married filing separately	Head of a household
66,000	66,050	12,278	8,976	12,278	10,804
66,050	66,100	12,290	8,984	12,290	10,816
66,100	66,150	12,303	8,991	12,303	10,829
66,150	66,200	12,315	8,999	12,315	10,841
66,200	66,250	12,328	9,006	12,328	10,854
66,250	66,300	12,340	9,014	12,340	10,866
66,300	66,350	12,353	9,021	12,353	10,879
66,350	66,400	12,365	9,029	12,365	10,891
66,400	66,450	12,378	9,036	12,378	10,904
66,450	66,500	12,390	9,044	12,390	10,916
66,500	66,550	12,403	9,051	12,403	10,929
66,550	66,600	12,415	9,059	12,415	10,941
66,600	66,650	12,428	9,066	12,428	10,954
66,650	66,700	12,440	9,074	12,440	10,966
66,700	66,750	12,453	9,081	12,453	10,979
66,750	66,800	12,465	9,089	12,465	10,991
66,800	66,850	12,478	9,096	12,478	11,004
66,850	66,900	12,490	9,104	12,490	11,016
66,900	66,950	12,503	9,111	12,503	11,029
66,950	67,000	12,515	9,119	12,515	11,041

67,000

At least	But less than	Single	Married filing jointly *	Married filing separately	Head of a household
67,000	67,050	12,528	9,126	12,528	11,054
67,050	67,100	12,540	9,134	12,540	11,066
67,100	67,150	12,553	9,141	12,553	11,079
67,150	67,200	12,565	9,149	12,565	11,091
67,200	67,250	12,578	9,156	12,578	11,104
67,250	67,300	12,590	9,164	12,590	11,116
67,300	67,350	12,603	9,171	12,603	11,129
67,350	67,400	12,615	9,179	12,615	11,141
67,400	67,450	12,628	9,186	12,628	11,154
67,450	67,500	12,640	9,194	12,640	11,166
67,500	67,550	12,653	9,201	12,653	11,179
67,550	67,600	12,665	9,209	12,665	11,191
67,600	67,650	12,678	9,216	12,678	11,204
67,650	67,700	12,690	9,224	12,690	11,216
67,700	67,750	12,703	9,231	12,703	11,229
67,750	67,800	12,715	9,239	12,715	11,241
67,800	67,850	12,728	9,246	12,728	11,254
67,850	67,900	12,740	9,254	12,740	11,266
67,900	67,950	12,753	9,261	12,753	11,279
67,950	68,000	12,765	9,269	12,765	11,291

68,000

At least	But less than	Single	Married filing jointly *	Married filing separately	Head of a household
68,000	68,050	12,778	9,276	12,778	11,304
68,050	68,100	12,790	9,284	12,790	11,316
68,100	68,150	12,803	9,291	12,803	11,329
68,150	68,200	12,815	9,299	12,815	11,341
68,200	68,250	12,828	9,306	12,828	11,354
68,250	68,300	12,840	9,314	12,840	11,366
68,300	68,350	12,853	9,321	12,853	11,379
68,350	68,400	12,865	9,329	12,865	11,391
68,400	68,450	12,878	9,336	12,878	11,404
68,450	68,500	12,890	9,344	12,890	11,416
68,500	68,550	12,903	9,351	12,903	11,429
68,550	68,600	12,915	9,359	12,915	11,441
68,600	68,650	12,928	9,366	12,928	11,454
68,650	68,700	12,940	9,374	12,940	11,466
68,700	68,750	12,953	9,381	12,953	11,479
68,750	68,800	12,965	9,389	12,965	11,491
68,800	68,850	12,978	9,396	12,978	11,504
68,850	68,900	12,990	9,404	12,990	11,516
68,900	68,950	13,003	9,411	13,003	11,529
68,950	69,000	13,015	9,419	13,015	11,541

69,000

At least	But less than	Single	Married filing jointly *	Married filing separately	Head of a household
69,000	69,050	13,028	9,426	13,028	11,554
69,050	69,100	13,040	9,434	13,040	11,566
69,100	69,150	13,053	9,441	13,053	11,579
69,150	69,200	13,065	9,449	13,065	11,591
69,200	69,250	13,078	9,456	13,078	11,604
69,250	69,300	13,090	9,464	13,090	11,616
69,300	69,350	13,103	9,471	13,103	11,629
69,350	69,400	13,115	9,479	13,115	11,641
69,400	69,450	13,128	9,486	13,128	11,654
69,450	69,500	13,140	9,494	13,140	11,666
69,500	69,550	13,153	9,501	13,153	11,679
69,550	69,600	13,165	9,509	13,165	11,691
69,600	69,650	13,178	9,516	13,178	11,704
69,650	69,700	13,190	9,524	13,190	11,716
69,700	69,750	13,203	9,531	13,203	11,729
69,750	69,800	13,215	9,539	13,215	11,741
69,800	69,850	13,228	9,546	13,228	11,754
69,850	69,900	13,240	9,554	13,240	11,766
69,900	69,950	13,253	9,561	13,253	11,779
69,950	70,000	13,265	9,569	13,265	11,791

70,000

At least	But less than	Single	Married filing jointly *	Married filing separately	Head of a household
70,000	70,050	13,278	9,576	13,278	11,804
70,050	70,100	13,290	9,584	13,290	11,816
70,100	70,150	13,303	9,591	13,303	11,829
70,150	70,200	13,315	9,599	13,315	11,841
70,200	70,250	13,328	9,606	13,328	11,854
70,250	70,300	13,340	9,614	13,340	11,866
70,300	70,350	13,353	9,621	13,353	11,879
70,350	70,400	13,365	9,629	13,365	11,891
70,400	70,450	13,378	9,636	13,378	11,904
70,450	70,500	13,390	9,644	13,390	11,916
70,500	70,550	13,403	9,651	13,403	11,929
70,550	70,600	13,415	9,659	13,415	11,941
70,600	70,650	13,428	9,666	13,428	11,954
70,650	70,700	13,440	9,674	13,440	11,966
70,700	70,750	13,453	9,681	13,453	11,979
70,750	70,800	13,465	9,689	13,465	11,991
70,800	70,850	13,478	9,696	13,478	12,004
70,850	70,900	13,490	9,704	13,490	12,016
70,900	70,950	13,503	9,711	13,503	12,029
70,950	71,000	13,515	9,719	13,515	12,041

71,000

At least	But less than	Single	Married filing jointly *	Married filing separately	Head of a household
71,000	71,050	13,528	9,726	13,528	12,054
71,050	71,100	13,540	9,734	13,540	12,066
71,100	71,150	13,553	9,741	13,553	12,079
71,150	71,200	13,565	9,749	13,565	12,091
71,200	71,250	13,578	9,756	13,578	12,104
71,250	71,300	13,590	9,764	13,590	12,116
71,300	71,350	13,603	9,771	13,603	12,129
71,350	71,400	13,615	9,779	13,615	12,141
71,400	71,450	13,628	9,786	13,628	12,154
71,450	71,500	13,640	9,794	13,640	12,166
71,500	71,550	13,653	9,801	13,653	12,179
71,550	71,600	13,665	9,809	13,665	12,191
71,600	71,650	13,678	9,816	13,678	12,204
71,650	71,700	13,690	9,824	13,690	12,216
71,700	71,750	13,703	9,831	13,703	12,229
71,750	71,800	13,715	9,839	13,715	12,241
71,800	71,850	13,728	9,846	13,728	12,254
71,850	71,900	13,740	9,854	13,740	12,266
71,900	71,950	13,753	9,861	13,753	12,279
71,950	72,000	13,765	9,869	13,765	12,291

72,000

At least	But less than	Single	Married filing jointly *	Married filing separately	Head of a household
72,000	72,050	13,778	9,876	13,778	12,304
72,050	72,100	13,790	9,884	13,790	12,316
72,100	72,150	13,803	9,891	13,803	12,329
72,150	72,200	13,815	9,899	13,815	12,341
72,200	72,250	13,828	9,906	13,828	12,354
72,250	72,300	13,840	9,914	13,840	12,366
72,300	72,350	13,853	9,921	13,853	12,379
72,350	72,400	13,865	9,929	13,865	12,391
72,400	72,450	13,878	9,936	13,878	12,404
72,450	72,500	13,890	9,944	13,890	12,416
72,500	72,550	13,903	9,951	13,903	12,429
72,550	72,600	13,915	9,959	13,915	12,441
72,600	72,650	13,928	9,966	13,928	12,454
72,650	72,700	13,940	9,974	13,940	12,466
72,700	72,750	13,953	9,981	13,953	12,479
72,750	72,800	13,965	9,989	13,965	12,491
72,800	72,850	13,978	9,996	13,978	12,504
72,850	72,900	13,990	10,004	13,990	12,516
72,900	72,950	14,003	10,011	14,003	12,529
72,950	73,000	14,015	10,019	14,015	12,541

73,000

At least	But less than	Single	Married filing jointly *	Married filing separately	Head of a household
73,000	73,050	14,028	10,026	14,028	12,554
73,050	73,100	14,040	10,034	14,040	12,566
73,100	73,150	14,053	10,041	14,053	12,579
73,150	73,200	14,065	10,049	14,065	12,591
73,200	73,250	14,078	10,056	14,078	12,604
73,250	73,300	14,090	10,064	14,090	12,616
73,300	73,350	14,103	10,071	14,103	12,629
73,350	73,400	14,115	10,079	14,115	12,641
73,400	73,450	14,128	10,086	14,128	12,654
73,450	73,500	14,140	10,094	14,140	12,666
73,500	73,550	14,153	10,101	14,153	12,679
73,550	73,600	14,165	10,109	14,165	12,691
73,600	73,650	14,178	10,116	14,178	12,704
73,650	73,700	14,190	10,124	14,190	12,716
73,700	73,750	14,203	10,131	14,203	12,729
73,750	73,800	14,215	10,139	14,215	12,741
73,800	73,850	14,228	10,146	14,228	12,754
73,850	73,900	14,240	10,154	14,240	12,766
73,900	73,950	14,253	10,161	14,253	12,779
73,950	74,000	14,265	10,169	14,265	12,791

74,000

At least	But less than	Single	Married filing jointly *	Married filing separately	Head of a household
74,000	74,050	14,278	10,176	14,278	12,804
74,050	74,100	14,290	10,184	14,290	12,816
74,100	74,150	14,303	10,191	14,303	12,829
74,150	74,200	14,315	10,199	14,315	12,841
74,200	74,250	14,328	10,206	14,328	12,854
74,250	74,300	14,340	10,214	14,340	12,866
74,300	74,350	14,353	10,221	14,353	12,879
74,350	74,400	14,365	10,229	14,365	12,891
74,400	74,450	14,378	10,236	14,378	12,904
74,450	74,500	14,390	10,244	14,390	12,916
74,500	74,550	14,403	10,251	14,403	12,929
74,550	74,600	14,415	10,259	14,415	12,941
74,600	74,650	14,428	10,266	14,428	12,954
74,650	74,700	14,440	10,274	14,440	12,966
74,700	74,750	14,453	10,281	14,453	12,979
74,750	74,800	14,465	10,289	14,465	12,991
74,800	74,850	14,478	10,296	14,478	13,004
74,850	74,900	14,490	10,304	14,490	13,016
74,900	74,950	14,503	10,311	14,503	13,029
74,950	75,000	14,515	10,319	14,515	13,041

* This column must also be used by a qualifying widow(er).

(Continued)

2016 Tax Table—Continued

If line 43 (taxable income) is—		And you are—			
At least	But less than	Single	Married filing jointly *	Married filing separately	Head of a household
		Your tax is—			

75,000

At least	But less than	Single	Married filing jointly *	Married filing separately	Head of a household
75,000	75,050	14,528	10,326	14,528	13,054
75,050	75,100	14,540	10,334	14,540	13,066
75,100	75,150	14,553	10,341	14,553	13,079
75,150	75,200	14,565	10,349	14,565	13,091
75,200	75,250	14,578	10,356	14,578	13,104
75,250	75,300	14,590	10,364	14,590	13,116
75,300	75,350	14,603	10,374	14,603	13,129
75,350	75,400	14,615	10,386	14,615	13,141
75,400	75,450	14,628	10,399	14,628	13,154
75,450	75,500	14,640	10,411	14,640	13,166
75,500	75,550	14,653	10,424	14,653	13,179
75,550	75,600	14,665	10,436	14,665	13,191
75,600	75,650	14,678	10,449	14,678	13,204
75,650	75,700	14,690	10,461	14,690	13,216
75,700	75,750	14,703	10,474	14,703	13,229
75,750	75,800	14,715	10,486	14,715	13,241
75,800	75,850	14,728	10,499	14,728	13,254
75,850	75,900	14,740	10,511	14,740	13,266
75,900	75,950	14,753	10,524	14,753	13,279
75,950	76,000	14,765	10,536	14,766	13,291

76,000

At least	But less than	Single	Married filing jointly *	Married filing separately	Head of a household
76,000	76,050	14,778	10,549	14,780	13,304
76,050	76,100	14,790	10,561	14,794	13,316
76,100	76,150	14,803	10,574	14,808	13,329
76,150	76,200	14,815	10,586	14,822	13,341
76,200	76,250	14,828	10,599	14,836	13,354
76,250	76,300	14,840	10,611	14,850	13,366
76,300	76,350	14,853	10,624	14,864	13,379
76,350	76,400	14,865	10,636	14,878	13,391
76,400	76,450	14,878	10,649	14,892	13,404
76,450	76,500	14,890	10,661	14,906	13,416
76,500	76,550	14,903	10,674	14,920	13,429
76,550	76,600	14,915	10,686	14,934	13,441
76,600	76,650	14,928	10,699	14,948	13,454
76,650	76,700	14,940	10,711	14,962	13,466
76,700	76,750	14,953	10,724	14,976	13,479
76,750	76,800	14,965	10,736	14,990	13,491
76,800	76,850	14,978	10,749	15,004	13,504
76,850	76,900	14,990	10,761	15,018	13,516
76,900	76,950	15,003	10,774	15,032	13,529
76,950	77,000	15,015	10,786	15,046	13,541

77,000

At least	But less than	Single	Married filing jointly *	Married filing separately	Head of a household
77,000	77,050	15,028	10,799	15,060	13,554
77,050	77,100	15,040	10,811	15,074	13,566
77,100	77,150	15,053	10,824	15,088	13,579
77,150	77,200	15,065	10,836	15,102	13,591
77,200	77,250	15,078	10,849	15,116	13,604
77,250	77,300	15,090	10,861	15,130	13,616
77,300	77,350	15,103	10,874	15,144	13,629
77,350	77,400	15,115	10,886	15,158	13,641
77,400	77,450	15,128	10,899	15,172	13,654
77,450	77,500	15,140	10,911	15,186	13,666
77,500	77,550	15,153	10,924	15,200	13,679
77,550	77,600	15,165	10,936	15,214	13,691
77,600	77,650	15,178	10,949	15,228	13,704
77,650	77,700	15,190	10,961	15,242	13,716
77,700	77,750	15,203	10,974	15,256	13,729
77,750	77,800	15,215	10,986	15,270	13,741
77,800	77,850	15,228	10,999	15,284	13,754
77,850	77,900	15,240	11,011	15,298	13,766
77,900	77,950	15,253	11,024	15,312	13,779
77,950	78,000	15,265	11,036	15,326	13,791

78,000

At least	But less than	Single	Married filing jointly *	Married filing separately	Head of a household
78,000	78,050	15,278	11,049	15,340	13,804
78,050	78,100	15,290	11,061	15,354	13,816
78,100	78,150	15,303	11,074	15,368	13,829
78,150	78,200	15,315	11,086	15,382	13,841
78,200	78,250	15,328	11,099	15,396	13,854
78,250	78,300	15,340	11,111	15,410	13,866
78,300	78,350	15,353	11,124	15,424	13,879
78,350	78,400	15,365	11,136	15,438	13,891
78,400	78,450	15,378	11,149	15,452	13,904
78,450	78,500	15,390	11,161	15,466	13,916
78,500	78,550	15,403	11,174	15,480	13,929
78,550	78,600	15,415	11,186	15,494	13,941
78,600	78,650	15,428	11,199	15,508	13,954
78,650	78,700	15,440	11,211	15,522	13,966
78,700	78,750	15,453	11,224	15,536	13,979
78,750	78,800	15,465	11,236	15,550	13,991
78,800	78,850	15,478	11,249	15,564	14,004
78,850	78,900	15,490	11,261	15,578	14,016
78,900	78,950	15,503	11,274	15,592	14,029
78,950	79,000	15,515	11,286	15,606	14,041

79,000

At least	But less than	Single	Married filing jointly *	Married filing separately	Head of a household
79,000	79,050	15,528	11,299	15,620	14,054
79,050	79,100	15,540	11,311	15,634	14,066
79,100	79,150	15,553	11,324	15,648	14,079
79,150	79,200	15,565	11,336	15,662	14,091
79,200	79,250	15,578	11,349	15,676	14,104
79,250	79,300	15,590	11,361	15,690	14,116
79,300	79,350	15,603	11,374	15,704	14,129
79,350	79,400	15,615	11,386	15,718	14,141
79,400	79,450	15,628	11,399	15,732	14,154
79,450	79,500	15,640	11,411	15,746	14,166
79,500	79,550	15,653	11,424	15,760	14,179
79,550	79,600	15,665	11,436	15,774	14,191
79,600	79,650	15,678	11,449	15,788	14,204
79,650	79,700	15,690	11,461	15,802	14,216
79,700	79,750	15,703	11,474	15,816	14,229
79,750	79,800	15,715	11,486	15,830	14,241
79,800	79,850	15,728	11,499	15,844	14,254
79,850	79,900	15,740	11,511	15,858	14,266
79,900	79,950	15,753	11,524	15,872	14,279
79,950	80,000	15,765	11,536	15,886	14,291

80,000

At least	But less than	Single	Married filing jointly *	Married filing separately	Head of a household
80,000	80,050	15,778	11,549	15,900	14,304
80,050	80,100	15,790	11,561	15,914	14,316
80,100	80,150	15,803	11,574	15,928	14,329
80,150	80,200	15,815	11,586	15,942	14,341
80,200	80,250	15,828	11,599	15,956	14,354
80,250	80,300	15,840	11,611	15,970	14,366
80,300	80,350	15,853	11,624	15,984	14,379
80,350	80,400	15,865	11,636	15,998	14,391
80,400	80,450	15,878	11,649	16,012	14,404
80,450	80,500	15,890	11,661	16,026	14,416
80,500	80,550	15,903	11,674	16,040	14,429
80,550	80,600	15,915	11,686	16,054	14,441
80,600	80,650	15,928	11,699	16,068	14,454
80,650	80,700	15,940	11,711	16,082	14,466
80,700	80,750	15,953	11,724	16,096	14,479
80,750	80,800	15,965	11,736	16,110	14,491
80,800	80,850	15,978	11,749	16,124	14,504
80,850	80,900	15,990	11,761	16,138	14,516
80,900	80,950	16,003	11,774	16,152	14,529
80,950	81,000	16,015	11,786	16,166	14,541

81,000

At least	But less than	Single	Married filing jointly *	Married filing separately	Head of a household
81,000	81,050	16,028	11,799	16,180	14,554
81,050	81,100	16,040	11,811	16,194	14,566
81,100	81,150	16,053	11,824	16,208	14,579
81,150	81,200	16,065	11,836	16,222	14,591
81,200	81,250	16,078	11,849	16,236	14,604
81,250	81,300	16,090	11,861	16,250	14,616
81,300	81,350	16,103	11,874	16,264	14,629
81,350	81,400	16,115	11,886	16,278	14,641
81,400	81,450	16,128	11,899	16,292	14,654
81,450	81,500	16,140	11,911	16,306	14,666
81,500	81,550	16,153	11,924	16,320	14,679
81,550	81,600	16,165	11,936	16,334	14,691
81,600	81,650	16,178	11,949	16,348	14,704
81,650	81,700	16,190	11,961	16,362	14,716
81,700	81,750	16,203	11,974	16,376	14,729
81,750	81,800	16,215	11,986	16,390	14,741
81,800	81,850	16,228	11,999	16,404	14,754
81,850	81,900	16,240	12,011	16,418	14,766
81,900	81,950	16,253	12,024	16,432	14,779
81,950	82,000	16,265	12,036	16,446	14,791

82,000

At least	But less than	Single	Married filing jointly *	Married filing separately	Head of a household
82,000	82,050	16,278	12,049	16,460	14,804
82,050	82,100	16,290	12,061	16,474	14,816
82,100	82,150	16,303	12,074	16,488	14,829
82,150	82,200	16,315	12,086	16,502	14,841
82,200	82,250	16,328	12,099	16,516	14,854
82,250	82,300	16,340	12,111	16,530	14,866
82,300	82,350	16,353	12,124	16,544	14,879
82,350	82,400	16,365	12,136	16,558	14,891
82,400	82,450	16,378	12,149	16,572	14,904
82,450	82,500	16,390	12,161	16,586	14,916
82,500	82,550	16,403	12,174	16,600	14,929
82,550	82,600	16,415	12,186	16,614	14,941
82,600	82,650	16,428	12,199	16,628	14,954
82,650	82,700	16,440	12,211	16,642	14,966
82,700	82,750	16,453	12,224	16,656	14,979
82,750	82,800	16,465	12,236	16,670	14,991
82,800	82,850	16,478	12,249	16,684	15,004
82,850	82,900	16,490	12,261	16,698	15,016
82,900	82,950	16,503	12,274	16,712	15,029
82,950	83,000	16,515	12,286	16,726	15,041

83,000

At least	But less than	Single	Married filing jointly *	Married filing separately	Head of a household
83,000	83,050	16,528	12,299	16,740	15,054
83,050	83,100	16,540	12,311	16,754	15,066
83,100	83,150	16,553	12,324	16,768	15,079
83,150	83,200	16,565	12,336	16,782	15,091
83,200	83,250	16,578	12,349	16,796	15,104
83,250	83,300	16,590	12,361	16,810	15,116
83,300	83,350	16,603	12,374	16,824	15,129
83,350	83,400	16,615	12,386	16,838	15,141
83,400	83,450	16,628	12,399	16,852	15,154
83,450	83,500	16,640	12,411	16,866	15,166
83,500	83,550	16,653	12,424	16,880	15,179
83,550	83,600	16,665	12,436	16,894	15,191
83,600	83,650	16,678	12,449	16,908	15,204
83,650	83,700	16,690	12,461	16,922	15,216
83,700	83,750	16,703	12,474	16,936	15,229
83,750	83,800	16,715	12,486	16,950	15,241
83,800	83,850	16,728	12,499	16,964	15,254
83,850	83,900	16,740	12,511	16,978	15,266
83,900	83,950	16,753	12,524	16,992	15,279
83,950	84,000	16,765	12,536	17,006	15,291

* This column must also be used by a qualifying widow(er).

(Continued)

If line 43 (taxable income) is—		And you are—			
At least	But less than	Single	Married filing jointly *	Married filing separately	Head of a household
		Your tax is—			

84,000

At least	But less than	Single	MFJ *	MFS	HoH
84,000	84,050	16,778	12,549	17,020	15,304
84,050	84,100	16,790	12,561	17,034	15,316
84,100	84,150	16,803	12,574	17,048	15,329
84,150	84,200	16,815	12,586	17,062	15,341
84,200	84,250	16,828	12,599	17,076	15,354
84,250	84,300	16,840	12,611	17,090	15,366
84,300	84,350	16,853	12,624	17,104	15,379
84,350	84,400	16,865	12,636	17,118	15,391
84,400	84,450	16,878	12,649	17,132	15,404
84,450	84,500	16,890	12,661	17,146	15,416
84,500	84,550	16,903	12,674	17,160	15,429
84,550	84,600	16,915	12,686	17,174	15,441
84,600	84,650	16,928	12,699	17,188	15,454
84,650	84,700	16,940	12,711	17,202	15,466
84,700	84,750	16,953	12,724	17,216	15,479
84,750	84,800	16,965	12,736	17,230	15,491
84,800	84,850	16,978	12,749	17,244	15,504
84,850	84,900	16,990	12,761	17,258	15,516
84,900	84,950	17,003	12,774	17,272	15,529
84,950	85,000	17,015	12,786	17,286	15,541

85,000

At least	But less than	Single	MFJ *	MFS	HoH
85,000	85,050	17,028	12,799	17,300	15,554
85,050	85,100	17,040	12,811	17,314	15,566
85,100	85,150	17,053	12,824	17,328	15,579
85,150	85,200	17,065	12,836	17,342	15,591
85,200	85,250	17,078	12,849	17,356	15,604
85,250	85,300	17,090	12,861	17,370	15,616
85,300	85,350	17,103	12,874	17,384	15,629
85,350	85,400	17,115	12,886	17,398	15,641
85,400	85,450	17,128	12,899	17,412	15,654
85,450	85,500	17,140	12,911	17,426	15,666
85,500	85,550	17,153	12,924	17,440	15,679
85,550	85,600	17,165	12,936	17,454	15,691
85,600	85,650	17,178	12,949	17,468	15,704
85,650	85,700	17,190	12,961	17,482	15,716
85,700	85,750	17,203	12,974	17,496	15,729
85,750	85,800	17,215	12,986	17,510	15,741
85,800	85,850	17,228	12,999	17,524	15,754
85,850	85,900	17,240	13,011	17,538	15,766
85,900	85,950	17,253	13,024	17,552	15,779
85,950	86,000	17,265	13,036	17,566	15,791

86,000

At least	But less than	Single	MFJ *	MFS	HoH
86,000	86,050	17,278	13,049	17,580	15,804
86,050	86,100	17,290	13,061	17,594	15,816
86,100	86,150	17,303	13,074	17,608	15,829
86,150	86,200	17,315	13,086	17,622	15,841
86,200	86,250	17,328	13,099	17,636	15,854
86,250	86,300	17,340	13,111	17,650	15,866
86,300	86,350	17,353	13,124	17,664	15,879
86,350	86,400	17,365	13,136	17,678	15,891
86,400	86,450	17,378	13,149	17,692	15,904
86,450	86,500	17,390	13,161	17,706	15,916
86,500	86,550	17,403	13,174	17,720	15,929
86,550	86,600	17,415	13,186	17,734	15,941
86,600	86,650	17,428	13,199	17,748	15,954
86,650	86,700	17,440	13,211	17,762	15,966
86,700	86,750	17,453	13,224	17,776	15,979
86,750	86,800	17,465	13,236	17,790	15,991
86,800	86,850	17,478	13,249	17,804	16,004
86,850	86,900	17,490	13,261	17,818	16,016
86,900	86,950	17,503	13,274	17,832	16,029
86,950	87,000	17,515	13,286	17,846	16,041

87,000

At least	But less than	Single	MFJ *	MFS	HoH
87,000	87,050	17,528	13,299	17,860	16,054
87,050	87,100	17,540	13,311	17,874	16,066
87,100	87,150	17,553	13,324	17,888	16,079
87,150	87,200	17,565	13,336	17,902	16,091
87,200	87,250	17,578	13,349	17,916	16,104
87,250	87,300	17,590	13,361	17,930	16,116
87,300	87,350	17,603	13,374	17,944	16,129
87,350	87,400	17,615	13,386	17,958	16,141
87,400	87,450	17,628	13,399	17,972	16,154
87,450	87,500	17,640	13,411	17,986	16,166
87,500	87,550	17,653	13,424	18,000	16,179
87,550	87,600	17,665	13,436	18,014	16,191
87,600	87,650	17,678	13,449	18,028	16,204
87,650	87,700	17,690	13,461	18,042	16,216
87,700	87,750	17,703	13,474	18,056	16,229
87,750	87,800	17,715	13,486	18,070	16,241
87,800	87,850	17,728	13,499	18,084	16,254
87,850	87,900	17,740	13,511	18,098	16,266
87,900	87,950	17,753	13,524	18,112	16,279
87,950	88,000	17,765	13,536	18,126	16,291

88,000

At least	But less than	Single	MFJ *	MFS	HoH
88,000	88,050	17,778	13,549	18,140	16,304
88,050	88,100	17,790	13,561	18,154	16,316
88,100	88,150	17,803	13,574	18,168	16,329
88,150	88,200	17,815	13,586	18,182	16,341
88,200	88,250	17,828	13,599	18,196	16,354
88,250	88,300	17,840	13,611	18,210	16,366
88,300	88,350	17,853	13,624	18,224	16,379
88,350	88,400	17,865	13,636	18,238	16,391
88,400	88,450	17,878	13,649	18,252	16,404
88,450	88,500	17,890	13,661	18,266	16,416
88,500	88,550	17,903	13,674	18,280	16,429
88,550	88,600	17,915	13,686	18,294	16,441
88,600	88,650	17,928	13,699	18,308	16,454
88,650	88,700	17,940	13,711	18,322	16,466
88,700	88,750	17,953	13,724	18,336	16,479
88,750	88,800	17,965	13,736	18,350	16,491
88,800	88,850	17,978	13,749	18,364	16,504
88,850	88,900	17,990	13,761	18,378	16,516
88,900	88,950	18,003	13,774	18,392	16,529
88,950	89,000	18,015	13,786	18,406	16,541

89,000

At least	But less than	Single	MFJ *	MFS	HoH
89,000	89,050	18,028	13,799	18,420	16,554
89,050	89,100	18,040	13,811	18,434	16,566
89,100	89,150	18,053	13,824	18,448	16,579
89,150	89,200	18,065	13,836	18,462	16,591
89,200	89,250	18,078	13,849	18,476	16,604
89,250	89,300	18,090	13,861	18,490	16,616
89,300	89,350	18,103	13,874	18,504	16,629
89,350	89,400	18,115	13,886	18,518	16,641
89,400	89,450	18,128	13,899	18,532	16,654
89,450	89,500	18,140	13,911	18,546	16,666
89,500	89,550	18,153	13,924	18,560	16,679
89,550	89,600	18,165	13,936	18,574	16,691
89,600	89,650	18,178	13,949	18,588	16,704
89,650	89,700	18,190	13,961	18,602	16,716
89,700	89,750	18,203	13,974	18,616	16,729
89,750	89,800	18,215	13,986	18,630	16,741
89,800	89,850	18,228	13,999	18,644	16,754
89,850	89,900	18,240	14,011	18,658	16,766
89,900	89,950	18,253	14,024	18,672	16,779
89,950	90,000	18,265	14,036	18,686	16,791

90,000

At least	But less than	Single	MFJ *	MFS	HoH
90,000	90,050	18,278	14,049	18,700	16,804
90,050	90,100	18,290	14,061	18,714	16,816
90,100	90,150	18,303	14,074	18,728	16,829
90,150	90,200	18,315	14,086	18,742	16,841
90,200	90,250	18,328	14,099	18,756	16,854
90,250	90,300	18,340	14,111	18,770	16,866
90,300	90,350	18,353	14,124	18,784	16,879
90,350	90,400	18,365	14,136	18,798	16,891
90,400	90,450	18,378	14,149	18,812	16,904
90,450	90,500	18,390	14,161	18,826	16,916
90,500	90,550	18,403	14,174	18,840	16,929
90,550	90,600	18,415	14,186	18,854	16,941
90,600	90,650	18,428	14,199	18,868	16,954
90,650	90,700	18,440	14,211	18,882	16,966
90,700	90,750	18,453	14,224	18,896	16,979
90,750	90,800	18,465	14,236	18,910	16,991
90,800	90,850	18,478	14,249	18,924	17,004
90,850	90,900	18,490	14,261	18,938	17,016
90,900	90,950	18,503	14,274	18,952	17,029
90,950	91,000	18,515	14,286	18,966	17,041

91,000

At least	But less than	Single	MFJ *	MFS	HoH
91,000	91,050	18,528	14,299	18,980	17,054
91,050	91,100	18,540	14,311	18,994	17,066
91,100	91,150	18,553	14,324	19,008	17,079
91,150	91,200	18,566	14,336	19,022	17,091
91,200	91,250	18,580	14,349	19,036	17,104
91,250	91,300	18,594	14,361	19,050	17,116
91,300	91,350	18,608	14,374	19,064	17,129
91,350	91,400	18,622	14,386	19,078	17,141
91,400	91,450	18,636	14,399	19,092	17,154
91,450	91,500	18,650	14,411	19,106	17,166
91,500	91,550	18,664	14,424	19,120	17,179
91,550	91,600	18,678	14,436	19,134	17,191
91,600	91,650	18,692	14,449	19,148	17,204
91,650	91,700	18,706	14,461	19,162	17,216
91,700	91,750	18,720	14,474	19,176	17,229
91,750	91,800	18,734	14,486	19,190	17,241
91,800	91,850	18,748	14,499	19,204	17,254
91,850	91,900	18,762	14,511	19,218	17,266
91,900	91,950	18,776	14,524	19,232	17,279
91,950	92,000	18,790	14,536	19,246	17,291

92,000

At least	But less than	Single	MFJ *	MFS	HoH
92,000	92,050	18,804	14,549	19,260	17,304
92,050	92,100	18,818	14,561	19,274	17,316
92,100	92,150	18,832	14,574	19,288	17,329
92,150	92,200	18,846	14,586	19,302	17,341
92,200	92,250	18,860	14,599	19,316	17,354
92,250	92,300	18,874	14,611	19,330	17,366
92,300	92,350	18,888	14,624	19,344	17,379
92,350	92,400	18,902	14,636	19,358	17,391
92,400	92,450	18,916	14,649	19,372	17,404
92,450	92,500	18,930	14,661	19,386	17,416
92,500	92,550	18,944	14,674	19,400	17,429
92,550	92,600	18,958	14,686	19,414	17,441
92,600	92,650	18,972	14,699	19,428	17,454
92,650	92,700	18,986	14,711	19,442	17,466
92,700	92,750	19,000	14,724	19,456	17,479
92,750	92,800	19,014	14,736	19,470	17,491
92,800	92,850	19,028	14,749	19,484	17,504
92,850	92,900	19,042	14,761	19,498	17,516
92,900	92,950	19,056	14,774	19,512	17,529
92,950	93,000	19,070	14,786	19,526	17,541

* This column must also be used by a qualifying widow(er).

(Continued)

2016 Tax Table—*Continued*

93,000

If line 43 (taxable income) is—		And you are—			
At least	But less than	Single	Married filing jointly *	Married filing separately	Head of a household
		Your tax is—			
93,000	93,050	19,084	14,799	19,540	17,554
93,050	93,100	19,098	14,811	19,554	17,566
93,100	93,150	19,112	14,824	19,568	17,579
93,150	93,200	19,126	14,836	19,582	17,591
93,200	93,250	19,140	14,849	19,596	17,604
93,250	93,300	19,154	14,861	19,610	17,616
93,300	93,350	19,168	14,874	19,624	17,629
93,350	93,400	19,182	14,886	19,638	17,641
93,400	93,450	19,196	14,899	19,652	17,654
93,450	93,500	19,210	14,911	19,666	17,666
93,500	93,550	19,224	14,924	19,680	17,679
93,550	93,600	19,238	14,936	19,694	17,691
93,600	93,650	19,252	14,949	19,708	17,704
93,650	93,700	19,266	14,961	19,722	17,716
93,700	93,750	19,280	14,974	19,736	17,729
93,750	93,800	19,294	14,986	19,750	17,741
93,800	93,850	19,308	14,999	19,764	17,754
93,850	93,900	19,322	15,011	19,778	17,766
93,900	93,950	19,336	15,024	19,792	17,779
93,950	94,000	19,350	15,036	19,806	17,791

94,000

At least	But less than	Single	Married filing jointly *	Married filing separately	Head of a household
94,000	94,050	19,364	15,049	19,820	17,804
94,050	94,100	19,378	15,061	19,834	17,816
94,100	94,150	19,392	15,074	19,848	17,829
94,150	94,200	19,406	15,086	19,862	17,841
94,200	94,250	19,420	15,099	19,876	17,854
94,250	94,300	19,434	15,111	19,890	17,866
94,300	94,350	19,448	15,124	19,904	17,879
94,350	94,400	19,462	15,136	19,918	17,891
94,400	94,450	19,476	15,149	19,932	17,904
94,450	94,500	19,490	15,161	19,946	17,916
94,500	94,550	19,504	15,174	19,960	17,929
94,550	94,600	19,518	15,186	19,974	17,941
94,600	94,650	19,532	15,199	19,988	17,954
94,650	94,700	19,546	15,211	20,002	17,966
94,700	94,750	19,560	15,224	20,016	17,979
94,750	94,800	19,574	15,236	20,030	17,991
94,800	94,850	19,588	15,249	20,044	18,004
94,850	94,900	19,602	15,261	20,058	18,016
94,900	94,950	19,616	15,274	20,072	18,029
94,950	95,000	19,630	15,286	20,086	18,041

95,000

At least	But less than	Single	Married filing jointly *	Married filing separately	Head of a household
95,000	95,050	19,644	15,299	20,100	18,054
95,050	95,100	19,658	15,311	20,114	18,066
95,100	95,150	19,672	15,324	20,128	18,079
95,150	95,200	19,686	15,336	20,142	18,091
95,200	95,250	19,700	15,349	20,156	18,104
95,250	95,300	19,714	15,361	20,170	18,116
95,300	95,350	19,728	15,374	20,184	18,129
95,350	95,400	19,742	15,386	20,198	18,141
95,400	95,450	19,756	15,399	20,212	18,154
95,450	95,500	19,770	15,411	20,226	18,166
95,500	95,550	19,784	15,424	20,240	18,179
95,550	95,600	19,798	15,436	20,254	18,191
95,600	95,650	19,812	15,449	20,268	18,204
95,650	95,700	19,826	15,461	20,282	18,216
95,700	95,750	19,840	15,474	20,296	18,229
95,750	95,800	19,854	15,486	20,310	18,241
95,800	95,850	19,868	15,499	20,324	18,254
95,850	95,900	19,882	15,511	20,338	18,266
95,900	95,950	19,896	15,524	20,352	18,279
95,950	96,000	19,910	15,536	20,366	18,291

96,000

At least	But less than	Single	Married filing jointly *	Married filing separately	Head of a household
96,000	96,050	19,924	15,549	20,380	18,304
96,050	96,100	19,938	15,561	20,394	18,316
96,100	96,150	19,952	15,574	20,408	18,329
96,150	96,200	19,966	15,586	20,422	18,341
96,200	96,250	19,980	15,599	20,436	18,354
96,250	96,300	19,994	15,611	20,450	18,366
96,300	96,350	20,008	15,624	20,464	18,379
96,350	96,400	20,022	15,636	20,478	18,391
96,400	96,450	20,036	15,649	20,492	18,404
96,450	96,500	20,050	15,661	20,506	18,416
96,500	96,550	20,064	15,674	20,520	18,429
96,550	96,600	20,078	15,686	20,534	18,441
96,600	96,650	20,092	15,699	20,548	18,454
96,650	96,700	20,106	15,711	20,562	18,466
96,700	96,750	20,120	15,724	20,576	18,479
96,750	96,800	20,134	15,736	20,590	18,491
96,800	96,850	20,148	15,749	20,604	18,504
96,850	96,900	20,162	15,761	20,618	18,516
96,900	96,950	20,176	15,774	20,632	18,529
96,950	97,000	20,190	15,786	20,646	18,541

97,000

At least	But less than	Single	Married filing jointly *	Married filing separately	Head of a household
97,000	97,050	20,204	15,799	20,660	18,554
97,050	97,100	20,218	15,811	20,674	18,566
97,100	97,150	20,232	15,824	20,688	18,579
97,150	97,200	20,246	15,836	20,702	18,591
97,200	97,250	20,260	15,849	20,716	18,604
97,250	97,300	20,274	15,861	20,730	18,616
97,300	97,350	20,288	15,874	20,744	18,629
97,350	97,400	20,302	15,886	20,758	18,641
97,400	97,450	20,316	15,899	20,772	18,654
97,450	97,500	20,330	15,911	20,786	18,666
97,500	97,550	20,344	15,924	20,800	18,679
97,550	97,600	20,358	15,936	20,814	18,691
97,600	97,650	20,372	15,949	20,828	18,704
97,650	97,700	20,386	15,961	20,842	18,716
97,700	97,750	20,400	15,974	20,856	18,729
97,750	97,800	20,414	15,986	20,870	18,741
97,800	97,850	20,428	15,999	20,884	18,754
97,850	97,900	20,442	16,011	20,898	18,766
97,900	97,950	20,456	16,024	20,912	18,779
97,950	98,000	20,470	16,036	20,926	18,791

98,000

At least	But less than	Single	Married filing jointly *	Married filing separately	Head of a household
98,000	98,050	20,484	16,049	20,940	18,804
98,050	98,100	20,498	16,061	20,954	18,816
98,100	98,150	20,512	16,074	20,968	18,829
98,150	98,200	20,526	16,086	20,982	18,841
98,200	98,250	20,540	16,099	20,996	18,854
98,250	98,300	20,554	16,111	21,010	18,866
98,300	98,350	20,568	16,124	21,024	18,879
98,350	98,400	20,582	16,136	21,038	18,891
98,400	98,450	20,596	16,149	21,052	18,904
98,450	98,500	20,610	16,161	21,066	18,916
98,500	98,550	20,624	16,174	21,080	18,929
98,550	98,600	20,638	16,186	21,094	18,941
98,600	98,650	20,652	16,199	21,108	18,954
98,650	98,700	20,666	16,211	21,122	18,966
98,700	98,750	20,680	16,224	21,136	18,979
98,750	98,800	20,694	16,236	21,150	18,991
98,800	98,850	20,708	16,249	21,164	19,004
98,850	98,900	20,722	16,261	21,178	19,016
98,900	98,950	20,736	16,274	21,192	19,029
98,950	99,000	20,750	16,286	21,206	19,041

99,000

At least	But less than	Single	Married filing jointly *	Married filing separately	Head of a household
99,000	99,050	20,764	16,299	21,220	19,054
99,050	99,100	20,778	16,311	21,234	19,066
99,100	99,150	20,792	16,324	21,248	19,079
99,150	99,200	20,806	16,336	21,262	19,091
99,200	99,250	20,820	16,349	21,276	19,104
99,250	99,300	20,834	16,361	21,290	19,116
99,300	99,350	20,848	16,374	21,304	19,129
99,350	99,400	20,862	16,386	21,318	19,141
99,400	99,450	20,876	16,399	21,332	19,154
99,450	99,500	20,890	16,411	21,346	19,166
99,500	99,550	20,904	16,424	21,360	19,179
99,550	99,600	20,918	16,436	21,374	19,191
99,600	99,650	20,932	16,449	21,388	19,204
99,650	99,700	20,946	16,461	21,402	19,216
99,700	99,750	20,960	16,474	21,416	19,229
99,750	99,800	20,974	16,486	21,430	19,241
99,800	99,850	20,988	16,499	21,444	19,254
99,850	99,900	21,002	16,511	21,458	19,266
99,900	99,950	21,016	16,524	21,472	19,279
99,950	100,000	21,030	16,536	21,486	19,291

$100,000 or over — use the Tax Computation Worksheet

2016 OPTIONAL SALES TAX TABLES

When Used

The election to deduct state and local general sales taxes requires that the taxpayer forgo any deduction for state and local income taxes. Whether this is advisable or not depends on a comparison of the amounts involved. In making the choice, however, the outcome could be influenced by the additional sales tax incurred due to certain "big ticket" purchases that were made. For example, a taxpayer who chose to deduct state and local income taxes for 2015 might well prefer the sales tax deduction in 2016 if a new boat was purchased or home improvements were made during the year. To make the sales tax election, the taxpayer must enter the amount on Schedule A, line 5, and check box b.

If the sales tax election is made, the amount of the deduction can be determined by use of the *actual expense method* or the *optional sales tax tables* issued by the IRS. The actual expense method can be used only when the taxpayer has actual receipts to support the deduction claimed. In the absence of receipts, the usual case with most taxpayers, resorting to the optional sales tax tables is necessary. Under neither method, however, is the purchase of items used in a taxpayer's trade or business to be considered.

Adjustments Necessary

The optional sales tax tables are based on a number of assumptions that require adjustments to be made. As the starting point for the use of the tables is AGI, nontaxable receipts have not been included. Examples of receipts that should be added include: tax-exempt interest, veterans' benefits, nontaxable combat pay, public assistance payments, workers' compensation, nontaxable Social Security, and other retirement benefits. They do not include any large nontaxable items that are not likely to be spent. For example, a $100,000 inheritance should not be added if it was invested in a certificate of deposit.

The tables represent the sales tax on the average (and recurring) expenditures based on level of income by family size and do not include exceptional purchases. Therefore, add to the table amount any sales taxes on major purchases (such as motor vehicles, aircraft, boats, and home building materials, etc.).

When the optional sales tax tables are utilized, special adjustments may be needed when a taxpayer has lived in more than one taxing jurisdiction (e.g., state, county, city) during the year. The adjustments involve apportionment of taxes based on days involved and are illustrated in Instructions for Schedule A (Form 1040), pages A-3 to A-6.

Local Sales Taxes

Local sales taxes (i.e., those imposed by counties, cities, transit authorities) may or may not require a separate determination. In those states where they are not imposed, no further computations are necessary. This is also the case where the local taxes are uniform and are incorporated into the state sales tax table. In other situations, another step is necessary to arrive at the optional sales tax table deduction. Depending on where the taxpayer lives, one of two procedures needs to be used. In one procedure, the local sales tax is arrived at by using the **state table** amount—see Example 1 and the related worksheet. In the other procedure, special **local tables** issued by the IRS for specified state and local jurisdictions are modified (if necessary) and used—see Example 2 and the related worksheet.

Use Illustrated

EXAMPLE 1 The Archers file a joint return for 2016 reflecting AGI of $88,000 and claiming three exemptions. They have tax-exempt interest of $3,000, and during the year they incurred sales tax of $1,650 on the purchase of an automobile for their dependent teenage son. They live in Bellaire, Texas, where the general sales tax rates are 6.25% for state and 2% for local. Since the IRS *has not issued* optional local sales tax tables for Texas, use the Worksheet below to arrive at the Archers' general sales tax deduction of $3,094.

Sales Tax Deduction Worksheet
(To be used when *no* IRS Optional Local Sales Tax Table Available)

Adjusted Gross Income (AGI) as listed on line 38 of Form 1040		$88,000
Add nontaxable items		3,000
Table income to be used for purposes of line 1 below		$91,000
1. Use table income to determine table amount—go to state of residence and find applicable range of table income and exemption column* for *state* sales tax		$ 1,094
2a. Enter local general sales tax rate	2.00	
2b. Enter state general sales tax rate	6.25	
2c. Divide 2a by 2b	0.32	
2d. Multiply line 1 by line 2c for the local sales tax		350
3. Enter general sales tax on large purchases		1,650
4. Deduction for general sales tax (add lines 1 + 2d + 3) and report on line 5 of Schedule A of Form 1040		$ 3,094

*Use total of personal and dependency exemptions as reported in item 6d of Form 1040.

EXAMPLE 2 The Hardys file a joint return for 2016, reporting AGI of $42,000 and claiming four exemptions (two personal and two dependency). They received $30,000 in nontaxable pension benefits. Although the Hardys do not keep sales tax receipts, they can prove that they paid $1,185 in sales tax on the purchase of a new boat in 2016. The Hardys are residents of Georgia and live in a jurisdiction that imposes a 2% local sales tax. Since the IRS *has issued* optional local sales tax tables for Georgia, use the Worksheet below to arrive at the Hardys' general sales tax deduction of $2,051.

Sales Tax Deduction Worksheet
(To be used for Alaska, Arizona, Arkansas,
Colorado, Georgia, Illinois, Louisiana, Missouri, New York,
North Carolina, South Carolina, Tennessee, Utah, and Virginia)

Adjusted Gross Income (AGI) as listed on line 38 of Form 1040		$42,000
Add nontaxable income		30,000
Table income to be used for purposes of line 1 below		$72,000
1. Use the table income to determine *state* sales tax amount—go to table for state of residence and find applicable income range and exemption column*		$ 538
2a. Enter local general sales tax rate	2.0	
2b. Enter IRS *local* sales tax table amount (based on a 1% tax rate)	$164	
2c. Multiply line 2b by 2a for the local sales tax		328
3. Enter general sales tax on large purchases		1,185
4. Deduction for general sales tax (add lines 1 + 2c + 3) and report on line 5 of Schedule A of Form 1040		$ 2,051

*Use total of personal and dependency exemptions as reported in item 6d of Form 1040.

2016 Optional State Sales Tax Tables *(State Sales Tax Rate Shown Next to State Name)*

Income At least	But less than	Alabama 1	2	3	4	5	Over 5	Arizona 1	2	3	4	5	Over 5	Arkansas 1	2	3	4	5	Over 5
		1 4.0000%						**2 5.6000%**						**2 6.5000%**					
$0	$20,000	223	255	277	294	309	329	231	250	262	271	279	290	314	344	364	378	391	407
$20,000	$30,000	337	384	416	441	462	492	378	408	428	444	456	473	500	549	580	604	624	651
$30,000	$40,000	397	452	489	518	543	577	460	496	520	538	553	574	602	660	698	727	751	783
$40,000	$50,000	449	510	552	584	611	650	532	573	601	622	640	664	690	757	801	834	862	899
$50,000	$60,000	496	562	608	643	673	715	598	644	675	699	718	745	771	846	895	932	962	1004
$60,000	$70,000	538	609	658	697	729	774	658	709	743	769	790	820	844	926	980	1021	1054	1100
$70,000	$80,000	577	653	705	746	780	828	715	770	806	834	857	889	912	1001	1059	1104	1140	1189
$80,000	$90,000	613	693	748	792	827	878	768	827	866	896	921	955	976	1072	1134	1181	1220	1273
$90,000	$100,000	647	732	789	835	872	925	818	881	923	955	981	1017	1037	1138	1204	1255	1296	1352
$100,000	$120,000	693	782	844	892	932	988	887	954	999	1034	1062	1101	1118	1228	1299	1353	1398	1459
$120,000	$140,000	753	849	915	966	1009	1070	977	1051	1100	1138	1169	1212	1225	1345	1423	1483	1532	1599
$140,000	$160,000	808	910	980	1036	1081	1146	1062	1142	1195	1236	1270	1317	1325	1455	1540	1605	1657	1730
$160,000	$180,000	860	967	1041	1100	1148	1217	1141	1227	1284	1328	1364	1414	1418	1558	1649	1718	1774	1852
$180,000	$200,000	908	1021	1099	1160	1211	1283	1217	1308	1369	1416	1454	1507	1507	1656	1752	1826	1886	1969
$200,000	$225,000	959	1077	1159	1223	1277	1352	1297	1394	1458	1508	1549	1605	1600	1758	1861	1939	2003	2091
$225,000	$250,000	1014	1138	1223	1291	1347	1426	1383	1486	1555	1608	1651	1712	1701	1868	1978	2061	2129	2223
$250,000	$275,000	1065	1195	1284	1355	1413	1496	1465	1574	1647	1703	1749	1812	1796	1973	2089	2177	2249	2348
$275,000	$300,000	1114	1249	1342	1415	1477	1563	1545	1659	1736	1794	1843	1910	1887	2074	2196	2288	2364	2468
$300,000	or more	1409	1573	1687	1777	1852	1958	2027	2176	2275	2351	2413	2500	2439	2681	2839	2959	3057	3192

Income At least	But less than	California 1	2	3	4	5	Over 5	Colorado 1	2	3	4	5	Over 5	Connecticut 1	2	3	4	5	Over 5
		3 7.5000%						**2 2.9000%**						**4 6.3500%**					
$0	$20,000	292	312	326	336	345	357	113	121	127	131	134	138	272	293	307	317	325	337
$20,000	$30,000	481	514	536	553	567	586	183	195	203	209	214	221	440	475	497	514	528	547
$30,000	$40,000	585	626	653	673	690	713	220	235	245	252	258	266	532	574	602	622	639	662
$40,000	$50,000	678	725	756	779	799	825	253	270	281	290	296	306	613	662	694	718	737	763
$50,000	$60,000	763	815	850	876	898	928	284	302	314	324	331	342	687	742	778	804	826	856
$60,000	$70,000	841	899	936	966	989	1022	311	331	345	355	363	375	754	815	854	884	908	941
$70,000	$80,000	915	976	1018	1049	1075	1110	337	359	373	384	393	405	817	884	926	958	984	1020
$80,000	$90,000	984	1050	1094	1128	1155	1194	361	384	399	411	421	434	877	948	994	1028	1056	1095
$90,000	$100,000	1049	1120	1166	1202	1232	1273	384	408	425	437	447	461	933	1009	1058	1094	1124	1165
$100,000	$120,000	1137	1214	1264	1303	1335	1379	415	441	458	472	483	498	1008	1091	1144	1184	1216	1260
$120,000	$140,000	1254	1338	1394	1436	1471	1520	456	484	503	517	529	546	1108	1199	1257	1301	1337	1386
$140,000	$160,000	1365	1455	1516	1562	1600	1652	494	524	545	560	573	591	1202	1300	1364	1412	1451	1504
$160,000	$180,000	1468	1565	1630	1679	1720	1776	530	562	584	600	614	633	1289	1395	1464	1515	1557	1614
$180,000	$200,000	1567	1670	1739	1792	1835	1895	564	598	621	639	653	673	1373	1486	1559	1614	1658	1719
$200,000	$225,000	1671	1781	1854	1910	1956	2020	600	636	660	679	694	715	1461	1581	1659	1717	1765	1830
$225,000	$250,000	1783	1900	1978	2038	2087	2155	638	676	702	722	738	761	1555	1684	1767	1829	1880	1949
$250,000	$275,000	1891	2015	2097	2160	2212	2284	675	715	742	763	780	804	1645	1782	1870	1936	1989	2063
$275,000	$300,000	1994	2125	2211	2278	2332	2408	710	752	781	802	820	845	1732	1876	1969	2038	2095	2172
$300,000	or more	2626	2795	2907	2994	3065	3164	924	977	1013	1041	1064	1095	2258	2447	2568	2660	2734	2836

Income At least	But less than	District of Columbia 1	2	3	4	5	Over 5	Florida 1	2	3	4	5	Over 5	Georgia 1	2	3	4	5	Over 5
		4 5.7500%						**1 6.0000%**						**2 4.0000%**					
$0	$20,000	171	184	194	201	207	216	254	272	284	293	301	311	155	167	175	181	186	193
$20,000	$30,000	284	307	323	335	345	360	418	447	467	482	494	510	251	270	282	292	299	310
$30,000	$40,000	348	376	395	410	422	440	509	544	568	586	600	621	304	326	341	352	361	374
$40,000	$50,000	404	437	459	476	491	511	589	630	657	678	695	718	350	375	392	405	415	430
$50,000	$60,000	456	493	518	537	553	576	662	708	739	762	781	807	392	420	439	453	465	481
$60,000	$70,000	504	544	572	593	611	637	730	780	814	839	860	889	431	461	482	497	510	528
$70,000	$80,000	549	592	622	646	666	693	793	848	884	912	934	966	467	500	521	538	552	571
$80,000	$90,000	591	638	670	696	717	747	852	911	950	980	1004	1038	501	536	559	577	592	612
$90,000	$100,000	631	681	716	743	766	797	909	972	1013	1045	1071	1106	533	570	595	614	629	651
$100,000	$120,000	686	740	778	807	832	866	985	1053	1098	1132	1160	1199	576	616	642	663	680	703
$120,000	$140,000	758	818	859	892	919	957	1085	1160	1210	1247	1278	1321	633	676	705	728	746	771
$140,000	$160,000	826	891	936	972	1001	1043	1180	1261	1315	1356	1390	1436	687	733	765	789	808	836
$160,000	$180,000	889	960	1009	1047	1079	1123	1269	1356	1414	1458	1494	1543	737	786	820	845	867	896
$180,000	$200,000	951	1026	1078	1119	1153	1200	1354	1447	1508	1555	1593	1646	784	837	872	900	922	953
$200,000	$225,000	1015	1095	1151	1195	1231	1282	1443	1542	1607	1657	1698	1755	835	890	928	957	980	1013
$225,000	$250,000	1085	1171	1230	1277	1315	1370	1540	1645	1715	1768	1812	1872	889	948	988	1018	1043	1078
$250,000	$275,000	1152	1243	1306	1355	1396	1454	1632	1743	1817	1873	1920	1983	940	1003	1044	1077	1103	1140
$275,000	$300,000	1216	1312	1379	1431	1474	1535	1721	1838	1916	1975	2024	2091	990	1055	1099	1133	1161	1199
$300,000	or more	1610	1737	1825	1894	1951	2032	2261	2415	2516	2594	2657	2745	1291	1374	1430	1473	1509	1558

Income At least	But less than	Hawaii 1	2	3	4	5	Over 5	Idaho 1	2	3	4	5	Over 5	Illinois 1	2	3	4	5	Over 5
		1,6 4.0000%						**1 6.0000%**						**2 6.2500%**					
$0	$20,000	263	298	322	340	355	376	338	385	417	442	463	493	241	262	276	287	296	309
$20,000	$30,000	402	456	492	520	543	575	514	584	631	668	699	742	386	418	440	457	471	490
$30,000	$40,000	476	540	582	615	642	680	607	688	743	787	822	873	466	503	529	549	566	589
$40,000	$50,000	540	612	660	697	728	770	688	778	840	889	929	985	535	578	607	630	649	675
$50,000	$60,000	597	677	730	770	804	851	760	859	927	980	1024	1086	599	646	678	703	724	753
$60,000	$70,000	649	735	793	837	873	924	826	932	1005	1062	1110	1177	657	708	743	770	793	825
$70,000	$80,000	696	789	851	898	937	992	886	1000	1078	1139	1189	1260	711	766	803	833	857	891
$80,000	$90,000	741	839	905	956	997	1055	943	1063	1145	1210	1263	1338	762	820	860	891	917	953
$90,000	$100,000	783	887	956	1009	1053	1115	996	1122	1209	1276	1332	1411	810	871	913	946	974	1012
$100,000	$120,000	838	950	1024	1081	1128	1194	1067	1201	1293	1365	1425	1509	874	940	985	1021	1050	1091
$120,000	$140,000	911	1032	1113	1175	1226	1297	1160	1304	1403	1481	1545	1636	959	1031	1080	1118	1150	1195
$140,000	$160,000	979	1109	1195	1262	1317	1393	1246	1401	1506	1589	1658	1754	1040	1116	1169	1210	1245	1293
$160,000	$180,000	1042	1180	1272	1342	1401	1482	1327	1490	1601	1689	1761	1864	1114	1196	1252	1296	1332	1384
$180,000	$200,000	1101	1247	1344	1419	1480	1566	1403	1574	1691	1783	1859	1967	1186	1271	1331	1377	1416	1470
$200,000	$225,000	1163	1317	1419	1498	1563	1654	1482	1662	1785	1881	1962	2075	1260	1351	1414	1463	1504	1561
$225,000	$250,000	1230	1392	1500	1584	1652	1748	1567	1756	1885	1987	2071	2190	1341	1437	1503	1555	1598	1659
$250,000	$275,000	1293	1463	1577	1664	1736	1837	1648	1845	1980	2086	2175	2299	1418	1518	1588	1642	1688	1752
$275,000	$300,000	1353	1531	1650	1741	1817	1922	1725	1930	2071	2182	2274	2403	1492	1597	1669	1727	1774	1841
$300,000	or more	1710	1934	2083	2199	2294	2426	2186	2438	2611	2747	2861	3021	1940	2071	2162	2234	2295	2379

(Continued)

2016 Optional State Sales Tax Tables *(Continued)*

Income At least	But less than	Indiana 1	2	3	4	5	Over 5	Iowa 1	2	3	4	5	Over 5	Kansas 1	2	3	4	5	Over 5
		7.0000% (4)						*6.0000%* (1)						*6.5000%* (1)					
$0	$20,000	294	318	334	345	355	368	268	292	308	320	330	343	394	454	494	525	551	588
$20,000	$30,000	464	502	526	544	559	580	433	473	499	518	534	557	597	686	747	793	832	887
$30,000	$40,000	555	600	630	651	669	694	523	572	603	627	646	673	703	808	879	934	979	1044
$40,000	$50,000	635	687	720	745	765	793	602	658	695	723	745	776	795	913	992	1054	1106	1178
$50,000	$60,000	707	764	802	830	852	883	675	738	778	810	835	870	877	1006	1094	1162	1219	1298
$60,000	$70,000	773	835	876	906	931	965	741	810	855	889	917	955	951	1091	1186	1260	1321	1407
$70,000	$80,000	834	901	945	978	1005	1041	802	878	926	964	994	1036	1019	1169	1270	1349	1415	1507
$80,000	$90,000	891	963	1010	1045	1073	1113	860	941	994	1034	1066	1111	1082	1241	1349	1433	1502	1600
$90,000	$100,000	944	1021	1071	1108	1138	1180	915	1001	1057	1100	1134	1182	1142	1309	1423	1511	1584	1687
$100,000	$120,000	1016	1099	1152	1193	1225	1270	989	1082	1143	1189	1227	1278	1221	1400	1521	1615	1694	1803
$120,000	$140,000	1111	1201	1260	1304	1339	1388	1086	1189	1256	1307	1348	1405	1324	1518	1649	1751	1836	1955
$140,000	$160,000	1200	1297	1360	1408	1446	1499	1178	1289	1362	1417	1462	1524	1420	1628	1768	1877	1968	2095
$160,000	$180,000	1282	1386	1453	1504	1545	1602	1263	1383	1461	1520	1569	1635	1509	1729	1878	1994	2090	2225
$180,000	$200,000	1360	1471	1542	1596	1640	1700	1344	1473	1556	1619	1670	1741	1593	1825	1982	2104	2205	2348
$200,000	$225,000	1442	1559	1635	1692	1739	1802	1430	1566	1655	1722	1777	1853	1680	1925	2090	2219	2325	2475
$225,000	$250,000	1530	1655	1735	1796	1845	1913	1522	1668	1763	1834	1893	1973	1774	2031	2206	2341	2454	2612
$250,000	$275,000	1614	1745	1830	1894	1946	2017	1610	1764	1865	1941	2003	2088	1862	2132	2315	2457	2575	2741
$275,000	$300,000	1694	1832	1921	1988	2042	2117	1695	1857	1963	2043	2108	2198	1947	2228	2419	2568	2691	2864
$300,000	or more	2175	2352	2466	2552	2622	2719	2206	2419	2558	2663	2748	2866	2446	2798	3036	3221	3375	3592

Income At least	But less than	Kentucky 1	2	3	4	5	Over 5	Louisiana 1	2	3	4	5	Over 5	Maine 1	2	3	4	5	Over 5
		6.0000% (4)						*4.7514%* (2)						*5.5000%* (4)					
$0	$20,000	237	255	267	276	284	295	204	219	229	236	243	251	181	194	203	209	215	223
$20,000	$30,000	384	413	432	447	459	476	333	358	374	386	397	411	296	316	330	341	350	362
$30,000	$40,000	465	499	522	540	555	575	405	435	454	469	481	498	359	383	400	413	423	438
$40,000	$50,000	536	576	602	622	639	662	468	502	525	542	556	576	415	443	462	477	489	506
$50,000	$60,000	601	645	674	697	715	741	526	564	590	609	625	647	466	497	518	535	548	567
$60,000	$70,000	661	709	741	765	786	814	579	621	649	670	687	711	512	547	570	588	603	623
$70,000	$80,000	716	768	803	829	851	881	629	674	704	727	746	772	556	593	618	637	653	676
$80,000	$90,000	768	824	861	889	913	945	676	724	757	781	801	829	597	637	663	684	701	725
$90,000	$100,000	818	877	916	946	971	1005	720	772	806	832	854	883	636	678	707	729	747	772
$100,000	$120,000	885	948	990	1023	1049	1086	780	836	873	901	924	956	689	734	765	788	808	835
$120,000	$140,000	973	1042	1088	1123	1153	1193	859	920	961	992	1018	1053	759	808	841	867	889	918
$140,000	$160,000	1056	1130	1180	1218	1250	1294	933	1000	1044	1078	1105	1144	824	877	913	941	965	997
$160,000	$180,000	1133	1213	1266	1307	1341	1387	1003	1074	1122	1158	1187	1229	886	942	981	1011	1035	1070
$180,000	$200,000	1207	1292	1348	1391	1427	1477	1069	1145	1196	1234	1266	1310	944	1004	1045	1077	1103	1140
$200,000	$225,000	1285	1374	1434	1480	1518	1571	1139	1220	1274	1315	1348	1395	1006	1069	1113	1147	1174	1213
$225,000	$250,000	1369	1464	1527	1576	1616	1672	1215	1301	1358	1402	1438	1487	1072	1140	1186	1222	1251	1293
$250,000	$275,000	1449	1549	1616	1667	1710	1769	1287	1378	1438	1485	1523	1575	1136	1207	1256	1293	1325	1368
$275,000	$300,000	1526	1631	1701	1755	1800	1861	1356	1452	1516	1564	1604	1659	1197	1272	1323	1362	1395	1441
$300,000	or more	1994	2127	2217	2287	2344	2423	1778	1903	1986	2049	2101	2173	1569	1665	1730	1781	1823	1883

Income At least	But less than	Maryland 1	2	3	4	5	Over 5	Massachusetts 1	2	3	4	5	Over 5	Michigan 1	2	3	4	5	Over 5
		6.0000% (4)						*6.2500%* (4)						*6.0000%* (4)					
$0	$20,000	218	238	251	261	270	282	210	222	229	235	240	247	228	245	257	265	272	282
$20,000	$30,000	358	389	410	426	440	459	336	354	365	374	382	392	367	394	412	426	437	453
$30,000	$40,000	436	472	498	517	534	557	404	425	439	450	459	471	444	476	497	513	527	545
$40,000	$50,000	504	546	575	598	616	643	464	488	503	516	526	540	511	547	571	590	605	627
$50,000	$60,000	566	613	646	671	692	721	519	544	562	576	587	602	572	612	639	660	677	700
$60,000	$70,000	624	675	711	738	761	793	568	596	615	630	642	659	628	672	701	724	742	768
$70,000	$80,000	678	733	771	801	826	861	614	645	665	681	694	712	680	727	759	783	803	831
$80,000	$90,000	728	787	828	860	887	924	658	690	712	728	742	762	729	780	813	839	860	890
$90,000	$100,000	776	839	883	916	945	984	699	733	756	773	788	809	776	829	865	892	915	946
$100,000	$120,000	841	909	956	992	1023	1065	754	790	815	834	850	872	838	895	934	963	987	1021
$120,000	$140,000	927	1001	1052	1092	1125	1172	827	866	893	913	930	954	921	983	1025	1057	1083	1120
$140,000	$160,000	1008	1088	1143	1186	1222	1273	895	937	966	988	1006	1032	998	1065	1110	1145	1173	1213
$160,000	$180,000	1083	1169	1228	1274	1313	1367	958	1003	1034	1057	1077	1104	1071	1142	1190	1227	1257	1299
$180,000	$200,000	1156	1246	1309	1358	1399	1457	1019	1066	1098	1123	1144	1173	1140	1215	1266	1305	1337	1382
$200,000	$225,000	1232	1328	1394	1447	1490	1552	1082	1132	1166	1193	1214	1245	1212	1292	1346	1387	1421	1469
$225,000	$250,000	1314	1416	1487	1542	1589	1654	1151	1203	1239	1267	1290	1323	1291	1375	1432	1476	1512	1562
$250,000	$275,000	1393	1500	1575	1634	1682	1751	1216	1271	1309	1338	1362	1396	1365	1454	1514	1560	1598	1651
$275,000	$300,000	1468	1581	1660	1721	1773	1845	1278	1336	1375	1406	1432	1467	1437	1530	1593	1641	1681	1736
$300,000	or more	1929	2074	2175	2255	2321	2414	1655	1728	1778	1816	1849	1894	1872	1990	2069	2131	2182	2253

Income At least	But less than	Minnesota 1	2	3	4	5	Over 5	Mississippi 1	2	3	4	5	Over 5	Missouri 1	2	3	4	5	Over 5
		6.8750% (1)						*7.0000%* (2)						*4.2250%* (2)					
$0	$20,000	271	285	294	301	306	314	438	496	536	566	591	625	174	192	204	214	221	232
$20,000	$30,000	440	464	479	491	500	512	669	758	817	863	901	953	281	309	328	343	355	372
$30,000	$40,000	533	562	581	595	606	622	790	895	965	1019	1064	1126	340	373	396	413	427	448
$40,000	$50,000	615	649	671	687	701	719	895	1014	1093	1154	1205	1275	391	429	455	475	491	514
$50,000	$60,000	690	729	753	772	787	807	989	1120	1208	1275	1330	1408	438	480	509	531	549	575
$60,000	$70,000	759	801	829	849	865	888	1074	1216	1311	1384	1444	1528	481	527	558	582	602	630
$70,000	$80,000	823	869	899	921	939	964	1153	1305	1407	1485	1550	1640	520	570	604	630	652	682
$80,000	$90,000	883	933	965	989	1009	1035	1226	1388	1496	1579	1648	1743	558	611	647	675	698	730
$90,000	$100,000	940	994	1028	1054	1075	1103	1295	1466	1579	1667	1740	1840	594	650	688	717	742	776
$100,000	$120,000	1017	1076	1113	1141	1163	1194	1387	1569	1691	1785	1862	1970	641	702	743	774	801	837
$120,000	$140,000	1119	1184	1225	1256	1281	1315	1506	1704	1837	1938	2022	2139	704	770	815	850	878	918
$140,000	$160,000	1215	1286	1331	1364	1391	1428	1618	1830	1972	2081	2171	2297	764	835	883	920	951	995
$160,000	$180,000	1305	1381	1429	1465	1495	1534	1721	1947	2097	2213	2309	2442	819	895	946	986	1019	1065
$180,000	$200,000	1390	1472	1523	1562	1593	1636	1818	2057	2216	2338	2439	2580	872	952	1007	1049	1084	1133
$200,000	$225,000	1480	1567	1622	1664	1697	1743	1920	2172	2339	2469	2575	2724	927	1012	1070	1115	1152	1204
$225,000	$250,000	1577	1670	1730	1774	1810	1858	2029	2295	2472	2608	2721	2878	987	1077	1138	1186	1225	1281
$250,000	$275,000	1670	1769	1832	1879	1917	1968	2132	2411	2597	2740	2858	3023	1044	1139	1203	1254	1295	1353
$275,000	$300,000	1759	1864	1930	1980	2020	2074	2231	2522	2716	2866	2989	3162	1099	1198	1266	1319	1362	1423
$300,000	or more	2301	2439	2528	2593	2647	2719	2815	3181	3425	3613	3769	3985	1430	1557	1644	1711	1767	1845

2016 Optional State Sales Tax Tables

Nebraska — 5.5000% (Exemption 1)

Income At least	But less than	1	2	3	4	5	Over 5
$0	$20,000	247	268	282	292	301	312
$20,000	$30,000	398	433	456	473	486	506
$30,000	$40,000	481	523	551	571	588	611
$40,000	$50,000	554	603	634	658	678	704
$50,000	$60,000	620	675	710	737	759	789
$60,000	$70,000	681	741	780	809	833	866
$70,000	$80,000	737	802	845	877	903	939
$80,000	$90,000	790	860	906	940	968	1007
$90,000	$100,000	840	915	964	1000	1030	1071
$100,000	$120,000	908	989	1042	1081	1114	1158
$120,000	$140,000	997	1086	1144	1188	1223	1272
$140,000	$160,000	1081	1178	1240	1288	1327	1380
$160,000	$180,000	1159	1263	1330	1381	1423	1480
$180,000	$200,000	1233	1344	1416	1471	1515	1576
$200,000	$225,000	1311	1430	1506	1564	1611	1676
$225,000	$250,000	1396	1522	1604	1666	1716	1785
$250,000	$275,000	1476	1610	1696	1762	1815	1888
$275,000	$300,000	1553	1694	1785	1854	1911	1988
$300,000	or more	2020	2205	2325	2415	2488	2589

Nevada — 6.8500% (Exemption 5)

Income At least	But less than	1	2	3	4	5	Over 5
$0	$20,000	261	281	294	304	312	323
$20,000	$30,000	421	451	472	487	500	518
$30,000	$40,000	508	544	569	587	602	624
$40,000	$50,000	585	626	654	675	692	716
$50,000	$60,000	655	701	731	755	774	801
$60,000	$70,000	719	769	802	828	849	878
$70,000	$80,000	779	832	868	896	918	950
$80,000	$90,000	835	892	930	960	984	1017
$90,000	$100,000	888	948	989	1020	1046	1081
$100,000	$120,000	960	1024	1068	1101	1129	1167
$120,000	$140,000	1054	1125	1172	1208	1238	1280
$140,000	$160,000	1143	1219	1270	1309	1341	1386
$160,000	$180,000	1226	1306	1361	1403	1437	1485
$180,000	$200,000	1305	1390	1448	1492	1529	1579
$200,000	$225,000	1388	1478	1539	1586	1625	1678
$225,000	$250,000	1477	1573	1637	1687	1728	1785
$250,000	$275,000	1562	1663	1731	1783	1827	1887
$275,000	$300,000	1645	1750	1821	1876	1921	1984
$300,000	or more	2141	2275	2366	2435	2493	2573

New Jersey — 7.0000% (Exemption 4)

Income At least	But less than	1	2	3	4	5	Over 5
$0	$20,000	273	285	293	299	304	311
$20,000	$30,000	448	468	482	492	500	512
$30,000	$40,000	545	570	586	598	608	622
$40,000	$50,000	631	659	678	693	704	721
$50,000	$60,000	709	741	763	779	792	810
$60,000	$70,000	781	817	840	858	872	892
$70,000	$80,000	849	887	912	932	948	969
$80,000	$90,000	912	954	981	1002	1019	1042
$90,000	$100,000	972	1017	1046	1068	1086	1111
$100,000	$120,000	1054	1102	1133	1157	1177	1204
$120,000	$140,000	1161	1214	1249	1275	1297	1327
$140,000	$160,000	1262	1320	1358	1386	1410	1443
$160,000	$180,000	1357	1419	1460	1491	1516	1551
$180,000	$200,000	1448	1514	1557	1590	1617	1654
$200,000	$225,000	1543	1613	1660	1695	1724	1763
$225,000	$250,000	1646	1721	1771	1808	1839	1881
$250,000	$275,000	1745	1824	1876	1916	1949	1994
$275,000	$300,000	1839	1923	1978	2020	2055	2102
$300,000	or more	2416	2526	2598	2654	2699	2761

New Mexico — 5.1250% (Exemption 1)

Income At least	But less than	1	2	3	4	5	Over 5
$0	$20,000	257	276	289	298	306	316
$20,000	$30,000	409	441	461	476	488	505
$30,000	$40,000	492	530	554	572	587	607
$40,000	$50,000	564	608	636	657	673	697
$50,000	$60,000	630	678	710	733	752	778
$60,000	$70,000	689	743	777	803	823	852
$70,000	$80,000	745	803	840	868	890	921
$80,000	$90,000	797	859	899	929	953	985
$90,000	$100,000	847	912	955	986	1012	1047
$100,000	$120,000	913	984	1029	1064	1091	1129
$120,000	$140,000	1000	1078	1128	1165	1195	1237
$140,000	$160,000	1081	1166	1220	1260	1293	1338
$160,000	$180,000	1157	1248	1306	1349	1384	1432
$180,000	$200,000	1230	1326	1388	1434	1471	1522
$200,000	$225,000	1306	1408	1473	1522	1562	1616
$225,000	$250,000	1387	1496	1566	1618	1660	1718
$250,000	$275,000	1465	1580	1653	1709	1753	1814
$275,000	$300,000	1539	1660	1738	1796	1843	1907
$300,000	or more	1988	2145	2245	2320	2381	2464

New York — 4.0000% (Exemption 2)

Income At least	But less than	1	2	3	4	5	Over 5
$0	$20,000	159	167	173	177	180	185
$20,000	$30,000	260	273	282	289	294	301
$30,000	$40,000	316	332	342	350	357	366
$40,000	$50,000	365	383	395	404	412	422
$50,000	$60,000	409	430	444	454	462	474
$60,000	$70,000	450	473	488	499	509	522
$70,000	$80,000	489	513	529	542	552	566
$80,000	$90,000	525	551	569	582	593	608
$90,000	$100,000	559	587	606	620	631	647
$100,000	$120,000	605	635	656	671	683	701
$120,000	$140,000	666	699	721	738	752	771
$140,000	$160,000	723	760	783	802	817	837
$160,000	$180,000	777	816	841	861	877	899
$180,000	$200,000	828	869	897	918	935	958
$200,000	$225,000	882	926	955	977	996	1021
$225,000	$250,000	940	987	1018	1042	1061	1088
$250,000	$275,000	995	1045	1078	1103	1124	1152
$275,000	$300,000	1049	1101	1136	1162	1184	1214
$300,000	or more	1373	1441	1486	1521	1549	1588

North Carolina — 4.7500% (Exemption 2)

Income At least	But less than	1	2	3	4	5	Over 5
$0	$20,000	247	274	292	306	317	333
$20,000	$30,000	385	427	455	477	494	518
$30,000	$40,000	459	509	542	568	588	617
$40,000	$50,000	523	580	618	647	670	703
$50,000	$60,000	580	644	686	718	744	781
$60,000	$70,000	633	702	748	783	811	851
$70,000	$80,000	681	756	805	843	874	916
$80,000	$90,000	727	806	859	899	932	977
$90,000	$100,000	769	854	909	952	987	1035
$100,000	$120,000	827	917	977	1023	1060	1112
$120,000	$140,000	901	1000	1065	1115	1156	1212
$140,000	$160,000	971	1078	1148	1202	1245	1306
$160,000	$180,000	1036	1150	1225	1282	1329	1393
$180,000	$200,000	1098	1218	1297	1358	1407	1476
$200,000	$225,000	1162	1290	1373	1437	1490	1562
$225,000	$250,000	1231	1366	1455	1523	1578	1655
$250,000	$275,000	1297	1439	1532	1604	1662	1743
$275,000	$300,000	1360	1509	1606	1681	1743	1828
$300,000	or more	1735	1924	2049	2145	2223	2331

North Dakota — 5.0000% (Exemption 1)

Income At least	But less than	1	2	3	4	5	Over 5
$0	$20,000	183	200	212	221	229	239
$20,000	$30,000	295	322	340	355	367	383
$30,000	$40,000	357	389	411	428	442	462
$40,000	$50,000	411	447	472	492	508	531
$50,000	$60,000	461	501	528	550	568	593
$60,000	$70,000	506	549	580	603	623	650
$70,000	$80,000	548	595	627	653	674	704
$80,000	$90,000	588	638	672	699	722	754
$90,000	$100,000	626	678	715	743	767	801
$100,000	$120,000	676	733	772	803	828	864
$120,000	$140,000	743	805	847	881	909	948
$140,000	$160,000	806	872	918	954	984	1027
$160,000	$180,000	865	935	984	1023	1055	1100
$180,000	$200,000	921	995	1047	1088	1122	1170
$200,000	$225,000	980	1059	1113	1156	1192	1243
$225,000	$250,000	1044	1127	1185	1230	1269	1322
$250,000	$275,000	1104	1192	1253	1301	1341	1397
$275,000	$300,000	1163	1254	1318	1368	1410	1470
$300,000	or more	1516	1632	1713	1777	1831	1907

Ohio — 5.7500% (Exemption 1)

Income At least	But less than	1	2	3	4	5	Over 5
$0	$20,000	248	266	278	287	294	304
$20,000	$30,000	403	432	451	466	477	494
$30,000	$40,000	488	523	546	564	578	598
$40,000	$50,000	564	604	630	650	667	690
$50,000	$60,000	632	677	707	729	748	773
$60,000	$70,000	695	744	777	801	822	849
$70,000	$80,000	754	807	842	869	891	921
$80,000	$90,000	810	866	904	932	956	988
$90,000	$100,000	862	922	962	992	1017	1052
$100,000	$120,000	933	998	1041	1073	1100	1137
$120,000	$140,000	1026	1097	1144	1180	1209	1250
$140,000	$160,000	1114	1191	1242	1281	1312	1357
$160,000	$180,000	1196	1278	1333	1374	1409	1456
$180,000	$200,000	1274	1362	1420	1464	1500	1551
$200,000	$225,000	1356	1449	1511	1558	1597	1650
$225,000	$250,000	1445	1544	1610	1660	1701	1758
$250,000	$275,000	1530	1635	1704	1757	1800	1860
$275,000	$300,000	1612	1721	1794	1850	1895	1958
$300,000	or more	2106	2248	2343	2415	2474	2555

Oklahoma — 4.5000% (Exemption 1)

Income At least	But less than	1	2	3	4	5	Over 5
$0	$20,000	252	285	308	326	341	362
$20,000	$30,000	392	443	478	505	528	559
$30,000	$40,000	468	528	568	600	627	664
$40,000	$50,000	533	601	647	683	713	755
$50,000	$60,000	592	667	718	757	790	837
$60,000	$70,000	646	727	782	825	861	911
$70,000	$80,000	696	782	841	887	926	980
$80,000	$90,000	743	834	897	946	987	1044
$90,000	$100,000	787	883	949	1001	1044	1104
$100,000	$120,000	846	949	1020	1075	1121	1185
$120,000	$140,000	924	1035	1111	1171	1221	1291
$140,000	$160,000	996	1115	1197	1261	1315	1390
$160,000	$180,000	1064	1190	1277	1345	1402	1481
$180,000	$200,000	1128	1261	1353	1424	1484	1568
$200,000	$225,000	1195	1335	1432	1507	1570	1659
$225,000	$250,000	1267	1415	1517	1596	1663	1756
$250,000	$275,000	1335	1490	1597	1681	1750	1849
$275,000	$300,000	1401	1563	1674	1762	1834	1937
$300,000	or more	1794	1996	2136	2245	2336	2465

Pennsylvania — 6.0000% (Exemption 1)

Income At least	But less than	1	2	3	4	5	Over 5
$0	$20,000	214	228	237	244	250	258
$20,000	$30,000	346	368	383	394	404	417
$30,000	$40,000	419	445	463	476	487	503
$40,000	$50,000	482	512	533	548	561	579
$50,000	$60,000	540	574	596	614	628	648
$60,000	$70,000	593	630	654	674	689	711
$70,000	$80,000	642	682	709	730	747	770
$80,000	$90,000	688	731	760	782	800	826
$90,000	$100,000	732	778	808	832	851	878
$100,000	$120,000	792	840	873	899	920	949
$120,000	$140,000	869	923	959	987	1010	1042
$140,000	$160,000	943	1000	1039	1069	1094	1129
$160,000	$180,000	1011	1073	1114	1147	1173	1210
$180,000	$200,000	1076	1142	1186	1220	1249	1288
$200,000	$225,000	1144	1214	1261	1298	1328	1369
$225,000	$250,000	1218	1292	1342	1381	1413	1457
$250,000	$275,000	1289	1367	1420	1460	1494	1541
$275,000	$300,000	1356	1438	1494	1537	1572	1621
$300,000	or more	1765	1871	1943	1998	2044	2108

Rhode Island — 7.0000% (Exemption 4)

Income At least	But less than	1	2	3	4	5	Over 5
$0	$20,000	283	301	312	321	328	337
$20,000	$30,000	448	477	495	509	520	535
$30,000	$40,000	538	572	594	610	624	642
$40,000	$50,000	616	655	680	699	715	736
$50,000	$60,000	686	730	759	780	797	821
$60,000	$70,000	751	799	830	853	872	898
$70,000	$80,000	810	863	896	921	942	970
$80,000	$90,000	866	922	958	985	1007	1037
$90,000	$100,000	919	979	1017	1046	1069	1101
$100,000	$120,000	990	1055	1096	1127	1152	1187
$120,000	$140,000	1084	1154	1199	1233	1261	1299
$140,000	$160,000	1171	1247	1296	1333	1363	1404
$160,000	$180,000	1252	1334	1387	1426	1458	1502
$180,000	$200,000	1329	1416	1472	1514	1548	1595
$200,000	$225,000	1410	1503	1562	1607	1643	1693
$225,000	$250,000	1498	1596	1659	1707	1745	1798
$250,000	$275,000	1580	1684	1751	1801	1842	1898
$275,000	$300,000	1660	1769	1839	1892	1935	1994
$300,000	or more	2137	2279	2370	2439	2494	2570

South Carolina — 6.0000% (Exemption 2)

Income At least	But less than	1	2	3	4	5	Over 5
$0	$20,000	263	283	296	306	314	324
$20,000	$30,000	421	454	475	490	503	520
$30,000	$40,000	507	546	572	591	606	627
$40,000	$50,000	583	628	657	679	696	721
$50,000	$60,000	651	702	734	759	778	806
$60,000	$70,000	713	769	805	832	853	883
$70,000	$80,000	772	832	871	900	923	956
$80,000	$90,000	826	891	932	964	989	1023
$90,000	$100,000	878	947	991	1024	1051	1088
$100,000	$120,000	948	1022	1070	1105	1134	1174
$120,000	$140,000	1039	1120	1173	1212	1244	1288
$140,000	$160,000	1125	1213	1270	1313	1347	1394
$160,000	$180,000	1205	1299	1360	1406	1443	1494
$180,000	$200,000	1281	1382	1447	1495	1535	1589
$200,000	$225,000	1361	1468	1537	1589	1631	1688
$225,000	$250,000	1447	1561	1634	1690	1734	1795
$250,000	$275,000	1529	1650	1727	1785	1833	1897
$275,000	$300,000	1607	1734	1816	1877	1927	1995
$300,000	or more	2082	2247	2353	2433	2498	2586

South Dakota (footnote 1, 4.2923%) · Tennessee (footnote 2, 7.0000%) · Texas (footnote 1, 6.2500%)

Income At least	But less than	SD 1	SD 2	SD 3	SD 4	SD 5	SD Over 5	TN 1	TN 2	TN 3	TN 4	TN 5	TN Over 5	TX 1	TX 2	TX 3	TX 4	TX 5	TX Over 5
$0	$20,000	269	307	332	352	368	391	384	429	459	483	502	529	276	303	321	334	345	360
$20,000	$30,000	412	469	508	537	562	596	602	671	718	754	784	826	445	489	518	540	558	583
$30,000	$40,000	487	555	600	635	664	704	719	801	857	899	935	984	537	590	625	652	674	704
$40,000	$50,000	552	628	679	719	752	797	821	915	977	1026	1066	1122	618	680	720	751	777	812
$50,000	$60,000	610	694	751	794	830	881	914	1017	1086	1140	1184	1246	691	761	806	841	870	909
$60,000	$70,000	663	754	815	863	902	956	998	1110	1185	1243	1291	1359	759	835	885	924	955	998
$70,000	$80,000	711	809	875	926	967	1026	1076	1196	1277	1339	1391	1463	821	905	959	1001	1035	1082
$80,000	$90,000	757	861	930	984	1029	1091	1149	1277	1363	1429	1484	1561	881	970	1028	1073	1109	1160
$90,000	$100,000	799	909	983	1039	1086	1152	1218	1353	1444	1514	1572	1653	936	1032	1094	1141	1180	1234
$100,000	$120,000	856	973	1052	1113	1163	1233	1310	1455	1552	1628	1690	1777	1012	1115	1182	1234	1276	1334
$120,000	$140,000	930	1057	1143	1209	1263	1340	1431	1588	1694	1776	1844	1939	1111	1224	1298	1355	1401	1465
$140,000	$160,000	999	1136	1227	1298	1357	1438	1545	1714	1827	1915	1988	2090	1204	1327	1408	1469	1519	1589
$160,000	$180,000	1063	1208	1305	1381	1443	1530	1650	1830	1951	2044	2122	2230	1291	1423	1510	1576	1630	1704
$180,000	$200,000	1123	1277	1379	1459	1524	1616	1751	1940	2068	2167	2249	2363	1373	1514	1607	1677	1735	1815
$200,000	$225,000	1186	1348	1456	1540	1609	1706	1856	2056	2191	2295	2382	2503	1460	1610	1709	1784	1845	1930
$225,000	$250,000	1254	1425	1539	1628	1701	1803	1969	2180	2323	2433	2525	2653	1554	1714	1819	1899	1965	2055
$250,000	$275,000	1318	1497	1617	1710	1787	1894	2076	2298	2448	2564	2660	2794	1643	1813	1924	2009	2078	2174
$275,000	$300,000	1379	1566	1692	1789	1869	1981	2178	2411	2568	2689	2790	2930	1729	1908	2025	2114	2187	2288
$300,000	or more	1741	1976	2134	2256	2357	2498	2795	3088	3286	3440	3567	3745	2248	2482	2636	2753	2848	2980

Utah (footnote 2, 4.7000%) · Vermont (footnote 1, 6.0000%) · Virginia (footnote 2, 4.3000%)

Income At least	But less than	UT 1	UT 2	UT 3	UT 4	UT 5	UT Over 5	VT 1	VT 2	VT 3	VT 4	VT 5	VT Over 5	VA 1	VA 2	VA 3	VA 4	VA 5	VA Over 5
$0	$20,000	249	277	296	311	323	340	163	169	173	175	178	181	181	199	211	221	228	239
$20,000	$30,000	392	436	466	489	507	533	259	269	275	280	284	289	287	314	333	348	360	376
$30,000	$40,000	470	522	557	584	606	637	312	323	331	336	341	348	344	377	399	416	430	450
$40,000	$50,000	537	596	636	667	692	728	357	371	379	386	392	399	394	431	457	476	492	515
$50,000	$60,000	599	664	708	742	770	809	399	414	424	431	437	446	440	481	509	530	548	573
$60,000	$70,000	654	725	773	810	841	883	436	453	464	472	479	488	481	526	556	579	599	626
$70,000	$80,000	706	782	834	874	906	952	472	490	502	511	518	528	520	568	600	625	646	675
$80,000	$90,000	754	836	891	933	968	1017	504	524	537	546	554	565	556	607	641	668	690	721
$90,000	$100,000	800	886	944	989	1026	1078	536	557	570	580	589	600	590	644	680	709	732	765
$100,000	$120,000	862	954	1016	1064	1104	1159	577	600	615	626	635	648	636	694	733	763	788	823
$120,000	$140,000	942	1043	1110	1162	1206	1266	632	657	674	686	696	710	697	759	802	834	862	900
$140,000	$160,000	1018	1126	1198	1255	1301	1366	684	711	729	742	753	768	754	821	866	901	931	972
$160,000	$180,000	1088	1203	1280	1340	1390	1459	732	761	780	795	806	822	806	878	926	964	995	1038
$180,000	$200,000	1155	1276	1358	1421	1474	1547	778	809	829	845	857	874	857	932	983	1023	1056	1102
$200,000	$225,000	1225	1353	1440	1507	1562	1639	826	859	881	897	910	928	910	989	1043	1085	1120	1168
$225,000	$250,000	1300	1436	1527	1598	1657	1739	877	913	936	953	968	987	967	1050	1107	1152	1188	1240
$250,000	$275,000	1372	1514	1611	1685	1747	1833	926	964	988	1007	1022	1043	1021	1109	1168	1215	1254	1308
$275,000	$300,000	1440	1590	1690	1768	1833	1923	973	1013	1039	1058	1074	1096	1073	1165	1227	1276	1316	1373
$300,000	or more	1853	2042	2170	2268	2350	2465	1257	1309	1343	1369	1390	1418	1386	1501	1580	1642	1693	1764

Washington (footnote 1, 6.5000%) · West Virginia (footnote 1, 6.0000%) · Wisconsin (footnote 1, 5.0000%)

Income At least	But less than	WA 1	WA 2	WA 3	WA 4	WA 5	WA Over 5	WV 1	WV 2	WV 3	WV 4	WV 5	WV Over 5	WI 1	WI 2	WI 3	WI 4	WI 5	WI Over 5
$0	$20,000	280	304	320	333	343	357	269	293	309	321	331	345	228	246	258	266	274	283
$20,000	$30,000	457	496	523	543	559	582	434	474	501	520	537	559	367	396	416	430	442	458
$30,000	$40,000	554	602	634	658	678	706	525	573	605	630	649	676	443	479	502	520	534	553
$40,000	$50,000	641	695	732	760	783	815	604	661	698	726	748	780	509	551	578	598	615	637
$50,000	$60,000	719	781	821	853	879	915	677	740	782	813	839	874	570	617	647	670	688	714
$60,000	$70,000	791	859	904	938	966	1006	743	813	859	893	921	960	625	677	710	735	756	784
$70,000	$80,000	859	932	980	1018	1048	1091	805	881	930	968	999	1041	677	733	769	797	819	849
$80,000	$90,000	922	1000	1052	1093	1125	1171	863	945	998	1038	1071	1117	726	786	825	854	878	910
$90,000	$100,000	983	1066	1121	1164	1199	1247	918	1005	1062	1105	1140	1188	772	836	877	908	934	968
$100,000	$120,000	1064	1153	1213	1259	1297	1350	992	1087	1148	1195	1233	1285	834	903	948	982	1009	1046
$120,000	$140,000	1171	1269	1335	1385	1427	1485	1090	1194	1261	1313	1355	1412	915	992	1041	1078	1108	1149
$140,000	$160,000	1272	1379	1450	1504	1550	1612	1182	1295	1368	1424	1470	1532	992	1075	1128	1169	1201	1246
$160,000	$180,000	1366	1480	1557	1616	1664	1731	1268	1389	1468	1528	1577	1644	1064	1153	1210	1253	1288	1336
$180,000	$200,000	1456	1578	1659	1722	1773	1845	1349	1479	1563	1627	1679	1751	1132	1227	1288	1334	1371	1423
$200,000	$225,000	1551	1680	1767	1833	1888	1964	1435	1573	1663	1731	1787	1863	1203	1304	1370	1419	1458	1513
$225,000	$250,000	1654	1791	1883	1954	2012	2093	1528	1675	1771	1844	1903	1985	1281	1388	1458	1510	1553	1611
$250,000	$275,000	1751	1897	1994	2069	2130	2216	1616	1772	1874	1951	2013	2100	1354	1468	1542	1597	1642	1704
$275,000	$300,000	1845	1998	2101	2179	2244	2334	1701	1865	1972	2053	2120	2211	1425	1545	1622	1681	1728	1793
$300,000	or more	2416	2615	2748	2850	2934	3052	2215	2430	2571	2677	2764	2884	1852	2009	2111	2187	2249	2334

Wyoming (footnote 1, 4.0000%)

Income At least	But less than	1	2	3	4	5	Over 5
$0	$20,000	171	183	192	198	203	210
$20,000	$30,000	280	300	313	323	332	343
$30,000	$40,000	340	364	380	392	402	416
$40,000	$50,000	393	421	439	453	465	481
$50,000	$60,000	441	472	493	509	522	540
$60,000	$70,000	485	520	543	560	574	594
$70,000	$80,000	527	564	589	608	623	645
$80,000	$90,000	566	606	633	653	669	692
$90,000	$100,000	603	646	674	695	713	737
$100,000	$120,000	653	699	730	753	772	798
$120,000	$140,000	719	770	803	829	850	879
$140,000	$160,000	781	836	872	900	923	954
$160,000	$180,000	839	898	937	967	991	1025
$180,000	$200,000	895	957	999	1031	1057	1092
$200,000	$225,000	953	1020	1064	1098	1125	1163
$225,000	$250,000	1017	1087	1134	1170	1200	1240
$250,000	$275,000	1077	1152	1201	1239	1270	1313
$275,000	$300,000	1135	1214	1266	1306	1338	1384
$300,000	or more	1487	1590	1658	1710	1752	1811

Note: Residents of **Alaska** do not have a state sales tax, but should follow the instructions on the next page to determine their local sales tax amount.

1 Use the Ratio Method to determine your local sales tax deduction, then add that to the appropriate amount in the state table. Your state sales tax rate is provided next to the state name.

2 Follow the instructions on the next page to determine your local sales tax deduction, then add that to the appropriate amount in the state table.

3 The California table includes the 1.25% uniform local sales tax rate in addition to the 6.25% state sales tax rate for a total of 7.50%. Some California localities impose a larger local sales tax. Taxpayers who reside in those jurisdictions should use the Ratio Method to determine their local sales tax deduction, then add that to the appropriate amount in the state table. The denominator of the correct ratio is 7.50%, and the numerator is the total sales tax rate minus 7.50%.

4 This state does not have a local general sales tax, so the amount in the state table is the only amount to be deducted.

5 The Nevada table includes the 2.25% uniform local sales tax rate in addition to the 4.6000% state sales tax rate for a total of 6.85%. Some Nevada localities impose a larger local sales tax. Taxpayers who reside in those jurisdictions should use the Ratio Method to determine their local sales tax deduction, then add that to the appropriate amount in the state table. The denominator of the correct ratio is 6.85%, and the numerator is the total sales tax rate minus 6.85%.

6 The 4.0% rate for Hawaii is actually an excise tax but is treated as a sales tax for purpose of this deduction.

Which Optional Local Sales Tax Table Should I Use?

IF you live in the state of...	AND you live in...	THEN use Local Table...
Alaska	Any locality	C
Arizona	Mesa, Phoenix	A
	Chandler, Glendale, Gilbert, Peoria, Scottsdale, Tempe, Tucson, Yuma, or any other locality	B
Arkansas	Any Locality	B
Colorado	Adams County, Arapahoe County, Boulder County, Centennial, Colorado Springs, Denver City/Denver County, El Paso County, Larimer County, Pueblo County, or any other locality	A
	Aurora, Boulder, Fort Collins, Greeley, Jefferson County, Lakewood, Longmont, or Pueblo City	B
	Arvada, Thornton, or Westminster	C
Georgia	Any locality	B
Illinois	Aurora, Elgin, or Waukegan	B
	Arlington Heights, Bloomington, Champaign, Chicago, Cicero, Decatur, Evanston, Joliet, Palatine, Peoria, Schaumburg, Skokie, Springfield, or any other locality	A
Louisiana	Ascension Parish, Bossier Parish, Caddo Parish, East Baton Rouge Parish, Iberia Parish, Jefferson Parish, Lafayette Parish, Lafourche Parish, Livingston Parish, Orleans Parish, Ouachita Parish, Rapides Parish, St. Bernard Parish, St. Landry Parish, St Tammany Parish, Tangipahoa Parish, or Terrebonne Parish	C
	Calcasieu Parish or any other locality	B
Mississippi	City of Jackson only	A
	City of Tupelo only	B
Missouri	Any locality	B
New York	Counties: Albany, Allegany, Broome, Cattaraugus, Cayuga, Chemung, Clinton, Cortland, Dutchess, Erie, Essex, Franklin, Fulton, Genesee, Herkimer, Jefferson, Lewis, Livingston, Madison, Monroe, Montgomery, Nassau, Niagara, Oneida, Onondaga, Ontario, Orange, Orleans, Oswego, Otsego, Putnam, Rensselaer, Rockland, St. Lawrence, Saratoga, Schenectady, Schoharie, Schuyler, Seneca, Steuben, Suffolk, Sullivan, Tompkins, Ulster, Warren, Washington, Westchester, Wyoming, or Yates Cities: Olean, Salamanca, Auburn, Gloversville, Johnstown, Oneida (Madison County), Rome, Utica, Oswego, Saratoga Springs, Ithaca, Glens Falls, Mount Vernon, New Rochelle, White Plains, Yonkers	B
	Counties: Chautauqua, Chenango, Columbia, Columbia, Delaware, Greene, Hamilton, Tioga, Wayne Cities: New York or Norwich (Chenango County)	A
	Any other locality	D*
North Carolina	Any locality	A
South Carolina	Aiken County, Andersonn County, Bamberg County, Charleston County, Cherokee County, Chesterfield County, Colleton County, Darlington County, Dillon County, Florence County, Georgetown County, Hampton County, Horry County, Jasper County, Lee County, Lexington County, Marion County, Marlboro County, Newberry County, Orangeburg County, York County, or any other locality	B
Tennessee	Any locality	B
Utah	Any locality	A
Virginia	Any locality	B

* Note: Local Table D is just 25% of the NY State table.

2016 Optional Local Sales Tax Tables

Income		Exemptions						Exemptions						Exemptions						Exemptions					
At least	But less than	1	2	3	4	5	Over 5	1	2	3	4	5	Over 5	1	2	3	4	5	Over 5	1	2	3	4	5	Over 5
		Local Table A						Local Table B						Local Table C						Local Table D					
$0	$20,000	37	40	42	43	44	46	48	54	58	61	63	67	60	68	73	77	80	85	40	42	43	44	45	46
20,000	30,000	60	64	67	69	71	73	75	83	89	94	98	103	92	104	112	118	123	130	65	68	71	72	74	75
30,000	40,000	72	77	81	83	86	88	89	99	106	111	116	122	110	123	132	140	145	154	79	83	86	88	89	92
40,000	50,000	83	89	93	96	98	102	101	113	121	127	132	139	124	140	150	158	165	174	91	96	99	101	103	106
50,000	60,000	93	100	104	107	110	114	112	125	134	140	146	153	138	155	166	175	182	193	102	108	111	114	116	119
60,000	70,000	103	110	114	118	121	125	123	136	146	153	159	167	150	168	181	190	198	209	113	118	122	125	127	131
70,000	80,000	111	119	124	127	131	135	132	147	157	164	171	180	161	181	194	204	213	225	122	128	132	136	138	142
80,000	90,000	119	127	133	137	140	145	141	156	167	175	182	191	172	193	207	218	227	239	131	138	142	146	148	152
90,000	100,000	127	135	141	145	149	154	149	165	177	185	192	202	182	204	218	230	239	253	140	147	152	155	158	162
100,000	120,000	137	146	152	157	161	166	160	178	190	199	206	217	195	218	234	246	256	271	151	159	164	168	171	175
120,000	140,000	151	160	167	172	176	182	174	194	206	216	225	236	212	238	255	268	279	294	167	175	180	185	188	193
140,000	160,000	163	174	181	187	191	198	188	208	222	233	242	254	228	255	274	288	300	316	181	190	196	201	204	209
160,000	180,000	175	187	194	200	205	212	200	222	237	248	258	271	243	272	291	307	319	336	194	204	210	215	219	225
180,000	200,000	187	199	207	213	218	225	212	235	251	263	273	287	257	288	308	324	337	356	207	217	224	230	234	240
200,000	225,000	198	211	220	226	232	239	225	249	265	278	289	303	272	304	326	343	356	376	221	232	239	244	249	255
225,000	250,000	211	225	234	241	247	255	238	264	281	294	305	321	288	322	345	362	377	397	235	247	255	261	265	272
250,000	275,000	224	238	247	255	261	269	251	278	296	310	321	338	303	338	362	381	396	418	249	261	270	276	281	288
275,000	300,000	235	250	260	268	274	283	263	291	310	325	337	354	317	354	379	399	415	437	262	275	284	291	296	304
300,000	or more	307	325	338	348	356	368	336	371	394	413	428	449	403	449	481	505	525	553	343	360	372	380	387	397

Appendix B

Tax Forms

(Tax forms can be obtained from the IRS website: **www.irs.gov**)

Form **1040**   Department of the Treasury—Internal Revenue Service   (99)
U.S. Individual Income Tax Return   **2016**   OMB No. 1545-0074   IRS Use Only—Do not write or staple in this space.

For the year Jan. 1–Dec. 31, 2016, or other tax year beginning ____ , 2016, ending ____ , 20 ____   See separate instructions.

Your first name and initial	Last name	Your social security number

If a joint return, spouse's first name and initial	Last name	Spouse's social security number

Home address (number and street). If you have a P.O. box, see instructions.   Apt. no.

▲ Make sure the SSN(s) above and on line 6c are correct.

City, town or post office, state, and ZIP code. If you have a foreign address, also complete spaces below (see instructions).

Presidential Election Campaign
Check here if you, or your spouse if filing jointly, want $3 to go to this fund. Checking a box below will not change your tax or refund.   ☐ You   ☐ Spouse

Foreign country name	Foreign province/state/county	Foreign postal code

Filing Status

Check only one box.

1 ☐ Single
2 ☐ Married filing jointly (even if only one had income)
3 ☐ Married filing separately. Enter spouse's SSN above and full name here. ▶
4 ☐ Head of household (with qualifying person). (See instructions.) If the qualifying person is a child but not your dependent, enter this child's name here. ▶
5 ☐ Qualifying widow(er) with dependent child

Exemptions

6a ☐ **Yourself.** If someone can claim you as a dependent, **do not** check box 6a . . . . .
  b ☐ **Spouse** . . . .

Boxes checked on 6a and 6b ____
No. of children on 6c who:
• lived with you ____
• did not live with you due to divorce or separation (see instructions) ____
Dependents on 6c not entered above ____
Add numbers on lines above ▶ ____

c **Dependents:**

(1) First name Last name	(2) Dependent's social security number	(3) Dependent's relationship to you	(4) ✓ if child under age 17 qualifying for child tax credit (see instructions)
			☐
			☐
			☐
			☐

If more than four dependents, see instructions and check here ▶ ☐

d   Total number of exemptions claimed

Income

Attach Form(s) W-2 here. Also attach Forms W-2G and 1099-R if tax was withheld.

If you did not get a W-2, see instructions.

7	Wages, salaries, tips, etc. Attach Form(s) W-2	7
8a	**Taxable** interest. Attach Schedule B if required	8a
b	**Tax-exempt** interest. **Do not** include on line 8a 8b	
9a	Ordinary dividends. Attach Schedule B if required	9a
b	Qualified dividends 9b	
10	Taxable refunds, credits, or offsets of state and local income taxes	10
11	Alimony received	11
12	Business income or (loss). Attach Schedule C or C-EZ	12
13	Capital gain or (loss). Attach Schedule D if required. If not required, check here ▶ ☐	13
14	Other gains or (losses). Attach Form 4797	14
15a	IRA distributions 15a b Taxable amount	15b
16a	Pensions and annuities 16a b Taxable amount	16b
17	Rental real estate, royalties, partnerships, S corporations, trusts, etc. Attach Schedule E	17
18	Farm income or (loss). Attach Schedule F	18
19	Unemployment compensation	19
20a	Social security benefits 20a b Taxable amount	20b
21	Other income. List type and amount	21
22	Combine the amounts in the far right column for lines 7 through 21. This is your **total income** ▶	22

Adjusted Gross Income

23	Educator expenses 23	
24	Certain business expenses of reservists, performing artists, and fee-basis government officials. Attach Form 2106 or 2106-EZ 24	
25	Health savings account deduction. Attach Form 8889 25	
26	Moving expenses. Attach Form 3903 26	
27	Deductible part of self-employment tax. Attach Schedule SE 27	
28	Self-employed SEP, SIMPLE, and qualified plans 28	
29	Self-employed health insurance deduction 29	
30	Penalty on early withdrawal of savings 30	
31a	Alimony paid b Recipient's SSN ▶ 31a	
32	IRA deduction 32	
33	Student loan interest deduction 33	
34	Tuition and fees. Attach Form 8917 34	
35	Domestic production activities deduction. Attach Form 8903 35	
36	Add lines 23 through 35	36
37	Subtract line 36 from line 22. This is your **adjusted gross income** ▶	37

For Disclosure, Privacy Act, and Paperwork Reduction Act Notice, see separate instructions.   Cat. No. 11320B   Form **1040** (2016)

Form 1040 (2016)

Page **2**

Tax and Credits	38	Amount from line 37 (adjusted gross income)	38	

	39a	Check if: ☐ **You** were born before January 2, 1952, ☐ Blind. ☐ **Spouse** was born before January 2, 1952, ☐ Blind. **Total boxes** checked ▶ 39a ☐	
	b	If your spouse itemizes on a separate return or you were a dual-status alien, check here▶ 39b☐	

Standard Deduction for—

- People who check any box on line 39a or 39b **or** who can be claimed as a dependent, see instructions.
- All others:

Single or Married filing separately, $6,300

Married filing jointly or Qualifying widow(er), $12,600

Head of household, $9,300

40	**Itemized deductions** (from Schedule A) **or** your **standard deduction** (see left margin) . .	40
41	Subtract line 40 from line 38	41
42	**Exemptions.** If line 38 is $155,650 or less, multiply $4,050 by the number on line 6d. Otherwise, see instructions	42
43	**Taxable income.** Subtract line 42 from line 41. If line 42 is more than line 41, enter -0- . .	43
44	**Tax** (see instructions). Check if any from: **a** ☐ Form(s) 8814 **b** ☐ Form 4972 **c** ☐	44
45	**Alternative minimum tax** (see instructions). Attach Form 6251	45
46	Excess advance premium tax credit repayment. Attach Form 8962	46
47	Add lines 44, 45, and 46 . . . . ▶	47

48	Foreign tax credit. Attach Form 1116 if required . .	48	
49	Credit for child and dependent care expenses. Attach Form 2441	49	
50	Education credits from Form 8863, line 19	50	
51	Retirement savings contributions credit. Attach Form 8880	51	
52	Child tax credit. Attach Schedule 8812, if required . . .	52	
53	Residential energy credits. Attach Form 5695 . . .	53	
54	Other credits from Form: **a** ☐ 3800 **b** ☐ 8801 **c** ☐	54	
55	Add lines 48 through 54. These are your **total credits**	55	
56	Subtract line 55 from line 47. If line 55 is more than line 47, enter -0- . . . . ▶	56	

Other Taxes

57	Self-employment tax. Attach Schedule SE	57
58	Unreported social security and Medicare tax from Form: **a** ☐ 4137 **b** ☐ 8919 . .	58
59	Additional tax on IRAs, other qualified retirement plans, etc. Attach Form 5329 if required . .	59
60a	Household employment taxes from Schedule H	60a
b	First-time homebuyer credit repayment. Attach Form 5405 if required	60b
61	Health care: individual responsibility (see instructions) Full-year coverage ☐	61
62	Taxes from: **a** ☐ Form 8959 **b** ☐ Form 8960 **c** ☐ Instructions; enter code(s)	62
63	Add lines 56 through 62. This is your **total tax** . . . . ▶	63

Payments

If you have a qualifying child, attach Schedule EIC.

64	Federal income tax withheld from Forms W-2 and 1099 . .	64	
65	2016 estimated tax payments and amount applied from 2015 return	65	
66a	**Earned income credit (EIC)**	66a	
b	Nontaxable combat pay election 66b ☐		
67	Additional child tax credit. Attach Schedule 8812 . . .	67	
68	American opportunity credit from Form 8863, line 8 . .	68	
69	Net premium tax credit. Attach Form 8962	69	
70	Amount paid with request for extension to file . . .	70	
71	Excess social security and tier 1 RRTA tax withheld . .	71	
72	Credit for federal tax on fuels. Attach Form 4136 . .	72	
73	Credits from Form: **a** ☐ 2439 **b** ☐ Reserved **c** ☐ 8885 **d** ☐	73	
74	Add lines 64, 65, 66a, and 67 through 73. These are your **total payments** . . . . ▶	74	

Refund

Direct deposit? See instructions.

75	If line 74 is more than line 63, subtract line 63 from line 74. This is the amount you **overpaid**	75
76a	Amount of line 75 you want **refunded to you.** If Form 8888 is attached, check here . . ▶ ☐	76a
▶ b	Routing number ┃┃┃┃┃┃┃┃┃ ▶ **c** Type: ☐ Checking ☐ Savings	
▶ d	Account number ┃┃┃┃┃┃┃┃┃┃┃┃┃┃┃┃┃	
77	Amount of line 75 you want **applied to your 2017 estimated tax** ▶ 77	

Amount You Owe

78	**Amount you owe.** Subtract line 74 from line 63. For details on how to pay, see instructions ▶	78
79	Estimated tax penalty (see instructions) 79	

Third Party Designee

Do you want to allow another person to discuss this return with the IRS (see instructions)? ☐ **Yes.** Complete below. ☐ **No**

Designee's name ▶	Phone no. ▶	Personal identification number (PIN) ▶

Sign Here

Joint return? See instructions. Keep a copy for your records.

Under penalties of perjury, I declare that I have examined this return and accompanying schedules and statements, and to the best of my knowledge and belief, they are true, correct, and accurately list all amounts and sources of income I received during the tax year. Declaration of preparer (other than taxpayer) is based on all information of which preparer has any knowledge.

Your signature	Date	Your occupation	Daytime phone number
Spouse's signature. If a joint return, **both** must sign.	Date	Spouse's occupation	If the IRS sent you an Identity Protection PIN, enter it here (see inst.)

Paid Preparer Use Only

Print/Type preparer's name	Preparer's signature	Date	Check ☐ if self-employed	PTIN
Firm's name ▶			Firm's EIN ▶	
Firm's address ▶			Phone no.	

Form **1040** (2016)

SCHEDULE A
(Form 1040)

Department of the Treasury
Internal Revenue Service (99)

Itemized Deductions

▶ Information about Schedule A and its separate instructions is at *www.irs.gov/schedulea*.
▶ **Attach to Form 1040.**

OMB No. 1545-0074

20**16**

Attachment
Sequence No. **07**

Name(s) shown on Form 1040

Your social security number

Caution: Do not include expenses reimbursed or paid by others.

Medical and Dental Expenses	**1** Medical and dental expenses (see instructions)	**1**
	2 Enter amount from Form 1040, line 38 `2`	
	3 Multiply line 2 by 10% (0.10). But if either you or your spouse was born before January 2, 1952, multiply line 2 by 7.5% (0.075) instead	**3**
	4 Subtract line 3 from line 1. If line 3 is more than line 1, enter -0-	**4**
Taxes You Paid	**5** State and local (**check only one box**):	
	a ☐ Income taxes, **or**	**5**
	b ☐ General sales taxes	
	6 Real estate taxes (see instructions)	**6**
	7 Personal property taxes	**7**
	8 Other taxes. List type and amount ▶ _____	**8**
	9 Add lines 5 through 8	**9**
Interest You Paid **Note:** Your mortgage interest deduction may be limited (see instructions).	**10** Home mortgage interest and points reported to you on Form 1098	**10**
	11 Home mortgage interest not reported to you on Form 1098. If paid to the person from whom you bought the home, see instructions and show that person's name, identifying no., and address ▶ _____	**11**
	12 Points not reported to you on Form 1098. See instructions for special rules	**12**
	13 Mortgage insurance premiums (see instructions)	**13**
	14 Investment interest. Attach Form 4952 if required. (See instructions.)	**14**
	15 Add lines 10 through 14	**15**
Gifts to Charity If you made a gift and got a benefit for it, see instructions.	**16** Gifts by cash or check. If you made any gift of $250 or more, see instructions	**16**
	17 Other than by cash or check. If any gift of $250 or more, see instructions. You **must** attach Form 8283 if over $500 . . .	**17**
	18 Carryover from prior year	**18**
	19 Add lines 16 through 18	**19**
Casualty and Theft Losses	**20** Casualty or theft loss(es). Attach Form 4684. (See instructions.)	**20**
Job Expenses and Certain Miscellaneous Deductions	**21** Unreimbursed employee expenses—job travel, union dues, job education, etc. Attach Form 2106 or 2106-EZ if required. (See instructions.) ▶ _____	**21**
	22 Tax preparation fees	**22**
	23 Other expenses—investment, safe deposit box, etc. List type and amount ▶ _____	**23**
	24 Add lines 21 through 23	**24**
	25 Enter amount from Form 1040, line 38 `25`	
	26 Multiply line 25 by 2% (0.02)	**26**
	27 Subtract line 26 from line 24. If line 26 is more than line 24, enter -0-	**27**
Other Miscellaneous Deductions	**28** Other—from list in instructions. List type and amount ▶ _____	**28**
Total Itemized Deductions	**29** Is Form 1040, line 38, over $155,650?	
	☐ **No.** Your deduction is not limited. Add the amounts in the far right column for lines 4 through 28. Also, enter this amount on Form 1040, line 40.	**29**
	☐ **Yes.** Your deduction may be limited. See the Itemized Deductions Worksheet in the instructions to figure the amount to enter.	
	30 If you elect to itemize deductions even though they are less than your standard deduction, check here . . . . ▶ ☐	

For Paperwork Reduction Act Notice, see Form 1040 instructions.

Cat. No. 17145C

Schedule A (Form 1040) 2016

SCHEDULE B
(Form 1040A or 1040)

Department of the Treasury
Internal Revenue Service (99)

Interest and Ordinary Dividends

▶ **Attach to Form 1040A or 1040.**
▶ **Information about Schedule B and its instructions is at** *www.irs.gov/scheduleb*.

OMB No. 1545-0074

2016

Attachment
Sequence No. **08**

Name(s) shown on return

Your social security number

			Amount
Part I **Interest** (See instructions on back and the instructions for Form 1040A, or Form 1040, line 8a.) **Note:** If you received a Form 1099-INT, Form 1099-OID, or substitute statement from a brokerage firm, list the firm's name as the payer and enter the total interest shown on that form.	**1**	List name of payer. If any interest is from a seller-financed mortgage and the buyer used the property as a personal residence, see instructions on back and list this interest first. Also, show that buyer's social security number and address ▶ -- -- -- -- -- -- -- -- -- -- -- --	**1**	
	2	Add the amounts on line 1	**2**	
	3	Excludable interest on series EE and I U.S. savings bonds issued after 1989. Attach Form 8815	**3**	
	4	Subtract line 3 from line 2. Enter the result here and on Form 1040A, or Form 1040, line 8a . . . . ▶	**4**	
Note: If line 4 is over $1,500, you must complete Part III.				Amount
Part II **Ordinary Dividends** (See instructions on back and the instructions for Form 1040A, or Form 1040, line 9a.) **Note:** If you received a Form 1099-DIV or substitute statement from a brokerage firm, list the firm's name as the payer and enter the ordinary dividends shown on that form.	**5**	List name of payer ▶ --------------------------------- -- -- -- -- -- -- -- -- -- -- -- -- --	**5**	
	6	Add the amounts on line 5. Enter the total here and on Form 1040A, or Form 1040, line 9a . . . . ▶	**6**	
Note: If line 6 is over $1,500, you must complete Part III.				

		You must complete this part if you **(a)** had over $1,500 of taxable interest or ordinary dividends; **(b)** had a foreign account; or **(c)** received a distribution from, or were a grantor of, or a transferor to, a foreign trust.	Yes	No
Part III **Foreign** **Accounts** **and Trusts** (See instructions on back.)	**7a**	At any time during 2016, did you have a financial interest in or signature authority over a financial account (such as a bank account, securities account, or brokerage account) located in a foreign country? See instructions		
		If "Yes," are you required to file FinCEN Form 114, Report of Foreign Bank and Financial Accounts (FBAR), to report that financial interest or signature authority? See FinCEN Form 114 and its instructions for filing requirements and exceptions to those requirements		
	b	If you are required to file FinCEN Form 114, enter the name of the foreign country where the financial account is located ▶		
	8	During 2016, did you receive a distribution from, or were you the grantor of, or transferor to, a foreign trust? If "Yes," you may have to file Form 3520. See instructions on back		

For Paperwork Reduction Act Notice, see your tax return instructions.   Cat. No. 17146N   **Schedule B (Form 1040A or 1040) 2016**

SCHEDULE C
(Form 1040)

Department of the Treasury
Internal Revenue Service (99)

Profit or Loss From Business
(Sole Proprietorship)

▶ Information about Schedule C and its separate instructions is at *www.irs.gov/schedulec.*
▶ Attach to Form 1040, 1040NR, or 1041; partnerships generally must file Form 1065.

OMB No. 1545-0074

2016

Attachment
Sequence No. **09**

Name of proprietor

Social security number (SSN)

A	Principal business or profession, including product or service (see instructions)	**B** Enter code from instructions ▶
C	Business name. If no separate business name, leave blank.	**D** Employer ID number (EIN), (see instr.)

E Business address (including suite or room no.) ▶ _____
      City, town or post office, state, and ZIP code

F   Accounting method: **(1)** ☐ Cash   **(2)** ☐ Accrual   **(3)** ☐ Other (specify) ▶ _____

G   Did you "materially participate" in the operation of this business during 2016? If "No," see instructions for limit on losses   ☐ Yes ☐ No

H   If you started or acquired this business during 2016, check here   . . . . ▶ ☐

I   Did you make any payments in 2016 that would require you to file Form(s) 1099? (see instructions) . . . . ☐ Yes ☐ No

J   If "Yes," did you or will you file required Forms 1099? . . . . ☐ Yes ☐ No

Part I   Income

1	Gross receipts or sales. See instructions for line 1 and check the box if this income was reported to you on Form W-2 and the "Statutory employee" box on that form was checked . . . . ▶ ☐	**1**	
2	Returns and allowances	**2**	
3	Subtract line 2 from line 1	**3**	
4	Cost of goods sold (from line 42)	**4**	
5	**Gross profit.** Subtract line 4 from line 3	**5**	
6	Other income, including federal and state gasoline or fuel tax credit or refund (see instructions)	**6**	
7	**Gross income.** Add lines 5 and 6 . . . . ▶	**7**	

Part II   Expenses. Enter expenses for business use of your home **only** on line 30.

8	Advertising	**8**		**18**	Office expense (see instructions)	**18**	
9	Car and truck expenses (see instructions)	**9**		**19**	Pension and profit-sharing plans .	**19**	
10	Commissions and fees .	**10**		**20**	Rent or lease (see instructions):		
11	Contract labor (see instructions)	**11**		**a**	Vehicles, machinery, and equipment	**20a**	
12	Depletion	**12**		**b**	Other business property . . .	**20b**	
13	Depreciation and section 179 expense deduction (not included in Part III) (see instructions)	**13**		**21**	Repairs and maintenance . . .	**21**	
				22	Supplies (not included in Part III) .	**22**	
				23	Taxes and licenses	**23**	
				24	Travel, meals, and entertainment:		
14	Employee benefit programs (other than on line 19) . .	**14**		**a**	Travel	**24a**	
15	Insurance (other than health)	**15**		**b**	Deductible meals and entertainment (see instructions) .	**24b**	
16	Interest:			**25**	Utilities	**25**	
a	Mortgage (paid to banks, etc.)	**16a**		**26**	Wages (less employment credits) .	**26**	
b	Other	**16b**		**27a**	Other expenses (from line 48) . .	**27a**	
17	Legal and professional services	**17**		**b**	**Reserved for future use** . . .	**27b**	

28	**Total expenses** before expenses for business use of home. Add lines 8 through 27a . . . . ▶	**28**	
29	Tentative profit or (loss). Subtract line 28 from line 7	**29**	

30   Expenses for business use of your home. Do not report these expenses elsewhere. Attach Form 8829 unless using the simplified method (see instructions).

     Simplified method filers only: enter the total square footage of: (a) your home: _____

     and (b) the part of your home used for business: _____ . Use the Simplified Method Worksheet in the instructions to figure the amount to enter on line 30 . . . . | **30** |

31   **Net profit or (loss).** Subtract line 30 from line 29.

     • If a profit, enter on both **Form 1040, line 12** (or **Form 1040NR, line 13**) and on **Schedule SE, line 2.** (If you checked the box on line 1, see instructions). Estates and trusts, enter on **Form 1041, line 3.** | **31** |

     • If a loss, you **must** go to line 32.

32   If you have a loss, check the box that describes your investment in this activity (see instructions).

     • If you checked 32a, enter the loss on both **Form 1040, line 12,** (or **Form 1040NR, line 13**) and on **Schedule SE, line 2.** (If you checked the box on line 1, see the line 31 instructions). Estates and trusts, enter on **Form 1041, line 3.**

     • If you checked 32b, you **must** attach **Form 6198.** Your loss may be limited.

32a ☐ All investment is at risk.
32b ☐ Some investment is not at risk.

For Paperwork Reduction Act Notice, see the separate instructions.   Cat. No. 11334P   Schedule C (Form 1040) 2016

Part III   **Cost of Goods Sold**   (see instructions)

33   Method(s) used to value closing inventory: **a** ☐ Cost   **b** ☐ Lower of cost or market   **c** ☐ Other (attach explanation)

34   Was there any change in determining quantities, costs, or valuations between opening and closing inventory? If "Yes," attach explanation   .   .   .   .   ☐ Yes   ☐ No

35 Inventory at beginning of year. If different from last year's closing inventory, attach explanation . . .	**35**	
36 Purchases less cost of items withdrawn for personal use	**36**	
37 Cost of labor. Do not include any amounts paid to yourself	**37**	
38 Materials and supplies	**38**	
39 Other costs	**39**	
40 Add lines 35 through 39	**40**	
41 Inventory at end of year	**41**	
42 **Cost of goods sold.** Subtract line 41 from line 40. Enter the result here and on line 4	**42**	

Part IV   **Information on Your Vehicle.**   Complete this part **only** if you are claiming car or truck expenses on line 9 and are not required to file Form 4562 for this business. See the instructions for line 13 to find out if you must file Form 4562.

43   When did you place your vehicle in service for business purposes? (month, day, year)   ▶ _____ / _____ / _____

44   Of the total number of miles you drove your vehicle during 2016, enter the number of miles you used your vehicle for:

   a Business _____   **b** Commuting (see instructions) _____   **c** Other _____

45   Was your vehicle available for personal use during off-duty hours?   .   .   .   .   ☐ Yes   ☐ No

46   Do you (or your spouse) have another vehicle available for personal use?.   .   .   .   .   ☐ Yes   ☐ No

47a   Do you have evidence to support your deduction?   .   .   .   .   ☐ Yes   ☐ No

   b   If "Yes," is the evidence written?   .   .   .   .   ☐ Yes   ☐ No

Part V   **Other Expenses.**   List below business expenses not included on lines 8–26 or line 30.

-----------------------------------		
48 **Total other expenses.** Enter here and on line 27a	**48**	

SCHEDULE D (Form 1040)	**Capital Gains and Losses**	OMB No. 1545-0074
Department of the Treasury Internal Revenue Service (99)	▶ Attach to Form 1040 or Form 1040NR. ▶ Information about Schedule D and its separate instructions is at *www.irs.gov/scheduled*. ▶ Use Form 8949 to list your transactions for lines 1b, 2, 3, 8b, 9, and 10.	20**16** Attachment Sequence No. **12**

Name(s) shown on return | Your social security number

Part I Short-Term Capital Gains and Losses—Assets Held One Year or Less

See instructions for how to figure the amounts to enter on the lines below. This form may be easier to complete if you round off cents to whole dollars.	(d) Proceeds (sales price)	(e) Cost (or other basis)	(g) Adjustments to gain or loss from Form(s) 8949, Part I, line 2, column (g)	(h) Gain or (loss) Subtract column (e) from column (d) and combine the result with column (g)
1a Totals for all short-term transactions reported on Form 1099-B for which basis was reported to the IRS and for which you have no adjustments (see instructions). However, if you choose to report all these transactions on Form 8949, leave this line blank and go to line 1b .				
1b Totals for all transactions reported on Form(s) 8949 with **Box A** checked				
2 Totals for all transactions reported on Form(s) 8949 with **Box B** checked				
3 Totals for all transactions reported on Form(s) 8949 with **Box C** checked				

4 Short-term gain from Form 6252 and short-term gain or (loss) from Forms 4684, 6781, and 8824 .	**4**	
5 Net short-term gain or (loss) from partnerships, S corporations, estates, and trusts from Schedule(s) K-1	**5**	
6 Short-term capital loss carryover. Enter the amount, if any, from line 8 of your **Capital Loss Carryover Worksheet** in the instructions	**6**	( )
7 **Net short-term capital gain or (loss).** Combine lines 1a through 6 in column (h). If you have any long-term capital gains or losses, go to Part II below. Otherwise, go to Part III on the back	**7**	

Part II Long-Term Capital Gains and Losses—Assets Held More Than One Year

See instructions for how to figure the amounts to enter on the lines below. This form may be easier to complete if you round off cents to whole dollars.	(d) Proceeds (sales price)	(e) Cost (or other basis)	(g) Adjustments to gain or loss from Form(s) 8949, Part II, line 2, column (g)	(h) Gain or (loss) Subtract column (e) from column (d) and combine the result with column (g)
8a Totals for all long-term transactions reported on Form 1099-B for which basis was reported to the IRS and for which you have no adjustments (see instructions). However, if you choose to report all these transactions on Form 8949, leave this line blank and go to line 8b .				
8b Totals for all transactions reported on Form(s) 8949 with **Box D** checked				
9 Totals for all transactions reported on Form(s) 8949 with **Box E** checked				
10 Totals for all transactions reported on Form(s) 8949 with **Box F** checked.				

11 Gain from Form 4797, Part I; long-term gain from Forms 2439 and 6252; and long-term gain or (loss) from Forms 4684, 6781, and 8824	**11**	
12 Net long-term gain or (loss) from partnerships, S corporations, estates, and trusts from Schedule(s) K-1	**12**	
13 Capital gain distributions. See the instructions	**13**	
14 Long-term capital loss carryover. Enter the amount, if any, from line 13 of your **Capital Loss Carryover Worksheet** in the instructions	**14**	( )
15 **Net long-term capital gain or (loss).** Combine lines 8a through 14 in column (h). Then go to Part III on the back	**15**	

For Paperwork Reduction Act Notice, see your tax return instructions.   Cat. No. 11338H   Schedule D (Form 1040) 2016

Part III   **Summary**

16   Combine lines 7 and 15 and enter the result **16**

   • If line 16 is a **gain,** enter the amount from line 16 on Form 1040, line 13, or Form 1040NR, line 14. Then go to line 17 below.

   • If line 16 is a **loss,** skip lines 17 through 20 below. Then go to line 21. Also be sure to complete line 22.

   • If line 16 is **zero,** skip lines 17 through 21 below and enter -0- on Form 1040, line 13, or Form 1040NR, line 14. Then go to line 22.

17   Are lines 15 and 16 **both** gains?
   ☐ **Yes.** Go to line 18.
   ☐ **No.** Skip lines 18 through 21, and go to line 22.

18   Enter the amount, if any, from line 7 of the **28% Rate Gain Worksheet** in the instructions . . ▶   **18**

19   Enter the amount, if any, from line 18 of the **Unrecaptured Section 1250 Gain Worksheet** in the instructions . . . . ▶   **19**

20   Are lines 18 and 19 **both** zero or blank?
   ☐ **Yes.** Complete the **Qualified Dividends and Capital Gain Tax Worksheet** in the instructions for Form 1040, line 44 (or in the instructions for Form 1040NR, line 42). **Don't** complete lines 21 and 22 below.

   ☐ **No.** Complete the **Schedule D Tax Worksheet** in the instructions. **Don't** complete lines 21 and 22 below.

21   If line 16 is a loss, enter here and on Form 1040, line 13, or Form 1040NR, line 14, the **smaller** of:

   • The loss on line 16 or
   • ($3,000), or if married filing separately, ($1,500)   } . . . .   **21** (   )

   Note: When figuring which amount is smaller, treat both amounts as positive numbers.

22   Do you have qualified dividends on Form 1040, line 9b, or Form 1040NR, line 10b?

   ☐ **Yes.** Complete the **Qualified Dividends and Capital Gain Tax Worksheet** in the instructions for Form 1040, line 44 (or in the instructions for Form 1040NR, line 42).

   ☐ **No.** Complete the rest of Form 1040 or Form 1040NR.

SCHEDULE E
(Form 1040)

Department of the Treasury
Internal Revenue Service (99)

Supplemental Income and Loss

(From rental real estate, royalties, partnerships, S corporations, estates, trusts, REMICs, etc.)

▶ Attach to Form 1040, 1040NR, or Form 1041.

▶ Information about Schedule E and its separate instructions is at *www.irs.gov/schedulee.*

OMB No. 1545-0074

2016

Attachment
Sequence No. **13**

Name(s) shown on return

Your social security number

Part I **Income or Loss From Rental Real Estate and Royalties** **Note:** If you are in the business of renting personal property, use **Schedule C** or **C-EZ** (see instructions). If you are an individual, report farm rental income or loss from **Form 4835** on page 2, line 40.

A Did you make any payments in 2016 that would require you to file Form(s) 1099? (see instructions) ☐ Yes ☐ No

B If "Yes," did you or will you file required Forms 1099? ☐ Yes ☐ No

1a Physical address of each property (street, city, state, ZIP code)

A	
B	
C	

1b	Type of Property (from list below)	2	For each rental real estate property listed above, report the number of fair rental and personal use days. Check the **QJV** box only if you meet the requirements to file as a qualified joint venture. See instructions.		Fair Rental Days	Personal Use Days	QJV
A				A			☐
B				B			☐
C				C			☐

Type of Property:

1 Single Family Residence   3 Vacation/Short-Term Rental   5 Land   7 Self-Rental
2 Multi-Family Residence   4 Commercial   6 Royalties 8 Other (describe)

Income:	Properties:		A	B	C
3 Rents received	3				
4 Royalties received	4				
Expenses:					
5 Advertising	5				
6 Auto and travel (see instructions)	6				
7 Cleaning and maintenance	7				
8 Commissions.	8				
9 Insurance	9				
10 Legal and other professional fees	10				
11 Management fees	11				
12 Mortgage interest paid to banks, etc. (see instructions)	12				
13 Other interest.	13				
14 Repairs.	14				
15 Supplies	15				
16 Taxes	16				
17 Utilities	17				
18 Depreciation expense or depletion	18				
19 Other (list) ▶ _____	19				
20 Total expenses. Add lines 5 through 19	20				
21 Subtract line 20 from line 3 (rents) and/or 4 (royalties). If result is a (loss), see instructions to find out if you must file **Form 6198**	21				
22 Deductible rental real estate loss after limitation, if any, on **Form 8582** (see instructions)	22	(	) (	) (	)

23a	Total of all amounts reported on line 3 for all rental properties	23a		
b	Total of all amounts reported on line 4 for all royalty properties	23b		
c	Total of all amounts reported on line 12 for all properties	23c		
d	Total of all amounts reported on line 18 for all properties	23d		
e	Total of all amounts reported on line 20 for all properties	23e		
24	**Income.** Add positive amounts shown on line 21. **Do not** include any losses	24		
25	**Losses.** Add royalty losses from line 21 and rental real estate losses from line 22. Enter total losses here	25	(	)
26	**Total rental real estate and royalty income or (loss).** Combine lines 24 and 25. Enter the result here. If Parts II, III, IV, and line 40 on page 2 do not apply to you, also enter this amount on Form 1040, line 17, or Form 1040NR, line 18. Otherwise, include this amount in the total on line 41 on page 2 . . .	26		

For Paperwork Reduction Act Notice, see the separate instructions.   Cat. No. 11344L   Schedule E (Form 1040) 2016

Name(s) shown on return. Do not enter name and social security number if shown on other side.	Your social security number

Caution: The IRS compares amounts reported on your tax return with amounts shown on Schedule(s) K-1.

Part II	**Income or Loss From Partnerships and S Corporations** **Note:** If you report a loss from an at-risk activity for which **any** amount is **not** at risk, you **must** check the box in column **(e)** on line 28 and attach **Form 6198**. See instructions.

27   Are you reporting any loss not allowed in a prior year due to the at-risk, excess farm loss, or basis limitations, a prior year unallowed loss from a passive activity (if that loss was not reported on Form 8582), or unreimbursed partnership expenses? If you answered "Yes," see instructions before completing this section.   ☐ **Yes**   ☐ **No**

28	**(a)** Name	**(b)** Enter **P** for partnership; **S** for S corporation	**(c)** Check if foreign partnership	**(d)** Employer identification number	**(e)** Check if any amount is not at risk
A			☐		☐
B			☐		☐
C			☐		☐
D			☐		☐

	Passive Income and Loss		**Nonpassive Income and Loss**		
	(f) Passive loss allowed (attach **Form 8582** if required)	**(g)** Passive income from **Schedule K-1**	**(h)** Nonpassive loss from **Schedule K-1**	**(i)** Section 179 expense deduction from **Form 4562**	**(j)** Nonpassive income from **Schedule K-1**
A					
B					
C					
D					
29a	Totals				
b	Totals				

30	Add columns (g) and (j) of line 29a	30	
31	Add columns (f), (h), and (i) of line 29b	31	( )
32	**Total partnership and S corporation income or (loss).** Combine lines 30 and 31. Enter the result here and include in the total on line 41 below	32	

Part III	**Income or Loss From Estates and Trusts**

33	**(a)** Name	**(b)** Employer identification number
A		
B		

	Passive Income and Loss		**Nonpassive Income and Loss**	
	(c) Passive deduction or loss allowed (attach **Form 8582** if required)	**(d)** Passive income from **Schedule K-1**	**(e)** Deduction or loss from **Schedule K-1**	**(f)** Other income from **Schedule K-1**
A				
B				
34a	Totals			
b	Totals			

35	Add columns (d) and (f) of line 34a	35	
36	Add columns (c) and (e) of line 34b	36	( )
37	**Total estate and trust income or (loss).** Combine lines 35 and 36. Enter the result here and include in the total on line 41 below	37	

Part IV	**Income or Loss From Real Estate Mortgage Investment Conduits (REMICs)—Residual Holder**

38	**(a)** Name	**(b)** Employer identification number	**(c)** Excess inclusion from **Schedules Q**, line 2c (see instructions)	**(d)** Taxable income (net loss) from **Schedules Q**, line 1b	**(e)** Income from **Schedules Q**, line 3b

39	Combine columns (d) and (e) only. Enter the result here and include in the total on line 41 below	39	

Part V	**Summary**

40	Net farm rental income or (loss) from **Form 4835**. Also, complete line 42 below	40	
41	**Total income or (loss).** Combine lines 26, 32, 37, 39, and 40. Enter the result here and on Form 1040, line 17, or Form 1040NR, line 18 ▶	41	

42   **Reconciliation of farming and fishing income.** Enter your **gross** farming and fishing income reported on Form 4835, line 7; Schedule K-1 (Form 1065), box 14, code B; Schedule K-1 (Form 1120S), box 17, code V; and Schedule K-1 (Form 1041), box 14, code F (see instructions) . . | 42 | |

43   **Reconciliation for real estate professionals.** If you were a real estate professional (see instructions), enter the net income or (loss) you reported anywhere on Form 1040 or Form 1040NR from all rental real estate activities in which you materially participated under the passive activity loss rules . . | 43 | |

SCHEDULE SE
(Form 1040)

Department of the Treasury
Internal Revenue Service (99)

Self-Employment Tax

▶ Information about Schedule SE and its separate instructions is at *www.irs.gov/schedulese*.

▶ **Attach to Form 1040 or Form 1040NR.**

OMB No. 1545-0074

2016

Attachment
Sequence No. **17**

Name of person with **self-employment** income (as shown on Form 1040 or Form 1040NR)

Social security number of person
with **self-employment** income ▶

Before you begin: To determine if you must file Schedule SE, see the Instructions.

May I Use Short Schedule SE or Must I Use Long Schedule SE?

Note. Use this flowchart **only if** you must file Schedule SE. If unsure, see *Who Must File Schedule SE* in the instructions.

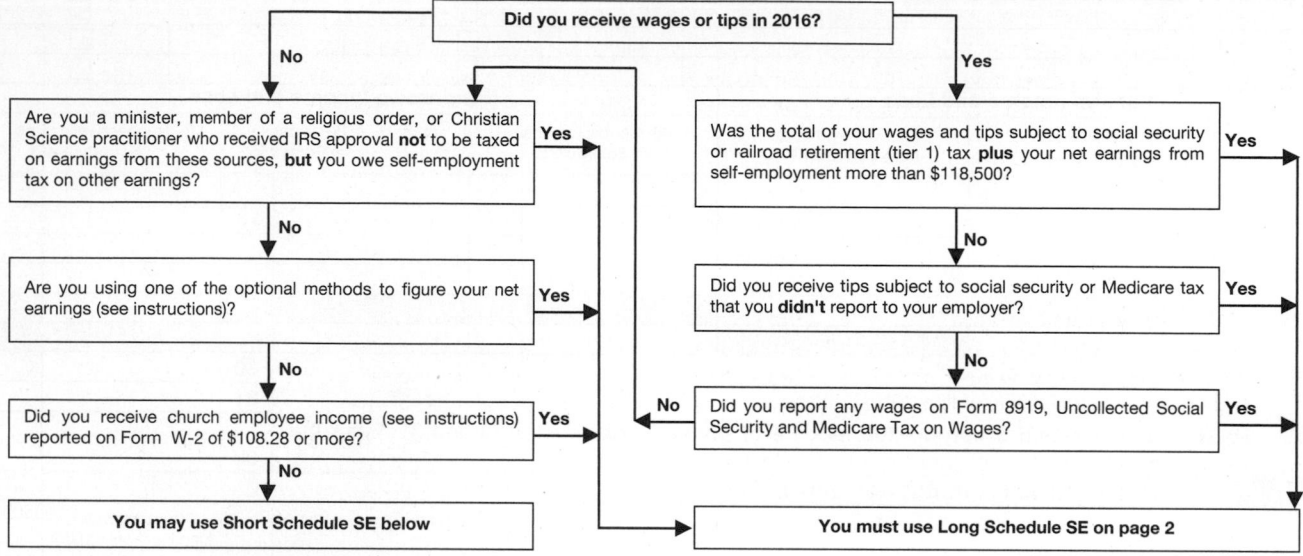

Section A—Short Schedule SE.   Caution. Read above to see if you can use Short Schedule SE.

1a	Net farm profit or (loss) from Schedule F, line 34, and farm partnerships, Schedule K-1 (Form 1065), box 14, code A	**1a**
b	If you received social security retirement or disability benefits, enter the amount of Conservation Reserve Program payments included on Schedule F, line 4b, or listed on Schedule K-1 (Form 1065), box 20, code Z	**1b** ( )
2	Net profit or (loss) from Schedule C, line 31; Schedule C-EZ, line 3; Schedule K-1 (Form 1065), box 14, code A (other than farming); and Schedule K-1 (Form 1065-B), box 9, code J1. Ministers and members of religious orders, see instructions for types of income to report on this line. See instructions for other income to report	**2**
3	Combine lines 1a, 1b, and 2	**3**
4	Multiply line 3 by 92.35% (0.9235). If less than $400, you don't owe self-employment tax; **don't** file this schedule unless you have an amount on line 1b . . . . ▶	**4**
	Note. If line 4 is less than $400 due to Conservation Reserve Program payments on line 1b, see instructions.	
5	**Self-employment tax.** If the amount on line 4 is:	
	• $118,500 or less, multiply line 4 by 15.3% (0.153). Enter the result here and on **Form 1040, line 57,** or **Form 1040NR, line 55**	
	• More than $118,500, multiply line 4 by 2.9% (0.029). Then, add $14,694 to the result.	
	Enter the total here and on **Form 1040, line 57,** or **Form 1040NR, line 55**	**5**
6	**Deduction for one-half of self-employment tax.** Multiply line 5 by 50% (0.50). Enter the result here and on **Form 1040, line 27,** or **Form 1040NR, line 27**	**6**

For Paperwork Reduction Act Notice, see your tax return instructions.   Cat. No. 11358Z   **Schedule SE (Form 1040) 2016**

Schedule SE (Form 1040) 2016 | Attachment Sequence No. **17** | Page **2**

Name of person with **self-employment** income (as shown on Form 1040 or Form 1040NR) | Social security number of person with **self-employment** income ▶

Section B—Long Schedule SE

Part I Self-Employment Tax

Note. If your only income subject to self-employment tax is **church employee income,** see instructions. Also see instructions for the definition of church employee income.

A If you are a minister, member of a religious order, or Christian Science practitioner **and** you filed Form 4361, but you had $400 or more of **other** net earnings from self-employment, check here and continue with Part I . . . . . . ▶ ☐

1a Net farm profit or (loss) from Schedule F, line 34, and farm partnerships, Schedule K-1 (Form 1065), box 14, code A. **Note.** Skip lines 1a and 1b if you use the farm optional method (see instructions) | **1a**

b If you received social security retirement or disability benefits, enter the amount of Conservation Reserve Program payments included on Schedule F, line 4b, or listed on Schedule K-1 (Form 1065), box 20, code Z | **1b** (|)

2 Net profit or (loss) from Schedule C, line 31; Schedule C-EZ, line 3; Schedule K-1 (Form 1065), box 14, code A (other than farming); and Schedule K-1 (Form 1065-B), box 9, code J1. Ministers and members of religious orders, see instructions for types of income to report on this line. See instructions for other income to report. **Note.** Skip this line if you use the nonfarm optional method (see instructions) . . . . | **2**

3 Combine lines 1a, 1b, and 2 . . . . | **3**

4a If line 3 is more than zero, multiply line 3 by 92.35% (0.9235). Otherwise, enter amount from line 3 | **4a**
Note. If line 4a is less than $400 due to Conservation Reserve Program payments on line 1b, see instructions.

b If you elect one or both of the optional methods, enter the total of lines 15 and 17 here . . | **4b**

c Combine lines 4a and 4b. If less than $400, **stop;** you do not owe self-employment tax.
Exception. If less than $400 and you had **church employee income,** enter -0- and continue ▶ | **4c**

5a Enter your **church employee income** from Form W-2. See instructions for definition of church employee income . . . | **5a** |

b Multiply line 5a by 92.35% (0.9235). If less than $100, enter -0- . . . . | **5b**

6 Add lines 4c and 5b . . . . | **6**

7 Maximum amount of combined wages and self-employment earnings subject to social security tax or the 6.2% portion of the 7.65% railroad retirement (tier 1) tax for 2016 . . . . . | **7** | 118,500 | 00

8a Total social security wages and tips (total of boxes 3 and 7 on Form(s) W-2) and railroad retirement (tier 1) compensation. If $118,500 or more, skip lines 8b through 10, and go to line 11 | **8a** |

b Unreported tips subject to social security tax (from Form 4137, line 10) | **8b** |

c Wages subject to social security tax (from Form 8919, line 10) | **8c** |

d Add lines 8a, 8b, and 8c . . . . | **8d**

9 Subtract line 8d from line 7. If zero or less, enter -0- here and on line 10 and go to line 11 . ▶ | **9**

10 Multiply the **smaller** of line 6 or line 9 by 12.4% (0.124) . . . . | **10**

11 Multiply line 6 by 2.9% (0.029) . . . . | **11**

12 **Self-employment tax.** Add lines 10 and 11. Enter here and on **Form 1040, line 57,** or **Form 1040NR, line 55** | **12**

13 **Deduction for one-half of self-employment tax.**
Multiply line 12 by 50% (0.50). Enter the result here and on **Form 1040, line 27,** or **Form 1040NR, line 27** . . . . . . | **13** |

Part II Optional Methods To Figure Net Earnings (see instructions)

Farm Optional Method. You may use this method **only if (a)** your gross farm income[1] was not more than $7,560, **or (b)** your net farm profits[2] were less than $5,457.

14 Maximum income for optional methods . . . . | **14** | 5,040 | 00

15 Enter the **smaller** of: two-thirds (2/3) of gross farm income[1] (not less than zero) **or** $5,040. Also include this amount on line 4b above . . . . | **15**

Nonfarm Optional Method. You may use this method **only if (a)** your net nonfarm profits[3] were less than $5,457 and also less than 72.189% of your gross nonfarm income,[4] **and (b)** you had net earnings from self-employment of at least $400 in 2 of the prior 3 years. **Caution.** You may use this method no more than five times.

16 Subtract line 15 from line 14 . . . . | **16**

17 Enter the **smaller** of: two-thirds (2/3) of gross nonfarm income[4] (not less than zero) **or** the amount on line 16. Also include this amount on line 4b above . . . . | **17**

[1] From Sch. F, line 9, and Sch. K-1 (Form 1065), box 14, code B.

[2] From Sch. F, line 34, and Sch. K-1 (Form 1065), box 14, code A—minus the amount you would have entered on line 1b had you not used the optional method.

[3] From Sch. C, line 31; Sch. C-EZ, line 3; Sch. K-1 (Form 1065), box 14, code A; and Sch. K-1 (Form 1065-B), box 9, code J1.

[4] From Sch. C, line 7; Sch. C-EZ, line 1; Sch. K-1 (Form 1065), box 14, code C; and Sch. K-1 (Form 1065-B), box 9, code J2.

Schedule SE (Form 1040) 2016

Form **8949**

Department of the Treasury
Internal Revenue Service

Sales and Other Dispositions of Capital Assets

▶ Information about Form 8949 and its separate instructions is at *www.irs.gov/form8949*.

▶ File with your Schedule D to list your transactions for lines 1b, 2, 3, 8b, 9, and 10 of Schedule D.

OMB No. 1545-0074

20**16**

Attachment
Sequence No. **12A**

Name(s) shown on return	Social security number or taxpayer identification number

Before you check Box A, B, or C below, see whether you received any Form(s) 1099-B or substitute statement(s) from your broker. A substitute statement will have the same information as Form 1099-B. Either will show whether your basis (usually your cost) was reported to the IRS by your broker and may even tell you which box to check.

Part I   **Short-Term.** Transactions involving capital assets you held 1 year or less are short term. For long-term transactions, see page 2.

Note: You may aggregate all short-term transactions reported on Form(s) 1099-B showing basis was reported to the IRS and for which no adjustments or codes are required. Enter the totals directly on Schedule D, line 1a; you aren't required to report these transactions on Form 8949 (see instructions).

You *must* check Box A, B, *or* C below. Check only one box. If more than one box applies for your short-term transactions, complete a separate Form 8949, page 1, for each applicable box. If you have more short-term transactions than will fit on this page for one or more of the boxes, complete as many forms with the same box checked as you need.

☐ **(A)** Short-term transactions reported on Form(s) 1099-B showing basis was reported to the IRS (see **Note** above)

☐ **(B)** Short-term transactions reported on Form(s) 1099-B showing basis **wasn't** reported to the IRS

☐ **(C)** Short-term transactions not reported to you on Form 1099-B

1 (a) Description of property (Example: 100 sh. XYZ Co.)	(b) Date acquired (Mo., day, yr.)	(c) Date sold or disposed of (Mo., day, yr.)	(d) Proceeds (sales price) (see instructions)	(e) Cost or other basis. See the **Note** below and see *Column (e)* in the separate instructions	Adjustment, if any, to gain or loss. If you enter an amount in column (g), enter a code in column (f). See the separate instructions. (f) Code(s) from instructions	(g) Amount of adjustment	(h) Gain or (loss). Subtract column (e) from column (d) and combine the result with column (g)

2 Totals. Add the amounts in columns (d), (e), (g), and (h) (subtract negative amounts). Enter each total here and include on your Schedule D, **line 1b** (if **Box A** above is checked), **line 2** (if **Box B** above is checked), or **line 3** (if **Box C** above is checked) ▶

Note: If you checked Box A above but the basis reported to the IRS was incorrect, enter in column (e) the basis as reported to the IRS, and enter an adjustment in column (g) to correct the basis. See *Column (g)* in the separate instructions for how to figure the amount of the adjustment.

For Paperwork Reduction Act Notice, see your tax return instructions.   Cat. No. 37768Z   Form **8949** (2016)

Form 8949 (2016)

Name(s) shown on return. Name and SSN or taxpayer identification no. not required if shown on other side	Social security number or taxpayer identification number

Before you check Box D, E, or F below, see whether you received any Form(s) 1099-B or substitute statement(s) from your broker. A substitute statement will have the same information as Form 1099-B. Either will show whether your basis (usually your cost) was reported to the IRS by your broker and may even tell you which box to check.

Part II   **Long-Term.** Transactions involving capital assets you held more than 1 year are long term. For short-term transactions, see page 1.

Note: You may aggregate all long-term transactions reported on Form(s) 1099-B showing basis was reported to the IRS and for which no adjustments or codes are required. Enter the totals directly on Schedule D, line 8a; you aren't required to report these transactions on Form 8949 (see instructions).

You *must* check Box D, E, *or* F below. Check only one box. If more than one box applies for your long-term transactions, complete a separate Form 8949, page 2, for each applicable box. If you have more long-term transactions than will fit on this page for one or more of the boxes, complete as many forms with the same box checked as you need.

- ☐ **(D)** Long-term transactions reported on Form(s) 1099-B showing basis was reported to the IRS (see **Note** above)
- ☐ **(E)** Long-term transactions reported on Form(s) 1099-B showing basis **wasn't** reported to the IRS
- ☐ **(F)** Long-term transactions not reported to you on Form 1099-B

1 (a) Description of property (Example: 100 sh. XYZ Co.)	(b) Date acquired (Mo., day, yr.)	(c) Date sold or disposed of (Mo., day, yr.)	(d) Proceeds (sales price) (see instructions)	(e) Cost or other basis. See the **Note** below and see *Column (e)* in the separate instructions	Adjustment, if any, to gain or loss. If you enter an amount in column (g), enter a code in column (f). See the separate instructions.		(h) Gain or (loss). Subtract column (e) from column (d) and combine the result with column (g)
					(f) Code(s) from instructions	(g) Amount of adjustment	
2 Totals. Add the amounts in columns (d), (e), (g), and (h) (subtract negative amounts). Enter each total here and include on your Schedule D, **line 8b** (if **Box D** above is checked), **line 9** (if **Box E** above is checked), or **line 10** (if **Box F** above is checked) ▶							

Note: If you checked Box D above but the basis reported to the IRS was incorrect, enter in column (e) the basis as reported to the IRS, and enter an adjustment in column (g) to correct the basis. See *Column (g)* in the separate instructions for how to figure the amount of the adjustment.

Form **8958**
(Rev. November 2014)
Department of the Treasury
Internal Revenue Service (99)

Allocation of Tax Amounts Between
Certain Individuals in Community Property States
▶ Attach to Form 1040.
▶ **Information about Form 8958 and its instructions is at *www.irs.gov/form8958*.**

OMB No. 1545-0074

Attachment
Sequence No. **63**

Your first name and initial	Your last name	Your social security number

Spouse's or partner's first name and initial	Spouse's or partner's last name	Spouse's or partner's social security number

	A Total Amount	B Allocated to Spouse or RDP SSN ____-__-____	C Allocated to Spouse or RDP SSN ____-__-____
1 Wages (each employer)			
2 Interest Income (each payer)			
3 Dividends (each payer)			
4 State Income Tax Refund			
5 Self-Employment Income (See instructions)			
6 Capital Gains and Losses			
7 Pension Income			
8 Rents, Royalties, Partnerships, Estates, Trusts			

For Paperwork Reduction Act Notice, see your tax return instructions.   Cat. No. 37779G   Form **8958** (Rev. 11-2014)

Form 8958 (Rev. 11-2014)

	A Total Amount	B Allocated to Spouse or RDP SSN _____ - ___ - _____	C Allocated to Spouse or RDP SSN _____ - ___ - _____
9 Deductible part of Self-Employment Tax (See instructions)			
10 Self-Employment Tax (See instructions)			
11 Taxes Withheld			
12 Other items such as: Social Security Benefits, Unemployment Compensation, Deductions, Credits, etc.			

Form **8958** (Rev. 11-2014)

Form **8959**

Department of the Treasury
Internal Revenue Service

Additional Medicare Tax

▶ If any line does not apply to you, leave it blank. See separate instructions.
▶ Attach to Form 1040, 1040NR, 1040-PR, or 1040-SS.
▶ Information about Form 8959 and its instructions is at *www.irs.gov/form8959.*

OMB No. 1545-0074

20**16**

Attachment
Sequence No. **71**

Name(s) shown on return

Your social security number

Part I	**Additional Medicare Tax on Medicare Wages**				
1	Medicare wages and tips from Form W-2, box 5. If you have more than one Form W-2, enter the total of the amounts from box 5	**1**			
2	Unreported tips from Form 4137, line 6	**2**			
3	Wages from Form 8919, line 6	**3**			
4	Add lines 1 through 3	**4**			
5	Enter the following amount for your filing status: Married filing jointly . . . . $250,000 Married filing separately . . . . $125,000 Single, Head of household, or Qualifying widow(er) $200,000	**5**			
6	Subtract line 5 from line 4. If zero or less, enter -0-			**6**	
7	Additional Medicare Tax on Medicare wages. Multiply line 6 by 0.9% (0.009). Enter here and go to Part II			**7**	

Part II	**Additional Medicare Tax on Self-Employment Income**				
8	Self-employment income from Schedule SE (Form 1040), Section A, line 4, or Section B, line 6. If you had a loss, enter -0- (Form 1040-PR and Form 1040-SS filers, see instructions.)	**8**			
9	Enter the following amount for your filing status: Married filing jointly . . . . $250,000 Married filing separately . . . . $125,000 Single, Head of household, or Qualifying widow(er) $200,000	**9**			
10	Enter the amount from line 4	**10**			
11	Subtract line 10 from line 9. If zero or less, enter -0-	**11**			
12	Subtract line 11 from line 8. If zero or less, enter -0-			**12**	
13	Additional Medicare Tax on self-employment income. Multiply line 12 by 0.9% (0.009). Enter here and go to Part III			**13**	

Part III	**Additional Medicare Tax on Railroad Retirement Tax Act (RRTA) Compensation**				
14	Railroad retirement (RRTA) compensation and tips from Form(s) W-2, box 14 (see instructions)	**14**			
15	Enter the following amount for your filing status: Married filing jointly . . . . $250,000 Married filing separately . . . . $125,000 Single, Head of household, or Qualifying widow(er) $200,000	**15**			
16	Subtract line 15 from line 14. If zero or less, enter -0-			**16**	
17	Additional Medicare Tax on railroad retirement (RRTA) compensation. Multiply line 16 by 0.9% (0.009). Enter here and go to Part IV			**17**	

Part IV	**Total Additional Medicare Tax**				
18	Add lines 7, 13, and 17. Also include this amount on Form 1040, line 62, (Form 1040NR, 1040-PR, and 1040-SS filers, see instructions) and go to Part V			**18**	

Part V	**Withholding Reconciliation**				
19	Medicare tax withheld from Form W-2, box 6. If you have more than one Form W-2, enter the total of the amounts from box 6	**19**			
20	Enter the amount from line 1	**20**			
21	Multiply line 20 by 1.45% (0.0145). This is your regular Medicare tax withholding on Medicare wages	**21**			
22	Subtract line 21 from line 19. If zero or less, enter -0-. This is your Additional Medicare Tax withholding on Medicare wages			**22**	
23	Additional Medicare Tax withholding on railroad retirement (RRTA) compensation from Form W-2, box 14 (see instructions)			**23**	
24	**Total Additional Medicare Tax withholding.** Add lines 22 and 23. Also include this amount with federal income tax withholding on Form 1040, line 64 (Form 1040NR, 1040-PR, and 1040-SS filers, see instructions)			**24**	

For Paperwork Reduction Act Notice, see your tax return instructions.   Cat. No. 59475X   Form **8959** (2016)

Form **8960**

Department of the Treasury
Internal Revenue Service (99)

Net Investment Income Tax—
Individuals, Estates, and Trusts

▶ Attach to your tax return.

▶ **Information about Form 8960 and its separate instructions is at** *www.irs.gov/form8960.*

OMB No. 1545-2227

2016

Attachment
Sequence No. **72**

Name(s) shown on your tax return

Your social security number or EIN

Part I	Investment Income	☐ Section 6013(g) election (see instructions)		
		☐ Section 6013(h) election (see instructions)		
		☐ Regulations section 1.1411-10(g) election (see instructions)		

1	Taxable interest (see instructions)	**1**		
2	Ordinary dividends (see instructions)	**2**		
3	Annuities (see instructions)	**3**		
4a	Rental real estate, royalties, partnerships, S corporations, trusts, etc. (see instructions)	**4a**		
b	Adjustment for net income or loss derived in the ordinary course of a non-section 1411 trade or business (see instructions)	**4b**		
c	Combine lines 4a and 4b	**4c**		
5a	Net gain or loss from disposition of property (see instructions)	**5a**		
b	Net gain or loss from disposition of property that is not subject to net investment income tax (see instructions)	**5b**		
c	Adjustment from disposition of partnership interest or S corporation stock (see instructions)	**5c**		
d	Combine lines 5a through 5c	**5d**		
6	Adjustments to investment income for certain CFCs and PFICs (see instructions)	**6**		
7	Other modifications to investment income (see instructions)	**7**		
8	Total investment income. Combine lines 1, 2, 3, 4c, 5d, 6, and 7	**8**		

Part II	Investment Expenses Allocable to Investment Income and Modifications			
9a	Investment interest expenses (see instructions)	**9a**		
b	State, local, and foreign income tax (see instructions)	**9b**		
c	Miscellaneous investment expenses (see instructions)	**9c**		
d	Add lines 9a, 9b, and 9c	**9d**		
10	Additional modifications (see instructions)	**10**		
11	Total deductions and modifications. Add lines 9d and 10	**11**		

Part III	Tax Computation			
12	Net investment income. Subtract Part II, line 11 from Part I, line 8. Individuals complete lines 13– 17. Estates and trusts complete lines 18a–21. If zero or less, enter -0-	**12**		
	Individuals:			
13	Modified adjusted gross income (see instructions)	**13**		
14	Threshold based on filing status (see instructions)	**14**		
15	Subtract line 14 from line 13. If zero or less, enter -0-	**15**		
16	Enter the smaller of line 12 or line 15	**16**		
17	Net investment income tax for individuals. Multiply line 16 by 3.8% (.038). **Enter here and include on your tax return** (see instructions)	**17**		
	Estates and Trusts:			
18a	Net investment income (line 12 above)	**18a**		
b	Deductions for distributions of net investment income and deductions under section 642(c) (see instructions)	**18b**		
c	Undistributed net investment income. Subtract line 18b from 18a (see instructions). If zero or less, enter -0-	**18c**		
19a	Adjusted gross income (see instructions)	**19a**		
b	Highest tax bracket for estates and trusts for the year (see instructions)	**19b**		
c	Subtract line 19b from line 19a. If zero or less, enter -0-	**19c**		
20	Enter the smaller of line 18c or line 19c	**20**		
21	Net investment income tax for estates and trusts. Multiply line 20 by 3.8% (.038). **Enter here and include on your tax return** (see instructions)	**21**		

For Paperwork Reduction Act Notice, see your tax return instructions.   Cat. No. 59474M   Form **8960** (2016)

Form **8962**	**Premium Tax Credit (PTC)**	OMB No. 1545-0074
Department of the Treasury Internal Revenue Service	▶ Attach to Form 1040, 1040A, or 1040NR. ▶ Information about Form 8962 and its separate instructions is at *www.irs.gov/form8962*.	20**16** Attachment Sequence No. **73**

Name shown on your return | Your social security number

You cannot claim the PTC if your filing status is married filing separately unless you qualify for an exception (see instructions). If you qualify, check the box. ☐

Part I Annual and Monthly Contribution Amount

1	Tax family size. Enter the number of exemptions from Form 1040 or Form 1040A, line 6d, or Form 1040NR, line 7d	1	
2a	Modified AGI. Enter your modified AGI (see instructions) . . . . . **2a** ⬚ **b** Enter the total of your dependents' modified AGI (see instructions) . . .	2b	
3	Household income. Add the amounts on lines 2a and 2b (see instructions)	3	
4	Federal poverty line. Enter the federal poverty line amount from Table 1-1, 1-2, or 1-3 (see instructions). Check the appropriate box for the federal poverty table used. **a** ☐ Alaska **b** ☐ Hawaii **c** ☐ Other 48 states and DC	4	
5	Household income as a percentage of federal poverty line (see instructions)	5	%
6	Did you enter 401% on line 5? (See instructions if you entered less than 100%.) ☐ **No.** Continue to line 7. ☐ **Yes.** You are not eligible to take the PTC. If advance payment of the PTC was made, see the instructions for how to report your excess advance PTC repayment amount.		
7	Applicable Figure. Using your line 5 percentage, locate your "applicable figure" on the table in the instructions . .	7	
8a	Annual contribution amount. Multiply line 3 by line 7. Round to nearest whole dollar amount **8a** ⬚ **b** Monthly contribution amount. Divide line 8a by 12. Round to nearest whole dollar amount	8b	

Part II Premium Tax Credit Claim and Reconciliation of Advance Payment of Premium Tax Credit

9	Are you allocating policy amounts with another taxpayer or do you want to use the alternative calculation for year of marriage (see instructions)? ☐ **Yes.** Skip to Part IV, Allocation of Policy Amounts, or Part V, Alternative Calculation for Year of Marriage. ☐ **No.** Continue to line 10.
10	See the instructions to determine if you can use line 11 or must complete lines 12 through 23. ☐ **Yes.** Continue to line 11. Compute your annual PTC. Then skip lines 12–23 and continue to line 24. ☐ **No.** Continue to lines 12–23. Compute your monthly PTC and continue to line 24.

Annual Calculation	**(a)** Annual enrollment premiums (Form(s) 1095-A, line 33A)	**(b)** Annual applicable SLCSP premium (Form(s) 1095-A, line 33B)	**(c)** Annual contribution amount (line 8a)	**(d)** Annual maximum premium assistance (subtract (c) from (b), if zero or less, enter -0-)	**(e)** Annual premium tax credit allowed (smaller of (a) or (d))	**(f)** Annual advance payment of PTC (Form(s) 1095-A, line 33C)
11 Annual Totals						

Monthly Calculation	**(a)** Monthly enrollment premiums (Form(s) 1095-A, lines 21–32, column A)	**(b)** Monthly applicable SLCSP premium (Form(s) 1095-A, lines 21–32, column B)	**(c)** Monthly contribution amount (amount from line 8b or alternative marriage monthly calculation)	**(d)** Monthly maximum premium assistance (subtract (c) from (b), if zero or less, enter -0-)	**(e)** Monthly premium tax credit allowed (smaller of (a) or (d))	**(f)** Monthly advance payment of PTC (Form(s) 1095-A, lines 21–32, column C)
12 January						
13 February						
14 March						
15 April						
16 May						
17 June						
18 July						
19 August						
20 September						
21 October						
22 November						
23 December						

24	Total premium tax credit. Enter the amount from line 11(e) or add lines 12(e) through 23(e) and enter the total here	24	
25	Advance payment of PTC. Enter the amount from line 11(f) or add lines 12(f) through 23(f) and enter the total here	25	
26	Net premium tax credit. If line 24 is greater than line 25, subtract line 25 from line 24. Enter the difference here and on Form 1040, line 69; Form 1040A, line 45; or Form 1040NR, line 65. If line 24 equals line 25, enter zero. Stop here. If line 25 is greater than line 24, leave this line blank and continue to line 27	26	

Part III Repayment of Excess Advance Payment of the Premium Tax Credit

27	Excess advance payment of PTC. If line 25 is greater than line 24, subtract line 24 from line 25. Enter the difference here	27	
28	Repayment limitation (see instructions)	28	
29	Excess advance premium tax credit repayment. Enter the smaller of line 27 or line 28 here and on Form 1040, line 46; Form 1040A, line 29; or Form 1040NR, line 44	29	

For Paperwork Reduction Act Notice, see your tax return instructions. Cat. No. 37784Z Form **8962** (2016)

Part IV Allocation of Policy Amounts

Complete the following information for up to four shared policy allocations. See instructions for allocation details.

Allocation 1

30	(a) Policy Number (Form 1095-A, line 2)	(b) SSN of other taxpayer	(c) Allocation start month	(d) Allocation stop month

Allocation percentage applied to monthly amounts	(e) Premium Percentage	(f) SLCSP Percentage	(g) Advance Payment of the PTC Percentage

Allocation 2

31	(a) Policy Number (Form 1095-A, line 2)	(b) SSN of other taxpayer	(c) Allocation start month	(d) Allocation stop month

Allocation percentage applied to monthly amounts	(e) Premium Percentage	(f) SLCSP Percentage	(g) Advance Payment of the PTC Percentage

Allocation 3

32	(a) Policy Number (Form 1095-A, line 2)	(b) SSN of other taxpayer	(c) Allocation start month	(d) Allocation stop month

Allocation percentage applied to monthly amounts	(e) Premium Percentage	(f) SLCSP Percentage	(g) Advance Payment of the PTC Percentage

Allocation 4

33	(a) Policy Number (Form 1095-A, line 2)	(b) SSN of other taxpayer	(c) Allocation start month	(d) Allocation stop month

Allocation percentage applied to monthly amounts	(e) Premium Percentage	(f) SLCSP Percentage	(g) Advance Payment of the PTC Percentage

34 Have you completed all policy amount allocations?

☐ **Yes.** Multiply the amounts on Form 1095-A by the allocation percentages entered by policy. Add all allocated policy amounts and non-allocated policy amounts from Forms 1095-A, if any, to compute a combined total for each month. Enter the combined total for each month on lines 12–23, columns (a), (b), and (f). Compute the amounts for lines 12–23, columns (c)–(e), and continue to line 24.

☐ **No.** See the instructions to report additional policy amount allocations.

Part V Alternative Calculation for Year of Marriage

Complete line(s) 35 and/or 36 to elect the alternative calculation for year of marriage. For eligibility to make the election, see the instructions for line 9. To complete line(s) 35 and/or 36 and compute the amounts for lines 12–23, see the instructions for this Part V.

		(a) Alternative family size	(b) Alternative monthly contribution amount	(c) Alternative start month	(d) Alternative stop month
35	**Alternative entries for your SSN**				
36	**Alternative entries for your spouse's SSN**				

Form **8962** (2016)

Appendix C

Glossary

The key terms in this glossary have been defined to reflect their conventional use in the field of taxation. The definitions may therefore be incomplete for other purposes.

A

AAA bypass election. In the context of a distribution by an S corporation, an election made by the entity to designate that the distribution is first from accumulated earnings and profits (AEP) and only then from the accumulated adjustments account (AAA).

Abandoned spouse. The abandoned spouse provision enables a married taxpayer with a dependent child whose spouse did not live in the taxpayer's home during the last six months of the tax year to file as a head of household rather than as married filing separately.

Accelerated cost recovery system (ACRS). A method in which the cost of tangible property is recovered (depreciated) over a prescribed period of time. This depreciation approach disregards salvage value, imposes a period of cost recovery that depends upon the classification of the asset into one of various recovery periods, and prescribes the applicable percentage of cost that can be deducted each year. A modified system is currently the default cost recovery method; it is referred to as MACRS. § 168.

Accelerated death benefits. The amount received from a life insurance policy by the insured who is terminally ill or chronically ill. Any realized gain may be excluded from the gross income of the insured if the policy is surrendered to the insurer or is sold to a licensed viatical settlement provider. § 101(g).

Acceleration rule. Treatment of an intercompany transaction on a consolidated return, when a sold asset leaves the group.

Accident and health benefits. Employee fringe benefits provided by employers through the payment of health and accident insurance premiums or the establishment of employer-funded medical reimbursement plans. Employers generally are entitled to a deduction for such payments, whereas employees generally exclude such fringe benefits from gross income. §§ 105 and 106.

Accident and health insurance benefits. See *accident and health benefits.*

Accountable plan. A type of expense reimbursement plan that requires an employee to render an adequate accounting to the employer and return any excess reimbursement or allowance. If the expense qualifies, it will be treated as a deduction *for* AGI.

Accounting income. The accountant's concept of income is generally based upon the realization principle. Financial accounting income may differ from taxable income (e.g., accelerated depreciation might be used for Federal income tax and straight-line depreciation for financial accounting purposes). Differences are included in a reconciliation of taxable and accounting income on Schedule M–1 or Schedule M–3 of Form 1120 for corporations.

Accounting method. The method under which income and expenses are determined for tax purposes. Important accounting methods include the cash basis and the accrual basis. Special methods are available for the reporting of gain on installment sales, recognition of income on construction projects (the completed contract and percentage of completion methods), and the valuation of inventories (last-in, first-out and first-in, first-out). §§ 446–474.

Accounting period. The period of time, usually a year, used by a taxpayer for the determination of tax liability. Unless a fiscal year is chosen, taxpayers must determine and pay their income tax liability by using the calendar year (January 1 through December 31) as the period of measurement. An example of a fiscal year is July 1 through June 30. A change in accounting period (e.g., from a calendar year to a fiscal year) generally requires the consent of the IRS. Usually, taxpayers are free to select either an initial calendar or a fiscal year without the consent of the IRS. §§ 441–444.

Accrual method. A method of accounting that reflects expenses incurred and income earned for any one tax year. In contrast to the cash basis of accounting, expenses need not be paid to be deductible, nor need income be received to be taxable. Unearned income (e.g., prepaid interest and rent) generally is taxed in the year of receipt regardless of the method of accounting used by the taxpayer. § 446(c)(2).

Accumulated adjustments account (AAA). An account that aggregates an S corporation's post-1982 income, loss, and deductions for the tax year (including nontaxable income and nondeductible losses and expenses). After the year-end income and expense adjustments are made, the account is reduced by distributions made during the tax year.

Accumulated E & P. See *accumulated earnings and profits (AEP)*.

Accumulated earnings and profits (AEP). Net undistributed tax-basis earnings of a corporation aggregated from March 1, 1913, to the end of the prior tax year. Used to determine the amount of dividend income associated with a distribution to shareholders. § 316 and Reg. § 1.316–2.

Accumulated earnings credit. A reduction allowed in arriving at accumulated taxable income, in determining the accumulated earnings tax.

Accumulated earnings tax. A special tax imposed on C corporations that accumulate (rather than distribute) their earnings beyond the reasonable needs of the business. The accumulated earnings tax and related interest are imposed on accumulated taxable income in addition to the corporate income tax. §§ 531–537.

Accumulated taxable income (ATI). The base upon which the accumulated earnings tax is imposed. Generally, it is the taxable income of the corporation as adjusted for certain items (e.g., the Federal income tax, excess charitable contributions, the dividends received deduction) less the dividends paid deduction and the accumulated earnings credit. § 535.

Accuracy-related penalties. Major civil taxpayer penalties relating to the accuracy of tax return data, including misstatements stemming from taxpayer negligence and improper valuation of income and deductions, are coordinated under this umbrella term. The penalty usually equals 20 percent of the understated tax liability.

ACE adjustment. An adjustment in computing corporate alternative minimum taxable income (AMTI), computed at 75 percent of the excess of adjusted current earnings (ACE) over unadjusted AMTI. ACE computations reflect longer and slower cost recovery deductions and other restrictions on the timing of certain recognition events. Exempt interest, life insurance proceeds, and other receipts that are included in earnings and profits but not in taxable income also increase the ACE adjustment. If unadjusted AMTI exceeds ACE, the ACE adjustment is negative. The negative adjustment is limited to the aggregate of the positive adjustments under ACE for prior years, reduced by any previously claimed negative adjustments.

Acquiescence. Agreement by the IRS on the results reached in certain judicial decisions; sometimes abbreviated *Acq.* or *A*.

Acquisition indebtedness. Debt incurred in acquiring, constructing, or substantially improving a qualified residence of the taxpayer. The interest on such loans is deductible as qualified residence interest. However, interest on such debt is deductible only on the portion of the indebtedness that does not exceed $1,000,000 ($500,000 for married persons filing separate returns). § 163(h)(3).

Active income. Wages, salary, commissions, bonuses, profits from a trade or business in which the taxpayer is a material participant, gain on the sale or other disposition of assets used in an active trade or business, and income from intangible property if the taxpayer's personal efforts significantly contributed to the creation of the property. The passive activity loss rules require classification of income and losses into three categories with active income being one of them.

Ad valorem taxes. A tax imposed on the value of property. The most common ad valorem tax is that imposed by states, counties, and cities on real estate. Ad valorem taxes can be imposed on personal property as well.

Additional first-year depreciation. This provision, effective for property acquired after December 31, 2011, and placed in service before January 1, 2020, provides for an additional cost recovery deduction of 50 percent in the tax year the qualified property is placed in service. (The bonus depreciation percentage is reduced to 40 percent in 2018 and 30 percent in 2019.) Qualified property includes most types of new property other than buildings. The taxpayer can elect to forgo this bonus depreciation. Different rules applied between 2008 and 2011.

Adjusted basis. The cost or other basis of property reduced by depreciation allowed or allowable and increased by capital improvements. Other special adjustments are provided in § 1016 and the related Regulations.

Adjusted current earnings (ACE). Used to determine an adjustment in computing corporate alternative minimum taxable income (AMTI). ACE reflects restrictions on the timing of certain recognition events. Exempt interest, life insurance proceeds, and other receipts that are included in earnings and profits but not in taxable income also increase ACE.

Adjustments. See *AMT adjustments*.

Adoption expenses credit. A provision intended to assist taxpayers who incur nonrecurring costs directly associated with the adoption process, such as legal costs, social service review costs, and transportation costs. Up to $13,570 of costs incurred to adopt an eligible child qualify for the credit (unique rules apply when adopting a special needs child). A taxpayer may claim the credit in the year qualifying expenses are paid or incurred if the expenses are paid during or after the year in which the adoption is finalized. For qualifying expenses paid or incurred in a tax year prior to the year the adoption is finalized, the credit must be claimed in the tax year following the tax year during which the expenses are paid or incurred. § 23.

Affiliated group. A parent-subsidiary group of corporations that is eligible to elect to file on a consolidated basis. Eighty percent ownership of the voting power and value of all of the corporations must be achieved every day of the tax year, and an identifiable parent corporation must exist (i.e., it must own at least 80 percent of another group member without applying attribution rules).

Aggregate (or conduit) concept. The theory of partnership taxation under which, in certain cases, a partnership is treated as a mere collection of the activities of each partner. See also *entity concept*.

Alimony and separate maintenance payments. Alimony deductions result from the payment of a legal obligation arising from the termination of a marital relationship.

Payments designated as alimony generally are included in the gross income of the recipient and are deductible *for AGI* by the payor.

Alimony recapture. The amount of alimony that previously has been included in the gross income of the recipient and deducted by the payor that now is deducted by the recipient and included in the gross income of the payor as the result of front-loading. § 71(f).

All events test. For accrual method taxpayers, income is earned when (1) all of the events have occurred that fix the right to receive the income and (2) the amount can be determined with reasonable accuracy. Accrual of income cannot be postponed simply because a portion of the income may have to be returned in a subsequent period. The all events test also is utilized to determine when expenses can be deducted by an accrual basis taxpayer. The application of the test could cause a variation between the treatment of an item for accounting and for tax purposes. For example, a reserve for warranty expense may be properly accruable under Generally Accepted Accounting Principles but not be deductible under the Federal income tax law. Because of the application of the all events test, the deduction becomes available in the year the warranty obligation becomes fixed and the amount is determinable with reasonable certainty. Reg. §§ 1.446–1(c)(1)(ii) and 1.461–1(a)(2).

Allocate. The assignment of income for various tax purposes. A multistate corporation's nonbusiness income usually is allocated to the state where the nonbusiness assets are located; it is not apportioned with the rest of the entity's income. The income and expense items of an estate or a trust are allocated between income and corpus components. Specific items of income, expense, gain, loss, and credit can be allocated to specific partners if a substantial economic nontax purpose for the allocation is established.

Alternate valuation date. Property passing from a decedent by death may be valued for estate tax purposes as of the date of death or the alternate valuation date. The alternate valuation date is six months after the date of death or the date the property is disposed of by the estate, whichever comes first. To use the alternate valuation date, the executor or administrator of the estate must make an affirmative election. Election of the alternate valuation date is not available unless it decreases the amount of the gross estate and reduces the estate tax liability.

Alternative depreciation system (ADS). A cost recovery system in which the cost or other initial basis of an asset is recovered using the straight-line method over recovery periods similar to those used in MACRS. The alternative system must be used in certain instances and can be elected in other instances. § 168(g).

Alternative minimum tax (AMT). The AMT is a fixed percentage of alternative minimum taxable income (AMTI). AMTI generally starts with the taxpayer's adjusted gross income (for individuals) or taxable income (for other taxpayers). To this amount, the taxpayer (1) adds designated preference items (e.g., tax-exempt interest income on private activity bonds), (2) makes other specified adjustments (e.g., to reflect a slower cost recovery method), (3) adjusts certain AMT itemized deductions for individuals (e.g., interest incurred on housing), and (4) subtracts an exemption amount. The taxpayer must pay the greater of the resulting AMT (reduced for larger corporations by only the foreign tax credit) or the regular income tax (reduced by all allowable tax credits). The AMT does not apply to certain small C corporations. AMT preferences and adjustments are assigned to partners, LLC members, and S corporation shareholders.

Alternative minimum tax credit. The AMT can result from timing differences that give rise to positive adjustments in calculating the AMT base. To provide equity for the taxpayer when these timing differences reverse, the regular tax liability may be reduced by a tax credit for a prior year's minimum tax liability attributable to timing differences. § 53.

Alternative minimum taxable income (AMTI). The base (prior to deducting the exemption amount) for computing a taxpayer's alternative minimum tax. This consists of the taxable income for the year modified for AMT adjustments and AMT preferences. § 55(b)(2).

Alternative tax. An option that is allowed in computing the tax on net capital gain. For the corporate taxpayer, the rate is 35 percent (the same as the highest regular corporate tax rate). Thus, for corporate taxpayers, the alternative tax does not produce a beneficial result. For noncorporate taxpayers, the rate is usually 15 percent (but is 25 percent for unrecaptured § 1250 gain and 28 percent for collectibles and § 1202 gain). However, if the noncorporate taxpayer is in either the 10 percent or the 15 percent tax bracket, the alternative tax rate is 0 percent (rather than 15 percent). Certain high-income taxpayers (i.e., in the 39.6 percent tax bracket) have an alternative tax rate of 20 percent. §§ 1(h) and 1201.

Alternative tax NOL deduction (ATNOLD). In calculating the AMT, the taxpayer is allowed to deduct NOL carryovers and carrybacks. However, for this purpose, a special calculation is required that is referred to as the ATNOLD. The regular income tax is modified for AMT adjustments and preferences to produce the ATNOLD. § 56(d).

American Opportunity credit. This credit replaces the HOPE scholarship credit for years after 2008 and applies for qualifying expenses for the first four years of postsecondary education. Qualified expenses include tuition and related expenses and books and other course materials. Room and board are ineligible for the credit. The maximum credit available per student is $2,500 (100 percent of the first $2,000 of qualified expenses and 25 percent of the next $2,000 of qualified expenses). Eligible students include the taxpayer, taxpayer's spouse, and taxpayer's dependents. To qualify for the credit, a student must take at least one-half of the full-time course load for at least one academic term at a qualifying educational institution. The credit is phased out for higher-income taxpayers. § 25A.

Amortization. The tax deduction for the cost or other basis of an intangible asset over the asset's estimated useful life. Examples of amortizable intangibles include patents, copyrights, and leasehold interests. Most purchased intangible assets (e.g., goodwill) can be amortized for income tax purposes over a 15-year period.

Amount realized. The amount received by a taxpayer upon the sale or exchange of property. Amount realized is the sum of the cash and the fair market value of any property or services received by the taxpayer plus any related debt assumed by the buyer. Determining the amount realized is the starting point for arriving at realized gain or loss. § 1001(b).

AMT adjustments. In calculating AMTI, certain adjustments are added to or deducted from taxable income. These adjustments generally reflect timing differences. § 56.

AMT exemption. An amount deducted from alternative minimum taxable income to determine the alternative minimum tax base. The exemption amount is phased out when AMTI exceeds specified threshold amounts.

AMT preferences. In calculating alternative minimum taxable income (AMTI), certain preference items are added to the taxable income starting point of the AMT calculation. AMT preferences generally reflect differences between the regular tax and the alternative minimum tax (AMT) computational bases. For instance, interest income from certain state and local bonds may be an AMT preference item.

Annual exclusion. In computing the taxable gifts for the year, each donor excludes the first $14,000 (for 2017) of a gift to each donee. Usually, the annual exclusion is not available for gifts of future interests. § 2503(b).

Annuity. A fixed sum of money payable to a person at specified times for a specified period of time or for life. If the party making the payment (i.e., the obligor) is regularly engaged in this type of business (e.g., an insurance company), the arrangement is classified as a commercial annuity. A so-called private annuity involves an obligor that is not regularly engaged in selling annuities (e.g., a charity or family member).

Apportion. The assignment of the business income of a multistate corporation to specific states for income taxation. Usually, the apportionment procedure accounts for the property, payroll, and sales activity levels of the various states, and a proportionate assignment of the entity's total income is made using a three-factor apportionment formula. These activities indicate the commercial domicile of the corporation relative to that income. Some states exclude nonbusiness income from the apportionment procedure; they allocate nonbusiness income to the states where the nonbusiness assets are located.

Appreciated inventory. In partnership taxation, appreciated inventory is a hot asset, and a partner's share of its ordinary income potential must be allocated. If a partner sells an interest in the partnership, ordinary income is recognized to the extent of the partner's share in the partnership's inventory and unrealized receivables. The definition of "inventory" here is broad enough to include any accounts receivable, including unrealized receivables.

Arm's length. See *arm's length price.*

Arm's length price. The standard under which unrelated parties would determine an exchange price for a transaction. Suppose, for example, Cardinal Corporation sells property to its sole shareholder for $10,000. In testing whether the $10,000 is an "arm's length" price, one would ascertain the price that would have been negotiated between the corporation and an unrelated party in a bargained exchange.

ASC 740 (SFAS 109). Under Generally Accepted Accounting Principles, the rules for the financial reporting of the tax expense of an enterprise. Permanent differences affect the enterprise's effective tax rate. Temporary differences create a deferred tax asset or a deferred tax liability on the balance sheet.

ASC 740-10 (FIN 48). An interpretation by the Financial Accounting Standards Board. When an uncertain tax return position exists, this interpretation is used to determine the financial reporting treatment, if any, for the taxpayer. If it is more likely than not (i.e., a greater than 50 percent probability) that the uncertain return position will be sustained (e.g., by the courts) on its technical merits, it must be reported on the financial statements. The amount to be reported then is computed based on the probabilities of the outcome of the technical review, and the amounts at which the dispute would be resolved. If the more-likely-than-not test is failed, no current financial disclosure of the results of the return position is required.

ASC 740-30 (APB 23). Under Generally Accepted Accounting Principles, the rules for the financial reporting of the tax expense relative to a U.S. corporation's non-U.S. subsidiary. If the parent documents that it is permanently reinvesting the non-U.S. earnings of a non-U.S. subsidiary, the parent does not record as an expense any U.S. income tax the parent might pay on such earnings (i.e., the book tax expense is deferred until such earnings are, if ever, repatriated to the United States).

Asset use test. In the context of a corporate reorganization, a means by which to determine if the continuity of business enterprise requirement is met. The acquiring corporation must continue to use the target entity's assets in the acquiror's business going forward; if this is not the case, the requirement is failed.

Assignment of income. A taxpayer attempts to avoid the recognition of income by assigning to another the property that generates the income. Such a procedure will not avoid income recognition by the taxpayer making the assignment if the income was earned at the point of the transfer. In this case, the income is taxed to the person who earns it.

At-risk limitation. Generally, a taxpayer can deduct losses related to a trade or business, S corporation, partnership, or investment asset only to the extent of the at-risk amount. The taxpayer has an amount at risk in a business or investment venture to the extent that personal assets have been subjected to the risks of the business. Typically, the taxpayer's at-risk amount includes (1) the amount of money or other property that the investor contributed to the venture for the investment, (2) the amount of any of the entity's liabilities for which the taxpayer personally is liable and that relate to the investment, and (3) an allocable share of nonrecourse debts incurred by the venture from third parties in arm's length transactions for real estate investments.

Attribution. Under certain circumstances, the tax law applies attribution (constructive ownership) rules to assign to one taxpayer the ownership interest of another taxpayer. If, for example, the stock of Gold Corporation is held 60 percent by Marsha and 40 percent by Sidney, Marsha may be deemed to own 100 percent of Gold Corporation if Marsha and Sidney are mother and child. In that case, the stock owned by Sidney is attributed to Marsha. Stated differently, Marsha has a 60 percent direct and a 40 percent indirect interest in Gold Corporation. It can also be said that Marsha is the constructive owner of Sidney's interest.

Automatic mileage method. Automobile expenses are generally deductible only to the extent the automobile is used in business or for the production of income. Personal commuting expenses are not deductible. The taxpayer may deduct actual expenses (including depreciation and insurance), or the standard (automatic) mileage rate may be used (53.5 cents per mile for 2017 and 54 cents per mile for 2016). Automobile expenses incurred for medical purposes or in connection with job-related moving expenses are deductible to the extent of actual out-of-pocket expenses or at the rate of 17 cents per mile for 2017 and 19 cents per mile for 2016. For charitable activities, the rate is 14 cents per mile.

B

Bad debt. A deduction is permitted if a business account receivable subsequently becomes partially or completely worthless, providing the income arising from the debt previously was included in income. Available methods are the specific charge-off method and the reserve method. However, except for certain financial institutions, TRA of 1986 repealed the use of the reserve method for 1987 and thereafter. If the reserve method is used, partially or totally worthless accounts are charged to the reserve. A nonbusiness bad debt deduction is allowed as a short-term capital loss if the loan did not arise in connection with the creditor's trade or business activities. Loans between related parties (family members) generally are classified as nonbusiness. § 166.

Balance sheet approach. The process under ASC 740 (SFAS 109) by which an entity's deferred tax expense or deferred tax benefit is determined as a result of the reporting period's changes in the balance sheet's deferred tax asset and deferred tax liability accounts.

Basis in partnership interest. The acquisition cost of the partner's ownership interest in the partnership. Includes purchase price and associated debt acquired from other partners and in the course of the entity's trade or business.

Benchmarking. The tax professional's use of two or more entities' effective tax rates and deferred tax balance sheet accounts. Used chiefly to compare the effectiveness of the entities' tax planning techniques, and to suggest future tax-motivated courses of action.

Blockage rule. A factor to be considered in valuing a large block of corporate stock. Application of this rule generally justifies a discount in the asset's fair market value, because the disposition of a large amount of stock at any one time may depress the value of the shares in the marketplace.

Boot. Cash or property of a type not included in the definition of a tax-deferred exchange. The receipt of boot causes an otherwise tax-deferred transfer to become immediately taxable to the extent of the lesser of the fair market value of the boot or the realized gain on the transfer. For example, see transfers to controlled corporations under § 351(b), reorganizations under § 368, and like-kind exchanges under § 1031(b).

Branch profits tax. A tax on the effectively connected earnings and profits of the U.S. branch of a foreign corporation. The tax is levied in addition to the usual § 11 tax in an amount equal to 30 percent of the dividend equivalent amount. Treaties can override the tax or reduce the withholding percentage. Earnings reinvested in the U.S. operations of the entity are not subject to the tax until repatriation.

Built-in gains tax. A penalty tax designed to discourage a shift of the incidence of taxation on unrealized gains from a C corporation to its shareholders, via an S election. Under this provision, any recognized gain during the first 10 (or seven or five) years of S status generates a corporate-level tax on a base not to exceed the aggregate untaxed built-in gains brought into the S corporation upon its election from C corporation taxable years.

Built-in loss property. Property contributed to a corporation under § 351 or as a contribution to capital that has a basis in excess of its fair market value. An adjustment is necessary to step down the basis of the property to its fair market value. The adjustment prevents the corporation and the contributing shareholder from obtaining a double tax benefit. The corporation allocates the adjustment proportionately among the assets with the built-in loss. As an alternative to the corporate adjustment, the shareholder may elect to reduce the basis in the stock.

Business bad debt. A tax deduction allowed for obligations obtained in connection with a trade or business that have become either partially or completely worthless. In contrast to nonbusiness bad debts, business bad debts are deductible as business expenses. § 166.

Business purpose. A justifiable business reason for carrying out a transaction. Mere tax avoidance is not an acceptable business purpose. The presence of a business purpose is crucial in the area of corporate reorganizations and certain liquidations.

Buy-sell agreement. An arrangement, particularly appropriate in the case of a closely held corporation or a partnership, whereby the surviving owners (shareholders or partners) or the entity agrees to purchase the interest of a withdrawing owner. The buy-sell agreement provides for an orderly disposition of an interest in a business and may aid in setting the value of the interest for estate tax purposes.

Bypass amount. The amount that can be transferred by gift or at death free of any unified transfer tax. For 2017, the bypass amount is $5.49 million for estate tax and $5.49 million for gift tax.

Bypass election. In the context of a distribution by an S corporation, an election made by the entity to designate that the distribution is first from accumulated earnings and profits and only then from the accumulated adjustments account (AAA).

C

C corporation. A separate taxable entity subject to the rules of Subchapter C of the Code. This business form may create a double taxation effect relative to its shareholders. The entity is subject to the regular corporate tax and a number of penalty taxes at the Federal level.

Cafeteria benefit plans. See *cafeteria plan*.

Cafeteria plan. An employee benefit plan under which an employee is allowed to select from among a variety of employer-provided fringe benefits. Some of the benefits may be taxable, and some may be statutory nontaxable benefits (e.g., health and accident insurance and group term life insurance). The employee is taxed only on the taxable benefits selected. A cafeteria benefit plan is also referred to as a flexible benefit plan. § 125.

Capital account. The financial accounting analog of a partner's tax basis in the entity.

Capital account maintenance. Under the § 704(b) Regulations, partnership allocations will be respected only if capital accounts are maintained in accordance with those regulations. These so-called "§ 704(b) book capital accounts" are properly maintained if they reflect the partner's contributions and distributions of cash, increases and decreases for the fair market value of contributed/distributed property, and adjustments for the partner's share of income, gains, losses, and deductions. Certain other adjustments are also required. See also *economic effect test*.

Capital asset. Broadly speaking, all assets are capital except those specifically excluded from that definition by the Code. Major categories of noncapital assets include property held for resale in the normal course of business (inventory), trade accounts and notes receivable, and depreciable property and real estate used in a trade or business (§ 1231 assets). § 1221.

Capital contribution. Various means by which a shareholder makes additional funds available to the corporation (placed at the risk of the business), sometimes without the receipt of additional stock. If no stock is received, the contributions are added to the basis of the shareholder's existing stock investment and do not generate gross income to the corporation. § 118.

Capital gains. The gain from the sale or exchange of a capital asset.

Capital gain property. Property contributed to a charitable organization that if sold rather than contributed, would have resulted in long-term capital gain to the donor.

Capital interest. Usually, the percentage of the entity's net assets that a partner would receive on liquidation. Typically determined by the partner's capital sharing ratio.

Capital losses. The loss from the sale or exchange of a capital asset.

Capital sharing ratio. A partner's percentage ownership of the entity's capital.

Carbon tax. A tax on fossil fuels to help reduce greenhouse gas emissions.

Cash balance plan. A hybrid form of pension plan similar in some aspects to a defined benefit plan. Such a plan is funded by the employer, and the employer bears the investment risks and rewards. But like defined contribution plans, a cash balance plan establishes allocations to individual employee accounts, and the payout for an employee depends on investment performance.

Cash method. See *cash receipts method*.

Cash receipts method. A method of accounting that reflects deductions as paid and income as received in any one tax year. However, deductions for prepaid expenses that benefit more than one tax year (e.g., prepaid rent and prepaid interest) usually are spread over the period benefited rather than deducted in the year paid. § 446(c)(1).

Casualty loss. A casualty is defined as "the complete or partial destruction of property resulting from an identifiable event of a sudden, unexpected or unusual nature" (e.g., floods, storms, fires, auto accidents). Individuals may deduct a casualty loss only if the loss is incurred in a trade or business or in a transaction entered into for profit or arises from fire, storm, shipwreck, or other casualty or from theft. Individuals usually deduct personal casualty losses as itemized deductions subject to a $100 nondeductible amount and to an annual floor equal to 10 percent of adjusted gross income that applies after the $100 per casualty floor has been applied. Special rules are provided for the netting of certain casualty gains and losses.

Charitable contribution. Contributions are deductible (subject to various restrictions and ceiling limitations) if made to qualified nonprofit charitable organizations. A cash basis taxpayer is entitled to a deduction solely in the year of payment. Accrual basis corporations may accrue contributions at year-end if payment is properly authorized before the end of the year and payment is made within two and one-half months after the end of the year. § 170.

Check-the-box Regulations. By using the check-the-box rules prudently, an entity can select the most attractive tax results offered by the Code, without being bound by legal forms. By default, an unincorporated entity with more than one owner is taxed as a partnership; an unincorporated entity with one owner is a disregarded entity, taxed as a sole proprietorship or corporate division. No action is necessary by the taxpayer if the legal form or default status is desired. Form 8832 is used to "check a box" and change the tax status. Not available if the entity is incorporated under state law.

Child tax credit. A tax credit based solely on the number of qualifying children under age 17. The maximum credit available is $1,000 per child. A qualifying child must be claimed as a dependent on a parent's tax return to qualify for the credit. Taxpayers who qualify for the child tax credit may also qualify for a supplemental credit. The supplemental credit is treated as a component of the earned income credit and is therefore refundable. The credit is phased out for higher-income taxpayers. § 24.

Circuit Court of Appeals. Any of 13 Federal courts that consider tax matters appealed from the U.S. Tax Court, a U.S. District Court, or the U.S. Court of Federal Claims. Appeal from a U.S. Court of Appeals is to the U.S. Supreme Court by Certiorari.

Circular 230. A portion of the Federal tax Regulations that describes the levels of conduct at which a tax preparer must operate. Circular 230 dictates, for instance, that a tax preparer may not charge an unconscionable fee or delay the execution of a tax audit with inappropriate delays. Circular 230 requires that there be a reasonable basis for a tax return position and that no frivolous returns be filed.

Citator. A tax research resource that presents the judicial history of a court case and traces the subsequent references to the case. When these references include the citing cases' evaluations of the cited case's precedents, the research can obtain some measure of the efficacy and reliability of the original holding.

Claim of right doctrine. A judicially imposed doctrine applicable to both cash and accrual basis taxpayers that holds that an amount is includible in income upon actual or constructive receipt if the taxpayer has an unrestricted claim to the payment. For the tax treatment of amounts repaid when previously included in income under the claim of right doctrine, see § 1341.

Closely held C corporation. A regular corporation (i.e., the S election is not in effect) for which more than 50 percent of the value of its outstanding stock is owned, directly or indirectly, by five or fewer individuals at any time during the tax year. The term is relevant in identifying C corporations that are subject to the passive activity loss provisions. § 469.

Closely held corporation. A corporation where stock ownership is not widely dispersed. Rather, a few shareholders are in control of corporate policy and are in a position to benefit personally from that policy.

Closing agreement. In a tax dispute, the parties sign a closing agreement to spell out the terms under which the matters are settled. The agreement is binding on both the Service and the taxpayer.

Collectibles. A special type of capital asset, the gain from which is taxed at a maximum rate of 28 percent if the holding period is more than one year. Examples include art, rugs, antiques, gems, metals, stamps, some coins and bullion, and alcoholic beverages held for investment.

Combined return. In multistate taxation, a group of unitary corporations may elect or be required to file an income tax return that includes operating results for all of the affiliates, not just those with nexus in the state. Thus, apportionment data is reported for the group's worldwide or water's-edge operations.

Community property. Louisiana, Texas, New Mexico, Arizona, California, Washington, Idaho, Nevada, and Wisconsin have community property systems. Alaska residents can elect community property status for assets. The rest of the states are common law property jurisdictions. The difference between common law and community property systems centers around the property rights possessed by married persons. In a common law system, each spouse owns whatever he or she earns. Under a community property system, one-half of the earnings of each spouse is considered owned by the other spouse. Assume, for example, that Jeff and Alice are husband and wife and that their only income is the $50,000 annual salary Jeff receives. If they live in New York (a common law state), the $50,000 salary belongs to Jeff. If, however, they live in Texas (a community property state), the $50,000 salary is owned one-half each by Jeff and Alice.

Compensatory damages. Damages received or paid by the taxpayer can be classified as compensatory damages or as punitive damages. Compensatory damages are paid to compensate one for harm caused by another. Compensatory damages received on account of physical injuries are excludible from the recipient's gross income.

Complete termination redemption. Sale or exchange treatment is available relative to this type of redemption. The shareholder must retire all of his or her outstanding shares in the corporation (ignoring family attribution rules) and cannot hold an interest, other than that of a creditor, for the 10 years following the redemption. § 302(b)(3).

Completed contract method. A method of reporting gain or loss on certain long-term contracts. Under this method of accounting, all gross income and expenses are recognized in the tax year in which the contract is completed. Reg. § 1.451–3.

Complex trust. Not a simple trust. Such trusts may have charitable beneficiaries, accumulate income, and distribute corpus. §§ 661–663.

Composite return. In multistate taxation, an S corporation may be allowed to file a single income tax return that assigns pass-through items to resident and nonresident shareholders. The composite or "block" return allows the entity to remit any tax that is attributable to the nonresident shareholders.

Conduit concept. A perspective taken towards a venture that regards the venture as an aggregation of its owners joined together in an agency relationship rather than as a separate entity. For tax purposes, this results in the income of the venture being taxable directly to its owners. For example, items of income and expense, capital gains and losses, tax credits, etc., realized by a partnership pass through the partnership (a conduit) and are subject to taxation at the partner level. Also, in an S corporation, certain items pass through and are reported on the returns of the shareholders.

Conduit perspective. See *conduit concept.*

Conservatism principle. The theory behind much of Generally Accepted Accounting Principles, under which assurance is provided that an entity's balance sheet assets are not overstated, nor liabilities understated. For instance, under ASC 740 (SFAS 109), a deferred tax asset is not recorded until it is more likely than not that the future tax benefit will be realized.

Consolidated returns. A procedure whereby certain affiliated corporations may file a single return, combine the tax transactions of each corporation, and arrive at a single income tax liability for the group. The election to file a consolidated return usually is binding on future years. §§ 1501–1505 and related Regulations.

Consolidation. The combination of two or more corporations into a newly created corporation. Thus, Black Corporation and White Corporation combine to form Gray Corporation. A consolidation may qualify as a nontaxable reorganization if certain conditions are satisfied. §§ 354 and 368(a)(1)(A).

Constructive dividend. A taxable benefit derived by a shareholder from his or her corporation that is not actually initiated by the board of directors as a dividend. Examples include unreasonable compensation, excessive rent payments, bargain purchases of corporate property, and shareholder use of corporate property. Constructive dividends generally are found in closely held corporations.

Constructive liquidation scenario. The means by which recourse debt is shared among partners in basis determination.

Constructive receipt. If income is unqualifiedly available although not physically in the taxpayer's possession, it still is subject to the income tax. An example is accrued interest on a savings account. Under the constructive receipt concept, the interest is taxed to a depositor in the year available, rather than the year actually withdrawn. The fact that the depositor uses the cash basis of accounting for tax purposes is irrelevant. See Reg. § 1.451–2.

Continuity of business enterprise. In a tax-favored reorganization, the acquiring corporation must continue the historic business of the target or use a significant portion of the target's assets in the new business.

Continuity of interest. In a tax-favored reorganization, a shareholder or corporation that has substantially the same investment after an exchange as before should not be taxed on the transaction. Specifically, the target shareholders must acquire an equity interest in the acquiring corporation equal in value to at least 40 percent of all the outstanding stock of the target entity.

Control. Holding a specified level of stock ownership in a corporation. For § 351, the new shareholder(s) must hold at least 80 percent of the total combined voting power of all voting classes of stock and at least 80 percent of the shares of all nonvoting classes. Other tax provisions require different levels of control to bring about desired effects, such as 50 or 100 percent.

Controlled foreign corporation (CFC). A non-U.S. corporation in which more than 50 percent of the total combined voting power of all classes of stock entitled to vote or the total value of the stock of the corporation is owned by U.S. shareholders on any day during the taxable year of the foreign corporation. For purposes of this definition, a U.S. shareholder is any U.S. person who owns, or is considered to own, 10 percent or more of the total combined voting power of all classes of voting stock of the foreign corporation. Stock owned directly, indirectly, and constructively is used in this measure. See *U.S. shareholder.*

Controlled group. A controlled group of corporations is required to share the lower corporate tax rates and various other tax benefits among the members of the group. A controlled group may be either a brother-sister or a parent-subsidiary group.

Corporate liquidation. Occurs when a corporation distributes its net assets to its shareholders and ceases to be a going concern. Generally, a shareholder recognizes capital gain or loss upon the liquidation of the entity, regardless of the corporation's balance in its earnings and profits account. The liquidating corporation recognizes gain and loss on assets that it sells during the liquidation period and on assets that it distributes to shareholders in kind.

Corpus. The body or principal of a trust. Suppose, for example, Grant transfers an apartment building into a trust, income payable to Ruth for life, remainder to Shawn upon Ruth's death. Corpus of the trust is the apartment building.

Correspondence audit. An audit conducted by the IRS by the U.S. mail. Typically, the IRS writes to the taxpayer requesting the verification of a particular deduction or exemption. The remittance of copies of records or other support is requested of the taxpayer.

Cost depletion. Depletion that is calculated based on the adjusted basis of the asset. The adjusted basis is divided by the expected recoverable units to determine the depletion per unit. The depletion per unit is multiplied by the units sold during the tax year to calculate cost depletion.

Cost recovery. The system by which a taxpayer is allowed to recover their investment in an asset by reducing their taxable income by the asset's cost or initial basis. Cost recovery methods include MACRS, § 179 expense, additional first-year depreciation, amortization, and depletion. §§ 168, 179, and 613.

Court of Federal Claims. A trial court (court of original jurisdiction) that decides litigation involving Federal tax matters. Appeal from this court is to the Court of Appeals for the Federal Circuit.

Court of original jurisdiction. The Federal courts are divided into courts of original jurisdiction and appellate courts. A dispute between a taxpayer and the IRS is first considered by a court of original jurisdiction (i.e., a trial court). The four Federal courts of original jurisdiction are the U.S. Tax Court, the U.S. District Court, the Court of Federal Claims, and the Small Cases Division of the U.S. Tax Court.

Coverdell education savings account (§ 530 plan). Coverdell education savings account exempts from tax the earnings on amounts placed in a qualified account for the education expenses of a named beneficiary. Contributions are limited to $2,000 per year per beneficiary and the proceeds can be withdrawn without tax provided the funds are used to pay qualified educational expenses for primary, secondary, or higher education. The account is named for the late Senator Paul Coverdell (R-GA), who sponsored the legislation in Congress. § 530.

Credit for certain retirement plan contributions. A nonrefundable credit is available based on eligible contributions of up to $2,000 to certain qualified retirement plans, such as traditional and Roth IRAs and § 401(k) plans. The benefit provided by this credit is in addition to any deduction or exclusion that otherwise is available resulting from the qualifying contribution. The amount of the credit depends on the taxpayer's AGI and filing status. § 25B.

Credit for child and dependent care expenses. A tax credit ranging from 20 percent to 35 percent of employment-related expenses (child and dependent care expenses) for amounts of up to $6,000 is available to individuals who are employed (or deemed to be employed) and maintain a household for a dependent child under age 13, disabled spouse, or disabled dependent. § 21.

Credit for employer-provided child care. A nonrefundable credit is available to employers who provide child care facilities to their employees during normal working hours. The credit, limited to $150,000, is comprised of two components. The portion of the credit for qualified child care expenses is equal to 25 percent of these expenses, while the portion of the credit for qualified child care resource and referral services is equal to 10 percent of these expenses. Any qualifying expenses otherwise deductible by the taxpayer must be reduced by the amount of the credit. In addition, the taxpayer's basis for any property used for qualifying purposes is reduced by the amount of the credit. § 45F.

Credit for small employer pension plan startup costs. A nonrefundable credit available to small businesses based on administrative costs associated with establishing and maintaining certain qualified plans. While such qualifying costs generally are deductible as ordinary and necessary business expenses, the availability of the credit is intended to lower the costs of starting a qualified retirement program and therefore encourage qualifying businesses to establish retirement plans for their employees. The credit is available for eligible employers at the rate of 50 percent of qualified startup costs. The maximum credit is $500 (based on a maximum $1,000 of qualifying expenses). § 45E.

Crop insurance proceeds. The proceeds received when an insured crop is destroyed. Section 451(d) permits the farmer to defer reporting the income from the insurance proceeds until the tax year following the taxable year of the destruction.

Crop method. A method of accounting for agricultural crops that are planted in one year but harvested in a subsequent year. Under this method, the costs of raising the crop are accumulated as inventory and are deducted when the income from the crop is realized.

Cross-purchase buy-sell agreement. Under this arrangement, the surviving owners of the business agree to buy out the withdrawing owner. Assume, for example, Ron and Sara are equal shareholders in Tip Corporation. Under a cross-purchase buy-sell agreement, Ron and Sara would contract to purchase the other's interest, should that person decide to withdraw from the business.

Current distribution. A payment made by a partnership to a partner when the partnership's legal existence does not cease thereafter. The partner usually assigns a basis in the distributed property that is equal to the lesser of the partner's basis in the partnership interest or the basis of the distributed asset to the partnership. The partner first assigns basis to any cash that he or she receives in the distribution. A cash distribution in excess of the partner's basis triggers a gain. The partner's remaining basis, if any, is assigned to the noncash assets according to their relative bases to the partnership.

Current E & P. Net tax-basis earnings of a corporation aggregated during the current tax year. A corporate distribution is deemed to be first from the entity's current earnings and profits and then from accumulated earnings and profits. Shareholders recognize dividend income to the extent of the earnings and profits of the corporation. A dividend results to the extent of current earnings and profits, even if there is a larger negative balance in accumulated earnings and profits.

Current tax expense. Under ASC 740 (SFAS 109), the book tax expense that relates to the current reporting period's net income and is actually payable (or creditable) to the appropriate governmental agencies for the current period. Also known as "cash tax" or "tax payable."

D

De minimis fringe. Benefits provided to employees that are too insignificant to warrant the time and effort required to account for the benefits received by each employee and the value of those benefits. Such amounts are excludible from the employee's gross income. § 132.

De minimis fringe benefits. See *de minimis fringe*.

Death benefits. A payment made by an employer to the beneficiary or beneficiaries of a deceased employee on account of the death of the employee.

Debt-financed income. Included in computations of the unrelated business income of an exempt organization, the gross income generated from debt-financed property.

Deceased spouse's unused exclusion (DSUE). In computing the Federal estate tax, the decedent uses the exclusion amount to shelter an amount of the gross estate from taxation. When the first spouse to die fails to use a portion of his/her exclusion amount, the unused portion is "portable," and becomes available to the surviving spouse. The surviving spouse can use the DSUE only of his/her last spouse to predecease.

Deduction for qualified tuition and related expenses. Taxpayers are allowed a deduction of up to $4,000 for higher education expenses. Certain taxpayers are not eligible for the deduction: those whose gross AGI exceeds a specified amount and those who can be claimed as a dependent by another taxpayer. These expenses are classified as a deduction *for* AGI, and they need not be employment-related. § 222.

Deductions *for* adjusted gross income. The Federal income tax is not imposed upon gross income. Rather, it is imposed upon taxable income. Congressionally identified deductions for individual taxpayers are subtracted either from gross income to arrive at adjusted gross income or from adjusted gross income to arrive at the tax base, taxable income.

Deductions *from* adjusted gross income. See *deductions for adjusted gross income*.

Deductions in respect of a decedent. Deductions accrued at the moment of death but not recognizable on the final income tax return of a decedent because of the method of accounting used. Such items are allowed as deductions on the estate tax return and on the income tax return of the estate (Form 1041) or the heir (Form 1040). An example of a deduction in respect of a decedent is interest expense accrued to the date of death by a cash basis debtor.

Deemed-paid credit. A foreign tax credit allowed to a U.S. taxpayer that has received an actual or constructive dividend from a non-U.S. corporation that has paid foreign income taxes. The credit is computed using the proportion of foreign income taxes paid by the payor corporation to its post-1986 undistributed earnings. Under § 78, the U.S. taxpayer claiming a deemed-paid credit includes the same amount in gross income for the tax year.

Deferred compensation. Compensation that will be taxed when received or upon the removal of certain restrictions on receipt and not when earned. Contributions by an employer to a qualified pension or profit sharing plan on behalf of an employee are an example. The contributions will not be taxed to the employee until the funds are made available or distributed to the employee (e.g., upon retirement).

Deferred tax asset. Under ASC 740 (SFAS 109), an item created on an enterprise's balance sheet by a temporary book-tax difference, such that a tax benefit is not recognized until a later date, although it already has been reported in the financial statements (e.g., the carryforward of a disallowed deduction).

Deferred tax benefit. Under ASC 740 (SFAS 109), a reduction in the book tax expense that relates to the current reporting period's net income but will not be realized until a future reporting period. Creates or adds to the entity's deferred tax asset balance sheet account. For instance, the carryforward of a net operating loss is a deferred tax benefit.

Deferred tax expense. Under ASC 740 (SFAS 109), a book tax expense that relates to the current reporting period's net income but will not be realized until a future reporting period. Creates or adds to the entity's deferred tax liability balance sheet account. For instance, a deferred tax expense is created when tax depreciation deductions for the period are "accelerated" and exceed the corresponding book depreciation expense.

Deferred tax liability. As determined under the rules of ASC 740 (SFAS 109), an item created on an enterprise's balance sheet by a temporary book-tax difference, such that a tax benefit is recognized earlier for tax purposes than it is in the financial accounting records (e.g., the use of an accelerated cost recovery deduction).

Defined benefit plan. Qualified plans can be dichotomized into defined benefit plans and defined contribution plans. Under a defined benefit plan, a formula defines the benefits employees are to receive. The formula usually includes years of service, employee compensation, and some stated percentage. The employer must make annual contributions based on actuarial computations that will be sufficient to pay the vested retirement benefits.

Defined contribution pension plan. Qualified plans can be dichotomized into defined benefit plans and defined contribution plans. Under a defined contribution plan, a separate account is maintained for each covered employee. The employee's benefits under the plan are based solely on (1) the amount contributed and (2) income from the fund that accrues to the employee's account. The plan defines the amount the employer is required to contribute (e.g., a flat dollar amount, an amount based on a special formula, or an amount equal to a certain percentage of compensation).

Dependency exemption. See *personal and dependency exemptions.*

Depletion. The process by which the cost or other basis of a natural resource (e.g., an oil or gas interest) is recovered upon extraction and sale of the resource. The two ways to determine the depletion allowance are the cost and percentage (or statutory) methods. Under cost depletion, each unit of production sold is assigned a portion of the cost or other basis of the interest. This is determined by dividing the cost or other basis by the total units expected to be recovered. Under percentage (or statutory) depletion, the tax law provides a special percentage factor for different types of minerals and other natural resources. This percentage is multiplied by the gross income from the interest to arrive at the depletion allowance. §§ 613 and 613A.

Depreciation. The system by which a taxpayer allocates for financial reporting purposes the cost of an asset to periods benefited by the asset.

Determination letter. Upon the request of a taxpayer, the IRS will comment on the tax status of a completed transaction. Determination letters frequently are used to determine whether a retirement or profit sharing plan qualifies under the Code, and to determine the tax-exempt status of certain nonprofit organizations.

Disabled access credit. A tax credit designed to encourage small businesses to make their facilities more accessible to disabled individuals. The credit is equal to 50 percent of the eligible expenditures that exceed $250 but do not exceed $10,250. Thus, the maximum amount for the credit is $5,000. The adjusted basis for depreciation is reduced by the amount of the credit. To qualify, the facility must have been placed in service before November 6, 1990. § 44.

Disaster area losses. A casualty sustained in an area designated as a disaster area by the president of the United States. In such an event, the disaster loss may be treated as having occurred in the taxable year immediately preceding the year in which the disaster actually occurred. Thus, immediate tax benefits are provided to victims of a disaster. § 165(i).

Disclaimer. Rejections, refusals, or renunciations of claims, powers, or property. Section 2518 sets forth the conditions required to avoid gift tax consequences as the result of a disclaimer.

Disguised sale. When a partner contributes property to the entity and soon thereafter receives a distribution from the partnership, the transactions are collapsed and the distribution is seen as a purchase of the asset by the partnership. § 707(a)(2)(B).

Disproportionate distribution. A distribution from a partnership to one or more of its partners in which at least one partner's interest in partnership hot assets is increased or decreased. For example, a distribution of cash to one partner and hot assets to another changes both partners' interest in hot assets and is disproportionate. The intent of rules for taxation of disproportionate distributions is to ensure that each partner eventually recognizes his or her proportionate share of partnership ordinary income.

Disproportionate redemption. Sale or exchange treatment is available relative to this type of redemption. After the exchange, the shareholder owns less than 80 percent of his or her pre-redemption interest in the corporation and only a minority interest in the entity. § 302(b)(2).

Disregarded entity. The Federal income tax treatment of business income usually follows the legal form of the taxpayer (i.e., an individual's sole proprietorship is reported on the Form 1040); a C corporation's taxable income is computed on Form 1120. The check-the-box Regulations are used if the unincorporated taxpayer wants to use a different tax regime. Under these rules, a disregarded entity is taxed as an individual or a corporate division; other tax regimes are not available. For instance, a one-member limited liability company is a disregarded entity.

Distributable net income (DNI). The measure that determines the nature and amount of the distributions from estates and trusts that the beneficiaries must include in income. DNI also limits the amount that estates and trusts can claim as a deduction for such distributions. § 643(a).

District Court. See *Federal District Court.*

Dividend. A nondeductible distribution to the shareholders of a corporation. A dividend constitutes gross income to the recipient if it is paid from the current or accumulated earnings and profits of the corporation.

Dividend equivalent amount (DEA). The amount subject to the branch profits tax, it is equal to the effectively connected E & P of the U.S. branch of a foreign corporation, reduced/(increased) by an increase/(reduction) in U.S. net equity.

Dividends received deduction. A deduction allowed a shareholder that is a corporation for dividends received from a domestic corporation. The deduction usually is 70 percent of the dividends received, but it could be 80 or 100 percent depending upon the ownership percentage held by the recipient corporation. §§ 243–246.

Divisive reorganization. A "Type D" spin-off, split-off, or split-up, reorganization in which the original corporation divides its active business (in existence for at least five years) assets among two or more corporations. The stock received by the original corporation shareholders must be at least 80 percent of the other corporations.

Dock sales. A purchaser uses its owned or rented vehicles to take possession of the product at the seller's shipping dock. In most states, the sale is apportioned to the operating state of the purchaser, rather than the seller. See also *apportion* and *sales factor*.

Dollar-value LIFO. An inventory technique that focuses on the dollars invested in the inventory rather than the particular items on hand each period. Each inventory item is assigned to a pool. A pool is a collection of similar items and is treated as a separate inventory. At the end of the period, each pool is valued in terms of prices at the time LIFO was adopted (base period prices), whether or not the particular items were actually on hand in the year LIFO was adopted, to compare with current prices to determine if there has been an increase or decrease in inventories.

Domestic production activities deduction (DPAD). A deduction based on a percentage of the lesser of (a) qualified production activities income (QPAI) or (b) taxable income (modified adjusted gross income for individuals). The deduction is further limited to 50 percent of the wages related to generating QPAI. § 199.

Domestic production gross receipts (DPGR). A key component in computing the domestic production activities deduction (DPAD). Includes receipts from the sale and other disposition of qualified production property produced in significant part within the United States. DPGR is defined in § 199(c)(4).

E

Earned income credit. A tax credit designed to provide assistance to certain low-income individuals who generally have a qualifying child. This is a refundable credit. To receive the most beneficial treatment, the taxpayer must have qualifying children. However, it is possible to qualify for the credit without having a child. See the text chapter on credits for the computation procedure required in order to determine the amount of the credit allowed.

Earnings and profits (E & P). Measures the economic capacity of a corporation to make a distribution to shareholders that is not a return of capital. Such a distribution results in dividend income to the shareholders to the extent of the corporation's current and accumulated earnings and profits.

Economic effect test. Requirements that must be met before a special allocation may be used by a partnership. The premise behind the test is that each partner who receives an allocation of income or loss from a partnership bears the economic benefit or burden of the allocation.

Economic income. The change in the taxpayer's net worth, as measured in terms of market values, plus the value of the assets the taxpayer consumed during the year. Because of the impracticality of this income model, it is not used for tax purposes.

Economic performance test. One of the requirements that must be satisfied for an accrual basis taxpayer to deduct an expense. Economic performance occurs when property or services are provided to the taxpayer, or in the case in which the taxpayer is required to provide property or services, whenever the property or services are actually provided by the taxpayer.

Education expenses. Employees may deduct education expenses that are incurred either (1) to maintain or improve existing job-related skills or (2) to meet the express requirements of the employer or the requirements imposed by law to retain employment status. The expenses are not deductible if the education is required to meet the minimum educational standards for the taxpayer's job or if the education qualifies the individual for a new trade or business. Reg. § 1.162–5.

Educational savings bonds. U.S. Series EE bonds whose proceeds are used for qualified higher educational expenses for the taxpayer, the taxpayer's spouse, or a dependent. The interest may be excluded from gross income, provided the taxpayer's adjusted gross income does not exceed certain amounts. § 135.

Effective tax rate. The financial statements for an entity include several footnotes, one of which reconciles the expected (statutory) income tax rate (e.g., 35 percent for a C corporation) with the effective tax rate (i.e., total tax expense as a percentage of book income). The reconciliation often is done in dollar and/or percentage terms.

Effectively connected income. Income of a nonresident alien or foreign corporation that is attributable to the operation of a U.S. trade or business under either the asset-use or the business-activities test.

E-file. The electronic filing of a tax return. The filing is either direct or indirect. As to direct, the taxpayer goes online using a computer and tax return preparation software. Indirect filing occurs when a taxpayer utilizes an authorized IRS e-file provider. The provider often is the tax return preparer.

E-filing. See *e-file*.

Employment taxes. Taxes that an employer must pay on account of its employees. Employment taxes include FICA (Federal Insurance Contributions Act) and FUTA (Federal Unemployment Tax Act) taxes. Employment taxes are paid to the IRS in addition to income tax withholdings at specified intervals. Such taxes can be levied on the employees, the employer, or both.

Energy credits. See *energy tax credits*.

Energy tax credits. Various tax credits are available to those who invest in certain energy property. The purpose of the credit is to create incentives for conservation and to develop alternative energy sources.

Enrolled agents (EAs). A tax practitioner who has gained admission to practice before the IRS by passing an IRS examination and maintaining a required level of continuing professional education.

Entertainment expenses. Expenses that are deductible only if they are directly related to or associated with a trade or business. Various restrictions and documentation requirements have been imposed upon the deductibility of entertainment expenses to prevent abuses by taxpayers. See, for example, the provision contained in § 274(n) that disallows

50 percent (20 percent prior to 1994) of entertainment expenses. § 274.

Entity accounting income. Entity accounting income is not identical to the taxable income of a trust or estate, nor is it determined in the same manner as the entity's financial accounting income would be. The trust document or will determines whether certain income, expenses, gains, or losses are allocated to the corpus of the entity or to the entity's income beneficiaries. Only the items that are allocated to the income beneficiaries are included in entity accounting income.

Entity buy-sell agreement. An arrangement whereby the entity is to purchase a withdrawing owner's interest. When the entity is a corporation, the agreement generally involves a stock redemption on the part of the withdrawing shareholder. See also *buy-sell agreement* and *cross-purchase buy-sell agreement*.

Entity concept. A perspective taken towards a venture that regards the venture as an entity separate and distinct from its owners. For tax purposes, this results in the venture being directly responsible for the tax on the income it generates. The entity perspective taken toward C corporations results in the double taxation of income distributed to the corporation's owners.

Entity perspective. See *entity concept*.

Equity method. Under Generally Accepted Accounting Principles, the method of financial reporting for the operations of a subsidiary when the parent corporation owns between 20 and 50 percent of the subsidiary's stock. Creates a book-tax difference, as the two entities' operating results are combined for book purposes, but a Federal income tax consolidated return cannot be filed.

Estate tax. A tax imposed on the right to transfer property by death. Thus, an estate tax is levied on the decedent's estate and not on the heir receiving the property.

Estimated tax. The amount of tax (including alternative minimum tax and self-employment tax) a taxpayer expects to owe for the year after subtracting tax credits and income tax withheld. The estimated tax must be paid in installments at designated intervals (e.g., for the individual taxpayer, by April 15, June 15, September 15, and January 15 of the following year).

Excess lobbying expenditures. An excise tax is applied on otherwise tax-exempt organizations with respect to the excess of total lobbying expenditures over grass roots lobbying expenditures for the year.

Excess loss account. When a subsidiary has generated more historical losses than its parent has invested in the entity, the parent's basis in the subsidiary is zero, and the parent records additional losses in an excess loss account. This treatment allows the parent to continue to deduct losses of the subsidiary, even where no basis reduction is possible, while avoiding the need to show a negative stock basis on various financial records. If the subsidiary stock is sold while an excess loss account exists, capital gain income usually is recognized to the extent of the balance in the account.

Excise taxes. A tax on the manufacture, sale, or use of goods; on the carrying on of an occupation or activity; or on the transfer of property. Thus, the Federal estate and gift taxes are, theoretically, excise taxes.

Exclusion amount. The value of assets that is exempt from transfer tax due to the credit allowed for gifts or transfers by death. For gifts and deaths in 2017, the exclusion amount is $5.49 million. An exclusion amount unused by a deceased spouse may be used by the surviving spouse. See also *exemption equivalent amount*.

Exempt organizations. An organization that is either partially or completely exempt from Federal income taxation. § 501.

Exemption amount. See *AMT exemption*.

Exemption equivalent. The maximum value of assets that can be transferred to another party without incurring any Federal gift or estate tax because of the application of the unified tax credit. See also *exemption equivalent amount*.

Exemption equivalent amount. The nontaxable amount (in 2017, $5.49 million for gift tax and estate tax) that is the equivalent of the unified transfer tax credit allowed.

F

Fair market value. The amount at which property would change hands between a willing buyer and a willing seller, neither being under any compulsion to buy or to sell and both having reasonable knowledge of the relevant facts. Reg. §§ 1.1001–1(a) and 20.2031–1(b).

Farm price method. A method of accounting for agricultural crops. The inventory of crops is valued at its market price less the estimated cost of disposition (e.g., freight and selling expense).

FDAP. Income of a nonresident alien or non-U.S. corporation that is received in the form of dividends, interest, rents, royalties, certain compensation, premiums, annuities, and other "fixed, determinable, annual, or periodic" forms. FDAP income usually is subject to U.S. income taxation at a flat 30 percent tax rate.

Federal District Court. A trial court for purposes of litigating Federal tax matters. It is the only trial court in which a jury trial can be obtained.

Feeder organization. An entity that carries on a trade or business for the benefit of an exempt organization. However, such a relationship does not result in the feeder organization itself being tax-exempt. § 502.

FICA tax. An abbreviation that stands for Federal Insurance Contributions Act, commonly referred to as the Social Security tax. The FICA tax is comprised of the Social Security tax (old age, survivors, and disability insurance) and the Medicare tax (hospital insurance) and is imposed on both employers and employees. The employer is responsible for withholding from the employee's wages the Social Security tax at a rate of 6.2 percent on a maximum wage base and the Medicare tax at a rate of 1.45 percent (no maximum wage base). The maximum Social Security wage base for 2017 is $127,200 and for 2016 is $118,500.

Fiduciary. One who holds a legal obligation to act on another's behalf. A *trustee* and an *executor* take fiduciary relationships relative to the *grantor* and the *decedent*, respectively. The fiduciary is assigned specific duties by the principal party, e.g., to file tax returns, manage assets, satisfy debt and other obligations, and to make investment decisions. The fiduciary often possesses specialized knowledge and experience. A fiduciary must avoid conflicts of interest in which the principal's goals are compromised in some way.

Field audit. An audit conducted by the IRS on the business premises of the taxpayer or in the office of the tax practitioner representing the taxpayer.

Filing status. Individual taxpayers are placed in one of five filing statuses each year (single, married filing jointly, married filing separately, surviving spouse, or head of household). Marital status and household support are key determinants. Filing status is used to determine the taxpayer's filing requirements, standard deduction, eligibility for certain deductions and credits, and tax liability.

Final Regulations. The U.S. Treasury Department Regulations (abbreviated Reg.) represent the position of the IRS as to how the Internal Revenue Code is to be interpreted. Their purpose is to provide taxpayers and IRS personnel with rules of general and specific application to the various provisions of the tax law. Regulations are published in the *Federal Register* and in all tax services.

Financial Accounting Standards Board (FASB). See *Generally Accepted Accounting Principles (GAAP).*

Financial transaction tax. A tax imposed on some type of financial transaction, such as stock sales.

Fiscal year. A 12-month period ending on the last day of a month other than December. In certain circumstances, a taxpayer is permitted to elect a fiscal year instead of being required to use a calendar year.

Flat tax. A form of consumption tax designed to alleviate the regressivity of a value added tax (VAT). It is imposed on individuals and businesses at the same, single (flat) rate.

Flexible spending plans. An employee benefit plan that allows the employee to take a reduction in salary in exchange for the employer paying benefits that can be provided by the employer without the employee being required to recognize income (e.g., medical and child care benefits). Contributions to a flexible spending plan are limited to $2,600 for 2017.

Flow-through entity. The entity is a tax reporter rather than a taxpayer. The owners are subject to tax. Examples are partnerships, S corporations, and limited liability companies.

Foreign earned income exclusion. The Code allows exclusions for earned income generated outside the United States to alleviate any tax base and rate disparities among countries. In addition, the exclusion is allowed for housing expenditures incurred by the taxpayer's employer with respect to the non-U.S. assignment, and self-employed individuals can deduct foreign housing expenses incurred in a trade or business. The exclusion is limited to $102,100 per year for 2017 ($101,300 in 2016). § 911.

Foreign Investment in Real Property Tax Act (FIRPTA). Under the Foreign Investment in Real Property Tax Act, gains or losses realized by nonresident aliens and non-U.S. corporations on the disposition of U.S. real estate creates U.S. source income and are subject to U.S. income tax.

Foreign tax credit (FTC). A U.S. citizen or resident who incurs or pays income taxes to a foreign country on income subject to U.S. tax may be able to claim some of these taxes as a credit against the U.S. income tax. §§ 27 and 901–905.

Franchise. An agreement that gives the transferee the right to distribute, sell, or provide goods, services, or facilities within a specified area. The cost of obtaining a franchise may be amortized over a statutory period of 15 years. In general, the franchisor's gain on the sale of franchise rights is an ordinary gain because the franchisor retains a significant power, right, or continuing interest in the subject of the franchise. §§ 197 and 1253.

Franchise tax. A tax levied on the right to do business in a state as a corporation. Although income considerations may come into play, the tax usually is based on the capitalization of the corporation.

Fraud. Tax fraud falls into two categories: civil and criminal. Under civil fraud, the IRS may impose as a penalty an amount equal to as much as 75 percent of the underpayment [§ 6651(f)]. Fines and/or imprisonment are prescribed for conviction of various types of criminal tax fraud (§§ 7201–7207). Both civil and criminal fraud involve a specific intent on the part of the taxpayer to evade the tax; mere negligence is not enough. Criminal fraud requires the additional element of willfulness (i.e., done deliberately and with evil purpose). In practice, it becomes difficult to distinguish between the degree of intent necessary to support criminal, rather than civil, fraud. In either situation, the IRS has the burden of proof to show the taxpayer committed fraud.

Fringe benefits. Compensation or other benefit received by an employee that is not in the form of cash. Some fringe benefits (e.g., accident and health plans, group term life insurance) may be excluded from the employee's gross income and therefore are not subject to the Federal income tax.

Fruit and tree metaphor. The courts have held that an individual who earns income from property or services cannot assign that income to another. For example, a father cannot assign his earnings from commissions to his child and escape income tax on those amounts.

Functional currency. The currency of the economic environment in which the taxpayer carries on most of its activities and in which the taxpayer transacts most of its business.

FUTA tax. An employment tax levied on employers. Jointly administered by the Federal and state governments, the tax provides funding for unemployment benefits. FUTA applies at a rate of 6.0 percent on the first $7,000 of covered wages paid during the year for each employee in 2017. The Federal government allows a credit for FUTA paid (or allowed under a merit rating system) to the state. The credit cannot exceed 5.4 percent of the covered wages.

Future interest. An interest that will come into being at some future time. It is distinguished from a present interest, which already exists. Assume that Dan transfers securities to a newly created trust. Under the terms of the trust instrument, income from the securities is to be paid each year to Wilma for her life, with the securities passing to Sam upon Wilma's death. Wilma has a present interest in the trust because she is entitled to current income distributions. Sam has a future interest because he must wait for Wilma's death to benefit from the trust. The annual exclusion of $14,000 (in 2017) is not allowed for a gift of a future interest. § 2503(b).

G

General business credit. The summation of various nonrefundable business credits, including the tax credit for rehabilitation expenditures, business energy credit, work opportunity credit, research activities credit, low-income housing credit, and disabled access credit. The amount of general business credit that can be used to reduce the tax liability is limited to the taxpayer's net income tax reduced by the greater of (1) the tentative minimum tax or (2) 25 percent of the net regular tax liability that exceeds $25,000. Unused general business credits can be carried back one year and forward 20 years. § 38.

General partners. A partner who is fully liable in an individual capacity for the debts owed by the partnership to third parties. A general partner's liability is not limited to the investment in the partnership. See also *limited partner*.

General partnership (GP). A partnership that is owned by one or more general partners. Creditors of a general partnership can collect amounts owed them from both the partnership assets and the assets of the partners individually.

Generally Accepted Accounting Principles (GAAP). Guidelines relating to how to construct the financial statements of enterprises doing business in the United States. Promulgated chiefly by the Financial Accounting Standards Board (FASB).

Gift tax. A tax imposed on the transfer of property by gift. The tax is imposed upon the donor of a gift and is based on the fair market value of the property on the date of the gift.

Golden parachute payments. A severance payment to employees that meets the following requirements: (1) the payment is contingent on a change of ownership of a corporation through a stock or asset acquisition and (2) the aggregate present value of the payment equals or exceeds three times the employee's average annual compensation. To the extent the severance payment meets these conditions, a deduction is disallowed to the employer for the excess of the payment over a statutory base amount (a five-year average of compensation if the taxpayer was an employee for the entire five-year period). In addition, a 20 percent excise tax is imposed on the employee who receives the excess severance pay. §§ 280G and 4999.

Goodwill. The reputation and built-up business of a company. For accounting purposes, goodwill has no basis unless it is purchased. In the purchase of a business, goodwill generally is the difference between the purchase price and the fair market value of the assets acquired. The intangible asset goodwill can be amortized for tax purposes over a 15-year period. § 197 and Reg. § 1.167(a)–3.

Grantor. A transferor of property. The creator of a trust is usually referred to as the grantor of the entity.

Grantor trust. A trust under which the grantor retains control over the income or corpus (or both) to such an extent that he or she is treated as the owner of the property and its income for income tax purposes. Income from a grantor trust is taxable to the grantor and not to the beneficiary who receives it. §§ 671–679.

Grass roots expenditures. Exempt organizations are prohibited from engaging in political activities, but spending incurred to influence the opinions of the general public relative to specific legislation is permitted by the law.

Gross estate. The property owned or previously transferred by a decedent that is subject to the Federal estate tax. The gross estate can be distinguished from the probate estate, which is property actually subject to administration by the administrator or executor of an estate. §§ 2031–2046.

Gross income. Income subject to the Federal income tax. Gross income does not include all economic income. That is, certain exclusions are allowed (e.g., interest on municipal bonds). For a manufacturing or merchandising business, gross income usually means gross profit (gross sales or gross receipts less cost of goods sold). § 61 and Reg. § 1.61–3(a).

Group term life insurance. Life insurance coverage provided by an employer for a group of employees. Such insurance is renewable on a year-to-year basis, and typically no cash surrender value is built up. The premiums paid by the employer on the insurance are not taxed to the employees on coverage of up to $50,000 per person. § 79 and Reg. § 1.79–1(b).

Guaranteed payments. Payments made by a partnership to a partner for services rendered or for the use of capital to the extent the payments are determined without regard to the income of the partnership. The payments are treated as though they were made to a nonpartner and thus are deducted by the entity.

H

H.R. 10 plans. See *Keogh plans*.

Half-year convention. A cost recovery convention that assumes that property is placed in service at mid-year and thus provides for a half-year's cost recovery for that year.

Head of household. An unmarried individual who maintains a household for another and satisfies certain conditions set forth in § 2(b). This status enables the taxpayer to use a set of income tax rates that are lower than those applicable to other unmarried individuals but higher than those applicable to surviving spouses and married persons filing a joint return.

Health Savings Account (HSA). A medical savings account created in legislation enacted in December 2003 that is designed to replace and expand Archer Medical Savings Accounts.

Highly compensated employee. The employee group is generally divided into two categories for fringe benefit (including pension and profit sharing plans) purposes. These are (1) highly compensated employees and (2) non-highly compensated employees. For most fringe benefits, if the fringe benefit plan discriminates in favor of highly compensated employees, it will not be a qualified plan with respect, at a minimum, to the highly compensated employees.

Historic business test. In a corporate reorganization, a means by which to determine if the continuity of business enterprise requirement is met. The acquiring corporation must continue to operate the target entity's existing business(es) going forward; if this is not the case, the requirement is failed.

Hobby losses. Losses from an activity not engaged in for profit. The Code restricts the amount of losses that an individual can deduct for hobby activities so that these transactions cannot be used to offset income from other sources. § 183.

Holding period. The period of time during which property has been held for income tax purposes. The holding period is significant in determining whether gain or loss from the sale or exchange of a capital asset is long or short term. § 1223.

Home equity loans. Loans that utilize the personal residence of the taxpayer as security. The interest on such loans is deductible as qualified residence interest. However, interest is deductible only on the portion of the loan that does not exceed the lesser of (1) the fair market value of the residence, reduced by the acquisition indebtedness, or (2) $100,000 ($50,000 for married persons filing separate returns). A major benefit of a home equity loan is that there are no tracing rules regarding the use of the loan proceeds. § 163(h)(3).

Hot assets. Unrealized receivables and substantially appreciated inventory under § 751. When hot assets are present, the sale of a partnership interest or the disproportionate distribution of the assets can cause ordinary income to be recognized.

Hybrid method. A combination of the accrual and cash methods of accounting. That is, the taxpayer may account for some items of income on the accrual method (e.g., sales and cost of goods sold) and other items (e.g., interest income) on the cash method.

I

Imputed interest. For certain long-term sales of property, the IRS can convert some of the gain from the sale into interest income if the contract does not provide for a minimum rate of interest to be paid by the purchaser. The seller recognizes less long-term capital gain and more ordinary income (interest income). § 483 and the related Regulations.

Inbound taxation. U.S. tax effects when a non-U.S. person begins an investment or business activity in the United States.

Incentive stock options (ISOs). A type of stock option that receives favorable tax treatment. If various qualification requirements can be satisfied, stock option grants do not create taxable income for the recipient. However, the spread (the excess of the fair market value at the date of exercise over the option price) is a tax preference item for purposes of the alternative minimum tax. The gain on disposition of the stock resulting from the exercise of the stock option will be classified as long-term capital gain if certain holding period requirements are met (the employee must not dispose of the stock within two years after the option is granted or within one year after acquiring the stock). § 422.

Income. For tax purposes, an increase in wealth that has been realized.

Income in respect of a decedent (IRD). Income earned by a decedent at the time of death but not reportable on the final income tax return because of the method of accounting that appropriately is utilized. Such income is included in the gross estate and is taxed to the eventual recipient (either the estate or heirs). The recipient is, however, allowed an income tax deduction for the estate tax attributable to the income. § 691.

Income tax provision. Under ASC 740 (SFAS 109), a synonym for the book tax expense of an entity for the financial reporting period. Following the "matching principle," all book tax expense that relates to the net income for the reporting period is reported on that period's financial statements, including not only the current tax expense, but also any deferred tax expense and deferred tax benefit.

Income tax treaties. See *tax treaty*.

Independent contractor. A self-employed person as distinguished from one who is employed as an employee.

Indexation. A procedure whereby adjustments are made by the IRS to key tax components (e.g., standard deduction, tax brackets, personal and dependency exemptions) to reflect inflation. The adjustments usually are made annually and are based on the change in the consumer price index.

Individual Retirement Account (IRA). A type of retirement plan to which an individual with earned income can contribute a statutory maximum of $5,500 in 2017. IRAs can be classified as traditional IRAs or Roth IRAs. With a traditional IRA, an individual can contribute and deduct a maximum of $5,500 per tax year in 2017. The deduction is a deduction *for* AGI. However, if the individual is an active participant in another qualified retirement plan, the deduction is phased out proportionally between certain AGI ranges (note that the phaseout limits the amount of the deduction and not the amount of the contribution). With a Roth IRA, an individual can contribute a maximum of $5,500 per tax year in 2017. No deduction is permitted. However, if a five-year holding period requirement is satisfied and if the distribution is a qualified distribution, the taxpayer can make tax-free withdrawals from a Roth IRA. The maximum annual contribution is phased out proportionally between certain AGI ranges. §§ 219 and 408A.

Individual Shared Responsibility Payment (ISRP). A mandate or penalty tax that individuals owe starting in 2014 for any month in which they do not have health coverage and do not qualify for an exemption. This mandate was created as part of the Affordable Care Act to encourage individuals to obtain health care coverage. If owed, the penalty is the greater of a "flat dollar amount" or a percentage of household income less the filing threshold. For 2017, the flat dollar amount is $695 and the percent applied to household income is 2.5 percent. For a family, the flat dollar amount cannot exceed three times the flat dollar amount. The overall cap on the penalty is the national average cost of a bronze level plan (this amount is published by the IRS). Worksheets for computing the penalty are included in the instructions to Form 8965 (Health Coverage Exemptions). § 5000A.

Inheritance tax. A tax imposed on the right to receive property from a decedent. Thus, theoretically, an inheritance tax is imposed on the heir. The Federal estate tax is imposed on the estate.

Inside basis. A partnership's basis in the assets it owns.

Installment method. A method of accounting enabling certain taxpayers to spread the recognition of gain on the sale of property over the collection period. Under this procedure, the seller arrives at the gain to be recognized by computing the gross profit percentage from the sale (the gain divided by the contract price) and applying it to each payment received. § 453.

Intangible drilling and development costs (IDCs). Taxpayers may elect to expense or capitalize (subject to amortization) intangible drilling and development costs. However, ordinary income recapture provisions apply to oil and gas properties on a sale or other disposition if the expense method is elected. §§ 263(c) and 1254(a).

Intermediate sanctions. The IRS can assess excise taxes on disqualified persons and organization management associated with so-called public charities engaging in excess benefit transactions. An excess benefit transaction is one in which a disqualified person engages in a non-fair market value transaction with the exempt organization or receives unreasonable compensation. Prior to the idea of intermediate sanctions, the only option available to the IRS was to revoke the organization's exempt status.

International Accounting Standards Board (IASB). The body that promulgates International Financial Reporting Standards (IFRS). Based in London, representing accounting standard setting bodies in over 100 countries, the IASB develops accounting standards that can serve as the basis for harmonizing conflicting reporting standards among nations.

International Financial Reporting Standards (IFRS). Produced by the International Accounting Standards Board (IASB), guidelines developed since 2001 as to revenue recognition, accounting for business combinations, and a conceptual framework for financial reporting. IFRS provisions are designed so that they can be used by all entities, regardless of where they are based or conduct business. IFRS have gained widespread acceptance throughout the world, and the SEC is considering how to require U.S. entities to use IFRS in addition to, or in lieu of, the accounting rules of the Financial Accounting Standards Board.

Interpretive Regulations. A Regulation issued by the Treasury Department that purports to explain the meaning of a particular Code Section. An interpretive Regulation is given less deference than a legislative Regulation.

Inventory. Under § 1221(a)(1), a taxpayer's stock in trade or property held for resale. For partnership tax purposes, inventory is defined in § 751(d) as inventory (per the above definition) or any partnership asset other than capital or § 1231 assets. See also *appreciated inventory.*

Investment income. Consisting of virtually the same elements as portfolio income, a measure by which to justify a deduction for interest on investment indebtedness.

Investment interest. Payment for the use of funds used to acquire assets that produce investment income. The deduction for investment interest is limited to net investment income for the tax year.

Investor loss. Losses on stock and securities. If stocks and bonds are capital assets in the hands of the holder, a capital loss materializes as of the last day of the taxable year in which the stocks or bonds become worthless. Under certain circumstances involving stocks and bonds of affiliated corporations, an ordinary loss is permitted upon worthlessness.

Involuntary conversion. The loss or destruction of property through theft, casualty, or condemnation. Gain realized on an involuntary conversion can, at the taxpayer's election, be deferred for Federal income tax purposes if the owner reinvests the proceeds within a prescribed period of time in property that is similar or related in service or use. § 1033.

Itemized deductions. Personal and employee expenditures allowed by the Code as deductions from adjusted gross income. Examples include certain medical expenses, interest on home mortgages, state income taxes, and charitable contributions. Itemized deductions are reported on Schedule A of Form 1040. Certain miscellaneous itemized deductions are reduced by 2 percent of the taxpayer's adjusted gross income. In addition, a taxpayer whose adjusted gross income exceeds a certain level (indexed annually) must reduce the itemized deductions by 3 percent of the excess of adjusted gross income over that level. Medical, casualty and theft, and investment interest deductions are not subject to the 3 percent reduction. The 3 percent reduction may not reduce itemized deductions that are subject to the reduction to below 20 percent of their initial amount.

J

Joint tenants. Two or more persons having undivided ownership of property with the right of survivorship. Right of survivorship gives the surviving owner full ownership of the property. Suppose Bob and Tami are joint tenants of a tract of land. Upon Bob's death, Tami becomes the sole owner of the property. For the estate tax consequences upon the death of a joint tenant, see § 2040.

K

Keogh plans. Retirement plans available to self-employed taxpayers. They are also referred to as H.R. 10 plans. Under such plans, a taxpayer may deduct each year up to 100 percent of net earnings from self-employment or $54,000 for 2017, whichever is less. If the plan is a profit sharing plan, the percentage is 25 percent.

Kiddie tax. Passive income, such as interest and dividends, that is recognized by a child under age 19 (or under age 24 if a full-time student) is taxed to him or her at the rates that would have applied had the income been incurred by the child's parents, generally to the extent the income exceeds $2,100 for 2017. The additional tax is assessed regardless of the source of the income or the income's underlying property. If the child's parents are divorced, the custodial parent's rates are used. The parents' rates reflect any applicable alternative minimum tax and the phaseouts of lower tax brackets and other deductions. § 1(g).

L

Least aggregate deferral method. An algorithm set forth in the Regulations to determine the tax year for a partnership or an S corporation with owners whose tax years differ. The tax year selected is the one that produces the least aggregate deferral of income for the owners.

Least aggregate deferral rule. See *least aggregate deferral method.*

Legislative Regulations. Some Code Sections give the Secretary of the Treasury or his delegate the authority to prescribe Regulations to carry out the details of administration or to otherwise complete the operating rules. Regulations issued pursuant to this type of authority truly possess the force and effect of law. In effect, Congress is almost delegating its legislative powers to the Treasury Department.

Lessee. One who rents property from another. In the case of real estate, the lessee is also known as the tenant.

Lessor. One who rents property to another. In the case of real estate, the lessor is also known as the landlord.

Letter ruling. The written response of the IRS to a taxpayer's request for interpretation of the revenue laws with respect to a proposed transaction (e.g., concerning the tax-free status of a reorganization). Not to be relied on as precedent by other than the party who requested the ruling.

Liabilities in excess of basis. On the contribution of capital to a corporation, an investor recognizes gain on the exchange to the extent contributed assets carry liabilities with a face amount in excess of the tax basis of the contributed assets. This rule keeps the investor from holding the investment asset received with a negative basis. § 357(c).

Life insurance proceeds. A specified sum (the face value or maturity value of the policy) paid to the designated beneficiary of the policy by the life insurance company upon the death of the insured.

Lifetime learning credit. A tax credit for qualifying expenses for taxpayers pursuing education beyond the first two years of postsecondary education. Individuals who are completing their last two years of undergraduate studies, pursuing graduate or professional degrees, or otherwise seeking new job skills or maintaining existing job skills are all eligible for the credit. Eligible individuals include the taxpayer, taxpayer's spouse, and taxpayer's dependents. The maximum credit is 20 percent of the first $10,000 of qualifying expenses and is computed per taxpayer. The credit is phased out for higher-income taxpayers. § 25A.

Like-kind exchanges. An exchange of property held for productive use in a trade or business or for investment (except inventory and stocks and bonds) for other investment or trade or business property. Unless non-like-kind property (boot) is received, the exchange is fully tax-deferred. § 1031.

Limited liability company (LLC). A legal entity in which all owners are protected from the entity's debts but which may lack other characteristics of a corporation (i.e., centralized management, unlimited life, free transferability of interests). LLCs are treated as partnerships (or disregarded entities if they have only one owner) for tax purposes.

Limited liability partnership (LLP). A legal entity allowed by many of the states, where a general partnership registers with the state as an LLP. All partners are at risk with respect to any contractual liabilities of the entity as well as any liabilities arising from their own malpractice or torts or that of their subordinates. However, all partners are protected from any liabilities resulting from the malpractice or torts of other partners.

Limited partners. A partner whose liability to third-party creditors of the partnership is limited to the amounts invested in the partnership. See also *general partner* and *limited partnership.*

Limited partnership (LP). A partnership in which some of the partners are limited partners. At least one of the partners in a limited partnership must be a general partner.

Liquidating distribution. A distribution by a partnership that is in complete liquidation of the entity's trade or business activities or in complete liquidation of a partner's interest in the partnership. A liquidating distribution is generally a tax-deferred transaction if it is proportionate with respect to the partnership's hot assets. In a proportionate liquidating distribution, the partnership recognizes no gain or loss. The partner only recognizes gain if the distributed cash (and cash equivalents, such as debt relief or certain marketable securities) exceeds the partner's basis in the partnership. The partner recognizes a loss if *only* cash and hot assets are distributed, and their combined inside (partnership) basis is less than the partner's basis in the partnership interest. In any case where no gain or loss is recognized, the partner's basis in the partnership interest is fully assigned to the basis of the assets received in the distribution.

Listed property. Property that includes (1) any passenger automobile; (2) any other property used as a means of transportation; (3) any property of a type generally used for purposes of entertainment, recreation, or amusement; (4) any computer or peripheral equipment (with an exception for exclusive business use); and (5) any other property of a type specified in the Regulations. If listed property is predominantly used for business, the taxpayer is allowed to use the statutory percentage method of cost recovery. Otherwise, the straight-line cost recovery method must be used. § 280F.

Lobbying expenditures. An expenditure made for the purpose of influencing legislation. Such payments can result in the loss of the exempt status of, and the imposition of Federal income tax on, an exempt organization.

Long-term care insurance. Insurance that helps pay the cost of care when the insured is unable to care for himself or herself. Such insurance is generally thought of as insurance against the cost of an aged person entering a nursing home. The employer can provide the insurance, and the premiums may be excluded from the employee's gross income. § 7702B.

Long-term contract. A building, installation, construction, or manufacturing contract that is entered into but not completed within the same tax year. A manufacturing contract is a long-term contract only if the contract is to manufacture (1) a unique item not normally carried in finished goods inventory or (2) items that normally require more than 12 calendar months to complete. The two available methods to account for long-term contracts are the percentage of completion method and the completed contract method. The completed contract method can be used only in limited circumstances. § 460.

Long-term nonpersonal use capital assets. Includes investment property with a long-term holding period. Such property disposed of by casualty or theft may receive § 1231 treatment.

Long-term tax-exempt rate. Used in deriving the yearly limitation on net operating loss and other tax benefits that carry over from the target to the acquiring when there is a more than 50-percentage-point ownership change (by value). The highest of the Federal long-term interest rates in effect for any of the last three months. § 382.

Lower of cost or market (replacement cost). An elective inventory method, whereby the taxpayer may value inventories at the lower of the taxpayer's actual cost or the current replacement cost of the goods. This method cannot be used in conjunction with the LIFO inventory method.

Low-income housing credit. Beneficial treatment to owners of low-income housing is provided in the form of a tax credit. The calculated credit is claimed in the year the building is placed in service and in the following nine years. § 42.

Lump-sum distribution. Payment of the entire amount due at one time rather than in installments. Such distributions often occur from qualified pension or profit sharing plans upon the retirement or death of a covered employee. The recipient of a lump-sum distribution may recognize both long-term capital gain and ordinary income upon the receipt of the distribution. The ordinary income portion may be subject to a special 10-year income averaging provision. § 402(e).

M

Majority interest partners. Partners who have more than a 50 percent interest in partnership profits and capital, counting only those partners who have the same taxable year. The term is of significance in determining the appropriate taxable year of a partnership. § 706(b).

Marital deduction. A deduction allowed against the taxable estate or taxable gifts upon the transfer of property from one spouse to another.

Marriage penalty. The additional tax liability that results for a married couple when compared with what their tax liability would be if they were not married and filed separate returns.

Matching rule. Treatment of an intercompany transaction on a consolidated return, when a sold asset remains within the group.

Material participation. If an individual taxpayer materially participates in a nonrental trade or business activity, any loss from that activity is treated as an active loss that can be offset against active income. Material participation is achieved by meeting any one of seven tests provided in the Regulations. § 469(h).

Meaningful reduction test. A decrease in the shareholder's voting control. Used to determine whether a stock redemption qualifies for sale or exchange treatment.

Medical expenses. Medical expenses of an individual, a spouse, and dependents are allowed as an itemized deduction to the extent such amounts (less insurance reimbursements) exceed 10 percent (or 7.5 percent if at least age 65) of adjusted gross income. § 213.

Merger. The absorption of one corporation by another with the corporation being absorbed losing its legal identity. Flow Corporation is merged into Jobs Corporation, and the shareholders of Flow receive stock in Jobs in exchange for their stock in Flow. After the merger, Flow ceases to exist as a separate legal entity. If a merger meets certain conditions, it is not currently taxable to the parties involved. § 368(a)(1).

Mid-month convention. A cost recovery convention that assumes that property is placed in service in the middle of the month that it is actually placed in service.

Mid-quarter convention. A cost recovery convention that assumes that property placed in service during the year is placed in service at the middle of the quarter in which it is actually placed in service. The mid-quarter convention applies if more than 40 percent of the value of property (other than eligible real estate) is placed in service during the last quarter of the year.

Minimum tax credit. See *alternative minimum tax credit.*

Miscellaneous itemized deductions. A special category of itemized deductions that includes expenses such as professional dues, tax return preparation fees, job-hunting costs, unreimbursed employee business expenses, and certain investment expenses. Such expenses are deductible only to the extent they exceed 2 percent of adjusted gross income. § 67.

Modified accelerated cost recovery system (MACRS). A method in which the cost of tangible property is recovered over a prescribed period of time. Enacted by the Economic Recovery Tax Act (ERTA) of 1981 and substantially modified by the Tax Reform Act (TRA) of 1986 (the modified system is referred to as MACRS), the approach disregards salvage value, imposes a period of cost recovery that depends upon the classification of the asset into one of various recovery periods, and prescribes the applicable percentage of cost that can be deducted each year. § 168.

Modified adjusted gross income. A key determinant in computing the domestic production activities deduction (DPAD) and certain other tax provisions (e.g., deduction for higher education tuition, exclusion of interest on education savings bonds). §§ 135, 144, and 199.

Moving expenses. A deduction *for* AGI is permitted to employees and self-employed individuals provided certain tests are met. The taxpayer's new job must be at least 50 miles farther from the old residence than the old residence was from the former place of work. In addition, an employee must be employed on a full-time basis at the new location for 39 weeks in the 12-month period following the move. Deductible moving expenses include the cost of moving the household and personal effects, transportation, and lodging expenses during the move. The cost of meals during the move is not deductible. Qualified moving expenses that are paid (or reimbursed) by the employer can be excluded from the employee's gross income. In this case, the related deduction by the employee is not permitted. §§ 62(a)(15), 132(a)(6), and 217.

Multiple support agreement. To qualify for a dependency exemption, the support test must be satisfied. This requires that over 50 percent of the support of the potential dependent be provided by the taxpayer. Where no one person provides more than 50 percent of the support, a multiple support agreement enables a taxpayer to still qualify for the dependency exemption. Any person who contributed more than 10 percent of the support is entitled to claim the exemption if each person in the group who contributed more than 10 percent files a written consent (Form 2120). Each person who is a party to the multiple support agreement must meet all of the other requirements for claiming the dependency exemption. § 152(c).

Multistate Tax Commission (MTC). A regulatory body of the states that develops operating rules and regulations for the implementation of the UDITPA and other provisions that assign the total taxable income of a multistate corporation to specific states.

N

National sales tax. Intended as a replacement for the current Federal income tax. Unlike a value added tax (VAT), which is levied on the manufacturer, it would be imposed on the consumer upon the final sale of goods and services. To reduce regressivity, individuals would receive a rebate to offset a portion of the tax.

Negligence. Failure to exercise the reasonable or ordinary degree of care of a prudent person in a situation that results in harm or damage to another. A penalty is assessed on taxpayers who exhibit negligence or intentional disregard of rules and Regulations with respect to the underpayment of certain taxes.

Net capital gain (NCG). The excess of the net long-term capital gain for the tax year over the net short-term capital loss. The net capital gain of an individual taxpayer is eligible for the alternative tax. § 1222(11).

Net capital loss (NCL). The excess of the losses from sales or exchanges of capital assets over the gains from sales or exchanges of such assets. Up to $3,000 per year of the net capital loss may be deductible by noncorporate taxpayers against ordinary income. The excess net capital loss carries over to future tax years. For corporate taxpayers, the net capital loss cannot be offset against ordinary income, but it can be carried back three years and forward five years to offset net capital gains. §§ 1211, 1212, and 1221(10).

Net investment income. The excess of investment income over investment expenses. Investment expenses are those deductible expenses directly connected with the production of investment income. Investment expenses do not include investment interest. The deduction for investment interest for the tax year is limited to net investment income. § 163(d).

Net operating loss (NOL). To mitigate the effect of the annual accounting period concept, § 172 allows taxpayers to use an excess loss of one year as a deduction for certain past or future years. In this regard, a carryback period of two (or more) years and a carryforward period of 20 years currently are allowed.

Nexus. The degree of activity that must be present before a taxing jurisdiction has the right to impose a tax on an out-of-state entity. The rules for income tax nexus are not the same as for sales tax nexus.

Ninety-day letter. This notice is sent to a taxpayer upon request, upon the expiration of the 30-day letter, or upon exhaustion by the taxpayer of his or her administrative remedies before the IRS. The notice gives the taxpayer 90 days in which to file a petition with the U.S. Tax Court. If a petition is not filed, the IRS will demand payment of the assessed deficiency. §§ 6211–6216.

No-additional-cost service. Services the employer may provide the employee at no additional cost to the employer. Generally, the benefit is the ability to utilize the employer's excess capacity (e.g., vacant seats on an airliner). Such amounts are excludible from the recipient's gross income.

Nonaccountable plan. An expense reimbursement plan that does not have an accountability feature. The result is that employee expenses must be claimed as deductions *from* AGI. An exception is moving expenses that are deductions *for* AGI.

Nonacquiescence. Disagreement by the IRS on the result reached in certain judicial decisions. *Nonacq.* or *NA*.

Nonbusiness bad debt. A bad debt loss that is not incurred in connection with a creditor's trade or business. The loss is classified as a short-term capital loss and is allowed only in the year the debt becomes entirely worthless. In addition to family loans, many investor losses are nonbusiness bad debts. § 166(d).

Nonqualified deferred compensation (NQDC). Compensation arrangements that are frequently offered to executives. Such plans may include stock options, restricted stock, etc. Often, an executive may defer the recognition of taxable income. The employer, however, does not receive a tax deduction until the employee is required to include the compensation in income.

Nonqualified stock option (NQSO). A type of stock option that does not satisfy the statutory requirements of an incentive stock option. If the NQSO has a readily ascertainable fair market value (e.g., the option is traded on an established exchange), the value of the option must be included in the employee's gross income at the date of the grant. Otherwise, the employee does not recognize income at the grant date. Instead, ordinary income is recognized in the year of exercise of the option.

Nonrecourse debt. Debt secured by the property that it is used to purchase. The purchaser of the property is not personally liable for the debt upon default. Rather, the creditor's recourse is to repossess the related property. Nonrecourse debt generally does not increase the purchaser's at-risk amount.

Nonrefundable credits. A credit that is not paid if it exceeds the taxpayer's tax liability. Some nonrefundable credits qualify for carryback and carryover treatment.

Nonresident alien (NRA). An individual who is neither a citizen nor a resident of the United States. Citizenship is determined under the immigration and naturalization laws of the United States. Residency is determined under § 7701(b) of the Internal Revenue Code.

Nontaxable exchange. A transaction in which realized gains or losses are not recognized. The recognition of gain or loss is postponed (deferred) until the property received in the nontaxable exchange is subsequently disposed of in a taxable transaction. Examples are § 1031 like-kind exchanges and § 1033 involuntary conversions.

Not essentially equivalent redemption. Sale or exchange treatment is given to this type of redemption. Although various safe-harbor tests are failed, the nature of the redemption is such that dividend treatment is avoided, because it represents a meaningful reduction in the shareholder's interest in the corporation. § 302(b)(1).

O

Occupational fee. A tax imposed on various trades or businesses. A license fee that enables a taxpayer to engage in a particular occupation.

Occupational taxes. See *occupational fee.*

Offer in compromise. A settlement agreement offered by the IRS in a tax dispute, especially where there is doubt as to the collectibility of the full deficiency. Offers in compromise can include installment payment schedules, as well as reductions in the tax and penalties owed by the taxpayer.

Office audit. An audit conducted by the IRS in the agent's office.

Office in the home expenses. Employment and business-related expenses attributable to the use of a residence (e.g., den or office) are allowed only if the portion of the residence is exclusively used on a regular basis as a principal place of business of the taxpayer or as a place of business that is used by patients, clients, or customers. If the expenses are incurred by an employee, the use must be for the convenience of the employer as opposed to being merely appropriate and helpful. In computing the office in the home expenses, a taxpayer can use either the regular method or simplified method. As a general rule, the regular method requires more effort and recordkeeping but results in a larger deduction. § 280A.

One-year rule for prepaid expenses. Taxpayers who use the cash method are required to use the accrual method for deducting certain prepaid expenses (i.e., must capitalize the item and can deduct only when used). If a prepayment will not be consumed or expire by the end of the tax year following the year of payment, the prepayment must be capitalized and prorated over the benefit period. Conversely, if the prepayment will be consumed by the end of the tax year following the year of payment, it can be expensed when paid. To obtain the current deduction under the one-year rule, the payment must be a required payment rather than a voluntary payment.

Operating agreement. The governing document of a limited liability company. This document is similar in structure, function, and purpose to a partnership agreement.

Optional adjustment election. See *Section 754 election.*

Options. The sale or exchange of an option to buy or sell property results in capital gain or loss if the property is a capital asset. Generally, the closing of an option transaction results in short-term capital gain or loss to the writer of the call and the purchaser of the call option. § 1234.

Ordinary and necessary. An ordinary expense is common and accepted in the general industry or type of activity in which the taxpayer is engaged. It comprises one of the tests for the deductibility of expenses incurred or paid in connection with a trade or business; for the production or collection of income; for the management, conservation, or maintenance of property held for the production of income; or in connection with the determination, collection, or refund of any tax. §§ 162(a) and 212. A necessary expense is appropriate and helpful in furthering the taxpayer's business or income-producing activity. §§ 162(a) and 212.

Ordinary income property. Property contributed to a charitable organization that, if sold rather than contributed, would have resulted in other than long-term capital gain to the donor (i.e., ordinary income property and short-term capital gain property). Examples are inventory and capital assets held for less than the long-term holding period. A contribution of ordinary income property must generally be valued at its fair market value less the gain, if any, that would have been realized if sold.

Organizational costs. See *organizational expenditures.*

Organizational expenditures. Items incurred early in the life of a corporation or partnership that are eligible for a $5,000 limited expensing (subject to phaseout) and an amortization of the balance over 180 months. Organizational expenditures exclude those incurred to obtain capital (underwriting fees) or assets (subject to cost recovery). Typically, eligible expenditures include legal and accounting fees and state incorporation payments. Such items must be incurred by the end of the entity's first tax year. §§ 248 and 709(b).

Original issue discount (OID). The difference between the issue price of a debt obligation (e.g., a corporate bond) and the maturity value of the obligation when the issue price is less than the maturity value. OID represents interest and must be amortized over the life of the debt obligation using the effective interest method. The difference is not considered to be original issue discount for tax purposes when it is less than one-fourth of 1 percent of the redemption price at maturity multiplied by the number of years to maturity. §§ 1272 and 1273(a)(3).

Other adjustments account (OAA). Used in the context of a distribution from an S corporation. The net accumulation of the entity's exempt income (e.g., municipal bond interest).

Other property. In a corporate reorganization, any property in the exchange that is not stock or securities, such as cash or land. This amount constitutes boot. This treatment is similar to that in a like-kind exchange.

Outbound taxation. U.S. tax effects when a U.S. person begins an investment or business activity outside the United States.

Outside basis. A partner's basis in his or her partnership interest.

Ownership change. An event that triggers a § 382 limitation for the acquiring corporation.

P

Parent-subsidiary controlled group. A controlled or affiliated group of corporations where at least one corporation is at least 80 percent owned by one or more of the others. The affiliated group definition is more difficult to meet.

Partial liquidation. A stock redemption where noncorporate shareholders are permitted sale or exchange treatment. In certain cases, an active business must have existed for at least five years. Only a portion of the outstanding stock in the entity is retired.

Partnership. For income tax purposes, a partnership includes a syndicate, group, pool, or joint venture, as well as ordinary partnerships. In an ordinary partnership, two or more parties combine capital and/or services to carry on a business for profit as co-owners. § 7701(a)(2).

Partnership agreement. The governing document of a partnership. A partnership agreement should describe the rights and obligations of the partners; the allocation of entity income, deductions, and cash flows; initial and future capital contribution requirements; conditions for terminating the partnership; and other matters.

Passive activity loss. Any loss from (1) activities in which the taxpayer does not materially participate or (2) rental activities (subject to certain exceptions). Net passive losses cannot be used to offset income from nonpassive sources. Rather, they are suspended until the taxpayer either generates net passive income (and a deduction of such losses is allowed) or disposes of the underlying property (at which time the loss deductions are allowed in full). One relief provision allows landlords who actively participate in the rental activities to deduct up to $25,000 of passive losses annually. However, a phaseout of the $25,000 amount commences when the landlord's AGI exceeds $100,000. Another relief provision applies for material participation in a real estate trade or business.

Passive investment company. A means by which a multistate corporation can reduce the overall effective tax rate by isolating investment income in a low- or no-tax state.

Passive investment income (PII). Gross receipts from royalties, certain rents, dividends, interest, annuities, and gains from the sale or exchange of stock and securities. When earnings and profits (E & P) also exists, if the passive investment income of an S corporation exceeds 25 percent of the corporation's gross receipts for three consecutive years, S status is lost.

Pass-through entity. A form of business structure for which the income and other tax items are attributed directly to the owners and generally no separate tax is levied upon the entity itself. Examples include sole proprietorships, partnerships, and S corporations. Also referred to as a flow-through entity.

Patent. An intangible asset that may be amortized over a statutory 15-year period as a § 197 intangible. The sale of a patent usually results in favorable long-term capital gain treatment. §§ 197 and 1235.

Payroll factor. The proportion of a multistate corporation's total payroll that is traceable to a specific state. Used in determining the taxable income that is to be apportioned to that state.

Pension plan. A type of deferred compensation arrangement that provides for systematic payments of definitely determinable retirement benefits to employees who meet the requirements set forth in the plan.

Percentage depletion. Depletion based on a statutory percentage applied to the gross income from the property. The taxpayer deducts the greater of cost depletion or percentage depletion. § 613.

Percentage of completion method. A method of reporting gain or loss on certain long-term contracts. Under this method of accounting, the gross contract price is included in income as the contract is completed. Reg. § 1.451–3.

Permanent and total disability. A person is considered permanently and totally disabled if he or she is unable to engage in any substantial gainful activity due to a physical or mental impairment. In addition, this impairment must be one that can be expected to result in death or that has lasted or can be expected to last for a continuous period of not less than 12 months. The taxpayer generally must provide the IRS a physician's statement documenting this condition.

Permanent differences. Under ASC 740 (SFAS 109), tax-related items that appear in the entity's financial statements or its tax return but not both. For instance, interest income from a municipal bond is a permanent book-tax difference.

Permanent establishment (PE). A level of business activity, as defined under an income tax treaty, that subjects the taxpayer to taxation in a country other than that in which the taxpayer is based. Often evidenced by the presence of a plant, an office, or other fixed place of business. Inventory storage and temporary activities do not rise to the level of a PE. PE is the treaty's equivalent to nexus.

Permanently reinvesting. Under ASC 740-30 (APB 23) of Generally Accepted Accounting Principles, a special rule that relates to the book tax expense of non-U.S. subsidiaries. If a parent corporation documents that it is permanently reinvesting the non-U.S. earning of a non-U.S. subsidiary, the parent does not record as an expense any U.S. income tax that the parent might pay on such earnings, i.e., the book tax expense is deferred until such earnings are (if ever) repatriated to the United States.

Personal and dependency exemptions. The tax law provides an exemption for each individual taxpayer and an additional exemption for the taxpayer's spouse if a joint return is filed. An individual may also claim a dependency exemption for each dependent, provided certain tests are met. The amount of the personal and dependency exemptions is $4,050 in 2017 ($4,050 in 2016). The exemption is subject to phaseout once adjusted gross income exceeds certain statutory threshold amounts.

Personal exemptions. See *personal and dependency exemptions.*

Personal holding company tax. A penalty tax imposed on certain closely held corporations with excessive investment income. Assessed at the top individual tax rate on personal holding company income, reduced by dividends paid and other adjustments. § 541.

Personal residence. If a residence has been owned and used by the taxpayer as the principal residence for at least two years during the five-year period ending on the date of sale, up to $250,000 of realized gain is excluded from gross income. For a married couple filing a joint return, the $250,000 is increased to $500,000 if either spouse satisfies the ownership requirement and both spouses satisfy the use requirement. § 121.

Personal service corporation (PSC). A corporation whose principal activity is the performance of personal services (e.g., health, law, engineering, architecture, accounting, actuarial science, performing arts, or consulting) and where such services are substantially performed by the employee-owners. The 35 percent statutory income tax rate applies to PSCs.

Personalty. All property that is not attached to real estate (realty) and is movable. Examples of personalty are machinery, automobiles, clothing, household furnishings, and personal effects.

Points. Loan origination fees that may be deductible as interest by a buyer of property. A seller of property who pays points reduces the selling price by the amount of the points paid for the buyer. While the seller is not permitted to deduct this amount as interest, the buyer may do so.

Portfolio income. Income from interest, dividends, rentals, royalties, capital gains, or other investment sources. Net passive losses cannot be used to offset net portfolio income.

Precedents. A previously decided court decision that is recognized as authority for the disposition of future decisions.

Precontribution gain or loss. Partnerships allow for a variety of special allocations of gain or loss among the partners, but gain or loss that is "built in" on an asset contributed to the partnership is assigned specifically to the contributing partner. § 704(c)(1)(A).

Preferences. See *AMT preferences.*

Preferred stock bailout. A process where a shareholder used the issuance and sale, or later redemption, of a preferred stock dividend to obtain long-term capital gains, without any loss of voting control over the corporation. In effect, the shareholder received corporate profits without suffering the consequences of dividend income treatment. This procedure led Congress to enact § 306, which, if applicable, converts the prior long-term capital gain on the sale or redemption of the tainted stock to dividend income.

Premium Tax Credit (PTC). A tax credit that is refundable and available in advance of filing a return for the year. The PTC serves to reduce the cost of health coverage obtained on the Marketplace (Exchange). A PTC is available to individuals who purchase coverage on the Exchange and have household income equal to or greater than 100 percent of the Federal poverty line (FPL) and no greater than 400 percent of the FPL. Also, an individual must not have been able to obtain affordable coverage from his or her employer. If obtained in advance, the PTC is given to the insurance provider to lower the monthly premium cost to the individual. The PTC is reconciled on Form 8962 (Premium Tax Credit) filed with Form 1040 or 1040-A (not Form 1040-EZ). Individuals who obtain insurance through the Marketplace receive Form 1095-A (Health Insurance Marketplace Statement) by January 31 of the following year. This form provides information necessary to claim or reconcile the PTC, including the monthly cost of premiums and the amount of PTC received in advance each month. § 36B.

Previously taxed income (PTI). Under prior law, the undistributed taxable income of an S corporation was taxed to the shareholders as of the last day of the corporation's tax year and usually could be withdrawn by the shareholders without tax consequences at some later point in time. The role of PTI has been taken over by the accumulated adjustments account. See also *accumulated adjustments account (AAA).*

Principal partner. A partner with a 5 percent or greater interest in partnership capital or profits. § 706(b)(3).

Private activity bonds. Interest on state and local bonds is excludible from gross income. Certain such bonds are labeled private activity bonds. Although the interest on such bonds is excludible for regular income tax purposes, it is treated as a tax preference in calculating the AMT. §§ 57(a)(5) and 103.

Private foundations. An exempt organization that is subject to additional statutory restrictions on its activities and on contributions made to it. Excise taxes may be levied on certain prohibited transactions, and the Code places more stringent restrictions on the deductibility of contributions to private foundations. § 509.

Probate costs. The costs incurred in administering a decedent's estate.

Probate estate. The property of a decedent that is subject to administration by the executor or administrator of an estate.

Procedural Regulations. A Regulation issued by the Treasury Department that is a housekeeping-type instruction indicating information that taxpayers should provide the IRS as well as information about the internal management and conduct of the IRS itself.

Profit and loss sharing ratios. Specified in the partnership agreement and used to determine each partner's allocation of ordinary taxable income and separately stated items. Profits and losses can be shared in different ratios. The ratios can be changed by amending the partnership agreement or by using a special allocation. § 704(a).

Profit sharing plan. A deferred compensation plan established and maintained by an employer to provide for employee participation in the company's profits. Contributions are paid from the employer's current or accumulated profits to a trustee. Separate accounts are maintained for each participant employee. The plan must provide a definite, predetermined formula for allocating the contributions among the participants. It also must include a definite, predetermined formula for distributing the accumulated funds after a fixed number of years, on the attainment of a stated age, or on the occurrence of certain events such as illness, layoff, or retirement.

Profits (loss) interest. The extent of a partner's entitlement to an allocation of the partnership's operating results. This interest is measured by the profit and loss sharing ratios.

Property. Assets defined in the broadest legal sense. Property includes the unrealized receivables of a cash basis taxpayer, but not services rendered. § 351.

Property dividend. Generally treated in the same manner as a cash distribution, measured by the fair market value of the property on the date of distribution. Distribution of appreciated property causes the distributing C or S corporation to recognize gain. The distributing corporation does not recognize loss on property that has depreciated in value.

Property factor. The proportion of a multistate corporation's total property that is traceable to a specific state. Used in determining the taxable income that is to be apportioned to that state.

Proportionate distribution. A distribution in which the partners' interests in hot assets does not change. This can happen, for instance, when no hot assets are distributed (e.g., a proportionate cash distribution) or when each partner in a partnership receives a pro rata share of hot assets being distributed. For example, a distribution of $10,000 of hot assets equally to two 50 percent partners is a proportionate distribution.

Proposed Regulations. A Regulation issued by the Treasury Department in proposed, rather than final, form. The interval between the proposal of a Regulation and its finalization permits taxpayers and other interested parties to comment on the propriety of the proposal.

Proprietorship. A business entity for which there is a single owner. The net profit of the entity is reported on the owner's Federal income tax return (Schedule C of Form 1040).

Public Law 86–272. A congressional limit on the ability of the state to force a multistate corporation to assign taxable income to that state. Under P.L. 86–272, where orders for tangible personal property are both filled and delivered outside the state, the entity must establish more than the mere solicitation of such orders before any income can be apportioned to the state.

Punitive damages. Damages received or paid by the taxpayer can be classified as compensatory damages or as punitive damages. Punitive damages are those awarded to punish the defendant for gross negligence or the intentional infliction of harm. Such damages are includible in gross income. § 104.

Q

Qualified ABLE program. A state program that allows funds to be set aside for the benefit of an individual who became disabled or blind before age 26. Cash may be put into the fund annually up to the annual gift tax exclusion amount. Distributions to the designated beneficiary are not taxable provided they do not exceed qualified disability expenses for the year. § 529A.

Qualified business unit (QBU). A subsidiary, branch, or other business entity that conducts business using a currency other than the U.S. dollar.

Qualified dividend income (QDI). See *qualified dividends*.

Qualified dividends. Distributions made by domestic (and certain non-U.S.) corporations to noncorporate shareholders that are subject to tax at the same rates as those applicable to net long-term capital gains (i.e., 0 percent, 15 percent, or 20 percent). The 20 percent rate applies to certain high-income taxpayers (i.e., whose tax bracket is 39.6 percent). The dividend must be paid out of earnings and profits, and the shareholders must meet certain holding period requirements as to the stock. §§ 1(h)(1) and (11).

Qualified employee discount. Discounts offered employees on merchandise or services that the employer ordinarily sells or provides to customers. The discounts must be generally available to all employees. In the case of property, the discount cannot exceed the employer's gross profit (the sales price cannot be less than the employer's cost). In the case of services, the discounts cannot exceed 20 percent of the normal sales price. § 132.

Qualified joint venture. At the election of the taxpayers, certain joint ventures between spouses can avoid partnership classification. Known as a qualified joint venture, the spouses generally report their share of the business activities from the venture as sole proprietors (using two Schedule C forms). This would be reported on Schedule E if the venture relates to a rental property. § 761(f).

Qualified nonrecourse debt. Debt issued on realty by a bank, retirement plan, or governmental agency. Included in the at-risk amount by the investor. § 465(b)(6).

Qualified production activities income (QPAI). A key determinant in computing the domestic production activities deduction (DPAD). It consists of domestic production gross receipts (DPGR) reduced by cost of goods sold and other assignable expenses. Thus, QPAI represents the profit derived from domestic production activities. § 199.

Qualified real property business indebtedness. Indebtedness that was incurred or assumed by the taxpayer in connection with real property used in a trade or business and is secured by such real property. The taxpayer must not be a C corporation. For qualified real property business indebtedness, the taxpayer may elect to exclude some or all of the income realized from cancellation of debt on qualified real property. If the election is made, the basis of the property must be reduced by the amount excluded. The amount excluded cannot be greater than the excess of the principal amount of the outstanding debt over the fair market value (net of any other debt outstanding on the property) of the property securing the debt. § 108(c).

Qualified residence interest. A term relevant in determining the amount of interest expense the individual taxpayer may deduct as an itemized deduction for what otherwise would be disallowed as a component of personal interest (consumer interest). Qualified residence interest consists of interest paid on qualified residences (principal residence and one other residence) of the taxpayer. Debt that qualifies as qualified residence interest is limited to $1 million of debt to acquire, construct, or substantially improve qualified residences (acquisition indebtedness) plus $100,000 of other debt secured by qualified residences (home equity indebtedness). The home equity indebtedness may not exceed the fair market value of a qualified residence reduced by the acquisition indebtedness for that residence. § 163(h)(3).

Qualified small business corporation. For purposes of computing an exclusion upon the sale of qualified small business stock, a C corporation that has aggregate gross assets not exceeding $50 million and that is conducting an active trade or business. § 1202.

Qualified small business stock. Stock in a qualified small business corporation, purchased as part of an original issue after August 10, 1993. The shareholder may exclude from gross income 50 (or 75 or 100) percent of the realized gain on the sale of the stock if he or she held the stock for more than five years. § 1202.

Qualified terminable interest property (QTIP). Generally, the marital deduction (for gift and estate tax purposes) is not available if the interest transferred will terminate upon the death of the transferee spouse and pass to someone else. Thus, if Jim (the husband) places property in trust, life estate to Mary (the wife), and remainder to their children upon Mary's death, this is a terminable interest that will not provide Jim (or Jim's estate) with a marital deduction. If, however, the transfer in trust is treated as qualified terminable interest property (the QTIP election is made), the terminable interest restriction is waived and the marital deduction becomes available. In exchange for this deduction, the surviving spouse's gross estate must include the value of the QTIP election assets, even though he or she has no control over the ultimate disposition of the asset. Terminable interest property qualifies for this election if the donee (or heir) is the only beneficiary of the asset during his or her lifetime and receives income distributions relative to the property at least annually. For gifts, the donor spouse is the one who makes the QTIP election. For property transferred by death, the executor of the estate of the deceased spouse makes the election. §§ 2056(b)(7) and 2523(f).

Qualified transportation fringes. Transportation benefits provided by the employer to the employee. Such benefits include (1) transportation in a commuter highway vehicle between the employee's residence and the place of employment, (2) a transit pass, and (3) qualified parking. Qualified transportation fringes are excludible from the employee's gross income to the extent categories (1) and (2) above do not exceed $255 per month in 2017 and category (3) does not exceed $255 per month in 2017. These amounts are indexed annually for inflation. § 132.

Qualified tuition program. A program that allows college tuition to be prepaid for a beneficiary. When amounts in the plan are used, nothing is included in gross income provided they are used for qualified higher education expenses. § 529.

Qualifying child. An individual who, as to the taxpayer, satisfies the relationship, abode, and age tests. To be claimed as a dependent, such individual must also meet the citizenship and joint return tests and not be self-supporting. §§ 152(a)(1) and (c).

Qualifying relative. An individual who, as to the taxpayer, satisfies the relationship, gross income, support, citizenship, and joint return tests. Such an individual can be claimed as a dependent of the taxpayer. §§ 152(a)(2) and (d).

R

Rate reconciliation. Under Generally Accepted Accounting Principles, a footnote to the financial statements often includes a table that accounts for differences in the statutory income tax rate that applies to the entity (say, 35 percent) and the higher or lower effective tax rate that the entity realized for the reporting period. The rate reconciliation includes only permanent differences between the book tax expense and the entity's income tax provision. The rate reconciliation table often is expressed in dollar and/or percentage terms.

Realized gain. See *realized gain or loss*.

Realized gain or loss. The difference between the amount realized upon the sale or other disposition of property and the adjusted basis of the property. § 1001.

Realized loss. See *realized gain or loss*.

Realty. Real estate.

Reasonable cause. Relief from taxpayer and preparer penalties often is allowed where reasonable cause is found for the taxpayer's actions. For example, reasonable cause for the late filing of a tax return might be a flood that damaged the taxpayer's record-keeping systems and made a timely completion of the return difficult.

Reasonable needs of the business. A means of avoiding the penalty tax on an unreasonable accumulation of earnings. In determining the base for this tax (accumulated taxable income), § 535 allows a deduction for "such part of earnings and profits for the taxable year as are retained for the reasonable needs of the business." § 537.

Reasonableness. See *reasonableness requirement*.

Reasonableness requirement. The Code includes a reasonableness requirement with respect to the deduction of salaries and other compensation for services. The courts have expanded this requirement to all business expenses, ruling that an expense must be reasonable in order to be ordinary and necessary. What constitutes reasonableness is a question of fact. If an expense is unreasonable, the amount that is classified as unreasonable is not allowed as a deduction. The question of reasonableness generally arises with respect to closely held corporations where there is no separation of ownership and management. § 162(a)(1).

Recapitalization. A "Type E" reorganization, constituting a major change in the character and amount of outstanding equity of a corporation. Tax-free exchanges are stock for stock, bonds for bonds, and bonds for stock. For example, common stock exchanged for preferred stock can qualify as a tax-free "Type E" reorganization.

Recognized gain. See *recognized gain or loss*.

Recognized gain or loss. The portion of realized gain or loss subject to income taxation.

Recognized loss. See *recognized gain or loss*.

Recourse debt. Debt for which the lender may both foreclose on the property and assess a guarantor for any payments due under the loan. A lender also may make a claim against the assets of any general partner in a partnership to which debt is issued, without regard to whether the partner has guaranteed the debt.

Recovery of capital doctrine. When a taxable sale or exchange occurs, the seller may be permitted to recover his or her investment (or other adjusted basis) in the property before gain or loss is recognized.

Redemption to pay death taxes. Sale or exchange treatment is available relative to this type of stock redemption, to the extent of the proceeds up to the total amount paid by the estate or heir for estate/inheritance taxes and administration expenses. The stock value must exceed 35 percent of the value of the decedent's adjusted gross estate. In meeting this test, shareholdings in corporations where the decedent held at least 20 percent of the outstanding shares are combined.

Refundable credits. A credit that is paid to the taxpayer even if the amount of the credit (or credits) exceeds the taxpayer's tax liability.

Regular corporations. See *C corporation*.

Rehabilitation expenditures credit. A credit that is based on expenditures incurred to rehabilitate industrial and commercial buildings and certified historic structures. The credit is intended to discourage businesses from moving from older, economically distressed areas to newer locations and to encourage the preservation of historic structures. § 47.

Rehabilitation expenditures credit recapture. When property that qualifies for the rehabilitation expenditures credit is disposed of or ceases to be used in the trade or business of the taxpayer, some or all of the tax credit claimed on the property may be recaptured as additional tax liability. The amount of the recapture is the difference between the amount of the credit claimed originally and what should have been claimed in light of the length of time the property was actually held or used for qualifying purposes. § 50.

Related party. Various Code Sections define related parties and often include a variety of persons within this (usually detrimental) category. Generally, related parties are accorded different tax treatment from that applicable to other taxpayers who enter into similar transactions. For instance, realized losses that are generated between related parties are not recognized in the year of the loss. However, these deferred losses can be used to offset recognized gains that occur upon the subsequent sale of the asset to a nonrelated party. Other uses of a related-party definition include the conversion of gain upon the sale of a depreciable asset into all ordinary income (§ 1239) and the identification of constructive ownership of stock relative to corporate distributions, redemptions, liquidations, reorganizations, and compensation.

Related-party transactions. The tax law places restrictions upon the recognition of gains and losses between related parties because of the potential for abuse. For example, restrictions are placed on the deduction of losses from the sale or exchange of property between related parties. In addition, under certain circumstances, related-party gains that would otherwise be classified as capital gain are classified as ordinary income. §§ 267, 707(b), and 1239.

Rental activity. Any activity where payments are received principally for the use of tangible property is a rental activity. Temporary Regulations provide that in certain circumstances, activities involving rentals of real and personal property are not to be treated as rental activities. The Temporary Regulations list six exceptions.

Reorganization. Any corporate restructuring, including when one corporation acquires another, a single corporation divides into two or more entities, a corporation makes a substantial change in its capital structure, a corporation undertakes a change in its legal name or domicile, or a corporation goes through a bankruptcy proceeding and continues to exist. The exchange of stock and other securities in a corporate reorganization can be effected favorably for tax purposes if certain statutory requirements are followed strictly. Tax consequences include the nonrecognition of any gain that is realized by the shareholders except to the extent of boot received. § 368.

Repatriation. To return assets to the owner's country. In Federal income taxation, the term refers to a foreign corporation issuing a dividend to its U.S. parent corporation. The income represented by the dividend generally is not subject to U.S. tax until it is paid to the U.S. corporation (the shareholder of the foreign subsidiary).

Required taxable year. A partnership or limited liability company must use a required tax year as its tax accounting period, or one of three allowable alternative tax year-ends. The required tax year is determined using the least aggregate deferral rule. But if there is a common tax year used by owners holding a majority of the entity's capital or profits interests, or used by all of the owners who hold 5 percent or more of the capital or profits interests, then that tax year-end is used by the entity.

Research activities credit. A tax credit whose purpose is to encourage research and development. It consists of three components: the incremental research activities credit, the basic research credit, and the energy credit. The incremental research activities credit is equal to 20 percent of the excess qualified research expenditures over the base amount. The basic research credit is equal to 20 percent of the excess of basic research payments over the base amount. § 41.

Research and experimental expenditures. Costs incurred to develop a product or process for which there exists uncertainty regarding its viability. The Code provides three alternatives for the tax treatment of research and experimentation expenditures. They may be expensed in the year paid or incurred, deferred subject to amortization, or capitalized. If the taxpayer does not elect to expense such costs or to defer them subject to amortization (over 60 months), the expenditures must be capitalized. § 174. Three types of research activities credits are available: the basic research credit, the incremental research activities credit, and the energy credit. The rate for each type is 20 percent. § 41.

Reserve method. A method of accounting whereby an allowance is permitted for estimated uncollectible accounts. Actual write-offs are charged to the reserve, and recoveries of amounts previously written off are credited to the reserve. The Code permits only certain financial institutions to use the reserve method. § 166.

Residential rental real estate. Buildings for which at least 80 percent of the gross rents are from dwelling units (e.g., an apartment building). This type of building is distinguished from nonresidential (commercial or industrial) buildings in applying the recapture of depreciation provisions. The term also is relevant in distinguishing between buildings that are eligible for a 27.5-year life versus a 39-year life for MACRS purposes. Generally, residential buildings receive preferential treatment.

Restricted property plan. An arrangement whereby an employer transfers property (usually stock) to an employee at a bargain price (for less than the fair market value). If the transfer is accompanied by a substantial risk of forfeiture and the property is not transferable, no compensation results to the employee until the restrictions disappear. An example of a substantial risk of forfeiture would be a requirement that the employee return the property if his or her employment is terminated within a specified period of time. § 83.

Revenue Agent's Report (RAR). A Revenue Agent's Report (RAR) reflects any adjustments made by the agent as a result of an audit of the taxpayer. The RAR is mailed to the taxpayer along with the 30-day letter, which outlines the appellate procedures available to the taxpayer.

Revenue neutrality. A description that characterizes tax legislation when it neither increases nor decreases the total revenue collected by the taxing jurisdiction. Thus, any tax revenue losses are offset by tax revenue gains.

Revenue Procedures. A matter of procedural importance to both taxpayers and the IRS concerning the administration of the tax laws is issued as a Revenue Procedure (abbreviated Rev.Proc.). A Revenue Procedure is published in an *Internal Revenue Bulletin* (I.R.B.).

Revenue Rulings. A Revenue Ruling (abbreviated Rev.Rul.) is issued by the National Office of the IRS to express an official interpretation of the tax law as applied to specific transactions. It is more limited in application than a Regulation. A Revenue Ruling is published in an *Internal Revenue Bulletin* (I.R.B.).

Reversionary interest. The trust property that reverts to the grantor after the expiration of an intervening income interest. Assume that Phil places real estate in trust with income to Junior for 11 years, and upon the expiration of this term, the property returns to Phil. Under these circumstances, Phil holds a reversionary interest in the property. A reversionary interest is the same as a remainder interest, except that, in the latter case, the property passes to someone other than the original owner (e.g., the grantor of a trust) upon the expiration of the intervening interest.

Roth IRA. See *Individual Retirement Account (IRA)*.

S

S corporation. The designation for a corporation that elects to be taxed similarly to a partnership. See also *Subchapter S*.

Sale or exchange. A requirement for the recognition of capital gain or loss. Generally, the seller of property must receive money or relief from debt to have sold the property. An exchange involves the transfer of property for other property. Thus, collection of a debt is neither a sale nor an exchange. The term *sale or exchange* is not defined by the Code.

Sales factor. The proportion of a multistate corporation's total sales that is traceable to a specific state. Used in determining the taxable income that is to be apportioned to that state.

Sales tax. A state- or local-level tax on the retail sale of specified property. Generally, the purchaser pays the tax, but the seller collects it, as an agent for the government. Various taxing jurisdictions allow exemptions for purchases of specific items, including certain food, services, and manufacturing equipment. If the purchaser and seller are in different states, a use tax usually applies.

Schedule K–1. A tax information form prepared for each partner in a partnership, each shareholder of an S corporation, and some beneficiaries of certain trusts. The Schedule K–1 reports the owner's share of the entity's ordinary income or loss from operations, as well as the owner's share of separately stated items.

Schedule M–1. On the Form 1120, a reconciliation of book net income with Federal taxable income. Accounts for temporary and permanent differences in the two computations, such as depreciation differences, exempt income, and nondeductible items. On Forms 1120S and 1065, the Schedule M–1 reconciles book income with the owners' aggregate ordinary taxable income.

Schedule M–3. An *expanded* reconciliation of book net income with Federal taxable income (see *Schedule M–1*). Required of C and S corporations and partnerships/LLCs with total assets of $10 million or more.

Scholarship. Scholarships are generally excluded from the gross income of the recipient unless the payments are a disguised form of compensation for services rendered. However, the Code imposes restrictions on the exclusion. The recipient must be a degree candidate. The excluded amount is limited to amounts used for tuition, fees, books, supplies, and equipment required for courses of instruction. Amounts received for room and board are not eligible for the exclusion. § 117.

Section 121 exclusion. If a residence has been owned and used by the taxpayer as the principal residence for at least two years during the five-year period ending on the date of sale, up to $250,000 of realized gain is excluded from gross income. For a married couple filing a joint return, the $250,000 is increased to $500,000 if either spouse satisfies the ownership requirement and both spouses satisfy the use requirement.

Section 179 expensing. The ability to deduct the cost of qualified property in the year the property is placed in service rather than over the asset's useful life or cost recovery period. The annual ceiling on the deduction is $510,000 in 2017 ($500,000 in 2016). However, the deduction is reduced dollar for dollar when § 179 property placed in service during the taxable year exceeds $2,030,000 ($2,010,000 in 2016). In addition, the amount expensed under § 179 cannot exceed the aggregate amount of taxable income derived from the conduct of any trade or business by the taxpayer.

Section 179 expensing election. See *Section 179 expensing*.

Section 338 election. When a corporation acquires at least 80 percent of a subsidiary within a 12-month period, it can elect to treat the acquisition of such stock as an asset purchase. The acquiring corporation's basis in the subsidiary's assets then is the cost of the stock. The subsidiary is deemed to have sold its assets for an amount equal to the grossed-up basis in its stock.

Section 382 limitation. When one corporation acquires another, the acquiring corporation's ability to use the loss and credit carryovers of the target may be limited by this anti-abuse provision. For instance, the maximum NOL deduction available to the acquiring is the value of the target when acquired times the long-term tax-exempt interest rate on that date.

Section 401(k) plan. A cash or deferred arrangement plan that allows participants to elect to receive up to $18,000 in 2017 in cash (taxed currently) or to have a contribution made on their behalf to a profit sharing or stock bonus plan (excludible from gross income). The plan may also be in the form of a salary reduction agreement between the participant and the employer.

Section 754 election. An election that may be made by a partnership to adjust the basis of partnership assets to reflect a purchasing partner's outside basis in interest or to reflect a gain, loss, or basis adjustment of a partner receiving a distribution from a partnership. The intent of the election is to maintain the equivalence between outside and inside basis for that partner. Once the election is made, the partnership must make basis adjustments for all future transactions, unless the IRS consents to revoke the election.

Section 1231 gains and losses. If the combined gains and losses from the taxable dispositions of § 1231 assets plus the net gain from business involuntary conversions (of both § 1231 assets and long-term capital assets) is a gain, the gains and losses are treated as long-term capital gains and losses. In arriving at § 1231 gains, however, the depreciation recapture provisions (e.g., § 1245) are applied first to produce ordinary income. If the net result of the combination is a loss, the gains and losses from § 1231 assets are treated as ordinary gains and losses. § 1231(a).

Section 1231 lookback. For gain to be classified as § 1231 gain, the gain must survive the § 1231 lookback. To the extent of nonrecaptured § 1231 losses for the five prior tax years, the gain is classified as ordinary income. § 1231(c).

Section 1231 property. Depreciable assets and real estate used in trade or business and held for the required long-term holding period. § 1231(b).

Section 1244 stock. Stock issued under § 1244 by qualifying small business corporations. If § 1244 stock becomes worthless, the shareholders may claim an ordinary loss rather than the usual capital loss, within statutory limitations.

Section 1245 property. Property that is subject to the recapture of depreciation under § 1245. For a definition of § 1245 property, see § 1245(a)(3).

Section 1245 recapture. Upon a taxable disposition of § 1245 property, all depreciation claimed on the property is recaptured as ordinary income (but not to exceed any recognized gain from the disposition).

Section 1250 property. Real estate that is subject to the recapture of depreciation under § 1250. For a definition of § 1250 property, see § 1250(c).

Section 1250 recapture. Upon a taxable disposition of § 1250 property, accelerated depreciation or cost recovery claimed on the property may be recaptured as ordinary income.

Securities. Stock, debt, and other financial assets. To the extent securities other than the stock of the transferee corporation are received in a § 351 exchange, the new shareholder recognizes a gain. For purposes of corporate reorganizations, securities are generally debt with terms longer than 10 years. To the extent stock and securities are transferred in a corporate reorganization under § 368, no gain or loss is recognized.

Self-employment tax. A tax of 12.4 percent is levied on individuals with net earnings from self-employment (up to $127,200 in 2017) to provide Social Security benefits (i.e., the old age, survivors, and disability insurance portion) for such individuals. In addition, a tax of 2.9 percent is levied on individuals with net earnings from self-employment (with no statutory ceiling) to provide Medicare benefits (i.e., the hospital insurance portion) for such individuals. If a self-employed individual also receives wages from an employer that are subject to FICA, the self-employment tax will be reduced. A partial deduction is allowed in calculating the self-employment tax. Individuals with net earnings of $400 or more from self-employment are subject to this tax. §§ 1401 and 1402.

Separate foreign tax credit income categories. The foreign tax credit of a taxpayer is computed for each of several types of income sources, as specified by the Code to limit the results of tax planning. FTC income "baskets" include general and passive. The FTC for the year is the sum of the credits as computed within all of the taxpayer's separate FTC baskets used for the tax year.

Separate return limitation year (SRLY). A series of rules limits the amount of an acquired corporation's net operating loss carryforwards that can be used by the acquiror. Generally, a consolidated return can include the acquiree's net operating loss carryforward only to the extent of the lesser of the subsidiary's (1) current-year or (2) cumulative positive contribution to consolidated taxable income.

Separately stated items. Any item of a partnership or an S corporation that might be taxed differently to any two owners of the entity. These amounts are not included in the ordinary income of the entity, but are instead reported separately to the owners; tax consequences are determined at the owner level.

Severance taxes. A tax imposed upon the extraction of natural resources.

Short period. See *short taxable year*.

Short sale. A sale that occurs when a taxpayer sells borrowed property (usually stock) and repays the lender with substantially identical property either held on the date of the short sale or purchased after the sale. No gain or loss is recognized until the short sale is closed, and such gain or loss is generally short-term. § 1233.

Short taxable year. A tax year that is less than 12 months. A short taxable year may occur in the initial reporting period, in the final tax year, or when the taxpayer changes tax years.

Significant participation activity. Seven tests determine whether an individual has achieved material participation in an activity, one of which is based on more than 500 hours of participation in significant participation activities. A significant participation activity is one in which the individual's participation exceeds 100 hours during the year. Temp.Reg. § 1.469–5T.

Simple trust. Trusts that are not complex trusts. Such trusts may not have a charitable beneficiary, accumulate income, or distribute corpus.

Simplified employee pension (SEP) plans. An employer may make contributions to an employee's IRA in amounts not exceeding the lesser of 15 percent of compensation or $54,000 per individual in 2017. These employer-sponsored simplified employee pensions are permitted only if the contributions are nondiscriminatory and are made on behalf of all employees who have attained age 21 and have worked for the employer during at least three of the five preceding calendar years. § 219(b).

Small business corporation. A corporation that satisfies the definition of § 1361(b), § 1244(c), or both. Satisfaction of § 1361(b) permits an S election, and satisfaction of § 1244 enables the shareholders of the corporation to claim an ordinary loss on the worthlessness of stock.

Small business stock (§ 1244 stock). See *Section 1244 stock*.

Small Cases Division. A division within the U.S. Tax Court where jurisdiction is limited to claims of $50,000 or less. There is no appeal from this court.

Solicitation. A level of activity brought about by the taxpayer within a specific state. Under Public Law 86-272, certain types of solicitation activities do not create nexus with the state. Exceeding mere solicitation, though, creates nexus.

Special allocation. Any amount for which an agreement exists among the partners of a partnership outlining the method used for spreading the item among the partners.

Special use value. Permits the executor of an estate to value, for estate tax purposes, real estate used in a farming activity or in connection with a closely held business at its current use value rather than at its most suitable or optimal use value. Under this option, a farm is valued for farming purposes even though, for example, the property might have a higher potential value as a shopping center. For the executor of an estate to elect special use valuation, the conditions of § 2032A must be satisfied.

Specific charge-off method. A method of accounting for bad debts in which a deduction is permitted only when an account becomes partially or completely worthless.

Spin-off. A type of reorganization where, for example, Apple Corporation transfers some assets to Core Corporation in exchange for Core stock representing control. Apple then distributes the Core stock to its shareholders.

Split-off. A type of reorganization where, for example, Apple Corporation transfers some assets to Core Corporation in exchange for Core stock representing control. Apple then distributes the Core stock to its shareholders in exchange for some of their Apple stock. Not all shareholders need to exchange stock.

Split-up. A type of reorganization where, for example, Firefly Corporation transfers some assets to Fire Corporation and the remainder to Fly Corporation. In return, Firefly receives enough Fire and Fly stock representing control of each corporation. Firefly then distributes the Fire and Fly stock to its shareholders in return for all of their Firefly stock. Firefly then liquidates, and its shareholders now have control of Fire and Fly.

Sprinkling trust. When a trustee has the discretion to either distribute or accumulate the entity accounting income of the trust and to distribute it among the trust's income beneficiaries in varying magnitudes. The trustee can "sprinkle" the income of the trust.

Standard deduction. The individual taxpayer can either itemize deductions or take the standard deduction. The amount of the standard deduction depends on the taxpayer's filing status (single, head of household, married filing jointly, surviving spouse, or married filing separately). For 2017, the amount of the standard deduction ranges from $6,350 (for single) to $12,700 (for married, filing jointly). Additional standard deductions of either $1,250 (for married taxpayers) or $1,550 (for single taxpayers) are available if the taxpayer is blind or age 65 or over. Limitations exist on the amount of the standard deduction of a taxpayer who is another taxpayer's dependent. The standard deduction amounts are adjusted for inflation each year. § 63(c).

Startup expenditures. Expenditures paid or incurred prior to the beginning of the business that would have been deductible as an ordinary and necessary business expense if business operations had begun. Examples of such expenditures include advertising; salaries and wages; travel and other expenses incurred in lining up prospective distributors, suppliers, or customers; and salaries and fees to executives, consultants, and professional service providers. A taxpayer will immediately expense the first $5,000 (subject to phaseout) of startup expenditures and amortize the balance over a period of 180 months, unless the taxpayer elects to not do so.

Statute of limitations. Provisions of the law that specify the maximum period of time in which action may be taken concerning a past event. Code §§ 6501–6504 contain the limitation periods applicable to the IRS for additional assessments, and §§ 6511–6515 relate to refund claims by taxpayers.

Statutory employees. Statutory employees are considered self-employed independent contractors for purposes of reporting income and expenses on their tax returns. Generally, a statutory employee must meet three tests:

- It is understood from a service contract that the services will be performed by the person.

- The person does not have a substantial investment in facilities (other than transportation used to perform the services).

- The services involve a continuing relationship with the person for whom they are performed.

For further information on statutory employees, see Circular E, *Employer's Tax Guide* (IRS Publication 15).

Step down. See *step-down in basis.*

Step transaction. Disregarding one or more transactions to arrive at the final result. Assume, for example, Beta Corporation creates Alpha Corporation by transferring assets desired by Beta's sole shareholder, Carl. Carl then causes Alpha to liquidate to obtain the assets. Under these circumstances, the IRS may contend that the creation and liquidation of Alpha be disregarded. What really happened was a dividend distribution from Beta to Carl.

Step up. See *step-up in basis.*

Step-down in basis. A reduction in the tax basis of property. See also *step-up in basis.*

Step-up in basis. An increase in the income tax basis of property. In an estate context, a step-up in basis occurs when a decedent dies owning appreciated property. Since the estate or heir acquires a basis in the property equal to the property's fair market value on the date of death (or alternate valuation date if available and elected), any appreciation is not subject to the income tax. Thus, a step-up in basis is the result, with no immediate income tax consequences. In the partnership context, a step-up arises when a § 754 election is in effect and when one of several transactions arises: (1) a partner purchases a partnership interest for an amount that exceeds the partner's share of the partnership's inside basis, (2) the partner recognizes a gain on a distribution of cash from the partnership, or (3) the partnership takes a basis in a partnership property that is less than the partnership's basis in that asset. In the opposite situations (e.g., loss recognition), a step-down can arise. See also *step-down in basis.*

Stock bonus plan. A type of deferred compensation plan in which the employer establishes and maintains the plan and contributes employer stock to the plan for the benefit of employees. The contributions need not be dependent on the employer's profits. Any benefits of the plan are distributable in the form of employer stock, except that distributable fractional shares may be paid in cash.

Stock dividend. Not taxable if pro rata distributions of stock or stock rights on common stock. Section 305 governs the taxability of stock dividends and sets out five exceptions to the general rule that stock dividends are nontaxable.

Stock option. The right to purchase a stated number of shares of stock from a corporation at a certain price within a specified period of time. §§ 421 and 422.

Stock redemption. A corporation buys back its own stock from a specified shareholder. Typically, the corporation recognizes any realized gain on the noncash assets that it uses to effect a redemption, and the shareholder obtains a capital gain or loss upon receipt of the purchase price.

Stock rights. Assets that convey to the holder the power to purchase corporate stock at a specified price, often for a limited period of time. Stock rights received may be taxed as a distribution of earnings and profits. After the right is exercised, the basis of the acquired share includes the investor's purchase price or gross income, if any, to obtain the right. Disposition of the right also can be taxable.

Subchapter S. Sections 1361–1379 of the Internal Revenue Code. An elective provision permitting certain small business corporations (§ 1361) and their shareholders (§ 1362) to elect to be treated for income tax purposes in accordance with the operating rules of §§ 1363–1379. However, some S corporations usually avoid the corporate income tax, and corporate losses can be claimed by the shareholders.

Subpart F. Identifies the current tax treatment of income earned by a controlled foreign corporation. Certain types of income are included in U.S. gross income by U.S. shareholders of such an entity as they are generated, not when they are repatriated.

Subpart F income. See *Subpart F.*

Substance over form. A standard used when one must ascertain the true reality of what has occurred. Suppose, for example, a father sells stock to his daughter for $1,000. If the stock is really worth $50,000 at the time of the transfer, the substance of the transaction is probably a gift to her of $49,000.

Substantial authority. Taxpayer and tax preparer understatement penalties are waived where substantial authority existed for the disputed position taken on the return.

Substantial risk of forfeiture (SRF). A term that is associated with a restricted property plan. Generally, an employee who receives property (e.g., stock of the employer-corporation) from the employer at a bargain price or at no cost must include the bargain element in gross income. However, the employee currently does not have to do so if there is a substantial risk of forfeiture. A substantial risk of forfeiture exists if a person's rights to full enjoyment of property are conditioned upon the future performance, or the refraining from the performance, of substantial services by the individual. § 83.

Sunset provision. A provision attached to new tax legislation that will cause such legislation to expire at a specified date. Sunset provisions are attached to tax cut bills for long-term budgetary reasons to make their effect temporary. Once the sunset provision comes into play, the tax cut is rescinded and former law is reinstated. An example of a sunset provision is contained in the Tax Relief Reconciliation Act of 2001 that related to the estate tax. After the estate tax was phased out in 2010, a sunset provision called for the reinstatement of the estate tax as of January 1, 2011.

Supreme Court. See *U.S. Supreme Court.*

Surviving spouse. When a husband or wife predeceases the other spouse, the survivor is known as a surviving spouse. Under certain conditions, a surviving spouse may be entitled to use the income tax rates in § 1(a) (those applicable to married persons filing a joint return) for the two years after the year of death of his or her spouse. § 2(a).

Syndication costs. Incurred in promoting and marketing partnership interests for sale to investors. Examples include legal and accounting fees, printing costs for prospectus and placement documents, and state registration fees. These items are capitalized by the partnership as incurred, with no amortization thereof allowed.

T

Tax avoidance. The minimization of one's tax liability by taking advantage of legally available tax planning opportunities. Tax avoidance can be contrasted with tax evasion, which entails the reduction of tax liability by illegal means.

Tax benefit rule. A provision that limits the recognition of income from the recovery of an expense or a loss properly deducted in a prior tax year to the amount of the deduction that generated a tax saving. Assume that last year Gary had medical expenses of $4,000 and adjusted gross income of $30,000. Because of the AGI limitation, Gary could deduct only $1,000 of these expenses [$4,000 − (10% × $30,000)]. If this year Gary is reimbursed in full by his insurance company for the $4,000 of expenses, the tax benefit rule limits the amount of income from the reimbursement to $1,000 (the amount previously deducted with a tax saving).

Tax Court. See *U.S. Tax Court.*

Tax credit for the elderly or disabled. An elderly (age 65 and over) or disabled taxpayer may receive a tax credit amounting to 15 percent of $5,000 ($7,500 for qualified married individuals filing jointly). This amount is reduced by Social Security benefits, excluded pension benefits, and one-half of the taxpayer's adjusted gross income in excess of $7,500 ($10,000 for married taxpayers filing jointly). § 22.

Tax credits. Amounts that directly reduce a taxpayer's tax liability. The tax benefit received from a tax credit is not dependent on the taxpayer's marginal tax rate, whereas the benefit of a tax deduction or exclusion is dependent on the taxpayer's tax bracket.

Tax evasion. The reduction of taxes by the use of subterfuge or fraud or other nonlegal means. For example, a cash basis taxpayer tries to increase his or her charitable contribution deduction by prepaying next year's church pledge with a pre-dated check issued in the following year.

Tax haven. A country in which either locally sourced income or residents of the country are subject to a low rate of taxation.

Tax preferences. See *AMT preferences.*

Tax preparer. One who prepares tax returns for compensation. A tax preparer must register with the IRS and receive a special ID number to practice before the IRS and represent taxpayers before the agency in tax audit actions. The conduct of a tax preparer is regulated under Circular 230. Tax preparers also are subject to penalties for inappropriate conduct when working in the tax profession.

Tax Rate Schedules. Rate schedules that are used by upper-income taxpayers and those not permitted to use the tax table. Separate rate schedules are provided for married individuals filing jointly, heads of households, single tax-payers, estates and trusts, and married individuals filing separate returns. § 1.

Tax research. The method used to determine the best available solution to a situation that possesses tax consequences. Both tax and nontax factors are considered.

Tax shelters. The typical tax shelter generated large losses in the early years of the activity. Investors would offset these losses against other types of income and therefore avoid paying income taxes on this income. These tax shelter investments could then be sold after a few years and produce capital gain income, which is taxed at a lower rate compared to ordinary income. The passive activity loss rules and the at-risk rules now limit tax shelter deductions.

Tax Table. A table that is provided for taxpayers with less than $100,000 of taxable income. Separate columns are provided for single taxpayers, married taxpayers filing jointly, heads of households, and married taxpayers filing separately. § 3.

Tax treaties. An agreement between the U.S. Department of State and another country designed to alleviate double taxation of income and asset transfers and to share administrative information useful to tax agencies in both countries. The United States has income tax treaties with almost 70 countries and transfer tax treaties with about 20.

Taxable estate. The taxable estate is the gross estate of a decedent reduced by the deductions allowed by §§ 2053–2057 (e.g., administration expenses, marital and charitable deductions). The taxable estate is subject to the unified transfer tax at death. § 2051.

Taxable gift. The amount of a gift that is subject to the unified transfer tax. Thus, a taxable gift has been adjusted by the annual exclusion and other appropriate deductions (e.g., marital and charitable). § 2053.

Taxable year. The annual period over which income is measured for income tax purposes. Most individuals use a calendar year, but many businesses use a fiscal year based on the natural business year.

Technical Advice Memoranda (TAM). TAMs are issued by the IRS in response to questions raised by IRS field personnel during audits. They deal with completed rather than proposed transactions and are often requested for questions related to exempt organizations and employee plans.

Technical termination of a partnership. The entity is treated for tax purposes as though it has terminated, even though it continues its activities. When there has been a sale or exchange of more than 50 percent of the capital interests of the partnership within 12 months, the partnership is deemed to have terminated when the 50 percent threshold is crossed. A new partnership immediately is formed through asset contributions by the partners. These activities can affect the entity's tax year and its bases in the assets it holds.

Temporary differences. Under ASC 740 (SFAS 109), tax-related items that appear in the entity's financial statements and its tax return, but in different time periods. For instance, doubtful accounts receivable often create a temporary book-tax difference, as a bad debt reserve is used to compute an expense for financial reporting purposes, but a bad debt often is deductible only under the specific write-off rule for tax purposes, and the difference observed for the current period creates a temporary difference.

Temporary Regulations. A Regulation issued by the Treasury Department in temporary form. When speed is critical, the Treasury Department issues Temporary Regulations that take effect immediately. These Regulations have the same authoritative value as Final Regulations and may be cited as precedent for three years. Temporary Regulations are also issued as proposed Regulations.

Tenants by the entirety. Essentially, a joint tenancy between husband and wife.

Tenants in common. A form of ownership where each tenant (owner) holds an undivided interest in property. Unlike a joint tenancy or a tenancy by the entirety, the interest of a tenant in common does not terminate upon that individual's death (there is no right of survivorship). Assume that Tim and Cindy acquire real estate as equal tenants in common. Upon Tim's death, his one-half interest in the property passes to his estate or heirs, not automatically to Cindy.

Terminable interests. An interest in property that terminates upon the death of the holder or upon the occurrence of some other specified event. The transfer of a terminable interest by one spouse to the other may not qualify for the marital deduction. §§ 2056(b) and 2523(b).

Theft losses. A loss from larceny, embezzlement, or robbery. It does not include misplacement of items.

Thin capitalization. When debt owed by a corporation to the shareholders becomes too large in relation to the corporation's capital structure (i.e., stock and shareholder equity), the IRS may contend that the corporation is thinly capitalized. In effect, some or all of the debt is reclassified as equity. The immediate result is to disallow any interest deduction to the corporation on the reclassified debt. To the extent of the corporation's earnings and profits, interest payments and loan repayments on the reclassified debt are treated as dividends to the shareholders.

Thirty-day letter. A letter that accompanies an RAR (Revenue Agent's Report) issued as a result of an IRS audit of a taxpayer (or the rejection of a taxpayer's claim for refund). The letter outlines the taxpayer's appeal procedure before the IRS. If the taxpayer does not request any such procedures within the 30-day period, the IRS issues a statutory notice of deficiency (the 90-day letter).

Throwback rule. If there is no income tax in the state to which a sale otherwise would be apportioned, the sale essentially is exempt from state income tax, even though the seller is domiciled in a state that levies an income tax. Nonetheless, if the seller's state has adopted a throwback rule, the sale is attributed to the seller's state and the transaction is subjected to a state-level tax.

Traditional IRA. See *Individual Retirement Account (IRA)*.

Transfer pricing. The process of setting internal prices for transfers of goods and services among related taxpayers. For example, what price should be used when Subsidiary purchases management services from Parent? The IRS can adjust transfer prices when it can show that the taxpayers were attempting to avoid tax by, say, shifting losses, deductions, or credits from low-tax to high-tax entities or jurisdictions.

Transportation expenses. Transportation expenses for an employee include only the cost of transportation (e.g., taxi fares and automobile expenses) in the course of employment when the employee is not away from home in travel status. Commuting expenses are not deductible.

Travel expenses. Expenses that include meals (generally subject to a 50 percent disallowance) and lodging and transportation expenses while away from home in the pursuit of a trade or business (including that of an employee).

Treaty shopping. An international investor attempts to use the favorable aspects of a tax treaty to his or her advantage, often elevating the form of the transaction over its substance (e.g., by establishing only a nominal presence in the country offering the favorable treaty terms).

U

UDITPA. The Uniform Division of Income for Tax Purposes Act has been adopted in some form by many of the states. The Act develops criteria by which the total taxable income of a multistate corporation can be assigned to specific states.

Unclaimed property. A U.S. state may have the right to acquire property that has been made available to an individual or legal entity for a fixed period of time, where the claimant has not taken possession of the property after a notice period. Examples of such property that a state could acquire are an uncashed payroll check, or an unused gift card.

Undistributed PHCI. The tax base for the personal holding company tax. § 545.

Unearned income. Income received but not yet earned. Normally, such income is taxed when received, even for accrual basis taxpayers.

Unified transfer tax. Rates applicable to transfers by gift and death made after 1976. § 2001(c).

Unified transfer tax credit. A credit allowed against any unified transfer tax. §§ 2010 and 2505.

Uniform capitalization (UNICAP) rules. Under § 263A, the Regulations provide a set of rules that all taxpayers (regardless of the particular industry) can use to determine the items of cost (and means of allocating those costs) that must be capitalized with respect to the production of tangible property.

Unitary approach. See *unitary theory.*

Unitary theory. Sales, property, and payroll of related corporations are combined for nexus and apportionment purposes, and the worldwide income of the unitary entity is apportioned to the state. Subsidiaries and other affiliated corporations found to be part of the corporation's unitary business (because they are subject to overlapping ownership, operation, or management) are included in the apportionment procedure. This approach can be limited if a water's-edge election is in effect.

Unit-livestock-price method. A method of accounting for the cost of livestock. The livestock are valued using a standard cost of raising an animal with the characteristics of the animals on hand to the same age as those animals.

Unrealized receivables. Amounts earned by a cash basis taxpayer but not yet received. Because of the method of accounting used by the taxpayer, these amounts have a zero income tax basis. When unrealized receivables are distributed to a partner, they generally convert a transaction from nontaxable to taxable or an otherwise capital gain to ordinary income (i.e., as a "hot asset").

Unreasonable compensation. A deduction is allowed for "reasonable" salaries or other compensation for personal services actually rendered. To the extent compensation is "excessive" ("unreasonable"), the distribution could be treated as a dividend, such that no deduction is allowed. The problem of unreasonable compensation usually is limited to closely held corporations, where the motivation is to pay out profits in some form that is deductible to the corporation.

Unreasonable position. A tax preparer penalty is assessed regarding the understatement of a client's tax liability due to a tax return position that is found to be too aggressive. The penalty is avoided if there is substantial authority for the position or if the position is disclosed adequately on the tax return. The penalty equals the greater of $1,000 or one-half of the tax preparer's fee that is traceable to the aggressive position.

Unrecaptured § 1250 gain. Gain from the sale of depreciable real estate held more than one year. The gain is equal to or less than the depreciation taken on such property and is reduced by § 1245 and § 1250 gain.

Unrelated business income (UBI). Income recognized by an exempt organization that is generated from activities not related to the exempt purpose of the entity. For instance, the gift shop located in a hospital may generate unrelated business income. § 511.

Unrelated business income tax (UBIT). Levied on the unrelated business income of an exempt organization.

U.S. Court of Federal Claims. A trial court (court of original jurisdiction) that decides litigation involving Federal tax matters. Appeal from this court is to the Court of Appeals for the Federal Circuit.

U.S. shareholder. For purposes of classification of an entity as a controlled foreign corporation, a U.S. person who owns, or is considered to own, 10 percent or more of the total combined voting power of all classes of voting stock of a foreign corporation. Stock owned directly, indirectly, and constructively is counted for this purpose.

U.S. Supreme Court. The highest appellate court or the court of last resort in the Federal court system and in most states. Only a small number of tax decisions of the U.S. Courts of Appeal are reviewed by the U.S. Supreme Court under its certiorari procedure. The Supreme Court usually grants certiorari to resolve a conflict among the Courts of Appeal (e.g., two or more appellate courts have assumed opposing positions on a particular issue) or when the tax issue is extremely important (e.g., size of the revenue loss to the Federal government).

U.S. Tax Court. One of four trial courts of original jurisdiction that decides litigation involving Federal income, death, or gift taxes. It is the only trial court where the taxpayer must not first pay the deficiency assessed by the IRS. The Tax Court will not have jurisdiction over a case unless a statutory notice of deficiency (90-day letter) has been issued by the IRS and the taxpayer files the petition for hearing within the time prescribed.

U.S. trade or business. A set of activities that is carried on in a regular, continuous, and substantial manner. A non-U.S.

taxpayer is subject to U.S. tax on the taxable income that is effectively connected with a U.S. trade or business.

Use tax. A sales tax that is collectible by the seller where the purchaser is domiciled in a different state.

V

Vacation homes. The Code places restrictions upon taxpayers who rent their residences or vacation homes for part of the tax year. The restrictions may result in a scaling down of expense deductions for the taxpayers. § 280A.

Valuation allowance. Under ASC 740 (SFAS 109), a tax-related item is reported for book purposes only when it is more likely than not that the item actually will be realized. When the "more likely than not" test is failed, a contra-asset account is created to offset some or all of the related deferred tax asset. For instance, if the entity projects that it will not be able to use all of its net operating loss carryforward due to a lack of future taxable income, a valuation allowance is created to reduce the net deferred tax asset that corresponds to the carryforward. If income projections later change and it appears that the carryforward will be used, the valuation allowance is reversed or "released." Creation of a valuation allowance usually increases the current tax expense and thereby reduces current book income, and its release often increases book income in the later reporting period.

Value added tax (VAT). A national sales tax that taxes the increment in value as goods move through the production process. A VAT is much used in other countries but has not yet been incorporated as part of the U.S. Federal tax structure.

Vesting requirements. A qualified deferred compensation arrangement must satisfy a vesting requirement. Under this provision, an employee's right to accrued plan benefits derived from employer contributions must be nonforfeitable in accordance with one of two vesting time period schedules (or two required alternate vesting schedules for certain employer matching contributions).

Voluntary revocation. The owners of a majority of shares in an S corporation elect to terminate the S status of the entity as of a specified date. The day on which the revocation is effective is the first day of the corporation's C tax year.

W

W–2 wages. The domestic production activities deduction (DPAD) cannot exceed 50 percent of the W–2 wages paid for any particular year. Prop.Reg. § 199–2(f)(2) provides several methods for calculating the W–2 wages, but the payments must involve common law employees. To qualify, employees need to be involved in the production process. § 199.

Wash sale. A loss from the sale of stock or securities that is disallowed because the taxpayer, within 30 days before or after the sale, has acquired stock or securities substantially identical to those sold. § 1091.

Water's edge. A limitation on the worldwide scope of the unitary theory. If a corporate water's-edge election is in effect, the state can consider in the apportionment procedure only the activities that occur within the boundaries of the United States.

Water's-edge election. See *water's edge.*

Wherewithal to pay. This concept recognizes the inequity of taxing a transaction when the taxpayer lacks the means with which to pay the tax. Under it, there is a correlation between the imposition of the tax and the ability to pay the tax. It is particularly suited to situations in which the taxpayer's economic position has not changed significantly as a result of the transaction.

Whistleblower Program. An IRS initiative that offers special rewards to informants who provide evidence regarding tax evasion activities of businesses or high-income individuals. More than $2 million of tax, interest, and penalty must be at stake. The reward can reach 30 percent of the tax recovery that is attributable to the whistleblower's information.

Withholding allowances. The number of withholding allowances serves as the basis for determining the amount of income taxes withheld from an employee's salary or wages. The more withholding allowances claimed, the less income tax withheld by an employer. An employee may claim withholding allowances for personal exemptions for self and spouse (unless claimed as a dependent of another person), dependency exemptions, and special withholding allowances.

Work opportunity tax credit. Employers are allowed a tax credit equal to 40 percent of the first $6,000 of wages (per eligible employee) for the first year of employment. Eligible employees include certain hard-to-employ individuals (e.g., qualified ex-felons, high-risk youth, food stamp recipients, and veterans). The employer's deduction for wages is reduced by the amount of the credit taken. For qualified summer youth employees, the 40 percent rate is applied to the first $3,000 of qualified wages.

Working condition fringes. A type of fringe benefit received by the employee that is excludible from the employee's gross income. It consists of property or services provided (paid or reimbursed) by the employer for which the employee could take a tax deduction if the employee had paid for them. § 132.

Worthless securities. A loss (usually capital) is allowed for a security that becomes worthless during the year. The loss is deemed to have occurred on the last day of the year. Special rules apply to securities of affiliated companies and small business stock. § 165.

Writ of Certiorari. Appeal from a U.S. Court of Appeals to the U.S. Supreme Court is by Writ of Certiorari. The Supreme Court need not accept the appeal, and it usually does not (*cert. den.*) unless a conflict exists among the lower courts that must be resolved or a constitutional issue is involved.

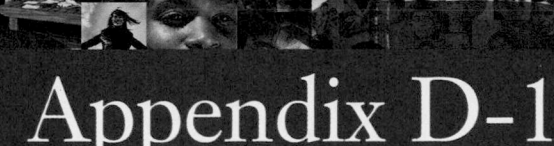

Appendix D-1

Table of Code Sections Cited

[See Title 26 U.S.C.A.]

Appendix D-2

Table of Regulations Cited

Table of Revenue Procedures and Revenue Rulings Cited

Appendix E

Practice Set Assignments—Comprehensive Tax Return Problems

PROBLEM 1

Steven B. (age 42) and Debra S. (age 41) Marshall are married and live at 426 East Twin Oaks Road, Sioux Falls, SD 57105. Steven is the regional manager for a restaurant chain (Moveable Feast), and Debra is a self-employed architect. They are calendar year, cash basis taxpayers.

1. Steven's annual salary from Moveable Feast is $82,000. He also earns an annual bonus. The amount is determined in late December, and Steven receives it in January of the next year. Steven's 2015 bonus was $6,000 (received in 2016), and his 2016 bonus was $7,000 (received in 2017). Steven is also paid a flat travel allowance of $16,000 per year. The allowance is to cover his expenses in visiting restaurants in his region to conduct inspections, consult with the local managers, and recruit potential hires. Although Steven maintains substantiation of his travel, he is not required to account for these expenses to Moveable Feast. Steven participates in his employer's group health insurance plan to which he contributed $3,600 in 2016 for medical coverage. These contributions are made with after-tax dollars. The health plan covers Steven, Debra, and their two dependent children. Moveable Feast does not provide any retirement benefits, but it has established a § 401(k) plan to enable its employees to save for retirement. Steven contributed $10,000 to the plan in 2016. The company provides an office for Steven's use that is located at 110 North Reid Street, Suite 217, Sioux Falls.

2. On March 5, 2015, Steven purchased a new Ford Focus for use in his job. The car cost $24,000 (including sales tax), with no trade-in involved. The car was driven 14,000 miles in 2015 and 18,000 in 2016 with usage as follows: 20% for his commute to the office and 80% for business trips. The mileage for 2016 was evenly distributed throughout the year. Steven deducts actual operating costs for his vehicle, using the 200% declining-balance method with a half-year convention to compute MACRS depreciation. In addition, Steven did not claim any § 179 expensing or

additional first-year depreciation last year when he bought the car. Steven's expenses related to operating the Focus for 2016 are as follows:

Gasoline	$2,900
Oil change and lubrication	150
Auto insurance	1,800
Repairs	400
Auto club dues	160
License and registration	120
Interest on car loan	900

3. Steven also incurred the following out-of-pocket employment-related expenses during 2016:

Airfare	$2,600
Lodging	3,200
Meals	3,400
Entertainment	800
Car rentals, limos, taxis	600
Parking and tolls	300
Subscriptions to trade journals	120
Dues to trade association	80
Business gifts	550
Speeding tickets	620

Steven made the business gifts in late December to managers of the top 11 restaurants in his region, with each manager receiving a $50 gift card to a national retailer. While on business trips in his car, Steven was cited for speeding several times and paid related fines totaling $620.

4. Debra Marshall is a licensed architect who works part-time on a consulting basis. Her professional activity code is 541310. Her major clients are real estate developers (both residential and commercial) for whom she prepares structural designs and construction plans. She also advises on building code requirements regarding the renovation and remodeling of existing structures. Debra does her work at the client's location or in her office at home (see item 5 below).

Debra collected $52,000 in consulting fees during 2016. This total includes a $3,000 payment for work she performed in 2015 and does not include $5,000 she billed in December for work performed in late 2016. In addition, Debra has an unpaid invoice for $6,000 from a client for work done in 2014. This client was convicted of arson in August 2013 and is now serving a five-year sentence in state prison. Debra is certain she will never collect the $6,000 she is owed. Her business expenses for 2016 are:

Drafting supplies	$4,800
Reproduction materials (e.g., molds, models, photos, blueprints, copies)	3,200
On-site work clothing (e.g., hip boots, safety glasses, safety helmet)	800
Professional license fee	400
Subscriptions to professional journals	250
Dues to professional organizations	240

In addition, Debra drove the family Acura (purchased on June 7, 2015) 940 miles on her job assignments. She uses the standard mileage method to deduct business costs related to the Acura. During 2016, Debra drove the car a total of 10,000 miles.

5. When the Marshalls purchased their home on February 2, 2015, they set aside 300 square feet (out of a total of 2,400 square feet) of living space for Debra's office. As of January 1, 2016, the home had an adjusted basis of $240,000 for purposes of line 36 of Form 8829 (of which $40,000 is attributable to the land)—the fair market

value of the property is in excess of this amount. Relevant information concerning the residence for all of 2016 appears below.

Homeowner's insurance	$3,200
Repairs and maintenance	1,800
Utilities	6,200
Painting (office area only)	2,500

The cost of Debra's office furniture and equipment was previously deducted under § 179 in the years these assets were acquired. On June 29, 2016, she purchased a fireproof file cabinet for $800 to safeguard the blueprints of her structural designs and construction plans. If possible, Debra prefers to avoid depreciating capital expenditures.

6. One of Debra's clients was interested in building a shopping center on a tract of land Debra owned in Lincoln County. She inherited the property from her uncle when he died on June 6, 1996. At that time, the land was worth $40,000. It has since been rezoned for commercial use and has a current value of $200,000. On February 10, 2016, Debra exchanged the Lincoln parcel for a similar tract in Minnehaha County worth $190,000 and cash of $10,000.

7. On September 2, 2016, Debra sold a tract of land in McCook County to a farmer who owned the adjoining property. The land was inherited from the same uncle who died in 1996, and it was worth $30,000 on June 6, 1996. Under the terms of the sale, Debra received cash of $20,000 and four notes to be received at one-year intervals. Each note calls for the payment of $25,000 plus simple interest of 8%. To the extent allowed by law, Debra wants to defer recognition of gain as long as possible.

8. In early 2015, Steven learned that one of his restaurant managers, Mindy Smith, was suffering domestic abuse at the hands of her husband, Billy. When Billy started to abuse their 5-year-old daughter too, Mindy decided it was time to get away. Before they left on April 14, 2015, Steven loaned Mindy $5,500 to help her and her daughter relocate. Steven had her sign an interest-free note due in one year. Steven never heard from Mindy again. In late 2016, Steven learned that Billy had tracked down Mindy and their daughter and killed both of them before he committed suicide. Given these tragic circumstances, Steven has no expectation that the loan will ever be repaid.

9. On August 5, 2014, Steven purchased 1,000 shares of Farmer's Markets America (FMA) common stock for $16 a share as part of its initial public offering. The corporation was formed to establish and operate farmers' markets in midsize cities throughout the United States. Although some market locations were profitable, the venture as a whole proved to be a failure. In November 2016, FMA's remaining assets were seized by its creditors, and FMA stock became worthless.

10. In addition to the items previously noted, the Marshalls had the following receipts for 2016:

Interest income:		
General Motors corporate bonds	$1,900	
City of Sioux Falls, SD bonds	1,400	
Castle Bank certificate of deposit	210	$ 3,510
Qualified dividends from MG&E Inc.		3,100
Refund from HomeStuff		430
Loan repayment by Sarah Marshall-Caine		4,500
Cash gifts from Debra's parents		32,000
2015 Federal income tax refund		290

In December 2015, the Marshalls made a major purchase of household items (e.g., appliances, furniture, etc.) at HomeStuff (a discount big box store). They called the manager when they realized they did not receive the advertised sale price. Consequently, the store corrected the mistake and sent a $430 refund that the Marshalls received in January 2016. Four years ago when his sister Sarah married, Steven lent her $4,000 to help pay for her honeymoon. Steven was pleasantly surprised when Sarah paid him back (plus interest of $500) on December 20, 2016. On March 20 of each year, Debra's parents send a generous gift of cash as a birthday present. Just as she has done for the past seven years, Debra immediately invested the cash in her children's § 529 college savings plans.

11. The Marshalls had the following expenditures for 2016:

Debra's contribution to her traditional IRA		$5,500
Net gambling loss		1,000
Life insurance premiums		2,700
Medical and dental expenses not covered by insurance		6,200
Taxes:		
Ad valorem taxes on personal residence	$4,800	
State and local sales taxes from receipts	3,200	8,000
Interest on home mortgage		4,000
Cash Contributions:		
Goodwill (Sioux Falls branch)	1,200	
South Dakota governor's election campaign fund	300	1,500

The $1,000 net gambling loss for 2016 is the difference between the Marshalls' gambling winnings of $1,200 and losses of $2,200. The life insurance premiums relate to the universal life insurance policies that Steven and Debra own. The first beneficiary on both policies is the other spouse, with the second beneficiaries being the children. Included in the medical expenses are $1,200 incurred in 2015, which were paid in early February 2016. The Marshalls can substantiate the $3,200 in sales taxes paid based on their purchase receipts for the year. The local sales tax rate in Sioux Falls is 2%. (HINT: Check to see if the Optional Sales Tax Tables provide the Marshalls with a greater deduction.) Debra contributed to the governor's campaign fund because she thinks his influence was key in getting the Lincoln County land rezoned for commercial use (see item 6 above).

12. The Marshalls maintain a household that includes their two children, Nickolas (age 16) and Kaleigh (age 19). Nickolas, a junior in high school, is a talented wrestler. In hopes of competing at the state tournament, he spends all of his free time on weight training when he's not at wrestling practice. Kaleigh graduated from high school on June 7, 2016, and is undecided about college. She is an accomplished vocalist and during 2016 earned $7,200 performing at various events (e.g., weddings, funerals). Kaleigh placed most of her earnings in a savings account for future use and kept only a small amount to spend on herself.

13. Steven's Form W–2 from Moveable Feast shows $13,800 withheld for Federal income tax. The Marshalls have made total quarterly income tax payments of $4,000.

14. Relevant Social Security numbers are noted below:

Name	Social Security Number
Steven B. Marshall	123-45-6786
Debra S. Marshall	123-45-6787
Kaleigh J. Marshall	123-45-6788
Nickolas W. Marshall	123-45-6789

Requirements

Prepare an income tax return (with appropriate schedules) for the Marshalls for 2016, using the following guidelines:

- The Marshalls choose to file a joint income tax return.
- The Marshalls do not want to contribute to the Presidential Election Campaign Fund.
- The Marshalls do not own any foreign bank accounts or other investments.
- The Marshalls prefer to receive any refund of overpaid taxes.
- The taxpayers are preparing their own return (i.e., no preparer is involved).
- For the past several years, the Marshalls have itemized their deductions from AGI.
- The taxpayers have the necessary substantiation (e.g., records, receipts) to support all transactions reported in their tax return.
- Make necessary assumptions for information not given in the problem but needed to complete the return.

PROBLEM 2

Neil B. (age 42) and Mae R. (age 48) King are married and live at 7605 Walnut Street, Kansas City, MO 64114. Neil is a chemist employed by Sargent Pharmaceuticals, Inc., and Mae is a self-employed doctor of anesthesiology. They are calendar year, cash basis taxpayers.

1. Sargent Pharmaceuticals develops and produces injectable medicines used in chemotherapy treatments for cancer patients. Neil manages the Kansas City facility for an annual salary of $90,000. Sargent makes contributions to a qualified defined contribution pension plan for all of its full-time employees. Although Neil also has the opportunity to make contributions to the plan, he chose not to do so in 2016. Neil participates in his employer's group health insurance plan, to which he contributed $4,000 in 2016 for medical coverage. These contributions are made with pre-tax dollars. The health plan covers Neil, Mae, and their two dependent children. Because of the risk associated with Neil's work (i.e., processing chemotherapy drugs), Sargent provides all of its employees with $200,000 of group term life insurance. An additional $180 of income is included in Neil's Form W–2 to report the taxable value of this insurance.

2. In late 2015, three employees at Sargent's Chicago facility were seriously injured while processing a customer order. While the injuries occurred in what the company called a "freak accident," Neil began to look for a safer job in the chemical industry. He incurred the following expenses during 2016:

Employment agency fee	$3,200
Résumé consultation, preparation, and distribution	1,800
Expenses in connection with job interviews	4,100

Neil received several attractive offers but ultimately decided against changing jobs. Influential in his choice was a promotion to regional manager and a $20,000 pay raise starting in 2017.

3. Sargent generally reimburses Neil for expenses related to his work for the company. However, as a matter of policy, Sargent does not reimburse for the following:

Monthly dinner meetings of the Midwestern Chemists Association [MCA]	$825
Dues to professional organizations	240
Subscriptions to professional journals	180
MIA correspondence study course	230

Neil attended 11 MCA dinner meetings in 2016. Each dinner involved the following costs: $40 (fee for speaker), $25 (price of meal), and $10 (parking). Neil goes to the meetings from work and returns home the same night. The MIA (Management Institute of America) charge was for an online home study course on ways to improve safety measures and avoid accidents in the industrial workplace.

4. Mae King is a board-certified doctor of anesthesiology. She provides anesthesiology services at a number of hospitals and surgical centers in the greater Kansas City area on a part-time basis. Mae is well respected by the surgeons with whom she works. She uses her home as her business address. She keeps her records there and otherwise conducts business (e.g., conducts pre-surgery appointments, renders professional advice, bills patients) on the premises. Because Mae does not maintain a specific area for exclusive business use, she does not claim an office in the home for tax purposes. Mae's receipts from her practice during 2016 were $245,000, $16,000 of which was for services performed in 2015. Not included in these amounts is $17,500 she received in January 2017 for services rendered in December 2016. Mae's professional activity code is 621111.

5. Mae had the following business expenses in 2016:

Medical clothing (e.g., lab coats, surgical scrubs)	$2,200
Medical malpractice insurance	9,500
State medical license fee	450
Dues to professional organizations	350
Subscriptions to professional journals	340

In addition, she drove the family Suburban (purchased on March 2, 2015) 2,900 miles in connection with her work. She uses the standard mileage method for computing deductible vehicle costs. Total mileage for the Suburban is 9,000 miles for the year.

6. Neil's widowed mother, Lucy, suffered a stroke on December 30, 2015, and died in the hospital on February 3, 2016. Most of Lucy's medical expenses were covered by Medicare, with Neil paying the remainder. On February 18, 2016, he paid $9,800 to the hospital, half of which was attributable to expenses incurred in 2015. At the same time, Neil also paid the funeral expenses of $16,000. Although Lucy lived in her own home prior to the stroke, Neil and Mae have properly claimed her as a dependent for the past few years.

7. As Lucy's sole heir, Neil inherited her home and its furnishings (located at 1420 Chickadee Lane, Topeka, KS 66546). The costs and values involved are as follows:

	Cost Basis	FMV on 2/3/16
Lot	$ 10,000	$ 30,000
House	110,000	250,000
Furnishings	55,000	25,000

Because the real estate market was depressed and the home was located in an attractive rental area, Neil decided not to sell. Instead, he rented the property fully furnished on May 1, 2016. The terms of the lease (executed on April 30) provide for the following: one-year lease at $2,500 per month (payable on the first of each month), last month's rent payable in advance, and damage deposit of $3,000. In total, Neil received $25,500 from the tenants in 2016 for their use of the property. Besides depreciation, his expenses were:

Property taxes	$4,800
Insurance	3,900
Repairs	2,100
Real estate renter's location service	400

For MACRS depreciation purposes, Neil plans to use the straight-line method with the mid-month convention to compute the deduction for the realty and the 200% declining-balance method with a half-year convention for the personalty.

8. While walking the family dogs in late July, Mae was struck by a delivery van and seriously injured. After being hospitalized for a week, she was released—bruised and sore but with no permanent injuries. The driver of the van was arrested and ticketed by the police for reckless operation of a vehicle and was later prosecuted for drug use. To prevent adverse publicity related to a lawsuit, the owner of the delivery service paid for Mae's medical expenses and sent her a check on August 16, 2016, for $90,000. The check was accompanied by a letter that stated "This $90,000 is a settlement for physical injuries sustained by Mae King." Mae was represented in the negotiations with the delivery company by her brother, a practicing attorney. He did not charge the Kings for his services.

9. The Kings had the following property transactions during 2016:

   a.   On May 5, the City Council condemned unimproved land owned by Neil for the construction of a fire station. He purchased the land (two vacant lots at 3400 and 3402 Sycamore Lane) as an investment on May 25, 2009, for $14,000. In exchange for the lots, the city gave Neil a large unimproved lot at 440 Genoa Street that was valued at $20,000. All in all, he was satisfied with the exchange because the Genoa Street property is in a better neighborhood and has a greater potential for appreciation.

   b.   On August 22, Neil sold a gun collection for $32,000 to an avid collector. The collection was a gift from Neil's father on December 25, 2011, when it was worth $22,000. His father bought the collection in 1997 for $14,000. Neil's sale of the collection was documented by a bill of sale, signed by both Neil and the buyer.

   c.   On September 9, the Kings sold 3,000 shares of Dove Pharmaceuticals for $2,000. The couple purchased the stock on December 4, 2015, for $25,000. The investment was motivated by the rumor that Dove was developing a new drug for infertility. On September 7, the FDA announced that it would not approve the drug due to adverse side effects, and the Dove stock price plummeted. The Kings' broker provided them with a Form 1099–B, which reported the gross proceeds from the sale and their basis in the stock.

10. The Kings have a long-term capital loss carryover of $1,500 from 2015.

11. In March 2016, the Kings were audited by the Missouri Department of Revenue for tax years 2013 and 2014. The audit proposed no changes for the 2013 tax return. However, the Kings were assessed $2,250 additional income tax for 2014 (no interest or penalties were included). The Kings agreed with the assessment and paid the $2,250 immediately.

12. During 2016, Neil served on a jury for a civil case that was litigated at the county courthouse. As a result of the service, he was paid $700 and incurred unreimbursed parking expenses of $60. In conformance with company policy, Neil remitted the $700 of jury duty fees to Sargent.

13. In addition to the items already noted, the Kings had the following receipts in 2016:

Life insurance proceeds		$50,000
2015 Missouri state income tax refund		450
Proceeds from garage sale		2,600
Interest income—		
Kansas City general purpose bonds	$480	
CitiBank certificate of deposit	600	1,080

The insurance proceeds were paid to Neil as the designated beneficiary of Lucy's life insurance policy. At the garage sale, the Kings sold personal items (e.g., camper, furniture, hunting and fishing equipment) that belonged to Neil's father and Neil's mother, Lucy. Neil and Mae estimated that the items they sold originally cost $7,100. The garage sale proceeds were donated to the Alzheimer's Association (a qualified charity) in memory of Neil's father.

14. The Kings had additional expenditures for 2016 of:

Dentist bills not covered by insurance	$3,100
Ad valorem property taxes on personal residence	4,100
Interest on home mortgage	2,600
Contributions to Goodwill (a qualified charity)	3,600

As part of a program sponsored by their church (a qualified charity), the Kings used the family Suburban to transport senior citizens to religious services, for a total of 900 miles. The Suburban also was used for numerous visits to an orthodontist for both of the Kings' children, for a total of 480 miles.

15. The Kings' household includes two dependent children: Ethan (age 15) and Bella (age 14), both of whom are full-time students. Relevant Social Security numbers appear below:

Name	Social Security Number
Neil B. King	123-45-6785
Mae R. King	123-45-6786
Lucy E. King	123-45-6787
Ethan M. King	123-45-6788
Bella A. King	123-45-6789

16. Neil's Form W–2 from Sargent Pharmaceuticals reflects income tax withholding of $6,500 (Federal) and $4,000 (state). The Kings made quarterly income tax payments of $20,000 (Federal) and $9,000 (state), for total payments of $80,000 (Federal) and $36,000 (state). They had their Federal income tax refund of $3,000 (for 2015) applied toward their 2016 income tax.

Requirements

Prepare an income tax return (with appropriate schedules) for the Kings for 2016, using the following guidelines:

- The Kings choose to file a joint income tax return.
- The Kings do not want to contribute to the Presidential Election Campaign Fund.
- The Kings do not own any foreign bank accounts or other investments.
- The Kings want to apply any Federal tax refund to their 2017 tax liability.
- The taxpayers are preparing their own return (i.e., no preparer is involved).
- For the past several years, the Kings have itemized their deductions from AGI instead of using the standard deduction. In addition, the Kings have deducted state income taxes (not sales taxes) for the past several years.
- The taxpayers have the necessary substantiation (e.g., records, receipts) to support all transactions reported in their tax return.
- Make necessary assumptions for information not given in the problem but needed to complete the return.

Appendix F

Table of Cases Cited

Appendix G

Tax Formulas

2016 Tax Rate Schedules

Single—Schedule X

If taxable income is: Over—	But not over—	The tax is:	of the amount over—
$ 0	$ 9,275	.........10%	$ 0
9,275	37,650	$ 927.50 + 15%	9,275
37,650	91,150	5,183.75 + 25%	37,650
91,150	190,150	18,558.75 + 28%	91,150
190,150	413,350	46,278.75 + 33%	190,150
413,350	415,050	119,934.75 + 35%	413,350
415,050	....	120,529.75 + 39.6%	415,050

Head of household—Schedule Z

If taxable income is: Over—	But not over—	The tax is:	of the amount over—
$ 0	$ 13,250	.........10%	$ 0
13,250	50,400	$ 1,325.00 + 15%	13,250
50,400	130,150	6,897.50 + 25%	50,400
130,150	210,800	26,835.00 + 28%	130,150
210,800	413,350	49,417.00 + 33%	210,800
413,350	441,000	116,258.50 + 35%	413,350
441,000	....	125,936.00 + 39.6%	441,000

Married filing jointly or Qualifying widow(er)—Schedule Y–1

If taxable income is: Over—	But not over—	The tax is:	of the amount over—
$ 0	$ 18,550	.........10%	$ 0
18,550	75,300	$ 1,855.00 + 15%	18,550
75,300	151,900	10,367.50 + 25%	75,300
151,900	231,450	29,517.50 + 28%	151,900
231,450	413,350	51,791.50 + 33%	231,450
413,350	466,950	111,818.50 + 35%	413,350
466,950	....	130,578.50 + 39.6%	466,950

Married filing separately—Schedule Y–2

If taxable income is: Over—	But not over—	The tax is:	of the amount over—
$ 0	$ 9,275	.........10%	$ 0
9,275	37,650	$ 927.50 + 15%	9,275
37,650	75,950	5,183.75 + 25%	37,650
75,950	115,725	14,758.75 + 28%	75,950
115,725	206,675	25,895.75 + 33%	115,725
206,675	233,475	55,909.25 + 35%	206,675
233,475	....	65,289.25 + 39.6%	233,475

2017 Tax Rate Schedules

Single—Schedule X

If taxable income is: Over—	But not over—	The tax is:	of the amount over—
$ 0	$ 9,325	.........10%	$ 0
9,325	37,950	$ 932.50 + 15%	9,325
37,950	91,900	5,226.25 + 25%	37,950
91,900	191,650	18,713.75 + 28%	91,900
191,650	416,700	46,643.75 + 33%	191,650
416,700	418,400	120,910.25 + 35%	416,700
418,400	....	121,505.25 + 39.6%	418,400

Head of household—Schedule Z

If taxable income is: Over—	But not over—	The tax is:	of the amount over—
$ 0	$ 13,350	.........10%	$ 0
13,350	50,800	$ 1,335.00 + 15%	13,350
50,800	131,200	6,952.50 + 25%	50,800
131,200	212,500	27,052.50 + 28%	131,200
212,500	416,700	49,816.50 + 33%	212,500
416,700	444,550	117,202.50 + 35%	416,700
444,550	....	126,950.00 + 39.6%	444,550

Married filing jointly or Qualifying widow(er)—Schedule Y–1

If taxable income is: Over—	But not over—	The tax is:	of the amount over—
$ 0	$ 18,650	.........10%	$ 0
18,650	75,900	$ 1,865.00 + 15%	18,650
75,900	153,100	10,452.50 + 25%	75,900
153,100	233,350	29,752.50 + 28%	153,100
233,350	416,700	52,222.50 + 33%	233,350
416,700	470,700	112,728.00 + 35%	416,700
470,700	....	131,628.00 + 39.6%	470,700

Married filing separately—Schedule Y–2

If taxable income is: Over—	But not over—	The tax is:	of the amount over—
$ 0	$ 9,325	.........10%	$ 0
9,325	37,950	$ 932.50 + 15%	9,325
37,950	76,550	5,226.25 + 25%	37,950
76,550	116,675	14,876.25 + 28%	76,550
116,675	208,350	26,111.25 + 33%	116,675
208,350	235,350	56,364.00 + 35%	208,350
235,350	....	65,814.00 + 39.6%	235,350

Tax Formula for Individuals

Income (broadly defined)	$xx,xxx
Less: Exclusions	(x,xxx)
Gross income	$xx,xxx
Less: Deductions *for* adjusted gross income	(x,xxx)
Adjusted gross income	$xx,xxx
Less: The greater of—	
Total itemized deductions	
or standard deduction	(x,xxx)
Less: Personal and dependency exemptions	(x,xxx)
Taxable income	$xx,xxx
Tax on taxable income	$ x,xxx
Less: Tax credits (including Federal income tax	
withheld and prepaid)	(xxx)
Tax due (or refund)	$ xxx

Basic Standard Deduction Amounts

Filing Status	2016	2017
Single	$ 6,300	$ 6,350
Married, filing jointly	12,600	12,700
Surviving spouse	12,600	12,700
Head of household	9,300	9,350
Married, filing separately	6,300	6,350

Amount of Each Additional Standard Deduction

Filing Status	2016	2017
Single	$1,550	$1,550
Married, filing jointly	1,250	1,250
Surviving spouse	1,250	1,250
Head of household	1,550	1,550
Married, filing separately	1,250	1,250

Personal and Dependency Exemption

2016	2017
$4,050	$4,050

AMT Formula for Individuals

Taxable income (increased by any standard deduction and personal or dependency exemptions)

Plus or minus: Adjustments

Plus: Preferences

Equals: Alternative minimum taxable income (AMTI)

Minus: Exemption

Equals: Alternative minimum tax (AMT) base

Multiplied by: 26% or 28% rate

Equals: Tentative minimum tax before foreign tax credit

Minus: AMT foreign tax credit

Equals: Tentative minimum tax (TMT)

Minus: Regular tax liability (less any foreign tax credit)

Equals: AMT (if TMT > regular tax liability)

2016 AMT Exemption and Phaseout for Individuals

| | | Phaseout | |
Filing Status	Exemption	Begins at	Ends at
Married, filing jointly	$83,800	$159,700	$494,900
Single or head of household	53,900	119,700	335,300
Married, filing separately	41,900	79,850	247,450

2017 AMT Exemption and Phaseout for Individuals

| | | Phaseout | |
Filing Status	Exemption	Begins at	Ends at
Married, filing jointly	$84,500	$160,900	$498,900
Single or head of household	54,300	120,700	337,900
Married, filing separately	42,250	80,450	249,450

AMT Formula for Corporations

Taxable income prior to any regular tax NOL deduction

Plus or minus: Adjustments

Plus: Preferences

Equals: Pre-ACE alternative minimum taxable income (AMTI)

Plus or minus: ACE adjustment

Equals: AMTI before ATNOLD

Minus: ATNOLD (limited to 90% of AMTI before ATNOLD)

Equals: AMTI

Minus: Exemption

Equals: Alternative minimum tax (AMT) base

Multiplied by: 20%

Equals: Tentative minimum tax before AMT foreign tax credit

Minus: AMT foreign tax credit

Equals: Tentative minimum tax (TMT)

Minus: Regular tax liability (less any foreign tax credit)

Equals: AMT (if TMT > regular tax liability)

Income Tax Rates—Corporations

Taxable Income	Tax Rate
Not over $50,000	15%
Over $50,000 but not over $75,000	25%
Over $75,000 but not over $100,000	34%
Over $100,000 but not over $335,000	39%*
Over $335,000 but not over $10,000,000	34%
Over $10,000,000 but not over $15,000,000	35%
Over $15,000,000 but not over $18,333,333	38%**
Over $18,333,333	35%

* Five percent of this rate represents a phaseout of the benefits of the lower tax rates on the first $75,000 of taxable income.

**Three percent of this rate represents a phaseout of the benefits of the lower tax rate (34% rather than 35%) on the first $10 million of taxable income.

Appendix H

Present Value and Future Value Tables

Present Value of $1

N/R	1%	2%	3%	4%	5%	6%	7%	8%	9%	10%	11%	12%
1	0.9901	0.9804	0.9709	0.9615	0.9524	0.9434	0.9346	0.9259	0.9174	0.9091	0.9009	0.8929
2	0.9803	0.9612	0.9426	0.9246	0.9070	0.8900	0.8734	0.8573	0.8417	0.8264	0.8116	0.7972
3	0.9706	0.9423	0.9151	0.8890	0.8638	0.8396	0.8163	0.7938	0.7722	0.7513	0.7312	0.7118
4	0.9610	0.9238	0.8885	0.8548	0.8227	0.7921	0.7629	0.7350	0.7084	0.6830	0.6587	0.6355
5	0.9515	0.9057	0.8626	0.8219	0.7835	0.7473	0.7130	0.6806	0.6499	0.6209	0.5935	0.5674
6	0.9420	0.8880	0.8375	0.7903	0.7462	0.7050	0.6663	0.6302	0.5963	0.5645	0.5346	0.5066
7	0.9327	0.8706	0.8131	0.7599	0.7107	0.6651	0.6227	0.5835	0.5470	0.5132	0.4817	0.4523
8	0.9235	0.8535	0.7894	0.7307	0.6768	0.6274	0.5820	0.5403	0.5019	0.4665	0.4339	0.4039
9	0.9143	0.8368	0.7664	0.7026	0.6446	0.5919	0.5439	0.5002	0.4604	0.4241	0.3909	0.3606
10	0.9053	0.8203	0.7441	0.6756	0.6139	0.5584	0.5083	0.4632	0.4224	0.3855	0.3522	0.3220
11	0.8963	0.8043	0.7224	0.6496	0.5847	0.5268	0.4751	0.4289	0.3875	0.3505	0.3173	0.2875
12	0.8874	0.7885	0.7014	0.6246	0.5568	0.4970	0.4440	0.3971	0.3555	0.3186	0.2858	0.2567
13	0.8787	0.7730	0.6810	0.6006	0.5303	0.4688	0.4150	0.3677	0.3262	0.2897	0.2575	0.2292
14	0.8700	0.7579	0.6611	0.5775	0.5051	0.4423	0.3878	0.3405	0.2992	0.2633	0.2320	0.2046
15	0.8613	0.7430	0.6419	0.5553	0.4810	0.4173	0.3624	0.3152	0.2745	0.2394	0.2090	0.1827
16	0.8528	0.7284	0.6232	0.5339	0.4581	0.3936	0.3387	0.2919	0.2519	0.2176	0.1883	0.1631
17	0.8444	0.7142	0.6050	0.5134	0.4363	0.3714	0.3166	0.2703	0.2311	0.1978	0.1696	0.1456
18	0.8360	0.7002	0.5874	0.4936	0.4155	0.3503	0.2959	0.2502	0.2120	0.1799	0.1528	0.1300
19	0.8277	0.6864	0.5703	0.4746	0.3957	0.3305	0.2765	0.2317	0.1945	0.1635	0.1377	0.1161
20	0.8195	0.6730	0.5537	0.4564	0.3769	0.3118	0.2584	0.2145	0.1784	0.1486	0.1240	0.1037

Present Value of an Ordinary Annuity of $1

N/R	1%	2%	3%	4%	5%	6%	7%	8%	9%	10%	11%	12%
1	0.9901	0.9804	0.9709	0.9615	0.9524	0.9434	0.9346	0.9259	0.9174	0.9091	0.9009	0.8929
2	1.9704	1.9416	1.9135	1.8861	1.8594	1.8334	1.8080	1.7833	1.7591	1.7355	1.7125	1.6901
3	2.9410	2.8839	2.8286	2.7751	2.7232	2.6730	2.6243	2.5771	2.5313	2.4869	2.4437	2.4018
4	3.9020	3.8077	3.7171	3.6299	3.5460	3.4651	3.3872	3.3121	3.2397	3.1699	3.1024	3.0373
5	4.8534	4.7135	4.5797	4.4518	4.3295	4.2124	4.1002	3.9927	3.8897	3.7908	3.6959	3.6048
6	5.7955	5.6014	5.4172	5.2421	5.0757	4.9173	4.7665	4.6229	4.4859	4.3553	4.2305	4.1114
7	6.7282	6.4720	6.2303	6.0021	5.7864	5.5824	5.3893	5.2064	5.0330	4.8684	4.7122	4.5638
8	7.6517	7.3255	7.0197	6.7327	6.4632	6.2098	5.9713	5.7466	5.5348	5.3349	5.1461	4.9676
9	8.5660	8.1622	7.7861	7.4353	7.1078	6.8017	6.5152	6.2469	5.9952	5.7590	5.5370	5.3282
10	9.4713	8.9826	8.5302	8.1109	7.7217	7.3601	7.0236	6.7101	6.4177	6.1446	5.8892	5.6502
11	10.3676	9.7868	9.2526	8.7605	8.3064	7.8869	7.4987	7.1390	6.8052	6.4951	6.2065	5.9377
12	11.2551	10.5753	9.9540	9.3851	8.8633	8.3838	7.9427	7.5361	7.1607	6.8137	6.4924	6.1944
13	12.1337	11.3484	10.6350	9.9856	9.3936	8.8527	8.3577	7.9038	7.4869	7.1034	6.7499	6.4235
14	13.0037	12.1062	11.2961	10.5631	9.8986	9.2950	8.7455	8.2442	7.7862	7.3667	6.9819	6.6282
15	13.8651	12.8493	11.9379	11.1184	10.3797	9.7122	9.1079	8.5595	8.0607	7.6061	7.1909	6.8109
16	14.7179	13.5777	12.5611	11.6523	10.8378	10.1059	9.4466	8.8514	8.3126	7.8237	7.3792	6.9740
17	15.5623	14.2919	13.1661	12.1657	11.2741	10.4773	9.7632	9.1216	8.5436	8.0216	7.5488	7.1196
18	16.3983	14.9920	13.7535	12.6593	11.6896	10.8276	10.0591	9.3719	8.7556	8.2014	7.7016	7.2497
19	17.2260	15.6785	14.3238	13.1339	12.0853	11.1581	10.3356	9.6036	8.9501	8.3649	7.8393	7.3658
20	18.0456	16.3514	14.8775	13.5903	12.4622	11.4699	10.5940	9.8181	9.1285	8.5136	7.9633	7.4694

Future Value of $1

N/R	1%	2%	3%	4%	5%	6%	7%	8%	9%	10%	11%	12%
1	1.0100	1.0200	1.0300	1.0400	1.0500	1.0600	1.0700	1.0800	1.0900	1.1000	1.1100	1.1200
2	1.0201	1.0404	1.0609	1.0816	1.1025	1.1236	1.1449	1.1664	1.1881	1.2100	1.2321	1.2544
3	1.0303	1.0612	1.0927	1.1249	1.1576	1.1910	1.2250	1.2597	1.2950	1.3310	1.3676	1.4049
4	1.0406	1.0824	1.1255	1.1699	1.2155	1.2625	1.3108	1.3605	1.4116	1.4641	1.5181	1.5735
5	1.0510	1.1041	1.1593	1.2167	1.2763	1.3382	1.4026	1.4693	1.5386	1.6105	1.6851	1.7623
6	1.0615	1.1262	1.1941	1.2653	1.3401	1.4185	1.5007	1.5869	1.6771	1.7716	1.8704	1.9738
7	1.0721	1.1487	1.2299	1.3159	1.4071	1.5036	1.6058	1.7138	1.8280	1.9487	2.0762	2.2107
8	1.0829	1.1717	1.2668	1.3686	1.4775	1.5938	1.7182	1.8509	1.9926	2.1436	2.3045	2.4760
9	1.0937	1.1951	1.3048	1.4233	1.5513	1.6895	1.8385	1.9990	2.1719	2.3579	2.5580	2.7731
10	1.1046	1.2190	1.3439	1.4802	1.6289	1.7908	1.9672	2.1589	2.3674	2.5937	2.8394	3.1058
11	1.1157	1.2434	1.3842	1.5395	1.7103	1.8983	2.1049	2.3316	2.5804	2.8531	3.1518	3.4785
12	1.1268	1.2682	1.4258	1.6010	1.7959	2.0122	2.2522	2.5182	2.8127	3.1384	3.4985	3.8960
13	1.1381	1.2936	1.4685	1.6651	1.8856	2.1329	2.4098	2.7196	3.0658	3.4523	3.8833	4.3635
14	1.1495	1.3195	1.5126	1.7317	1.9799	2.2609	2.5785	2.9372	3.3417	3.7975	4.3104	4.8871
15	1.1610	1.3459	1.5580	1.8009	2.0789	2.3966	2.7590	3.1722	3.6425	4.1772	4.7846	5.4736
16	1.1726	1.3728	1.6047	1.8730	2.1829	2.5404	2.9522	3.4259	3.9703	4.5950	5.3109	6.1304
17	1.1843	1.4002	1.6528	1.9479	2.2920	2.6928	3.1588	3.7000	4.3276	5.0545	5.8951	6.8660
18	1.1961	1.4282	1.7024	2.0258	2.4066	2.8543	3.3799	3.9960	4.7171	5.5599	6.5436	7.6900
19	1.2081	1.4568	1.7535	2.1068	2.5270	3.0256	3.6165	4.3157	5.1417	6.1159	7.2633	8.6128
20	1.2202	1.4859	1.8061	2.1911	2.6533	3.2071	3.8697	4.6610	5.6044	6.7275	8.0623	9.6463

Future Value of an Ordinary Annuity of $1

N/R	1%	2%	3%	4%	5%	6%	7%	8%	9%	10%	11%	12%
1	1.0000	1.0000	1.0000	1.0000	1.0000	1.0000	1.0000	1.0000	1.0000	1.0000	1.0000	1.0000
2	2.0100	2.0200	2.0300	2.0400	2.0500	2.0600	2.0700	2.0800	2.0900	2.1000	2.1100	2.1200
3	3.0301	3.0604	3.0909	3.1216	3.1525	3.1836	3.2149	3.2464	3.2781	3.3100	3.3421	3.3744
4	4.0604	4.1216	4.1836	4.2465	4.3101	4.3746	4.4399	4.5061	4.5731	4.6410	4.7097	4.7793
5	5.1010	5.2040	5.3091	5.4163	5.5256	5.6371	5.7507	5.8666	5.9847	6.1051	6.2278	6.3528
6	6.1520	6.3081	6.4684	6.6330	6.8019	6.9753	7.1533	7.3359	7.5233	7.7156	7.9129	8.1152
7	7.2135	7.4343	7.6625	7.8983	8.1420	8.3938	8.6540	8.9228	9.2004	9.4872	9.7833	10.0890
8	8.2857	8.5830	8.8923	9.2142	9.5491	9.8975	10.2598	10.6366	11.0285	11.4359	11.8594	12.2997
9	9.3685	9.7546	10.1591	10.5828	11.0266	11.4913	11.9780	12.4876	13.0210	13.5795	14.1640	14.7757
10	10.4622	10.9497	11.4639	12.0061	12.5779	13.1808	13.8164	14.4866	15.1929	15.9374	16.7220	17.5487
11	11.5668	12.1687	12.8078	13.4864	14.2068	14.9716	15.7836	16.6455	17.5603	18.5312	19.5614	20.6546
12	12.6825	13.4121	14.1920	15.0258	15.9171	16.8699	17.8885	18.9771	20.1407	21.3843	22.7132	24.1331
13	13.8093	14.6803	15.6178	16.6268	17.7130	18.8821	20.1406	21.4953	22.9534	24.5227	26.2116	28.0291
14	14.9474	15.9739	17.0863	18.2919	19.5986	21.0151	22.5505	24.2149	26.0192	27.9750	30.0949	32.3926
15	16.0969	17.2934	18.5989	20.0236	21.5786	23.2760	25.1290	27.1521	29.3609	31.7725	34.4054	37.2797
16	17.2579	18.6393	20.1569	21.8245	23.6575	25.6725	27.8881	30.3243	33.0034	35.9497	39.1899	42.7533
17	18.4304	20.0121	21.7616	23.6975	25.8404	28.2129	30.8402	33.7502	36.9737	40.5447	44.5008	48.8837
18	19.6147	21.4123	23.4144	25.6454	28.1324	30.9057	33.9990	37.4502	41.3013	45.5992	50.3959	55.7497
19	20.8109	22.8406	25.1169	27.6712	30.5390	33.7600	37.3790	41.4463	46.0185	51.1591	56.9395	63.4397
20	22.0190	24.2974	26.8704	29.7781	33.0660	36.7856	40.9955	45.7620	51.1601	57.2750	64.2028	72.0524

Index